HOLT McDOUGAL

Mathematics
Course 1

Virginia

Jennie M. Bennett
Edward B. Burger
David J. Chard
Earlene J. Hall
Paul A. Kennedy
Freddie L. Renfro
Tom W. Roby
Janet K. Scheer
Bert K. Waits

HOLT McDOUGAL
a division of Houghton Mifflin Harcourt

OAK VALLEY CENTER
11230 WAPLES MILL ROAD
SUITE 100
FAIRFAX, VA 22030

Cover Photo: Dazzling Dozen by Charles Bell
©Louis K. Meisel Gallery, Inc./CORBIS

Copyright © 2012 by Houghton Mifflin Harcourt Publishing Company

All rights reserved. No part of this work may be reproduced or transmitted in any form or by any means, electronic or mechanical, including photocopying or recording, or by any information storage and retrieval system, without the prior written permission of the copyright owner unless such copying is expressly permitted by federal copyright law. Requests for permission to make copies of any part of the work should be addressed to Houghton Mifflin Harcourt Publishing Company, Attn: Contracts, Copyrights, and Licensing, 9400 South Park Center Loop, Orlando, Florida 32819.

Printed in Canada

If you have received these materials as examination copies free of charge, Houghton Mifflin Harcourt Publishing Company retains title to the materials and they may not be resold. Resale of examination copies is strictly prohibited.

Possession of this publication in print format does not entitle users to convert this publication, or any portion of it, into electronic format.

ISBN 978-0-547-48545-4

2 3 4 5 6 7 8 9 10 1774 19 18 17 16 15 14 13 12 11

4500305219   A B C D E F G

Authors

Jennie M. Bennett, Ed.D., is a recently retired mathematics teacher at Hartman Middle School in Houston, Texas. She is past president of the Benjamin Banneker Association, the former First Vice-President of NCSM, and a former board member of NCTM.

Edward B. Burger, Ph.D., is Professor of Mathematics and Chair at Williams College and is the author of numerous articles, books, and videos. He has won many prestigious writing and teaching awards offered by the Mathematical Association of America. In 2006, Dr. Burger was named Reader's Digest's "Best Math Teacher" in its "100 Best of America" issue. He has made numerous television and radio appearances and has given countless mathematical presentations around the world.

David J. Chard, Ph.D., is the Leon Simmons Dean of the School of Education and Human Development at Southern Methodist University. He is a Past President of the Division for Research at the Council for Exceptional Children, a member of the International Academy for Research on Learning Disabilities, and has been the Principal Investigator on numerous research projects for the U.S. Department of Education. He is the author of several research articles and books on instructional strategies for students struggling in school.

Earlene J. Hall, Ed.D., is the Middle School Mathematics Supervisor for the Detroit Public Schools district. She teaches graduate courses in Mathematics Leadership at University of Michigan Dearborn. Dr. Hall has traveled extensively throughout Africa and China and has made numerous presentations including topics such as Developing Standards Based Professional Development and Culture Centered Education. She is a member of the NCTM 2009 Yearbook Panel.

Paul A. Kennedy, Ph.D., is a professor in the Department of Mathematics at Colorado State University. Dr. Kennedy is a leader in mathematics education. His research focuses on developing algebraic thinking by using multiple representations and technology. He is the author of numerous publications.

Freddie L. Renfro, MA, has 35 years of experience in Texas education as a classroom teacher and director/coordinator of Mathematics PreK-12 for school districts in the Houston area. She has served as a reviewer and TXTEAM trainer for Texas Math Institutes and has presented at numerous math workshops.

Tom W. Roby, Ph.D., is Associate Professor of Mathematics and Director of the Quantitative Learning Center at the University of Connecticut. He founded and co-directed the Bay Area-based ACCLAIM professional development program. He also chaired the advisory board of the California Mathematics Project and reviewed content for the California Standards Tests.

Janet K. Scheer, Ph.D., Executive Director of Create A Vision™, is a motivational speaker and provides customized K-12 math staff development. She has taught and supervised internationally and nationally at all grade levels.

Bert K. Waits, Ph.D., is a Professor Emeritus of Mathematics at The Ohio State University and cofounder of T^3 (Teachers Teaching with Technology), a national professional development program. Dr. Waits is also a former board member of NCTM and an author of the original NCTM Standards.

Virginia Teacher Reviewers

Jen Farrey
Leesburg, VA

Sharon E. Laarz, M.Ed
Instructional Specialist
Newport News Public Schools

Jack Plonkey
Arlington, VA

Molly Sullivan
Oscar Smith Middle School
Chesapeake Public Schools

Meredith L. Zirkle
M.A. in Education
Admiral Richard E. Byrd Middle School
Frederick County Public Schools

Field Test Participants

Wendy Black
Southmont Jr. High
Crawfordsville, IN

Barbara Broeckelman
Oakley Middle School
Oakley, KS

Cindy Bush
Riverside Middle School
Greer, SC

Cadian Collman
Cutler Ridge Middle School
Miami, FL

Dora Corcini
Eisenhower Middle School
Oregon, OH

Deborah Drinkwalter
Sedgefield Middle School
Goose Creek, SC

Susan Gomez
Glades Middle School
Miami, FL

LaChandra Hogan
Apollo Middle School
Hollywood, FL

Ty Inlow
Oakley Middle School
Oakley, KS

Leighton Jenkins
Glades Middle School
Miami, FL

Heather King
Clever Middle School
Clever, MO

Dianne Marrett
Pines Middle School
Pembroke Pines, FL

Angela J. McNeal
Audubon Middle School
Los Angeles, CA

Wendy Misner
Lakeland Middle School
LaGrange, IN

Vanessa Nance
Pines Middle School
Pembroke Pines, FL

Teresa Patterson
Damonte Ranch High School
Reno, NV

Traci Peters
Cario Middle School
Mount Pleasant, SC

Ashley Piatt
East Forsyth Middle School
Kernersville, NC

Jeannine Quigley
Wilbur Wright Middle School
Dayton, OH

Shioban Smith-Haye
Apollo Middle School
Hollywood, FL

Jill Snipes
Bunn Middle School
Bunn, NC

Cathy Spencer
Oakridge Junior High
Oakridge, OR

Connie Vaught
K.D. Waldo School
Aurora, IL

Shelley Weeks
Lewis Middle School
Valparaiso, FL

Jennie Woo
Gaithersburg Middle School
Gaitersburg, MD

Reggie Wright
West Hopkins School
Nebo, KY

Program Reviewers

Judy Broughton
Math Teacher
Poplar Street Sixth Grade Center
North Little Rock, Arkansas

Troy Deckebach
Math Teacher
Tredyffrin-Easttown Middle
   School
Berwyn, PA

Maridith Gebhart
Math Teacher
Ramay Junior High School
Fayetteville, AR

Ruth Harbin-Miles
District Math Coordinator—
   Retired
Instructional Resource Center
Olathe, KS

Kim Hayden
Math Teacher
Clermont County School District
Milford, OH

Rhoni Herell
Math Teacher
Enid Waller Junior High
Enid, Oklahoma

Becky Lowe
Math Teacher
Bartlesville Mid-High
Bartlesville, Oklahoma

George Maguschak
Math Teacher/Building
   Chairperson
Wilkes-Barre Area
Wilkes-Barre, PA

Samantha McGlennen
Math Teacher/Department
   Coordinator
Summit Middle School
Fort Wayne, Indiana

Diane McIntire
Math Teacher
Garfield School
Kearny, NJ

Kenneth McIntire
Math Teacher
Lincoln School
Kearny, NJ

Tim Messal
Math Teacher/Math Department
   Chair
Woodside Middle School
Fort Wayne, Indiana

Vicki Perryman Petty
Math Teacher
Central Middle School
Murfreesboro, TN

Laronda Raines-Langham
Math Teacher
North Jefferson Middle School
Kimberly, Alabama

Rene Rush
Math Teacher
Colonial Heights Middle School
Colonial Heights, VA

Jennifer Sawyer
Math Teacher
Shawboro, NC

Shelly Schram
Math Teacher
East Grand Rapids Middle School
East Grand Rapids, Michigan

Richard Seavey
Math Teacher—Retired
Metcalf Junior High
Eagan, MN

Gail M. Sigmund
Math Teacher—Retired
Charles A. Mooney Preparatory
   School
Cleveland, OH

Jeffrey Slagel
Math Department Chair
South Eastern Middle School
Fawn Grove, PA

Paul Turney
Math Teacher
Ladue School District
St. Louis, MO

Dave Warren
Math Teacher
Meridian Middle School
Meridian, Idaho

Marilyn Wheeler
Math Teacher
Cityside Middle School
Zeeland, Michigan

CHAPTER 1
Whole Numbers and Patterns

ARE YOU READY? 3

Whole Numbers and Exponents
- 1-1 Estimating with Whole Numbers 6
- 6.5 1-2 Exponents 10
- READY TO GO ON? QUIZ 14
- Focus on Problem Solving: Solve 15

Using Whole Numbers
- LAB Explore the Order of Operations 16
- 6.8 1-3 Order of Operations 18
- 1-4 Properties and Mental Math 22
- 1-5 Choosing a Method of Computation 26
- 6.17 1-6 Patterns and Sequences 29
- LAB Find a Pattern in Sequences 33
- READY TO GO ON? QUIZ 34
- REAL-WORLD CONNECTION: CONNECTICUT 35

Study Guide: Preview 4
Reading and Writing Math 5
Game Time: Palindromes 36
It's in the Bag! Picture This 37
Study Guide: Review 38
Chapter Test 41

6.FPC.5: Algebra
See pp. C2–C3 for text.

Tools for Success

Reading and Writing Math
- Reading Math 5
- Writing Math 9, 13, 21, 25, 28, 32
- Vocabulary 6, 10, 18, 22, 29

Study Skills
- Know-It Notebook Chapter 1
- Homework Help Online 8, 12, 20, 24, 27, 31
- Student Help 6, 18, 22, 23, 29

Test Prep
- Countdown to Testing Weeks 1, 2
- Test Prep and Spiral Review 9, 13, 25, 28, 32
- Test Tackler 42
- Standardized Test Prep 44

Introduction to Algebra

CHAPTER 2

ARE YOU READY? 47

Understanding Variables and Expressions
- 2-1 Variables and Expressions 50
- 2-2 Translating Between Words and Math 54
- 2-3 Translating Between Tables and Expressions 58
- **LAB** Explore Area and Perimeter of Rectangles 62
- READY TO GO ON? QUIZ 64
- Focus on Problem Solving: Understand the Problem 65

Understanding Equations
- 6.18 2-4 Equations and Their Solutions 66
- 6.18 2-5 Addition Equations 70
- 6.18 2-6 Subtraction Equations 74
- 6.18 2-7 Multiplication Equations 77
- 6.18 2-8 Division Equations 81
- READY TO GO ON? QUIZ 84
- REAL-WORLD CONNECTION: PENNSYLVANIA 85

Study Guide: Preview 48
Reading and Writing Math 49
Game Time: Math Magic 86
It's in the Bag! Tri-Sided Equations 87
Study Guide: Review 88
Chapter Test 91

Learn It Online
Online Resources go.hrw.com,
keyword MR10 TOC

Focal Points
6.FP.3: Algebra
See pp. C2–C3 for text.

Tools for Success

Reading and Writing Math
- Reading Math 66
- Writing Math 49, 51, 53, 61, 69, 73, 76, 80, 83
- Vocabulary 50, 66, 70

Study Skills
- Know-It Notebook Chapter 2
- Homework Help Online 52, 56, 60, 68, 72, 75, 79, 82
- Student Help 59, 77

Test Prep
- Countdown to Testing Weeks 2, 3
- Test Prep and Spiral Review 53, 57, 61, 69, 73, 76, 80, 83
- Standardized Test Prep 92

CHAPTER 3

Decimals

		Are You Ready? 95
		Understanding Decimals
	LAB	Model Decimals 98
6.2d	3-1	Representing, Comparing, and Ordering Decimals 100
	3-2	Estimating Decimals 104
	LAB	Explore Decimal Addition and Subtraction 108
6.7	3-3	Adding and Subtracting Decimals 110
		Ready to Go On? Quiz 114
		Focus on Problem Solving: Solve 115
		Multiplying and Dividing Decimals
	3-4	Scientific Notation 116
	LAB	Explore Decimal Multiplication and Division 120
6.7	3-5	Multiplying Decimals 122
6.7	3-6	Dividing Decimals by Whole Numbers 126
6.7	3-7	Dividing by Decimals 129
6.7	3-8	Interpreting the Quotient 133
	3-9	Solving Decimal Equations 136
		Ready to Go On? Quiz 140
		Real World Connection: Washington 141

Study Guide: Preview 96
Reading and Writing Math 97
Game Time: Jumbles 142
It's in the Bag! Project E Z 2 C Decimals 143
Study Guide: Review 144
Chapter Test 147

Focal Points

6.FP.1: Number and Operations
6.FP.3: Algebra
6.FPC.4: Number and Operations
See pp. C2–C3 for text.

Tools for Success

Reading and Writing Math

Reading Math 100
Writing Math 97, 103, 107, 113, 119, 128, 132, 135, 139
Vocabulary 104, 116

Study Skills

Know-It Notebook Chapter 3
Homework Help Online 102, 106, 112, 118, 124, 127, 131, 134, 138
Student Help 101, 104, 105, 110, 111, 122, 123, 126, 127, 129, 133, 136, 137

Test Prep

Countdown to Testing Weeks 3, 4, 5
Test Prep and Spiral Review 103, 107, 113, 119, 125, 128, 132, 135, 139
Test Tackler 148
Standardized Test Prep 150

Number Theory and Fractions

CHAPTER 4

		ARE YOU READY?	153
		Number Theory	
	4-1	Divisibility	156
	LAB	Explore Factors	160
	4-2	Factors and Prime Factorization	161
	4-3	Greatest Common Factor	165
	LAB	Greatest Common Factor	169
	EXT	Sets of Numbers	170
		READY TO GO ON? QUIZ	172
		Focus on Problem Solving: Understand the Problem	173
		Understanding Fractions	
	LAB	Explore Decimals and Fractions	174
6.2c	4-4	Decimals and Fractions	175
	LAB	Model Equivalent Fractions	179
6.2c	4-5	Equivalent Fractions	180
	LAB	Explore Fraction Measurement	184
6.2c	4-6	Mixed Numbers and Improper Fractions	186
		READY TO GO ON? QUIZ	190
		Focus on Problem Solving: Understand the Problem	191
		Introduction to Fraction Operations	
6.2d	4-7	Comparing and Ordering Fractions	192
	4-8	Adding and Subtracting with Like Denominators	196
6.6b	4-9	Estimating Fraction Sums and Differences	200
		READY TO GO ON? QUIZ	204
		REAL-WORLD CONNECTION: MONTANA	205
		Study Guide: Preview	154
		Reading and Writing Math	155
		Game Time: Riddle Me This	206
		It's in the Bag! Spec-Tag-Ular Number Theory	207
		Study Guide: Review	208
		Chapter Test	211

Learn It Online
Online Resources go.hrw.com,
keyword MR10 TOC

Focal Points
6.FPC.4: Number and Operations
See pp. C2–C3 for text.

Tools for Success

Reading and Writing Math
Reading Math 155, 186
Writing Math 159, 164, 168, 176, 178, 183, 189, 195, 199, 203
Vocabulary 156, 161, 165, 170, 175, 180, 186, 192

Study Skills
Know-It Notebook Chapter 4
Homework Help Online 158, 163, 167, 177, 182, 188, 194, 198, 202
Student Help 156, 161, 162, 166, 171, 175, 181, 192, 193, 196, 197, 201

Test Prep
Countdown to Testing Weeks 6, 7, 8
Test Prep and Spiral Review 159, 164, 168, 178, 183, 189, 195, 199, 203
Standardized Test Prep 212

CHAPTER 5
Fraction Operations

ARE YOU READY? 215

Adding and Subtracting Fractions

	5-1	Least Common Multiple 218
	LAB	Model Fraction Addition and Subtraction 222
	5-2	Adding and Subtracting with Unlike Denominators 224
6.6b	5-3	Adding and Subtracting Mixed Numbers 228
	LAB	Model Subtraction with Regrouping 232
6.6b	5-4	Regrouping to Subtract Mixed Numbers 234
	5-5	Solving Fraction Equations: Addition and Subtraction... 238

READY TO GO ON? QUIZ 242
Focus on Problem Solving: Solve 243

Multiplying and Dividing Fractions

6.6a	5-6	Multiplying Fractions by Whole Numbers 244
	LAB	Model Fraction Multiplication 248
6.6a	5-7	Multiplying Fractions 250
6.6a	5-8	Multiplying Mixed Numbers 254
	LAB	Model Fraction Division 258
6.6a	5-9	Dividing Fractions and Mixed Numbers 260
	5-10	Solving Fraction Equations: Multiplication and Division .. 264

READY TO GO ON? QUIZ 268
REAL-WORLD CONNECTION: MISSOURI 269

Study Guide: Preview 216
Reading and Writing Math 217
Game Time: Fraction Riddles 270
It's in the Bag! Flipping over Fractions 271
Study Guide: Review 272
Chapter Test 275

Focal Points
6.FP.1: Number and Operations
6.FP.3: Algebra
6.FPC.4: Number and Operations
See pp. C2–C3 for text.

Tools for Success

Reading and Writing Math
Writing Math 221, 227, 231, 237, 241, 247, 253, 263, 267
Vocabulary 218, 224, 260

Study Skills
Know-It Notebook Chapter 5
Study Strategy 227
Homework Help Online 220, 226, 230, 236, 240, 246, 252, 256, 262, 266
Student Help 218, 219, 224, 229, 245, 251, 254, 255, 261, 264

Test Prep
Countdown to Testing Weeks 8, 9, 10
Test Prep and Spiral Review 221, 227, 231, 237, 241, 247, 253, 257, 263, 267
Test Tackler 276
Standardized Test Prep 278

Collecting and Displaying Data

CHAPTER 6

ARE YOU READY? 281

Organizing Data

	6-1	Making a Table 284
	LAB	Collect Data to Explore Mean 287
6.15a	6-2	Mean, Median, Mode, and Range 288
	6-3	Additional Data and Outliers 292
		READY TO GO ON? QUIZ 296
		Focus on Problem Solving: Make a Plan 297

Displaying and Interpreting Data

	6-4	Bar Graphs 298
	LAB	Create Bar Graphs 302
	6-5	Line Plots, Frequency Tables, and Histograms 304
	EXT	Frequency Distribution 308
	LAB	Use a Survey to Collect Data 310
6.11a	6-6	Ordered Pairs 311
	6-7	Line Graphs 314
	6-8	Misleading Graphs 318
	6-9	Stem-and-Leaf Plots 322
6.14c	6-10	Choosing an Appropriate Display 325
		READY TO GO ON? QUIZ 328
		REAL-WORLD CONNECTION: OKLAHOMA 329

Study Guide: Preview 282
Reading and Writing Math 283
Game Time: A Thousand Words 330
It's in the Bag! Graphing According to Me 331
Study Guide: Review 332
Chapter Test 335

Learn It Online
Online Resources go.hrw.com,
keyword MR10 TOC

Tools for Success

Reading and Writing Math
Reading Math 283, 299, 304, 308
Writing Math 286, 295, 301, 307, 313, 317, 321, 327
Vocabulary 288, 292, 298, 304, 308, 311, 314, 322

Study Skills
Know-It Notebook Chapter 6
Homework Help Online 285, 290, 294, 300, 306, 312, 316, 320, 323, 326
Student Help 292, 314, 315, 322, 323

Test Prep
Countdown to Testing
Weeks 10, 11, 12, 13
Test Prep and Spiral Review 286, 291, 295, 301, 307, 313, 317, 321, 324, 327
Standardized Test Prep 336

CHAPTER 7
Proportional Relationships

ARE YOU READY? 339

Virginia Mathematics Standards of Learning

Understanding Ratios and Proportions

6.1	7-1	Ratios and Rates	342
6.2a	7-2	Using Tables to Explore Equivalent Ratios and Rates	346
	LAB	Explore Proportions	350
	7-3	Proportions	352
	7-4	Similar Figures	356
	7-5	Indirect Measurement	360
	LAB	Sketch Scale Drawings	363
	7-6	Scale Drawings and Maps	364

READY TO GO ON? QUIZ 368
Focus on Problem Solving: Make a Plan 369

Understanding Percents

	LAB	Model Percents	370
6.2c	7-7	Percents	371
6.2c	7-8	Percents, Decimals, and Fractions	375
	LAB	Convert Between Percents, Decimals, and Fractions	379
	7-9	Percent Problems	380
	7-10	Applying Percents	384
	EXT	Simple Interest	388

READY TO GO ON? QUIZ 390
REAL-WORLD CONNECTION: MICHIGAN 391

Study Guide: Preview 340
Reading and Writing Math 341
Game Time: The Golden Rectangle 392
It's in the Bag! Double-Door Fractions,
Decimals, and Percents 393
Study Guide: Review 394
Chapter Test 397

Learn It Online
Online Resources go.hrw.com,
keyword MR10 TOC Go

Focal Points

6.FP.2: Number and Operations
6.FP.3: Algebra
6.FPC.4: Number and Operations
See pp. C2–C3 for text.

Tools for Success

Reading and Writing Math

Reading Math 342, 346, 352
Writing Math 341, 345, 349, 355, 359, 362, 367, 374, 378, 383, 387, 389
Vocabulary 342, 352, 356, 360, 364, 371, 384, 388

Study Skills

Know-It Notebook Chapter 7
Homework Help Online 344, 348, 354, 358, 361, 366, 373, 377, 382, 386
Student Help 346, 353, 357, 364, 372, 376, 380, 384

Test Prep

Countdown to Testing
Weeks 13, 14, 15
Test Prep and Spiral Review 345, 349, 355, 359, 362, 367, 374, 378, 383, 387
Test Tackler 398
Standardized Test Prep 400

Geometric Relationships

CHAPTER 8

ARE YOU READY? 403

Lines and Angles
- 8-1 Building Blocks of Geometry 406
- 8-2 Measuring and Classifying Angles 410
- LAB Construct Congruent Segments and Angles 414
- 8-3 Angle Relationships 416
- 8-4 Classifying Pairs of Lines 420
- LAB Parallel Line Relationships 424
- **READY TO GO ON? QUIZ** 426
- **Focus on Problem Solving:** Solve 427

Polygons
- LAB Triangle Inequality 428
- 6.12 8-5 Triangles 429
- LAB Angles in Triangles 433
- 6.13 8-6 Quadrilaterals 434
- 8-7 Polygons 438
- LAB Intersecting Polygons 442
- 8-8 Geometric Patterns 444
- **READY TO GO ON? QUIZ** 448
- **Focus on Problem Solving:** Make a Plan 449

Polygon Relationships
- 6.12 8-9 Congruent Polygons 450
- 8-10 Transformations 453
- 8-11 Symmetry 457
- LAB Create Tessellations 462
- **READY TO GO ON? QUIZ** 464
- **REAL-WORLD CONNECTION: OHIO** 465

Study Guide: Preview 404
Reading and Writing Math 405
Game Time: Tangrams 466
It's in the Bag! Geometry Grab Bag 467
Study Guide: Review 468
Chapter Test 471

Virginia Mathematics Standards of Learning

Online Resources go.hrw.com, keyword MR10 TOC

Focal Points
6.FPC.5: Algebra
See pp. C2–C3 for text.

Tools for Success

Reading and Writing Math
Reading Math 405, 410, 411, 420, 439
Writing Math 409, 413, 419, 423, 432, 437, 441, 447, 452, 456, 461
Vocabulary 406, 410, 416, 420, 429, 434, 438, 450, 453, 457

Study Skills
Know-It Notebook Chapter 8
Homework Help Online 408, 412, 418, 422, 431, 436, 440, 446, 451, 455, 459
Student Help 430, 444, 450

Test Prep
Countdown to Testing Weeks 15, 16, 17
Test Prep and Spiral Review 409, 413, 419, 423, 432, 437, 441, 447, 452, 456, 461
Standardized Test Prep 478

CHAPTER 9

Measurement and Geometry

ARE YOU READY? **475**

Customary and Metric Measurement

LAB	Select and Use Appropriate Measuring Tools **478**
9-1	Understanding Customary Units of Measure **480**
9-2	Understanding Metric Units of Measure **484**
9-3	Converting Customary Units **488**
9-4	Converting Metric Units **492**
9-5	Time and Temperature **496**

READY TO GO ON? QUIZ **500**
Focus on Problem Solving: Look Back **501**

Measurement and Geometric Figures

	9-6	Finding Angle Measures in Polygons **502**
6.10c	9-7	Perimeter **506**
	LAB	Explore Circumference **510**
6.10b	9-8	Circles and Circumference **512**
	LAB	Construct Circle Graphs **516**

READY TO GO ON? QUIZ **518**
REAL-WORLD CONNECTION: TENNESSEE **519**

Study Guide: Preview **476**
Reading and Writing Math **477**
Game Time: Logic Puzzle **520**
It's in the Bag! Perfectly Packaged Perimeters **521**
Study Guide: Review **522**
Chapter Test **525**

Learn It Online
Online Resources **go.hrw.com**,
keyword MR10 TOC

Virginia Mathematics Standards of Learning

Focal Points

6.FP.1: Number and Operations
6.FP.2: Number and Operations
6.FP.3: Algebra
See pp. C2–C3 for text.

Tools for Success

Reading and Writing Math

Writing Math 483, 487, 491, 495, 499, 505, 509, 515
Vocabulary 480, 484, 506, 512

Study Skills

Know-It Notebook Chapter 9
Study Strategy 477
Homework Help Online 482, 486, 490, 494, 498, 504, 508, 514
Student Help 481, 488, 489, 492, 493, 497, 502, 503

Test Prep

Countdown to Testing Weeks 18, 19
Test Prep and Spiral Review 483, 487, 491, 495, 499, 505, 509, 515
Test Tackler 526
Standardized Test Prep 528

Measurement: Area and Volume

CHAPTER 10

Virginia Mathematics Standards of Learning

		ARE YOU READY?	531
		Area	
6.10c	10-1	Area of Rectangles and Parallelograms	534
	LAB	Squares and Square Roots	538
6.10c	10-2	Area of Triangles and Trapezoids	540
	LAB	Explore Perimeter and Area	544
6.10c	10-3	Area of Composite Figures	545
6.10c	10-4	Changing Dimensions	548
	LAB	Explore Area of Circles	551
6.10b	10-5	Area of Circles	552
		READY TO GO ON? QUIZ	556
		Focus on Problem Solving: Solve	557
		Volume and Surface Area	
	LAB	Draw Views of Three-Dimensional Figures	558
	10-6	Three-Dimensional Figures	560
	LAB	Explore Volume of Prisms and Cylinders	564
6.10d	10-7	Volume of Prisms	566
	10-8	Volume of Cylinders	570
	LAB	Model Three-Dimensional Figures	574
6.10d	10-9	Surface Area	576
		READY TO GO ON? QUIZ	580
		REAL-WORLD CONNECTION: RHODE ISLAND	581
		Study Guide: Preview	532
		Reading and Writing Math	533
		Game Time: Polygon Hide-and-Seek	582
		It's in the Bag! Area and Volume Suitcase	583
		Study Guide: Review	584
		Chapter Test	587

Learn It Online
Online Resources go.hrw.com,
keyword MR10 TOC

Focal Points

6.FP.1: Number and Operations
6.FP.3: Algebra
6.FPC.6: Measurement and Geometry

See pp. C2–C3 for text.

Tools for Success

Reading and Writing Math

Reading Math 533
Writing Math 537, 543, 547, 550, 555, 563, 569, 573, 579
Vocabulary 534, 560, 566, 576

Study Skills

Know-It Notebook Chapter 10
Homework Help Online 536, 542, 546, 549, 554, 562, 568, 572, 578
Student Help 545, 546, 561, 566, 571, 577

Test Prep

Countdown to Testing Weeks 20, 21
Test Prep and Spiral Review 537, 543, 547, 550, 555, 563, 569, 573, 579
Standardized Test Prep 588

CHAPTER 11

Integers

ARE YOU READY? 591

Understanding Integers

6.3c	11-1	Integers and Absolute Value	594
6.3b	11-2	Comparing and Ordering Integers	598
	EXT	Negative Rational Numbers	602
6.11a	11-3	The Coordinate Plane	604
	11-4	Transformations in the Coordinate Plane	608

READY TO GO ON? QUIZ 612
Focus on Problem Solving: Understand the Problem 613

Integer Operations

LAB	Model Integer Addition	614
11-5	Adding Integers	615
LAB	Model Integer Subtraction	619
11-6	Subtracting Integers	620
11-7	Multiplying Integers	623
11-8	Dividing Integers	626
LAB	Model Integer Equations	630
11-9	Solving Integer Equations	632

READY TO GO ON? QUIZ 636
REAL-WORLD CONNECTION: NEW JERSEY 637

Study Guide: Preview 592
Reading and Writing Math 593
Game Time: A Math Riddle 638
It's in the Bag! Positive-Negative Pull Out 639
Study Guide: Review 640
Chapter Test 643

Tools for Success

Reading Math 595, 608
Writing Math 593, 597, 601, 607, 611, 615, 618, 622, 625, 629, 635
Vocabulary 594, 602, 604, 646

Know-It Notebook Chapter 11
Homework Help Online 596, 600, 606, 610, 617, 621, 624, 628, 634
Student Help 594, 598, 602, 604, 609, 623, 624, 626, 627, 632

Countdown to Testing Weeks 21, 22, 23
Test Prep and Spiral Review 597, 601, 607, 611, 618, 622, 625, 629, 635
Test Tackler 644
Standardized Test Prep 646

Probability

CHAPTER 12

	ARE YOU READY?	649

Understanding Probability

6.2c	12-1	Introduction to Probability	652
	12-2	Experimental Probability	656
	LAB	Simulations	660
	12-3	Counting Methods and Sample Spaces	662
	12-4	Theoretical Probability	666
		READY TO GO ON? QUIZ	670
		Focus on the Problem: Look Back	671

Using Probability

12-5	Compound Events	672
EXT	Independent and Dependent Events	676
LAB	Explore Permutations and Combinations	678
12-6	Making Predictions	680
	READY TO GO ON? QUIZ	684
	REAL-WORLD CONNECTION: LOUISIANA	685

Study Guide: Preview ... 650
Reading and Writing Math ... 651
Game Time: Probability Brain Teasers ... 686
It's in the Bag! CD Spinner ... 687
Study Guide: Review ... 688
Chapter Test ... 691

Tools for Success

Reading Math 656
Writing Math 655, 657, 659, 665, 669, 675, 677, 683
Vocabulary 652, 656, 662, 666, 672, 676, 680

Know-It Notebook Chapter 12
Study Strategy 651
Homework Help Online 654, 658, 664, 668, 674, 682
Student Help 652, 653, 666, 673

Countdown to Testing Weeks 23, 24
Test Prep and Spiral Review 655, 659, 665, 669, 675, 683
Standardized Test Prep 692

CHAPTER 13

Functions, Equations, and Inequalities

ARE YOU READY? 695

Equations and Functions

- 13-1 Tables and Functions 698
- 13-2 Graphing Functions 702
- 13-3 Slope and Rate of Change 706
- **LAB** Explore Linear and Nonlinear Relationships 710
- READY TO GO ON? QUIZ 712
- Focus on Problem Solving: Make a Plan 713

Equations and Inequalities

- 13-4 Two-Step Equations 714
- 6.20 13-5 Inequalities 718
- 13-6 Two-Step Inequalities 722
- READY TO GO ON? QUIZ 726
- REAL-WORLD CONNECTION: ALASKA 727

Study Guide: Preview 696
Reading and Writing Math 697
Game Time: Try Angles 728
It's in the Bag! Picture Envelopes 729
Study Guide: Review 730
Chapter Test 733

Focal Points

6.FP.3: Algebra
See pp. C2–C3 for text.

Tools for Success

Reading and Writing Math
Reading Math 707
Writing Math 701, 705, 717, 721, 725
Vocabulary 698, 702, 706, 718

Study Skills
Know-It Notebook Chapter 13
Study Strategy 697
Homework Help Online 700, 704, 708, 716, 720, 724
Student Help 698, 706, 714, 715, 722

Test Prep
Test Prep and Spiral Review 701, 705, 709, 717, 721, 725
Test Tackler 734
Standardized Test Prep 736

Virginia Mathematics Standards of Learning
Grade Six

Number and Number Sense
Focus: Relationships among Fractions, Decimals, and Percents

Themes
1. Ratios
2. Equivalent Forms of Numbers
3. Comparing and Ordering
4. Integers
5. Absolute Value
6. Fractions
7. Exponents
8. Perfect Squares

What It Means To You

In the study of mathematics, understanding the relationships and properties of numbers is essential and provides a solid foundation in mathematical thinking and reasoning. To develop number sense means to build an intuitive understanding for numbers and their uses. This includes relationships among numbers and how basic operations change numbers. A solid grasp of number sense also includes the ability to manipulate numbers and expressions for a particular situation.

6.1 The student will describe and compare data, using ratios, and will use appropriate notations, such as $\frac{a}{b}$, a to b, and a:b.

6.2a The student will investigate and describe fractions, decimals, and percents as ratios.

6.2b The student will identify a given fraction, decimal, or percent from a representation.

6.2c The student will demonstrate equivalent relationships among fractions, decimals, and percents.

6.2d The student will compare and order fractions, decimals, and percents.

6.3a The student will identify and represent integers.

6.3b The student will order and compare integers.

6.3c The student will identify and describe absolute value of integers.

6.4 The student will demonstrate multiple representations of multiplication and division of fractions.

6.5 The student will investigate and describe concepts of positive exponents and perfect squares.

Virginia

Computation and Estimation
Focus: Applications of Operations with Rational Numbers

Themes
1. Fractions and Mixed Numbers
2. Decimals
3. Estimation Strategies
4. Evaluating Numerical Expressions
5. Computation
6. Order of Operations

What It Means To You

Estimation is an integral part of mastering mental math skills. Being comfortable and confident to estimate solutions involving mathematical situations results in faster and more efficient problem solving. Strong estimation skills are also pivotal in checking computations, for evaluating reasonableness, and verifying accuracy.

6.6a The student will multiply and divide fractions and mixed numbers.

6.6b The student will estimate solutions and then solve single-step and multistep practical problems involving addition, subtraction, multiplication, and division of fractions.

6.7 The student will solve single-step and multistep practical problems involving addition, subtraction, multiplication, and division of decimals.

6.8 The student will evaluate whole number numerical expressions, using the order of operations.

Measurement
Focus: Problem Solving with Area, Perimeter, Volume, and Surface Area

Themes
1. Comparing Measurement Systems
2. Properties of Circles
3. Area and Perimeter
4. Volume and Surface Area

What It Means To You

Measurement is the assignment of a numeric value and appropriate unit to an attribute of a figure or object. Measurement also involves aspects of geometry, including knowledge of geometric properties, unit recognition and analysis, and computation using properties and units. Measurement is used daily in many aspects of life, from grocery shopping to buying a house, and paying for utilities; its extent is endless. Therefore, an appreciation for measurement further enhances the development of number sense and the acquisition of mathematical skills.

6.9 The student will make ballpark comparisons between measurements in the U.S. Customary System of measurement and measurements in the metric system.

6.10a The student will define π (pi) as the ratio of the circumference of a circle to its diameter.

6.10b The student will solve practical problems involving circumference and area of a circle, given the diameter or radius.

6.10c The student will solve practical problems involving area and perimeter.

6.10d The student will describe and determine the volume and surface area of a rectangular prism.

Geometry
Focus: Properties and Relationships

Themes
1. The Coordinate Plane
2. Ordered Pairs
3. Congruence
4. Properties of Quadrilaterals

What It Means To You

Geometry is a branch of mathematics that focuses on the relationship among geometric properties, measurement, and geometric figures. Geometric figures extend from simple lines and points, including those on a coordinate grid, to the shapes of polygons and the existence of three-dimensional figures, known as solids. A coordinate grid is a functional method of assigning and determining locations. It is a useful skill that is transferred to the understanding of maps and global positioning systems (GPS).

6.11a The student will identify the coordinates of a point in a coordinate plane.

6.11b The student will graph ordered pairs in a coordinate plane.

6.12 The student will determine congruence of segments, angles, and polygons.

6.13 The student will describe and identify properties of quadrilaterals.

Virginia

Probability and Statistics
Focus: Practical Applications of Statistics

Themes
1. Circle Graphs
2. Comparing and Contrasting Data Displays
3. Measures of Central Tendency
4. Dependent and Independent Events
5. Probability

What It Means To You
Probability and statistics is the study of events, populations, samples, and data collected from various sources. Probability is a ratio used to describe the likelihood that an event will occur. Statistics are numbers that are used to describe populations and are often displayed in graphs and other types of visual displays. Probabilities and statistics are utilized in both work and life as individuals and companies analyze data of past performances to make predictions for the future.

6.14a The student, given a problem situation, will construct circle graphs.

6.14b The student, given a problem situation, will draw conclusions and make predictions, using circle graphs.

6.14c The student, given a problem situation, will compare and contrast graphs that present information from the same data set.

6.15a The student will describe mean as balance point.

6.15b The student will decide which measure of center is appropriate for a given purpose.

6.16a The student will compare and contrast dependent and independent events.

6.16b The student will determine probabilities for dependent and independent events.

Virginia Grade Six Mathematics Standards

Patterns, Functions, and Algebra
Focus: Variable Equations and Properties

Themes
1. Geometric and Arithmetic Sequences
2. Solving Linear Equations
3. Identity Properties
4. Multiplicative Property of Zero
5. Inverse Property for Multiplication
6. Graphing Inequalities

What It Means To You

Algebra is the branch of mathematics where symbols or variables are used to represent unknown values and equations are written and solved for generalized situations. Algebra examines the relationships between quantities and relationships that vary. The use of algebra is widely used in professional fields from carpentry to engineering.

6.17 The student will identify and extend geometric and arithmetic sequences.

6.18 The student will solve one-step linear equations in one variable involving whole number coefficients and positive rational solutions.

6.19a The student will investigate and recognize the identity properties for addition and multiplication.

6.19b The student will investigate and recognize the multiplicative property of zero.

6.19c The student will investigate and recognize the inverse property for multiplication.

6.20 The student will graph inequalities on a number line.

Countdown to SOL

WEEK 1

DAY 1

Each week, Yoshio adds some baseball cards to his collection. The table shows the number of cards in his collection. Assuming the pattern continues, in which week will he have 150 cards in his collection?

Week	1	2	3	4
Number of Cards	15	30	45	60

A 10
B 15
C 20
D 75

6.17

DAY 2

What is the value of the expression $3 \times 4 + 5 \times 7$?

F 47
G 56
H 68
J 119

6.8

DAY 3

What is the value of the expression $9^2 - 45 \div 9$?

A 4
B 12
C 76
D 105

6.8

DAY 4

Jerome uses metal strips to make rectangular frames that are 8 inches long and 4 inches wide. What is the total length of the metal needed to make 5 frames?

F 17 inches
G 60 inches
H 120 inches
J 160 inches

6.10c

DAY 5

In a school auditorium, the first row has 15 seats. The second row has 18 seats, the third row has 21 seats, and the fourth row has 24 seats. Suppose the pattern continues. How many seats are in the sixth row?

A 27
B 30
C 33
D 36

6.17

VA20 Countdown to SOL

Countdown to SOL

WEEK 2

DAY 1

A marching band has 8 musicians in the first row, 11 musicians in the second row, and 14 musicians in the third row. Assuming the pattern continues, how many musicians are in the seventh row?

A 17
B 23
C 26
D 56

6.17

DAY 2

The table shows the number of passengers that traveled through four airports in 2007. Which of the airports had the fewest passengers in 2007?

Airport Statistics, 2007	
Airport	Number of Passengers
Detroit Metropolitan	36,126,555
London Gatwick	35,218,399
Narita International	35,530,035
Singapore Changi	36,701,556

F Detroit Metropolitan
G London Gatwick
H Narita International
J Singapore Changi

6.3b

DAY 3

If the pattern below continues, what will be the 7th term?

$$16, 8, 4, 2, \frac{1}{2}, \ldots$$

A 2
B $\frac{1}{4}$
C $\frac{1}{8}$
D $\frac{1}{16}$

6.17

DAY 4

Jill drew a diagram of her room. What is the area of Jill's room?

F 18 square feet
G 36 square feet
H 40 square feet
J 80 square feet

8 ft
10 ft

6.10c

DAY 5

Which of the following numbers is NOT a perfect square?

A 25
B 38
C 49
D 64

6.5

Countdown to SOL — WEEK 3

DAY 1

Which of the following describes the relationship between the numbers in this sequence?

$$\frac{1}{2}, \frac{1}{4}, \frac{1}{8}, \frac{1}{16}, \ldots$$

A Each number is twice the number before it.

B Each number is two more than the number before it.

C Each number is one-half the number before it.

D Each number is two less than the number before it.

6.17

DAY 2

A supermarket has a display of stacked soup cans. Starting at the bottom, the first row has 25 cans, the second row has 23 cans, and the third row has 21 cans. Assuming the pattern continues, how many cans are in the 11th row?

F 3
G 5
H 7
J 9

6.17

DAY 3

The distance around Amy's pool is 398 feet. The width w of the pool is 41 feet. Which is the best estimate for the length ℓ of the pool?

A 10 feet
B 160 feet
C 320 feet
D 360 feet

6.10c

DAY 4

The cost for roast beef was $4.79 per pound and the cost for turkey was $5.19 per pound. Arlene bought 2.5 pounds of roast beef and 1.25 pounds of turkey. How much did Arlene pay? Round to the nearest cent.

F $9.98
G $13.73
H $15.92
J $18.46

6.7

DAY 5

Which of the following shows the decimals in order from least to greatest?

A 0.35, 0.75, 0.4, 0.8
B 0.35, 0.4, 0.75, 0.8
C 0.4, 0.8, 0.35, 0.75
D 0.8, 0.4, 0.35, 0.75

6.2d

Countdown to SOL

WEEK 4

DAY 1

Which decimal shows the ratio of shaded squares to total squares in the figure at the right?

- A 0.32
- B 0.38
- C 0.62
- D 0.68

6.2b

DAY 2

Cara wants to cover a wall with fabric. The wall is 19 feet by 49 feet. About how much fabric should Cara buy?

19 ft
49 ft

- F 450 square feet
- G 600 square feet
- H 850 square feet
- J 1000 square feet

6.10c

DAY 3

Blake works in a cheese store. The table shows how many cheese tidbits he has made at the end of each hour. If he continues at the same pace, how many tidbits will Blake have made in 6 hours?

Hours	2	3	4
Cheese Tidbits	234	351	468

- A 585
- B 702
- C 819
- D 1404

6.17

DAY 4

Keenan creates a sequence using blocks. The pattern of the sequence is shown in the table. How many blocks will he use for the fourteenth figure in the sequence?

Figure	1	2	3	4
Blocks	1	4	7	10

- F 37
- G 40
- H 42
- J 46

6.17

DAY 5

Solve the equation for x: $56 = \frac{x}{2}$.

- A 14
- B 28
- C 56
- D 112

6.18

Countdown to SOL

WEEK 5

DAY 1

Solve the equation for t: $4t = 64$.

A 16
B 32
C 60
D 256

6.18

DAY 2

A serving of 10 strawberries contains 0.8 gram of protein. What is the total amount of protein you consume by eating 10 strawberries on Monday, 30 strawberries on Tuesday, and 20 strawberries on Wednesday?

F 0.8 gram
G 2.4 grams
H 4.8 grams
J 8 grams

6.7

DAY 3

Kris has four pet turtles. Last week he measured the length of each turtle. What is the order of the turtles from shortest to longest?

A Carly, Patty, Bennie, Charley
B Patty, Bennie, Charley, Carly
C Patty, Carly, Bennie, Charley
D Bennie, Patty, Carly, Charley

Turtle	Length (in.)
Bennie	5.67
Charley	5.75
Patty	5.07
Carly	5.5

6.2d

DAY 4

Kim made this flag. What is the area of the shaded region of her flag?

6 cm
10 cm   10 cm
16 cm

F 25 square centimeters
G 50 square centimeters
H 110 square centimeters
J 160 square centimeters

6.10c

DAY 5

There are 9^3 species of birds and 4^4 species of mammals at a local zoo. How many more species of birds are there than species of mammals?

A 11
B 65
C 473
D 713

6.5

VA24   Countdown to SOL

Countdown to SOL

WEEK 6

DAY 1

The table shows the lengths of several hiking trails at Olympic National Park in Washington. The Chavez family hikes the three shortest trails. What is the total distance they hike?

A 3.45 miles
B 3.55 miles
C 3.7 miles
D 4.6 miles

Trails at Olympic National Park	
Trail	Length (mi)
Terrace Loop	1.5
Second Beach	0.8
Mt. Storm King	1.7
Third Beach	1.4
Spruce Nature	1.25

6.7

DAY 2

The table shows the number of students in four different classes at Park Street Middle School who take the bus to school. Which class has the greatest fraction of students who take the bus to school?

Class	A	B	C	D
Students Who Take Bus	$\frac{15}{20}$	$\frac{20}{25}$	$\frac{12}{18}$	$\frac{12}{24}$

F Class A
G Class B
H Class C
J Class D

6.2d

DAY 3

If Sarah wants to buy a dozen roses and two dozen irises, how much will she spend?

Flower prices (dozen)	
Roses	$15.99
Irises	$6.75

A $9.24
B $22.74
C $29.49
D $31.98

6.7

DAY 4

Which expression has the greatest value?

F $4^2 + 4 \times 2 - 1$
G $(4^2 + 4) \times 2 - 1$
H $4^2 + (4 \times 2) - 1$
J $4^2 + 4 \times (2 - 1)$

6.8

DAY 5

At a frozen yogurt shop, $\frac{1}{5}$ of the yogurts sold on Monday were peach yogurts. What decimal of the yogurts sold on Monday were peach?

A 0.15
B 0.2
C 0.5
D 0.95

6.2c

Countdown to SOL

WEEK 7

DAY 1

Kendra shades additional squares in the figure so that 30% of the figure is shaded. How many additional squares does she shade?

A 1
B 2
C 4
D 6

6.2b

DAY 2

Michael bought art supplies for his painting class. He spent $3.98 on a brush, $20.08 on paints, $10.49 on paint thinner, and $17.47 for some canvas. How much did Michael spend on art supplies?

F $48.62
G $50.09
H $52.02
J $52.74

6.7

DAY 3

Which shows the expanded form of 5^3?

A 3×5
B $3 \times 3 \times 3 \times 3 \times 3$
C 5×3
D $5 \times 5 \times 5$

6.5

DAY 4

Which statement is NOT correct?

F $0.2 = \frac{1}{5}$
G $0.54 = \frac{27}{50}$
H $0.67 = \frac{6}{7}$
J $0.85 = \frac{17}{20}$

6.2c

DAY 5

The table shows the distances Margo walked during one week. How many miles did she walk in all?

A 2.71
B 2.79
C 3.37
D 3.42

Day	M	T	W	Th	F
Distance Walked (mi)	0.725	0.7	0.62	0.665	0.71

6.7

VA26 Countdown to SOL

Countdown to SOL

WEEK 8

DAY 1

Use the table of Andrea's chores. How much time does it take Andrea to complete all three chores?

Andrea's Chores	
Chore	Time (hours)
Mow lawn	1.35
Do dishes	0.25
Clean room	0.9

A 1.6 hours
B 1.7 hours
C 2.5 hours
D 2.6 hours

6.7

DAY 2

To make biscuits, Lilly needs 16.45 ounces of butter. She needs 9.7 ounces of butter to make muffins. How much more butter does Lilly need for the biscuits than she needs for the muffins?

F 6.75 ounces
G 7.38 ounces
H 16.35 ounces
J 26.15 ounces

6.7

DAY 3

Eric's science class grew plants from bean seeds. The table shows how much each student's plant grew in two weeks. Put the plants in order from least change to greatest change.

A $\frac{1}{2}, \frac{5}{12}, \frac{3}{16}, \frac{1}{8}, \frac{4}{5}$

B $\frac{1}{8}, \frac{3}{16}, \frac{5}{12}, \frac{1}{2}, \frac{4}{5}$

C $\frac{1}{2}, \frac{4}{5}, \frac{1}{8}, \frac{5}{12}, \frac{3}{16}$

D $\frac{1}{8}, \frac{1}{2}, \frac{3}{16}, \frac{4}{5}, \frac{5}{12}$

Student	Miguel	Eric	Jane	Trisha	Cindy
Plant Heights (in.)	$\frac{1}{2}$	$\frac{5}{12}$	$\frac{3}{16}$	$\frac{1}{8}$	$\frac{4}{5}$

6.2d

DAY 4

Solve the equation for a: $a - 16 = 48$.

F 3
G 32
H 64
J 768

6.18

DAY 5

A geologist has four rock samples whose masses are 1.2 kilograms, 1.48 kilograms, 1.55 kilograms, and 1.6 kilograms. She needs a sample whose mass is as close as possible to $1\frac{1}{2}$ kilograms. Which sample should she use?

A 1.2 kilograms
B 1.48 kilograms
C 1.55 kilograms
D 1.6 kilograms

6.2d

Countdown to SOL — WEEK 9

DAY 1

The table shows the amount of water needed to cook $\frac{1}{6}$ cup of several different grains. Which grain requires the greatest amount of water?

A Buckwheat
B Millet
C Oats
D Wild Rice

Cooking Instructions	
Grain	Amount of Water
Buckwheat	$\frac{1}{3}$ cup
Millet	$\frac{5}{12}$ cup
Oats	$\frac{2}{3}$ cup
Wild Rice	$\frac{1}{2}$ cup

6.2d

DAY 2

How many feet of wood molding would Jeremy need to trim all the walls of his bedroom?

16 ft | Bedroom
20 ft

F 4 feet
G 32 feet
H 72 feet
J 320 feet

6.10c

DAY 3

What multiplication expression does the model at the right represent?

A $\frac{1}{3} \times \frac{1}{2}$
B $\frac{2}{3} \times \frac{1}{2}$
C $\frac{1}{2} \times \frac{1}{2}$
D $\frac{2}{3} \times \frac{1}{3}$

6.4

DAY 4

What is the value of the expression $58 - [16 + (5 - 2^2)]$?

F 33
G 41
H 43
J 51

6.8

DAY 5

It takes $1\frac{3}{4}$ cups of sauce to make one pizza. How many cups of sauce are needed to make $5\frac{1}{2}$ pizzas?

A $5\frac{3}{8}$ cups
B $7\frac{1}{4}$ cups
C $9\frac{5}{8}$ cups
D $12\frac{5}{6}$ cups

6.6a

Countdown to SOL

WEEK 10

DAY 1

Mr. Reyes wants to fence in the area behind his house. How many meters of fencing does he need to buy?

30.75 m
20.5 m
House

A 51.25
B 71.75
C 102.5
D 630.38

6.10c

DAY 2

The table shows the results of a survey of 40 people who were asked to choose their favorite fruit. Which ratio shows the number of people who named strawberry to the total number of people surveyed?

Fruit	Number of People
Apple	18
Orange	10
Strawberry	12

F $\frac{1}{4}$ H $\frac{9}{20}$

G $\frac{3}{10}$ J $\frac{11}{20}$

6.1

DAY 3

Which property is demonstrated by the statement below?

$-12 \times 1 = -12$

A Identity Property for Addition
B Identity Property for Multiplication
C Multiplicative Property of Zero
D Inverse Property of Multiplication

6.19a

DAY 4

Angelo has $\frac{7}{8}$ pound of cherries. He wants to divide the cherries into bags that each weigh $\frac{3}{10}$ pound. What expression can he use to find how many bags he will need?

F $\frac{3}{10} \div \frac{7}{8}$

G $\frac{3}{10} \times \frac{7}{8}$

H $\frac{7}{8} \div \frac{10}{3}$

J $\frac{7}{8} \div \frac{3}{10}$

6.4

DAY 5

An orange contains $2\frac{1}{2}$ grams of fiber. Each day, Ricardo eats an orange at breakfast and another orange as an afternoon snack. How many grams of fiber does Ricardo get from eating oranges each week?

A $2\frac{1}{2}$ grams
B $7\frac{1}{2}$ grams
C $17\frac{1}{2}$ grams
D 35 grams

6.6a

Countdown to SOL

WEEK 11

DAY 1

Ryan is making $7\frac{1}{2}$ cups of rice to serve at dinner with his friends. If he wants to give $\frac{3}{4}$ cup of rice to each guest, how many people will the rice serve?

A 8
B 10
C 12
D 14

6.6a

DAY 2

If a car is traveling at a speed of 48 miles per hour, how far can it travel in $1\frac{7}{8}$ hours?

F 50 miles
G 80 miles
H 90 miles
J 100 miles

6.6a

DAY 3

Dante recorded the following information about a seedling's growth for science class. How many inches did the seedling grow in three weeks?

A $1\frac{1}{6}$ inches
B $1\frac{17}{24}$ inches
C 2 inches
D 48 inches

Week	1	2	3
Inches Grown	$\frac{7}{8}$	$\frac{5}{6}$	$\frac{7}{24}$

6.6b

DAY 4

Graciela has a piece of clay that weighs $12\frac{1}{2}$ pounds. She divides the clay into 5 equal pieces. What is the weight of 3 of the pieces?

F $2\frac{1}{5}$ pounds
G $4\frac{1}{6}$ pounds
H $7\frac{1}{2}$ pounds
J $8\frac{3}{5}$ pounds

6.6a

DAY 5

The price of a meal came to $12 without a tip. What is the best estimate of the total cost of the meal plus a tip that is $\frac{1}{5}$ the amount of the meal?

A $10
B $12
C $15
D $20

6.6b

Countdown to SOL

WEEK 12

DAY 1

A hot-air balloon rises at 42.1 feet per minute. It descends at twice the rate that it rises. If it descends at a constant rate, how many feet will the hot-air balloon descend in 20 minutes?

A 842 feet
C 2105 feet
B 1684 feet
D 4210 feet

6.7

DAY 2

Trevor has a piece of yarn that is $6\frac{2}{3}$ feet long. He cuts off pieces that are $1\frac{3}{4}$ feet long. What is the maximum number of such pieces he can cut from the yarn?

F 3
G 4
H 5
J 6

6.6a

DAY 3

Janika surveyed her class to find out what kind of pets they owned. She placed her results in two graphs, shown below.

Which statement is NOT true?

A The circle graph shows the percent of students that own each type of pet.

B The bar graph shows the number of students that own each type of pet.

C The height of the bar in the bar graph is equal to the percent shown in the circle graph.

D More students owned dogs than any other pet.

Types of Pets (circle graph)
- Other 7%
- Fish 14%
- Snake 9%
- Rodent 18%
- Dog 29%
- Cat 23%

Types of Pets (bar graph: Number of Students vs Pet)

6.14c

DAY 4

Which property is demonstrated by the statement below?

$49 + 0 = 49$

F Identity Property for Addition
G Identity Property for Multiplication
H Multiplicative Property of Zero
J Inverse Property of Multiplication

6.19a

DAY 5

Which measure is often referred to as a balance point of the data in the set it describes?

A mean
B median
C mode
D range

6.15a

Countdown to SOL

WEEK 13

DAY 1

Quinton has a piece of poster board shaped like a trapezoid. Which statement is true about the piece of poster board?

A The poster board has four congruent sides.

B The poser board has four right angles.

C The poster board has exactly one pair of parallel sides.

D The poster board has opposite sides that are parallel and congruent.

6.13

DAY 2

The lines below are intersecting lines and are not perpendicular. Which two angles are congruent?

F ∠AEB and ∠BEC

G ∠BEC and ∠AED

H ∠CED and ∠AED

J ∠BED and ∠AED

6.12

DAY 3

Bruce and Jhang conduct a science experiment where they measure the temperature of a solution every minute as it boils. Their results show that the temperature of the solution decreases as the time increases. They decide to put their results in a data display. Which statement should they consider when choosing their graph?

A A stem-and-leaf plot would group the temperatures in intervals.

B A circle graph would show the percent of minutes the temperature was unchanged.

C A bar graph would show the type of solution and the maximum temperature it reached.

D A line graph would show the temperature changes over time.

6.14c

DAY 4

Sandy bought 2.75 liters of cranberry juice, 3.5 liters of pineapple juice, and 4.2 liters of orange juice two make punch. How much punch will this make?

F 3.52 liters

G 9.45 liters

H 7.7 liters

J 10.45 liters

6.7

DAY 5

In a frog-jumping contest, Ben's frog jumped 20.75 centimeters in one hop. Billy's frog jumped 24.09 centimeters in one hop. How much farther did Billy's frog jump than Ben's frog?

A 2.34 centimeters

B 3.34 centimeters

C 3.35 centimeters

D 4.66 centimeters

6.7

VA32 *Countdown to SOL*

Countdown to SOL

WEEK 14

DAY 1

Rectangles *ABCD* and *EFGH* are congruent. What is the length of $\overline{GH}$?

```
A   12 cm   B        E          F
┌────────────┐       ┌──────────┐
│        4 cm│       │          │
└────────────┘       └──────────┘
D            C        H          G
```

- **A** 4 cm
- **B** 8 cm
- **C** 12 cm
- **D** 24 cm

6.12

DAY 2

A regular hexagon was divided into two congruent quadrilaterals. Which type of quadrilateral was formed?

- **F** square
- **G** rectangle
- **H** trapezoid
- **J** parallelogram

6.13

DAY 3

Malcolm made 6 liters of lemonade for his sister's birthday party. About how many gallons of lemonade did he make?

- **A** 1
- **B** $1\frac{1}{2}$
- **C** 2
- **D** $2\frac{1}{2}$

6.9

DAY 4

The ratio of girls to boys at a summer camp is $\frac{2}{3}$. What is the ratio of girls to students?

- **F** $\frac{3}{5}$
- **G** $\frac{2}{5}$
- **H** $\frac{5}{3}$
- **J** $\frac{5}{2}$

6.2a

DAY 5

Terri runs about 3 miles a day. About how many kilometers is this?

- **A** 8
- **B** 5
- **C** 3
- **D** 2

6.9

Countdown to SOL

WEEK 15

DAY 1

Which point on the number line represents −41?

(Number line with points A at −43, B at −41, C at −39, D at −38; labels −44, −42, −40, −38, −36)

- A A
- B B
- C C
- D D

6.3a

DAY 2

What does point R on the number line represent?

(Number line with R between −5 and 0; labels −5, 0, 5)

- F −5
- G −2
- H 2
- J 5

6.3a

DAY 3

The table shows how much a seedling grew each day for five days. On which days did the seedling grow less than $\frac{3}{4}$ in.?

- A Monday and Friday
- B Tuesday and Wednesday
- C Wednesday and Thursday
- D Thursday and Friday

Day	M	T	W	Th	F
Growth (in.)	$\frac{4}{5}$	$\frac{5}{6}$	$\frac{7}{10}$	$\frac{5}{8}$	$\frac{4}{5}$

6.2d

DAY 4

Jonathan bought a video game for $39.99 and a CD for $19.49. He had a coupon for $\frac{1}{10}$ off the total price. About how much did Jonathan pay for the video game and CD?

- F $6
- G $54
- H $60
- J $66

6.6b

DAY 5

What is the value of |−5|?

- A −5
- B −3
- C 3
- D 5

6.3c

VA34   Countdown to SOL

Countdown to SOL

WEEK 16

DAY 1

The figure shows a pattern of tiles on the top of a table. Jared writes the ratio of black tiles to white tiles as *n*:6. What is the value of *n*?

A 1
B 2
C 3
D 12

6.1

DAY 2

Which describes |–11|?

F –11 is 11 units from its opposite on a number line.
G –11 is 22 units from 0 on a number line.
H –11 is to the right of 0 on a number line.
J –11 is 11 units from 0 on a number line.

6.3c

DAY 3

A canal boat went through a series of locks with the following rises and drops. A positive number shows a rise. A negative number shows a drop. At which lock was there the greatest rise?

Lock	1	2	3	4
Rise or Fall (ft)	–17	11	–8	6

A 1
B 2
C 3
D 4

6.3b

DAY 4

While making jewelry, Carolyn cuts out 12 pieces of metal in the shape below. What is the total area of the metal needed to make the shapes?

6 mm
4 mm
12 mm

F 216 square millimeters
G 432 square millimeters
H 576 square millimeters
J 864 square millimeters

6.10c

DAY 5

Carrie is designing a mosaic wall for her school's library. The wall measures 4 meters by 8 meters. The tiles she is using are 10 centimeters by 10 centimeters. If the tiles come 600 to a package, how many packages will Carrie need to cover the wall?

A 4
B 5
C 6
D 7

6.10c

Countdown to SOL   VA35

Countdown to SOL — WEEK 17

DAY 1

A rope is 17 feet long. Natasha cuts the rope into pieces that are each $1\frac{3}{8}$ feet long. What is the maximum number of such pieces that she can cut from the rope?

A 9
B 12
C 13
D 15

6.6a

DAY 2

Kenny is building a compost bin. What is the best estimate of the volume of the bin?

Dimensions: $4\frac{2}{3}$ ft, $2\frac{2}{5}$ ft, $3\frac{5}{8}$ ft

F 11 cubic feet
G 24 cubic feet
H 40 cubic feet
J 60 cubic feet

6.6b

DAY 3

Louis received the scores shown in the table on his English quizzes this semester. Which description of this data set would make Louis' results look best?

A the mean of his scores
B the median of his scores
C the mode of his scores
D the range of his scores

Quiz	Score
Poetry	95
Hamlet	95
Great Gatsby	80
Tale of Two Cities	70
Sherlock Holmes	60

6.15b

DAY 4

Rosa walked on a nature trail that was 3.25 miles long. She took a photo at the beginning and end of the trail and every 0.25 mile along the way. How many photos did she take?

F 4
G 12
H 13
J 14

6.7

DAY 5

Which is greatest for this set of data—the mean, median, mode, or range?

(Line plot: value 1 has 2 X's; value 2 has 3 X's; value 3 has 2 X's; value 4 has 2 X's)

A mean
B median
C mode
D range

6.15b

VA36 Countdown to SOL

Countdown to SOL

WEEK 18

DAY 1

A student added a point P to the figure. Then she connected the four points and formed a rectangle. What are the coordinates of point P?

A (−1, 4)

B (1, 4)

C (2, 4)

D (4, 4)

6.11a

DAY 2

Alex kept track of the number of telemarketing calls he received each month for 6 months.

   14, 10, 17, 12, 11, 15

Which of the following would NOT change if Alex decided to add the data value 11 for a seventh month?

F median

G range

H mode

J mean

6.15b

DAY 3

The figure shows the dimensions of a circular fountain. A bug crawls around the circumference of the fountain at a rate of 2 feet per minute. About how long does it take the bug to go once around the fountain?

A 13 minutes

B 25 minutes

C 50 minutes

D 100 minutes

8 ft

6.10b

DAY 4

In Alfred's drawer of shirts, there are 3 striped shirts, 5 solid-colored shirts, and 2 plaid shirts. What is the probability that Alfred will choose a solid-colored shirt and then a striped shirt without putting the first shirt back?

F $\frac{1}{6}$

G $\frac{1}{10}$

H $\frac{1}{18}$

J $\frac{1}{90}$

6.16b

DAY 5

A bag contains 20 red marbles, 16 blue marbles, and 14 yellow marbles. Jacob chooses a marble from the bag without looking. What is the probability that he chooses a red marble?

A 20%

B 28%

C 40%

D 60%

6.16b

Countdown to SOL   VA37

Countdown to SOL

WEEK 19

DAY 1

In Derek's class, 18 of the 25 students belong to an after-school club. Which of the following describes the ratio of students not in an after-school club to students in an after-school club?

A $\frac{7}{18}$

B 18 to 25

C 25:18

D $\frac{7}{25}$

6.1

DAY 2

The radius of a circle is 18 inches. A snail crawls along the circumference of the circle at a rate of 3 inches per minute. About how long does it take the snail to make the trip?

F 19 minutes

G 38 minutes

H 57 minutes

J 76 minutes

6.10b

DAY 3

The picture shows the shirts Teresa owns. What is the ratio of red shirts to blue shirts?

A 3 to 9   C 6 to 3

B 9 to 6   D 6 to 9

6.1

DAY 4

Jorge recorded the following information while studying the effects of sunlight on plant growth. Which plant grew the most?

Plant	1	2	3	4
Change in Height (cm)	1	−3	−2	3

F 1   H 3

G 2   J 4

6.3b

DAY 5

A fountain is a circle with a diameter of 80 ft. For a ceremony, candles are placed approximately every 25 ft around the edge of the fountain. How many candles are needed?

A 5

B 10

C 20

D 200

6.10b

Countdown to SOL

WEEK 20

DAY 1

Which best describes the definition of pi (π)?

A the ratio of the circumference of a circle to its radius

B the ratio of the circumference of a circle to its diameter

C the ratio of the area of a circle to its radius

D the ratio of the area of a circle to its diameter

6.10a

DAY 2

A chandelier uses three different sizes of bulbs. Each bulb has a diameter that is twice as large as the previous one. What is the diameter of the largest bulb?

C = 6.28 in.   1x   2x   4x

F 2 inches

G 3.14 inches

H 8 inches

J 12.56 inches

6.10b

DAY 3

In Katie's class, 65% of the students have a pet. What fraction of the class does NOT have a pet?

A $\frac{7}{50}$

B $\frac{7}{20}$

C $\frac{1}{2}$

D $\frac{13}{20}$

6.2a

DAY 4

The width of a rectangle is 75% of the length. The length of the rectangle is 12 feet. What is the perimeter of the rectangle?

F 9 feet

G 21 feet

H 42 feet

J 108 feet

6.10c

DAY 5

Christina wants to paint a circle with a radius of 4 feet on her bedroom wall. If 1 can of paint covers 26 square feet, how many cans of paint will Christina need to buy?

4 ft

A 1   B 2.   C 3   D 4

6.10b

Countdown to SOL

WEEK 21

DAY 1

Paola drew a circle with four congruent circles inside it. If the area of the large circle is 167.2 square meters, what is the area of one small circle?

- A 5.65 square meters
- B 10.46 square meters
- C 18.54 square meters
- D 41.83 square meters

6.10b

DAY 2

The triangles shown here are congruent. What is the perimeter of △MNP?

(Triangle BCD with BD = 10 m, CD = 8 m; Triangle PMN with MN = 6 m)

- F 6 meters
- G 14 meters
- H 18 meters
- J 24 meters

6.10c

DAY 3

Brianna is making a circular patio in her back yard. She wants the diameter of the patio to be 6 feet. She is paying $9.75 per square foot for the concrete to be poured. How much will it cost for the concrete to be poured? Round to the nearest 10 dollars.

- A $100
- B $180
- C $280
- D $370

6.10c

DAY 4

Alicia has a bag of 26 unique letter tiles labeled A through Z. She randomly chooses a letter from the bag. It is the letter T. She then chooses a second letter tile without putting the first tile back. Which statement below is NOT true?

- F The probability of picking the B on the second draw is $\frac{1}{25}$.
- G The probability of picking the T on the second draw is 0.
- H Picking the two tiles, one at a time without replacement, are independent events.
- J Picking the two tiles, one at a time without replacement, are dependent events.

6.16a

DAY 5

Mark wants to frame a painting. If the painting is 2.75 feet by 4.25 feet, what is the best estimate for the number of feet of wood Mark will need?

- A 7 feet
- B 12 feet
- C 14 feet
- D 16 feet

6.7

Countdown to SOL — WEEK 22

DAY 1

An artist uses wood to make this circle. Approximately how much wood is needed to make the circle?

6 in.

A 6 square inches
B 9 square inches
C 19 square inches
D 28 square inches

6.10b

DAY 2

A box of crackers is a rectangular prism with a volume of 128 cubic inches. The length of the box is 8 inches and the width is 4 inches. What is the height of the box?

F 2 inches
G 4 inches
H 8 inches
J 16 inches

6.10d

DAY 3

Nico is setting up a probability experiment using dependent events. What option below should he choose?

A Pick a marble from a bag, replace it, and then pick another.
B Flip a coin twice.
C Spin a spinner and roll a 6-sided number cube.
D Choose a name from a hat, and do not replace it before choosing another name.

6.16a

DAY 4

Jose plots the points A, B, C, and D as shown and connects them to form a square. Then he moves the square one unit to the right. Which of these is NOT a point on the square after it is moved?

F (6, 5)
G (6, 7)
H (7, 6)
J (8, 5)

6.11b

DAY 5

Which location has an ordered pair of the form (a, a), for some number a?

A Bank
B Library
C City Hall
D Theater

6.11b

Countdown to SOL

WEEK 23

DAY 1

Each card in a set of 12 cards is marked with the letter *A* or *B*. When you choose a card at random, the probability of choosing a card marked *A* is $\frac{2}{3}$. How many cards are marked *A*?

- **A** 4
- **B** 6
- **C** 8
- **D** 9

6.16b

DAY 2

Randy was helping his brother study his multiplication facts, when he noticed that whenever a number is multiplied by zero, the product was zero. What property does this demonstrate?

- **F** Identity Property for Addition
- **G** Identity Property for Multiplication
- **H** Multiplicative Property of Zero
- **J** Distributive Property

6.19b

DAY 3

What inequality is graphed on the number line?

←|—⊙—|—|—|—|—|—|—|—|—|→
−5 −4 −3 −2 −1 0 1 2 3 4 5

- **A** $2x < -8$
- **B** $2x \leq -8$
- **C** $2x \geq -8$
- **D** $2x > -8$

6.20

DAY 4

A blue plate has a radius of 1.74 centimeters. A red plate has a radius that is twice as long as the blue plate. What is the diameter of the red plate?

- **F** 0.87 centimeter
- **G** 3.48 centimeters
- **H** 6.96 centimeters
- **J** 13.92 centimeters

6.7

DAY 5

Which property is demonstrated with the equation $\frac{3}{4} \times \frac{4}{3} = 1$?

- **A** Associative Property of Multiplication
- **B** Distributive Property
- **C** Inverse Property of Multiplication
- **D** Identity Property for Multiplication

6.19c

Countdown to SOL

WEEK 24

DAY 1

Sandra surveyed 50 of her classmates to find a favorite type of food in the cafeteria. She found that 15 of her classmates like pizza best. What should be the angle measure for the section of a circle graph labeled *pizza*?

A 15°
B 30°
C 33°
D 108°

6.14a

DAY 2

A grocery store manager surveyed every fifth customer to see what items customers would like to have available in the store. If 48 of the 120 customers surveyed would like to see organic produce available, what percent should the *organics* section be labeled in a circle graph?

F 5%
G 40%
H 48%
J 144%

6.14a

DAY 3

A group of students were asked to name their main after-school activity. The results are shown in the graph. If 12 students named soccer as their main after-school activity, how many students were surveyed?

A 24
B 36
C 48
D 60

Main After-School Activities
Guitar Lessons 15%
Chores 40%
Soccer 20%
Library 25%

6.14b

DAY 4

Ted wants to make a small fountain in his garden. The diagram shows the dimensions of the fountain. How much water will Ted need to fill the fountain?

3 ft, 5 ft, 8 ft

F 18 cubic feet
G 40 cubic feet
H 80 cubic feet
J 120 cubic feet

6.10d

DAY 5

On a winter day, the temperature rose 6°F between 1 pm and 5 pm. Then the temperature dropped 8°F between 5 pm and 8 pm. The temperature at 8 pm was −5°F. What was the temperature at 1 pm?

A −7°F
B −3°F
C 1°F
D 9°F

6.3a

Focal Points

The National Council of Teachers of Mathematics recommends the following curriculum focal points and related connections as the most important math topics to be learned in Grade 6. You can learn more about the focal points by visiting http://www.nctm.org.

Grade 6 Curriculum Focal Points

6.FP.1: GRADE 6 FOCAL POINT 1

Number and Operations: Developing an understanding of and fluency with multiplication and division of fractions and decimals.

Students use the meanings of fractions, multiplication and division, and the inverse relationship between multiplication and division to make sense of procedures for multiplying and dividing fractions and explain why they work. They use the relationship between decimals and fractions, as well as the relationship between finite decimals and whole numbers (i.e., a finite decimal multiplied by an appropriate power of 10 is a whole number), to understand and explain the procedures for multiplying and dividing decimals. Students use common procedures to multiply and divide fractions and decimals efficiently and accurately. They multiply and divide fractions and decimals to solve problems, including multistep problems and problems involving measurement. CHAPTERS 3, 5, 9, AND 10

6.FP.2: GRADE 6 FOCAL POINT 2

Number and Operations: Connecting ratio and rate to multiplication and division.

Students use simple reasoning about multiplication and division to solve ratio and rate problems (e.g., "If 5 items cost $3.75 and all items are the same price, then I can find the cost of 12 items by first dividing $3.75 by 5 to find out how much one item costs and then multiplying the cost of a single item by 12"). By viewing equivalent ratios and rates as deriving from, and extending, pairs of rows (or columns) in the multiplication table, and by analyzing simple drawings that indicate the relative sizes of quantities, students extend whole number multiplication and division to ratios and rates. Thus, they expand the repertoire of problems that they can solve by using multiplication and division, and they build on their understanding of fractions to understand ratios. Students solve a wide variety of problems involving ratios and rates. CHAPTERS 7 AND 9

6.FP.3: GRADE 6 FOCAL POINT 3

Algebra: Writing, interpreting, and using mathematical expressions and equations.

Students write mathematical expressions and equations that correspond to given situations, they evaluate expressions, and they use expressions and formulas to solve problems. They understand that variables represent numbers whose exact values are not yet specified, and they use variables appropriately. Students understand that expressions in different forms can be equivalent, and they can rewrite an expression to represent a quantity in a different way (e.g., to make it more compact or to feature different information). Students know that the solutions of an equation are the values of the variables that make the equation true. They solve simple one-step equations by using number sense, properties of operations, and the idea of maintaining equality on both sides of an equation. They construct and analyze tables (e.g., to show quantities that are in equivalent ratios), and they use equations to describe simple relationships (such as $3x = y$) shown in a table. CHAPTERS 2, 3, 5, 7, 9, 10, AND 13

Connections to the Focal Points

● **6.FPC.4:** GRADE 6 FOCAL POINT CONNECTION 4

Number and Operations: Students' work in dividing fractions shows them that they can express the result of dividing two whole numbers as a fraction (viewed as parts of a whole). Students then extend their work in grade 5 with division of whole numbers to give mixed number and decimal solutions to division problems with whole numbers. They recognize that ratio tables not only derive from rows in the multiplication table but also connect with equivalent fractions. Students distinguish multiplicative comparisons from additive comparisons. CHAPTERS 3, 4, 5, AND 7

● **6.FPC.5:** GRADE 6 FOCAL POINT CONNECTION 5

Algebra: Students use the commutative, associative, and distributive properties to show that two expressions are equivalent. They also illustrate properties of operations by showing that two expressions are equivalent in a given context (e.g., determining the area in two different ways for a rectangle whose dimensions are x + 3 by 5). Sequences, including those that arise in the context of finding possible rules for patterns of figures or stacks of objects, provide opportunities for students to develop formulas. CHAPTERS 1 AND 8

● **6.FPC.6:** GRADE 6 FOCAL POINT CONNECTION 6

Measurement and Geometry: Problems that involve areas and volumes, calling on students to find areas or volumes from lengths or to find lengths from volumes or areas and lengths, are especially appropriate. These problems extend the students' work in grade 5 on area and volume and provide a context for applying new work with equations. CHAPTER 10

Are You Ready?
Pre-Course Test

✓ Place Value of Whole Numbers
Identify the place value of each underlined digit.
1. 6<u>4</u>,253
2. 8<u>1</u>3,479

✓ Round Whole Numbers
Round each number to the nearest hundred.
3. 8,297
4. 42,631

✓ Compare Whole Numbers
Compare. Write <, >, or =.
5. 512 ■ 521
6. 417 ■ 328

✓ Multiples
List the first four multiples of each number.
7. 9
8. 14

✓ Factors
Find all the whole-number factors of each number.
9. 20
10. 121

✓ Exponents
Find each value.
11. 3^4
12. 16^2

✓ Write and Read Decimals
Write each decimal in word form.
13. 6.29
14. 9.834

✓ Simplify Fractions
Write each fraction in simplest form.
15. $\frac{3}{15}$
16. $\frac{8}{12}$
17. $\frac{18}{30}$
18. $\frac{15}{21}$

✓ Write a Mixed Number as an Improper Fraction
Write each mixed number as an improper fraction.
19. $4\frac{2}{5}$
20. $8\frac{5}{6}$

✓ Write Equivalent Fractions
Write three equivalent fractions for each given fraction.
21. $\frac{1}{3}$
22. $\frac{2}{9}$

✓ Compare Fractions
Compare. Write >, <, or =.
23. $\frac{3}{7}$ ■ $\frac{7}{3}$
24. $\frac{2}{6}$ ■ $\frac{3}{9}$

✓ Write Fractions as Decimals
Write each fraction as a decimal.
25. $\frac{3}{4}$
26. $\frac{7}{8}$

Write Ratios

Write the ratio.

27. red squares to all squares
28. blue squares to red squares

Whole Number Operations

Add, subtract, multiply, or divide.

29. $34 + 42$
30. 28×16
31. $545 - 217$
32. $6\overline{)174}$
33. 317×25
34. $245 + 576$
35. $31\overline{)1426}$
36. $905 - 438$

Decimal Operations

Multiply.

37. 3.27×41
38. 7.4×6.3

Simplify Numerical Expressions

Simplify each expression.

39. $\frac{1}{2}(7 + 9)$
40. $2.6(4)^2$

Evaluate Expressions

Evaluate each expression for the given value of the variable.

41. $2(5 - x)$ for $x = 2.7$
42. $4y^2$ for $y = 3.1$

Solve One-Step Equations

Solve each equation.

43. $t + 4.8 = 7.0$
44. $\frac{h}{3} = 24$

Solve Proportions

Solve for n.

45. $\frac{4}{6} = \frac{n}{15}$
46. $\frac{n}{5} = \frac{21}{15}$

Graph Ordered Pairs

Graph each ordered pair.

47. $(3, 7)$
48. $(8, 1)$

Identify Polygons

Tell how many sides and angles each polygon has.

49.
50.

ADDITIONAL TOPIC A-1

Mean as a Fair Share and a Balancing Point

The mean is one way to describe or represent a data set. You learned earlier that the formula for the mean is the sum of all the items in the set divided by the number of items in the set.

To help you interpret the mean of a data set, you can think of the mean as representing a fair share. In this context, a fair share is an equal part of something being shared.

EXAMPLE 1 Mean as a Fair Share

Six members of the Science Club raised $38, $21, $56, $63, $38, and $24 through fund-raising. The money will be divided among the students and used to pay for a trip to the Science Museum. What is each student's fair share of the funds?

$$\frac{38 + 21 + 56 + 63 + 38 + 24}{6}$$

$$\frac{240}{6}$$

$$40$$

Think: The mean is the total amount raised divided by the number of students who get a share.

Each student's fair share is $40.00.

You can also think of the mean as a balancing point.

EXAMPLE 2 Mean as a Balancing Point

The greatest drop of a roller coaster is the vertical distance in feet from the top of the largest drop to the bottom of that drop. The eight greatest drops for steel roller coasters are shown in the graph. Find the mean drop of the roller coasters and explain why it represents a balancing point.

Eight Greatest Steel Roller Coaster Drops

Drop (ft): Phantom's Revenge 228, Fujiyama 230, Titan 255, Goliath 255, Millenium Force 300, Steel Dragon 2000 306, Top Thrill Dragster 400, Kingda Ka 418

$$\frac{228 + 230 + 255 + 255 + 300 + 306 + 400 + 418}{8}$$

$$\frac{2392}{8}$$

$$299$$

Use the formula for mean.

The mean drop of the roller coasters is 299 feet.

Eight Greatest Steel Roller Coaster Drops

Draw a horizontal line through all the bars on the graph at 299 feet.

Find the difference between the value represented by each bar and the value represented by the horizontal line.

$299 - 228 = 71$ $299 - 255 = 44$ $300 - 299 = 1$ $400 - 299 = 101$
$299 - 230 = 69$ $299 - 255 = 44$ $306 - 299 = 7$ $418 - 299 = 119$

Total difference below dashed line:
  $71 + 69 + 44 + 44 = 228$
Total difference above dashed line:
  $1 + 7 + 101 + 119 = 228$

The total difference below the line is equal to the total difference above the line, so the differences are balanced. This is why the mean can be thought of as a balancing point.

Exercises

Find the mean. Tell whether a fair share or a balancing point makes sense in each situation. Justify your reasoning.

1. The lengths of 5 garter snakes are given in the bar graph.

2. Kenny brought 24 mini muffins and Terica brought 12 mini muffins to share with the 18 students in their class.

3. Jamie, Katie, and April are sharing the costs of hosting a party for their coworkers. When they bought food and decorations, Jamie spent $12.78, Katie spent $29.32, and April spent $21.53.

4. The distances Jarrod ran on 6 days are given in the table.

Lengths of Garter Snakes

Snake	Length (cm)
Snake 1	46
Snake 2	49
Snake 3	57
Snake 4	63
Snake 5	75

Distances Jarrod Ran (mi)

3	5.5
3.5	6
4.5	7.5

A-1 Mean as a Fair Share and a Balancing Point

Focus on Problem Solving

The Problem Solving Process

In order to be a good problem solver, you first need a good problem-solving process. The process used in this book is detailed below.

UNDERSTAND the Problem

- **What are you asked to find?** — Restate the question in your own words.
- **What information is given?** — Identify the facts in the problem.
- **What information do you need?** — Determine which facts are needed to answer the question.
- **Is all the information given?** — Determine whether all the facts are given.
- **Is there any information given that you will not use?** — Determine which facts, if any, are unnecessary to solve the problem.

Make a PLAN

- **Have you ever solved a similar problem?** — Think about other problems like this that you successfully solved.
- **What strategy or strategies can you use?** — Determine a strategy that you can use and how you will use it.

SOLVE

- **Follow your plan.** — Show the steps in your solution. Write your answer as a complete sentence.

LOOK BACK

- **Have you answered the question?** — Be sure that you answered the question that is being asked.
- **Is your answer reasonable?** — Your answer should make sense in the context of the problem.
- **Is there another strategy you could use?** — Solving the problem using another strategy is a good way to check your work.
- **Did you learn anything while solving this problem that could help you solve similar problems in the future?** — Try to remember the problems you have solved and the strategies you used to solve them.

Using the Problem Solving Process

During summer vacation, Nicholas will visit first his cousin and then his grandmother. He will be gone for 5 weeks and 2 days, and he will spend 9 more days with his cousin than with his grandmother. How long will he stay with each family member?

UNDERSTAND the Problem

Identify the important information.
- Nicholas's visits will total 5 weeks and 2 days.
- He will spend 9 more days with his cousin than with his grandmother.

The answer will be how long he will stay with each family member.

Make a PLAN

You can draw a diagram to show how long Nicholas will stay. Use boxes for the length of each stay. The length of each box will represent the length of each stay.

SOLVE

Think: There are 7 days in a week, so 5 weeks and 2 days is 37 days in all. Your diagram might look like this:

Cousin | ? days | 9 days | = 37 days

Grandmother | ? days

Cousin | 14 days | 9 days | $37 - 9 = 28$

Grandmother | 14 days | $28 \div 2 = 14$

So Nicholas will stay with his cousin for 23 days and with his grandmother for 14 days.

LOOK BACK

Twenty-three days is 9 days longer than 14 days. The total of the two stays is 23 + 14, or 37 days, which is the same as 5 weeks and 2 days. This solution fits the description of Nicholas's trip given in the problem.

Focus on Problem Solving

Using Your Book for Success

This book has many features designed to help you learn and study math. Becoming familiar with these features will prepare you for greater success on your exams.

Learn

Before starting a chapter, read the **Study Guide: Preview** to help you understand the concepts that are taught in the chapter.

Review the **Reading and Writing Math** to learn about reading, writing, and study strategies.

Preview new **vocabulary** terms listed at the beginning of the lesson.

Look for the **Student Help** for hints, reminders, cautions, and help with reading math.

Study the **examples** to learn new math ideas and skills. The examples include step-by-step solutions.

VA52   Using Your Book for Success

Practice

Look back at examples from the lesson to help with the **Guided Practice** and **Independent Practice** exercises.

Use the Internet for **Homework Help Online**.

Complete the **Real-World Connections** to practice skills from the chapter in a real-world context.

Review

As you finish each section, test your knowledge with **practice problems** before you continue.

Review important **examples** from every lesson in the chapter.

Study and review the **vocabulary** from the entire chapter.

Test your knowledge with **practice problems**.

Using Your Book for Success **VA53**

CHAPTER 1
Whole Numbers and Patterns

1A Whole Numbers and Exponents
- 1-1 Estimating with Whole Numbers
- 1-2 Exponents

1B Using Whole Numbers
- LAB Explore the Order of Operations
- 1-3 Order of Operations
- 1-4 Properties and Mental Math
- 1-5 Choosing a Method of Computation
- 1-6 Patterns and Sequences
- LAB Find a Pattern in Sequences

Why Learn This?

Patterns are visible all around us. In nature, we see patterns in the lines formed by strata in rock formations over millions of years and exposed by erosion.

Learn It Online
Chapter Project Online go.hrw.com,
keyword MR10 Ch1

Chapter Focus
- Use properties to find equivalent expressions.
- Find possible rules for sequences.

Are You Ready?

Vocabulary

Choose the best term from the list to complete each sentence.

1. The answer in a multiplication problem is called the ___?___.
2. 5,000 + 400 + 70 + 5 is a number written in ___?___ form.
3. A(n) ___?___ tells about how many.
4. The number 70,562 is written in ___?___ form.
5. Ten thousands is the ___?___ of the 4 in 42,801.

place value
estimate
product
expanded
standard
period

Complete these exercises to review skills you will need for this chapter.

Compare Whole Numbers

Compare. Write <, >, or =.

6. 245 ■ 219
7. 5,320 ■ 5,128
8. 64 ■ 67
9. 784 ■ 792

Round Whole Numbers

Round each number to the nearest hundred.

10. 567
11. 827
12. 1,642
13. 12,852
14. 1,237
15. 135
16. 15,561
17. 452,801

Round each number to the nearest thousand.

18. 4,709
19. 3,399
20. 9,825
21. 26,419
22. 12,434
23. 4,561
24. 11,784
25. 468,201

Whole Number Operations

Add, subtract, multiply, or divide.

26. 18 × 22
27. 135 ÷ 3
28. 247 + 96
29. 358 − 29

Simplify Numerical Expressions

Simplify each expression.

30. 3 × 4 × 2
31. 20 + 100 − 40
32. 5 × 20 ÷ 4
33. 6 × 12 × 5

Whole Numbers and Patterns

Chapter 1 Study Guide: Preview

Where You've Been

Previously, you

- compared and ordered whole numbers to the hundred thousands.
- used the order of operations without exponents.
- looked for patterns.

In This Chapter

You will study

- using the order of operations, including exponents.
- how to recognize and extend sequences.
- using properties to compute whole-number operations mentally.
- representing whole numbers by using exponents.

Where You're Going

You can use the skills learned in this chapter

- to express numbers in scientific and standard notation in science classes.
- to recognize and extend geometric sequences.

Key Vocabulary/Vocabulario

Associative Property	propiedad asociativa
base	base (en numeración)
Commutative Property	propiedad conmutativa
Distributive Property	propiedad distributiva
exponent	exponente
numerical expression	expresión numérica
order of operations	orden de las operaciones
sequence	sucesión
term	término (en una sucesión)

Vocabulary Connections

To become familiar with some of the vocabulary terms in the chapter, consider the following. You may refer to the chapter, the glossary, or a dictionary if you like.

1. An *order* is the way things are arranged one after the other. How do you think an **order of operations** will help you solve math problems?

2. The word *numerical* means "of numbers." The word *expression* can refer to a mathematical symbol or combination of symbols. What do you think a **numerical expression** is?

3. A *sequence* is a list or arrangement that is in a particular order. What kind of **sequence** do you expect to see in this chapter?

Reading and Writing Math

Reading Strategy: Use Your Book for Success

Understanding how your textbook is organized will help you locate and use helpful information.

As you read through an example problem, pay attention to the **margin notes**, such as Reading Math notes, Writing Math notes, Helpful Hints, and Caution notes. These notes will help you understand concepts and avoid common mistakes.

Reading Math
A group of four ta[lly] marks with a line through it means [five]

Writing Math
To write a repeati[ng] decimal, you can show three dots

Helpful Hint
Estimating before you add or subtra[ct] will help you che[ck]

Caution!
When you write a[n] expression for dat[a in] a table, check tha[t]

The **Glossary** is found in the back of your textbook. Use it as a resource when you need the definition of an unfamiliar word or property.

The **Index** is located at the end of your textbook. Use it to locate the page where a particular concept is taught.

The **Skills Bank** is found in the back of your textbook. These pages review concepts from previous math courses, including geometry skills.

Glossary/Glosari[o]
A
ENGLISH
absolute value The distance of a number from zero on a number line; shown by | |.

valor
está u[n]
numér[o]
absol[uto]

Index
A
Aaron, Hank, 36
Abacus, 9
Absolute value, 762
Accuracy, 767

in sca[...]
37[...]
in sim[...]
solvi[ng]
tiles, 63[...]
variable[...]
Algebra ti[les]
Algebra[ic]
writing,
Alternate
Alternate
Alvin sub[...]

Skills Bank
Place Value—Trillions
You can use a place-value chart to read and write numbers.

Try This

Use your textbook.

1. Use the glossary to find the definitions of *bisect* and *factor tree*.

2. Where in the Skills Bank can you review how to round whole numbers and decimals?

3. Use the Problem Solving Handbook to list the four steps of the problem-solving plan and two different problem-solving strategies.

4. Use the index to find the pages where *angles* and *histogram* appear.

Whole Numbers and Patterns

1-1 Estimating with Whole Numbers

Learn to estimate with whole numbers.

Vocabulary
estimate
compatible number
underestimate
overestimate

Sometimes in math you do not need an exact answer. Instead, you can use an *estimate*. **Estimates** are close to the exact answer but are usually easier and faster to find.

When estimating, you can round the numbers in the problem to *compatible numbers*. **Compatible numbers** are close to the numbers in the problem, and they can help you do math mentally.

"WELL, MAYBE UMPTEEN ZILLION WAS TOO GENERAL A COST ESTIMATE."

Remember!

When rounding, look at the digit to the right of the place to which you are rounding.
- If that digit is 5 or greater, round up.
- If that digit is less than 5, round down.

See Skills Bank p. SB2

EXAMPLE 1 Estimating a Sum or Difference by Rounding

Estimate each sum or difference by rounding to the place value indicated.

A 5,439 + 7,516; thousands

$$\begin{array}{r} 5,000 \\ +\,8,000 \\ \hline 13,000 \end{array}$$

Round 5,439 down.
Round 7,516 up.

The sum is about 13,000.

B 62,167 − 47,511; ten thousands

$$\begin{array}{r} 60,000 \\ -\,50,000 \\ \hline 10,000 \end{array}$$

Round 62,167 down.
Round 47,511 up.

The difference is about 10,000.

An estimate that is less than the exact answer is an **underestimate**.

An estimate that is greater than the exact answer is an **overestimate**.

EXAMPLE 2 Estimating a Product by Rounding

Ms. Escobar is planning a graduation celebration for the entire eighth grade. There are 9 eighth-grade homeroom classes of 27 students. Estimate how many cups Ms. Escobar needs to buy for the students if they all attend the celebration.

Find the number of students in the eighth grade.

$9 \times 27 \rightarrow 9 \times 30$ *Overestimate the number of students.*

$9 \times 30 = 270$ *The actual number of students is less than 270.*

If Ms. Escobar buys 270 cups, she will have enough for every student.

EXAMPLE 3 Estimating a Quotient Using Compatible Numbers

Mrs. Byrd will drive 120 miles to take Becca to the state fair. She can drive 65 mi/h. About how long will the trip take?

To find how long the trip will be, divide the miles Mrs. Byrd has to travel by how many miles per hour she can drive.

miles ÷ miles per hour

$120 \div 65 \rightarrow 120 \div 60$ *120 and 60 are compatible numbers. Underestimate the speed.*

$120 \div 60 = 2$ *Because she underestimated the speed, the actual time will be less than 2 hours.*

It will take Mrs. Byrd about two hours to reach the state fair.

Think and Discuss

1. **Suppose** you are buying items for a party and you have $50. Would it be better to overestimate or underestimate the cost of the items?

2. **Suppose** your car can travel between 20 and 25 miles on a gallon of gas. You want to go on a 100-mile trip. Would it be better to overestimate or underestimate the number of miles per gallon your car can travel?

3. **Describe** situations in which you might want to estimate.

1-1 Exercises

Learn It Online
Homework Help Online go.hrw.com,
keyword MR10 1-1
Exercises 1–12, 15, 17, 19, 21, 23, 25, 27

GUIDED PRACTICE

See Example 1 Estimate each sum or difference by rounding to the place value indicated.

1. 4,689 + 2,469; thousands
2. 50,498 − 35,798; ten thousands

See Example 2
3. The graph shows the number of bottles of water used in three bicycle races last year. If the same number of riders enter the races each year, estimate the number of bottles that will be needed for races held in May over the next five years.

Bicycle-Race Bottled-Water Use

See Example 3
4. If a local business provided half the bottled water needed for the August bicycle race, about how many bottles did the company provide?

5. Carla drives 80 miles on her scooter. If the scooter gets about 42 miles per gallon of gas, about how much gas did she use?

INDEPENDENT PRACTICE

See Example 1 Estimate each sum or difference by rounding to the place value indicated.

6. 6,570 + 3,609; thousands
7. 49,821 − 11,567; ten thousands
8. 3,912 + 1,269; thousands
9. 37,097 − 20,364; ten thousands

See Example 2
10. The recreation center has provided softballs every year to the city league. Use the table to estimate the number of softballs the league will use in 5 years.

Recreation Center Balls Supplied	
Sport	Number of Balls
Basketball	21
Golf	324
Softball	28
Table tennis	95

See Example 3
11. The recreation center has a girls' golf team with 8 members. About how many golf balls will each girl on the team get?

12. If the recreation center loses about 4 table tennis balls per year, and they are not replaced, about how many years will it take until the center has none left?

PRACTICE AND PROBLEM SOLVING

Extra Practice
See page EP1.

Estimate each sum or difference by rounding to the greatest place value.

13. 152 + 269
14. 797 − 234
15. 242 − 179
16. 6,152 − 3,195
17. 9,179 + 2,206
18. 10,982 + 4,821
19. 82,465 − 38,421
20. 38,347 + 17,039
21. 51,201 + 16,492
22. 639,069 + 283,136
23. 777,060 − 410,364
24. 998,927 − 100,724

Chapter 1 Whole Numbers and Patterns

Social Studies LINK

Use the bar graph for Exercises 25–31.

25. On one summer day there were 2,824 sailboats on Lake Erie. Estimate the number of square miles available to each boat.

26. If the areas of all the Great Lakes are rounded to the nearest thousand, which two of the lakes would be the closest in area?

27. About how much larger is Lake Huron than Lake Ontario?

28. The Great Lakes are called "great" because of the huge amount of fresh water they contain. Estimate the total area of all the Great Lakes combined.

29. **What's the Question?** Lake Erie is about 50,000 square miles smaller. What is the question?

30. **Write About It** Explain how you would estimate the areas of Lake Huron and Lake Michigan to compare their sizes.

31. **Challenge** Estimate the average area of the Great Lakes.

Areas of the Great Lakes

Area includes the water surface and drainage basin within the United States and Canada.

Test Prep and Spiral Review

32. **Multiple Choice** Which number is the best estimate for 817 + 259?

    (A) 10,000   (B) 2,000   (C) 1,100   (D) 800

33. **Short Response** The National Football League requires home teams to have 36 new footballs for outdoor games and 24 new footballs for indoor games. Estimate how many new footballs the Washington Redskins must buy for 8 outdoor games. Explain how you determined your estimate.

Find each product or quotient. (Previous Course)

34. 148 ÷ 4   35. 523 × 5   36. 1,054 ÷ 31   37. 312 × 8

Write each number in expanded form. (Previous Course)

38. 269   39. 1,354   40. 32,498   41. 416,703

1-1 Estimating with Whole Numbers

1-2 Exponents

Learn to represent numbers by using exponents.

Vocabulary
exponent
base
exponential form

Since 1906, the height of Mount Vesuvius in Italy has increased by about 7^3 feet. How many feet is this?

The number 7^3 is written with an exponent. An **exponent** tells how many times a number called the **base** is used as a factor.

Base → 7^3 ← Exponent
$= 7 \times 7 \times 7 = 343$

The most recent eruption of Mount Vesuvius took place in 1944.

So the height of Mount Vesuvius has increased by about 343 ft.

Interactivities Online ▶ A number is in **exponential form** when it is written with a base and an exponent.

Exponential Form	Read	Multiply	Value
10^1	"10 to the 1st power"	10	10
10^2	"10 squared," or "10 to the 2nd power"	10×10	100
10^3	"10 cubed," or "10 to the 3rd power"	$10 \times 10 \times 10$	1,000
10^4	"10 to the 4th power"	$10 \times 10 \times 10 \times 10$	10,000

EXAMPLE 1 Writing Numbers in Exponential Form

Write each expression in exponential form.

A $4 \times 4 \times 4$
4^3 *4 is a factor 3 times.*

B $9 \times 9 \times 9 \times 9 \times 9$
9^5 *9 is a factor 5 times.*

EXAMPLE 2 Finding the Value of Numbers in Exponential Form

Find each value.

A 2^7
$2^7 = 2 \times 2 \times 2 \times 2 \times 2 \times 2 \times 2$
$= 128$

B 6^4
$6^4 = 6 \times 6 \times 6 \times 6$
$= 1,296$

10 Chapter 1 Whole Numbers and Patterns

EXAMPLE 3 **PROBLEM SOLVING APPLICATION**

If Dana's school closes, a phone tree is used to contact each student's family. The secretary calls 3 families. Then each family calls 3 other families, and so on. How many families will be notified during the 6th round of calls?

1. Understand the Problem

The **answer** will be the number of families called in the 6th round.

List the **important information:**
- The secretary calls 3 families.
- Each family calls 3 families.

2. Make a Plan

You can draw a diagram to see how many calls are in each round.

Secretary

1st round—3 calls

2nd round—9 calls

3. Solve

Notice that in each round, the number of calls is a power of 3.
1st round: 3 calls = 3 = 3^1
2nd round: 9 calls = 3 × 3 = 3^2

So during the 6th round there will be 3^6 calls.
$3^6 = 3 \times 3 \times 3 \times 3 \times 3 \times 3 = 729$
During the 6th round of calls, 729 families will be notified.

4. Look Back

Drawing a diagram helps you visualize the pattern, but the numbers become too large for a diagram after the third round of calls. Solving this problem by using exponents can be easier and faster.

Think and Discuss

1. **Read** each number: 4^8, 12^3, 3^2.
2. **Explain** which has the greater value, 3^4 or 4^3.

1-2 Exercises

GUIDED PRACTICE

See Example 1 Write each expression in exponential form.
1. $8 \times 8 \times 8$
2. 7×7
3. $6 \times 6 \times 6 \times 6 \times 6$
4. $4 \times 4 \times 4 \times 4$
5. $5 \times 5 \times 5 \times 5 \times 5$
6. 1×1

See Example 2 Find each value.
7. 4^2
8. 3^3
9. 5^4
10. 8^2
11. 7^3

See Example 3
12. At Russell's school, one person will contact 4 people and each of those people will contact 4 other people, and so on. How many people will be contacted in the fifth round?

INDEPENDENT PRACTICE

See Example 1 Write each expression in exponential form.
13. $2 \times 2 \times 2 \times 2 \times 2 \times 2$
14. $9 \times 9 \times 9 \times 9$
15. 8×8
16. $1 \times 1 \times 1$
17. $6 \times 6 \times 6 \times 6 \times 6$
18. $5 \times 5 \times 5$
19. $7 \times 7 \times 7 \times 7 \times 7 \times 7 \times 7$
20. $3 \times 3 \times 3 \times 3$
21. 4×4

See Example 2 Find each value.
22. 2^4
23. 3^5
24. 6^2
25. 9^2
26. 7^4
27. 8^3
28. 1^4
29. 16^2
30. 10^8
31. 12^2

See Example 3
32. To save money for a video game, you put one dollar in an envelope. Each day for 5 days you double the number of dollars in the envelope from the day before. How much will be saved on the fifth day?

PRACTICE AND PROBLEM SOLVING

Extra Practice
See page EP1.

Write each expression as repeated multiplication.
33. 16^3
34. 22^2
35. 31^6
36. 46^5
37. 50^3
38. 4^1
39. 1^9
40. 17^6
41. 8^5
42. 12^4

Find each value.
43. 10^6
44. 73^1
45. 9^4
46. 80^2
47. 10^5
48. 19^2
49. 2^9
50. 57^1
51. 5^3
52. 11^3

Compare. Write <, >, or =.
53. 6^1 ☐ 5^1
54. 9^2 ☐ 20^1
55. 10^1 ☐ $1{,}000{,}000^1$
56. 7^3 ☐ 3^7
57. 5^5 ☐ 25^1
58. 100^2 ☐ 10^4

Chapter 1 Whole Numbers and Patterns

Life Science LINK

You are able to grow because your body produces new cells. New cells are made when old cells divide. Single-celled bodies, such as bacteria, divide by *binary fission*, which means "splitting into two parts." A cycle is the length of time a cell needs to divide once.

59. In science lab, Carol has a dish containing 4^5 cells. How many cells are represented by this number?

60. A certain colony of bacteria triples in length every 15 minutes. Its length is now 1 mm. How long will it be in 1 hour? (*Hint:* There are four cycles of 15 minutes in 1 hour.)

Use the bar graph for Exercises 61–64.

61. Determine how many times cell type A will divide in a 24-hour period. If you begin with one type A cell, how many cells will be produced in 24 hours?

62. Multi-Step If you begin with one type B cell and one type C cell, what is the difference between the number of type B cells and the number of type C cells produced in 24 hours?

63. Write About It Explain how to find the number of type A cells produced in 48 hours.

64. Challenge How many hours will it take one C cell to divide into at least 100 C cells?

This plant cell shows the anaphase stage of mitosis. Mitosis is the process of nuclear division in complex cells called eukaryotes.

Test Prep and Spiral Review

65. Multiple Choice Which of the following shows the expression $4 \times 4 \times 4$ in exponential form?

Ⓐ 64   Ⓑ 444   Ⓒ 3^4 Ⓓ 4^3

66. Multiple Choice Which expression has the greatest value?

Ⓕ 2^5 Ⓖ 3^4 Ⓗ 4^3 Ⓙ 5^2

Order the numbers from least to greatest. (Previous Course)

67. 8,452; 8,732; 8,245   **68.** 991; 1,010; 984   **69.** 12,681; 11,901; 12,751

Estimate each sum or difference by rounding to the place value indicated. (Lesson 1-1)

70. 12,876 + 17,986; thousands   **71.** 72,876 − 15,987; ten thousands

Ready To Go On?

Quiz for Lessons 1-1 Through 1-2

1-1 Estimating with Whole Numbers

Estimate each sum or difference by rounding to the place value indicated.

1. 61,582 + 13,281; ten thousands
2. 86,125 − 55,713; ten thousands
3. 7,903 + 2,654; thousands
4. 34,633 − 32,087; thousands
5. 1,896,345 + 3,567,194; hundred thousands
6. 56,129,482 − 37,103,758; ten millions

7. Marcus wants to make a stone walkway in his garden. The rectangular walkway will be 3 feet wide and 21 feet long. Each 2-foot by 3-foot stone covers an area of 6 square feet. How many stones will Marcus need?

8. Jenna's sixth-grade class is taking a bus to the zoo. The zoo is 156 miles from the school. If the bus travels an average of 55 mi/h, about how long will it take the class to get to the zoo?

9. Robin's class is contacting families from her school as part of a fundraiser. If there are 471 families at the school and 27 students in Robin's class, about how many families will each student contact?

1-2 Exponents

Write each expression in exponential form.

10. $7 \times 7 \times 7$
11. $5 \times 5 \times 5 \times 5$
12. $3 \times 3 \times 3 \times 3 \times 3 \times 3$
13. $10 \times 10 \times 10 \times 10$
14. $1 \times 1 \times 1 \times 1 \times 1$
15. $4 \times 4 \times 4 \times 4$

Find each value.

16. 3^3
17. 2^4
18. 6^2
19. 8^3

20. To start reading a novel for English class, Sara read 1 page. Each day for 4 days she reads double the number of pages she read the day before. How many pages will she read on the fourth day?

Focus on Problem Solving

Solve
- **Choose the operation: addition or subtraction**

Read the whole problem before you try to solve it. Determine what action is taking place in the problem. Then decide whether you need to add or subtract in order to solve the problem.

If you need to combine or put numbers together, you need to add. If you need to take away or compare numbers, you need to subtract.

Action	Operation	Picture
Combining Putting together	Add	
Removing Taking away	Subtract	
Comparing Finding the difference	Subtract	

Read each problem. Determine the action in each problem. Choose an operation in order to solve the problem. Then solve.

Most hurricanes that occur over the Atlantic Ocean, the Caribbean Sea, or the Gulf of Mexico occur between June and November. Since 1886, a hurricane has occurred in every month except April.

Number of Out-of-Season Hurricanes Since 1886

Month	Number
Jan	1
Feb	1
Mar	1
May	14
Dec	10

Use the table for problems 1 and 2.

1. How many out-of-season hurricanes have occurred in all?

2. How many more hurricanes have occurred in May than in December?

3. There were 14 named storms during the 2000 hurricane season. Eight of these became hurricanes, and three others became major hurricanes. How many of the named storms were not hurricanes or major hurricanes?

Focus on Problem Solving **15**

Technology LAB 1-3

Explore the Order of Operations

Use with Lesson 1-3

Learn It Online
Lab Resources Online go.hrw.com,
keyword MR10 Lab1 Go

Look at the expression 3 + 2 · 8. To evaluate this expression, decide whether to add first or multiply first. Knowing the correct *order of operations* is important. Without this knowledge, you could get an incorrect result.

Activity 1

Use pencil and paper to evaluate 3 + 2 · 8 two different ways.

Add first, and   3 + 2 = 5
then multiply by 8.   5 · 8 = 40

Multiply first, and   2 · 8 = 16
then add 3.   16 + 3 = 19

Now evaluate 3 + 2 · 8 using a graphing or scientific calculator.

The result, 19, shows that this calculator multiplied first, even though addition came first in the expression.

If there are no parentheses, then multiplication and division are done before addition or subtraction. If the addition is to be done first, parentheses *must* be used.

When you evaluate (3 + 2) · 8 on a calculator, the result is 40. Because of the parentheses, the calculator adds before multiplying.

Graphing and scientific calculators follow a logical system called the algebraic order of operations. The order of operations tells you to multiply and divide before you add or subtract.

Think and Discuss

1. In 4 + 15 ÷ 5, which operation do you perform first? How do you know?
2. Tell the order in which you would perform the operations in the expression 8 ÷ 2 + 6 · 3 − 4.

Try This

Evaluate each expression with pencil and paper. Check your answer with a calculator.

1. 4 · 12 − 7
2. 15 ÷ 3 + 10
3. 4 + 2 · 6
4. 10 − 4 ÷ 2

Activity 2

What should you do if the same operation appears twice in an expression? Use a calculator to decide which subtraction is done first in the expression $7 - 3 - 2$.

If $7 - 3$ is done first, the value of the expression is $4 - 2 = 2$.

If $3 - 2$ is done first, the value of the expression is $7 - 1 = 6$.

On the calculator, the value of $7 - 3 - 2$ is 2. The subtraction on the left, $7 - 3$, is done first.

Addition and subtraction (or multiplication and division) are done from left to right.

Think and Discuss

1. In $15 + 5 + 4$, does it matter which operation you perform first? Explain.
2. Does it matter which operation you perform first in $15 - 5 + 4$? Explain.

Try This

Evaluate each expression. Check your answer with a calculator.

1. $8 - 6 - 1$
2. $20 \div 5 \div 2$
3. $3 \cdot 6 \cdot 2$
4. $19 + 6 + 5$

Activity 3

Without parentheses, the expression $8 + 2 \cdot 10 - 3$ equals 25. Insert parentheses to make the value of the expression 22.

What happens if you add first?	What happens if you subtract first?
$(8 + 2) \cdot 10 - 3$	$8 + 2 \cdot (10 - 3)$
$10 \cdot 10 - 3$	$8 + 2 \cdot 7$
$100 - 3$	$8 + 14$
97	22

For the expression to equal 22, the subtraction must be done first.

Think and Discuss

1. To evaluate $13 + 5 \cdot 255$ on a calculator, you type $13 + 5$ and then press the ⨯ key. But before you can type in the 255, the display changes to 18!
   a. Does this calculator follow the correct order of operations? Why?
   b. How could you use this calculator to evaluate $13 + 5 \cdot 255$?

Try This

Insert parentheses to make the value of each expression 12.

1. $56 - 40 + 4$
2. $3 - 1 \cdot 10 - 4$
3. $18 \div 2 + 1 + 6$
4. $100 + 8 \div 2 \cdot 2 + 5$

1-3 Order of Operations

Learn to use the order of operations.

A **numerical expression** is a mathematical phrase that includes only numbers and operation symbols.

Numerical Expressions	$4 + 8 \div 2 \times 6$	$371 - 203 + 2$	$5{,}006 \times 19$

Vocabulary
numerical expression
simplify
order of operations

When you **simplify** a numerical expression, you find its value.

Erika and Jamie each simplified $3 + 4 \times 6$. Their work is shown below. Whose answer is correct?

When an expression has more than one operation, you must know which operation to do first. To make sure that everyone gets the same answer, we use the **order of operations**.

Erika
$3 + 4 \times 6$
$3 + 24$
27
$3 + 4 \times 6 = 27$

Jamie
$3 + 4 \times 6$
7×6
42
$3 + 4 \times 6 = 42$

Remember!
The first letters of these words can help you remember the order of operations.

Please	Parentheses
Excuse	Exponents
My	Multiply/
Dear	Divide
Aunt	Add/
Sally	Subtract

ORDER OF OPERATIONS
1. Perform operations in **parentheses**.
2. Find the values of numbers with **exponents**.
3. **Multiply** or **divide** from left to right as ordered in the problem.
4. **Add** or **subtract** from left to right as ordered in the problem.

$3 + 4 \times 6$ There are no parentheses or exponents. Multiply first.
$3 + 24$ Add.
27 Erika has the correct answer.

EXAMPLE 1   Using the Order of Operations

Simplify each expression.

A $9 + 12 \times 2$

$9 + 12 \times 2$ There are no parentheses or exponents.
$9 + \quad 24$ Multiply.
$\quad 33$ Add.

18   Chapter 1 Whole Numbers and Patterns

Simplify each expression.

B $7 + (12 \times 3) \div 6$

$7 + (12 \times 3) \div 6$	
$7 + \quad 36 \quad \div 6$	*Perform operations within parentheses.*
$7 + \qquad\quad 6$	*Divide.*
13	*Add.*

EXAMPLE 2 Using the Order of Operations with Exponents

Simplify each expression.

A $3^3 + 8 - 16$

$3^3 + 8 - 16$	*There are no parentheses.*
$27 + 8 - 16$	*Find the values of numbers with exponents.*
$35 \quad - 16$	*Add*
19	*Subtract.*

B $8 \div (1 + 3) \times 5^2 - 2$

$8 \div (1 + 3) \times 5^2 - 2$	
$8 \div \quad 4 \quad \times 5^2 - 2$	*Perform operations within parentheses.*
$8 \div \quad 4 \quad \times 25 - 2$	*Find the values of numbers with exponents.*
$2 \quad \times 25 - 2$	*Divide.*
$50 \quad - 2$	*Multiply.*
48	*Subtract.*

EXAMPLE 3 Consumer Application

Regina bought 5 carved wooden beads for $3 each and 8 glass beads for $2 each. Simplify $5 \times 3 + 8 \times 2$ to find the amount Regina spent for beads.

$5 \times 3 + 8 \times 2$
$\quad 15 \ + \ 16$
$\qquad 31$

Regina spent $31 for beads.

Think and Discuss

1. Explain why $6 + 7 \times 10 = 76$ but $(6 + 7) \times 10 = 130$.

2. Tell how you can add parentheses to the numerical expression $2^2 + 5 \times 3$ so that 27 is the correct answer.

1-3 Exercises

Learn It Online
Homework Help Online go.hrw.com,
keyword MR10 1-3 Go
Exercises 1–21, 25, 27, 31, 39, 41, 43, 45

GUIDED PRACTICE

See Example 1 Simplify each expression.
1. $36 - 18 \div 6$
2. $7 + 24 \div 6 \times 2$
3. $62 - 4 \times (15 \div 5)$

See Example 2
4. $11 + 2^3 \times 5$
5. $5 \times (28 \div 7) - 4^2$
6. $5 + 3^2 \times 6 - (10 - 9)$

See Example 3
7. Coach Milner fed the team after the game by buying 24 Chicken Deals for $4 each and 7 Burger Deals for $6 each. Simplify $24 \times 4 + 7 \times 6$ to find the cost of the food.

INDEPENDENT PRACTICE

See Example 1 Simplify each expression.
8. $9 + 27 \div 3$
9. $2 \times 7 - 32 \div 8$
10. $45 \div (3 + 6) \times 3$
11. $(6 + 2) \times 4$
12. $9 \div 3 + 6 \times 2$
13. $5 + 3 \times 2 + 12 \div 4$

See Example 2
14. $4^2 + 48 \div (10 - 4)$
15. $100 \div 5^2 + 7 \times 3$
16. $6 \times 2^2 + 28 - 5$
17. $6^2 - 12 \div 3 + (15 - 7)$
18. $21 \div (3 + 4) \times 9 - 2^3$
19. $(3^2 + 6 \div 2) \times (36 \div 6 - 4)$

See Example 3
20. The nature park has a pride of 5 adult lions and 3 cubs. The adults eat 8 lb of meat each day and the cubs eat 4 lb. Simplify $5 \times 8 + 3 \times 4$ to find the amount of meat consumed each day by the lions.

21. Angie read 4 books that were each 150 pages long and 2 books that were each 325 pages long. Simplify $4 \times 150 + 2 \times 325$ to find the total number of pages Angie read.

PRACTICE AND PROBLEM SOLVING

Extra Practice
See page EP1.

Simplify each expression.
22. $12 + 3 \times 4$
23. $25 - 21 \div 3$
24. $1 + 7 \times 2$
25. $60 \div (10 + 2) \times 4^2 - 23$
26. $10 \times (28 - 23) + 7^2 - 37$
27. $(5 - 3) \div 2$
28. $72 \div 9 - 2 \times 4$
29. $12 + (1 + 7^2) \div 5$
30. $25 - 5^2$
31. $(15 - 6)^2 - 34 \div 2$
32. $(2 \times 4)^2 - 3 \times (5 + 3)$
33. $16 + 2 \times 3$

Add parentheses so that each equation is correct.
34. $2^3 + 6 - 5 \times 4 = 12$
35. $7 + 2 \times 6 - 4 - 3 = 53$
36. $3^2 + 6 + 3 \times 3 = 36$
37. $5^2 - 10 + 5 + 4^2 = 36$
38. $2 \times 8 + 5 - 3 = 23$
39. $9^2 - 2 \times 15 + 16 - 8 = 11$
40. $5 + 7 \times 2 - 3 = 21$
41. $4^2 \times 3 - 2 \div 4 = 4$

42. **Critical Thinking** Jon says the answer to $1 + 3 \times (6 + 2) - 7$ is 25. Julie says the answer is 18. Who is correct? Explain.

Chapter 1 Whole Numbers and Patterns

Social Studies LINK

Archaeologists study cultures of the past by uncovering items from ancient cities. An archaeologist has chosen a site in Colorado for her team's next dig. She divides the location into rectangular plots and labels each plot so that uncovered items can be identified by the plot in which they were found.

43. The archaeologist must order a cover for the plot where the team is digging. Simplify the expression $3 \times (2^2 + 6)$ to find the area of the plot in square meters.

Tourists assist archaeologists at Shields Pueblo in Colorado.

44. In the first week, the archaeology team digs down 2 meters and removes a certain amount of dirt. Simplify the expression $3 \times (2^2 + 6) \times 2$ to find the volume of the dirt removed from the plot in the first week.

45. Over the next two weeks, the archaeology team digs down an additional 2^3 meters. Simplify the expression $3 \times (2^2 + 6) \times (2 + 2^3)$ to find the total volume of dirt removed from the plot after 3 weeks.

46. ✏️ **Write About It** Explain why the archaeologist must follow the order of operations to determine the area of each plot.

47. ⭐ **Challenge** Write an expression for the volume of dirt that would be removed if the archaeologist's team were to dig down an additional 3^2 meters after the first three weeks.

Test Prep and Spiral Review

48. Multiple Choice Which operation should you perform first when you simplify $81 - (6 + 30 \div 2) \times 5$?

Ⓐ Addition Ⓑ Division Ⓒ Multiplication Ⓓ Subtraction

49. Multiple Choice Which expression does NOT have a value of 5?

Ⓕ $2^2 + (3 - 2)$ Ⓖ $(2^2 + 3) - 2$ Ⓗ $2^2 + 3 - 2$ Ⓙ $2^2 - (3 + 2)$

50. Gridded Response What is the value of the expression $3^2 + (9 \div 3 - 2)$?

Write each number in standard form. (Previous Course)

51. $3,000 + 200 + 70 + 3$ **52.** $10,000 + 500 + 20 + 1$ **53.** $70,000 + 7$

Find each value. (Lesson 1-2)

54. 8^5 **55.** 5^3 **56.** 3^8 **57.** 4^4 **58.** 7^2

1-4 Properties and Mental Math

Learn to use number properties to compute mentally.

Vocabulary
Commutative Property
Associative Property
Distributive Property

Mental math means "doing math in your head." Shakuntala Devi is extremely good at mental math. When she was asked to multiply 7,686,369,774,870 by 2,465,099,745,779, she took only 28 seconds to multiply the numbers mentally and gave the correct answer of 18,947,668,177,995,426,462,773,730!

Many mental math strategies use number properties that you already know to make equivalent expressions that may be easier to simplify.

Caution!
The Commutative and Associative Properties do not apply to subtraction or division.

COMMUTATIVE PROPERTY (Ordering)	
Words	Numbers
You can add or multiply numbers in any order.	$18 + 9 = 9 + 18$ $15 \times 2 = 2 \times 15$

ASSOCIATIVE PROPERTY (Grouping)	
Words	Numbers
When you are only adding or only multiplying, you can group any of the numbers together.	$(17 + 2) + 9 = 17 + (2 + 9)$ $(12 \times 2) \times 4 = 12 \times (2 \times 4)$

EXAMPLE 1 Using Properties to Add and Multiply Whole Numbers

A Simplify $12 + 4 + 18 + 46$.

$12 + 4 + 18 + 46$
$12 + 18 + 4 + 46$
$(12 + 18) + (4 + 46)$
$\quad 30 \quad + \quad 50$
$\quad\quad\quad 80$

Look for sums that are multiples of 10.
Use the Commutative Property.
Use the Associative Property to make groups of compatible numbers.
Use mental math to add.

22 *Chapter 1 Whole Numbers and Patterns*

Video Lesson Tutorials Online my.hrw.com

Helpful Hint

The expressions in each row of Example 1B are equivalent expressions because they have the same value.

B Simplify $5 \times 12 \times 2$.

$5 \times 12 \times 2$	*Look for products that are multiples of 10.*
$12 \times 5 \times 2$	*Use the Commutative Property.*
$12 \times (5 \times 2)$	*Use the Associative Property to group compatible numbers.*
12×10	
120	*Use mental math to multiply.*

To multiply a number by a sum, such as $6 \times (10 + 4)$, you can use the order of operations, or you can use the *Distributive Property*.

DISTRIBUTIVE PROPERTY

Words	Numbers
To multiply a number by a sum, multiply by each number in the sum and then add.	$6 \times (10 + 4) = (6 \times 10) + (6 \times 4)$ $= 60 + 24$ $= 84$

When you multiply two numbers, you can "break apart" one of the numbers into a sum and then use the Distributive Property.

EXAMPLE 2 Using the Distributive Property to Multiply

Use the Distributive Property to find each product.

A 4×23

$4 \times 23 = 4 \times (20 + 3)$	*"Break apart" 23 into 20 + 3.*
$= (4 \times 20) + (4 \times 3)$	*Use the Distributive Property.*
$= 80 + 12$	*Use mental math to multiply.*
$= 92$	*Use mental math to add.*

B 8×74

$8 \times 74 = 8 \times (70 + 4)$	*"Break apart" 74 into 70 + 4.*
$= (8 \times 70) + (8 \times 4)$	*Use the Distributive Property.*
$= 560 + 32$	*Use mental math to multiply.*
$= 592$	*Use mental math to add.*

Think and Discuss

1. **Give examples** of the Commutative Property and the Associative Property.
2. **Name** some situations in which you might use mental math.

1-4 Exercises

Learn It Online
Homework Help Online go.hrw.com,
keyword MR10 1-4
Exercises 1–30, 31, 39, 41, 45, 51

GUIDED PRACTICE

See Example 1 Simplify.

1. $13 + 9 + 7 + 11$
2. $19 + 18 + 11 + 32$
3. $25 + 7 + 13 + 5$
4. $5 \times 14 \times 4$
5. $4 \times 16 \times 5$
6. $5 \times 17 \times 2$

See Example 2 Use the Distributive Property to find each product.

7. 5×24
8. 8×52
9. 4×39
10. 6×14
11. 3×33
12. 2×78
13. 9×12
14. 2×87

INDEPENDENT PRACTICE

See Example 1 Simplify.

15. $15 + 17 + 3 + 5$
16. $14 + 7 + 16 + 13$
17. $6 + 21 + 14 + 9$
18. $5 \times 25 \times 2$
19. $2 \times 32 \times 10$
20. $6 \times 12 \times 5$

See Example 2 Use the Distributive Property to find each product.

21. 3×36
22. 4×42
23. 6×71
24. 2×94
25. 6×23
26. 5×25
27. 6×62
28. 7×21
29. 8×41
30. 2×94

PRACTICE AND PROBLEM SOLVING

Extra Practice See page EP2.

Use mental math to find each sum or product.

31. $8 + 13 + 7 + 12$
32. $2 \times 25 \times 4$
33. $4 + 22 + 16 + 18$
34. $5 \times 8 \times 12$
35. $5 + 98 + 95$
36. $6 \times 5 \times 14$
37. $11 + 75 + 25$
38. $8 \times 11 \times 5$
39. $19 + 1 + 11 + 39$

40. Paul is writing a story for the school newspaper about the landscaping done by his class. The students planted 15 vines, 12 hedges, 8 trees, and 35 flowering plants. How many plants were used in the project?

41. **Earth Science** The temperature on Sunday was 58 °F. The temperature is predicted to rise 4 °F on Monday, then rise 2 °F more on Tuesday, and then rise another 6 °F by Saturday. What is the predicted temperature on Saturday?

42. **Multi-Step** Janice wants to order disks for her computer. She needs to find the total cost, including shipping and handling. If Janice orders 7 disks, what will her total cost be?

Description	Number	Unit Cost with Tax	Price
Computer Disk	7	$24.00	
		Shipping & Handling	$7.00
		Total	

24 Chapter 1 Whole Numbers and Patterns

Life Science

Poison-dart frogs are members of the family Dendrobatidae, which includes about 170 species. Many are brightly colored.

Multiply using the Distributive Property.

43. 9 × 17   **44.** 4 × 27   **45.** 11 × 18   **46.** 7 × 51

Determine if each pair of expressions is equivalent. If so, state the property shown.

47. 8 × 35 and (8 × 30)(8 × 5)   **48.** 14 + 7 + 6 and 6 + 14 + 7

49. (9 × 7) × 6 and 9 × (7 × 6)   **50.** 24 ÷ 6 ÷ 2 and 6 ÷ 24 ÷ 2

51. Life Science Poison-dart frogs can breed underwater, and the females lay from 4 to 30 eggs. What would be the total number of eggs if four female poison-dart frogs each laid 27 eggs?

Use the table for Exercises 52 and 53.

52. Rickie wants to buy 3 garden hoses. How much will they cost?

53. The boys in Josh's family are saving money to buy 4 ceiling fans. How much will they need to save?

Home Center Clearance Sale	
Table lamp	$15
Garden hose	$16
Ceiling fan	$52

54. Critical Thinking Give a problem that you could simplify using the Commutative and Associative Properties. Then, show the steps to solve the problem and label the Commutative and Associative Properties.

55. What's The Error? A student wrote 5 + 24 + 25 + 6 = 5 + 25 + 24 + 6 by the Associative Property. What error did the student make?

56. Write About It Why can you simplify 5(50 + 3) using the Distributive Property? Why can't you simplify 5(50) + 3 using the Distributive Property?

57. Challenge Explain how you could find the product of 5^2 × 112 using the Distributive Property. Simplify the expression.

Test Prep and Spiral Review

58. Multiple Choice Which expression does NOT have the same value as 7 × (4 + 23)?

Ⓐ 7 × 27   Ⓑ (7 × 4) + (7 × 23)   Ⓒ 7 × 4 + 23   Ⓓ 28 + (7 × 23)

59. Gridded Response Michelle flew 1,240 miles from Los Angeles to Dallas, and another 718 miles from Dallas to Atlanta. From Atlanta, she flew 760 miles to New York City. How many miles did Michelle fly in all?

Estimate each sum or difference by rounding to the nearest thousands place. (Lesson 1-1)

60. 5,237 − 1,586   **61.** 915,178 + 451,836   **62.** 39,187 − 24,999

Simplify each expression. (Lesson 1-3)

63. 4 × 14 + 12 ÷ 2   **64.** 16 ÷ 4^2 + 15 − 2   **65.** 62 + 14 − (5 × 4)

1-4 Properties and Mental Math

1-5 Choosing a Method of Computation

Learn to choose an appropriate method of computation and justify your choice.

Earth has one moon. Scientists have determined that other planets in our solar system have as many as 63 moons. Mercury and Venus have no moons at all.

Triton is the largest of Neptune's 13 moons.

EXAMPLE 1

Astronomy Application

Choose a solution method and solve. Explain your choice.

A How many known moons are in our solar system?

It might be hard to keep track of all of these numbers if you tried to add mentally. But the numbers themselves are small. You can use paper and pencil.

```
  1
  2
 63
 60
 27
+13
───
166
```

Planet	Moons
Mercury	0
Venus	0
Earth	1
Mars	2
Jupiter	63
Saturn	60
Uranus	27
Neptune	13

Source: The Planetary Society, 2006

There are 166 known moons in our solar system.

B The average temperature on Earth is 59 °F. The average temperature on Venus is 867 °F. How much hotter is Venus's average temperature?

Venus temperature − Earth temperature
867 − 59

These numbers are small, and 59 is close to a multiple of 10. You can use mental math.

$(867 + 1) - (59 + 1)$
$868 - 60$
808

Think: Add 1 to 59 to make 60. Add 1 to 867 to compensate.

The average temperature on Venus is 808 °F hotter than the average temperature on Earth.

Choose a solution method and solve. Explain your choice.

C Every day, about 120 tons of cosmic dust—debris from outer space—enter Earth's atmosphere. How many tons of cosmic dust enter Earth's atmosphere each year?

<u>tons per day</u> × <u>days per year</u>   *Think: There are 365 days in a year.*
   120   ×   365

These numbers are not compatible, so mental math is not a good choice.

You could use paper and pencil. But finding a product of 3-digit numbers requires several steps. Using a calculator will probably be faster.

Carefully enter the numbers on a calculator. Record the product.
120 × 365 = 43,800

Each year, about 43,800 tons of cosmic dust enter Earth's atmosphere.

Think and Discuss

1. Give an example of a situation in which you would use mental math to solve a problem. When would you use paper and pencil?

2. Tell how you could use mental math in Example 1B if the problem were 867 + 59.

1-5 Exercises

GUIDED PRACTICE

See Example **1**   Choose a solution method and solve. Explain your choice.

1. Astronomy What is the total number of astronauts who have space flight experience?

U.S.	Germany	France	Canada	Japan	Italy	Russia
244	9	8	7	5	3	88

2. Sports In the 2004 Summer Olympic Games, 929 medals were given. The U.S. team brought home the most medals, 103. How many medals were not won by the U.S. team?

3. A factory produces 126 golf balls per minute. How many golf balls can be produced in 515 minutes?

INDEPENDENT PRACTICE

See Example 1 Choose a solution method and solve. Explain your choice.
For 4 and 5, use the diagram at right.

6	9	5
10	20	8
3	7	4

4. The highest score is a total of all the squares on the board. What is that score?

5. What score is higher, the total of the squares in the middle row or middle column?

6. If each store in a chain of 108 furniture stores sells 135 sofas a year, what is the total number of sofas sold?

PRACTICE AND PROBLEM SOLVING

Extra Practice
See page EP2.

Simplify the expression, and state the method of computation you used.

7. $5 + 24 + 7 + 1 + 64 + 2 + 8$
8. $16 + 2 + 4 + 13 + 5 + 1 + 14$
9. 828×623
10. $742 - 167$
11. $41 + 169$
12. $499 - 201$
13. $338 + 12$

14. A satellite travels 985,200 miles per year. How many miles will it travel if it stays in space for 12 years?

15. **What's the Question?** An astronaut has spent the following minutes training in a tank that simulates weightlessness: 2, 15, 5, 40, 10, and 55. The answer is 127. What is the question?

16. **Write About It** Explain how you can decide whether to use pencil and paper, mental math, or a calculator to solve a subtraction problem.

17. **Challenge** A list of possible astronauts was narrowed down by two committees. The first committee selected 93 people to complete a written form. The second selected 31 of those people to come to an interview. If 837 were not asked to complete a form, how many were on the original list?

Test Prep and Spiral Review

18. **Multiple Choice** It takes Mars 687 days to revolve around the Sun. It takes Venus only 225 days to revolve around the Sun. How many more days does it take Mars to revolve around the Sun than it takes Venus?

    Ⓐ 462 days   Ⓑ 500 days   Ⓒ 900 days   Ⓓ 912 days

19. **Short Response** Hector biked 13 miles on Monday, Wednesday, and Friday of every week for 24 weeks. Find the total number of miles he biked during the 24 weeks. Explain your answer.

Simplify each expression. (Lesson 1-3)
20. $(2 + 7 - 5) \div 2$
21. $10(6 - 3)$
22. $5 + 8 \times 7 - 1$
23. $5 + (8 + 2) - 3$

Identify the property illustrated by each equation. (Lesson 1-4)
24. $3 + (4 + 5) = (3 + 4) + 5$
25. $19(24) = 19(20) + 19(4)$
26. $2(13) = 13(2)$

1-6 Patterns and Sequences

Learn to find patterns and to recognize, describe, and extend patterns in sequences.

Vocabulary
sequence
term
arithmetic sequence

Each month, Eva chooses 3 new DVDs from her DVD club.

Eva's DVDs

Position ⇨

Month	DVDs
1	3
2	6
3	9
4	12

⇦ Value of Term

+3
+3
+3

The number of DVDs Eva has after each month shows a pattern: Add 3. This pattern can be written as a sequence. 3, 6, 9, 12, 15, . . .

A **sequence** is an ordered set of numbers. Each number in the sequence is called a **term**. In this sequence, the first term is 3, the second term is 6, and the third term is 9.

When the terms of a sequence change by the same amount each time, the sequence is an **arithmetic sequence**.

EXAMPLE 1   Extending Arithmetic Sequences

Identify a pattern in each arithmetic sequence and then find the missing terms.

A 3, 15, 27, 39, ▢, ▢, . . .

Look for a pattern.
A pattern is to add 12 to each term to get the next term.

3, 15, 27, 39, ▢, ▢, . . .
+12 +12 +12 +12 +12

$39 + 12 = 51$ $51 + 12 = 63$
So 51 and 63 are the missing terms.

Helpful Hint
Look for a relationship between the 1st term and the 2nd term. Check if this relationship works between the 2nd term and the 3rd term, and so on.

B 12, 21, 30, 39, ▢, ▢, . . .

Use a table to find a pattern.

Position	1	2	3	4	5	6
Value of Term	12	21	30	39	▢	▢

+9 +9 +9 +9 +9

A pattern is to add 9 to each term to get the next term.
$39 + 9 = 48$ $48 + 9 = 57$
So 48 and 57 are the missing terms.

Interactivities Online ▶

Video   Lesson Tutorials Online   my.hrw.com

Not all sequences are arithmetic sequences.

Arithmetic Sequences	Not Arithmetic Sequences

2, 4, 6, 8,...   20, 35, 50, 65,...
  +2 +2 +2   +15 +15 +15
	1, 3, 6, 10,... 2, 6, 18, 54,...
	  +2 +3 +4 ×3 ×3 ×3

In nonarithmetic sequences, look for patterns that involve multiplication or division. Some sequences may even be combinations of different operations.

EXAMPLE 2 Completing Other Sequences

Identify a pattern in each sequence. Name the missing terms.

A 4, 15, 8, 19, 12, 23, 16, ▪, ▪, ▪, ...

4 15 8 19 12 23 16 ▪ ▪ ▪
 +11 −7 +11 −7 +11 −7 +11 −7 +11

A pattern is to add 11 to one term and subtract 7 from the next.

$16 + 11 = 27 \quad 27 - 7 = 20 \quad 20 + 11 = 31$

So 27, 20, and 31 are the missing terms.

B

Position	1	2	3	4	5	6	7	8	9
Value of Term	1	6	2	12	▪	24	8	▪	16

Position	1	2	3	4	5	6	7	8	9
Value of Term	1	6	2	12	▪	24	8	▪	16

×6 ÷3 ×6 ÷3 ×6 ÷3 ×6 ÷3

A pattern is to multiply one term by 6 and divide the next by 3.

$12 \div 3 = 4 \qquad 8 \times 6 = 48$

So 4 and 48 are the missing terms.

Think and Discuss

1. **Tell** how you could check whether the next two terms in the arithmetic sequence 5, 7, 9, 11, . . . are 13 and 15.

2. **Explain** how to find the next term in the sequence 16, 8, 4, 2, ▪, ...

3. **Explain** how to determine whether 256, 128, 64, 32, . . . is an arithmetic or nonarithmetic sequence.

1-6 Exercises

GUIDED PRACTICE

See Example 1 Identify a pattern in each arithmetic sequence and then find the missing terms.

1. 12, 24, 36, 48, ▪, ▪, ▪, ...
2. 105, 90, 75, 60, 45, ▪, ▪, ▪, ...

3.
Position	1	2	3	4	5	6
Value of Term	7	18	29	40	▪	▪

4.
Position	1	2	3	4	5	6
Value of Term	44	38	32	26	▪	▪

See Example 2 Identify a pattern in each sequence. Name the missing terms.

5. 2, 9, 7, 14, ▪, ▪, ...
6. 80, 8, 40, 4, ▪, 2, 10, ▪, ...

7.
Position	1	2	3	4	5	6	7	8
Value of Term	1	6	3	18	▪	54	27	▪

INDEPENDENT PRACTICE

See Example 1 Identify a pattern in each arithmetic sequence and then find the missing terms.

8. 9, 19, 29, 39, 49, ▪, ▪, ▪, ...
9. 98, 84, 70, 56, 42, ▪, ▪, ▪, ...

10.
Position	1	2	3	4	5	6
Value of Term	45	38	31	24	▪	▪

11.
Position	1	2	3	4	5	6
Value of Term	8	11	14	17	▪	▪

See Example 2 Identify a pattern in each sequence. Name the missing terms.

12. 50, 40, 43, 33, ▪, 26, ▪, ...
13. 7, 28, 24, 45, ▪, ▪, ▪, ...

14.
Position	1	2	3	4	5	6	7
Value of Term	120	60	180	90	▪	▪	405

15.
Position	1	2	3	4	5	6	7
Value of Term	400	100	200	50	▪	▪	50

1-6 Patterns and Sequences

PRACTICE AND PROBLEM SOLVING

Extra Practice
See page EP2.

Use the pattern to write the first five terms of the sequence.

16. Start with 1; multiply by 3. **17.** Start with 5; add 9. **18.** Start with 100; subtract 7.

19. Social Studies The Chinese lunar calendar is based on a 12-year cycle, with each of the 12 years named after a different animal. The year 2006 was the year of the dog.
   a. When will the next year of the dog occur?
   b. When was the last year of the dog?
   c. Will the year 2030 be a year of the dog? Explain.

Identify whether each given sequence could be arithmetic. If not, identify the pattern of the sequence.

20. 10, 16, 22, 28, 34, ... **21.** 60, 56, 61, 57, 62, ... **22.** 111, 121, 131, 141, 151, ...

23. Choose a Strategy The * shows where a piece is missing from the pattern. What piece is missing?

   Ⓐ y   Ⓑ B   Ⓒ y   Ⓓ Y

24. Whole numbers raised to the second power are called perfect squares. This is because they can be represented by objects arranged in the shape of a square. Perfect squares can be written as the sequence 1, 4, 9, 16, ...
   a. Find the next two perfect squares in the sequence.
   b. Explain how can you know whether a number is a perfect square?

25. Write About It Explain how to determine if a sequence is arithmetic.

26. Challenge Find the missing terms in the following sequence:
   ▓, 2^3, 27, 4^3, 125, ▓, 343, ...

Test Prep and Spiral Review

27. Multiple Choice Identify the pattern in the sequence 6, 11, 16, 21, 26, ...

   Ⓐ Add 5.   Ⓑ Add 6.   Ⓒ Multiply by 5.   Ⓓ Multiply by 6.

28. Extended Response Identify the first term and a pattern for the sequence 5, 8, 11, 14, 17, ... Is the sequence arithmetic? Explain why or why not. Find the next three terms in the sequence.

Use mental math to find each sum or product. *(Lesson 1-4)*

29. 13 + 6 + 17 + 24   **30.** 4 × 11 × 5   **31.** 45 + 11 + 35 + 29

Choose a solution method and solve. Explain your choice. *(Lesson 1-5)*

32. As of 2006, Hank Aaron was Major League Baseball's career home run leader with 755 home runs. Sadaharu Oh was the career home run leader of Japanese baseball with 868 home runs. How many more home runs did Oh hit than Aaron?

Technology Lab 1-6
Find a Pattern in Sequences

Use with Lesson 1-6

Learn It Online
Lab Resources Online go.hrw.com,
keyword MR10 Lab1

The numbers 4, 7, 10, 13, 16, 19, … form an arithmetic sequence. To continue the sequence, identify a pattern. Here is a possible pattern:

$$4, \quad 4 + 3 = 7, \quad 7 + 3 = 10, \quad 10 + 3 = 13, \ldots$$

Activity

Use a spreadsheet to generate the first seven terms of the sequence above.

To start with 4, type **4** in cell A1.

To add 3 to the value in cell A1, type **=A1 + 3** in cell B1.

Press ENTER.

To continue the sequence, click the square in the lower right corner of cell B1, hold down the mouse button, and drag the cursor across through cell G1.

When you release the mouse button, A1 through G1 will list the first seven terms of the sequence.

Think and Discuss

1. How do you use a sequence's pattern when you use your spreadsheet to generate the terms?

Try This

Identify a pattern in each sequence. Then use a spreadsheet to generate the first 12 terms.

1. 9, 14, 19, 24, 29, 34, …
2. 7, 13, 19, 25, 31, 37, …
3. 105, 98, 91, 84, 77, 70, …
4. 21, 29, 37, 45, 53, 61, …
5. 150, 174, 198, 222, 246, 270, …
6. 600, 550, 500, 450, 400, 350, …

Ready To Go On?

Quiz for Lessons 1-3 Through 1-6

1-3 Order of Operations

Simplify each expression.

1. $3 \times 4 \div (10 - 4)$
2. $5^2 + 10 \div 2 - 1$
3. $4 + (12 - 8) \times 6$
4. $(2^3 + 2) \times 10$

5. Mrs. Webb buys 7 cards for $2 each, 3 metallic pens for $1 each, and 1 pad of writing paper for $4. Simplify $7 \times 2 + 3 \times 1 + 1 \times 4$ to find the total amount Mrs. Webb spends.

1-4 Properties and Mental Math

Simplify.

6. $4 + 21 + 9 + 6$
7. $5 \times 17 \times 2$
8. $45 + 19 + 1 + 55$
9. $2 \times 17 \times 10$

Use the Distributive Property to find each product.

10. 5×62
11. 9×41
12. 4×23
13. 7×14
14. 5×34

1-5 Choosing a Method of Computation

Choose a solution method and solve. Explain your choice.

15. How many Texas state parks are shown in the table?

16. How many more parks are there in the Prairies and Lakes region than in the Big Bend region?

Texas State Parks	
Region	Number of Parks
Big Bend	7
Gulf Coast	11
Hill Country	11
Panhandle Plains	12
Pineywoods	13
Prairies and Lakes	22
South Texas Plains	5

1-6 Patterns and Sequences

Identify a pattern in the arithmetic sequence and then find the missing terms.

17.

Position	1	2	3	4	5	6	7
Value of Term	5	14	23	32	■	■	■

Identify a pattern in each sequence. Name the missing terms.

18. 4, 20, 15, 31, ■, ■, 37, …

19. 16, 32, 8, 16, ■, 8, 2, ■, 1, …

20. A concert hall has 5 seats in the front row, 9 seats in the second row, 13 seats in the third row, and 17 seats in the fourth row. If this pattern continues, how many seats are in the sixth row?

Real-World Connections

CHAPTER 1

UConn Women's Basketball The University of Connecticut, located in Storrs, is home to one of the nation's best women's basketball teams. In fact, the Huskies won the national championship in 2002, 2003, and 2004. The team's success has made them a favorite of sports fans throughout Connecticut and around the country.

CONNECTICUT

Storrs

1. The table shows the number of field goals and free throws that were made by some of the team's players during the 2007–2008 season. Estimate the total number of free throws that were made by these players. Explain how you made your estimate.

UConn Women's Basketball: 2007–2008 Season			
Player	Two-Point Field Goals	Three-Point Field Goals	Free Throws
Tina Charles	202	0	86
Renee Montgomery	91	63	96
Mel Thomas	22	35	17
Ketia Swanier	47	39	13
Meghan Gardler	17	5	21

2. To find the total number of points a player scored, multiply the number of two-point field goals by 2, multiply the number of three-point field goals by 3, and multiply the number of free throws by 1. Then add these values.

    a. To find the number of points scored by Ketia Swanier, a fan writes the expression 47 × 2 + 39 × 3 + 13 × 1. Explain how to evaluate this expression. Then find the number of points Ketia Swanier scored.

    b. Which of the five players scored the greatest number of points?

3. In a 2008 game against Georgetown, the UConn team scored $2^6 + 4^2$ points. The two teams scored a total of 2^7 points. What was the final score of the game?

Real-World Connections **35**

Game Time

Palindromes

A *palindrome* is a word, phrase, or number that reads the same forward and backward.

Examples:
race car   Madam, I'm Adam.   3710173

You can turn almost any number into a palindrome with this trick.

Think of any number.
Now add that number in reverse.

```
  283
+ 382
  665
```

Use the sum to repeat the previous step and keep repeating until the final sum is a palindrome.

```
   665
 + 566
 1,231
```

```
  1,231
+ 1,321
  2,552
```

It took only three steps to create a palindrome by starting with the number 283. What happens if you start with the number 196? Do you think you will ever create a palindrome if you start with 196? One man who started with 196 did these steps until he had a number with 70,928 digits and he still had not created a palindrome!

Spin-a-Million

The object of this game is to create the number closest to 1,000,000.

Taking turns, spin the pointer and write the number on your place-value chart. The number cannot be moved once it has been placed.

After six turns, the player whose number is closest to one million wins the round and scores a point. The first player to get five points wins the game.

A complete copy of the rules and game pieces are available online.

Learn It Online
Game Time Extra go.hrw.com,
keyword MR10 Games

It's in the Bag!

Materials
- plastic DVD case
- card stock
- markers
- scissors
- glue stick
- library pocket
- index cards
- brass fastener
- large paper clip

PROJECT Picture This

Make a game in an empty DVD case to review concepts from this chapter.

Directions

1. Cut a piece of card stock that can be folded in half to fit inside the DVD case. Lay the card stock flat and draw a path for a board game. Be sure to have a start and a finish. **Figure A**

2. Close the game board and decorate the front. Glue a library pocket onto the front to hold the index cards. **Figure B**

3. On the index cards, write problems that can be solved using math from the chapter. Place the cards in the pocket.

4. Cut a piece of card stock to fit the other side of the DVD box. Glue directions for your game at the top. At the bottom, make a spinner the size of a DVD. Attach a brass fastener to the middle of the spinner, and then attach a paper clip to the fastener. **Figure C**

Putting the Math into Action

Play your game with a partner. Use buttons or coins as playing pieces. Players should take turns spinning the spinner and then be required to solve a problem correctly in order to move their piece.

It's in the Bag! 37

CHAPTER 1 Study Guide: Review

Vocabulary

arithmetic sequence 29	exponential form 10
Associative Property 22	numerical expression 18
base 10	order of operations 18
Commutative Property 22	overestimate 6
compatible numbers 6	sequence 29
Distributive Property 23	simplify 18
estimate 6	term 29
exponent 10	underestimate 6

Complete the sentences below with vocabulary words from the list above.

1. An ordered set of numbers is called a(n) ___?___. Each number in a sequence is called a(n) ___?___.

2. In the expression 8^5, 8 is the ___?___, and 5 is the ___?___.

3. The ___?___ is a set of rules used to evaluate an expression that contains more than one operation.

4. When you ___?___ a numerical expression, you find its value.

EXAMPLES / EXERCISES

1-1 Estimating with Whole Numbers (pp. 6–9)

■ **Estimate the sum 837 + 710 by rounding to the hundreds place.**
800 + 700 = 1,500
The sum is about 1,500.

■ **Estimate the quotient of 148 and 31.**
150 ÷ 30 = 5
The quotient is about 5.

Estimate each sum or difference by rounding to the place value indicated.

5. 4,671 − 3,954; thousands

6. 3,123 + 2,987; thousands

7. 53,465 − 27,465; ten thousands

8. Ralph has 38 photo album sheets with 22 baseball cards in each sheet. About how many baseball cards does he have?

38 Chapter 1 Whole Numbers and Patterns

EXAMPLES | EXERCISES

1-2 Exponents (pp. 10–13)

■ Write 6 × 6 in exponential form.

6^2 *6 is a factor 2 times.*

Find each value.

■ 5^2 ■ 6^3
$5^2 = 5 × 5$ $6^3 = 6 × 6 × 6$
    = 25   = 216

Write each expression in exponential form.

9. 5 × 5 × 5
10. 3 × 3 × 3 × 3 × 3
11. 7 × 7 × 7 × 7
12. 8 × 8
13. 4 × 4 × 4 × 4
14. 1 × 1 × 1

Find each value.

15. 4^4
16. 2^4
17. 6^3
18. 3^3
19. 1^5
20. 7^4
21. 5^3
22. 10^2
23. 9^2

1-3 Order of Operations (pp. 18–21)

■ Simplify $8 ÷ (7 − 5) × 2^2 − 2 + 9$.

$8 ÷ (7 − 5) × 2^2 − 2 + 9$
$8 ÷ 2 × 2^2 − 2 + 9$ *Subtract in parentheses.*
$8 ÷ 2 × 4 − 2 + 9$ *Simplify the exponent.*
$4 × 4 − 2 + 9$ *Divide.*
$16 − 2 + 9$ *Multiply.*
$14 + 9$ *Subtract.*
23 *Add.*

Simplify each expression.

24. 9 × 8 − 13
25. 21 ÷ 3 + 4
26. 6 + 4 × 5
27. 19 − 12 ÷ 6
28. 30 ÷ 2 − 5 × 2
29. $(7 + 3) ÷ 2 × 3^2$
30. Jerome bought 4 shirts for $12 each and 5 pairs of pants for $18 each. The tax for his purchase was $11. Simplify 4 × 12 + 5 × 18 + 11 to find the amount Jerome spent for clothes.

1-4 Properties and Mental Math (pp. 22–25)

Simplify.

■ 4 + 13 + 6 + 7   ■ 5 × 9 × 6
   4 + 6 + 13 + 7   5 × 6 × 9
   (4 + 6) + (13 + 7)   (5 × 6) × 9
     10   +   20   30 × 9
         30   270

■ Use the Distributive Property to find 3 × 16.

$3 × 16 = 3 × (10 + 6)$
$= (3 × 10) + (3 × 6)$
$= 30 + 18 = 48$

Simplify.

31. 9 + 5 + 1 + 15
32. 8 × 13 × 5
33. 31 + 16 + 19 + 14
34. 6 × 12 × 15
35. 17 + 12 + 8 + 3
36. 16 × 5 × 4

Use the Distributive Property to find each product.

37. 7 × 24
38. 9 × 15
39. 6 × 34
40. 8 × 19

EXAMPLES / EXERCISES

1-5 Choosing a Method of Computation (pp. 26–28)

■ Choose a solution method and solve. Explain your choice.

The average annual rainfall in Washington, D.C., is 39 inches. How much rain does Washington, D.C., average in 8 years?

These numbers are not so big that you must use a calculator. Use pencil and paper to find the answer. 39 × 8 = 312 inches

Choose a solution method and solve. Explain your choice.

41. The average high temperature for Washington, D.C., in January is 42 °F. The record high temperature for Washington, D.C., is 104 °F. How much higher is the record temperature than the average high temperature in January?

42. There are 14 players on Emily's softball team. If each player's family bought 5 tickets to a tournament, how many tickets did Emily's team buy in all?

43. If the National Debt of the United States is $8,951,056,150,180.66 and there are 302,634,238 people in the country, what is each person's share of the debt, rounded to the nearest penny?

44. At 5:00 A.M., the temperature was 41 °F. By noon, the temperature was 69 °F. By how many degrees did the temperature increase?

1-6 Patterns and Sequences (pp. 29–32)

Identify a pattern in the sequence. Name the missing terms.

■ 1, 3, 5, 7, ▨, ▨, ...
  +2 +2 +2 +2 +2

The pattern is to add 2 to each term. The missing terms are 9 and 11.

■ 6, 12, 11, 22, ▨, 42, ▨, ...
  ×2 −1 ×2 −1 ×2 −1

The pattern is to multiply one term by 2 and subtract the next by 1. The missing terms are 21 and 41.

Identify a pattern in each arithmetic sequence and then find the missing terms.

45. 4, 9, 14, 19, ▨, ▨, ...
46. 21, 19, 17, 15, ▨, ▨, ...

Identify a pattern in each sequence. Name the missing terms.

47. 16, 20, 18, 22, ▨, 24, ▨, ...
48. 1, 3, 9, 27, ▨, ▨, ...
49. 65, 70, 68, 73, ▨, 76, ▨, ...

Chapter Test

CHAPTER 1

Estimate each sum or difference by rounding to the place value indicated.

1. 8,743 + 3,198; thousands
2. 62,524 − 17,831; ten thousands

Estimate.

3. Kaitlin's family is planning a trip from Washington, D.C., to New York City. New York City is 227 miles from Washington, D.C., and the family can drive an average of 55 mi/h. About how long will the trip take?

4. An auditorium can hold 572 people. If 109 people have come in through the north entrance, and 218 people have come in through the south entrance, about how many more people can fit in the auditorium?

Write each expression in exponential form.

5. $4 \times 4 \times 4 \times 4 \times 4$
6. $10 \times 10 \times 10$
7. $6 \times 6 \times 6 \times 6$

Find each value.

8. 2^3
9. 5^2
10. 4^4
11. 11^2
12. 9^3

Simplify each expression.

13. $12 + 8 \div 2$
14. $3^2 \times 5 + 10 - 7$
15. $12 + (28 - 15) + 4 \times 2$

Simplify.

16. $15 + 23 + 47 + 5$
17. $5 \times 48 \times 2$
18. $2 \times 5 \times 11$
19. $44 + 18 + 12 + 6$

Use the Distributive Property to find each product.

20. 3×32
21. 52×6
22. 24×5
23. 81×6
24. 6×21

Choose a solution method and solve. Explain your choice.

25. During a performance, a middle school choir stands on risers in 4 rows. There are 11 singers in the first row, 13 in the second row, 14 in the third row, and 17 in the last row. How many singers are there in the choir?

26. Earth is approximately 93,000,000 miles from the Sun. Neptune is approximately 2,794,000,000 miles from the Sun. How many times the distance from Earth to the Sun is the distance from Neptune to the Sun?

Identify a pattern in each sequence. Name the missing terms.

27. 8, 22, 36, 50, ■, ■, ■, . . .
28. 2, 10, 7, 15, ■, 20, ■, . . .

29. A tile pattern has 1 tile in the first row, 3 tiles in the second row, and 5 tiles in the third row. If this pattern continues, how many tiles are in the fifth row?

Test Tackler
Standardized Test Strategies

Multiple Choice: Eliminate Answer Choices

You can solve some math problems without doing detailed calculations. You can use mental math, estimation, or logical reasoning to help you eliminate answer choices and save time.

EXAMPLE 1

Which number is the closest estimate for 678 + 189?

- Ⓐ 700
- Ⓑ 900
- Ⓒ 1,000
- Ⓓ 5,000

You can use logical reasoning to eliminate choice A because it is too small. The estimated sum has to be greater than 700 because 678 + 189 is greater than 700.

Choice D may also be eliminated because the value is too large. The estimated sum will be less than 5,000.

Round 678 up to 700 and 189 up to 200. Then find the sum of 700 and 200: 700 + 200 = 900. You can eliminate choice C because it is greater than 900.

Choice B is the closest estimate.

EXAMPLE 2

Which of the following numbers is the standard form of four million, six hundred eight thousand, fifteen?

- Ⓕ 468,015
- Ⓖ 4,608,015
- Ⓗ 4,068,150
- Ⓙ 4,600,815,000

Logical reasoning can be used to eliminate choices. Numbers that have a place value in the millions must have at least seven but no more than nine digits. Choices F and J can be eliminated because they do not have the correct number of digits.

Both choices G and H have the correct range of digits, so narrow it down further. The number must end in 15. Choice H ends in 50, so it cannot be correct. Eliminate it.

The correct answer choice is G.

HOT TIP! Some answer choices, called distracters, may seem correct because they are based on common errors made in calculations.

Read each item and answer the questions that follow.

Item A
Which number is the greatest?

- Ⓐ 599,485
- Ⓑ 5,571,987
- Ⓒ 5,569,003
- Ⓓ 5,399,879

1. Are there any answer choices you can eliminate immediately? If so, which ones and why?

2. Describe how you can find the correct answer.

City Middle School Populations	
Central Middle School	652
Eastside Middle School	718
Northside Middle School	663
Southside Middle School	731
Westside Middle School	842

Item B
The school district receives $30 a day in state funding for every student enrolled in a public school. Find the approximate number of students that attend all of the city middle schools.

- Ⓕ 2,000
- Ⓖ 3,300
- Ⓗ 3,600
- Ⓙ 4,000

3. Can F be eliminated? Why or why not?

4. Can H be eliminated? Why or why not?

5. Explain how to use mental math to solve this problem.

Item C
Which expression does NOT have the same value as $8 \times (52 + 12)$?

- Ⓐ 8×64
- Ⓑ $(8 \times 52) + (8 \times 12)$
- Ⓒ $8(60) + 8(4)$
- Ⓓ $8 \times 52 + 12$

6. Which answer choice can be eliminated immediately? Explain.

7. Explain how you can use the Distributive Property to solve this problem.

Item D
Stacey is beginning a new exercise program. She plans to cycle 2 kilometers on her first day. Each day after that, she will double the number of kilometers she cycled from the day before. Which expression shows how many kilometers she will cycle on the sixth day?

- Ⓕ 2×6
- Ⓖ $2 + 2 + 2 + 2 + 2 + 2$
- Ⓗ 2^6
- Ⓙ 6^2

8. Are there any answer choices you can eliminate immediately? If so, which choices and why?

9. Explain how you can use a table to help you solve this problem.

Item E
James is driving to his aunt's house. If he drives about 55 miles per hour for 5 hours, about how many miles will he have driven?

- Ⓐ 12 miles
- Ⓑ 300 miles
- Ⓒ 60 miles
- Ⓓ 600 miles

10. Which answer choice(s) can be immediately eliminated and why?

11. Explain how to solve this problem.

Test Tackler

Cumulative Assessment, Chapter 1

Multiple Choice

1. Jonah has 31 boxes of baseball cards. If each box contains 183 cards, about how many baseball cards does Jonah have in his collection?

   (A) 3,000 cards   (C) 9,000 cards
   (B) 6,000 cards   (D) 12,000 cards

2. Which of the following does NOT have a value of 27?

   (F) 3^3 (H) $3 \times 3 + 18$
   (G) $3^2 + 3 \times 7$ (J) $9^2 \div 3$

3. What are the next two terms in the following sequence?

   6, 3, 12, 6, 24, …

   (A) 3, 12   (C) 12, 48
   (B) 6, 36   (D) 18, 72

4. Which of the following correctly shows the use of the Distributive Property to find the product of 64 and 8?

   (F) $64 \times 8 = (8 \times 60) + (8 \times 4)$
   (G) $64 \times 8 = 8 \times 64$
   (H) $64 \times 8 = 8 + (60 + 4)$
   (J) $64 \times 8 = (8 \times 4) \times 60$

5. What is five billion, two hundred fifty-two million, six hundred thousand, three hundred eleven in standard form?

   (A) 5,252,603,011   (C) 5,252,600,311
   (B) 52,526,311   (D) 5,252,060,311

6. The attendance at a local library is shown in the table below. How many people visited the library last week?

Last Week's Attendance	
Sunday	Closed
Monday	78
Tuesday	125
Wednesday	122
Thursday	96
Friday	104
Saturday	225

   (F) 450   (H) 650
   (G) 550   (J) 750

7. Which number is the greatest?

   (A) 5,432,873   (C) 5,221,754
   (B) 5,201,032   (D) 5,332,621

8. What is $6 \times 6 \times 6 \times 6$ written in exponential form?

   (F) 24^4
   (G) 1,296
   (H) 6^4
   (J) $1000 + 200 + 90 + 6$

9. The expression $6 \times 3 \times 4 = 3 \times 6 \times 4$ is an example of which property?

   (A) Associative   (C) Distributive
   (B) Commutative   (D) Exponential

44   *Chapter 1 Whole Numbers and Patterns*

10. Which list of numbers is in order from least to greatest?

   F. 1,231; 1,543; 1,267; 1,321
   G. 3,210; 3,357; 3,366; 3,401 ✓
   H. 4,321; 4,312; 4,211; 4,081
   J. 5,019; 5,187; 5,143; 5,314

11. There are 2,347 seats in the town theater. A ticket to the Friday night concert costs $32. Which method of computation should be used to find how much money the theater will make if the Friday night concert sells out?

   A. Paper and pencil
   B. Calculator
   C. Mental Math
   D. Estimation

HOT TIP! When you read a word problem, underline the information you need to help you answer the question.

Gridded Response

12. What is the value of $3 + 8 \times 6 - (12 \div 4)$?

13. What is the value of 2^4?

14. Martha walked 4 minutes on Monday, 7 minutes on Tuesday, and 10 minutes on Wednesday. If the pattern continues, how many minutes will she walk on Saturday?

15. At 2:00 P.M., the water temperature in the pool was 88 °F. By 10:00 P.M. the water temperature in the pool was 75 °F. By how many degrees did the water temperature drop?

16. Estimate the sum of 3,820 and 4,373 by rounding to the nearest thousand.

17. What is the base of 6^3?

Short Response

S1. Megan deposited $2 into her savings account on the first Friday of the month. Each week she doubles her deposit from the week before.

   a. If this pattern continues, how much money will she deposit in week 4?
   b. What is the total amount in Megan's account after her fourth deposit? Explain how you found your answer.

S2. Create a numerical expression that can be simplified in four steps. Include one set of parentheses and an exponent. The same mathematical operation may be used no more than two times. Show how to simplify your expression.

Extended Response

E1. The student population at Southside Middle School is listed in the table below.

Student Population at Southside Middle School		
	Boys	Girls
6th Grade	98	102
7th Grade	89	105
8th Grade	123	117

   a. Use the information in the table to find the total number of students who attend Southside Middle School. Show your work.
   b. About how many more girls are enrolled in the school than boys? Show your work. Explain how you found your answer.
   c. The school board wants the school to have one teacher for every 20 students. If there are 8 sixth-grade teachers, does the school need to hire more sixth-grade teachers? If so, how many more? Explain your answer.

Cumulative Assessment, Chapter 1   **45**

CHAPTER 2
Introduction to Algebra

2A **Understanding Variables and Expressions**
2-1 Variables and Expressions
2-2 Translating Between Words and Math
2-3 Translating Between Tables and Expressions
LAB Explore Area and Perimeter of Rectangles

2B **Understanding Equations**
2-4 Equations and Their Solutions
2-5 Addition Equations
2-6 Subtraction Equations
2-7 Multiplication Equations
2-8 Division Equations

Chapter Focus
- Write expressions and equations for given situations.
- Evaluate expressions.
- Solve one-step equations.

Why Learn This

Rafting is a popular activity in many parts of the country. If you know how long you rafted and the distance you traveled, you can solve an equation to find the average speed of the river.

Learn It Online
Chapter Project Online go.hrw.com,
keyword MR10 Ch2 Go

Are You Ready?

Vocabulary

Choose the best term from the list to complete each sentence.

1. Multiplication is the ___?___ of division.
2. The ___?___ of 12 and 3 is 36.
3. The ___?___ of 12 and 3 is 15.
4. Addition, subtraction, multiplication, and division are called ___?___.
5. The answer to a division problem is called the ___?___.

dividend
factor
inverse
operations
product
quotient
sum

Complete these exercises to review skills you will need for this chapter.

Multiplication Facts

Multiply.

6. 7×4
7. 8×9
8. 9×6
9. 7×7
10. 6×5
11. 3×8
12. 5×5
13. 2×9

Division Facts

Divide.

14. $64 \div 8$
15. $63 \div 9$
16. $56 \div 7$
17. $54 \div 6$
18. $49 \div 7$
19. $30 \div 5$
20. $32 \div 4$
21. $18 \div 3$

Whole Number Operations

Add, subtract, multiply, or divide.

22. $28 + 15$
23. $71 + 38$
24. $1{,}218 + 430$
25. $2{,}218 + 1{,}135$

26. $72 - 35$
27. $98 - 45$
28. $1{,}642 - 249$
29. $3{,}408 - 1{,}649$

30. 6×13
31. 8×15
32. 16×22
33. 20×35

34. $9\overline{)72}$
35. $7\overline{)84}$
36. $16\overline{)112}$
37. $23\overline{)1{,}472}$

Introduction to Algebra

Chapter 2 Study Guide: Preview

Where You've Been

Previously, you

- wrote numerical expressions involving whole numbers.
- solved problems using addition, subtraction, multiplication, and division of whole numbers.

In This Chapter

You will study

- writing algebraic expressions involving whole numbers.
- using addition, subtraction, multiplication, and division to solve one-step equations involving whole numbers.
- determining whether a number is a solution to an equation.

Where You're Going

You can use the skills learned in this chapter

- to solve one-step equations involving decimals and fractions.
- to solve one-step inequalities.

Key Vocabulary/Vocabulario

algebraic expression	expresión algebraica
constant	constante
equation	ecuación
solution of an equation	solución de una ecuación
variable	variable

Vocabulary Connections

To become familiar with some of the vocabulary terms in the chapter, consider the following. You may refer to the chapter, the glossary, or a dictionary if you like.

1. *Algebra* is a type of math that uses letters to represent numbers. The word *algebraic* means "relating to algebra." What do you think an **algebraic expression** contains?

2. When something is *constant*, it does not change. If there is a **constant** in an expression, do you think the number changes? Explain.

3. When something is *variable*, it is able to vary, or change. What do you think a **variable** in an expression is able to do?

4. An *equation* shows that two expressions are equal. What mathematical symbol would you expect to see in an **equation**?

Reading and Writing Math

CHAPTER 2

Writing Strategy: Use Your Own Words

Sometimes when you are reading about a new math concept for the first time from a textbook, the concept is difficult to understand.

As you go through each lesson, do the following:

- Look for the key ideas.
- Rewrite explanations given as paragraphs as steps or a list.
- Add an example when possible.

What Lupe Reads

When you multiply two numbers, you can "break apart" one of the numbers into a sum and then use the Distributive Property.

What Lupe Writes

Multiply Using Mental Math

Step 1: Break one of the numbers into a sum.
Step 2: Use the Distributive Property.
Step 3: Use mental math to multiply; then add.

Example: 5×27

Break one number into a sum: $5 \times (20 + 7)$

Use the Distributive Property: $(5 \times 20) + (5 \times 7)$

Use mental math to multiply; $100 + 35$
then add: 135

Try This

Rewrite the paragraph in your own words.

1. Sometimes in math you do not need an exact answer. Instead, you can use an estimate. Estimates are close to the exact answer but are usually easier and faster to find. When estimating, you can round the numbers in the problem to compatible numbers. Compatible numbers are close to the numbers in the problem, and they can help you do math mentally.

Introduction to Algebra

2-1 Variables and Expressions

Learn to identify and evaluate expressions.

Vocabulary
variable
constant
algebraic expression
evaluate

Inflation is the rise in prices that occurs over time. For example, you would have paid about $7 in the year 2000 for something that cost only $1 in 1950.

With this information, you can convert prices in 1950 to their equivalent prices in 2000.

1950	2000
$1	$7
$2	$14
$3	$21
$p	$p × 7

A **variable** is a letter or symbol that represents a quantity that can change. In the table above, p is a variable that stands for any price in 1950. A **constant** is a quantity that does not change. For example, the price of something in 2000 is always 7 times the price in 1950.

An **algebraic expression** contains one or more variables and may contain operation symbols. So $p \times 7$ is an algebraic expression.

Algebraic Expressions	NOT Algebraic Expressions
150 + y	85 ÷ 5
35 × w + z	10 + 3 × 5

To **evaluate** an algebraic expression, substitute a number for the variable and then find the value by simplifying.

EXAMPLE 1 Evaluating Algebraic Expressions

Evaluate each expression to find the missing values in the tables.

A

w	w ÷ 11
55	5
66	▪
77	▪

Substitute for w in w ÷ 11.

w = 55; 55 ÷ 11 = 5
w = 66; 66 ÷ 11 = 6
w = 77; 77 ÷ 11 = 7

The missing values are 6 and 7.

Chapter 2 Introduction to Algebra

Evaluate each expression to find the missing values in the tables.

B

n	4 × n + 6²
1	40
2	
3	

Substitute for n in 4 × n + 6².
Use the order of operations.
n = 1; 4 × 1 + 36 = 40
n = 2; 4 × 2 + 36 = **44**
n = 3; 4 × 3 + 36 = **48**

The missing values are 44 and 48.

Writing Math

When you are multiplying a number times a variable, the number is written first. Write "3x" and not "x3." Read 3x as "three x."

You can write multiplication and division expressions without using the symbols × and ÷.

Instead of . . .	You can write . . .
x × 3	x · 3 x(3) 3x
35 ÷ y	$\frac{35}{y}$

EXAMPLE 2 Evaluating Expressions with Two Variables

A rectangle is 2 units wide. What is the area of the rectangle if it is 4, 5, 6, or 7 units long?

You can multiply length and width to find area, which is measured in square units. Let ℓ be length and w be width.

ℓ	w	ℓ × w
4	2	8
5	2	
6	2	
7	2	

Make a table to help you find the number of square units for each length.
ℓ = 4; 4 × 2 = 8 square units
ℓ = 5; 5 × 2 = **10** square units
ℓ = 6; 6 × 2 = **12** square units
ℓ = 7; 7 × 2 = **14** square units

The rectangle will cover 8, 10, 12, or 14 square units.

Check
Draw a rectangle 2 units wide. Then count the total number of square units when the rectangle is 4, 5, 6, and 7 units long.

Think and Discuss

1. **Name** a quantity that is a variable and a quantity that is a constant.

2. **Explain** why 45 + x is an algebraic expression.

2-1 Exercises

GUIDED PRACTICE

See Example 1   Evaluate each expression to find the missing values in the tables.

1.

n	n + 7
38	45
49	
58	

2.

x	$12x + 2^3$
8	104
9	
10	

See Example 2   3. A rectangle is 4 units wide. How many square units does the rectangle cover if it is 6, 7, 8, or 9 units long?

INDEPENDENT PRACTICE

See Example 1   Evaluate each expression to find the missing values in the tables.

4.

x	4x
50	200
100	
150	

5.

n	$2n - 3^2$
10	11
16	
17	

See Example 2   6. A builder is designing a rectangular patio that has a length of 12 units. Find the total number of square units the patio will cover if the width is 4, 5, 6, or 7 units.

PRACTICE AND PROBLEM SOLVING

Extra Practice
See page EP3.

7. **Estimation** Bobby drives his truck at a rate of 50 to 60 miles per hour.
   a. Approximately how far can Bobby drive in 2, 3, 4, and 5 hours?
   b. Bobby plans to take an 8-hour trip, which will include a 1-hour stop for lunch. What is a reasonable distance for Bobby to drive?

8. **Multi-Step** Each table in the cafeteria seats 8 people. Find the total number of people that can be seated at 7, 8, 9, and 10 tables. If the average bill per person is $12, how much money can the cafeteria expect from 7, 8, 9, and 10 tables that have no empty seats?

9. **Measurement** When traveling in Europe, Jessika converts the temperature given in degrees Celsius to a Fahrenheit temperature by using the expression $9x \div 5 + 32$, where x is the Celsius temperature. Find the temperature in degrees Fahrenheit when it is 0 °C, 10 °C, and 25 °C.

10. **Geometry** To find the area of a triangle, you can use the expression $b \times h \div 2$, where b is the base of the triangle and h is its height. Find the area of a triangle with a base of 5 and a height of 6.

52   Chapter 2 Introduction to Algebra

Money

Why does a Polish coin show Australia and a kangaroo? This coin honors Pawel Edmund Strzelecki, a Pole who explored and mapped much of Australia.

Evaluate each expression for the given value of the variable.

11. $3h + 2$ for $h = 10$
12. $2x^2$ for $x = 3$
13. $t - 7$ for $t = 20$
14. $4p - 3$ for $p = 20$
15. $\frac{c}{7}$ for $c = 56$
16. $10 + 2r$ for $r = 5$
17. $3x + 17$ for $x = 13$
18. $5p$ for $p = 12$
19. $s^2 - 15$ for $s = 5$
20. $14 - 2c$ for $c = 2$
21. $10x$ for $x = 11$
22. $4j + 12$ for $j = 9$

23. **Money** The zloty is the currency in Poland. In 2005, 1 U.S. dollar was worth 3 zlotys. How many zlotys were equivalent to 8 U.S. dollars?

24. Use the graph to complete the table.

Cups of Water	Number of Lemons
8	
12	
16	
w	

Lemonade

25. **What's the Error?** A student evaluated the expression $x \div 2$ for $x = 14$ and gave an answer of 28. What did the student do wrong?

26. **Write About It** How would you evaluate the expression $2x + 5$ for $x = 1, 2, 3,$ and 4?

27. **Challenge** Using the algebraic expression $3n - 5$, what is the smallest whole-number value for n that will give you a result greater than 100?

Test Prep and Spiral Review

28. **Multiple Choice** Evaluate $8m - 5$ for $m = 9$.

    Ⓐ 67   Ⓑ 83   Ⓒ 84   Ⓓ 94

29. **Gridded Response** Evaluate the expression $4p + 18$ for $p = 5$.

Write each expression in exponential form. (Lesson 1-2)

30. $3 \times 3 \times 3$
31. $5 \times 5 \times 5 \times 5 \times 5 \times 5$
32. $10 \times 10 \times 10 \times 10$

Choose a computation method and solve. Explain your choice. (Lesson 1-5)

33. Al earns $16 per hour for his work at a factory. He works 32 hours per week and gets paid every 2 weeks. If the factory takes $105 out of each check for taxes, how much money will Al be paid for two weeks of work?

2-1 Variables and Expressions 53

2-2 Translating Between Words and Math

Learn to translate between words and math.

The distance from Charlotte, North Carolina, to Charlotte, Tennessee, is 470 miles. Beth drove c miles from Charlotte, NC, toward Charlotte, TN. How many more miles must she drive to reach Charlotte, TN?

In word problems, you may need to identify the action to translate words to math.

Interactivities Online ▶

Action	Put together or combine	Find how much more or less	Put together groups of equal parts	Separate into equal groups
Operation	Add	Subtract	Multiply	Divide

To solve this problem, you need to find how many more miles Beth must drive. To find *how much more,* subtract.

$$470 - c$$

Beth must drive $470 - c$ more miles to reach Charlotte, TN.

EXAMPLE 1 Social Studies Applications

A The Nile River is the world's longest river. Let n stand for the length in miles of the Nile. The Amazon River is 4,000 miles long. Write an expression to show how much longer the Nile is than the Amazon.

To *find how much longer,* subtract the **length of the Amazon** from the **length of the Nile**.

$$n \quad - \quad 4{,}000$$

The Nile is $n - 4{,}000$ miles longer than the Amazon.

B Let s represent the number of senators that each of the 50 states has in the U.S. Senate. Write an expression for the total number of senators.

To *put together 50 equal groups of s,* multiply 50 times s.

$$50s$$

There are $50s$ senators in the U.S. Senate.

There are several different ways to write math expressions with words.

Operation	+	−	×	÷
Numerical Expression	37 + 28	90 − 12	8 × 48 or 8 · 48 or (8)(48) or 8(48) or (8)48	327 ÷ 3 or $\frac{327}{3}$
Words	• 28 **added** to 37 • 37 **plus** 28 • the **sum** of 37 and 28 • 28 **more than** 37	• 12 **subtracted** from 90 • 90 **minus** 12 • the **difference** of 90 and 12 • 12 **less than** 90 • **take away** 12 from 90	• 8 **times** 48 • 48 **multiplied** by 8 • the **product** of 8 and 48 • 8 **groups of** 48	• 327 **divided** by 3 • the **quotient** of 327 and 3
Algebraic Expression	x + 28	k − 12	8 · w or (8)(w) or 8w	n ÷ 3 or $\frac{n}{3}$
Words	• 28 **added** to x • x **plus** 28 • the **sum** of x and 28 • 28 **more than** x	• 12 **subtracted** from k • k **minus** 12 • the **difference** of k and 12 • 12 **less than** k • **take away** 12 from k	• 8 **times** w • w **multiplied** by 8 • the **product** of 8 and w • 8 **groups of** w	• n **divided** by 3 • the **quotient** of n and 3

EXAMPLE 2   **Translating Words into Math**

Write each phrase as a numerical or algebraic expression.

A 287 plus 932
287 + 932

B b divided by 14
b ÷ 14 or $\frac{b}{14}$

EXAMPLE 3   **Translating Math into Words**

Write two phrases for each expression.

A a − 45
• a **minus** 45
• **take away** 45 from a

B (34)(7)
• the **product** of 34 and 7
• 7 **multiplied** by 34

Think and Discuss

1. Tell how to write each of the following phrases as a numerical or algebraic expression: 75 less than 1,023; the product of 125 and z.

2. Give two examples of "a ÷ 17" expressed with words.

2-2 Translating Between Words and Math

2-2 Exercises

Learn It Online
Homework Help Online go.hrw.com,
keyword MR10 2-2
Exercises 1–27, 29, 31, 33, 37

GUIDED PRACTICE

See Example 1
1. **Social Studies** The Big Island of Hawaii is the largest Hawaiian island, with an area of 4,028 mi^2. The next biggest island is Maui. Let m represent the area of Maui. Write an expression for the difference between the two areas.

See Example 2
Write each phrase as a numerical or algebraic expression.
2. 279 minus 125
3. the product of 15 and x
4. 17 plus 4
5. p divided by 5
6. the sum of 9 and q
7. 149 times 2

See Example 3
Write two phrases for each expression.
8. $r + 87$
9. 345×196
10. $476 \div 28$
11. $d - 5$

INDEPENDENT PRACTICE

See Example 1
12. **Social Studies** In 2005, California had 21 more seats in the U.S. Congress than Texas had. If t represents the number of seats Texas had, write an expression for the number of seats California had.

13. Let x represent the number of television show episodes that are taped in a season. Write an expression for the number of episodes taped in 5 seasons.

See Example 2
Write each phrase as a numerical or algebraic expression.
14. 25 less than k
15. the quotient of 325 and 25
16. 34 times w
17. 675 added to 137
18. the sum of 135 and p
19. take away 14 from j

See Example 3
Write two phrases for each expression.
20. $h + 65$
21. $243 - 19$
22. $125 \div n$
23. $342(75)$
24. $\frac{d}{27}$
25. $45 \cdot 23$
26. $629 + c$
27. $228 - b$

PRACTICE AND PROBLEM SOLVING

Extra Practice
See page EP3.

Translate each phrase into a numerical or algebraic expression.
28. 13 less than z
29. 15 divided by d
30. 874 times 23
31. m multiplied by 67
32. the sum of 35, 74, and 21
33. 319 less than 678

34. **Critical Thinking** Paula and Manda were asked to write an expression to find the total number of shoes in a closet. Let s represent the number of pairs of shoes. Paula wrote s and Manda wrote $2s$. Who is correct? Explain.

35. **Write About It** Write a situation that could be modeled by the expression $x + 5$.

56 Chapter 2 Introduction to Algebra

Science Link

The graph shows the number of U.S. space exploration missions from 1961 to 2005.

U.S. Space Exploration Missions

(Bar graph showing Number of missions vs. Years: 1961–1965, 1966–1970, 1971–1975, 1976–1980, 1981–1985, 1986–1990, 1991–1995, 1996–2000, 2001–2005)

36. Between 1966 and 1970, the Soviet Union had m fewer space missions than the United States. Write an algebraic expression for this situation.

37. Let d represent the number of dollars that the United States spent on space missions from 1986 to 1990. Write an expression for the cost per mission.

38. ✏️ **Write a Problem** Use the data in the graph to write a word problem that can be answered with a numerical or algebraic expression.

39. **Critical Thinking** Let p stand for the number of missions between 1996 and 2000 that had people aboard. What operation would you use to write an expression for the number of missions without people? Explain.

40. ⭐ **Challenge** Write an expression for the following: two more than the number of missions from 1971 to 1975, minus the number of missions from 1986 to 1990. Then evaluate the expression.

Test Prep and Spiral Review

41. Multiple Choice Which expression represents the product of 79 and x?

Ⓐ $79 + x$ Ⓑ $x - 79$ Ⓒ $79x$ Ⓓ $\frac{x}{79}$

42. Extended Response Tim is driving from Ames, Iowa to Canton, Ohio. He is 280 miles from Ames when he stops for gas. Write an expression to represent the number of miles Tim has left to drive. Explain. Translate your expression into two different word phrases.

Use mental math to find each sum or product. (Lesson 1-4)

43. $8 \times 5 \times 9$ **44.** $49 + 26 + 11 + 14$ **45.** $4 \times 15 \times 6$

Evaluate each expression for the given value of the variable. (Lesson 2-1)

46. $2y + 6$ for $y = 4$ **47.** $\frac{z}{5}$ for $z = 40$ **48.** $7r - 3$ for $r = 18$ **49.** $\frac{p}{7} + 12$ for $p = 28$

2-2 Translating Between Words and Math

2-3 Translating Between Tables and Expressions

Learn to write expressions for tables and sequences.

In 2004, International Chess Master Andrew Martin broke a world record by playing 321 games of chess at the same time. Each game required 32 chess pieces. The table shows the number of pieces needed for different numbers of games.

Games	Pieces
1	32
2	64
3	96
n	$32n$

The number of pieces is always 32 times the number of games. For n games, the expression $32n$ gives the number of pieces that are needed.

EXAMPLE 1 — Writing an Expression

Write an expression for the missing value in each table.

A

Reilly's Age	Ashley's Age
9	11
10	12
11	13
12	14
n	■

Ashley's age is Reilly's age plus 2.
$9 + 2 = 11$
$10 + 2 = 12$
$11 + 2 = 13$
$12 + 2 = 14$
$n + 2$

When Reilly's age is n, Ashley's age is $n + 2$.

B

Eggs	Dozens
12	1
24	2
36	3
48	4
e	■

The number of dozens is the number of eggs divided by 12.
$12 \div 12 = 1$
$24 \div 12 = 2$
$36 \div 12 = 3$
$48 \div 12 = 4$
$e \div 12$

When there are e eggs, the number of dozens is $e \div 12$, or $\frac{e}{12}$.

You can look for a pattern in a table to help you write an expression.

EXAMPLE 2   Writing an Expression for a Sequence

Write an expression for the sequence in the table.

Position	1	2	3	4	5	n
Value of Term	3	5	7	9	11	

Look for a relationship between the positions and the values of the terms in the sequence. Use guess and check.

Guess $2n$.
Check by substituting 3.
$2 \times 3 \neq 7$ ✗

Guess $2n + 1$.
Check by substituting 3.
$2 \times 3 + 1 = 7$ ✓

The expression $2n + 1$ works for the entire sequence.
$2 \times 1 + 1 = 3, 2 \times 2 + 1 = 5, 2 \times 3 + 1 = 7,$
$2 \times 4 + 1 = 9, 2 \times 5 + 1 = 11$

The expression for the sequence is $2n + 1$.

Caution!
When you write an expression for data in a table, check that the expression works for *all* of the data in the table.

EXAMPLE 3   Writing an Expression for the Area of a Figure

A triangle has a base of 8 inches. The table shows the area of the triangle for different heights. Write an expression that can be used to find the area of the triangle when its height is h inches.

Base (in.)	Height (in.)	Area (in²)
8	1	4
8	2	8
8	3	12
8	4	16
8	h	

$8 \times 1 = 8, \quad 8 \div 2 = 4$
$8 \times 2 = 16, \quad 16 \div 2 = 8$
$8 \times 3 = 24, \quad 24 \div 2 = 12$
$8 \times 4 = 32, \quad 32 \div 2 = 16$
$8 \times h = 8h, \quad 8h \div 2$

In each row of the table, the area is half the product of the base and the height. The expression is $\frac{8h}{2}$, or $4h$.

Think and Discuss

1. **Describe** how to write an expression for a sequence given in a table.
2. **Explain** why it is important to check your expression for all of the data in a table.

2-3 Exercises

GUIDED PRACTICE

See Example 1 — Write an expression for the missing value in each table.

1.

Go-Carts	1	2	3	4	n
Wheels	4	8	12	16	

See Example 2 — Write an expression for the sequence in the table.

2.

Position	1	2	3	4	5	n
Value of Term	9	10	11	12	13	

See Example 3

3. A rectangle has a length of 5 inches. The table shows the area of the rectangle for different widths. Write an expression that can be used to find the area of the rectangle when its width is w inches.

Length (in.)	Width (in.)	Area (in²)
5	2	10
5	4	20
5	6	30
5	8	40
5	w	

INDEPENDENT PRACTICE

See Example 1 — Write an expression for the missing value in each table.

4.

Players	Soccer Teams
22	2
44	4
66	6
88	8
n	

5.

Weeks	Days
4	28
8	56
12	84
16	112
n	

See Example 2 — Write an expression for the sequence in the table.

6.

Position	1	2	3	4	5	n
Value of Term	7	12	17	22	27	

See Example 3

7. The table shows the area of a square with different side lengths. Write an expression that can be used to find the area of a square when its side length is s feet.

Length (ft)	2	4	6	8	s
Area (ft²)	4	16	36	64	

Chapter 2 Introduction to Algebra

PRACTICE AND PROBLEM SOLVING

Extra Practice
See page EP3.

Make a table for each sequence. Then write an expression for the sequence.

8. 2, 4, 6, 8, ...
9. 6, 7, 8, 9, ...
10. 10, 20, 30, 40, ...

11. **Earth Science** The planet Mercury takes 88 days to make a complete orbit of the Sun. The table shows the number of orbits and the number of days it takes to make the orbits. Write an expression for the number of days it takes Mercury to make n orbits.

Orbits	Days
1	88
2	176
3	264
n	▇

12. **Multi-Step** The entry fee for a county fair is $10. Each ride at the fair costs $2. The table shows the total cost to go on various numbers of rides. Write an expression for the cost of r rides. Then use the expression to find the cost of 12 rides.

Number of Rides	1	3	5	8	10	r
Total Cost ($)	12	16	20	26	30	▇

13. **Critical Thinking** Write two different expressions that describe the relationship in the table.

Position (n)	Value of Term
3	10

14. **Write About It** Explain how you can make a table of values for the expression $4n + 3$.

15. **Challenge** Can there be more than one expression that describes a set of data in a table? Explain.

Test Prep and Spiral Review

16. **Multiple Choice** Which expression describes the sequence in the table?

Position	1	2	3	4	5	n
Value of Term	6	11	16	21	26	▇

Ⓐ $n + 5$ Ⓑ $5n + 1$ Ⓒ $6n$ Ⓓ $6n - 1$

17. **Multiple Choice** Find the missing value in the sequence 1, 3, 5, ▇, 9, ...

Ⓕ 6 Ⓖ 7 Ⓗ 8 Ⓙ 9

Simplify each expression. (Lesson 1-3)
18. $14 + 8 \times 2$
19. $6^2 - (4 + 3)$
20. $5 \times 8 \div (3 + 1)$
21. $45 \div 3^2 + 16$

Use the Distributive Property to find each product. (Lesson 1-4)
22. 3×21
23. 7×35
24. 6×19
25. 2×63

Hands-on LAB 2-3

Explore Area and Perimeter of Rectangles

Use with Lesson 2-3

Learn It Online
Lab Resources Online go.hrw.com,
keyword MR10 Lab2 Go

REMEMBER
- Perimeter is the distance around a figure.
- Area is the amount of space a figure covers. It is measured in square units.

You can use graph paper to model the area of different rectangles.

Activity 1

Sarita is digging rectangular vegetable gardens. To prevent weeds from growing she will cover each garden with a mesh sheet the exact size of the garden before planting the vegetables. Complete the table to find the size of sheet needed for each garden.

Each sheet will be the same size as the garden it covers. Complete the table at right to show the area of each garden.

Garden A   Garden B

Garden C   Garden D

Areas of Gardens			
Garden	Length (ℓ)	Width (w)	Area (A)
A	4	2	8
B	4	3	▪
C	▪	▪	▪
D	▪	▪	▪

Think and Discuss

1. If you had a garden with a length of 4 and an area of 24, what would the width be? How did you get your answer?

2. The area of each garden is equal to its length times its width. Using the variables ℓ and w, what expression can you use to find the area of a rectangle? $A =$ _____.

Try This

Complete a table like the one in Activity 1 to find the area of each rectangle.

1. length = 10, width = 5
2. length = 10, width = 6
3. length = 10, width = 7

You can use graph paper to model the perimeters of different rectangles.

Activity 2

Jorge's family has many pictures that they want to frame, and they decide to make their own frames. The amount of wood needed for each frame is the perimeter of the frame. Complete the table to find the amount of wood needed for each frame.

Frame A

Frame B

Frame C

Frame D

Perimeters of Picture Frames			
Frame	Length (ℓ)	Width (w)	Perimeter (P)
A	4	2	12
B	4	3	▧
C	▧	▧	▧
D	▧	▧	▧

Think and Discuss

1. How did you find the perimeter of each frame?

2. A rectangle has one pair of sides with the same measure, called the length, and another pair with the same measure, called the width. We can say two lengths and two widths equal the perimeter. Using the variables ℓ and w, what expression can you use to find the perimeter of a rectangle?
$P =$ _____.

3. Use the Distributive Property to write another expression for the perimeter of a rectangle:
$P =$ _____.

Try This

Complete a table like the one in Activity 2 to find the perimeter of each rectangle.

1. length = 8, width = 3
2. length = 20, width = 4
3. length = 7, width = 7

2-3 Hands-On Lab

CHAPTER 2 SECTION 2A

Ready To Go On?

Quiz for Lessons 2-1 Through 2-3

2-1 Variables and Expressions

Evaluate each expression to find the missing values in the tables.

1.
y	$23 + y$
17	40
27	
37	

2.
w	$w \times 3 + 10$
4	22
5	
6	

3. Stephanie's CD holder holds 6 CDs per page. How many CDs does Stephanie have if she fills 2, 3, 4, or 5 pages?

2-2 Translating Between Words and Math

4. The small and large intestines are part of the digestive system. The small intestine is longer than the large intestine. Let n represent the length in feet of the small intestine. The large intestine is 5 feet long. Write an expression to show how much longer the small intestine is than the large intestine.

5. Let h represent the number of times your heart beats in 1 minute. Write an expression for the total number of times it beats in 1 hour. (*Hint:* 1 hour = 60 minutes)

Write each phrase as a numerical or algebraic expression.

6. 719 plus 210
7. t multiplied by 7
8. the sum of n and 51

Write two phrases for each expression.

9. $n + 19$
10. $12 \cdot 13$
11. $72 - x$
12. $\frac{t}{12}$
13. $15s$

2-3 Translating Between Tables and Expressions

Write an expression for the missing value in the table.

14.
Position	1	2	3	4	5	n
Value of Term	8	16	24	32	40	

Make a table for each sequence. Then write an expression for the sequence.

15. 3, 4, 5, 6, . . .
16. 4, 7, 10, 13, . . .

Focus on Problem Solving

Understand the Problem

• **Identify too much or too little information**

Problems often give too much or too little information. You must decide whether you have enough information to work the problem.

Read the problem and identify the facts that are given. Can you use any of these facts to arrive at an answer? Are there facts in the problem that are not necessary to find the answer? These questions can help you determine whether you have too much or too little information.

If you cannot solve the problem with the information given, decide what information you need. Then read the problem again to be sure you haven't missed the information in the problem.

Copy each problem. Circle the important facts. Underline any facts that you do not need to answer the question. If there is not enough information, list the additional information you need.

1. The reticulated python is one of the longest snakes in the world. One was found in Indonesia in 1912 that was 33 feet long. At birth, a reticulated python is 2 feet long. Suppose an adult python is 29 feet long. Let f represent the number of feet the python grew since birth. What is the value of f?

2. The largest flying flag in the world is 7,410 square feet and weighs 180 pounds. There are a total of 13 horizontal stripes on it. Let h represent the height of each stripe. What is the value of h?

3. The elevation of Mt. McKinley is 20,320 ft. People who climb Mt. McKinley are flown to a base camp located at 7,200 ft. From there, they begin a climb that may last 20 days or longer. Let d represent the distance from the base camp to the summit of Mt. McKinley. What is the value of d?

4. Let c represent the cost of a particular computer in 1981. Six years later, in 1987, the price of the computer had increased to $3,600. What is the value of c?

2-4 Equations and Their Solutions

Learn to determine whether a number is a solution of an equation.

An **equation** is a mathematical statement that two expressions are equal. You can think of a correct equation as a balanced scale.

$4 \cdot 2$ 6 $3 + 2$ 5

Vocabulary

equation
solution

Equations may contain variables. If a value for a variable makes an equation true, that value is a **solution** of the equation.

You can test a value to see whether it is a solution of an equation by substituting the value for the variable.

Interactivities Online ▶

$s + 15 = 27$

$s = 12$ $s = 10$

$12 + 15$ 27 $10 + 15$ 27

$s = 12$ is a solution because $12 + 15 = 27$. $s = 10$ is not a solution because $10 + 15$ 27.

Reading Math

The symbol $\neq$ means "is not equal to."

EXAMPLE 1   Determining Solutions of Equations

Determine whether the given value of the variable is a solution.

A $a + 23 = 82$ for $a = 61$

$a + 23 = 82$
$61 + 23 \stackrel{?}{=} 82$ *Substitute 61 for a.*
$84 \stackrel{?}{=} 82$ *Add.*

84   82

Since $84 \neq 82$, 61 is not a solution of $a + 23 = 82$.

Determine whether the given value of the variable is a solution.

B $60 \div c = 6$ for $c = 10$

$60 \div c = 6$

$60 \div 10 \stackrel{?}{=} 6$ Substitute 10 for c.

$6 \stackrel{?}{=} 6$ Divide.

| 6 | 6 |

Because $6 = 6$, 10 is a solution of $60 \div c = 6$.

You can use equations to check whether measurements given in different units are equal.

For example, there are 12 inches in one foot. If you have a measurement in feet, multiply by 12 to find the measurement in inches: $12 \cdot \text{feet} = \text{inches}$, or $12f = i$.

If you have one measurement in feet and another in inches, check whether the two numbers make the equation $12f = i$ true.

EXAMPLE 2

Life Science Application

One science book states that a male giraffe can grow to be 19 feet tall. According to another book, a male giraffe may grow to 228 inches. Determine if these two measurements are equal.

$12f = i$

$12 \cdot 19 \stackrel{?}{=} 228$ Substitute.

$228 \stackrel{?}{=} 228$ Multiply.

Because $228 = 228$, 19 feet is equal to 228 inches.

Reading Math

An equation has an equal sign, but an expression does not. An equation can be solved, but an expression can only be evaluated or simplified.

Think and Discuss

1. Tell which of the following is the solution of $y \div 2 = 9$: $y = 14$, $y = 16$, or $y = 18$. How do you know?

2. Give an example of an equation with a solution of 15.

2-4 Exercises

Learn It Online
Homework Help Online go.hrw.com, keyword MR10 2-4
Exercises 1–21, 25, 27, 29, 35, 37, 39, 41

GUIDED PRACTICE

See Example 1 Determine whether the given value of the variable is a solution.

1. $c + 23 = 48$ for $c = 35$
2. $z + 31 = 73$ for $z = 42$
3. $96 = 130 - d$ for $d = 34$
4. $85 = 194 - a$ for $a = 105$
5. $75 \div y = 5$ for $y = 15$
6. $78 \div n = 13$ for $n = 5$

See Example 2

7. **Social Studies** An almanac states that the Minnehaha Waterfall in Minnesota is 53 feet tall. A tour guide said the Minnehaha Waterfall is 636 inches tall. Determine if these two measurements are equal.

INDEPENDENT PRACTICE

See Example 1 Determine whether the given value of the variable is a solution.

8. $w + 19 = 49$ for $w = 30$
9. $d + 27 = 81$ for $d = 44$
10. $g + 34 = 91$ for $g = 67$
11. $k + 16 = 55$ for $k = 39$
12. $101 = 150 - h$ for $h = 49$
13. $89 = 111 - m$ for $m = 32$
14. $116 = 144 - q$ for $q = 38$
15. $92 = 120 - t$ for $t = 28$
16. $80 \div b = 20$ for $b = 4$
17. $91 \div x = 7$ for $x = 12$
18. $55 \div j = 5$ for $j = 10$
19. $49 \div r = 7$ for $r = 7$

See Example 2

20. **Money** Kent earns $6 per hour at his after-school job. One week, he worked 12 hours and received a paycheck for $66. Determine if Kent was paid the correct amount of money. (*Hint:* $6 · hours = total pay)

21. **Measurement** The Eiffel Tower in Paris, France, is 300 meters tall. A fact page states that it is 30,000 centimeters tall. Determine if these two measurements are equal. (*Hint:* 1 m = 100 cm)

PRACTICE AND PROBLEM SOLVING

Extra Practice
See page EP4.

Determine whether the given value of the variable is a solution.

22. $93 = 48 + u$ for $u = 35$
23. $112 = 14 \times f$ for $f = 8$
24. $13 = m \div 8$ for $m = 104$
25. $79 = z - 23$ for $z = 112$
26. $64 = l - 34$ for $l = 98$
27. $105 = p \times 7$ for $p = 14$
28. $94 \div s = 26$ for $s = 3$
29. $v + 79 = 167$ for $v = 88$
30. $m + 36 = 54$ for $m = 18$
31. $x - 35 = 96$ for $x = 112$
32. $12y = 84$ for $y = 7$
33. $7x = 56$ for $x = 8$

34. **Estimation** A large pizza has 8 slices. Determine whether 6 large pizzas will be enough for 24 people, if each person eats 2 to 3 slices of pizza.

68   Chapter 2 Introduction to Algebra

35. Multi-Step Rebecca has 17 one-dollar bills. Courtney has 350 nickels. Do the two girls have the same amount of money? (*Hint*: First find how many nickels are in a dollar.)

Replace each ■ with a number that makes the equation correct.

36. $4 + 1 = \blacksquare + 2$

37. $2 + \blacksquare = 6 + 2$

38. $\blacksquare - 5 = 9 - 2$

39. $5(4) = 10(\blacksquare)$

40. $3 + 6 = \blacksquare - 4$

41. $12 \div 4 = 9 \div \blacksquare$

42. Critical Thinking Linda is building a rectangular playhouse. The width is x feet. The length is $x + 3$ feet. The distance around the base of the playhouse is 36 feet. Is 8 the value of x? Explain.

43. Choose a Strategy What should replace the question mark to keep the scale balanced?

Ⓐ ●   Ⓑ ▮ ●   Ⓒ ●●●   Ⓓ ●●●●

44. Write About It Explain how to determine if a value is a solution to an equation.

45. Challenge Is $n = 4$ a solution for $n^2 + 79 = 88$? Explain.

Test Prep and Spiral Review

46. Multiple Choice For which equation is $b = 8$ a solution?

Ⓐ $13 - b = 8$ Ⓑ $8 + b = 21$ Ⓒ $b - 13 = 21$ Ⓓ $b + 13 = 21$

47. Multiple Choice When Paul gets 53 more postcards, he will have 82 cards in his collection. Solve the equation $n + 53 = 82$ to find how many postcards Paul has in his collection now.

Ⓕ 135   Ⓖ 125   Ⓗ 29   Ⓙ 27

Write each expression in exponential form. (Lesson 1-2)

48. $3 \times 3 \times 3 \times 3 \times 3$ **49.** $9 \times 9 \times 9 \times 9$ **50.** $13 \times 13 \times 13$ **51.** 8×8

Write an expression for the sequence in the table. (Lesson 2-3)

52.

Position	1	2	3	4	5	n
Value of Term	4	7	10	13	16	

2-4 Equations and Their Solutions

2-5 Addition Equations

Learn to solve whole-number addition equations.

Vocabulary
inverse operations

Some surfers recommend that the length of a beginner's surfboard be 14 inches greater than the surfer's height. If a surfboard is 82 inches, how tall should the surfer be to ride it?

The height of the surfer *combined* with 14 inches equals 82 inches. To combine amounts, you need to add.

Let h stand for the surfer's height. You can use the equation $h + 14 = 82$.

The equation $h + 14 = 82$ can be represented as a balanced scale.

To find the value of h, you need h by itself on one side of a balanced scale.

To get h by itself, first take away 14 from the left side of the scale. Now the scale is unbalanced.

To rebalance the scale, take away 14 from the other side.

Taking away 14 from both sides of the scale is the same as subtracting 14 from both sides of the equation.

$$\begin{aligned} h + 14 &= 82 \\ -14 & -14 \\ h &= 68 \end{aligned}$$

A surfer using an 82-inch surfboard should be 68 inches tall.

Inverse operations undo each other. Addition and subtraction are inverse operations. If an equation contains addition, solve it by subtracting from both sides to "undo" the addition.

EXAMPLE 1 Solving Addition Equations

Interactivities Online ▶

Solve each equation. Check your answers.

A $x + 62 = 93$

$$x + 62 = 93$$
$$\underline{-62 \quad -62}$$
$$x \quad = 31$$

62 is added to x.
Subtract 62 from both sides to undo the addition.

Check $x + 62 = 93$
$$31 + 62 \stackrel{?}{=} 93$$
$$93 \stackrel{?}{=} 93 \checkmark$$

Substitute 31 for x in the equation.
31 is the solution.

B $81 = 17 + y$

$$81 = 17 + y$$
$$\underline{-17 \quad -17}$$
$$64 = \quad y$$

17 is added to y.
Subtract 17 from both sides to undo the addition.

Check $81 = 17 + y$
$$81 \stackrel{?}{=} 17 + 64$$
$$81 \stackrel{?}{=} 81 \checkmark$$

Substitute 64 for y in the equation.
64 is the solution.

EXAMPLE 2 Social Studies Application

Tulsa, Oklahoma City, and Lawton are located in Oklahoma, as shown on the map. Find the distance d between Oklahoma City and Tulsa.

distance between Tulsa and Lawton	=	distance between Oklahoma City and Lawton	+	distance between Oklahoma City and Tulsa
175	=	75	+	d

$$175 = 75 + d$$
$$\underline{-75 \quad -75}$$
$$100 = d$$

75 is added to d.
Subtract 75 from both sides to undo the addition.

The distance between Oklahoma City and Tulsa is 100 miles.

Think and Discuss

1. **Tell** whether the solution of $c + 4 = 21$ will be less than 21 or greater than 21. Explain.

2. **Describe** how you could check your answer in Example 2.

2-5 Exercises

Learn It Online
Homework Help Online go.hrw.com,
keyword MR10 2-5
Exercises 1–17, 21, 23, 25, 27, 29, 31, 33

GUIDED PRACTICE

See Example 1 Solve each equation. Check your answers.

1. $x + 54 = 90$
2. $49 = 12 + y$
3. $n + 27 = 46$
4. $22 + t = 91$
5. $31 = p + 13$
6. $c + 38 = 54$

See Example 2

7. Lou, Michael, and Georgette live on Mulberry Street, as shown on the map. Lou lives 10 blocks from Georgette. Georgette lives 4 blocks from Michael. How many blocks does Michael live from Lou?

INDEPENDENT PRACTICE

See Example 1 Solve each equation. Check your answers.

8. $x + 19 = 24$
9. $10 = r + 3$
10. $s + 11 = 50$
11. $b + 17 = 42$
12. $12 + m = 28$
13. $z + 68 = 77$
14. $72 = n + 51$
15. $g + 28 = 44$
16. $27 = 15 + y$

See Example 2

17. What is the length of a killer whale?

PRACTICE AND PROBLEM SOLVING

Extra Practice
See page EP4.

Solve each equation.

18. $x + 12 = 16$
19. $n + 32 = 39$
20. $23 + q = 34$
21. $52 + y = 71$
22. $73 = c + 35$
23. $93 = h + 15$
24. $125 = n + 85$
25. $87 = b + 18$
26. $12 + y = 50$
27. $t + 17 = 43$
28. $k + 9 = 56$
29. $25 + m = 47$

72 Chapter 2 Introduction to Algebra

Write an equation for each statement.

30. The number of eggs e increased by 3 equals 14.

31. The number of new photos taken p added to 20 equals 36.

32. **Physical Science** Temperature can be measured in degrees Fahrenheit, degrees Celsius, or kelvins. To convert from degrees Celsius to kelvins, add 273 to the Celsius temperature. Complete the table.

	Kelvins (K)	°C + 273 = K	Celsius (°C)
Water Freezes	273	°C + 273 = 273	
Body Temperature	310		
Water Boils	373		

This ice sculpture, called Ice Dragon, was carved by Steve Rose and David Patterson as part of the First Night celebrations in Boston, Massachusetts.

33. **History** In 1520, the explorer Ferdinand Magellan tried to measure the depth of the ocean. He weighted a 370 m rope and lowered it into the ocean. This rope was not long enough to reach the ocean floor. Suppose the depth at this location was 1,250 m. How much longer would Magellan's rope have to have been to reach the ocean floor?

34. **Write a Problem** Use data from your science book to write a problem that can be solved using an addition equation. Solve your problem.

35. **Write About It** Why are addition and subtraction called inverse operations?

36. **Challenge** In the magic square at right, each row, column, and diagonal has the same sum. Find the values of x, y, and z.

7	61	x
y	37	1
31	z	67

Test Prep and Spiral Review

37. **Multiple Choice** Pauline hit 6 more home runs than Danielle. Pauline hit 18 home runs. How many home runs did Danielle hit?

    (A) 3   (B) 12   (C) 18   (D) 24

38. **Multiple Choice** Which is the solution to the equation $79 + r = 118$?

    (F) $r = 39$ (G) $r = 52$ (H) $r = 79$ (J) $r = 197$

Order the numbers from least to greatest. (Previous course)

39. 798; 648; 923   40. 1,298; 876; 972   41. 1,498; 2,163; 1,036

Evaluate each expression to find the missing values in the table. (Lesson 2-1)

42.
x	5	6	7	8
$9x$	45			

43.
y	121	99	77	55
$y \div 11$	11			

2-5 Addition Equations 73

2-6 Subtraction Equations

Learn to solve whole-number subtraction equations.

When Theodore Roosevelt became president of the United States, he was 42 years old. He was 27 years younger than Ronald Reagan was when Reagan became president. How old was Reagan when he became president?

Let a represent Ronald Reagan's age.

Ronald Reagan's age	−	27	=	Theodore Roosevelt's age
a	−	27	=	42

Recall that addition and subtraction are inverse operations. When an equation contains subtraction, use addition to "undo" the subtraction. Remember to add the same amount to both sides of the equation.

$$\begin{aligned} a - 27 &= 42 \\ +\,27 &+27 \\ \hline a &= 69 \end{aligned}$$

Ronald Reagan was 69 years old when he became president.

EXAMPLE 1 Solving Subtraction Equations

Solve each equation. Check your answers.

A $p - 2 = 5$

$$\begin{aligned} p - 2 &= 5 \\ +\,2 &+2 \\ \hline p &= 7 \end{aligned}$$

2 is subtracted from p.
Add 2 to both sides to undo the subtraction.

Check $p - 2 = 5$

$7 - 2 \stackrel{?}{=} 5$ *Substitute 7 for p in the equation.*

$5 \stackrel{?}{=} 5$ ✓ *7 is the solution.*

74 Chapter 2 Introduction to Algebra

Solve each equation. Check your answers.

B $40 = x - 11$

$$40 = x - 11$$
$$\underline{+11 \qquad +11}$$
$$51 = x$$

11 is subtracted from x.
Add 11 to both sides to undo the subtraction.

Check $40 = x - 11$
$$40 \stackrel{?}{=} 51 - 11$$
$$40 \stackrel{?}{=} 40 \checkmark$$

Substitute 51 for x in the equation.
51 is the solution.

C $x - 56 = 19$

$$x - 56 = 19$$
$$\underline{+56 \quad +56}$$
$$x \quad\quad = 75$$

56 is subtracted from x.
Add 56 to both sides to undo the subtraction.

Check $x - 56 = 19$
$$75 - 56 \stackrel{?}{=} 19$$
$$19 \stackrel{?}{=} 19 \checkmark$$

Substitute 75 for x in the equation.
75 is the solution.

Think and Discuss

1. Tell whether the solution of $b - 14 = 9$ will be less than 9 or greater than 9. Explain.

2. Explain how you know what number to add to both sides of an equation containing subtraction.

2-6 Exercises

GUIDED PRACTICE

See Example 1 Solve each equation. Check your answers.

1. $p - 8 = 9$ **2.** $3 = x - 16$ **3.** $a - 13 = 18$

4. $15 = y - 7$ **5.** $n - 24 = 9$ **6.** $39 = d - 2$

INDEPENDENT PRACTICE

See Example 1 Solve each equation. Check your answers.

7. $y - 18 = 7$ **8.** $8 = n - 5$ **9.** $a - 34 = 4$

10. $c - 21 = 45$ **11.** $a - 40 = 57$ **12.** $31 = x - 14$

13. $28 = p - 5$ **14.** $z - 42 = 7$ **15.** $s - 19 = 12$

PRACTICE AND PROBLEM SOLVING

Extra Practice
See page EP4.

Solve each equation.

16. $r - 57 = 7$
17. $11 = x - 25$
18. $8 = y - 96$
19. $a - 6 = 15$
20. $q - 14 = 22$
21. $f - 12 = 2$
22. $18 = j - 19$
23. $109 = r - 45$
24. $d - 8 = 29$
25. $g - 71 = 72$
26. $p - 13 = 111$
27. $13 = m - 5$

28. **Geography** Mt. Rainier, in Washington, has a higher elevation than Mt. Shasta. The difference between their elevations is 248 feet. What is the elevation of Mt. Rainier? Write an equation and solve.

U.S. Mountains
- Yale (CO): 14,196
- Shasta (CA): 14,162
- Sill (CA): 14,153
- Augusta (AK): 14,070

29. **Social Studies** In 2004, the population of New York City was 5 million less than the population of Shanghai, China. The population of New York City was 8 million. Solve the equation $8 = s - 5$ to find the population of Shanghai.

30. **Write About It** Suppose $n - 15$ is a whole number. What do you know about the value of n? Explain.

31. **What's the Error?** Look at the student paper at right. What did the student do wrong? What is the correct answer?

$$51 = n - 17$$
$$-17 \quad\quad -17$$
$$34 = n$$

32. **Challenge** Write "the difference between n and 16 is 5" as an algebraic equation. Then find the solution.

Test Prep and Spiral Review

33. **Multiple Choice** Which is a solution to the equation $j - 39 = 93$?
    - Ⓐ $j = 54$
    - Ⓑ $j = 66$
    - Ⓒ $j = 93$
    - Ⓓ $j = 132$

34. **Short Response** When 17 is subtracted from a number, the result is 64. Write an equation that can be used to find the original number. Then find the original number.

Simplify each expression. (Lesson 1-3)

35. $81 - 4 \times 3 + 18 \div (6 + 3)$
36. $17 \times (5 - 3) + 16 \div 8$
37. $3^2 - (15 - 8) + 4 \times 5$

Solve each equation. (Lesson 2-5)

38. $a + 3 = 18$
39. $y + 7 = 45$
40. $x + 16 = 71$
41. $87 = b + 31$

2-7 Multiplication Equations

Learn to solve whole-number multiplication equations.

Nine-banded armadillos are always born in groups of 4. If you count 32 babies, what is the number of mother armadillos?

To put together equal groups of 4, multiply. Let m represent the number of mother armadillos. There will be m equal groups of 4.

You can use the equation $4m = 32$.

Multiplication and division are inverse operations. To solve an equation that contains multiplication, use division to "undo" the multiplication.

Caution!
$4m$ means "$4 \times m$."

$$4m = 32$$
$$\frac{4m}{4} = \frac{32}{4}$$
$$m = 8$$

There are 8 mother armadillos.

EXAMPLE 1   Solving Multiplication Equations

Interactivities Online ▶

Solve each equation. Check your answers.

A $3x = 12$

$3x = 12$ *x is multiplied by 3.*

$\frac{3x}{3} = \frac{12}{3}$ *Divide both sides by 3 to undo the multiplication.*

$x = 4$

Check $3x = 12$

$3(4) \stackrel{?}{=} 12$ *Substitute 4 for x in the equation.*

$12 \stackrel{?}{=} 12$ ✔   *4 is the solution.*

B $8 = 4w$

$8 = 4w$ *w is multiplied by 4.*

$\frac{8}{4} = \frac{4w}{4}$ *Divide both sides by 4 to undo the multiplication.*

$2 = w$

Check $8 = 4w$

$8 \stackrel{?}{=} 4(2)$ *Substitute 2 for w in the equation.*

$8 \stackrel{?}{=} 8$ ✔   *2 is the solution.*

EXAMPLE 2 **PROBLEM SOLVING APPLICATION**

The area of a rectangle is 36 square inches. Its length is 9 inches. What is its width?

1. Understand the Problem

The **answer** will be the width of the rectangle in inches.

List the **important information:**
- The area of the rectangle is 36 square inches.
- The length of the rectangle is 9 inches.

Draw a diagram to represent this information.

2. Make a Plan

You can write and solve an equation using the formula for area. To find the area of a rectangle, multiply its length by its width.

$$A = \ell w$$
$$36 = 9w$$

3. Solve

$36 = 9w$ *w is multiplied by 9.*

$\dfrac{36}{9} = \dfrac{9w}{9}$ *Divide both sides by 9 to undo the multiplication.*

$4 = w$

So the width of the rectangle is 4 inches.

4. Look Back

Arrange 36 identical squares in a rectangle. The length is 9, so line up the squares in rows of 9. You can make 4 rows of 9, so the width of the rectangle is 4.

Think and Discuss

1. **Tell** what number you would use to divide both sides of the equation $15x = 60$.

2. **Tell** whether the solution of $10c = 90$ will be less than 90 or greater than 90. Explain.

2-7 Exercises

Learn It Online
Homework Help Online go.hrw.com,
keyword MR10 2-7 Go
Exercises 1–17, 21, 27, 29, 33, 37, 39, 41

GUIDED PRACTICE

See Example 1 Solve each equation. Check your answers.

1. $7x = 21$
2. $27 = 3w$
3. $90 = 10a$
4. $56 = 7b$
5. $3c = 33$
6. $12 = 2n$

See Example 2
7. The area of a rectangular deck is 675 square feet. The deck's width is 15 feet. What is its length?

INDEPENDENT PRACTICE

See Example 1 Solve each equation. Check your answers.

8. $12p = 36$
9. $52 = 13a$
10. $64 = 8n$
11. $20 = 5x$
12. $6r = 30$
13. $77 = 11t$
14. $14s = 98$
15. $12m = 132$
16. $9z = 135$

See Example 2
17. Marcy spreads out a rectangular picnic blanket with an area of 24 square feet. Its width is 4 feet. What is its length?

PRACTICE AND PROBLEM SOLVING

Extra Practice
See page EP4.

Solve each equation.

18. $5y = 35$
19. $18 = 2y$
20. $54 = 9y$
21. $15y = 120$
22. $4y = 0$
23. $22y = 440$
24. $3y = 63$
25. $z - 6 = 34$
26. $6y = 114$
27. $161 = 7y$
28. $135 = 3y$
29. $y - 15 = 3$
30. $81 = 9y$
31. $4 + y = 12$
32. $7y = 21$
33. $a + 12 = 26$
34. $10x = 120$
35. $36 = 12x$
36. $s - 2 = 7$
37. $15 + t = 21$

38. **Estimation** Colorado is almost a perfect rectangle on a map. Its border from east to west is about 387 mi, and its area is about 104,247 mi². Estimate the length of Colorado's border from north to south. (Area = length × width)

2-7 Multiplication Equations

Life Science LINK

Arthropods make up the largest group of animals on Earth. They include insects, spiders, crabs, and centipedes. Arthropods have segmented bodies. In centipedes and millipedes, all of the segments are identical.

39. Centipedes have 2 legs per segment. They can have from 30 to 354 legs. Find a range for the number of segments a centipede can have.

40. Millipedes have 4 legs per segment. The record number of legs on a millipede is 752. How many segments did this millipede have?

Millipedes kept as pets can live for up to 7 years and grow to be up to 15 inches long.

Many arthropods have compound eyes. Compound eyes are made up of tiny bundles of identical light-sensitive cells.

41. A dragonfly has 7 times as many light-sensitive cells as a housefly. How many of these cells does a housefly have?

42. Find how many times more light-sensitive cells a dragonfly has than a butterfly.

43. ✏️ **Write About It** A trapdoor spider can pull with a force that is 140 times its own weight. What other information would you need to find the spider's weight? Explain.

44. ⭐ **Challenge** There are about 6 billion humans in the world. Scientists estimate that there are a billion billion arthropods in the world. About how many times larger is the arthropod population than the human population?

Test Prep and Spiral Review

45. Multiple Choice Solve the equation $25x = 175$.

Ⓐ $x = 5$ Ⓑ $x = 6$ Ⓒ $x = 7$ Ⓓ $x = 8$

46. Multiple Choice The area of a rectangle is 42 square inches. Its width is 6 inches. What is its length?

Ⓕ 5 inches   Ⓖ 7 inches   Ⓗ 9 inches   Ⓙ 11 inches

Estimate each sum or difference by rounding to the place value indicated. (Lesson 1-1)

47. $4{,}798 + 2{,}118$; thousands   **48.** $49{,}169 - 13{,}919$; ten thousands

Solve each equation. (Lessons 2-5 and 2-6)

49. $b + 53 = 95$ **50.** $a - 100 = 340$ **51.** $n - 24 = 188$ **52.** $w + 20 = 95$

2-8 Division Equations

Learn to solve whole-number division equations.

Recreational scuba divers go as deep as 130 feet underwater to view fish and coral. At this depth, the pressure on a diver is much greater than at the water's surface. Water pressure can be described using equations containing division.

Recall that multiplication and division are inverse operations. If an equation contains division, solve it by multiplying on both sides to "undo" the division.

EXAMPLE 1 Solving Division Equations

Interactivities Online ▶

Solve each equation. Check your answers.

A $\dfrac{y}{5} = 4$

$\dfrac{y}{5} = 4$ *y is divided by 5.*

$5 \cdot \dfrac{y}{5} = 5 \cdot 4$ *Multiply both sides by 5 to undo the division.*

$y = 20$

Check

$\dfrac{y}{5} = 4$

$\dfrac{20}{5} \stackrel{?}{=} 4$ *Substitute 20 for y in the equation.*

$4 \stackrel{?}{=} 4$ ✔   *20 is the solution.*

B $12 = \dfrac{z}{4}$

$12 = \dfrac{z}{4}$ *z is divided by 4.*

$4 \cdot 12 = 4 \cdot \dfrac{z}{4}$ *Multiply both sides by 4 to undo the division.*

$48 = z$

Check

$12 = \dfrac{z}{4}$

$12 \stackrel{?}{=} \dfrac{48}{4}$ *Substitute 48 for z in the equation.*

$12 \stackrel{?}{=} 12$ ✔   *48 is the solution.*

Video   Lesson Tutorials Online   my.hrw.com

EXAMPLE 2 **Physical Science Application**

Pressure is the amount of force exerted on an area. Pressure can be measured in pounds per square inch, or psi.

The pressure at the surface of the water is half the pressure at 30 ft underwater.

pressure at surface = $\dfrac{\text{pressure at 30 ft underwater}}{2}$

The pressure at the surface is 15 psi. What is the water pressure at 30 ft underwater?

Let p represent the pressure at 30 ft underwater.

$15 = \dfrac{p}{2}$ Substitute 15 for pressure at the surface. p is divided by 2.

$2 \cdot 15 = 2 \cdot \dfrac{p}{2}$ Multiply both sides by 2 to undo the division.

$30 = p$

The water pressure at 30 ft underwater is 30 psi.

Think and Discuss

1. **Tell** whether the solution of $\dfrac{c}{10} = 70$ will be less than 70 or greater than 70. Explain.
2. **Describe** how you would check your answer to Example 2.
3. **Explain** why $13 \cdot \dfrac{x}{13} = x$.

2-8 Exercises

GUIDED PRACTICE

See Example 1 Solve each equation. Check your answers.

1. $\dfrac{y}{4} = 3$
2. $14 = \dfrac{z}{2}$
3. $\dfrac{r}{9} = 7$
4. $\dfrac{s}{10} = \dfrac{4}{40}$
5. $12 = \dfrac{j}{3}$
6. $9 = \dfrac{x}{5}$
7. $\dfrac{f}{12} = 5$
8. $\dfrac{g}{2} = 1$

See Example 2 9. Irene mowed the lawn and planted flowers. The amount of time she spent mowing the lawn was one-third the amount of time it took her to plant flowers. It took her 30 minutes to mow the lawn. Find the amount of time Irene spent planting flowers.

82 Chapter 2 Introduction to Algebra

INDEPENDENT PRACTICE

See Example 1 Solve each equation. Check your answers.

10. $\frac{d}{3} = 12$
11. $\frac{c}{2} = 13$
12. $7 = \frac{m}{7}$
13. $\frac{g}{7} = 14$
14. $6 = \frac{f}{4}$
15. $\frac{x}{12} = 12$
16. $\frac{j}{20} = 10$
17. $9 = \frac{r}{9}$

See Example 2
18. The area of Danielle's garden is one-twelfth the area of her entire yard. The area of the garden is 10 square feet. Find the area of the yard.

PRACTICE AND PROBLEM SOLVING

Extra Practice See page EP4.

Find the value of c in each equation.

19. $\frac{c}{12} = 8$
20. $4 = \frac{c}{9}$
21. $\frac{c}{15} = 11$
22. $c + 21 = 40$
23. $14 = \frac{c}{5}$
24. $\frac{c}{4} = 12$
25. $\frac{c}{4} = 15$
26. $5c = 120$

27. **Multi-Step** The Empire State Building is 381 m tall. At the Grand Canyon's widest point, 76 Empire State Buildings would fit end to end. Write and solve an equation to find the width of the Grand Canyon at this point.

28. **Earth Science** You can estimate the distance of a thunderstorm in kilometers by counting the number of seconds between the lightning flash and the thunder and then dividing this number by 3. If a storm is 5 km away, how many seconds will you count between the lightning flash and the thunder?

29. **Write a Problem** Write a problem about money that can be solved with a division equation.

30. **Write About It** Use a numerical example to explain how multiplication and division undo each other.

31. **Challenge** A number halved and then halved again is equal to 2. What was the original number?

Test Prep and Spiral Review

32. **Multiple Choice** Carl has n action figures in his collection. He wants to place them in 6 bins with 12 figures in each bin. Solve the equation $\frac{n}{6} = 12$ to determine the number of action figures Carl has.

    (A) $n = 2$
    (B) $n = 6$
    (C) $n = 18$
    (D) $n = 72$

33. **Multiple Choice** Which equation does NOT have $k = 28$ as a solution?

    (F) $\frac{k}{14} = 2$
    (G) $\frac{k}{7} = 4$
    (H) $\frac{k}{28} = 1$
    (J) $\frac{k}{6} = 12$

Identify a pattern in each sequence. Name the next three terms. (Lesson 1-6)

34. 3, 10, 17, 24, ...
35. 5, 10, 15, 20, ...
36. 1, 4, 2, 5, 3, ...

Solve each equation. (Lesson 2-7)

37. $4r = 52$
38. $8k = 128$
39. $81 = 9p$
40. $119 = 17q$

Ready To Go On?

Quiz for Lessons 2-4 Through 2-8

2-4 Equations and Their Solutions

Determine whether the given value of the variable is a solution.

1. $c - 13 = 54$ for $c = 67$
2. $5r = 65$ for $r = 15$
3. $48 \div x = 6$ for $x = 8$
4. Brady buys 2 notebooks and should get $3 back in change. The cashier gives him 12 quarters. Determine if Brady was given the correct amount of change.

2-5 Addition Equations

Solve each equation. Check your answers.

5. $p + 51 = 76$
6. $107 = 19 + j$
7. $45 = s + 27$
8. A large section of the original Great Wall of China is now in ruins. As measured today, the length of the wall is about 6,350 kilometers. When the length of the section now in ruins is included, the length of the wall is about 6,850 kilometers. Write and solve an equation to find the approximate length of the section of the Great Wall that is now in ruins.

2-6 Subtraction Equations

Solve each equation. Check your answers.

9. $k - 5 = 17$
10. $150 = p - 30$
11. $n - 24 = 72$
12. The Kingda Ka roller coaster at Six Flags® Great Adventure in New Jersey is taller than the Top Thrill Dragster located at Cedar Point™ in Ohio. The difference between their heights is 36 feet. The Top Thrill Dragster is 420 feet high. Write and solve an equation to find the height of Kingda Ka.

2-7 Multiplication Equations

Solve each equation. Check your answers.

13. $6f = 18$
14. $105 = 5d$
15. $11x = 99$
16. Taryn buys 8 identical glasses. Her total is $48 before tax. Write and solve an equation to find out how much Taryn pays per glass.

2-8 Division Equations

Solve each equation. Check your answers.

17. $10 = \frac{j}{9}$
18. $5 = \frac{t}{6}$
19. $\frac{r}{15} = 3$
20. Paula is baking peach pies for a bake sale. Each pie requires 2 pounds of peaches. She bakes 6 pies. Write and solve an equation to find how many pounds of peaches Paula had to buy.

Real-World CONNECTIONS

CHAPTER 2

The First Oil Well In 1859, Edwin Drake drilled the world's first oil well, beside Oil Creek near Titusville, Pennsylvania. Almost overnight, towns sprang up in the area and people came from everywhere to be part of the oil boom. Until 1901, Pennsylvania produced half of the world's oil.

PENNSYLVANIA
Titusville

1. Before Drake drilled his well, about 5 gallons of oil could be collected aboveground each day near Oil Creek. Drake's well produced 210 times as much oil each day as could be collected aboveground.

   a. Given that there are 42 gallons in one barrel, find the daily production in barrels of Drake's well.

   b. Let x represent the number of days. Write an expression for the number of barrels of oil produced in x days.

   c. How many days did it take the well to produce 500 barrels of oil? How do you know?

2. In 3 days, Drake's well produced oil worth $1,500. What was the value of the oil produced in one week?

3. The surface of the ground at Drake's well is 1,200 ft above sea level. To reach oil, Drake first drilled through gravel to a point 1,168 ft above sea level. He then drilled an additional 38 ft through shale. What was the total depth of the well?

Real-World Connections

Game Time

Math Magic

Guess what your friends are thinking with this math magic trick.

Copy the following number charts.

1	10	19
2, 2	11, 11	20, 20
4	13	22
5, 5	14, 14	23, 23
7	16	25
8, 8	17, 17	26, 26

3	12	21
4	13	22
5	14	23
6, 6	15, 15	24, 24
7, 7	16, 16	25, 25
8, 8	17, 17	26, 26

9	15	21, 21
10	16	22, 22
11	17	23, 23
12	18, 18	24, 24
13	19, 19	25, 25
14	20, 20	26, 26

Step 1: Ask a friend to think of a number from 1 to 26.
Example: Your friend thinks of 26.

Step 2: Show your friend the first chart and ask how many times the chosen number appears. Remember the answer.
Your friend says the chosen number appears twice on the first chart.   2

Step 3: Show the second chart and ask the same question. Multiply the answer by 3. Add your result to the answer from step 2. Remember this answer.
Your friend says the chosen number appears twice. $3 \cdot 2 = 6$
The answer from step 2 is 2. $6 + 2 = 8$

Step 4: Show the third chart and ask the same question. Multiply the answer by 9. Add your result to the answer from step 3. The answer is your friend's number.
Your friend says the chosen number appears twice. $9 \cdot 2 = 18$
The answer from step 3 is 8. $18 + 8 = 26$
↑
Your friend's number

How does it work?

Your friend's number will be the following:

(answer from step 2) + (3 · answer from step 3) + (9 · answer from step 4)

This is an expression with three variables: $a + 3b + 9c$. A number will be on a particular chart 0, 1, or 2 times, so a, b, and c will always be 0, 1, or 2. With these values, you can write expressions for each number from 1 to 26.

a	b	c	$a + 3b + 9c$
1	0	0	1 + 3(0) + 9(0) = **1**
2	0	0	2 + 3(0) + 9(0) = **2**
0	1	0	0 + 3(1) + 9(0) = **3**

Can you complete the table for 4–26?

86   Chapter 2 Introduction to Algebra

Materials
- file folder
- 3 small pockets
- card stock
- scissors
- glue stick
- markers

It's in the Bag!

PROJECT Tri-Sided Equations

Use a colorful file folder to prepare a three-sided review of algebra!

Directions

1. Close the file folder. Fold one side down to the folded edge. Turn the folder over and fold the other side down to the folded edge. **Figure A**

2. Open the folder. It will be divided into four sections. On the top section, cut off $\frac{1}{4}$ inch from each edge. On the bottom section, make a 1 inch diagonal slit in the top left corner and in the top right corner. **Figure B**

3. Fold the folder so that the corners of the smaller top section fit into the slits. This will create your three-sided holder for notes. **Figure C**

4. Write the definition of an equation on one side of your note holder. Write the order of operations on another side. Write examples of expressions on the third side.

Taking Note of the Math

Glue a small pocket made from construction paper or card stock onto each side of your note holder. On rectangular slips of card stock, write problems that demonstrate your knowledge of equations, order of operations, and expressions. Store the note cards in the appropriate pockets.

It's in the Bag!

CHAPTER 2 Study Guide: Review

Vocabulary

algebraic expression 50	inverse operations 70
constant 50	solution 66
equation 66	variable 50
evaluate 50	

Complete the sentences below with vocabulary words from the list above.

1. A(n) ___?___ contains one or more variables.

2. A(n) ___?___ is a mathematical statement that says two quantities are equal.

3. In the equation $12 + t = 22$, t is a ___?___.

EXAMPLES

EXERCISES

2-1 Variables and Expressions (pp. 50–53)

■ Evaluate the expression to find the missing values in the table.

n	3n + 4
1	7
2	■
3	■

$n = 1$; $3 \times 1 + 4 = 7$
$n = 2$; $3 \times 2 + 4 = 10$
$n = 3$; $3 \times 3 + 4 = 13$

The missing values are 10 and 13.

■ A rectangle is 3 units wide. How many square units does the rectangle cover if it is 5, 6, 7, or 8 units long?

ℓ	w	ℓ × w
5	3	15
6	3	■
7	3	■
8	3	■

$5 \times 3 = 15$ square units
$6 \times 3 = 18$ square units
$7 \times 3 = 21$ square units
$8 \times 3 = 24$ square units

The rectangle will cover a total of 15, 18, 21, or 24 square units.

Evaluate each expression to find the missing values in the tables.

4.
y	y ÷ 7
56	8
49	■
42	■

5.
k	k × 4 − 6
2	2
3	■
4	■

6. A rectangle is 9 units long. How many square units does the rectangle cover if it is 1, 2, 3, or 4 units wide?

7. Karen buys 3 bouquets of flowers. How many flowers does she buy if each bouquet contains 10, 11, 12, or 13 flowers?

8. Ron buys 5 bags of marbles. How many marbles does he buy if each bag contains 15, 16, 17, or 18 marbles?

EXAMPLES | EXERCISES

2-2 Translating Between Words and Math (pp. 54–57)

Write each phrase as a numerical or algebraic expression.

- 617 minus 191
  $617 - 191$

- d multiplied by 5
  $5d$ or $5 \cdot d$ or $(5)(d)$

Write two phrases for each expression.

- $a \div 5$
  - a divided by 5
  - the quotient of a and 5

- $67 + 19$
  - the sum of 67 and 19
  - 19 more than 67

Write each phrase as a numerical or algebraic expression.

9. 15 plus b
10. the product of 6 and 5
11. 9 times t
12. the quotient of g and 9

Write two phrases for each expression.

13. $4z$
14. $15 + x$
15. $54 \div 6$
16. $\frac{m}{20}$
17. $3 - y$
18. $5{,}100 + 64$
19. $y - 3$
20. $g - 20$

2-3 Translating Between Tables and Expressions (pp. 58–61)

- Write an expression for the sequence in the table.

Position	1	2	3	4	n
Value of Term	9	18	27	36	

To go from the position to the value of the term, multiply the position by 9. The expression is $9n$.

Write an expression for the sequence in each table.

21.

Position	1	2	3	4	n
Value of Term	4	7	10	13	

22.

Position	1	2	3	4	n
Value of Term	0	1	2	3	

2-4 Equations and Their Solutions (pp. 66–69)

- Determine whether the given value of the variable is a solution.

  $f + 14 = 50$ for $f = 34$
  $f + 14 = 50$
  $34 + 14 \stackrel{?}{=} 50$ Substitute 34 for f.
  $48 \neq 50$ Add.
  34 is not a solution.

Determine whether the given value of the variable is a solution.

23. $28 + n = 39$ for $n = 11$
24. $12t = 74$ for $t = 6$
25. $y - 53 = 27$ for $y = 80$
26. $96 \div w = 32$ for $w = 3$

EXAMPLES

EXERCISES

2-5 Addition Equations (pp. 70–73)

■ Solve the equation $x + 18 = 31$.

$$\begin{aligned} x + 18 &= 31 \\ -18 & -18 \\ x &= 13 \end{aligned}$$

18 is added to x. Subtract 18 from both sides to undo the addition.

Solve each equation.

27. $4 + x = 10$ **28.** $n + 10 = 24$
29. $c + 71 = 100$ **30.** $y + 16 = 22$
31. $44 = p + 17$ **32.** $94 + w = 103$

33. Melinda's new HD radio will play 93 channels. This is 26 more channels than her old radio played. How many channels could she listen to with her old radio?

2-6 Subtraction Equations (pp. 74–76)

■ Solve the equation $c - 7 = 16$.

$$\begin{aligned} c - 7 &= 16 \\ +7 & +7 \\ c &= 23 \end{aligned}$$

7 is subtracted from c. Add 7 to each side to undo the subtraction.

Solve each equation.

34. $28 = k - 17$ **35.** $d - 8 = 1$
36. $p - 55 = 8$ **37.** $n - 31 = 36$
38. $3 = r - 11$ **39.** $97 = w - 47$

40. There are 14 Winter Olympics sports. This is 17 fewer than the number of Summer Olympics sports. How many Summer sports are there?

2-7 Multiplication Equations (pp. 77–80)

■ Solve the equation $6x = 36$.

$$6x = 36$$
$$\frac{6x}{6} = \frac{36}{6}$$
$$x = 6$$

x is multiplied by 6. Divide both sides by 6 to undo the multiplication.

Solve each equation.

41. $5v = 40$ **42.** $27 = 3y$
43. $12c = 84$ **44.** $18n = 36$
45. $72 = 9s$ **46.** $11t = 110$

47. The average American eats about 30 pounds of cheese per year. This is $\frac{3}{5}$ the amount eaten by the average French person. How many pounds of cheese does a French person eat in one year?

2-8 Division Equations (pp. 81–83)

■ Solve the equation $\frac{k}{4} = 8$.

$$\frac{k}{4} = 8$$
$$4 \cdot \frac{k}{4} = 4 \cdot 8$$
$$k = 32$$

k is divided by 4. Multiply both sides by 4 to undo the division.

Solve each equation.

48. $\frac{r}{7} = 6$ **49.** $\frac{t}{5} = 3$
50. $6 = \frac{y}{3}$ **51.** $12 = \frac{n}{6}$
52. $\frac{z}{13} = 4$ **53.** $20 = \frac{b}{5}$

Chapter Test

CHAPTER 2

Evaluate each expression to find the missing values in the tables.

1.
a	a + 18
10	28
12	
14	

2.
y	y ÷ 6
18	3
30	
42	

3.
n	n ÷ 5 + 7
10	9
20	
30	

4. A van can seat 6 people. How many people can ride in 3, 4, 5, and 6 vans?

5. A rectangle is 5 units wide. How many square units does the rectangle cover if it is 10, 11, 12, or 13 units long?

Write an expression for the missing value in each table.

6.
Packages	Rolls
1	8
2	16
3	24
4	32
p	

7.
Students	Groups
5	1
10	2
15	3
20	4
s	

Write an expression for the sequence in the table.

8.
Position	1	2	3	4	5	n
Value of Term	4	7	10	13	16	

9. There are more reptile species than amphibian species. There are 3,100 living species of amphibians. Write an expression to show how many more reptile species there are than amphibian species.

Write each phrase as a numerical or algebraic expression.

10. 26 more than n
11. g multiplied by 4
12. the quotient of 180 and 15

Write two phrases for each expression.

13. $(14)(16)$
14. $n \div 8$
15. $p + 11$
16. $s - 6$

Determine whether the given value of the variable is a solution.

17. $5d = 70$ for $d = 12$
18. $29 = 76 - n$ for $n = 46$
19. $108 \div a = 12$ for $a = 9$
20. $15 + m = 27$ for $m = 12$

Solve each equation.

21. $a + 7 = 25$
22. $121 = 11d$
23. $3 = t - 8$
24. $6 = \frac{k}{9}$

25. Air typically has about 4,000 bacteria per cubic meter. If your room is 30 cubic meters, about how many bacteria would there be in the air in your room?

Cumulative Assessment, Chapters 1–2

Multiple Choice

1. Which is an algebraic expression for the product of 15 and x?

   (A) $15 - x$
   (B) $15x$
   (C) $x + 15$
   (D) $15 \div x$

2. Max earned $560 working as a landscaper. If he worked a total of 80 hours, which expression can be used to find how much he earned each hour?

   (F) $560 - 80$
   (G) $560 \div 80$
   (H) $560 + 80$
   (J) $560 \cdot 80$

3. Find the expression for the table.

x	
3	9
8	19
11	25
15	33

   (A) $3x$
   (B) $x + 18$
   (C) $2x + 3$
   (D) $3x - 5$

4. A rectangular classroom has an area of 252 square feet. The width of the classroom is 14 feet. What is its length?

   (F) 14 feet
   (G) 16 feet
   (H) 18 feet
   (J) 20 feet

5. What is the difference between 82,714 and 54,221 rounded to the nearest hundred?

   (A) 28,500
   (B) 27,700
   (C) 26,900
   (D) 26,000

6. What is the value of 8^3?

   (F) 11
   (G) 24
   (H) 192
   (J) 512

7. Zane biked 23 miles this week. This is 8 miles more than he biked the week before. Solve the equation $x + 8 = 23$ to find how many miles Zane biked last week.

   (A) 15 miles
   (B) 23 miles
   (C) 31 miles
   (D) 33 miles

8. Which team sold the most fund-raising products?

Fund-raising Results by Team	
Team	Products Sold
Golf	6,536
Soccer	6,421
Swim	6,879
Track	6,019

   (F) Soccer team
   (G) Golf team
   (H) Swim team
   (J) Track team

9. Which equation is an example of the Associative Property?

   (A) $3 + (4 + 6) = (3 + 4) + 6$
   (B) $(42 + 6) + 18 = (42 + 18) + 6$
   (C) $(3 \times 20) + (3 \times 4) = 3 \times 24$
   (D) $8(2 \times 6) = (8 \times 2) + (8 \times 6)$

10. Nicole is 15 years old. She is 3 years younger than her sister Jan. Solve the equation $j - 3 = 15$ to find Jan's age.

    F. 18 years H. 12 years
    G. 17 years J. 5 years

11. Ling created an arithmetic sequence that starts with 5 and then adds 8. Find the 6th term in this sequence.

    A. 30 C. 40
    B. 38 D. 45

HOT TIP! Substitute the values given in the answers into an equation to see which value makes the equation true.

Gridded Response

12. Use the table to find the unknown value.

t	$11 \times t + 3$
5	58
8	

13. What is the value of $5^2 - (18 \div 6) \times 7$?

14. Scott spends 16 minutes in the pool treading water during swim practice. This is $\frac{1}{3}$ of his practice time. How many total minutes is Scott's swim practice?

15. A case of pencils costs $15. If the academic team spends $135 on pencils for the school tournament, how many cases of pencils did the academic team buy?

16. What value of x will make each of the following expressions equal 12?

    $2x + 4$ $5x - 8$

17. What is the solution to the equation $8a = 48$?

Short Response

S1. Every week Brandi runs 7 more miles than her sister Jamie.

   a. Write an expression for the number of miles that Brandi runs each week. Identify the variable.

   b. Evaluate your expression to find the number of miles Brandi runs when Jamie runs 5 miles.

S2. A vacation tour costs $450. Additional outings cost $25 each. The table shows the total cost to go on additional outings.

Outings	1	2	3	n
Total Cost ($)	475	500	525	

Write an expression for the cost of n outings. Use the expression to find how much it costs to go on 5 outings.

Extended Response

E1. Chrissy and Kathie are sisters. Chrissy was born on Kathie's birthday and is exactly 8 years younger. Chrissy celebrated her 16th birthday on December 8, 2005.

   a. Complete the table to show the ages of the sisters in the years 2005, 2008, and 2011.

Year	Kathie's Age	Chrissy's Age
2005		
2008		
2011		

   b. Write an equation that could be used to find Kathie's age in 2011. Identify the variable in the equation.

   c. Solve the equation. Show your work. Compare your answer to the value in the table. Are the two solutions the same? Explain your answer.

Cumulative Assessment, Chapters 1–2

Chapter 3: Decimals

3A Understanding Decimals
- **LAB** Model Decimals
- **3-1** Representing, Comparing, and Ordering Decimals
- **3-2** Estimating Decimals
- **LAB** Explore Decimal Addition and Subtraction
- **3-3** Adding and Subtracting Decimals

3B Multiplying and Dividing Decimals
- **3-4** Scientific Notation
- **LAB** Explore Decimal Multiplication and Division
- **3-5** Multiplying Decimals
- **3-6** Dividing Decimals by Whole Numbers
- **3-7** Dividing by Decimals
- **3-8** Interpreting the Quotient
- **3-9** Solving Decimal Equations

Chapter Focus
- Use common procedures to multiply and divide decimals.
- Evaluate expressions and solve equations with decimals.

Why Learn This

Most statistics in sports are reported as decimals. In basketball, for example, a player who has made 52 out of 60 free throws would have a "free throw percentage" of 0.867. In this chapter, you will learn about decimals and how to use them to solve problems.

Learn It Online
Chapter Project Online go.hrw.com,
keyword MR10 Ch3

Are You Ready?

✓ Vocabulary

Choose the best term from the list to complete each sentence.

1. The first place value to the left of the decimal point is the ___?___ place, and the place value two places to the left of the decimal point is the ___?___ place.
2. In the expression 72 ÷ 9, 72 is the ___?___, and 9 is the ___?___.
3. The answer to a subtraction expression is the ___?___.
4. A(n) ___?___ is a mathematical statement that says two quantities are equivalent.

difference
dividend
divisor
equation
ones
quotient
tens

Complete these exercises to review skills you will need for this chapter.

✓ Place Value of Whole Numbers

Identify the place value of each underlined digit.

5. 1<u>5</u>2
6. <u>7</u>,903
7. <u>1</u>45,072
8. 4,8<u>9</u>3,025
9. 1<u>3</u>,796,020
10. 1<u>4</u>5,683,032

✓ Add and Subtract Whole Numbers

Find each sum or difference.

11. $425 − $75
12. 532 + 145
13. 160 − 82

✓ Multiply and Divide Whole Numbers

Find each product or quotient.

14. $320 × 5
15. 125 ÷ 5
16. 54 × 3

✓ Exponents

Find each value.

17. 10^3
18. 3^6
19. 10^5
20. 4^5
21. 8^3
22. 2^7

✓ Solve One-Step Equations

Solve each equation.

23. $y + 382 = 743$
24. $n - 150 = 322$
25. $9x = 108$

Decimals

CHAPTER 3 Study Guide: Preview

Where You've Been

Previously, you
- compared and ordered whole numbers.
- wrote large whole numbers in standard form.
- rounded numbers to a given place value.
- used addition, subtraction, multiplication, and division of whole numbers to solve problems.

In This Chapter

You will study
- reading, writing, comparing, and ordering decimals.
- writing large whole numbers in scientific notation.
- using rounding to estimate answers to problems that involve decimals.
- solving decimal equations.

Where You're Going

You can use the skills learned in this chapter
- to solve two-step decimal equations in higher-level math classes, such as Algebra 1.
- to solve problems using scientific notation in science classes, such as Astronomy.

Key Vocabulary/Vocabulario

clustering	aproximación
front-end estimation	estimación por partes
scientific notation	notación científica

Vocabulary Connections

To become familiar with some of the vocabulary terms in the chapter, consider the following. You may refer to the chapter, the glossary, or a dictionary if you like.

1. When you estimate, you approximate the value of something. What part of a decimal do you think you are using to approximate a value when you use **front-end estimation**?

2. *Notation* is a way of expressing something. In what other classes do you think you will use **scientific notation**?

3. A *cluster* is a close grouping of similar items. When do you think **clustering** might be a good method of estimation?

96 Chapter 3

Reading and Writing Math

CHAPTER 3

Writing Strategy: Keep a Math Journal

You can help improve your writing and reasoning skills by keeping a math journal. When you express your thoughts on paper, you can make sense of confusing math concepts.

You can also record your thoughts about each lesson and reflect on what you learned in class. Your journal will become a personal math reference book from which to study.

Journal Entry: Read the entry Jaime wrote in his math journal about translating between math and words.

> Journal Entry 2   October
>
> Today's lesson was on translating between words and math. I understand that a math expression like 18 × 2 can be written as "18 multiplied by 2." However, I am confused which symbol to use when translating from words to math. My teacher suggested that I make a list in this journal of common terms and their symbols.
>
> | Words | Symbols |
> |---|---|
> | sum, added, plus | + |
> | difference, less than | − |
> | product, times | × or · |
> | divide, quotient | ÷ |
>
> Now I understand! This list will help me when I need to know which symbol goes with which word.

Try This

Begin a math journal. Make an entry every day for one week. Use the following ideas to start your journal entries. Be sure to date each entry.

- What I already know about this lesson is . . .
- The skills I used to complete this lesson were . . .
- What problems did I have? How did I deal with these problems?
- What I liked/did not like about this lesson . . .

Decimals

Hands-on LAB 3-1

Model Decimals

Use with Lesson 3-1

Learn It Online
Lab Resources Online go.hrw.com,
keyword MR10 Lab3

KEY

| 1 one | 0.1 one tenth | 0.01 one hundredth |

You can use decimal grids to model decimals. The grid is divided into 100 small squares. One square represents one hundredth, or 0.01. Ten squares form a column, which represents one tenth, or 0.1. Ten columns make up the grid, which represents one whole, or 1. By shading hundredths, tenths, or whole grids, you can model decimal numbers.

Activity 1

Write the decimal that is represented by each model.

a. *2 columns and 24 squares are shaded.*

So the model represents 0.24.

b. *1 whole grid and 8 columns are shaded.*

So the model represents 1.8.

c. *2 whole grids, 3 columns, and 7 squares are shaded.*

So the model represents 2.37.

Think and Discuss

1. Explain how a decimal grid can show that 0.30 = 0.3.

Try This

Write the decimal that is represented by each model.

1.
2.
3.

Activity 2

Use a decimal grid to model each decimal.

a. 0.42

Shade 4 columns and 2 squares.

b. 1.88

Shade 1 whole grid, 8 columns, and 8 squares.

c. 2.75

Shade 2 whole grids, 7 columns, and 5 squares.

Think and Discuss

1. Explain how to model 0.46 by shading only 10 sections on the grid. (Hint: A section is a grid, column, or square.)

Try This

Use a decimal grid to model each decimal.

1. 1.02 **2.** 0.04 **3.** 0.4 **4.** 2.14 **5.** 0.53

3-1 Hands-On Lab

3-1 Representing, Comparing, and Ordering Decimals

Learn to write, compare, and order decimals using place value and number lines.

The smaller the apparent magnitude of a star, the brighter the star appears when viewed from Earth. The magnitudes of some stars are listed in the table as decimal numbers.

Apparent Magnitudes of Stars	
Star	Magnitude
Procyon	0.38
Proxima Centauri	11.0
Wolf 359	13.5
Vega	0.03

Decimal numbers represent combinations of whole numbers and numbers between whole numbers.

Interactivities Online ▶ Place value can help you understand and write and compare decimal numbers.

Place Value

Hundreds	Tens	Ones	Tenths	Hundredths	Thousandths	Ten-Thousandths	Hundred-Thousandths
	2	3 .	0	0	5	0	3

EXAMPLE 1 Reading and Writing Decimals

Write each decimal in standard form, expanded form, and words.

A 1.05

Expanded form: 1 + 0.05
Word form: one *and* five hundredths

Reading Math
Read the decimal point as "and."

B 0.05 + 0.001 + 0.0007

Standard form: 0.0517
Word form: five hundred seventeen ten-thousandths

C sixteen and nine hundredths

Standard form: 16.09
Expanded form: 10 + 6 + 0.09

You can use place value to compare decimal numbers.

EXAMPLE 2 **Earth Science Application**

Rigel and Betelgeuse are two stars in the constellation Orion. The apparent magnitude of Rigel is 0.12. The apparent magnitude of Betelgeuse is 0.50. Which star has the smaller magnitude? Which star appears brighter?

0.1̃2 *Line up the decimal points. Start from the left and compare the digits.*

0.5̃0 *Look for the first place where the digits are different.*

1 is less than 5.
0.12 < 0.50

Rigel has a smaller apparent magnitude than Betelgeuse. The star with the smaller magnitude appears brighter. When seen from Earth, Rigel appears brighter than Betelgeuse.

EXAMPLE 3 **Comparing and Ordering Decimals**

Order the decimals from least to greatest.
14.35, 14.3, 14.05

14.3**5**	14.30 < 14.35	*Compare two of the numbers at a time. Write 14.3 as "14.30."*
14.3**0**		
14.**3**5	14.05 < 14.35	*Start at the left and compare the digits.*
14.**0**5		
14.**3**0	14.05 < 14.30	*Look for the first place where the digits are different.*
14.**0**5		

Helpful Hint

Writing zeros at the end of a decimal does not change the value of the decimal.

0.3 = 0.30 = 0.300

Graph the numbers on a number line.

14.05 14.30 14.35
← ●——●—●——————————→
14 14.1 14.2 14.3 14.4 14.5 14.6 14.7 14.8 14.9 15

The numbers are ordered when you read the number line from left to right. The numbers in order from least to greatest are 14.05, 14.3, and 14.35.

Think and Discuss

1. Explain why 0.5 is greater than 0.29 even though 29 is greater than 5.

2. Name the decimal with the least value: 0.29, 2.09, 2.009, 0.029

3. Name three numbers between 1.5 and 1.6.

3-1 Exercises

Learn It Online
Homework Help Online go.hrw.com, keyword MR10 3-1
Exercises 1–16, 19, 23, 27, 29, 31, 37, 41

GUIDED PRACTICE

See Example 1 Write each decimal in standard form, expanded form, and words.
1. 1.98
2. ten and forty-one thousandths
3. 0.07 + 0.006 + 0.0005
4. 0.0472

See Example 2
5. **Physical Science** Osmium and iridium are precious metals. The density of osmium is 22.58 g/cm^3, and the density of iridium is 22.56 g/cm^3. Which metal is denser?

See Example 3 Order the decimals from least to greatest.
6. 9.5, 9.35, 9.65
7. 4.18, 4.1, 4.09
8. 12.39, 12.09, 12.92

INDEPENDENT PRACTICE

See Example 1 Write each decimal in standard form, expanded form, and words.
9. 7.0893
10. 12 + 0.2 + 0.005
11. seven and fifteen hundredths
12. 3 + 0.1 + 0.006

See Example 2
13. **Astronomy** Two meteorites landed in Mexico. The one found in Bacuberito weighed 24.3 tons, and the one found in Chupaderos weighed 26.7 tons. Which meteorite weighed more?

See Example 3 Order the decimals from least to greatest.
14. 15.25, 15.2, 15.5
15. 1.56, 1.62, 1.5
16. 6.7, 6.07, 6.23

PRACTICE AND PROBLEM SOLVING

Extra Practice See page EP6.

Write each number in words.
17. 9.007
18. 5 + 0.08 + 0.004
19. 10.022
20. 4.28
21. 142.6541
22. 0.001 + 0.0007
23. 0.92755
24. 1.02

Compare. Write <, >, or =.
25. 8.04 ■ 8.403
26. 0.907 ■ 0.6801
27. 1.246 ■ 1.29
28. one and fifty-two ten-thousandths ■ 1.0052
29. ten and one hundredth ■ 10.100

Write the value of the red digit in each number.
30. 3.02**6**
31. 17.5**3**703
32. 0.000**5**98
33. 425.**1**055

Order the numbers from greatest to least.
34. 32.525, 32.5254, 31.6257
35. 0.34, 1.43, 4.034, 1.043, 1.424
36. 1.01, 1.1001, 1.101, 1.0001
37. 652.12, 65.213, 65.135, 61.53

102 Chapter 3 Decimals

Astronomy Link

Proxima Centauri, the closest star to Earth other than the Sun, was discovered in 1913. It would take about 115,000 years for a spaceship traveling from Earth at 25,000 mi/h to reach Proxima Centauri.

Use the table for Exercises 38–44.

38. Order the stars Sirius, Luyten 726-8, and Lalande 21185 from closest to farthest from Earth.

39. Which star in the table is farthest from Earth?

40. How far in light-years is Ross 154 from Earth? Write the answer in words and expanded form.

41. List the stars that are less than 5 light-years from Earth.

42. **What's the Error?** A student wrote the distance of Proxima Centauri from Earth as "four hundred and twenty-two hundredths." Explain the error. Write the correct answer.

43. **Write About It** Which star is closer to Earth, Alpha Centauri or Proxima Centauri? Explain how you can compare the distances of these stars. Then answer the question.

44. **Challenge** Wolf 359 is located 7.75 light-years from Earth. If the stars in the table were listed in order from closest to farthest from Earth, between which two stars would Wolf 359 be located?

Distance of Stars from Earth	
Star	Distance (light-years)
Alpha Centauri	4.35
Barnard's Star	5.98
Lalande 21185	8.22
Luyten 726-8	8.43
Proxima Centauri	4.22
Ross 154	9.45
Sirius	8.65

Test Prep and Spiral Review

45. **Multiple Choice** What is the standard form of "five and three hundred twenty-one hundred-thousandths"?

    Ⓐ 5.321   Ⓑ 5.0321   Ⓒ 5.00321   Ⓓ 5.000321

46. **Gridded Response** Write $30 + 2 + 0.8 + 0.009$ in standard form.

Estimate each sum or difference by rounding to the place value indicated. (Lesson 1-1)

47. $6,832 + 2,078$; thousands

48. $52,854 - 25,318$; ten thousands

Solve each equation. (Lesson 2-6)

49. $n - 52 = 71$

50. $30 = k - 15$

51. $c - 22 = 30$

3-1 Representing, Comparing, and Ordering Decimals

3-2 Estimating Decimals

Learn to estimate decimal sums, differences, products, and quotients.

Vocabulary
clustering
front-end estimation

Billy's health class is learning about fitness and nutrition. The table shows the approximate number of calories burned by someone who weighs 90 pounds.

Activity (45 min)	Calories Burned (Approx.)
Cycling	198.45
Playing ice hockey	210.6
Rowing	324
Water skiing	194.4

When numbers are about the same value, you can use *clustering* to estimate. **Clustering** means rounding the numbers to the same value.

EXAMPLE 1 Health Application

Billy wants to cycle, play ice hockey, and water ski. If Billy weighs 90 pounds and spends 45 minutes doing each activity, *about* how many calories will he burn in all?

$$\begin{array}{rcl} 198.45 & \rightarrow & 200 \\ 210.6 & \rightarrow & 200 \\ +194.4 & \rightarrow & +200 \\ \hline & & 600 \end{array}$$

The addends cluster around 200. To estimate the total number of calories, round each addend to 200. Add.

Billy will burn about 600 calories.

EXAMPLE 2 Rounding Decimals to Estimate Sums and Differences

Estimate by rounding to the indicated place value.

A 3.92 + 6.48; ones

3.92 + 6.48
4 + 6 = 10

Round to the nearest whole number.
The sum is about 10.

B 8.6355 − 5.039; hundredths

$$\begin{array}{r} 8.6355 \\ -5.039 \end{array} \qquad \begin{array}{r} 8.64 \\ -5.04 \\ \hline 3.60 \end{array}$$

Round to the hundredths.
Align the decimals.
Subtract.

Caution!
Look at the digit to the right of the place to which you are rounding.
• If it is *5 or greater*, round *up*.
• If it is *less than 5*, round *down*.
See Skills Bank p. SB3.

EXAMPLE 3 Using Compatible Numbers to Estimate Products and Quotients

Estimate each product or quotient.

A 26.76 × 2.93

25 × 3 = 75 *25 and 3 are compatible.*

So 26.76 × 2.93 is about 75.

B 42.64 ÷ 16.51

45 ÷ 15 = 3 *45 and 15 are compatible.*

So 42.64 ÷ 16.51 is about 3.

Remember!
Compatible numbers are close to the numbers that are in the problem and are helpful when you are solving the problem mentally.
See Skills Bank p. SB8.

You can also use *front-end estimation* to estimate with decimals. **Front-end estimation** means to use only the whole-number part of the decimal.

EXAMPLE 4 Using Front-End Estimation

Estimate a range for the sum.

9.99 + 22.89 + 8.3

Use front-end estimation.

```
   9.99  →    9        Add the whole numbers only.
  22.89  →   22        The whole-number values of the decimals
 + 8.30  →  + 8        are less than the actual numbers, so the
 at least  39           answer is an underestimate.
```

The exact answer of 9.99 + 22.89 + 8.3 is greater than 39.

You can estimate a range for the sum by adjusting the decimal part of the numbers. Round the decimals to 0.5 or 1.

```
   0.99  →   1.00      Add the adjusted decimal part of the numbers.
   0.89  →   1.00      Add the whole-number estimate and this
 + 0.30  → + 0.50      sum.
             2.50      The adjusted decimals are greater than the
 39.00 + 2.50 = 41.50  actual decimals, so 41.50 is an overestimate.
```

The estimated range for the sum is between 39.00 and 41.50.

Think and Discuss

1. **Tell** what number the following decimals cluster around: 34.5, 36.78, and 35.234.

2. **Determine** whether a front-end estimation without adjustment is always an overestimation or an underestimation.

3-2 Exercises

Learn It Online
Homework Help Online go.hrw.com,
keyword MR10 3-2 Go
Exercises 1–21, 23, 25, 27, 29

GUIDED PRACTICE

See Example 1
1. Elba runs every Monday, Wednesday, and Friday. Last week she ran 3.62 miles on Monday, 3.8 miles on Wednesday, and 4.3 miles on Friday. About how many miles did she run last week?

See Example 2
Estimate by rounding to the indicated place value.
2. 2.746 − 0.866; tenths
3. 6.735 + 4.9528; ones
4. 10.8071 + 5.392; hundredths
5. 5.9821 − 0.48329; ten-thousandths

See Example 3
Estimate each product or quotient.
6. 38.92 ÷ 4.06
7. 14.51 × 7.89
8. 22.47 ÷ 3.22

See Example 4
Estimate a range for each sum.
9. 7.8 + 31.39 + 6.95
10. 14.27 + 5.4 + 21.86

INDEPENDENT PRACTICE

See Example 1
11. **Multi-Step** Before Mike's trip, the odometer in his car read 146.8 miles. He drove 167.5 miles to a friend's house and 153.9 miles to the beach. About how many miles did the odometer read when he arrived at the beach?

12. The rainfall in July, August, and September was 16.76 cm, 13.97 cm, and 15.24 cm, respectively. About how many total centimeters of rain fell during those three months?

See Example 2
Estimate by rounding to the indicated place value.
13. 2.0993 + 1.256; tenths
14. 7.504 − 2.3792; hundredths
15. 0.6271 + 4.53027; thousandths
16. 13.274 − 8.5590; tenths

See Example 3
Estimate each product or quotient.
17. 9.64 × 1.769
18. 11.509 ÷ 4.258
19. 19.03 ÷ 2.705

See Example 4
Estimate a range for each sum.
20. 17.563 + 4.5 + 2.31
21. 1.620 + 10.8 + 3.71

PRACTICE AND PROBLEM SOLVING

Extra Practice
See page EP6.

Estimate by rounding to the nearest whole number.
22. 8.456 + 7.903
23. 12.43 × 3.72
24. 1,576.2 − 150.50

25. Estimate the quotient of 67.55 and 3.83.

26. Estimate $84.85 divided by 17.

106 Chapter 3 Decimals

Use the table for Exercises 27–31.

Long-Distance Costs for Callers in the United States

Country	Cost per Minute (¢)
Venezuela	22
Russia	9.9
Japan	7.9
United States	3.7

27. **Money** Round each cost in the table to the nearest cent. Write your answer using a dollar sign and decimal point.

28. About how much does it cost to phone someone in Russia and talk for 8 minutes?

29. About how much more does it cost to make a 12-minute call to Japan than to make an 18-minute call within the United States?

30. Will the cost of a 30-minute call to someone within the United States be greater or less than $1.20? Explain.

31. **Multi-Step** Kim is in New York. She calls her grandmother in Venezuela and speaks for 20 minutes, then calls a friend in Japan and talks for 15 minutes, and finally calls her mother in San Francisco and talks for 30 minutes. Estimate the total cost of all her calls.

32. **Health** The recommended daily allowance (RDA) for iron is 15 mg/day for teenage girls. Julie eats a hamburger that contains 3.88 mg of iron. About how many more milligrams of iron does she need to meet the RDA?

33. **Write a Problem** Write a problem with three decimal numbers that have a total sum between 30 and 32.5.

34. **Write About It** How do you adjust a front-end estimation? Why is this done?

35. **Challenge** Place a decimal point in each number so that the sum of the numbers is between 124 and 127: 1059 + 725 + 815 + 1263.

Test Prep and Spiral Review

36. **Multiple Choice** Which is the estimated difference of 34.45 − 24.71 by rounding to the nearest whole number?

    Ⓐ 11   Ⓑ 10   Ⓒ 9   Ⓓ 8

37. **Short Response** The average rainfall in Oklahoma City is 2.8 inches in April, 5.3 inches in May, and 4.3 inches in June. A weather forecaster predicts that the rainfall one year will double the average in April and May and half the average in June. Estimate the predicted rainfall each month to the nearest inch.

Solve each equation. (Lesson 2-5)

38. $83 + n = 157$
39. $x + 23 = 92$
40. $25 + c = 145$

Order the decimals from least to greatest. (Lesson 3-1)

41. 8.304, 8.009, 8.05
42. 5.62, 15.34, 1.589
43. 30.211, 30.709, 30.75

Hands-on LAB 3-3

Explore Decimal Addition and Subtraction

Use with Lesson 3-3

Learn It Online
Lab Resources Online go.hrw.com,
keyword MR10 Lab3 Go

KEY

| 1 | 0.1 | 0.01 |
| one | 1 tenth | 1 hundredth |

You can model addition and subtraction of decimals with decimal grids.

Activity 1

Use decimal grids to find each sum.

a. 0.24 + 0.32

To represent 0.24, shade 24 squares.

To represent 0.32, shade 32 squares in another color.

There are 56 shaded squares.

0.24 + 0.32 = 0.56

b. 1.56 + 0.4

To represent 1.56, shade a whole grid and 56 squares of another.

To represent 0.4, shade 4 columns in another color.

One whole grid and 96 squares are shaded.

1.56 + 0.4 = 1.96

c. 0.75 + 0.68

To represent 0.75, shade 75 squares.

To represent 0.68, shade 68 squares in another color. You will need to use another grid.

One whole grid and 43 squares are shaded.

0.75 + 0.68 = 1.43

Chapter 3 Decimals

Think and Discuss

1. How would you shade a decimal grid to represent 0.2 + 0.18?

Try This

Use decimal grids to find each sum.

1. 0.2 + 0.6
2. 1.07 + 0.03
3. 1.62 + 0.08
4. 0.45 + 0.29
5. 0.88 + 0.12
6. 1.29 + 0.67
7. 0.07 + 0.41
8. 0.51 + 0.51
9. 1.01 + 0.23

Activity 2

Use a decimal grid to find each difference.

a. 0.6 − 0.38

To represent 0.6, shade 6 columns.

Subtract 0.38 by removing 38 squares.

There are 22 remaining squares.

0.6 − 0.38 = 0.22

b. 1.22 − 0.41

To represent 1.22, shade an entire decimal grid and 22 squares of another.

Subtract 0.41 by removing 41 squares.

There are 81 remaining squares.

1.22 − 0.41 = 0.81

Think and Discuss

1. How would you shade a decimal grid to represent 1.3 − 0.6?

Try This

Use decimal grids to find each difference.

1. 0.9 − 0.3
2. 1.2 − 0.98
3. 0.6 − 0.41
4. 1.6 − 0.07
5. 0.35 − 0.03
6. 2.12 − 0.23
7. 2.0 − 0.86
8. 0.78 − 0.76
9. 1.06 − 0.55

3-3 Adding and Subtracting Decimals

Learn to add and subtract decimals.

At the 2004 U.S. Gymnastics Championships, Carly Patterson and Courtney Kupets tied for the All-Around title.

Carly Patterson's Preliminary Scores	
Event	Points
Floor exercise	9.7
Balance beam	9.7
Vault	9.3
Uneven bars	9.45

To find the total number of points, you can add all of the scores.

Carly Patterson also won a gold medal in the Women's Individual All-Around in the 2004 Olympic Games.

EXAMPLE 1 Sports Application

A What was Carly Patterson's preliminary total score in the 2004 U.S. Championships?

First estimate the sum of 9.7, 9.7, 9.3, and 9.45.

$$9.7 + 9.7 + 9.3 + 9.45$$
$$\downarrow \quad \downarrow \quad \downarrow \quad \downarrow$$
$$10 + 10 + 9 + 9 = 38$$

Estimate by rounding to the nearest whole number.
The total is about 38 points.

Then add.

```
  9.70      Align the decimal points.
  9.70
  9.30      Use zeros as placeholders.
+ 9.45
─────
 38.15      Add. Then place the decimal point.
```

Since 38.15 is close to the estimate of 38, the answer is reasonable. Patterson's total preliminary score was 38.15 points.

B How many more points did Patterson need on the uneven bars to have a perfect score of 10?

Find the difference between 10 and 9.45.

```
 10.00      Align the decimal points.
− 9.45      Use zeros as placeholders.
─────
  0.55      Subtract. Then place the decimal point.
```

Patterson needed another 0.55 points to have a perfect score.

Helpful Hint

Estimating before you add or subtract will help you check whether your answer is reasonable.

EXAMPLE 2 **Using Mental Math to Add and Subtract Decimals**

Find each sum or difference.

A $1.6 + 0.4$
$1.6 + 0.4$ *Think: 0.6 + 0.4 = 1*
$1.6 + 0.4 = 2$

B $3 - 0.8$
$3 - 0.8$ *Think: 0.8 + 0.2 = 1,*
$3 - 0.8 = 2.2$ *so 1 − 0.8 = 0.2.*

EXAMPLE 3 **Evaluating Decimal Expressions**

Evaluate $7.52 - s$ for each value of s.

A $s = 2.9$

$7.52 - s$
$7.52 - 2.9$ *Substitute 2.9 for s.*

$$\begin{array}{r} 7.52 \\ -\,2.90 \\ \hline 4.62 \end{array}$$

Align the decimal points.
Use a zero as a placeholder.
Subtract.
Place the decimal point.

Remember!
You can place any number of zeros at the end of a decimal number without changing its value.

B $s = 4.5367$

$7.52 - s$
$7.52 - 4.5367$ *Substitute 4.5367 for s.*

$$\begin{array}{r} 7.5200 \\ -\,4.5367 \\ \hline 2.9833 \end{array}$$

Align the decimal points.
Use zeros as placeholders.
Subtract.
Place the decimal point.

Think and Discuss

1. **Show** how you would write $2.678 + 124.5$ to find the sum.
2. **Tell** why it is a good idea to estimate the answer before you add and subtract.
3. **Explain** how you can use mental math to find how many more points Carly Patterson would have needed to have scored a perfect 10 on the floor exercise.

3-3 Exercises

Learn It Online
Homework Help Online go.hrw.com, keyword MR10 3-3
Exercises 1–29, 31, 33, 35, 37, 39, 43, 45

GUIDED PRACTICE

See Example 1 Use the table for Exercises 1–3.

1. How many miles in all is Rea's triathlon training?
2. How many miles did Rea run and swim in all?
3. How much farther did Rea cycle than swim?

Rea's Triathlon Training	
Sport	Distance (mi)
Cycling	14.25
Running	4.35
Swimming	1.6

See Example 2 Find each sum or difference.

4. $2.7 + 0.3$
5. $6 - 0.4$
6. $5.2 + 2.8$
7. $8.9 - 4$

See Example 3 Evaluate $5.35 - m$ for each value of m.

8. $m = 2.37$
9. $m = 1.8$
10. $m = 4.7612$
11. $m = 0.402$

INDEPENDENT PRACTICE

See Example 1

12. **Sports** During a diving competition, Phil performed two reverse dives and two dives from a handstand position. He received the following scores: 8.765, 9.45, 9.875, and 8.025. What was Phil's total score?

13. Brad works after school at a local grocery store. How much did he earn in all for the month of October?

Brad's Earnings for October				
Week	1	2	3	4
Earnings	$123.48	$165.18	$137.80	$140.92

See Example 2 Find each sum or difference.

14. $7.2 + 1.8$
15. $8.5 - 7$
16. $3.3 + 0.7$
17. $15.9 + 2.1$
18. $7 - 0.6$
19. $7.55 - 3.25$
20. $21.4 + 3.6$
21. $5 - 2.7$

See Example 3 Evaluate $9.67 - x$ for each value of x.

22. $x = 1.52$
23. $x = 3.8$
24. $x = 7.21$
25. $x = 0.635$
26. $x = 6.9$
27. $x = 1.001$
28. $x = 8$
29. $x = 9.527$

PRACTICE AND PROBLEM SOLVING

Extra Practice See page EP6.

Add or subtract.

30. $5.62 + 4.19$
31. $10.508 - 6.73$
32. $13.009 + 12.83$

33. Find the sum of 0.0679 and 3.75.
34. Subtract 3.0042 from 7.435.

35. **Sports** Terin Humphrey was ranked third at the 2004 U.S. Gymnastics Championships with a score of 75.45. What was the difference between her score and Courtney Kupet's and Carly Patterson's score of 76.45?

112 Chapter 3 Decimals

Career

The risk of death in a house fire can be reduced by up to 50% if the home has a working smoke alarm.

Evaluate each expression.

36. $8.09 - a$ for $a = 4.5$

37. $7.03 + 33.8 + n$ for $n = 12.006$

38. $b + (5.68 - 3.007)$ for $b = 6.134$

39. $(2 \times 14) - a + 1.438$ for $a = 0.062$

40. $5^2 - w$ for $w = 3.5$

41. $100 - p$ for $p = 15.034$

42. Career A fire helmet must be sturdy enough to protect the firefighter's head from dangerous objects and extremely hot temperatures while still being as lightweight as possible. One fire helmet weighs 1.616 kg, and another fire helmet weighs 1.403 kg. What is the difference in weights?

43. Multi-Step Logan wants to buy a new bike that costs $135.00. He started with $14.83 in his savings account. Last week, he deposited $15.35 into his account. Today, he deposited $32.40. How much more money does he need to buy the bike?

44. Swimming With a time of 60.35 seconds, Martina Moracova broke Jennifer Thompson's world record time in the women's 100-meter medley. How much faster was Thompson than Moracova when, in the next heat, she reclaimed the record with a time of 59.30 seconds?

45. Sports The highest career batting average ever achieved by a professional baseball player is 0.366. Bill Bergen finished with a career 0.170 average. How much lower is Bergen's career average than the highest career average?

46. What's the Question? A cup of rice contains 0.8 mg of iron, and a cup of lima beans contains 4.4 mg of iron. If the answer is 6 mg, what is the question?

47. Write About It Why is it important to align the decimal points before adding or subtracting decimal numbers?

48. Challenge Evaluate $(5.7 + a) \times (9.75 - b)$ for $a = 2.3$ and $b = 7.25$.

Test Prep and Spiral Review

49. Multiple Choice What is the sum of 24.91 and 35.8?

Ⓐ 28.49 Ⓑ 59.99 Ⓒ 60.71 Ⓓ 60.99

50. Multiple Choice Lead has an atomic weight of 207.19. Mercury has an atomic weight of 200.6. How much greater is the atomic weight of lead than mercury?

Ⓕ 6.59 Ⓖ 7.41 Ⓗ 7.59 Ⓙ 187.13

Solve each equation. (Lesson 2-6)

51. $s - 47 = 23$

52. $73 = a - 78$

53. $823 = t - 641$

Estimate each product or quotient. (Lesson 3-2)

54. 15.72×4.08

55. 14.87×3.78

56. $53.67 \div 9.18$

3-3 Adding and Subtracting Decimals

Ready To Go On?

Quiz for Lessons 3-1 Through 3-3

3-1 Representing, Comparing, and Ordering Decimals

Write each decimal in standard form, expanded form, and words.

1. 4.012
2. ten and fifty-four thousandths
3. On Monday Jamie ran 3.54 miles. On Wednesday he ran 3.6 miles. On which day did he run farther?

Order the decimals from least to greatest.

4. 3.406, 30.08, 3.6
5. 10.10, 10.01, 101.1
6. 16.782, 16.59, 16.79
7. 62.0581, 62.148, 62.0741
8. 123.05745, 132.05628, 123.05749

3-2 Estimating Decimals

9. Matt drove 106.8 miles on Monday, 98.3 miles on Tuesday, and 103.5 miles on Wednesday. About how many miles did he drive in all?

Estimate.

10. $8.345 - 0.6051$; round to the hundredths
11. $16.492 - 2.613$; round to the tenths
12. 18.79×4.68
13. $71.378 \div 8.13$
14. 52.055×7.18

Estimate a range for each sum.

15. $7.42 + 13.87 + 101.2$
16. $1.79 + 3.45 + 7.92$

3-3 Adding and Subtracting Decimals

17. Greg's scores at four gymnastic meets were 9.65, 8.758, 9.884, and 9.500. What was his total score for all four meets?
18. Mrs. Henry buys groceries each week and uses a spreadsheet to keep track of how much she spends. How much did she spend in all for the month of December?

Grocery Spending for December				
Week	1	2	3	4
Amount Spent ($)	52.35	77.97	90.10	42.58

19. Sally walked 1.2 miles on Monday, 1.6 miles on Wednesday, and 2.1 miles on Friday. How many miles did she walk in all?

Find each sum or difference.

20. $0.47 + 0.03$
21. $8 - 0.6$
22. $2.2 + 1.8$

Evaluate $8.67 - s$ for each value of s.

23. $s = 3.4$
24. $s = 2.0871$
25. $s = 7.205$

Focus on Problem Solving

Solve
- Write an equation

Read the whole problem before you try to solve it. Sometimes you need to solve the problem in more than one step.

Read the problem. Determine the steps needed to solve the problem.

Brian buys erasers and pens for himself and 4 students in his class. The erasers cost $0.79 each, and the pens cost $2.95 each. What is the total amount that Brian spends on the erasers and pens?

Here is one way to solve the problem.

5 erasers cost	5 pens cost
5 · $0.79	5 · $2.95

(5 · $0.79) + (5 · $2.95)

Read each problem. Decide whether you need more than one step to solve the problem. List the possible steps. Then choose an equation with which to solve the problem.

1 Joan is making some costumes. She cuts 3 pieces of fabric, each 3.5 m long. She has 5 m of fabric left. Which equation can you use to find f, the amount of fabric she had to start with?

A) $(3 \cdot 3.5) + 5 = f$
B) $3 + 3.5 + 5 = f$
C) $(5 \times 3.5) \div 3 = f$
D) $5 - (3 \cdot 3.5) = f$

2 Mario buys 4 chairs and a table. He spends $245.99 in all. If each chair costs $38.95, which equation can you use to find T, the cost of the table?

F) $4 + \$245.99 + \$38.95 = T$
G) $(4 \cdot \$38.95) + \$245.99 = T$
H) $\$245.99 - (4 \cdot \$38.95) = T$
J) $\$245.99 \div (4 \cdot \$38.95) = T$

3 Mya skis down Ego Bowl three times and down Fantastic twice. Ego Bowl is 5.85 km long, and Fantastic is 8.35 km long. Which equation can you use to estimate d, the distance Mya skis in all?

A) $(6 \cdot 3) + (8 \cdot 2) = d$
B) $(6 + 8) + (3 + 2) = d$
C) $3(6 + 8) = d$
D) $(6 \div 3) + (8 \div 2) = d$

Focus on Problem Solving

3-4 Scientific Notation

Learn to write large numbers in scientific notation.

Vocabulary
scientific notation

Artist Georges Seurat used the technique *pointillism* in his 1884 painting *A Sunday on La Grande Jatte*.

In pointillism, an artist places many small dots close together to create a picture. Seurat's painting is made up of about 3,456,000 dots.

The dots in the painting are as small as $\frac{1}{16}$ inch. It took Seurat about two years to complete the painting.

You can write large numbers such as 3,456,000 as the product of a number and a power of 10. Look for a pattern in the table below.

Number	×	Power of 10	Product	Number of Places the Decimal Point Moves
3.456	×	10	34.56	1
3.456	×	100	345.6	2
3.456	×	1,000	3,456	3
3.456	×	10,000	34,560	4

EXAMPLE 1 Multiplying by Powers of Ten

Find each product.

A $4{,}325 \times 1{,}000$

$\quad 4{,}325.000$ *There are 3 zeros in 1,000.*
                    To multiply, move the decimal point 3 places right.
$= 4{,}325{,}000$ *Write 3 placeholder zeros.*

B $2.54 \times 10{,}000$

$\quad 2.5400$ *There are 4 zeros in 10,000.*
              To multiply, move the decimal point 4 places right.
$= 25{,}400$ *Write 2 placeholder zeros.*

Scientific notation is a shorthand method that can be used to write large numbers.

A number written in scientific notation has two numbers that are multiplied.

$$4.123 \times 10^5$$

The first part is a number that is greater than or equal to 1 and less than 10.

The second part is a power of 10.

116 Chapter 3 Decimals

EXAMPLE 2 **Writing Numbers in Scientific Notation**

Write 8,296,000 in scientific notation.

8,296,000

8,296,000   *Move the decimal point 6 places left. The power of 10 is 6.*

$8{,}296{,}000 = 8.296 \times 10^6$

You can write a large number written in scientific notation in standard form. Look at the power of 10 and move the decimal point that number of places to the right.

EXAMPLE 3 **Writing Numbers in Standard Form**

Write 3.2×10^7 in standard form.

3.2×10^7 *The power of 10 is 7.*

3.2000000   *Move the decimal point 7 places right. Use zeros as placeholders.*

$3.2 \times 10^7 = 32{,}000{,}000$

EXAMPLE 4 **Art Application**

Write the number of dots in Seurat's painting *A Sunday on La Grande Jatte*, 3,456,000, in scientific notation.

3,456,000   *Move the decimal point left to form a number that is greater than 1 and less than 10.*

3,456,000   *Multiply that number by a power of ten.*

3.456×10^6 *The power of 10 is 6, because the decimal point is moved 6 places left.*

The number of dots in Seurat's painting is 3.456×10^6.

Think and Discuss

1. **Explain** how you can check whether a number is written correctly in scientific notation.

2. **Tell** why 782.5×10^8 is not correctly written in scientific notation.

3. **Tell** the advantages of writing a number in scientific notation over writing it in standard form. Explain any disadvantages.

3-4 Exercises

GUIDED PRACTICE

See Example 1 Find each product.
1. $5{,}937 \times 100$
2. $719.25 \times 1{,}000$
3. $6.0912 \times 100{,}000$

See Example 2 Write each number in scientific notation.
4. $62{,}000$
5. $500{,}000$
6. $6{,}913{,}000$

See Example 3 Write each number in standard form.
7. 6.793×10^6
8. 1.4×10^4
9. 3.82×10^5

See Example 4 10. **Geography** The Atlantic Ocean has a surface area of 31,660,000 square miles. Write the surface area of the Atlantic Ocean in scientific notation.

INDEPENDENT PRACTICE

See Example 1 Find each product.
11. $278 \times 1{,}000$
12. 74.1×100
13. $381.8 \times 10{,}000$
14. $1.97 \times 10{,}000$
15. $4{,}129 \times 100$
16. $62.4 \times 1{,}000$

See Example 2 Write each number in scientific notation.
17. $90{,}000$
18. $186{,}000$
19. $1{,}607{,}000$
20. $240{,}000$
21. $6{,}000{,}000$
22. $16{,}900{,}000$

See Example 3 Write each number in standard form.
23. 3.211×10^5
24. 1.63×10^6
25. 7.7×10^3
26. 2.14×10^4
27. 4.03×10^6
28. 8.1164×10^8

See Example 4 29. **Entertainment** *Star Wars: Episode III—Revenge of the Sith* made $6,200,000 from its opening-night midnight screenings. Write this amount in scientific notation.

PRACTICE AND PROBLEM SOLVING

Extra Practice
See page EP6.

Write each number in standard form.
30. 7.21×10^3
31. 1.234×10^5
32. 7.200×10^2
33. 2.08×10^5
34. 6.954×10^3
35. 5.43×10^1

Write each number in scientific notation.
36. $112{,}050$
37. $150{,}000$
38. $4{,}562$
39. 652
40. $1{,}000$
41. $65{,}342$
42. 95
43. $28{,}001$

44. **Technology** In the year 2005, there were about 1 billion computers in the world. Write this number in standard form and scientific notation.

118 Chapter 3 Decimals

Earth Science

This F/A-18 Hornet makes a vapor cloud by flying at Mach 0.98, just under the speed of sound.

45. **Life Science** Genes carry the codes used for making proteins that are necessary for life. No one knows yet how many human genes there are. Estimates range from 2.0×10^4 to 2.5×10^4. Write a number in standard form that is within this range.

46. **Earth Science** The speed of light is about 300,000 km/s. The speed of sound in air that has a temperature of 20°C is 1,125 ft/s. Write both of these values in scientific notation.

Use the pictograph for Exercises 47 and 48.

47. Write the capacity of Rungnado Stadium in scientific notation.

48. **Estimation** Estimate the capacity of the largest stadium shown. Write the estimate in scientific notation.

Stadium Seating Capacities

Strahov - Czech Republic
Maracana Municipal - Brazil
Rungnado - North Korea

= 25,000 seats

49. **Social Studies** The Library of Congress, in Washington, D.C., is the largest library in the world. At one time, it had 24,616,867 books. Round the number of books to the nearest hundred thousand, and write that number in scientific notation.

50. **What's the Error?** A student said 56,320,000 written in scientific notation is 56.32×10^6. Describe the error. Then write the correct answer.

51. **Write About It** How does writing numbers in scientific notation make it easier to compare and order the numbers?

52. **Challenge** What is 5.32 written in scientific notation?

Test Prep and Spiral Review

53. **Multiple Choice** What is 23,600,000 in scientific notation?

    Ⓐ 236×10^5 Ⓑ 23.6×10^6 Ⓒ 2.36×10^6 Ⓓ 2.36×10^7

54. **Gridded Response** Rhode Island has an area of 1.045×10^3 square miles. What is this number in standard form?

Identify the property illustrated by each equation. (Lesson 1-4)

55. $4 + 5 = 5 + 4$ 56. $3(4 - 1) = 3(4) - 3(1)$ 57. $(9 \times 80) \times 72 = 9 \times (80 \times 72)$

Evaluate each expression for $a = 4$, $b = 2.8$, and $c = 0.9$. (Lesson 3-3)

58. $a + b$ 59. $b - c$ 60. $a + c$ 61. $a - b$ 62. $a - c$

3-4 Scientific Notation

Hands-On Lab 3-5: Explore Decimal Multiplication and Division

Use with Lessons 3-5 and 3-6

KEY

1	0.1	0.01
one	1 tenth	1 hundredth

You can use decimal grids to model multiplication and division of decimals.

Activity 1

Use decimal grids to find each product.

a. $3 \cdot 0.32$

To represent $3 \cdot 0.32$, shade 32 small squares three times.

Use a different color to shade a different group of 32 small squares each time.

There are 96 shaded squares.

$3 \cdot 0.32 = 0.96$

b. $0.3 \cdot 0.5$

To represent 0.3, shade 3 columns.

To represent 0.5, shade 5 rows in another color.

There are 15 squares in the area where the shading overlaps.

$0.3 \cdot 0.5 = 0.15$

Think and Discuss

1. How is multiplying a decimal by a decimal different from multiplying a decimal by a whole number?

2. Why can you shade 5 rows to represent 0.5?

Try This

Use decimal grids to find each product.

1. $3 \cdot 0.14$
2. $5 \cdot 0.18$
3. $0.7 \cdot 0.5$
4. $0.6 \cdot 0.4$
5. $4 \cdot 0.25$
6. $0.2 \cdot 0.9$
7. $9 \cdot 0.07$
8. $8 \cdot 0.15$

Activity 2

Use decimal grids to find each quotient.

a. 3.66 ÷ 3

Shade 3 grids and 66 small squares of a fourth grid to represent 3.66.

Divide the shaded wholes into 3 equal groups. Use scissors to divide the 66 hundredths into 3 equal groups.

3.66 ÷ 3 = 1.22   *One whole grid and 22 small squares are in each group.*

b. 3.6 ÷ 1.2

Shade 3 grids and 6 columns of a fourth grid to represent 3.6. Cut apart the 6 tenths.

Divide the grids and tenths into equal groups of 1.2.

3.6 ÷ 1.2 = 3   *There are 3 equal groups of 1.2.*

Think and Discuss

1. Find 36 ÷ 12. How does this problem and its quotient compare to 3.6 ÷ 1.2?

Try This

Use decimal grids to find each quotient.

1. 4.04 ÷ 4   **2.** 3.25 ÷ 5   **3.** 7.8 ÷ 1.3   **4.** 5.6 ÷ 0.8

5. 6.24 ÷ 2   **6.** 5.1 ÷ 1.7   **7.** 5.7 ÷ 3   **8.** 5.4 ÷ 0.9

3-5 Multiplying Decimals

Learn to multiply decimals by whole numbers and by decimals.

Because the Moon has less mass than Earth, it has a smaller gravitational effect. An object that weighs 1 pound on Earth weighs only 0.17 pound on the Moon.

You can multiply the weight of an object on Earth by 0.17 to find its weight on the Moon.

Gravity on Earth is about six times the gravity on the surface of the Moon.

You can multiply decimals by first multiplying as you would whole numbers. Then place the decimal point by finding the total of the number of decimal places in the factors. The product will have the same number of decimal places.

EXAMPLE 1 Science Application

A flag weighs 3 pounds on Earth. What is the weight of the flag on the Moon?

Multiply 3 by 0.17, since 1 pound on Earth is 0.17 pound on the Moon.

$$\begin{array}{r} 17 \\ \times\ 3 \\ \hline 51 \end{array}$$

Multiply as you would with whole numbers.

Place the decimal point by adding the number of decimal places in the numbers multiplied.

0.17	2 decimal places
× 3	+ 0 decimal places
0.51	2 decimal places

A 3 lb flag on Earth weighs 0.51 lb on the Moon.

EXAMPLE 2 Multiplying a Decimal by a Decimal

Helpful Hint
You can use a decimal grid to model multiplication of decimals.

Find each product.

A 0.2 × 0.6

Multiply. Then place the decimal point.

0.2	1 decimal place
× 0.6	+ 1 decimal place
0.12	2 decimal places

122 Chapter 3 Decimals

Find each product.

B 3.25 × 4.8

3 × 5 = 15   *Estimate the product. Round each factor to the nearest whole number.*

```
   3.25
 × 4.8
  ─────
   2600
  13000
  ─────
  15.600
```

Multiply. Then place the decimal point.

2 + 1 = 3 decimal places

15.600 is close to the estimate of 15. The answer is reasonable.

C 0.05 × 0.9

0.05 × 1 = 0.05   *Estimate the product. 0.9 is close to 1.*

Multiply. Then place the decimal point.

```
   0.05        2 decimal places
 × 0.9       + 1 decimal place
 ─────
  0.045       3 decimal places; use a placeholder zero.
```

0.045 is close to the estimate of 0.05. The answer is reasonable.

EXAMPLE 3   Evaluating Decimal Expressions

Evaluate 3x for each value of x.

Remember!
These notations all mean multiply 3 times x.
3 · x 3x 3(x)

A $x = 4.047$

3x = 3(4.047)   *Substitute 4.047 for x.*

```
   4.047        3 decimal places
 ×     3      + 0 decimal places
 ──────
  12.141        3 decimal places
```

B $x = 2.95$

3x = 3(2.95)   *Substitute 2.95 for x.*

```
   2.95         2 decimal places
 ×    3       + 0 decimal places
 ─────
   8.85         2 decimal places
```

Think and Discuss

1. Tell how many decimal places are in the product of 235.2 and 0.24.

2. Show how to use the Distributive Property to find 1.7 × 2.

3. Describe how the products of 0.3 × 0.5 and 3 × 5 are similar. How are they different?

3-5 Exercises

Learn It Online
Homework Help Online go.hrw.com,
keyword MR10 3-5 Go
Exercises 1–28, 29, 37, 39, 45, 47, 49, 51

GUIDED PRACTICE

See Example 1
1. Each can of cat food costs $0.28. How much will 6 cans of cat food cost?
2. Jorge buys 8 baseballs for $9.29 each. How much does he spend in all?

See Example 2 Find each product.

3. 0.6 × 0.4
4. 0.008 × 0.5
5. 3.0 × 0.07
6. 0.12 × 0.6

See Example 3 Evaluate $5x$ for each value of x.

7. $x = 3.304$
8. $x = 4.58$
9. $x = 7.126$
10. $x = 1.9$

INDEPENDENT PRACTICE

See Example 1
11. Gwenyth walks her dog each morning. If she walks 0.37 kilometers each morning, how many kilometers will she have walked in 7 days?
12. **Consumer Math** Apples are on sale for $0.49 per pound. What is the price for 4 pounds of apples?

See Example 2 Find each product.

13. 0.9 × 0.03
14. 4.5 × 0.5
15. 0.31 × 0.7
16. 1.6 × 0.08

17. 0.007 × 0.06
18. 0.04 × 3.0
19. 2.0 × 0.006
20. 0.005 × 0.003

See Example 3 Evaluate $7x$ for each value of x.

21. $x = 1.903$
22. $x = 2.461$
23. $x = 3.72$
24. $x = 4.05$
25. $x = 0.164$
26. $x = 5.89$
27. $x = 0.3702$
28. $x = 1.82$

PRACTICE AND PROBLEM SOLVING

Extra Practice
See page EP7.

Multiply.

29. 0.3 × 0.03
30. 1.4 × 0.21
31. 0.06 × 1.02
32. 8.2 × 4.1
33. 12.6 × 2.1
34. 3.04 × 0.6
35. 0.66 × 2.52
36. 3.08 × 0.7
37. 0.2 × 0.94 × 1.3
38. 1.54 × 3.05 × 2.6
39. 1.98 × 0.4 × 5.2
40. 1.7 × 2.41 × 0.5
41. 2.5 × 1.52 × 3.7
42. 6.5 × 0.15 × 3.8

Evaluate.

43. $6n$ for $n = 6.23$
44. $5t + 0.462$ for $t = 3.04$
45. $8^2 - 2b$ for $b = 0.95$
46. $4^3 + 5c$ for $c = 1.9$
47. $3h - 15 + h$ for $h = 5.2$
48. $5^2 + 6j + j$ for $j = 0.27$

Physical Science LINK

Saturn is the second-largest planet in the solar system. Saturn is covered by thick clouds. Saturn's density is very low. Suppose you weigh 180 pounds on Earth. If you were able to stand on Saturn, you would weigh only 165 pounds. To find the weight of an object on another planet, multiply its weight on Earth by the gravitational pull listed in the table.

Gravitational Pull of Planets (Compared with Earth)	
Planet	Gravitational Pull
Mercury	0.38
Venus	0.91
Mars	0.38
Jupiter	2.54
Saturn	0.93
Neptune	1.2

49. Christopher found a rock that weighs 5 pounds on Earth. How much would the rock weigh on Saturn?

50. On which two planets would the weight of an object be the same?

51. Multi-Step An object weighs 9 pounds on Earth. How much more would this object weigh on Neptune than on Mars?

52. Write a Problem Use the data in the table to write a word problem that can be answered by evaluating an expression with multiplication. Solve your problem.

53. What's the Error? A student said that his new baby brother, who weighs 10 pounds, would weigh 120 pounds on Neptune. What is the error? Write the correct answer.

54. Challenge An object weighs between 2.79 lb and 5.58 lb on Saturn. Give a range for the object's weight on Earth.

Galileo Galilei was the first person to look at Saturn through a telescope. He thought there were groups of stars on each side of the planet, but it was later determined that he had seen Saturn's rings.

Test Prep and Spiral Review

55. Multiple Choice Max uses 1.6 liters of gasoline each hour mowing lawns. How much gas does he use in 5.8 hours?

- Ⓐ 7.4 liters
- Ⓑ 9.28 liters
- Ⓒ 92.8 liters
- Ⓓ 928 liters

56. Multiple Choice What is the value of $5x$ when $x = 3.2$?

- Ⓕ 16
- Ⓖ 1.6
- Ⓗ 0.16
- Ⓙ 8.2

Solve each equation. (Lesson 2-8)

57. $\frac{x}{8} = 4$ **58.** $\frac{y}{12} = 5$ **59.** $3 = \frac{t}{17}$ **60.** $2 = \frac{s}{21}$

Write each decimal in expanded form. (Lesson 3-1)

61. 1.23   **62.** 0.45   **63.** 26.07   **64.** 116.2   **65.** 80.002

3-6 Dividing Decimals by Whole Numbers

Learn to divide decimals by whole numbers.

Emily and two of her friends are going to share equally the cost of making pottery for the art fair.

To find how much each person should pay for the materials, you will need to divide a decimal by a whole number.

Remember!

Quotient
$$0.15 \\ 5)\overline{0.75}$$
Divisor Dividend

For more on dividing with whole numbers, see Skills Bank page SB5.

EXAMPLE 1 Dividing a Decimal by a Whole Number

Find each quotient.

A $0.75 \div 5$

$$\begin{array}{r} 0.15 \\ 5)\overline{0.75} \\ -\,5\downarrow \\ \hline 25 \\ -25 \\ \hline 0 \end{array}$$

Place a decimal point in the quotient directly above the decimal point in the dividend.
Divide as you would with whole numbers.

B $2.52 \div 3$

$$\begin{array}{r} 0.84 \\ 3)\overline{2.52} \\ -24\downarrow \\ \hline 12 \\ -12 \\ \hline 0 \end{array}$$

Place a decimal point in the quotient directly above the decimal point in the dividend.
Divide as you would with whole numbers.

EXAMPLE 2 Evaluating Decimal Expressions

Evaluate $0.435 \div x$ for each given value of x.

A $x = 3$

$0.435 \div x$
$0.435 \div 3$ *Substitute 3 for x.*

$$\begin{array}{r} 0.145 \\ 3)\overline{0.435} \\ -\,3\downarrow \\ \hline 13 \\ -12\downarrow \\ \hline 15 \\ -15 \\ \hline 0 \end{array}$$

Divide as you would with whole numbers.

B $x = 15$

$0.435 \div x$
$0.435 \div 15$ *Substitute 15 for x.*

$$\begin{array}{r} 0.029 \\ 15)\overline{0.435} \\ -\,0\downarrow \\ \hline 43 \\ -30\downarrow \\ \hline 135 \\ -135 \\ \hline 0 \end{array}$$

Sometimes you need to use a zero as a placeholder.
$15 > 4$, so place a zero in the quotient and divide 15 into 43.

EXAMPLE 3 Consumer Math Application

Emily and two of her friends are making pottery using clay, glaze, and paint. The materials cost $11.61. If they share the cost equally, how much should each person pay?

$11.61 should be divided into three equal groups.
Divide $11.61 by 3.

```
    3.87
3)11.61
   -9↓
    2 6
   -2 4↓
      21
     -21
       0
```

Place a decimal point in the quotient directly above the decimal point in the dividend.

Divide as you would with whole numbers.

Check
3.87 × 3 = 11.61
Each person should pay $3.87.

Remember!
Multiplication can "undo" division. To check your answer to a division problem, multiply the divisor by the quotient.

Think and Discuss

1. **Tell** how you know where to place the decimal point in the quotient.
2. **Explain** why you can use multiplication to check your answer to a division problem.

3-6 Exercises

Learn It Online
Homework Help Online go.hrw.com,
keyword MR10 3-6
Exercises 1–18, 19, 21, 23

GUIDED PRACTICE

See Example 1 Find each quotient.
1. $1.38 \div 6$
2. $0.96 \div 8$
3. $1.75 \div 5$
4. $0.72 \div 4$

See Example 2 Evaluate $0.312 \div x$ for each given value of x.
5. $x = 4$
6. $x = 6$
7. $x = 3$
8. $x = 12$

See Example 3
9. **Consumer Math** Mr. Richards purchased 8 T-shirts for the volleyball team. The total cost of the T-shirts was $70.56. How much did each shirt cost?

INDEPENDENT PRACTICE

See Example 1 Find each quotient.
- **10.** $0.91 \div 7$
- **11.** $1.32 \div 6$
- **12.** $4.68 \div 9$
- **13.** $0.81 \div 3$

See Example 2 Evaluate $0.684 \div x$ for each given value of x.
- **14.** $x = 3$
- **15.** $x = 4$
- **16.** $x = 18$
- **17.** $x = 9$

See Example 3
- **18. Consumer Math** Charles, Kate, and Kim eat lunch in a restaurant. The bill is $27.12. If they share the bill equally, how much will each person pay?

PRACTICE AND PROBLEM SOLVING

Extra Practice
See page EP7.

Find the value of each expression.
- **19.** $(0.49 + 0.045) \div 5$
- **20.** $(4.9 - 3.125) \div 5$
- **21.** $(13.28 - 7.9) \div 4$

Evaluate the expression $x \div 4$ for each value of x.
- **22.** $x = 0.504$
- **23.** $x = 0.944$
- **24.** $x = 57.484$
- **25.** $x = 1.648$

26. Multi-Step At the grocery store, a 6 lb bag of oranges costs $2.04. Is this more or less expensive than the price shown at the farmers' market?

27. Critical Thinking How could you use rounding to check your answer to the problem $5.58 \div 6$?

28. Choose a Strategy Sarah had $1.19 in coins. Jeff asked her for change for a dollar, but she did not have the correct change. What coins did she have?

29. Write About It When do you use a placeholder zero in the quotient?

30. Challenge Evaluate the expression $x \div 2$ for the following values of $x = 520$, 52, and 5.2. Try to predict the value of the same expression for $x = 0.52$.

Test Prep and Spiral Review

31. Multiple Choice What is the value of $0.98 \div x$ when $x = 2$?
- Ⓐ 49
- Ⓑ 4.9
- Ⓒ 0.49
- Ⓓ 0.049

32. Gridded Response Danika spent $89.24 on two pairs of shoes. Each pair of shoes cost the same amount. How much, in dollars, did each pair cost?

Identify a pattern in each sequence. Name the missing term. (Lesson 1-6)
- **33.** 85, 80, 75, 70, 65, ■, …
- **34.** 2, 6, 5, 9, 8, ■, …
- **35.** 10, 17, 12, 19, 14, ■, …

Write each number in standard form. (Lesson 3-4)
- **36.** 6.479×10^3
- **37.** 0.208×10^2
- **38.** 13.507×10^4
- **39.** 7.1×10^5

3-7 Dividing by Decimals

Learn to divide whole numbers and decimals by decimals.

Julie and her family traveled to the Grand Canyon. They stopped to refill their gas tank with 13.4 gallons of gasoline after they had driven 368.5 miles.

To find the miles that they drove per gallon, you will need to divide a decimal by a decimal.

EXAMPLE 1 Dividing a Decimal by a Decimal

Find each quotient.

A $3.6 \div 1.2$

$1.2\overline{)3.6}$

Helpful Hint

Multiplying the divisor and the dividend by the same number does not change the quotient.

$42 \div 6 = 7$
$\times 10 \downarrow \quad \times 10 \downarrow$
$420 \div 60 = 7$

$42 \div 6 = 7$
$\times 100 \downarrow \quad \times 100 \downarrow$
$4{,}200 \div 600 = 7$

Multiply the divisor by 10^1, or 10, to make it a whole number. Multiply the dividend by the same power of 10.

There is one decimal place in the divisor. Multiply by 10^1, or 10.

Think: $1.2 \times 10 = 12 \quad 3.6 \times 10 = 36$

3
$12\overline{)36}$
$\underline{-36}$
0

Divide as with whole numbers.

$3.6 \div 1.2 = 3$

B $42.3 \div 0.12$

$0.12\overline{)42.3}$

Multiply the divisor by 10^2, or 100, to make it a whole number. Multiply the dividend by the same power of 10.
Think: $0.12 \times 100 = 12 \quad 42.3 \times 100 = 4{,}230$

352.5
$12\overline{)4230.0}$
$\underline{-36}$
63
$\underline{-60}$
30
$\underline{-24}$
60
$\underline{-60}$
0

Place the decimal point in the quotient. Divide as with whole numbers.

When there is a remainder, place a zero after the decimal point in the dividend and continue to divide.

$42.3 \div 0.12 = 352.5$

EXAMPLE 2 PROBLEM SOLVING APPLICATION

After driving 368.5 miles, Julie and her family refilled the tank of their car with 13.4 gallons of gasoline. On average, how many miles did they drive per gallon of gas?

1. Understand the Problem

The **answer** will be the average number of miles per gallon.

List the **important information:**

- They drove 368.5 miles.
- They used 13.4 gallons of gas.

2. Make a Plan

Solve a simpler problem by replacing the decimals in the problem with whole numbers.

If they drove 10 miles using 2 gallons of gas, they averaged 5 miles per gallon. You need to divide miles by gallons to solve the problem.

3. Solve

First estimate the answer. You can use compatible numbers.
$368.5 \div 13.4 \longrightarrow 360 \div 12 = 30$

$13.4 \overline{)368.5}$ *Multiply the divisor and the dividend by 10. Think: 13.4 × 10 = 134   368.5 × 10 = 3,685*

$$\begin{array}{r} 27.5 \\ 134{\overline{\smash{\big)}\,3685.0}} \\ -268\downarrow \\ \hline 1005 \\ -938\downarrow \\ \hline 67\,0 \\ -67\,0 \\ \hline 0 \end{array}$$

Place the decimal point in the quotient. Divide as with whole numbers.

Julie and her family averaged 27.5 miles per gallon.

4. Look Back

The answer is reasonable, since 27.5 is close to the estimate of 30.

Think and Discuss

1. Tell how the quotient of 48 ÷ 12 is similar to the quotient of 4.8 ÷ 1.2. How is it different?

3-7 Exercises

Learn It Online
Homework Help Online go.hrw.com,
keyword MR10 3-7 Go
Exercises 1–20, 23, 27, 29, 31, 35, 37, 39

GUIDED PRACTICE

See Example 1 Find each quotient.

1. $6.5 \div 1.3$
2. $20.7 \div 0.6$
3. $25.5 \div 1.5$
4. $5.4 \div 0.9$
5. $13.2 \div 2.2$
6. $63.39 \div 0.24$

See Example 2

7. Marcus drove 354.9 miles in 6.5 hours. On average, how many miles per hour did he drive?

8. **Consumer Math** Anthony spends $87.75 on shrimp. The shrimp cost $9.75 per pound. How many pounds of shrimp does Anthony buy?

INDEPENDENT PRACTICE

See Example 1 Find each quotient.

9. $3.6 \div 0.6$
10. $8.2 \div 0.5$
11. $18.4 \div 2.3$
12. $4.8 \div 1.2$
13. $52.2 \div 0.24$
14. $32.5 \div 2.6$
15. $49.5 \div 4.5$
16. $96.6 \div 0.42$
17. $6.5 \div 1.3$

See Example 2

18. Jen spends $5.98 on ribbon. Ribbon costs $0.92 per meter. How many meters of ribbon does Jen buy?

19. Kyle's family drove 329.44 miles. Kyle calculated that the car averaged 28.4 miles per gallon of gas. How many gallons of gas did the car use?

20. **Consumer Math** Peter is saving $4.95 each week to buy a DVD that costs $24.75, including tax. For how many weeks will he have to save?

PRACTICE AND PROBLEM SOLVING

Extra Practice
See page EP7.

Divide.

21. $2.52 \div 0.4$
22. $12.586 \div 0.35$
23. $0.5733 \div 0.003$
24. $10.875 \div 1.2$
25. $92.37 \div 0.5$
26. $8.43 \div 0.12$

Evaluate.

27. $0.732 \div n$ for $n = 0.06$
28. $73.814 \div c$ for $c = 1.3$
29. $b \div 0.52$ for $b = 6.344$
30. $r \div 4.17$ for $r = 10.5918$

Find the value of each expression.

31. $6.35 \times 10^2 \div 0.5$
32. $8.1 \times 10^2 \div 0.9$
33. $4.5 \times 10^3 \div 4$
34. $20.1 \times 10^3 \div 0.1$
35. $2.76 \times 10^2 \div 0.3$
36. $6.2 \times 10^3 \div 8$

37. **Multi-Step** Find the value of $6.45 \times 10^6 \div 0.3$. Write your answer in scientific notation.

3-7 Dividing by Decimals   131

History

The U.S. Mint was established by the Coinage Act in 1792. The first coins were copper and were made in Philadelphia.

38. Earth Science A planet's year is the time it takes that planet to revolve around the Sun. A Mars year is 1.88 Earth years. If you are 13 years old in Earth years, about how old would you be in Mars years?

39. History The U.S. Treasury first printed paper money in 1862. The paper money we use today is 0.0043 inch thick. Estimate the number of bills you would need to stack to make a pile that is 1 inch thick. If you stacked $20 bills, what would be the total value of the money in the pile?

Use the map for Exercises 40 and 41.

40. Multi-Step Bill drove from Washington, D.C., to Charlotte in 6.5 hours. What was his average speed in miles per hour?

41. Estimation Betty drove a truck from Richmond to Washington, D.C. It took her about 2.5 hours. Estimate the average speed she was driving.

42. What's the Error? A student incorrectly answered the division problem below. Explain the error and write the correct quotient.

$$0.004 \overline{)53.824} = 13.456$$

43. Write About It Explain how you know where to place the decimal point in the quotient when you divide by a decimal number.

44. Challenge Find the value of a in the division problem.

$$4a3 \overline{)0417.13} = 1.01$$

Test Prep and Spiral Review

45. Multiple Choice Nick bought 2.5 pounds of popcorn for $8.35. How much did he pay for each pound of popcorn?

Ⓐ $20.88   Ⓑ $3.43   Ⓒ $3.34   Ⓓ $33.40

46. Extended Response In the 2006–2007 NBA season, Kevin Garnett earned a salary of $21,000,000. He played in 76 games and averaged 39.4 minutes per game. How much money did Kevin Garnett earn each minute he played? Round your answer to the nearest dollar. Explain how you solved the problem.

Compare. Write <, >, or =. (Previous Course)

47. 56,902 ▨ 56,817   **48.** 14,562 ▨ 14,581   **49.** 1,240,518 ▨ 1,208,959

Evaluate 4y for each value of y. (Lesson 3-5)

50. $y = 2.13$ **51.** $y = 4.015$ **52.** $y = 3.6$ **53.** $y = 0.78$ **54.** $y = 1.4$

132   Chapter 3 Decimals

3-8 Interpreting the Quotient

Learn to solve problems by interpreting the quotient.

In science lab, Ken learned to make slime from corn starch, water, and food coloring. He has 0.87 kg of corn starch, and the recipe for one bag of slime calls for 0.15 kg. To find the number of bags of slime Ken can make, you need to divide.

EXAMPLE 1   Measurement Application

Ken will use 0.87 kg of corn starch to make gift bags of slime for his friends. If each bag requires 0.15 kg of corn starch, how many bags of slime can he make?

The question asks how many whole bags of slime can be made when the corn starch is divided into groups of 0.15 kg.

$0.87 \div 0.15 = ?$
$87 \div 15 = 5.8$

Think: The quotient shows that there is not enough to make 6 bags of slime that are 0.15 kg each. There is only enough for 5 bags. The decimal part of the quotient will not be used in the answer.

Ken can make **5** gift bags of slime.

Remember!
To divide decimals, first write the divisor as a whole number. Multiply the divisor and dividend by the same power of ten.

EXAMPLE 2   Photography Application

There are 246 students in the sixth grade. If Ms. Lee buys rolls of film with 24 exposures each, how many rolls will she need to take every student's picture?

The question asks how many whole rolls are needed to take a picture of every one of the students.

$246 \div 24 = ?$
$246 \div 24 = 10.25$

Think: Ten rolls of film will not be enough to take every student's picture. Ms. Lee will need to buy another roll of film. The quotient must be rounded up to the next highest whole number.

Ms. Lee will need **11** rolls of film.

EXAMPLE 3 **Social Studies Application**

Marissa is drawing a time line of the Stone Age. She plans for 6 equal sections, two each for the Paleolithic, Mesolithic, and Neolithic periods. If she has 7.8 meters of paper, how long is each section?

The question asks exactly how long each section will be when the paper is divided into 6 sections.

$7.8 \div 6 = 1.3$ *Think: The question asks for an exact answer, so do not estimate. Use the entire quotient.*

Each section will be **1.3** meters long.

When the question asks	→ You should
How many whole groups can be made when you divide?	→ Drop the decimal part of the quotient.
How many whole groups are needed to put all items from the dividend into a group?	→ Round the quotient up to the next highest whole number.
What is the exact number when you divide?	→ Use the entire quotient as the answer.

Think and Discuss

1. **Tell** how you would interpret the quotient: A group of 27 students will ride in vans that carry 12 students each. How many vans are needed?

3-8 Exercises

Learn It Online
Homework Help Online go.hrw.com,
keyword MR10 3-8
Exercises 1–6, 7, 13

GUIDED PRACTICE

See Example 1
1. Kay is making beaded belts for her friends from 6.5 meters of cord. One belt uses 0.625 meter of cord. How many belts can she make?

See Example 2
2. Julius is supplying cups for a party of 136 people. If cups are sold in packs of 24, how many packs of cups will he need?

See Example 3
3. Miranda is decorating for a party. She has 13 balloons and 29.25 meters of ribbon. She wants to tie the same length of ribbon on each balloon. How long will each ribbon be?

INDEPENDENT PRACTICE

See Example 1
4. There are 0.454 kg of corn starch in a container. How many 0.028 kg portions are in one container?

See Example 2
5. Tina needs 36 flowers for her next project. The flowers are sold in bunches of 5. How many bunches will she need?

See Example 3
6. Bobby's goal is to run 27 miles a week. If he runs the same distance 6 days a week, how many miles would he have to run each day?

PRACTICE AND PROBLEM SOLVING

Extra Practice
See page EP7.

7. Nick wants to write thank-you notes to 15 of his friends. The cards are sold in packs of 6. How many packs does Nick need to buy?

8. **Multi-Step** The science teacher has 7 packs of seeds and 36 students. If the students should each plant the same number of seeds, how many can each student plant?

9. **Critical Thinking** How do you know when to round your answer up to the next whole number?

10. **Write a Problem** Create a problem that is solved by interpreting the quotient.

11. **Write About It** Explain how a calculator shows the remainder when you divide 145 by 8.

12. **Challenge** Leonard wants to place a fence on both sides of a 10-meter walkway. If he puts a post at both ends and at every 2.5 meters in between, how many posts does he use?

Test Prep and Spiral Review

13. **Multiple Choice** There are 375 students going on a field trip. Each bus holds 65 students. How many buses are needed for the field trip?

   (A) 4   (B) 5   (C) 6   (D) 7

14. **Multiple Choice** Mrs. Neal has 127 stickers. She wants to give each of the 22 students in her class the same number of stickers. Which expression can be used to find how many stickers each student will get?

   (F) $127 - 22$ (G) $127 \div 22$ (H) $127 + 22$ (J) 127×22

Solve for y. (Lessons 2-4, 2-5, 2-6)

15. $y - 23 = 40$ 16. $14y = 168$ 17. $36 + y = 53$ 18. $\frac{y}{5} = 7$

Find each quotient. (Lesson 3-7)

19. $45.5 \div 5$ 20. $103.7 \div 2$ 21. $35 \div 2.5$ 22. $4.25 \div 0.25$

3-9 Solving Decimal Equations

Learn to solve equations involving decimals.

Felipe has earned $45.20 by mowing lawns for his neighbors. He wants to buy inline skates that cost $69.95. Write and solve an equation to find how much more money Felipe must earn to buy the skates.

Let m be the amount of money Felipe needs. $\$45.20 + m = \$69.95$

Interactivities Online ▶

You can solve equations with decimals using inverse operations just as you solved equations with whole numbers.

$$\$45.20 + m = \$69.95$$
$$-\$45.20 \quad\quad -\$45.20$$
$$m = \$24.75$$

Felipe needs $24.75 more to buy the inline skates.

EXAMPLE 1 Solving One-Step Equations with Decimals

Solve each equation. Check your answer.

Remember!
Use inverse operations to get the variable alone on one side of the equation.

A $g - 3.1 = 4.5$

$\quad g - 3.1 = 4.5$ *3.1 is subtracted from g.*
$\quad \underline{+ 3.1 \quad + 3.1}$ *Add 3.1 to both sides to undo the subtraction.*
$\quad\quad\quad g = 7.6$

Check
$\quad g - 3.1 = 4.5$
$7.6 - 3.1 \stackrel{?}{=} 4.5$ *Substitute 7.6 for g in the equation.*
$\quad\quad 4.5 \stackrel{?}{=} 4.5$ ✔   *7.6 is the solution.*

B $3k = 8.1$

$\quad 3k = 8.1$ *k is multiplied by 3.*
$\quad \dfrac{3k}{3} = \dfrac{8.1}{3}$ *Divide both sides by 3 to undo the multiplication.*
$\quad k = 2.7$

Check
$\quad\quad 3k = 8.1$
$\quad 3(2.7) \stackrel{?}{=} 8.1$ *Substitute 2.7 for k in the equation.*
$\quad\quad 8.1 \stackrel{?}{=} 8.1$ ✔   *2.7 is the solution.*

Solve each equation. Check your answer.

C $\frac{m}{5} = 1.5$

$\frac{m}{5} = 1.5$ *m is divided by 5.*

$\frac{m}{5} \cdot 5 = 1.5 \cdot 5$ *Multiply both sides by 5 to undo the division.*

$m = 7.5$

Check

$\frac{m}{5} = 1.5$

$\frac{7.5}{5} \stackrel{?}{=} 1.5$ *Substitute 7.5 for m in the equation.*

$1.5 \stackrel{?}{=} 1.5$ ✓   *7.5 is the solution.*

EXAMPLE 2 Measurement Application

A The area of the floor in Jonah's bedroom is 28 square meters. If its length is 3.5 meters, what is the width of the bedroom?

Remember!
The area of a rectangle is its length times its width.

$A = \ell w$

area = length · width

28 = 3.5 · w

$28 = 3.5w$ *Write the equation for the problem. Let w be the width of the room. w is multiplied by 3.5.*

$\frac{28}{3.5} = \frac{3.5w}{3.5}$ *Divide both sides by 3.5 to undo the multiplication.*

$8 = w$

The width of Jonah's bedroom is 8 meters.

B Jonah is carpeting his bedroom. The carpet costs $22.50 per square meter. What is the total cost to carpet the bedroom?

total cost = area · cost of carpet per square meter

$C = 28 \cdot 22.50$ *Let C be the total cost. Write the equation for the problem.*

$C = 630$ *Multiply.*

The cost of carpeting the bedroom is $630.

Think and Discuss

1. **Explain** whether the value of m will be less than or greater than 1 when you solve $5m = 4.5$.

2. **Tell** how you can check the answer in Example 2A.

3-9 Exercises

Learn It Online
Homework Help Online go.hrw.com,
keyword MR10 3-9
Exercises 1–19, 21, 23, 25, 27, 29, 31, 33

GUIDED PRACTICE

See Example 1 Solve each equation. Check your answer.

1. $a - 2.3 = 4.8$
2. $6n = 8.4$
3. $\frac{c}{4} = 3.2$
4. $8.5 = 2.49 + x$
5. $\frac{d}{3.2} = 1.09$
6. $1.6 = m \cdot 4$

See Example 2

7. The length of a window is 10.5 meters, and the width is 5.75 meters. Solve the equation $a \div 10.5 = 5.75$ to find the area of the window.

8. Gretchen wants to add a wallpaper border along the top of the walls of her square room. The distance around her room is 20.4 meters.
   a. What is the length of each wall of Gretchen's room?
   b. The price of wallpaper border is $1.25 per meter. What is the total cost to add the border to her room?

INDEPENDENT PRACTICE

See Example 1 Solve each equation. Check your answer.

9. $b - 5.6 = 3.7$
10. $1.6 = \frac{p}{7}$
11. $3r = 62.4$
12. $9.5 = 5x$
13. $a - 4.8 = 5.9$
14. $\frac{n}{8} = 0.8$
15. $8 + f = 14.56$
16. $5.2s = 10.4$
17. $1.95 = z - 2.05$

See Example 2

18. **Geometry** The area of a rectangle is 65.8 square units. The length is 7 units. Solve the equation $7 \cdot w = 65.8$ to find the width of the rectangle.

19. Ken wants to fence his square garden. He will need 6.4 meters of fence to enclose all four sides of the garden.
    a. How long is each side of his garden?
    b. The price of fencing is $2.25 per meter. What is the total cost to fence Ken's garden?

PRACTICE AND PROBLEM SOLVING

Extra Practice
See page EP7.

Solve each equation and check your answer.

20. $9.8 = t - 42.1$
21. $q \div 2.6 = 9.5$
22. $45.36 = 5.6 \cdot m$
23. $1.3b = 5.46$
24. $4.93 = 0.563 + m$
25. $\frac{a}{5} = 2.78$
26. $w - 64.99 = 13.044$
27. $6.205z = 80.665$
28. $74.2 = 38.06 + c$

29. **Geometry** The shortest side of the triangle is 10 units long.
    a. What are the lengths of the other two sides of the triangle?
    b. What is the perimeter of the triangle?

    $s - 3.5 = 10$
    $s + 6$
    $s + 7.5$

138 Chapter 3 Decimals

The London Eye is the world's largest Ferris wheel. Use the table for Exercises 30–32.

30. Write the height of the wheel in kilometers.

31. Multi-Step There are 1,000 kilograms in a metric ton. What is the weight of the wheel in kilograms written in scientific notation?

32. a. How many seconds does it take for the wheel to make one revolution?
   b. The wheel moves at a rate of 0.26 meters per second. Use the equation $d \div 0.26 = 1,800$ to find the distance of one revolution.

33. Each capsule can hold 25 passengers. How many capsules are needed to hold 210 passengers?

Weight of wheel	1,900 metric tons
Time to revolve	30 minutes
Height of wheel	135 meters

34. In 2007, 15 standard flight adult tickets for the London Eye cost £217.50 (about $432.43). What is the cost for one ticket? Give the answer in both pounds sterling (£) and U.S. dollars.

35. What's the Error? When solving the equation $b - 12.98 = 5.03$, a student said that $b = 7.95$. Describe the error. What is the correct value for b?

36. Write About It Explain how you solve for the variable in a multiplication equation such as $2.3a = 4.6$.

37. Challenge Solve $1.45n \times 3.2 = 23.942 + 4.13$.

Test Prep and Spiral Review

38. Multiple Choice Solve the equation $d \div 4 = 6.7$ for d.

   Ⓐ $d = 26.8$ Ⓑ $d = 10.7$ Ⓒ $d = 2.7$ Ⓓ $d = 1.675$

39. Multiple Choice Kelly bought 2.8 pounds of beef for $5.04. How much did she pay for each pound of beef?

   Ⓕ $18.00   Ⓖ $7.84   Ⓗ $1.80   Ⓙ $0.18

Write each phrase as a numerical or algebraic expression. (Lesson 2-2)

40. 103 less than 739   **41.** the product of 7 and z **42.** the difference of 12 and n

Find each quotient. (Lesson 3-6)

43. $25.5 \div 5$ **44.** $44.7 \div 3$ **45.** $96.48 \div 6$ **46.** $0.0378 \div 9$

Ready To Go On?

Quiz for Lessons 3-4 Through 3-9

3-4 Scientific Notation

Find each product.

1. $516 \times 10{,}000$
2. 16.82×100
3. $5{,}217 \times 1{,}000$

Write each number in scientific notation.

4. $102{,}000$
5. $5{,}480{,}000$
6. $100{,}000{,}000$

3-5 Multiplying Decimals

Evaluate $5x$ for each value of x.

7. $x = 1.025$
8. $x = 6.2$
9. $x = 2.64$

10. Neptune has a gravitational pull 1.2 times that of Earth. If an object weighs 15 pounds on Earth, how much would it weigh on Neptune?

3-6 Dividing Decimals by Whole Numbers

Find each quotient.

11. $17.5 \div 5$
12. $11.6 \div 8$
13. $23.4 \div 6$
14. $35.5 \div 5$

15. Five apples cost $4.90. How much does each apple cost?

3-7 Dividing by Decimals

Find each quotient.

16. $2.226 \div 0.42$
17. $13.49 \div 7.1$
18. $35.34 \div 6.2$
19. $178.64 \div 81.2$

20. Peri spent $21.89 on material to make a skirt. The material cost $3.98 per yard. How many yards did Peri buy?

3-8 Interpreting the Quotient

21. There are 352 students graduating from high school. The photographer takes one picture of each student as the student receives his or her diploma. If the photographer has 36 exposures on each roll of film, how many rolls will she have to buy to take each student's picture?

3-9 Solving Decimal Equations

Solve each equation.

22. $t - 6.3 = 8.9$
23. $4h = 20.4$
24. $\dfrac{p}{7} = 4.6$
25. $d + 2.8 = 9.5$

Real-World Connections

CHAPTER 3

Puget Sound Ferries Puget Sound is an arm of the Pacific Ocean with about 2,000 miles of coastline. Not surprisingly, ferries play an important role for Washington residents who live near Puget Sound. The sound's state-run ferry system is the largest in the United States.

1. Estimate the total length of the five ferry routes shown on the map.

2. Which route is longer, Kingston-Edmonds or Southworth-Fauntleroy?

3. How much longer is the Seattle-Bremerton route than the Seattle-Bainbridge Island route?

4. The Anacortes-Orcas route (not shown on the map) is 8.5 times as long as the Tahlequah-Pt. Defiance route. Find the length of the Anacortes-Orcas route.

5. A one-way trip on the Southworth-Fauntleroy ferry takes 0.75 hours.

   a. How many one-way trips can the ferry make in 12 hours? (Assume the ferry departs immediately after reaching its destination.) Explain which operation you used to solve this problem.

   b. What is the total distance that the ferry travels while making these one-way trips?

WASHINGTON

Map distances:
- Kingston–Edmonds: 5.15 mi
- Bremerton–Seattle: 17.8 mi
- Bainbridge Island–Seattle: 7.9 mi
- Southworth–Fauntleroy: 5.2 mi
- Tahlequah–Pt. Defiance: 1.7 mi

Game Time

Jumbles

Do you know what eleven plus two equals?

Use your calculator to evaluate each expression. Keep the letters under the expressions with the answers you get. Then order the answers from least to greatest, and write down the letters in that order. You will spell the answer to the riddle.

$4 - 1.893$	$0.21 \div 0.3$	$0.443 - 0.0042$	$4.509 - 3.526$	$3.14 \cdot 2.44$	$1.56 \cdot 3.678$
E	L	E	V	E	N

$6.34 \div 2.56$	$1.19 + 1.293$	$8.25 \div 2.5$	$7.4 - 2.356$
P	L	U	S

$0.0003 + 0.003$	$0.3 \cdot 0.04$	$2.17 + 3.42$
T	W	O

Make A Buck

The object of the game is to win the most points by adding decimal numbers to make a sum close to but not over $1.00.

Most cards have a decimal number on them representing an amount of money. Others are wild cards: The person who receives a wild card decides its value.

The dealer gives each player four cards. Taking turns, players add the numbers in their hand. If the sum is less than $1.00, a player can either draw a card from the top of the deck or pass.

When each player has taken a turn or passed, the player whose sum is closest to but not over $1.00 scores a point. If players tie for the closest sum, each of those players scores a point. All cards are then discarded and four new cards are dealt to each player.

When all of the cards have been dealt, the player with the most points wins.
A complete copy of the rules and game pieces are available online.

Materials
- 2 plastic slide holders
- squares of card stock
- clear tape
- permanent marker

It's in the Bag!

PROJECT ## Project E Z 2 C Decimals

Practice reading decimals by making this see-through decimal holder.

Directions

1. Cut out about 40 small squares of colored card stock. Remove ten of the squares. On these squares, write "Ones," "Tens," "Hundreds," "Thousands," "Ten-Thousands," "Tenths," "Hundredths," "Thousandths," "Ten-Thousandths," and "Hundred-Thousandths." **Figure A**

2. On each of the remaining squares, write a number from 0 to 9.

3. Tape the two slide holders together. Using a permanent marker, draw decimal points down the middle where the holders are taped together. **Figure B**

4. Put the squares with the names of the place values in the correct slots along the top row.

Putting the Math into Action

Put numbered squares in the remaining slots. Work with a partner to practice reading the resulting decimals. Mix up the numbered squares and repeat the process several more times, sometimes using all of the slots in a row and sometimes making shorter decimals.

It's in the Bag!

CHAPTER 3 Study Guide: Review

Vocabulary

clustering 104

front-end estimation 105

scientific notation 116

Complete the sentences below with vocabulary words from the list above.

1. When you estimate a sum by using only the whole-number part of the decimals, you are using ___?___.

2. ___?___ is a shorthand method that can be used to write large numbers.

3. ___?___ means rounding all the numbers to the same value.

EXAMPLES / EXERCISES

3-1 Representing, Comparing, and Ordering Decimals (pp. 100–103)

■ Write 4.025 in expanded form and words.

Expanded form: 4 + 0.02 + 0.005

Word form: four and twenty-five thousandths

■ Order the decimals from least to greatest.
7.8, 7.83, 7.08

7.08 < 7.80 < 7.83   Compare the numbers.
7.08, 7.8, 7.83   Then order the numbers.

Write each in expanded form and words.

4. 5.68
5. 1.0076
6. 1.203
7. 23.005
8. 71.038
9. 99.9999

Order the decimals from least to greatest.

10. 1.2, 1.3, 1.12
11. 11.17, 11.7, 11.07
12. 0.3, 0.303, 0.033
13. 5.009, 5.950, 5.5
14. 101.52, 101.25, 101.025

3-2 Estimating Decimals (pp. 104–107)

■ Estimate.

5.35 − 0.7904; round to tenths

$$\begin{array}{r} 5.4 \\ -0.8 \\ \hline 4.6 \end{array}$$ Align the decimals. Subtract.

■ Estimate 49.67 × 2.88.

49.67 × 2.88
50 × 3 = 150

Estimate.

15. 8.0954 + 3.218; round to the hundredths
16. 6.8356 − 4.507; round to the tenths
17. 9.258 + 4.97; round to the ones

Estimate each product or quotient.

18. 21.19 × 4.23
19. 53.98 ÷ 5.97
20. 102.89 × 19.95

144 Chapter 3 Decimals

3-3 Adding and Subtracting Decimals (pp. 110–113)

EXAMPLES

■ Find the sum.

7.62 + 0.563

```
  7.620
+ 0.563
-------
  8.183
```

Align the decimal points. Use zeros as placeholders. Add. Place the decimal point.

EXERCISES

Find each sum or difference.

21. 7.08 + 4.5 + 13.27
22. 6 − 0.7
23. 6.21 + 5.8 + 21.01
24. 7.001 − 2.0785

Evaluate 6.48 − s for each value of s.

25. $s = 3.9$
26. $s = 3.6082$
27. $s = 5.01$
28. $s = 0.057$

29. Rodney bought a new book for $15.75 and two new CDs for $12.99 each. How much did Rodney spend?

3-4 Scientific Notation (pp. 116–119)

EXAMPLES

■ Find the product.

326 × 10,000
= 326.0000
= 3,260,000

Move the decimal point 4 places right. Write 4 placeholder zeros.

■ Write the number in scientific notation.

60,000

Move the decimal point 4 places to the left.

= 6.0×10^4

■ Write each number in standard form.

7.18×10^5
= 718,000

Move the decimal point 5 places right.

EXERCISES

Find each product.

30. 12.6 × 10,000
31. 546 × 100
32. 67 × 100,000
33. 180.6 × 1,000

Write each number in scientific notation.

34. 550,000
35. 7,230
36. 1,300,000
37. 14.8

Write each number in standard form.

38. 3.02×10^4
39. 4.293×10^5
40. 1.7×10^6
41. 5.39×10^3

42. During a single day, the average person loses around 50,400,000 dead skin cells. Write this number in scientific notation.

3-5 Multiplying Decimals (pp. 122–125)

EXAMPLES

■ Find the product.

```
   0.3       1 decimal place
× 0.08     + 2 decimal places
-------
  0.024      3 decimal places
```

EXERCISES

Find each product.

43. 4 × 2.36
44. 0.5 × 1.73
45. 0.6 × 0.012
46. 8 × 3.052
47. 1.2 × 0.45
48. 9.7 × 1.084

49. An object on the surface of the Sun would weigh around 28 times as much as it weighs on Earth. How much would a 202.8-pound man weigh on the Sun?

EXAMPLES	EXERCISES

3-6 Dividing Decimals by Whole Numbers (pp. 126–128)

■ **Find the quotient.**

$0.95 \div 5$

Place a decimal point directly above the decimal point in the dividend. Then divide.

$$5 \overline{)0.95} = 0.19$$

Find each quotient.

50. $6.18 \div 6$
51. $2.16 \div 3$
52. $34.65 \div 9$
53. $20.72 \div 8$

54. If four people equally share a bill for $14.56, how much should each person pay?

3-7 Dividing by Decimals (pp. 129–132)

■ **Find the quotient.**

$9.65 \div 0.5$

Make the divisor a whole number.

Place the decimal point in the quotient.

$$5 \overline{)96.5} = 19.3$$

Find each quotient.

55. $4.86 \div 0.6$
56. $1.85 \div 0.3$
57. $34.89 \div 9$
58. $62.73 \div 1.2$

59. Ana cuts some wood that is 3.75 meters long into 5 pieces of equal length. How long is each piece?

3-8 Interpreting the Quotient (pp. 133–135)

■ Ms. Ald needs 26 stickers for her preschool class. Stickers are sold in packs of 8. How many packs should she buy?

$26 \div 8 = 3.25$

3.25 is between 3 and 4.

3 packs will not be enough.

Ms. Ald should buy 4 packs of stickers.

60. Billy has 3.6 liters of juice. How many 0.25 L containers can he fill?

61. There are 34 people going on a field trip. If each car holds 4 people, how many cars will they need for the field trip?

62. Mr. Paxton has 16.5 feet of twine. If he is wrapping 3 packages, how much twine can he use on each package?

3-9 Solving Decimal Equations (pp. 136–139)

■ **Solve $4x = 20.8$.**

$4x = 20.8$ x is multiplied by 4.

$\dfrac{4x}{4} = \dfrac{20.8}{4}$ Divide both sides by 4.

$x = 5.2$

Solve each equation.

63. $a - 6.2 = 7.18$
64. $3y = 7.86$
65. $n + 4.09 = 6.38$
66. $\dfrac{p}{7} = 8.6$

67. Jasmine buys 2.25 kg of apples for $11.25. How much does 1 kg of apples cost?

Chapter Test

CHAPTER 3

1. The New York Philharmonic Orchestra performs at Avery Fisher Hall in New York City. It seats 2,738 people. The Boston Symphony Orchestra performs at Symphony Hall in Boston, Massachusetts. It seats 2,625 people. Which hall seats more people?

Order the decimals from least to greatest.

2. 12.6, 12.07, 12.67
3. 3.5, 3.25, 3.08
4. 0.10301, 0.10318, 0.10325

Estimate by rounding to the indicated place value.

5. 6.178 − 0.2805; hundredths
6. 7.528 + 6.075; ones

Estimate.

7. 21.35 × 3.18
8. 98.547 ÷ 4.93
9. 11.855 × 8.45

Estimate a range for each sum.

10. 3.89 + 42.71 + 12.32
11. 20.751 + 2.55 + 17.4
12. 4.987 + 28.27 + 0.098

13. Britney wants to exercise in a step aerobics class. The class uses the 4-inch step for 15 minutes and the 6-inch step for 15 minutes. About how many calories will she burn in all?

Step Height (in.)	Calories Burned in 15 minutes
4	67.61
6	82.2
8	96

Evaluate.

14. 0.76 + 2.24
15. 7 − 0.4
16. 0.12 × 0.006
17. 5.85 ÷ 3.9

Find each product.

18. 516 × 10,000
19. 16.82 × 100
20. 521.7 × 100,000
21. 423.6 × 1,000

Write each number in scientific notation.

22. 16,900
23. 180,500
24. 3,190,000

Write each number in standard form.

25. 3.08×10^5
26. 1.472×10^6
27. 2.973×10^4

Solve each equation.

28. $b - 4.7 = 2.1$
29. $5a = 4.75$
30. $\frac{y}{6} = 7.2$
31. $c + 1.9 = 26.04$

32. The school band is going to a competition. There are 165 students in the band. If each bus holds 25 students, how many buses will be needed?

33. Marisol bought six sweaters on sale for a total of $126.24. How much did each sweater cost if they were all marked down to the same price?

Test Tackler
Standardized Test Strategies

Short Response: Write Short Responses

Short-response test items require a solution to the problem and the reasoning or work used to get that solution. Short-response test items are scored according to a 2-point scoring rubric. A sample scoring rubric is provided below.

EXAMPLE 1

Short Response Coach Mott needs to order jackets for the boys' basketball team. Each jacket costs $28.75. The team has $125 from their fund-raiser to go toward the total cost of the jackets. If there are 10 players on the team, how much money will each player need to give to Coach Mott for a jacket so he can place the order? Explain.

Scoring Rubric

2 points: The student correctly answers the question, shows all work, and provides a complete and correct explanation.

1 point: The student correctly answers the question but does not show all work or does not provide a complete explanation; or the student makes minor errors resulting in an incorrect solution but shows all work and provides a complete explanation.

0 points: The student gives an incorrect answer and shows no work or explanation, or the student gives no response.

2-point response:

Cost of one jacket: $28.75
Total cost for team jackets (10 players):
$28.75 × 10 = $287.50

Subtract the money the team already has from the total cost.
$287.50 − $125 = $162.50

Divide the remaining cost by the number of players on the team.
$162.50 ÷ 10 = $16.25

Each player needs to give Coach Mott $16.25 so he can place the order for the jackets.

1-point response:

($287.50 − $125) ÷ $10 = $16.25
He will need $16.25 from each player.

The student correctly solved the problem but did not show all of his or her work or did not provide an explanation.

0-point response:

$16.25

The student gave a correct answer but did not show any work or give an explanation.

HOT TIP! Never leave a short-response test item blank. Showing your work and providing a reasonable explanation will result in at least some credit.

Read each test item and answer the questions that follow by using the scoring rubric below.

Item A
Short Response Write two equations that each have a solution of 12. You cannot use the same mathematical operation for both equations. Explain how to solve both equations.

Student's Answer

One equation that has a solution of 12 is $\frac{x}{6} = 2$. To solve this equation, I must undo the division by multiplying by 6 on both sides.

$$\frac{x}{6} = 2$$
$$6 \cdot \left(\frac{x}{6}\right) = 6 \cdot 2$$
$$x = 12$$

Another equation with a solution of 12 is $x - 8 = 20$.
To solve this equation, I must add the opposite of 8 to both sides.

$$x - 8 = 20$$
$$-8 = -8$$
$$x = 12$$

1. The student's answer will not receive full credit. Find the error in the student's answer.

2. Rewrite the student's answer so that it receives full credit.

Item B
Short Response June is 8 years older than her cousin Liv. Write an expression to find June's age. Identify the variable and list three possible solutions showing the ages of June and Liv.

Student's Answer

Let x = Liv's age. Since June is 8 years older, the expression $x + 8$ can be used to find June's age.
Three possible solutions for Liv and June follow:
$x = 3, 3 + 8 = 11$; Liv: 3, June: 11
$x = 8, 8 + 8 = 16$; Liv: 8, June: 16
$x = 11, 11 + 8 = 19$; Liv: 11, June: 19

3. What score should the student's answer receive? Explain your reasoning.

4. What additional information, if any, should the student's answer include in order to receive full credit?

Item C
Short Response Write an equation to represent the following situation. Define the variable. Solve the problem. *Sam has two kittens. The larger kitten weighs 3.2 kg. The other kitten needs to gain 1.9 kg to weigh as much as the larger kitten. How much does the smaller kitten weigh?*

Student's Answer

Let x = the weight of the smaller kitten.
$x + 1.9 = 3.2$
$3.2 + 1.9 = 5.1$

5. How would you score the student's response? Explain.

6. Rewrite the response so that it receives full credit.

Test Tackler

Cumulative Assessment, Chapters 1–3

Multiple Choice

1. Which of the following is the standard form for six and eighty-six thousandths?

   Ⓐ 6.860
   Ⓑ 6.086
   Ⓒ 6.0086
   Ⓓ 6.00086

2. The weights of three backpacks are 15.8 pounds, 18.1 pounds, and 16.7 pounds. About how many pounds do the backpacks weigh all together?

   Ⓕ 30 pounds
   Ⓖ 40 pounds
   Ⓗ 50 pounds
   Ⓙ 60 pounds

3. For which equation is $c = 8$ NOT a solution?

   Ⓐ $\frac{c}{4} = 2$
   Ⓑ $c + 4 = 12$
   Ⓒ $4c = 28$
   Ⓓ $c - 5 = 3$

4. Jerah scored 15 more points in a basketball game than his brother Jim did. Jim scored 7 points. Which expression can be used to find the number of points Jerah scored?

   Ⓕ $15 - 7$
   Ⓖ 15×7
   Ⓗ $15 \div 7$
   Ⓙ $15 + 7$

5. Find the sum of 1.4 and 0.9.

   Ⓐ 0.1
   Ⓑ 0.5
   Ⓒ 1.3
   Ⓓ 2.3

6. Which number is the greatest?

   Ⓕ 18.095
   Ⓖ 18.9
   Ⓗ 18.907
   Ⓙ 18.75

7. The heights of four different plants are listed below. Which statement is supported by the data?

Plant Height (in.)				
Plant	T	S	U	W
Week 1	15.9	23.6	17.1	12.5
Week 2	21.4	27.4	22.9	16.4

   Ⓐ Plant T was the shortest during week 1.
   Ⓑ Plant S grew more than 4 inches between week 1 and week 2.
   Ⓒ Plant U grew the most between week 1 and week 2.
   Ⓓ Plant W is the tallest.

8. What is the value of 3^4?

   Ⓕ 7
   Ⓖ 12
   Ⓗ 81
   Ⓙ 96

9. There are 58,000 seats in a football stadium. Which of the following is the correct way to write 58,000 in scientific notation?

   Ⓐ 580×10^2
   Ⓑ 58×10^3
   Ⓒ 5.8×10^4
   Ⓓ 0.58×10^5

10. Tomas needs 42 cups for a party. The cups are sold in packages of 5. How many packages should he buy?

    Ⓕ 10 packages
    Ⓖ 9 packages
    Ⓗ 8 packages
    Ⓙ 7 packages

11. What is $7.89 \div 3$?

    Ⓐ 263
    Ⓑ 26.3
    Ⓒ 0.263
    Ⓓ 2.63

12. Which set of numbers is in order from least to greatest?

    F. 23.7, 23.07, 23.13, 23.89

    G. 21.4, 21.45, 21.79, 21.8

    H. 22, 22.09, 21.9, 22.1

    J. 25.4, 25.09, 25.6, 25.7

13. Megan is beginning an exercise routine. She plans to walk 1 mile on day 1 and increase her distance each day by 0.25 mile. How many miles will she be walking on day 10?

    A. 2.5 miles
    C. 4.75 miles
    B. 3.25 miles
    D. 6.0 miles

HOT TIP! Estimate your answer before solving the question. Use your estimate to check the reasonableness of your answer.

Gridded Response

14. What is the value of c in the equation $\frac{c}{6} = 3.4$?

15. What is the missing term in the following sequence?

    5, 12, 26, 47, ▓, 110, . . .

16. Sam has 10 boxes full of computer games. Each box holds 13 games. How many games does Sam own?

17. Cindy bought 3 bunches of daisies and 4 bunches of carnations. There are 6 daisies and 10 carnations in a bunch. How many flowers does she have in all?

18. Bart and his 2 friends buy lunch. The total is $13.74. If they share the cost equally, how much, in dollars, should each person pay?

19. Daisy buys a shirt that costs $21.64 after tax. She gives the cashier $25. How much, in dollars, does she get back in change?

Short Response

S1. Kevin buys 5 steaks for $43.75. Let b equal the cost of one steak. Write and solve the equation to find the cost of one steak.

S2. Ms. Maier has 8 packs of pencils to give out to students taking a state test. Each pack has 8 pencils. There are 200 students taking the test who need pencils.

   a. How many more packs of pencils does Ms. Maier need to buy? Explain your answer and show your work.

   b. If each pack of pencils costs $0.79, how much money will Ms. Maier need to spend to buy the extra pencils? Show your work.

Extended Response

E1. Admission to the Children's Museum is listed below. Use the chart to answer the following questions.

Admission Costs ($)	
Adult	7.50
Child	5.75

   a. Write an expression to find the cost of admission for 2 adults and c children.

   b. Use your expression to find the total cost for Mr. and Mrs. Chu and their 8-year-old triplets. Show your work.

   c. If Mr. Chu pays for admission using a $50 bill, how much change does he get back? Show your work.

   d. On the Chu's next visit, Mrs. Chu plans to use a coupon and will only pay $28.50 for the family. How much will she save using the coupon?

CHAPTER 4
Number Theory and Fractions

4A Number Theory
- 4-1 Divisibility
- LAB Explore Factors
- 4-2 Factors and Prime Factorization
- 4-3 Greatest Common Factor
- LAB Greatest Common Factor
- EXT Sets of Numbers

4B Understanding Fractions
- LAB Explore Decimals and Fractions
- 4-4 Decimals and Fractions
- LAB Model Equivalent Fractions
- 4-5 Equivalent Fractions
- LAB Explore Fraction Measurement
- 4-6 Mixed Numbers and Improper Fractions

4C Introduction to Fraction Operations
- 4-7 Comparing and Ordering Fractions
- 4-8 Adding and Subtracting with Like Denominators
- 4-9 Estimating Fraction Sums and Differences

Chapter Focus
- Know that a fraction can be viewed as parts of a whole.
- Use multiplication and division to determine equivalent fractions.

Why Learn This?
Recipes often list quantities of ingredients as fractions and mixed numbers. Professional chefs must be able to work with these numbers in order to follow recipes.

Learn It Online
Chapter Project Online **go.hrw.com**,
keyword MR10 Ch4 Go

Are You Ready?

Vocabulary

Choose the best term from the list to complete each sentence.

1. To find the sum of two numbers, you should __?__.
2. Fractions are written as a __?__ over a __?__.
3. In the equation 4 · 3 = 12, 12 is the __?__.
4. The __?__ of 18 and 10 is 8.
5. The numbers 18, 27, and 72 are __?__ of 9.

add
denominator
difference
multiples
numerator
product
quotient

Complete these exercises to review skills you will need for this chapter.

Write and Read Decimals

Write each decimal in word form.

6. 0.5
7. 2.78
8. 0.125
9. 12.8
10. 125.49
11. 8.024

Multiples

List the first four multiples of each number.

12. 6
13. 8
14. 5
15. 12
16. 7
17. 20
18. 14
19. 9

Evaluate Expressions

Evaluate each expression for the given value of the variable.

20. $y + 4.3$ for $y = 3.2$
21. $\frac{x}{5}$ for $x = 6.4$
22. $3c$ for $c = 0.75$
23. $a + 4 \div 8$ for $a = 3.75$
24. $27.8 - d$ for $d = 9.25$
25. $2.5b$ for $b = 8.4$

Factors

Find all the whole-number factors of each number.

26. 8
27. 12
28. 24
29. 30
30. 45
31. 52
32. 75
33. 150

Number Theory and Fractions

CHAPTER 4

Study Guide: Preview

Where You've Been

Previously, you
- identified a number as prime or composite.
- identified common factors of a set of whole numbers.
- generated equivalent fractions.
- compared two fractions with common denominators.

In This Chapter

You will study
- writing the prime factorization of a number.
- finding the greatest common factor (GCF) of a set of whole numbers.
- generating equivalent forms of numbers, including whole numbers, fractions, and decimals.
- comparing and ordering fractions, decimals, and whole numbers.

Where You're Going

You can use the skills learned in this chapter
- to double or halve recipes when cooking.
- to add together fractions when determining volume in a science class.

Key Vocabulary/Vocabulario

common denominator	común denominador
composite number	número compuesto
equivalent fractions	fracciones equivalentes
factor	factor
greatest common factor (GCF)	máximo común divisor (MCD)
improper fraction	fracción impropia
prime factorization	factorización prima
prime number	número primo
terminating decimal	decimal cerrado

Vocabulary Connections

To become familiar with some of the vocabulary terms in the chapter, consider the following. You may refer to the chapter, the glossary, or a dictionary if you like.

1. The word *equivalent* means "equal in value." What do you think **equivalent fractions** are?

2. To *terminate* something means to bring it to an end. If a decimal is a **terminating decimal**, what do you think happens to it? Explain.

3. When people have something in *common*, they have something that they share. What do you think **common denominators** share?

4. If something is *improper*, it is not right. In fractions, it is *improper* to have the numerator be greater than the denominator. How would you expect an **improper fraction** to look?

Reading and Writing Math

CHAPTER 4

Reading Strategy: Read a Lesson for Understanding

Reading ahead will prepare you for new ideas and concepts presented in class. As you read a lesson, make notes. Write down the main points of the lesson, math terms that you do not understand, examples that need more explanation, and questions you can ask during class.

Learn to solve equations involving decimals. → The objective tells you the main idea of the lesson.

Work through the examples and write down any questions you have.

Solving One-Step Equations with Decimals

Solve each equation. Check your answer.

A $g - 3.1 = 4.5$

$$g - 3.1 = 4.5$$
$$\underline{+\ 3.1\quad +3.1}$$
$$g = 7.6$$

3.1 is subtracted from g.
Add 3.1 to both sides to undo the subtraction.

Check

$g - 3.1 = 4.5$
$7.6 - 3.1 \stackrel{?}{=} 4.5$ *Substitute 7.6 for g in the equation.*
$4.5 \stackrel{?}{=} 4.5$ ✓   *7.6 is the solution.*

Questions:
- How do I know what operation to use?
- What should I do if I check my answer and the two sides are not equal?

→ Write down questions you have as you read the lesson.

Try This

Read Lesson 4-1 before your next class and answer the following questions.

1. What is the objective of the lesson?
2. Are there new vocabulary terms, formulas, or symbols? If so, what are they?

Number Theory and Fractions

4-1 Divisibility

Learn to use divisibility rules.

This year, 42 girls signed up to play soccer for the Junior Girls League, which has 6 teams. To find whether each team can have the same number of girls, decide if 42 is divisible by 6.

Vocabulary
divisible
composite number
prime number

A number is **divisible** by another number if the quotient is a whole number with no remainder.

$42 \div 6 = 7 \leftarrow$ Quotient

Since there is no remainder, 42 is divisible by 6. The Junior Girls League can have 6 teams with 7 girls each.

Remember!
Division by 0 is undefined.

Divisibility Rules

A number is divisible by...	Divisible	Not Divisible
2 if the last digit is even (0, 2, 4, 6, or 8).	3,978	4,975
3 if the sum of the digits is divisible by 3.	315	139
4 if the last two digits form a number divisible by 4.	8,512	7,518
5 if the last digit is 0 or 5.	14,975	10,978
6 if the number is divisible by both 2 and 3.	48	20
9 if the sum of the digits is divisible by 9.	711	93
10 if the last digit is 0.	15,990	10,536

EXAMPLE 1 Checking Divisibility

A Tell whether 610 is divisible by 2, 3, 4, and 5.

2	The last digit, 0, is even.	Divisible
3	The sum of the digits is 6 + 1 + 0 = 7. 7 is not divisible by 3.	Not divisible
4	The last two digits form the number 10. 10 is not divisible by 4.	Not divisible
5	The last digit is 0.	Divisible

So 610 is divisible by 2 and 5.

B Tell whether 387 is divisible by 6, 9, and 10.

6	*The last digit, 7, is odd, so 387 is not divisible by 2.*	Not divisible
9	*The sum of the digits is 3 + 8 + 7 = 18. 18 is divisible by 9.*	Divisible
10	*The last digit is 7, not 0.*	Not divisible

So 387 is divisible by 9.

Any number greater than 1 is divisible by at least two numbers—1 and the number itself. Numbers that are divisible by more than two numbers are called **composite numbers**.

A **prime number** is divisible by only the numbers 1 and itself. For example, 11 is a prime number because it is divisible by only 1 and 11. The numbers 0 and 1 are neither prime nor composite.

EXAMPLE 2 Identifying Prime and Composite Numbers

Tell whether each number is prime or composite.

A 45

divisible by 1, 3, 5, 9, 15, 45
composite

B 13

divisible by 1, 13
prime

C 19

divisible by 1, 19
prime

D 49

divisible by 1, 7, 49
composite

The prime numbers from 1 through 50 are highlighted below.

1	2	3	4	5	6	7	8	9	10
11	12	13	14	15	16	17	18	19	20
21	22	23	24	25	26	27	28	29	30
31	32	33	34	35	36	37	38	39	40
41	42	43	44	45	46	47	48	49	50

Think and Discuss

1. **Tell** which whole numbers are divisible by 1.
2. **Explain** how you know that 87 is a composite number.
3. **Tell** how the divisibility rules help you identify composite numbers.

4-1 Exercises

Learn It Online
Homework Help Online go.hrw.com,
keyword MR10 4-1 Go
Exercises 1–32, 33, 35, 41, 43, 45

GUIDED PRACTICE

See Example 1 Tell whether each number is divisible by 2, 3, 4, 5, 6, 9, and 10.
1. 508
2. 432
3. 247
4. 189

See Example 2 Tell whether each number is prime or composite.
5. 75
6. 17
7. 27
8. 63
9. 72
10. 83
11. 99
12. 199

INDEPENDENT PRACTICE

See Example 1 Tell whether each number is divisible by 2, 3, 4, 5, 6, 9, and 10.
13. 741
14. 810
15. 675
16. 480
17. 908
18. 146
19. 514
20. 405

See Example 2 Tell whether each number is prime or composite.
21. 34
22. 29
23. 61
24. 81
25. 51
26. 23
27. 97
28. 93
29. 77
30. 41
31. 67
32. 39

PRACTICE AND PROBLEM SOLVING

Extra Practice
See page EP7.

Copy and complete the table. Write *yes* if the number is divisible by the given number. Write *no* if it is not.

		2	3	4	5	6	9	10
33.	677	no	■	■	no	■	■	no
34.	290	yes	■	■	■	■	■	■
35.	1,744	■	■	■	■	■	■	■
36.	12,180	■	■	■	■	■	■	■

Tell whether each statement is true or false. Explain your answers.

37. All even numbers are divisible by 2.
38. All odd numbers are divisible by 3.
39. Some even numbers are divisible by 5.
40. All odd numbers are prime.

Replace each box with a digit that will make the number divisible by 3.

41. 74■
42. 8,10■
43. 3,■41
44. ■,335
45. 67,■11
46. 10,0■1

158 Chapter 4 Number Theory and Fractions

47. Make a table that shows the prime numbers from 50 to 100.

48. **Astronomy** Earth has a diameter of 7,926 miles. Tell whether this number is divisible by 2, 3, 4, 5, 6, 9, and 10.

49. On which of the bridges in the table could a light fixture be placed every 6 meters so that the first light is at the beginning of the bridge and the last light is at the end of the bridge? Explain.

Verrazano-Narrows Bridge

Longest Bridges in the U.S.	
Name and State	Length (m)
Verrazano-Narrows, NY	1,298
Golden Gate, CA	1,280
Mackinac Straits, MI	1,158
George Washington, NY	1,067

50. **Critical Thinking** A number is between 80 and 100 and is divisible by both 5 and 6. What is the number?

51. **Choose a Strategy** Find the greatest four-digit number that is divisible by 1, 2, 3, and 4.

52. **What's the Error?** To find whether 3,463 is divisible by 4, a student added the digits. The sum, 16, is divisible by 4, so the student stated that 3,463 is divisible by 4. Explain the error.

53. **Write About It** If a number is divisible by both 4 and 9, by what other numbers is it divisible? Explain.

54. **Challenge** Find a number that is divisible by 2, 3, 4, 5, 6, and 10, but not 9.

Test Prep and Spiral Review

55. **Multiple Choice** ___?___ numbers are divisible by more than two numbers.

    (A) Whole (B) Prime (C) Equivalent (D) Composite

56. **Short Response** What is the least three-digit number that is divisible by both 5 and 9? Show your work.

Use the pattern to write the first five terms of each sequence. (Lesson 1-6)

57. Start with 7; add 4.
58. Start with 78; subtract 9.
59. Start with 6; multiply by 5.

Evaluate each expression for the given value of the variable. (Lesson 2-1)

60. $2x + 28$ for $x = 4$
61. $x + 18$ for $x = 12$
62. $\frac{x}{5}$ for $x = 25$

4-1 Divisibility

Hands-on LAB 4-2

Explore Factors

Use with Lesson 4-2

Learn It Online
Lab Resources Online go.hrw.com,
keyword MR10 Lab4 Go

You can use graph paper or unit cubes to model *factors* of a number and determine whether the number is a prime number or a composite number.

Activity

Use graph paper to show the different ways the number 16 can be modeled.

1 The number 16 can be modeled by drawing a rectangle 2 units wide and 8 units long. The dimensions, 2 and 8, are factors of 16. This means that 2 × 8 = 16.

What other ways can 16 be modeled?
A rectangle 1 unit wide and 16 units long and a 4-unit-by-4 unit square can also model 16.

The factors of 16 are 1, 2, 4, 8, and 16. Because you can model 16 in more than one way, 16 is a composite number.

Use graph paper to show the different ways the number 3 can be modeled.

2 The number 3 can be modeled by drawing a rectangle 1 unit wide and 3 units long. The dimensions, 1 and 3, are factors of 3. This means that 1 × 3 = 3.
Because 3 cannot be modeled any other way, 3 is a prime number.

Think and Discuss

1. How can you use the rules of divisibility to determine whether there is more than one way to model a number?

2. Find the factors of 2. Is 2 prime or composite? Explain.

Try This

1. Use graph paper to model two prime numbers and two composite numbers. Find their factors.

160 Chapter 4 Number Theory and Fractions

4-2 Factors and Prime Factorization

Learn to write prime factorizations of composite numbers.

Whole numbers that are multiplied to find a product are called **factors** of that product. A number is divisible by its factors.

$2 \cdot 3 = 6$ $6 \div 3 = 2$

Factors Product

$6 \div 2 = 3$

6 is divisible by 3 and 2.

Vocabulary
factor
prime factorization

EXAMPLE 1 Finding Factors

Interactivities Online

List all of the factors of each number.

A 18

Begin listing factors in pairs.

$18 = 1 \cdot 18$ — 1 is a factor.
$18 = 2 \cdot 9$ — 2 is a factor.
$18 = 3 \cdot 6$ — 3 is a factor.
— 4 and 5 are not factors.
$18 = 6 \cdot 3$ — 6 and 3 have already been listed, so stop here.

1 2 3 6 9 18 — You can draw a diagram to illustrate the factor pairs.

The factors of 18 are 1, 2, 3, 6, 9, and 18.

Helpful Hint

When the pairs of factors begin to repeat, then you have found all of the factors of the number you are factoring.

B 13

$13 = 1 \cdot 13$ — Begin listing factors in pairs. 13 is not divisible by any other whole numbers.

The factors of 13 are 1 and 13.

You can use factors to write a number in different ways.

Factorization of 12			
$1 \cdot 12$	$2 \cdot 6$	$3 \cdot 4$	$3 \cdot 2 \cdot 2$

← Notice that these factors are all prime.

The **prime factorization** of a number is the number written as the product of its prime factors.

Video Lesson Tutorials Online my.hrw.com

EXAMPLE 2 Writing Prime Factorizations

Write the prime factorization of each number.

A 36

Method 1: Use a factor tree.

Choose any two factors of 36 to begin. Keep finding factors until each branch ends at a prime factor.

```
      36                    36
     /  \                  /  \
   ③ • 12               ② • 18
        /  \                  /  \
       4 • ③                9 • ②
      / \                   / \
     ② • ②               ③ • ③
```

36 = 3 • 2 • 2 • 3   36 = 2 • 3 • 3 • 2

The prime factorization of 36 is 2 • 2 • 3 • 3, or $2^2 • 3^2$.

Helpful Hint

You can use exponents to write prime factorizations. Remember that an exponent tells you how many times the base is a factor.

B 54

Method 2: Use a ladder diagram.

Choose a prime factor of 54 to begin. Keep dividing by prime factors until the quotient is 1.

```
  2 | 54            3 | 54
    3 | 27            3 | 18
      3 | 9             2 | 6
        3 | 3             3 | 3
            1                 1
```

54 = 2 • 3 • 3 • 3   54 = 3 • 3 • 2 • 3

The prime factorization of 54 is 2 • 3 • 3 • 3, or $2 • 3^3$.

In Example 2, notice that the prime factors may be written in a different order, but they are still the same factors. Except for changes in the order, there is only one way to write the prime factorization of a number.

Think and Discuss

1. **Tell** how you know when you have found all of the factors of a number.

2. **Tell** how you know when you have found the prime factorization of a number.

3. **Explain** the difference between factors of a number and prime factors of a number.

4-2 Exercises

Learn It Online
Homework Help Online go.hrw.com,
keyword MR10 4-2 Go
Exercises 1–24, 33, 35, 37, 39, 43, 45, 47

GUIDED PRACTICE

See Example 1 List all of the factors of each number.
  1. 12
  2. 21
  3. 52
  4. 75

See Example 2 Write the prime factorization of each number.
  5. 48
  6. 20
  7. 66
  8. 34

INDEPENDENT PRACTICE

See Example 1 List all of the factors of each number.
  9. 24
  10. 37
  11. 42
  12. 56
  13. 67
  14. 72
  15. 85
  16. 92

See Example 2 Write the prime factorization of each number.
  17. 49
  18. 38
  19. 76
  20. 60
  21. 81
  22. 132
  23. 140
  24. 87

PRACTICE AND PROBLEM SOLVING

Extra Practice
See page EP7.

Write each number as a product in two different ways.
  25. 34
  26. 82
  27. 88
  28. 50
  29. 15
  30. 78
  31. 94
  32. 35

33. **Sports** Little League Baseball began in 1939 in Pennsylvania. When it first started, there were 45 boys on 3 teams.
  a. If the teams were equally sized, how many boys were on each team?
  b. Name another way the boys could have been divided into equally sized teams. (Remember that a baseball team must have at least 9 players.)

34. **Critical Thinking** Use the divisibility rules to list the factors of 171. Explain how you determined the factors.

Find the prime factorization of each number.
  35. 99
  36. 249
  37. 284
  38. 620
  39. 840
  40. 150
  41. 740
  42. 402

43. The prime factorization of 50 is $2 \cdot 5^2$. Without dividing or using a diagram, find the prime factorization of 100.

44. **Geometry** The area of a rectangle is the product of its length and width. Suppose the area of a rectangle is 24 in^2. What are the possible whole number measurements of its length and width?

45. **Physical Science** The speed of sound at sea level at 20 °C is 343 meters per second. Write the prime factorization of 343.

4-2 Factors and Prime Factorization

Life Science LINK

Climate changes, habitat destruction, and overhunting can cause animals and plants to die in large numbers. When the entire population of a species begins to die out, the species is considered endangered.

The graph shows the number of endangered species in each category of animal.

Endangered Species

Mammals: 324, Birds: 251, Reptiles: 78, Insects: 51, Amphibians: 20, Clams: 64

46. How many species of mammals are endangered? Write this number as the product of prime factors.

47. Which category of animal has a prime number of endangered species?

48. How many species of reptiles and amphibians combined are endangered? Write the answer as the product of prime factors.

Most white tigers are found in zoos or sanctuaries for big cats. They are very rarely seen in the wild.

49. **What's the Error?** When asked to write the prime factorization of the number of endangered amphibian species, a student wrote 4 × 5. Explain the error and write the correct answer.

50. **Write About It** A team of five scientists is going to study endangered insect species. The scientists want to divide the species evenly among them. Will they be able to do this? Why or why not?

51. **Challenge** Add the number of endangered mammal species to the number of endangered bird species. Find the prime factorization of this number.

Test Prep and Spiral Review

52. Multiple Choice Which expression shows the prime factorization of 50?

Ⓐ 2×5^2 Ⓑ 2×5^{10} Ⓒ 10^5 Ⓓ 5×10

53. Gridded Response What number has a prime factorization of 2 × 2 × 3 × 5?

54. Damien's favorite song is 4.2 minutes long. Jan's favorite song is 2.89 minutes long. Estimate the difference in the lengths of the songs by rounding to the nearest whole number. (Lesson 3-2)

Tell whether each number is divisible by 2, 3, 4, 5, 6, 9, and 10. (Lesson 4-1)

55. 105   **56.** 198   **57.** 360   **58.** 235
59. 100   **60.** 92   **61.** 540   **62.** 441

4-3 Greatest Common Factor

Learn to find the greatest common factor (GCF) of a set of numbers.

Vocabulary
greatest common factor (GCF)

Factors shared by two or more whole numbers are called common factors. The largest of the common factors is called the **greatest common factor**, or **GCF**.

Factors of 24: 1, 2, 3, 4, 6, 8, 12, 24

Factors of 36: 1, 2, 3, 4, 6, 9, 12, 18, 36

Common factors: 1, 2, 3, 4, 6, ⑫

The greatest common factor (GCF) of 24 and 36 is 12.

Example 1 shows three different methods for finding the GCF.

EXAMPLE 1 Finding the GCF

Find the GCF of each set of numbers.

A 16 and 24

Method 1: List the factors.

factors of 16: 1, 2, 4, ⑧, 16   *List all the factors.*
factors of 24: 1, 2, 3, 4, 6, ⑧, 12, 24   *Circle the GCF.*

The GCF of 16 and 24 is 8.

B 12, 24, and 32

Method 2: Use prime factorization.

$12 = 2 \cdot 2 \cdot 3$ *Write the prime factorization of each number.*
$24 = 2 \cdot 2 \cdot 2 \cdot 3$
$32 = 2 \cdot 2 \cdot 2 \cdot 2 \cdot 2$ *Find the common prime factors.*

$2 \cdot 2 = 4$ *Find the prime factors common to all the numbers.*

The GCF of 12, 24, and 32 is 4.

C 12, 18, and 60

Method 3: Use a ladder diagram.

```
2 | 12 | 18 | 60
3 |  6 |  9 | 30
        2    3   10
```

Begin with a factor that divides into each number. Keep dividing until the three numbers have no common factors.

$2 \cdot 3 = 6$ *Find the product of the numbers you divided by.*

The GCF is 6.

EXAMPLE 2

PROBLEM SOLVING APPLICATION

There are 12 boys and 18 girls in Ms. Ruiz's science class. The students must form lab groups. Each group must have the same number of boys and the same number of girls. What is the greatest number of groups Ms. Ruiz can make if every student must be in a group?

1. Understand the Problem

The **answer** will be the *greatest* number of groups 12 boys and 18 girls can form so that each group has the same number of boys, and each group has the same number of girls.

2. Make a Plan

You can make an organized list of the possible groups.

3. Solve

There are more girls than boys in the class, so there will be more girls than boys in each group.

Helpful Hint

If more students are put in each group, there will be fewer groups. You need the most groups possible, so put the smallest possible number of students in each team. Start with 1 boy in each group.

Boys	Girls	Groups
1	2	(B/GG) (B/GG) (B/GG) (B/GG) (B/GG) (B/GG) (B/GG) (B/GG) (B/GG) 9 boys, 18 girls: There are 3 boys not in groups. ✗
2	3	(BB/GGG) (BB/GGG) (BB/GGG) (BB/GGG) (BB/GGG) (BB/GGG) 12 boys, 18 girls: Every student is in a group. ✓

The greatest number of groups is 6.

4. Look Back

The number of groups will be a common factor of the number of boys and the number of girls. To form the largest number of groups, find the GCF of 12 and 18.

factors of 12: 1, 2, 3, 4, ⑥, 12   factors of 18: 1, 2, 3, ⑥, 9, 18

The GCF of 12 and 18 is 6.

Think and Discuss

1. **Explain** what the GCF of two prime numbers is.
2. **Tell** what the least common factor of a group of numbers would be.

166 Chapter 4 Number Theory and Fractions

4-3 Exercises

Learn It Online
Homework Help Online go.hrw.com,
keyword MR10 4-3
Exercises 1–18, 23, 25, 27, 29, 31, 35, 37

GUIDED PRACTICE

See Example 1 Find the GCF of each set of numbers.
1. 18 and 27
2. 32 and 72
3. 21, 42, and 56
4. 15, 30, and 60
5. 18, 24, and 36
6. 9, 36, and 81

See Example 2
7. Kim is making flower arrangements. She has 16 red roses and 20 pink roses. Each arrangement must have the same number of red roses and the same number of pink roses. What is the greatest number of arrangements Kim can make if every flower is used?

INDEPENDENT PRACTICE

See Example 1 Find the GCF of each set of numbers.
8. 10 and 35
9. 28 and 70
10. 36 and 72
11. 26, 48, and 62
12. 16, 40, and 88
13. 12, 60, and 68
14. 30, 45, and 75
15. 24, 48, and 84
16. 16, 48, and 72

See Example 2
17. The local recreation center held a scavenger hunt. There were 15 boys and 9 girls at the event. The group was divided into the greatest number of teams possible with the same number of boys on each team and the same number of girls on each team. How many teams were made if each person was on a team?

18. Ms. Kline makes balloon arrangements. She has 32 blue balloons, 24 yellow balloons, and 16 white balloons. Each arrangement must have the same number of each color. What is the greatest number of arrangements that Ms. Kline can make if every balloon is used?

PRACTICE AND PROBLEM SOLVING

Extra Practice
See page EP7.

Write the GCF of each set of numbers.
19. 60 and 84
20. 14 and 17
21. 10, 35, and 110
22. 21 and 306
23. 630 and 712
24. 16, 24, and 40
25. 75, 225, and 150
26. 42, 112, and 105
27. 12, 16, 20, and 24

28. Jared has 12 jars of grape jam, 16 jars of strawberry jam, and 24 jars of raspberry jam. He wants to place the jam into the greatest possible number of boxes so that each box has the same number of jars of each kind of jam. How many boxes does he need?

29. Pam is making fruit baskets. She has 30 apples, 24 bananas, and 12 oranges. What is the greatest number of baskets she can make if each type of fruit is distributed equally among the baskets?

30. **Critical Thinking** Write a set of three different numbers that have a GCF of 9. Explain your method.

4-3 Greatest Common Factor 167

Life Science

The biggest flower in the world is the Rafflesia. It grows in the Indonesian rain forest. Blossoms can measure four feet across, weigh about 15 pounds, and contain about 1.5 gallons of water.

Write the GCF of each set of numbers.

31. 16, 24, 30, and 42
32. 25, 90, 45, and 100
33. 27, 90, 135, and 72
34. $2 \times 2 \times 3$ and 2×2
35. $2 \times 3^2 \times 7$ and $2^2 \times 3$
36. $3^2 \times 7$ and $2 \times 3 \times 5^2$

37. Mr. Chu is planting 4 types of flowers in his garden. He wants each row to contain the same number of each type of flower. What is the greatest number of rows Mr. Chu can plant if every bulb is used?

Flower Types

Number of bulbs — Irises 42, Daffodils 36, Tulips 18, Lilies 12

38. In a parade, one school band will march directly behind another school band. All rows must have the same number of students. The first band has 36 students, and the second band has 60 students. What is the greatest number of students who can be in each row?

39. **Social Studies** Branches of the U.S. Mint in Denver and Philadelphia make all U.S. coins for circulation. A tiny *D* or *P* on the coin tells you where the coin was minted. Suppose you have 32 *D* quarters and 36 *P* quarters. What is the greatest number of groups you can make with the same number of *D* quarters in each group and the same number of *P* quarters in each group so that every quarter is placed in a group?

40. **What's the Error?** Mike says if $12 = 2^2 \cdot 3$ and $24 = 2^3 \cdot 3$, then the GCF of 12 and 24 is $2 \cdot 3$, or 6. Explain Mike's error.

41. **Write About It** What method do you like best for finding the GCF? Why?

42. **Challenge** The GCF of three numbers is 9. The sum of the numbers is 90. Find the three numbers.

Test Prep and Spiral Review

43. **Multiple Choice** For which set of numbers is 16 the GCF?

    Ⓐ 16, 32, 48 Ⓑ 12, 24, 32 Ⓒ 24, 48, 60 Ⓓ 8, 80, 100

44. **Multiple Choice** Mrs. Lyndon is making baskets of muffins. She has 48 lemon muffins, 120 blueberry muffins, and 112 banana nut muffins. How many baskets can Mrs. Lyndon make with each type of muffin distributed evenly?

    Ⓕ 4 Ⓖ 6 Ⓗ 8 Ⓙ 12

Solve each equation. (Lessons 2-4, 2-5, 2-6, 2-7)

45. $y + 37 = 64$
46. $c - 5 = 19$
47. $72 \div z = 9$
48. $3v = 81$

Write the prime factorization of each number. (Lesson 4-2)

49. 42
50. 62
51. 51
52. 132
53. 200

168 Chapter 4 Number Theory and Fractions

Technology Lab 4-3: Greatest Common Factor

Use with Lesson 4-3

You can use a graphing calculator to quickly find the greatest common factor (GCF) of two or more numbers. A calculator is particularly useful when you need to find the GCF of large numbers.

Activity

Find the GCF of 504 and 3,150.

The GCF is also known as the *greatest common divisor,* or GCD. The GCD function is found on the **MATH** menu.

To find the GCD on a graphing calculator, press **MATH**. Press ▶ to highlight **NUM**, and then use ▼ to scroll down and highlight **9:**.

Press **ENTER** 504 **,** 3150 **)** **ENTER**.

The greatest common factor of 504 and 3,150 is 126.

Think and Discuss

1. Suppose your calculator will not allow you to enter three numbers into the GCD function. How could you still use your calculator to find the GCF of the three following numbers: 4,896; 2,364; and 656? Explain your strategy and why it works.

2. Would you use your calculator to find the GCF of 6 and 18? Why or why not?

Try This

Find the GCF of each set of numbers.

1. 14, 48
2. 18, 54
3. 99, 121
4. 144, 196
5. 200, 136
6. 246, 137
7. 72, 860
8. 55, 141, 91

LESSON 4-3 EXTENSION
Sets of Numbers

Learn to make Venn diagrams to describe number sets.

Vocabulary
set
element
intersection
union

A group of items is called a **set**. The items in a set are called **elements**. In this chapter, you saw several sets of numbers, such as prime numbers, composite numbers, and factors.

In a Venn diagram, circles are used to show relationships between sets. The overlapped region represents elements that are in both set A *and* set B. This set is called the **intersection** of A and B. Elements that are in set A *or* set B make up the **union** of A and B.

EXAMPLE 1 Identifying Elements and Drawing Venn Diagrams

Identify the elements in each set. Then draw a Venn diagram. What is the intersection? What is the union?

A Set A: prime numbers   Set B: composite numbers
Elements of A: 2, 3, 5, 7, …   Elements of B: 4, 6, 8, 9, …

The circles do not overlap because no number is both prime and composite.

Intersection: none. When a set has no elements, it is called an *empty set*. The intersection of A and B is empty.

Union: all numbers that are prime *or* composite—all whole numbers except 0 and 1.

B Set A: factors of 36   Set B: factors of 24
Elements of A: 1, 2, 3, 4, 6, 9, 12, 18, 36
Elements of B: 1, 2, 3, 4, 6, 8, 12, 24

The circles overlap because some factors of 36 are also factors of 24.

Intersection: 1, 2, 3, 4, 6, 12   *factors of 36 and 24*
Union: 1, 2, 3, 4, 6, 8, 9, 12, 18, 24, 36   *factors of 36 or 24*

Identify the elements in each set. Then draw a Venn diagram. What is the intersection? What is the union?

C Set A: factors of 36   Set B: factors of 12

Elements of A: 1, 2, 3, 4, 6, 9, 12, 18, 36
Elements of B: 1, 2, 3, 4, 6, 12

The circle for set B is entirely inside the circle for set A because all factors of 12 are also factors of 36.

Intersection: 1, 2, 3, 4, 6, 12   *factors of 36 and 12*
Union: 1, 2, 3, 4, 6, 9, 12, 18, 36   *factors of 36 or 12*

Helpful Hint
To decide whether set B is a subset of set A, ask yourself, "Is every element of B also in A?" If the answer is yes, then B is a subset of A.

Look at Example 1C. When one set is entirely contained in another set, we say the first set is a *subset* of the second set.

B is a subset of A.

EXTENSION Exercises

Identify the elements in each set. Then draw a Venn diagram. What is the intersection? What is the union?

1. Set A: even numbers
   Set B: odd numbers

2. Set A: factors of 18
   Set B: factors of 40

3. Set A: factors of 72
   Set B: factors of 36

4. Set A: even numbers
   Set B: composite numbers

Tell whether set A is a subset of set B.

5. Set A: whole numbers less than 10
   Set B: whole numbers less than 12

6. Set A: whole numbers less than 8
   Set B: whole numbers greater than 9

7. Set A: prime numbers
   Set B: odd numbers

8. Set A: numbers divisible by 6
   Set B: numbers divisible by 3

9. **Write About It** How could you use a Venn diagram to help find the greatest common factor of two numbers? Give an example.

10. **Challenge** How could you use a Venn diagram to help find the greatest common factor of three numbers? Give an example.

Ready To Go On?

Quiz for Lessons 4-1 Through 4-3

4-1 Divisibility

Tell whether each number is divisible by 2, 3, 4, 5, 6, 9, and 10.

1. 708
2. 514
3. 470
4. 338

5. A highway loop around a city is 45 miles long. If exits are placed every 5 miles, will the exits be evenly spaced around the loop? Explain.

6. Hoover Dam is 1,244 feet across at the top. Tell whether this number is divisible by 2, 3, 4, 5, 6, 9, and 10.

Tell whether each number is prime or composite.

7. 76
8. 59
9. 69
10. 33

4-2 Factors and Prime Factorization

List all of the factors of each number.

11. 26
12. 32
13. 39
14. 84

15. Mr. Collins's bowling league has 48 members. If the league splits into teams of 12 members each, how many equally sized teams will there be?

Write the prime factorization of each number.

16. 96
17. 50
18. 104
19. 63

20. Scientists classify many sunflowers in the genus *Helianthus*. There are approximately 67 species of *Helianthus*. Write the prime factorization of 67.

4-3 Greatest Common Factor

Find the GCF of each set of numbers.

21. 16 and 36
22. 22 and 88
23. 65 and 91
24. 20, 55, and 85

25. There are 36 sixth-graders and 40 seventh-graders. What is the greatest number of teams that the students can form if each team has the same number of sixth-graders and the same number of seventh-graders and every student must be on a team?

26. There are 14 girls and 21 boys in Mrs. Sutter's gym class. To play a certain game, the students must form teams. Each team must have the same number of girls and the same number of boys. What is the greatest number of teams Mrs. Sutter can make if every student is on a team?

27. Mrs. Young, an art teacher, is organizing the art supplies. She has 76 red markers, 52 blue markers, and 80 black markers. She wants to divide the markers into boxes with the same number of red, the same number of blue, and the same number of black markers in each box. What is the greatest number of boxes she can have if every marker is placed in a box?

Focus on Problem Solving

Understand the Problem
• Interpret unfamiliar words

You must understand the words in a problem in order to solve it. If there is a word you do not know, try to use context clues to figure out its meaning. Suppose there is a problem about red, green, blue, and chartreuse fabric. You may not know the word *chartreuse*, but you can guess that it is probably a color. To make the problem easier to understand, you could replace *chartreuse* with the name of a familiar color, like *white*.

In some problems, the name of a person, place, or thing might be difficult to pronounce, such as *Mr. Joubert*. When you see a proper noun that you do not know how to pronounce, you can use another proper noun or a pronoun in its place. You could replace *Mr. Joubert* with *he*. You could replace *Koenisburg Street* with *K Street*.

Copy each problem. Underline any words that you do not understand. Then replace each word with a more familiar word.

1. Grace is making flower bouquets. She has 18 chrysanthemums and 42 roses. She wants to arrange them in groups that each have the same number of chrysanthemums and the same number of roses. What is the fewest number of flowers that Grace can have in each group? How many chrysanthemums and how many roses will be in each group?

2. Most marbles are made from glass. The glass is liquefied in a furnace and poured. It is then cut into cylinders that are rounded off and cooled. Suppose 1,200 cooled marbles are put into packages of 8. How many packages could be made? Would there be any marbles left over?

3. In ancient times, many civilizations used calendars that divided the year into months of 30 days. A year has 365 days. How many whole months were in these ancient calendars? Were there any days left over? If so, how many?

4. Mrs. LeFeubre is tiling her garden walkway. It is a rectangle that is 4 feet wide and 20 feet long. Mrs. LeFeubre wants to use square tiles, and she does not want to have to cut any tiles. What is the size of the largest square tile that Mrs. LeFeubre can use?

Focus on Problem Solving

Hands-on LAB 4-4

Explore Decimals and Fractions

Use with Lesson 4-4

Learn It Online
Lab Resources Online go.hrw.com,
keyword MR10 Lab4 Go

KEY

0.01   0.1   1

You can use decimal grids to show the relationship between fractions and decimals.

Activity

Write the number represented on each grid as a fraction and as a decimal.

1 Seven hundredths squares are shaded → 0.07
How many squares are shaded? $\frac{7}{100}$ ← numerator
How many squares are in the whole?   ← denominator

$0.07 = \frac{7}{100}$

2 Three tenths columns are shaded →   0.3
How many complete columns are shaded? $\frac{3}{10}$
How many columns are in the whole?

$0.3 = \frac{3}{10}$

Think and Discuss

1. Is 0.09 the same as $\frac{9}{10}$? Use decimal grids to support your answer.

Try This

Use decimal grids to represent each number.

1. 0.8   2. $\frac{37}{100}$ 3. 0.53   4. $\frac{1}{10}$ 5. $\frac{67}{100}$

6. For 1–5, write each decimal as a fraction and each fraction as a decimal.

174   Chapter 4 Number Theory and Fractions

4-4 Decimals and Fractions

Learn to convert between decimals and fractions.

Vocabulary
mixed number
terminating decimal
repeating decimal

Decimals and fractions can often be used to represent the same number.

For example, a baseball player's or baseball team's batting average can be represented as a fraction:

$$\frac{\text{number of hits}}{\text{number of times at bat}}$$

The Oregon State University baseball team won the College World Series in 2006 and 2007.

In 2007, the Oregon State University baseball team won its second College World Series title. During that season, the team had 659 hits and 2,297 at bats. The team's batting average was $\frac{659}{2,297}$.

$$659 \div 2,297 = 0.2868959512\ldots$$

The 2007 batting average for the Oregon State baseball team is reported as .287.

Interactivities Online

Decimals can be written as fractions or mixed numbers. A number that contains both a whole number greater than 0 and a fraction, such as $1\frac{3}{4}$, is called a **mixed number**.

Mixed numbers

$\frac{1}{4}$ $\frac{1}{2}$ $\frac{3}{4}$ $1\frac{1}{4}$ $1\frac{1}{2}$ $1\frac{3}{4}$ $2\frac{1}{4}$ $2\frac{1}{2}$

0   0.25   0.5   0.75   1   1.25   1.5   1.75   2   2.25   2.5

EXAMPLE 1 Writing Decimals as Fractions or Mixed Numbers

Remember!

Place Value
Ones · Tenths Hundredths Thousandths

Write each decimal as a fraction or mixed number.

A 0.23

0.2**3** *Identify the place value of the digit farthest to the right.*

$\frac{23}{100}$ *The 3 is in the **hundred**ths place, so use **100** as the denominator.*

B 1.7

1.**7** *Identify the place value of the digit farthest to the right.*

$1\frac{7}{10}$ *Write the whole number, 1. The 7 is in the **ten**ths place, so use **10** as the denominator.*

EXAMPLE 2 Writing Fractions as Decimals

Write each fraction or mixed number as a decimal.

A $\frac{3}{4}$

$$
\begin{array}{r}
0.75 \\
4\overline{)3.00} \\
-28 \\
\hline
20 \\
-20 \\
\hline
0
\end{array}
$$

Divide 3 by 4.
Add zeros after the decimal point.
The remainder is 0.

$\frac{3}{4} = 0.75$

B $5\frac{2}{3}$

$$
\begin{array}{r}
0.666 \\
3\overline{)2.000} \\
-18 \\
\hline
20 \\
-18 \\
\hline
20 \\
-18 \\
\hline
2
\end{array}
$$

Divide 2 by 3.
Add zeros after the decimal point.
The 6 repeats in the quotient.

$5\frac{2}{3} = 5.666... = 5.\overline{6}$

Writing Math

To write a repeating decimal, you can show three dots or draw a bar over the repeating part: $0.666... = 0.\overline{6}$

A **terminating decimal**, such as 0.75, has a finite number of decimal places. A **repeating decimal**, such as 0.666..., has a block of one or more digits that repeat without end.

Common Fractions and Equivalent Decimals

$\frac{1}{5}$	$\frac{1}{4}$	$\frac{1}{3}$	$\frac{2}{5}$	$\frac{1}{2}$	$\frac{3}{5}$	$\frac{2}{3}$	$\frac{3}{4}$	$\frac{4}{5}$
0.2	0.25	$0.\overline{3}$	0.4	0.5	0.6	$0.\overline{6}$	0.75	0.8

EXAMPLE 3 Comparing and Ordering Fractions and Decimals

Order the fractions and decimals from least to greatest.

$0.5, \frac{1}{5}, 0.37$

First rewrite the fraction as a decimal. $\frac{1}{5} = 0.2$

Order the three decimals.

The numbers in order from least to greatest are $\frac{1}{5}$, 0.37, and 0.5.

Think and Discuss

1. **Tell** how reading the decimal 6.9 as "six and nine tenths" helps you to write 6.9 as a mixed number.

2. **Look** at the decimal 0.121122111222.... If the pattern continues, is this a repeating decimal? Why or why not?

4-4 Exercises

Learn It Online
Homework Help Online go.hrw.com,
keyword MR10 4-4 Go
Exercises 1–33, 37, 41, 43, 49, 53, 57, 63

GUIDED PRACTICE

See Example 1 Write each decimal as a fraction or mixed number.
1. 0.15
2. 1.25
3. 0.43
4. 2.6

See Example 2 Write each fraction or mixed number as a decimal.
5. $\frac{2}{5}$
6. $2\frac{7}{8}$
7. $\frac{1}{8}$
8. $4\frac{1}{10}$

See Example 3 Order the fractions and decimals from least to greatest.
9. $\frac{2}{3}$, 0.78, 0.21
10. $\frac{5}{16}$, 0.67, $\frac{1}{6}$
11. 0.52, $\frac{1}{9}$, 0.3

INDEPENDENT PRACTICE

See Example 1 Write each decimal as a fraction or mixed number.
12. 0.31
13. 5.71
14. 0.13
15. 3.23
16. 0.5
17. 2.7
18. 0.19
19. 6.3

See Example 2 Write each fraction or mixed number as a decimal.
20. $\frac{1}{9}$
21. $1\frac{3}{5}$
22. $\frac{8}{9}$
23. $3\frac{11}{40}$
24. $2\frac{5}{6}$
25. $\frac{3}{8}$
26. $4\frac{4}{5}$
27. $\frac{5}{8}$

See Example 3 Order the fractions and decimals from least to greatest.
28. 0.49, 0.82, $\frac{1}{2}$
29. $\frac{3}{8}$, 0.29, $\frac{1}{9}$
30. 0.94, $\frac{4}{5}$, 0.6
31. 0.11, $\frac{1}{10}$, 0.13
32. $\frac{2}{3}$, 0.42, $\frac{2}{5}$
33. $\frac{3}{7}$, 0.76, 0.31

PRACTICE AND PROBLEM SOLVING

Extra Practice
See page EP7.

Write each decimal in expanded form and use a whole number or fraction for each place value.
34. 0.81
35. 92.3
36. 13.29
37. 107.17

Write each fraction as a decimal. Tell whether the decimal terminates or repeats.
38. $\frac{7}{9}$
39. $\frac{1}{6}$
40. $\frac{17}{20}$
41. $\frac{5}{12}$
42. $\frac{7}{8}$
43. $\frac{4}{5}$
44. $\frac{9}{5}$
45. $\frac{15}{18}$
46. $\frac{7}{3}$
47. $\frac{11}{12}$

Compare. Write <, >, or =.
48. 0.75 ▨ $\frac{3}{4}$
49. $\frac{5}{8}$ ▨ 0.5
50. 0.78 ▨ $\frac{7}{9}$
51. $\frac{1}{3}$ ▨ 0.35
52. $\frac{2}{5}$ ▨ 0.4
53. 0.75 ▨ $\frac{4}{5}$
54. $\frac{3}{8}$ ▨ 0.25
55. 0.8 ▨ $\frac{5}{6}$

56. **Multi-Step** Peter walked $1\frac{3}{5}$ miles on a treadmill. Sally walked 1.5 miles on the treadmill. Who walked farther? Explain.

4-4 Decimals and Fractions

Order the mixed numbers and decimals from greatest to least.

57. 4.48, 3.92, $4\frac{1}{2}$

58. $10\frac{5}{9}$, 10.5, $10\frac{1}{5}$

59. 125.205, 125.25, $125\frac{1}{5}$

Sports The table shows batting averages for two baseball seasons. Use the table for Exercises 60–62.

Player	Season 1	Season 2
Pedro	0.360	$\frac{3}{10}$
Jill	0.380	$\frac{3}{8}$
Lamar	0.290	$\frac{1}{3}$
Britney	0.190	$\frac{3}{20}$

60. Which players had higher batting averages in season 1 than they had in season 2?

61. Who had the highest batting average in either season?

62. Multi-Step Whose batting average changed the most between season 1 and season 2?

63. Life Science Most people with color deficiency (often called color blindness) have trouble distinguishing shades of red and green. About 0.05 of men in the world have color deficiency. What fraction of men have color deficiency?

64. What's the Error? A student found the decimal equivalent of $\frac{7}{18}$ to be $0.\overline{38}$. Explain the error. What is the correct answer?

People with normal color vision will see "7" in this color-blindness test.

65. Write About It The decimal for $\frac{1}{25}$ is 0.04, and the decimal for $\frac{2}{25}$ is 0.08. Without dividing, find the decimal for $\frac{6}{25}$. Explain how you found your answer.

66. Challenge Write $\frac{1}{999}$ as a decimal.

Test Prep and Spiral Review

67. Multiple Choice Which numbers are listed from least to greatest?

Ⓐ 0.65, 0.81, $\frac{4}{5}$ Ⓑ 0.81, 0.65, $\frac{4}{5}$ Ⓒ $\frac{4}{5}$, 0.81, 0.65   Ⓓ 0.65, $\frac{4}{5}$, 0.81

68. Gridded Response Write $5\frac{1}{8}$ as a decimal.

Find each sum or difference. (Lesson 3-3)

69. 12.56 + 8.91   **70.** 19.05 − 2.27   **71.** 5 + 8.25 + 10.2

Find the GCF of each set of numbers. (Lesson 4-3)

72. 235 and 35   **73.** 28 and 154   **74.** 90 and 56   **75.** 16 and 112

Hands-on LAB 4-5A

Model Equivalent Fractions

Use with Lesson 4-5

Learn It Online
Lab Resources Online go.hrw.com,
keyword MR10 Lab4 Go

KEY

🟡🟡 = 1   🟡 = $\frac{1}{2}$ 🔶 = $\frac{1}{4}$ 🔷 = $\frac{1}{6}$ 🔺 = $\frac{1}{12}$

Pattern blocks can be used to model equivalent fractions. To find a fraction that is equivalent to $\frac{1}{2}$, first choose the pattern block that represents $\frac{1}{2}$. Then find all the pieces of one color that will fit evenly on the $\frac{1}{2}$ block. Count these pieces to find the equivalent fraction. You may be able to find more than one equivalent fraction.

$\frac{1}{2}$ = $\frac{2}{4}$ = $\frac{3}{6}$ = $\frac{6}{12}$

Activity

Use pattern blocks to find an equivalent fraction for $\frac{8}{12}$.

First show $\frac{8}{12}$.

You can cover $\frac{8}{12}$ with four of the $\frac{1}{6}$ pieces.

$\frac{8}{12} = \frac{4}{6}$

Think and Discuss

1. Can you find a combination of pattern blocks for $\frac{1}{3}$? Find an equivalent fraction for $\frac{1}{3}$.

2. Are $\frac{9}{12}$ and $\frac{3}{6}$ equivalent? Use pattern blocks to support your answer.

Try This

Write the fraction that is modeled. Then find an equivalent fraction.

1.

2.

4-5A Hands-On Lab   179

4-5 Equivalent Fractions

Learn to write equivalent fractions.

Vocabulary
equivalent fractions
simplest form

Rulers often have marks for inches, $\frac{1}{2}$, $\frac{1}{4}$, and $\frac{1}{8}$ inches.

Notice that $\frac{1}{2}$ in., $\frac{2}{4}$ in., and $\frac{4}{8}$ in. all name the same length. Fractions that represent the same value are **equivalent fractions**. So $\frac{1}{2}$, $\frac{2}{4}$, and $\frac{4}{8}$ are equivalent fractions.

$$\frac{1}{2} = \frac{2}{4} = \frac{4}{8}$$

EXAMPLE 1 — Finding Equivalent Fractions

Interactivities Online

Find two equivalent fractions for $\frac{6}{8}$.

$$\frac{6}{8} = \frac{9}{12} = \frac{3}{4}$$

The same area is shaded when the rectangle is divided into 8 parts, 12 parts, and 4 parts.

So $\frac{6}{8}$, $\frac{9}{12}$, and $\frac{3}{4}$ are all equivalent fractions.

EXAMPLE 2 — Multiplying and Dividing to Find Equivalent Fractions

Find the missing number that makes the fractions equivalent.

A $\frac{2}{3} = \frac{\square}{18}$

$\frac{2 \cdot 6}{3 \cdot 6} = \frac{12}{18}$

In the denominator, 3 is multiplied by 6 to get 18. Multiply the numerator, 2, by the same number, 6.

So $\frac{2}{3}$ is equivalent to $\frac{12}{18}$.

$$\frac{2}{3} = \frac{12}{18}$$

Chapter 4 Number Theory and Fractions

Find the missing number that makes the fractions equivalent.

B $\dfrac{70}{100} = \dfrac{7}{\square}$

$\dfrac{70 \div 10}{100 \div 10} = \dfrac{7}{10}$ *In the numerator, 70 is divided by 10 to get 7. Divide the denominator by the same number, 10.*

So $\dfrac{70}{100}$ is equivalent to $\dfrac{7}{10}$.

$\dfrac{70}{100} = \dfrac{7}{10}$

Every fraction has one equivalent fraction that is called the simplest form of the fraction. A fraction is in **simplest form** when the GCF of the numerator and the denominator is 1.

Example 3 shows two methods for writing a fraction in simplest form.

EXAMPLE 3   Writing Fractions in Simplest Form

Write each fraction in simplest form.

A $\dfrac{18}{24}$

The GCF of 18 and 24 is 6, so $\dfrac{18}{24}$ is not in simplest form.

Method 1: Use the GCF.

$\dfrac{18 \div 6}{24 \div 6} = \dfrac{3}{4}$ *Divide 18 and 24 by their GCF, 6.*

Method 2: Use prime factorization.

$\dfrac{18}{24} = \dfrac{2 \cdot 3 \cdot 3}{2 \cdot 2 \cdot 2 \cdot 3} = \dfrac{3}{4}$ *Write the prime factors of 18 and 24. Simplify.*

So $\dfrac{18}{24}$ written in simplest form is $\dfrac{3}{4}$.

B $\dfrac{8}{9}$

The GCF of 8 and 9 is 1, so $\dfrac{8}{9}$ is already in simplest form.

Helpful Hint

Method 2 is useful when you know that the numerator and denominator have common factors, but you are not sure what the GCF is.

Think and Discuss

1. **Explain** whether a fraction is equivalent to itself.
2. **Tell** which of the following fractions are in simplest form: $\dfrac{9}{21}$, $\dfrac{20}{25}$, and $\dfrac{5}{13}$. Explain.
3. **Explain** how you know that $\dfrac{7}{16}$ is in simplest form.

4-5 Exercises

Learn It Online
Homework Help Online go.hrw.com,
keyword MR10 4-5
Exercises 1–36, 37, 39, 41, 43, 47

GUIDED PRACTICE

See Example 1 Find two equivalent fractions for each fraction.

1. $\frac{4}{6}$
2. $\frac{3}{12}$
3. $\frac{3}{6}$
4. $\frac{6}{16}$

See Example 2 Find the missing numbers that make the fractions equivalent.

5. $\frac{2}{5} = \frac{10}{\square}$
6. $\frac{7}{21} = \frac{1}{\square}$
7. $\frac{3}{4} = \frac{\square}{28}$
8. $\frac{8}{12} = \frac{\square}{3}$

See Example 3 Write each fraction in simplest form.

9. $\frac{2}{10}$
10. $\frac{6}{18}$
11. $\frac{4}{16}$
12. $\frac{9}{15}$

INDEPENDENT PRACTICE

See Example 1 Find two equivalent fractions for each fraction.

13. $\frac{3}{9}$
14. $\frac{2}{10}$
15. $\frac{3}{21}$
16. $\frac{3}{18}$
17. $\frac{12}{15}$
18. $\frac{4}{10}$
19. $\frac{10}{12}$
20. $\frac{6}{10}$

See Example 2 Find the missing numbers that make the fractions equivalent.

21. $\frac{3}{7} = \frac{\square}{35}$
22. $\frac{6}{48} = \frac{1}{\square}$
23. $\frac{2}{5} = \frac{28}{\square}$
24. $\frac{12}{18} = \frac{\square}{3}$
25. $\frac{2}{7} = \frac{\square}{21}$
26. $\frac{8}{32} = \frac{\square}{4}$
27. $\frac{2}{7} = \frac{40}{\square}$
28. $\frac{3}{5} = \frac{21}{\square}$

See Example 3 Write each fraction in simplest form.

29. $\frac{2}{8}$
30. $\frac{10}{15}$
31. $\frac{6}{30}$
32. $\frac{6}{14}$
33. $\frac{12}{16}$
34. $\frac{4}{28}$
35. $\frac{4}{8}$
36. $\frac{10}{35}$

PRACTICE AND PROBLEM SOLVING

Extra Practice
See page EP7.

Write the equivalent fractions represented by each picture.

37.

38.

39.

40.

Write each fraction in simplest form. Show two ways to simplify.

41. $\frac{10}{40}$
42. $\frac{4}{52}$
43. $\frac{28}{70}$
44. $\frac{112}{220}$

182 Chapter 4 Number Theory and Fractions

Social Studies LINK

The Old City Market is a public market in Charleston, South Carolina. Local artists, craftspeople, and vendors display and sell their goods in open-sided booths.

45. You can buy food, such as southern sesame seed cookies, at $\frac{1}{10}$ of the booths. Write two equivalent fractions for $\frac{1}{10}$.

46. Handwoven sweetgrass baskets are a regional specialty. About 8 out of every 10 baskets sold are woven at the market. Write a fraction for "8 out of 10." Then write this fraction in simplest form.

47. Suppose the circle graph shows the number of each kind of craft booth at the Old City Market. For each type of booth, tell what fraction it represents of the total number of craft booths. Write these fractions in simplest form.

Craft Booth Types
- Baskets & wreaths 12
- Paintings 12
- Glass & pottery 16
- Jewelry 32

48. Customers can buy packages of dried rice and black-eyed peas, which can be made into black-eyed pea soup. One recipe for black-eyed pea soup calls for $\frac{1}{2}$ tsp of basil. How could you measure the basil if you had only a $\frac{1}{4}$ tsp measuring spoon? What if you had only a $\frac{1}{8}$ tsp measuring spoon?

49. 🖊 **Write About It** The recipe for soup also calls for $\frac{1}{4}$ tsp of pepper. How many fractions are equivalent to $\frac{1}{4}$? Explain.

50. ⭐ **Challenge** Silver jewelry is a popular item at the market. Suppose there are 28 bracelets at one jeweler's booth and that $\frac{3}{7}$ of these bracelets have red stones. How many bracelets have red stones?

Test Prep and Spiral Review

51. Multiple Choice Which fraction is NOT equivalent to $\frac{1}{6}$?

 Ⓐ $\frac{2}{12}$ Ⓑ $\frac{6}{1}$ Ⓒ $\frac{3}{18}$ Ⓓ $\frac{6}{36}$

52. Multiple Choice Which denominator makes the fractions $\frac{7}{28}$ and $\frac{21}{\blacksquare}$ equivalent?

 Ⓕ 3   Ⓖ 4   Ⓗ 84   Ⓙ 112

Solve each equation. Check your answer. (Lesson 2-7)

53. $\frac{x}{3} = 15$ **54.** $8 = \frac{h}{8}$ **55.** $\frac{w}{2} = 9$ **56.** $\frac{p}{5} = 10$

Write each fraction or mixed number as a decimal. (Lesson 4-4)

57. $\frac{2}{3}$ **58.** $\frac{7}{8}$ **59.** $3\frac{1}{5}$ **60.** $2\frac{9}{16}$

Hands-on LAB 4-5B

Explore Fraction Measurement

Use with Lesson 4-5

Learn It Online
Lab Resources Online go.hrw.com,
keyword MR10 Lab4 Go

Look at a standard ruler. It probably has marks for inches, half inches, quarter inches, eighth inches, and sixteenth inches.

In this activity, you will make some of your own rulers and use them to help you find and understand equivalent fractions.

Activity

1 You will need four strips of paper. On one strip, use your ruler to make a mark for every half inch. Number each mark, beginning with 0. Label this strip "half-inch ruler."

0 1 2 3 4 5 6 7 8
$\frac{1}{2}$-inch ruler

On a second strip, make a mark for every quarter inch. Again, number each mark, beginning with 0. Label this strip "quarter-inch ruler."

0 1 2 3 4 5 6 7 8 9 10 11 12 13 14 15 16
$\frac{1}{4}$-inch ruler

Do the same thing for eighth inches and sixteenth inches.

0 2 4 6 8 10 12 14 16 18 20 22 24 26 28 30 32
$\frac{1}{8}$-inch ruler

0 4 8 12 16 20 24 28 32 36 40 44 48 52 56 60 64
$\frac{1}{16}$-inch ruler

184 Chapter 4 Number Theory and Fractions

2 Now use the half-inch ruler you made to measure the green line segment at right. How many half inches long is the segment?

Use your quarter-inch ruler to measure the line segment again. How many quarter inches long is the segment?

How many eighth inches long is the segment?

How many sixteenth inches?

Fill in the blanks: $\dfrac{1}{2} = \dfrac{\Box}{4} = \dfrac{\Box}{8} = \dfrac{\Box}{16}$.

3 Use your quarter-inch ruler to measure the green line segment below.

How long is the segment?

Now use your eighth-inch ruler to measure the line segment again. How many eighth inches long is the segment?

How many sixteenth inches?

Fill in the blanks: $\dfrac{3}{4} = \dfrac{\Box}{8} = \dfrac{\Box}{16}$.

Think and Discuss

1. How does a ruler show that equivalent fractions have the same value?

2. Look at your lists of equivalent fractions from **2** and **3**. Do you notice any patterns? Describe them.

3. Use your rulers to measure an object longer than 1 inch. Use your measurements to write equivalent fractions. What do you notice about these fractions?

Try This

1. Use your rulers to measure the length of the items below. Use your measurements to write equivalent fractions.

2. Use your rulers to measure several items in your classroom. Use your measurements to write equivalent fractions.

4-5B Hands-On Lab

4-6 Mixed Numbers and Improper Fractions

Learn to convert between mixed numbers and improper fractions.

Vocabulary
improper fraction
proper fraction

Reading Math
$\frac{11}{4}$ is read as "eleven-fourths."

Have you ever witnessed a total eclipse of the sun? It occurs when the sun's light is completely blocked out. A total eclipse is rare—only three have been visible in the continental United States since 1963.

The graph shows that the eclipse in 2017 will last $2\frac{3}{4}$ minutes. There are eleven $\frac{1}{4}$-minute sections, so $2\frac{3}{4} = \frac{11}{4}$.

An **improper fraction** is a fraction in which the numerator is greater than or equal to the denominator, such as $\frac{11}{4}$.

Approximate Length of U.S. Total Solar Eclipses

Year	
1963	
1970	
1979	
2017	

= $\frac{1}{4}$ minute

Whole numbers can be written as improper fractions. The whole number is the numerator, and the denominator is 1. For example, $7 = \frac{7}{1}$.

Interactivities Online ▶

When the numerator is less than the denominator, the fraction is called a **proper fraction**.

Improper and Proper Fractions

Improper Fractions
- Numerator equals denominator → fraction is equal to 1 $\frac{3}{3} = 1$ $\frac{102}{102} = 1$
- Numerator greater than denominator → fraction is greater than 1 $\frac{9}{5} > 1$ $\frac{13}{1} > 1$

Proper Fractions
- Numerator less than denominator → fraction is less than 1 $\frac{2}{5} < 1$ $\frac{102}{351} < 1$

You can write an improper fraction as a mixed number.

EXAMPLE 1 Astronomy Application

The longest total solar eclipse in the next 200 years will take place in 2186. It will last about $\frac{15}{2}$ minutes. Write $\frac{15}{2}$ as a mixed number.

Method 1: Use a model.
Draw squares divided into half sections. Shade 15 of the half sections.

There are 7 whole squares and 1 half square, or $7\frac{1}{2}$ squares, shaded.

186   Chapter 4 Number Theory and Fractions   Video Lesson Tutorials Online   my.hrw.com

Method 2: Use division.

$$2\overline{)15}^{\,7\frac{1}{2}}$$
$$\underline{-14}$$
$$1$$

Divide the numerator by the denominator.

To form the fraction part of the quotient, use the remainder as the numerator and the divisor as the denominator.

The 2186 eclipse will last about $7\frac{1}{2}$ minutes.

Mixed numbers can be written as improper fractions.

EXAMPLE 2 Writing Mixed Numbers as Improper Fractions

Write $2\frac{1}{5}$ as an improper fraction.

Method 1: Use a model.

You can draw a diagram to illustrate the whole and fractional parts.

There are 11 fifths, or $\frac{11}{5}$.   *Count the fifths in the diagram.*

Method 2: Use multiplication and addition.

When you are changing a mixed number to an improper fraction, spiral clockwise as shown in the picture. The order of operations will help you remember to multiply before you add.

Then add.

First multiply.

$2\frac{1}{5} = \frac{(5 \cdot 2) + 1}{5}$ *Multiply the whole number by the denominator and add the numerator. Keep the same denominator.*

$= \frac{10 + 1}{5}$

$= \frac{11}{5}$

Think and Discuss

1. **Read** each improper fraction: $\frac{10}{7}, \frac{25}{9}, \frac{31}{16}$.
2. **Tell** whether each fraction is less than 1, equal to 1, or greater than 1: $\frac{21}{21}, \frac{54}{103}, \frac{9}{11}, \frac{7}{3}$.
3. **Explain** why any mixed number written as a fraction will be improper.

4-6 Exercises

GUIDED PRACTICE

See Example 1
1. The fifth largest meteorite found in the United States is named the Navajo. The Navajo weighs $\frac{12}{5}$ tons. Write $\frac{12}{5}$ as a mixed number.

See Example 2 Write each mixed number as an improper fraction.
2. $1\frac{1}{4}$
3. $2\frac{2}{3}$
4. $1\frac{2}{7}$
5. $2\frac{2}{5}$

INDEPENDENT PRACTICE

See Example 1
6. **Astronomy** Saturn is the sixth planet from the Sun. It takes Saturn $\frac{59}{2}$ years to revolve around the Sun. Write $\frac{59}{2}$ as a mixed number.

7. **Astronomy** Pluto has low surface gravity. A person who weighs 143 pounds on Earth weighs $\frac{43}{5}$ pounds on Pluto. Write $\frac{43}{5}$ as a mixed number.

See Example 2 Write each mixed number as an improper fraction.
8. $1\frac{3}{5}$
9. $2\frac{2}{9}$
10. $3\frac{1}{7}$
11. $4\frac{1}{3}$
12. $2\frac{3}{8}$
13. $4\frac{1}{6}$
14. $1\frac{4}{9}$
15. $3\frac{4}{5}$

PRACTICE AND PROBLEM SOLVING

Extra Practice See page EP8.

Write each improper fraction as a mixed number or whole number. Tell whether your answer is a mixed number or whole number.
16. $\frac{21}{4}$
17. $\frac{32}{8}$
18. $\frac{20}{3}$
19. $\frac{43}{5}$
20. $\frac{108}{9}$
21. $\frac{87}{10}$
22. $\frac{98}{11}$
23. $\frac{105}{7}$

Write each mixed number as an improper fraction.
24. $9\frac{1}{4}$
25. $4\frac{9}{11}$
26. $11\frac{4}{9}$
27. $18\frac{3}{5}$

28. **Measurement** The actual dimensions of a piece of lumber called a 2-by-4 are $1\frac{1}{2}$ inches and $3\frac{1}{2}$ inches. Write these numbers as improper fractions.

Replace each shape with a number that will make the equation correct.
29. $\blacksquare \frac{2}{5} = \frac{17}{\bullet}$
30. $\blacksquare \frac{6}{11} = \frac{83}{\bullet}$
31. $\blacksquare \frac{1}{9} = \frac{118}{\bullet}$
32. $\blacksquare \frac{6}{7} = \frac{55}{\bullet}$
33. $\blacksquare \frac{9}{10} = \frac{29}{\bullet}$
34. $\blacksquare \frac{1}{3} = \frac{55}{\bullet}$

35. Daniel is a costume designer for movies and music videos. He recently purchased $\frac{256}{9}$ yards of metallic fabric for space-suit costumes. Write a mixed number to represent the number of yards of fabric Daniel purchased.

Write the improper fraction as a decimal. Then use <, >, or = to compare.
36. $\frac{7}{5}$ ■ 1.8
37. 6.875 ■ $\frac{55}{8}$
38. $\frac{27}{2}$ ■ 13
39. $\frac{20}{5}$ ■ 4.25

188 Chapter 4 Number Theory and Fractions

Life Science The table lists the lengths of the longest bones in the human body. Use the table for Exercises 40–42.

Longest Human Bones	
Fibula (outer lower leg)	$\frac{81}{2}$ cm
Ulna (inner lower arm)	$28\frac{1}{5}$ cm
Femur (upper leg)	$\frac{101}{2}$ cm
Humerus (upper arm)	$36\frac{1}{2}$ cm
Tibia (inner lower leg)	43 cm

40. Write the length of the ulna as an improper fraction. Then do the same for the length of the humerus.

41. Write the length of the fibula as a mixed number. Then do the same for the length of the femur.

42. Use the mixed-number form of each length. Compare the whole-number part of each length to write the bones in order from longest to shortest.

X-rays are used to produce images of bones.

43. **Social Studies** The European country of Monaco, with an area of only $1\frac{4}{5}$ km², is one of the smallest countries in the world. Write $1\frac{4}{5}$ as an improper fraction.

44. For a disc to be approved by the Professional Disc Golf Association, it must not weigh more than $8\frac{3}{10}$ gram for each centimeter of its diameter. Write $8\frac{3}{10}$ as an improper fraction.

45. **What's the Question?** The lengths of Victor's three favorite movies are $\frac{11}{4}$ hours, $\frac{9}{4}$ hours, and $\frac{7}{4}$ hours. The answer is $2\frac{1}{4}$ hours. What is the question?

46. **Write About It** Draw models representing $\frac{4}{4}$, $\frac{5}{5}$, and $\frac{9}{9}$. Use your models to explain why a fraction whose numerator is the same as its denominator is equal to 1.

47. **Challenge** Write $\frac{65}{12}$ as a decimal.

Test Prep and Spiral Review

48. **Multiple Choice** What is $3\frac{2}{11}$ written as an improper fraction?

   Ⓐ $\frac{35}{11}$ Ⓑ $\frac{35}{3}$ Ⓒ $\frac{33}{22}$ Ⓓ $\frac{70}{11}$

49. **Multiple Choice** It takes $\frac{24}{5}$ new pencils placed end to end to be the same length as one yardstick. What is this improper fraction written as a mixed number?

   Ⓕ $3\frac{4}{5}$ Ⓖ $4\frac{1}{4}$ Ⓗ $4\frac{1}{5}$ Ⓙ $4\frac{4}{5}$

Order the numbers from least to greatest. (Previous Course)

50. 1,497; 2,560; 1,038
51. 10,462; 9,198; 11,320
52. 4,706; 11,765; 1,765

Estimate a range for each sum. (Lesson 3-2)

53. 19.85 + 6.7 + 12.4
54. 2.456 + 8.3 + 11.05
55. 15.36 + 10.75 + 6.1

List all the factors of each number. (Lesson 4-2)

56. 57
57. 36
58. 54

4-6 Mixed Numbers and Improper Fractions 189

Ready To Go On?

Quiz for Lessons 4-4 Through 4-6

4-4 Decimals and Fractions

Write each decimal as a fraction.

1. 0.67
2. 0.9
3. 0.43

Write each fraction as a decimal.

4. $\frac{2}{5}$
5. $\frac{1}{6}$
6. $\frac{3}{4}$

Compare. Write <, >, or =.

7. $\frac{7}{10}$ ■ 0.9
8. 0.4 ■ $\frac{2}{5}$
9. $\frac{3}{5}$ ■ 0.5

10. Jamal got $\frac{4}{5}$ of the questions correct on his quiz. Dominic got 0.75 of the questions correct. Who got more questions correct?

4-5 Equivalent Fractions

Write two equivalent fractions for each fraction.

11. $\frac{9}{12}$
12. $\frac{18}{42}$
13. $\frac{25}{30}$

Write each fraction in simplest form.

14. $\frac{20}{24}$
15. $\frac{14}{49}$
16. $\frac{12}{28}$

17. Mandy ate $\frac{1}{6}$ of a pizza. Write two equivalent fractions for $\frac{1}{6}$.

18. Liane is making fruit salad. The recipe calls for $\frac{1}{2}$ cup shredded coconut. Liane has only a $\frac{1}{4}$-cup measure. How can she measure the correct $\frac{1}{2}$-cup amount?

4-6 Mixed Numbers and Improper Fractions

Replace each shape with a number that will make the equation correct.

19. ■$\frac{2}{7}$ = $\frac{9}{●}$
20. $6\frac{■}{8}$ = $\frac{49}{●}$
21. ■$\frac{4}{9}$ = $\frac{157}{●}$

Use the table for Exercises 22–24.

22. Write the lengths of *1900* and *Empire* as mixed numbers in simplest form.

23. Write the lengths of *Fanny and Alexander* and *War and Peace* as improper fractions.

24. Write the movies in order from longest to shortest.

25. The proboscis bat, with a length of $\frac{19}{5}$ cm, is one of the smallest bats. Write $\frac{19}{5}$ as a mixed number.

World's Longest Movies	
Title	Length (h)
1900	$\frac{318}{60}$
Empire	$\frac{480}{60}$
Fanny and Alexander	$5\frac{1}{5}$
War and Peace	$8\frac{31}{60}$

Focus on Problem Solving

Understand the Problem

• Write the problem in your own words

One way to understand a problem better is to write it in your own words. Before you do this, you may need to read it over several times, perhaps aloud so that you can hear yourself say the words.

When you write a problem in your own words, try to make the problem simpler. Use smaller words and shorter sentences. Leave out any extra information, but make sure to include all the information you need to answer the question.

Write each problem in your own words. Check that you have included all the information you need to answer the question.

1 Martin is making muffins for his class bake sale. The recipe calls for $2\frac{1}{3}$ cups of flour, but Martin's only measuring cup holds $\frac{1}{3}$ cup. How many of his measuring cups should he use?

2 Mariko sold an old book to a used bookstore. She had hoped to sell it for $0.80, but the store gave her $\frac{3}{4}$ of a dollar. What is the difference between the two amounts?

3 Koalas of eastern Australia feed mostly on eucalyptus leaves. They select certain trees over others to find the $1\frac{1}{4}$ pounds of food they need each day. Suppose a koala has eaten $1\frac{1}{8}$ pounds of food. Has the koala eaten enough food for the day?

4 The first day of the Tour de France is called the prologue. Each of the days after that is called a stage, and each stage covers a different distance. The total distance covered in the race is about 3,600 km. If a cyclist has completed $\frac{1}{3}$ of the race, how many kilometers has he ridden?

Focus on Problem Solving

4-7 Comparing and Ordering Fractions

Learn to use pictures and number lines to compare and order fractions.

Vocabulary
like fractions
unlike fractions
common denominator

Rachel and Hannah are making a kind of dumpling called a *potsticker*. They have $\frac{1}{2}$ cup of green onion, but the recipe requires $\frac{1}{3}$ cup.

To determine if they have enough for the recipe, they need to compare the fractions $\frac{1}{2}$ and $\frac{1}{3}$.

Potstickers
3/4 cup ground pork
1 1/2 cup chopped cabbage
1/3 cup chopped green onion
1 tablespoon minced garlic
2 tablespoons minced ginger
1/2 cup soy sauce
48 dumpling wrappers

When you are comparing fractions, first check their denominators. When fractions have the same denominator, they are called **like fractions**. For example, $\frac{1}{8}$ and $\frac{5}{8}$ are like fractions. When two fractions have different denominators, they are called **unlike fractions**. For example, $\frac{7}{10}$ and $\frac{1}{2}$ are unlike fractions.

EXAMPLE 1 Comparing Fractions

Compare. Write <, >, or =.

Helpful Hint
When two fractions have the same denominator, the one with the larger numerator is greater.
$\frac{2}{5} < \frac{3}{5}$ $\frac{3}{8} > \frac{1}{8}$

A $\frac{1}{8}$ ☐ $\frac{5}{8}$

Model $\frac{1}{8}$ and $\frac{5}{8}$.

From the model, $\frac{1}{8} < \frac{5}{8}$.

B $\frac{7}{10}$ ☐ $\frac{1}{2}$

Model $\frac{7}{10}$ and $\frac{1}{2}$.

From the model, $\frac{7}{10} > \frac{1}{2}$.

Chapter 4 Number Theory and Fractions

Video Lesson Tutorials Online   my.hrw.com

To compare unlike fractions without models, first rename the fractions so they have the same denominator. This is called finding a **common denominator**. This method can be used to compare mixed numbers as well.

EXAMPLE 2 Cooking Application

Rachel and Hannah have $1\frac{2}{3}$ cups of cabbage. They need $1\frac{1}{2}$ cups to make potstickers. Do they have enough for the recipe?

Compare $1\frac{2}{3}$ and $1\frac{1}{2}$.

Compare the whole-number parts of the numbers.
$1 = 1$ The whole-number parts are equal.

Compare the fractional parts. Find a common denominator by multiplying the denominators. $2 \cdot 3 = 6$

Find equivalent fractions with 6 as the denominator.

$$\frac{2}{3} = \frac{\square}{6} \qquad\qquad \frac{1}{2} = \frac{\square}{6}$$

$$\frac{2 \cdot 2}{3 \cdot 2} = \frac{4}{6} \qquad\qquad \frac{1 \cdot 3}{2 \cdot 3} = \frac{3}{6}$$

$$\frac{2}{3} = \frac{4}{6} \qquad\qquad \frac{1}{2} = \frac{3}{6}$$

Compare the like fractions. $\frac{4}{6} > \frac{3}{6}$, so $\frac{2}{3} > \frac{1}{2}$.

Therefore, $1\frac{2}{3}$ is greater than $1\frac{1}{2}$.

Since $1\frac{2}{3}$ cups is more than $1\frac{1}{2}$ cups, they have enough cabbage.

EXAMPLE 3 Ordering Fractions

Order $\frac{3}{7}$, $\frac{3}{4}$, and $\frac{1}{4}$ from least to greatest.

$$\frac{3 \cdot 4}{7 \cdot 4} = \frac{12}{28} \qquad \frac{3 \cdot 7}{4 \cdot 7} = \frac{21}{28} \qquad \frac{1 \cdot 7}{4 \cdot 7} = \frac{7}{28}$$

Rename with like denominators.

Remember!
Numbers increase in value as you move from left to right on a number line.

The fractions in order from least to greatest are $\frac{1}{4}, \frac{3}{7}, \frac{3}{4}$.

Think and Discuss

1. **Tell** whether the values of the fractions change when you rename two fractions so that they have common denominators.

2. **Explain** how to compare $\frac{2}{5}$ and $\frac{4}{5}$.

4-7 Exercises

Learn It Online
Homework Help Online go.hrw.com,
keyword MR10 4-7
Exercises 1–26, 27, 29, 39, 41, 43, 45, 47

GUIDED PRACTICE

See Example 1 Compare. Write <, >, or =.

1. $\frac{3}{5}$ ▪ $\frac{2}{5}$
2. $\frac{1}{9}$ ▪ $\frac{2}{9}$
3. $\frac{6}{8}$ ▪ $\frac{3}{4}$
4. $\frac{3}{7}$ ▪ $\frac{6}{7}$

See Example 2

5. Arsenio has $\frac{2}{3}$ cup of brown sugar. The recipe he is using requires $\frac{1}{4}$ cup of brown sugar. Does he have enough brown sugar for the recipe? Explain.

See Example 3 Order the fractions from least to greatest.

6. $\frac{3}{8}, \frac{1}{5}, \frac{2}{3}$
7. $\frac{1}{4}, \frac{2}{5}, \frac{1}{3}$
8. $\frac{5}{9}, \frac{1}{8}, \frac{2}{7}$
9. $\frac{1}{2}, \frac{1}{6}, \frac{2}{3}$

INDEPENDENT PRACTICE

See Example 1 Compare. Write <, >, or =.

10. $\frac{2}{5}$ ▪ $\frac{4}{5}$
11. $\frac{1}{10}$ ▪ $\frac{3}{10}$
12. $\frac{3}{4}$ ▪ $\frac{3}{8}$
13. $\frac{5}{6}$ ▪ $\frac{4}{6}$
14. $\frac{4}{5}$ ▪ $\frac{5}{5}$
15. $\frac{2}{4}$ ▪ $\frac{1}{2}$
16. $\frac{4}{8}$ ▪ $\frac{16}{24}$
17. $\frac{11}{16}$ ▪ $\frac{9}{16}$

See Example 2

18. Kelly needs $\frac{2}{3}$ gallon of paint to finish painting her deck. She has $\frac{5}{8}$ gallon of paint. Does she have enough paint to finish her deck? Explain.

See Example 3 Order the fractions from least to greatest.

19. $\frac{1}{2}, \frac{3}{5}, \frac{3}{7}$
20. $\frac{1}{6}, \frac{2}{5}, \frac{1}{4}$
21. $\frac{4}{9}, \frac{3}{8}, \frac{1}{3}$
22. $\frac{1}{4}, \frac{5}{6}, \frac{5}{9}$
23. $\frac{3}{4}, \frac{7}{10}, \frac{2}{3}$
24. $\frac{13}{18}, \frac{5}{9}, \frac{5}{6}$
25. $\frac{3}{8}, \frac{1}{4}, \frac{2}{3}$
26. $\frac{3}{10}, \frac{2}{3}, \frac{5}{11}$

PRACTICE AND PROBLEM SOLVING

Extra Practice
See page EP8.

Compare. Write <, >, or =.

27. $\frac{4}{15}$ ▪ $\frac{3}{10}$
28. $\frac{7}{12}$ ▪ $\frac{13}{30}$
29. $\frac{5}{9}$ ▪ $\frac{4}{11}$
30. $\frac{8}{14}$ ▪ $\frac{8}{9}$
31. $\frac{3}{5}$ ▪ $\frac{26}{65}$
32. $\frac{3}{5}$ ▪ $\frac{2}{21}$
33. $\frac{24}{41}$ ▪ $\frac{2}{7}$
34. $\frac{10}{38}$ ▪ $\frac{1}{4}$

Order the fractions from least to greatest.

35. $\frac{2}{5}, \frac{1}{2}, \frac{3}{10}$
36. $\frac{3}{4}, \frac{3}{5}, \frac{7}{10}$
37. $\frac{7}{15}, \frac{2}{3}, \frac{1}{5}$
38. $\frac{3}{4}, \frac{1}{3}, \frac{8}{15}$
39. $\frac{2}{5}, \frac{4}{9}, \frac{11}{15}$
40. $\frac{7}{12}, \frac{5}{8}, \frac{1}{2}$
41. $\frac{5}{8}, \frac{3}{4}, \frac{5}{12}$
42. $\frac{2}{3}, \frac{7}{8}, \frac{7}{15}$

43. Laura and Kim receive the same amount of allowance each week. Laura spends $\frac{3}{5}$ of it on going to the movies. Kim spends $\frac{4}{7}$ of it on a CD. Which girl spent more of her allowance? Explain.

44. Kyle operates a hot dog cart in a large city. He spends $\frac{2}{5}$ of his budget on supplies, $\frac{1}{12}$ on advertising, and $\frac{2}{25}$ on taxes and fees. Does Kyle spend more on advertising or more on taxes and fees?

194 Chapter 4 Number Theory and Fractions

Agriculture

Order the numbers from least to greatest.

45. $1\frac{2}{5}, 1\frac{1}{8}, 3\frac{4}{5}, 3, 3\frac{2}{5}$

46. $7\frac{1}{2}, 9\frac{4}{7}, 9\frac{1}{2}, 8, 8\frac{3}{4}$

47. $\frac{1}{2}, 3\frac{1}{5}, 3\frac{1}{10}, \frac{3}{4}, 3\frac{1}{15}$

48. $2\frac{1}{5}, 2\frac{5}{6}, 1\frac{1}{4}, 2, \frac{7}{8}$

49. $4\frac{3}{4}, 5, 3\frac{5}{7}, 4\frac{2}{3}, 5\frac{1}{3}$

50. $6\frac{1}{3}, 5\frac{1}{4}, 5\frac{7}{8}, 6, 5\frac{1}{2}$

51. **Agriculture** The table shows the fraction of the world's total corn each country produces.

   a. List the countries in order from the country that produces the most corn to the country that produces the least corn.

World's Corn Production	
United States	$\frac{39}{100}$
China	$\frac{1}{5}$
Canada	$\frac{7}{500}$

   b. Brazil produces $\frac{1}{10}$ of the world's corn. Tell whether Brazil's corn production is more than or less than Canada's corn production.

There are over 3,500 different uses for corn products, from ethanol fuel and industrial products to the household items you see above.

52. **Multi-Step** The Dixon Dragons must win at least $\frac{3}{7}$ of their remaining games to qualify for their district playoffs. If they have 15 games left and they win 7 of them, will the Dragons compete in the playoffs? Explain.

53. **Write a Problem** Write a problem that involves comparing two fractions with different denominators.

54. **Write About It** Compare the fractions below. What do you notice about two fractions that have the same numerator but different denominators? Which one is greater?

   $\frac{1}{2} \blacksquare \frac{1}{4}$ $\frac{2}{3} \blacksquare \frac{2}{5}$ $\frac{3}{4} \blacksquare \frac{3}{7}$ $\frac{4}{5} \blacksquare \frac{4}{9}$

55. **Challenge** Name a fraction that would make the inequality true.

   $\frac{1}{4} > \blacksquare > \frac{1}{5}$

Test Prep and Spiral Review

56. **Multiple Choice** Which fraction has the least value?

   Ⓐ $\frac{1}{5}$ Ⓑ $\frac{3}{11}$ Ⓒ $\frac{2}{15}$ Ⓓ $\frac{4}{18}$

57. **Extended Response** Kevin is making potato soup. The recipe shows that he needs $\frac{1}{2}$ gallon of milk and 3.5 pounds of potatoes. He has $\frac{2}{5}$ gallon of milk and $\frac{21}{5}$ pounds of potatoes. Does Kevin have enough milk and potatoes to make the soup? Show your work and explain your answer.

Write each number in scientific notation. (Lesson 3-4)

58. 45   59. 405,000   60. 1,600,000   61. 23,000,000

Write each fraction in simplest form. (Lesson 4-5)

62. $\frac{3}{36}$ 63. $\frac{4}{42}$ 64. $\frac{6}{20}$ 65. $\frac{12}{30}$ 66. $\frac{5}{55}$

4-8 Adding and Subtracting with Like Denominators

Learn to add and subtract fractions with like denominators.

You can estimate the age of an oak tree by measuring around the trunk at four feet above the ground.

The distance around a young oak tree's trunk increases at a rate of approximately $\frac{1}{8}$ inch per month.

EXAMPLE 1   Life Science Application

Sophie plants a young oak tree in her backyard. The distance around the trunk grows at a rate of $\frac{1}{8}$ inch per month. Use pictures to model how much this distance will increase in two months, then write your answer in simplest form.

$\frac{1}{8} + \frac{1}{8}$

$\frac{1}{8} + \frac{1}{8} = \frac{2}{8}$ Add the numerators. Keep the same denominator.

$= \frac{1}{4}$ Write your answer in simplest form.

The distance around the trunk will increase by $\frac{1}{4}$ inch.

EXAMPLE 2   Subtracting Like Fractions and Mixed Numbers

Subtract. Write each answer in simplest form.

A $1 - \frac{2}{3}$

$\frac{3}{3} - \frac{2}{3} = \frac{1}{3}$ To get a common denominator, rewrite 1 as a fraction with a denominator of 3.
Subtract the numerators. Keep the same denominator.

Check

Remember!
When the numerator equals the denominator, the fraction is equal to 1.
$\frac{3}{3} = 1$ $\frac{173}{173} = 1$

Chapter 4 Number Theory and Fractions

Subtract. Write each answer in simplest form.

B $3\frac{7}{12} - 1\frac{1}{12}$

$3\frac{7}{12} - 1\frac{1}{12}$ *Subtract the fractions. Then subtract the whole numbers.*

$2\frac{6}{12}$

$2\frac{1}{2}$ *Write your answer in simplest form.*

Check

EXAMPLE 3 Evaluating Expressions with Fractions

Evaluate each expression for $x = \frac{3}{8}$. Write each answer in simplest form.

A $\frac{5}{8} - x$

$\frac{5}{8} - x$ *Write the expression.*

$\frac{5}{8} - \frac{3}{8} = \frac{2}{8}$ *Substitute $\frac{3}{8}$ for x and subtract the numerators. Keep the same denominator.*

$= \frac{1}{4}$ *Write your answer in simplest form.*

Helpful Hint

When adding a fraction to a mixed number, you can think of the fraction as having a whole number of 0.
$\frac{3}{8} = 0\frac{3}{8}$

B $x + 1\frac{1}{8}$

$x + 1\frac{1}{8}$ *Write the expression.*

$\frac{3}{8} + 1\frac{1}{8} = 1\frac{4}{8}$ *Substitute $\frac{3}{8}$ for x. Add the fractions. Then add the whole numbers.*

$= 1\frac{1}{2}$ *Write your answer in simplest form.*

C $x + \frac{7}{8}$

$x + \frac{7}{8}$ *Write the expression.*

$\frac{3}{8} + \frac{7}{8} = \frac{10}{8}$ *Substitute $\frac{3}{8}$ for x and add the numerators. Keep the same denominator.*

$= \frac{5}{4}$ or $1\frac{1}{4}$ *Write your answer in simplest form.*

Think and Discuss

1. **Explain** how to add or subtract like fractions.
2. **Tell** why the sum of $\frac{1}{5}$ and $\frac{3}{5}$ is not $\frac{4}{10}$. Give the correct sum.
3. **Describe** how you would add $2\frac{3}{8}$ and $1\frac{1}{8}$. How would you subtract $1\frac{1}{8}$ from $2\frac{3}{8}$?

4-8 Exercises

Learn It Online
Homework Help Online go.hrw.com,
keyword MR10 4-8 Go
Exercises 1–18, 23, 25, 27, 31, 33, 39

GUIDED PRACTICE

See Example 1
1. Marta is filling a bucket with water. The height of the water is increasing $\frac{1}{6}$ foot each minute. Use pictures to model how much the height of the water will change in three minutes, and then write your answer in simplest form.

See Example 2
Subtract. Write each answer in simplest form.
2. $2 - \frac{3}{5}$
3. $8 - \frac{6}{7}$
4. $4\frac{2}{3} - 1\frac{1}{3}$
5. $8\frac{7}{12} - 3\frac{5}{12}$

See Example 3
Evaluate each expression for $x = \frac{3}{10}$. Write each answer in simplest form.
6. $\frac{9}{10} - x$
7. $x + \frac{1}{10}$
8. $x + \frac{9}{10}$
9. $x - \frac{1}{10}$

INDEPENDENT PRACTICE

See Example 1
10. Wesley drinks $\frac{2}{13}$ gallon of juice each day. Use pictures to model the number of gallons of juice Wesley drinks in 5 days, and then write your answer in simplest form.

See Example 2
Subtract. Write each answer in simplest form.
11. $1 - \frac{5}{7}$
12. $1 - \frac{3}{8}$
13. $2\frac{4}{5} - 1\frac{1}{5}$
14. $9\frac{9}{14} - 5\frac{3}{14}$

See Example 3
Evaluate each expression for $x = \frac{11}{20}$. Write each answer in simplest form.
15. $x + \frac{13}{20}$
16. $x - \frac{3}{20}$
17. $x - \frac{9}{20}$
18. $x + \frac{17}{20}$

PRACTICE AND PROBLEM SOLVING

Extra Practice
See page EP8.

Write each sum or difference in simplest form.
19. $\frac{1}{16} + \frac{9}{16}$
20. $\frac{15}{26} - \frac{11}{26}$
21. $\frac{10}{33} + \frac{4}{33}$
22. $1 - \frac{9}{10}$
23. $\frac{26}{75} + \frac{24}{75}$
24. $\frac{100}{999} + \frac{899}{999}$
25. $37\frac{13}{18} - 24\frac{7}{18}$
26. $\frac{1}{20} + \frac{7}{20} + \frac{3}{20}$
27. $\frac{11}{24} + \frac{1}{24} + \frac{5}{24}$

28. Lily took $\frac{5}{6}$ lb of peanuts to a baseball game. She ate $\frac{2}{6}$ lb. How many pounds of peanuts does she have left? Write the answer in simplest form.

Evaluate. Write each answer in simplest form.
29. $a + \frac{7}{18}$ for $a = \frac{1}{18}$
30. $\frac{6}{13} - j$ for $j = \frac{4}{13}$
31. $c + c$ for $c = \frac{5}{14}$
32. $m - \frac{6}{17}$ for $m = 1$
33. $8\frac{14}{15} - z$ for $z = \frac{4}{15}$
34. $13\frac{1}{24} + y$ for $y = 2\frac{5}{24}$

35. Sheila spent x hour studying on Tuesday and $\frac{1}{4}$ hour studying on Thursday. What was the total amount of time in hours Sheila spent studying if $x = \frac{2}{4}$?

198 Chapter 4 Number Theory and Fractions

Life Science

Bamboo is a type of grass that grows very fast; some species can grow 1 meter per day. Because bamboo is a renewable resource, it is an environmentally friendly building material.

36. Carlos had 7 cups of chocolate chips. He used $1\frac{2}{3}$ cups to make a chocolate sauce and $3\frac{1}{3}$ cups to make cookies. How many cups of chocolate chips does Carlos have now?

37. A concert was $2\frac{1}{4}$ hr long. The first musical piece lasted $\frac{1}{4}$ hr. The intermission also lasted $\frac{1}{4}$ hr. How long was the rest of the concert?

38. A flight from Washington, D.C., stops in San Francisco and then continues to Seattle. The trip to San Francisco takes $4\frac{5}{8}$ hr. The trip to Seattle takes $1\frac{1}{8}$ hr. What is the total flight time?

Life Science Use the graph for Exercises 39–41. Sheila performed an experiment to find the most effective plant fertilizer. She used a different fertilizer on each of 5 different plants. The heights of the plants at the end of her experiment are shown in the graph.

39. What is the combined height of plants C and E?

40. What is the difference in height between the tallest plant and the shortest plant?

41. **What's the Error?** Sheila found the combined heights of plants B and E to be $1\frac{6}{24}$ feet. Explain the error and give the correct answer in simplest form.

42. **Write About It** When writing 1 as a fraction in a subtraction problem, how do you know what the numerator and denominator should be? Give an example.

43. **Challenge** Explain how you might estimate the difference between $\frac{3}{4}$ and $\frac{6}{23}$.

Test Prep and Spiral Review

44. **Multiple Choice** Solve. $x - \frac{6}{11} = \frac{5}{11}$

    Ⓐ $\frac{1}{22}$ Ⓑ $\frac{1}{11}$ Ⓒ 1   Ⓓ 11

45. **Short Response** Your friend was absent from school and asked you for help with the math assignment. Give your friend detailed instructions on how to subtract $4\frac{7}{12}$ from $13\frac{11}{12}$.

Find two equivalent fractions for each fraction. (Lesson 4-5)

46. $\frac{4}{7}$ 47. $\frac{3}{4}$ 48. $\frac{2}{9}$ 49. $\frac{3}{5}$ 50. $\frac{1}{10}$

Order the fractions from least to greatest. (Lesson 4-7)

51. $\frac{3}{7}, \frac{5}{4}, \frac{2}{6}$ 52. $\frac{2}{3}, \frac{4}{11}, \frac{5}{8}$ 53. $\frac{3}{10}, \frac{3}{8}, \frac{1}{3}$

4-8 Adding and Subtracting with Like Denominators

4-9 Estimating Fraction Sums and Differences

Learn to estimate sums and differences of fractions and mixed numbers.

Members of the Nature Club went mountain biking in Shenandoah National Park, Virginia. They biked $10\frac{3}{10}$ miles on Monday.

You can estimate fractions by rounding to 0, $\frac{1}{2}$, or 1.

The fraction $\frac{3}{4}$ is halfway between $\frac{1}{2}$ and 1, but we usually round up. So the fraction $\frac{3}{4}$ rounds to 1.

You can round fractions by comparing the numerator and denominator.

closer to 0	closer to $\frac{1}{2}$	closer to 1
$\frac{1}{5}$ $\frac{2}{11}$ $\frac{2}{15}$	$\frac{5}{11}$ $\frac{4}{7}$ $\frac{9}{20}$	$\frac{9}{10}$ $\frac{16}{19}$ $\frac{6}{7}$
Each numerator is much less than half the denominator, so the fractions are close to 0.	Each numerator is about half the denominator, so the fractions are close to $\frac{1}{2}$.	Each numerator is about the same as the denominator, so the fractions are close to 1.

EXAMPLE 1   Estimating Fractions

Estimate each sum or difference by rounding to 0, $\frac{1}{2}$, or 1.

A $\frac{8}{9} + \frac{2}{11}$

$\frac{8}{9} + \frac{2}{11}$ *Think: $\frac{8}{9}$ rounds to 1 and $\frac{2}{11}$ rounds to 0.*

$1 + 0 = 1$

$\frac{8}{9} + \frac{2}{11}$ is about 1.

B $\frac{7}{12} - \frac{8}{15}$

$\frac{7}{12} - \frac{8}{15}$ *Think: $\frac{7}{12}$ rounds to $\frac{1}{2}$ and $\frac{8}{15}$ rounds to $\frac{1}{2}$.*

$\frac{1}{2} - \frac{1}{2} = 0$

$\frac{7}{12} - \frac{8}{15}$ is about 0.

You can also estimate by rounding mixed numbers. Compare the mixed number to the two nearest whole numbers and the nearest $\frac{1}{2}$.

Does $10\frac{3}{10}$ round to 10, $10\frac{1}{2}$, or 11?

$$\begin{array}{c} 10 \quad\quad 10\frac{3}{10} \quad 10\frac{1}{2} \quad\quad\quad\quad 11 \\ \leftarrow\!\!+\!\!+\!\!+\!\!+\!\!+\!\!+\!\!+\!\!+\!\!+\!\!+\!\!\rightarrow \\ 10\frac{1}{10}\ 10\frac{2}{10}\quad 10\frac{4}{10}\quad 10\frac{6}{10}\ 10\frac{7}{10}\ 10\frac{8}{10}\ 10\frac{9}{10} \end{array}$$

The mixed number $10\frac{3}{10}$ rounds to $10\frac{1}{2}$.

EXAMPLE 2 **Sports Application**

Nature Club's Biking Distances

Day	Distances (mi)
Monday	$10\frac{3}{10}$
Tuesday	$9\frac{3}{4}$
Wednesday	$12\frac{1}{4}$
Thursday	$4\frac{7}{10}$

A About how far did the Nature Club ride on Monday and Tuesday?

$10\frac{3}{10} + 9\frac{3}{4}$
$\downarrow \quad\quad \downarrow$
$10\frac{1}{2} + 10 = 20\frac{1}{2}$

They rode about $20\frac{1}{2}$ miles.

Helpful Hint

$\frac{1}{4}$ is halfway between 0 and $\frac{1}{2}$. Round $\frac{1}{4}$ up to $\frac{1}{2}$.

B About how much farther did the Nature Club ride on Wednesday than on Thursday?

$12\frac{1}{4} - 4\frac{7}{10}$
$\downarrow \quad\quad \downarrow$
$12\frac{1}{2} - 4\frac{1}{2} = 8$

They rode about 8 miles farther on Wednesday than on Thursday.

C Estimate the total distance that the Nature Club rode on Monday, Tuesday, and Wednesday.

$10\frac{3}{10} + 9\frac{3}{4} + 12\frac{1}{4}$
$\downarrow \quad\quad \downarrow \quad\quad \downarrow$
$10\frac{1}{2} + 10 + 12\frac{1}{2} = 33$

They rode about 33 miles.

Think and Discuss

1. Tell whether each fraction rounds to 0, $\frac{1}{2}$, or 1: $\frac{5}{6}, \frac{2}{15}, \frac{7}{13}$.

2. Explain how to round mixed numbers to the nearest whole number.

3. Determine whether the Nature Club met their goal to ride at least 35 total miles.

4-9 Exercises

Learn It Online
Homework Help Online go.hrw.com,
keyword MR10 4-9
Exercises 1–17, 19, 21, 23, 25, 27, 29, 33

GUIDED PRACTICE

See Example 1 Estimate each sum or difference by rounding to 0, $\frac{1}{2}$, or 1.

1. $\frac{8}{9} + \frac{1}{6}$
2. $\frac{11}{12} - \frac{4}{9}$
3. $\frac{3}{7} + \frac{1}{12}$
4. $\frac{6}{13} - \frac{2}{5}$

See Example 2 Use the table for Exercises 5 and 6.

5. About how far did Mark run during week 1 and week 2?

6. About how much farther did Mark run during week 2 than during week 3?

Mark's Running Distances	
Week	Distance (mi)
1	$8\frac{3}{4}$
2	$7\frac{1}{5}$
3	$5\frac{5}{6}$

INDEPENDENT PRACTICE

See Example 1 Estimate each sum or difference by rounding to 0, $\frac{1}{2}$, or 1.

7. $\frac{7}{8} - \frac{3}{8}$
8. $\frac{3}{10} + \frac{3}{4}$
9. $\frac{5}{6} - \frac{7}{8}$
10. $\frac{7}{10} + \frac{1}{6}$
11. $\frac{3}{4} + \frac{7}{10}$
12. $\frac{9}{20} - \frac{1}{6}$
13. $\frac{8}{9} + \frac{4}{5}$
14. $\frac{19}{20} + \frac{9}{10}$

See Example 2 Use the table for Exercises 15–17.

15. About how much do the meteorites in Brenham and Goose Lake weigh together?

16. About how much more does the meteorite in Willamette weigh than the meteorite in Norton County?

17. About how much do the two meteorites in Kansas weigh together?

Meteorites in the United States	
Location	Weight (tons)
Willamette, AZ	$16\frac{1}{2}$
Brenham, KS	$2\frac{3}{5}$
Goose Lake, CA	$1\frac{3}{10}$
Norton County, KS	$1\frac{1}{10}$

PRACTICE AND PROBLEM SOLVING

Extra Practice
See page EP8.

Estimate each sum or difference to compare. Write < or >.

18. $\frac{5}{6} + \frac{7}{9}$ ■ 3
19. $2\frac{8}{15} - 1\frac{1}{11}$ ■ 1
20. $1\frac{2}{21} + \frac{3}{7}$ ■ 2
21. $1\frac{7}{13} - \frac{8}{9}$ ■ 1
22. $3\frac{2}{10} + 2\frac{2}{5}$ ■ 6
23. $4\frac{6}{9} - 2\frac{3}{19}$ ■ 2

24. **Critical Thinking** Describe a situation in which it is better to round a mixed number up to the next whole number even if the fraction in the mixed number is closer to $\frac{1}{2}$ than 1.

Estimate.

25. $\frac{7}{8} + \frac{4}{7} + \frac{7}{13}$
26. $\frac{6}{11} + \frac{9}{17} + \frac{3}{5}$
27. $\frac{8}{9} + \frac{3}{4} + \frac{9}{10}$
28. $1\frac{5}{8} + 2\frac{1}{15} + 2\frac{12}{13}$
29. $4\frac{11}{12} + 3\frac{1}{19} + 5\frac{4}{7}$
30. $10\frac{1}{9} + 8\frac{5}{9} + 11\frac{13}{14}$

202 Chapter 4 Number Theory and Fractions

Life Science Use an inch ruler for Exercises 31–32. Measure to the nearest $\frac{1}{4}$ inch.

cetonid beetle

chrysomeliad beetle

harlequin beetle

31. About how much longer is the harlequin beetle than the cetonid beetle?

32. About how much longer is the harlequin beetle than the chrysomeliad beetle?

33. Use the table to estimate the total weekly snowfall.

Day	Mon	Tue	Wed	Thu	Fri	Sat	Sun
Snowfall (in.)	$3\frac{4}{7}$	$\frac{7}{8}$	0	$2\frac{1}{6}$	$\frac{2}{11}$	$1\frac{9}{20}$	$1\frac{4}{7}$

34. Write a Problem Write a problem about a trip that can be solved by estimating fractions. Exchange with a classmate and solve.

35. Write About It Explain how to estimate the sum of two mixed numbers. Give an example to explain your answer.

36. Challenge Estimate. $\left[5\frac{7}{8} - 2\frac{3}{20}\right] + 1\frac{4}{7}$

Test Prep and Spiral Review

37. Multiple Choice Larry ran $3\frac{1}{3}$ miles on Monday and $5\frac{3}{4}$ miles on Tuesday. About how many miles did Larry run on Monday and Tuesday?

Ⓐ 8   Ⓑ 9   Ⓒ 10   Ⓓ 11

38. Multiple Choice Marie used $2\frac{4}{5}$ cups of flour for a recipe. Linda used $1\frac{1}{4}$ cups of flour for a recipe. About how many more cups of flour did Marie use than Linda?

Ⓕ 1   Ⓖ 2   Ⓗ 3   Ⓙ 4

Simplify each expression. (Lesson 1-3)

39. $6 \times (21 - 15) \div 12$ **40.** $72 \div 8 + 2^3 \times 5 - 19$ **41.** $5 + (6 - 1) \times 2 \div 2$

Write an expression for the missing value in each table. (Lesson 2-3)

42.

Games Played	2	4	6	8	n
Points Scored	14	28	42	56	

43.

Month	1	3	5	7	n
Hours Worked	6	8	10	12	

4-9 Estimating Fraction Sums and Differences

Ready To Go On?

Quiz for Lessons 4-7 Through 4-9

4-7 Comparing and Ordering Fractions

Compare. Write <, >, or =.

1. $\frac{3}{4}$ ▪ $\frac{2}{3}$
2. $\frac{7}{9}$ ▪ $\frac{5}{6}$
3. $\frac{4}{9}$ ▪ $\frac{4}{7}$
4. $\frac{5}{11}$ ▪ $\frac{3}{5}$

Order the fractions from least to greatest.

5. $\frac{5}{8}, \frac{1}{2}, \frac{3}{4}$
6. $\frac{3}{4}, \frac{3}{5}, \frac{7}{10}$
7. $\frac{1}{3}, \frac{3}{8}, \frac{1}{4}$
8. $\frac{2}{5}, \frac{4}{9}, \frac{11}{15}$

9. Mrs. Wilson split a bag of marbles between her three sons. Ralph got $\frac{1}{10}$, Pete got $\frac{1}{2}$, and Jon got $\frac{8}{20}$. Who got the most marbles?

4-8 Adding and Subtracting with Like Denominators

10. The average growth rate for human hair is $\frac{1}{2}$ inch per month. On average, how long will a person's hair grow in 3 months? Write your answer in simplest form.

11. A recipe for fruit salad calls for $\frac{1}{5}$ cup coconut. Ryan wants to double the recipe. How much coconut should he use? Write your answer in simplest form.

Subtract. Write each answer in simplest form.

12. $1 - \frac{3}{4}$
13. $6\frac{5}{9} - 5\frac{1}{9}$
14. $10\frac{7}{16} - 4\frac{3}{16}$
15. $5\frac{8}{9} - 1\frac{7}{9}$
16. $8\frac{4}{17} - 6\frac{2}{17}$
17. $1 - \frac{7}{8}$

Evaluate each expression for $x = \frac{5}{7}$. Write your answer in simplest form.

18. $x + 2\frac{1}{7}$
19. $x - \frac{3}{7}$
20. $10 + x$
21. $3\frac{2}{7} + x$
22. $6\frac{6}{7} - x$
23. $x + \frac{2}{7}$

4-9 Estimating Fraction Sums and Differences

Estimate each sum or difference.

24. $\frac{3}{4} - \frac{1}{10}$
25. $\frac{7}{9} + \frac{7}{9}$
26. $\frac{15}{16} - \frac{4}{5}$
27. $3\frac{7}{8} - 1\frac{1}{10}$

Use the table for problems 28–30.

28. About how far did Mrs. Ping walk during week 1 and week 2?

29. About how much farther did Mrs. Ping walk in week 2 than in week 3?

30. About how far did Mrs. Ping walk during the three weeks?

Mrs. Ping's Walking Distances	
Week	Distance (mi)
1	$2\frac{3}{4}$
2	$3\frac{1}{8}$
3	$2\frac{4}{7}$

Chapter 4 Number Theory and Fractions

Real-World Connections

CHAPTER 4

Glacier National Park Glacier National Park stretches across nearly 1,600 square miles of northwestern Montana. With more than 130 lakes, 1,000 species of plants, and 700 miles of hiking trails, the park offers something for everyone who loves the outdoors.

MONTANA
Glacier National Park

1. A visitor to the park plans to hike either Snyder Lake Trail or Ptarmigan Lake Trail. She wants to choose the longer of the two trails. Which trail should she choose?

2. List the following four trails from shortest to longest: Ptarmigan Lake, Iceberg Lake, Trout Lake, Mt. Brown Lookout.

3. a. Write the length of Swiftcurrent Pass Trail as a mixed number.

   b. A visitor hikes Swiftcurrent Pass Trail one day and Snyder Lake Trail the next day. Find the total distance he hikes.

4. Write the length of Grinnell Lake Trail as a decimal.

5. A family plans to hike Iceberg Lake Trail and Grinnell Lake Trail.

   a. Estimate the total distance the family will hike.

   b. The family can usually hike one mile in 30 minutes. About how long will it take them to hike the two trails?

Trails at Glacier National Park	
Trail Name	Length (mi)
Snyder Lake	$4\frac{2}{5}$
Ptarmigan Lake	$4\frac{3}{10}$
Iceberg Lake	4.7
Trout Lake	$4\frac{1}{5}$
Mt. Brown Lookout	5.4
Swiftcurrent Pass	6.6
Grinnell Lake	$3\frac{2}{5}$

Game Time

Riddle Me This

"When you go from there to here,
you'll find I disappear.
Go from here to there, and then
you'll see me again.
What am I?"

To solve this riddle, copy the square below. If a number is divisible by 3, color that box red. Remember the divisibility rule for 3. If a number is not divisible by 3, color that box blue.

102	981	210	6,015	72
79	1,204	576	10,019	1,771
548	3,416	12,300	904	1,330
217	2,662	1,746	3,506	15,025
34,351	725	2,352	5,675	6,001

On a Roll

The object is to be the first person to fill in all the squares on your game board.

On your turn, roll a number cube and record the number rolled in any blank square on your game board. Once you have placed a number in a square, you cannot move that number. If you cannot place the number in a square, then your turn is over. The winner is the first player to complete their game board correctly.

A complete copy of the rules and game pieces are available online.

It's in the Bag!

Materials
- tan card stock
- scissors
- reinforcements
- hole punch
- wire ring
- markers

PROJECT Spec-Tag-Ular Number Theory

Tags will help you keep notes about number theory and fractions on an easy-to-use reference ring.

Directions

1. Make tags by cutting ten rectangles from card stock, each approximately $2\frac{3}{4}$ inches by $1\frac{1}{2}$ inches.

2. Use scissors to clip off two corners at the end of each tag. **Figure A**

3. Punch a hole between the clipped corners of each tag. Put a reinforcement around the hole on both sides of the tag. **Figure B**

4. Hook all of the tags together on a wire ring. On one of the tags, write the number and name of the chapter. **Figure C**

Taking Note of the Math

On each tag, write a divisibility rule from the chapter. You can also use the tags to record important facts about fractions.

It's in the Bag! 207

CHAPTER 4 Study Guide: Review

Vocabulary

common denominator 193	mixed number 175
composite number 157	prime factorization 161
divisible 156	prime number 157
equivalent fractions 180	proper fraction 186
factor 161	repeating decimal 176
greatest common factor (GCF) 165	simplest form 181
improper fraction 186	terminating decimal 176
like fractions 192	unlike fractions 192

Complete the sentences below with vocabulary words from the list above.

1. The number $\frac{11}{9}$ is an example of a(n) __?__, and $3\frac{1}{6}$ is an example of a(n) __?__.

2. A(n) __?__, such as 0.3333…, has a block of one or more digits that repeat without end. A(n) __?__, such as 0.25, has a finite number of decimal places.

3. A(n) __?__ is divisible by only two numbers, 1 and itself. A(n) __?__ is divisible by more than two numbers.

EXAMPLES | EXERCISES

4-1 Divisibility (pp. 156–159)

■ Tell whether 210 is divisible by 2, 3, 4, and 6.

2	The last digit, 0, is even.	Divisible
3	The sum of the digits is divisible by 3.	Divisible
4	The number formed by the last two digits is not divisible by 4.	Not divisible
6	210 is divisible by 2 and 3.	Divisible

■ Tell whether each number is prime or composite.

17 only divisible by 1 and 17   prime
25 divisible by 1, 5, and 25   composite

Tell whether each number is divisible by 2, 3, 4, 5, 6, 9, and 10.

4. 118
5. 90
6. 342
7. 284
8. 170
9. 393

Tell whether each number is prime or composite.

10. 121
11. 77
12. 13
13. 118
14. 67
15. 93
16. 39
17. 97
18. 85
19. 61

208 Chapter 4 Number Theory and Fractions

EXAMPLES

EXERCISES

4-2 Factors and Prime Factorization (pp. 161–164)

■ List all the factors of 10.
$10 = 1 \cdot 10 \qquad 10 = 2 \cdot 5$
The factors of 10 are 1, 2, 5, and 10.

■ Write the prime factorization of 30.

```
      30
     /  \
   (2) · 15
        /  \
      (3) · (5)
```

$30 = 2 \cdot 3 \cdot 5$

List all the factors of each number.

20. 60   **21.** 72
22. 29   **23.** 56
24. 85   **25.** 71

Write the prime factorization of each number.

26. 65   **27.** 94   **28.** 110
29. 81   **30.** 99   **31.** 76
32. 77   **33.** 55   **34.** 46

4-3 Greatest Common Factor (pp. 165–168)

■ Find the GCF of 35 and 50.
factors of 35: 1, (5), 7, 35
factors of 50: 1, 2, (5), 10, 25, 50
The GCF of 35 and 50 is 5.

Find the GCF of each set of numbers.

35. 36 and 60
36. 50, 75, and 125
37. 45, 81, and 99
38. Mr. Rojo needs to put 12 trumpets and 8 trombones in groups with the same number of each instrument in each group. What is the greatest number of groups he can make?

4-4 Decimals and Fractions (pp. 175–178)

■ Write 1.29 as a mixed number.
$1.29 = 1\frac{29}{100}$

■ Write $\frac{3}{5}$ as a decimal.
$5\overline{)3.0}$ → 0.6 $\frac{3}{5} = 0.6$

Write as a fraction or mixed number.

39. 0.37   **40.** 1.8   **41.** 0.4

Write as a decimal.

42. $\frac{7}{8}$ **43.** $\frac{2}{5}$ **44.** $\frac{7}{9}$

4-5 Equivalent Fractions (pp. 180–183)

■ Find an equivalent fraction for $\frac{4}{5}$.
$\frac{4}{5} = \frac{\square}{15} \qquad \frac{4 \cdot 3}{5 \cdot 3} = \frac{12}{15}$

■ Write $\frac{8}{12}$ in simplest form.
$\frac{8 \div 4}{12 \div 4} = \frac{2}{3}$

Find two equivalent fractions.

45. $\frac{4}{6}$ **46.** $\frac{4}{5}$ **47.** $\frac{3}{12}$

Write each fraction in simplest form.

48. $\frac{14}{16}$ **49.** $\frac{9}{30}$ **50.** $\frac{7}{10}$

EXAMPLES | EXERCISES

4-6 Mixed Numbers and Improper Fractions (pp. 186–189)

■ Write $3\frac{5}{6}$ as an improper fraction.

$$3\frac{5}{6} = \frac{(3 \cdot 6) + 5}{6} = \frac{18 + 5}{6} = \frac{23}{6}$$

■ Write $\frac{19}{4}$ as a mixed number.

$$4)\overline{19} \quad \text{4R3} \qquad \frac{19}{4} = 4\frac{3}{4}$$

Write as an improper fraction.

51. $3\frac{7}{9}$ **52.** $2\frac{5}{12}$ **53.** $5\frac{2}{7}$

Write as a mixed number.

54. $\frac{23}{6}$ **55.** $\frac{17}{5}$ **56.** $\frac{41}{8}$

57. Katie gathered all her leftover clay and found that she had $\frac{15}{4}$ blocks of clay. Write $\frac{15}{4}$ as a mixed number.

4-7 Comparing and Ordering Fractions (pp. 192–195)

■ Order from least to greatest.

$\frac{3}{5}, \frac{2}{3}, \frac{1}{3}$ *Rename with like denominators.*

$\frac{3 \cdot 3}{5 \cdot 3} = \frac{9}{15} \qquad \frac{2 \cdot 5}{3 \cdot 5} = \frac{10}{15} \qquad \frac{1 \cdot 5}{3 \cdot 5} = \frac{5}{15}$

$\frac{1}{3}, \frac{3}{5}, \frac{2}{3}$

Compare. Write <, >, or =.

58. $\frac{6}{8}$ ▢ $\frac{3}{6}$ **59.** $\frac{7}{9}$ ▢ $\frac{2}{3}$

60. $\frac{4}{5}$ ▢ $\frac{8}{10}$ **61.** $\frac{2}{5}$ ▢ $\frac{2}{3}$

Order from least to greatest.

62. $\frac{3}{8}, \frac{2}{3}, \frac{7}{8}$ **63.** $\frac{4}{6}, \frac{3}{12}, \frac{1}{3}$

64. $\frac{1}{2}, \frac{3}{8}, \frac{1}{3}$ **65.** $\frac{5}{6}, \frac{9}{10}, \frac{7}{8}$

4-8 Adding and Subtracting with Like Denominators (pp. 196–199)

■ Subtract $4\frac{5}{6} - 2\frac{1}{6}$. Write your answer in simplest form.

$4\frac{5}{6} - 2\frac{1}{6} = 2\frac{4}{6} = 2\frac{2}{3}$

Add or subtract. Write each answer in simplest form.

66. $\frac{1}{5} + \frac{4}{5}$ **67.** $1 - \frac{3}{12}$

68. $\frac{9}{10} - \frac{3}{10}$ **69.** $4\frac{2}{7} + 2\frac{3}{7}$

70. Lydia painted $\frac{3}{8}$ of her bedroom one afternoon. How much of the room still needs to be painted?

4-9 Estimating Fraction Sums and Differences (pp. 200–203)

■ Estimate the sum or difference by rounding fractions to 0, $\frac{1}{2}$, or 1.

$\frac{7}{8} + \frac{1}{7}$ *Think: 1 + 0.*

$\frac{7}{8} + \frac{1}{7}$ is about 1.

Estimate each sum or difference by rounding fractions to 0, $\frac{1}{2}$, or 1.

71. $\frac{3}{5} + \frac{3}{7}$ **72.** $\frac{6}{7} - \frac{5}{9}$

73. $4\frac{9}{10} + 6\frac{1}{5}$ **74.** $7\frac{5}{11} - 4\frac{3}{4}$

Chapter Test

CHAPTER 4

List all the factors of each number. Then tell whether each number is prime or composite.

1. 98   **2.** 40   **3.** 45

Write the prime factorization of each number.

4. 64   **5.** 130   **6.** 49

Find the GCF of each set of numbers.

7. 24 and 108   **8.** 45, 18, and 39   **9.** 49, 77, and 84

10. Ms. Arrington is making supply boxes for her students. She has 63 pencils, 42 pens, and 21 packs of markers. Each type of supply must be evenly distributed. What is the greatest number of supply boxes she can make if every supply is used?

Write each decimal as a fraction or mixed number.

11. 0.37   **12.** 1.9   **13.** 0.92

Write each fraction or mixed number as a decimal.

14. $\frac{3}{8}$ **15.** $9\frac{3}{5}$ **16.** $\frac{2}{3}$

Write each fraction in simplest form.

17. $\frac{4}{12}$ **18.** $\frac{6}{9}$ **19.** $\frac{3}{15}$

Write each mixed number as an improper fraction.

20. $4\frac{7}{8}$ **21.** $7\frac{5}{12}$ **22.** $3\frac{5}{7}$

Compare. Write <, >, or =.

23. $\frac{5}{6}$ ☐ $\frac{3}{6}$ **24.** $\frac{3}{4}$ ☐ $\frac{7}{8}$ **25.** $\frac{4}{5}$ ☐ $\frac{7}{10}$

Order the fractions and decimals from least to greatest.

26. 2.17, 2.3, $2\frac{1}{9}$ **27.** 0.1, $\frac{3}{8}$, 0.3   **28.** 0.9, $\frac{2}{8}$, 0.35

29. On Monday, it snowed $2\frac{1}{4}$ inches. On Tuesday, an additional $3\frac{3}{4}$ inches of snow fell. How much snow fell altogether on Monday and Tuesday?

Estimate each sum or difference by rounding to 0, $\frac{1}{2}$, or 1.

30. $\frac{1}{8} + \frac{4}{7}$ **31.** $\frac{11}{12} - \frac{4}{9}$ **32.** $\frac{4}{5} + \frac{1}{9}$ **33.** $2\frac{9}{10} - 2\frac{1}{7}$

Chapter 4 Test

Standardized Test Prep

Cumulative Assessment, Chapters 1–4

Multiple Choice

1. Which of the following numbers is divisible by 3, 4, and 8?
   - (A) 12
   - (B) 16
   - (C) 20
   - (D) 24

2. When June sits down today to read, she notices she is on page 20 of a 200-page book. She decides to read 4 pages of this book every day until she is finished. If this pattern continues, what page of the book will June be on in 10 more days?
   - (F) 24
   - (G) 44
   - (H) 60
   - (J) 120

3. Alice is using three different colors of beads to make necklaces. She has 48 blue beads, 56 pink beads, and 32 white beads. She wants to use the same number of pink, same number of blue, and same number of white beads on each necklace. What is the greatest number of necklaces she can make if she uses all of the beads?
   - (A) 16
   - (B) 12
   - (C) 8
   - (D) 4

4. A writer spends $144.75 on 5 ink cartridges. Which equation can be used to find the cost c of one ink cartridge?
   - (F) $5c = 144.75$
   - (G) $\frac{c}{144.75} = 5$
   - (H) $5 + c = 144.75$
   - (J) $144.75 - c = 5$

5. Which fraction is equal to 0.25?
   - (A) $\frac{1}{3}$
   - (B) $\frac{1}{4}$
   - (C) $\frac{2}{5}$
   - (D) $\frac{1}{25}$

6. Which fraction is NOT equivalent to $\frac{4}{6}$?
   - (F) $\frac{2}{3}$
   - (G) $\frac{10}{15}$
   - (H) $\frac{8}{12}$
   - (J) $\frac{16}{18}$

7. Which fraction is equivalent to the shaded area of the model?

   - (A) $\frac{2}{4}$
   - (B) $\frac{3}{24}$
   - (C) $\frac{6}{32}$
   - (D) $\frac{4}{40}$

8. Steve bought a movie ticket for $6.25, a box of popcorn for $2.25, and a large drink for $4.75. How much money did he spend at the movie?
   - (F) $12.00
   - (G) $12.75
   - (H) $13.25
   - (J) $13.50

9. Four boys each order their own small pizza. William eats $\frac{2}{3}$ of his pizza. Mike eats $\frac{2}{5}$ of his pizza. Julio eats $\frac{1}{2}$ of his pizza. Lee eats $\frac{3}{8}$ of his pizza. Who ate the least amount of pizza?
   - (A) Lee
   - (B) Mike
   - (C) Julio
   - (D) William

10. There are 78 students going on a field trip to the state capitol. The students are in groups of 4. Each group must have an adult leader. How many adult leaders are needed for each student group to have an adult leader?

    Ⓕ 15 　Ⓗ 20
    Ⓖ 19 　Ⓙ 22

11. Which of the following is equivalent to 2.52?

    Ⓐ $2\frac{52}{100}$ 　Ⓒ $\frac{52}{200}$
    Ⓑ $2\frac{52}{10}$ 　Ⓓ $\frac{2}{52}$

HOT TIP! You can answer some problems without doing many calculations. Use mental math, estimation, or logical reasoning to eliminate answer choices and save time.

Gridded Response

12. What prime number is greater than 90 but less than 100?

13. Find the least common multiple of 4 and 6.

14. Suppose you are making fruit baskets that contain 6 bananas, 4 oranges, and 5 apples each. If you need to make 100 fruit baskets, how many apples do you need?

15. What is the solution to the equation $97.56 + x = 143.07$?

16. The prime factorization of a number is $2^3 \times 3 \times 5$. What is the number?

17. The table below shows the number of days it rained each month. How many total days did it rain during the 3-month period?

Month	Rainy Days
January	6
February	5
March	7

Short Response

S1. Stacie has $16\frac{3}{8}$ yards of material. She uses $7\frac{1}{8}$ yards for a skirt. How much material does she have left? Write your answer as a mixed number in simplest form. Then give three other equivalent answers, including one decimal.

S2. Maggie says that 348 is divisible by 2, 4, and 8. Is she correct? Give any other number by which 348 is divisible. Explain.

S3. Write the numbers 315 and 225 as products of prime factors. Then list all the factors of each number and find the GCF. Are 315 and 225 prime or composite? Explain.

S4. Suzanne has 317 flyers to mail. Each flyer requires 1 stamp. If she buys books of stamps that contain 20 stamps each, how many books will she need to mail the flyers?

Extended Response

E1. Mr. Peters needs to build a rectangular pig pen $14\frac{4}{5}$ meters long and $5\frac{1}{5}$ meters wide.

   a. How much fencing does Mr. Peters need to buy? Show how you found your answer. Write your answer in simplest form.

   b. Mr. Peters's pig pen will need 6 meters more fencing than the rectangular pig pen his neighbor is building. Write and solve an equation to find how much fencing his neighbor needs to buy. Show your work.

   c. If the neighbor's pig pen is going to be 4 meters wide, how long will it be? Show your work.

CHAPTER 5
Fraction Operations

5A Adding and Subtracting Fractions
- **5-1** Least Common Multiple
- **LAB** Model Fraction Addition and Subtraction
- **5-2** Adding and Subtracting with Unlike Denominators
- **5-3** Adding and Subtracting Mixed Numbers
- **LAB** Model Subtraction with Regrouping
- **5-4** Regrouping to Subtract Mixed Numbers
- **5-5** Solving Fraction Equations: Addition and Subtraction

5B Multiplying and Dividing Fractions
- **5-6** Multiplying Fractions by Whole Numbers
- **LAB** Model Fraction Multiplication
- **5-7** Multiplying Fractions
- **5-8** Multiplying Mixed Numbers
- **LAB** Model Fraction Division
- **5-9** Dividing Fractions and Mixed Numbers
- **5-10** Solving Fraction Equations: Multiplication and Division

Why Learn This?
Fractions are a very important part of music. Musical notes even have fractional names, which tell you how long each note is. For example, an eighth note is held for one eighth the length of a four-beat measure.

Learn It Online
Chapter Project Online go.hrw.com,
keyword MR10 Ch5

Chapter Focus
- Understand the procedures for multiplying and dividing fractions.
- Evaluate expressions and solve equations with fractions.

Are You Ready?

Vocabulary

Choose the best term from the list to complete each sentence.

1. The first five __?__ of 6 are 6, 12, 18, 24, and 30. The __?__ of 6 are 1, 2, 3, and 6.
2. Fractions with the same denominator are called __?__.
3. A fraction is in __?__ when the GCF of the numerator and the denominator is 1.
4. The fraction $\frac{13}{9}$ is a(n) __?__ because the __?__ is greater than the __?__.

denominator
factors
improper fraction
like fractions
multiples
numerator
proper fraction
simplest form
unlike fractions

Complete these exercises to review skills you will need for this chapter.

Simplify Fractions

Write each fraction in simplest form.

5. $\frac{6}{10}$
6. $\frac{5}{15}$
7. $\frac{14}{8}$
8. $\frac{8}{12}$
9. $\frac{10}{100}$
10. $\frac{12}{144}$
11. $\frac{33}{121}$
12. $\frac{15}{17}$

Write a Mixed Number as an Improper Fraction

Write each mixed number as an improper fraction.

13. $1\frac{1}{8}$
14. $2\frac{3}{4}$
15. $2\frac{4}{5}$
16. $1\frac{7}{9}$
17. $3\frac{1}{5}$
18. $5\frac{2}{3}$
19. $4\frac{4}{7}$
20. $3\frac{11}{12}$

Add and Subtract Like Fractions

Add or subtract. Write each answer in simplest form.

21. $\frac{5}{8} + \frac{1}{8}$
22. $\frac{3}{7} + \frac{5}{7}$
23. $\frac{9}{10} - \frac{3}{10}$
24. $\frac{5}{9} - \frac{2}{9}$
25. $\frac{1}{2} + \frac{1}{2}$
26. $\frac{7}{12} - \frac{5}{12}$
27. $\frac{3}{5} + \frac{4}{5}$
28. $\frac{4}{15} - \frac{1}{15}$

Multiplication Facts

Multiply.

29. 8×11
30. 7×8
31. 4×12
32. 12×7
33. 10×13
34. 9×7
35. 6×8
36. 11×12

Fraction Operations

CHAPTER 5 Study Guide: Preview

Where You've Been

Previously, you
- modeled addition and subtraction of fractions with like denominators.
- estimated sums and differences of whole numbers.
- wrote equivalent fractions.

In This Chapter

You will study
- modeling addition and subtraction situations involving fractions.
- estimating sums and differences of fractions.
- adding, subtracting, multiplying, and dividing fractions and mixed numbers with unlike denominators.
- solving equations with fractions.

Where You're Going

You can use the skills learned in this chapter
- to solve measurement problems that involve fractions and mixed numbers.
- to estimate sums and differences between distances that involve fractions.

Key Vocabulary/Vocabulario

least common denominator (LCD)	mínimo común denominador (MCD)
least common multiple (LCM)	mínimo común múltiplo (MCM)
reciprocals	recíproco

Vocabulary Connections

To become familiar with some of the vocabulary terms in the chapter, consider the following. You may refer to the chapter, the glossary, or a dictionary if you like.

1. The word *reciprocal* means "inversely related or opposite." What do you think the **reciprocal** of a fraction will look like?

2. When people have something in *common*, they have something that they share. What do you think two numbers with a common multiple share? What do you think the **least common multiple** of two numbers is?

3. Fractions with the same denominator have a common denominator. What do you think the **least common denominator** of two fractions is?

Reading and Writing Math

CHAPTER 5

Study Strategy: Make Flash Cards

Create flash cards to help you learn a sequence of steps, vocabulary, math symbols, formulas, or mathematical rules. Study your flash cards often.

Use these suggestions to make flash cards.

- Label each card with the lesson number so you can look back at your textbook when studying.
- Write the name of the formula, term, or rule on one side of the card, and the meaning or an example on the other side of the card.
- Write definitions using your own words.

From Lesson 4-8

Life Science Application

Sophie plants a young oak tree in her backyard. The distance around the trunk grows at a rate of $\frac{1}{8}$ inch per month. Use pictures to model how much this distance will increase in two months, then write your answer in simplest form.

$$\frac{1}{8} + \frac{1}{8}$$

$$\frac{1}{8} + \frac{1}{8} = \frac{2}{8}$$ Add the numerators. Keep the same denominator.

$$= \frac{1}{4}$$ Write your answer in simplest form.

The distance around the trunk will increase by $\frac{1}{4}$ inch.

Sample Flash Card

Front:

Lesson 4-8
Pages 202–205

Adding and Subtracting Fractions with Like Denominators

Back:

$$\frac{1}{8} + \frac{1}{8}$$

Keep the denominators. $\frac{1}{8} + \frac{1}{8} = \frac{}{8}$

Add the numerators. $\frac{1}{8} + \frac{1}{8} = \frac{2}{8}$

Write in simplest form. $\frac{1}{4}$

Try This

1. Use Lesson 4-6 to make flash cards for the rules for writing mixed numbers as improper fractions.

Fraction Operations

5-1 Least Common Multiple

Learn to find the least common multiple (LCM) of a group of numbers.

Vocabulary

least common multiple (LCM)

After games in Lydia's basketball league, one player's family brings snacks for both teams to share. This week Lydia's family will provide juice boxes and granola bars for 24 players.

You can make a model to help you find the least number of juice and granola packs Lydia's family should buy. Use colored counters, drawings, or pictures to illustrate the problem.

EXAMPLE 1

Remember!

A multiple of a number is the product of the number and any nonzero whole number. See Skills Bank p. SB6.

Consumer Application

Juice comes in packs of 6, and granola bars in packs of 8. If there are 24 players, what is the least number of packs needed so that each player has a drink and granola bar and there are none left over?

Draw juice boxes in groups of 6. Draw granola bars in groups of 8. Stop when you have drawn the same number of each.

There are 24 juice boxes and 24 granola bars.

Lydia's family should buy 4 packs of juice and 3 packs of granola bars.

The smallest number that is a multiple of two or more numbers is the **least common multiple (LCM)**. In Example 1, the LCM of 6 and 8 is 24.

Chapter 5 Fraction Operations

EXAMPLE 2 **Using Multiples to Find the LCM**

Find the least common multiple (LCM).

Method 1: Use a number line.

A 6 and 9

Use a number line to skip count by 6 and 9.

[number line from 0 to 18 showing skip counts of 6 and 9]

The least common multiple (LCM) of 6 and 9 is 18.

Method 2: Use a list.

B 3, 5, and 6

3: 3, 6, 9, 12, 15, 18, 21, 24, 27, 30, 33, . . .
5: 5, 10, 15, 20, 25, 30, 35, . . .
6: 6, 12, 18, 24, 30, 36, . . .

List multiples of 3, 5, and 6.

Find the smallest number that is in all the lists.

LCM: 30

Method 3: Use prime factorization.

C 8 and 12

$8 = 2 \cdot 2 \cdot 2$
$12 = 2 \cdot 2 \cdot   3$

$2 \cdot 2 \cdot 2 \cdot 3$
$2 \cdot 2 \cdot 2 \cdot 3 = 24$

Write the prime factorization of each number. Line up the common factors.

To find the LCM, multiply one number from each column.

LCM: 24

D 12, 10, and 15

$12 = 2^2 \cdot 3$
$10 = 2 \cdot 5$
$15 = 3 \cdot 5$

$2^2 \cdot 3 \cdot 5$
$2^2 \cdot 3 \cdot 5 = 60$

Write the prime factorization of each number in exponential form.

To find the LCM, multiply each prime factor once with the greatest exponent used in any of the prime factorizations.

LCM: 60

> **Remember!**
> The prime factorization of a number is the number written as a product of its prime factors.

Think and Discuss

1. **Explain** why you cannot find a greatest common multiple for a group of numbers.

2. **Tell** whether the LCM of a set of numbers can ever be smaller than any of the numbers in the set.

5-1 Exercises

GUIDED PRACTICE

See Example 1
1. Pencils are sold in packs of 12, and erasers in packs of 9. Mr. Joplin wants to give each of 36 students a pencil and an eraser. What is the least number of packs he should buy so there are none left over?

See Example 2 Find the least common multiple (LCM).

2. 3 and 5
3. 4 and 9
4. 2, 3, and 6
5. 2, 4, and 5
6. 4 and 12
7. 6 and 16
8. 4, 6, and 8
9. 2, 5, and 8
10. 6 and 10
11. 21 and 63
12. 3, 5, and 9
13. 5, 6, and 25

INDEPENDENT PRACTICE

See Example 1
14. String-cheese sticks are sold in packs of 10, and celery sticks in packs of 15. Ms. Sobrino wants to give each of 30 students one string-cheese stick and one celery stick. What is the least number of packs she should buy so there are none left over?

See Example 2 Find the least common multiple (LCM).

15. 2 and 8
16. 3 and 7
17. 4 and 10
18. 3 and 9
19. 3, 6, and 9
20. 4, 8, and 10
21. 4, 6, and 12
22. 4, 6, and 7
23. 3, 8, and 12
24. 3, 7, and 10
25. 2, 6, and 11
26. 2, 3, 6, and 9
27. 2, 4, 5, and 6
28. 10 and 11
29. 4, 5, and 7
30. 2, 3, 6, and 8

PRACTICE AND PROBLEM SOLVING

Extra Practice
See page EP10.

31. What is the LCM of 6 and 12?
32. What is the LCM of 5 and 11?

33. The diagram at right is a Venn diagram. The numbers in the red circle are multiples of 4. The numbers in the blue circle are multiples of 6. The numbers in the purple section are multiples of both 4 and 6.

    Find the missing numbers in the Venn diagram.
    a. a two-digit multiple of 4 that is not a multiple of 6
    b. a two-digit multiple of 6 that is not a multiple of 4
    c. the LCM of 4 and 6
    d. a three-digit common multiple of 4 and 6

Find a pair of numbers that has the given characteristics.

34. The LCM of the two numbers is 26. One number is even and one is odd.
35. The LCM of the two numbers is 48. The sum of the numbers is 28.
36. The LCM of the two numbers is 60. The difference of the two numbers is 3.

Chapter 5 Fraction Operations

37. During its grand opening weekend, a restaurant offered the specials shown in order to attract new customers.

   a. Which customer was the first to receive all three free items?

   b. Which customer was the first to receive a free appetizer and frozen yogurt?

   c. If the restaurant served 500 customers that weekend, how many of those customers received all three free items?

GRAND OPENING SPECIALS
Every 8th customer: FREE APPETIZER!
Every 12th customer: FREE BEVERAGE!
Every 15th customer: FREE DESSERT!

38. **Choose a Strategy** Sophia gave $\frac{1}{2}$ of her semi-precious-rock collection to her son. She gave $\frac{1}{2}$ of what she had left to her grandson. Then she gave $\frac{1}{2}$ of what she had left to her great-grandson. She kept 10 rocks for herself. How many rocks did she have in the beginning?

   Ⓐ 40   Ⓑ 80   Ⓒ 100   Ⓓ 160

39. **Write About It** Explain the steps you can use to find the LCM of two numbers. Choose two numbers to show an example of your method.

40. **Challenge** Find the LCM of each pair of numbers.

   a. 4 and 6   b. 8 and 9   c. 5 and 7   d. 8 and 10

   When is the LCM of two numbers equal to the product of the two numbers?

Test Prep and Spiral Review

41. **Multiple Choice** Cheese cubes are sold in packs of 60. Crackers are sold in packs of 12. To make 60 snacks of 2 cheese cubes and 1 cracker, what is the least number of packs of each type needed?

   Ⓐ 2 cheese, 1 cracker   Ⓒ 2 cheese, 2 cracker
   Ⓑ 2 cheese, 5 cracker   Ⓓ 5 cheese, 2 cracker

42. **Multiple Choice** What is the least common multiple of 5 and 8?

   Ⓕ 40   Ⓖ 20   Ⓗ 80   Ⓙ 60

Multiply. (Lesson 3-6)

43. 0.3×0.1 44. 0.16×0.5 45. 1.2×0.2 46. 0.7×9

Compare. Write <, >, or =. (Lesson 4-7)

47. $\frac{2}{9}$ ■ $\frac{2}{13}$ 48. $\frac{10}{11}$ ■ $\frac{100}{110}$ 49. $5\frac{2}{7}$ ■ $3\frac{5}{7}$

Add or subtract. (Lesson 4-8)

50. $\frac{5}{6} + \frac{11}{6}$ 51. $\frac{3}{7} + 4\frac{2}{7}$ 52. $6\frac{2}{3} - 3\frac{1}{3}$

Hands-on LAB 5-2

Model Fraction Addition and Subtraction

Use with Lessons 5-2 and 5-3

Learn It Online
Lab Resources Online go.hrw.com,
keyword: MR10 Lab5

When fractions have different denominators, you need to find a common denominator before you can add or subtract them. Write equivalent fractions with the same denominator and then perform the operation.

Activity 1

1 Find $\frac{1}{8} + \frac{1}{4}$.

$\frac{1}{8} + \frac{2}{8} = \frac{3}{8}$

Use fraction bars to represent both fractions.
Use the same size fraction bar to model both fractions.
$\frac{1}{8} = \frac{1}{8}$ and $\frac{1}{4}$ is equivalent to $\frac{2}{8}$.
Find the total number of $\frac{1}{8}$ fraction bars.

2 Find $\frac{2}{3} + \frac{1}{2}$.

$\frac{2}{6} + \frac{2}{6} + \frac{3}{6}$
$\frac{7}{6} = 1\frac{1}{6}$

Use fraction bars to represent both fractions.
Use the same size fraction bar to model both fractions.
$\frac{1}{3}$ is equivalent to $\frac{2}{6}$ and $\frac{1}{2}$ is equivalent to $\frac{3}{6}$.
Find the total number of $\frac{1}{6}$ fraction bars.

Think and Discuss

1. Explain what the denominators of $\frac{1}{6}, \frac{1}{4}, \frac{2}{3}$, and $\frac{1}{2}$ have in common? (Hint: Think of common multiples.)

Try This

Model each addition expression with fraction bars, draw the model, and find the sum.

1. $\frac{1}{4} + \frac{1}{2}$
2. $\frac{3}{8} + \frac{1}{4}$
3. $\frac{1}{2} + \frac{2}{5}$
4. $\frac{3}{4} + \frac{1}{6}$
5. $\frac{1}{3} + \frac{1}{6}$
6. $\frac{7}{8} + \frac{3}{4}$
7. $\frac{2}{3} + \frac{1}{4}$
8. $\frac{5}{8} + \frac{1}{4}$

Activity 2

1 Find $\frac{1}{3} - \frac{1}{6}$.

Use fraction bars to represent both fractions.

Use the same size fraction bar to model both fractions.

$\frac{1}{3}$ is equivalent to $\frac{2}{6}$ and $\frac{1}{6} = \frac{1}{6}$.

Take away $\frac{1}{6}$ from $\frac{2}{6}$.

$\frac{2}{6} - \frac{1}{6} = \frac{1}{6}$

2 Find $\frac{1}{2} - \frac{1}{3}$.

Use fraction bars to represent both fractions.

Use the same size fraction bar to model both fractions.

$\frac{1}{2}$ is equivalent to $\frac{3}{6}$ and $\frac{1}{3}$ is equivalent to $\frac{2}{6}$.

Take away $\frac{2}{6}$ from $\frac{3}{6}$.

$\frac{3}{6} - \frac{2}{6} = \frac{1}{6}$

Think and Discuss

1. What size fraction bar would you use to model $\frac{1}{2} - \frac{1}{4}$? Is there another size fraction bar you could use? Explain.

2. What size fraction bar would you use to model $\frac{4}{5} - \frac{1}{2}$? Explain.

Try This

Model each subtraction expression with fraction bars, draw the model, and find the difference.

1. $\frac{3}{4} - \frac{1}{3}$
2. $\frac{1}{3} - \frac{1}{4}$
3. $\frac{1}{2} - \frac{2}{5}$
4. $\frac{5}{6} - \frac{1}{3}$
5. $\frac{1}{2} - \frac{5}{12}$
6. $\frac{7}{8} - \frac{3}{4}$
7. $\frac{1}{4} - \frac{1}{8}$
8. $\frac{1}{4} - \frac{1}{6}$

5-2 Hands-On Lab

5-2 Adding and Subtracting with Unlike Denominators

Learn to add and subtract fractions with unlike denominators.

Vocabulary

least common denominator (LCD)

Remember!
Fractions that represent the same value are equivalent.

The Pacific Ocean covers $\frac{1}{3}$ of Earth's surface. The Atlantic Ocean covers $\frac{1}{5}$ of Earth's surface. To find the fraction of Earth's surface that is covered by both oceans, you can add $\frac{1}{3}$ and $\frac{1}{5}$, which are unlike fractions.

To add or subtract unlike fractions, first rewrite them as equivalent fractions with a common denominator.

EXAMPLE 1 Social Studies Application

What fraction of Earth's surface is covered by the Atlantic and Pacific Oceans? Add $\frac{1}{3}$ and $\frac{1}{5}$.

$\frac{1}{3}$
$+ \frac{1}{5}$

Find a common denominator for 3 and 5: $3 \times 5 = 15$.

$\frac{1}{3} \rightarrow \frac{5}{15}$

Write equivalent fractions with 15 as the common denominator.

$+ \frac{1}{5} \rightarrow \frac{3}{15}$

$\frac{8}{15}$

Add the numerators. Keep the common denominator.

The Pacific and Atlantic Oceans cover $\frac{8}{15}$ of Earth's surface.

You can use *any* common denominator or the *least common denominator* to add and subtract unlike fractions. The **least common denominator (LCD)** is the least common multiple of the denominators.

224 Chapter 5 Fraction Operations

EXAMPLE 2 Adding and Subtracting Unlike Fractions

Add or subtract. Write each answer in simplest form.

Method 1: Multiply the denominators.

A) $\dfrac{9}{10} - \dfrac{7}{8}$

$\dfrac{9}{10} - \dfrac{7}{8}$ *Multiply the denominators. 10 · 8 = 80*

$\dfrac{72}{80} - \dfrac{70}{80}$ *Write equivalent fractions with a common denominator.*

$\dfrac{2}{80}$ *Subtract.*

$\dfrac{1}{40}$ *Write the answer in simplest form.*

Method 2: Use the LCD.

B) $\dfrac{9}{10} - \dfrac{7}{8}$

$\dfrac{9}{10} - \dfrac{7}{8}$ *Multiples of 10: 10, 20, 30, 40, . . .*

$\dfrac{9}{10} - \dfrac{7}{8}$ *Multiples of 8: 8, 16, 24, 32, 40, . . . The LCD is 40.*

$\dfrac{36}{40} - \dfrac{35}{40}$ *Write equivalent fractions with a common denominator.*

$\dfrac{1}{40}$ *Subtract.*

Method 3: Use mental math.

C) $\dfrac{5}{12} + \dfrac{1}{6}$

$\dfrac{5}{12} + \dfrac{1}{6}$ *Think: 12 is a multiple of 6, so the LCD is 12.*

$\dfrac{5}{12} + \dfrac{2}{12}$ *Rewrite $\dfrac{1}{6}$ with a denominator of 12.*

$\dfrac{7}{12}$ *Add.*

D) $\dfrac{1}{3} - \dfrac{2}{9}$

$\dfrac{1}{3} - \dfrac{2}{9}$ *Think: 9 is a multiple of 3, so the LCD is 9.*

$\dfrac{3}{9} - \dfrac{2}{9}$ *Rewrite $\dfrac{1}{3}$ with a denominator of 9.*

$\dfrac{1}{9}$ *Subtract.*

Think and Discuss

1. **Explain** an advantage of using the least common denominator (LCD) when adding unlike fractions.

2. **Tell** when the least common denominator (LCD) of two fractions is the product of their denominators.

3. **Explain** how you can use mental math to subtract $\dfrac{1}{12}$ from $\dfrac{3}{4}$.

5-2 Adding and Subtracting with Unlike Denominators

5-2 Exercises

GUIDED PRACTICE

See Example 1
1. A trailer hauling wood weighs $\frac{2}{3}$ ton. The trailer weighs $\frac{1}{4}$ ton without the wood. What is the weight of the wood?

See Example 2
Add or subtract. Write each answer in simplest form.
2. $\frac{1}{3} + \frac{1}{9}$
3. $\frac{7}{10} - \frac{2}{5}$
4. $\frac{2}{3} - \frac{2}{5}$
5. $\frac{1}{2} + \frac{3}{7}$

INDEPENDENT PRACTICE

See Example 1
6. **Social Studies** Approximately $\frac{1}{5}$ of the world's population lives in China. The people of India make up about $\frac{1}{6}$ of the world's population. What fraction of the world's people live in either China or India?

7. Cedric is making an Italian dish using a recipe that calls for $\frac{2}{3}$ cup of grated mozarella cheese. If Cedric has grated $\frac{1}{2}$ cup of mozarella cheese, how much more does he need to grate?

See Example 2
Add or subtract. Write each answer in simplest form.
8. $\frac{3}{4} - \frac{1}{2}$
9. $\frac{1}{6} + \frac{5}{12}$
10. $\frac{5}{6} - \frac{3}{4}$
11. $\frac{1}{5} + \frac{1}{4}$
12. $\frac{7}{10} + \frac{1}{8}$
13. $\frac{1}{3} + \frac{4}{5}$
14. $\frac{8}{9} - \frac{2}{3}$
15. $\frac{5}{8} + \frac{1}{2}$

PRACTICE AND PROBLEM SOLVING

Extra Practice
See page EP10.

Find each sum or difference. Write your answer in simplest form.
16. $\frac{3}{10} + \frac{1}{2}$
17. $\frac{4}{5} - \frac{1}{3}$
18. $\frac{5}{8} - \frac{1}{6}$
19. $\frac{1}{6} + \frac{2}{9}$
20. $\frac{2}{7} + \frac{2}{5}$
21. $\frac{7}{12} - \frac{1}{4}$
22. $\frac{7}{8} - \frac{2}{3}$
23. $\frac{2}{11} + \frac{2}{3}$

Evaluate each expression for $b = \frac{1}{2}$. Write your answer in simplest form.
24. $b + \frac{1}{3}$
25. $\frac{8}{9} - b$
26. $b - \frac{2}{11}$
27. $\frac{7}{10} - b$
28. $\frac{2}{7} + b$
29. $b + b$
30. $b - b$
31. $b + \frac{5}{8}$

Evaluate. Write each answer in simplest form.
32. $\frac{1}{3} + \frac{1}{9} + \frac{1}{3}$
33. $\frac{9}{10} - \frac{2}{10} - \frac{1}{5}$
34. $\frac{1}{2} + \frac{1}{4} - \frac{1}{8}$
35. $\frac{3}{7} + \frac{1}{14} + \frac{2}{28}$
36. $\frac{5}{6} - \frac{2}{3} + \frac{7}{12}$
37. $\frac{2}{3} + \frac{1}{4} - \frac{1}{6}$
38. $\frac{2}{9} + \frac{1}{6} + \frac{1}{3}$
39. $\frac{1}{2} - \frac{1}{4} + \frac{5}{8}$

40. Bailey spent $\frac{2}{3}$ of his monthly allowance at the movies and $\frac{1}{5}$ of it on baseball cards. What fraction of Bailey's allowance is left?

41. **Multi-Step** Betty is making punch for a party. She needs a total of $\frac{9}{10}$ gallon of water to add to fruit juice. In one container she has $\frac{1}{3}$ gallon water, and in another she has $\frac{2}{5}$ gallon. How much more water does she need?

226 Chapter 5 Fraction Operations

Life Science LINK

The red lorikeet, galah cockatoo, and green-cheeked Amazon are three very colorful birds. The African grey parrot is known for its ability to mimic sounds it hears. In fact, one African grey named Prudle had a vocabulary of almost 1,000 words.

42. Which bird weighs more, the green-cheeked Amazon or the red lorikeet?

43. What is the difference in weights between the green-cheeked Amazon and the red lorikeet?

44. Does the red lorikeet weigh more or less than $\frac{1}{2}$ lb? Explain.

45. **What's the Error?** A student found the difference in weight between the African grey parrot and the galah cockatoo to be 1 lb. Explain the error. Then find the correct difference between the weights of these birds.

46. **Write About It** Explain how you find the difference in weight between the galah cockatoo and green-cheeked Amazon.

47. **Challenge** Find the average weight of the birds.

Red lorikeet, $\frac{3}{8}$ lb, $11\frac{2}{5}$ in.

Galah cockatoo, $\frac{3}{4}$ lb, $13\frac{9}{10}$ in.

Green-cheeked Amazon, $\frac{3}{5}$ lb, $13\frac{1}{5}$ in.

African grey parrot, $\frac{7}{8}$ lb, 13 in.

Test Prep and Spiral Review

48. Multiple Choice One apple weighs $\frac{1}{4}$ lb and another apple weighs $\frac{3}{16}$ lb. Find the difference in their weights.

Ⓐ $\frac{1}{16}$ lb   Ⓑ $\frac{1}{6}$ lb   Ⓒ $\frac{1}{4}$ lb   Ⓓ $\frac{7}{16}$ lb

49. Short Response Wanda walked $\frac{7}{24}$ mile more than Lori. Lori walked $\frac{5}{6}$ mile less than Jack. Wanda walked $\frac{3}{8}$ mile. How many miles did Jack walk? Give your answer in simplest form. Explain how you solved the problem.

Divide. (Lesson 3-7)

50. $1.40 \div 2$ **51.** $3.3 \div 3$ **52.** $0.85 \div 5$ **53.** $0.375 \div 3$

Estimate each sum or difference to compare. Write < or >. (Lesson 4-9)

54. $\frac{4}{5} + \frac{2}{3}$ ▨ 1   **55.** $6\frac{1}{3} - 2\frac{1}{9}$ ▨ 4   **56.** $8\frac{7}{10} - 1\frac{3}{7}$ ▨ 8   **57.** $5\frac{1}{5} + \frac{8}{9}$ ▨ 6

5-2 Adding and Subtracting with Unlike Denominators

5-3 Adding and Subtracting Mixed Numbers

Learn to add and subtract mixed numbers with unlike denominators.

Chameleons can change color at any time to camouflage themselves. They live high in trees and are seldom seen on the ground.

A Parsons chameleon, which is the largest kind of chameleon, can extend its tongue $1\frac{1}{2}$ times the length of its body. This allows the chameleon to capture food it otherwise would not be able to reach.

To add or subtract mixed numbers with unlike denominators, you must first find a common denominator for the fractions.

The chameleon is the only animal capable of moving each eye independently of the other. A chameleon can turn its eyes about 360°.

EXAMPLE 1 Adding and Subtracting Mixed Numbers

Find each sum or difference. Write the answer in simplest form.

A $2\frac{3}{4} + 1\frac{1}{6}$

$3 + 1 = 4$

$2\frac{3}{4} \longrightarrow 2\frac{18}{24}$
$+ 1\frac{1}{6} \longrightarrow + 1\frac{4}{24}$
$\phantom{+ 1\frac{1}{6} \longrightarrow} 3\frac{22}{24} = 3\frac{11}{12}$

Estimate the sum. Round each fraction to the nearest whole number.
Multiply the denominators. 4 • 6 = 24
Write equivalent fractions with a common denominator of 24.
Add the fractions and then the whole numbers, and simplify.

$3\frac{11}{12}$ is close to the estimate of 4. The answer is reasonable.

B $4\frac{5}{6} - 2\frac{2}{9}$

$5 - 2 = 3$

$4\frac{5}{6} \longrightarrow 4\frac{15}{18}$
$- 2\frac{2}{9} \longrightarrow - 2\frac{4}{18}$
$\phantom{- 2\frac{2}{9} \longrightarrow} 2\frac{11}{18}$

Estimate the difference.
The LCD of 6 and 9 is 18.
Write equivalent fractions with a common denominator of 18.
Subtract the fractions and then the whole numbers.

$2\frac{11}{18}$ is close to the estimate of 3. The answer is reasonable.

Find each sum or difference. Write the answer in simplest form.

C $8\frac{2}{5} - 6\frac{3}{10}$

$8 - 6 = 2$ *Estimate the difference.*

$$8\frac{2}{5} \longrightarrow 8\frac{4}{10}$$
$$-6\frac{3}{10} \longrightarrow -6\frac{3}{10}$$
$$\overline{} \qquad \overline{2\frac{1}{10}}$$

Think: 10 is a multiple of 5, so 10 is the LCD.
Write equivalent fractions with a common denominator of 10.
Subtract the fractions and then the whole numbers.

$2\frac{1}{10}$ is close to the estimate of 2. The answer is reasonable.

EXAMPLE 2   **Life Science Application**

The length of a Parsons chameleon's body is $23\frac{1}{2}$ inches. The chameleon can extend its tongue $35\frac{1}{4}$ inches. What is the total length of its body and its tongue?

Add $23\frac{1}{2}$ and $35\frac{1}{4}$.

$$23\frac{1}{2} \longrightarrow 23\frac{2}{4}$$
$$+35\frac{1}{4} \longrightarrow +35\frac{1}{4}$$
$$\overline{} \qquad \overline{58\frac{3}{4}}$$

Find a common denominator. Write equivalent fractions with the LCD, 4, as the denominator. Add the fractions and then the whole numbers.

Helpful Hint

You can use mental math to find an LCD. *Think:* 4 is a multiple of 2 and 4.

The total length of the chameleon's body and tongue is $58\frac{3}{4}$ inches.

Think and Discuss

1. **Tell** what mistake was made when subtracting $2\frac{1}{2}$ from $5\frac{3}{5}$ gave the following result: $5\frac{3}{5} - 2\frac{1}{2} = 3\frac{2}{3}$. Then find the correct answer.

2. **Explain** why you first find equivalent fractions when adding $1\frac{1}{5}$ and $1\frac{1}{2}$.

3. **Tell** how you know that $5\frac{1}{2} - 3\frac{1}{4}$ is more than 2.

5-3 Exercises

GUIDED PRACTICE

See Example 1 Find each sum or difference. Write the answer in simplest form.

1. $7\frac{1}{12} + 3\frac{1}{3}$
2. $2\frac{1}{6} + 2\frac{3}{8}$
3. $8\frac{5}{6} - 2\frac{3}{4}$
4. $6\frac{6}{7} - 1\frac{1}{2}$

See Example 2

5. **Life Science** A sea turtle traveled $7\frac{3}{4}$ hours in two days. It traveled $3\frac{1}{2}$ hours on the first day. How many hours did it travel on the second day?

INDEPENDENT PRACTICE

See Example 1 Find each sum or difference. Write the answer in simplest form.

6. $3\frac{9}{10} - 1\frac{2}{5}$
7. $2\frac{1}{6} + 4\frac{5}{12}$
8. $5\frac{9}{11} + 5\frac{1}{3}$
9. $9\frac{3}{4} - 3\frac{1}{2}$
10. $6\frac{3}{10} + 3\frac{2}{5}$
11. $10\frac{2}{3} - 2\frac{1}{12}$
12. $14\frac{3}{4} - 6\frac{5}{12}$
13. $19\frac{1}{10} + 10\frac{1}{2}$

See Example 2

14. **School** The drama club rehearsed $1\frac{3}{4}$ hours Friday and $3\frac{1}{6}$ hours Saturday. How many total hours did the students rehearse?

PRACTICE AND PROBLEM SOLVING

Extra Practice
See page EP10.

Add or subtract. Write each answer in simplest form.

15. $15\frac{5}{6} + 18\frac{2}{3}$
16. $17\frac{1}{6} + 12\frac{1}{4}$
17. $23\frac{9}{10} - 20\frac{3}{9}$
18. $32\frac{5}{7} - 13\frac{2}{5}$
19. $28\frac{11}{12} - 8\frac{5}{9}$
20. $12\frac{2}{11} + 20\frac{2}{3}$
21. $36\frac{5}{8} - 24\frac{5}{12}$
22. $48\frac{9}{11} + 2\frac{1}{4}$

23. **Measurement** Kyle's backpack weighs $14\frac{7}{20}$ lb. Kirsten's backpack weighs $12\frac{1}{4}$ lb.
    a. How much do the backpacks weigh together?
    b. How much more does Kyle's backpack weigh than Kirsten's backpack?
    c. Kyle takes his $3\frac{1}{4}$ lb math book out of his backpack. How much does his backpack weigh now?

Add or subtract. Write each answer as a fraction in simplest form.

24. $0.3 + \frac{2}{5}$
25. $\frac{4}{5} + 0.9$
26. $5\frac{4}{5} - 3.2$
27. $14\frac{1}{4} + 9.5$
28. $6.3 + \frac{4}{5}$
29. $23\frac{3}{4} - 10.5$
30. $18.9 - 6\frac{1}{2}$
31. $21.8 - 3\frac{3}{5}$

32. A wheelbarrow can hold $52\frac{1}{2}$ lb. Five rocks that weigh $9\frac{5}{8}$ lb, $12\frac{1}{6}$ lb, $9\frac{1}{4}$ lb, $11\frac{1}{8}$ lb, and $10\frac{1}{2}$ lb are to be loaded into the wheelbarrow. Can the wheelbarrow hold all five rocks? Explain.

33. The route Jo usually takes to work is $4\frac{2}{5}$ mi. After heavy rains, when that road is flooded, she must take a different route that is $4\frac{9}{10}$ mi. How much longer is Jo's alternate route?

34. **Multi-Step** Mr. Hansley used $1\frac{2}{3}$ c of flour to make muffins and $4\frac{1}{2}$ c to make bread. If he has $3\frac{5}{6}$ c left, how much flour did Mr. Hansley have before making the muffins and bread?

Chapter 5 Fraction Operations

Evaluate each expression for $n = 2\frac{1}{3}$. Write your answer in simplest form.

35. $2\frac{2}{3} + n$
36. $5 - \left(1\frac{2}{3} + n\right)$
37. $n - 1\frac{1}{4}$
38. $5 - n$
39. $n + 5\frac{7}{9}$
40. $6 + \left(3\frac{4}{9} + n\right)$
41. $2\frac{1}{3} - n$
42. $3 + \left(2\frac{3}{4} - n\right)$

43. **Life Science** Elephants can communicate through low-frequency infrasonic rumbles. Such sounds can travel from $\frac{1}{8}$ km to $9\frac{1}{2}$ km. Find the difference between these two distances.

Use the drawing for Exercises 44–47.

44. Sarah is a landscape architect designing a garden. Based on her drawing, how much longer is the south side of the building than the west side?

45. Sarah needs to determine how many azalea bushes she can plant along both sides of the path. What is the sum of the lengths of the two sides of the path?

46. How wide is the path?

47. **What's the Question?** The answer is $63\frac{2}{3}$ yd. What is the question?

48. **Write About It** Explain how you would use the sum of $\frac{2}{5}$ and $\frac{1}{3}$ to find the sum of $10\frac{2}{5}$ and $6\frac{1}{3}$.

49. **Challenge** Find each missing numerator.

   a. $3\frac{x}{9} + 4\frac{2}{9} = 7\frac{7}{9}$

   b. $1\frac{3}{10} + 9\frac{x}{2} = 10\frac{4}{5}$

Research shows that elephants hear through their feet. The feet act as drums, sending vibrations through the bones to the elephant's ears.

Test Prep and Spiral Review

50. **Multiple Choice** Which expression does NOT have a sum of $6\frac{3}{10}$?

   Ⓐ $1\frac{1}{20} + 5\frac{1}{4}$
   Ⓑ $3\frac{1}{5} + 3\frac{1}{10}$
   Ⓒ $3\frac{2}{5} + 3\frac{1}{5}$
   Ⓓ $4\frac{3}{20} + 2\frac{3}{20}$

51. **Multiple Choice** A bumblebee bat is $1\frac{1}{5}$ inches in length. A thread snake is $4\frac{1}{4}$ inches in length. How much longer is a thread snake than a bumblebee bat?

   Ⓕ $3\frac{1}{4}$ inches
   Ⓖ $3\frac{1}{5}$ inches
   Ⓗ $3\frac{1}{10}$ inches
   Ⓙ $3\frac{1}{20}$ inches

Write each decimal as a fraction or mixed number. (Lesson 4-4)

52. 0.35
53. 1.5
54. 0.7
55. 1.4

Evaluate each expression for $x = \frac{2}{5}$. Write your answer in simplest form. (Lesson 5-2)

56. $x - \frac{3}{10}$
57. $x + \frac{5}{12}$
58. $\frac{7}{8} - x$
59. $\frac{2}{3} + x$

Hands-On Lab 5-4: Model Subtraction with Regrouping

Use with Lesson 5-4

Sometimes you need to regroup a mixed number before you can subtract. To regroup a mixed number, divide one or more of the whole numbers into fractional parts.

Activity

1 Find $1\frac{1}{3} - \frac{2}{3}$.

Use fraction bars to model the first mixed number, $1\frac{1}{3}$.

You need to rename $1\frac{1}{3}$ as $\frac{4}{3}$.

Now you can subtract $\frac{2}{3}$ from $\frac{4}{3}$.

$$1\frac{1}{3} - \frac{2}{3} \rightarrow \frac{4}{3} - \frac{2}{3} = \frac{2}{3}$$

2 Find $1\frac{1}{6} - \frac{5}{12}$.

Use fraction bars to model the first mixed number, $1\frac{1}{6}$.

Write an equivalent fraction with a denominator of 12: $1\frac{1}{6} = 1\frac{2}{12}$.

You need to rename $1\frac{2}{12}$ as $\frac{14}{12}$.

Now you can subtract $\frac{5}{12}$ from $\frac{14}{12}$.

$$1\frac{1}{6} - \frac{5}{12} \rightarrow \frac{14}{12} - \frac{5}{12} = \frac{9}{12}, \text{ or } \frac{3}{4}$$

232 Chapter 5 Fraction Operations

3 Find $1\frac{1}{3} - \frac{1}{2}$.

Use fraction bars to model the first mixed number, $1\frac{1}{3}$.

Write an equivalent fraction with a denominator of 6: $1\frac{1}{3} = 1\frac{2}{6}$.

You need to rename $1\frac{2}{6}$ as $\frac{8}{6}$.

Now you can subtract $\frac{1}{2}$ from $\frac{8}{6}$.

$1\frac{1}{3} - \frac{1}{2} \rightarrow \frac{8}{6} - \frac{3}{6} = \frac{5}{6}$

Think and Discuss

1. Tell whether you need to regroup before you subtract $3\frac{3}{8} - 1\frac{1}{8}$.

2. Tell whether you need to regroup before you subtract $4\frac{3}{5} - 1\frac{7}{10}$.

Try This

Give the subtraction expression that is modeled.

1.

2.

3.

4.

Model each subtraction expression with fraction bars, draw the model, and find the difference.

5. $1\frac{3}{4} - 1\frac{1}{8}$
6. $1\frac{1}{2} - \frac{3}{4}$
7. $1\frac{2}{6} - \frac{5}{6}$
8. $1\frac{1}{6} - \frac{3}{4}$
9. $2\frac{3}{8} - 1\frac{1}{2}$
10. $3\frac{1}{3} - 1\frac{2}{3}$
11. $4\frac{1}{4} - 2\frac{5}{6}$
12. $3\frac{1}{6} - 1\frac{1}{4}$

5-4 Hands-On Lab

5-4 Regrouping to Subtract Mixed Numbers

Learn to regroup mixed numbers to subtract.

Jimmy and his mother planted a tree when it was $1\frac{3}{4}$ ft tall. Now the tree is $2\frac{1}{4}$ ft tall. How much has the tree grown since it was planted?

The difference in the heights can be represented by the expression $2\frac{1}{4} - 1\frac{3}{4}$.

You will need to regroup $2\frac{1}{4}$ because the fraction in $1\frac{3}{4}$ is greater than $\frac{1}{4}$.

Divide *one whole* of $2\frac{1}{4}$ into fourths.

Regroup $2\frac{1}{4}$ as $1\frac{5}{4}$.

$$2\frac{1}{4} \rightarrow 1\frac{5}{4}$$
$$-1\frac{3}{4} \rightarrow -1\frac{3}{4}$$
$$\frac{2}{4} = \frac{1}{2}$$

Remove $1\frac{3}{4}$.

The tree has grown $\frac{1}{2}$ ft since it was planted.

EXAMPLE 1 Regrouping Mixed Numbers

Subtract. Write each answer in simplest form.

A $6\frac{5}{12} - 2\frac{7}{12}$

$6 - 3 = 3$ *Estimate the difference.*

$$6\frac{5}{12} \longrightarrow 5\frac{17}{12}$$
$$-2\frac{7}{12} \longrightarrow -2\frac{7}{12}$$
$$\overline{\phantom{-2\frac{7}{12}}\,3\frac{10}{12}}$$
$$= 3\frac{5}{6}$$

Regroup $6\frac{5}{12}$ as $5 + 1\frac{5}{12} = 5 + \frac{12}{12} + \frac{5}{12}$. Subtract the fractions and then the whole numbers.

Write the answer in simplest form.

$3\frac{5}{6}$ is close to the estimate of 3. The answer is reasonable.

234 Chapter 5 Fraction Operations   Lesson Tutorials Online my.hrw.com

Subtract. Write each answer in simplest form.

B $8 - 5\frac{3}{4}$

$8 - 6 = 2$ *Estimate the difference.*

$$8 \longrightarrow 7\frac{4}{4}$$
$$-5\frac{3}{4} \longrightarrow -5\frac{3}{4}$$
$$\overline{} \quad \overline{2\frac{1}{4}}$$

Write 8 as a mixed number with a denominator of 4. Regroup 8 as $7 + \frac{4}{4}$.
Subtract the fractions and then the whole numbers.

$2\frac{1}{4}$ is close to the estimate of 2. The answer is reasonable.

EXAMPLE 2 Measurement Application

Dave is re-covering an old couch and cushions. He determines that he needs 17 yards of fabric for the job.

A Dave has $1\frac{2}{3}$ yards of fabric. How many more yards does he need?

$$17 \longrightarrow 16\frac{3}{3}$$
$$-1\frac{2}{3} \longrightarrow -1\frac{2}{3}$$
$$\overline{} \quad \overline{15\frac{1}{3}}$$

Write 17 as a mixed number with a denominator of 3. Regroup 17 as $16 + \frac{3}{3}$.
Subtract the fractions and then the whole numbers.

Dave needs another $15\frac{1}{3}$ yards of material.

B If Dave uses $9\frac{5}{6}$ yards of fabric to cover the couch frame, how much of the 17 yards will he have left?

$$17 \longrightarrow 16\frac{6}{6}$$
$$-9\frac{5}{6} \longrightarrow -9\frac{5}{6}$$
$$\overline{} \quad \overline{7\frac{1}{6}}$$

Write 17 as a mixed number with a denominator of 6. Regroup 17 as $16 + \frac{6}{6}$.
Subtract the fractions and then the whole numbers.

Dave will have $7\frac{1}{6}$ yards of material left.

Think and Discuss

1. **Explain** why you regroup 2 as $1\frac{8}{8}$ instead of $1\frac{3}{3}$ when you find $2 - 1\frac{3}{8}$.

2. **Give an example** of a subtraction expression in which you would need to regroup the first mixed number to subtract.

3. **Explain** whether you would need to regroup to simplify the expression $7\frac{7}{8} - 2\frac{5}{8} - 1\frac{3}{8}$.

5-4 Exercises

Learn It Online
Homework Help Online go.hrw.com, keyword MR10 5-4
Exercises 1–15, 19, 23, 25, 27, 37, 39, 41

GUIDED PRACTICE

See Example 1 Subtract. Write each answer in simplest form.

1. $2\frac{1}{2} - 1\frac{3}{4}$
2. $8\frac{2}{9} - 2\frac{7}{9}$
3. $3\frac{2}{6} - 1\frac{2}{3}$
4. $7\frac{1}{4} - 4\frac{11}{12}$

See Example 2

5. Mr. Jones purchased a 4-pound bag of flour. He used $1\frac{2}{5}$ pounds of flour to make bread. How many pounds of flour are left?

INDEPENDENT PRACTICE

See Example 1 Subtract. Write each answer in simplest form.

6. $6\frac{3}{11} - 3\frac{10}{11}$
7. $9\frac{2}{5} - 5\frac{3}{5}$
8. $4\frac{3}{10} - 3\frac{3}{5}$
9. $10\frac{1}{2} - 2\frac{5}{8}$
10. $11\frac{1}{4} - 9\frac{3}{8}$
11. $7\frac{5}{9} - 2\frac{5}{6}$
12. $6 - 2\frac{2}{3}$
13. $5\frac{3}{10} - 3\frac{1}{2}$

See Example 2

14. **Measurement** A standard piece of notebook paper has a length of 11 inches and a width of $8\frac{1}{2}$ inches. What is the difference between these two measures?

15. Chad opened a 10-pound bag of birdseed to refill his feeders. He used $3\frac{1}{3}$ pounds to fill them. How many pounds of birdseed were left?

PRACTICE AND PROBLEM SOLVING

Extra Practice
See page EP10.

Find each difference. Write the answer in simplest form.

16. $8 - 6\frac{4}{7}$
17. $13\frac{1}{9} - 11\frac{2}{3}$
18. $10\frac{3}{4} - 6\frac{1}{2}$
19. $13 - 4\frac{2}{11}$
20. $15\frac{2}{5} - 12\frac{3}{4}$
21. $17\frac{5}{9} - 6\frac{1}{3}$
22. $18\frac{1}{4} - 14\frac{3}{8}$
23. $20\frac{1}{6} - 7\frac{4}{9}$

24. **Economics** A single share of stock in a company cost $23\frac{2}{5}$ on Monday. By Tuesday, the cost of a share in the company had fallen to $19\frac{1}{5}$. By how much did the price of a share fall?

25. Jasmine is $62\frac{1}{2}$ inches tall. Her brother, Antoine, is $69\frac{3}{4}$ inches tall. What is the difference, in inches, in their heights?

Simplify each expression. Write the answer in simplest form.

26. $4\frac{2}{3} + 5\frac{1}{3} - 7\frac{1}{8}$
27. $12\frac{5}{9} - 6\frac{2}{3} + 1\frac{4}{9}$
28. $7\frac{7}{8} - 4\frac{1}{8} + 1\frac{1}{4}$
29. $7\frac{4}{11} - 2\frac{8}{11} - \frac{10}{11}$
30. $8\frac{1}{3} - 5\frac{8}{9} + 8\frac{1}{2}$
31. $5\frac{2}{7} - 2\frac{1}{14} + 8\frac{5}{14}$

32. **Multi-Step** Octavio used a brand new 6-hour tape to record some television shows. He recorded a movie that is $1\frac{1}{2}$ hours long and a cooking show that is $1\frac{1}{4}$ hours long. How much time is left on the tape?

236 Chapter 5 Fraction Operations

Evaluate each expression for $a = 6\frac{2}{3}$, $b = 8\frac{1}{2}$, and $c = 1\frac{3}{4}$. Write the answer in simplest form.

33. $a - c$ **34.** $b - c$ **35.** $b - a$ **36.** $10 - b$

37. $b - (a + c)$ **38.** $c + (b - a)$ **39.** $(a + b) - c$ **40.** $(10 - c) - a$

Use the table for Exercises 41–44.

41. Gustavo is working at a gift wrap center. He has 2 yd² of wrapping paper to wrap a small box. How much wrapping paper will be left after he wraps the gift?

42. Gustavo must now wrap two extra-large boxes. If he has 6 yd² of wrapping paper, how much more wrapping paper will he need to wrap the two gifts?

43. To wrap a large box, Gustavo used $\frac{3}{4}$ yd² less wrapping paper than the amount listed in the table. How many square yards did he use to wrap the gift?

Gustavo's Gift Wrap Table	
Gift Size	Paper Needed (yd²)
Small	$\frac{11}{12}$
Medium	$1\frac{5}{9}$
Large	$2\frac{2}{3}$
X-large	$3\frac{1}{9}$

44. What's the Error? Gustavo calculated the difference between the amount needed to wrap an extra-large box and the amount needed to wrap a medium box to be $2\frac{4}{9}$ yd². Explain his error and find the correct answer.

45. Write About It Explain why you write equivalent fractions before you regroup them. Explain why you do not regroup them first.

46. Challenge Fill in the box with a mixed number that makes the inequality true.

$$12\frac{1}{2} - 8\frac{3}{4} > 10 - \Box$$

Test Prep and Spiral Review

47. Multiple Choice Find the difference of $5 - \frac{4}{9}$.

Ⓐ $5\frac{5}{9}$ Ⓑ $5\frac{1}{9}$ Ⓒ $4\frac{5}{9}$ Ⓓ $4\frac{1}{9}$

48. Gridded Response Tami worked 4 hours on Saturday at the city pool. She spent $1\frac{3}{4}$ hours cleaning the pool and the remaining time working as a lifeguard. How many hours did Tami spend working as a lifeguard?

Find the missing numbers that make the fractions equivalent. (Lesson 4-5)

49. $\frac{1}{2} = \frac{8}{a}$ **50.** $\frac{x}{5} = \frac{3}{15}$ **51.** $\frac{3}{z} = \frac{7}{21}$ **52.** $\frac{7}{8} = \frac{d}{56}$

Estimate. (Lesson 4-9)

53. $6\frac{7}{8} + 3\frac{2}{15} + 7\frac{1}{20}$ **54.** $2\frac{3}{4} + 8\frac{9}{10} + 3\frac{1}{9}$ **55.** $12\frac{8}{15} + 2\frac{1}{6} + 7\frac{3}{5}$

5-4 Regrouping to Subtract Mixed Numbers

5-5 Solving Fraction Equations: Addition and Subtraction

Learn to solve equations by adding and subtracting fractions.

Sugarcane is the main source of the sugar we use to sweeten our foods. It grows in tropical areas, such as Costa Rica and Brazil.

In one year, the average person in Costa Rica consumes $24\frac{1}{4}$ lb less sugar than the average person in the United States consumes.

EXAMPLE 1 Solving Equations by Adding and Subtracting

Solve each equation. Write the solution in simplest form.

A $x + 6\frac{2}{3} = 11$

$$x + 6\frac{2}{3} = 11$$
$$\underline{-6\frac{2}{3}} \quad \underline{-6\frac{2}{3}}$$

Subtract $6\frac{2}{3}$ from both sides to undo the addition.

$$x = 10\frac{3}{3} - 6\frac{2}{3}$$

Regroup 11 as $10\frac{3}{3}$.

$$x = 4\frac{1}{3}$$

Subtract.

B $2\frac{1}{4} = x - 3\frac{1}{2}$

$$2\frac{1}{4} = x - 3\frac{1}{2}$$
$$\underline{+3\frac{1}{2}} \quad \underline{+3\frac{1}{2}}$$

Add $3\frac{1}{2}$ to both sides to undo the subtraction.

$$2\frac{1}{4} + 3\frac{2}{4} = x$$

Find a common denominator. $3\frac{1}{2} = 3\frac{2}{4}$

$$5\frac{3}{4} = x$$

Add.

C $5\frac{3}{5} = m + \frac{7}{10}$

$$5\frac{3}{5} = m + \frac{7}{10}$$
$$\underline{-\frac{7}{10}} \quad \underline{-\frac{7}{10}}$$

Subtract $\frac{7}{10}$ from both sides to undo the addition.

$$5\frac{6}{10} - \frac{7}{10} = m$$

Find a common denominator. $5\frac{3}{5} = 5\frac{6}{10}$

$$4\frac{16}{10} - \frac{7}{10} = m$$

Regroup $5\frac{6}{10}$ as $4\frac{10}{10} + \frac{6}{10}$.

$$4\frac{9}{10} = m$$

Subtract.

Solve each equation. Write the solution in simplest form.

D $w - \frac{1}{2} = 2\frac{3}{4}$

$$w - \frac{1}{2} = 2\frac{3}{4}$$
$$\underline{+\frac{1}{2} \quad +\frac{1}{2}}$$ *Add $\frac{1}{2}$ to both sides to undo the subtraction.*
$$w = 2\frac{3}{4} + \frac{1}{2}$$
$$w = 2\frac{3}{4} + \frac{2}{4}$$ *Find a common denominator. $\frac{1}{2} = \frac{2}{4}$*
$$w = 2\frac{5}{4}$$ *Add.*
$$w = 3\frac{1}{4}$$ *Regroup: $2\frac{5}{4} = 2 + 1\frac{1}{4}$*

EXAMPLE 2 Social Studies Application

On average, a person in Costa Rica consumes $132\frac{1}{4}$ lb of sugar per year. If the average person in Costa Rica consumes $24\frac{1}{4}$ lb less than the average person in the U.S., what is the average sugar consumption per year by a person in the U.S.?

$$u - 24\frac{1}{4} = 132\frac{1}{4}$$ *Let u represent the average amount of sugar consumed in the U.S.*

$$\underline{+24\frac{1}{4} \quad +24\frac{1}{4}}$$ *Add $24\frac{1}{4}$ to both sides to undo the subtraction.*
$$u = 156\frac{2}{4} = 156\frac{1}{2}$$ *Simplify.*

Check

$$u - 24\frac{1}{4} = 132\frac{1}{4}$$
$$156\frac{1}{2} - 24\frac{1}{4} \stackrel{?}{=} 132\frac{1}{4}$$ *Substitute $156\frac{1}{2}$ for u.*
$$156\frac{2}{4} - 24\frac{1}{4} \stackrel{?}{=} 132\frac{1}{4}$$ *Find a common denominator.*
$$132\frac{1}{4} \stackrel{?}{=} 132\frac{1}{4} ✓$$ *$156\frac{1}{2}$ is the solution.*

On average, a person in the U.S. consumes $156\frac{1}{2}$ lb of sugar per year.

Think and Discuss

1. **Explain** how regrouping a mixed number when subtracting is similar to regrouping when subtracting whole numbers.

2. **Give an example** of an addition equation with a solution that is a fraction between 3 and 4.

5-5 Exercises

GUIDED PRACTICE

See Example 1 Solve each equation. Write the solution in simplest form.

1. $x + 2\frac{1}{2} = 7$
2. $3\frac{1}{3} = x - 5\frac{1}{9}$
3. $9\frac{3}{4} = x + 4\frac{1}{8}$
4. $x + 1\frac{1}{5} = 5\frac{3}{10}$
5. $3\frac{2}{5} + x = 7\frac{1}{2}$
6. $8\frac{7}{10} = x - 4\frac{1}{4}$

See Example 2

7. A tailor increased the length of a robe by $2\frac{1}{4}$ inches. The new length of the robe is 60 inches. What was the original length?

INDEPENDENT PRACTICE

See Example 1 Solve each equation. Write the solution in simplest form.

8. $x - 4\frac{3}{4} = 1\frac{1}{12}$
9. $x + 5\frac{3}{8} = 9$
10. $3\frac{1}{2} = 1\frac{3}{10} + x$
11. $4\frac{2}{3} = x - \frac{1}{6}$
12. $6\frac{3}{4} + x = 9\frac{1}{8}$
13. $x - 3\frac{7}{9} = 5$

See Example 2

14. Robert is taking a movie-making class in school. He edited his short video and cut $3\frac{2}{5}$ minutes. The new length of the video is $12\frac{1}{10}$ minutes. How long was his video before he cut it?

15. An extension for a table increased its length by $2\frac{1}{2}$ feet. The new length of the table is $8\frac{3}{4}$ feet. What was the original length?

PRACTICE AND PROBLEM SOLVING

Extra Practice
See page EP10.

Find the solution to each equation. Check your answers.

16. $y + 8\frac{2}{4} = 10$
17. $p - 1\frac{2}{5} = 3\frac{7}{10}$
18. $6\frac{2}{3} + n = 7\frac{5}{6}$
19. $5\frac{3}{5} = s - 2\frac{3}{10}$
20. $k - 8\frac{1}{4} = 1\frac{1}{3}$
21. $\frac{23}{24} = c + \frac{5}{8}$

22. The difference between Cristina's and Erin's heights is $\frac{1}{2}$ foot. Erin's height is $4\frac{1}{4}$ feet, and she is shorter than Cristina. How tall is Cristina?

23. **Measurement** Lori used $2\frac{5}{8}$ ounces of shampoo to wash her dog. When she was finished, the bottle contained $13\frac{3}{8}$ ounces of shampoo. How many ounces of shampoo were in the bottle before Lori washed her dog?

24. **Sports** Jack decreased his best time in the 400-meter race by $1\frac{3}{10}$ seconds. His new best time is $52\frac{3}{5}$ seconds. What was Jack's old time in the 400-meter race?

25. **Crafts** Juan makes bracelets to sell at his mother's gift shop. He alternates between green and blue beads.

    What is the length of the green bead?

240 Chapter 5 Fraction Operations

Find the solution to each equation. Check your answers.

26. $m + 4 = 6\frac{3}{8} - 1\frac{1}{4}$
27. $3\frac{2}{9} - 1\frac{1}{3} = p - 5\frac{1}{2}$
28. $q - 4\frac{1}{4} = 1\frac{1}{6} + 1\frac{1}{2}$
29. $a + 5\frac{1}{4} + 2\frac{1}{2} = 13\frac{1}{6}$
30. $11\frac{2}{7} = w + 3\frac{1}{2} - 1\frac{1}{7}$
31. $9 - 5\frac{7}{8} = x - 1\frac{1}{8}$

32. **Music** A string quartet is performing Antonio Vivaldi's *The Four Seasons*. The concert is scheduled to last 45 minutes.

   a. After playing "Spring," "Summer," and "Autumn," how much time will be left in the concert?

   b. Is the concert long enough to play the four movements and another piece that is $6\frac{1}{2}$ minutes long? Explain.

33. **Write a Problem** Use the pictograph to write a subtraction problem with two mixed numbers.

34. **Choose a Strategy** How can you draw a line that is 5 inches long using only one sheet of $8\frac{1}{2}$ in. × 11 in. notebook paper?

35. **Write About It** Explain how you know whether to add a number to or subtract a number from both sides of an equation in order to solve the equation.

36. **Challenge** Use the numbers 1, 2, 3, 4, 5, and 6 to write a subtraction problem with two mixed numbers that have a difference of $4\frac{13}{20}$.

Test Prep and Spiral Review

37. **Multiple Choice** Solve $4\frac{1}{2} + x = 6\frac{1}{6}$ for x.

   (A) $x = 1\frac{1}{4}$
   (B) $x = 1\frac{2}{3}$
   (C) $x = 2\frac{1}{4}$
   (D) $x = 2\frac{2}{3}$

38. **Multiple Choice** Ambra's hair was $7\frac{2}{3}$ inches long. After she got her hair cut, the length of her hair was $5\frac{4}{5}$ inches. How many inches of hair were cut?

   (F) $1\frac{13}{15}$
   (G) $2\frac{2}{5}$
   (H) $2\frac{2}{3}$
   (J) $2\frac{13}{15}$

Find the least common multiple (LCM). (Lesson 5-1)

39. 4 and 12
40. 7, 14, and 21
41. 6, 9, and 24

Simplify. Write each answer as a fraction in simplest form. (Lesson 5-3)

42. $2.5 + 5\frac{3}{8}$
43. $3.1 - 2\frac{3}{4}$
44. $15\frac{1}{5} - 8.2$
45. $6\frac{1}{6} + 1.4$

Ready To Go On?

Quiz for Lessons 5-1 Through 5-5

5-1 Least Common Multiple

1. Markers are sold in packs of 8, and crayons are sold in packs of 16. If there are 32 students in Mrs. Reading's art class, what is the least number of packs needed so that each student can have one marker and one crayon and none will be left over?

2. Cans of soup are sold in packs of 24, and packets of crackers are sold in groups of 4. If there are 120 people to be fed and each will get one can of soup and one packet of crackers, what is the least number of packs needed to feed everyone such that no crackers or soup are left over?

Find the least common multiple (LCM).

3. 4 and 6
4. 2 and 15
5. 3, 5, and 9
6. 4, 6, and 10

5-2 Adding and Subtracting with Unlike Denominators

Add or subtract. Write each answer in simplest form.

7. $\frac{5}{7} - \frac{3}{14}$
8. $\frac{7}{8} + \frac{1}{24}$
9. $\frac{8}{9} - \frac{1}{10}$
10. $\frac{1}{6} + \frac{1}{2}$

11. Alexia needs to add $\frac{2}{3}$ cup of sugar for the recipe she is making. She has added $\frac{1}{2}$ cup already. How much more sugar does she need to add?

5-3 Adding and Subtracting Mixed Numbers

Find each sum or difference. Write each answer in simplest form.

12. $2\frac{9}{13} - 1\frac{1}{26}$
13. $9\frac{5}{10} + 11\frac{4}{5}$
14. $7\frac{8}{9} - 1\frac{1}{18}$
15. $2\frac{4}{5} + 1\frac{1}{10}$

5-4 Regrouping to Subtract Mixed Numbers

Subtract. Write each answer in simplest form.

16. $2\frac{1}{13} - 1\frac{1}{26}$
17. $7\frac{1}{3} - 5\frac{7}{9}$
18. $3\frac{3}{10} - 1\frac{4}{5}$
19. $10\frac{1}{2} - 5\frac{2}{3}$

20. Mary Ann buys $4\frac{2}{5}$ pounds of bananas. She uses $1\frac{1}{2}$ pounds making banana bread. How many pounds of bananas does she have left?

5-5 Solving Fraction Equations: Addition and Subtraction

Solve each equation. Write the solution in simplest form.

21. $t + 2\frac{5}{8} = 9$
22. $5\frac{1}{6} = x - \frac{7}{8}$
23. $g + \frac{1}{4} = 2\frac{9}{10}$
24. $a + \frac{3}{5} = 1\frac{7}{10}$

25. Bryn bought $5\frac{1}{8}$ yards of material. She used $3\frac{7}{9}$ yards to make a dress. How much material does she have left?

Focus on Problem Solving

Solve
- **Choose the operation: multiplication or division**

Read the whole problem before you try to solve it. Determine what action is taking place in the problem. Then decide whether you need to multiply or divide in order to solve the problem.

If you are asked to combine equal groups, you need to multiply. If you are asked to share something equally or to separate something into equal groups, you need to divide.

Action	Operation	
Combining equal groups	Multiplication	
Sharing things equally or separating into equal groups	Division	

Read each problem, and determine the action taking place. Choose an operation to solve the problem. Then solve, and write the answer in simplest form.

1. Jason picked 30 cups of raspberries. He put them in giant freezer bags with 5 cups in each bag. How many bags does he have?

2. When the cranberry flowers start to open in June, cranberry growers usually bring in about $2\frac{1}{2}$ beehives per acre of cranberries to pollinate the flowers. A grower has 36 acres of cranberries. About how many beehives does she need?

3. A recipe that makes 3 cranberry banana loaves calls for 4 cups of cranberries. Linh wants to make only 1 loaf. How many cups of cranberries does she need?

4. Clay wants to double a recipe for blueberry muffins that calls for 1 cup of blueberries. How many blueberries will he need?

5-6 Multiplying Fractions by Whole Numbers

Learn to multiply fractions by whole numbers.

Recall that multiplication by a whole number can be represented as repeated addition. For example, $4 \cdot 5 = 5 + 5 + 5 + 5$. You can multiply a whole number by a fraction using the same method.

$$3 \cdot \frac{1}{4} = \frac{1}{4} + \frac{1}{4} + \frac{1}{4} = \frac{3}{4}$$

Interactivities Online

There is another way to multiply with fractions. Remember that a whole number can be written as an improper fraction with 1 in the denominator. So $3 = \frac{3}{1}$.

$$\frac{3}{1} \cdot \frac{1}{4} = \frac{3 \cdot 1}{1 \cdot 4} = \frac{3}{4}$$ ← Multiply numerators.
← Multiply denominators.

Notice that when you multiply a proper fraction and a number greater than 1, the product is between the factors.

EXAMPLE 1 Multiplying Fractions and Whole Numbers

Multiply. Write each answer in simplest form.

Method 1: Use repeated addition.

A $5 \cdot \frac{1}{8}$

$5 \cdot \frac{1}{8} = \frac{1}{8} + \frac{1}{8} + \frac{1}{8} + \frac{1}{8} + \frac{1}{8}$ *Write $5 \cdot \frac{1}{8}$ as addition. Add the numerators.*

$= \frac{5}{8}$

B $3 \cdot \frac{1}{9}$

$3 \cdot \frac{1}{9} = \frac{1}{9} + \frac{1}{9} + \frac{1}{9}$ *Write $3 \cdot \frac{1}{9}$ as addition. Add the numerators.*

$= \frac{3}{9}$

$= \frac{1}{3}$ *Write your answer in simplest form.*

Method 2: Multiply.

C $4 \cdot \frac{7}{8}$

$\frac{4}{1} \cdot \frac{7}{8} = \frac{28}{8}$ *Multiply.*

$= \frac{7}{2}$ or $3\frac{1}{2}$ *Write your answer in simplest form.*

244 Chapter 5 Fraction Operations

EXAMPLE 2 Evaluating Fraction Expressions

Evaluate 6x for each value of x. Write each answer in simplest form.

A $x = \frac{1}{8}$

$6x$ — Write the expression.

$6 \cdot \frac{1}{8}$ — Substitute $\frac{1}{8}$ for x.

$\frac{6}{1} \cdot \frac{1}{8} = \frac{6}{8}$ — Multiply.

$= \frac{3}{4}$ — Write your answer in simplest form.

B $x = \frac{2}{3}$

$6x$ — Write the expression.

$6 \cdot \frac{2}{3}$ — Substitute $\frac{2}{3}$ for x.

$\frac{6}{1} \cdot \frac{2}{3} = \frac{12}{3}$ — Multiply.

$= \frac{4}{1}$

$= 4$

Remember!
$\frac{12}{3}$ means $12 \div 3$.

Sometimes the denominator of an improper fraction will divide into the numerator without a remainder, as in Example 2B. When this happens, the improper fraction is equivalent to a whole number, not a mixed number.

$$\frac{12}{3} = 4$$

EXAMPLE 3 Social Studies Application

Any proposed amendment to the U.S. Constitution must be ratified, or approved, by $\frac{3}{4}$ of the states. When the 13th Amendment abolishing slavery was proposed in 1865, there were 36 states. How many states needed to ratify this amendment in order for it to pass?

To find $\frac{3}{4}$ of 36, multiply.

$\frac{3}{4} \cdot 36 = \frac{3}{4} \cdot \frac{36}{1}$

$= \frac{108}{4}$

$= 27$ — Divide 108 by 4 and write your answer in simplest form.

For the 13th Amendment to pass, 27 states had to ratify it.

Think and Discuss

1. Describe a model you could use to show the product of $4 \cdot \frac{1}{5}$.

2. Choose the expression that is correctly multiplied.

$2 \cdot \frac{3}{7} = \frac{6}{7}$ $2 \cdot \frac{3}{7} = \frac{6}{14}$

3. Explain how you know without actually multiplying that $\frac{5}{8} \cdot 16$ is greater than 8.

5-6 Exercises

GUIDED PRACTICE

See Example 1 Multiply. Write each answer in simplest form.

1. $8 \cdot \frac{1}{9}$
2. $2 \cdot \frac{1}{5}$
3. $12 \cdot \frac{1}{4}$
4. $7 \cdot \frac{4}{9}$
5. $3 \cdot \frac{1}{7}$
6. $4 \cdot \frac{2}{11}$
7. $8 \cdot \frac{3}{4}$
8. $18 \cdot \frac{1}{3}$

See Example 2 Evaluate $12x$ for each value of x. Write each answer in simplest form.

9. $x = \frac{2}{3}$
10. $x = \frac{1}{2}$
11. $x = \frac{3}{4}$
12. $x = \frac{5}{6}$

See Example 3

13. The school Community Service Club has 45 members. Of these 45 members, $\frac{3}{5}$ are boys. How many boys are members of the Community Service Club?

INDEPENDENT PRACTICE

See Example 1 Multiply. Write each answer in simplest form.

14. $4 \cdot \frac{1}{10}$
15. $6 \cdot \frac{1}{8}$
16. $3 \cdot \frac{1}{12}$
17. $2 \cdot \frac{2}{5}$
18. $6 \cdot \frac{10}{11}$
19. $2 \cdot \frac{3}{11}$
20. $15 \cdot \frac{2}{15}$
21. $20 \cdot \frac{1}{2}$

See Example 2 Evaluate $8x$ for each value of x. Write each answer in simplest form.

22. $x = \frac{1}{2}$
23. $x = \frac{3}{4}$
24. $x = \frac{1}{8}$
25. $x = \frac{1}{4}$
26. $x = \frac{2}{5}$
27. $x = \frac{5}{7}$
28. $x = \frac{7}{8}$
29. $x = \frac{4}{9}$

See Example 3

30. **School** Kiesha spent 120 minutes completing her homework last night. Of those minutes, $\frac{1}{6}$ were spent on Spanish. How many minutes did Kiesha spend on her Spanish homework?

PRACTICE AND PROBLEM SOLVING

Extra Practice See page EP10.

Evaluate each expression. Write each answer in simplest form.

31. $12b$ for $b = \frac{7}{12}$
32. $20m$ for $m = \frac{1}{20}$
33. $33z$ for $z = \frac{5}{11}$
34. $\frac{2}{3}y$ for $y = 18$
35. $\frac{1}{4}x$ for $x = 20$
36. $\frac{3}{5}a$ for $a = 30$
37. $\frac{4}{5}c$ for $c = 12$
38. $14x$ for $x = \frac{3}{8}$
39. $\frac{9}{10}n$ for $n = 50$

Compare. Write <, >, or =.

40. $9 \cdot \frac{1}{16}$ ▢ $\frac{1}{2}$
41. $15 \cdot \frac{2}{5}$ ▢ 5
42. $\frac{8}{13}$ ▢ $4 \cdot \frac{2}{13}$
43. $3 \cdot \frac{2}{9}$ ▢ $\frac{2}{3}$
44. $6 \cdot \frac{4}{15}$ ▢ $\frac{11}{24}$
45. 5 ▢ $12 \cdot \frac{3}{4}$
46. $3 \cdot \frac{1}{7}$ ▢ $3 \cdot \frac{1}{5}$
47. $7 \cdot \frac{3}{4}$ ▢ $6 \cdot \frac{3}{7}$
48. $2 \cdot \frac{5}{6}$ ▢ $6 \cdot \frac{2}{5}$

49. Denise spent $55 shopping. Of that $55, she spent $\frac{3}{5}$ on a pair of shoes. How much money did Denise spend on the pair of shoes?

246 Chapter 5 Fraction Operations

Life Science LINK

The General Sherman, a giant sequoia tree in California's Sequoia National Park, is one of the largest trees in the world at 275 ft tall.

California also has some of the nation's tallest grand firs, ponderosa pines, and sugar pines. The table shows how the heights of these trees compare with the height of the General Sherman. For example, the grand fir is $\frac{23}{25}$ the height of the General Sherman.

50. Find the heights of the trees in the table. Write your answers in simplest form.

51. The world's tallest bluegum eucalyptus tree is $\frac{3}{5}$ the height of the General Sherman tree. How tall is this bluegum eucalyptus?

52. **What's the Question?** Joshua trees can grow to be 40 ft tall. The answer is $\frac{8}{55}$. What is the question?

53. **Write About It** Find $\frac{1}{5}$ the height of the General Sherman. Then divide the height of the General Sherman by 5. What do you notice? Why does this make sense?

54. **Challenge** The world's tallest incense cedar tree is 152 ft tall. What is $\frac{1}{5}$ of $\frac{1}{2}$ of $\frac{1}{4}$ of 152?

Tree Heights Compared with the General Sherman	
Tallest Grand Fir	$\frac{23}{25}$
Tallest Ponderosa Pine	$\frac{41}{50}$
Tallest Sugar Pine	$\frac{21}{25}$

Source: The Top 10 of Everything 2000

Test Prep and Spiral Review

55. **Multiple Choice** A recipe uses $\frac{1}{3}$ cup of sugar. Daniela doubled the recipe. How much sugar did she use?

    (A) $\frac{1}{4}$ cup   (B) $\frac{1}{3}$ cup   (C) $\frac{2}{3}$ cup   (D) $\frac{3}{4}$ cup

56. **Extended Response** Mario bought $\frac{1}{5}$ pound of turkey. Rose bought four times as much turkey as Mario. And Celia bought 2 times as much as Rose. How many pounds of turkey did Rose buy? How many pounds did Celia buy? How much more did Celia buy than Mario? Show your work.

Write each phrase as a numerical or algebraic expression. (Lesson 2-2)

57. w less than 75   58. the product of n and 16   59. the quotient of p and 7

Subtract. Write each answer in simplest form. (Lesson 5-4)

60. $5\frac{2}{3} - 4\frac{5}{6}$ 61. $12\frac{4}{7} - 3\frac{6}{7}$ 62. $9\frac{7}{12} - 2\frac{1}{3}$ 63. $11\frac{5}{8} - 5\frac{1}{4}$

5-6 Multiplying Fractions by Whole Numbers

Hands-on Lab 5-7: Model Fraction Multiplication

Use with Lessons 5-7 and 5-8

You can use grids to help you understand fraction multiplication.

Activity 1

1 Think of $\frac{1}{2} \cdot \frac{1}{3}$ as $\frac{1}{2}$ of $\frac{1}{3}$.

Shade $\frac{1}{3}$ of a square.   Divide the square into halves.

Look at $\frac{1}{2}$ of the part you shaded.

What fraction of the whole is this? $\frac{1}{2}$ of $\frac{1}{3}$ is $\frac{1}{6}$.

2 Think of $\frac{2}{3} \cdot \frac{1}{2}$ as $\frac{2}{3}$ of $\frac{1}{2}$.

Shade $\frac{1}{2}$ of a square.   Divide the square into thirds. $\frac{2}{3}$ of $\frac{1}{2}$ is $\frac{2}{6}$, or $\frac{1}{3}$.

Think and Discuss

1. Tell whether the product is greater than or less than the fractions you started with.

Try This

Write the multiplication expression modeled on each grid.

1.

2.

3.

Use a grid to model each multiplication expression.

4. $\frac{1}{3} \cdot \frac{1}{2}$
5. $\frac{2}{3} \cdot \frac{1}{3}$
6. $\frac{1}{4} \cdot \frac{2}{3}$
7. $\frac{1}{3} \cdot \frac{3}{4}$

You can also use grids to model multiplication of mixed numbers.

Activity 2

Think of $\frac{1}{2} \cdot 2\frac{1}{2}$ as $\frac{1}{2}$ of $2\frac{1}{2}$.

Shade $2\frac{1}{2}$ squares.

Divide the squares into halves.

Look at $\frac{1}{2}$ of the part you shaded.

What fraction of the model is this?

$\frac{1}{2}$ of $2\frac{1}{2}$ is $\frac{5}{4}$, or $1\frac{1}{4}$.

Think and Discuss

1. Describe how modeling multiplication of mixed numbers is like modeling multiplication of fractions.

Try This

Write the multiplication expression modeled on each grid.

1.
2.
3.

Use a grid to model each multiplication expression.

4. $\frac{1}{3} \cdot 1\frac{1}{2}$
5. $\frac{2}{3} \cdot 2\frac{1}{3}$
6. $\frac{1}{4} \cdot 2\frac{2}{3}$
7. $\frac{1}{3} \cdot 1\frac{3}{4}$
8. $\frac{3}{4} \cdot 1\frac{1}{3}$
9. $\frac{1}{2} \cdot 3\frac{1}{3}$
10. $\frac{2}{3} \cdot 1\frac{3}{4}$
11. $\frac{1}{4} \cdot 2\frac{1}{2}$

5-7 Hands-On Lab

5-7 Multiplying Fractions

Learn to multiply fractions.

On average, people spend $\frac{1}{3}$ of their lives asleep. About $\frac{1}{4}$ of the time they sleep, they dream. What fraction of a lifetime does a person typically spend dreaming?

One way to find $\frac{1}{4}$ of $\frac{1}{3}$ is to make a model.

Find $\frac{1}{4}$ of $\frac{1}{3}$.

Interactivities Online ▶

$$\frac{1}{4} \cdot \frac{1}{3} = \frac{1}{12}$$

Your brain keeps working even when you're asleep. It makes sure that you keep breathing and that your heart keeps beating.

You can also multiply fractions without making a model.

$$\frac{1}{4} \cdot \frac{1}{3} = \frac{1 \cdot 1}{4 \cdot 3}$$ ← Multiply the numerators.
← Multiply the denominators.

$$= \frac{1}{12}$$ The answer is in simplest form.

A person typically spends $\frac{1}{12}$ of his or her lifetime dreaming.

Notice that when you multiply two proper fractions, the product is less than either factor.

EXAMPLE 1 Multiplying Fractions

Multiply. Write each answer in simplest form.

A $\frac{1}{3} \cdot \frac{3}{5}$

$\frac{1}{3} \cdot \frac{3}{5} = \frac{1 \cdot 3}{3 \cdot 5}$ *Multiply numerators. Multiply denominators.*

$= \frac{3}{15}$ *The GCF of 3 and 15 is 3.*

$= \frac{1}{5}$ *The answer is in simplest form.*

B $\frac{6}{7} \cdot \frac{2}{3}$

$\frac{\overset{2}{\cancel{6}}}{7} \cdot \frac{2}{\underset{1}{\cancel{3}}} = \frac{2}{7} \cdot \frac{2}{1}$ *Use the GCF to simplify the fractions before multiplying. The GCF of 6 and 3 is 3.*

$= \frac{2 \cdot 2}{7 \cdot 1}$ *Multiply numerators. Multiply denominators.*

$= \frac{4}{7}$ *The answer is in simplest form.*

250 Chapter 5 Fraction Operations

Multiply. Write each answer in simplest form.

C $\frac{3}{8} \cdot \frac{2}{9}$

$\frac{3}{8} \cdot \frac{2}{9} = \frac{3 \cdot 2}{8 \cdot 9}$ *Multiply numerators. Multiply denominators.*

$= \frac{6}{72}$ *The GCF of 6 and 72 is 6.*

$= \frac{1}{12}$ *The answer is in simplest form.*

EXAMPLE 2 **Evaluating Fraction Expressions**

Evaluate the expression $a \cdot \frac{1}{3}$ for each value of a. Write the answer in simplest form.

A $a = \frac{5}{8}$ $a \cdot \frac{1}{3}$

$\frac{5}{8} \cdot \frac{1}{3}$ *Substitute $\frac{5}{8}$ for a.*

$\frac{5 \cdot 1}{8 \cdot 3}$ *Multiply.*

$\frac{5}{24}$ *The answer is in simplest form.*

Helpful Hint

You can look for a common factor in a numerator and a denominator to determine whether you can simplify before multiplying.

B $a = \frac{9}{10}$ $a \cdot \frac{1}{3}$

$\frac{9}{10} \cdot \frac{1}{3}$ *Substitute $\frac{9}{10}$ for a.*

$\frac{\overset{3}{\cancel{9}}}{10} \cdot \frac{1}{\underset{1}{\cancel{3}}}$ *Use the GCF to simplify.*

$\frac{3 \cdot 1}{10 \cdot 1}$ *Multiply.*

$\frac{3}{10}$ *The answer is in simplest form.*

C $a = \frac{3}{4}$ $a \cdot \frac{1}{3}$

$\frac{3}{4} \cdot \frac{1}{3}$ *Substitute $\frac{3}{4}$ for a.*

$\frac{3 \cdot 1}{4 \cdot 3}$ *Multiply numerators. Multiply denominators.*

$\frac{3}{12}$ *The GCF of 3 and 12 is 3.*

$\frac{1}{4}$ *The answer is in simplest form.*

Think and Discuss

1. **Determine** whether the product of two proper fractions is greater than or less than each factor.
2. **Name** the missing denominator in the equation $\frac{1}{\blacksquare} \cdot \frac{2}{3} = \frac{2}{21}$.
3. **Tell** how to find the product of $\frac{4}{12} \cdot \frac{6}{10}$ in two different ways.

5-7 Exercises

GUIDED PRACTICE

See Example 1   Multiply. Write each answer in simplest form.

1. $\frac{1}{2} \cdot \frac{1}{3}$
2. $\frac{2}{5} \cdot \frac{1}{4}$
3. $\frac{4}{7} \cdot \frac{3}{4}$
4. $\frac{5}{6} \cdot \frac{3}{5}$

See Example 2   Evaluate the expression $b \cdot \frac{1}{5}$ for each value of b. Write the answer in simplest form.

5. $b = \frac{2}{3}$
6. $b = \frac{5}{8}$
7. $b = \frac{1}{4}$
8. $b = \frac{3}{5}$

INDEPENDENT PRACTICE

See Example 1   Multiply. Write each answer in simplest form.

9. $\frac{1}{3} \cdot \frac{2}{7}$
10. $\frac{1}{3} \cdot \frac{1}{5}$
11. $\frac{5}{6} \cdot \frac{2}{3}$
12. $\frac{1}{3} \cdot \frac{6}{7}$
13. $\frac{3}{10} \cdot \frac{5}{6}$
14. $\frac{7}{9} \cdot \frac{3}{5}$
15. $\frac{1}{2} \cdot \frac{10}{11}$
16. $\frac{3}{5} \cdot \frac{3}{4}$

See Example 2   Evaluate the expression $x \cdot \frac{1}{6}$ for each value of x. Write the answer in simplest form.

17. $x = \frac{4}{5}$
18. $x = \frac{6}{7}$
19. $x = \frac{3}{4}$
20. $x = \frac{5}{6}$
21. $x = \frac{8}{9}$
22. $x = \frac{9}{10}$
23. $x = \frac{5}{8}$
24. $x = \frac{3}{8}$

PRACTICE AND PROBLEM SOLVING

Extra Practice
See page EP11.

Find each product. Simplify the answer.

25. $\frac{3}{5} \cdot \frac{4}{9}$
26. $\frac{5}{12} \cdot \frac{9}{10}$
27. $\frac{2}{5} \cdot \frac{2}{7} \cdot \frac{5}{8}$
28. $\frac{2}{7} \cdot \frac{1}{8}$
29. $\frac{6}{7} \cdot \frac{9}{10}$
30. $\frac{4}{9} \cdot \frac{2}{3}$
31. $\frac{1}{2} \cdot \frac{2}{5} \cdot \frac{9}{11}$
32. $\frac{1}{12} \cdot \frac{3}{7}$

33. A walnut muffin recipe calls for $\frac{3}{4}$ cup walnuts. Mrs. Hooper wants to make $\frac{1}{3}$ of the recipe. What fraction of a cup of walnuts will she need?

34. Jim spent $\frac{5}{6}$ of an hour doing chores. He spent $\frac{2}{5}$ of that time washing dishes. What fraction of an hour did he spend washing dishes?

Compare. Write <, >, or =.

35. $\frac{2}{3} \cdot \frac{1}{4}$ ■ $\frac{1}{3} \cdot \frac{3}{4}$
36. $\frac{3}{5} \cdot \frac{3}{4}$ ■ $\frac{1}{2} \cdot \frac{9}{10}$
37. $\frac{5}{6} \cdot \frac{2}{3}$ ■ $\frac{1}{3} \cdot \frac{2}{3}$
38. $\frac{5}{8} \cdot \frac{1}{4}$ ■ $\frac{2}{9} \cdot \frac{1}{7}$
39. $\frac{2}{5} \cdot \frac{1}{10}$ ■ $\frac{3}{5} \cdot \frac{2}{3}$
40. $\frac{1}{2} \cdot \frac{4}{5}$ ■ $\frac{10}{20} \cdot \frac{16}{20}$

41. A multiplying number machine uses a rule to change one fraction into another fraction. The machine changed $\frac{1}{2}$ into $\frac{1}{8}$, $\frac{1}{5}$ into $\frac{1}{20}$, and $\frac{5}{7}$ into $\frac{5}{28}$.

   a. What is the rule?
   b. Into what fraction will the machine change $\frac{1}{3}$?

42. Alex exercised for $\frac{3}{4}$ hour. He lifted weights for $\frac{1}{5}$ of that time. What fraction of an hour did he spend lifting weights?

43. **Life Science** A bat can eat half its weight in insects in one night. If a bat weighing $\frac{3}{4}$ lb eats half its weight in insects, how much do the insects weigh?

44. **Multi-Step** The number of American bison has steadily declined throughout the years. Once, 20 million bison roamed the United States. Now, there are only $\frac{1}{40}$ of that number of bison. Of those, only $\frac{1}{25}$ roam in the wild. The number of American bison currently roaming in the wild is what fraction of 20 million? How many bison is that?

45. The seating plan shows Oak School's theater. The front section has $\frac{3}{4}$ of the seats, and the rear section has $\frac{1}{4}$ of the seats. The school has reserved $\frac{1}{2}$ of the seats in the front section for students. What fraction of the seating is reserved for students?

46. **Write a Problem** Use the seating plan to write a problem in which you need to multiply two fractions. Then solve the problem.

47. **Write About It** Explain how you can use the GCF before multiplying so that the product of two fractions is in simplest form.

48. **Challenge** Simplify the expression.

$$\frac{(2+6)}{5} \cdot \frac{1}{4} \cdot 6$$

There are about 1,000 species of bats in the world. Bats make up about $\frac{1}{4}$ of the world's mammals.

Test Prep and Spiral Review

49. **Multiple Choice** Which shows the product of $\frac{4}{5}$ and $\frac{3}{5}$ in simplest form?

    Ⓐ $1\frac{2}{5}$ Ⓑ $1\frac{1}{3}$ Ⓒ $\frac{3}{5}$ Ⓓ $\frac{12}{25}$

50. **Multiple Choice** Julie spent $\frac{1}{3}$ of her birthday money on new clothes. She spent $\frac{3}{10}$ of that money on shoes. What fraction of her birthday money did Julie spend on shoes?

    Ⓕ $\frac{1}{30}$ Ⓖ $\frac{1}{10}$ Ⓗ $\frac{2}{15}$ Ⓙ $\frac{3}{13}$

Solve each equation. (Lesson 2-7)

51. $15n = 45$ 52. $7t = 147$ 53. $6a = 78$ 54. $12b = 216$

Find each sum or difference. (Lesson 5-2)

55. $\frac{1}{9} + \frac{1}{3}$ 56. $\frac{11}{12} - \frac{5}{6}$ 57. $\frac{2}{7} + \frac{6}{21}$ 58. $\frac{1}{5} + \frac{3}{10} - \frac{1}{15}$

5-7 Multiplying Fractions

5-8 Multiplying Mixed Numbers

Learn to multiply mixed numbers.

Janice and Carla are making homemade pasta from a recipe that calls for $1\frac{1}{2}$ cups of flour. They want to make $\frac{1}{3}$ of the recipe.

You can find $\frac{1}{3}$ of $1\frac{1}{2}$, or multiply $\frac{1}{3}$ by $1\frac{1}{2}$, to find how much flour Janice and Carla need.

EXAMPLE 1 Multiplying Fractions and Mixed Numbers

Multiply. Write each answer in simplest form.

Remember!
To write a mixed number as an improper fraction, start with the denominator, multiply by the whole number, and add the numerator. Use the same denominator.

$$1\frac{1}{5} = \frac{1 \cdot 5 + 1}{5} = \frac{6}{5}$$

A $\frac{1}{3} \cdot 1\frac{1}{2}$

$\frac{1}{3} \cdot \frac{3}{2}$ *Write $1\frac{1}{2}$ as an improper fraction. $1\frac{1}{2} = \frac{3}{2}$*

$\frac{1 \cdot 3}{3 \cdot 2}$ *Multiply numerators. Multiply denominators.*

$\frac{3}{6}$

$\frac{1}{2}$ *Write the answer in simplest form.*

B $1\frac{1}{5} \cdot \frac{2}{3}$

$\frac{6}{5} \cdot \frac{2}{3}$ *Write $1\frac{1}{5}$ as an improper fraction. $1\frac{1}{5} = \frac{6}{5}$*

$\frac{6 \cdot 2}{5 \cdot 3}$ *Multiply numerators. Multiply denominators.*

$\frac{12}{15}$

$\frac{4}{5}$ *Write the answer in simplest form.*

C $\frac{3}{4} \cdot 2\frac{1}{3}$

$\frac{3}{4} \cdot \frac{7}{3}$ *Write $2\frac{1}{3}$ as an improper fraction. $2\frac{1}{3} = \frac{7}{3}$*

$\frac{\cancel{3}^1}{4} \cdot \frac{7}{\cancel{3}_1}$ *Use the GCF to simplify before multiplying.*

$\frac{1 \cdot 7}{4 \cdot 1}$

$\frac{7}{4} = 1\frac{3}{4}$ *You can write the answer as a mixed number.*

EXAMPLE 2 Multiplying Mixed Numbers

Find each product. Write the answer in simplest form.

Remember!
You can estimate the product to see whether your answer is reasonable.

A $2\frac{1}{2} \cdot 1\frac{1}{3}$

$\frac{5}{2} \cdot \frac{4}{3}$ *Write the mixed numbers as improper fractions.* $2\frac{1}{2} = \frac{5}{2}$ $1\frac{1}{3} = \frac{4}{3}$

$\frac{5 \cdot 4}{2 \cdot 3}$ *Multiply numerators.*
Multiply denominators.

$\frac{20}{6}$

$3\frac{2}{6}$ *Write the improper fraction as a mixed number.*

$3\frac{1}{3}$ *Simplify.*

B $1\frac{1}{4} \cdot 1\frac{1}{3}$

$\frac{5}{4} \cdot \frac{4}{3}$ *Write the mixed numbers as improper fractions.* $1\frac{1}{4} = \frac{5}{4}$ $1\frac{1}{3} = \frac{4}{3}$

$\frac{5}{4} \cdot \frac{\overset{1}{4}}{3}$ *Use the GCF to simplify before multiplying.*
$\underset{1}{}$

$\frac{5 \cdot 1}{1 \cdot 3}$ *Multiply numerators. Multiply denominators.*

$\frac{5}{3}$

$1\frac{2}{3}$ *Write the answer as a mixed number.*

C $5 \cdot 3\frac{2}{11}$

$5 \cdot 3\frac{2}{11}$

$5 \cdot \left(3 + \frac{2}{11}\right)$

$(5 \cdot 3) + \left(5 \cdot \frac{2}{11}\right)$ *Use the Distributive Property.*

$(5 \cdot 3) + \left(\frac{5}{1} \cdot \frac{2}{11}\right)$

$15 + \frac{10}{11}$ *Multiply.*

$15\frac{10}{11}$ *Add.*

Think and Discuss

1. **Tell** how you multiply a mixed number by a mixed number.
2. **Explain** two ways you would multiply a mixed number by a whole number.
3. **Explain** whether the product of a proper fraction and a mixed number is less than, between, or greater than the two factors.

5-8 Exercises

Learn It Online
Homework Help Online go.hrw.com,
keyword MR10 5-8
Exercises 1–28, 31, 35, 37, 49, 51

GUIDED PRACTICE

See Example 1 Multiply. Write each answer in simplest form.

1. $1\frac{1}{4} \cdot \frac{2}{3}$
2. $2\frac{2}{3} \cdot \frac{1}{4}$
3. $\frac{3}{7} \cdot 1\frac{5}{6}$
4. $1\frac{1}{3} \cdot \frac{6}{7}$
5. $\frac{2}{3} \cdot 1\frac{3}{10}$
6. $2\frac{6}{11} \cdot \frac{2}{7}$

See Example 2 Find each product. Write the answer in simplest form.

7. $1\frac{5}{6} \cdot 1\frac{1}{8}$
8. $2\frac{2}{5} \cdot 1\frac{1}{12}$
9. $4 \cdot 5\frac{3}{7}$
10. $2\frac{3}{4} \cdot 1\frac{5}{6}$
11. $2\frac{3}{8} \cdot 5\frac{1}{5}$
12. $10\frac{1}{2} \cdot 1\frac{1}{4}$

INDEPENDENT PRACTICE

See Example 1 Multiply. Write each answer in simplest form.

13. $1\frac{1}{4} \cdot \frac{3}{4}$
14. $\frac{4}{7} \cdot 1\frac{1}{4}$
15. $1\frac{1}{6} \cdot \frac{2}{5}$
16. $2\frac{1}{6} \cdot \frac{3}{7}$
17. $\frac{5}{9} \cdot 1\frac{9}{10}$
18. $2\frac{2}{9} \cdot \frac{3}{5}$
19. $1\frac{3}{10} \cdot \frac{5}{7}$
20. $\frac{3}{4} \cdot 1\frac{2}{5}$

See Example 2 Find each product. Write the answer in simplest form.

21. $1\frac{1}{3} \cdot 1\frac{5}{7}$
22. $1\frac{2}{3} \cdot 2\frac{3}{10}$
23. $4 \cdot 3\frac{7}{8}$
24. $6 \cdot 2\frac{1}{3}$
25. $5 \cdot 4\frac{7}{10}$
26. $2\frac{2}{3} \cdot 3\frac{5}{8}$
27. $1\frac{1}{2} \cdot 2\frac{2}{5}$
28. $3\frac{5}{6} \cdot 2\frac{3}{4}$

PRACTICE AND PROBLEM SOLVING

Extra Practice See page EP11.

Write each product in simplest form.

29. $1\frac{2}{3} \cdot \frac{2}{9}$
30. $3\frac{1}{3} \cdot \frac{7}{10}$
31. $2 \cdot \frac{5}{8}$
32. $2\frac{8}{11} \cdot \frac{3}{10}$
33. $\frac{3}{8} \cdot \frac{4}{9}$
34. $2\frac{1}{12} \cdot 1\frac{3}{5}$
35. $3\frac{3}{10} \cdot 4\frac{1}{6}$
36. $2\frac{1}{4} \cdot 1\frac{2}{9}$
37. $2 \cdot \frac{4}{5} \cdot 1\frac{2}{3}$
38. $3\frac{5}{6} \cdot \frac{9}{10} \cdot 4\frac{2}{3}$
39. $1\frac{7}{8} \cdot 2\frac{1}{3} \cdot 4$
40. $1\frac{2}{7} \cdot 3 \cdot 2\frac{5}{8}$

41. **Multi-Step** Jared used $1\frac{2}{5}$ bags of soil for his garden. He is digging another garden that will need $\frac{1}{5}$ as much soil as the original. How much will he use total?

42. Milo is making $1\frac{1}{2}$ batches of muffins. If one batch calls for $1\frac{3}{4}$ cups flour, how much flour will he need?

43. **Critical Thinking** Is the product of two mixed numbers less than, between, or greater than the two factors?

Evaluate each expression.

44. $\frac{1}{2} \cdot c$ for $c = 4\frac{2}{5}$
45. $1\frac{5}{7} \cdot x$ for $x = \frac{5}{6}$
46. $1\frac{3}{4} \cdot b$ for $b = 1\frac{1}{7}$
47. $1\frac{5}{9} \cdot n$ for $n = 18$
48. $2\frac{5}{9} \cdot t$ for $t = 4$
49. $3\frac{3}{4} \cdot p$ for $p = \frac{1}{2}$
50. $\frac{4}{5} \cdot m$ for $m = 2\frac{2}{3}$
51. $6y$ for $y = 3\frac{5}{8}$
52. $2\frac{3}{5} \cdot c$ for $c = 1\frac{1}{5}$

Cooking LINK

Muffins probably started out as a form of cake, or possibly as a variety of cornbread. Early muffins didn't have nearly as much variety as is available today.

Fresh Fruit Muffins

1 3/4 cups all-purpose flour
1/3 cup granulated sugar
2 1/2 teaspoons baking powder
1/2 teaspoon salt
3/4 cup milk
1 egg
1/3 cup butter, melted
1 cup fresh fruit

In a large bowl, whisk together dry ingredients. Add milk, egg, and butter, and mix until ingredients are moistened – do not over-beat. Stir in fruit and pour into greased muffin cups. Bake at 400°F for 20-25 minutes, or until tops spring back when lightly touched. Makes 12 muffins.

Use the recipe for Exercises 53–57.

53. How much flour and baking powder would you need if you doubled the recipe?

54. How much baking powder is needed for half of the recipe?

55. Raquel is baking muffins for a bake sale at school. She plans on multiplying the recipe by $3\frac{1}{2}$.
    a. How much flour will she need?
    b. How much sugar will she need?
    c. How much salt will she need?

56. Each muffin contains $22\frac{1}{5}$ grams of carbohydrates. How many grams of carbohydrates are contained in 12 muffins?

57. ★ **Challenge** What is the smallest number by which you could multiply the entire recipe so that the amount of each ingredient would be a whole number?

Test Prep and Spiral Review

58. **Multiple Choice** A chef uses $2\frac{1}{4}$ cups of water for a recipe. The chef doubled the recipe. How much water did the chef use?

    Ⓐ 4 cups   Ⓑ $4\frac{1}{4}$ cups   Ⓒ $4\frac{1}{2}$ cups   Ⓓ $4\frac{3}{4}$ cups

59. **Gridded Response** Keith ate $\frac{1}{3}$ pound of grapes last week. Jamal ate five times as many grapes as Keith last week. How many pounds of grapes did Jamal eat?

60. **Short Response** Josh is training to run in a half-marathon. So far this week, he has run $6\frac{3}{8}$ miles on each of three days. What is the total distance Josh has run this week?

Write each number in scientific notation. (Lesson 3-4)

61. 540   62. 1,400   63. 54,000   64. 508,000,000

Multiply. Write each answer in simplest form. (Lesson 5-6)

65. $5 \times \frac{1}{10}$ 66. $21 \times \frac{1}{3}$ 67. $\frac{2}{7} \times 14$ 68. $\frac{5}{12} \times 2$

Hands-On Lab 5-9

Model Fraction Division

Use with Lesson 5-9

Learn It Online
Lab Resources Online go.hrw.com,
keyword: MR10 Lab5

You can use grids to help you understand division of fractions.

Activity 1

Find $4\frac{1}{2} \div 3$.

Think of $4\frac{1}{2} \div 3$ as dividing $4\frac{1}{2}$ into 3 equal groups.

Shade $4\frac{1}{2}$ squares.

Divide the shaded parts into 3 equal groups.

Look at one of the shaded groups.

What fraction is this?

$$4\frac{1}{2} \div 3 = 1\frac{1}{2}$$

Think and Discuss

1. Explain how you know the number of groups into which you must divide the squares.

Try This

Write the division expression modeled on each grid.

1. = 1

Draw a model for each division expression. Then find the value of the expression.

2. $9\frac{1}{3} \div 4$ 3. $3\frac{3}{4} \div 5$ 4. $4\frac{2}{3} \div 2$ 5. $4\frac{1}{5} \div 3$

Activity 2

1. Find $2\frac{2}{3} \div \frac{2}{3}$.

Shade $2\frac{2}{3}$ squares.

258 Chapter 5 Fraction Operations

$2\frac{2}{3} \div \frac{2}{3} = 4$

Divide the shaded squares and shaded thirds into equal groups of $\frac{2}{3}$.

There are 4 groups of $\frac{2}{3}$ in $2\frac{2}{3}$.

2 *To find $3 \div \frac{3}{4}$, think, "How many groups of $\frac{3}{4}$ are in 3?"*

Shade 3 squares. Then divide the squares into fourths because the denominator of $\frac{3}{4}$ is 4.

Divide the shaded squares into equal groups of $\frac{3}{4}$.

There are 4 groups of $\frac{3}{4}$ in 3.

$3 \div \frac{3}{4} = 4$

Think and Discuss

1. Explain what prediction you can make about the value of $6 \div \frac{3}{4}$ if you know that $3 \div \frac{3}{4}$ is 4.

Try This

Write the division expression modeled by each grid.

1. = 1

2. = 1

Draw a model for each division expression. Then find the value of the expression.

3. $4 \div 1\frac{1}{3}$
4. $3\frac{3}{4} \div \frac{3}{4}$
5. $5\frac{1}{3} \div \frac{2}{3}$
6. $6\frac{2}{3} \div 1\frac{2}{3}$

5-9 Hands-On Lab 259

5-9 Dividing Fractions and Mixed Numbers

Learn to divide fractions and mixed numbers.

Vocabulary
reciprocal
multiplicative inverse

Curtis is making sushi rolls. First, he will place a sheet of seaweed, called *nori*, on the sushi rolling mat. Then, he will use the mat to roll up rice, cucumber, avocado, and crabmeat. Finally, he will slice the roll into smaller pieces.

Curtis has 2 cups of rice and will use $\frac{1}{3}$ cup for each sushi roll. How many sushi rolls can he make?

Think: How many $\frac{1}{3}$ pieces equal 2 wholes?

There are six $\frac{1}{3}$ pieces in 2 wholes, so Curtis can make 6 sushi rolls.

Reciprocals can help you divide by fractions. Two numbers are **reciprocals** or *multiplicative inverses*, if their product is 1.

Multiplicative Inverse Property	
Words	Numbers
The product of a nonzero number and its reciprocal, or **multiplicative inverse**, is 1.	$\frac{3}{4} \cdot \frac{4}{3} = 1$

EXAMPLE 1 Finding Reciprocals

Find the reciprocal.

A $\frac{1}{5}$

$\frac{1}{5} \cdot \blacksquare = 1$ *Think: $\frac{1}{5}$ of what number is 1?*

$\frac{1}{5} \cdot 5 = 1$ *$\frac{1}{5}$ of $\frac{5}{1}$ is 1.*

The reciprocal of $\frac{1}{5}$ is 5.

B $2\frac{1}{3}$

$\frac{7}{3} \cdot \blacksquare = 1$ *Write $2\frac{1}{3}$ as $\frac{7}{3}$.*

$\frac{7}{3} \cdot \frac{3}{7} = \frac{21}{21} = 1$ *$\frac{7}{3}$ of $\frac{3}{7}$ is 1.*

The reciprocal of $\frac{7}{3}$ is $\frac{3}{7}$.

Look at the relationship between the fractions $\frac{3}{4}$ and $\frac{4}{3}$. If you switch the numerator and denominator of a fraction, you will find its reciprocal. Dividing by a number is the same as multiplying by its reciprocal.

$$24 \div 4 = 6 \qquad 24 \cdot \tfrac{1}{4} = 6$$

EXAMPLE 2 Using Reciprocals to Divide Fractions and Mixed Numbers

Divide. Write each answer in simplest form.

A $\frac{4}{5} \div 5$

$\frac{4}{5} \div 5 = \frac{4}{5} \cdot \frac{1}{5}$ *Rewrite as multiplication using the reciprocal of 5, $\frac{1}{5}$.*

$\quad = \frac{4 \cdot 1}{5 \cdot 5}$ *Multiply by the reciprocal.*

$\quad = \frac{4}{25}$ *The answer is in simplest form.*

B $\frac{3}{4} \div \frac{1}{2}$

$\frac{3}{4} \div \frac{1}{2} = \frac{3}{4} \cdot \frac{2}{1}$ *Rewrite as multiplication using the reciprocal of $\frac{1}{2}$, $\frac{2}{1}$.*

$\quad = \frac{3 \cdot \overset{1}{\cancel{2}}}{\underset{2}{\cancel{4}} \cdot 1}$ *Simplify before multiplying.*

$\quad = \frac{3}{2}$ *Multiply.*

$\quad = 1\frac{1}{2}$ *You can write the answer as a mixed number.*

C $2\frac{2}{3} \div 1\frac{1}{6}$

$2\frac{2}{3} \div 1\frac{1}{6} = \frac{8}{3} \div \frac{7}{6}$ *Write the mixed numbers as improper fractions. $2\frac{2}{3} = \frac{8}{3}$ and $1\frac{1}{6} = \frac{7}{6}$*

$\quad = \frac{8}{3} \cdot \frac{6}{7}$ *Rewrite as multiplication.*

$\quad = \frac{8 \cdot \overset{2}{\cancel{6}}}{\underset{1}{\cancel{3}} \cdot 7}$ *Simplify before multiplying.*

$\quad = \frac{16}{7}$ *Multiply.*

$\quad = 2\frac{2}{7}$ *You can write the answer as a mixed number.*

Caution!

When you divide by a proper fraction, the quotient will be greater than the dividend. For example, since there are 8 halves in 4, $4 \div \frac{1}{2} = 8$.

Think and Discuss

1. **Explain** how you can use mental math to find the value of n in the equation $\frac{5}{8} \cdot n = 1$.
2. **Explain** how to find the reciprocal of $3\frac{6}{11}$.

5-9 Exercises

GUIDED PRACTICE

See Example 1 Find the reciprocal.

1. $\frac{2}{7}$
2. $\frac{5}{9}$
3. $\frac{1}{9}$
4. $\frac{3}{11}$
5. $2\frac{3}{5}$

See Example 2 Divide. Write each answer in simplest form.

6. $\frac{5}{6} \div 3$
7. $2\frac{1}{7} \div 1\frac{1}{4}$
8. $\frac{5}{12} \div 5$
9. $1\frac{5}{8} \div \frac{3}{4}$
10. $\frac{2}{3} \div \frac{1}{6}$
11. $\frac{3}{10} \div 1\frac{2}{3}$
12. $\frac{4}{7} \div 1\frac{1}{7}$
13. $4 \div \frac{7}{8}$

INDEPENDENT PRACTICE

See Example 1 Find the reciprocal.

14. $\frac{7}{8}$
15. $\frac{1}{10}$
16. $\frac{3}{8}$
17. $\frac{11}{12}$
18. $2\frac{5}{8}$
19. $\frac{8}{11}$
20. $\frac{5}{6}$
21. $\frac{6}{7}$
22. $\frac{2}{9}$
23. $5\frac{1}{4}$

See Example 2 Divide. Write each answer in simplest form.

24. $\frac{7}{8} \div 4$
25. $2\frac{3}{8} \div 1\frac{3}{4}$
26. $\frac{8}{9} \div 12$
27. $9 \div \frac{3}{4}$
28. $3\frac{5}{6} \div 1\frac{5}{9}$
29. $\frac{9}{10} \div 3$
30. $2\frac{4}{5} \div 1\frac{5}{7}$
31. $3\frac{1}{5} \div 1\frac{2}{7}$
32. $\frac{5}{8} \div \frac{1}{2}$
33. $1\frac{1}{2} \div 2\frac{1}{4}$
34. $\frac{7}{12} \div 2\frac{5}{8}$
35. $\frac{1}{8} \div 5$

PRACTICE AND PROBLEM SOLVING

Extra Practice
See page EP11.

Multiply or divide. Write each answer in simplest form.

36. $2\frac{3}{4} \div 2\frac{1}{5}$
37. $4\frac{4}{5} \div 2\frac{6}{7}$
38. $\frac{3}{8} \cdot \frac{5}{12}$
39. $6 \cdot \frac{7}{9}$
40. $3\frac{1}{7} \div 5$
41. $\frac{9}{14} \cdot \frac{1}{6}$

42. At Lina's restaurant, one serving of chili is $1\frac{1}{2}$ cups. The chef makes 48 cups of chili each night. How many servings of chili are in 48 cups?

43. Rhula bought 12 lb of raisins. She packed them into freezer bags so that each bag weighs $\frac{3}{4}$ lb. How many freezer bags did she pack?

Decide whether the fractions in each pair are reciprocals. If not, write the reciprocal of each fraction.

44. $\frac{1}{2}, 2$
45. $\frac{3}{8}, \frac{16}{6}$
46. $\frac{7}{9}, \frac{21}{27}$
47. $\frac{5}{6}, \frac{12}{10}$
48. $1\frac{1}{2}, \frac{2}{3}$
49. $\frac{2}{5}, \frac{4}{25}$
50. $\frac{3}{7}, 2\frac{1}{3}$
51. $5, \frac{5}{1}$

52. Lisa had some wood that was $12\frac{1}{2}$ feet long. She cut it into 5 pieces that are equal in length. How long is each piece of wood?

53. **Critical Thinking** How can you recognize the reciprocal of a fraction?

Multiply or divide. Write each answer in simplest form.

54. $\frac{11}{12} \cdot \frac{9}{10} \div 1\frac{1}{4}$

55. $2\frac{3}{4} \cdot 1\frac{2}{3} \div 5$

56. $1\frac{1}{2} \div \frac{3}{4} \cdot \frac{2}{5}$

57. $\frac{3}{4} \cdot \left(\frac{5}{7} \div \frac{1}{2}\right)$

58. $4\frac{2}{3} \div \left(6 \cdot \frac{3}{5}\right)$

59. $5\frac{1}{5} \cdot \left(3\frac{2}{5} \cdot 2\frac{1}{3}\right)$

Life Science The bar graph shows the lengths of some species of snakes found in the United States. Use the bar graph for Exercises 60–62.

Lengths of Snakes

- Eastern garter snake: $20\frac{1}{3}$
- Diamondback water snake: $29\frac{2}{3}$
- Western ribbon snake: $22\frac{2}{3}$

Length (in.)

60. Is the length of the eastern garter snake greater than or less than $\frac{1}{2}$ yd? Explain.

61. What is the average length of all the snakes?

62. Jim measured the length of a rough green snake. It was $27\frac{1}{3}$ in. long. What would the average length of the snakes be if Jim's measure of a rough green snake were added?

63. What's the Error? A student said the reciprocal of $6\frac{2}{3}$ is $6\frac{3}{2}$. Explain the error. Then write the correct reciprocal.

64. Write About It Explain how to divide fractions to find $\frac{3}{4} \div 2\frac{1}{3}$.

65. Challenge Evaluate the expression $\frac{(6-3)}{4} \div \frac{1}{8} \cdot 5$.

Test Prep and Spiral Review

66. Multiple Choice A piece of wood was 12 feet long. Gene cut the wood into pieces $\frac{2}{3}$ foot long. How many pieces did Gene have?

Ⓐ 4   Ⓑ 8   Ⓒ 16   Ⓓ 18

67. Multiple Choice Which product is NOT equal to 1?

Ⓕ $\frac{2}{3} \cdot \frac{3}{2}$ Ⓖ $8 \cdot \frac{1}{8}$ Ⓗ $\frac{1}{9} \cdot \frac{9}{3}$ Ⓙ $\frac{2}{13} \cdot \frac{13}{2}$

Find the number of decimal places in each product. Then multiply. (Lesson 3-5)

68. 2.4×1.8 **69.** 19×0.5 **70.** 7.04×2.3 **71.** 0.4×0.1

Find each product. (Lesson 5-8)

72. $2\frac{2}{3} \cdot \frac{1}{8}$ **73.** $\frac{1}{4} \cdot 3\frac{1}{2}$ **74.** $1\frac{1}{4} \cdot 1\frac{2}{5}$ **75.** $2\frac{1}{5} \cdot 2\frac{2}{3}$

5-9 Dividing Fractions and Mixed Numbers

5-10 Solving Fraction Equations: Multiplication and Division

Learn to solve equations by multiplying and dividing fractions.

Josef is building a fish pond for koi in his backyard. He makes the width of the pond $\frac{2}{3}$ of the length. The width of the pond is 14 feet. You can use the equation $\frac{2}{3}\ell = 14$ to find the length of the pond.

Small koi in a backyard pond usually grow 2 to 4 inches per year.

EXAMPLE 1   Solving Equations by Multiplying and Dividing

Solve each equation. Write the answer in simplest form.

Interactivities Online ▶

Remember!
Dividing by a number is the same as multiplying by its reciprocal.

A $\frac{2}{3}\ell = 14$

$\frac{2}{3}\ell = 14$

$\frac{2}{3}\ell \div \frac{2}{3} = 14 \div \frac{2}{3}$ Divide both sides of the equation by $\frac{2}{3}$.

$\frac{2}{3}\ell \cdot \frac{3}{2} = 14 \cdot \frac{3}{2}$ Multiply by $\frac{3}{2}$, the reciprocal of $\frac{2}{3}$.

$\ell = 14 \cdot \frac{3}{2}$

$\ell = \frac{14 \cdot 3}{1 \cdot 2}$

$\ell = \frac{42}{2}$, or 21

B $2x = \frac{1}{3}$

$2x = \frac{1}{3}$

$\frac{2x}{1} \cdot \frac{1}{2} = \frac{1}{3} \cdot \frac{1}{2}$ Multiply both sides by the reciprocal of 2.

$x = \frac{1 \cdot 1}{3 \cdot 2}$

$x = \frac{1}{6}$ The answer is in simplest form.

C $\frac{5x}{6} = 4$

$\frac{5x}{6} = 4$

$\frac{5x}{6} \div \frac{5}{6} = \frac{4}{1} \div \frac{5}{6}$ Divide both sides by $\frac{5}{6}$.

$\frac{5x}{6} \cdot \frac{6}{5} = \frac{4}{1} \cdot \frac{6}{5}$ Multiply by the reciprocal of $\frac{5}{6}$.

$x = \frac{24}{5}$, or $4\frac{4}{5}$

EXAMPLE 2　PROBLEM SOLVING APPLICATION

Dexter makes dog biscuits for the animal shelter. He makes $\frac{3}{4}$ of a recipe and uses 15 cups of powdered milk. How many cups of powdered milk are in the recipe?

1. Understand the Problem

The **answer** will be the number of cups of powdered milk in the recipe.

List the **important information**:
- He makes $\frac{3}{4}$ of the recipe.
- He uses 15 cups of powdered milk.

2. Make a Plan

You can write and solve an equation. Let x represent the number of cups in the recipe.

He uses 15 cups, which is three-fourths of the amount in the recipe. $15 = \frac{3}{4}x$

3. Solve

$$15 = \frac{3}{4}x$$

$$15 \cdot \frac{4}{3} = \frac{3}{4}x \cdot \frac{4}{3} \quad \text{Multiply both sides by } \frac{4}{3}, \text{ the reciprocal of } \frac{3}{4}.$$

$$\frac{\overset{5}{\cancel{15}}}{1} \cdot \frac{4}{\underset{1}{\cancel{3}}} = x \quad \text{Simplify. Then multiply.}$$

$$20 = x$$

There are 20 cups of powdered milk in the recipe.

4. Look Back

Check　$15 = \frac{3}{4}x$

$15 \stackrel{?}{=} \frac{3}{4}(20)$　　Substitute 20 for x.

$15 \stackrel{?}{=} \frac{\overset{15}{\cancel{60}}}{\underset{1}{\cancel{4}}}$　　Multiply and simplify.

$15 \stackrel{?}{=} 15$ ✓　　20 is the solution.

Pets

No more than $\frac{1}{10}$ of a dog's diet should consist of treats and biscuits.

Think and Discuss

1. **Explain** whether $\frac{2}{3}x = 4$ is the same as $\frac{2}{3} = 4x$.
2. **Tell** how you know which numbers to divide by in the following equations: $\frac{2}{3}x = 4$ and $\frac{4}{5} = 8x$.

5-10 Exercises

Learn It Online
Homework Help Online go.hrw.com,
keyword MR10 5-10
Exercises 1–15, 17, 21, 27, 29, 31, 33

GUIDED PRACTICE

See Example 1 Solve each equation. Write the answer in simplest form.

1. $\frac{3}{4}z = 12$
2. $4n = \frac{3}{5}$
3. $\frac{2x}{3} = 5$
4. $2c = \frac{9}{10}$

See Example 2
5. **School** In PE class, $\frac{3}{8}$ of the students want to play volleyball. If 9 students want to play volleyball, how many students are in the class?

INDEPENDENT PRACTICE

See Example 1 Solve each equation. Write the answer in simplest form.

6. $3t = \frac{2}{7}$
7. $\frac{1}{3}x = 3$
8. $\frac{3r}{5} = 9$
9. $8t = \frac{4}{5}$
10. $\frac{4}{5}a = 1$
11. $\frac{y}{4} = 5$
12. $2b = \frac{6}{7}$
13. $\frac{7}{9}j = 10$

See Example 2
14. Jason uses 2 cans of paint to paint $\frac{1}{2}$ of his room. How many cans of paint will he use to paint the whole room?

15. Cassandra baby-sits for $\frac{4}{5}$ of an hour and earns $8. What is her hourly rate?

PRACTICE AND PROBLEM SOLVING

Extra Practice
See page EP11.

Solve each equation. Write the answer in simplest form.

16. $m = \frac{3}{8} \cdot 4$
17. $\frac{3y}{5} = 6$
18. $4z = \frac{7}{10}$
19. $t = \frac{4}{5} \cdot 20$
20. $\frac{3}{5}a = \frac{3}{5}$
21. $\frac{1}{6}b = 2\frac{1}{3}$
22. $5c = \frac{2}{3} \div \frac{2}{3}$
23. $\frac{3}{4}x = 7$
24. $\frac{1}{2} = \frac{w}{4}$
25. $8 = \frac{2n}{3}$
26. $\frac{1}{4} \cdot \frac{1}{2} = 4d$
27. $2y = \frac{4}{5} \div \frac{3}{5}$

Write each equation. Then solve, and check the solution.

28. A number n is divided by 4 and the quotient is $\frac{1}{2}$.

29. A number n is multiplied by $1\frac{1}{2}$ and the product is 9.

30. A recipe for a loaf of bread calls for $\frac{3}{4}$ cup of oatmeal.
    a. How much oatmeal do you need if you make half the recipe?
    b. How much oatmeal do you need if you double the recipe?

31. **Entertainment** Connie rode the roller coaster at the amusement park. After 3 minutes, the ride was $\frac{3}{4}$ complete. How long did the entire ride take?

32. Zac moved $\frac{1}{5}$ of the things from his old bedroom to his new dorm room in $32\frac{1}{2}$ minutes. How long will it take in minutes for him to move all of his things to his new dorm room?

33. A dress pattern requires $3\frac{1}{8}$ yards of fabric. Jody wants to make matching dresses for the girls in her sewing club so she purchased $34\frac{3}{8}$ yards of fabric. How many dresses can Jody make using this pattern?

266 Chapter 5 Fraction Operations

Life Science

The northwest corner of Madagascar is home to black lemurs. These primates live in groups of 7–10, and they have an average life span of 20–25 years.

34. **Multi-Step** Alder cut 3 pieces of fabric from a roll. Each piece of fabric she cut is $1\frac{1}{2}$ yd long. She has 2 yards of fabric left on the roll. How much fabric was on the roll before she cut it?

35. **Life Science** Sasha's book report is about animals in Madagascar. She writes 10 pages, which represents $\frac{1}{3}$ of her report, about lemurs. How many more pages does Sasha have to write to complete her book report?

36. **Critical Thinking** How can you tell, without solving the equation $\frac{1}{2}x = 4\frac{7}{8}$, that x is greater that $4\frac{7}{8}$?

Use the circle graph for Exercises 37 and 38.

37. The circle graph shows the results of a survey of people who were asked to choose their favorite kind of bagel.

   a. One hundred people chose plain bagels as their favorite kind of bagel. How many people were surveyed in all?

   b. One-fifth of the people who chose sesame bagels also chose plain cream cheese as their favorite spread. How many people chose plain cream cheese? (*Hint*: Use the answer to part **a** to help you solve this problem.)

Favorite Bagels: $\frac{1}{4}$ Sesame, $\frac{1}{2}$ Plain, $\frac{1}{8}$ Poppy, $\frac{1}{8}$ Raisin

38. **What's the Question?** If the answer is 25 people, what is the question?

39. **Write About It** Explain how to solve $\frac{3}{5}x = 4$.

40. **Challenge** Solve $2\frac{3}{4}n = \frac{11}{12}$

Test Prep and Spiral Review

41. **Multiple Choice** Solve $\frac{3}{10}x = 9$.

    Ⓐ $x = 15$ Ⓑ $x = 30$ Ⓒ $x = 60$ Ⓓ $x = 90$

42. **Multiple Choice** Which of the following is a solution to $4x = \frac{3}{4}$?

    Ⓕ $x = \frac{3}{16}$ Ⓖ $x = \frac{3}{4}$ Ⓗ $x = 3$ Ⓙ $x = 5\frac{1}{3}$

43. **Gridded Response** What value of y is a solution to $\frac{4}{5}y = 28$?

Find the GCF of each set of numbers. (Lesson 4-3)

44. 6 and 15   45. 18 and 56   46. 12, 16, and 32   47. 24, 63, and 81

Divide. Write each answer in simplest form. (Lesson 5-9)

48. $\frac{2}{3} \div \frac{1}{3}$ 49. $\frac{9}{10} \div \frac{3}{4}$ 50. $2\frac{3}{8} \div \frac{1}{4}$ 51. $1\frac{1}{4} \div 2\frac{1}{3}$

CHAPTER 5 SECTION 5B

Ready To Go On?

Quiz for Lessons 5-6 Through 5-10

5-6 Multiplying Fractions by Whole Numbers

1. Multiply $4 \cdot \frac{2}{3}$. Write your answer in simplest form.

2. Michelle ordered 5 lb of fruit for a family picnic. Of that fruit, $\frac{1}{3}$ was watermelon. How much of the fruit was watermelon?

3. Philip has 35 comic books. Of those comics, $\frac{2}{10}$ take place in space. How many of Philip's comic books take place in space?

5-7 Multiplying Fractions

Multiply. Write each answer in simplest form.

4. $\frac{2}{7} \cdot \frac{3}{4}$
5. $\frac{3}{5} \cdot \frac{2}{3}$
6. $\frac{7}{12} \cdot \frac{4}{5}$

Evaluate the expression $t \cdot \frac{1}{8}$ for each value of t. Write the answer in simplest form.

7. $t = \frac{4}{9}$
8. $t = \frac{4}{5}$
9. $t = \frac{2}{3}$

5-8 Multiplying Mixed Numbers

Multiply. Write each answer in simplest form.

10. $\frac{1}{4} \cdot 2\frac{1}{3}$
11. $1\frac{1}{6} \cdot \frac{2}{3}$
12. $\frac{7}{8} \cdot 2\frac{2}{3}$

Find each product. Write the answer in simplest form.

13. $2\frac{1}{4} \cdot 1\frac{1}{6}$
14. $1\frac{2}{3} \cdot 2\frac{1}{5}$
15. $3 \cdot 4\frac{2}{7}$

5-9 Dividing Fractions and Mixed Numbers

Find the reciprocal.

16. $\frac{2}{7}$
17. $\frac{5}{12}$
18. $\frac{3}{5}$

Divide. Write each answer in simplest form.

19. $\frac{3}{5} \div 4$
20. $1\frac{3}{10} \div 3\frac{1}{4}$
21. $1\frac{1}{5} \div 2\frac{1}{3}$

5-10 Solving Fraction Equations: Multiplication and Division

Solve each equation.

22. $\frac{2y}{3} = 10$
23. $6p = \frac{3}{4}$
24. $\frac{2x}{3} = 9$

25. Michael has a black cat and a gray kitten. The black cat weighs 12 pounds. The gray kitten weighs $\frac{3}{5}$ the weight of the black cat. How much does the gray kitten weigh?

Real-World Connections

CHAPTER 5

The American Royal Barbecue Since 1980, Kansas City has hosted one of the "hottest" events of the year. The annual American Royal Barbecue is the world's largest barbecue contest, with nearly 500 grilling teams from around the world. Each year, 70,000 visitors sample barbecued ribs, chicken, turkey, and much more.

1. Anne's team is using the recipe for barbecue sauce shown here. She starts by stirring together the steak sauce and the hot pepper sauce. How many tablespoons of this mixture will she have?

2. Miguel's team uses a different recipe for barbecue sauce. It makes $3\frac{3}{4}$ cups of sauce.

   a. How much more sauce does Miguel's recipe make than the recipe shown here?

   b. Miguel's recipe calls for $\frac{2}{3}$ of the amount of peanut oil that is in the recipe shown here. How much peanut oil is in Miguel's recipe?

3. Ray's team uses the recipe shown here to make a large amount of barbecue sauce for the contest. He multiplies all the quantities in the recipe by 5.

   a. How many cups of sauce will Ray make?

   b. Ray plans to divide the sauce equally among 7 storage containers. How much sauce will be in each container?

Kansas City Barbecue Sauce

- 2 cups apple cider vinegar
- 4 ounces tomato paste
- 1 1/2 tablespoons sugar
- 1 1/2 tablespoons peanut oil
- 1 1/2 tablespoons salt
- 3/4 tablespoon steak sauce
- 3/4 tablespoon Worcestershire sauce
- 1/2 tablespoon hot pepper sauce

Mix ingredients together in a saucepan. Simmer for 10 minutes. Makes 3 1/2 cups.

Game Time

Fraction Riddles

1. What is the value of one-half of two-thirds of three-fourths of four-fifths of five-sixths of six-sevenths of seven-eighths of eight-ninths of nine-tenths of one thousand?

2. What is the next fraction in the sequence below?

   $\frac{1}{12}, \frac{1}{6}, \frac{1}{4}, \frac{1}{3}, \ldots$

3. I am a three-digit number. My hundreds digit is one-third of my tens digit. My tens digit is one-third of my ones digit. What number am I?

4. A *splorg* costs three-fourths of a dollar plus three-fourths of a *splorg*. How much does a *splorg* cost?

5. How many cubic inches of dirt are in a hole that measures $\frac{1}{3}$ feet by $\frac{1}{4}$ feet by $\frac{1}{2}$ feet?

Fraction Bingo

The object is to be the first player to cover five squares in a row horizontally, vertically, or diagonally.

One person is the caller. On each of the caller's cards, there is an expression containing fractions. When the caller draws a card, he or she reads the expression aloud for the players.

The players must find the value of the expression. If a square on the player's card has that value or a fraction equivalent to that value, they cover the square.

The first player to cover five squares in a row is the winner. Take turns being the caller. A variation can be played in which the winner is the first person to cover all their squares.

A complete copy of the rules and game pieces are available online.

Materials
- file folder
- scissors
- white paper
- hole punch
- chenille stem
- surveyor's flagging tape
- tape

It's in the Bag!

PROJECT: Flipping over Fractions

Make a flip-flop book to take notes and work sample problems related to fraction operations.

Directions

1. Cut the folder in half from the fold to the edge. Then cut out a flip-flop shape, with the "toe" of the flip-flop along the folded edge. **Figure A**

2. Cut about ten flip-flop shapes out of the white paper. They should be slightly smaller than the flip-flop you cut out of the file folder.

3. Put the white flip-flops inside the file-folder flip-flop. Punch a hole at the top through all the layers. Also punch holes at the sides of the flip-flip cover. These side holes should go through only the cover. **Figure B**

4. Insert the chenille stem into the hole at the top, make a loop, and trim. Insert the surveyor's flagging tape through the loop, and insert the ends into the holes at the sides of the flip-flop. Tape the surveyor's flagging tape to the back of the cover to hold it in place. **Figure C**

Taking Note of the Math

Write the chapter number and title on the flip-flop. Then use the inside pages to work problems from the chapter. Choose problems that will help you remember the most important concepts.

It's in the Bag!

CHAPTER 5 Study Guide: Review

Vocabulary

least common denominator (LCD) 224
least common multiple (LCM) 218
reciprocals 260
multiplicative inverse 260

Complete the sentences below with vocabulary words from the list above.

1. Two numbers are ___?___ if their product is 1.

2. The ___?___ is the smallest number that is a common multiple of two or more denominators.

EXAMPLES | EXERCISES

5-1 Least Common Multiple (pp. 218–221)

■ Find the least common multiple (LCM) of 4, 6, and 8.

4: 4, 8, 12, 16, 20, 24, 28, ...
6: 6, 12, 18, 24, 30, ...
8: 8, 16, 24, 32, ...
LCM: 24

Find the least common multiple (LCM).

3. 3, 5, and 10
4. 6, 8, and 16
5. 3, 9, and 27
6. 4, 12, and 30
7. 25 and 45
8. 12, 22, and 30

5-2 Adding and Subtracting with Unlike Denominators (pp. 224–227)

■ Add. Write the answer in simplest form.

$\frac{7}{9} + \frac{2}{3}$

$\frac{7}{9} + \frac{2}{3}$ *Write equivalent fractions. Add.*

$\frac{7}{9} + \frac{6}{9} = \frac{13}{9} = 1\frac{4}{9}$

Add or subtract. Write each answer in simplest form.

9. $\frac{1}{5} + \frac{5}{8}$
10. $\frac{1}{6} + \frac{7}{12}$
11. $\frac{13}{15} - \frac{4}{5}$
12. $\frac{7}{8} - \frac{2}{3}$

5-3 Adding and Subtracting Mixed Numbers (pp. 228–231)

■ Find the difference. Write the answer in simplest form.

$5\frac{5}{8} - 3\frac{1}{6}$

$5\frac{15}{24} - 3\frac{4}{24}$ *Write equivalent fractions.*

$2\frac{11}{24}$ *Subtract.*

Find each sum or difference. Write the answer in simplest form.

13. $1\frac{3}{10} + 3\frac{2}{5}$
14. $4\frac{5}{9} - 1\frac{1}{2}$

15. Angela had $\frac{7}{10}$ gallon of paint. She used $\frac{1}{3}$ gallon for a project. How much paint did she have left?

272 Chapter 5 Fraction Operations

EXAMPLES

EXERCISES

5-4 Regrouping to Subtract Mixed Numbers (pp. 234–237)

■ Subtract. Write the answer in simplest form.

$4\frac{7}{10} - 2\frac{9}{10}$

$3\frac{17}{10} - 2\frac{9}{10}$ *Regroup $4\frac{7}{10}$. Subtract.*

$1\frac{8}{10}$

$1\frac{4}{5}$

Subtract. Write each answer in simplest form.

16. $7\frac{2}{9} - 3\frac{5}{9}$
17. $3\frac{1}{5} - 1\frac{7}{10}$
18. $8\frac{7}{12} - 2\frac{11}{12}$
19. $5\frac{3}{8} - 2\frac{3}{4}$
20. $11\frac{6}{7} - 4\frac{13}{14}$
21. $10 - 8\frac{7}{8}$

22. Georgette needs 8 feet of ribbon to decorate gifts. She has $3\frac{1}{4}$ feet of ribbon. How many more feet of ribbon does Georgette need?

5-5 Solving Fraction Equations: Addition and Subtraction (pp. 238–241)

■ Solve $n + 2\frac{5}{7} = 8$. Write the solution in simplest form.

$n + 2\frac{5}{7} - 2\frac{5}{7} = 8 - 2\frac{5}{7}$

$n = 8 - 2\frac{5}{7}$

$n = 7\frac{7}{7} - 2\frac{5}{7}$

$n = 5\frac{2}{7}$

Solve each equation. Write the solution in simplest form.

23. $x - 12\frac{3}{4} = 17\frac{2}{5}$
24. $t + 6\frac{11}{12} = 21\frac{5}{6}$
25. $3\frac{2}{3} = m - 1\frac{3}{4}$
26. $5\frac{2}{3} = p + 2\frac{2}{9}$
27. $y - 1\frac{2}{3} = 3\frac{4}{5}$
28. $4\frac{2}{5} + j = 7\frac{7}{10}$

29. Jon poured $1\frac{1}{2}$ oz of lemon juice onto a salad. He has $5\frac{1}{2}$ oz lemon juice left in the bottle. How many ounces of lemon juice were in the bottle before Jon poured some on the salad?

30. Abigail is walking to her grandparents' house. If she has walked $1\frac{1}{3}$ miles and her grandparents live 3 miles away, how much farther does Abigail have to walk?

5-6 Multiplying Fractions by Whole Numbers (pp. 244–247)

■ Multiply $3 \cdot \frac{3}{5}$. Write your answer in simplest form.

$3 \cdot \frac{3}{5} = \frac{3}{5} + \frac{3}{5} + \frac{3}{5} = \frac{9}{5}$ or $1\frac{4}{5}$

Multiply. Write each answer in simplest form.

31. $5 \cdot \frac{1}{7}$
32. $2 \cdot \frac{3}{8}$
33. $3 \cdot \frac{6}{7}$
34. $4 \cdot \frac{5}{8}$
35. $6 \cdot \frac{1}{2}$
36. $2 \cdot \frac{3}{5}$

37. There are 105 members of the high school band. Of these members, $\frac{1}{5}$ play percussion instruments. How many members play percussion?

EXAMPLES

EXERCISES

5-7 Multiplying Fractions (pp. 250–253)

■ Multiply. Write the answer in simplest form.

$\frac{3}{4} \cdot \frac{1}{3}$ *Multiply. Then simplify.*

$\frac{3 \cdot 1}{4 \cdot 3} = \frac{3}{12} = \frac{1}{4}$

Multiply. Write each answer in simplest form.

38. $\frac{5}{6} \cdot \frac{2}{5}$ 39. $\frac{5}{7} \cdot \frac{3}{4}$ 40. $\frac{4}{5} \cdot \frac{1}{8}$

41. $\frac{7}{10} \cdot \frac{2}{5}$ 42. $\frac{1}{9} \cdot \frac{5}{9}$ 43. $\frac{1}{4} \cdot \frac{6}{7}$

44. Andrew's hockey team won $\frac{4}{5}$ of their games. Andrew scored in $\frac{2}{3}$ of the games his team won. In what fraction of his team's games did Andrew score?

5-8 Multiplying Mixed Numbers (pp. 254–257)

■ Multiply. Write the answer in simplest form.

$\frac{2}{5} \cdot 1\frac{2}{3} = \frac{2}{5} \cdot \frac{5}{3} = \frac{10}{15} = \frac{2}{3}$

Multiply. Write each answer in simplest form.

45. $\frac{2}{5} \cdot 2\frac{1}{4}$ 46. $\frac{3}{4} \cdot 1\frac{2}{3}$ 47. $3\frac{1}{3} \cdot \frac{3}{5}$

5-9 Dividing Fractions and Mixed Numbers (pp. 260–263)

■ Divide. Write the answer in simplest form.

$\frac{3}{4} \div 6 = \frac{3 \cdot 1}{4 \cdot 6} = \frac{3}{24} = \frac{1}{8}$

Divide. Write each answer in simplest form.

48. $\frac{4}{7} \div 3$ 49. $\frac{3}{10} \div 2$ 50. $1\frac{1}{3} \div 2\frac{2}{5}$

51. Beverly needs to measure $2\frac{2}{3}$ cups of bread crumbs. She has a $\frac{1}{3}$ cup measuring scoop. How many times must she fill the $\frac{1}{3}$ cup measuring scoop to get $2\frac{2}{3}$ cups of bread crumbs?

5-10 Solving Fraction Equations: Multiplication and Division (pp. 264–267)

■ Solve the equation.

$\frac{4}{5}n = 12$

$\frac{4}{5}n \div \frac{4}{5} = 12 \div \frac{4}{5}$ *Divide both sides by $\frac{4}{5}$.*

$\frac{4}{5}n \cdot \frac{5}{4} = 12 \cdot \frac{5}{4}$ *Multiply by the reciprocal.*

$n = \frac{60}{4} = 15$

Solve each equation.

52. $4a = \frac{1}{2}$ 53. $\frac{3b}{4} = 1\frac{1}{2}$

54. $\frac{2m}{7} = 5$ 55. $6g = \frac{4}{5}$

56. $\frac{5}{6}r = 9$ 57. $\frac{s}{8} = 6\frac{1}{4}$

58. $6p = \frac{2}{3}$ 59. $\frac{8j}{9} = 1\frac{5}{8}$

60. Marcus is $66\frac{2}{3}$ inches tall. If Marcus is $\frac{5}{6}$ as tall as his father, how tall is Marcus's father?

Chapter Test

CHAPTER 5

Find the least common multiple (LCM).

1. 10 and 15
2. 4, 6, and 18
3. 9, 10, and 12
4. 6, 15, and 20

Add or subtract. Write the answer in simplest form.

5. $4\frac{1}{9} - 2\frac{4}{9}$
6. $1\frac{7}{10} + 3\frac{3}{4}$
7. $\frac{2}{3} - \frac{3}{8}$
8. $2\frac{1}{3} - \frac{5}{6}$
9. $4 + 2\frac{2}{7}$
10. $\frac{1}{12} + \frac{5}{6}$
11. $\frac{3}{8} + \frac{3}{4}$
12. $\frac{5}{6} - \frac{2}{3}$

13. On Saturday, Cecelia ran $3\frac{3}{7}$ miles. On Sunday, she ran $4\frac{5}{6}$ miles. How much farther did Cecelia run on Sunday than on Saturday?

14. Michael studied social studies for $\frac{3}{4}$ of an hour, Spanish for $1\frac{1}{2}$ hours, and math for $1\frac{1}{4}$ hours. How many hours did Michael spend studying all three subjects?

15. Quincy needs $6\frac{1}{3}$ feet of rope to tie down the things he is hauling in his truck. He finds a 9 foot long rope in his garage. How much extra rope does Quincy have?

Find the reciprocal.

16. $\frac{3}{5}$
17. $\frac{7}{11}$
18. $\frac{5}{9}$
19. $\frac{1}{8}$

Multiply or divide. Write the answer in simplest form.

20. $\frac{3}{7} \cdot \frac{4}{9}$
21. $1\frac{3}{8} \cdot \frac{6}{11}$
22. $2\frac{1}{4} \cdot 2\frac{2}{3}$
23. $\frac{7}{8} \div 2$
24. $3\frac{1}{3} \div 1\frac{5}{12}$
25. $\frac{4}{5} \cdot 1\frac{1}{3}$
26. $3\frac{1}{8} \div 1\frac{1}{4}$
27. $\frac{3}{8} \cdot \frac{2}{3}$

Evaluate the expression $n \cdot \frac{1}{4}$ for each value of n. Write the answer in simplest form.

28. $n = \frac{7}{8}$
29. $n = \frac{2}{5}$
30. $n = \frac{8}{9}$
31. $n = \frac{4}{11}$

32. Twenty-four students tried out for the cheerleading squad. Only $\frac{5}{6}$ of the students will be chosen. How many students will be chosen for the squad?

33. A recipe for granola bars require $1\frac{1}{2}$ cups of flour. How much flour is needed to make a triple batch of granola bars?

Solve each equation. Write the solution in simplest form.

34. $3r = \frac{9}{10}$
35. $n + 3\frac{1}{6} = 12$
36. $5\frac{5}{6} = x - 3\frac{1}{4}$
37. $\frac{2}{5}t = 9$
38. $\frac{4}{5}m = 7$
39. $y - 15\frac{3}{5} = 2\frac{1}{3}$

40. Jessica purchased a bag of cat food. She feeds her cat 1 cup of cat food each day. After 7 days, she has fed her cat $\frac{2}{3}$ of the food in the bag. How many cups of food were in the bag of cat food when Jessica bought it?

CHAPTER 5

Test Tackler
STANDARDIZED TEST STRATEGIES

Gridded Response: Write Gridded Responses

When responding to a test item that has an answer grid, you must fill out the grid correctly, or the item will be marked as incorrect.

EXAMPLE 1

Gridded Response: Simplify the expression $(8 \times 3) - 5 \times (6 - 3)$.

$(8 \times 3) - 5 \times (6 - 3)$
$24 - 5 \times 3$ *Perform operations within parentheses.*
$24 - 15$ *Multiply.*
9 *Subtract.*

The expression simplifies to 9.

- Use a pencil to write your answer in the answer boxes at the top of the grid.
- The answer can be entered starting in the far left column, or in the far right column, but not in the middle.
- Write only one digit in each box. Do not leave a blank box in the middle of an answer.
- Shade the correct bubble below your written digit.

EXAMPLE 2

Gridded Response: Evaluate $2\frac{1}{4} + 1\frac{1}{4} + 3\frac{3}{4}$.

$2\frac{1}{4} + 1\frac{1}{4} + 3\frac{3}{4}$
$6\frac{5}{4}$ *Add the fractions and then add the whole numbers.*
$6\frac{5}{4} = 6 + 1\frac{1}{4} = 7\frac{1}{4}$ or 7.25 or $\frac{29}{4}$ *Simplify.*

- You cannot fill in mixed numbers. You must fill in the answer as an improper fraction or a decimal.
- Use a pencil to write your answer in the answer boxes at the top of the grid.
- Write only one digit or symbol in each box. On some grids, the fraction bar and the decimal point have a special box. If so, write your fraction or decimal around it correctly. Do not leave a blank box in the middle of an answer.
- Shade the correct bubble below your written digit.

276   Chapter 5 Fraction Operations

Hot Tip! When filling out a grid be sure to use a pencil and completely fill in the bubbles directly below each digit or symbol you wrote.

Read each sample and then answer the questions that follow.

Sample A
A student divided two fractions and got $\frac{4}{25}$ as a result. Then the student filled in the grid as shown.

1. What error did the student make when filling in the grid?
2. Explain how to fill in the answer correctly.

Sample B
A student solved the equation $x + 2.1 = 5$, and found that $x = 2.9$. This answer is displayed in the grid as shown.

3. What error did the student make when filling in the grid?
4. Explain how to fill in the answer correctly.

Sample C
A student correctly simplified the expression $6\frac{7}{8} + 1\frac{3}{8} - 2\frac{5}{8}$. Then the student filled in the grid as shown.

5. What answer does the grid show?
6. Explain why you cannot grid a mixed number.
7. Write the answer $5\frac{5}{8}$ in two forms that could be entered in the grid correctly.

Sample D
A student wrote the standard form of the decimal one and twenty-five hundredths and then filled in the grid as shown.

8. What error did the student make when filling in the grid?
9. Explain how to fill in the answer correctly.

Test Tackler 277

Standardized Test Prep

Cumulative Assessment, Chapters 1–5

Multiple Choice

1. Which number is less than $\frac{3}{4}$?
   - Ⓐ $\frac{2}{3}$
   - Ⓑ $\frac{4}{5}$
   - Ⓒ $\frac{5}{6}$
   - Ⓓ $\frac{9}{10}$

2. Mr. Ledden's briefcase has a mass of 9.4 kilograms on Earth. How much would his briefcase weigh on Jupiter?

Gravitational Pull of Planets (Compared with Earth)	
Planet	Gravitational Pull
Mercury	0.38
Venus	0.91
Mars	0.38
Jupiter	2.54
Saturn	0.93
Neptune	1.2

   - Ⓕ 8.554 kg
   - Ⓖ 11.28 kg
   - Ⓗ 11.94 kg
   - Ⓙ 23.876 kg

3. Brandon's family is planning a trip from Dallas to San Antonio. Dallas is about 272 miles from San Antonio. If Brandon's dad drives an average of 60 miles per hour, about how long will the trip take?
   - Ⓐ 3 hours
   - Ⓑ 5 hours
   - Ⓒ 6 hours
   - Ⓓ 7 hours

4. What is the value of 5^4?
   - Ⓕ 9
   - Ⓖ 20
   - Ⓗ 625
   - Ⓙ 1,000

5. A recipe calls for $\frac{1}{4}$ cup of sugar and $\frac{2}{3}$ cup of flour. How much more flour than sugar is needed for this recipe?
   - Ⓐ $\frac{1}{7}$ cup
   - Ⓑ $\frac{5}{12}$ cup
   - Ⓒ $\frac{1}{2}$ cup
   - Ⓓ $\frac{3}{4}$ cup

6. Maggie needs $15\frac{3}{8}$ yards of blue rope, $24\frac{1}{3}$ yards of white rope, and $8\frac{3}{4}$ yards of red rope. About how many yards of rope does she need in all?
   - Ⓕ 38 yards
   - Ⓖ 45 yards
   - Ⓗ 48 yards
   - Ⓙ 55 yards

7. Let d represent the number of dogs that Max walks in 1 day. Which expression shows the number of dogs Max walks in 7 days?
   - Ⓐ $7 + d$
   - Ⓑ $d - 7$
   - Ⓒ $7d$
   - Ⓓ $\frac{d}{7}$

8. Charlie eats $\frac{5}{8}$ of a pizza. One-fifth of the pizza he eats is covered with mushrooms. How much of Charlie's pizza is covered with mushrooms?
   - Ⓕ $\frac{1}{8}$ pizza
   - Ⓖ $\frac{5}{13}$ pizza
   - Ⓗ $\frac{1}{5}$ pizza
   - Ⓙ $3\frac{1}{8}$ pizza

9. Which of the following sets of decimals is ordered from least to greatest?
   - Ⓐ 3.8, 3.89, 3.08, 3.9
   - Ⓑ 3.89, 3.8, 3.9, 3.08
   - Ⓒ 3.08, 3.89, 3.8, 3.9
   - Ⓓ 3.08, 3.8, 3.89, 3.9

10. Samantha gets to choose a number for her soccer jersey. She picks a number that is divisible by 3, 5, and 9, but not by 2, 4, or 6. Which of the following can be Samantha's jersey number?

    F 15
    G 27
    H 30
    J 45

11. A theater has 145 rows of seats. There are 12 seats in each row. The sixth grade class from Brookpark Middle School has 168 students and 15 chaperones that are attending a play next week. How many rows will they need to reserve for the upcoming play?

    A 14 rows
    B 15 rows
    C 16 rows
    D 17 rows

HOT TIP! Underline key words given in the test question so you know for certain what the question is asking.

Gridded Response

12. What is the least common denominator for the following fractions: $\frac{4}{5}$, $\frac{3}{4}$, and $\frac{1}{10}$?

13. During a walk-a-thon, Brian walks $3\frac{1}{4}$ kilometers, and Stacey walks $2\frac{7}{8}$ kilometers. How many more kilometers does Brian walk than Stacy?

14. What is the reciprocal of $6\frac{1}{7}$?

15. Ying caught a fish that measured 62.5 centimeters. This fish measured 8.2 centimeters less than the fish Ying caught yesterday. How many centimeters did the fish Ying caught yesterday measure?

16. Name the decimal that is equivalent to $\frac{3}{5}$.

17. Natalie lives $\frac{1}{6}$ mile from school. Peter lives $\frac{3}{10}$ mile from school. How many miles further does Peter live from the school than Natalie?

Short Response

S1. Jane is building a tank for her pet snake. The tank's minimum length should equal two-thirds of the snake's length, and the tank's width should be equal to half the snake's length. Jane's snake is $2\frac{1}{2}$ feet long. Calculate and explain how to find the dimensions of the tank.

S2. Lucy has $\frac{5}{6}$ yard of ribbon to wrap gifts for her friends. The bow on each gift requires $\frac{1}{6}$ yard of ribbon. Write an equation to determine how many b bows Lucy can make. Solve and interpret your answer.

Extended Response

E1. Garrett attends a summer day camp for 6 hours each day. The circle graph below shows what fraction of each day he spends doing different activities.

Camp Activities

Reading $\frac{1}{12}$, Swimming $\frac{1}{3}$, Crafts $\frac{1}{6}$, Sports activities $\frac{1}{6}$, Playground games $\frac{1}{8}$, Lunch $\frac{1}{8}$

a. How long does Garrett spend doing each activity? Write the activities in order from longest to shortest.

b. Sports activities and playground games are all held on the camp fields. What fraction of the day does Garrett spend on the fields? Write your answer in simplest form.

c. Lunch and crafts are held in the cafeteria. How many hours does Garrett spend in the cafeteria during a 5-day week at day camp? Write your answer in simplest form, and show the work necessary to determine the correct answer.

Cumulative Assessment, Chapters 1–5

CHAPTER 6
Collecting and Displaying Data

6A Organizing Data
- 6-1 Making a Table
- LAB Collect Data to Explore Mean
- 6-2 Mean, Median, Mode, and Range
- 6-3 Additional Data and Outliers

6B Displaying and Interpreting Data
- 6-4 Bar Graphs
- LAB Create Bar Graphs
- 6-5 Line Plots, Frequency Tables, and Histograms
- EXT Frequency Distribution
- LAB Use a Survey to Collect Data
- 6-6 Ordered Pairs
- 6-7 Line Graphs
- 6-8 Misleading Graphs
- 6-9 Stem-and-Leaf Plots
- 6-10 Choosing an Appropriate Display

Why Learn This?

Scientists can use data to make predictions about populations of animals such as these King penguins on South Georgia Island in the southern Atlantic Ocean.

Learn It Online
Chapter Project Online go.hrw.com,
keyword MR10 Ch6

Chapter Focus
- Use mean, median, mode, and range to summarize data sets.
- Make and interpret a variety of graphs.

Are You Ready?

Vocabulary

Choose the best term from the list to complete each sentence.

1. The answer to an addition problem is called the ___?___.
2. The ___?___ of the 6 in 5,672 is hundreds.
3. When you move ___?___, you move left or right.
   When you move ___?___, you move up or down.

horizontally
place value
quotients
sum
vertically

Complete these exercises to review skills you will need for this chapter.

Place Value of Whole Numbers

Write the digit in the tens place of each number.

4. 718
5. 989
6. 55
7. 7,709

Compare and Order Whole Numbers

Order the numbers from least to greatest.

8. 40, 32, 51, 78, 26, 43, 27
9. 132, 150, 218, 176, 166
10. 92, 91, 84, 92, 87, 90
11. 23, 19, 33, 27, 31, 31, 28, 18

Find the greatest number in each set.

12. 452, 426, 502, 467, 530, 512
13. 711, 765, 723, 778, 704, 781
14. 143, 122, 125, 137, 140, 118, 139
15. 1,053; 1,106; 1,043; 1,210; 1,039; 1,122

Write Fractions as Decimals

Write each fraction as a decimal.

16. $\frac{1}{4}$
17. $\frac{5}{8}$
18. $\frac{1}{6}$
19. $\frac{2}{5}$
20. $\frac{5}{6}$
21. $\frac{1}{2}$
22. $\frac{3}{4}$
23. $\frac{9}{11}$

Locate Points on a Number Line

Name the point on the number line that corresponds to each given value.

24. 5
25. 12
26. 8
27. 1

Collecting and Displaying Data

CHAPTER 6 Study Guide: Preview

Where You've Been

Previously, you

- described characteristics of data such as the shape of the data and the middle number.
- graphed a given set of data using an appropriate graphical representation.
- used tables of related number pairs to make line graphs.

In This Chapter

You will study

- using mean, median, mode, and range to describe data.
- solving problems by collecting, organizing, and displaying data.
- drawing and comparing different graphical representations of the same data.

Where You're Going

You can use the skills learned in this chapter

- to recognize misuses of graphical information and evaluate conclusions based on data analysis.
- to display data correctly for projects in social studies and science.

Key Vocabulary/Vocabulario

bar graph	gráfica de barras
coordinate grid	cuadrícula de coordenadas
line graph	gráfica lineal
mean	media
median	mediana
mode	moda
ordered pair	par ordenado
outlier	valor extremo
range	rango (en estadística)
stem-and-leaf plot	diagrama de tallo y hojas

Vocabulary Connections

To become familiar with some of the vocabulary terms in the chapter, consider the following. You may refer to the chapter, the glossary, or a dictionary if you like.

1. A *bar* can be a straight stripe or band. What do you think a **bar graph** uses to display data?

2. A *grid* is a network of uniformly spaced horizontal and perpendicular lines. What do you think a **coordinate grid** looks like?

3. *Ordered* means "to be arranged." The word *pair* can mean "two things designed for use together." What do you think an **ordered pair** is made up of?

4. A *range* can mean the distance between possible extremes. If you are looking for the **range** of a set of numbers, what do you think you are looking for?

5. The *stem* is the main trunk of a plant. The *leaves* are the outgrowth from the stem. How do you think a **stem-and-leaf plot** is made?

Reading and Writing Math

CHAPTER 6

Reading Strategy: Read and Interpret Graphics

Figures, diagrams, charts, and graphs are used to illustrate data. Knowing how to understand these visual aids will help you learn the important facts and details of a problem.

Chart

Gustavo's Gift Wrap Table

Gift Size	Paper Needed (yd^2)
Small	$\frac{11}{12}$
Medium	$1\frac{5}{9}$
Large	$2\frac{2}{3}$
X-large	$3\frac{1}{9}$

Read and understand each column head and each row head.

- **Title:** Gustavo's Gift Wrap Table
- **Gift Size:** Small, Medium, Large, and X-large
- **Paper Needed (yd^2):** Tells how much paper is needed to wrap the given gift size.

Graph

U.S. Space Exploration Missions

(Bar graph: Number of missions vs. Years in 5-year intervals from 1961–1965 through 2001–2005)

The titles of the graph describe what information is being graphed. Read the label on each axis.

- **Title:** U.S. Space Exploration Missions
- **x-axis:** Years (given as 5-year intervals)
- **y-axis:** Number of missions

Try This

Look up each exercise in your textbook and answer the following questions.

1. Lesson 5-5, Exercise 32: What type of graph is shown? How many minutes long is "Winter"? Explain.

2. Lesson 5-10, Exercise 37: What is the title of the circle graph? What types of bagels are listed?

Collecting and Displaying Data

6-1 Making a Table

Learn to use tables to record and organize data.

Weather forecasters collect data about weather. By organizing and interpreting this data, they can often warn people of severe weather before it happens. This advance warning can save lives.

This satellite image shows a hurricane approaching Florida's coastline.

One way to organize data is to make a table. By looking at a table, you may see patterns and relationships.

EXAMPLE 1

Weather Application

Use the data about Hurricane Dean to make a table. Then use your table to describe how the hurricane's strength changed over time.

On August 16, 2007, Hurricane Dean's wind speed was 75 mi/h. On August 17, its wind speed was 100 mi/h. On August 18, its wind speed was 150 mi/h. On August 21, its wind speed was 160 mi/h. On August 22, its wind speed was 85 mi/h.

Date (2007)	Wind Speed (mi/h)
August 16	75
August 17	100
August 18	150
August 21	160
August 22	85

Make a table. Write the dates in order so that you can see how the hurricane's strength changed over time.

From the table, you can see that Hurricane Dean became stronger from August 16 to August 21 and then weakened from August 21 to August 22.

Weather

Hurricane Dean was the first Category 5 Hurricane to make land-fall in the Atlantic Basin since 1992, when Hurricane Andrew struck the Bahamas and southern Florida.

EXAMPLE 2 Organizing Data in a Table

Use the temperature data to make a table. Then use your table to find a pattern in the data and draw a conclusion.

At 10 A.M., the temperature was 62°F. At noon, it was 65°F. At 2 P.M., it was 68°F. At 4 P.M., it was 70°F. At 6 P.M., it was 66°F.

Time	Temperature (°F)
10 A.M.	62
Noon	65
2 P.M.	68
4 P.M.	70
6 P.M.	66

The temperature rose until 4 P.M., and then it dropped. One conclusion is that the high temperature on this day was at least 70°F.

Think and Discuss

1. **Tell** how a table helps you organize data.
2. **Explain** why the data in Example 2 was arranged from earliest to latest time instead of from lowest to highest temperature.

6-1 Exercises

GUIDED PRACTICE

See Example 1
1. On Monday, the high temperature was 72°F. On Tuesday, the high was 75°F. On Wednesday, the high was 68°F. On Thursday, the high was 62°F. On Friday, the high was 55°F. Use this data to make a table.

See Example 2
2. Use your table from Exercise 1 to find a pattern in the data and draw a conclusion.

INDEPENDENT PRACTICE

See Example 1
3. On his first math test, Joe made a grade of 70. On the second test, Joe made a grade of 75. On the third test, Joe made a grade of 80. On the fourth test, Joe made a grade of 85. On the fifth test, Joe made a grade of 90. Use this data to make a table.

See Example 2
4. Use your table from Exercise 3 to find a pattern in the data and draw a conclusion.

PRACTICE AND PROBLEM SOLVING

Extra Practice
See page EP11.

5. Multi-Step For ice-skating on a frozen pond to be safe, the ice should be at least 7 inches thick. Use the data below to make a table, and estimate the date on which it first became safe to ice-skate.
On December 3, the ice was 1 in. thick. On December 18, the ice was 2 in. thick. On January 3, the ice was 5 in. thick. On January 18, the ice was 11 in. thick. On February 3, the ice was 17 in. thick.

6. Write About It Use the data in the table below to make a second table that organizes the same information in a different way. Explain when each table might be useful.

Time	2 A.M.	6 A.M.	10 A.M.	2 P.M.	6 P.M.	10 P.M.
Temperature (°F)	51	55	68	75	62	58

7. Challenge Arthur, Victoria, and Jeffrey are in the sixth, seventh, and eighth grades, although not necessarily in that order. Victoria is not in eighth grade. The sixth-grader is in choir with Arthur and in band with Victoria. Which student is in which grade? Use a yes/no table like the one at right to help you answer this question.

	Arthur	Victoria	Jeffrey
6th			
7th			
8th		No	

Test Prep and Spiral Review

8. Multiple Choice In 1999, an earthquake that measured 7.4 on the Richter scale occurred in Turkey. In 2001, an earthquake that measured 7.9 on the Richter scale occurred in India. In 2003, an earthquake that measured 6.5 on the Richter scale occurred in Iran. Which shows the data accurately in a table?

A
Country	Turkey	India	Iran
Measure	7.4	6.5	7.9

B
Country	Turkey	India	Iran
Measure	7.9	7.4	6.5

C
Country	Turkey	India	Iran
Measure	6.5	7.4	7.9

D
Country	Turkey	India	Iran
Measure	7.4	7.9	6.5

9. Short Response Make a table to show the following data: Ty builds model cars. He built 2 the first week, 5 the second week, 8 the third week, and 11 the fourth week. Use your table to find a pattern in the data and draw a conclusion.

Simplify. (Lesson 1-2)

10. 5^3 **11.** 3^4 **12.** 2^6 **13.** 6^3

Write two phrases for each expression. (Lesson 2-2)

14. $b + 13$ **15.** $(2)(12)$ **16.** $26 - c$ **17.** $m \div 3$

Hands-On Lab 6-2: Collect Data to Explore Mean

Use with Lesson 6-2

Learn It Online
Lab Resources Online go.hrw.com,
keyword MR10 Lab6

You can use counters to find a single number that describes an entire set of data. Consider the set of data in the table.

| 2 | 5 | 4 | 3 | 6 |

First use counters to make stacks that match the data.

Now move some of the counters so that all of the stacks are the same height.

All of the stacks have 4 counters. The set of data can be described by the number 4. It is the *mean* (average) of the set of data.

Activity

1. Ella surveys five people to find out how many brothers and sisters they have.
2. She collects the data and records the results.
3. Use counters to show the data.
4. Move counters so that all of the stacks are the same height. The mean is 2.

Number of Siblings

| 2 | 3 | 1 | 1 | 3 |

Think and Discuss

1. Suppose one of the people surveyed had 8 brothers and sisters instead of 3. How would this change the mean?

2. All of the students in a classroom have 3 textbooks. What is the mean of the set of data? How do you know?

Try This

1. Collect data by surveying four friends to find out how many pets they have. Use counters to find the mean of the set of data.

6-2 Mean, Median, Mode, and Range

Learn to find the mean, median, mode, and range of a data set.

Vocabulary
mean
median
mode
range

Players on a volleyball team measured how high they could jump. The results in inches are recorded in the table.

| 13 | 23 | 21 | 20 | 21 | 24 | 18 |

One way to describe this data set is to find the *mean*. The **mean** is the sum of all the items divided by the number of items in the set. Sometimes the mean is also called the *average*. The mean of this set of data is the average height that the volleyball team could jump.

EXAMPLE 1 Finding the Mean of a Data Set

Find the mean of each data set.

A

Heights of Vertical Jumps (in.)						
13	23	21	20	21	24	18

$13 + 23 + 21 + 20 + 21 + 24 + 18 = 140$ *Add all values.*
$140 \div 7 = 20$ *Divide the sum by the number of items.*

The mean is 20 inches.

B

Numbers of Pets Owned				
2	4	1	1	2

$2 + 4 + 1 + 1 + 2 = 10$ *Add all values.*
$10 \div 5 = 2$ *Divide the sum by the number of items.*

The mean is 2. The average number of pets that these five people own is 2.

Check

Use counters to make stacks that match the data.

    2   4   1   1   2

Move the chips so that each stack has the same number.

Each stack has 2 counters. The mean is 2.

Interactivities Online ▶ Some other descriptions of a set of data are called the *median*, *mode*, and *range*.

- The **median** is the middle value when the data are in numerical order, or the mean of the two middle values if there are an even number of items.

- The **mode** is the value or values that occur most often. There may be more than one mode for a data set. When all values occur an equal number of times, the data set has no mode.

- The **range** is the difference between the greatest and least values in the set.

EXAMPLE 2 Finding the Mean, Median, Mode, and Range of a Data Set

Find the mean, median, mode, and range of each data set.

NFL Career Touchdowns			
Marcus Allen	145	Franco Harris	100
Jim Brown	126	Walter Payton	125

mean: $\frac{145 + 126 + 100 + 125}{4}$ *Add all values. Divide the sum by the number of items.*

$= 124$

Write the data in numerical order: 100, 125, 126, 145

median: 100, (125, 126), 145   *There are an even number of items, so find the mean of the two middle values.*

$\frac{125 + 126}{2} = 125.5$

mode: none   *No value occurs most often.*

range: $145 - 100 = 45$ *Subtract least value from greatest value.*

The mean is 124 touchdowns; the median is 125.5 touchdowns; there is no mode; and the range is 45 touchdowns.

Think and Discuss

1. Describe what you can say about the values in a data set if the set has a small range.

2. Tell how many modes are in the following data set. Explain your answer. 15, 12, 13, 15, 12, 11

3. Describe how adding 20 inches to the data set in Example 1A would affect the mean.

6-2 Exercises

GUIDED PRACTICE

See Example 1 Find the mean of the data set.

1.
| Number of Petals | 13 | 24 | 35 | 18 | 15 | 27 |

See Example 2 Find the mean, median, mode, and range of the data set.

2.
| Heights of Students (in.) | 51 | 67 | 63 | 52 | 49 | 48 | 48 |

INDEPENDENT PRACTICE

See Example 1 Find the mean of the data set.

3.
| Numbers of Books Read | 6 | 4 | 10 | 5 | 6 | 8 |

See Example 2 Find the mean, median, mode, and range of each data set.

4.
| Ages of Students (yr) | 14 | 16 | 15 | 17 | 16 | 12 |

5. **Ages of Recent Presidents at Election**
- George W. Bush: 54
- Bill Clinton: 46
- George Bush: 64
- Ronald Reagan: 69
- Jimmy Carter: 52

PRACTICE AND PROBLEM SOLVING

Extra Practice See page EP11.

6. Frank has 3 nickels, 5 dimes, and 2 quarters. Find the range, mean, median, and mode of the values of Frank's coins.

7. **Education** For the six New England states, the mean scores on the math section of the SAT one year were as follows: Connecticut, 509; Maine, 500; Massachusetts, 513; New Hampshire, 519; Rhode Island, 500; and Vermont, 508. Create a table using this data. Then find the range, mean, median, and mode.

8. **Critical Thinking** Gina spent $4, $5, $7, $7, and $6 over the past 5 days buying lunch. Is the mean, median, mode, or range the most useful way to describe this data set? Explain.

Find each missing value.

9. 3, 5, 7, 9, ▨; mean: 7

10. 15, 17, ▨, 28, 30; mean: 23

11. 10, 9, ▨, 4, 8, 8, 4, 7; mode: 4

12. 7, 2, ▨, 15, 20, 8, 14, 29; median: 13

13. 50, 100, 75, 60, ▨, 25, 105, 40; median: 65

14. 14, 8, 17, 21, ▨, 11, 3, 13; range: 20

15. **Critical Thinking** Find the set of 5 items of data that has a range of 9, a mean of 11, a median of 12, and a mode of 15.

16. **What's the Error?** Joey says that the mean of the set of data is 23.5. Describe Joey's error.

Numbers of Flowers in Bouquets	25	20	21	22	25	25

17. **What's the Question?** On an exam, three students scored 75, four students scored 82, three students scored 88, four students scored 93, and one student scored 99. If the answer is 88, what is the question?

18. **Challenge** In the Super Bowls from 2002 to 2007, the winning team won by a mean of $9\frac{5}{6}$ points. By how many points did the New England Patriots win in 2002?

Year	Super Bowl Champion	Points Won By
2007	Indianapolis Colts	12
2006	Pittsburgh Steelers	11
2005	New England Patriots	3
2004	New England Patriots	3
2003	Tampa Bay Buccaneers	27
2002	New England Patriots	▨

Test Prep and Spiral Review

19. **Multiple Choice** Over 5 days, Pedro jogged 6.5 miles, 5 miles, 2 miles, 2 miles, and 4.5 miles. Find the mean distance that Pedro jogged.

    Ⓐ 2 miles   Ⓑ 3.5 miles   Ⓒ 4 miles   Ⓓ 4.75 miles

20. **Multiple Choice** Which value is NOT always a number in the data set it represents?

    Ⓕ Mode   Ⓖ Mean   Ⓗ Least value   Ⓙ Greatest value

21. **Gridded Response** The mean of 12, 15, 20 and x is 18. Find the value of x.

Tell whether each number is divisible by 2, 3, or 5. (Lesson 4-1)

22. 155   23. 14   24. 99   25. 2,345

26. Make a table to show the number of days in each month of a non-leap year. (Lesson 6-1)

6-3 Additional Data and Outliers

Learn the effect of additional data and outliers.

The mean, median, and mode may change when you add data to a data set.

USA's Shani Davis at the 2007 ISU World Single Distances Speed Skating Championships.

EXAMPLE 1   Sports Application

Vocabulary
outlier

A Find the mean, median, and mode of the data in the table.

U.S. Winter Olympic Medals Won								
Year	2006	2002	1998	1994	1992	1988	1984	1980
Medals	25	34	13	13	11	6	8	12

mean = 15.25   mode = 13   median = 12.5

B The United States also won 10 medals in 1976 and 8 medals in 1972. Add this data to the data in the table and find the mean, median, and mode.

mean = 14   *The mean decreased by 1.25.*
modes = 8, 13   *There is an additional mode.*
median = 11.5   *The median decreased by 1.*

Interactivities Online ▶ An **outlier** is a value in a set that is very different from the other values.

EXAMPLE 2   Social Studies Application

In 2001, 64-year-old Sherman Bull became the oldest American to reach the top of Mount Everest. Other climbers to reach the summit that day were 33, 31, 31, 32, 33, and 28 years old. Find the mean, median, and mode without and with Bull's age, and explain the changes.

Data without Bull's age: mean ≈ 31.3   modes = 31, 33   median = 31.5

Data with Bull's age: mean = 36   modes = 31, 33   median = 32

When you add Bull's age, the mean increases by 4.7, the modes stay the same, and the median increases by 0.5. The mean is the most affected by the outlier.

Helpful Hint

In Example 2, Sherman Bull's age is an outlier because he is much older than the others in the group.

Sometimes one or two data values can greatly affect the mean, median, or mode. When one of these values is affected like this, you should choose a different value to best describe the data set.

EXAMPLE 3 **Describing a Data Set**

The Seawells are shopping for a DVD player. They found ten DVD players with the following prices:

$175, $180, $130, $150, $180, $500, $160, $180, $150, $160

What are the mean, median, and mode of this data set? Which one best describes the data set?

mean:

$$\frac{175 + 180 + 130 + 150 + 180 + 500 + 160 + 180 + 150 + 160}{10} = \frac{1965}{10}$$
$$= 196.50$$

The mean is $196.50.

Most of the DVD players cost less than $200, so the mean does not describe the data set best.

median:
130, 150, 150, 160, 160, 175, 180, 180, 180, 500

$$\frac{160 + 175}{2} = 167.50$$

The median is $167.50.

The median best describes the data set because a majority of the data is clustered around the value $167.50.

mode:
The value $180 occurs 3 times, more than any other value. The mode is $180.

The mode represents only 3 of the 10 values. The mode does not describe the entire data set.

Some data sets, such as {red, blue, red}, do not contain numbers. In this case, the only way to describe the data set is with the mode.

Think and Discuss

1. **Explain** how an outlier with a large value will affect the mean of a data set. What is the effect of a small outlier value?

2. **Explain** why the mean would not be a good description of the following high temperatures that occurred over 7 days: 72°F, 73°F, 70°F, 68°F, 70°F, 71°F, and 39°F.

6-3 Exercises

Learn It Online
Homework Help Online go.hrw.com,
keyword MR10 6-3
Exercises 1–6, 7, 13

GUIDED PRACTICE

See Example 1
1. **Sports** The graph shows how many times some countries have won the Davis Cup in tennis from 1900 to 2000.
   a. Find the mean, median, and mode of the data.
   b. The United States won 31 Davis Cups between 1900 and 2000. Add this number to the data in the graph and find the mean, median, and mode.

Davis Cup Wins 1900 to 2000
- France
- Germany
- Sweden
- Spain

🎾 = 2 wins

See Example 2
2. In 1998, 77-year-old John Glenn became the oldest person to travel into space. Other astronauts traveling on that same mission were 43, 37, 38, 46, 35, and 42 years old. Find the mean, median, and mode of all their ages with and without Glenn's age, and explain the changes.

See Example 3
3. Kate read books that were 240, 450, 180, 160, 195, 170, 240, and 165 pages long. What are the mean, median, and mode of this data set? Which one best describes the data set?

INDEPENDENT PRACTICE

See Example 1
4. **History** The table shows the ages of the 10 youngest signers of the Declaration of Independence.
   a. Find the mean, median, and mode of the data.
   b. Benjamin Franklin was 70 years old when he signed the Declaration of Independence. Add his age to the data in the table and find the mean, median, and mode.

Ages of 10 Youngest Signers of Declaration of Independence						
Age	26	29	30	31	33	34
Number Of Signers	//	/	/	/	///	//

See Example 2
5. **Geography** The map shows the population densities of several states along the Atlantic coast. Find the mean, median, and mode of the data with and without Maine's population density, and explain the changes.

Population Density (people per square mile)
- Maine 41
- Massachusetts 810
- New Jersey 1,138
- Rhode Island 1,003
- Connecticut 702

See Example 3
6. The passengers in a van are 16, 19, 17, 18, 15, 14, 32, 32, and 41 years old. What are the mean, median, and mode of this data set? Which one best describes the data set?

Extra Practice
See page EP11.

294 Chapter 6 Collecting and Displaying Data

Earth Science LINK

On September 13, 1922, the temperature in El Azizia, Libya, reached 136°F, the record high for the planet. (*Source: The World Almanac and Book of Facts*)

Continent	Highest Temperature (°F)
Africa	136
Antarctica	59
Asia	129
Australia	128
Europe	122
North America	134
South America	120

Erg Murzuq Dunes in the Libyan Desert

7. What are the mean, median, and mode of the highest recorded temperatures on each continent?

8. a. Which temperature is an outlier?
   b. What are the mean, median, and mode of the temperatures if the outlier is not included?

9. **What's the Error?** A student stated that the median temperature would rise to 120.6°F if a new record high of 75°F were recorded in Antarctica. Explain the error. How would the median temperature actually be affected if a high of 75°F were recorded in Antarctica?

10. **Write About It** Is the data in the table best described by the mean, median, or mode? Explain.

11. **Challenge** Suppose a new high temperature were recorded in Europe, and the new mean temperature became 120°F. What is Europe's new high temperature?

Test Prep and Spiral Review

12. **Multiple Choice** Which value will change the most when 5 is added to the data set 0, 1, 4, 0, 3, 4, 2, and 1?

    Ⓐ Range   Ⓑ Median   Ⓒ Mode   Ⓓ Mean

13. **Gridded Response** The table shows the speeds, in miles per hour, of certain animals. Which speed is an outlier?

Animal	House cat	Rabbit	Cheetah	Reindeer	Zebra	Elk	Elephant
Speed (mi/h)	30	35	70	32	40	45	25

Solve each equation. Check your answer. (Lesson 5-5)

14. $\frac{1}{2} + m = 2$ 15. $n - \frac{4}{5} = \frac{1}{10}$ 16. $\frac{1}{3} + x = \frac{2}{3}$

17. Find the median, mode, and range of the animal speeds in Exercise 13. (Lesson 6-2)

6-3 Additional Data and Outliers

Ready To Go On?

Quiz for Lessons 6-1 Through 6-3

6-1 Making a Table

1. The local dance studio holds a spring recital each year. Five years ago, 220 people attended the recital. Four years ago, 235 people attended. Three years ago, 250 people attended. Two years ago, 242 people attended. Last year, 258 people attended. Use the attendance data to make a table. Then use your table to describe how attendance changed over time.

6-2 Mean, Median, Mode, and Range

Find the mean, median, mode, and range of each data set.

2.

Distance (mi)					
5	6	4	7	3	5

3.

Test Scores				
78	80	85	92	90

4.

Ages of Students (yr)							
11	13	12	12	12	13	9	14

5.

Number of Pages in Each Book						
145	119	156	158	125	128	135

6-3 Additional Data and Outliers

6. The table shows the number of people who attended each monthly meeting from January to May.

Number of People Attending				
Jan	Feb	Mar	Apr	May
27	26	32	30	30

   a. Find the mean, median, and mode of the attendances.
   b. In June, 39 people attended the meeting, and in July, 26 people attended the meeting. Add this data to the table and find the mean, median, and mode with the new data.

7. The four states with the longest coastlines are Alaska, Florida, California, and Hawaii. Alaska's coastline is 6,640 miles. Florida's coastline is 1,350 miles. California's coastline is 840 miles, and Hawaii's coastline is 750 miles. Find the mean, median, and mode of the lengths with and without Alaska's, and explain the changes.

8. The daily snowfall amounts for the first ten days of December are listed below.

   2 in., 5 in., 0 in., 0 in., 15 in., 1 in., 0 in., 3 in., 1 in., 4 in.

   What are the mean, median, and mode of this data set? Which one best describes the data set?

Focus on Problem Solving

Make a Plan

- **Prioritize and sequence information**

Some problems give you a lot of information. Read the entire problem carefully to be sure you understand all of the facts. You may need to read it over several times, perhaps aloud so that you can hear yourself say the words.

Then decide which information is most important (prioritize). Is there any information that is absolutely necessary to solve the problem? This information is important.

Finally, put the information in order (sequence). Use comparison words like *before, after, longer, shorter,* and so on to help you. Write the sequence down before you try to solve the problem.

Read the problems below and answer the questions that follow.

1 The portable MP3 player appeared 300 years after the piano. The tape recorder was invented in 1898. Thomas Edison invented the phonograph 21 years before the tape recorder and 122 years before the portable MP3 player. What is the date of each invention?

  a. Which invention's date can you use to find the dates of all the others?

  b. Can you solve the problem without this date? Explain.

  c. List the inventions in order from earliest invention to latest invention.

2 Jon recorded the heights of his family members. There are 4 people in Jon's family, including Jon. Jon's mother is 2 inches taller than Jon's father. Jon is 56 inches tall. Jon's sister is 4 inches taller than Jon and 5 inches shorter than Jon's father. What are the heights of Jon and his family members?

  a. Whose height can you use to find the heights of all the others?

  b. Can you solve the problem without this height? Explain.

  c. List Jon's family members in order from shortest to tallest.

6-4 Bar Graphs

Learn to display and analyze data in bar graphs.

Vocabulary
bar graph
double-bar graph

A biome is a large region characterized by a specific climate. There are ten land biomes on Earth. Some are pictured at right. Each gets a different amount of rainfall.

A *bar graph* can be used to display and compare data about rainfall. A **bar graph** displays data with vertical or horizontal bars.

EXAMPLE 1 Reading a Bar Graph

Use the bar graph to answer each question.

A Which biome in the graph has the most rainfall?

Find the highest bar.

The rain forest has the most rainfall.

B Which biomes in the graph have an average yearly rainfall less than 40 inches?

Find the bar or bars whose heights measure less than 40.

The tundra has an average yearly rainfall less than 40 inches.

EXAMPLE 2 Making a Bar Graph

Use the given data to make a bar graph.

Coal Reserves (billion metric tons)		
Asia	Europe	Africa
695	404	66

Step 1: Find an appropriate scale and interval. The scale must include all of the data values. The interval separates the scale into equal parts.

Step 2: Use the data to determine the lengths of the bars. Draw bars of equal width. The bars cannot touch.

Step 3: Title the graph and label the axes.

A **double-bar graph** shows two sets of related data.

EXAMPLE 3   PROBLEM SOLVING APPLICATION

Make a double-bar graph to compare the data in the table.

Life Expectancies in Atlantic South America				
	Brazil	Argentina	Uruguay	Paraguay
Male (yr)	59	71	73	70
Female (yr)	69	79	79	74

1. Understand the Problem

You are asked to use a graph to compare the data given in the table. You will need to use all of the information given.

2. Make a Plan

You can make a double-bar graph to display the two sets of data.

3. Solve

Determine an appropriate scale for both sets of data.

Use the data to determine the lengths of the bars. Draw bars of equal width. Bars should be in pairs. Use a different color for male ages and female ages.

Title the graph and label both axes.

Include a key to show what each bar represents.

4. Look Back

You could make two separate graphs, one of male ages and one of female ages. However, it is easier to compare the two data sets when they are on the same graph.

Reading Math

This symbol means there is a break in the scale. Some intervals were left out because they were not needed for the graph.

Think and Discuss

1. **Give** comparisons you can make by looking at a bar graph.
2. **Describe** the kind of data you would display in a bar graph.
3. **Tell** why the graph in Example 3 needs a key.

6-4 Exercises

GUIDED PRACTICE

See Example 1   Use the bar graph to answer each question.

1. Which color was the least common among the cars in the parking lot?

2. Which colors appeared more than ten times in the parking lot?

Cars in the Parking Lot (bar graph: Black ≈ 18, White ≈ 14, Red ≈ 11, Green ≈ 8)

See Example 2   3. Use the given data to make a bar graph.

Students in Mr. Jones's History Classes			
Period 1	28	Period 6	22
Period 2	27	Period 7	7

See Example 3   4. Make a double-bar graph to compare the data in the table.

Movie Preferences of Men and Women Polled at the Mall						
	Comedy	Action	Sci-Fi	Horror	Drama	Other
Men	16	27	16	23	12	6
Women	21	14	8	18	30	9

INDEPENDENT PRACTICE

See Example 1   Use the bar graph to answer each question.

5. Which fruit was liked the best?

6. Which fruits were liked by equal numbers of people?

Favorite Fruits (bar graph: Banana = 12, Apple = 12, Orange = 16, Grapes = 7)

See Example 2   7. Use the given data to make a bar graph.

Days with Rainfall			
January	14	March	16
February	12	April	23

See Example 3   8. Make a double-bar graph to compare the data in the table.

Heart Rates Before and After Exercise (beats per minute)						
	Jason	Jamal	Ray	Tonya	Peter	Brenda
Before	60	62	61	65	64	65
After	131	140	128	140	135	120

300   Chapter 6 Collecting and Displaying Data

PRACTICE AND PROBLEM SOLVING

Extra Practice
See page EP11.

Social Studies Use the bar graph for Exercises 9–12.

9. What is the range of the land area of the continents?

10. What is the mode of the land area of the continents?

11. What is the mean of the land area of the continents?

12. What is the median of the land area of the continents?

Land Area of the Continents

13. The basketball coach divided the team into two practice squads, the Blue Squad and the Green Squad. The table shows the scores from 6 weeks of practice games.

    a. Draw a double bar graph.

    b. Find the mean score and range for each squad.

    c. Which squad would you pick to play in an upcoming tournament? Explain your reasoning.

14. **Write About It** Explain how you would make a bar graph of the five most populated cities in the United States.

15. **Challenge** Create a bar graph displaying the number of A's, B's, C's, D's, and F's in Ms. Walker's class if the grades were the following: 81, 87, 80, 75, 77, 98, 52, 78, 75, 82, 74, 95, 76, 52, 76, 53, 86, 77, 90, 83, 96, 83, 74, 67, 90, 65, 69, 93, 68, and 76.

Scores of Practice Games

	Blue	Green
Week 1	62	40
Week 2	40	44
Week 3	42	44
Week 4	54	48
Week 5	36	52
Week 6	50	56

Grading System

A	90–100
B	80–89
C	70–79
D	60–69
F	0–59

Test Prep and Spiral Review

Use the bar graph for Exercises 16 and 17.

16. **Multiple Choice** Which animal has the longest life span?

    Ⓐ Lion   Ⓑ Horse   Ⓒ Squirrel   Ⓓ Cow

17. **Multiple Choice** Which two animals have the same life span?

    Ⓕ Lion and horse   Ⓖ Squirrel and cow   Ⓗ Horse and squirrel   Ⓙ Lion and cow

Life Spans of Animals

Find each sum or difference. Write the answer in simplest form. *(Lessons 5-2 and 5-3)*

18. $\frac{1}{7} + \frac{1}{4}$

19. $\frac{1}{2} - \frac{3}{10}$

20. $1\frac{3}{4} + 2\frac{1}{8}$

21. $8\frac{2}{5} - 6\frac{1}{15}$

6-4 Bar Graphs

Technology LAB 6-4

Create Bar Graphs

Use with Lesson 6-4

Learn It Online
Lab Resources Online go.hrw.com,
keyword MR10 Lab6

You can use a computer spreadsheet to draw bar graphs. The Chart Wizard icon, on a spreadsheet menu looks like a bar graph. The Chart Wizard allows you to create different types of graphs.

Activity

The U.S. Census Bureau has projected the population of North Carolina through 2030. Make a bar graph of this data.

North Carolina Population

Year	Population
2000	8,049,313
2005	8,829,902
2010	9,345,823
2015	10,010,770
2020	10,709,289
2025	11,449,153
2030	12,227,739

1. Type the titles *Year* and *Population* into cells A1 and B1. Then type the data into columns A (year) and B (population.)

2. Select the cells containing the titles and the data. Do this by placing your pointer in A1, clicking and holding the mouse button, and dragging the pointer down to B8.

3. Click the Chart Wizard icon. Highlight **Column** to make a vertical bar graph. Click **Next**.

④ **The next screen shows where the data from the graph comes from. Click the tab titled "Series" to specify the labels for each bar. (Category (x) axis labels) Click Next.**

⑤ **Title your graph and both axes. Click the Legend tab. Click the box next to Show Legend to turn off the key. (You would need a key if you were making a double-bar graph). Click Next when you are finished.**

⑥ **The next screen asks you where you want to place your chart. Click Finish to place it in your spreadsheet.**

Think and Discuss

1. Do you think the population of North Carolina will be 10,709,289 in the year 2020 as shown in the graph? Explain.

Try This

1. Find the number of North Carolina counties that begin with the letter A, B, C, or D. Make a bar graph of the data.

6-4 Technology Lab

6-5 Line Plots, Frequency Tables, and Histograms

Learn to organize data in line plots, frequency tables, and histograms.

Your fingerprints are unlike anyone else's. Even identical twins have slightly different fingerprint patterns.

All fingerprints have one of three patterns: whorl, loop, or arch.

The **frequency** of a data value is the number of times it occurs.

A **frequency table** tells the number of items an event, category, or group occurs.

Vocabulary
frequency
frequency table
line plot
histogram

Whorl   Loop   Arch

EXAMPLE 1 Using Tally Marks to Make a Frequency Table

Each student in Mrs. Choe's class recorded their fingerprint pattern. Which type is most common in Mrs. Choe's class?

| whorl | loop | loop | loop | loop | arch | loop |
| whorl | arch | loop | arch | loop | arch | whorl |

Make a table to show each type of fingerprint.

Step 1: For each fingerprint, make a tally mark in the appropriate row.

Step 2: Count the number of tally marks for each pattern. This is the frequency.

Fingerprint Patterns

Pattern	Tallies	Frequency
Whorl	|||	3
Arch	||||	4
Loop	ЖН ||	7

Reading Math
A group of four tally marks with a line through it means five.
ЖН = 5
ЖН ЖН = 10

The loop pattern is the most common in Mrs. Choe's class.

A **line plot** uses a number line and *x*'s or other symbols to show frequencies of values.

EXAMPLE 2 Making a Line Plot

Students in Mr. Lee's class each ran several miles in a week. Make a line plot of the data.

Number of Miles Run

| 8 | 3 | 5 | 6 | 7 | 8 | 5 | 5 | 3 | 6 | 10 | 7 | 5 |

Step 1: Draw a number line.
Step 2: For each student, use an *x* on the number line to represent how many miles he or she ran.

```
                X
                X
    X       X X X X
    X       X X X X       X
    +---+---+---+---+---+---+---+
    3   4   5   6   7   8   9   10
         Number of miles run
```

Chapter 6 Collecting and Displaying Data

EXAMPLE 3 Making a Frequency Table with Intervals

Use the data in the table to make a frequency table with intervals.

Number of Representatives per State in the U.S. House of Representatives												
7	1	6	4	52	6	6	1	1	23	11	2	2
20	10	5	4	6	7	2	8	10	16	8	5	9
1	3	2	2	13	3	31	12	1	19	6	5	21
2	6	1	9	30	3	1	11	9	3	9		

Step 1: Choose equal intervals.

Step 2: Find the number of data values in each interval. Write these numbers in the "Frequency" row.

Number of Representatives per State in the U.S. House of Representatives									
Number	0–5	6–11	12–17	18–23	24–29	30–35	36–41	42–47	48–53
Frequency	22	18	3	4	0	2	0	0	1

This table shows that 22 states have between 0 and 5 representatives, 18 states have between 6 and 11 representatives, and so on.

A **histogram** is a bar graph that shows the number of data items that occur within each interval.

EXAMPLE 4 Making a Histogram

Use the frequency table in Example 3 to make a histogram.

Step 1: Choose an appropriate scale and interval.

Step 2: Draw a bar for the number of states in each interval. The bars should touch but not overlap.

Step 3: Title the graph and label the axes.

Number of Representatives by State

(Histogram with Frequency on y-axis from 0 to 24, Number of representatives on x-axis with intervals 0–5, 6–11, 12–17, 18–23, 24–29, 30–35, 36–41, 42–47, 48–53)

Think and Discuss

1. Describe a data set that can appropriately be displayed using a histogram.

6-5 Exercises

GUIDED PRACTICE

See Example 1

1. Each student in the band recorded the type of instrument he or she plays. The results are shown in the box. Make a frequency table to organize the data. Which instrument do the fewest students play?

trumpet	tuba	French horn	drums	trombone
drums	trombone	trombone	trumpet	trumpet
trumpet	French horn	trumpet	French horn	French horn

See Example 2

2. Make a line plot of the data.

Length of Each U.S. Presidency (yr)
8 4 8 8 8 4 8 4 0 4 4 1 3 4 4 4 8 4 0 4
4 4 4 4 8 4 8 2 6 4 12 8 8 2 6 5 3 4 8 4 8

See Example 3

3. Use the data in the table in Exercise 2 to make a frequency table with intervals.

See Example 4

4. Use your frequency table from Exercise 3 to make a histogram.

INDEPENDENT PRACTICE

See Example 1

5. Students recorded the type of pet they own. The results are shown in the box. Make a frequency table. Which type of pet do most students own?

cat	cat	bird	dog	dog
dog	bird	dog	bird	fish
bird	cat	fish	dog	cat
fish	hamster	cat	hamster	dog

See Example 2

6. Make a line plot of the data.

Number of Olympic Medals Won by 27 Countries
8 88 59 12 11 57 38 17 14 28 28 26 25 23
18 8 29 34 14 17 13 13 58 12 97 10 9

See Example 3

7. Use the data in the table in Exercise 6 to make a frequency table with intervals.

See Example 4

8. Use your frequency table from Exercise 7 to make a histogram.

PRACTICE AND PROBLEM SOLVING

Extra Practice
See page EP12.

9. **Critical Thinking** Would a bar graph or a histogram be more appropriate to display the state test scores for an entire sixth grade class? Explain.

10. **Multi-Step** Gather data on the number of pairs of shoes your classmates own. Make two line plots of the data, one for the boys and one for the girls. Compare the data.

11. **Social Studies** The map shows the populations of Australia's states and territories. Use the data to make a frequency table with intervals.

    Northern Territory 187,100
    Queensland 3,401,200
    New South Wales 6,274,400
    Australian Capital Territory 309,800
    Victoria 4,605,100
    Tasmania 473,500
    Western Australia 1,798,100
    South Australia 1,479,800

12. **Social Studies** Use your frequency table from Exercise 11 to make a histogram.

13. **Critical Thinking** Can a frequency table have intervals of 0–5, 5–10, and 10–15? Why or why not?

14. **What's the Error?** Reading from the line plot, Kathryn says that there are 10 campers who are three years old. What is Kathryn's error?

    Ages of campers

15. **Write About It** Choose one of the histograms you made for this lesson and redraw it using different intervals. How did the histogram change? Explain.

16. **Challenge** Can you find the mean, median, and mode price using this frequency table? If so, find them. If not, explain why not.

Cost of Video Game Rentals at Different Stores				
Price	$2.00–$2.99	$3.00–$3.99	$4.00–$4.99	$5.00–$5.99
Frequency	5	12	8	5

Echidnas are egg-laying mammals found only in Australia and New Guinea. A baby echidna is called a puggle.

Test Prep and Spiral Review

17. **Multiple Choice** Emily is making a histogram for the data 12, 24, 56, 7, 34, 75, 34, 86, 34, 78, and 96. Which is the most appropriate first interval?

    Ⓐ 0–5   Ⓑ 0–10   Ⓒ 0–50   Ⓓ 0–100

18. **Short Response** Use the data in the table to make a frequency table with three-goal intervals. How many times were 6–8 goals scored?

Number of Goals Scored Each Game
3 5 2 5 4 7 1 0 6 4 8 5 3 2 4 5 9

Write each decimal in expanded form and word form. (Lesson 3-1)

19. 1.23   20. 0.45   21. 26.07   22. 80.002

Find the outlier in each data set. (Lesson 6-3)

23. 3, 6, 19, 4, 2, and 5   24. 564, 514, 723, and 573   25. 34, 37, 41, 9, and 34

LESSON 6-5 EXTENSION
Frequency Distribution

Learn to describe the frequency distribution of a data set and to make a cumulative frequency table and histogram.

In the previous lesson you learned how to make frequency tables and histograms. These represent the *frequency distribution* of a data set. **Frequency distribution** describes the number of values in a data set that fall into each interval. The shape of a histogram may also help you find the median and any outliers.

EXAMPLE 1 Describing Frequency Distribution

Vocabulary
frequency distribution
cumulative frequency

Reading Math
In this data set, most of the values are near the lower part of the range.

The histogram shows the number of students who have given numbers of first cousins in their family.

A Around what value(s) does the data cluster?

The data clusters around the values 3–6.

Number of First Cousins (histogram with Number of Cousins on x-axis: 1–2, 3–4, 5–6, 7–8, 9–10, 11–12, 13–14, 15–16; Number of Students on y-axis: 0–6)

B Explain whether the histogram shows the median or outliers of the data set.

There are 19 values shown in the histogram, so the 10th value is the median. The median falls in the interval 5–6. The histogram does not show whether 5 or 6 is the median.

One data value is in the interval 15–16. It is an outlier because it is very different from the other values.

Recall that a frequency table shows the number of times a category or group occurs. If you add a third column to a frequency table, you can make a *cumulative frequency* table. **Cumulative frequency** is the frequency of all data values that are less than or equal to a given value.

EXAMPLE 2 Making a Cumulative Frequency Table

The best jumps in inches in a high-jump contest are given below.

60, 54, 63, 56, 45, 62, 58, 60, 61, 60, 54, 62

A Use the data to make a cumulative frequency table.

Step 1 Title the table.
Step 2 Choose intervals for the first column of the table.
Step 3 Put the frequency of each interval in the second column.

Chapter 6 Collecting and Displaying Data

Step 4 Add the frequency of each interval to the frequencies of all the intervals above it. Put the sum in the third column.

Best High Jumps		
Height (in.)	Frequency	Cumulative Frequency
45–50	1	1
51–55	2	3
56–60	5	8
61–65	4	12

B How many of the jumps are less than 61 inches?

All jumps below 61 in. are in the top three rows. The cumulative frequency in the third row is 8, so 8 of the jumps are below 61 in.

C Make a histogram and a line graph of the data in the cumulative frequency table in part A.

To make a histogram, draw a bar for the cumulative frequency for each interval.

To make a line graph, place points in the lower left corner and upper right corner of each bar. Then connect those points with line segments, as shown.

EXTENSION
Exercises

The histogram shows the number of times Jaime deposits given amounts of money in his account.

1. Around what value(s) does the data cluster?

2. Does the histogram show the median or any outliers? Explain.

3. Make a cumulative frequency table of the data set.

4. **What's the Error** Explain the error in the table.

CDs Sold		
Price ($)	Frequency	Cumulative Frequency
6–9	5	12
10–13	7	19
14–17	4	23
17–20	2	25

6-5 Extension

Hands-on LAB 6-5

Use a Survey to Collect Data

Use with Lesson 6-5

Learn It Online
Lab Resources Online go.hrw.com,
keyword MR10 Lab6 Go

You can use a survey to collect data. In this lab, you will split into teams and ask your classmates how long it takes them to get to school.

Work in teams of 2 or 3 students. Each team will survey students as they arrive at school, but the teams will work in different locations:

- Half the teams should survey students outside as they get off the school buses.
- The other teams should survey students as they enter their homerooms.

Each team should follow the steps below for their survey.

Activity

1. Ask students if they have been surveyed by any other team. If not, ask them what time they left their house that morning. Try to get 10 to 15 responses.

2. After you've finished surveying, calculate the time between when each student left the house and the time that first period of school starts. Record your data in a table like the one at right.

3. Calculate the mean travel time for the students you surveyed.

Time Student Left Home	Total Time Spent Getting to First Period (min)
6:57 A.M.	33
7:05 A.M.	25

Think and Discuss

1. Do you think the mean times will be longer for the bus teams or for the homeroom teams? Explain why.

2. As a class, find the mean time of all the students surveyed by the bus teams. Then find the mean time of all the students surveyed by the homeroom teams. Do the results match your prediction from problem **1**?

3. Do you think the bus mean or the homeroom mean is a more accurate estimate of the average time students take to get to school? Why?

Try This

1. Draw a histogram to display your team's data.

2. Think of something you'd like to know about the students in your school and write a survey question to find the answer. Explain how you would conduct the survey to get accurate results.

6-6 Ordered Pairs

Learn to graph ordered pairs on a coordinate grid.

Vocabulary
coordinate grid
ordered pair

Interactivities Online ▶

Cities, towns, and neighborhoods are often laid out on a grid. This makes it easier to map and find locations.

A **coordinate grid** is formed by horizontal and vertical lines and is used to locate points.

Each point on a coordinate grid can be located by using an **ordered pair** of numbers, such as (4, 6). The starting point is (0, 0).

San Diego, CA. Image courtesy of spaceimaging.com.

- The first number tells how far to move horizontally from (0, 0).
- The second number tells how far to move vertically.

EXAMPLE 1 Identifying Ordered Pairs

Name the ordered pair for each location.

A library

Start at (0, 0). Move right 2 units and then up 3 units.

The library is located at (2, 3).

B school

Start at (0, 0). Move right 6 units and then up 5 units.

The school is located at (6, 5).

C pool

Start at (0, 0). Move right 12 units and up 1 unit.

The pool is located at (12, 1).

EXAMPLE 1 **Graphing Ordered Pairs**

Graph and label each point on a coordinate grid.

A $Q\left(4\frac{1}{2}, 6\right)$ Start at (0, 0).
Move right $4\frac{1}{2}$ units.
Move up 6 units.

B $S(0, 4)$ Start at (0, 0).
Move right 0 units.
Move up 4 units.

Think and Discuss

1. **Tell** what point is the starting location when you are graphing on a coordinate grid.
2. **Describe** how to graph $\left(2\frac{1}{2}, 8\right)$ on a coordinate grid.

6-6 Exercises

Learn It Online
Homework Help Online go.hrw.com,
keyword MR10 6-6
Exercises 1–22, 23, 25, 27, 29, 31, 33

GUIDED PRACTICE

See Example 1   Name the ordered pair for each location.

1. school
2. store
3. hospital
4. mall
5. office
6. hotel

See Example 2   Graph and label each point on a coordinate grid.

7. $T\left(3\frac{1}{2}, 4\right)$
8. $S(2, 8)$
9. $U(5, 5)$
10. $V\left(4\frac{1}{2}, 1\right)$

INDEPENDENT PRACTICE

See Example 1   Name the ordered pair for each location.

11. diner
12. library
13. store
14. bank
15. theater
16. town hall

312   Chapter 6 Collecting and Displaying Data

See Example 2   Graph and label each point on a coordinate grid.

17. $P\left(5\frac{1}{2}, 1\right)$ **18.** $R(2, 4)$ **19.** $Q\left(3\frac{1}{2}, 2\right)$

20. $V(6, 5)$ **21.** $X\left(1\frac{1}{2}, 3\right)$ **22.** $Y(7, 4)$

PRACTICE AND PROBLEM SOLVING

Extra Practice
See page EP12.

Use the coordinate grid for Exercises 23–35.
Name the point found at each location.

23. $(1, 7)$ **24.** $\left(5, 9\frac{1}{2}\right)$ **25.** $(3, 3)$

26. $\left(4\frac{1}{2}, 7\right)$ **27.** $(7, 4)$ **28.** $\left(7\frac{1}{2}, 7\right)$

Give the ordered pair for each point.

29. D **30.** H **31.** K

32. Q **33.** M **34.** B

35. Multi-Step The coordinates of points B, J, and M in the coordinate grid above form three of the corners of a rectangle. What are the coordinates of the fourth corner? Explain how you found your answer.

36. Write About It Explain the difference between the points $(3, 2)$ and $(2, 3)$.

37. What's the Question? If the answer is "Start at $(0, 0)$ and move 3 units to the right," what is the question?

38. Challenge Locate and graph points that can be connected to form your initials. What are the ordered pairs for these points?

Test Prep and Spiral Review

Use the coordinate grid for Exercises 39 and 40.

39. Multiple Choice At which ordered pair is the airport located?

   Ⓐ $(7, 9)$ Ⓑ $(3, 4)$ Ⓒ $(6, 3)$ Ⓓ $(9, 7)$

40. Multiple Choice Which location is at $(1, 2)$?

   Ⓕ Airport   Ⓗ Supermarket

   Ⓖ Library   Ⓙ Train station

Write each expression in exponential form. (Lesson 1-2)

41. $3 \times 3 \times 3 \times 5 \times 5$ **42.** $7 \times 7 \times 4 \times 4$ **43.** $2 \times 2 \times 3 \times 3 \times 5$

Find each product. Write each answer in simplest form. (Lesson 5-7)

44. $\frac{2}{3} \cdot \frac{1}{5}$ **45.** $\frac{3}{7} \cdot \frac{1}{4}$ **46.** $\frac{2}{9} \cdot \frac{3}{8}$ **47.** $\frac{1}{4} \cdot \frac{6}{7}$

6-7 Line Graphs

Learn to display and analyze data in line graphs.

Vocabulary
line graph
double-line graph

The first permanent English settlement in the New World was founded in 1607. It contained 104 colonists. Population increased quickly as more and more immigrants left Europe for North America.

The table shows the estimated population of English American colonies from 1650 to 1700.

Population of American Colonies				
Year	1650	1670	1690	1700
Population	50,400	111,900	210,400	250,900

Data that shows change over time is best displayed in a *line graph*. A **line graph** displays a set of data using line segments.

EXAMPLE 1 Making a Line Graph

Use the data in the table above to make a line graph.

Step 1: Place *years* on the horizontal axis and *population* on the vertical axis. Label the axes.

Step 2: Determine an appropriate scale and interval for each axis.

Step 3: Mark a point for each data value. Connect the points with straight lines.

Step 4: Title the graph.

Caution!
Because time passes whether or not the population changes, time is *independent* of population. Always put the independent quantity on the horizontal axis.

314 Chapter 6 Collecting and Displaying Data

EXAMPLE 2 Reading a Line Graph

Use the line graph to answer each question.

A In which year did mountain bikes cost the least? 2004

B About how much did mountain bikes cost in 2006? about $300

C Did mountain bike prices increase or decrease from 2004 through 2008? They increased.

Line graphs that display two sets of data are called **double-line graphs**.

EXAMPLE 3 Making a Double-Line Graph

Use the data in the table to make a double-line graph.

United States Trade (Billions of $)						
	1980	1985	1990	1995	2000	2005
Export	272	289	535	794	1,071	1,289
Import	291	411	616	890	1,450	1,997

Helpful Hint

Use different colors of lines to connect the export and import values so you will easily be able to tell the data apart.

Step 1: Determine an appropriate scale and interval.

Step 2: Mark a point for each export value and connect the points.

Step 3: Mark a point for each import value and connect the points.

Step 4: Title the graph and label both axes. Include a key.

Think and Discuss

1. **Explain** when it would be helpful to use a line graph instead of a bar graph to display data.
2. **Describe** how you might use a line graph to make predictions.
3. **Tell** why the graph in Example 3 needs a key.

6-7 Exercises

Learn It Online
Homework Help Online go.hrw.com,
keyword MR10 6-7
Exercises 1–9, 15

GUIDED PRACTICE

See Example 1

1. Use the data in the table to make a line graph.

School Enrollment				
Year	2005	2006	2007	2008
Students	2,000	2,500	2,750	3,500

See Example 2

Use the line graph to answer each question.

2. In which year did the most students participate in the science fair?

3. About how many students participated in 2007?

4. Did the number of students increase or decrease from 2005 to 2006?

See Example 3

5. Use the data in the table to make a double-line graph.

	January	February	March	April	May
Stock A	$10	$12	$20	$25	$22
Stock B	$8	$8	$12	$20	$30

INDEPENDENT PRACTICE

See Example 1

6. Use the data in the table to make a line graph.

Winning Times in the Iditarod Trail Sled Dog Race								
Year	2000	2001	2002	2003	2004	2005	2006	2007
Time (hr)	217	236	215	232	228	235	227	222

See Example 2

Use the line graph to answer each question.

7. About how many people used the Internet in the United States in 2004?

8. When was the number of Internet users about 205 million?

316 Chapter 6 Collecting and Displaying Data

See Example 3

9. Use the data in the table to make a double-line graph.

Soccer Team's Total Fund-Raising Sales						
Day	0	1	2	3	4	5
Team A	$0	$100	$225	$300	$370	$450
Team B	$0	$50	$100	$150	$200	$250

PRACTICE AND PROBLEM SOLVING

Extra Practice
See page EP12.

Use the line graph for Exercises 10 and 11.

10. **Life Science** Estimate the difference in the dogs' weights in March.

11. **Life Science** One of Dion's dogs is a Great Dane, and the other is a Jack Russell Terrier. Which dog is probably the Great Dane? Justify your answer.

12. **Life Science** The table shows the weights in pounds for Sara Beth's two pets. Use the data to make a line graph that is similar to Dion's.

	Jan	Feb	Mar	Apr	May	Jun	Jul	Aug	Sep	Oct	Nov	Dec
Ginger	3	9	15	21	24	25	26	25	26	27	26	28
Toto	4	8	13	17	24	26	27	29	25	26	28	28

Life Science

Larger dogs usually have shorter life spans than smaller dogs. Great Danes live an average of 8.4 years, and Jack Russell terriers live an average of 13.6 years.

13. **Write About It** You have a bowl of soup for lunch. Draw a line graph that could represent the changes in the soup's temperature during lunch. Explain.

14. **Challenge** Describe a situation that this graph could represent.

Test Prep and Spiral Review

15. **Multiple Choice** Which type of graph would you use to display two sets of data that change over time?

    Ⓐ Bar graph   Ⓑ Pictograph   Ⓒ Double-line graph   Ⓓ Line graph

16. **Short Response** Use the graph from Exercises 10 and 11. Did Max's weight increase or decrease between September and October? Explain.

Solve each equation. (Lesson 2-7)

17. $5s = 90$ 18. $4g = 128$ 19. $8m = 120$ 20. $17a = 544$

21. A survey of 100 people found that 48 of the people have had 0 speeding tickets, 34 have had 1 ticket, 10 have had 2 tickets, 5 have had 3 tickets, and 2 have had 4 or more tickets. Create a bar graph to display the data. (Lesson 6-4)

6-8 Misleading Graphs

Learn to recognize misleading graphs.

Data can be displayed in many different ways. Sometimes people who make graphs choose to display data in a misleading way.

This bar graph was created by a group of students who believe their school should increase support of the football team. How could this bar graph be misleading?

Interactivities Online ▶ At a glance, you might conclude that about three times as many students prefer football to basketball. But if you look at the values of the bars, you can see that only 20 students chose football over basketball.

EXAMPLE 1 Misleading Bar Graphs

A Why is this bar graph misleading?

Because the lower part of the horizontal scale is missing, the differences in seating capacities are exaggerated.

B What might people believe from the misleading graph?

People might believe that the Wachovia Complex holds 2–4 times as many people as Quicken Loans Arena and the Rose Garden. In reality, the Wachovia Complex holds only one to two thousand more people than the other two arenas.

EXAMPLE 2 **Misleading Line Graphs**

Fall Temperatures

September: Temperature (°F) axis from 75 to 90; Week 1: ~89, Week 2: 85, Week 3: 83, Week 4: 76.

October: Temperature (°F) axis from 50 to 70; Week 1: 65, Week 2: 59, Week 3: 52, Week 4: 50.

A Why are these line graphs misleading?

If you look at the scale for each graph, you will notice that the September graph goes from 75°F to 90°F and the October graph goes from 50°F to 65°F.

B What might people believe from these misleading graphs?

People might believe that the temperatures in October were about the same as the temperatures in September. In reality, the temperatures in September were 20–30 degrees higher.

C Why is this line graph misleading?

Average Number of Sit-ups in One Minute

Number of sit-ups axis: 0, 30, 35, 36, 40, 50 (Sep–Dec)
- Morning P.E. classes
- Afternoon P.E. classes

The scale does not have equal intervals. So, for example, an increase from 35 sit-ups to 40 sit-ups looks greater than an increase from 30 sit-ups to 35 sit-ups.

Think and Discuss

1. **Give an example** of a situation in which you think someone would intentionally try to make a graph misleading.
2. **Tell** who might have made the misleading graph in Example 2C.
3. **Tell** how you could change the graph in Example 2C so that it is not misleading.

6-8 Exercises

Learn It Online
Homework Help Online go.hrw.com,
keyword MR10 6-8
Exercises 1–8, 9

GUIDED PRACTICE

See Example 1
1. Why is this bar graph misleading?
2. What might people believe from the misleading graph?

Volunteers at Community Center
Years: 1940–1980, 1981–1990, 1991–2000
Number of volunteers: 0, 500, 1,000, 1,500, 2,000, 2,500, 3,000

See Example 2
3. Why is this line graph misleading?
4. What might people believe from the misleading graph?

Distance Biked
Distance from home (mi): 0, 2, 4, 6, 8
Time (min): 0, 5, 10, 15, 20, 25, 30
■ Wanda ■ Kerry

INDEPENDENT PRACTICE

See Example 1
5. Why is this bar graph misleading?
6. What might people believe from the misleading graph?

Books Read
Number of books: 430, 440, 450, 460, 470, 480
6th graders, 7th graders, 8th graders

See Example 2
7. Why is this line graph misleading?
8. What might people believe from the misleading graph?

U.S. Minimum Wage
Dollars: 0, 1, 2, 3, 4, 5, 6
Year: 1970, 1980, 1990, 1992, 1997, 2000, 2002, 2004, 2006, 2007

PRACTICE AND PROBLEM SOLVING

Extra Practice
See page EP12.

9. **Critical Thinking** In a survey, people were asked which teeth-whitening product they found worked best. The results stated that 1,007 people chose strips, 995 people chose paste, and 998 chose paint. Make two bar graphs, one to show that the strips are significantly more effective than the paste or paint, and the other to show that the paste is the most effective.

320   Chapter 6 Collecting and Displaying Data

Health Link

A research company has developed a cholesterol medication. The table shows the mean monthly cholesterol levels for patients who have been taking the medication for 5 months.

Mean Cholesterol Level	
Month	Cholesterol
1	300
2	275
3	240
4	230
5	210

10. What kind of graph would you make to display this data? Why?

11. Make a graph that suggests the medication greatly reduces cholesterol levels. Explain how your graph does this.

12. Make a graph that suggests the medication has little effect on cholesterol levels. Explain how your graph does this.

13. **What's the Question?** Look at the entries in the table. If the answer is 90, what is the question?

14. **Write About It** Suppose you saw your graph from Exercise 12 in an advertisement. What do you think it might be an advertisement for? Explain.

15. **Challenge** What additional information could the research company gather and use to make a double-line graph that shows how its medication affects cholesterol levels?

A heart with coronary artery disease, caused by buildup of fatty deposits

An artery that has been narrowed by high levels of blood cholesterol

Test Prep and Spiral Review

16. **Multiple Choice** Which statement is supported by the information in the bar graph?

    A Damon scored twice as high as Kyle on the test.
    B Kyle scored the highest on the test.
    C Brent scored twice as high as Julie on the test.
    D Deb scored the second-highest on the test.

17. **Short Response** What might readers believe from the misleading bar graph? Explain how to redraw the graph so that it is not as misleading.

Simplify each expression. (Lesson 1-3)

18. $6 \times 2^3 + 17 - 3 \times 2$

19. $85 - (44 + 33) \div 7 + (62 - 12)$

Plot each point on a coordinate grid. (Lesson 6-6)

20. $A(3, 5)$ 21. $B(6, 2)$ 22. $C(0, 4)$ 23. $D(1, 0)$ 24. $E(5.5, 7)$

6-8 Misleading Graphs

6-9 Stem-and-Leaf Plots

Learn to make and analyze stem-and-leaf plots.

Vocabulary
stem-and-leaf plot

A **stem-and-leaf plot** shows data arranged by place value. You can use a stem-and-leaf plot when you want to display data in an organized way that allows you to see each value.

Bryan Berg holds the Guinness World Record for cardstacking. The Explorer Scouts had a competition to see who could build the highest card tower. The table shows the number of levels reached by each scout.

Number of Card-Tower Levels									
12	23	31	50	14	17	25	44	51	20
23	18	35	15	19	15	23	42	21	13

EXAMPLE 1 Creating Stem-and-Leaf Plots

Use the data in the table above to make a stem-and-leaf plot.

Step 1: Group the data by tens digits.
Step 2: Order the data from least to greatest.

```
12 13 14 15 15 17 18 19
20 21 23 23 23 25
31 35
42 44
50 51
```

Step 3: List the tens digits of the data in order from least to greatest. Write these in the "stems" column.

Step 4: For each tens digit, record the ones digits of each data value in order from least to greatest. Write these in the "leaves" column.

Step 5: Title the graph and add a key.

Helpful Hint
To write 42 in a stem-and-leaf plot, write each digit in a separate column.

4 | 2
Stem   Leaf

Number of Card Tower Levels

Stems	Leaves
1	2 3 4 5 5 7 8 9
2	0 1 3 3 3 5
3	1 5
4	2 4
5	0 1

Key: 1|5 means 15

Chapter 6 Collecting and Displaying Data

EXAMPLE 2 Reading Stem-and-Leaf Plots

Find the least value, greatest value, mean, median, mode, and range of the data.

Stems	Leaves
5	8
6	8 9
7	2 4 8
8	0 4 5 6 8
9	0 0 2 3 6 7 8
10	
11	7

Key: 5|8 means 58

The least stem and least leaf give the least value, 58.

The greatest stem and greatest leaf give the greatest value, 117.

Use the data values to find the mean.
(58 + ... + 117) ÷ 19 = 85

The median is the middle value in the table, 86.

To find the mode, look for the number that occurs most often in a row of leaves. Then identify its stem. The mode is 90.

The range is the difference between the greatest and least value.
117 − 58 = 59

Caution!
If a stem has no leaves, there are no data points with that stem. In the stem-and-leaf plot in Example 2, there are no data values between 100 and 109.

Think and Discuss

1. **Describe** how to show 25 on a stem-and-leaf plot.

6-9 Exercises

Learn It Online
Homework Help Online go.hrw.com,
keyword MR10 6-9
Exercises 1–14, 15, 17

GUIDED PRACTICE

See Example 1

1. Use the data in the table to make a stem-and-leaf plot.

Daily High Temperatures (°F)	45	56	40	39	37	48	51

See Example 2

Find each value of the data.

2. smallest value
3. largest value
4. mean
5. median
6. mode
7. range

Stems	Leaves
1	0 2
2	
3	2
4	1 4

Key: 1|0 means 10

INDEPENDENT PRACTICE

See Example 1

8. Use the data in the table to make a stem-and-leaf plot.

Heights of Plants (cm)	30	12	27	28	15	47	37	28	40	20

See Example 2 Find each value of the data.

9. least value
10. greatest value
11. mean
12. median
13. mode
14. range

Stems	Leaves
4	1 2 2
5	1 3
6	7 8

Key: 4|1 means 41

PRACTICE AND PROBLEM SOLVING

Extra Practice
See page EP12.

For Exercises 15 and 16, write the letter of the stem-and-leaf plot described.

A.
Stems	Leaves
1	0 3 4
2	0 0 1 1 1 3
3	4 5 9
4	8

Key: 1|0 means 10

B.
Stems	Leaves
1	6
2	2 3
3	0 1 4
4	1 4 8

Key: 1|6 means 16

C.
Stems	Leaves
1	4
2	
3	6
4	3 6 8

Key: 1|4 means 14

15. The data set has a mode of 21.
16. The data set has a median of 31.

Use the table for Exercises 17 and 18.

17. Karla recorded the number of cars with only one passenger that came through a toll booth each day. Use Karla's data to make a stem-and-leaf plot.

Cars with Only One Passenger						
82	103	95	125	88	94
89	92	94	99	87	80
109	101	100	83	124	81

18. **What's the Error?** Karla's classmate looked at the stem-and-leaf plot and said that the mean number of cars with only one passenger is 4. Explain Karla's classmate's error. What is the correct mean?

19. **Challenge** Josh is the second youngest of 4 teenage boys, all 2 years apart in age. Josh's mother is 3 times as old as Josh is, and she is 24 years younger than her father. Make a stem-and-leaf plot to show the ages of Josh, his brothers, his mother, and his grandfather.

Test Prep and Spiral Review

20. **Multiple Choice** What is the value of 1|2 in the stem-and-leaf plot?

    Ⓐ 12
    Ⓑ 1,200
    Ⓒ 100,002
    Ⓓ 100,200

Stems	Leaves
1	0 1 2 3
2	7 9 9 9

Key: 1|1 means 1,100

21. **Gridded Response** What is the median of the data in Exercise 20?

Order the numbers from least to greatest. (Previous Course)

22. 3,673,809; 3,708,211; 3,671,935
23. 2,004,801; 225,971; 298,500,004

Find the reciprocal. (Lesson 5-9)

24. 6
25. $\frac{4}{7}$
26. $\frac{2}{9}$
27. $\frac{1}{5}$
28. $\frac{9}{8}$

Chapter 6 Collecting and Displaying Data

6-10 Choosing an Appropriate Display

Learn to choose an appropriate way to display data.

A neighborhood community center offers programs for people of all ages. Its recent brochure includes a bar graph that shows the number of people, by age, enrolled in various programs.

Depending on the data to be displayed, some types of graphs are more useful than others.

	Common Uses of Data Displays		
	You can use a line plot to show how often each number occurs.		You can use a bar graph to display and compare data in separate categories.
	You can use a line graph to show how data change over a period of time.		You can use a stem-and-leaf plot to show how often data values occur and how they are distributed.

EXAMPLE 1 Choosing an Appropriate Data Display

A The table shows the number of miles of coastline for states bordering the Gulf of Mexico. Which graph would be more appropriate to show the data—a bar graph or a line graph? Draw the more appropriate graph.

State	AL	FL	LA	MS	TX
Miles of Coastline	33	770	397	44	367

Think: Is the information in the table describing a change over time? Is the information in the table divided into different categories?

The table shows the number of miles of coastline in different states. The data should be displayed in separate categories. So a bar graph is more appropriate than a line graph.

Gulf Coast States' Coastlines

Video Lesson Tutorials Online my.hrw.com

B The table shows the lengths of some animals. Which graph would be more appropriate to show the data—a stem-and-leaf plot or a line graph? Draw the more appropriate graph.

Lengths of Animals (in.)					
70	43	42	50	35	32
32	45	61	35	40	30

Think: The table shows a number of different lengths. It does not show data changing over time.

A stem-and-leaf plot shows how often data values occur. So a stem-and-leaf plot is more appropriate than a line graph.

Lengths of Animals (in.)

Stems	Leaves
3	0 2 2 5 5
4	0 2 3 5
5	0
6	1
7	0

Key: 3|2 means 32

Think and Discuss

1. **Describe** a situation when a line graph would be a more appropriate choice than a bar graph to show data.

2. **Describe** another type of graph that could be used to display the data shown in the table in Example 1B.

6-10 Exercises

Learn It Online
Homework Help Online go.hrw.com,
keyword MR10 6-10 Go
Exercises 1, 2, 3

GUIDED PRACTICE

See Example 1

1. The table shows the average high temperatures in Atlanta for six months of one year. Which graph would be more appropriate to show the data—a bar graph or a line graph? Draw the more appropriate graph.

Month	Jan	Mar	May	Jul	Sep	Nov
Temp. (°F)	54	63	81	88	83	62

INDEPENDENT PRACTICE

See Example 1

2. The table shows the percentages of students who bought a hot lunch from the school cafeteria. Which graph would be more appropriate to show the data—a bar graph or a line graph? Draw the more appropriate graph.

September	30%	November	27%	January	45%
October	28%	December	27%	February	42%

PRACTICE AND PROBLEM SOLVING

Extra Practice
See page EP12.

3. **Social Studies** The table shows the U.S. population from 1900 through 2000.

   a. What graph would be most appropriate to show the data? Why?

   b. Make a graph of the data.

Year	Population
1900	76,094,000
1925	115,829,000
1950	152,271,417
1975	215,973,199
2000	281,421,906

4. **Critical Thinking** The total wins that teams in the Western Conference of the National Hockey League had in a recent year are as follows: 48, 39, 38, 25, 20, 43, 40, 42, 36, 30, 43, 22, 29, 41, 28. Which graph would be more appropriate to show the data—a line plot or a bar graph? Draw the more appropriate graph. Then explain how to use the graph to find the median and mode.

5. **Write a Problem** Use the information in the table to write a problem that can be solved by drawing a graph. Tell which type of graph you would use.

Animal	Life Span (yr)
Bear	40
Carp	100
Elephant	70
Tiger	22

6. **Write About It** Explain the similarities and differences between a bar graph and a line graph.

7. **Challenge** The stem-and-leaf plot shows the number of hours 20 students spent studying over a two-week period. Make a line plot to show the data. What does the line plot show more clearly than a stem-and-leaf plot would?

Study Times

Stems	Leaves
1	5 6 6 6 7 7 9 9
2	0 0 1 1 1 1 2 2 3
3	5 7 9

Key: 1|5 means 15

Test Prep and Spiral Review

8. **Multiple Choice** Which graph would be most appropriate to show the number of miles each student walked in one week for a charity walk-a-thon?

   A Circle graph   B Stem-and-leaf plot   C Line graph   D Bar graph

9. **Extended Response** People leaving a gym were asked how long they exercised. The results in minutes are: 15, 10, 35, 35, 60, 65, 15, 60, 20, 35. Which type of graph would be most appropriate to show the data? Explain. Make a graph of the data. What is the median amount of time spent exercising?

Find the GCF of each set of numbers. (Lesson 4-3)

10. 4 and 16
11. 15 and 50
12. 15, 60, and 75
13. 4, 8, and 80

14. Ashlee spent 50 minutes washing and waxing her car. She spent $\frac{2}{5}$ of that time washing the car. How many minutes did Ashlee spend washing her car? (Lesson 5-6)

6-10 Choosing an Appropriate Display

CHAPTER 6 SECTION 6B

Ready To Go On?

Quiz for Lessons 6-4 Through 6-10

6-4 Bar Graphs

The students in Ms. Bain's class voted on their favorite fruit juice. Use the bar graph to answer each question.

1. How many more students prefer orange juice than prefer grape juice?
2. How many students in all voted?

Favorite Juices
(Orange: 12, Apple: 7, Grape: 5 — Number of students)

6-5 Line Plots, Frequency Tables, and Histograms

Shoppers leaving Midtown Mall were each asked to give their age. Use the line plot to answer each question.

3. What are the range and mode of the data?
4. How many of the shoppers surveyed were older than 20?

Shoppers at Midtown Mall — Ages of shoppers (15–22)

6-6 Ordered Pairs

Graph and label each point on a coordinate grid.

5. $A\,(4, 5)$
6. $B\left(0, 3\frac{1}{2}\right)$

6-7 Line Graphs

7. Use the data in the table to make a line graph.

Graphicworks

Year	Numbers of Employees
2003	852
2004	1,098
2005	1,150
2006	1,150

6-8 Misleading Graphs

8. Bob drew a line graph of the Graphicworks data. For the vertical scale representing the number of employees, he used these intervals: 0; 800; 1,000; and 1,500. Explain why his graph is misleading.

6-9 Stem-and-Leaf Plots

9. Use the data in the line plot in problems 3 and 4 to make a stem-and-leaf plot.

6-10 Choosing an Appropriate Display

10. Would it also be appropriate to use a line graph to represent the data that is shown in the bar graph in problems 1 and 2? Explain.

Real-World Connections

CHAPTER 6

Tornado Alley Oklahoma lies at the heart of Tornado Alley, the region of the central United States where tornadoes are most likely to occur. The state has survived some of the world's most powerful tornadoes, including a 1999 twister with the greatest wind speeds ever recorded on earth—318 mi/h!

OKLAHOMA

1. The table shows the number of tornadoes in Oklahoma from 2000 to 2007. Make a bar graph of the data.

Tornadoes in Oklahoma								
Year	2000	2001	2002	2003	2004	2005	2006	2007
Number of Tornadoes	44	61	18	78	62	27	27	49

2. Explain how you can find the mode of the data by looking at the bar graph.

3. Find the mean number of tornadoes per year.

4. Find the median number of tornadoes per year.

5. In 1999, there were 145 tornadoes in Oklahoma. Suppose this value is included in the data set shown in the table.

   a. Find the mean, median, and mode when the 1999 data is included.

   b. Explain how the mean, median, and mode change when the 1999 data is included.

   c. Does the mean, median, or mode best describe the data set when the 1999 data is included? Why?

Game Time

A Thousand Words

Did you ever hear the saying "A picture is worth a thousand words"? A graph can be worth a thousand words too!

Each of the graphs below tells a story about a student's trip to school. Read each story and think about what each graph is showing. Can you match each graph with its story?

Kyla:
I rode my bike to school at a steady pace. I had to stop and wait for the light to change at two intersections.

Tom:
I walked to my bus stop and waited there for the bus. After I boarded the bus, it was driven straight to school.

Megan:
On my way to school, I stopped at my friend's house. She wasn't ready yet, so I waited for her. Then we walked to school.

Spinnermeania

Round 1: On your turn, spin the spinner four times and record the results. After everyone has had a turn, find the mean, median, and mode of your results. For every category in which you have the highest number, you get one point. If there is a tie in a category, each player with that number gets a point. If your data set has more than one mode, use the greatest one.

Spin five times in round 2, eight times in round 3, ten times in round 4, and twelve times in round 5. The player with the highest score at the end of five rounds is the winner.

Learn It Online
Game Time Extra go.hrw.com,
keyword MR10 Games

A complete copy of the rules and game pieces are available online.

Materials
- 2 pieces of card stock
- 6 sandwich-size zipper bags
- clear packaging tape
- graph paper
- scissors

It's in the Bag!

PROJECT Graphing According to Me

Create different types of graphs and make a zippered accordion book to hold them all.

Directions

1. Place one piece of card stock that is $6\frac{1}{2}$ inches by 7 inches next to one of the bags. The opening of the bag should be at the top, and there should be a small space between the card stock and the bag. Tape the card stock and bag together on the front and back sides. **Figure A**

2. Lay another bag down next to the first, keeping a small space between them. Tape them together, front and back. **Figure B**

3. Continue with the rest of the bags. At the end of the chain, tape a second piece of card stock that is $6\frac{1}{2}$ inches by 7 inches to the last bag. **Figure C**

4. Fold the bags accordion-style, back and forth, with the two card stock covers on the front and back.

5. Cut out squares of graph paper so they will fit in the bags.

Taking Note of the Math

Write the number and title of the chapter on the cover. On each piece of graph paper, draw and label an example of one type of graph from the chapter. Store the graphs in the bags.

It's in the Bag!

CHAPTER 6 Study Guide: Review

Vocabulary

bar graph 298	histogram 305	mode 289
coordinate grid 311	line graph 314	ordered pair 311
double-bar graph 299	line plot 304	outlier 292
double-line graph 315	mean 288	range 289
frequency 304	median 289	stem-and-leaf plot 322
frequency table 304		

Complete the sentences below with vocabulary words from the list above.

1. A(n) __?__ uses vertical or horizontal bars to show the number of items within each interval.

2. A point can be located by using a(n) __?__ of numbers such as (3, 5).

3. In a data set, the __?__ is the value or values that occur most often.

EXAMPLES / EXERCISES

6-1 Making a Table (pp. 284–286)

■ Make a table using the data.

Day	Snowfall
Mon	2 in.
Tue	3.5 in.
Thu	4.25 in.

Monday it snowed 2 inches. Tuesday it snowed 3.5 inches. Thursday it snowed 4.25 inches.

4. Make a table using the data on snake lengths.

An anaconda can be up to 35 ft long. A diamond python can be up to 21 ft long. A king cobra can be up to 19 ft long. A boa constrictor can be up to 16 ft long.

6-2 Mean, Median, Mode, and Range (pp. 288–291)

■ Find the mean, median, mode, and range. 7, 8, 12, 10, 8

mean: $7 + 8 + 8 + 10 + 12 = 45$
$45 \div 5 = 9$
median: 8
mode: 8
range: $12 - 7 = 5$

Find the mean, median, mode, and range.

5. **Hours Worked Each Week**

32	39	39	38	36	39	36

6. **Amount Saved Each Month ($)**

50	120	75	30	40	50	35	100

332 Chapter 6 Collecting and Displaying Data

EXAMPLES

6-3 Additional Data and Outliers (pp. 292–295)

■ Find the mean, median, and mode with and without the outlier.

10, 4, 7, 8, 34, 7, 7, 12, 5, 8   *The outlier is 34.*

With: mean = 10.2,
     mode = 7,
     median = 7.5

Without: mean ≈ 7.555,
        mode = 7,
        median = 7

6-4 Bar Graphs (pp. 298–301)

■ Which grades have more than 200 students? 6th grade and 8th grade

Number of Students in Each Grade
(Bar graph showing 8th, 7th, 6th grade with Number of students on x-axis from 0 to 200)

6-5 Line Plots, Frequency Tables, and Histograms (pp. 304–307)

■ Make a frequency table with intervals.

Ages of people at Irene's birthday party:
37, 39, 18, 15, 13

Ages of People at Irene's Birthday Party				
Ages	13–19	20–26	27–33	34–40
Frequency	3	0	0	2

6-6 Ordered Pairs (pp. 311–313)

■ Name the ordered pair for A.

(Coordinate grid showing point A at (3, 2))

A is at (3, 2).

EXERCISES

Find the mean, median, and mode of each data set with and without the outlier.

7. 12, 11, 9, 38, 10, 8, 12
8. 34, 12, 32, 45, 32
9. 16, 12, 15, 52, 10, 13

Use the bar graph at left for Exercise 10.

10. Which grade has the most students?
11. Use the data to make a bar graph.

Test	Math	English	History	Science
Grade	95	85	90	80

12. Make a frequency table with intervals.

Points Scored					
6	4	5	4	7	10

13. Use the frequency table from Exercise 12 to make a histogram.

Name the ordered pair for each location.

14. Bob's house
15. toy store

(Coordinate grid showing Toy store at (3, 3) and Bob's house at (4, 1))

Study Guide: Review

EXAMPLES | EXERCISES

6-7 Line Graphs (pp. 314–317)

■ Use the temperature data to make a line graph.

Day 1: 32°F; Day 2: 36°F; Day 3: 38°F; Day 4: 40°F; Day 5: 36°F

Temperature Recording (line graph showing Temp. (°F) on y-axis from 0 to 44, Days 1–5 on x-axis)

16. Use the bookstore sales data to make a line graph.

    Jan: $425; Feb: $320; Mar: $450; Apr: $530

    Use your line graph from Exercise 16.

17. When were bookstore sales the greatest?

18. Describe the trend in bookstore sales over the four months.

6-8 Misleading Graphs (pp. 318–321)

■ Why is this graph misleading?

Extra Credit (bar graph with Points 60–100 for Tony, Shelly, Hakeem, Alicia)

The lower part of the scale is missing.

19. Explain why this graph is misleading.

    Walter's Walk (line graph with Distance (mi) 0, 1, 2, 10, 15, 20 on y-axis, Time (hr) 1–5 on x-axis)

6-9 Stem-and-Leaf Plots (pp. 322–324)

■ Make a stem-and-leaf plot of the following test scores.
80, 75, 92, 88, 86, 85, 94, 77

Stems	Leaves
7	5 7
8	0 5 6 8
9	2 4

Key: 8|0 means 80

20. Make a stem-and-leaf plot of the following basketball scores.

    22, 26, 34, 46, 20, 44, 40, 28

21. List the least value, greatest value, mean, median, mode, and range of the data from Exercise 20.

6-10 Choosing an Appropriate Display (pp. 325–327)

■ Which graph would be more appropriate to show time spent shopping—a stem-and-leaf plot or a line graph?

Use a stem-and-leaf plot to see how often data values occur.

22. Which graph would be more appropriate to show the number of books read over the school year by a class—a bar graph or a line graph?

Chapter Test

CHAPTER 6

1. Use the data about sound to make a table.

   The loudness of a sound is measured by the size of its vibrations. The unit of measurement is the decibel (dB). A soft whisper is 30 dB. Conversation is 60 dB. A loud shout is 100 dB. The pain threshold for humans is 130 dB. An airplane takeoff at 100 ft is 140 dB.

Use the bar graph for Exercises 2–4.

2. Find the mean, median, mode, and range of the rainfall amounts.

3. Which month had the lowest average rainfall?

4. Which months had rainfall amounts greater than 2 inches?

5. The table shows the number of strawberries picked by customers at a pick-your-own strawberry patch. Organize the data in a line plot.

   Number of Strawberries Picked

28	33	35	27	35	28	35	29
30	27	30	35	28	27	31	32

Name the ordered pair for each point on the grid.

6. A
7. B
8. C
9. D
10. E
11. F
12. G
13. H

Graph and label each point on a coordinate grid.

14. $T(3, 4)$
15. $M\left(\frac{1}{2}, 6\right)$
16. $P(5, 1)$
17. $S\left(3\frac{1}{2}, 2\right)$
18. $N(0, 5)$

19. Make a stem-and-leaf plot of the push-up data. Use your stem-and-leaf plot to find the mean, median, and mode of the data.

    Number of Push-ups Performed

35	33	25	45	52	21	18
41	27	35	40	53	24	38

20. The table shows the population of a small town over several years. Which graph would be more appropriate to show the data—a bar graph or a line graph? Draw the more appropriate graph.

Year	2002	2003	2004	2005
Population	852	978	1,125	1,206

Chapter 6 Test

Cumulative Assessment, Chapters 1–6

Multiple Choice

1. The stem-and-leaf plot shows the ages of the volunteers who work at a local food bank. What is the median of this set of data?

Stems	Leaves
1	6
2	2 3
3	0 1 4
4	1 4 8

   Key: 1|6 means 16

   (A) 31
   (B) 32.1
   (C) 41
   (D) 48

2. In a vacuum, light travels at a speed of 299,792,458 meters per second. Which of the following approximates this rate in scientific notation?

   (F) 2.9×10^7 meters per second
   (G) 2.9×10^8 meters per second
   (H) 2.9×10^9 meters per second
   (J) 2.9×10^{10} meters per second

3. Harrison spends $3\frac{1}{2}$ hours a week working in his yard. He spends $1\frac{1}{3}$ hours pulling weeds. He spends the rest of the time mowing the yard. How much time does he spend mowing the yard?

   (A) $1\frac{1}{6}$ hours
   (B) $2\frac{1}{6}$ hours
   (C) $2\frac{1}{3}$ hours
   (D) $3\frac{1}{3}$ hours

4. Which value is equivalent to 4^4?

   (F) 8
   (G) 16
   (H) 64
   (J) 256

5. Jamie is making a fruit salad. She needs $2\frac{1}{4}$ cups of crushed pineapple, $3\frac{3}{4}$ cups of sliced apples, $1\frac{1}{3}$ cups of mandarin oranges, and $2\frac{2}{3}$ cups of red grapes. How many cups total of fruit does she need for the fruit salad?

   (A) 6 cups
   (B) 8 cups
   (C) 10 cups
   (D) 12 cups

6. The line plot shows the ages of the number of participants in a science fair. Which of the following statements is NOT supported by the line plot?

   Ages of Science Fair Participants

   ```
                  X
          X       X
      X   X       X       X
      X X X       X   X X X
      X X X       X X X X X
      ┼───┼───┼───┼───┼───┼───┼
      12  13  14  15  16  17  18
   ```

   (F) The range is 6.
   (G) The mean age of the participants in the science fair is 15.1.
   (H) The mode of the ages of the participants in the science fair is 16.
   (J) The median age of the participants in the science fair is 15.

7. What is the mode of the following data? 17, 13, 14, 13, 21, 18, 16, 19

   (A) 13
   (B) 16
   (C) 16.5
   (D) 16.375

8. Which is a type of graph that uses bars and intervals to display data?

   F Stem-and-leaf plot

   G Histogram

   H Double-line graph

   J Line plot

9. Which equation has a solution of 8?

   A $2x = 18$

   B $x - 4 = 12$

   C $x + 6 = 24$

   D $\frac{x}{4} = 2$

HOT TIP! Read graphs and diagrams carefully. Look at the labels for important information.

Gridded Response

Use the following data set for items 10 and 11.

   4, 13, 7, 26, 6, 7, 3, 4, 2, 8, 10, 9

10. Which number in the data set is an outlier?

11. What is the mean of the data set?

12. Greg is separating his marbles into sets. He has 16 green marbles and 20 red marbles. Each set must have the same number of green marbles and the same number of red marbles. What is the greatest number of marble sets that Greg can make if he wants to use every marble?

13. What is the least common multiple of 5, 6, and 8?

14. Miguel has a piece of lumber that is 48.6 centimeters long. How many centimeters does he need to cut off if he wants the piece of lumber to measure 32.8 centimeters?

15. Write $4\frac{3}{8}$ as a decimal.

Short Response

S1. Look at the bar graph of favorite flavors of frozen fruit bars. Explain why the graph is misleading. Use the same data to make a graph that is not misleading.

S2.

Stems	Leaves
2	1 3 6
3	2 2 5 9
4	0 3
5	1 5 5 5

Key: 2|1 means 21

a. Find the range, mean, median, and mode of the data in the stem-and-leaf plot.

b. How does adding 82, 18, and 42 to the data change the range, mean, median, and mode?

Extended Response

E1. The high temperature on Monday was 54°F. On Tuesday, it was 62°F. On Wednesday, it was 65°F. On Thursday, it was 60°F. On Friday, it was 62°F.

a. Organize this data in a table. Find the range, mean, median, and mode of the data.

b. Which graph would be more appropriate to show the data—a bar graph or a line graph? Explain.

c. Make a graph of the data.

CHAPTER 7
Proportional Relationships

Chapter Focus
- Use tables to determine whether quantities are in equivalent ratios.
- Use proportional reasoning to solve rate and ratio problems.

7A Understanding Ratios and Proportions
- 7-1   Ratios and Rates
- 7-2   Using Tables to Explore Equivalent Ratios and Rates
- LAB   Explore Proportions
- 7-3   Proportions
- 7-4   Similar Figures
- 7-5   Indirect Measurement
- LAB   Sketch Scale Drawings
- 7-6   Scale Drawings and Maps

7B Understanding Percents
- LAB   Model Percent
- 7-7   Percents
- 7-8   Percents, Decimals, and Fractions
- LAB   Convert Between Percents, Decimals, and Fractions
- 7-9   Percent Problems
- 7-10 Applying Percents
- EXT   Simple Interest

Why Learn This?
Scale models use proportional relationships to make smaller versions of large objects and larger versions of small objects. This scale model of Shanghai, China, is $\frac{1}{2,000}$ the size of the actual city.

Learn It Online
Chapter Project Online go.hrw.com,
keyword MR10 Ch7

Are You Ready?

Vocabulary

Choose the best term from the list to complete each sentence.

1. A(n) __?__ is a three-sided polygon, and a(n) __?__ is a four-sided polygon.
2. A(n) __?__ is used to name a part of a whole.
3. When two numbers have the same value, they are said to be __?__.
4. When writing 0.25 as a fraction, 25 is the __?__ and 100 is the __?__.

angle
denominator
equivalent
fraction
numerator
pentagon
quadrilateral
triangle

Complete these exercises to review skills you will need for this chapter.

Simplify Fractions

Write each fraction in simplest form.

5. $\frac{6}{10}$
6. $\frac{9}{12}$
7. $\frac{8}{6}$

Write Equivalent Fractions

Write three equivalent fractions for each given fraction.

8. $\frac{4}{16}$
9. $\frac{5}{10}$
10. $\frac{5}{6}$

Compare Fractions

Compare. Write >, <, or =.

11. $\frac{3}{10}$ ■ $\frac{2}{5}$
12. $1\frac{3}{4}$ ■ $1\frac{5}{7}$
13. $\frac{5}{8}$ ■ $\frac{1}{2}$
14. $2\frac{11}{12}$ ■ $\frac{35}{12}$

Write Fractions as Decimals

Write each fraction as a decimal.

15. $\frac{1}{2}$
16. $\frac{7}{20}$
17. $\frac{2}{25}$
18. $\frac{3}{25}$

Multiply Decimals

Multiply.

19. $0.42 \cdot 10$
20. $0.3 \cdot 52$
21. $20.5 \cdot 0.25$
22. $6.75 \cdot 0.40$
23. $9.8 \cdot 0.2$
24. $0.8 \cdot 7.4$
25. $0.52 \cdot 0.64$
26. $0.75 \cdot 8.9$

Proportional Relationships

CHAPTER 7 Study Guide: Preview

Where You've Been

Previously, you
- used fractions to represent situations involving division.
- generated equivalent fractions and decimals.
- used multiplication and division to find equivalent fractions.

In This Chapter

You will study
- using ratios to describe proportional situations.
- representing ratios and percents with concrete models, fractions, and decimals.
- using multiplication and division to solve problems involving equivalent ratios and rates.
- using ratios to make predictions in proportional situations.

Where You're Going

You can use the skills learned in this chapter
- to find discounts and sales tax on retail items at stores.
- to know how much of a tip to leave at restaurants.

Key Vocabulary/Vocabulario

corresponding angles	ángulos correspondientes (en polígonos)
equivalent ratios	razones equivalentes
indirect measurement	medición indirecta
percent	porcentaje
proportion	proporción
rate	tasa
ratio	razón
scale drawing	dibujo a escala
similar	semejantes
unit rate	tasa unitaria

Vocabulary Connections

To become familiar with some of the vocabulary terms in the chapter, consider the following. You may refer to the chapter, the glossary, or a dictionary if you like.

1. *Equivalent* can mean "equal in value." How do you think **equivalent ratios** are related?

2. *Indirect* means "not direct." Do you think you will use a ruler to find an **indirect measurement**?

3. *Percent* comes from *per* and the Latin word *centum*, meaning "hundred." What do you think **percent** means?

4. *Ratio* can mean "the relationship in quantity, amount, or size between two things." How many numbers do you think a **ratio** will have?

5. A *scale* shows the relationship in size between two or more things. If you are making a **scale drawing** of a room, what do you think you would include on the drawing to show the room's actual size?

340 Chapter 7 Proportional Relationships

Reading and Writing Math

CHAPTER 7

Writing Strategy: Write a Convincing Explanation

You will see the Write About It icons throughout the book. These icons show exercises that require you to write a convincing explanation.

A convincing explanation should include

- a restatement of the question or problem.
- a complete solution to the problem.
- any work, definitions, diagrams, or charts needed to answer the problem.

From Lesson 6-8

C Why is this line graph misleading?

Average Number of Sit-ups in One Minute

Step 1 **Restate the question.**
The graph is misleading because the scale does not have equal intervals.

Step 2 **Provide a complete solution to the problem with facts and an explanation.**
For example, an increase from 35 sit-ups to 40 sit-ups appears greater than an increase from 30 sit-ups to 35 sit-ups. By reading the scale, you know that this is incorrect. Therefore, the graph is misleading.

Try This

Use your textbook.

1. Write a convincing explanation to explain why there are two modes in the data set 4, 6, 1, 0, 4, 8, 9, 0.

2. Look at one of your previous Write About It exercises. Does your answer follow the method outlined above? If so, label the items that should be included. If not, rewrite the explanation.

Proportional Relationships

7-1 Ratios and Rates

Learn to write ratios and rates and to find unit rates.

Vocabulary
ratio
equivalent ratios
rate
unit rate

Reading Math
Read the ratio $\frac{29}{12}$ as "twenty-nine to twelve."

For a time, a local symphony orchestra was made up of 95 musicians.

Violins	29	Violas	12
Cellos	10	Basses	9
Flutes	5	Trumpets	3
Double reeds	8	Percussion	5
Clarinets	4	Harp	1
Horns	6	Trombones	3

You can compare the different groups by using ratios. A **ratio** is a comparison of two quantities using division.

For example, you can use a ratio to compare the number of violins with the number of violas. This ratio can be written in three ways.

Terms $\frac{29}{12}$ 29 to 12   29:12

Notice that the ratio of violins to violas, $\frac{29}{12}$, is different from the ratio of violas to violins, $\frac{12}{29}$. The order of the terms is important.

Ratios can be written to compare a part to a part, a part to the whole, or the whole to a part.

EXAMPLE 1 Writing Ratios

Use the table above to write each ratio.

A flutes to clarinets

$\frac{5}{4}$ or   5 to 4   or   5:4   *Part to part*

B trumpets to total instruments

$\frac{3}{95}$ or   3 to 95   or   3:95   *Part to whole*

C total instruments to basses

$\frac{95}{9}$ or   95 to 9   or   95:9   *Whole to part*

Equivalent ratios are ratios that name the same comparison. You can find an equivalent ratio by multiplying or dividing both terms of a ratio by the same number.

EXAMPLE 2 **Writing Equivalent Ratios**

Write three equivalent ratios to compare the number of stars with the number of moons in the pattern.

$\dfrac{\text{number of stars}}{\text{number of moons}} = \dfrac{4}{6}$ There are 4 stars and 6 moons.

$\dfrac{4}{6} = \dfrac{4 \div 2}{6 \div 2} = \dfrac{2}{3}$ There are 2 stars for every 3 moons.

$\dfrac{4}{6} = \dfrac{4 \cdot 2}{6 \cdot 2} = \dfrac{8}{12}$ If you double the pattern, there will be 8 stars and 12 moons.

So $\dfrac{4}{6}$, $\dfrac{2}{3}$, and $\dfrac{8}{12}$ are equivalent ratios.

Interactivities Online ▶ A **rate** compares two quantities that have different units of measure.

Suppose a 2-liter bottle of soda costs $1.98.

$\text{rate} = \dfrac{\text{price}}{\text{number of liters}} = \dfrac{\$1.98}{2 \text{ liters}}$ $1.98 for 2 liters

When the comparison is to one unit, the rate is called a **unit rate**.

Divide both terms by the second term to find the unit rate.

$\text{unit rate} = \dfrac{\$1.98}{2} = \dfrac{\$1.98 \div 2}{2 \div 2} = \dfrac{\$0.99}{1}$ $0.99 for 1 liter

When the prices of two or more items are compared, the item with the lowest unit rate is the best deal.

EXAMPLE 3 **Consumer Math Application**

A 2-liter bottle of soda costs $2.02. A 3-liter bottle of the same soda costs $2.79. Which is the better deal?

2-liter bottle

$\dfrac{\$2.02}{2 \text{ liters}}$ Write the rate.

$\dfrac{\$2.02 \div 2}{2 \text{ liters} \div 2}$ Divide both terms by 2.

$\dfrac{\$1.01}{1 \text{ liter}}$ $1.01 for 1 liter

3-liter bottle

$\dfrac{\$2.79}{3 \text{ liters}}$ Write the rate.

$\dfrac{\$2.79 \div 3}{3 \text{ liters} \div 3}$ Divide both terms by 3.

$\dfrac{\$0.93}{1 \text{ liter}}$ $0.93 for 1 liter

The 3-liter bottle is the better deal.

Think and Discuss

1. **Explain** why the ratio 2:5 is different from the ratio 5:2.
2. **Tell** whether the ratios $\dfrac{4}{5}$ and $\dfrac{16}{25}$ are equivalent. If they are not, give a ratio that is equivalent to $\dfrac{4}{5}$.

7-1 Exercises

Learn It Online
Homework Help Online go.hrw.com,
keyword MR10 7-1
Exercises 1–11, 13, 15, 17, 19, 27

GUIDED PRACTICE

See Example 1 Use the table to write each ratio.
1. music programs to art programs
2. arcade games to entire collection
3. entire collection to educational games

Jacqueline's Software Collection	
Educational games	16
Word processing	2
Art programs	10
Arcade games	10
Music programs	3

See Example 2 4. Write three equivalent ratios to compare the number of red hearts in the picture with the total number of hearts.

See Example 3 5. **Consumer Math** An 8-ounce bag of sunflower seeds costs $1.68. A 4-ounce bag of sunflower seeds costs $0.88. Which is the better deal?

INDEPENDENT PRACTICE

See Example 1 Use the table to write each ratio.
6. Redbirds to Blue Socks
7. right-handed Blue Socks to left-handed Blue Socks
8. left-handed Redbirds to total Redbirds

	Redbirds	Blue Socks
Left-Handed Batters	8	3
Right-Handed Batters	11	19

See Example 2 9. Write three equivalent ratios to compare the number of stars in the picture with the number of stripes.

See Example 3 10. Gina charges $28 for 3 hours of swimming lessons. Hector charges $18 for 2 hours of swimming lessons. Which instructor offers a better deal?

11. **Consumer Math** A 12-pound bag of dog food costs $12.36. A 15-pound bag of dog food costs $15.30. Which is the better deal?

PRACTICE AND PROBLEM SOLVING

Extra Practice
See page EP14.

Write each ratio two different ways.
12. 10 to 7
13. $\frac{24}{11}$
14. 4 to 30
15. $\frac{7}{10}$
16. 16 to 20
17. $\frac{5}{9}$
18. 50 to 79
19. 100 to 101

20. A florist can create 16 bouquets during an 8-hour work day. How many bouquets can the florist create per hour?

344 Chapter 7 Proportional Relationships

Use the diagram of an oxygen atom and a boron atom for Exercises 21–24. Find each ratio. Then give two equivalent ratios.

21. oxygen protons to boron protons

22. boron neutrons to boron protons

23. boron electrons to oxygen electrons

24. oxygen electrons to oxygen protons

25. A lifeguard received 16 hours of first aid training and 8 hours of cardiopulmonary resuscitation (CPR) training. Write the ratio of hours of CPR training to hours of first aid training.

26. **Critical Thinking** Cassandra has three pictures on her desk. The pictures measure 4 in. long by 6 in. wide, 24 mm long by 36 mm wide, and 6 cm long by 7 cm wide. Which photos have a length-to-width ratio equivalent to 2:3?

27. **Multi-Step** On which day did Alfonso run faster?

Day	Distance (m)	Time (min)
Monday	1,020	6
Wednesday	1,554	9

28. **Earth Science** Water rushes over Niagara Falls at the rate of 180 million cubic feet every 30 minutes. How much water goes over the falls in 1 minute?

29. **What's the Question?** The ratio of total students in Mr. Avalon's class to students in the class who have a blue backpack is 3 to 1. The answer is 1:2. What is the question?

30. **Write About It** How are equivalent ratios like equivalent fractions?

31. **Challenge** There are 36 performers in a dance recital. The ratio of men to women is 2:7. How many men are in the dance recital?

Test Prep and Spiral Review

32. **Multiple Choice** Which ratio is equivalent to $\frac{1}{20}$?

    Ⓐ 9:180   Ⓑ 180 to 9   Ⓒ 4 to 100   Ⓓ 100:4

33. **Short Response** A 24-ounce box of raisins costs $4.56. A 15-ounce box of raisins costs $3.15. Which is the better deal? Explain.

Find the GCF of each set of numbers. (Lesson 4-3)

34. 12, 36   35. 15, 24   36. 18, 24, 42   37. 5, 14, 17

Solve each equation. Write the solution in simplest form. (Lesson 5-5)

38. $g + \frac{3}{10} = \frac{2}{5}$ 39. $m - \frac{1}{2} = \frac{1}{9}$ 40. $\frac{2}{3} = p + \frac{1}{6}$ 41. $h - \frac{1}{4} = \frac{5}{12}$

7-2 Using Tables to Explore Equivalent Ratios and Rates

Learn to use a table to find equivalent ratios and rates.

Mrs. Kennedy's students are painting a mural in their classroom. They mixed yellow and blue paints for a green background and found that the ratio of the amount of yellow to the amount of blue is 3 to 2.

Now they need to make more green paint, using the same ratio as before.

Use a table to find ratios equivalent to 3 to 2.

	Original ratio	3 · 2 ↓	3 · 3 ↓	3 · 4 ↓
Pints of yellow	3	6	9	12
Pints of blue	2	4	6	8
		↑ 2 · 2	↑ 2 · 3	↑ 2 · 4

Reading Math

Finding equivalent ratios is sometimes referred to as "scaling up" or "scaling down."

You can increase amounts but keep them in the same ratio by multiplying both the numerator and denominator of the ratio by the same number.

The ratios 3 to 2, 6 to 4, 9 to 6, and 12 to 8 are equivalent.

You can also decrease amounts in the same ratio by dividing the numerator and denominator by the same number.

EXAMPLE 1 Making a Table to Find Equivalent Ratios

Use a table to find three equivalent ratios.

A $\frac{8}{3}$

	Original ratio	8 · 2 ↓	8 · 3 ↓	8 · 4 ↓
	8	16	24	32
	3	6	9	12
		↑ 3 · 2	↑ 3 · 3	↑ 3 · 4

Multiply the numerator and the denominator by 2, 3, and 4.

Helpful Hint

Multiplying the ratio in Example 1A by 2, 3, and 4 will give you three equivalent ratios, but there are many other equivalent ratios that are correct.

The ratios $\frac{8}{3}$, $\frac{16}{6}$, $\frac{24}{9}$, and $\frac{32}{12}$ are equivalent.

Chapter 7 Proportional Relationships

Use a table to find three equivalent ratios.

B 4 to 7

Original ratio: 4·2, 4·3, 4·4

4	8	12	16
7	14	21	28

7·2, 7·3, 7·4

Multiply the numerator and the denominator by 2, 3, and 4.

The ratios 4 to 7, 8 to 14, 12 to 21, and 16 to 28 are equivalent.

C 40:16

Original ratio: 40÷2, 40÷4, 40÷8

40	20	10	5
16	8	4	2

16÷2, 16÷4, 16÷8

Divide the numerator and the denominator by 2.

The ratios 40:16, 20:8, 10:4, and 5:2 are equivalent.

Ratios in tables can be used to make estimates or predictions.

EXAMPLE 2 Entertainment Application

A group of 10 friends is in line to see a movie. The table shows how much different groups will pay in all. Predict how much the group of 10 will pay.

Number in Group	3	5	6	12
Amount Paid ($)	15	25	30	60

6 < 10 < 12; therefore, the group will pay between $30 and $60.

Use the amount paid by the group of 5.

The only factor of 10 in the table is 5.

2 · 5 = 10
2 · $25 = $50

Multiply the numerator and denominator by the same factor, 2.

A group of 10 friends would pay $50.00.

Think and Discuss

1. **Explain** how you can be sure that all the ratios you have written are correct when you have multiplied or divided a ratio to find equivalent ratios.

2. **Explain** how you can be sure that you have written the numerator and denominator in the correct order when rewriting ratios that have colons as fractions.

7-2 Exercises

Learn It Online
Homework Help Online go.hrw.com,
keyword MR10 7-2
Exercises 1–18, 19, 21, 27

GUIDED PRACTICE

See Example 1 Use a table to find three equivalent ratios.

1. $\frac{2}{7}$
2. 7 to 12
3. 96:48
4. $\frac{3}{5}$
5. 5 to 8
6. $\frac{9}{4}$
7. 24 to 16
8. 25:26

See Example 2

9. **Sports** Leo runs laps around a track. The table shows how long it takes him to run different numbers of laps. Predict how long it will take Leo to run 7 laps.

Number of Laps	2	4	6	8	10
Time (min)	10	20	30	40	50

INDEPENDENT PRACTICE

See Example 1 Use a table to find three equivalent ratios.

10. 6:5
11. 8 to 15
12. $\frac{12}{4}$
13. 6 to 7
14. $\frac{13}{20}$
15. 11:25
16. 5 to 18
17. $\frac{51}{75}$

See Example 2

18. Lee Middle School orders 15 textbooks for every 12 students. The table shows how many textbooks the school orders for certain numbers of students. Predict the number of textbooks that the school would order for 72 students.

Students	12	24	48	96	192
Textbooks	15	30	60	120	240

PRACTICE AND PROBLEM SOLVING

Extra Practice
See page EP14.

19. **Biology** Brown bats vary in length from 3 to 6 inches and have wing spans from 8 to 16 inches. Write a ratio in simplest form of a bat's wing span to the bat's body length.

20. Buy-A-Lot Market has tomatoes on sale. The table shows some sale prices. Predict how much a restaurant owner will pay for 25 pounds of tomatoes at the rate shown in the table.

Amount (lb)	30	20	15	10	5
Cost ($)	11.70	7.80	5.85	3.90	1.95

Complete each table to find the missing ratios.

21.

6	12	18	▇
5	10	▇	20

22.

96	48	24	▇
48	24	▇	6

348 Chapter 7 Proportional Relationships

History

President Lyndon Baines Johnson, often referred to as LBJ, was born in Stillwater, Texas, in 1908. President Johnson had no vice president from November 1963 to January 1965.

Multiply and divide each ratio to find two equivalent ratios.

23. 36:48
24. $\frac{4}{60}$
25. $\frac{128}{48}$
26. 15:100

27. **Multi-Step** Lyndon Johnson was elected president in 1964. The ratio of the number of votes he received to the number of votes that Barry Goldwater received was about 19:12. About how many votes were cast for both candiates?

Candidates	Number of Votes
Lyndon Johnson	43,121,085
Barry Goldwater	

28. **What's the Error?** A student said that 3:4 is equivalent to 9:16 and 18:64. What did the student do wrong? Correct the ratios so they are equivalent.

29. **Write About It** If Daniel drives the same distance each day, will he be able to complete a 4,500-mile trip in 2 weeks? Explain how you solved the problem.

Days	Distance (mi)
3	1,020
5	1,700
9	3,060

30. **Challenge** The table shows the regular and sale prices of CDs at Bargain Blast. How much money will you save if you buy 10 CDs on sale?

Number of CDs	Regular Price ($)	Sale Price ($)
2	17.00	14.40
3	25.50	21.60
6	51.00	43.20

Test Prep and Spiral Review

31. **Multiple Choice** Which ratio is NOT equivalent to 3 to 7?

    (A) 9:21   (B) 36:77   (C) 45:105   (D) 54:126

32. **Short Response** The table shows the distances traveled and the numbers of gallons of gas used on four automobile trips. Predict the number of gallons of gas that would be used for a trip of 483 miles.

Distance (mi)	552	414	276	138
Gas Used (gal)	24	18	12	6

33. In 2005, the heights of the world's tallest buildings were 509, 452, 452, 442, 421, and 415 meters. Find the mean, median, mode, and range of the data set. (Lesson 6-2)

34. Javier saved $65, $82, $58, $74, $65, and $72 each month from his part-time job for six months. The next month he worked full-time and saved $285. Find the mean, median, and mode of the amounts saved with and without the full-time savings. (Lesson 6-3)

7-2 Using Tables to Explore Equivalent Ratios and Rates

Hands-on LAB 7-3

Explore Proportions

Use with Lesson 7-3

You can use counters to model equivalent ratios.

Activity 1

Find three ratios that are equivalent to $\frac{6}{12}$.

1. Show 6 red counters and 12 yellow counters.

2. Separate the red counters into two equal groups. Then separate the yellow counters into two equal groups.

3. Write the ratio of red counters in each group to yellow counters in each group.

$$\frac{3 \text{ red counters}}{6 \text{ yellow counters}} = \frac{3}{6}$$

4. Now separate the red counters into three equal groups. Then separate the yellow counters into three equal groups.

5. Write the ratio of red counters in each group to yellow counters in each group.

$$\frac{2 \text{ red counters}}{4 \text{ yellow counters}} = \frac{2}{4}$$

6. Now separate the red counters into six equal groups. Then separate the yellow counters into six equal groups.

7. Write the ratio of red counters in each group to yellow counters in each group.

$$\frac{1 \text{ red counter}}{2 \text{ yellow counters}} = \frac{1}{2}$$

The three ratios you wrote are equivalent to $\frac{6}{12}$.

$$\frac{6}{12} = \frac{3}{6} = \frac{2}{4} = \frac{1}{2}$$

When you write an equation showing equivalent ratios, that equation is called a *proportion*.

Think and Discuss

1. How do the models show that the ratios are equivalent?

Try This

Use models to determine whether the ratios form a proportion.

1. $\frac{1}{3}$ and $\frac{4}{12}$
2. $\frac{3}{4}$ and $\frac{6}{9}$
3. $\frac{4}{10}$ and $\frac{2}{5}$

Activity 2

Write a proportion in which one of the ratios is $\frac{1}{3}$.

1 You must find a ratio that is equivalent to $\frac{1}{3}$. First show one red counter and three yellow counters.

2 Show one more group of one red counter and three yellow counters.

3 Write the ratio of red counters to yellow counters for the two groups.

$$\frac{2 \text{ red counters}}{6 \text{ yellow counters}} = \frac{2}{6}$$

4 The two ratios are equivalent. Write the proportion $\frac{1}{3} = \frac{2}{6}$.

You can find more equivalent ratios by adding more groups of one red counter and three yellow counters. Use your models to write proportions.

$$\frac{3 \text{ red counters}}{9 \text{ yellow counters}} = \frac{3}{9} \qquad \frac{4 \text{ red counters}}{12 \text{ yellow counters}} = \frac{4}{12}$$

$$\frac{3}{9} = \frac{1}{3} \qquad \frac{4}{12} = \frac{1}{3}$$

Think and Discuss

1. The models above show that $\frac{1}{3}, \frac{2}{6}, \frac{3}{9}$, and $\frac{4}{12}$ are equivalent ratios. Do you see a pattern in this list of ratios?

2. Use counters to find another ratio that is equivalent to $\frac{1}{3}$.

Try This

Use counters to write a proportion containing each given ratio.

1. $\frac{1}{4}$
2. $\frac{1}{5}$
3. $\frac{3}{7}$
4. $\frac{1}{6}$
5. $\frac{4}{9}$

7-3 Hands-On Lab

7-3 Proportions

Learn to write and solve proportions.

Vocabulary
proportion

Have you ever heard water called H_2O? H_2O is the scientific formula for water. One molecule of water contains two hydrogen atoms (H_2) and one oxygen atom (O). No matter how many molecules of water you have, hydrogen and oxygen will always be in the ratio 2 to 1.

Water Molecules	1	2	3	4
$\dfrac{\text{Hydrogen atoms}}{\text{Oxygen atoms}}$	$\dfrac{2}{1}$	$\dfrac{4}{2}$	$\dfrac{6}{3}$	$\dfrac{8}{4}$

"Remember everybody this is planet Earth So whatever you do, don't drink the water"

Reading Math

Read the proportion $\dfrac{2}{1} = \dfrac{4}{2}$ as "two is to one as four is to two."

Notice that $\dfrac{2}{1}, \dfrac{4}{2}, \dfrac{6}{3},$ and $\dfrac{8}{4}$ are equivalent ratios.

A **proportion** is an equation that shows two equivalent ratios.

$$\dfrac{2}{1} = \dfrac{4}{2} \qquad \dfrac{4}{2} = \dfrac{8}{4} \qquad \dfrac{2}{1} = \dfrac{6}{3}$$

EXAMPLE 1 Modeling Proportions

Write a proportion for the model.

First write the ratio of triangles to circles.

$$\dfrac{\text{number of triangles}}{\text{number of circles}} = \dfrac{4}{2}$$

Next separate the triangles and the circles into two equal groups.

Now write the ratio of triangles to circles in each group.

$$\dfrac{\text{number of triangles in each group}}{\text{number of circles in each group}} = \dfrac{2}{1}$$

A proportion shown by the model is $\dfrac{4}{2} = \dfrac{2}{1}$.

352 Chapter 7 Proportional Relationships

CROSS PRODUCTS

Cross products in proportions are equal.

$\dfrac{4}{8} = \dfrac{2}{4}$	$\dfrac{3}{5} = \dfrac{9}{15}$	$\dfrac{9}{6} = \dfrac{3}{2}$	$\dfrac{14}{7} = \dfrac{2}{1}$
$8 \cdot 2 = 4 \cdot 4$	$5 \cdot 9 = 3 \cdot 15$	$6 \cdot 3 = 9 \cdot 2$	$7 \cdot 2 = 14 \cdot 1$
$16 = 16$	$45 = 45$	$18 = 18$	$14 = 14$

Interactivities Online ▶

EXAMPLE 2 Using Cross Products to Complete Proportions

Find the missing value in the proportion $\dfrac{3}{4} = \dfrac{n}{16}$.

$\dfrac{3}{4} \bowtie \dfrac{n}{16}$ *Find the cross products.*

$4 \cdot n = 3 \cdot 16$ *The cross products are equal.*

$4n = 48$ *n is multiplied by 4.*

$\dfrac{4n}{4} = \dfrac{48}{4}$ *Divide both sides by 4 to undo the multiplication.*

$n = 12$

EXAMPLE 3 Measurement Application

The label from a bottle of pet vitamins shows recommended dosages. What dosage would you give an adult dog that weighs 15 lb?

$\dfrac{1 \text{ tsp}}{20 \text{ lb}} = \dfrac{v}{15 \text{ lb}}$ *Let v be the amount of vitamins for a 15 lb dog.*

$\dfrac{1 \text{ tsp}}{20 \text{ lb}} \bowtie \dfrac{v}{15 \text{ lb}}$ *Write a proportion.*

$20 \cdot v = 1 \cdot 15$ *The cross products are equal.*

$20v = 15$ *v is multiplied by 20.*

$\dfrac{20v}{20} = \dfrac{15}{20}$ *Divide both sides by 20 to undo the multiplication.*

$v = \dfrac{3}{4}$ tsp   *Write your answer in simplest form.*

You should give $\dfrac{3}{4}$ tsp of vitamins to a 15 lb dog.

Pet Vitamins
- Adult dogs:
  1 tsp per 20 lb body weight
- Puppies, pregnant dogs, or nursing dogs:
  1 tsp per 10 lb body weight
- Cats:
  1 tsp per 12 lb body weight

Caution!

In a proportion, the units must be in the same order in both ratios.

$\dfrac{\text{tsp}}{\text{lb}} = \dfrac{\text{tsp}}{\text{lb}}$

or $\dfrac{\text{lb}}{\text{tsp}} = \dfrac{\text{lb}}{\text{tsp}}$

Think and Discuss

1. **Tell** whether $\dfrac{7}{8} = \dfrac{4}{14}$ is a proportion. How do you know?

2. **Give an example** of a proportion. Tell how you know that it is a proportion.

7-3 Exercises

Learn It Online
Homework Help Online go.hrw.com,
keyword MR10 7-3
Exercises 1–12, 13, 15, 17, 19, 21, 23

GUIDED PRACTICE

See Example 1
1. Write a proportion for the model.

See Example 2   Find the missing value in each proportion.

2. $\frac{12}{9} = \frac{n}{3}$ 3. $\frac{t}{5} = \frac{28}{20}$ 4. $\frac{1}{c} = \frac{6}{12}$ 5. $\frac{6}{7} = \frac{30}{b}$

See Example 3
6. Ursula is entering a bicycle race for charity. Her mother pledges $0.75 for every 0.5 mile she bikes. If Ursula bikes 17.5 miles, how much will her mother donate?

INDEPENDENT PRACTICE

See Example 1
7. Write a proportion for the model.

See Example 2   Find the missing value in each proportion.

8. $\frac{3}{2} = \frac{24}{d}$ 9. $\frac{p}{40} = \frac{3}{8}$ 10. $\frac{6}{14} = \frac{x}{7}$ 11. $\frac{5}{p} = \frac{7}{77}$

See Example 3
12. According to Ty's study guidelines, how many minutes of science reading should he do if his science class is 90 minutes long?

Ty's Study Guidelines	
Class	Reading Time
Literature	35 minutes for every 50 minutes of class time
Science	20 minutes for every 60 minutes of class time
History	30 minutes for every 55 minutes of class time

PRACTICE AND PROBLEM SOLVING

Extra Practice
See page EP14.

Find the value of p in each proportion.

13. $\frac{18}{6} = \frac{6}{p}$ 14. $\frac{4}{p} = \frac{48}{60}$ 15. $\frac{p}{10} = \frac{15}{50}$ 16. $\frac{3}{5} = \frac{12}{p}$

17. $\frac{21}{15} = \frac{p}{5}$ 18. $\frac{3}{6} = \frac{p}{8}$ 19. $\frac{15}{5} = \frac{9}{p}$ 20. $\frac{6}{p} = \frac{4}{28}$

21. **Patterns** Given that the first term in a sequence is $\frac{7}{2}$, the second term is $\frac{14}{4}$, the fourth term is $\frac{28}{8}$, and the fifth term is $\frac{35}{10}$, find the value of the third term.

354   Chapter 7 Proportional Relationships

Social Studies LINK

The value of the U.S. dollar as compared to the values of currencies from other countries changes every day. The graph shows recent values of various currencies compared to the U.S. dollar. Use the graph for Exercises 22–26.

22. What is the value of 9.72 European euros in U.S. dollars?

23. Multi-Step You have $100 in U.S. dollars. Determine how much money this is in euros, Canadian dollars, yuan, shekels, and Mexican pesos.

24. What's the Error? A student set up the proportion $\frac{1}{7.52} = \frac{x}{30}$ to determine the value of 30 U.S. dollars in China. Why is this proportion incorrect? Write the correct proportion, and find the missing value.

25. Write About It Which is worth more: five U.S. dollars or five Canadian dollars? Why?

26. Challenge A dime is worth about how many Mexican pesos?

Currency Conversions

- Value of foreign currency in U.S. dollars
- Value of $1 U.S. in foreign currency

Europe (euro): 1.39, 0.72
Canada (dollar): 0.98, 1.02
China (yuan): 0.13, 7.52
Israel (shekel): 0.24, 4.08
Mexico (peso): 0.09, 11.08

Test Prep and Spiral Review

27. Multiple Choice A recipe calls for 4 cups of sugar and 16 cups of water. If the recipe is reduced, how many cups of water should be used with 1 cup of sugar?

Ⓐ 0.25 cups Ⓑ 1.6 cups Ⓒ 4 cups Ⓓ 16 cups

28. Multiple Choice Li mixes 3 units of red paint with 8 units of white paint to get pink. How many units of red paint should she mix with 12 units of white paint to get the same pink shade?

Ⓕ $2\frac{3}{4}$ Ⓖ 3 Ⓗ $3\frac{1}{4}$ Ⓙ $4\frac{1}{2}$

Compare. Write <, >, or =. (Lesson 4-7)

29. $\frac{4}{7}$ ☐ $\frac{7}{10}$ **30.** $\frac{3}{5}$ ☐ $\frac{14}{15}$ **31.** $\frac{9}{27}$ ☐ $\frac{6}{18}$ **32.** $\frac{45}{18}$ ☐ $\frac{18}{9}$

Write each ratio two different ways. (Lesson 7-1)

33. 4:9 **34.** eight to eleven **35.** $\frac{6}{13}$ **36.** 7:5

7-4 Similar Figures

Learn to use proportions to find missing measures in similar figures.

Matching sides of two or more polygons are called **corresponding sides**, and matching angles are called **corresponding angles**.

Vocabulary
corresponding sides
corresponding angles
similar

Similar figures have the same shape but not necessarily the same size.

SIMILAR FIGURES

Two figures are similar if
- the measures of the corresponding angles are equal.
- the ratios of the lengths of the corresponding sides are proportional.

In the rectangles above, one proportion is $\frac{AB}{WX} = \frac{AD}{WZ}$, or $\frac{2}{6} = \frac{3}{9}$.

EXAMPLE 1 Finding Missing Measures in Similar Figures

The two triangles are similar. Find the missing length x and the measure of $\angle A$.

$\frac{8}{12} = \frac{6}{x}$ Write a proportion using corresponding side lengths.

$12 \cdot 6 = 8 \cdot x$ The cross products are equal.

$72 = 8x$ x is multiplied by 8.

$\frac{72}{8} = \frac{8x}{8}$ Divide both sides by 8 to undo the multiplication.

$9 \text{ cm} = x$

Angle A corresponds to angle B, and the measure of $\angle B = 37°$. The measure of $\angle A = 37°$.

EXAMPLE 2

PROBLEM SOLVING APPLICATION

Children at the Ice Cream Stand was painted by American artist William H. Johnson. This reduction is similar to the actual painting. The height of the actual painting is 32 cm. To the nearest centimeter, what is the width of the actual painting?

1. Understand the Problem

The **answer** will be the width of the actual painting.

List the **important information:**
- The actual painting and the reduction above are similar.
- The reduced painting is 5.1 cm tall and 6 cm wide.
- The actual painting is 32 cm tall.

2. Make a Plan

Draw a diagram to represent the situation.
Use the corresponding sides to write a proportion.

3. Solve

$\dfrac{5.1 \text{ cm}}{32 \text{ cm}} = \dfrac{6 \text{ cm}}{w \text{ cm}}$ *Write a proportion.*

$32 \cdot 6 = 5.1 \cdot w$ *The cross products are equal.*

$192 = 5.1w$ *w is multiplied by 5.1.*

$\dfrac{192}{5.1} = \dfrac{5.1}{5.1}$ *Divide both sides by 5.1 to undo the multiplication.*

$38 \approx w$ *Round to the nearest centimeter.*

The width of the actual painting is about 38 cm.

4. Look Back

Estimate to check your answer. The ratio of the heights is about 5:30, or 1:6. The ratio of the widths is about 6:36, or 1:6. Since these ratios are equal, 38 cm is a reasonable answer.

Remember!
The symbol ≈ means "is approximately equal to."

Think and Discuss

1. Name two items in your classroom that appear to be similar figures.

2. Explain whether all squares are similar.

7-4 Exercises

GUIDED PRACTICE

See Example 1

1. The two triangles are similar. Find the missing length x and the measure of $\angle G$.

See Example 2

2. Pat's school photo package includes one large photo and several smaller photos. The large photo is similar to the photo at right. If the height of the large photo is 10 in., what is its width?

INDEPENDENT PRACTICE

See Example 1

3. The two triangles are similar. Find the missing length n and the measure of $\angle M$.

See Example 2

4. LeJuan swims in a pool that is similar to an Olympic-sized pool. LeJuan's pool is 30 m long by 8 m wide. The length of an Olympic-sized pool is 50 m. To the nearest meter, what is the width of an Olympic-sized pool?

PRACTICE AND PROBLEM SOLVING

Extra Practice
See page EP14.

Name the corresponding sides and angles for each pair of similar figures.

5.

6.

7. **Critical Thinking** The ratio of the lengths of two similar paintings is $\frac{100}{32}$. If the length of one painting is 100 cm, is the length of the other less than or greater than 100 cm? Explain.

358 Chapter 7 Proportional Relationships

The figures in each pair are similar. Find the unknown measures.

8.

E, 7 in., 7 in., F, ?, D, 10 in., 51°, 51°, M, ?, 30 in., 51°, N, L, 78°, 21 in., ?

9. 100°, 80°, X, 4 yd, Y, ?, ?, W, ?, Z, 80°, 11 yd, G, 8 yd, H, 100°, ?, 11 yd, ?, 100°, J, 8 yd, I

Tell whether the figures in each pair are similar. Explain your answers.

10. 90°, 125°, 5, 4, 5, 8, 90°, 55°; 90°, 7.5, 125°, 6, 7.5, 12, 90°, 55°

11. 53°, 5, 3, 4, 90°; 90°, 6, 6, 45°

12. Graphic Art Lenny sketches designs for billboards. The sketch and the billboard are similar. If the height of the billboard is 30 ft, what is the width to the nearest foot of the billboard?

13. What's the Error? A student drew two rectangles with dimensions 10 in. by 9 in. and 5 in. by 3 in. The student said that the rectangles are similar. What's the error?

14. Write About It Are all triangles that have one 90° angle similar? Explain your answer.

15. Challenge Draw two similar rectangles whose sides are in a ratio of 5:2.

1.5 in., 2.5 in., Visit SCORPION VALLEY

Test Prep and Spiral Review

16. Multiple Choice The triangles are similar. Find the missing angle measure.

8 cm, 120°, 30°, x, y; 6 cm, 30°, 30°, 4 cm, 120°

Ⓐ 30°   Ⓑ 60°   Ⓒ 120°   Ⓓ 180°

17. Multiple Choice Use the similar triangles in Exercise 16. Find the missing length y.

Ⓕ 4 cm   Ⓖ 12 cm   Ⓗ 18 cm   Ⓙ 24 cm

Identify the property that is illustrated by each equation. (Lesson 1-4)

18. $3 + (4 + 5) = (3 + 4) + 5$ **19.** $19(24) = 19(20) + 19(4)$ **20.** $(2)(13) = (13)(2)$

Find the value of n in each proportion. (Lesson 7-3)

21. $\frac{n}{7} = \frac{30}{42}$ **22.** $\frac{4}{n} = \frac{16}{8}$ **23.** $\frac{1}{9} = \frac{n}{6.3}$

7-4 Similar Figures

7-5 Indirect Measurement

Learn to use proportions and similar figures to find unknown measures.

Vocabulary
indirect measurement

The Statue of Liberty has been standing in New York Harbor since 1876. How could you measure the height of the statue?

One way to find a height that you cannot measure directly is to use similar figures and proportions. This method is called **indirect measurement**.

Suppose that on a sunny day, the statue cast a shadow that was 610 feet long. A 6-foot-tall person standing by the statue cast a 12-foot-long shadow.

Both the person and the statue form 90° angles with the ground, and their shadows are cast at the same angle. This means we can form two similar triangles and use proportions to find the missing height.

EXAMPLE 1 Using Indirect Measurement

Use the similar triangles above to find the height of the Statue of Liberty.

$\frac{6}{h} = \frac{12}{610}$ *Write a proportion using corresponding sides.*

$12 \cdot h = 6 \cdot 610$ *The cross products are equal.*

$12h = 3,660$ *h is multiplied by 12.*

$\frac{12h}{12} = \frac{3,660}{12}$ *Divide both sides by 12 to undo the multiplication.*

$h = 305$

The Statue of Liberty is about 305 feet tall.

EXAMPLE 2   **Measurement Application**

A lighthouse casts a shadow that is 36 m long when a meterstick casts a shadow that is 3 m long. How tall is the lighthouse?

$\dfrac{h}{1} = \dfrac{36}{3}$ *Write a proportion using corresponding sides.*

$1 \cdot 36 = 3 \cdot h$ *The cross products are equal.*

$36 = 3h$ *h is multiplied by 3.*

$\dfrac{36}{3} = \dfrac{3h}{3}$ *Divide both sides by 3 to undo the multiplication.*

$12 = h$

The lighthouse is 12 m tall.

Measurement

The Cape Hatteras lighthouse, located on Hatteras Island, North Carolina, is the tallest lighthouse in America at 225 ft tall. You can climb the 268 steps to the top for a magnificent view of the Atlantic.

Think and Discuss

1. **Name** two items for which it would make sense to use indirect measurement to find their heights.
2. **Name** two items for which it would **not** make sense to use indirect measurement to find their heights.

7-5 Exercises

Learn It Online
Homework Help Online go.hrw.com,
keyword MR10 7-5
Exercises 1–4, 5, 7

GUIDED PRACTICE

See Example 1
1. Use the similar triangles to find the height of the flagpole.

See Example 2
2. A tree casts a shadow that is 26 ft long. At the same time, a 3-foot-tall sunflower casts a shadow that is 4 ft long. How tall is the tree?

INDEPENDENT PRACTICE

See Example 1
3. Use the similar triangles to find the height of the lamppost.

See Example 2
4. The Eiffel Tower casts a shadow that is 328 feet long. A 6-foot-tall person standing by the tower casts a 2-foot-long shadow. How tall is the Eiffel Tower?

PRACTICE AND PROBLEM SOLVING

Extra Practice
See page EP14.

Find the unknown heights.

5. [palm tree, h, 84 in., 105 in., 130 in.]

6. [flag, h, 2.5 m, 28 m, 3.5 m]

7. A statue casts a shadow that is 360 m long. At the same time, a person who is 2 m tall casts a shadow that is 6 m long. How tall is the statue?

8. **Write About It** How are indirect measurements useful?

9. **Challenge** A 5.5-foot-tall girl stands so that her shadow lines up with the shadow of a telephone pole. The tip of her shadow is even with the tip of the pole's shadow. If the length of the pole's shadow is 40 feet and the girl is standing 27.5 feet away from the pole, how tall is the telephone pole?

Test Prep and Spiral Review

10. **Multiple Choice** An 18-foot-tall telephone pole casts a shadow that is 28.8 feet long. At the same time, a woman casts a shadow that is 8.8 feet long. How tall is the woman?

  (A) 4.4 feet   (B) 5.5 feet   (C) 14.08 feet   (D) 158.4 feet

11. **Gridded Response** A 4-foot-tall girl casts a shadow that is 7.2 feet long. A nearby tree casts a shadow that is 25.56 feet long. How tall, in feet, is the tree?

Estimate by rounding to the indicated place value. (Lesson 3-2)

12. $4.325 - 1.895$; tenths   13. $5.121 - 0.1568$; tenths   14. $7.592 + 9.675$; hundredths

Solve each equation. Write the solution in simplest form. (Lesson 5-5)

15. $x - 1\frac{1}{4} = 7$ 16. $4\frac{1}{3} = x + \frac{5}{6}$ 17. $x - 8\frac{1}{2} = \frac{3}{10}$ 18. $6\frac{2}{3} = 4\frac{1}{6} + x$

362 Chapter 7 Proportional Relationships

Hands-On Lab 7-6: Sketch Scale Drawings

Use with Lesson 7-6

REMEMBER
- Similar figures are exactly the same shape, but they may be different sizes.

You can use a *scale factor* to sketch scale drawings. A *scale drawing* is a drawing of an object that is proportionally smaller or larger than the object. A *scale factor* is the ratio that describes how much a figure is enlarged or reduced.

Activity

Draw triangle A on graph paper with height 1 and base 3 as shown.

To draw a similar triangle using a scale factor of 3, draw another triangle whose sides are 3 times as long as the corresponding sides of the original.

To find the height of the new triangle, multiply the height of triangle A by 3.
height = 1 × 3 = 3; the new height will be 3 units.

To find the base of the new triangle, multiply the base of triangle A by 3.
base = 3 × 3 = 9; the new base will be 9 units.

Label the new figure triangle B.

For every 1 unit of length on the original triangle, the second triangle has 3 units of length.

Think and Discuss

1. How does knowing the scale factor help you find the dimensions of a similar figure?

2. If you use a scale factor of $\frac{3}{2}$, will the new figure be larger or smaller than the original? Explain.

Try This

Use the given scale factor to draw a figure similar to triangle A.

1. 4
2. $\frac{1}{2}$
3. 2
4. $\frac{3}{2}$

7-6 Scale Drawings and Maps

Learn to read and use map scales and scale drawings.

Vocabulary
scale drawing
scale

The map of Chicago shown above is a *scale drawing*. A **scale drawing** is a drawing of a real object that is proportionally smaller or larger than the real object. In other words, measurements on a scale drawing are in proportion to the measurements of the real object.

Interactivities Online ▶ A **scale** is a ratio between two sets of measurements. In the map above, the scale is 1 in:2 mi. This ratio means that 1 inch on the map represents 2 miles in Chicago.

EXAMPLE 1 Finding Actual Distances

On the map, the distance between Wrigley Field and the Shedd Aquarium is approximately 3.3 inches. What is the actual distance?

Helpful Hint
In Example 1, think "1 inch is 2 miles, so 3.3 inches is how many miles?" This approach will help you set up proportions in similar problems.

$$\frac{1 \text{ in.}}{2 \text{ mi}} = \frac{3.3 \text{ in.}}{x \text{ mi}}$$

Write a proportion using the scale. Let x be the actual number of miles from Wrigley Field to the Shedd Aquarium.

$2 \cdot 3.3 = 1 \cdot x$ The cross products are equal.
$6.6 = x$ Identify Property of Multiplication

The actual distance from Wrigley Field to the Shedd Aquarium is approximately 6.6 miles.

EXAMPLE 2 **Astronomy Application**

Mercury
Earth
1 in:30 million km

A **What is the actual distance from Mercury to Earth?**

Use your inch ruler to measure the distance from the center of Mercury to the center of Earth on the drawing. Mercury and Earth are about 3 inches apart.

$$\frac{1 \text{ in.}}{30 \text{ million km}} = \frac{3 \text{ in.}}{x \text{ million km}}$$ *Write a proportion. Let x be the actual distance from Mercury to Earth.*

$$30 \cdot 3 = 1 \cdot x$$ *The cross products are equal.*

$$90 = x$$

The actual distance from Mercury to Earth is about 90 million km.

B **The actual distance from Mercury to Venus is 50 million kilometers. How far apart should Mercury and Venus be drawn?**

$$\frac{1 \text{ in.}}{30 \text{ million km}} = \frac{x \text{ in.}}{50 \text{ milllion km}}$$ *Write a proportion. Let x be the distance from Mercury to Venus on the drawing.*

$$30 \cdot x = 1 \cdot 50$$ *The cross products are equal.*

$$30x = 50$$ *x is multiplied by 30.*

$$\frac{30x}{30} = \frac{50}{30}$$ *Divide both sides by 30 to undo the multiplication.*

$$x = 1\frac{2}{3}$$

Mercury and Venus should be drawn $1\frac{2}{3}$ inches apart.

Think and Discuss

1. **Give an example** of when you would use a scale drawing.

2. **Suppose** that you are going to make a scale drawing of your classroom with a scale of 1 inch:3 feet. Select a distance in your classroom and measure it. What will this distance be on your drawing?

7-6 Exercises

Learn It Online
Homework Help Online go.hrw.com,
keyword MR10 7-6
Exercises 1–6, 9, 17

GUIDED PRACTICE

See Example 1
1. On the map, the distance between the post office and the fountain is 6 cm. What is the actual distance?

Scale 1 cm:50 ft

See Example 2
2. What is the actual length of the car?

3. The actual height of the car is 1.6 meters. Is the car's height in the drawing correct?

Scale: 1 cm:0.8 m

INDEPENDENT PRACTICE

See Example 1
4. On the map of California, Los Angeles is 1.25 inches from Malibu. Find the actual distance from Los Angeles to Malibu.

See Example 2
5. Riverside, California, is 50 miles from Los Angeles. On the map, how far should Riverside be from Los Angeles?

Scale: 1 in:20 mi

6. **Life Science** A paramecium is a one-celled organism. The scale drawing at right is larger than an actual paramecium. Find the actual length of the paramecium.

Scale: 1 in:0.005 in.

PRACTICE AND PROBLEM SOLVING

Extra Practice
See page EP14.

7. Suppose you are asked to make a scale drawing of a room. The room has four walls. The lengths of the walls are as follows: north wall, 8 ft; west wall, 12 ft; south wall, 20 ft; slanted east wall, 17 ft. The scale for the drawing is 1 in:4 ft.

   a. Use the actual lengths of the walls to find the lengths in the drawing.
   b. Sketch the room and label each wall. What shape does the room resemble?
   c. Mark a 2.5 ft wide window on the west wall, and a 3.5 ft wide door on the south wall. Give the width of each on the scale drawing.

8. **Hobbies** A popular scale used in model trains is called HO. The scale for HO is 1 ft:87 ft. If a model train is 3 feet long, how long is the actual train?

366 Chapter 7 Proportional Relationships

Social Studies LINK

Florida is the 22nd largest state in the country. It has 663 miles of beaches, which makes it a popular vacation destination.

Scale: 1 cm = 84 km

9. What is the distance in kilometers from Miami to Orlando?

10. What is the distance in kilometers from West Palm Beach to Tampa?

11. Name two cities on the map that are more than 700 kilometers apart.

12. St. Augustine is about 244 kilometers from Tampa.
    a. How far apart should these cities be on the map?
    b. What else would you need to know to be able to place St. Augustine on the map?

13. **Write a Problem** Write a problem using the map and its scale.

14. **Write About It** Explain how to find the actual distance between two cities if you know the distance on a map and the scale of the map.

15. **Challenge** If you travel over water at a constant speed of 50 kilometers per hour, about how long will it take you to travel from Key West to Pensacola?

Test Prep and Spiral Review

16. **Multiple Choice** The distance between towns A and C on a map is 13 centimeters. What is the actual distance between towns B and C?

    Scale: 1 cm:30 km

    Ⓐ 0.27 kilometers Ⓑ 150 kilometers Ⓒ 240 kilometers Ⓓ 390 kilometers

17. **Gridded Response** Tanya has a 1 in:32 in. scale model car. The length of the model car is 2 inches. What is the actual length of the car?

Find each sum or difference. (Lesson 3-3)

18. $8.3 - 6.7$ 19. $25.6 + 12.8$ 20. $14 - 5.9$ 21. $8.62 - 4.75$ 22. $15.75 + 9.38$

Find the missing value in each proportion. (Lesson 7-3)

23. $\frac{9}{15} = \frac{x}{5}$ 24. $\frac{b}{20} = \frac{3}{15}$ 25. $\frac{1}{7} = \frac{6}{k}$ 26. $\frac{8}{3} = \frac{a}{9}$ 27. $\frac{p}{4} = \frac{11}{44}$

7-6 Scale Drawings and Maps

Chapter 7 Ready To Go On?

Quiz for Lessons 7-1 Through 7-6

7-1 Ratios and Rates

Types of CDs in Mark's Music Collection			
Classical	4	Jazz	3
Country	9	Pop	14
Dance	8	Rock	10

Use the table to write each ratio.

1. classical CDs to rock CDs
2. country to total CDs
3. A package containing 6 pairs of socks costs $6.89. A package containing 4 pairs of socks costs $4.64. Which is the better deal?

7-2 Using Tables to Explore Equivalent Ratios and Rates

Use a table to find three equivalent ratios.

4. $\frac{21}{30}$
5. 15:6
6. 3 to 101

7. The table shows the wait time for different groups at a restaurant. Predict how long a group of 8 will wait.

Number in Group	1	2	5	7	10
Wait Time (min)	3	6	15	21	30

7-3 Proportions

Find the missing value in each proportion.

8. $\frac{1}{4} = \frac{n}{12}$
9. $\frac{3}{n} = \frac{15}{25}$
10. $\frac{n}{4} = \frac{18}{6}$
11. $\frac{10}{4} = \frac{5}{n}$

7-4 Similar Figures

12. The two triangles are similar. Find the missing length n and the measure of ∠R.

7-5 Indirect Measurement

13. A tree casts a shadow that is 18 feet long. At the same time, a 5-foot-tall person casts a shadow that is 3.6 feet long. How tall is the tree?

7-6 Scale Drawings and Maps

Use the scale drawing and a metric ruler to answer each question.

14. What is the actual length of the kitchen?
15. What are the actual length and width of bedroom 1?

Scale: 1cm:8ft

Focus on Problem Solving

Make a Plan

- **Estimate or find an exact answer**

Sometimes an estimate is all you need to solve a problem, and sometimes you need to find an exact answer.

One way to decide whether you can estimate is to see if you can rewrite the problem using the words *at most, at least,* or *about*. For example, suppose Laura has $30. Then she could spend *at most* $30. She would not have to spend *exactly* $30. Or, if you know it takes 15 minutes to get to school, you must leave your house *at least* (not exactly) 15 minutes before school starts.

Read the problems below. Decide whether you can estimate or whether you must find the exact answer. How do you know?

1. Alex is a radio station disc jockey. He is making a list of songs that should last no longer than 30 minutes total when played in a row. His list of songs and their playing times are given in the table. Does Alex have the right amount of music?

Song Title	Length (min)
Color Me Blue	4.5
Hittin' the Road	7.2
Stand Up, Shout	2.6
Top Dog	3.6
Kelso Blues	4.3
Smile on Me	5.7
A Long Time Ago	6.4

2. For every 10 minutes of music, Alex has to play 1.5 minutes of commercials. If Alex plays the songs on the list, how much time does he need to allow for commercials?

3. If Alex must play the songs on the list and the commercials in 30 minutes, how much music time does he need to cut to allow for commercials?

Focus on Problem Solving **369**

Hands-on LAB 7-7

Model Percents

Use with Lesson 7-7

Learn It Online
Lab Resources Online go.hrw.com,
keyword MR10 Lab7 Go

A *percent* shows the ratio of a number to 100. You can model percents by using a 10-by-10 grid on graph paper.

Activity

1 Model 55% on a 10-by-10 grid.

Write 55% as a ratio comparing 55 to 100.

$55\% = \frac{55}{100}$

Since there are 100 squares in a 10 × 10 grid, shade in 55 squares.

$\frac{\text{number of squares shaded}}{\text{total number of squares}} = \frac{55}{100} = 55\%$

The model represents 55%.

2 What percent of grid A is shaded?

Find the number of squares shaded in grid A. Compare it with the total number of squares.

$\frac{\text{number of squares shaded}}{\text{total number of squares}} = \frac{42}{100}$

Since 42 out of 100 squares are shaded, the grid models 42%.

Grid A

Think and Discuss

1. Shade in $\frac{3}{4}$ of a 10-by-10 grid. What percent of the grid is shaded? Explain.

2. How can equivalent ratios help you find your answer to **1**?

3. How would you model 105%? 0.5%? Explain your answer.

Try This

Model each percent on a 10-by-10 grid.

1. 50%   2. 68%   3. 4%   4. 91%   5. 100%

7-7 Percents

Learn to write percents as decimals and as fractions.

Vocabulary
percent

Most states charge sales tax on items you purchase. Sales tax is a percent of the item's price. A **percent** is a ratio of a number to 100.

You can remember that *percent* means "per hundred." For example, 8% means "8 per hundred," or "8 out of 100."

If a sales tax rate is 8%, the following statements are true:
- For every $1.00 you spend, you pay $0.08 in sales tax.
- For every $10.00 you spend, you pay $0.80 in sales tax.
- For every $100 you spend, you pay $8 in sales tax.

At a sales tax rate of 8%, the tax on this wakeskate would be $12.80.

Because *percent* means "per hundred," 100% means "100 out of 100." This is why 100% is often used to mean "all" or "the whole thing."

EXAMPLE 1 Modeling Percents

Interactivities Online

Use a 10-by-10-square grid to model 8%.

A 10-by-10-square grid has 100 squares.
8% means "8 out of 100," or $\frac{8}{100}$.
Shade 8 squares out of 100 squares.

EXAMPLE 2 Writing Percents as Fractions

Write 40% as a fraction in simplest form.

$40\% = \frac{40}{100}$ Write the percent as a fraction with a denominator of 100.

$\frac{40 \div 20}{100 \div 20} = \frac{2}{5}$ Write the fraction in simplest form.

Written as a fraction, 40% is $\frac{2}{5}$.

Video Lesson Tutorials Online   my.hrw.com

EXAMPLE 3 Life Science Application

Up to 55% of the heat lost by your body can be lost through your head. Write 55% as a fraction in simplest form.

$55\% = \frac{55}{100}$ *Write the percent as a fraction with a denominator of 100.*

$\frac{55 \div 5}{100 \div 5} = \frac{11}{20}$ *Write the fraction in simplest form.*

Written as a fraction, 55% is $\frac{11}{20}$.

EXAMPLE 4 Writing Percents as Decimals

Write 24% as a decimal.

$24\% = \frac{24}{100}$ *Write the percent as a fraction with a denominator of 100.*

$$\begin{array}{r} 0.24 \\ 100\overline{)24.00} \\ -200 \\ \hline 400 \\ -400 \\ \hline 0 \end{array}$$

Write the fraction as a decimal.

Written as a decimal, 24% is 0.24.

Remember!

To divide by 100, move the decimal point two places to the left.

$.24 \div 100 = 0.24$

EXAMPLE 5 Earth Science Application

The water frozen in glaciers makes up almost 75% of the world's fresh water supply. Write 75% as a decimal.

$75\% = \frac{75}{100}$ *Write the percent as a fraction with a denominator of 100.*

$75 \div 100 = 0.75$ *Write the fraction as a decimal.*

Written as a decimal, 75% is 0.75.

Think and Discuss

1. **Give an example** of a situation in which you have seen percents.
2. **Tell** how much sales tax you would have to pay on $1, $10, and $100 if your state had a 5% sales tax rate.
3. **Explain** how to write a percent as a fraction.
4. **Write** 100% as a decimal and as a fraction.

7-7 Exercises

Learn It Online
Homework Help Online go.hrw.com,
keyword MR10 7-7
Exercises 1–33, 35, 37, 39, 41, 43, 45, 47

GUIDED PRACTICE

See Example 1 Use a 10-by-10-square grid to model each percent.
1. 45%   2. 3%   3. 61%

See Example 2 Write each percent as a fraction in simplest form.
4. 25%   5. 80%   6. 54%

See Example 3
7. **Social Studies** Belize is a country in Central America. Of the land in Belize, 92% is made up of forests and woodlands. Write 92% as a fraction in simplest form.

See Example 4 Write each percent as a decimal.
8. 72%   9. 4%   10. 90%

See Example 5
11. About 64% of the runways at airports in the United States are not paved. Write 64% as a decimal.

INDEPENDENT PRACTICE

See Example 1 Use a 10-by-10-square grid to model each percent.
12. 14%   13. 98%   14. 36%   15. 28%

See Example 2 Write each percent as a fraction in simplest form.
16. 20%   17. 75%   18. 11%   19. 72%
20. 5%   21. 64%   22. 31%   23. 85%

See Example 3
24. Nikki must answer 80% of the questions on her final exam correctly to pass her class. Write 80% as a fraction in simplest form.

See Example 4 Write each percent as a decimal.
25. 44%   26. 13%   27. 29%   28. 51%
29. 60%   30. 92%   31. 7%   32. 87%

See Example 5
33. Brett was absent 2% of the school year. Write 2% as a decimal.

PRACTICE AND PROBLEM SOLVING

Extra Practice
See page EP15.

Write each percent as a fraction in simplest form and as a decimal.
34. 23%   35. 1%   36. 49%   37. 70%   38. 10%
39. 37%   40. 85%   41. 8%   42. 63%   43. 75%
44. 94%   45. 100% 46. 0%   47. 52%   48. 12%

49. Model 15%, 52%, 71%, and 100% using different 10-by-10 grids. Then write each percent as a fraction in simplest form.

7-7 Percents   373

Music Link

The circle graph shows the percent of radio stations around the world that play each type of music listed. Use the graph for Exercises 50–57.

50. What fraction of the radio stations play easy listening music? Write this fraction in simplest form.

51. Use a 10-by-10-square grid to model the percent of radio stations that play country music. Then write this percent as a decimal.

52. Which type of music makes up $\frac{1}{20}$ of the graph?

53. Someone reading the graph said, "More than $\frac{1}{10}$ of the radio stations play top 40 music." Do you agree with this statement? Why or why not?

54. Suppose you converted all of the percents in the graph to decimals and added them. Without actually doing this, tell what the sum would be. Explain.

55. **Write a Problem** Write a question about the circle graph that involves changing a percent to a fraction. Then answer your question.

56. **Write About It** How does the percent of radio stations that play Spanish music compare with the fraction $\frac{1}{6}$? Explain.

57. **Challenge** Name a fraction that is greater than the percent of radio stations that play Spanish music but less than the percent of radio stations that play urban/rap music.

Radio Formats of the World

- Alternative rock 4%
- Classic rock 4%
- Other 15%
- Oldies 5%
- Spanish 6%
- Top 40 9%
- Urban/rap 7%
- Modern rock 7%
- Country 11%
- Easy listening 15%
- News/Talk 17%

Source: Scholastic Kid's Almanac for the 21st Century

Test Prep and Spiral Review

58. **Multiple Choice** Which decimal is equivalent to 85%?

   Ⓐ 85.0   Ⓑ 8.5   Ⓒ 0.85   Ⓓ 0.085

59. **Multiple Choice** Which term describes a number compared to 100?

   Ⓕ Rate   Ⓖ Ratio   Ⓗ Percent   Ⓙ Proportion

Simplify each expression. (Lesson 1-3)

60. $45 \div 5 + 2 - 10$
61. $25 - 4 \times 2$
62. $18 - 7 \times 2 + 8$
63. $48 - 9 \times 3 - 11$

64. The Sears Tower in Chicago casts a shadow 580 feet long. At the same time, a 5-foot-tall boy casts a 2-foot shadow. What is the height of the Sears Tower? (Lesson 7-5)

7-8 Percents, Decimals, and Fractions

Learn to write decimals and fractions as percents.

Percents, decimals, and fractions appear in newspapers, on television, and on the Internet. To fully understand the data you see in your everyday life, you should be able to change from one number form to another.

In Lesson 7-7, you learned how to write a percent as a fraction or as a decimal. You can also express decimals and fractions as percents.

$$\frac{1}{2} = 0.5 = 50\%$$

EXAMPLE 1 Writing Decimals as Percents

Interactivities Online ▶

Write each decimal as a percent.

Method 1: Use place value.

A 0.3

$0.3 = \frac{3}{10}$ *Write the decimal as a fraction.*

$\frac{3 \cdot 10}{10 \cdot 10} = \frac{30}{100}$ *Write an equivalent fraction with 100 as the denominator.*

$\frac{30}{100} = 30\%$ *Write the numerator with a percent symbol.*

B 0.43

$0.43 = \frac{43}{100}$ *Write the decimal as a fraction.*

$\frac{43}{100} = 43\%$ *Write the numerator with a percent symbol.*

Method 2: Multiply by 100.

C 0.7431

$0.7431 \cdot 100$ *Multiply by 100.*

74.31% *Add the percent symbol.*

D 0.023

$0.023 \cdot 100$ *Multiply by 100.*

2.3% *Add the percent symbol.*

Video Lesson Tutorials Online   my.hrw.com

EXAMPLE 2 Writing Fractions as Percents

Write each fraction as a percent.

Method 1: Write an equivalent fraction with a denominator of 100.

A $\frac{4}{5}$

$\frac{4 \cdot 20}{5 \cdot 20} = \frac{80}{100}$ *Write an equivalent fraction with a denominator of 100.*

$\frac{80}{100} = 80\%$ *Write the numerator with a percent symbol.*

Method 2: Use division to write the fraction as a decimal.

B $\frac{3}{8}$

$8\overline{)3.000}$ quotient 0.375   *Divide the numerator by the denominator.*

$0.375 = 37.5\%$ *Multiply by 100 by moving the decimal point right two places. Add the percent symbol.*

Helpful Hint
When the denominator is a factor of 100, it is often easier to use method 1. When the denominator is not a factor of 100, it is usually easier to use method 2.

EXAMPLE 3 Earth Science Application

About $\frac{39}{50}$ of Earth's atmosphere is made up of nitrogen. About what percent of the atmosphere is nitrogen?

$\frac{39}{50}$

$\frac{39 \cdot 2}{50 \cdot 2} = \frac{78}{100}$ *Write an equivalent fraction with a denominator of 100.*

$\frac{78}{100} = 78\%$ *Write the numerator with a percent symbol.*

About 78% of Earth's atmosphere is made up of nitrogen.

The number line below shows common equivalent fractions, decimals, and percents.

0	$\frac{1}{5}$	$\frac{1}{4}$	$\frac{1}{3}$	$\frac{2}{5}$	$\frac{1}{2}$	$\frac{3}{5}$	$\frac{2}{3}$	$\frac{3}{4}$	$\frac{4}{5}$	1
	0.2	0.25	$0.\overline{3}$	0.4	0.5	0.6	$0.\overline{6}$	0.75	0.8	
	20%	25%	$33.\overline{3}\%$	40%	50%	60%	$66.\overline{6}\%$	75%	80%	

Think and Discuss

1. **Tell** which method you prefer for converting decimals to percents—using equivalent fractions or multiplying by 100. Why?
2. **Give** two different ways to write three-tenths.
3. **Explain** how to write fractions as percents using two different methods.

7-8 Exercises

Learn It Online
Homework Help Online go.hrw.com, keyword MR10 7-8 Go
Exercises 1–26, 31, 33, 39, 43, 49, 55, 59

GUIDED PRACTICE

See Example 1 Write each decimal as a percent.
1. 0.39
2. 0.125
3. 0.8
4. 0.112

See Example 2 Write each fraction as a percent.
5. $\frac{11}{25}$
6. $\frac{7}{8}$
7. $\frac{7}{10}$
8. $\frac{1}{2}$
9. $\frac{9}{15}$

See Example 3
10. Patti spent $\frac{3}{4}$ of her allowance on a new backpack. What percent of her allowance did she spend?

INDEPENDENT PRACTICE

See Example 1 Write each decimal as a percent.
11. 0.6
12. 0.55
13. 0.34
14. 0.308
15. 0.62

See Example 2 Write each fraction as a percent.
16. $\frac{3}{5}$
17. $\frac{3}{10}$
18. $\frac{24}{25}$
19. $\frac{9}{20}$
20. $\frac{17}{20}$
21. $\frac{1}{8}$
22. $\frac{11}{16}$
23. $\frac{37}{50}$
24. $\frac{2}{5}$
25. $\frac{18}{45}$

See Example 3
26. About $\frac{1}{125}$ of the people in the United States have the last name *Johnson*. What percent of people in the United States have this last name?

PRACTICE AND PROBLEM SOLVING

Extra Practice See page EP15.

Write each decimal as a percent and a fraction.
27. 0.04
28. 0.32
29. 0.45
30. 0.59
31. 0.01
32. 0.81
33. 0.6
34. 0.39
35. 0.14
36. 0.62

Write each fraction as a percent and as a decimal. Round to the nearest hundredth, if necessary.
37. $\frac{4}{5}$
38. $\frac{1}{3}$
39. $\frac{5}{6}$
40. $\frac{7}{12}$
41. $\frac{17}{50}$
42. $\frac{2}{30}$
43. $\frac{1}{25}$
44. $\frac{8}{11}$
45. $\frac{4}{15}$
46. $\frac{22}{35}$

Compare. Write <, >, or =.
47. 70% ☐ $\frac{3}{4}$
48. $\frac{5}{8}$ ☐ 6.25%
49. 0.2 ☐ $\frac{1}{5}$
50. 1.25 ☐ $\frac{1}{8}$
51. 0.7 ☐ 7%
52. $\frac{9}{10}$ ☐ 0.3
53. 37% ☐ $\frac{3}{7}$
54. $\frac{17}{20}$ ☐ 0.85

55. **Language Arts** The longest word in all of Shakespeare's plays is *honorificabilitudinitatibus*. About what percent of the letters in this word are vowels? About what percent of the letters are consonants?

7-8 Percents, Decimals, and Fractions   377

Order the numbers from least to greatest.

56. 45%, $\frac{21}{50}$, 0.43, 89%

57. $\frac{7}{8}$, 90%, 0.098

58. 0.7, 26%, $\frac{1}{4}$, 34%

59. 38%, $\frac{7}{25}$, 0.21

60. $\frac{9}{20}$, 14%, 0.125, 24%

61. 0.605, 17%, $\frac{5}{9}$

62. **Entertainment** A record-company official estimates that 3 out of every 100 albums released become hits. What percent of albums do not become hits?

63. **Multi-Step** About 97 million households in the United States have at least one television. Use the table below to answer the questions that follow.

Television in the United States	
Fraction of households with at least one television	$\frac{49}{50}$
Percent of households with three televisions	38%
Fraction of television owners with basic cable	$\frac{2}{3}$

a. About what percent of television owners have basic cable?

b. Write a decimal to express the percent of television owners who have three televisions.

64. **What's the Question?** Out of 25 students, 12 prefer to take their test on Monday, and 5 prefer to take their test on Tuesday. The answer is 32%. What is the question?

65. **Write About It** Explain why 0.8 is equal to 80% and not 8%.

66. **Challenge** The dimensions of a rectangle are 0.5 yard and 24% of a yard. What is the area of the rectangle? Write your answer as a fraction in simplest form.

The Recording Industry Association of America awards gold records to artists who sell at least 500,000 copies of an album.

Test Prep and Spiral Review

67. **Multiple Choice** Which expression is NOT equal to half of n?

   Ⓐ 0.5n Ⓑ $\frac{n}{2}$ Ⓒ $n \div 2$ Ⓓ 5% of n

68. **Multiple Choice** Approximately $\frac{2}{3}$ of U.S. homeowners own a cell phone. What percent of homeowners do NOT own a cell phone?

   Ⓕ 0.67%   Ⓖ 2.3%   Ⓗ 33.3%   Ⓙ 66.7%

Add or subtract. Write each answer in simplest form. (Lesson 5-2)

69. $\frac{1}{2} + \frac{3}{4}$

70. $\frac{2}{3} - \frac{1}{5}$

71. $\frac{2}{5} + \frac{1}{2}$

72. $\frac{8}{9} - \frac{1}{6}$

The scale for blueprints of a house is 2 in:3 ft. Use the scale to determine the related actual lengths. (Lesson 7-6)

73. porch length: 2 in.

74. bedroom wall: 5 in.

75. window: 1.5 in.

Technology Lab 7-8

Convert Between Percents, Decimals, and Fractions

Use with Lesson 7-8

Learn It Online
Lab Resources Online go.hrw.com,
keyword MR10 Lab7

You can use your calculator to quickly change between percents, decimals, and fractions.

Activity

1 To write a decimal as a fraction on a graphing calculator, use the **FRAC** command from the **MATH** menu.

Find the fraction equivalent of 0.225 by pressing 0.225 MATH 1 ENTER.

2 To write a percent as a fraction, first write the percent as a fraction whose denominator is 100. Then use the **FRAC** command to find the simplest form of the fraction.

Find the fraction equivalent of 65% by pressing 65 ÷ 100 MATH 1 ENTER.

3 To write a fraction as a percent, multiply the fraction by 100.

Find the percent equivalent of $\frac{11}{25}$ by pressing 11 ÷ 25 × 100 ENTER.

$\frac{11}{25} = 44\%$

Think and Discuss

1. Use the **FRAC** command on a graphing calculator to find the fraction equivalent of 0.142857142857 by pressing 0.142857142857 MATH 1 ENTER. Describe what happens.

Try This

Write each percent as a fraction.

1. 57.5%   2. 32.5%   3. 3.25%   4. 1.65%   5. 81.25%

Write each fraction as a percent.

6. $\frac{7}{40}$ 7. $\frac{3}{8}$ 8. $\frac{19}{25}$ 9. $\frac{3}{16}$ 10. $\frac{17}{20}$

7-9 Percent Problems

Learn to find the missing value in a percent problem.

The frozen-yogurt stand in the mall sells 420 frozen-yogurt cups per day, on average. Forty-five percent of the frozen-yogurt cups are sold to teenagers. On average, how many frozen-yogurt cups are sold to teenagers each day?

To answer this question, you will need to find 45% of 420.

To find the percent one number is of another, use this proportion:

$$\frac{\%}{100} = \frac{\text{is}}{\text{of}}$$

Because you are looking for **45% of 420**, 45 replaces the **percent sign** and 420 replaces **"of."** The first denominator, 100, always stays the same. The "is" part is what you have been asked to find.

EXAMPLE 1 Consumer Math Application

How many frozen-yogurt cups are sold to teenagers each day?

First estimate your answer. Think: $45\% = \frac{45}{100}$, which is close to $\frac{50}{100}$, or $\frac{1}{2}$. So about $\frac{1}{2}$ of the 420 yogurt cups are sold to teenagers.

$\frac{1}{2} \cdot 420 = 210$ ← *This is the estimate.*

Now solve:

$\frac{45}{100} = \frac{y}{420}$ *Let y represent the number of yogurt cups sold to teenagers.*

$100 \cdot y = 45 \cdot 420$ *The cross products are equal.*

$100y = 18{,}900$ *y is multiplied by 100.*

$\frac{100y}{100} = \frac{18{,}900}{100}$ *Divide both sides of the equation by 100 to undo the multiplication.*

$y = 189$

Since 189 is close to your estimate of 210, 189 is a reasonable answer. About 189 yogurt cups per day are sold to teenagers.

Helpful Hint

Think: "45 out of 100 is how many out of 420?"

EXAMPLE 2 *Technology Application*

Heather is downloading a file from the Internet. So far, she has downloaded 75% of the file. If 30 minutes have passed since she started, how long will it take her to download the rest of the file?

$$\frac{\%}{100} = \frac{is}{of}$$

$$\frac{75}{100} = \frac{30}{m}$$

75% of the file has downloaded, so 30 minutes is 75% of the total time needed.

$100 \cdot 30 = 75 \cdot m$ *The cross products are equal.*

$3{,}000 = 75m$ *m is multiplied by 75.*

$$\frac{3{,}000}{75} = \frac{75m}{75}$$

Divide both sides by 75 to undo the multiplication.

$40 = m$

The time needed to download the entire file is 40 min. So far, the file has been downloading for 30 min. Because 40 − 30 = 10, the remainder of the file will be downloaded in 10 min.

Instead of using proportions, you can also multiply to find a percent of a number.

EXAMPLE 3 **Multiplying to Find a Percent of a Number**

Find 20% of 150.

$20\% = 0.20$ *Write the percent as a decimal.*
$0.20 \cdot 150$ *Multiply using the decimal.*
30

So 30 is 20% of 150.

Check
Use a model to check the answer.

0%	10%	20%	30%	40%	50%	60%	70%	80%	90%	100%
0	15	30	45	60	75	90	105	120	135	150

Think and Discuss

1. Explain why you must subtract 30 from 40 in Example 2.

2. Give an example of a time when you would need to find a percent of a number.

7-9 Exercises

Learn It Online
Homework Help Online go.hrw.com, keyword MR10 7-9
Exercises 1–18, 21, 23, 25, 27, 29, 31, 33

GUIDED PRACTICE

See Example 1
1. Members of the drama club sold T-shirts for their upcoming musical. Of the 80 T-shirts sold, 55% were size medium. How many of the T-shirts sold were size medium?

See Example 2
2. Loni has read 25% of a book. If she has been reading for 5 hours, how many more hours will it take her to complete the book?

See Example 3
3. Find 12% of 56.
4. Find 65% of 240.
5. Find 2% of 20.
6. Find 85% of 115.
7. Find 70% of 54.
8. Find 85% of 355.

INDEPENDENT PRACTICE

See Example 1
9. Tamara collects porcelain dolls. Of the 24 dolls that she has, 25% have blond hair. How many of her dolls have blond hair?

10. Mr. Green has a garden. Of the 40 seeds he planted, 35% were vegetable seeds. How many vegetable seeds did he plant?

See Example 2
11. Kevin has mowed 40% of the lawn. If he has been mowing for 20 minutes, how long will it take him to mow the rest of the lawn?

12. Maggie ordered a painting. She paid 30% of the total cost when she ordered it, and she will pay the remaining amount when it is delivered. If she has paid $15, how much more does she owe?

See Example 3
13. Find 22% of 130.
14. Find 78% of 350.
15. Find 28% of 65.
16. Find 9% of 50.
17. Find 45% of 210.
18. Find 54% of 602.

PRACTICE AND PROBLEM SOLVING

Extra Practice
See page EP15.

Find the percent of each number.

19. 6% of 38
20. 20% of 182
21. 13% of 40
22. 32% of 205
23. 14% of 88
24. 98% of 105
25. 78% of 52
26. 31% of 345
27. 62% of 50
28. 10% of 50
29. 1.5% of 800
30. 0.3% of 9

31. **Geometry** The width of a rectangular room is 75% of the length of the room. The room is 12 feet long.
    a. How wide is the room?
    b. The area of a rectangle is the product of the length and the width. What is the area of the room?

32. **Multi-Step** Marissa is shopping and finds a sales rack with items that are 25% off. If Marissa likes a shirt on the rack that originally cost $15, how much will she pay for the shirt before tax?

382 Chapter 7 Proportional Relationships

33. **Chemistry** Glucose is a type of sugar. A glucose molecule is composed of 24 atoms. Hydrogen atoms make up 50% of the molecule, carbon atoms make up 25% of the molecule, and oxygen atoms make up the other 25%. How many of each atom are in a molecule of glucose?

34. **Technology** Students were asked in a school survey about how they use their computers. The circle graph shows the results.

   What Do You Do Most Often on Your Computer?
   - E-mail 34%
   - Other Internet 21%
   - Homework 28%
   - Games 11%
   - Other

   a. If there are 850 students in the school, how many spend most of their computer time using e-mail?
   b. Fifty-one students selected "other." What percent of the school population does this represent?
   c. Which choices were selected by more than 200 students?
   d. How many more students chose Internet than chose playing games?

35. **What's the Error?** To find 80% of 130, a student set up the proportion $\frac{80}{100} = \frac{130}{x}$. Explain the error. Write the correct proportion, and find the missing value.

36. **Write About It** Suppose you were asked to find 48% of 300 and your answer was 6.25. Would your answer be reasonable? How do you know? What is the correct answer?

37. **Challenge** Mrs. Peterson makes ceramic figurines. She recently made 25 figurines. Of those figurines, 16 are animals. What percent of the figurines are NOT animals?

Technology

Someday you may do all of your schoolwork on a computer, if your school becomes a digital school, like the one pictured above.

Test Prep and Spiral Review

38. **Multiple Choice** Which of the following amounts is greatest?

    Ⓐ 45% of 200 Ⓑ 50% of 150 Ⓒ 60% of 190 Ⓓ 100% of 110

39. **Short Response** If Sara orders 8 sports magazines and 12 health magazines on sale, how much will she save compared to the regular price? Explain.

Magazine Type	Original Price	Sale
Sports	8 for $60	Save 60%
Health	12 for $72	Save 30%

Write each decimal as a fraction or mixed number. (Lesson 4-4)

40. 0.25   41. 0.78   42. 1.4   43. 0.99   44. 5.36

45. About $\frac{7}{8}$ of the flowers in Monica's garden are snapdragons. What percent of the flowers in the garden are snapdragons? (Lesson 7-8)

7-10 Applying Percents

Learn to solve percent problems that involve discounts, tips, and sales tax.

Percents show up often in daily life. Think of examples that you have seen of percents—sales at stores, tips in restaurants, and sales tax on purchases. You can estimate percents such as these to find amounts of money.

Vocabulary

discount

tip

sales tax

"Yogi always said '90% of the game is half mental' ... I think it's more like 95%."

© Cartoon Stock

	Common Uses of Percents
Discounts	A **discount** is an amount that is subtracted from the regular price of an item. discount = price · discount rate total cost = price − discount
Tips	A **tip** is an amount added to a bill for service. tip = bill · tip rate total cost = bill + tip
Sales tax	**Sales tax** is an amount added to the price of an item. sales tax = price · sales tax rate total cost = price + sales tax

EXAMPLE 1 Finding Discounts

A music store sign reads "10% off the regular price." If Nichole wants to buy a CD whose regular price is $14.99, about how much will she pay for her CD after the discount?

Step 1: First round $14.99 to $15.

Step 2: Find 10% of $15 by multiplying 0.10 · $15. (*Hint:* Moving the decimal point one place left is a shortcut.)

$$10\% \text{ of } 15 = 0.10 \cdot \$15 = \$1.50$$

The approximate discount is $1.50. Subtract this amount from $15.00 to estimate the cost of the CD.

$$\$15.00 - \$1.50 = \$13.50$$

Nichole will pay about $13.50 for the CD.

Remember!

To multiply by 0.10, move the decimal point one place left.

When estimating percents, use percents that you can calculate mentally.
- You can find 10% of a number by moving the decimal point one place to the left.
- You can find 1% of a number by moving the decimal point two places to the left.
- You can find 5% of a number by finding one-half of 10% of the number.

EXAMPLE 2 Finding Tips

Leslie's lunch bill is $13.95. She wants to leave a tip that is 15% of the bill. About how much should her tip be?

Step 1: First round $13.95 to $14.

Step 2: Think: 15% = 10% + 5%
    10% of $14 = 0.10 · $14 = $1.40

Step 3: 5% = 10% ÷ 2
           = $1.40 ÷ 2 = $0.70

Step 4: 15% = 10% + 5%
           = $1.40 + $0.70 = $2.10

Leslie should leave about $2.10 as a tip.

EXAMPLE 3 Finding Sales Tax

Marc is buying a scooter for $79.65. The sales tax rate is 6%. About how much will the total cost of the scooter be?

Step 1: First round $79.65 to $80.

Step 2: Think: 6% = 6 · 1%
    1% of $80 = 0.01 · $80 = $0.80

Step 3: 6% = 6 · 1%
         = 6 · $0.80 = $4.80

The approximate sales tax is $4.80. Add this amount to $80 to estimate the total cost of the scooter.

$$\$80 + \$4.80 = \$84.80$$

Marc will pay about $84.80 for the scooter.

Think and Discuss

1. **Tell** when it would be useful to estimate the percent of a number.
2. **Explain** how to estimate to find the sales tax of an item.

7-10 Exercises

GUIDED PRACTICE

See Example 1
1. Norine wants to buy a beaded necklace that is on sale for 10% off the marked price. If the marked price is $8.49, about how much will the necklace cost after the discount?

See Example 2
2. Alice and Wagner ordered a pizza to be delivered. The total bill was $12.15. They want to give the delivery person a tip that is 20% of the bill. About how much should the tip be?

See Example 3
3. A bicycle sells for $139.75. The sales tax rate is 8%. About how much will the total cost of the bicycle be?

INDEPENDENT PRACTICE

See Example 1
4. Peter has a coupon for 15% off the price of any item in a sporting goods store. He wants to buy a pair of sneakers that are priced at $36.99. About how much will the sneakers cost after the discount?

5. All DVDs are discounted 25% off the original price. The DVD that Marissa wants to buy was originally priced at $24.98. About how much will the DVD cost after the discount?

See Example 2
6. Michael's breakfast bill came to $7.65. He wants to leave a tip that is 15% of the bill. About how much should he leave for the tip?

7. Betty and her family went out for dinner. Their bill was $73.82. Betty's parents left a tip that was 15% of the bill. About how much was the tip that they left?

See Example 3
8. A computer game costs $36.85. The sales tax rate is 6%. About how much will the total cost be for this computer game?

9. Irene is buying party supplies. The cost of her supplies is $52.75. The sales tax rate is 5%. About how much will the total cost of her party supplies be?

PRACTICE AND PROBLEM SOLVING

Extra Practice
See page EP15.

10. **Multi-Step** Lenny, Robert, and Katrina went out for lunch. The items they ordered are listed on the receipt. The sales tax rate was 7%, and they left a tip that was 15% of the total bill. How much did the three friends spend in all?

```
**** Thank you ****
Chicken Sandwich - 1      $5.95
Hamburger - 1             $4.75
Roast Beef Sandwich - 1   $7.35
Milk - 2                  $2.40
Iced Tea - 1              $1.89
```

11. Jackie has $32.50 to buy a new pair of jeans. The pair she likes costs $38 but is marked "20% off ticketed price." The sales tax rate is 5%. Does Jackie have enough money to buy the jeans? Explain.

386 Chapter 7 Proportional Relationships

12. Evan buys a bike that is on sale for 20% off the original price of $95. His brother Kyle buys the same bike at a different store on sale for 15% off the original price of $90. Who paid more? Explain.

13. Multi-Step An electronics store is going out of business. The sign on the door reads "All items on sale for 60% off the ticketed price." A computer has a ticketed price of $649, and a printer has a ticketed price of $199. What is the total cost of both items after the discount?

14. Social Studies Use the table.

   a. A shirt costs $18.95. Will the shirt cost more after sales tax in Georgia or in Kentucky? About how much more?

   b. A video game in North Carolina costs $59.75. The same video game in New York costs $60. After sales tax, in which state will the video game cost less? How much less?

State	Sales Tax Rate
Georgia	4%
Kentucky	6%
New York	4%
North Carolina	4.25%

15. What's the Error? The original price of an item was $48.65. The item was discounted 40%. A customer calculated the price after the discount to be $19.46. What's the error? Give the correct price after the discount.

16. Write About It Discuss the difference between a discount, sales tax, and a tip, in relation to the total cost. How does each affect the total cost? Give examples of situations in which each one is used.

17. Challenge Suppose a jacket is discounted 50% off the original price and then discounted an additional 20%. Is this the same as discounting the jacket 70% off the original price? Explain.

Test Prep and Spiral Review

18. Multiple Choice Electric City is offering a 20% discount on all radios. Pedro would like to buy a radio that was originally priced at $36.50. What is the total cost after the discount?

   Ⓐ $7.30   Ⓑ $16.50   Ⓒ $29.20   Ⓓ $36.70

19. Extended Response Ann is researching the price of a CD. At Music Place, the CD that Ann wants was originally priced at $15.96 but is discounted 25%. At Awesome Sound, the CD was originally priced at $12.99 but is discounted 10%. What is the sale price of each CD? Which is the better deal? Explain.

Determine whether the given value of the variable is a solution. (Lesson 2-4)

20. $2x + 3 = 10$ for $x = 4$ **21.** $5(b - 3) = 25$ for $b = 8$ **22.** $18 = 3a - 9$ for $a = 3$

Find 20% of each number. (Lesson 7-9)

23. 15   **24.** 50   **25.** 65   **26.** 200   **27.** 3,000

LESSON 7-10 EXTENSION
Simple Interest

Learn to find simple interest.

When you save money in a savings account, you earn money that the bank adds to your account. When you borrow money, you pay money that is added to the amount you borrowed. In both cases, the added money is called **interest**. The original amount you put into the account is the **principal**. Interest is a percentage of the principal.

Vocabulary
- interest
- principal
- simple interest

One type of interest is called *simple interest*. **Simple interest** is a fixed percentage of the original principal and is often paid over a certain time period. For example, simple interest may be paid once per year or several times per year. In this section, we will assume that simple interest is paid once per year.

Simple Interest

$$I = P \cdot r \cdot t$$

- Interest
- Principal
- Annual interest rate (as a decimal)
- Time that the money earns interest (in years)

Note that interest rates are usually given as percents, but you must convert the rates to decimals when you use the simple interest formula above.

EXAMPLE 1 Finding Simple Interest

Alyssa put $250 in a savings account at a simple interest rate of 6% per year.

A If she does not add money to or take money from her account, how much interest will she have earned at the end of 3 years?

$I = P \cdot r \cdot t$ *P = $250, r = 0.06, t = 3 years*
$I = 250 \cdot 0.06 \cdot 3$ *Multiply.*
$I = \$45$

Alyssa will earn $45 in interest in 3 years.

B How much money will be in her account after 3 years?

To find the total amount in Alyssa's account after three years, add the interest to the principal.

$$\$250 + \$45 = \$295$$

Alyssa will have $295 in her account after 3 years.

388 Chapter 7 Proportional Relationships

EXTENSION Exercises

1. Tamara put $425 in a savings account at a simple interest rate of 7% per year. How much interest will she have earned after 5 years?

2. Jerome put $75 in a savings account at a simple interest rate of 3% per year. How much interest will Jerome have earned after 1 year? How much money will he have in his account after 1 year?

Use the equation $I = P \cdot r \cdot t$ to find the missing amount.

3. principal = $320
   interest rate = 5% per year
   time = 2 years
   interest = ■

4. principal = $150
   interest rate = 2% per year
   time = 7 years
   interest = ■

5. principal = ■
   interest rate = 4% per year
   time = 3 years
   interest = $30

6. principal = $456
   interest rate = 6% per year
   time = ■
   interest = $109.44

7. principal = $100
   interest rate = ■ per year
   time = 5 years
   interest = $15

8. principal = $750
   interest rate = ■ per year
   time = 10 years
   interest = $300

9. Mr. Bruckner is saving to go on a vacation. He put $340 in a savings account at a simple interest rate of 4% per year. How much money will he have in the savings account after 2 years?

10. When you borrow money, the amount borrowed is the principal. Instead of receiving interest, you pay interest on the principal. Kendra borrowed $1,500 from the bank to buy a home computer. The bank is charging her a simple interest rate of 7% per year. How much interest will Kendra owe the bank after 1 year?

11. Mr. Pei paid $7,500 in interest over 20 years at 1% per year on a loan. How much money did he borrow?

12. Hunter put $165 in a savings account at a simple interest rate of 6% per year. Nicholas put $145 in a savings account at a simple interest rate of 7% per year. Who will have earned more interest after 3 years? How much more?

13. **Write About It** Explain the difference between principal and interest.

14. **Write About It** Would you prefer a high or low interest rate when you are borrowing money? When you are saving money? Explain.

15. **Challenge** Madison put $200 in a savings account at an interest rate of 5%. Each year the interest is added to the principal, and then the new amount of interest is calculated. If Madison does not add money to or take money out of the account, how much will she have after 3 years?

Ready To Go On?

Quiz for Lessons 7-7 Through 7-10

7-7 Percents

Write each percent as a fraction in simplest form.

1. 60%
2. 15%
3. 75%

Write each percent as a decimal.

4. 34%
5. 77%
6. 6%

7. About 71% of Earth's surface is covered with water. Write 71% as a decimal.

7-8 Percents, Decimals, and Fractions

Write each fraction as a percent.

8. $\frac{9}{20}$
9. $\frac{2}{3}$
10. $\frac{21}{50}$

Write each decimal as a percent.

11. 0.28
12. 0.9
13. 0.02

14. Mike's baseball team won $\frac{17}{20}$ of its games. What percent of the games did Mike's baseball team win?

7-9 Percent Problems

Use the circle graph for problems 15 and 16.

In a survey, 300 students were asked how they contact their friends.

15. How many students said they use text messaging?

16. How many students said they use a cell phone?

17. Find 40% of 80.

18. Find 5% of 30.

How Do You Like to Contact Your Friends?
- Cell phone 25%
- E-mail 15%
- Text message on cell phone 60%

7-10 Applying Percents

19. Max and Dan order a pizza. The total bill is $11.60. If they give the delivery person a tip that is 20% of the bill, how much is the tip?

20. Mia wants to buy a poster that is 10% off the marked price. If the marked price is $15.99, about how much will the poster cost with the discount?

Real-World Connections

CHAPTER 7

Greenfield Village Greenfield Village in Dearborn, Michigan, is the largest outdoor museum in the country. Visitors to the village travel back in time to see how Americans have lived and worked. To create the village, nearly 100 historic buildings were moved to the site from their original locations.

MICHIGAN

Dearborn

Greenfield Village consists of seven historic districts. The table gives information on five of the districts. Use the table for Exercises 1–2.

1. What is the ratio of buildings at Railroad Junction to buildings at Liberty Craftworks?

2. The ratio of buildings in the Main Street district to buildings at Liberty Craftworks is 3:2.

   a. Write and solve a proportion to find the number of buildings in the Main Street district.

   b. In the Main Street district, the ratio of stores to other types of buildings is 1:2. How many stores are there in the district?

Greenfield Village Historic Districts	
District	Number of Buildings
Liberty Craftworks	12
Porches and Parlors	22
Working Farms	6
Railroad Junction	3
Edison at Work	7

3. Greenfield Village is spread across 240 acres of land. Only 37% of the land is used for the exhibits, while the rest of the land consists of forests, rivers, and pastures. How many acres are used for exhibits?

4. The village has a special walking tour with a garden theme. Six of the stops on the tour are at historic homes. This is 30% of the tour stops. How many stops are on the tour?

Game Time

The Golden Rectangle

Which rectangle do you find most visually pleasing?

Did you choose rectangle 3? If so, you agree with artists and architects throughout history. Rectangle 3 is a golden rectangle. Golden rectangles are said to be the most pleasing to the human eye.

In a golden rectangle, the ratio of the length of the longer side to the length of the shorter side is approximately equal to 1.6. In other words,

$$\frac{\text{length of longer side}}{\text{length of shorter side}} \approx \frac{1.6}{1}$$

Measure the length and width of each rectangle below. Which could be golden rectangles? Are they the most pleasing to your eye?

Triple Play

Number of players: 3–5

Deal five cards to each player. Place the remaining cards in a pile facedown. At any time, you may remove *triples* from your hand. A *triple* is a fraction card, a decimal card, and a percent card that are all equivalent.

On your turn, ask any other player for a specific card. For example, if you have the $\frac{3}{5}$ card, you might ask another player if he or she has the 60% card. If so, he or she must give it to you, and you repeat your turn. If not, take the top card from the deck, and your turn is over.

The first player to get rid of his or her cards is the winner.

Learn It Online
Game Time Extra go.hrw.com,
keyword MR10 Games

A complete copy of the rules and game pieces are available online.

Materials
- construction paper
- $\frac{1}{4}$ in. graph paper
- glue
- scissors
- markers

It's in the Bag!

PROJECT Double-Door Fractions, Decimals, and Percents

Open the door to fractions, decimals, and percents by making this handy converter.

Directions

1. Cut the construction paper to $6\frac{1}{2}$ inches by $8\frac{1}{2}$ inches. Fold it in half lengthwise and then unfold it. Fold the top and bottom edges to the middle crease to make a double door. **Figure A**

2. Cut a strip of graph paper that is 2 inches wide by $8\frac{1}{2}$ inches long. Make a percent number line along the middle of the strip. Include 0%, 5%, 10%, and so on, up to 100%. **Figure B**

3. Cut two 1-by-$8\frac{1}{2}$-inch strips of graph paper. On one strip, make a fraction number line that includes $\frac{0}{20}$, $\frac{1}{20}$, and so on, up to $\frac{20}{20}$. Write the fractions in simplest form. On the other strip, make a decimal number line that includes 0.0, 0.05, 0.1, and so on, up to 1. **Figure C**

4. Glue the percent number line along the center fold of the construction paper. **Figure D**

5. Close the double doors. Glue the remaining number lines to the outside of the doors, making sure the number lines match up.

Putting the Math into Action

Team up with a classmate. Use your double-door converters to quiz each other on equivalent fractions, decimals, and percents.

CHAPTER 7 Study Guide: Review

Vocabulary

corresponding angles	356	ratio	342
corresponding sides	356	sales tax	384
discount	384	scale	364
equivalent ratios	342	scale drawing	364
indirect measurement	360	similar	356
percent	371	tip	384
proportion	352	unit rate	343
rate	343		

Complete the sentences below with vocabulary words from the list above.

1. A(n) __?__ is an amount subtracted from the regular price of an item.

2. A __?__ is a ratio of a number to 100.

3. In similar figures, __?__ have the same measure.

EXAMPLES

7-1 Ratios and Rates (pp. 342–345)

■ Write the ratio of hearts to diamonds.

♥♥♥♥
♦♦♦♦♦♦♦♦ $\frac{hearts}{diamonds} = \frac{4}{8}$

7-2 Using Tables to Explore Equivalent Ratios and Rates (pp. 346–349)

■ Use a table to find three ratios equivalent to 6:7.

6	12	18	24
7	14	21	28

Multiply the numerator and denominator by 2, 3, and 4.

The ratios 6:7, 12:14, 18:21, and 24:28 are equivalent.

EXERCISES

4. Write three equivalent ratios for 4:8.

5. Which is the better deal—an 8 oz package of pretzels for $1.92 or a 12 oz package of pretzels for $2.64?

Use a table to find three equivalent ratios.

6. $\frac{3}{10}$ 7. 5 to 21   8. 15:7

9. The table below shows the cost of canoeing for different-sized groups. Predict how much a group of 9 will pay.

Number in Group	2	4	8	10
Cost ($)	10.50	21	42	52.50

394 Chapter 7 Proportional Relationships

EXAMPLES

EXERCISES

7-3 Proportions (pp. 352–355)

■ Find the value of n in $\frac{5}{6} = \frac{n}{12}$.

$6 \cdot n = 5 \cdot 12$ Cross products are equal.

$\frac{6n}{6} = \frac{60}{6}$ Divide both sides by 6.

$n = 10$

Find the value of n in each proportion.

10. $\frac{3}{5} = \frac{n}{15}$
11. $\frac{1}{n} = \frac{3}{9}$
12. $\frac{7}{8} = \frac{n}{16}$
13. $\frac{n}{4} = \frac{8}{16}$

14. A fruit salad recipe calls for 2 cups of bananas for every 3 cups of apples. If Shannon is using 9 cups of apples to make fruit salad for a party, how many cups of bananas does she need?

7-4 Similar Figures (pp. 356–359)

■ The triangles are similar. Find b.

1 cm, 2 cm; 32 cm, b

$\frac{1}{32} = \frac{2}{b}$ Write a proportion.

$32 \cdot 2 = 1 \cdot b$ Cross products are equal.

$64 \text{ cm} = b$

15. The shapes are similar. Find n and $m\angle A$.

6 in., 22 in.; A, n, 3 in.

7-5 Indirect Measurement (pp. 360–362)

■ A tree casts a 12 ft shadow when a 6 ft man casts a 4 ft shadow. How tall is the tree?

$\frac{h}{6} = \frac{12}{4}$ Write a proportion.

$6 \cdot 12 = 4 \cdot h$ The cross products are equal.

$\frac{72}{4} = \frac{4h}{4}$ Divide both sides by 4.

$18 = h$ The tree is 18 ft tall.

16. Find the height of the building.

h, 65.8 ft; yardstick, 2.1 ft

7-6 Scale Drawings and Maps (pp. 364–367)

■ Find the actual distance from A to B.

$A \leftarrow 3 \text{ cm} \rightarrow B$

Scale: 1 cm:35 m

$\frac{1 \text{ cm}}{35 \text{ m}} = \frac{3 \text{ cm}}{x \text{ m}}$ Write a proportion.

$35 \cdot 3 = 1 \cdot x$ Cross products are equal.

$105 = x$

The actual distance is 105 m.

Ferris, Mason; 1 in:25 mi

17. Find the actual distance from Ferris to Mason.

18. Renfield is 75 mi from Mason. About how far apart should Renfield and Mason be on the map?

Video   Lesson Tutorials Online   my.hrw.com

Study Guide: Review   **395**

EXAMPLES

EXERCISES

7-7 Percents (pp. 371–374)

- Write 48% as a fraction in simplest form.

  $48\% = \frac{48}{100}$ $\frac{48 \div 4}{100 \div 4} = \frac{12}{25}$

- Write 16% as a decimal.

  $16\% = \frac{16}{100}$ $16 \div 100 = 0.16$

Write each as a fraction in simplest form.

19. 75% **20.** 6% **21.** 30%

Write each percent as a decimal.

22. 8% **23.** 65% **24.** 20%

7-8 Percents, Decimals, and Fractions (pp. 375–378)

- Write 0.365 as a percent.

  $0.365 = 36.5\%$ *Multiply by 100.*

- Write $\frac{3}{5}$ as a percent.

  $\frac{3 \cdot 20}{5 \cdot 20} = \frac{60}{100} = 60\%$

Write each decimal or fraction as a percent.

25. 0.896 **26.** 0.70 **27.** 0.057

28. 0.12 **29.** $\frac{7}{10}$ **30.** $\frac{3}{12}$

31. $\frac{7}{8}$ **32.** $\frac{4}{5}$ **33.** $\frac{1}{16}$

34. Water constitutes approximately $\frac{13}{20}$ of the body of an average adult male. About what percent of the average adult male body is made of water?

7-9 Percent Problems (pp. 380–383)

- Find 30% of 85.

  $30\% = 0.30$ *Write 30% as a decimal.*
  $0.30 \cdot 85 = 25.5$ *Multiply.*

35. Find 25% of 48.

36. Find 33% of 18.

37. A total of 325 tickets were sold for the school concert, and 36% of these were sold to students. How many tickets were sold to students?

38. When paying for his lunch, Archie decides to leave a 15% tip. How much should he leave if his lunch totaled $11.90?

7-10 Applying Percents (pp. 384–387)

- A DVD costs $24.98. The sales tax is 5%. About how much is the tax?

  Step 1: Round $24.98 to $25.

  Step 2: 5% = 5 · **1%**
  1% of $25 = 0.01 · $25 = **$0.25**

  Step 3: 5% = 5 · **1%**
  = 5 · **$0.25** = $1.25

  The tax is about $1.25.

39. A sweater is marked 40% off the original price. The original price was $31.75. About how much is the sweater after the discount?

40. Barry and his friends went out for lunch. The bill was $28.68. About how much should they leave for a 15% tip?

41. Ana is purchasing a book for $17.89. The sales tax rate is 6%. About how much will she pay in sales tax?

Chapter Test

CHAPTER 7

Use the table to write each ratio.

1. three equivalent ratios to compare dramas to documentaries
2. documentaries to total videos
3. music videos to exercise videos
4. Which is a better deal—5 videos for $29.50 or 3 videos for $17.25?

Types of Videos in Richard's Collection			
Comedy	5	Cartoon	7
Drama	6	Exercise	3
Music	3	Documentary	2

Find the value of *n* in each proportion.

5. $\frac{5}{6} = \frac{n}{24}$
6. $\frac{8}{n} = \frac{12}{3}$
7. $\frac{n}{10} = \frac{3}{6}$
8. $\frac{3}{9} = \frac{4}{n}$

9. A cocoa recipe calls for 4 tbsp cocoa mix to make an 8 oz serving. How many tbsp of cocoa mix are needed to make a 15 oz serving?

10. A 3-foot-tall mailbox casts a shadow that is 1.8 feet long. At the same time, a nearby street lamp casts a shadow that is 12 feet long. How tall is the street lamp?

11. The table shows the time it takes Jenny to swim laps. Predict how long it will take her to swim 14 laps.

Number of Laps	4	8	12	16
Time (min)	3	6	9	12

Use the scale drawing for Problems 12 and 13.

12. The length of the court in the drawing is 6 cm. How long is the actual court?

13. The free-throw line is always 15 feet from the backboard. Is the distance between the backboard and the free-throw line correct in the drawing? Explain.

Scale: 1 cm : $15\frac{2}{3}$ ft

Write each percent as a fraction in simplest form and as a decimal.

14. 66%
15. 90%
16. 5%
17. 18%

Write each decimal or fraction as a percent.

18. 0.546
19. 0.092
20. $\frac{14}{25}$
21. $\frac{1}{8}$

Find each percent.

22. 55% of 218
23. 30% of 310
24. 25% of 78

25. A bookstore sells paperback books at 20% off the listed price. If Brandy wants to buy a paperback book whose listed price is $12.95, about how much will she pay for the book after the discount?

Chapter 7 Test 397

CHAPTER 7 Test Tackler
STANDARDIZED TEST STRATEGIES

Extended Response: Write Extended Responses

When you answer an extended-response test item, you need to explain your reasoning clearly. Extended-response items are scored using a 4-point scoring rubric like the one shown below.

EXAMPLE

Extended Response Amber tracks her math test scores. Her goal is to have a 92% average. Her 10 test scores are 94, 76, 90, 98, 91, 93, 88, 90, 89, and 85. Find the range, mean, median, and mode of the data set. If her lowest score is dropped, will she meet her goal? Explain your answer.

Here is an example of a 4-point response according to the scoring rubric at right.

Scoring Rubric

4 points: The student correctly answers all parts of the question, shows all work, and provides a complete and correct explanation.

3 points: The student answers all parts of the question, shows all work, and provides a complete explanation that demonstrates understanding, but the student makes minor errors in computation.

2 points: The student does not answer all parts of the question but shows all work and provides a complete and correct explanation for the parts answered, or the student correctly answers all parts of the question but does not show all work or does not provide an explanation.

1 point: The student gives incorrect answers and shows little or no work or explanation, or the student does not follow directions.

0 points: The student gives no response.

4-point response:

Range: $98 - 76 = 22$
The range is 22.
Mean:
$$\frac{94 + 76 + 90 + 98 + 91 + 93 + 88 + 90 + 89 + 85}{10} = \frac{894}{10} = 89.4$$
The mean is 89.4.

Median: There are an even number of values in this set. The two middle numbers are 90 and 90. The median is 90.

Mode: The value that occurs most often is 90. The mode is 90.

When the lowest score, 76, is dropped, the average is $\frac{894 - 76}{9} = \frac{818}{9} = 90.9$. This value is less than 92. Even if the lowest score is dropped, Amber will not meet her goal.

The student correctly calculates and shows how to find the range, mean, median, and mode of this data set.

The student correctly answers the questions and shows how the answer is calculated.

398 Chapter 7 Proportional Relationships

Hot Tip! Once you have answered an extended-response test item, double-check to make sure that you answered all of the different parts.

Read each test item and use the scoring rubric to answer the questions that follow.

Item A
Extended Response Use the table below to identify a pattern and find the next three terms. Is this sequence arithmetic? Explain.

Position	Value of Term
1	4
2	7
3	10
4	13
5	16
n	■

1. What needs to be included in a response that would receive 4 points?

2. Write a response that would receive full credit.

Item B
Extended Response Draw a polygon that has three congruent sides. What is true about the measures of the angles of this polygon? Find the measurement of each angle. Classify the type of polygon you drew. Explain your answer.

Kim wrote this response:

Each angle measures 60°.
This is an equilateral triangle.

3. Score Kim's response. Explain your scoring decision.

4. Rewrite Kim's response so that it receives full credit.

Item C
Extended Response Look at the graph. Why is this graph misleading? Explain your answer. What might someone believe from this graph? What changes would you make to the graph so it is not misleading?

Plant Growth
(bar graph showing Growth (cm) vs Week, weeks 1-4 with bars approximately at 25, 65, 92, 100)

5. What needs to be included in a response that would receive 4 points?

6. Write a response that would receive full credit.

Item D
Extended Response The ages of the employees at a discount store are shown below. Find the mean, median, and mode of the data set. Which one bests describes the data set? Explain your answer.

68	32	16	23	21
17	28	20	39	38
21	22	17	23	37

7. Should the response shown receive a score of 4 points? Why or why not?

The mean is 28.
The modes are 17 and 23.
The median is 22.
The best descriptor is the mode because there is more than one.

8. Correct or add any information, if necessary, for the response to receive full credit.

Test Tackler

Standardized Test Prep

Cumulative Assessment, Chapters 1–7

Multiple Choice

1. Janet has a flower garden with 6 rose bushes, 7 lilac bushes, and 5 azaleas. Which of the following shows the ratio of lilac bushes to the total number of plants in Janet's garden?

    A 7:11
    B 7:18
    C 11:18
    D 18:5

2. Jenny lives in Paris, Kentucky. She wants to visit Paris, France, this summer. The distance between the two cities is 6.715×10^3 kilometers. What is this distance in standard form?

    F 67.15 kilometers
    G 671.5 kilometers
    H 6,715 kilometers
    J 67,150 kilometers

3. Carina rode her exercise bike 30 minutes on Monday, 45 minutes on Tuesday, 30 minutes on Wednesday, 60 minutes on Thursday, and 50 minutes on Friday. Find the mean amount of time that Carina rode her bike in these 5 days.

    A 30 minutes
    B 43 minutes
    C 45 minutes
    D 215 minutes

4. The sixth grade chorus is going to a competition. There are 116 students in the sixth grade chorus. If each bus holds 35 students, how many buses will be needed to take the students to the competition?

    F 5 buses
    G 4 buses
    H 3 buses
    J 2 buses

5. Which of the following is NOT an example of a proportion?

    A $\frac{3}{4} = \frac{9}{12}$
    B $\frac{5}{9} = \frac{45}{81}$
    C $\frac{1}{3} = \frac{15}{42}$
    D $\frac{7}{8} = \frac{35}{40}$

6. On the map the distance between point R and point T is 1.125 inches. Find the actual distance between point R and point T.

    Scale: 1 in:10 mi

    F 10 miles
    G 11.25 miles
    H 12.5 miles
    J 15 miles

7. Esperanza has a puppy that weighs $3\frac{1}{4}$ pounds. In 3 months, the puppy should weigh 3 times as much as it weighs now. How much weight should the puppy gain in the next 3 months?

    A $6\frac{1}{2}$ pounds
    B $6\frac{3}{4}$ pounds
    C $8\frac{1}{4}$ pounds
    D $9\frac{3}{4}$ pounds

8. Which value is greatest?

    F $\frac{5}{6}$
    G 0.7
    H 80%
    J $\frac{6}{7}$

9. Max earns $7.25 per hour working for a florist. His weekly paycheck is $108.75 before taxes. If h equals the number of hours worked, which equation can be used to find the number of hours Max works each week?

   Ⓐ $7.25 + h = 108.75$

   Ⓑ $\frac{7.25}{h} = 108.75$

   Ⓒ $108.75 - h = 7.25$

   Ⓓ $7.25h = 108.75$

HOT TIP! Estimate your answer before solving the problem. You can often use your estimate to eliminate some of the answer choices.

Gridded Response

10. A school band is putting together music kits for the local music fair. They have 72 recorders, 96 kazoos, and 60 whistles. If each kit has the same number of each instrument, what is the greatest number of kits that can be made if the band uses all the instruments?

11. Find the value of $40 \div (3 + 5) \times 2$.

12. Rylee has a collection of music boxes. Of the 36 music boxes she owns, 25% of them have parts that move when the music plays. How many of her music boxes have moving parts?

13. What is $2\frac{3}{4} + \frac{1}{3}$ written as an improper fraction?

14. Ms. Chavez is ordering art supplies. She orders enough pencils for every student and then adds 20% more for extras. If she has 210 students, how many pencils does she need to order?

Short Response

S1. One of the oldest living oak trees is 105 feet tall. One sunny day it casts a shadow that is 75 feet long. At the same time, a younger oak tree casts a shadow that is 15 feet long.

   a. Draw a picture to explain how to find the height of the younger tree.

   b. Use your picture to write a proportion to find the height of the younger tree. Solve the proportion. Show your work.

S2. Chrissy is shopping for T-shirts for the pep club. Package A is 10 shirts for $15.50. Package B is 15 shirts for $20.50. Package C is 20 shirts for $25.50. Find the unit price for each package. Which T-shirt package is the best deal? Explain your reasoning and show your work.

S3. A computer is marked 30% off the original price. The computer originally cost $685. Find the amount of the discount and the sale price of the computer.

Extended Response

E1. A small purple rectangle is 8 millimeters wide and 18 millimeters tall. A larger purple rectangle is 18 millimeters wide and 25 millimeters tall.

   a. Are the two purple rectangles similar? Explain your answer.

   b. A third rectangle is similar to the smaller purple rectangle. The width of the third rectangle is 14 millimeters. Let x represent the height of the third rectangle. Write an equation that could be used to find x.

   c. Find the height of the third rectangle. Show your work.

CHAPTER 8
Geometric Relationships

Chapter Focus
- Use facts about two-dimensional figures to solve problems.
- Find possible rules for patterns of figures.

8A Lines and Angles
- 8-1 Building Blocks of Geometry
- 8-2 Measuring and Classifying Angles
- LAB Construct Congruent Segments and Angles
- 8-3 Angle Relationships
- 8-4 Classifying Pairs of Lines
- LAB Parallel Line Relationships

8B Polygons
- LAB Triangle Inequality
- 8-5 Triangles
- LAB Angles in Triangles
- 8-6 Quadrilaterals
- 8-7 Polygons
- LAB Explore Intersecting Polygons
- 8-8 Geometric Patterns

8C Polygon Relationships
- 8-9 Congruent Polygons
- 8-10 Transformations
- 8-11 Symmetry
- LAB Create Tessellations

Why Learn This?

This dragon is part of a fountain at the entrance of Parc Guell in Barcelona, Spain. The dragon is covered in mosaic tiles that are in the shapes of different polygons.

Learn It Online
Chapter Project Online go.hrw.com,
keyword MR10 Ch8

Are You Ready?

Learn It Online
Resources Online go.hrw.com,
keyword MR10 AYR8 Go

✓ Vocabulary

Choose the best term from the list to complete each sentence.

clockwise
counterclockwise
horizontal
protractor
quadrilateral
ruler
triangle
vertical

1. A closed figure with three sides is a __?__, and a closed figure with four sides is a __?__.
2. A __?__ is used to measure and draw angles.
3. The arrow inside the circle is moving __?__.
4. A line that extends left to right is __?__.

Complete these exercises to review skills you will need for this chapter.

✓ Graph Ordered Pairs

Use the coordinate plane for problems 5–8. Write the ordered pair for each point.

5. A
6. B
7. C
8. D

✓ Identify Polygons

Tell how many sides and angles each figure has.

9.
10.
11.

✓ Identify Congruent Figures

Which two figures are exactly the same size and shape but in different positions?

12.

A   B   C   D

Geometric Relationships 403

Chapter 8 Study Guide: Preview

Where You've Been

Previously, you
- defined geometric shapes.
- identified congruent and similar figures.
- located points on a coordinate plane.

In This Chapter

You will study
- measuring angles.
- using angle measurements to classify angles as acute, obtuse, or right.
- identifying relationships involving angles in triangles and quadrilaterals.
- using congruence and similarity to solve problems.
- transforming figures on the coordinate plane and describing the transformation.

Where You're Going

You can use the skills learned in this chapter
- to solve problems and create geometric proofs by using angle and line relationships in geometry.
- to use transformations to create patterns in art class.

Key Vocabulary/Vocabulario

angle	ángulo
congruent	congruentes
line symmetry	simetría axial
parallel lines	líneas paralelas
perpendicular lines	lineas perpendiculares
polygon	polígono
quadrilateral	cuadrilátero
rotation	rotación
transformation	transformación
vertex	vértice

Vocabulary Connections

To become familiar with some of the vocabulary terms in the chapter, consider the following. You may refer to the chapter, the glossary, or a dictionary if you like.

1. *Congruent* comes from the Latin word *congruere* meaning "to agree, correspond." If two figures are **congruent**, do you think they look the same or different?

2. *Parallel* comes from the Greek words *para* meaning "alongside" and *allenon* meaning "one another." If two lines are **parallel** where do you think they are located in relation to each other?

3. *Polygon* comes from the Greek words *polus* meaning "many" and *gonia* meaning "angle." According to this information, what do you think a shape called a **polygon** includes?

4. *Quadrilateral* comes from the Latin words *quadri* meaning "four" and *latus* meaning "sides." How many sides do you think a **quadrilateral** has?

Reading and Writing Math

CHAPTER 8

Reading Strategy: Read Problems for Understanding

It is important to read word problems carefully to make sure you understand the problem and identify all the parts of the problem that need to be answered.

Following these steps can help you understand and answer problems:

1. Read through the problem once.
2. Identify what you are supposed to answer and what skills are needed.
3. Read the problem again carefully and identify key information.
4. Make a plan to solve and answer ALL parts of the problem.
5. Solve.

Lesson 7-9 Percent Problems

Step 1. Read the problem.

> 10. Mr. Green has a garden. Of the 40 seeds he planted, 35% were vegetable seeds. How many vegetable seeds did he plant?

Step 2.	What are you supposed to answer, and what skills are needed?	• Find how many vegetable seeds were planted in the garden. • Find the percent of a number.
Step 3.	Identify the key information.	• There were a total of 40 seeds planted. • The vegetable seeds make up 35% of the total number of seeds.
Step 4.	Make a plan to solve and answer all parts of the problem.	• Write 35% as a fraction. • Set up a proportion and solve for the unknown value. • Check your answer by making sure the cross products are equal.
Step 5.	Solve.	

Try This

Read the problem for understanding. Use the steps above to answer the following question.

1. A garden has the shape of a square. The distance around the garden is 200 meters. What is the length of one side of the garden?

Geometric Relationships

8-1 Building Blocks of Geometry

Learn to describe figures by using the terms of geometry.

Vocabulary
point
line
plane
line segment
ray

The building blocks of geometry are *points*, *lines*, and *planes*.

A **point** is an exact location that has no size.	• P	point P, P
	A point is named by a capital letter.	
A **line** is a straight path that has no thickness and extends forever.	←•—•→ A B	line AB, $\overleftrightarrow{AB}$, line BA, $\overleftrightarrow{BA}$
	A line is named by two points on the line.	
A **plane** is a flat surface that has no thickness and extends forever.	•L •M •N	plane LMN, plane MLN, plane NLM
	A plane is named by three points on the plane that are not on the same line.	

Interactivities Online ▶

EXAMPLE 1 Identifying Points, Lines, and Planes

Use the diagram to name each geometric figure.

A three points
   A, C, and D
   Five points are labeled: points A, B, C, D, and E.

B two lines
   $\overleftrightarrow{AB}$ and $\overleftrightarrow{BE}$
   You can also write $\overleftrightarrow{BA}$ and $\overleftrightarrow{EB}$.

C a point shared by two lines
   point B
   Point B is a point on $\overleftrightarrow{AB}$ and $\overleftrightarrow{BE}$.

D a plane
   plane ADC
   Use any three points in the plane that are not on the same line. Write the three points in any order.

Line segments and *rays* are parts of lines. Use points on a line to name line segments and rays.

A **line segment** is a part of a line made of two endpoints and all the points between them.	line segment XY, $\overline{XY}$, line segment YX, $\overline{YX}$
	A line segment is named by its endpoints.
A **ray** is a part of a line that starts at an endpoint and extends forever in one direction.	ray JK, $\overrightarrow{JK}$
	A ray is named by its endpoint first followed by another point on the ray.

EXAMPLE 2 Identifying Line Segments and Rays

Use the diagram to give a possible name to each figure.

A three different line segments
$\overline{TU}$, $\overline{UV}$, and $\overline{TV}$
You can also write $\overline{UT}$, $\overline{VU}$, and $\overline{VT}$.

B three ways to name the line
$\overleftrightarrow{UT}$, $\overleftrightarrow{VU}$, and $\overrightarrow{VT}$
You can also write $\overrightarrow{TU}$, $\overrightarrow{UV}$, and $\overrightarrow{TV}$.

C six ways to name rays
$\overrightarrow{TU}$, $\overrightarrow{TV}$, $\overrightarrow{VT}$, $\overrightarrow{VU}$, $\overrightarrow{UV}$, and $\overrightarrow{UT}$

D another name for ray TU
$\overrightarrow{TV}$
T is still the endpoint. V is another point on the ray.

Think and Discuss

1. **Name** the geometric figure suggested by each of the following: a page of a book; a dot (also called a *pixel*) on a computer screen; the path of a jet across the sky.
2. **Explain** how $\overrightarrow{XY}$ is different from $\overleftrightarrow{XY}$.
3. **Explain** how $\overline{AB}$ is different from $\overleftrightarrow{AB}$.

8-1 Exercises

GUIDED PRACTICE

See Example 1 Use the diagram to name each geometric figure.
1. two points
2. a line
3. a point shared by two lines
4. a plane

See Example 2 Use the diagram to give a possible name to each figure.
5. two different ways to name the line
6. four ways to name rays
7. another name for $\overrightarrow{AC}$

INDEPENDENT PRACTICE

See Example 1 Use the diagram to name each geometric figure.
8. three points
9. one line
10. a point shared by a line and a ray
11. a plane

See Example 2 Use the diagram to give a possible name to each figure.
12. two different line segments
13. six ways to name rays
14. another name for $\overrightarrow{YX}$

PRACTICE AND PROBLEM SOLVING

Extra Practice
See page EP15.

Tell what figure is contained by the intersection of the given figures.

15. two lines
16. a plane and a line that does not lie in the plane
17. two planes

Draw each geometric figure.

18. $\overrightarrow{RS}$
19. $\overline{LM}$
20. $\overleftrightarrow{AB}$
21. $\overrightarrow{XY}$ on $\overrightarrow{YX}$
22. $\overrightarrow{JK}$ and $\overrightarrow{JH}$ on the same line

408   Chapter 8   Geometric Relationships

Geography Link

Mapmakers often include a *legend* on the maps they create. The legend explains what each symbol or location on the map represents.

23. Name the geometric figure suggested by each part of the map.
    a. City Hall and Gordon Middle School
    b. Highway 80
    c. the section of the road from the park to the post office
    d. the road from City Hall past the police station

24. A student rides her bike from Gordon Middle School to City Hall. She then rides to the city park, first passing the police station and then passing by the school. List the segments on the map that represent her route.

25. **Critical Thinking** Name a line segment, a ray, and a line that include the same two locations on the map, but do not include the city park.

26. **What's the Error?** A student described the road from Gordon Middle School to City Hall as $\overleftrightarrow{VY}$. What was the student's error?

27. **Write About It** Explain why the road from City Hall that goes past the police station suggests a ray named $\overrightarrow{VX}$ rather than a ray named $\overrightarrow{XV}$.

28. **Challenge** What are all the possible names for the line suggested by IH-45?

MAP LEGEND
V	City Hall
W	Post Office
X	Police Station
Y	Gordon Middle School
Z	City Park

Test Prep and Spiral Review

29. **Multiple Choice** Which figure is NOT found in the diagram?
    A) Line
    B) Point
    C) Line segment
    D) Ray

30. **Gridded Response** How many endpoints does a ray have?

Find the value of k in each equation. (Lesson 2-8)

31. $\frac{k}{3} = 7$

32. $\frac{k}{11} = 4$

33. $20 = \frac{k}{5}$

34. $21 = \frac{k}{7}$

Write each improper fraction as a mixed number. (Lesson 4-6)

35. $\frac{13}{4}$

36. $\frac{70}{9}$

37. $\frac{41}{3}$

38. $\frac{75}{6}$

39. $\frac{81}{7}$

8-2 Measuring and Classifying Angles

Learn to name, measure, draw, and classify angles.

Vocabulary
angle
vertex
acute angle
right angle
obtuse angle
straight angle

You can adjust the *angle* that a treadmill makes with the ground in order to have an easier or more intense workout.

An **angle** is formed by two rays with a common endpoint, called the **vertex**. An angle can be named by its vertex or by its vertex and a point from each ray. The middle point in the name must be the vertex. The angle of the treadmill can be called ∠F, ∠EFG, or ∠GFE.

Angles are measured in degrees. Use the symbol ° to show degrees.

EXAMPLE 1 Measuring an Angle with a Protractor

Use a protractor to measure the angle.

- Place the center point of the protractor on the vertex of the angle.
- Place the protractor so that ray YZ passes through the 0° mark.
- Using the scale that starts with 0° along ray YZ, read the measure where ray YX crosses.
- The measure of ∠XYZ is 75°. Write this as m∠XYZ = 75°.

Reading Math
m∠XYZ is read "the measure of angle XYZ."

EXAMPLE 2 Drawing an Angle with a Protractor

Use a protractor to draw an angle that measures 150°.

- Draw a ray, and place the center point of the protractor on the endpoint of the ray.
- Place the protractor so that the ray passes through the 0° mark.
- Make a mark at 150° above the scale on the protractor.
- Draw a ray from the endpoint of the first ray through the mark at 150°.

You can classify an angle by its measure.

Interactivities Online ▶

An **acute angle** measures greater than 0° and less than 90°.

Reading Math
Right angles are usually marked with a ⌐ symbol.

A **right angle** measures exactly 90°.

An **obtuse angle** measures greater than 90° and less than 180°.

A **straight angle** measures exactly 180°.

EXAMPLE 3 Classifying Angles

Classify each angle as acute, right, obtuse, or straight.

A

The angle measures greater than 90° and less than 180°, so it is an obtuse angle.

B

The angle measures less than 90°, so it is an acute angle.

EXAMPLE 4 Architectural Application

An architect designed this floor plan for a five-sided room of a house. Classify ∠A, ∠B, and ∠D in the floor plan.

∠A   right angle   The angle is marked as a right angle.
∠B   obtuse angle   The angle measures greater than 90° and less than 180°.
∠D   acute angle   The angle measures less than 90°.

Think and Discuss

1. **Explain** how you know which point is the vertex of ∠XYZ.
2. **Give an example** of a right angle in your classroom.
3. **Tell** what type of angle is suggested by each of the following.
   a. an open book lying flat
   b. the corner of a sheet of paper
   c. the point of a pencil
   d. the hands of a clock at 12:25

Video Lesson Tutorials Online my.hrw.com

8-2 Exercises

Learn It Online
Homework Help Online go.hrw.com,
keyword MR10 8-2
Exercises 1–23, 27, 29

GUIDED PRACTICE

See Example 1   Use a protractor to measure each angle.

    1.   **2.**   **3.**

See Example 2   Use a protractor to draw an angle with each given measure.

    4. 55°   **5.** 135°   **6.** 20°   **7.** 190°

See Example 3   Classify each angle as acute, right, obtuse, or straight.

    8.   **9.**   **10.**

See Example 4   **11.** Kendra is planning a flower bed for her garden, which is shown in the figure. Classify each angle of the flower bed.

INDEPENDENT PRACTICE

See Example 1   Use a protractor to measure each angle.

    12.   **13.**   **14.**

See Example 2   Use a protractor to draw an angle with each given measure.

    15. 150°   **16.** 38°   **17.** 90°   **18.** 72°   **19.** 45°

See Example 3   Classify each angle as acute, right, obtuse, or straight.

    20.   **21.**   **22.**

See Example 4   **23.** The figure shows the shape of a ceramic tile. Classify each of the tile's angles.

412   Chapter 8   Geometric Relationships

PRACTICE AND PROBLEM SOLVING

Extra Practice
See page EP15.

Use a protractor to draw each angle.

24. an acute angle whose measure is less than 45°

25. an obtuse angle whose measure is between 100° and 160°

26. a right angle

Classify the smallest angle formed by the hands on each clock.

27.   **28.**   **29.**

30. Critical Thinking Can two acute angles that share a vertex form a right angle? Justify your answer with a diagram.

31. What's the Error? A student wrote that the measure of this angle is 156°. Explain the error the student may have made, and give the correct measure of the angle. How can the student avoid making the same mistake again?

32. Write About It Describe how an acute angle and an obtuse angle are different.

33. Challenge How many times during the day do the hands of a clock form a straight angle?

Test Prep and Spiral Review

34. Multiple Choice The figure shows a plan for a skateboard ramp. What type of angle is ∠B?

Ⓐ Acute Ⓑ Right Ⓒ Obtuse Ⓓ Straight

35. Multiple Choice Which of the following is another name for ∠PQR?

Ⓕ ∠P Ⓖ ∠RQP Ⓗ ∠PRQ Ⓙ ∠QPR

Write each decimal as a percent and a fraction. (Lesson 7-8)

36. 0.09   **37.** 0.4   **38.** 0.65   **39.** 0.9   **40.** 0.76

Find the percent of each number. (Lesson 7-9)

41. 12% of 30   **42.** 30% of 60   **43.** 65% of 110   **44.** 82% of 360

Hands-on LAB 8-2

Construct Congruent Segments and Angles

Use with Lesson 8-2

Line segments are congruent if they are the same length. You can use a compass and straightedge to construct congruent line segments.

Activity 1

Draw a line segment congruent to line segment *AM*.

A•————————•M

1 Draw a ray that is longer than *AM* and label the endpoint *B*.

B•——————————→

2 Place your compass point on point *A*. Open the compass to the length of $\overline{AM}$. Use the same opening to draw an arc that intersects the ray. Label the intersection point *Y*.

$\overline{AM} \cong \overline{BY}$

Think and Discuss

1. Tell whether it is more accurate to use a ruler or a compass to construct congruent line segments. Explain your answer.

Try This

Construct a line segment congruent to the given line segment.

1.

2.

3.

414   Chapter 8 Geometric Relationships

Angles are congruent if they have the same measure. You can use a compass and straightedge to construct congruent angles.

Activity 2

Draw an angle congruent to ∠C.

1. Draw a ray and label the endpoint P.

2. Place your compass point on point C and draw an arc through ∠C. Label the points of intersection D and E.

3. Place the compass point on P and draw a similar arc through the ray. Label the point of intersection R.

4. Use the compass to measure the arc in ∠DCE. Then place the compass point on R and draw an arc that intersects the first one. Label the point of intersection Q. Draw $\overline{PQ}$.

∠DCE ≅ ∠QPR

Think and Discuss

1. Explain how drawing and constructing are different.

Try This

Construct a congruent angle for each given angle.

1.
2.
3.

8-2 Hands-On Lab   415

8-3 Angle Relationships

Learn to understand relationships of angles.

Angle relationships play an important role in many sports and games. Miniature-golf players must understand angles to know where to aim the ball. In the miniature-golf hole shown, m∠1 = m∠2, m∠3 = m∠4, and m∠5 = m∠6.

Vocabulary
congruent angles
vertical angles
adjacent angles
complementary angles
supplementary angles

Congruent angles have the same measure.

Vertical angles are formed opposite each other when two lines intersect. Vertical angles have the same measure, so they are always congruent.

∠MRP and ∠NRQ are vertical angles.
∠MRN and ∠PRQ are vertical angles.

Interactivities Online ▶

Adjacent angles are side by side and have a common vertex and ray. Adjacent angles may or may not be congruent.

∠MRN and ∠NRQ are adjacent angles. They share vertex R and $\overrightarrow{RN}$.
∠NRQ and ∠QRP are adjacent angles. They share vertex R and $\overrightarrow{RQ}$.

EXAMPLE 1 Identifying Types of Angle Pairs

Identify the type of each angle pair shown.

A
∠1 and ∠2 are opposite each other and are formed by two intersecting lines.
They are vertical angles.

B
∠3 and ∠4 are side by side and have a common vertex and ray.
They are adjacent angles.

Complementary angles are two angles whose measures have a sum of 90°.

65° + 25° = 90°
∠LMN and ∠NMP are complementary.

Supplementary angles are two angles whose measures have a sum of 180°.

65° + 115° = 180°
∠GHK and ∠KHJ are supplementary.

EXAMPLE 2 Identifying an Unknown Angle Measure

Find each unknown angle measure.

A The angles are complementary.

$55° + a = 90°$
$-55° -55°$ *The sum of the measures is 90°.*
$a = 35°$

B The angles are supplementary.

$75° + b = 180°$
$-75° -75°$ *The sum of the measures is 180°.*
$b = 105°$

C The angles are vertical angles.

$c = 51°$ *Vertical angles are congruent.*

D Angles JGF and KGH are congruent.

$d + e + 136° = 180°$ *The sum of the measures is 180°.*
$-136° -136°$
$d + e = 44°$ *Each angle measures half of 44°.*
$d = 22°$ and $e = 22°$

Think and Discuss

1. **Give** the measure of ∠2 if ∠1 and ∠2 are vertical angles and m∠1 = 40°.

2. **Give** the measure of ∠3 if ∠3 and ∠4 are supplementary and m∠4 = 150°.

3. **Use** supplementary angles to explain why vertical angles must be congruent.

8-3 Exercises

GUIDED PRACTICE

See Example 1 Identify the type of each angle pair shown.

1.

2.

See Example 2 Find each unknown angle measure.

3. The angles are complementary.

4. The angles are supplementary.

150°, b

81°, a

INDEPENDENT PRACTICE

See Example 1 Identify the type of each angle pair shown.

5.

6.

See Example 2 Find each unknown angle measure.

7. The angles are vertical angles.

c, 78°

8. The angles are supplementary.

62°, d

PRACTICE AND PROBLEM SOLVING

Extra Practice
See page EP15.

Use the figure for Exercises 9–12.

9. Which angles are not adjacent to ∠3?

10. Name all the pairs of vertical angles that include ∠8.

11. If the m∠6 is 72°, what are the measures of ∠5, ∠7, and ∠8?

12. What is the sum of the measures of ∠1, ∠2, ∠3, and ∠4?

418 Chapter 8 Geometric Relationships

Use the figure for Exercises 13–15.

13. Find the measure of ∠VYW.

14. Find the measure of ∠XYZ.

15. **Multi-Step** Use the measures of ∠VYW and ∠XYZ to find the measure of ∠WYX.

Find the measure of the angle that is complementary to each given angle. Use a protractor to draw both angles.

16. 47°   17. 62°   18. 55°   19. 31°

Find the measure of the angle that is supplementary to each given angle. Use a protractor to draw both angles.

20. 75°   21. 102°   22. 136°   23. 81°

24. Angles A and B are complementary. If the measure of angle A equals the measure of angle B, what is the measure of each angle?

25. Angles C and D are each complementary to angle F. How are angle C and angle D related?

26. **Write a Problem** Draw a pair of adjacent supplementary angles. Write a problem in which the measure of one of the angles must be found.

27. **Write About It** Two angles are supplementary to the same angle. Explain the relationship between the measures of these angles.

28. **Challenge** The measure of angle A is 38°. Angle B is complementary to angle A. Angle C is supplementary to angle B. What is the measure of angle C?

Test Prep and Spiral Review

29. **Multiple Choice** Which type of angles are always congruent?

    (A) Adjacent   (B) Complementary   (C) Supplementary   (D) Vertical

30. **Multiple Choice** Angle J and angle K are supplementary. What is the measure of ∠K if the measure of ∠J is 75°?

    (F) 15°   (G) 25°   (H) 105°   (J) 150°

Find the missing value in each proportion. (Lesson 7-3)

31. $\frac{n}{6} = \frac{5}{15}$ 32. $\frac{2}{m} = \frac{0.8}{3.6}$ 33. $\frac{1}{8} = \frac{p}{2}$ 34. $\frac{30}{8} = \frac{15}{s}$

Classify each angle as acute, right, obtuse, or straight. (Lesson 8-2)

35.   36.   37.   38.

8-4 Classifying Pairs of Lines

Learn to classify pairs of lines.

Vocabulary
parallel lines
perpendicular lines
skew lines

The photograph of the houses and the table below show some of the ways that lines can relate to each other. The blue lines are intersecting. The purple lines are *parallel*. The green lines are *perpendicular*. The red lines are *skew*.

Interactivities Online ▶

Reading Math
The red arrows on the lines show that the lines are parallel.

Intersecting lines are lines that cross at one common point.	*(diagram with points W, Y, Z, X)*	Line YZ intersects line WX. $\overleftrightarrow{YZ}$ intersects $\overleftrightarrow{WX}$.
Parallel lines are lines in the same plane that never intersect.	*(diagram with points A, B, L, M)*	Line AB is parallel to line ML. $\overleftrightarrow{AB} \parallel \overleftrightarrow{ML}$
Perpendicular lines intersect to form 90° angles, or right angles.	*(diagram with points R, T, S, U)*	Line RS is perpendicular to line TU. $\overleftrightarrow{RS} \perp \overleftrightarrow{TU}$
Skew lines are lines that lie in different planes. They are neither parallel nor intersecting.	*(diagram with points M, A, B, L)*	Line AB and line ML are skew. $\overleftrightarrow{AB}$ and $\overleftrightarrow{ML}$ are skew.

EXAMPLE 1 **Classifying Pairs of Lines**

Classify each pair of lines.

A

The lines are in the same plane. They do not appear to intersect.
They are parallel.

B

The lines cross at one common point.
They are intersecting.

C

The lines intersect to form right angles.
They are perpendicular.

D

The lines are in different planes and are not parallel or intersecting.
They are skew.

EXAMPLE 2 *Physical Science Application*

The particles in a transverse wave move up and down as the wave travels to the right. What type of line relationship does this represent?

Points along the ribbon move up and down.

This wave moves to the right.

The direction that the particles move forms a right angle with the direction that the wave is traveling. The lines are perpendicular.

Think and Discuss

1. **Give an example** of intersecting, parallel, perpendicular, and skew lines or line segments in your classroom.

2. **Determine** whether two lines must be parallel if they do not intersect. Explain.

8-4 Classifying Pairs of Lines

8-4 Exercises

GUIDED PRACTICE

See Example 1   Classify each pair of lines.

1.

2.

See Example 2

3. Croquet wickets may be round or have corners like this one. What type of relationship is formed by the lines?

INDEPENDENT PRACTICE

See Example 1   Classify each pair of lines.

4.

5.

6.

See Example 2

7. What type of relationship is formed by the lines?

PRACTICE AND PROBLEM SOLVING

Extra Practice
See page EP15.

Describe each pair of lines as parallel, skew, intersecting, or perpendicular.

8.

9.

10.

11. Capitol Street intersects 1st, 2nd, and 3rd Avenues, which are parallel to each other. West Street and East Street are perpendicular to 2nd Avenue.

   a. Draw a map showing the six streets.

   b. Suppose East and West Streets were perpendicular to Capitol Street rather than 2nd Avenue. Draw a map showing the streets.

422   Chapter 8   Geometric Relationships

The lines in the figure intersect to form a rectangular box.

12. Name all the lines that are parallel to $\overleftrightarrow{AD}$.

13. Name all the lines that are perpendicular to $\overleftrightarrow{FG}$.

14. Name a pair of lines that are skew.

15. Name all the lines that are not parallel to and do not intersect $\overleftrightarrow{DH}$.

Tell whether each statement is *always*, *sometimes*, or *never* true.

16. Intersecting lines are parallel.

17. Intersecting lines are perpendicular.

18. Perpendicular lines are intersecting.

19. Parallel lines are skew.

20. **Critical Thinking** Use *parallel, perpendicular, skew,* or a combination of these terms to describe the lines on a sheet of graph paper. Explain your answer.

21. **What's the Error?** A student drew two lines and claimed that the lines were both parallel and intersecting. Explain the error.

22. **Write About It** Explain the similarities and differences between perpendicular and intersecting lines.

23. **Challenge** Lines *x*, *y*, and *z* are in a plane. If lines *x* and *y* are parallel and line *z* intersects line *x*, does line *z* intersect line *y*? Explain.

Test Prep and Spiral Review

24. **Multiple Choice** Which types of lines never intersect when they are in the same plane?

    Ⓐ Intersecting   Ⓑ Parallel   Ⓒ Perpendicular   Ⓓ Skew

25. **Multiple Choice** Main Street and Elm Street meet at a 90° angle. Which term best describes the streets?

    Ⓕ Intersecting   Ⓖ Parallel   Ⓗ Perpendicular   Ⓙ Skew

26. **Extended Response** A student draws two lines on the same plane. He claims the lines are skew lines. Is he correct? Explain. What are the possible line types that the student drew?

Graph and label each point on a coordinate grid. (Lesson 6-6)

27. $A(3, 4)$
28. $B(1, 5)$
29. $C(7, 1)$
30. $D\left(8\frac{1}{2}, 5\right)$
31. $E\left(2, 3\frac{1}{2}\right)$

Find the measure of the angle that is complementary to each given angle. (Lesson 8-3)

32. 14°
33. 57°
34. 80°
35. 63°
36. 21°

Hands-On LAB 8-4

Parallel Line Relationships

Use with Lesson 8-4

Learn It Online
Lab Resources Online go.hrw.com,
keyword: MR10 Lab8 Go

Parallel lines are in the same plane and never intersect. You can use a straightedge, compass, and protractor to draw parallel lines.

Activity

1 Draw a line on your paper. Label two points A and B.

Use your protractor to measure and mark a 90° angle at each point.

Draw rays with endpoints A and B through the marks you made with the protractor.

Place the point of your compass on point A, and draw an arc through the ray.

Use the same compass opening to draw an arc through the ray at point B.

Label the points of intersection X and Y.

Now use your straightedge to draw a line through X and Y.

Use the symbol for parallel lines to indicate that $\overleftrightarrow{AB}$ is parallel to $\overleftrightarrow{XY}$.

$\overleftrightarrow{AB} \parallel \overleftrightarrow{XY}$

When a pair of parallel lines is intersected by a third line, the angles formed have special relationships.

2 Draw a pair of parallel lines and a third line that intersects them. Label the angles 1 through 8, as shown.

Angles inside the parallel lines are called *interior angles*. The interior angles here are angles 3, 4, 5, and 6.

Angles outside the parallel lines are called *exterior angles*. The exterior angles here are angles 1, 2, 7, and 8.

Measure each angle, and write its measurement inside the angle.

Shade angles with the same measure with the same color.

The interior angles with the same measure are called *alternate interior angles*. They are angles 3 and 6 and angles 4 and 5.

The exterior angles with the same measure are called *alternate exterior angles*. They are angles 1 and 8 and angles 2 and 7.

Angles in the same position when the third line intersects the parallel lines are called *corresponding angles*.

Think and Discuss

1. Name three pairs of corresponding angles.
2. Tell the relationship between the measure of interior angles and the measure of exterior angles.
3. **Make a Conjecture** Suppose two lines are intersected by a third line. The alternate interior angles are congruent, and the alternate exterior angles are congruent. Make a conjecture about the relationship between the two lines.

Try This

Follow the steps to construct and label the diagram.

1. Draw a pair of parallel lines, and draw a third line intersecting them where one angle measures 75°.
2. Label each angle on the diagram using the measure you know.

8-4 Hands-On Lab **425**

CHAPTER 8
SECTION 8A

Ready To Go On?

Learn It Online
Resources Online go.hrw.com,
keyword MR10 RTGO8A

Quiz for Lessons 8-1 Through 8-4

8-1 Building Blocks of Geometry

Use the diagram to name each geometric figure.

1. three points
2. two lines
3. a point shared by two lines
4. a plane
5. two different line segments
6. two different rays

8-2 Measuring and Classifying Angles

Use a protractor to measure each angle. Then classify each angle as acute, right, obtuse, or straight.

7. 8. 9. 10.

11. A football player throws a long pass, and the initial angle the path of the ball makes with the ground is 30°. Draw an angle with this measurement.

8-3 Angle Relationships

12. If two angles are supplementary and one angle measures 97°, what is the measure of the other angle?

Find each unknown angle measure.

13. a, 45°
14. b, 30°
15. c, 32°
16. d, 65°, 35°

8-4 Classifying Pairs of Lines

Classify each pair of lines.

17. 18. 19. 20.

426 Chapter 8 Geometric Relationships

Focus on Problem Solving

Solve
• **Eliminate answer choices**

Sometimes, when a problem has multiple answer choices, you can eliminate some of the choices to help you solve the problem.

For example, a problem reads, "The missing shape is not a red triangle." If one of the answer choices is a red triangle, you can eliminate that answer choice.

Read each problem, and look at the answer choices. Determine whether you can eliminate any of the answer choices before solving the problem. Then solve.

Smileys are letters and symbols that look like faces if you turn them around. When you write an e-mail to someone, you can use smileys to show how you are feeling.

Smileys	
Symbol	Meaning
:-(	Frown
:-D	Laugh
:-)	Smile
:-o	Shout
;-)	Wink

For 1–3, use the table.

1. Dora made a pattern with smileys. Which smiley will she probably use next?

   :-D :-) :-D :-) :-D :-) :-D :-) :-D ▇

   Ⓐ :-D   Ⓒ :-)
   Ⓑ :-)   Ⓓ :-D

2. Troy made a pattern with smileys. Identify a pattern. Which smiley is missing?

   :-(;-) :-o :-(;-) :-o :-(▇ :-o

   Ⓕ :-(Ⓗ ;-)
   Ⓖ :-o   Ⓙ ;-)

3. To end an e-mail, Mya typed four smileys in a row. The shout is first. The wink is between the frown and the smile. The smile is not last. In which order did Mya type the smileys?

   Ⓐ :-o :-(;-) :-)
   Ⓑ :-o :-) ;-) :-(
   Ⓒ :-) ;-) :-o :-(
   Ⓓ :-o ;-) :-(:-)

CarlyQ - Instant Message
File Edit View

Mindy2005: My mom says she will take us to the movie Fri. :-)

CarlyQ: Cool. Are Jaime and Rachel going too? :-D

Mindy2005: No, Rachel and Jaime are going to visit their grandmother. :-(

CarlyQ: We will have fun anyway. ;-)

Focus on Problem Solving

Hands-On LAB 8-5

Triangle Inequality

Use with Lesson 8-5

Learn It Online
Lab Resources Online go.hrw.com,
keyword MR10 Lab8 Go

REMEMBER
- A triangle is a polygon with three sides and three angles.

You can use pieces of straws to make triangles. Only some combinations of side lengths will make triangles.

Activity

1. Cut drinking straws into five pieces that have lengths of 3 cm, 4 cm, 5 cm, 6 cm, and 9 cm.

2. The table shows sets of three straw lengths, *a*, *b*, and *c*. For each set, the lengths of *a*, *b*, and *c* are shown in centimeters. Try to make a triangle with each set of straw lengths shown in the table. Write down whether each triangle can be made.

3. For each triangle, find the sum $a + b$ and record it in the table.

Straw 1 *a*	Straw 2 *b*	Straw 3 *c*	Can these straws form a triangle?	$a + b$
3	4	5		
3	4	6		
3	4	9		
3	5	9		
4	5	9		
5	6	9		

Think and Discuss

1. Which sets of straw lengths can make a triangle?

2. For each set of straw lengths, compare the sum of the lengths of the two sides $a + b$ with the third side length *c*. Make a conjecture about the relationship between the sides of a triangle based on your comparisons.

Try This

Use a centimeter ruler to measure the line segments. Tell whether the three segments could form a triangle.

1.

2.

428 Chapter 8 Geometric Relationships

8-5 Triangles

Learn to classify triangles and solve problems involving angle and side measures of triangles.

Vocabulary
- acute triangle
- obtuse triangle
- right triangle
- congruent line segments
- scalene triangle
- isosceles triangle
- equilateral triangle

A triangle is a closed figure with three line segments and three angles. Triangles can be classified by the measures of their angles. An **acute triangle** has only acute angles. An **obtuse triangle** has one obtuse angle. A **right triangle** has one right angle.

Acute triangle (75°, 50°, 55°)   Obtuse triangle (20°, 135°, 25°)   Right triangle (40°, 50°)

To decide whether a triangle is acute, obtuse, or right, you need to know the measures of its angles.

The sum of the measures of the angles in any triangle is 180°. You can see this if you tear the corners from a triangle and arrange them around a point on a line.

By knowing the sum of the measures of the angles in a triangle, you can find unknown angle measures.

EXAMPLE 1   Food Application

Interactivities Online ▶

This half of a sandwich is shaped like a triangle. The measure of ∠A is 90°, and the measure of ∠B is 30°. Classify the triangle.

To classify the triangle, find the measure of ∠C.

m∠C = 180° − (90° + 30°)
m∠C = 180° − 120°   *Subtract the sum of the known*
m∠C = 60°   *angle measures from 180°.*

So the measure of ∠C is 60°. Because △ABC has one right angle, the sandwich is a right triangle.

You can use what you know about vertical, adjacent, complementary, and supplementary angles to find the missing measures of angles.

EXAMPLE 2 Using Properties of Angles to Label Triangles

Use the diagram to find the measure of each indicated angle.

A ∠BDE

∠BDE and ∠ADC are vertical angles, so m∠BDE = m∠ADC.

m∠ADC = 180° − (30° + 35°)
= 180° − 65°
= 115°

B ∠ADB

∠BDE and ∠ADB are supplementary,
so m∠BDE + m∠ADB = 180°.

m∠ADB = 180° − 115°
= 65°

Congruent line segments have the same length. Triangles can be classified by the lengths of their sides. A **scalene triangle** has no congruent sides. An **isosceles triangle** has at least two congruent sides. An **equilateral triangle** has three congruent sides.

Helpful Hint

You can use tick marks to show congruent sides.

Scalene triangle   Isosceles triangle   Equilateral triangle

EXAMPLE 3 Classifying Triangles by Lengths of Sides

Classify the triangle. The perimeter of the triangle is 7.8 cm.

$a + (3.8 + 2) = 7.8$
$a + 5.8 = 7.8$
$a + 5.8 - 5.8 = 7.8 - 5.8$
$a = 2$

Side a is 2 centimeters long. Because △WXY has at least two sides, but not three, that are the same length, it is an isosceles triangle.

Think and Discuss

1. Explain why a triangle cannot have two obtuse angles.

2. Tell whether a right triangle can also be an acute triangle. Explain.

8-5 Exercises

Learn It Online
Homework Help Online go.hrw.com, keyword MR10 8-5
Exercises 1–10, 11, 13, 15, 19

GUIDED PRACTICE

See Example 1
1. Three stars form a triangular constellation. Two of the angles measure 20° and 50°. Classify the triangle.

See Example 2
Use the diagram to find the measure of each indicated angle.
2. ∠XZV
3. ∠VZW

See Example 3
Classify each triangle using the given information.
4. The perimeter of the triangle is 24 cm. (8 cm, 8 cm)
5. The perimeter of the triangle is 30 ft. (6 ft, 12 ft)

INDEPENDENT PRACTICE

See Example 1
6. Interstate highways connecting towns R, S, and T form a triangle. Two of the angles measure 40° and 42°. Classify the triangle.

See Example 2
Use the diagram to find the measure of each indicated angle.
7. ∠KNJ
8. ∠LKM

See Example 3
Classify each triangle using the given information.
9. The perimeter of the triangle is 10.5 in. (4 in., 3.2 in.)
10. The perimeter of the triangle is 231 km. (100 km, 58 km)

PRACTICE AND PROBLEM SOLVING

Extra Practice See page EP16.

If the angles can form a triangle, classify it as acute, obtuse, or right.
11. 45°, 90°, 45°
12. 51°, 88°, 41°
13. 71°, 40°, 59°
14. 55°, 102°, 33°
15. 37°, 40°, 103°
16. 90°, 30°, 50°

17. Find a triangle in your classroom or at home. Describe the triangle and classify it. Explain your classification.

8-5 Triangles   431

Social Studies

This stamp, issued in 2007, commemorates the 400th anniversary of the founding of the first permanent English settlement in the U.S. in Jamestown, Virginia Colony.

The lengths of two sides are given for △ABC. Use the sum of the lengths of the three sides to calculate the length of the third side and classify each triangle.

18. $AB = 7$ cm; $BC = 7$ cm; sum = 15.9 cm

19. $AB = 1\frac{1}{6}$ ft; $BC = 1\frac{1}{6}$ ft; sum = $3\frac{1}{2}$ ft

20. Social Studies Some triangular stamps are made by dividing a rectangle into two parts. Classify the triangle that is made by cutting on a line that connects one corner of a rectangle to the opposite corner.

Draw an example of each triangle described.

21. a scalene acute triangle

22. an isosceles right triangle

23. an isosceles obtuse triangle

24. a scalene right triangle

25. Critical Thinking Use a centimeter ruler to measure each side of triangle A. Add the lengths of any two sides and compare the sum to the length of the third side. Add a different pair of lengths and compare the sum to the third side. Do the same for triangles B and C. How does the sum of the lengths of any two sides of a triangle compare to the length of the third side?

26. Choose a Strategy How many triangles are in the figure at right?

27. Write About It *Equiangular* means "having equal angles." Which type(s) of triangles are equiangular?

28. Challenge Find the sum of the angles of a square. (*Hint*: Divide the square into two triangles.)

Test Prep and Spiral Review

29. Multiple Choice A triangle has one right angle. What could the measures of the other two angles be?

Ⓐ 20° and 70°   Ⓑ 30° and 15°   Ⓒ 60° and 120°   Ⓓ 90° and 100°

30. Multiple Choice The lengths of two sides of a triangle are 54 meters and 45 meters. The sum of the three sides is 126 meters. Find the missing third side.

Ⓕ 27 m   Ⓖ 72 m   Ⓗ 81 m   Ⓙ 99 m

Write each percent as a decimal. (Lesson 7-7)

31. 12%   **32.** 55%   **33.** 3%   **34.** 47%   **35.** 76%

Draw each geometric figure. (Lesson 8-1)

36. $\overleftrightarrow{CD}$ **37.** $\overrightarrow{GM}$ **38.** $\overline{XY}$ **39.** point A

Technology LAB 8-5

Angles in Triangles

Use with Lesson 8-5

Learn It Online
Lab Resources Online go.hrw.com,
keyword MR10 Lab8

The sum of the angle measures is the same for any triangle. You can use geometry software to find this sum and to check that the sum is the same for many different triangles.

Activity

1. Use the geometry software to make triangle *ABC*. Then use the angle measure tool to measure ∠*B*.

2. Use the angle measure tool to measure ∠*C* and ∠*A*. Then use the calculator tool to add the measures of the three angles. Notice that the sum is 180°.

3. Select vertex *A* and drag it around to change the shape of triangle *ABC*. Watch the angle sum. Change the shape of the triangle again and then again. Be sure to make acute and obtuse triangles.

   Notice that the sum of the angle measures is always 180°, regardless of the triangle's shape.

Think and Discuss

1. Can you use geometry software to draw a triangle with two obtuse angles? Explain.

Try This

Solve. Then use geometry software to check each answer.

1. In triangle *ABC*, m∠*B* = 49.15° and m∠*A* = 113.75°. Find m∠*C*.

2. Use geometry software to construct an acute triangle *XYZ*. Give the measures of its angles, and check that their sum is 180°.

8-6 Quadrilaterals

Learn to identify, classify, and compare quadrilaterals.

Vocabulary
quadrilateral
parallelogram
rectangle
rhombus
square
trapezoid

A **quadrilateral** is a plane figure with four sides and four angles.

Five special types of quadrilaterals and their properties are shown in the table below. The tick marks on two or more sides of a figure indicate that the sides are congruent.

Theo van Doesburg painted *Compostion 17*. Many of his abstract paintings consist of different-sized rectangles.

Interactivities Online ▶

Parallelogram	Opposite sides are parallel and congruent. Opposite angles are congruent.
Rectangle	Parallelogram with four right angles. Opposite sides are parallel and congruent.
Rhombus	Parallelogram with four congruent sides. Opposite angles are congruent.
Square	Rectangle with four congruent sides. All angles are right angles.
Trapezoid	Quadrilateral with exactly two parallel sides. May have two right angles.

EXAMPLE 1 Naming Quadrilaterals

Give the most descriptive name for each figure.

A There are four congruent sides, and opposite angles are congruent.

The figure is a quadrilateral, a parallelogram, and a rhombus.

Rhombus is the most descriptive name.

B There are two parallel sides. There are no congruent angles.

The figure is a quadrilateral and a trapezoid.

Trapezoid is the most descriptive name.

434   Chapter 8 Geometric Relationships

Give the most descriptive name for each figure.

C There are four congruent sides and four right angles.
The figure is a quadrilateral, parallelogram, rectangle, rhombus, and square.

Square is the most descriptive name.

D This figure is a plane figure, but it has more than 4 sides.

The figure is not a quadrilateral.

You can draw a diagram to classify quadrilaterals based on their properties.

Quadrilaterals
- Parallelograms
  - Rectangles
  - Squares
  - Rhombuses
- Trapezoids

EXAMPLE 2 Classifying Quadrilaterals

Complete each statement.

A A rhombus that is a rectangle is also a ___?___.

A rhombus has four congruent sides, and the opposite sides are parallel. If it is a rectangle, it has four right angles, which makes it a **square**.

B A square can also be called a ___?___, ___?___, and ___?___.

A square has opposite sides that are parallel; it can be called a **parallelogram**.
A square has four congruent sides; it can be called a **rhombus**.
A square has four right angles; it can be called a **rectangle**.

Think and Discuss

1. Tell whether all squares are rhombuses and whether all rhombuses are squares.

2. Compare a trapezoid with a rectangle.

8-6 Quadrilaterals

8-6 Exercises

GUIDED PRACTICE

See Example 1 — Give the most descriptive name for each figure.

1. 2. 3.

See Example 2 — Complete each statement.

4. A trapezoid is also a ___?___.
5. All ___?___ are also rectangles.
6. A square has four ___?___ angles.

INDEPENDENT PRACTICE

See Example 1 — Give the most descriptive name for each figure.

7. 8. 9.

See Example 2 — Complete each statement.

10. A rhombus with four right angles is a ___?___.
11. A parallelogram cannot be a ___?___.
12. A quadrilateral with four congruent sides and no right angles can be called a ___?___ and a ___?___.

PRACTICE AND PROBLEM SOLVING

Extra Practice
See page EP16.

Give all of the possible names for each figure. Circle the most exact name.

13. 14. 15.

Determine if the given statements are *sometimes*, *always*, or *never* true.

16. A square is a rectangle.
17. A trapezoid is a parallelogram.
18. A rhombus is a square.
19. A parallelogram is a quadrilateral.
20. A rectangle is a rhombus.
21. Four-sided figures are parallelograms.
22. A rectangle is a square.
23. A trapezoid has one right angle.

436 Chapter 8 Geometric Relationships

Sports

The first baseball game played at Shea Stadium was on April 17, 1964. In September 1974, the Mets played a 25-inning game, almost three times the length of a regulation game.

Draw each quadrilateral as described. If it is not possible to draw, explain why.

24. a rectangle that is also a square
25. a rhombus that is also a trapezoid
26. a parallelogram that is not a rectangle
27. a square that is not a rhombus

28. **Sports** A baseball diamond is in the shape of a square. The distance from home plate to first base is 90 ft. What is the distance around the baseball diamond?

29. A rectangular picture frame is 3 in. wider than it is tall. The total length of the four sides of the frame is 38 in.

   a. The dimensions of the frame could be 10 in. by 13 in. because one dimension is 3 in. longer than the other. Explain how you know the frame is not 10 in. by 13 in.

   b. **Critical Thinking** How can you use your answer from part **a** to find the dimensions of the frame?

   c. Using parts **a** and **b**, what are the dimensions of the frame?

30. Anika drew a quadrilateral. Then she drew a line segment connecting one pair of opposite corners. She saw that she had divided the original quadrilateral into two right isosceles triangles. Classify the quadrilateral she began with.

31. **What's the Error?** A student said that any quadrilateral with two right angles and a pair of parallel sides is a rectangle. What is the error in the statement?

32. **Write About It** Explain why a square is also a rectangle and a rhombus.

33. **Challenge** Part of a quadrilateral is hidden. What are the possible types of special quadrilaterals that the figure could be?

Test Prep and Spiral Review

34. **Multiple Choice** Which quadrilateral is NOT a parallelogram?

    (A) Rectangle   (B) Rhombus   (C) Square   (D) Trapezoid

35. **Short Response** List all of the names for the figure. Which is the most descriptive?

Use the pattern to write the first five terms of the sequence. (Lesson 1-6)

36. Start with 6; add 5.
37. Start with 2; multiply by 3.

Tell whether each statement is *always, sometimes,* or *never* true. (Lesson 8-4)

38. Perpendicular lines are intersecting lines.
39. Skew lines are on the same plane.

8-7 Polygons

Learn to identify regular and not regular polygons and to find the angle measures of regular polygons.

Vocabulary
polygon
regular polygon
diagonal

A **polygon** is a closed plane figure formed by three or more line segments. A **regular polygon** is a polygon in which all sides are congruent and all angles are congruent. Polygons are named by the number of their sides and angles.

	Triangle	Quadrilateral	Pentagon	Hexagon
Sides and Angles	3	4	5	6
Regular	△	□	⬠	⬡
Not Regular				

	Heptagon	Octagon	Nonagon	Decagon
Sides and Angles	7	8	9	10
Regular				
Not Regular				

EXAMPLE 1   Identifying Polygons

Tell whether each shape is a polygon. If so, give its name and tell whether it appears to be regular or not regular.

A
There are 4 sides and 4 angles.
quadrilateral
The sides and angles appear to be congruent.
regular

B
There are 4 sides and 4 angles.
quadrilateral
All 4 sides do not appear to be congruent.
not regular

You can divide any quadrilateral into two triangles by drawing a **diagonal**, a line segment that connects two non-adjacent vertices. The sum of the interior angle measures in a triangle is 180°, so the sum of the interior angle measures in a quadrilateral is 360°.

EXAMPLE 2 PROBLEM SOLVING APPLICATION

A stop sign is in the shape of a regular octagon. What is the measure of each angle of the stop sign?

1. Understand the Problem

The **answer** will be the measure of each angle in a regular octagon. List the **important information:**

- A regular octagon has 8 congruent sides and 8 congruent angles.

2. Make a Plan

Make a table to look for a pattern using regular polygons.

3. Solve

Draw some regular polygons and divide each into triangles.

Polygon	Sides	Triangles	Sum of Angle Measures
Triangle	3	1	1 × 180° = 180°
Quadrilateral	4	2	2 × 180° = 360°
Pentagon	5	3	3 × 180° = 540°
Hexagon	6	4	4 × 180° = 720°

The number of triangles is always 2 fewer than the number of sides. An octagon can be divided into 8 − 2 = 6 triangles.

The sum of the interior angle measures in an octagon is 6 × 180° = 1,080°.

So the measure of each angle is 1,080° ÷ 8 = 135°.

4. Look Back

Each angle in a regular octagon is obtuse. 135° is a reasonable answer, because an obtuse angle is between 90° and 180°.

Reading Math

The prefixes in the names of the polygons tell you how many sides and angles there are.

tri- = three
quad- = four
penta- = five
hexa- = six
octa- = eight

Think and Discuss

1. **Classify** the angles in each figure: a regular triangle, a regular hexagon, and a rectangle.
2. **Name** an object that is in the shape of a pentagon and an object that is in the shape of an octagon.

8-7 Exercises

GUIDED PRACTICE

See Example 1 Tell whether each shape is a polygon. If so, give its name and tell whether it appears to be regular or not regular.

1.
2.
3.

See Example 2 4. A carpenter is building a deck around a hot tub in the shape of a regular hexagon. What is the measure of each angle of the hexagon?

INDEPENDENT PRACTICE

See Example 1 Tell whether each shape is a polygon. If so, give its name and tell whether it appears to be regular or not regular.

5.
6.
7.

See Example 2 8. Janet made a sign for her room in the shape of a regular pentagon. What is the measure of each angle of the pentagon?

PRACTICE AND PROBLEM SOLVING

Extra Practice
See page EP16.

Explain why each shape is NOT a polygon.

9.
10.
11.

Use the diagram to find the measure of each indicated angle.

12. ∠BCD
13. ∠GFJ
14. ∠RST

440   Chapter 8   Geometric Relationships

Classify each of the following polygons as either *always* regular, *sometimes* regular, or *never* regular.

		Always	Sometimes	Never
15.	Trapezoid	?	?	?
16.	Right triangle	?	?	?
17.	Parallelogram	?	?	?
18.	Equilateral triangle	?	?	?

Critical Thinking For each figure below, one diagonal is shown.

19. **a.** How many diagonals does a rectangle have?

    b. How many diagonals does a pentagon have?

20. **What's the Error?** A student said a rectangle is never a regular polygon because the lengths of all the sides are not congruent. What error did the student make? Explain why a rectangle is sometimes a regular polygon.

21. **Write About It** What polygon is formed when two equilateral triangles are placed side by side, with one upside down? Draw examples, and explain whether the polygon formed by the two triangles is regular.

22. **Challenge** A figure is formed by placing 6 equilateral triangle tiles around a regular hexagon tile. The distance around the regular hexagon is 60 cm. A snail moves along the sides of the figure. How far will the snail travel until it gets back to its starting point?

Test Prep and Spiral Review

23. **Multiple Choice** Which quadrilateral is regular?

    (A) Triangle (B) Trapezoid (C) Square (D) Rhombus

24. **Gridded Response** What is the measure, in degrees, of each angle of a regular pentagon?

Solve each equation. (Lesson 3-9)

25. $5.5 = 5c$
26. $d + 4.96 = 9$
27. $j - 12.5 = 39.04$
28. $\frac{x}{2.4} = 3.5$

29. Can angles with measurements 34°, 53°, and 93° form a triangle? If so, classify the triangle as acute, obtuse, or right. (Lesson 8-5)

Hands-On LAB 8-7

Explore Intersecting Polygons

Use with Lesson 8-7

Learn It Online
Lab Resources Online go.hrw.com,
keyword MR10 Lab8

Two polygons in the same plane may intersect in one or more points.

Activity 1

1. Begin by drawing two squares that intersect in only one point.

   1 point of intersection

2. Now try drawing two squares that intersect at two points, three points, and four points.

   2 points of intersection   **3 points of intersection**   **4 points of intersection**

Think and Discuss

1. How many points of intersection would there be if two squares shared a side?

Try This

Draw two squares with the indicated number of intersection points.

1. 5 points
2. 6 points
3. 7 points
4. 8 points

5. **Make a Conjecture** What do you think the maximum number of intersection points for two squares is? Explain.

442 Chapter 8 Geometric Relationships

When two polygons in the same plane intersect, they may form overlapping regions in the shape of other polygons.

Activity 2

1. Begin by drawing two polygons that overlap to form a triangular region.

Triangle

2. Now try drawing two polygons that overlap to form a quadrilateral and a pentagon.

Quadrilateral   **Pentagon**

Think and Discuss

1. Can two polygons intersect so that the overlapping region is not a polygon? Explain.

2. Do you think that the maximum number of sides of the overlapping region is based on the two polygons you start with? Explain.

Try This

Draw the two given shapes so that they overlap to form the indicated polygon.

1. two squares; pentagon

2. two trapezoids; hexagon

3. two triangles; square

4. a triangle and a rectangle; trapezoid

5. **Make a Conjecture** Find the maximum number of sides that the overlapping region can have when two quadrilaterals overlap. Explain.

8-7 Hands-On Lab

8-8 Geometric Patterns

Learn to recognize, describe, and extend geometric patterns.

Central American art often involves geometric patterns. The patterns are based on the shape, color, size, position, or number of geometric figures.

This blanket has a geometric pattern. The colorful zig-zag lines are in groups of three, separated by black zig-zags. Within each group of three, the first and third lines are decorated with triangles. The middle zig-zag in each group is decorated with a square design. In this blanket, the colors used are not part of the geometric pattern.

EXAMPLE 1 Extending Geometric Patterns

Identify a possible pattern. Use the pattern to draw the next figure.

A

The small shapes within the figure are shaded one at a time from bottom to top. Then the figure is rotated and the top triangle is shaded.

So the next figure might look like this:

B

The figures from left to right are a 1 × 1 square, a 2 × 2 square, a 3 × 3 square, and a 4 × 4 square.

So the next figure might look like this:

Remember!

Perfect squares, such as 2^2, 3^2, and 4^2, are also called "square numbers" because they can be modeled as a square array.

444   Chapter 8 Geometric Relationships

EXAMPLE 2 Completing Geometric Patterns

Identify a possible pattern. Use the pattern to draw the missing figure.

A

The first figure from the bottom row to the top has 4 squares and then 3, 2, and 1 square. The next figure has 5 squares in the bottom row and then 4, 3, 2, and 1.

So the missing figure might look like this:

B

Each figure is an equilateral triangle. The first figure has 3 red triangles along the base. The third figure has 5 red triangles, and the last figure has 6.

So the missing figure might look like this:

EXAMPLE 3 Art Application

Dan is painting a clay pot. Identify a pattern in Dan's design and tell what the finished pot might look like.

The pattern from bottom to top is narrow stripe, wide stripe, narrow stripe, wide stripe. The color pattern from bottom to top is blue, green, yellow, blue, green.

If this pattern is followed, the finished pot might look like the pot at left.

Think and Discuss

1. **Explain** how you can use a pattern to find the number of squares in the next, or fifth, figure in Example 2A.

2. **Tell** how you can use a pattern to find the number of small red triangles in the sixth figure in Example 2B.

8-8 Exercises

Learn It Online
Homework Help Online go.hrw.com,
keyword MR10 8-8
Exercises 1–6, 7, 9

GUIDED PRACTICE

See Example 1 Identify a possible pattern. Use the pattern to draw the next figure.

1.

See Example 2 Identify a possible pattern. Use the pattern to draw the missing figure.

2.

See Example 3 3. Oscar is making a beaded necklace. Identify a pattern in Oscar's design. Then tell which five beads Oscar will probably use next.

INDEPENDENT PRACTICE

See Example 1 Identify a possible pattern. Use the pattern to draw the next figure.

4.

See Example 2 Identify a possible pattern. Use the pattern to draw the missing figure.

5.

See Example 3 6. Tamara is planting flowers in her garden. She makes groups of purple flowers and groups of pink flowers.

If she continues this pattern, how many flowers might Tamara plant in the next group of purple flowers? How many flowers might she plant in the next group of pink flowers?

PRACTICE AND PROBLEM SOLVING

Extra Practice
See page EP16.

Draw the next figure in the pattern.

7.

8.   9.

446   Chapter 8   Geometric Relationships

Social Studies LINK

In South Africa, Ndebele people paint their houses with brightly colored patterns made up of geometric shapes.

10. Look at the shapes found on the wall surrounding the Ndebele house. Identify a possible pattern that was used to paint the top band of the wall. Use the pattern to draw the shapes hidden by the Ndebele people. (You do not need to include color in the pattern.)

11. **Write About It** Look closely at the Ndebele house. Draw four geometric figures you see painted on the house. Then use those figures to make a pattern. Describe your pattern.

12. **Challenge** Look at the designs below, which were made using an African motif. Identify a possible pattern. If the pattern continues, how many motifs will be in the sixth design? If there are 45 motifs, what will the design number be?

Test Prep and Spiral Review

13. **Multiple Choice** Identify a possible pattern in the image. Use the pattern to determine the missing figure.

14. **Short Response** Determine the next figure in the pattern. Draw the figure. Explain your answer.

Simplify. (Lesson 1-2)

15. 9^2
16. 2^6
17. 3^3
18. 1^{12}
19. 4^5

Write the prime factorization of each number. (Lesson 4-2)

20. 38
21. 50
22. 120
23. 214
24. 75

8-8 Geometric Patterns 447

CHAPTER 8 SECTION 8B

Ready To Go On?

Quiz for Lessons 8-5 Through 8-8

8-5 Triangles

Use the diagram for problems 1 and 2.

1. Find m∠SUV.

2. Classify triangle STR by its angles and by its sides.

If the angles can form a triangle, classify it as acute, obtuse, or right.

3. 15°, 60°, 95°   4. 47°, 51°, 82°   5. 94°, 76°, 10°   6. 78°, 102°, 20°

8-6 Quadrilaterals

Give the most descriptive name for each figure.

7.   8.   9.   10.

8-7 Polygons

11. Nina cuts a regular hexagon out of poster board. What is the measure of each angle of the hexagon?

12. The perimeter of an equilateral triangle is 186 centimeters. What is the length of one side of the triangle?

Name each polygon, and tell whether it appears to be regular or not regular.

13.   14.   15.   16.

8-8 Geometric Patterns

Identify a possible pattern. Use the pattern to draw the missing figure.

17.   18.

19.   20.

Focus on Problem Solving

Make a Plan
• Draw a diagram

Sometimes a problem seems difficult because it is described in words only. You can draw a diagram to help you picture the problem. Try to label all the information you are given on your diagram. Then use the diagram to solve the problem.

Read each problem. Draw a diagram to help you solve the problem. Then solve.

1. Bob used a ruler to draw a quadrilateral. First he drew a line 3 in. long and labeled it $\overline{AB}$. From B, he drew a line 2 in. long and labeled the endpoint C. From A, he drew a line $2\frac{1}{2}$ in. long and labeled the endpoint D. What is the length of $\overline{CD}$ if the perimeter of Bob's quadrilateral is $12\frac{1}{2}$ in?

2. Karen has a vegetable garden that is 12 feet long and 10 feet wide. She plans to plant tomatoes in one-half of the garden. She will divide the other half of the garden equally into three beds, where she'll grow cabbage, pumpkins, and radishes. All the beds will be rectangles.
   a. What are the possible whole number dimensions of the tomato bed?
   b. What fraction of the garden will Karen use to grow cabbage?

3. Pam draws three parallel lines that are an equal distance apart. The two outside lines are 8 cm apart. How far apart is the middle line from the outside lines?

4. Jan connected the following points in order on a coordinate grid: (2, 4), (4, 6), (6, 6), (6, 2), (3, 2), and (2, 4).
   a. What figure did Jan draw?
   b. How many right angles does the figure have?

5. Triangle ABC is isoceles. The measure of angle B is equal to the measure of angle C. The measure of angle B equals 50°. What is the measure of angle A?

8-9 Congruent Polygons

Learn to identify congruent figures and to use congruence to solve problems.

You know that angles that have the same measure are congruent. **Congruent figures** have the same shape and same size. This means the corresponding sides and corresponding angles are congruent.

This geodesic dome at the Centre for Alternative Technology in the United Kingdom is made of congruent triangles.

Vocabulary
congruent figures

EXAMPLE 1   Identifying Congruent Figures

Interactivities Online ▶

Decide whether the figures in each pair are congruent. If not, explain.

A

These figures are both quadrilaterals. But they are neither the same size nor the same shape.

The figures are not congruent.

B

Each triangle has a 12 cm side, a 16 cm side, and a 20 cm side. The corresponding angles are congruent.

The triangles are congruent.

C

Each figure is a square, which means all angles are 90°. Each side of each square measures 2 inches.

The figures are congruent.

Remember!
Tick marks indicate that lengths or angle measures are equal.

450   Chapter 8   Geometric Relationships

EXAMPLE 2 Consumer Application

Landra needs a ground cloth that is congruent to the tent floor. Which ground cloth appears to be congruent to the tent floor?

Tent floor
3 ft
4 ft   4 ft
3 ft   3 ft
3 ft

Ground cloth A
3 ft
4 ft   3 ft
3 ft   3 ft
4 ft

Ground cloth B
1.5 ft
2 ft   2 ft
1.5 ft   1.5 ft
1.5 ft

Both cloths are hexagons. Only Cloth A has the same side lengths.

Cloth A appears to be congruent to the tent floor.

Think and Discuss

1. **Explain** whether you can determine that figures are congruent just by looking at them.
2. **Describe** how similar figures are different from congruent figures.

8-9 Exercises

GUIDED PRACTICE

See Example 1 Decide whether the figures in each pair are congruent. If not, explain.

1.

2.

See Example 2 3. Which quadrilateral appears to be congruent to the bottom of the box?

4 cm
4 cm A 4 cm
4 cm

8 cm
4 cm B 4 cm
8 cm

8 cm
8 cm C 8 cm
8 cm

8-9 Congruent Polygons 451

INDEPENDENT PRACTICE

See Example 1 Decide whether the figures in each pair are congruent. If not, explain.

4.

5.

See Example 2 6. Which puzzle piece will fit into the empty space?

a.   b.   c.

PRACTICE AND PROBLEM SOLVING

Extra Practice
See page EP17.

7. Copy the dot grid. Then draw three figures congruent to the given figure. The figures can have common sides but should not overlap.

8. **Measurement** Use an inch ruler to draw two congruent rectangles with side lengths that are longer than 2 in. and shorter than 6 in. Label each side length.

9. **Write About It** Explain how to tell whether two polygons are congruent.

10. **Challenge** Two quadrilaterals have side lengths 2 cm, 2 cm, 5 cm, and 5 cm. Are the two quadrilaterals congruent? Explain.

Test Prep and Spiral Review

11. **Multiple Choice** Squares $ABCD$ and $WXYZ$ are congruent. The length of $\overline{AB}$ is 5 in. What is the length of $\overline{WX}$?

    Ⓐ 5 in.   Ⓑ 9 in.   Ⓒ 20 in.   Ⓓ 25 in.

12. **Multiple Choice** Hexagons $FGHJKL$ and $RSTWXY$ are congruent and regular. The length of $\overline{FG}$ is 7 km. Find the perimeter of hexagon $RSTWXY$.

    Ⓕ 7 km   Ⓖ 35 km   Ⓗ 42 km   Ⓙ 49 km

Solve each equation. Check your answers. (Lesson 2-7)

13. $9y = 81$ 14. $70 = 10x$ 15. $64 = 8n$ 16. $60 = 12m$

Multiply. Write each answer in simplest form. (Lesson 5-7)

17. $\frac{2}{3} \cdot \frac{4}{7}$ 18. $\frac{1}{5} \cdot \frac{3}{8}$ 19. $\frac{3}{4} \cdot \frac{1}{2}$ 20. $\frac{4}{5} \cdot \frac{1}{3}$

8-10 Transformations

Learn to use translations, reflections, and rotations to transform geometric shapes.

Vocabulary
transformation
translation
rotation
reflection
line of reflection

Interactivities Online ▶

A rigid **transformation** moves a figure without changing its size or shape. So the original figure and the transformed figure are always congruent.

The illustrations of the truck show three transformations: a *translation*, a *rotation*, and a *reflection*. Notice the transformed truck does not change in size or shape.

A **translation** is the movement of a figure along a straight line.

Only the location of the figure changes with a translation.

A **rotation** is the movement of a figure around a point. A point of rotation can be on or outside a figure.

The location and position of a figure can change with a rotation.

When a figure flips over a line, creating a mirror image, it is called a **reflection**. The line the figure is flipped over is called the **line of reflection**.

The location and position of a figure change with a reflection.

EXAMPLE 1 Identifying Transformations

Tell whether each is a translation, rotation, or reflection.

A

The figure moves around a point.

It is a rotation.

Tell whether each is a translation, rotation, or reflection.

B) *The figure is flipped over a line.*
It is a reflection.

C) *The figure is moved along a line.*
It is a translation.

A full turn is a 360° rotation. So a $\frac{1}{4}$ turn is 90°, and a $\frac{1}{2}$ turn is 180°.

EXAMPLE 2 Drawing Transformations

Draw each transformation.

A) **Draw a 90° clockwise rotation about the point shown.**
Trace the figure and the point of rotation.
Place your pencil on the point of rotation.
Rotate the figure clockwise 90°.
Trace the figure in its new location.

B) **Draw a horizontal reflection.**
Trace the figure and the line of reflection.
Fold along the line of reflection.
Trace the figure in its new location.

Think and Discuss

1. **Give examples** of reflections that occur in the real world.
2. **Name** a figure that can be rotated so that it will land on top of itself.

8-10 Exercises

GUIDED PRACTICE

See Example 1 Tell whether each is a translation, rotation, or reflection.

1.
2.
3.

See Example 2 Draw each transformation.

4. Draw a 180° clockwise rotation about the point shown.

5. Draw a horizontal reflection across the line.

INDEPENDENT PRACTICE

See Example 1 Tell whether each is a translation, rotation, or reflection.

6.
7.
8.

See Example 2 Draw each transformation.

9. Draw a vertical reflection across the line.

10. Draw a 90° counterclockwise rotation about the point.

11. Draw a translation.

12. Draw a translation.

13. Draw a 90° clockwise rotation about the point.

14. Draw a horizontal reflection across the line.

8-10 Transformations 455

PRACTICE AND PROBLEM SOLVING

Extra Practice
See page EP17.

15. Which is a horizontal reflection of this red arrow?

16. Language Arts Which capital letters in the alphabet can be horizontally reflected and still look the same? Which letters can be vertically reflected and still look the same?

Use the chessboard for Exercises 17–20.

Hobbies Chess is a game of skill that is played on a board divided into 64 squares. Each chess piece is moved differently.

17. Copy the lower left corner of the chessboard. Then show the indicated knight moving in a translation of two forward and one right.

Knight   King   Pawn

In a game of chess, each player has 318,979,564,000 possible ways to make the first four moves.

18. Choose a Strategy If the knight, king, and pawn are placed in a straight line, how many ways can they be arranged?

Ⓐ 3   Ⓑ 4   Ⓒ 6   Ⓓ 12

19. Write About It Draw one of the chess pieces. Then draw a translation, rotation, and reflection of that piece. Describe each transformation.

20. Challenge Draw one of the chess pieces rotated 90° clockwise around the vertex of a square and then horizontally reflected.

Test Prep and Spiral Review

21. Multiple Choice What is the movement of a figure about a point?

Ⓐ Translation   Ⓑ Tessellation   Ⓒ Reflection   Ⓓ Rotation

22. Short Response Tell whether the picture shows a rotation, translation, or reflection. Explain.

Write each phrase as a numerical or algebraic expression. (Lesson 2-2)

23. 19 times 3   **24.** the quotient of g divided by 6   **25.** the sum of 5 and 9

Write each decimal as a fraction or mixed number. (Lesson 4-4)

26. 0.9   **27.** 6.71   **28.** 0.20   **29.** 2.88   **30.** 0.55

8-11 Symmetry

Learn to identify symmetry.

Vocabulary
line symmetry
line of symmetry
rotational symmetry

The patterns visible when you look through a kaleidoscope have two types of symmetry.

A figure has **line symmetry** if it can be folded or reflected so that the two parts of the figure match, or are congruent. The line of reflection is called the **line of symmetry**.

EXAMPLE 1 — Identifying Lines of Symmetry

Determine whether each dashed line appears to be a line of symmetry.

A

The two parts of the figure are congruent, but they do not match exactly when folded or reflected across the line.
The line does not appear to be a line of symmetry.

B

The two parts of the figure appear to match exactly when folded or reflected across the line.
The line appears to be a line of symmetry.

Some figures have more than one line of symmetry.

EXAMPLE 2 — Finding Multiple Lines of Symmetry

Find all of the lines of symmetry in each regular polygon.

A

Trace each figure and cut it out.
Fold the figure in half in different ways.
Count the lines of symmetry.

6 lines of symmetry

Find all of the lines of symmetry in each regular polygon.

B

4 lines of symmetry

Count the lines of symmetry.

C

3 lines of symmetry

Count the lines of symmetry.

EXAMPLE 3 Social Studies Application

Find all of the lines of symmetry in each flag design.

A Antigua and Barbuda

1 line of symmetry

B Macedonia

2 lines of symmetry

C Norway

1 line of symmetry

D Lesotho

There are no lines of symmetry.

A figure has **rotational symmetry** if it can be rotated about a point by an angle less than 360° so that it coincides with itself. When the pinwheel is rotated 72° about its center, the image looks the same as the original pinweel. So the pinwheel has rotational symmetry.

458   Chapter 8   Geometric Relationships

EXAMPLE 4 **Identifying Rotational Symmetry**

Tell whether each figure has rotational symmetry.

A. *Each time the figure is rotated 72° about its center, the image looks like the original figure.*
The figure has rotational symmetry.

B. *For any rotation less than 360°, the image never looks like the original figure.*
The figure does not have rotational symmetry.

Think and Discuss

1. **Explain** how you can use your knowledge of reflection to create a figure that has a line of symmetry.
2. **Determine** whether all hexagons have six lines of symmetry.
3. **Explain** why the angle of rotation must be less than 360° when determining whether a figure has rotational symmetry.

8-11 Exercises

GUIDED PRACTICE

See Example 1 — Determine whether each dashed line appears to be a line of symmetry.

1.
2.
3.

See Example 2 — Find all of the lines of symmetry in each regular polygon.

4.
5.
6.

See Example 3 — Find all of the lines of symmetry in each design.

7.
8.

See Example 4 Tell whether each figure has rotational symmetry.

9. 10. 11.

INDEPENDENT PRACTICE

See Example 1 Determine whether each dashed line appears to be a line of symmetry.

12. 13. 14.

See Example 2 Find all of the lines of symmetry in each regular polygon.

15. 16. 17.

See Example 3 Find all of the lines of symmetry in each object.

18. 19.

See Example 4 Tell whether each figure has rotational symmetry.

20. 21. 22.

PRACTICE AND PROBLEM SOLVING

Extra Practice
See page EP17.

23. How many lines of symmetry does an equilateral triangle have? an isosceles triangle? a scalene triangle? Draw diagrams to support your answer.

24. Round objects can also have rotational symmetry. Which of the circular items below does not have rotational symmetry? Explain.

25. Draw a figure that has both line symmetry and rotational symmetry.

460   Chapter 8   Geometric Relationships

Music Link

Many cultures play music on unique instruments. You might hear the sun drum or turtle drum in Native American music. In music made by people from the Appalachian Mountains, you might hear the strains of a dulcimer.

26. Determine whether the dashed line in each drawing is a line of symmetry.

a.

b.

27. Write About It The turtle drum is a regular octagon. How can you find all of the lines of symmetry in a regular polygon?

28. Challenge A student drew a drum in the shape of an octagon on a grid. What are the coordinates of the vertices of the unfolded half of the drum drawing if the fold shown is a line of symmetry?

Test Prep and Spiral Review

29. Multiple Choice How many lines of symmetry are in a rectangle that is NOT a square?

Ⓐ 1   Ⓑ 2   Ⓒ 4   Ⓓ 6

30. Short Response Draw the lines of symmetry in the figure.

Compare. Write <, >, or =. (Previous Course)

31. 4,897,204 ▨ 4,895,190

32. 133,099,588 ▨ 133,099,600

Find each sum or difference. (Lesson 3-3)

33. 30 − 5.32   **34.** 80.37 + 15.125   **35.** 100 − 25.65   **36.** 200.6 + 62.78

Hands-on Lab 8-11: Create Tessellations

Use with Lesson 8-11

Learn It Online
Lab Resources Online go.hrw.com, keyword MR10 Lab8

A repeating arrangement of one or more shapes that completely covers a plane, with no gaps or overlaps, is called a *tessellation*. You can make your own tessellations using paper, scissors, and tape.

Activity

1 Start with a square.

Use scissors to cut out a shape from one side of the square.

Translate the shape you cut out to the opposite side of the square and tape the two pieces together.

Trace this new shape to form at least two rows of a tessellation. You will need to translate, rotate, or reflect the shape.

2 Start again with a square.

Use scissors to cut out shapes and move them to the opposite sides of the square.

Trace this new shape to form at least two rows of a tessellation. You will need to translate, rotate, or reflect the shape.

Chapter 8 Geometric Relationships

3 You can base a tessellating shape on other polygons.

Try starting with a hexagon.

Use scissors to cut out a shape from one side of the hexagon. Translate the shape to the opposite side of the hexagon.

Try repeating these steps on other sides of the hexagon.

Trace the new shape to form a tessellation. You will need to translate, rotate, or reflect the shape.

Think and Discuss

1. Tell whether you can make a tessellation out of circles.
2. Tell whether any polygon can make a tessellation.

Try This

Make each tessellation shape described. Then form two rows of a tessellation.

1.
2.
3.

Tell whether each shape can be used to form a tessellation.

4.
5.
6.

7. Cut out a polygon, and then change it by cutting out a part of one side. Translate the cut-out part to the opposite side. Can your shape form a tessellation? Make a drawing to show your answer.

8-11 Hands-On Lab

Ready To Go On?

Quiz for Lessons 8-9 Through 8-11

8-9 Congruent Polygons

Decide whether the figures in each pair are congruent. If not, explain.

1.

2. 2 in. / 3 in.

3. Marcus needs a lid for his box. Which lid should he buy?

8-10 Transformations

Tell whether each is a translation, rotation, or reflection.

4.

5.

Draw each transformation.

6. Draw a 180° clockwise rotation about the point.

7. Draw a translation.

8-11 Symmetry

Determine whether each dashed line appears to be a line of symmetry. Then tell whether the figure has rotational symmetry.

8.

9.

10.

464   Chapter 8   Geometric Relationships

Real-World Connections

CHAPTER 8

Dresden Suspension Bridge The Dresden Suspension Bridge crosses the Muskingum River in central Ohio. Since its completion in 1914, it has been considered an important landmark. The structure is an example of an eyebar suspension bridge and is one of the few bridges of this type ever built in the United States.

The figure shows the support structure of one of the bridge's towers.

1. Angle *CAB* is a right angle. Classify ∠*CAG* as acute, right, obtuse, or straight. Explain how you know.

2. Name two pairs of vertical angles in the structure.

3. Angles *CEH* and *HEF* are complementary, and m∠*CEH* = 50°.

    a. Find m∠*HEF*.

    b. Angles *HEF* and *HFE* are congruent. Show how you can use this information to find m∠*EHF*.

    c. Classify triangle *EHF* based on its angles.

4. Consider the polygon *CGDFE*.

    a. What is the name for this type of polygon? Does it appear to be a regular polygon? Why or why not?

    b. What is the sum of the interior angles of the polygon?

5. How many lines of symmetry (if any) does the structure have? Sketch the structure and draw any lines of symmetry.

Game Time

Tangrams

A tangram is an ancient Chinese puzzle. The seven shapes that make this square can be arranged to make many other figures. Copy the shapes that make this square, and then cut them apart. See if you can arrange the pieces to make the figures below.

A complete copy of Tangram puzzle pieces is available online.

Learn It Online
Game Time Extra go.hrw.com,
keyword MR10 Games

466   Chapter 8   Geometric Relationships

Materials
- gift bag
- scissors
- tape
- white paper
- card stock
- glue
- markers

It's in the Bag!

PROJECT ## Geometry Grab Bag

Use a recycled gift bag to make a journal for your geometry notes.

Directions

1. Cut away the sides and bottom of the bag. This will leave two rectangles with handles attached. **Figure A**

2. Place the two halves of the bag face down and tape them together as shown, leaving a small space between them. This will form the covers of your journal. **Figure B**

3. Cut several sheets of white paper and the card stock so that they are all the same size and slightly smaller than the covers of the journal. Staple them together, with a piece of card stock on the top and bottom of the stack. **Figure C**

4. Glue the top piece of card stock to the inside front cover. Glue the bottom piece of card stock to the inside back cover.

Taking Note of the Math

Write the number and title of the chapter on the front of the journal. Then use the pages of the journal to take notes on angles, polygons, and transformations.

It's in the Bag! **467**

CHAPTER 8 Study Guide: Review

Vocabulary

acute angle 411	line symmetry 457	right angle 411
acute triangle 429	obtuse angle 411	right triangle 429
adjacent angles 416	obtuse triangle 429	rotation 453
angle 410	parallel lines 420	rotational symmetry 458
complementary angles .417	parallelogram 434	scalene triangle 430
congruent angles 416	perpendicular lines 420	skew lines 420
congruent figures 450	plane 406	square 434
congruent line segments 430	point 406	straight angle 411
diagonal 438	polygon 438	supplementary angles ..417
equilateral triangle 430	quadrilateral 434	transformation 453
isosceles triangle 430	ray 407	translation 453
line 406	rectangle 434	trapezoid 434
line of reflection 453	reflection 453	vertex 410
line of symmetry 457	regular polygon 438	vertical angles 416
line segment 407	rhombus 434	

Complete the sentences below with vocabulary words from the list above.

1. A quadrilateral with exactly two parallel sides is called a(n) ___?___.
2. A(n) ___?___ is a closed plane figure formed by three or more line segments.

EXAMPLES | EXERCISES

8-1 Building Blocks of Geometry (pp. 406–409)

■ Use the diagram.

Name a line. $\overleftrightarrow{RS}$
Name a line segment. $\overline{ST}$

Use the diagram.

3. Name two lines.
4. Name a ray.

8-2 Measuring and Classifying Angles (pp. 410–413)

■ Classify each angle as acute, right, obtuse, or straight.

m∠A = 80°
80° < 90°, so ∠A is acute.

Classify each angle as acute, right, obtuse, or straight.

5. m∠x = 60°
6. m∠x = 100°
7. m∠x = 45°
8. m∠x = 180°

468 Chapter 8 Geometric Relationships

EXAMPLES

EXERCISES

8-3 Angle Relationships (pp. 416–419)

- Find the unknown angle measure.

  m∠a = 40° *Vertical angles are congruent.*

Find each unknown angle measure.

9. (b, 63°)

10. (d, 82°)

8-4 Classifying Pairs of Lines (pp. 420–423)

- Classify each pair of lines.

  The red lines are parallel.
  The blue lines are perpendicular.

Classify each pair of lines.

11. (A, B, E, F)

12. (D, E, H, J)

8-5 Triangles (pp. 429–432)

- Classify the triangle using the given information.

  m∠G + 45° + 55° = 180°
  m∠G = 80°, so △EFG is an acute triangle.

Classify the triangle using the given information.

13. Triangle ABC: AB = 3 cm, BC = 4 cm, AC = 6 cm

14. Right triangle with two congruent legs

8-6 Quadrilaterals (pp. 434–437)

- Give the most exact name for the figure.

  The most exact name is rectangle.

Give the most exact name for the figure.

15.

16.

8-7 Polygons (pp. 438–441)

- Name the polygon and tell whether it appears to be regular or not regular.

  It is a regular octagon.

Name each polygon and tell whether it appears to be regular or not regular.

17. YIELD

18. MAIN STREET

Lesson Tutorials Online my.hrw.com

EXAMPLES

EXERCISES

8-8 Geometric Patterns (pp. 444–447)

■ Identify a possible pattern. Use the pattern to draw the missing figure.

The missing figure might be ⌂⌂.

Identify a possible pattern. Use the pattern to draw the missing figure.

19. △   △△   ?   △△△△

20. ○   ○○○   ?   (triangular stack of circles)

8-9 Congruent Polygons (pp. 450–452)

■ Decide whether the figures are congruent. If not, explain.

These figures are congruent.

Decide whether the figures in each pair are congruent. If not, explain.

21.

22.

8-10 Transformations (pp. 453–456)

■ Tell whether the transformation is a translation, rotation, or reflection.

The transformation is a reflection.

■ Draw the transformation.
Draw a horizontal reflection.

Tell whether the transformation is a translation, rotation, or reflection.

23.

Draw each transformation.

24. Draw a translation.

25. Draw a 90° clockwise rotation about the point.

8-11 Symmetry (pp. 457–461)

■ Determine whether the dashed line appears to be a line of symmetry. Does the figure have rotational symmetry?

The line appears to be a line of symmetry. The figure does not have rotational symmetry.

Determine whether the dashed line appears to be a line of symmetry. Then tell whether the figure has rotational symmetry.

26.

27.

470 Chapter 8 Geometric Relationships

Chapter Test

CHAPTER 8

Classify each pair of angles or lines.

1.
2.
3.

Classify the triangles by angle and side measures.

4. 25 cm, 20 cm, 25 cm
5. 4 ft, 5 ft, 3 ft
6. 16 km, 16 km, 16 km

Find the unknown angle measure.

7. 65°, a
8. b, 57°
9. 134°, c

10. Triangle ABC has sides of equal length. The measure of $\angle A$ is 60°, and the measure of $\angle B$ is 60°. What is the measure of $\angle C$? Classify the triangle based on the measures of the angles and lengths of the sides.

Draw each transformation.

11. Reflect across the line.

12. Rotate 270° clockwise about the point.

13. Translate $\frac{3}{4}$ in. right.

Determine whether each dashed line appears to be a line of symmetry. Then tell whether the figure has rotational symmetry.

14.
15.
16.

Decide whether the figures in each pair are congruent. If not, explain.

17.
18.

Identify a possible pattern. Use your pattern to draw the next figure.

19.
20.

Chapter 8 Test 471

Standardized Test Prep

Cumulative Assessment, Chapters 1–8

Multiple Choice

1. Which of the following is an example of an obtuse angle?

2. Hillary buys 6 flower bouquets for table decorations. Each bouquet costs $16. The sales tax is 6.5%. What is the total cost of her purchase?

   F $17.03
   G $95.94
   H $101.70
   J $102.24

3. Two angles are complementary. If the measure of one angle is 36°, what is the measure of the second angle?

   A 36°
   B 54°
   C 64°
   D 144°

4. Steve, Ashley, and Jeremy work at the same restaurant. Steve works every 4 days. Ashley works every 6 days. Jeremy works every 3 days. If on May 1 they are all working at the restaurant, what is the next date that the three of them will work together?

   F May 6
   G May 13
   H May 18
   J May 24

5. Terri is $60\frac{1}{2}$ inches tall. Steve is $65\frac{1}{4}$ inches tall. What is the difference, in inches, in their heights?

   A $4\frac{1}{4}$
   B $4\frac{1}{2}$
   C $4\frac{3}{4}$
   D $5\frac{1}{4}$

6. In the figure below, which of the following angle pairs are NOT adjacent?

   F ∠1 and ∠2
   G ∠5 and ∠8
   H ∠1 and ∠3
   J ∠6 and ∠7

7. Reggie is a long-distance runner. His daily $2\frac{1}{2}$-hour practice is divided evenly into three areas: warm-up, running, and cool-down. How many minutes total does Reggie spend warming up and cooling down each day at practice?

   A 100 min
   B 75 min
   C 60 min
   D 50 min

8. The arrow is being reflected over the black line. Which of the following correctly shows the arrow after it is reflected over the black line?

472 Chapter 8 Geometric Relationships

9. Shown below is a map of specific areas at Boone Park. Which of the following is located at the point (7, 6) on the map?

- A. Playground
- B. Parking lot
- C. Pond
- D. Soccer field

10. What is the most descriptive name for the figure below?

- F. Rhombus
- G. Rectangle
- H. Square
- J. Parallelogram

HOT TIP! Draw a picture to help in problem solving situations involving plane figures. Be sure to accurately label your drawings.

Gridded Response

11. What is the value of 9^3?

12. The distance around a square flower box is 128.4 inches. How many inches long is one side of the flower box?

13. Maggie tutors Anne after school. Maggie charges $7 per hour. If Anne pays Maggie $84, how many hours did Maggie tutor Anne?

14. There are 120 students trying out for the school play. Only 5% of those trying out will have a speaking part. Write this percent as a fraction in lowest terms.

Short Response

S1. Identify the figure shown.

Draw a figure that is congruent to this figure. Explain why your figure is congruent to the given figure.

S2. The table shows ten distances hit by a baseball player.

Distances (ft)				
334	360	350	343	330
320	265	327	335	270

Is the mean distance of this player's hits more than or less than the median distance? Explain how you found your answer.

S3. Triangle JKL is a right triangle.

a. What are the angle measurements of ∠JKM, ∠KLM, ∠KML, and ∠KMJ?

b. Name two other triangles. Classify these triangles by their angles. Explain your classifications.

Extended Response

E1. A student draws a trapezoid on a coordinate grid. The coordinates are A (3, 1), B (2, 2), C (2, 3), and D (3, 4).

a. Plot these points on a grid and connect the points.

b. Draw a line that passes through points A and D. Reflect the trapezoid over that line, label the points on the new trapezoid, and give the new coordinates.

c. What new plane figure is created? Does this new figure have line symmetry? Explain your answer.

Cumulative Assessment, Chapters 1–8

CHAPTER 9
Measurement and Geometry

9A Customary and Metric Measurement
- LAB Select and Use Appropriate Measuring Tools
- 9-1 Understanding Customary Units of Measure
- 9-2 Understanding Metric Units of Measure
- 9-3 Converting Customary Units
- 9-4 Converting Metric Units
- 9-5 Time and Temperature

9B Measurement and Geometric Figures
- 9-6 Finding Angle Measures in Polygons
- 9-7 Perimeter
- LAB Explore Circumference
- 9-8 Circles and Circumference
- LAB Construct Circle Graphs

Chapter Focus
- Use ratios to convert customary and metric units.
- Solve problems involving measurement and formulas.

Why Learn This?

Measurements help us describe and compare objects. For example, the Georgia Aquarium contains more than 8 million gallons of water, or enough to fill more than 12 Olympic-sized swimming pools.

Learn It Online
Chapter Project Online go.hrw.com,
keyword MR10 Ch9

Are You Ready?

Vocabulary

Choose the best term from the list to complete each sentence.

1. If you find how heavy an object is, you are finding the ___?___.
2. A ___?___ is used to measure an angle.
3. If you find the amount a container can hold when filled, you are finding the ___?___ of the container.
4. A ___?___ is an equation that shows two equivalent ratios.
5. A parallelogram with four right angles is a ___?___.

capacity
length
proportion
protractor
rectangle
temperature
weight

Complete these exercises to review skills you will need for this chapter.

Write and Read Decimals

Write each decimal in standard form.

6. 12 and 4 tenths
7. 150 and 18 hundredths
8. 1 thousand, 60 and 5 tenths

Simplify Fractions

Write each fraction in simplest form.

9. $\frac{8}{12}$
10. $\frac{4}{20}$
11. $\frac{6}{8}$
12. $\frac{8}{16}$

Write Ratios

Write each ratio three different ways.

13. Hearts to rectangles
14. Rectangles to circles

15. Triangles to squares
16. Hexagons to triangles

Solve Proportions

Solve for n.

17. $\frac{2}{n} = \frac{4}{10}$
18. $\frac{3}{8} = \frac{6}{n}$
19. $\frac{n}{7} = \frac{8}{14}$
20. $\frac{5}{9} = \frac{n}{18}$

Measurement and Geometry

CHAPTER 9

Study Guide: Preview

Where You've Been

Previously, you

- performed simple conversions within the metric system.
- used angle measurements to classify angles.
- classified polygons according to their sides.

In This Chapter

You will study

- converting measures within the same measurement system.
- identifying relationships involving angles in triangles and quadrilaterals.
- solving problems involving perimeter.
- describing the relationship between the radius, diameter, and circumference of a circle.

Where You're Going

You can use the skills learned in this chapter

- to understand the relationship between the perimeter and the area of a polygon.
- to determine how much fencing to buy to enclose an animal pen or garden.

Key Vocabulary/Vocabulario

center of a circle	centro de un círculo
circle	círculo
circumference	circunferencia
customary system	sistema usual de medidas
diameter	diámetro
metric system	sistema métrico
perimeter	perímetro
pi	pi
radius	radio

Vocabulary Connections

To become familiar with some of the vocabulary terms in the chapter, consider the following. You may refer to the chapter, the glossary, or a dictionary if you like.

1. The word *perimeter* has the prefix *peri-*, which means "all around or surrounding," and the root *meter*, which is the basic unit of length in the metric system. What do you think the **perimeter** of an object is?

2. The word *circumference* has the prefix *circum-*, which means "around a circle." What do you think you will measure if you find the **circumference** of a circle?

3. The word *radius* is related to the word *radiate*, which means to move outward in all directions from the center. What do you think the **radius** of a circle is?

4. The word *diameter* has the prefix *dia-*, which means "across." What do you think you will measure if you find the **diameter** of a circle?

Reading and Writing Math

CHAPTER 9

Study Strategy: Use Multiple Representations

Math concepts can be explained using multiple representations. As you study, pay attention to any tables, lists, graphs, diagrams, symbols, and words used to describe a concept.

From Lesson 8-4

In this example, the concept of classifying lines is explained using words, diagrams, symbols, and examples.

Words	Diagrams	Symbols/Examples
Intersecting lines are lines that cross at one common point.	(lines WX and YZ crossing)	Line YZ intersects line WX. $\overleftrightarrow{YZ}$ intersects $\overleftrightarrow{WX}$.
Parallel lines are lines in the same plane that never intersect.	(lines AB and ML parallel)	Line AB is parallel to line ML. $\overleftrightarrow{AB} \parallel \overleftrightarrow{ML}$
Perpendicular lines intersect to form 90° angles, or right angles.	(lines RS and TU perpendicular)	Line RS is perpendicular to line TU. $\overleftrightarrow{RS} \perp \overleftrightarrow{TU}$
Skew lines are lines that lie in different planes. They are neither parallel nor intersecting.	(box with lines AB and ML)	Line AB and line ML are skew. $\overleftrightarrow{AB}$ and $\overleftrightarrow{ML}$ are skew.

Try This

1. Classify one of the types of triangles in Lesson 8-5 using the four different representations shown above.
2. Review your notes from the previous chapter. Which different representations did you use to explain how to classify lines? Which representation do you prefer? Why?

Hands-on Lab 9-1

Select and Use Appropriate Measuring Tools

Use with Lessons 9-1 and 9-2

Learn It Online
Lab Resources Online go.hrw.com,
keyword: MR10 Lab9 Go

Activity 1

1. Measure the length of a paper clip to the nearest inch. Select an inch or millimeter ruler to measure the length of the paper clip.

2. Count the small markings from the first line on the left to the line that shows 1 inch. How many are there?

   Measure the paper clip to the nearest sixteenth of an inch.

3. Measure a pencil to the nearest fourth of an inch. Then measure the pencil to the nearest eighth of an inch.

4. Now using the metric ruler, measure the length of this line segment to the nearest centimeter.

5. Count the small markings from the first line on the left to the line that shows 1 centimeter. How many are there?

6. Each line shows 1 millimeter. How long is the line segment in millimeters?

7. Measure a pencil to the nearest centimeter. Then measure the pencil to the nearest millimeter.

Think and Discuss

1. Name 5 items that would be appropriate to measure with a ruler.

2. *Precision* is the level of detail an instrument can measure. The smaller the unit of measure on the instrument, the more precise the measurement will be. Is the measurement in ❶ or ❷ more precise? Explain.

Try This

Use a ruler to measure each object to the nearest sixteenth of an inch and to the nearest millimeter.

1. your pinky
2. your desktop
3. your shoe

478 Chapter 9 Measurement and Geometry

Activity 2

1 Find the weight of a bunch of grapes. Use a customary or metric scale to weigh the grapes.

What is the weight of the grapes in pounds?

What is the weight of the grapes in kilograms?

Pounds **Kilograms**

2 What is the weight of your math book in pounds and in kilograms?

Think and Discuss

1. Which is heavier, 1 pound of grapes or 1 kilogram of grapes?

Try This

Use a scale to measure each object in pounds and kilograms.

1. your shoe
2. 5 pencils
3. a tissue box

Activity 3

1 Use a measuring cup that shows fluid ounces and milliliters. Fill the cup with water up to the 8 fluid ounces mark. About how many milliliters is this?

2 Fill a measuring cup with 150 milliliters of water. About how many fluid ounces is this?

Think and Discuss

1. Explain how you can use a measuring cup and a metric scale to find the mass of 2 cups of water.

2. About how many milliliters are in 2 cups?

Try This

1. Place 25 tablespoons of water in a measuring cup. How many fluid ounces is this? how many milliliters?

2. Find the mass of 2 cups of water.

9-1 Hands-On Lab **479**

9-1 Understanding Customary Units of Measure

Learn to understand and select appropriate customary units of measure.

If you do not have an instrument, such as a ruler, scale, or measuring cup, you can estimate the length, weight, and capacity of an object by using a benchmark.

The **customary system** is the measurement system often used in the United States. It includes units of measurement for length, weight, and capacity.

Vocabulary

customary system

Customary Units of Length

Unit	Abbreviation	Benchmark
Inch	in.	Width of your thumb
Foot	ft	Distance from your elbow to your wrist
Yard	yd	Width of a classroom door
Mile	mi	Four times around a track

EXAMPLE 1 Choosing Appropriate Units of Length

What unit of measure provides the best estimate? Explain.

A A table is about 4 ___?___ long.
A table is about 4 ft long.

Think: The length of a table is about 4 times the distance from your elbow to your wrist.

B A ceiling is about 3 ___?___ high.
A ceiling is about 3 yd high.

Think: The height of a ceiling is about 3 times the width of a classroom door.

Customary Units of Weight

Unit	Abbreviation	Benchmark
Ounce	oz	A slice of bread
Pound	lb	A loaf of bread
Ton	T	A small car

EXAMPLE 2 Choosing Appropriate Units of Weight

What unit of measure provides the best estimate? Explain.

A A female elephant can weigh up to 4 ___?___.
A female elephant can weigh up to 4 T.

Think: An elephant has a weight of about 4 small cars.

What unit of measure provides the best estimate? Explain.

B A remote control weighs about 5 ___?___.

Think: A remote control has a weight of about 5 slices of bread.

A remote control weighs about 5 oz.

Capacity deals with volume, or the amount a container can hold.

Customary Units of Capacity

Unit	Abbreviation	Benchmark
Fluid Ounce	fl oz	A spoonful
Cup	c	A glass of juice
Pint	pt	A small bottle of salad dressing
Quart	qt	A small container of paint
Gallon	gal	A large container of milk

EXAMPLE 3 Choosing Appropriate Units of Capacity

What unit of measure provides the best estimate? Explain.

A bathtub holds about 50 ___?___ of water.

Think: A bathtub holds about 50 large containers of milk.

A bathtub holds about 50 gal of water.

Inch rulers are usually separated into sixteenths of an inch.

EXAMPLE 4 Finding Measurements

Helpful Hint

All measurements are approximate. Their precision depends on the tools being used, and on how the tools are used.

Use a ruler to measure the length of the golf tee to the nearest half, fourth, or eighth inch.

The golf tee is between $3\frac{1}{4}$ in. and $3\frac{3}{8}$ in. It is closer to $3\frac{1}{4}$ in.

The length of the golf tee is about $3\frac{1}{4}$ in.

Think and Discuss

1. **Give an example** of when you might need to estimate the weight of an object.

2. **Give an example** of when you might need to estimate the capacity of a container.

9-1 Exercises

Learn It Online
Homework Help Online go.hrw.com,
keyword MR10 9-1
Exercises 1–8, 9, 11, 13, 21

GUIDED PRACTICE

See Example 1 — **What unit of measure provides the best estimate? Explain.**
1. A pencil is about 7 __?__ long.

See Example 2
2. A tube of toothpaste weighs about 8 __?__.

See Example 3
3. A swimming pool holds about 20,000 __?__ of water.

See Example 4
4. Use a ruler to measure the length of the key to the nearest half, fourth, or eighth inch.

INDEPENDENT PRACTICE

See Example 1 — **What unit of measure provides the best estimate? Explain.**
5. The distance from New York City to Boston is about 200 __?__.

See Example 2
6. A small dog weighs about 12 __?__.

See Example 3
7. A pot for cooking soup holds about 10 __?__ of water.

See Example 4
8. Use a ruler to measure the length of the green bean to the nearest half, fourth, or eighth inch.

PRACTICE AND PROBLEM SOLVING

Extra Practice
See page EP19.

Which unit of measure would you use for each? Justify your answer.

9. the height of a flagpole
10. the width of a CD case
11. the capacity of a car's gas tank
12. the capacity of a baby's bottle
13. the weight of an egg
14. the weight of a chair

Use benchmarks to estimate each measure.

15. the width of your math textbook
16. the width of an armchair
17. the capacity of a flower pot
18. the weight of an alarm clock

19. **Critical Thinking** When would you choose to measure to the nearest eighth inch rather than the nearest fourth inch?

482 Chapter 9 Measurement and Geometry

History

Alfred the Great was one of the most famous Anglo-Saxon kings. He defended England from Viking raids and helped found the British Navy. He is the only English monarch to be awarded the label of "the Great."

Find the weight of the object to the nearest half, fourth, or eighth of a pound.

20.

21.

22. **History** The early Saxon kings of England wore a sash around their waist that they used as a benchmark for measuring length. The name of the sash eventually became the name of one of the customary units of length. What unit of length did the sash represent: the inch, foot, yard, or mile? Explain.

Find how much liquid is in each container to the nearest half, fourth, or eighth of a cup or quart.

23.

24.

25. **Write a Problem** Write a problem that can be answered using a pen as a benchmark.

26. **Write About It** Make up your own personal benchmarks for an inch, a cup, and a pound.

27. **Challenge** Look up the words *rod*, *peck*, and *dram* in a dictionary. Tell what each one is and what it is used to measure.

Test Prep and Spiral Review

28. **Multiple Choice** Which is the best estimate for the width of a classroom?

    Ⓐ 30 in. Ⓑ 30 ft Ⓒ 30 yd Ⓓ 30 mi

29. **Multiple Choice** Madison needs to buy a turkey to feed 12 people. What weight turkey should she buy?

    Ⓕ 16 lb Ⓖ 16 oz Ⓗ 16 c Ⓘ 16 T

List all the factors of each number. (Lesson 4-2)

30. 24   31. 45   32. 56   33. 80

Two angles of a triangle are given. Classify the triangle. (Lesson 8-5)

34. 55°, 35°   35. 18°, 82°   36. 47°, 26°   37. 95°, 45°

9-1 Understanding Customary Units of Measure

9-2 Understanding Metric Units of Measure

Learn to understand and select appropriate metric units of measure.

Vocabulary

metric system

The **metric system** of measurement is used almost everywhere in the world. Its advantage over the customary system is that all metric units are related by the decimal system.

The shortest Olympic track race is 100 meters. Use the length of your classroom as a benchmark. A classroom is about 10 meters long, so a 100-meter race is about the length of 10 classrooms.

Metric Units of Length

Unit	Abbreviation	Relation to a Meter	Benchmark
Millimeter	mm	0.001 m	Thickness of a dime
Centimeter	cm	0.01 m	Width of a fingernail
Decimeter	dm	0.1 m	Width of a CD case
Meter	m	1 m	Width of a single bed
Kilometer	km	1,000 m	Distance around a city block

EXAMPLE 1 Choosing Appropriate Units of Length

What unit of measure provides the best estimate? Explain.

A A TV remote control is about 19 ___?___ long.
Think: A TV remote control is about 19 times the width of a fingernail.
A TV remote control is about 19 cm long.

B A school auditorium is about 40 ___?___ long.
Think: An auditorium is about 40 times the width of a single bed.
A school auditorium is about 40 m long.

Metric Units of Mass

Unit	Abbreviation	Relation to a Gram	Benchmark
Milligram	mg	0.001 g	Very small insect
Gram	g	1 g	Paper clip
Kilogram	kg	1,000 g	Textbook

EXAMPLE 2 **Choosing Appropriate Units of Mass**

What unit of measure provides the best estimate? Explain.

A sandwich has a mass of about 400 ___?___.

Think: A sandwich has a mass of about 400 paperclips.

A sandwich has a mass of about 400 g.

Metric Units of Capacity

Unit	Abbreviation	Relation to a Liter	Benchmark
Milliliter	mL	0.001 L	Drop of water
Liter	L	1 L	Water pitcher

EXAMPLE 3 **Choosing Appropriate Units of Capacity**

What unit of measure provides the best estimate? Explain.

A bucket has a capacity of about 10 ___?___.

Think: A bucket has a capacity of about 10 water pitchers.

A bucket has a capacity of about 10 L.

EXAMPLE 4 **Finding Measurements**

Use a ruler to measure the length of the barrette to the nearest centimeter.

The barrette is between 6 and 7 cm. It is closer to 7 cm than 6 cm.

The length of the barrette is about 7 cm.

Think and Discuss

1. Explain how you would estimate the length of the board in your classroom using the barrette in Example 4 as a benchmark.

9-2 Exercises

Learn It Online
Homework Help Online go.hrw.com,
keyword MR10 9-2
Exercises 1–10, 11, 13, 15, 17

GUIDED PRACTICE

See Example **1** — What unit of measure provides the best estimate? Explain.
1. The height of a doorknob from the floor is about 1 __?__.

See Example **2** — 2. A greeting card has a mass of about 28 __?__.

See Example **3** — 3. A kitchen sink holds about 20 __?__ of water.
4. A bowl holds about 350 __?__ of soup.

See Example **4** — 5. Use a ruler to measure the length of the party favor to the nearest centimeter.

INDEPENDENT PRACTICE

See Example **1** — What unit of measure provides the best estimate? Explain.
6. The width of a desk is about 10 __?__.

See Example **2** — 7. The mass of a packet of sugar is about 3 __?__.

See Example **3** — 8. A bathtub holds about 50 __?__ of water.
9. A cooking pot holds about 1.5 __?__.

See Example **4** — 10. Use a ruler to measure the length of the feather to the nearest centimeter.

PRACTICE AND PROBLEM SOLVING

Extra Practice
See page EP19.

11. **Estimation** Felipe is estimating the length of his baseball bat using a benchmark. He gets an estimate of about 10 __?__. Which benchmark was Felipe most likely using: the width of his fist, the length of his foot, the distance from his elbow to his fingertip, or the length of his baseball cap?

486 Chapter 9 Measurement and Geometry

Which unit of measure would you use for each? Justify your answer.

12. the length of a movie screen
13. the length of a walk around a campus
14. the mass of a single flower
15. the mass of a CD case
16. the capacity of a jug
17. the capacity of a thimble

18. **Multi-Step** A shipment of DVD players contains 8 cartons. Each carton has 6 players in it. A single player weighs 1,500 g. All the players can be unpacked and placed on a shelf in the stockroom. A sign above the shelf reads "Maximum weight 80 ___?___." What is the missing unit of measure on the sign above the shelf?

19. **Physics** An empty balloon weighs 4.5 g. A filled balloon weighs 5.3 g. Find the mass of the air in the balloon. Does air have mass? Explain.

20. **What's the Error?** Ellis made a travel brochure for his social studies project. He wrote that the common highway speed in Canada is 8,000 km per hour. What error did Ellis make?

21. **Write About It** Measure the dimensions of a shoebox and estimate the mass of the box when it contains a pair of shoes. Describe which metric units of measure you used.

22. **Challenge** Jermaine is trying to limit the amount of fat in his diet to 50 g per day. At breakfast, Jermaine has one serving of milk, two servings of peanut butter, and a serving of apple, which has almost no fat. If his lunch and dinner contain the same amount of fat as his breakfast, is Jermaine likely to meet his goal for the day? Explain.

240 mL serving
2.5 g fat

16 g serving
8 g fat

Test Prep and Spiral Review

23. **Multiple Choice** Which unit could NOT reasonably be used to measure something involving a home aquarium?

    (A) A liter   (B) A meter   (C) A kilometer   (D) A kilogram

24. **Short Response** What metric unit of measure provides the best estimate of the width of a bedroom window? Explain your answer.

Find the greatest common factor (GCF) of each set of numbers. (Lesson 4-3)

25. 16 and 24
26. 84 and 28
27. 48 and 112
28. 5, 10, and 105

Find the least common multiple (LCM). (Lesson 5-1)

29. 4 and 9
30. 6 and 11
31. 15 and 20
32. 2, 8, and 10

9-3 Converting Customary Units

Learn to convert customary units of measure.

Jacques Freitag is the first athlete to win gold medals at the International Association of Athletic Federations (IAAF) Youth, Junior, and Senior Championships. His personal best in the high jump is over 93 inches. How many feet is this?

You can use the information in the table below to convert one customary unit to another.

Common Customary Measurements		
Length	Weight	Capacity
1 foot = 12 inches	1 pound = 16 ounces	1 cup = 8 fluid ounces
1 yard = 36 inches	1 ton = 2,000 pounds	1 pint = 2 cups
1 yard = 3 feet		1 quart = 2 pints
1 mile = 5,280 feet		1 quart = 4 cups
1 mile = 1,760 yards		1 gallon = 4 quarts
		1 gallon = 16 cups
		1 gallon = 128 fluid ounces

When you convert one unit of measure to another, you can multiply by a conversion factor.

EXAMPLE 1 Using a Conversion Factor

A Convert 93 inches to feet.

Set up a conversion factor.

93 in. × $\frac{1 \text{ ft}}{12 \text{ in.}}$

93 in. = 7.75 ft

Think: inches to feet—1 ft = 12 in., so use $\frac{1 \text{ ft}}{12 \text{ in.}}$. Multiply 93 in. by the conversion factor. Cancel the common unit, in.

Caution!
Write the unit you are converting *to* in the numerator and the unit you are converting *from* in the denominator.

B Convert 2 pounds to ounces.

Set up a conversion factor.

2 lb × $\frac{16 \text{ oz}}{1 \text{ lb}}$ = 32 oz

2 lb = 32 oz

Think: ounces to pounds—16 oz = 1 lb, so use $\frac{16 \text{ oz}}{1 \text{ lb}}$. Multiply 2 lb by the conversion factor. Cancel the common unit, lb.

Another way to convert units is to use proportions.

EXAMPLE 2 Converting Units of Measure by Using Proportions

Remember!
A proportion shows that two ratios are equivalent. Use a conversion factor for one of the ratios. See p. 352.

Convert 48 quarts to gallons.

48 qt = ■ gal

$\dfrac{4 \text{ qt}}{1 \text{ gal}} = \dfrac{48 \text{ qt}}{x \text{ gal}}$ *1 gallon is 4 quarts. Write a proportion. Use a variable for the value you are trying to find.*

$4 \cdot x = 1 \cdot 48$ *The cross products are equal.*
$4x = 48$ *Divide both sides by 4 to undo the multiplication.*
$x = 12$

48 qt = 12 gal

EXAMPLE 3 PROBLEM SOLVING APPLICATION

The Washington Monument is about 185 yards tall. This height is almost equal to the length of two football fields. About how many feet is this?

1. Understand the Problem

The **answer** will be the height of the Washington Monument in feet.

List the **important information:**

- The height of the Washington Monument is about 185 yards.

2. Make a Plan

Make a table from the information to show the number of feet in 1, 2, and 3 yards. Then find the number of feet in *n* yards.

3. Solve

Yards	Feet
1	3
2	6
3	9
n	3n

Look for a pattern.
$1 \cdot 3 = 3$
$2 \cdot 3 = 6$
$3 \cdot 3 = 9$
$n \cdot 3 = 3n$

$185 \cdot 3 = 555$ so, the Washington Monument is about 555 ft tall.

4. Look Back

Round 185 to 200. Then multiply by 3.
$200 \cdot 3 = 600$
The answer is reasonable because 555 is close to 600.

Think and Discuss

1. Explain how to set up a proportion to convert miles to yards.

9-3 Exercises

Learn It Online
Homework Help Online go.hrw.com,
keyword MR10 9-3 Go
Exercises 1–26, 31, 33, 35, 37, 39, 41, 47

GUIDED PRACTICE

See Example 1 **Convert.**
1. 9 ft = ☐ in.
2. 10 pt = ☐ qt
3. 14,000 lb = ☐ T
4. 5 yd = ☐ ft
5. 24 fl oz = ☐ c
6. 4 lb = ☐ oz

See Example 2
7. 32 qt = ☐ gal
8. 9 lb = ☐ oz
9. 36 in. = ☐ ft
10. 2 yd = ☐ in.
11. 11 qt = ☐ pt
12. 6 T = ☐ lb

See Example 3
13. **Biology** An adult male of average size normally has about 6 quarts of blood in his body. Approximately how many cups of blood does the average adult male have in his body?

INDEPENDENT PRACTICE

See Example 1 **Convert.**
14. 96 oz = ☐ lb
15. 6 c = ☐ fl oz
16. 3 mi = ☐ ft
17. 4,000 lb = ☐ T
18. 6 lb = ☐ oz
19. 3,520 yd = ☐ mi

See Example 2
20. 27 ft = ☐ yd
21. 3 T = ☐ lb
22. 16 qt = ☐ gal
23. 48 oz = ☐ lb
24. 3 yd = ☐ in.
25. 10 pt = ☐ c

See Example 3
26. **Architecture** The steel used to make the Statue of Liberty weighs about 125 tons. About how many pounds of steel were used to make the Statue of Liberty?

PRACTICE AND PROBLEM SOLVING

Extra Practice
See page EP19.

Compare. Use <, >, or =.
27. 18 ft ☐ 220 in.
28. 24 lb ☐ 388 oz
29. $\frac{1}{2}$ pt ☐ 1 c
30. 2 mi ☐ 10,000 ft
31. 12 pt ☐ 3 gal
32. 72 ft ☐ 24 yd
33. 9 c ☐ 72 fl oz
34. 30 yd ☐ 93 ft
35. 145 in. ☐ 4 yd

36. Linda cut off $1\frac{1}{2}$ feet of her hair to donate to an organization that makes wigs for children with cancer. How many inches of hair did Linda cut off?

37. **Geography** Lake Superior is about 1,302 feet deep at its deepest point. What is this depth in yards?

38. **Multi-Step** A company produces 3 tons of cereal each week. How many 12-ounce cereal boxes can be filled each week?

39. **Sports** The width of a singles tennis court is 27 feet.
    a. How many yards wide is a singles tennis court?
    b. How many inches wide is a singles tennis court?

490 Chapter 9 Measurement and Geometry

Art

Long-Term Parking is 65 feet tall and stands in front of a parking lot in Paris.

Convert.

40. 108 in. = ▮ ft = ▮ yd
41. 10,560 ft = ▮ yd = ▮ mi
42. 12 qt = ▮ c = ▮ fl oz
43. 2 gal = ▮ qt = ▮ pt

44. **Art** In Paris, the sculpture *Long-Term Parking,* created by Armand Fernandez, contains 60 cars embedded in 3.5 million pounds of concrete. How many tons of concrete is this?

45. **Multi-Step** If a half-gallon of milk sells for $1.60, what is the cost of a fluid ounce of milk? (Round your answer to the nearest cent.)

46. **Critical Thinking** Make a table to convert ounces to pounds. Write an expression for the number of pounds in n ounces. Then write an expression for the number of ounces in n pounds.

47. **Multi-Step** If you drink 14 quarts of water per week, on average, how many pints do you drink per day?

48. **What's the Error?** Sari said that she walked a total of 8,800 feet in a 5-mile walk-a-thon. Explain Sari's error.

49. **Write About It** Explain how to compare a length given in inches to a length given in feet.

50. **Challenge** In 1942, there were 15,000 troops on the ship *Queen Mary*. Each soldier was given 2 quarts of fresh water for the entire journey.
    a. How many gallons of fresh water did the soldiers have in all?
    b. **Estimation** If the journey took 5 days, about how many fluid ounces of fresh water should a soldier have rationed himself each day?

Test Prep and Spiral Review

51. **Multiple Choice** Which of the following amounts is NOT equivalent to 1 gal?

    Ⓐ 64 fl oz   Ⓑ 16 c   Ⓒ 8 pt   Ⓓ 4 qt

52. **Multiple Choice** The world's largest ice cream sundae weighed about 55,000 pounds. How many tons did it weigh?

    Ⓕ 2.7 T   Ⓖ 27.5 T   Ⓗ 275 T   Ⓙ 2,750 T

Solve each equation. (Lessons 2-5, 2-6)

53. $6 + x = 15$
54. $y - 17 = 29$
55. $43 = 26 + d$
56. $32 = w - 8$

Give the most descriptive name for each figure. (Lesson 8-6)

57.   58.   59.

9-4 Converting Metric Units

Learn to convert metric units of measure.

The first Tour de France was in 1903 and was 2,428 km long. It had only 6 stages. Compare that to the 2005 Tour de France, which had 21 stages and covered 3,607 km.

During the 2005 Tour de France, Lance Armstrong was the stage winner from Tours to Blois, which has a distance of 67.5 km. How many meters is this distance?

In the metric system, the value of each place is 10 times greater than the value of the place to its right. When you convert one unit of measure to another, you can multiply or divide by a power of 10.

kilo-
hecto-
deka-
meter
gram
liter
deci-
centi-
milli-

To convert from smaller to larger units, **divide** by 10 for each step.

To convert from larger to smaller units, **multiply** by 10 for each step.

EXAMPLE 1

Sports Application

Helpful Hint

To multiply by a power of 10, move the decimal to the right; to divide by a power of 10, move the decimal to the left.

During the 2005 Tour de France, Lance Armstrong was the stage winner from Tours to Blois, which has a distance of 67.5 km. How many meters is this distance?

67.5 km = ■ m

Think: Kilometer to meter is going from a bigger unit to a smaller unit. A meter is 3 places to the right of a kilometer in the chart, so 10 · 10 · 10 or 10^3 = 1,000.

67.5 km = (67.5 · 1,000) m

1 km = 1,000 m. You are converting a bigger unit to a smaller unit, so multiply by 1,000.

67.5 km = 67,500 m

Move the decimal point 3 places to the right.

EXAMPLE 2 Using Powers of Ten to Convert Metric Units of Measure

Caution!
Make sure you are multiplying or dividing by the correct power of ten.

Convert.

A The width of a book is about 22 cm. 22 cm = ▓ mm

22 cm = (22 · 10) mm   *1 cm = 10 mm, bigger unit to smaller unit, so multiply by 10.*

22 cm = 220 mm   *Move the decimal point 1 place right.*

B A backpack has a mass of about 6 kg. 6 kg = ▓ g

6 kg = (6 · 1,000) g   *1 kg = 1,000 g, bigger unit to smaller unit, so multiply by 1,000.*

6 kg = 6,000 g   *Move the decimal point 3 places right.*

C A water bottle holds about 400 mL. 400 mL = ▓ L

400 mL = (400 ÷ 1,000) L   *1,000 mL = 1 L, smaller unit to bigger unit, so divide by 1,000.*

400 mL = 0.4 L   *Move the decimal point 3 places left.*

Metric Measurements

Distance	Mass	Capacity
1 km = 1,000 m	1 kg = 1,000 g	1 L = 1,000 mL
1 m = 100 cm	1 g = 1,000 mg	
1 cm = 10 mm		

Convert metric measures by using a conversion factor or using proportions.

EXAMPLE 3 Converting Metric Units of Measure

Convert.

A Method 1: Use a conversion factor.

11 m = ▓ cm   *Think: 100 cm = 1 m so use $\frac{100 \text{ cm}}{1 \text{ m}}$.*

$11 \text{ m} \cdot \frac{100 \text{ cm}}{1 \text{ m}} = 1,100 \text{ cm}$ *Multiply 11 m by the conversion factor. Cancel the common unit, m.*

B Method 2: Use proportions.

190 mL = ▓ L

$\frac{190 \text{ mL}}{x \text{ L}} = \frac{1000 \text{ mL}}{1 \text{ L}}$ *Write a proportion.*

$1,000x = 190$ *The cross products are equal. Divide both sides by 1,000 to undo the multiplication.*

$x = 0.19 \text{ L}$

Think and Discuss

1. Describe how to convert 825 cm to mm.

9-4 Converting Metric Units

9-4 Exercises

Learn It Online
Homework Help Online go.hrw.com,
keyword MR10 9-4
Exercises 1–22, 23, 25, 27, 29, 31, 33, 35

GUIDED PRACTICE

See Example 1
1. The length of a school hallway is 115 meters. How many kilometers long is the hallway?

See Example 2
Convert.
2. The diameter of a ceiling fan is about 95 cm. 95 cm = ▢ m
3. A rock has a mass of about 852 g. 852 g = ▢ kg
4. A vase holds about 1.25 L of water. 1.25 L = ▢ mL
5. A sheet of paper has a mass of about 3.5 g. 3.5 g = ▢ mg

See Example 3
6. 3 kg = ▢ g
7. 4.4 L = ▢ mL
8. 1 kg = ▢ mg
9. 50 mm = ▢ m
10. 21 km = ▢ cm
11. 6 ml = ▢ L

INDEPENDENT PRACTICE

See Example 1
12. A juice container holds 300 milliliters. How many liters of juice are in the container?

See Example 2
Convert.
13. A teacup holds about 110 mL. 110 mL = ▢ L
14. The distance around a school is about 825 m. 825 m = ▢ km
15. A chair has a mass of about 22.5 kg. 22.5 kg = ▢ g
16. A gas tank holds about 85 L. 85 L = ▢ mL

See Example 3
17. 2,460 m = ▢ km
18. 842 mm = ▢ cm
19. 9,680 mg = ▢ g
20. 25 cm = ▢ mm
21. 782 g = ▢ kg
22. 1.2 km = ▢ m

PRACTICE AND PROBLEM SOLVING

Extra Practice
See page EP19.

23. **Multi-Step** There are 28 L of soup in a pot. Marshall serves 400 mL in each bowl. If he fills 16 bowls, how much soup is left in the pot? Write your answer two ways: as a number of liters and as a number of milliliters.

24. **Multi-Step** Joanie wants to frame a rectangular picture that is 1.7 m by 0.9 m. Joanie has 500 cm of wood to use for a frame. Does Joanie have enough wood to frame the picture? Explain.

Convert.

25. $\dfrac{23{,}850 \text{ cm}}{x \text{ km}} = \dfrac{100{,}000 \text{ cm}}{1 \text{ km}}$

26. $\dfrac{350 \text{ L}}{x \text{ mL}} = \dfrac{1 \text{ L}}{1{,}000 \text{ mL}}$

27. $7 \text{ km} \cdot \dfrac{1{,}000 \text{ m}}{\text{km}} = $ ▢ m

28. $9.5 \text{ L} \cdot \dfrac{1{,}000 \text{ mL}}{\text{L}} = $ ▢ mL

494 Chapter 9 Measurement and Geometry

Compare. Use <, >, or =.

29. 1,000 mm ▭ 1 m
30. 5.2 kg ▭ 60 g
31. 3 L ▭ 6,000 mL
32. 2 g ▭ 20,000 mg
33. 0.0065 m ▭ 6.5 mm
34. 0.1 km ▭ 10 mm

35. **Multi-Step** The St. Louis Gateway Arch in Missouri is about 19,200 centimeters tall. The San Jacinto Monument, outside of Houston, Texas, is about 174 m tall. Which structure is taller? by how much? Give your answer in meters.

St. Louis Gateway Arch   San Jacinto Monument

36. **Critical Thinking** A *millimicron* is equal to one-billionth of a meter. How many millimicrons are there in 2.5 meters?

37. **What's the Error?** Edgar wanted to know the mass of a package of cereal in kilograms. The label on the box says 672 g. Edgar said that the mass is 672,000 kg. Explain Edgar's error and give the correct answer.

38. **Write About It** Amy ran a 1,000-meter race. Explain how to find the number of centimeters in 1,000 meters.

39. **Challenge** The lemonade cooler at the class picnic holds 12.5 L. One liter is approximately equal to 0.26 gallons. Each plastic cup holds 7.5 fl oz. Estimate the number of cups that can be filled from the cooler.

Test Prep and Spiral Review

40. **Multiple Choice** Complete the statement with the most reasonable metric unit. A snail might crawl at a rate of about 0.01 __?__ per hour.

    Ⓐ mm   Ⓑ m   Ⓒ mL   Ⓓ km

41. **Extended Response** Liza, Toni, and Kim used a metric scale to weigh some shells they collected at the beach. The masses of the shells were 29 g, 52 g, 18 g, 103 g, 154 g, and 96 g. What was the combined mass of the shells in kilograms? in milligrams? What is the difference in kilograms between the heaviest and lightest shells?

If the angles can form a triangle, classify it as acute, obtuse, or right. (Lesson 8-5)

42. 49°, 41°, 90°
43. 92°, 41°, 47°
44. 57°, 63°, 60°

Determine if the given statements are *sometimes, always,* or *never* true. (Lesson 8-6)

45. A rhombus is a square.
46. A square is a rhombus.
47. A circle is a polygon.
48. A polygon has fewer than 3 sides.

9-4 Converting Metric Units

9-5 Time and Temperature

Learn to find measures of time and temperature.

Jamie took a tour of London on a double-decker bus. The tour started at 11:45 A.M. and ended at 3:15 P.M. Jamie was on the bus for 3 hours 30 minutes.

You can use the information in the table below to convert one unit of time to another.

Time	
1 year (yr) = 365 days	1 day = 24 hours (h)
1 year = 12 months (mo)	1 hour = 60 minutes (min)
1 year = 52 weeks	1 minute = 60 seconds (s)
1 week = 7 days	

EXAMPLE 1 Converting Time

Convert.

A ▢ min 45 s = ▢ s

1 minute 45 seconds
60 seconds + 45 seconds   *Think: 1 minute = 60 seconds.*
105 seconds
1 min 45 s = 105 s

B 450 min = ▢ h

$450 \text{ min} \cdot \frac{1 \text{ h}}{60 \text{ min}} = \frac{450}{60}$ h   *Think: 1 hour = 60 minutes.*

$450 \text{ min} = 7\frac{1}{2}$ h   *Write as a mixed number.*

C ▢ weeks = ▢ h

$6 \text{ wk} \cdot \frac{7 \text{ days}}{1 \text{ wk}} \cdot \frac{24 \text{ h}}{1 \text{ day}} = 1{,}008$ h   *Think: 1 week = 7 days and 1 day = 24 hours.*

6 weeks = 1,008 h

The time between the start of an activity and the end of an activity is called the *elapsed time*.

EXAMPLE 2 Finding Elapsed Time

A Jamie's flight to London was scheduled to arrive at 9:10 A.M. It was 4 hours 25 minutes late. When did it arrive?

Scheduled time: 9:10 A.M.
Arrival time: 1:35 P.M.

Think: 4 hours after 9:10 A.M. is 1:10 P.M. 25 minutes after 1:10 P.M. is 1:35 P.M.

The flight arrived at 1:35 P.M.

B Jamie's friend Tina joined her in London. Tina's flight arrived at 2:30 p.m. The flight was 3 hours 15 minutes long. At what time did Tina's plane depart?

Arrival time: 2:30 P.M.
Departure: 11:15 A.M.

*Think: 3 hours before 2:30 P.M. is 11:30 A.M.
15 minutes before 11:30 A.M. is 11:15 A.M.*

The plane departed at 11:15 A.M.

Celsius and Fahrenheit are the scales used to measure temperature. You can use these formulas to convert temperature.

Temperature Conversions	
To convert Celsius to Fahrenheit use $F = \frac{9}{5}C + 32$.	To convert Fahrenheit to Celsius use $C = \frac{5}{9}(F - 32)$.

EXAMPLE 3 Estimating Temperature

Remember!
Dividing by 2 is the same as multiplying by $\frac{1}{2}$.
See p. 261.

Estimate the temperature.

A 20 °C is about ▪ °F.

$F = \frac{9}{5} \cdot C + 32$ *Use the formula.*

Round $\frac{9}{5}$ to 2, and 32 to 30.

$F \approx 2 \cdot 20 + 30$ *Use the order of operations.*
$F \approx 40 + 30$
$F \approx 70$

20 °C is about 70 °F.

B 50 °F is about ▪ °C.

$C = \frac{5}{9}(F - 32)$ *Use the formula.*

Round $\frac{5}{9}$ to $\frac{1}{2}$, and 32 to 30.

$C \approx \frac{1}{2}(50 - 30)$ *Use the order of operations.*
$C \approx \frac{1}{2}(20)$
$C \approx 10$

50 °F is about 10 °C.

Think and Discuss

1. **Explain** how to find the number of minutes in a week.

2. **Explain** how to find the elapsed time between 7:45 A.M. and 10:30 P.M. if you know the elapsed time between 7:45 A.M. and 10:30 A.M.

9-5 Exercises

GUIDED PRACTICE

See Example 1 Convert.

1. 20 min = ■ s
2. 98 days = ■ weeks
3. 30 mo = ■ yr
4. 3 min 25 s = ■ s
5. 8 h = ■ min
6. 4,320 min = ■ days

See Example 2

7. A movie starts at 11:50 A.M. and runs for 2 hours 25 minutes. At what time does the movie end?

8. Nick drove to visit some friends. If he arrived at 1:30 P.M. and took 4 hours 10 minutes to get there, at what time did Nick start out?

See Example 3 Estimate the temperature.

9. 12 °C is about ■ °F
10. 78 °F is about ■ °C
11. 15 °C is about ■ °F

INDEPENDENT PRACTICE

See Example 1 Convert.

12. 2 h 25 min = ■ min
13. 96 h = ■ days
14. 1 yr 6 mo = ■ mo
15. 7,200 s = ■ h
16. 5 weeks 1 day = ■ days
17. 4,368 h = ■ weeks

See Example 2

18. A bus arrived at its destination at 2:15 P.M. If the trip took 3 hours 50 minutes, at what time did the bus depart?

19. **Multi-Step** The school play lasts 1 hour 25 minutes, and there is a 15-minute intermission. The play started at 10:30 A.M. When will it end?

See Example 3 Estimate the temperature.

20. 56 °F is about ■ °C
21. 84 °C is about ■ °F
22. 75 °F is about ■ °C

PRACTICE AND PROBLEM SOLVING

Extra Practice See page EP19.

Compare. Use <, >, or =.

23. 21 h ■ $\frac{5}{6}$ day
24. 2 yr ■ 104 weeks
25. 80,000 s ■ 1 day

26. **Patterns** The sequence below shows the times that a radio station gives a traffic report. When will the radio station give the next traffic report?
11:18 A.M., 11:30 A.M., 11:42 A.M., 11:54 A.M., …

For Exercises 27 and 28, use the table.

27. Which bus from Miami to Orlando would you take to spend the least amount of time on the bus? the greatest amount of time on the bus?

28. Bus 490 was delayed in traffic for 1 hour 15 minutes. At what time did the bus finally arrive?

Miami to Orlando Schedule		
Bus	Depart	Arrive
460	8:00 A.M.	2:45 P.M.
470	10:50 A.M.	5:45 P.M.
480	1:00 P.M.	7:40 P.M.
490	4:30 P.M.	11:20 P.M.

498 Chapter 9 Measurement and Geometry

Social Studies LINK

The United States and Jamaica are the only two countries in the world that use the Fahrenheit scale for daily temperature readings. All the other countries in the world use the Celsius scale.

29. **Estimation** Diana, who lives in Paris, France, is going to Jamaica on vacation. She read that the temperature in Jamaica is 86 °F. Estimate this temperature in degrees Celsius.

30. **Multi-Step** The table shows the average monthly temperatures from April to July in degrees Fahrenheit for New York City and in degrees Celsius for London. In which months is the average monthly temperature in New York City higher than it is in London?

Average Monthly Temperatures		
Month	New York City (°F)	London (°C)
April	50	10
May	61	13
June	70	16
July	76	19

31. Bobby's trip from Paris, Texas, to Paris, France, should have taken $10\frac{1}{2}$ hours, but it was 3 hours and 20 minutes longer. About how long was his trip?

32. **What's the Error?** David read in a travel book that the average temperature in Dublin in July is 15 °C. He estimated the temperature in degrees Fahrenheit by adding 30 to the Celsius temperature and then multiplying by 2. What did David do wrong?

33. **Write About It** Explain how to find the elapsed time between two given times.

34. **Challenge** Below is a list of the daily high temperatures in Glasgow, Scotland, for one week. What was the mean high temperature in degrees Fahrenheit? 7 °C, 12 °C, 9 °C, 10 °C, 14 °C, 10 °C, 8 °C

Test Prep and Spiral Review

35. **Multiple Choice** Which measure is NOT equivalent to the others?

    A) 8 h   B) 480 min   C) 28,000 s   D) $\frac{1}{3}$ day

36. **Multiple Choice** A flight departs at 11:35 A.M. The flight is 2 hours 45 minutes long, but it is delayed 30 minutes. What is the new arrival time?

    F) 2:20 P.M.   G) 2:50 P.M.   H) 3:05 P.M.   J) 3:15 P.M.

Compare. Write <, >, or =. (Lesson 3-1)

37. 9.17 ▨ 9.107   38. 3.456 ▨ 3.65   39. 0.051 ▨ 0.052   40. 12.5 ▨ 12.50

Evaluate $10.35 - w$ for each value of w. (Lesson 3-3)

41. $w = 4.8$ 42. $w = 8.62$ 43. $w = 0.903$ 44. $w = 5.075$

CHAPTER 9 SECTION 9A

Ready To Go On?

Learn It Online
Resources Online go.hrw.com,
keyword MR10 RTGO9A

Quiz for Lessons 9-1 Through 9-5

9-1 Understanding Customary Units of Measure

What unit of measure provides the best estimate? Explain.

1. A fishbowl can hold about 2 __?__ of water.
2. A Columbian mammoth, which was about the same size as an elephant, lived in Mexico about 1.5 million years ago. A mammoth weighed about 10 __?__ .

9-2 Understanding Metric Units of Measure

What unit of measure provides the best estimate? Explain.

3. A cat has a mass of about 3 __?__ .
4. The length of an airport runway is about 3 __?__ .

Measure the length of each line to the nearest centimeter.

5. •————•   6. •——————————•

9-3 Converting Customary Units

Use the table for Exercises 7 and 8.

7. Convert Ty's length to feet and inches.
8. How many ounces does Ty weigh?

Baby Ty Rodriguez	
Birth Date	July 8, 2005, 11:50 P.M.
Weight	9 lb 8 oz
Length	$21\frac{1}{2}$ in.

9-4 Converting Metric Units

Convert.

9. 8 m = ■ cm
10. 12 kg = ■ g
11. 2,000 mL = ■ L

9-5 Time and Temperature

Convert.

12. 5 min 32 s = ■ s
13. 3 days = ■ min
14. 24 mo = ■ yr
15. 330 s = ■ h

Estimate the temperature.

16. 30 °C is about ■ °F
17. 80 °F is about ■ °C
18. 54 °F is about ■ °C

19. What is the elapsed time between 8:45 P.M. and 12:15 A.M.?
20. A train scheduled to arrive at 10:35 A.M. was delayed 3 hours 20 minutes. What time did it arrive?

Focus on Problem Solving

Look Back
• **Check that the question is answered.**

Sometimes a problem requires you to go through a series of steps to find the answer. When you read a question, ask yourself what information you need to find in order to answer it. After you have solved the problem, reread the question to make sure you have answered it completely.

Read each problem and determine whether the given solution answers the question in the problem. If not, provide the correct answer.

1 The giant house spider has a leg span of 70 millimeters. The western black widow has a leg span of 4 centimeters. How many centimeters longer is the leg span of the giant house spider?
Solution: 3 centimeters

2 A recipe for fruit punch calls for 8 fluid ounces of pineapple juice. Daryl pours the required amount of pineapple juice into a bowl that holds 1 gallon. How many additional fluid ounces of liquid can the bowl hold?
Solution: 120 fluid ounces

3 The distance from Belleville to Cedar Falls is twice the distance from Appleton to Belleville. The distance from Cedar Falls to Donner is twice the distance from Belleville to Cedar Falls. What is the distance from Belleville to Donner?

2 km
Appleton Belleville Cedar Falls Donner

Solution: 8 kilometers

4 The 1939 film *Gone with the Wind* had a running time of 3 hours 50 minutes. The film was usually shown with one 15-minute intermission. An afternoon showing of the film started at 2:30 P.M. At what time did the film end?
Solution: 4 hr 5 min

5 A typical chicken egg weighs 2 ounces. A typical ostrich egg weighs 3 pounds. How many times greater is the weight of the ostrich egg than the chicken egg?
Solution: 48 ounces

Focus on Problem Solving

9-6 Finding Angle Measures in Polygons

Learn to find angle measures in polygons.

All softball and baseball diamonds have a home plate. Home plate is in the shape of a pentagon.

You can use a protractor and your knowledge of angles in polygons to find the measures of the angles in home plate.

EXAMPLE 1

Subtracting to Find Angle Measures

Use a protractor to find the measure of ∠ABC. Then classify the angle.

- Place the center point of the protractor on the vertex of the angle.
- Read the measures where ray BA and ray BC cross.
- Ray BA crosses at 40°, and ray BC crosses at 120°.
- The measure of ∠ABC is 120° − 40°, or 80°. Write this as m ∠ABC = 80°.
- Since 80° < 90°, the angle is acute.

Check

Use the other scale on the protractor to find the measure of ∠ABC.
140° − 60° = 80°

Caution!

Ray BA can also be read as crossing at 140°, and ray BC can be read as crossing at 60°. The angle measure is still 80°. Make sure that you read the measures on the same scale.

To estimate the measure of an angle, compare it with an angle whose measure you already know. A right angle has half the measure of a straight angle. A 45° angle has half the measure of a right angle.

180°   90°   45°   270°

502 Chapter 9 Measurement and Geometry

Video Lesson Tutorials Online   my.hrw.com

EXAMPLE 2 Estimating Angle Measures

Estimate the measure of ∠J in the parallelogram *JKLM*. Then use a protractor to check the reasonableness of your answer.

Think: The measure of the angle is close to 45°, but it is a little less. A good estimate would be about 35°.

Remember that in a parallelogram, opposite angles are congruent.

So use the angle opposite ∠J to find its measure.

Use the protractor. The measure of the angle is 38°.
m∠J = 38°, so the estimate of 35° is reasonable.

Caution!
Use the scale on the protractor that starts with 0°.

EXAMPLE 3 Sports Application

The shape of a softball home plate is shown at right. Find the measures of ∠A and ∠B.

Use a protractor to measure ∠A. $\vec{AB}$ crosses at 45°, and $\vec{AE}$ crosses at 135°.

Subtract.
135° − 45° = 90°.
m∠A = 90°

Estimate m∠B.

It is greater than 90°, so it is obtuse. It looks as if the angle measure is 90° + 45°. So, m∠B is about 135°.

Use a protractor to measure ∠B.
m∠B = 135°

Think and Discuss

1. Explain how you can find the measures of all three angles in a triangle while using a protractor only twice.

9-6 Exercises

GUIDED PRACTICE

See Example 1 Use a protractor to find the measure of each angle. Then classify the angle.

1. 2. 3.

See Example 2 Estimate the measure of ∠A in each figure. Then use a protractor to check the reasonableness of your answer.

4. 5. 6.

See Example 3 7. The shape of a pond is shown at right. Find the measures of ∠A and ∠B.

INDEPENDENT PRACTICE

See Example 1 Use a protractor to find the measure of each angle. Then classify the angle.

8. 9. 10.

See Example 2 Estimate the measure of ∠A in each figure. Then use a protractor to check the reasonableness of your answer.

11. 12. 13.

See Example 3 14. The shape of a park is shown at right. Find the measures of ∠A and ∠B.

Chapter 9 Measurement and Geometry

PRACTICE AND PROBLEM SOLVING

Extra Practice
See page EP20.

Find the measure of the given angle and the measure of the angle that makes up its supplement.

15.

16.

17. Architecture Most buildings are built at a 90° angle from the ground. The Leaning Tower of Pisa, in Pisa, Italy, is at an angle of approximately 84.5° from the ground. How many degrees is it leaning?

18. Critical Thinking Three angles form a 180° angle. If m∠3 = 80° and ∠1 and ∠2 are congruent, what is the measure of ∠1?

84.5°

19. What's the Error? Loni said that the measurement of ∠J was 20°. What is her error?

20. Write About It Describe how to measure an angle two different ways.

21. Challenge Another way to measure angles is in radians. 2π radians is equal to 360°. How many radians equal 90°?

Test Prep and Spiral Review

22. Multiple Choice Find the measure of ∠C to the nearest degree.

Ⓐ 30°   Ⓑ 60°   Ⓒ 75°   Ⓓ 115°

23. Short Response Use a protractor to find the measure of ∠A. Classify the angle. Explain.

Convert. (Lesson 9-3)

24. 6 ft = ▊ in.   **25.** 8 qt = ▊ gal   **26.** 7 lb = ▊ oz   **27.** 4 qt = ▊ pt

28. Pete got into the pool to swim laps at 2:10 P.M. He got out of the pool at 3:25 P.M. How long was he in the pool? (Lesson 9-5)

9-7 Perimeter

Learn to find the perimeter and missing side lengths of a polygon.

Vocabulary
perimeter

One of the largest jigsaw puzzles ever assembled depicted a painting titled *Portrait of a Young Venetian* by Albrecht Dürer. The puzzle was 20 meters long and 15 meters wide.

The **perimeter** of a figure is the distance around it. To find the perimeter of the puzzle, you can add the lengths of the sides.

20 + 15 + 20 + 15 = 70

The perimeter of the puzzle was 70 meters.

EXAMPLE 1   Finding the Perimeter of a Polygon

Find the perimeter of the figure.

2 + 2 + 2 + 2 + 2 = 10   *Estimate the perimeter.*

1.5 + 1.7 + 1.5 + 1.9 + 2 = 8.6   *Add all the side lengths.*

The perimeter is 8.6 cm.

PERIMETER OF A RECTANGLE

The opposite sides of a rectangle are equal in length. Find the perimeter of a rectangle by using the formula, in which ℓ is the length and w is the width.

$P = 2\ell + 2w$

$P = \ell + \ell + w + w$

EXAMPLE 2   Using a Formula to Find Perimeter

Find the perimeter P of the frame.

$P = 2\ell + 2w$

$P = (2 \cdot 3) + (2 \cdot 2)$ *Substitute 3 for ℓ and 2 for w.*

$P = 6 + 4$ *Multiply.*

$P = 10$ *Add.*

The perimeter is 10 feet.

EXAMPLE 3 Finding Unknown Side Lengths and the Perimeter of a Polygon

Find each unknown measure.

A What is the length of side a if the perimeter equals 105 m?

P = sum of side lengths
$105 = a + 26 + 16 + 7 + 29$ *Use the values you know.*
$105 = a + 78$ *Add the known lengths.*
$105 - 78 = a + 78 - 78$ *Subtract 78 from both sides.*
$27 = a$

Side a is 27 m long.

B What is the perimeter of the polygon?

First find the unknown side length.
Find the sides opposite side b.
The length of side b = 10 + 4.
Side b is 14 in. long.
Find the perimeter.
$P = 14 + 8 + 10 + 5 + 4 + 3$
$P = 44$

The perimeter of the polygon is 44 in.

C The width of a rectangle is 12 cm. What is the perimeter of the rectangle if the length is 3 times the width?

$\ell = 3w$ *Find the length.*
$\ell = (3 \cdot 12)$ *Substitute 12 for w.*
$\ell = 36$ *Multiply.*

$P = 2\ell + 2w$ *Use the formula for the perimeter of a rectangle.*
$P = 2(36) + 2(12)$ *Substitute 36 and 12.*
$P = 72 + 24$ *Multiply.*
$P = 96$ *Add.*

The perimeter of the rectangle is 96 cm.

Think and Discuss

1. **Explain** how to find the perimeter of a regular pentagon if you know the length of one side.
2. **Tell** what formula you can use to find the perimeter of a square.

9-7 Exercises

Learn It Online
Homework Help Online go.hrw.com,
keyword MR10 9-7
Exercises 1–12, 13, 15, 17, 19

GUIDED PRACTICE

See Example 1 Find the perimeter of each figure.

1. Rhombus with sides 0.5 in., 0.5 in., 0.5 in., 0.5 in.

2. Triangle with sides 7 cm, 9 cm, 12 cm.

See Example 2 Find the perimeter P of each rectangle.

3. Rectangle 12 m by 8 m.

4. Rectangle 7.3 in. by 4 in.

See Example 3 Find the unknown measure.

5. What is the length of side b if the perimeter equals 21 yd?
(Polygon with sides b, 3 yd, 4 yd, 3 yd, 4 yd)

INDEPENDENT PRACTICE

See Example 1 Find the perimeter of each figure.

6. Triangle with sides $1\frac{1}{4}$ ft, 3 ft, $2\frac{3}{4}$ ft.

7. regular octagon (side 12 in.)

See Example 2 Find the perimeter P of each rectangle.

8. Rectangle 11 in. by 5 in.

9. Square with side 1.75 cm.

10. Rectangle 7 m by $2\frac{1}{2}$ m.

See Example 3 Find each unknown measure.

11. What is the perimeter of the polygon?
(Polygon with sides 6 m, 5 m, b, 11 m, 4 m)

12. The width of a rectangle is 15 ft. What is the perimeter of the rectangle if the length is 5 ft longer than the width?

508 Chapter 9 Measurement and Geometry

PRACTICE AND PROBLEM SOLVING

Extra Practice
See page EP20.

Use the figure ACDEFG for Exercises 13–15.

13. What is the length of side FE?

14. If the perimeter of rectangle BCDE is 34 in., what is the length of side BC?

15. Use your answer from Exercise 14 to find the perimeter of figure ACDEFG.

Find the perimeter of each figure.

16. a triangle with side lengths 6 in., 8 in., and 10 in.

17. a regular pentagon with side length $\frac{2}{5}$ km

18. a regular dodecagon (12-sided figure) with side length 3 m.

19. **Sports** The diagram shows one-half of a badminton court.
    a. What are the dimensions of the whole court?
    b. What is the perimeter of the whole court?

20. **What's the Error?** A student found the perimeter of a 10-inch-by-13-inch rectangle to be 23 inches. Explain the student's error. Then find the correct perimeter.

21. **Write About It** Explain how to find the unknown length of a side of a triangle that has a perimeter of 24 yd and two sides that measure 6 yd and 8 yd.

22. **Challenge** The perimeter of a regular octagon is 20 m. What is the length of one side of the octagon?

Test Prep and Spiral Review

23. **Multiple Choice** Find the perimeter of the figure.
    - Ⓐ 17 cm
    - Ⓒ 21 cm
    - Ⓑ 19 cm
    - Ⓓ 25 cm

24. **Multiple Choice** The width of a rectangle is 16 m. What is the perimeter of the rectangle if the length is 2 times the width?
    - Ⓕ 16 m
    - Ⓖ 32 m
    - Ⓗ 64 m
    - Ⓙ 96 m

Find each sum or difference. (Lesson 3-3)

25. $30 - 5.32$

26. $80.31 + 15.125$

27. $100 - 25.65$

28. $200.6 + 1$

Find the missing value in each proportion. (Lesson 7-3)

29. $\frac{9}{15} = \frac{x}{5}$

30. $\frac{a}{20} = \frac{3}{15}$

31. $\frac{1}{7} = \frac{6}{k}$

32. $\frac{4}{5} = \frac{x}{5}$

Hands-on LAB 9-8A: Explore Circumference

Use with Lesson 9-8

Learn It Online
Lab Resources Online go.hrw.com,
keyword MR10 Lab9 Go

In this lab, you will measure objects to investigate the distance around a circle. The distance around a circle is called the *circumference*.

Activity 1

1. Choose a cylindrical object, such as a can or a mug. Tightly wrap a piece of string around the object, and mark the string where it meets itself. Measure this length on the string, and record it in a table like the one below as the circumference.

2. Using a ruler, measure the distance across the object through its center. Record this as the *diameter*.

3. Use a calculator to find the ratio of the circumference C to the diameter d. Round this value to the nearest hundredth, and record it in the table.

4. Repeat the process with three more cylindrical objects.

	Object 1	Object 2	Object 3	Object 4
Circumference C				
Diameter d				
$\frac{C}{d}$				

Think and Discuss

1. Describe what you notice about the ratio $\frac{C}{d}$ in your table.

Try This

Find the ratio $\frac{C}{d}$ for each circle.

1. $C = 12.57$ in.; 4 in.

2. $C = 9.42$ cm; 3 cm

3. $C = 15.71$ ft; 5 ft

510   Chapter 9   Measurement and Geometry

The ratio of the circumference of a circle to its diameter is called *pi*, which is represented by the Greek letter π. As you saw in Activity 1, the value of π is close to 3. You can approximate π as 3.14 or $\frac{22}{7}$.

For any circle, $\frac{C}{d} = \pi$. You can solve this equation for C to give an equation for the circumference of a circle in terms of the diameter. The equation is $C = \pi d$.

Activity 2

1. Open your compass to a width of 4 cm. Use the compass to draw a circle with a radius of 4 cm. What is the diameter of the circle?

2. Use the equation $C = \pi d$ and the approximation $\pi \approx 3.14$ to predict the circumference of the circle.

3. Carefully lay a piece of string on top of the circle. Make sure the string matches the circle as closely as possible.

4. Mark the string where it meets itself, and measure this length.

5. Repeat the process, this time starting with a circle whose radius is 3.5 cm. Use the equation $C = \pi d$ to predict the circle's circumference, and then check the prediction by using a string to measure the circumference.

Think and Discuss

1. In each case, how did the length of the string compare with the circumference that you predicted?

2. If you know the diameter of a circle, what should you do to find the circle's circumference?

3. If you know the circumference of a circle, what should you do to find the circle's diameter?

Try This

Find the circumference of each circle. Use 3.14 for π.

1. 9 in.
2. 5 ft
3. 10 cm

9-8 Circles and Circumference

Learn to identify the parts of a circle and to find the circumference of a circle.

Vocabulary
circle
center
chord
diameter
radius (radii)
circumference
pi

The shape of a drum is a *circle*. A **circle** is the set of all points in a plane that are the same distance from a given point, called the **center**.

Like a polygon, a circle is a plane figure. But a circle is not a polygon because it is not made of line segments.

Chord A line segment that has both endpoints on the circle.

Diameter A chord that passes through the center of the circle. Diameters are the longest chords in a circle.

Center

Radius (plural radii) A line segment with one endpoint at the center of the circle and the other endpoint on the circle.

The length of the diameter is twice the length of the radius.

EXAMPLE 1 Naming Parts of a Circle

Name the circle, two chords, a diameter, and three radii.

A circle is named by its center, so this is circle O.
$\overline{AB}$ and $\overline{DE}$ are chords.
$\overline{AB}$ is a diameter.
$\overline{OA}$, $\overline{OB}$, and $\overline{OC}$ are radii.

The distance around a circle is called the **circumference**.

The ratio of the circumference to the diameter, $\frac{C}{d}$, is the same for any circle. This ratio is represented by the Greek letter π, which is read "**pi**."

$$\frac{C}{d} = \pi$$

The decimal representation of *pi* starts with 3.14159265 . . . and goes on forever without repeating. Most people approximate π using either 3.14 or $\frac{22}{7}$. To make multiplying by *pi* easier, you can round π to 3.

The formula for the circumference of a circle is $C = \pi d$, or $C = 2\pi r$.

Circumference of a Circle	
Words	Formula
The circumference of any circle is equal to π times the diameter, or 2π times the radius.	$C = \pi d$ or $C = 2\pi r$

EXAMPLE 2 — Architecture Application

An architect is making a plan for a new circular theater. Find the circumference of the theater by rounding π to 3.

$C = \pi d$ *Use the formula.*

$C \approx 3 \cdot 32$ *Replace π with 3 and d with 32.*

$C \approx 96$ meters

The circumference of the circle is about 96 meters.

Theater — 32 m

EXAMPLE 3 — Using the Formula for the Circumference of a Circle

Find each missing value to the nearest hundredth. Use 3.14 for π.

A $d = 8$ ft; $C = ?$

$C = \pi d$ *Write the formula.*

$C \approx 3.14 \cdot 8$ *Replace π with 3.14 and d with 8.*

$C \approx 25.12$ ft

B $r = 3$ cm; $C = ?$

$C = 2\pi r$ *Write the formula.*

$C \approx 2 \cdot 3.14 \cdot 3$ *Replace π with 3.14 and r with 3.*

$C \approx 18.84$ cm

C $C = 37.68$ in.; $d = ?$

$C = \pi d$ *Write the formula.*

$37.68 \approx 3.14 d$ *Replace C with 37.68, and π with 3.14.*

$\dfrac{37.68}{3.14} \approx \dfrac{3.14 d}{3.14}$ *Divide both sides by 3.14.*

12.00 in. $\approx d$

Think and Discuss

1. **Explain** how to find the radius in Example 3C.
2. **Tell** whether rounding *pi* to 3 in Example 3B will result in an overestimation or an underestimation.
3. **Explain** why a circle is not a polygon.

9-8 Exercises

GUIDED PRACTICE

See Example 1
1. Point *G* is the center of the circle. Name the circle, two chords, a diameter, and three radii.

See Example 2
A builder is putting in a circular window. Find the circumference by rounding π to 3.
2. What is the circumference if the diameter is 8 feet?
3. What is the circumference if the radius is 2 feet?

See Example 3
Find each missing value to the nearest hundredth. Use 3.14 for π.
4. $C = $? $d = 10$ mm
5. $C = $? $r = 2$ in.

INDEPENDENT PRACTICE

See Example 1
6. Point *P* is the center of the circle. Name the circle, two chords, a diameter, and three radii.

See Example 2
A gardener is digging a circular pond and planting a circular herb garden around it. Find the circumference by rounding π to 3.
7. If the diameter of the pond is 5 yards, what is its circumference?
8. If the radius of the garden is 7 yards, what is its circumference?

See Example 3
Find each missing value to the nearest hundredth. Use 3.14 for π.
9. $C = $? $d = 1.5$ m
10. $C = $? $r = 0.8$ cm
11. $d = $? $C = 1.57$ in.

PRACTICE AND PROBLEM SOLVING

Extra Practice
See page EP20.

Fill in the blanks. Use 3.14 for π and round to the nearest hundredth.
12. If $r = 7$ m, then $d = $ ___?___, and $C = $ ___?___.
13. If $d = 11.5$ ft, then $r = $ ___?___, and $C = $ ___?___.
14. If $C = 7.065$ cm, then $d = $ ___?___, and $r = $ ___?___.
15. If $C = 16.956$ in., then $d = $ ___?___, and $r = $ ___?___.

514   Chapter 9 Measurement and Geometry

History

Performers like Thea Ulrich have learned to twirl multiple Hula Hoops around their bodies. The world record for most Hula Hoops kept in revolution is 100!

16. **Measurement** Draw a circle. Name the center P and make the radius 2 in. long.

    a. Draw the diameter $\overline{AB}$ and give its length.

    b. Find the circumference. Use 3.14 for π. Round your answer to the nearest hundredth.

17. **History** The first Hula Hoop® was introduced in 1958. What is the circumference of a Hula Hoop with a 3 ft diameter? Use 3.14 for π.

Use the cylinders for Exercises 18 and 19.

18. **Estimation** About how many times greater is the circumference of the top of the purple cylinder than the top of the blue cylinder?

19. **Choose a Strategy** If the circumference of the top of the yellow cylinder is 22.5 centimeters, which method can you use to find the radius?

    Ⓐ Divide 22.5 by π.

    Ⓑ Multiply 22.5 by π.

    Ⓒ Divide 22.5 by π and then divide the quotient by 2.

    Ⓓ Multiply 22.5 by π and then multiply the product by 2.

20. **Write About It** The circumference of a circle is 3.14 m. Explain how you can find the diameter and radius of the circle.

21. **Challenge** An Olympic outdoor archery target is made up of 10 equally spaced concentric circles. *Concentric* means that the center of each of the circles is the same. If the diameter of the biggest ring on the target is 122 cm and the diameter of the bullseye is 12.2 centimeters, what is the diameter of the fourth ring from the inside?

Test Prep and Spiral Review

22. **Multiple Choice** A mini-DVD has a radius of 4 centimeters. Which expression can you use to find the circumference of the mini-DVD?

    Ⓐ 4π Ⓑ 8π Ⓒ 16π Ⓓ $2 \cdot 2 \cdot \pi \cdot 8$

23. **Short Response** The wheels on Ryan's bike are each about 2 feet in diameter. If Ryan rides his bike for 1 mile, about how many times will each wheel rotate? Use 3 for π.

Order the fractions from greatest to least. (Lesson 4-7)

24. $\frac{1}{2}, \frac{3}{8}, \frac{5}{8}$ 25. $\frac{3}{4}, \frac{10}{12}, \frac{1}{12}$ 26. $\frac{3}{10}, \frac{3}{5}, \frac{7}{10}$ 27. $\frac{7}{16}, \frac{3}{4}, \frac{5}{8}$

Write each percent as a decimal. (Lesson 7-7)

28. 50%   29. 5%   30. 85%   31. 100%   32. 15%

Hands-on LAB 9-8B

Construct Circle Graphs

Use with Lesson 9-8

Learn It Online
Lab Resources Online go.hrw.com,
keyword MR10 Lab9 Go

REMEMBER
The sum of the measures of the angles in any circle is 360°.

A circle graph shows parts of a whole. If you think of a complete circle as 100%, you can express sections of a circle graph as percents.

- Ms. Shipley's class earned $400 at the school fair. What fraction of the $400 did the class earn at the bake sale?

- What percent of the $400 did the class earn at the bake sale?

Money Raised at School Fair
- Bake sale $200
- Drinks $50
- Crafts $100
- Games $50

Activity

At Mazel Middle School, students were surveyed about their favorite types of TV programs. Make a circle graph to represent the results.

Students' Favorite Programs	
Type of Program	Number of Students
Science	25
Cooking	15
Sports	50
Sitcoms	150
Movies	60
Cartoons	200

① Find the total number of students surveyed.

$$25 + 15 + 50 + 150 + 60 + 200 = 500$$

② Find the percent of the total represented by students who like science programs.

$$\frac{25}{500} = 5\%$$

③ Since there are 360° in a circle, multiply 5% by 360°. This will give you an angle measure in degrees.

$$0.05 \cdot 360° = 18°$$

④ Use a compass to draw a circle. Mark the center and use a straightedge to draw a line from the center to the edge of the circle.

5 Use your protractor to draw an angle measuring 18°. The vertex of the angle will be the center of the circle, and one side will be the line that you drew. The section formed represents the percent of students who prefer science programs.

6 Repeat **2** through **5** for each type of program. Label each section, and give the graph a title.

Favorite TV Programs
- Cooking 3%
- Cartoons 40%
- Science 5%
- Sitcoms 30%
- Sports 10%
- Movies 12%

Think and Discuss

1. Looking at your circle graph, discuss five pieces of information you have learned about the TV habits of students at Mazel Middle School.

2. What does the whole circle represent?

3. Why do you need to know that there are 360° in a circle?

4. How does the size of each section of your circle graph relate to the percent that it represents?

Try This

1. People at a mall were surveyed about their favorite pets. Make a circle graph to display the results of the survey. Round to the nearest tenth.

Favorite Pets	
Type of Pet	Number of People
Dog	225
Fish	150
Bird	112
Cat	198
Other	65

2. Collect data from your classmates about their favorite colors. Use the data to make a circle graph with no more than five sections.

3. The circle graph shows the results of a survey about what people in the United States like to eat for breakfast. If this survey included 1,500 people, how many people said they like to eat cereal for breakfast?

Favorite Breakfast Foods
- Cold cereal 26%
- Toast, roll 40%
- Eggs, meat 34%

9-8B Hands-On Lab

CHAPTER 9 SECTION 9B

Ready To Go On?

Learn It Online
Resources Online go.hrw.com,
keyword MR10 RTGO9B

Quiz for Lessons 9-6 Through 9-8

9-6 Finding Angle Measures in Polygons

Use a protractor to find the measure of each angle. Then classify the angle.

1.
2.
3.

4. A garden plot is shown at right. Find the measures of ∠A and ∠B.

9-7 Perimeter

Find the perimeter of each figure.

5. 18 cm, 12 cm, 14 cm
6. 17 ft, 12 ft, 7 ft, 9 ft, 13 ft
7. 18 cm, 8 cm, 8 cm, 8 cm, 4 cm, 2 cm

9-8 Circles and Circumference

Name the circle, a chord, and two radii, and then find the circumference for each circle. Use 3.14 for π and round to the nearest hundredth.

8. 7 cm (B, C, A, E, D)
9. 3 in. (G, D, H)
10. $8\frac{1}{4}$ km (F, G, H, I, J)
11. 42 cm (J, M, K, L)

12. An architect is making a plan for a new circular playground. Find the circumference of the playground by rounding π to 3.

$d = 64$ m

Find each missing value to the nearest hundredth. Use 3.14 for π.

13. $r = 9$ in.; $C = $ ___?___
14. $d = 20$ m; $C = $ ___?___
15. $C = 37.68$ ft; $d = $ ___?___

Real-World CONNECTIONS

CHAPTER 9

Bicentennial Capitol Mall A visit to Bicentennial Capitol Mall in Nashville is an ideal way to explore the history and geography of Tennessee. The 19-acre park features memorials, fountains, and a footpath containing a time capsule from each of the state's 95 counties.

TENNESSEE

Nashville

1. The park's World War II memorial includes a granite globe that weights 18,000 lb. Convert the weight of the globe to tons.

2. The mall's walkway has a large map of Tennessee on it. The map is 2,400 inches long.

    a. Convert the length of the map to feet.

    b. Each foot of the map represents 2.5 actual miles. What is the actual length of the state?

3. The mall has two clusters of Tennessee flags. Each cluster contains a large flag and several small flags. The dimensions of the flags are shown in the table. Find the missing values.

Tennessee Flags at Bicentennial Capitol Mall			
Size	Length (ft)	Width (ft)	Perimeter (ft)
Large	18	12	
Small	8		26

4. The Court of Three Stars is a circular area at one end of the park. The court's diameter is 180 ft.

    a. Find the circumference of the court. Use 3.14 for π and round to the nearest foot.

    b. A snail crawls around the edge of the court at a rate of 5 feet per minute. How long does it take the snail to crawl once around the court?

Real-World Connections 519

Game Time

Logic Puzzle

Each day from Monday through Friday, Mayuri, Naomi, Brett, Thomas, and Angela took turns picking a restaurant for lunch. They ate at restaurants that serve either Chinese food, hamburgers, pizza, seafood, or tacos. Use the clues below to determine which student picked the restaurant on each day and which restaurant the student picked.

1. Angela skipped Friday's lunch to play in a basketball game.
2. Brett picked the restaurant on Wednesday.
3. The students ate tacos on Friday.
4. Naomi is allergic to seafood and volunteered to pick the first restaurant.
5. Thomas picked a hamburger restaurant on the day before another student chose a pizza restaurant.

You can use a chart like the one below to help you solve this puzzle. Place an O in a square for something that is true and an X in a square for something that cannot be true. Remember that when you place an O in a square, you can put X's in the rest of the squares in that row and column. The information from the first two clues has been entered for you.

		Mayuri	Naomi	Brett	Thomas	Angela	Seafood	Pizza	Hamburger	Chinese	Tacos
Day	Monday			X							
	Tuesday			X							
	Wednesday	X	X	O	X	X					
	Thursday			X							
	Friday			X		X					
Restaurant	Seafood										
	Pizza										
	Hamburgers										
	Chinese										
	Tacos										

A copy of a blank logic puzzle chart is available online.

Materials
- Magnetic strip
- construction paper
- glue
- scissors
- 6 paint chips
- small metal box

It's in the Bag!

PROJECT ## Perfectly Packaged Perimeters

This metal box stores magnetic vocabulary tiles and small squares that you can use to create a variety of shapes.

Directions

1. Glue construction paper onto the magnetic strip.

2. Write vocabulary words from this chapter on the magnetic strip. Then cut the words apart to form magnetic vocabulary tiles. **Figure A**

3. Cut the paint chips into smaller squares, each approximately $1\frac{1}{4}$ inches by $1\frac{1}{4}$ inches.

4. Glue a small piece of construction paper onto the lid of the metal box. Label it with the number and title of the chapter. **Figure B**

5. Store the vocabulary tiles and the small squares in the metal box.

Putting the Math into Action

Place the vocabulary tiles on the outside of the box or on another metal surface to review key terms from the chapter. Arrange the small squares to form shapes with various perimeters. What is the greatest perimeter you can make?

It's in the Bag! 521

CHAPTER 9 Study Guide: Review

Vocabulary

center 512	diameter 512
chord 512	metric system 484
circle 512	perimeter 506
circumference 512	pi 512
customary system 480	radius (radii) 512

Complete the sentences below with vocabulary words from the list above.

1. The distance around a polygon is called the ___?___, and the distance around a circle is called the ___?___.

2. A line segment that passes through the center of a circle and has both endpoints on the circle is a ___?___.

3. The ___?___ is the measurement system often used in the United States.

EXAMPLES / EXERCISES

9-1 Understanding Customary Units of Measure (pp. 480–483)

■ What unit of measure provides the best estimate? Explain.

A desk is about 3 ___?___ long.

Think: The length of a desk is about 3 times the distance from your shoulder to your elbow.

A desk is about 3 ft long.

Measure the length of the arrow to the nearest half, fourth, or eighth inch.

The arrow is between $1\frac{1}{4}$ and $1\frac{3}{8}$ in. It is closer to $1\frac{3}{8}$.
The length of the arrow is about $1\frac{3}{8}$ in.

What unit of measure provides the best estimate? Explain.

4. A crayon is about 5 ___?___ long.

5. The distance from Denver, CO, to Dallas, TX, is about 800 ___?___.

6. A bunch of bananas weighs about 2 ___?___.

7. An eyedropper holds about 1 ___?___ of liquid.

8. Measure the length of the arrow to the nearest half, fourth, or eighth inch.

522 Chapter 9 Measurement and Geometry

EXAMPLES

EXERCISES

9-2 Understanding Metric Units of Measure (pp. 484–487)

■ **What unit of measure provides the best estimate? Explain.**

A sofa is about 3 __?__ long.

Think: The length of a sofa is about 3 times the width of a single bed.

A sofa is about 3 m long.

Measure the length of the arrow to the nearest centimeter.

The arrow is between 2 and 3 cm. It is closer to 2 cm.
The length of the arrow is about 2 cm.

What unit of measure provides the best estimate? Explain.

9. A paper clip is about 32 __?__ long.
10. A grain of rice has a mass of about 5 __?__.
11. A laptop computer has a mass of about 2 __?__.
12. A large pitcher has a capacity of about 2 __?__.
13. Measure the length of the arrow to the nearest centimeter.

9-3 Converting Customary Units (pp. 488–491)

■ **Convert 5 yards to feet.**

Set up a conversion factor.

$5 \text{ yd} \times \frac{3 \text{ ft}}{1 \text{ yd}}$ *Think: yards to feet—3 ft = 1 yd, so use $\frac{3 \text{ ft}}{yd}$.*

$5 \text{ yd} = 15 \text{ ft}$ *Multiply 5 yd by the conversion factor. Cancel the common unit, yd.*

Convert.

14. 3 mi to feet
15. 18 ft to yards
16. 3 qt to cups
17. 48 c to gal
18. 128 oz to pounds
19. 8,000 lb to tons
20. $\frac{64 \text{ oz}}{x \text{ lb}} = \frac{16 \text{ oz}}{1 \text{ lb}}$
21. $\frac{12 \text{ ft}}{x \text{ in.}} = \frac{1 \text{ ft}}{12 \text{ in.}}$
22. $\frac{8 \text{ pt}}{x \text{ qt}} = \frac{2 \text{ pt}}{1 \text{ qt}}$
23. $\frac{3 \text{ ft}}{1 \text{ yd}} = \frac{x \text{ ft}}{33 \text{ yd}}$
24. The Golden Gate Bridge, in San Francisco, has a tower height of 750 ft. How many yards tall is this?

9-4 Converting Metric Units (pp. 492–495)

■ **Convert.**

$29 \text{ cm} = \blacksquare \text{ m}$

$29 \text{ cm} \cdot \frac{1 \text{ m}}{100 \text{ cm}} = 0.29 \text{ m}$ *Cancel the common unit, cm.*

Convert.

25. 3.2 L = ▆ mL
26. 7 mL = ▆ L
27. 342 m = ▆ km
28. 42 g = ▆ kg
29. 51 mm = ▆ m
30. 71 km = ▆ m
31. The heaviest pumpkin ever grown weighed approximately 681.296 kilograms. How many grams is this?

EXAMPLES

9-5 Time and Temperature (pp. 496–499)

■ Convert.

14 hours = ▢ minutes

14 h̶r̶ · $\frac{60 \text{ min}}{1 \text{ h̶r̶}}$ = 840 min   1 hour = 60 minutes

9-6 Finding Angle Measures in Polygons (pp. 502–505)

■ Use a protractor to find the measure of ∠ABC. Then classify the angle.

∠ABC = 95° − 60° = 35°
Since 35° < 90°, the angle is acute.

9-7 Perimeter (pp. 506–509)

■ Find the perimeter of the figure.

Add all the side lengths.

P = 9 + 10 + 5 + 16 + 12 = 52
The perimeter is 52 cm.

9-8 Circles and Circumference (pp. 512–515)

■ Find the circumference of the circle. Use 3.14 for π.

C = πd
C ≈ 3.14 · 6
C ≈ 18.84 cm

d = 6 cm

EXERCISES

Convert.

32. 3,600 seconds = ▢ hours
33. 990 minutes = ▢ seconds
34. 15 weeks = ▢ days
35. Ariel arrived in Boston at 2:33 P.M. after a 2 hour 23 minute bus trip. At what time did Ariel's bus depart?

36. Use a protractor to find the measure of ∠ABC. Then classify the angle.

37. Estimate the measure of ∠P in pentagon PQRST. Then use a protractor to check the reasonableness of your answer.

38. Find the perimeter of the figure.

39. What is the length of n if the perimeter is 20 ft?

Find each missing value to the nearest hundredth. Use 3.14 for π.

40. d = 10 ft; C = $\underline{?}$
41. C = 28.26 m; d = $\underline{?}$
42. r = 8 cm; C = $\underline{?}$
43. C = 69.08 ft; r = $\underline{?}$

524 Chapter 9 Measurement and Geometry

Chapter Test

CHAPTER 9

What metric unit of measure provides the best estimate? Explain.

1. A flower pot can hold about 1 __?__ of water.
2. A baby bird has a mass of about 15 __?__.
3. The length of a cricket is about 3 __?__ long.

Use the table for Problems 4–6.

Baby Darian Cole	
Birth Date	May 1, 2005, 11:45 A.M.
Weight	7 lb
Length	1 ft 8 in.

4. If Darian was moved to the nursery at 2:25 P.M., how long was he in the hospital room?
5. Convert Darian's weight to ounces.
6. How long was Darian in inches?

Estimate the temperature.

7. 48 °C is about ▇ °F.
8. 70 °F is about ▇ °C.

Use a protractor to find the measure of each angle. Then classify the angle.

9.
10.

Find the perimeter of each figure.

11. 12 m, 8 m
12. 12 cm, 6 cm, 7 cm
13. 11 ft, 3 ft, 5 ft, 4 ft, 10 ft

Name the circle, a chord, and two radii, and then find the circumference for each circle. Use 3.14 for π and round to the nearest hundredth.

14. Circle P with $2\frac{1}{2}$ m; points A, V, R, T
15. Circle O with 10 in.; points J, D
16. Circle F with 9 cm; points B, H, L, S

Find each missing value to the nearest hundredth. Use 3.14 for π.

17. $r = 4$ cm; $C =$ __?__
18. $d = 10$ ft; $C =$ __?__
19. $C = 37.68$ ft; $d =$ __?__

20. A gardener is digging a rose garden. Find the circumference of the rose garden by rounding π to 3. $d = 21$ m

Chapter 9 Test

Test Tackler
STANDARDIZED TEST STRATEGIES

Any Question Type: Use a Diagram

Diagrams are a helpful tool. If a diagram is included in a test item, study it closely as it may contain useful information. Sometimes it is helpful to draw your own diagram.

EXAMPLE 1

Multiple Choice A small circle is inside a large circle. The diameter of the small circle is 10 feet. If the circumference of the large circle is 4 times greater than the circumference of the small circle, what is the radius of the large circle? (Round *pi* to 3.)

Ⓐ 20 ft   Ⓑ 30 ft   Ⓒ 40 ft   Ⓓ 120 ft

Draw a diagram to help you visualize the problem.
Draw two circles and label them with all the information given in the problem.

Diameter = 10 ft

The circumference of the small circle is about 30 feet. The circumference of the large circle is about 120 feet. Divide by 2π. $120 \div (3 \cdot 2) = 20$, so the radius is about 20 feet.

Choice A is correct.

EXAMPLE 2

Short Response $\triangle ABC$ is similar to $\triangle FDE$. Find the missing length.

These triangles do not look similar and are not drawn to scale, but the information in the problem says that they are.

Set up a proportion to find the missing length and solve for *x*. $\frac{x}{6} = \frac{15}{9}$

The unknown side length is 10 in.

526 Chapter 9 Measurement and Geometry

Hot Tip! If you have trouble understanding what a test item is asking, draw a diagram to help you visualize the question.

Read each test item and answer the questions that follow.

Item A
Multiple Choice The temperature at the ski lodge was 21°F at 9:00 P.M. At sunrise, the temperature was 34°F. How many degrees did the temperature rise overnight?

- Ⓐ 54 °F
- Ⓑ 25 °F
- Ⓒ 13 °F
- Ⓓ 4 °F

1. What information will help you solve the problem?

2. Sketch a diagram to help you solve this problem. Be sure to label the diagram with all of the information you know.

Item B
Short Answer Prove that the two rectangles below are similar. Explain your reasoning.

M 6 cm N
A 7.5 cm B
15 cm
3 cm
D C P O

3. What information can you get from the diagram to help you prove that the figures are similar?

4. Do you think the drawings accurately illustrate the given information? If not, why?

5. What is the length of $\overline{DC}$?

Item C
Gridded Response The longest side of a triangle is 14.4 centimeters. Its shortest side is 5.9 centimeters shorter than the longest side. If the perimeter of the triangle is 35.2 centimeters, what is the length of the third side?

6. How do you determine the perimeter of a triangle?

7. Sketch a diagram of the triangle. Explain how sketching the diagram can help you answer the problem.

8. Tell how you would fill in your response to this test item on a grid.

Item D
Multiple Choice Which angle pairs are vertical angles?

- Ⓕ ∠a and ∠f
- Ⓖ ∠b and ∠c
- Ⓗ ∠b and ∠e
- Ⓙ ∠c and ∠d

9. Which answer choice can you immediately eliminate? Why?

10. How can you use the diagram to help you eliminate the other choices?

11. Explain which answer choice is correct.

Test Tackler

Chapter 9 Standardized Test Prep

Cumulative Assessment, Chapters 1–9

Multiple Choice

1. The world's largest ball of twine is located in Cawker City, Kansas. It weighs 17,571 pounds. About how many tons does this ball of twine weigh?

   (A) 9 tons
   (B) 10 tons
   (C) 11 tons
   (D) 12 tons

2. The two triangles shown below are similar. What is the length of the unknown side n?

   (F) 7 in.
   (G) 8.5 in.
   (H) 15.75 in.
   (J) Not here

3. What is the most appropriate unit of measure for the length of a tractor?

   (A) Inches
   (B) Feet
   (C) Millimeters
   (D) Pounds

4. In 2002, the U.S. Census reported that 37.4 million Latinos were living in the United States. Approximately 3.2 million of these Latinos were from Puerto Rico. What percent of the Latino population in 2002 came from Puerto Rico?

   (F) 0.086%
   (G) 0.86%
   (H) 8.6%
   (J) 86%

5. Josh's violin lessons start at 8:55 A.M. and last 95 minutes. What time will Josh's lesson end?

   (A) 9:45 A.M.
   (B) 10:15 A.M.
   (C) 10:30 A.M.
   (D) 10:45 A.M.

6. An online survey by Kids' Money asked children to share how much money they receive for an allowance. The results from 6- to 12-year-olds are shown below. According to this survey, what is the average allowance for children between the ages of 8 and 12?

   (F) $6.06
   (G) $6.90
   (H) $7.18
   (J) $8.49

7. Shelly has a bookshelf that is $48\frac{3}{4}$ inches long. If Shelly's textbooks are each $3\frac{1}{2}$ inches wide, how many books can Shelly fit on a shelf?

   (A) 15 books
   (B) 14 books
   (C) 13 books
   (D) 12 books

8. Which metric unit should be used to show how much liquid a jar can hold?

   F. Kilograms
   G. Milligrams
   H. Millimeters
   J. Milliliters

9. Which of the following statements about plane figures is NOT true?

   A. A square is always a rhombus.
   B. A rectangle is always a square.
   C. A trapezoid is always a quadrilateral.
   D. A rhombus is always a parallelogram.

HOT TIP! When converting between metric units, multiply by a power of 10 when changing from larger units to smaller units. Divide by a power of 10 when changing from smaller units to larger units.

Gridded Response

10. Nicole gets on the train at 8:13 A.M. and gets off the train at 9:02 A.M. How many minutes is Nicole on the train?

11. Find the value of the expression $5(6x + 4y^2 - 2z)$ when $x = 4$, $y = 5$, and $z = 6$.

12. Jordan's locker number is greater than 225 but less than 250. It is divisible by 3 and 9, but not by 2, 4, or 5. What is Jordan's locker number?

13. In 1912, a reticulated python was found to be 10.7 meters long. How many centimeters long was this snake?

14. What is the 5th term in a sequence that begins on 6 and is divided each time by $\frac{1}{3}$?

15. Jessie is $1\frac{1}{2}$ times taller than her sister. If her sister is 4 feet tall, how many inches taller is Jessie than her sister?

Short Response

S1. Gene and Janice's gas tanks are empty. It cost Gene $74.27 to fill up his 25.7-gallon gas tank. At another gas station, Janice filled up her 13.8 gallon tank and paid $39.60. Who paid the most for a gallon of gas? Explain.

S2. Larry is making a model of an Olympic-size swimming pool. The scale is 2 cm = 5 m.

   a. An Olympic-size pool is 50 m long by 25 m wide. What are the dimensions of the model? Show your work.

   b. There are 8 lanes in the actual pool. Each lane is 2.5 m wide. How many centimeters wide are the lanes in the model? Show your work.

S3. A regulation football field is 160 feet wide and 420 feet long. These dimensions include the end zones.

   a. What is the perimeter of a regulation football field in yards? Show your work.

   b. A football field has two end zones at the end of each side of the playing field. If the playing field is 100 yards long, how many inches long is one end zone? Show your work.

Extended Response

E1. Teresa is planning to build a stone border around a large walnut tree. The stones are 6 inches long.

   a. How many stones will Teresa need if she creates a square border that is 8 feet long? Show your work.

   b. How many stones will Teresa need if she creates a circular border that has an 8-foot diameter? Use $\frac{22}{7}$ for π. Show your work.

   c. If the stones cost $2.69 each, how much money will Teresa save if she builds a circular border instead of a square border? Explain.

Cumulative Assessment, Chapters 1–9

CHAPTER 10
Measurement: Area and Volume

10A Area
- **10-1** Area of Rectangles and Parallelograms
- **LAB** Squares and Square Roots
- **10-2** Area of Triangles and Trapezoids
- **LAB** Explore Perimeter and Area
- **10-3** Area of Composite Figures
- **10-4** Changing Dimensions
- **LAB** Explore Area of Circles
- **10-5** Area of Circles

10B Volume and Surface Area
- **LAB** Draw Views of Three-Dimensional Figures
- **10-6** Three-Dimensional Figures
- **LAB** Explore Volume of Prisms and Cylinders
- **10-7** Volume of Prisms
- **10-8** Volume of Cylinders
- **LAB** Model Three-Dimensional Figures
- **10-9** Surface Area

Chapter Focus
- Solve problems that involve lengths, areas, and volumes.
- Use fractions and decimals to solve measurement problems.

Why Learn This?
Different three-dimensional figures can be seen in various architectural structures. Many buildings are simple rectangular prisms while others are in the shape of pyramids or cylinders.

Learn It Online
Chapter Project Online go.hrw.com,
keyword MR10 Ch10

Are You Ready?

Vocabulary

Choose the best term from the list to complete each sentence.

1. A(n) __?__ is a quadrilateral with opposite sides that are parallel and congruent.
2. Some customary units of length are __?__ and __?__. Some metric units of length are __?__ and __?__.
3. A(n) __?__ is a quadrilateral with side lengths that are all congruent and four right angles.
4. A(n) __?__ is a polygon with six sides.

centimeters
cube
feet
hexagon
inches
liters
meters
parallelogram
square
trapezoid

Complete these exercises to review skills you will need for this chapter.

Add and Multiply Whole Numbers, Fractions, and Decimals

Find each sum or product.

5. $1.5 + 2.4 + 3.6 + 2.5$
6. $2 \cdot 3.5 \cdot 4$
7. $\frac{22}{7} \cdot 21$
8. $\frac{1}{2} \cdot 5 \cdot 4$
9. $3.2 \cdot 5.6$
10. $\frac{1}{2} \cdot 10 \cdot 3$
11. $(2 \cdot 5) + (6 \cdot 8)$
12. $2(3.5) + 2(1.5)$
13. $9(20 + 7)$

Measure with Metric Units

Use a centimeter ruler to measure each line to the nearest centimeter.

14. _____

15. _____

Identify Polygons

Name each polygon. Determine whether it appears to be regular or not regular.

16. [square]
17. [hexagon, 2 cm]
18. [polygon, 2 cm, 3 cm]

Measurement: Area and Volume

CHAPTER 10 Study Guide: Preview

Where You've Been

Previously, you
- selected appropriate units to measure perimeter, area, and volume.
- classified polygons.
- identified three-dimensional figures.

In This Chapter

You will study
- solving problems involving area.
- identifying, drawing, and building three-dimensional figures.
- finding the surface area of prisms, pyramids, and cylinders.
- finding the volume of prisms and cylinders.

Where You're Going

You can use the skills learned in this chapter
- to find the volume of pyramids, cones, and spheres.
- to find the surface area of spheres.

Key Vocabulary/Vocabulario

area	área
base	base (de un polígono o figura tridimensional)
cylinder	cilindro
edge	arista
face	cara
polyhedron	poliedro
pyramid	pirámide
surface area	área total
vertex	vértice
volume	volumen

Vocabulary Connections

To become familiar with some of the vocabulary terms in the chapter, consider the following. You may refer to the chapter, the glossary, or a dictionary if you like.

1. The word *cylinder* comes from the Greek *kylindein,* meaning "to roll." What do you think the three-dimensional shape of a **cylinder** can do? What shape base do you expect it to have?

2. The word *polyhedron* comes from the Greek *polys,* meaning "many" and *hedra,* meaning "base." What do you think **polyhedrons** are made up of?

3. The Egyptian pyramids are huge stone structures whose outside walls, in the form of four triangles, meet in a point at the top. What shapes do you think make up a **pyramid**?

4. The word *vertex* can mean "highest point." Where do you think you can find one **vertex** of a three-dimensional figure?

532 Chapter 10

Reading and Writing Math

CHAPTER 10

Reading Strategy: Learn Math Vocabulary

Many new math terms fill the pages of your textbook. By learning these new terms and their meanings when they are introduced, you will be able to apply this knowledge to different concepts throughout your math classes.

Some ways that may help you learn vocabulary include the following:

- Try to find the meaning of the new term by its context.
- Use the prefix or suffix to figure out the meaning of the term.
- Relate the new term to familiar everyday words or situations.

Vocabulary Word	Definition	Study Tip
Origin	The point (0, 0) where the *x*-axis and *y*-axis intersect on the coordinate plane	The word begins with an "O" which can remind you that the coordinates of the origin are (0, 0).
Quadrants	The *x*- and *y*- axis divide the coordinate plane into four regions. Each region is called a quadrant.	The prefix *quad* means "four." A *quadrilateral* is a four-sided figure, for example.
Coordinate	One of the numbers of an ordered pair that locate a point on a coordinate graph	*Think:* x coordinates with y.

origin = "O" → (0,0)

quad = 4

coordinate = coordinates with

Try This

Complete the table as you work through the chapter to help you learn the vocabulary words.

	Vocabulary Word	Definition	Study Tip
1.	Area		
2.			
3.			

Measurement: Area and Volume

10-1 Area of Rectangles and Parallelograms

Learn to estimate the area of irregular figures and to find the area of rectangles and parallelograms.

Vocabulary
area

When colonists settled the land that would become the United States, ownership boundaries were sometimes natural landmarks such as rivers, trees, and hills. Landowners who wanted to know the size of their property needed to estimate the area of their land.

The **area** of a figure is the amount of surface it covers. We measure area in square units.

EXAMPLE 1 Estimating the Area of an Irregular Figure

Estimate the area of the figure.

☐ = 1 mi²

Count full squares: 16 red squares.
Count almost-full squares: 11 blue squares.
Count squares that are about half-full:
4 green squares ≈ 2 full squares.
Do not count almost empty yellow squares.
Add. 16 + 11 + 2 = 29

The area of the figure is about 29 mi².

AREA OF A RECTANGLE

To find the area of a rectangle, multiply the length by the width.

$A = \ell w$
$A = 4 \cdot 3 = 12$

The area of the rectangle is 12 square units.

EXAMPLE 2 Finding the Area of a Rectangle

Find the area of the rectangle.

13 m
8 m

$A = \ell w$ Write the formula.
$A = 13 \cdot 8$ Substitute 13 for ℓ and 8 for w.
$A = 104$ Multiply.

The area is 104 m².

You can use the formula for the area of a rectangle to write a formula for the area of a parallelogram. Imagine cutting off the triangle drawn in the parallelogram and sliding it to the right to form a rectangle.

The area of a parallelogram = bh.   The area of a rectangle = ℓw.

The **base** of the parallelogram is the **length** of the rectangle.
The **height** of the parallelogram is the **width** of the rectangle.

EXAMPLE 3   Finding the Area of a Parallelogram

Find the area of the parallelogram.

$A = bh$ *Write the formula.*

$A = 2\frac{1}{3} \cdot 3\frac{1}{2}$ *Substitute $2\frac{1}{3}$ for b and $3\frac{1}{2}$ for h.*

$A = \frac{7}{3} \cdot \frac{7}{2}$ *Multiply.*

$A = \frac{49}{6}$, or $8\frac{1}{6}$ The area is $8\frac{1}{6}$ in^2.

EXAMPLE 4   Recreation Application

A rectangular park is made up of a rectangular spring-fed pool and a limestone picnic ground that surrounds it. The rectangular park is 30 yd by 25 yd, and the pool is 10 yd by 4 yd. What is the area of the limestone picnic ground?

To find the area of the picnic ground, subtract the area of the pool from the area of the park.

park area	−	pool area	=	picnic ground area	
(30 · 25)	−	(10 · 4)	=	n	*Substitute for ℓ and w in $A = \ell w$.*
750	−	40	=	710	*Use the order of operations.*

The area of the limestone picnic ground is 710 yd^2.

Think and Discuss

1. Explain how the area of a parallelogram and the area of a rectangle that have the same base and the same height are related.

2. Give a formula for the area of a square.

10-1 Exercises

Learn It Online
Homework Help Online go.hrw.com,
keyword MR10 10-1
Exercises 1–20, 25

GUIDED PRACTICE

See Example 1 — Estimate the area of each figure.

1.
2.
3.

See Example 2 — Find the area of each rectangle.

4. 7 mm, 14 mm
5. 13 in., 7.7 in.
6. 4 cm, 6 cm

See Example 3 — Find the area of each parallelogram.

7. 4 ft, 12 ft
8. $2\frac{1}{3}$ cm, 9 cm
9. 2.5 in., 4 in.

See Example 4

10. Mindy is designing a rectangular fountain in a courtyard. The rest of the courtyard will be covered with stone. The rectangular courtyard is 12 ft by 15 ft. What is the area of the courtyard that will be covered with stone?

Courtyard — 2 ft, 6 ft — Fountain

INDEPENDENT PRACTICE

See Example 1 — Estimate the area of each figure.

11.
12.
13.

See Example 2 — Find the area of each rectangle.

14. 5 mi, 25 mi
15. 1.5 m, 8.5 m
16. 2 cm, 12 cm

See Example 3 — Find the area of each parallelogram.

17. 13 ft, 20 ft
18. 2.2 in., 4.1 in.
19. 0.5 cm, 1.5 cm

See Example 4

20. Bob is planting in a rectangular container. In the center of the container, he places a smaller rectangular tub with mint. The tub is 8 in. by 3 in. He plants flowers around the tub. What is the area of the container planted with flowers?

Flowers — 38 in., 25 in. — Mint

Extra Practice See page EP20.

536 Chapter 10 Measurement: Area and Volume

Social Studies LINK

Iceland has many active volcanoes and frequent earthquakes. There are more hot springs in Iceland than in any other country in the world.

Use the map for Exercises 21 and 22.

21. **Choose a Strategy** One square on the map represents 1,700 km². Which is a reasonable estimate for the area of Iceland?

    A. Less than 65,000 km²
    B. Between 90,000 and 105,000 km²
    C. Between 120,000 and 135,000 km²
    D. Greater than 150,000 km²

22. **Estimation** About 10% of the area of Iceland is covered with glaciers. Estimate the area covered by glaciers.

23. **Write About It** The House is Iceland's oldest building. When it was built in 1765, the builders measured length in *ells*. The base of the House is 14 ells wide and 20 ells long. Explain how to find the area in ells of the House.

24. **Challenge** The length of one ell varied from country to country. In England, one ell was equal to $1\frac{1}{4}$ yd. Suppose the House were measured in English ells. Find the area in yards of the House.

Test Prep and Spiral Review

25. **Multiple Choice** A small square is inside a larger square. The larger square is 14 feet long. The smaller square is 2 feet long. What is the area of the shaded region?

    A. 52 ft²   B. 192 ft²   C. 196 ft²   D. 200 ft²

26. **Multiple Choice** Find the area of a rectangle with length 3 in. and width 12 in.

    F. 9 in²   G. 18 in²   H. 36 in²   J. 144 in²

List all the factors of each number. (Lesson 4-2)

27. 20   28. 85   29. 59   30. 40

31. A tree casts a shadow that is 14 feet long. At the same time, a 5.5-foot-tall boy casts a shadow that is 11 feet long. How tall is the tree? (Lesson 7-5)

10-1 Area of Rectangles and Parallelograms

Hands-on Lab 10-1

Squares and Square Roots

Use with Lesson 10-1

Learn It Online
Lab Resources Online go.hrw.com,
keyword MR10 Lab10 Go

VOCABULARY
- perfect square
- square root

WHAT YOU NEED
- grid paper

When a number is raised to the second power, or multiplied by itself, we say that it is squared. Because the length of any two sides of a square are equal, the area of any square can be written as $x \cdot x$, or x^2.

$A = x^2$, x, x

You can use grid paper to model the relationship between the area of a square and the length of its sides.

Activity

1 Use grid paper to copy the figures below. When you have copied these figures, continue the pattern until you have drawn 10 figures.

Figure 1   Figure 2   Figure 3

2 Use your drawings to complete the table.

Area of Figure (units²)	Side Length of Figure (units)
1	1
4	2
9	▪
16	▪
25	▪
36	▪

The numbers 1, 4, 9, 16, 25, and 36 are called *perfect squares*. A perfect square is the square of a whole number.

538 Chapter 10 Measurement: Area and Volume

❸ When the area of a square is 4, the side length is 2. Because $2^2 = 4$, we call 2 a *square root* of 4. This is written as $\sqrt{4}$.

Use your drawings to find $\sqrt{49}$, $\sqrt{64}$, $\sqrt{81}$, and $\sqrt{100}$. Record your results in the table.

Number	Square Root
49	▪
64	▪
81	▪
100	▪

Think and Discuss

1. Why do you think squaring 3 and finding $\sqrt{9}$ are called inverse operations?

2. Explain why the square root of 12 is not a whole number.

3. Can the area of any rectangle be found by squaring one of the sides? Explain.

Try This

Find the side length of each square. Explain how you found your answer.

1. Area = 121 units^2

2. Area = 144 units^2

3. Area = 196 units^2

4. Area = 225 units^2

5. Area = 361 units^2

6. Area = 400 units^2

Complete each equation.

7. $\sqrt{\Box} = 13$

8. $\sqrt{\Box} = 16$

9. $\sqrt{\Box} = 18$

10. Find two perfect squares whose sum is 100.

10-1 Hands-On Lab 539

10-2 Area of Triangles and Trapezoids

Learn to find the area of triangles and trapezoids.

The Flatiron Building in New York City was built in 1902. Many people consider it to be New York's first skyscraper. The foundation of the building is shaped like a triangle. You can find the area of the triangle to find how much land the building occupies.

You can divide any parallelogram into two congruent triangles. The area of each triangle is half the area of the parallelogram.

AREA OF A TRIANGLE

The area A of a triangle is half the product of its base b and its height h.

$$A = \tfrac{1}{2}bh$$

When the legs of a triangle meet at a 90° angle, the lengths of the legs can be used as the base and height.

EXAMPLE 1   Finding the Area of a Triangle

Find the area of each triangle.

Reading Math
An altitude of a triangle is a perpendicular segment from one vertex to the line containing the opposite side. The length of the altitude is the height.

A 8 cm, 12 cm

$A = \tfrac{1}{2}bh$ Write the formula.
$A = \tfrac{1}{2}(12 \cdot 8)$ Substitute 12 for b. Substitute 8 for h.
$A = \tfrac{1}{2}(96)$ Multiply.
$A = 48$

The area is 48 cm².

B $4\tfrac{1}{2}$ yd, 6 yd

$A = \tfrac{1}{2}bh$ Write the formula.
$A = \tfrac{1}{2}\left(6 \cdot 4\tfrac{1}{2}\right)$ Substitute 6 for b. Substitute $4\tfrac{1}{2}$ for h.
$A = \tfrac{1}{2}(27)$ Multiply.
$A = 13\tfrac{1}{2}$

The area is $13\tfrac{1}{2}$ yd².

540   Chapter 10 Measurement: Area and Volume

EXAMPLE 2 Architecture Application

The diagram shows the outline of the foundation of the Flatiron Building. What is the area of the foundation?

$A = \frac{1}{2}bh$ *Write the formula.*

$A = \frac{1}{2}(190 \cdot 79.1)$ *Substitute 190 for b. Substitute 79.1 for h.*

$A = \frac{1}{2}(15{,}029) = 7{,}514.5$ *Multiply.*

The area of the foundation is 7,514.5 ft².

You can divide a parallelogram into two congruent trapezoids. The area of each trapezoid is half the area of the parallelogram.

AREA OF A TRAPEZOID

The area A of a trapezoid is half the product of its height h and the sum of its bases b_1 and b_2.

$A = \frac{1}{2}h(b_1 + b_2)$

EXAMPLE 3 Finding the Area of a Trapezoid

Find the area of the trapezoid.

$A = \frac{1}{2}h(b_1 + b_2)$ *Write the formula.*

$A = \frac{1}{2}(6)(4.3 + 10.5)$ *Substitute 6 for h, 4.3 for b_1, and 10.5 for b_2.*

$A = \frac{1}{2}(6)(14.8) = 44.4$ *Multiply.*

The area is 44.4 m².

Think and Discuss

1. **Explain** how the areas of a triangle and a parallelogram with the same base and height are related.

2. **Explain** whether this is correct: To find the area of a trapezoid, multiply the height by the top base and the height by the bottom base. Then add the two numbers together and divide the sum by 2.

10-2 Exercises

Learn It Online
Homework Help Online go.hrw.com,
keyword MR10 10-2
Exercises 1–15, 17, 19, 21

GUIDED PRACTICE

See Example 1 Find the area of each triangle.

1. (triangle: 3 yd base, 2 yd height)
2. (triangle: 6 cm base, 11 cm height)
3. (triangle: 9 m side, 6 m height)

See Example 2

4. Harry plans to paint the triangular portion of the side of his house. How many square feet does he need to paint? (triangle with 8 ft height on top of a 20 ft wide rectangle)

See Example 3 Find the area of each trapezoid.

5. (trapezoid: 4 ft top, 9 ft bottom, 4 ft height)
6. (trapezoid: 6 in. top, 8 in. bottom, 4 in. height)
7. (trapezoid: 15 cm top, 7 cm bottom, 8 cm height)

INDEPENDENT PRACTICE

See Example 1 Find the area of each triangle.

8. (triangle: 9.25 m base, 8 m height)
9. (triangle: 6 ft base, 1 ft height)
10. (triangle: 6 yd base, 5 yd height)

See Example 2

11. Sean is making pennants for the school football team. How many square inches of felt does he use for one pennant? (triangle: 18 in. base, 8 in. height)

12. Erin has a triangular garden plot that is 5 meters long and 3 meters tall. What is the area of the plot?

See Example 3 Find the area of each trapezoid.

13. (trapezoid: 2 yd top, 6 yd bottom, 4 yd height)
14. (trapezoid: 16 in. top, 21 in. bottom, 12 in. height)
15. (trapezoid: 10 m top, 14 m bottom, 8 m height)

PRACTICE AND PROBLEM SOLVING

Extra Practice See page EP20.

16. The water in a drainage canal is 4 feet deep. What is the area of a cross section of the water in the ditch, which is shaped like a trapezoid? (trapezoid: 18 ft top, 8 ft bottom, 4 ft height)

542 Chapter 10 Measurement: Area and Volume

For Exercises 17–21, find the area of each figure.

17.

18.

19.

20. triangle: $b = 2\frac{1}{2}$ in.; $h = 1\frac{3}{4}$ in.   **21.** trapezoid: $b_1 = 18$ m; $b_2 = 27$ m; $h = 15.4$ m

22. Social Studies The shape of the state of Nevada is similar to a trapezoid with the measurements shown. Estimate the area of the state in square miles.

320 mi
198 mi
490 mi

23. Critical Thinking The areas and heights of a triangle and a rectangle are the same. How do the lengths of their bases compare?

Find the missing measurement for each figure.

24. Area = 16 in²

3 in.
h
5 in.

25. Area = 5 cm²

2 cm
b

26. Area = 18 m²

h
6 m

27. Write a Problem Write a problem about a trapezoid with bases 12 ft and 18 ft and height 10 ft.

28. Write About It Two triangles have the same base. The height of one triangle is half the height of the other. How do the areas of the triangles compare?

29. Challenge Find the area of the unshaded portion of the trapezoid.

18 m
15 m
36 m

Social Studies

Nevada has many ghost towns scattered around the state. Many were once boom-towns built during the gold and silver mining rush.

Test Prep and Spiral Review

30. Multiple Choice A building sign in the shape of a trapezoid has the measurements shown. Which expression can be used to find the area of the sign?

10 ft
11 ft
18 ft

Ⓐ $\frac{1}{2}(11)(10 + 18)$ Ⓑ $\frac{1}{2}(18)(10)$ Ⓒ $\frac{1}{2}(11)(10)(18)$ Ⓓ $(11)(10 + 18)$

31. Short Response Find the area of a right triangle with legs measuring 14 cm and 25 cm.

Multiply. Write each answer in simplest form. (Lesson 5-6)

32. $3 \cdot \frac{2}{7}$ **33.** $4 \cdot \frac{3}{5}$ **34.** $12 \cdot \frac{9}{10}$ **35.** $15 \cdot \frac{1}{2}$

36. Zeb earned $24,000 last year. This year, his salary increased by 5%. How much will he earn? (Lesson 7-9)

10-2 Area of Triangles and Trapezoids   543

Hands-on Lab 10-2: Explore Perimeter and Area

Use with Lesson 10-2

WHAT YOU NEED:
- 1-inch grid paper
- corkboard
- 30-inch piece of string
- 4 push pins

REMEMBER
$P = 2l + 2w$
$A = lw$

Attach 1-inch grid paper to a piece of corkboard. Then use string and push pins to model the relationship between perimeters and areas.

Activity

1. Set push pins at grid intersections to model the first rectangle in the table below.

2. Use the string to measure the perimeter. Multiply to find the area of the rectangle. Model each of the rectangles in the table below and record its perimeter and area.

Length	Width	Perimeter (in.)	Area (in²)
2	10	24	20
3	9	24	27
4	8	24	32
5	7	24	35

3. Use push pins to model rectangles with the dimensions in the table below. Use the string to measure the perimeters. Multiply to find the areas. Record your results in the table below.

Length	Width	Perimeter (in.)	Area (in²)
1	12	26	12
2	6	16	12
3	4	14	12

Think and Discuss

1. Compare the perimeters and areas of each rectangle in the first table.

2. Compare the perimeters and areas of each rectangle in the second table.

Try This

1. List all the whole-number dimensions of rectangles with a perimeter of 16 inches.

2. List all the whole-number dimensions of rectangles with an area of 18 square inches.

10-3 Area of Composite Figures

Learn to break a polygon into simpler parts to find its area.

You can find the areas of irregular polygons by breaking them apart into rectangles, parallelograms, and triangles.

EXAMPLE 1 Finding Areas of Composite Figures

Find the area of each polygon.

A

Think: Break the polygon apart into rectangles.

Find the area of each rectangle.

$A = \ell w$ $A = \ell w$ *Write the formula for the area of a rectangle.*

$A = 1.8 \cdot 1.5$ $A = 2 \cdot 0.5$

$A = 2.7$ $A = 1$

$2.7 + 1 = 3.7$ *Add to find the total area.*

The area of the polygon is 3.7 cm².

Helpful Hint

In Example 1A, the figure could be broken apart as follows.

1.5 cm, 1.3 cm
3.5 cm, 0.5 cm

The area is the same.

B

Think: Break the figure apart into a triangle and a rectangle.

$A = \ell w$ $A = \frac{1}{2} bh$ *Find the area of each polygon.*

$A = 8 \cdot 10$ $A = \frac{1}{2} \cdot 8 \cdot 3$

$A = 80$ $A = 12$

$80 + 12 = 92$ *Add to find the total area of the figure.*

The area of the figure is 92 cm².

EXAMPLE 2

Art Application

Stan made a wall hanging. Use the coordinate grid to find its area.

Think: Divide the wall hanging into rectangles.

Find the area of each rectangle.

Rectangle 1
$\ell = 8, w = 4; A = 8 \cdot 4 = 32$

Rectangle 2
$\ell = 6, w = 2; A = 6 \cdot 2 = 12$

Rectangle 3
$\ell = 4, w = 6; A = 4 \cdot 6 = 24$

Add the areas of the three rectangles to find the total area of the wall hanging.

$32 + 12 + 24 = 68$ square units

The area of the wall hanging is 68 square units.

Helpful Hint

You can also count the squares and multiply by the area of one square.
1 square = 4 square units
$17 \cdot 4 = 68$ square units

Think and Discuss

1. **Explain** how you can find the area of a regular octagon by breaking it apart into congruent triangles, if you know the area of one triangle.

2. **Explain** another way that you can divide the wall hanging in Example 2.

10-3 Exercises

Learn It Online
Homework Help Online go.hrw.com,
keyword MR10 10-3
Exercises 1–6, 11

GUIDED PRACTICE

See Example 1 Find the area of each polygon.

1. 20 m, 70 m, 50 m, 90 m

2. 10.2 cm, 1 cm, 1.8 cm, 1 cm, 5.4 cm

See Example 2 3. Gina used tiles to create a design. Use the coordinate grid to find the area of Gina's design.

546 Chapter 10 Measurement: Area and Volume

INDEPENDENT PRACTICE

See Example 1 Find the area of each polygon.

4. [figure: L-shaped polygon with sides $9\frac{1}{2}$ in., 2 in., $4\frac{1}{3}$ in., $6\frac{1}{3}$ in., 3 in.]

5. [figure: polygon with 11 yd, 21 yd, 40 yd]

See Example 2

6. Edgar plants daffodils around a rectangular pond. The yellow part of the diagram shows where the daffodils are planted. Use the coordinate grid to find the area of the yellow part of the diagram.

[coordinate grid figure showing L-shaped yellow region with Pond labeled]

PRACTICE AND PROBLEM SOLVING

Extra Practice
See page EP20.

7. **Social Studies** The map shows the approximate dimensions of the state of South Australia, outlined in red.

   a. Estimate the area of the state of South Australia.

   b. The total area of Australia is about 7.7 million km². About what fraction of the total area of Australia is the area of the state of South Australia?

8. **Write About It** Draw a figure that can be broken up into two rectangles. Label the lengths of each side. Explain how you can find the area of the figure. Then find the area.

9. **Challenge** The perimeter of the figure is 42.5 cm. Find the area of this figure.

Test Prep and Spiral Review

10. **Multiple Choice** What is the area of the polygon?

    (F) 40 cm²   (G) 65 cm²   (H) 45 cm²   (J) 90 cm²

    [figure: pentagon/house shape with 9 cm, 4 cm, 10 cm]

11. **Gridded Response** Use the coordinate grid to find the area, in square units, of the polygon.

    [coordinate grid figure]

Find each sum or difference. Write the answer in simplest form. (Lesson 5-3)

12. $4\frac{1}{3} + 7\frac{5}{12}$

13. $8\frac{1}{2} - 3\frac{1}{3}$

14. $6\frac{2}{3} + 3\frac{1}{6}$

15. $8\frac{7}{10} - 2\frac{2}{5}$

Find the area of each polygon. (Lesson 10-1)

16. rectangle: $\ell = 14$ m; $w = 11$ m

17. parallelogram: $b = 18$ cm; $h = 8$ cm

10-3 Area of Composite Figures

10-4 Changing Dimensions

Learn to make a model to explore how area and perimeter are affected by changes in the dimensions of a figure.

Ms. Cohn wants to enlarge a photo by doubling its length and width.

Recall that similar figures have exactly the same shape but not necessarily the same size. Doubling the dimensions of the photo will create a larger photo similar to the original.

You can draw a model on graph paper to see how the perimeter and the area of a figure change when its dimensions change.

EXAMPLE 1

Interactivities Online

Comparing Perimeters and Areas

Find how the perimeter and the area of the figure change when its dimensions change.

Draw a model of the two figures on graph paper. Label the dimensions.

☐ = 1 in²

The original photo is a 3 in. × 2 in. rectangle.

Perimeter:

$P = 2(\ell + w)$
$= 2(3 + 2)$ *Substitute for ℓ and w.*
$= 2(5)$
$= 10$ *Simplify.*

The perimeter is 10 in.

Area:

$A = \ell w$
$= 3 \times 2$ *Substitute for ℓ and w.*
$= 6$ *Simplify.*

The area is 6 in².

The enlarged photo is a 6 in. × 4 in. rectangle.

Perimeter:

$P = 2(\ell + w)$
$= 2(6 + 4)$
$= 2(10)$
$= 20$

The perimeter is 20 in.

Area:

$A = \ell w$
$= 6 \times 4$
$= 24$

The area is 24 in².

When the dimensions of the rectangle are doubled, the perimeter is also doubled, and the area becomes four times as great.

548 Chapter 10 Measurement: Area and Volume

EXAMPLE 2 **Measurement Application**

Use a centimeter ruler to measure the photo. Draw a rectangle whose sides are 3 times as long to enlarge the photo. How do the perimeter and the area change?

$P = 6$ cm
$A = 2$ cm^2

Multiply each dimension by 3.
$P = 18$ cm
$A = 18$ cm^2

When the dimensions of the rectangle are multiplied by 3, the **perimeter** is multiplied by **3**, and the **area** is multiplied by **9**, or **3^2**.

Think and Discuss

1. **Explain** how the perimeter of a triangle changes when all the side lengths are doubled.
2. **Tell** how the area of a rectangle changes when all the side lengths are divided in half.

10-4 Exercises

Learn It Online
Homework Help Online go.hrw.com,
keyword MR10 10-4
Exercises 1–4, 5, 9

GUIDED PRACTICE

See Example 1
1. Find how the perimeter and the area of the figure change when its dimensions change.

See Example 2
2. Use a centimeter ruler to measure the rectangle. Draw a rectangle whose sides are 2 times as long to enlarge the rectangle. How do the perimeter and the area change?

10-4 Changing Dimensions   549

INDEPENDENT PRACTICE

See Example 1

3. Find how the perimeter and the area of the figure change when its dimensions change.

See Example 2

4. Use a centimeter ruler to measure the triangle. Draw a triangle whose sides are half as long to reduce the triangle. How do the perimeter and the area change?

PRACTICE AND PROBLEM SOLVING

Extra Practice
See page EP20.

5. The schoolyard is a rectangle with a length of 120 ft and a width of 80 ft. The PE teacher plans to make a field in the schoolyard.

   a. What will the area of the field be if she divides only one of the dimensions of the schoolyard in half?

   b. What will the perimeter of the field be if she divides only the length in half? the width in half?

6. **Critical Thinking** If George enlarges a 3 in. × 4 in. photo so that it is 12 in. × 16 in., how will its area change?

7. **Write About It** What happens to the area and the perimeter of a rectangle when the length and width are multiplied by 4?

8. **Challenge** A rectangle has a perimeter of 24 meters. If its length and width are whole numbers, what is its greatest possible area?

Test Prep and Spiral Review

9. **Multiple Choice** A photo is 4 in. × 6 in. long. To enlarge the photo, Lee doubles both the length and width. Find the perimeter of the enlarged photo.

   (A) 8 in.   (B) 12 in.   (C) 20 in.   (D) 40 in.

10. **Multiple Choice** If Jinny enlarges a 3 in. × 4 in. photo so that it is 12 in. × 16 in., how will its area change?

    (F) The area will increase by 2 times.   (H) The area will increase by 3^2.
    (G) The area will increase by 2^2 times.   (J) The area will increase by 4^2 times.

Write each fraction in simplest form. (Lesson 4-5)

11. $\frac{9}{12}$ 12. $\frac{4}{16}$ 13. $\frac{5}{10}$ 14. $\frac{25}{100}$ 15. $\frac{65}{100}$

Find the perimeter of each figure. (Lesson 9-7)

16. 125 ft, 30 ft

17. 18 cm, 8 cm, 8 cm, 8 cm, 4 cm, 2 cm

550   Chapter 10 Measurement: Area and Volume

Hands-On LAB 10-5

Explore Area of Circles

Use with Lesson 10-5

Learn It Online
Lab Resources Online go.hrw.com,
keyword MR10 Lab10 Go

You can use what you know about circles and *pi* to learn about the area of circles.

Activity

1. The *radius* of a circle is half of its diameter. Use a compass to draw a circle with a 2-inch radius. Cut your circle out and fold it three times as shown.

2. Unfold the circle, trace the folds, and shade one-half of the circle.

3. Cut along the folds, and fit the pieces together to make a figure that looks approximately like a parallelogram.

   Think of this figure as a parallelogram. The base and height of the parallelogram relate to the parts of the circle.

   base $b = \frac{1}{2}$ the circumference of the circle, or πr

   height $h =$ the radius of the circle, or r

   To find the area of a parallelogram, use the equation $A = bh$.

   To find the area of a circle, use the equation $A = \pi r(r) = \pi r^2$.

Think and Discuss

1. Compare the lengths of all the diameters of a circle.
2. Compare the lengths of all the radii of a circle.

Try This

Find the area of each circle with the given measure. Use 3.14 for π. Round to the nearest tenth.

1. $r = 4$ yd
2. 2.5 m
3. $d = 10$ m
4. 7.5 ft

10-5 Hands-On Lab **551**

10-5 Area of Circles

Learn to find the area of a circle.

In medieval times, circular shields were usually made from wood that was covered with leather or steel. The amount of leather or steel needed to cover a shield depended upon the shield's area.

AREA OF A CIRCLE

The area of a circle is equal to π times the radius squared.

$A = \pi r^2$

You can estimate the area of a circle by using 3 to approximate the value of π.

EXAMPLE 1 Estimating the Area of a Circle

Estimate the area of each circle. Use 3 to approximate π.

A 6 in.

$A = \pi r^2$ Write the formula for the area.
$A \approx 3 \cdot 6^2$ Replace π with 3 and r with 6.
$A \approx 3 \cdot 36$ Use the order of operations.
$A \approx 108$ in^2 Multiply.

B 50.4 m

$A = \pi r^2$ Write the formula for the area.
$r = d \div 2$ The length of the radius is half the
$r = 50.4 \div 2$ length of the diameter.
$r = 25.2$ Divide.
$r \approx 25$ Round 25.2 to 25.

$A \approx 3 \cdot 25^2$ Replace π with 3 and r with 25.
$A \approx 3 \cdot 625$ Use the order of operations.
$A \approx 1,875$ m^2 Multiply.

552   Chapter 10 Measurement: Area and Volume   Video   Lesson Tutorials Online   my.hrw.com

EXAMPLE 2 Using the Formula for the Area of a Circle

Find the area of each circle. Use $\frac{22}{7}$ for π.

A 14 in.

$A = \pi r^2$ — Write the formula for the area.
$r = d \div 2$ — The length of the radius is half
$r = 14 \div 2$ — the length of the diameter.
$r = 7$ — Divide.

$A \approx \frac{22}{7} \cdot 7^2$ — Replace π with $\frac{22}{7}$ and r with 7.
$A \approx \frac{22}{7_1} \cdot \overset{7}{\cancel{49}}$ — Use the GCF to simplify.
$A \approx 154$ in² — Multiply.

B 21 cm

$A = \pi r^2$ — Write the formula for the area.
$A \approx \frac{22}{7} \cdot 21^2$ — Replace π with $\frac{22}{7}$ and r with 21.
$A \approx \frac{22}{7} \cdot 441$ — Use the order of operations.
$A \approx \frac{9702}{7}$ — Multiply.
$A \approx 1386$ cm² — Divide.

EXAMPLE 3 History Application

A circular shield has a diameter of 20 inches. Find the area of the steel needed to cover one side of the shield. Use 3.14 for π.

20 in.

$A = \pi r^2$ — Write the formula for the area.
$r = d \div 2$ — The length of the radius is half
$r = 20 \div 2$ — the length of the diameter.
$r = 10$ — Divide.

$A \approx 3.14 \cdot 10^2$ — Replace π with 3.14 and r with 10.
$A \approx 3.14 \cdot 100$ — Use the order of operations.
$A \approx 314$ in² — Multiply.

Check Use 3 as an estimate for π. The area, πr^2, is approximately $3 \cdot 10^2 = 3 \cdot 100 = 300$, so the answer is reasonable.

Think and Discuss

1. **Describe** how you could estimate the area of a circle whose radius is 1 cm.

2. **Explain** why the area of a circle with a radius of 5 ft must be greater than 75 ft².

3. **Tell** how you can check that your answer is reasonable after you have calculated the area of a circle.

10-5 Exercises

Learn It Online
Homework Help Online go.hrw.com, keyword MR10 10-5
Exercises 1–14, 15, 17, 19

GUIDED PRACTICE

See Example 1 Estimate the area of each circle. Use 3 to approximate π.

1. 4 ft
2. 8.1 in.
3. 18.2 in.

See Example 2 Find the area of each circle. Use $\frac{22}{7}$ for π.

4. 7 ft
5. 28 cm
6. 3.5 m

See Example 3
7. **Architecture** A circular window has a diameter of 4 ft. Find the area of the glass needed to fill the window. Use 3.14 for π.

INDEPENDENT PRACTICE

See Example 1 Estimate the area of each circle. Use 3 to approximate π.

8. 12 m
9. 32.4 in.
10. 6.1 m

See Example 2 Find the area of each circle. Use $\frac{22}{7}$ for π.

11. 7 yd
12. 77 cm
13. 56 ft

See Example 3
14. **Cooking** A pizza recipe calls for the dough to be rolled out to form a circle with a diameter of 18 in. Find the area of the dough when it is rolled out. Use 3.14 for π.

PRACTICE AND PROBLEM SOLVING

Extra Practice
See page EP20.

Find the area and circumference of each circle. Use 3.14 for π and round to the nearest hundredth.

15. 5.7 cm
16. 63 ft
17. 14.9 in.

554 Chapter 10 Measurement: Area and Volume

Earth Science

Scientists estimate that the asteroid that struck the earth to form Meteor Crater was about 80 ft in diameter.

18. **Sports** The diameter of the circle that a shot-putter stands in is 7 ft. What is the area of the circle? Use $\frac{22}{7}$ for π.

19. **Earth Science** Meteor Crater in central Arizona was formed when an asteroid struck Earth between 20,000 and 50,000 years ago. The circular crater has a diameter of 1.2 km. Find the area of the crater to the nearest hundredth. Use 3.14 for π.

20. **Multi-Step** A restaurant makes pizzas with 6 in. diameters and 12 in. diameters.

    a. Estimate the difference between the areas of the two sizes of pizzas. (Use 3.14 for π. Round to the nearest whole number.)

    b. Is the area of the 12 in. pizza about twice the area of the 6 in. pizza? Explain.

21. **Critical Thinking** The area of a circular garden plot is 30 ft². Explain why the diameter of the plot must be greater than 6 ft.

22. **What's the Error?** A student estimated the area of this circle as shown. Explain the student's error.

    12 in.

    $A = \pi r^2$
    $A \approx 3 \cdot 12^2$
    $A \approx 3 \cdot 144$
    $A \approx 432$ in²

23. **Write About It** Describe a step-by-step process you can use to estimate the area of a circle.

24. **Challenge** What is the area of the shaded part of the figure? Use 3.14 for π. Round the answer to the nearest hundredth.

    2 m

Test Prep and Spiral Review

25. **Multiple Choice** Jerome knows the radius of a baking pan. He needs to estimate the pan's area. Which method can Jerome use to estimate the area?

    Ⓐ Multiply the radius by 3.

    Ⓑ Divide the radius by 2 and square the result.

    Ⓒ Square the radius and multiply the result by 3.

    Ⓓ Multiply the radius by 3 and square the result.

26. **Gridded Response** Find the area, in square inches, of a circle with a diameter of 10 in. Use 3.14 for π.

Multiply. Write each answer in simplest form. (Lesson 5-7)

27. $\frac{3}{8} \cdot \frac{4}{9}$

28. $\frac{7}{10} \cdot \frac{3}{14}$

29. $\frac{8}{9} \cdot \frac{5}{16}$

30. $\frac{6}{15} \cdot \frac{10}{21}$

Divide. Write each answer in simplest form. (Lesson 5-9)

31. $\frac{3}{5} \div 5$

32. $\frac{4}{9} \div 12$

33. $\frac{5}{6} \div \frac{2}{3}$

34. $2\frac{4}{5} \div 1\frac{1}{2}$

10-5 Area of Circles

Chapter 10 Ready To Go On?

Quiz for Lessons 10-1 Through 10-5

10-1 Area of Rectangles and Parallelograms

Find the area of each figure.

1. Rectangle with length 62 cm and width 41 cm.

2. Parallelogram with base $5\frac{1}{3}$ ft and height $2\frac{1}{4}$ ft.

3. Mark is making a rectangular vegetable garden in his backyard. The rest of the backyard is covered with gravel. What is the area of the backyard that is covered with gravel?

   Backyard: 75 ft by 120 ft; garden: 24 ft by 15 ft.

10-2 Area of Triangles and Trapezoids

Find the area of each figure.

4. Triangle with base 3 cm and height 2 cm.

5. Trapezoid with parallel sides 4.5 ft and 7.5 ft, height 3 ft.

6. Triangle with base 8 m and height 5.8 m.

10-3 Area of Composite Figures

7. Find the area of the polygon.

   Dimensions: 7 ft, 5 ft, 10 ft, 11 ft, 25 ft.

8. Using the approximate dimensions, estimate the area of the state of Oklahoma.

   Dimensions: 464 mi, 167 mi, 35 mi, 222 mi.

10-4 Changing Dimensions

9. The length and width of a rectangle are each multiplied by 4. Find how the perimeter and the area of the rectangle change.

10-5 Area of Circles

Find the area of each circle. Use 3.14 for π. Round to the nearest hundredth.

10. Circle with center A and radius AC = 7 cm.

11. Circle with center D and radius DG = 3 in.

12. Circle with center I and radius FG = $8\frac{1}{4}$ km.

13. Circle with center K and diameter JL = 42 cm.

Focus on Problem Solving

Solve
• **Choose the operation**

Read the whole problem before you try to solve it. Determine what action is taking place in the problem. Then decide whether you need to add, subtract, multiply, or divide in order to solve the problem.

Action	Operation
Combining or putting together	Add
Removing or taking away Comparing or finding the difference	Subtract
Combining equal groups	Multiply
Sharing equally or separating into equal groups	Divide

Read each problem and determine the action taking place. Choose an operation, and then solve the problem.

1 There are 3 lily ponds in the botanical gardens. They are identical in size and shape. The total area of the ponds is 165 ft^2. What is the area of each lily pond?

2 The greenhouse is made up of 6 rectangular rooms with an area of 4,800 ft^2 each. What is the total area of the greenhouse?

3 A shady area with 17 different varieties of magnolia trees, which bloom from March to June, surrounds the plaza in Magnolia Park. In the center of the plaza, there is a circular bed of shrubs as shown in the chart. If the total area of the park is 625 ft^2, what is the area of the plaza?

Magnolia Park

Plaza

Area of shrubs: 20 ft^2

Area of magnolia trees: 450 ft^2

Hands-on Lab 10-6: Draw Views of Three-Dimensional Figures

Use with Lesson 10-6

Activity 1

1. Draw a rectangular prism. Imagine that you are looking at the top of the prism, and draw what you would see. Draw the front and side views of the prism.

   Top   Front   Side

   All the faces of a rectangular prism are rectangles.

2. Stack centimeter cubes to make the three-dimensional figure shown. Draw the top, front, and side views.

   Top   Front   Side

   Each view shows a different configuration of squares representing the number of cubes you see.

Think and Discuss

1. Explain why a side view of a three-dimensional figure might change if you look at a different side.

Try This

Draw the top, front, and side views of each three-dimensional figure.

1.
2.
3.

558 Chapter 10 Measurement: Area and Volume

Activity 2

You can use different views of a solid to construct the figure.

Using centimeter cubes, construct a three-dimensional figure that has the given views.

Top   Front   Side

Step 1: Start with the top view of the solid and place the cubes.

Step 2: Use the front view to stack two more cubes on the left side.

Step 3: Check that the side view is correct. Since the side view is correct, there are no more cubes to add.

This is the three-dimensional figure that has the given views.

Think and Discuss

1. Explain why it is a good idea to start with the top view.

Try This

Using centimeter cubes, construct the three-dimensional figure that has the given views.

1. Top   Front   Side

2. Top   Front   Side

10-6 Hands-On Lab   **559**

10-6 Three-Dimensional Figures

Learn to name three-dimensional figures.

Vocabulary
polyhedron
face   edge
vertex
prism
base
cylinder
pyramid
cone
sphere

A **polyhedron** is a three-dimensional object with flat surfaces, called **faces**, that are polygons.

When two faces of a three-dimensional figure share a side, they form an **edge**. A point at which three or more edges meet is a **vertex** (plural: *vertices*).

A cube is formed by 6 square faces. It has 8 vertices and 12 edges. The polyhedrons in the photo each have 5 faces, 6 vertices, and 9 edges. Shapes like this are used to reflect light resulting in rainbows.

EXAMPLE 1   Identifying Faces, Edges, and Vertices

Interactivities Online ▶

Identify the number of faces, edges, and vertices on each three-dimensional figure.

A
5 faces
9 edges
6 vertices

B
6 faces
12 edges
8 vertices

A **prism** is a polyhedron with two congruent, parallel **bases**, and other faces that are all parallelograms. A prism is named for the shape of its bases. A **cylinder** also has two congruent, parallel bases, but bases of a cylinder are circular. A cylinder is not a polyhedron because not every surface is a polygon.

Rectangular prism   Hexagonal prism   Cylinder

Helpful Hint

Cones and spheres are not polyhedrons because they have curved surfaces.

A **pyramid** has one polygon-shaped base and three or more triangular faces that share a vertex. A pyramid is named for the shape of its base. A **cone** has a circular base and a curved surface that comes to a point. A **sphere** has no base and one curved surface. All points on the surface are the same distance from a point called the center of the sphere.

Square pyramid   **Triangular pyramid**   **Cone**   **Sphere**

EXAMPLE 2 Naming Three-Dimensional Figures

Name each three-dimensional figure represented by each object.

A
All the faces are flat and are squares.
The figure is a polyhedron.
There are two congruent, parallel bases, so the figure is a prism.
The bases are squares.
The figure is a cube.

B
There is a curved surface.
The figure is not a polyhedron.
There is a flat, circular base.
The curved surface comes to a point.
The figure represents a cone.

C
All the faces are flat and are polygons.
The figure is a polyhedron.
It has one base and the other faces are triangles that meet at a point, so the figure is a pyramid.
The base is a square.
The figure is a square pyramid.

Think and Discuss

1. **Compare** a pyramid and a prism.
2. **Compare** a cone and a pyramid.

10-6 Exercises

Learn It Online
Homework Help Online go.hrw.com, keyword MR10 10-6 Go
Exercises 1–12, 13, 15, 17, 19, 21, 23, 25

GUIDED PRACTICE

See Example 1 Identify the number of faces, edges, and vertices on each three-dimensional figure.

1.
2.
3.

See Example 2 Name each three-dimensional figure represented by each object.

4.
5.
6.

INDEPENDENT PRACTICE

See Example 1 Identify the number of faces, edges, and vertices on each three-dimensional figure.

7.
8.
9.

See Example 2 Name each three-dimensional figure represented by each object.

10.
11.
12.

PRACTICE AND PROBLEM SOLVING

Extra Practice
See page EP21.

Name each figure and tell whether it is a polyhedron.

13.
14.
15.

Write the letter of all the figures that match each description.

16. prism
17. has triangular faces
18. has 6 faces
19. has 5 vertices

562 Chapter 10 Measurement: Area and Volume

Write *true* or *false* for each statement.

20. A cone does not have a flat surface.

21. The bases of a cylinder are congruent.

22. All pyramids have five or more vertices.

23. All of the edges of a cube are congruent.

24. **Architecture** Name the three-dimensional figure represented by each building.

    a.   b.   c.

25. **Critical Thinking** Li makes candles with her mother. She made a candle in the shape of a pyramid that had 9 faces. How many sides did the base of the candle have? Name the polyhedron formed by the candle.

26. **What's the Error?** A student says that any polyhedron can be named if the number of faces it has is known. What is the student's error?

27. **Write About It** How are a cone and cylinder alike? How are they different?

28. **Challenge** A square pyramid is cut in half, and the cut is made parallel to the base of the pyramid. What are the shapes of the faces of the bottom half of the pyramid?

Test Prep and Spiral Review

29. **Multiple Choice** Which figure has the greatest number of faces?

    Ⓐ Cone   Ⓑ Cube   Ⓒ Octagonal prism   Ⓓ Triangular prism

30. **Multiple Choice** Which figure has a circular base?

    Ⓕ Cube   Ⓖ Cylinder   Ⓗ Square pyramid   Ⓙ Triangular prism

Compare. Write <, >, or =. (Lesson 3-1)

31. 9.04 ▨ 9.404   32. 12.7 ▨ 12.70   33. 0.03 ▨ 0.003   34. 5.12 ▨ 5.125

Classify each pair of lines. (Lesson 8-4)

35.   36.   37.

Hands-on LAB 10-7

Explore Volumes of Prisms and Cylinders

Use with Lesson 10-7

Learn It Online
Lab Resources Online go.hrw.com,
keyword MR10 Lab10

REMEMBER
- Volume is the number of cubic units needed to fill a space.

You can use centimeter cubes to help you find the volume of a *prism*.

Activity

Use the steps and diagrams below to fill in the table.

	Length (ℓ)	Width (w)	Height (h)	Total Number of Cubes (V)
Figure A				
Figure B				
Figure C				

1. Draw a 4 × 3 rectangle on centimeter graph paper. Place centimeter cubes on the rectangle. *(Figure A)* How many cubes did you use? What is the height of this prism?

2. Make a prism that is 2 units tall. *(Figure B)* How many cubes did you use?

3. Make a prism that is 5 units tall. *(Figure C)* How many cubes did you use?

Think and Discuss

1. How can you use the length, width, and height of a prism to find the total number of cubes without counting them?

2. Use your answer from Problem 1 to write a formula for the volume of a prism.

3. When the height of the prism is doubled, what happens to the volume?

Try This

Build each rectangular prism and find its volume.

1. $\ell = 4$; $w = 2$; $h = 3$
2. $\ell = 1$; $w = 4$; $h = 5$
3. $\ell = 3$; $w = 3$; $h = 3$
4. $\ell = 5$; $w = 10$; $h = 2$

5. Estimate the volume of a shoe box. Fill it with centimeter cubes. How close was your estimate?

You can use graph paper and centimeter cubes to estimate the volume of a *cylinder*.

Activity 2

Use the steps below to fill in the table to estimate the volume of a can.

	Estimated Area of Base (A)	Height (h)	Volume (V)
Can	■	■	■

1. Trace around the bottom of a can on graph paper. Count the squares inside the circle to estimate the area A of the bottom of the can.

2. Use centimeter cubes to find the height of the can.

3. Use centimeter cubes to build a prism that covers the area of the circle and is the height of the can. Find the volume of the can by counting the cubes used to build the prism or by using $V = A \times h$.

Think and Discuss

1. If you measure the radius of the base, what expression can you use to find the exact area of the circle?

2. Use the expression you found in Problem 1 to write a formula for the volume of a cylinder.

3. When the height of the cylinder is doubled, how does the volume change?

Try This

Estimate the volume of different-sized cans.

		Estimated Area of Base (A)	Height (h)	Volume (V)
1.	Tuna Can	■	■	■
2.		■	■	■
3.		■	■	■

10-7 Hands-On Lab   565

10-7 Volume of Prisms

Learn to estimate and find the volumes of rectangular prisms and triangular prisms.

Vocabulary
volume

Interactivities Online ▶

Volume is the number of cubic units needed to fill a space.

You need 10, or 5 · 2, centimeter cubes to cover the bottom of this rectangular prism.

You need 3 layers of 10 cubes each to fill the prism. It takes 30, or 5 · 2 · 3, cubes.

Volume is expressed in cubic units, so the volume of the prism is 5 cm · 2 cm · 3 cm = 30 cubic centimeters, or 30 cm³.

EXAMPLE 1 Finding the Volume of a Rectangular Prism

Find the volume of the rectangular prism.

20 in., 36 in., 80 in.

$V = \ell wh$ Write the formula.
$V = 80 \cdot 36 \cdot 20$ $\ell = 80; w = 36; h = 20$
$V = 57{,}600 \text{ in}^3$ Multiply.

To find the volume of any prism, you can use the formula $V = Bh$, where B is the area of the base, and h is the prism's height.

EXAMPLE 2 Finding the Volume of a Triangular Prism

Find the volume of each triangular prism.

A 2.8 m, 4.2 m, 5 m

$V = Bh$ Write the formula.
$V = \left(\frac{1}{2} \cdot 2.8 \cdot 4.2\right) \cdot 5$ $B = \frac{1}{2} \cdot 2.8 \cdot 4.2; h = 5$
$V = 29.4 \text{ m}^3$ Multiply.

B 4.3 ft, 9 ft, 8.2 ft

$V = Bh$ Write the formula.
$V = \left(\frac{1}{2} \cdot 8.2 \cdot 4.3\right) \cdot 9$ $B = \frac{1}{2} \cdot 8.2 \cdot 4.3; h = 9$
$V = 158.67 \text{ ft}^3$ Multiply.

Caution!
The bases of a prism are always two congruent, parallel polygons.

EXAMPLE 3 PROBLEM SOLVING APPLICATION

A toy maker ships 12 alphabet blocks in a box. What are the possible dimensions for a box of the alphabet blocks?

1. Understand the Problem

The **answer** will be all possible dimensions for a box of 12 cubic blocks.

List the **important information:**

- There are 12 blocks in a box.
- The blocks are cubic, or square prisms.

2. Make a Plan

You can make models using cubes to find the possible dimensions for a box of 12 blocks.

3. Solve

Make different arrangements of 12 cubes.

$12 \times 1 \times 1$

$4 \times 3 \times 1$

$6 \times 2 \times 1$

$3 \times 2 \times 2$

The possible dimensions for a box of 12 alphabet blocks are the following: $12 \times 1 \times 1$, $4 \times 3 \times 1$, $6 \times 2 \times 1$, and $3 \times 2 \times 2$.

4. Look Back

Notice that each dimension is a factor of 12. Also, the product of the dimensions (length · width · height) is 12, showing that the volume of each case is 12 cubes.

Think and Discuss

1. **Explain** how to find the height of a rectangular prism if you know its length, width, and volume.
2. **Describe** the difference between the units used to measure perimeter, area, and volume.

10-7 Exercises

Learn It Online
Homework Help Online go.hrw.com,
keyword MR10 10-7
Exercises 1–14, 15, 17, 19, 21, 23

GUIDED PRACTICE

See Example 1 Find the volume of each rectangular prism.

1. 2 cm, 9 cm, 9 cm
2. 4 in., 4 in., 4 in.
3. 1 ft, 5 ft, 2 ft

See Example 2 Find the volume of each triangular prism.

4. 6 m, 13 m, 9 m
5. 4 ft, 20 ft, 8 ft
6. 10 dm, 20 dm, 25 dm

See Example 3

7. A toy company packs 10 cubic boxes of toys in a case. What are the possible dimensions for a case of toys?

INDEPENDENT PRACTICE

See Example 1 Find the volume of each rectangular prism.

8. $2\frac{1}{2}$ in., 8 in., $2\frac{1}{2}$ in.
9. 3.2 in., 7.75 in., 3.2 in.
10. 12 ft, 12 ft, 2 ft

See Example 2 Find the volume of each triangular prism.

11. 3 m, 9 m, 4 m
12. $2\frac{1}{2}$ cm, 8 cm, $8\frac{3}{4}$ cm
13. 4.5 ft, 3.75 ft, 8.5 ft

See Example 3

14. A printing company packs 18 cubic boxes of business cards in a larger shipping box. What are the possible dimensions for the shipping box?

PRACTICE AND PROBLEM SOLVING

Extra Practice
See page EP21.

Find the volume of each figure.

15. 8 in., 6 in., 10 in.
16. 3.5 cm, 3.5 cm, 7.25 cm
17. 7.5 km, 11.5 km, 11 km

Find the missing measurement for each prism.

18. $\ell = \underline{\ ?\ }$; $w = 25$ m; $h = 4$ m; $V = 300$ m^3

19. $\ell = 9$ ft; $w = \underline{\ ?\ }$; $h = 5$ ft; $V = 900$ ft^3

20. $B = 9.28$ in.; $h = \underline{\ ?\ }$; $V = 55.68$ in^3

568 Chapter 10 Measurement: Area and Volume

Physical Science LINK

The density of a substance is a measure of its mass per unit of volume. The density of a particular substance is always the same. The formula for density D is the mass m of a substance divided by its volume V, or $D = \frac{m}{V}$.

21. Find the volume of each substance in the table.

22. Calculate the density of each substance.

23. Water has a density of 1 g/cm³. A substance whose density is less than that of water will float. Which of the substances in the table will float in water?

24. A fresh egg has a density of approximately 1.2 g/cm³. A spoiled egg has a density of about 0.9 g/cm³. How can you tell whether an egg is fresh without cracking it open?

25. **Multi-Step** Alicia has a solid rectangular prism of a substance she believes is gold. The dimensions of the prism are 2 cm by 1 cm by 2 cm, and the mass is 20.08 g. Is the substance that Alicia has gold? Explain.

26. **Write About It** In a science lab, you are given a prism of copper. You determine that its dimensions are 4 cm, 2 cm, and 6 cm. Without weighing the prism, how can you determine its mass? Explain your answer.

27. **Challenge** A solid rectangular prism of silver has a mass of 84 g. What are some possible dimensions of the prism?

Rectangular Prisms				
Substance	Length (cm)	Width (cm)	Height (cm)	Mass (g)
Copper	2	1	5	89.6
Gold	$\frac{2}{3}$	$\frac{3}{4}$	2	19.32
Iron pyrite	0.25	2	7	17.57
Pine	10	10	3	120
Silver	2.5	4	2	210

Test Prep and Spiral Review

28. **Multiple Choice** A rectangular prism has a volume of 1,080 ft³. The height of the prism is 8 ft, and the width is 9 ft. What is the length of the prism?

    Ⓐ 15 ft   Ⓑ 120 ft   Ⓒ 135 ft   Ⓓ 77,760 ft

29. **Gridded Response** The dimensions of a rectangular prism are 4.3 inches, 12 inches, and 1.5 inches. What is the volume, in cubic inches, of the prism?

Find the GCF of each set of numbers. (Lesson 4-3)

30. 12, 18, 24   31. 15, 18, 30   32. 16, 24, 42   33. 18, 54, 63

10-8 Volume of Cylinders

Learn to find volumes of cylinders.

Thomas Edison invented the first phonograph in 1877. The main part of this phonograph was a cylinder with a 4-inch diameter and a height of $3\frac{3}{8}$ inches.

To find the volume of a cylinder, you can use the same method as you did for prisms: Multiply the area of the base by the height.

Interactivities Online ▶

volume of a cylinder = area of base × height

The area of the circular base is πr^2, so the formula is $V = Bh = \pi r^2 h$.

EXAMPLE 1   Finding the Volume of a Cylinder

Find the volume V of each cylinder to the nearest cubic unit.

A 4 in., 15 in.

$V = \pi r^2 h$ — Write the formula.
$V \approx 3.14 \times 4^2 \times 15$ — Replace π with 3.14, r with 4, and h with 15.
$V \approx 753.6$ — Multiply.

The volume is about 754 in³.

B 6 ft, 18 ft

6 ft ÷ 2 = 3 ft — Find the radius.
$V = \pi r^2 h$ — Write the formula.
$V \approx 3.14 \times 3^2 \times 18$ — Replace π with 3.14, r with 3, and h with 18.
$V \approx 508.68$ — Multiply.

The volume is about 509 ft³.

C $r = \frac{h}{6} + 1$, $h = 24$ cm

$r = \frac{h}{6} + 1$ — Find the radius.
$r = \frac{24}{6} + 1 = 5$ — Substitute 24 for h.
$V = \pi r^2 h$ — Write the formula.
$V \approx 3.14 \times 5^2 \times 24$ — Replace π with 3.14, r with 5, and h with 24.
$V \approx 1{,}884$ — Multiply.

The volume is about 1,884 cm³.

EXAMPLE 2 **Music Application**

The cylinder in Edison's first phonograph had a 4 in. diameter and a height of about 3 in. The standard phonograph manufactured 21 years later had a 2 in. diameter and a height of 4 in. Estimate the volume of each cylinder to the nearest cubic inch.

Remember!
The value of π can be approximated as 3.14 or $\frac{22}{7}$.

A Edison's first phonograph

4 in. ÷ 2 = 2 in.   *Find the radius.*
$V = \pi r^2 h$ *Write the formula.*
$V \approx 3.14 \times 2^2 \times 3$ *Replace π with 3.14, r with 2, and h with 3.*
$V \approx 37.68$ *Multiply.*

The volume of Edison's first phonograph was about 38 in³.

B Edison's standard phonograph

2 in. ÷ 2 = 1 in.   *Find the radius.*
$V = \pi r^2 h$ *Write the formula.*
$V \approx \frac{22}{7} \times 1^2 \times 4$ *Replace π with $\frac{22}{7}$, r with 1, and h with 4.*
$V \approx \frac{88}{7} = 12\frac{4}{7}$ *Multiply.*

The volume of the standard phonograph was about 13 in³.

EXAMPLE 3 **Comparing Volumes of Cylinders**

Find which cylinder has the greater volume.

Cylinder 1: $V = \pi r^2 h$
$V \approx 3.14 \times 6^2 \times 12$
$V \approx 1{,}356.48 \text{ cm}^3$

12 cm
6 cm

Cylinder 2: $V = \pi r^2 h$
$V \approx 3.14 \times 4^2 \times 16$
$V \approx 803.84 \text{ cm}^3$

16 cm
8 cm

Cylinder 1 has the greater volume because 1,356.48 cm³ > 803.84 cm³.

Think and Discuss

1. **Explain** how the formula for the volume of a cylinder is similar to the formula for the volume of a rectangular prism.

2. **Explain** which parts of a cylinder are represented by πr^2 and h in the formula $V = \pi r^2 h$.

10-8 Exercises

GUIDED PRACTICE

See Example 1 Find the volume V of each cylinder to the nearest cubic unit.

1. 4 m; 15 m
2. 8 cm; 2.5 cm
3. 10 in.; 10 in.

See Example 2

4. A cylindrical bucket with a diameter of 4 inches is filled with rainwater to a height of 2.5 inches. Estimate the volume of the rainwater to the nearest cubic inch.

See Example 3

5. Find which cylinder, A or B, has the greater volume.

   A: 4 ft, 15 ft
   B: 5 ft, 10 ft

INDEPENDENT PRACTICE

See Example 1 Find the volume V of each cylinder to the nearest cubic unit.

6. 28 cm; 14 cm
7. 4 ft; 25 ft
8. 5 cm; 4 cm

See Example 2

9. Wooden dowels are solid cylinders of wood. One dowel has a radius of 1 cm, and another dowel has a radius of 3 cm. Both dowels have a height of 10 cm. Estimate the volume of each dowel to the nearest cubic centimeter.

See Example 3

10. Find which cylinder, X or Y, has the greater volume.

    X: 6 in., 3 in.
    Y: 3 in., 6 in.

PRACTICE AND PROBLEM SOLVING

Extra Practice
See page EP21.

Find the volume of each cylinder to the nearest cubic unit.

11. 2.8 in.; 5.6 in.
12. $5\frac{2}{3}$ cm; $1\frac{3}{4}$ cm
13. 4.5 m; 0.5 m

Find the volume of each cylinder using the information given.

14. $r = 6$ cm; $h = 6$ cm
15. $d = 4$ in.; $h = 8$ in.
16. $r = 2$ m; $h = 5$ m
17. $r = 7.5$ ft; $h = 11.25$ ft
18. $d = 12\frac{1}{4}$ yd; $h = 5\frac{3}{5}$ yd
19. $d = 20$ mm; $h = 40$ mm

572 Chapter 10 Measurement: Area and Volume

Multi-Step Find the volume of each shaded cylinder to the nearest cubic unit.

20. 8 m, 3 m, 9 m

21. 14 ft, 10 ft, 3 ft

22. 28 in., 7 in., 10 in.

23. **Measurement** Could this blue can hold 200 cm³ of juice? How do you know?

    5 cm, 10 cm

24. **Science** A scientist filled a cylindrical beaker with 942 mm³ of a chemical solution. The area of the base of the cylinder is 78.5 mm². What is the height of the solution?

25. **Choose a Strategy** Fran, Gene, Helen, and Ira have cylinders with different volumes. Gene's cylinder holds more than Fran's. Ira's cylinder holds more than Helen's, but less than Fran's. Whose cylinder has the largest volume? What color cylinder does each person have?

    5 in., 6 in. | 4 in., 10 in. | 6 in., 4 in. | 8 in., 12 in.

26. **Write About It** Explain why volume is expressed in cubic units of measurement.

27. **Challenge** Find the volume of the shaded area.

    $1\frac{1}{2}$ cm, 4 cm, 4 cm, 4 cm

Test Prep and Spiral Review

28. **Multiple Choice** Find the volume of a cylinder with a height of $2\frac{1}{3}$ feet and a radius of $1\frac{1}{2}$ feet.

    F 19.75 ft³   G 16.5 ft³   H 11 ft³   J 5.5 ft³

29. **Short Response** Chicken noodle soup is sold in a can that is 11 cm tall and has a radius of 2.5 cm. Tomato soup is sold in a can that is 7.5 cm tall and has a radius of 4 cm. Find the volume of both cans. Which can holds more soup?

Identify a pattern in each sequence. Name the missing terms. (Lesson 1-6)

30. 10, 13, 16, 19, ▮, ▮, ...   31. 5, 8, 7, 10, ▮, ▮, ...   32. 4, 16, 64, 256, ▮, ▮, ...

33. The diagram shows a school yard. What is the measure of $\angle W$? (Lesson 9-6)

10-8 Volume of Cylinders

Hands-on LAB 10-9

Model Three-Dimensional Figures

Use with Lesson 10-9

Learn It Online
Lab Resources Online go.hrw.com,
keyword MR10 Lab10 Go

You can build a solid figure by cutting its faces from paper, taping them together, and then folding them to form the solid. A pattern of shapes that can be folded to form a solid figure is called a *net*.

Activity

1 To make a pattern for a rectangular prism follow the steps below.

   a. Draw the following rectangles and cut them out:

   Two 2 in. × 3 in. rectangles

   Two 1 in. × 3 in. rectangles

   Two 1 in. × 2 in. rectangles

   b. Tape the pieces together to form the prism.

   c. Remove the tape from some of the edges so that the pattern lies flat.

2 Create a net for a cylinder.

Think: What shapes can make a cylinder?

If a cylinder is "unfolded," the bases of the cylinder are circles, and the curved surface is a rectangle.

The net is made up of two circles and a rectangle.

574 Chapter 10 Measurement: Area and Volume

3 Create a net for a square pyramid.

Think: What shapes can make a square pyramid?

If the square pyramid is "unfolded," the base is a square, and the sides are triangles.

The net is made up of a square and four triangles.

Think and Discuss

1. Compare the nets for a rectangular prism and a cube.
2. Tell what shapes will always appear in a net for a triangular pyramid.
3. Tell what shapes will always appear in a net for a hexagonal prism.

Try This

Tell whether each net can be folded to form a cube. If not, explain.

1.
2.
3.
4.

Name the three-dimensional figure that can be formed from each net.

5.
6.

7. Create a net for a cone.

10-9 Hands-On Lab   575

10-9 Surface Area

Learn to find the surface areas of prisms, pyramids, and cylinders.

The amount of wrapping paper needed to cover a present depends on the surface area of the present.

The **surface area** of a three-dimensional figure is the sum of the areas of its surfaces. To help you see all the surfaces of a three-dimensional figure, you can use a *net*. A **net** is the pattern made when the surface of a three-dimensional figure is layed out flat showing each face of the figure.

Vocabulary
surface area
net

EXAMPLE 1 Finding the Surface Area of a Prism

Find the surface area S of each prism.

A Method 1: Use a net.

Draw a net to help you see each face of the prism.

Use the formula $A = \ell w$ to find the area of each face.

A: $A = 11 \times 5 = 55$
B: $A = 21 \times 11 = 231$
C: $A = 21 \times 5 = 105$
D: $A = 21 \times 11 = 231$
E: $A = 21 \times 5 = 105$
F: $A = 11 \times 5 = 55$

$S = 55 + 231 + 105 + 231 + 105 + 55 = 782$ *Add the areas of each face.*

The surface area is 782 in².

B Method 2: Use a three-dimensional drawing.

Find the area of the front, top, and side, and multiply each by 2 to include the opposite faces.

Front: $6 \times 8 = 48 \longrightarrow 48 \times 2 = 96$
Top: $6 \times 4 = 24 \longrightarrow 24 \times 2 = 48$
Side: $4 \times 8 = 32 \longrightarrow 32 \times 2 = 64$

$S = 96 + 48 + 64 = 208$ *Add the areas of the faces.*

The surface area is 208 cm².

The surface area of a pyramid equals the sum of the area of the base and the areas of the triangular faces. To find the surface area of a pyramid, think of its net.

EXAMPLE 2 Finding the Surface Area of a Pyramid

Find the surface area S of the pyramid.

S = area of square + 4 × (area of triangular face)

$S = s^2 + 4 \times \left(\frac{1}{2}bh\right)$

$S = 6^2 + 4 \times \left(\frac{1}{2} \times 6 \times 5\right)$ *Substitute.*

$S = 36 + 4 \times 15$

$S = 36 + 60$

$S = 96$

The surface area is 96 ft².

The surface area of a cylinder equals the sum of the area of its bases and the area of its curved surface.

EXAMPLE 3 Finding the Surface Area of a Cylinder

Find the surface area S of the cylinder. Use 3.14 for π, and round to the nearest hundredth.

Helpful Hint

To find the area of the curved surface of a cylinder, multiply its height by the circumference of the base.

S = area of curved surface + 2 × (area of each base)

$S = h \times (2\pi r) + 2 \times (\pi r^2)$

$S = 5 \times (2 \times \pi \times 2) + 2 \times (\pi \times 2^2)$ *Substitute.*

$S = 5 \times 4\pi + 2 \times 4\pi$

$S \approx 5 \times 4(3.14) + 2 \times 4(3.14)$ *Use 3.14 for π.*

$S \approx 5 \times 12.56 + 2 \times 12.56$

$S \approx 62.8 + 25.12$

$S \approx 87.92$

The surface area is about 87.92 ft².

Think and Discuss

1. **Describe** how to find the surface area of a pentagonal prism.
2. **Tell** how to find the surface area of a cube if you know the area of one face.

10-9 Exercises

Learn It Online
Homework Help Online go.hrw.com,
keyword MR10 10-9
Exercises 1–18, 29

GUIDED PRACTICE

See Example 1 Find the surface area S of each prism.

1. 5 in., 3 in., 4 in.
2. 4 m, 8 m, 2 m
3. 2 cm, 6 cm, 2 cm

See Example 2 Find the surface area S of each pyramid.

4. 8 ft, 6 ft, 6 ft
5. 29 cm, 30 cm, 30 cm
6. 3 m, 2 m, 2 m

See Example 3 Find the surface area S of each cylinder. Use 3.14 for π, and round to the nearest hundredth.

7. 4 ft, 9 ft
8. 7 in., 10 in.
9. 6 m, 4 m

INDEPENDENT PRACTICE

See Example 1 Find the surface area S of each prism.

10. 5 cm, 3 cm, 8 cm, 4 cm
11. $1\frac{1}{2}$ m, 2 m, $1\frac{1}{2}$ m
12. 40.5 in., 78.25 in., 35 in.

See Example 2 Find the surface area S of each pyramid.

13. 6 cm, 7 cm, 7 cm
14. 13.6 ft, 10.2 ft, 10.2 ft
15. 5 km, 1 km, 1 km

See Example 3 Find the surface area S of each cylinder. Use 3.14 for π, and round to the nearest hundredth.

16. 22 in., 7 in.
17. 7.8 m, 6.75 m
18. $1\frac{3}{4}$ in., $9\frac{3}{4}$ in.

578 Chapter 10 Measurement: Area and Volume

PRACTICE AND PROBLEM SOLVING

Extra Practice
See page EP21.

Architecture

I. M. Pei is the architect of the pyramid-shaped addition to the Louvre in Paris, France.

19. You are designing a container for oatmeal. Your first design is a rectangular prism with a height of 12 in., a width of 8 in., and a depth of 3 in.
    a. What is the surface area of the package?
    b. You redesign the package as a cylinder with the same surface area as the prism from part **a**. If the radius of the cylinder is 2 in., what is the height of the cylinder? Round to the nearest tenth of an inch.

20. **Architecture** The entrance to the Louvre Museum is a glass-paned square pyramid. The width of the base is 34.2 m, and the height of the triangular sides is 27 m. What is the surface area of the glass?

Estimation Estimate the surface area of each figure.

21. 4.8 ft, 5.6 ft, 5.6 ft

22. 3 m, 7 m

23. 4.5 cm, 4.5 cm, 6.825 cm

24. **What's the Question?** The surface area of a cube is 150 cm^2. The answer is 5 cm. What is the question?

25. **Write About It** How is finding the surface area of a rectangular pyramid different from finding the surface area of a triangular prism?

26. **Challenge** This cube is made of 27 smaller cubes whose sides measure 1 in.
    a. What is the surface area of the large cube?
    b. Remove one small cube from each of the eight corners of the larger cube. What is the surface area of the solid formed?

Test Prep and Spiral Review

27. **Multiple Choice** Find the surface area of a cube with a side length of 9.4 yd.

    Ⓐ 56.4 yd^2 Ⓑ 88.36 yd^2 Ⓒ 338.4 yd^2 Ⓓ 530.16 yd^2

28. **Gridded Response** Find the surface area, in square meters, of a cylinder with a radius of 7 m and a height of 6 m. Use 3.14 for π and round to the nearest hundredth.

Solve each equation. (Lesson 2-5)

29. $12 + y = 23$
30. $38 + y = 80$
31. $y + 76 = 230$

Find each sum or difference. Write the answer in simplest form. (Lesson 5-3)

32. $5\frac{2}{3} - 1\frac{1}{9}$
33. $1\frac{1}{4} + 2\frac{3}{8}$
34. $2\frac{5}{6} - 2\frac{3}{4}$
35. $4\frac{2}{5} + 3\frac{3}{10}$

10-9 Surface Area

Ready To Go On?

Quiz for Lessons 10-6 Through 10-9

10-6 Three-Dimensional Figures

Identify the number of faces, edges, and vertices on each figure. Then name the figure and tell whether it is a polyhedron.

1.
2.
3.

10-7 Volume of Prisms

Find the volume of each prism.

4. 3 cm, 3 cm, 3 cm
5. 4 ft, 11 ft, 3 ft
6. 6 mm, 4.5 mm, 4.5 mm

7. There are 16 cubic boxes of erasers in a case. What are all the possible dimensions for a case of erasers?

10-8 Volume of Cylinders

Find the volume V of each cylinder to the nearest cubic unit. Use 3.14 for π.

8. 3 cm, 12 cm
9. 4 in., 8.5 in.
10. 5.5 ft, 12.5 ft

11. Which cylinder has the greater volume?

9 ft, 10 ft | 18 ft, 5 ft

10-9 Surface Area

Find the surface area S of each figure. Use 3.14 for π, and round to the nearest hundredth.

12. 8 m, 4 m, 5 m
13. 5 ft, 3 ft, 3 ft
14. 2.5 cm, 2.5 cm, 2.5 cm

580 Chapter 10 Measurement: Area and Volume

Real-World Connections

CHAPTER 10

Marble House In the late 1800s, some of America's wealthiest families built mansions in the coastal town of Newport, Rhode Island. Marble House is one of the most extravagant examples. Marble House got its name from the approximately 500,000 cubic feet of marble used in its construction.

RHODE ISLAND
Newport

1. A block of marble with a volume of 1 cubic foot weighs approximately 160 pounds. How much does all of the marble in Marble House weigh?

2. A block of marble is in the shape of a rectangular prism. The dimensions are 2 ft wide, 1 foot deep, and 18 inches high.

    a. What is the volume of the block of marble in cubic feet?

    b. Set up and solve a proportion to find out how much this block of marble weighs.

3. The Gold Ballroom in Marble House can be rented for private parties and corporate events. The room is 28 feet long by 46 feet wide.

    a. What is the area of the Gold Ballroom?

    b. A private party wants to fill the Gold Ballroom with rows of round tables. The tables are 4 feet in diameter, and each table must be 5 feet from any walls or other tables. How many tables can fit in the Ballroom?

    c. How much of the floor space will *not* be covered by tables? Round to the nearest square foot.

Game Time

Polygon Hide-and-Seek

Use the figure to name each polygon described.

1. an obtuse scalene triangle
2. a right isosceles triangle
3. a parallelogram with no right angles
4. a trapezoid with two congruent sides
5. a pentagon with three congruent sides

Poly-Cross Puzzle

You will use the names of the figures below to complete a crossword puzzle.

A copy of the crossword puzzle is available online.

Learn It Online
Game Time Extra go.hrw.com,
keyword MR10 Games

ACROSS
1. (pentagon)
2. (square)
3. (triangle)
4. (rectangular prism)
5. (pyramid)
6. (cone)

DOWN
1. (pentagonal pyramid)
7. (cylinder)
8. (triangular prism)

Materials
- colored file folder
- scissors
- 8 library pockets
- glue stick
- index cards
- black construction paper
- markers
- tag
- string

It's in the Bag!

PROJECT Area and Volume Suitcase

Carry your notes with you as you travel through Chapter 10.

Directions

1. Cut the tabs off a colored file folder to form a rectangular folder with straight sides.
Figure A

2. Open the folder. Glue library pockets inside the folder so that there are four on each side. Place an index card in each pocket.
Figure B

3. Cut out "handles" from the construction paper. Glue these to the folder as shown.
Figure C

4. Use a piece of string to attach a tag to one of the handles. Write your name and the name of your class on the tag. Write the name and number of the chapter on the front of the folder.

Taking Note of the Math

Write the names of the chapter's lessons on the library pockets. Then take notes on each lesson on the appropriate index card.

583

CHAPTER 10 Study Guide: Review

Vocabulary

area	534	polyhedron	560
base	560	prism	560
cone	561	pyramid	561
cylinder	560	sphere	561
edge	560	surface area	576
face	560	vertex	560
net	576	volume	566

Complete the sentences below with vocabulary words from the list above.

1. A ___?___ is a three-dimensional object with flat faces that are polygons.

2. The number of cubic units needed to fill a space is called ___?___.

3. The point at which three or more edges meet on a three-dimensional figure is called a ___?___.

EXAMPLES

EXERCISES

10-1 Area of Rectangles and Parallelograms (pp. 534–537)

■ Find the area of the rectangle.

4 ft, 15 ft

$A = \ell w$
$A = 15 \cdot 4 = 60$
The area is 60 ft².

■ Find the area of the parallelogram.

7 mm, 10 mm

$A = bh$
$A = 10 \cdot 7 = 70$
The area is 70 mm².

Find the area of each rectangle.

4. 3 ft, 6 ft

5. 1 m, 7 m

Find the area of each parallelogram.

6. 4 in., 3 in.

7. 2 in., 6 in.

584 Chapter 10 Measurement: Area and Volume

EXAMPLES

EXERCISES

10-2 Area of Triangles and Trapezoids (pp. 540–543)

■ Find the area of the trapezoid.

4 m
2 m
10 m

$A = \frac{1}{2}h(b_1 + b_2)$
$= \frac{1}{2}(2)(10 + 4)$ Substitute 10 for b_1, 4 for b_2, and 2 for h.
$= \frac{1}{2}(2)(14)$
$= \frac{1}{2}(28) = 14 \text{ m}^2$

Find the area of each triangle.

8. 11 in., 28 in.
9. 4 cm, 6 cm

Find the area of each trapezoid.

10. 8 cm, 5 cm, 4 cm
11. 3.5 ft, 3 ft, 4.5 ft

10-3 Area of Composite Figures (pp. 545–547)

■ Find the area of the polygon.

15 ft, 7 ft, 12 ft, 8 ft, 8 ft, 12 ft, 12 ft

$A_1 = 12 \cdot 8 = 96$
$A_2 = \frac{1}{2} \cdot 12 \cdot 7 = 42$
$42 \text{ ft}^2 + 96 \text{ ft}^2 = 138 \text{ ft}^2$

Find the area of each polygon.

12. 5 cm, 7 cm, 13 cm, 10 cm, 12 cm
13. 16 ft, 9 ft, 23 ft

10-4 Changing Dimensions (pp. 548–550)

■ Find how the perimeter and area of a rectangle change when its dimensions change.

When the dimensions of the rectangle are multiplied by x, the perimeter is multiplied by x, and the area is multiplied by x^2.

Find how the perimeter and area change when its dimensions change.

14. 4 cm, 5 cm, 5 cm, 6 cm; 10 cm, 10 cm, 8 cm, 12 cm

10-5 Area of Circles (pp. 552–555)

■ Find the area of the circle. Use 3.14 for π.

$A = \pi r^2$
$r = \frac{1}{2}d$
$= \frac{1}{2} \cdot 6 = 3$
$A \approx 3.14 \cdot 3^2$
$A \approx 3.14 \cdot 9 \approx 28.26 \text{ cm}^2$

$d = 6$ cm

Find the area of each circle. Use 3.14 for π.

15. $d = 10$ ft
16. $r = 8$ cm
17. $d = 4$ m
18. $r = 6$ ft
19. A circular window has a diameter of 14 ft. Find the area of the glass needed to fill the window. Use $\frac{22}{7}$ for π.

EXAMPLES

EXERCISES

10-6 Three-Dimensional Figures (pp. 560–563)

■ Identify the number of faces, edges, and vertices on the solid figure. Then name the solid.

5 faces; 9 edges; 6 vertices
There are two congruent parallel bases, so the figure is a prism. The bases are triangles. The solid is a triangular prism.

Identify the number of faces, edges, and vertices on each solid figure. Then name the solid.

20.

21.

10-7 Volume of Prisms (pp. 566–569)

■ Find the volume of the rectangular prism.
12 in.
23 in.
48 in.

$V = \ell wh$
$V = 48 \cdot 12 \cdot 23$
$V = 13{,}248$ in^3
The volume is 13,248 in^3.

Find the volume of each prism.

22.
16 cm
6 cm
8 cm

23.
14 in.
25 in.
18 in.

10-8 Volume of Cylinders (pp. 570–573)

■ Find the volume V of the cylinder to the nearest cubic unit.
$r = 4$ cm
$h = 16$ cm

$V \approx 3.14 \cdot 4^2 \cdot 16$
$V \approx 803.84$ cm^3
The volume is about 804 cm^3.

Find the volume V of each cylinder to the nearest cubic unit.

24. $h = 12.5$ m
$r = 3$ m

25. $r = 7$ ft
$h = 15$ ft

10-9 Surface Area (pp. 576–579)

■ Find the surface area S of the cylinder.
2 in.
6 in.

$S = h \cdot (2\pi r) + 2 \cdot (\pi r^2)$
$S \approx 6 \cdot (2 \cdot 3.14 \cdot 2) + 2 \cdot (3.14 \cdot 2^2)$
$S \approx 100.48$ in^2
The surface area is about 100.48 in^2.

Find the surface area S of each solid.

26.
$h = 10$ m
5 m 5 m

27.
2 cm
3 cm
9 cm

Chapter Test

CHAPTER 10

Find the area of each figure.

1. 12 m, 8 m (rectangle)

2. (figure on grid)

3. 11 ft, 10 ft, 3 ft, 5 ft, 4 ft

4. Find how the perimeter and the area of a rectangle change when the length and width are doubled.

5. A patio is in the shape of a trapezoid. What is the area of the patio?

   A—24 ft—B, 6 ft, D, 32 ft, C

Find the area of each circle. Use 3.14 for π. Round to the nearest hundredth.

6. Circle with A, V, P, $2\frac{1}{2}$ m

7. Circle with J, O, D, 10 in.

8. Circle with 9 cm, H, F, S

Identify the number of faces, edges, and vertices on each three-dimensional figure. Then name the figure and tell whether it is a polyhedron.

9. (triangular prism)

10. (pyramid)

11. (cone)

Find the volume V of each three-dimensional figure.

12. 8 m, 6 m, 4 m

13. 3 in., 4 in. (cylinder)

14. 12 cm, 10 cm, 18 cm

15. Patricia has two cylinder-shaped jars. Jar A has a radius of 6 cm and a height of 9 cm. Jar B has a diameter of 8 cm and a height of 17 cm. Which jar has the greater volume? How much greater?

Find the surface area S of each three-dimensional figure.

16. 3 in., 3 in., 6 in.

17. 4 ft, 2 ft, 2 ft (pyramid)

18. 7.2 cm, 5.2 cm, 5.4 cm

Chapter 10 Test **587**

Chapter 10 Standardized Test Prep

Cumulative Assessment, Chapters 1–10

Multiple Choice

1. Which of the following solid figures is NOT a polyhedron?
   - A (hexagonal prism)
   - B (hexagonal prism)
   - C (cylinder)
   - D (wedge)

2. On May 1, 2005, in Galveston, Texas, the sun rose at 6:37 A.M. The sun set at 7:56 P.M. How much time elapsed from sunrise to sunset?
   - F 1 hour and 39 minutes
   - G 12 hours and 29 minutes
   - H 13 hours and 9 minutes
   - J 13 hours and 19 minutes

3. A gallon of paint will cover 250 square feet. About how many gallons of paint are needed to paint a rectangular billboard that is 120 feet long and 85 feet tall?
   - A 2 gallons
   - B 10 gallons
   - C 22 gallons
   - D 41 gallons

4. Justin has 3 cups of sugar in a canister. He uses $\frac{1}{3}$ cup of sugar in a cookie recipe. He uses $\frac{3}{4}$ of what is remaining in the canister to make a pitcher of lemonade. How much sugar is left?
   - F $\frac{2}{3}$ cup
   - G 1 cup
   - H $1\frac{11}{12}$ cups
   - J 2 cups

5. What is the prime factorization of 324?
   - A $2^2 \times 3^4$
   - B $2^2 \times 9^2$
   - C $2^2 \times 3^2 \times 27$
   - D $2^2 \times 81$

6. Maysville Middle School is hosting a craft fair. The circle graph shows how many different types of booths will be at the craft fair. To the nearest whole number, what percent of the booths will be selling jewelry?

   Craft Booth Types
   - Baskets & wreaths: 12
   - Paintings: 12
   - Jewelry: 32
   - Glass & pottery: 16

   - F 80%
   - G 55%
   - H 44%
   - J 33%

7. An antique round tabletop has a diameter of 3 feet. What is the area of the tabletop? Use 3.14 for π. Round to the nearest tenth.
   - A 7.1 ft²
   - B 9.4 ft²
   - C 18.8 ft²
   - D 28.3 ft²

8. The scale on a map is 1 in:50 mi. If Cincinnati, Ohio, is about 300 miles from Chicago, Illinois, about how far apart are the two cities on the map?
   - F 5 in.
   - G 6 in.
   - H 7 in.
   - J 8 in.

588 Chapter 10 Measurement: Area and Volume

9. In March of 2005, Steve Fossett became the first man to complete the first solo, nonstop flight around the world. He did not even stop to refuel. The 36,818-kilometer voyage took 67 hours and 2 minutes. How many kilometers did he travel per minute? Round to the nearest kilometer.

   Ⓐ 5 km/min   Ⓒ 23 km/min
   Ⓑ 9 km/min   Ⓓ 26 km/min

HOT TIP! Pay attention to the units used in problems. If the units used in a problem do not match the units used in the answer choices, you will need to convert from one unit to another.

Gridded Response

The table shows the number of people who attended the Super Bowl from 1967 to 1971. Use the table for items 10 and 11.

10. What was the mean attendance? Round to the nearest whole number.

Superbowl Attendance					
Year	1967	1968	1969	1970	1971
Number of People	61,946	75,546	75,389	80,562	79,204

11. How many more people attended the Super Bowl in 1971 than in 1967? Round your answer to the nearest thousand.

12. The area of a triangle is 57.12 cm². If the height of the triangle is 8.4 cm, how many centimeters long is the base?

13. Solve the equation $\frac{2}{7}k = \frac{1}{6}$ for k.

14. Marcia is weighing her produce. A watermelon weighs 2.89 kg. How many grams are in 2.89 kg?

Short Response

S1. Triangle WXY is isosceles. The two short sides have a length of 18 mm. The other side has as length of 30 mm.
   a. Draw a triangle that is similar to triangle WXY.
   b. Write a proportion to prove that the two triangles are similar.

S2. A company's rectangular parking lot is 35 m long and 60 m wide. The company is planning on expanding the area. If the dimensions are doubled, how many times greater will the area of the new parking lot be compared to the area of the original parking lot? Explain how you found your answer.

S3. Carole has a piece of fabric that is 2 yards long. She wants to cut the fabric into 2.4-inch strips. Let s equal one of the fabric strips. Write and solve an equation to find how many 2.4-inch strips Carole can cut from the piece of fabric.

Extended Response

E1. There are 3 pools in Marcie's neighborhood where she can go swimming. The dimensions are listed below. Pool 2 is a circular pool. The width is its radius.

Pool	Length (ft)	Depth (ft)	Width (ft)
1	25	5	8
2	–	6	9
3	15	4	9

   a. Find the volume of each pool. Which pool has the greatest volume? Show your work. Use 3.14 for π.
   b. What is the circumference of pool 2?
   c. Samantha's pool has the same volume as pool 1. However, her pool is in the shape of a cube. What are the dimensions of Samantha's pool?

CHAPTER 11
Integers

11A Understanding Integers
- 11-1 Integers and Absolute Value
- 11-2 Comparing and Ordering Integers
- Ext Negative Rational Numbers
- 11-3 The Coordinate Plane
- 11-4 Transformations in the Coordinate Plane

11B Integer Operations
- LAB Model Integer Addition
- 11-5 Adding Integers
- LAB Model Integer Subtraction
- 11-6 Subtracting Integers
- 11-7 Multiplying Integers
- 11-8 Dividing Integers
- LAB Model Integer Equations
- 11-9 Solving Integer Equations

Chapter Focus
- Use negative numbers in everyday contexts.
- Add, subtract, multiply, and divide integers.

Why Learn This?
Integers are useful in finding and comparing distances both above and below ground level, such as what you encounter in caves and the countryside surrounding them.

Learn It Online
Chapter Project Online **go.hrw.com**,
keyword MR10 Ch 11

Are You Ready?

Vocabulary

Choose the best term from the list to complete each sentence.

1. When you ___?___ a numerical expression, you find its value.
2. ___?___ are the set of numbers 0, 1, 2, 3, 4, ...
3. A(n) ___?___ is an exact location in space.
4. A(n) ___?___ is a mathematical statement that two quantities are equal.

equation
evaluate
exponents
less than
point
whole numbers

Complete these exercises to review skills you will need for this chapter.

Compare Whole Numbers

Write <, >, or = to compare the numbers.

5. 9 ▢ 2
6. 4 ▢ 5
7. 8 ▢ 1
8. 3 ▢ 3
9. 412 ▢ 214
10. 1,076 ▢ 1,074
11. 502 ▢ 520
12. 9,123 ▢ 9,001

Whole-Number Operations

Add, subtract, multiply, or divide.

13. $7 + 6$
14. $15 - 8$
15. $6 \cdot 7$
16. $25 \div 5$
17. $129 + 30$
18. $32 - 25$
19. $119 \cdot 5$
20. $156 \div 6$

Solve One-Step Equations

Solve each equation.

21. $4t = 32$
22. $b - 4 = 12$
23. $24 = 6r$
24. $3x = 72$
25. $8 = 4a$
26. $m + 3 = 63$

Graph Ordered Pairs

Graph each ordered pair.

27. (1, 3)
28. (0, 5)
29. (3, 2)
30. (4, 0)
31. (6, 4)
32. (2, 5)
33. (0, 1)
34. (1, 0)

Integers

CHAPTER 11 Study Guide: Preview

Where You've Been

Previously, you

- graphed and located ordered pairs of whole numbers on a coordinate grid.
- graphed a given set of data.
- used equations to represent real-life situations.

In This Chapter

You will study

- using integers to represent real-life situations.
- using tables and symbols to represent sequences.
- using data tables to generate formulas representing relationships like perimeter.
- graphing and locating ordered pairs on four quadrants of a coordinate plane.

Where You're Going

You can use the skills learned in this chapter

- to interpret graphs of functions that represent real-world situations.
- to solve multi-step equations with integers and positive and negative fractions and decimals.

Key Vocabulary/Vocabulario

coordinates	coordenadas
integer	entero
linear equation	ecuación lineal
opposites	opuestos
origin	origen
quadrants	cuadrante

Vocabulary Connections

To become familiar with some of the vocabulary terms in the chapter, consider the following. You may refer to the chapter, the glossary, or a dictionary if you like.

1. The word *linear* means "relating to a straight line." What do you think the graph of a **linear equation** will look like?

2. The word *opposite* can mean "across from." Where do you think **opposites** will lie on a number line?

3. The word *origin* can mean "the point at which something begins." At what coordinates do you think the **origin** is?

4. The word *quadrant* comes from the Latin *quattuor,* meaning "four." How many **quadrants** do you think a coordinate plane has?

Reading and Writing Math

CHAPTER 11

Writing Strategy: Write a Convincing Argument

Being able to write a convincing argument about a math concept proves that you have a solid understanding of the concept.

A good argument should include
- an answer.
- support to prove the statement (including examples if necessary).
- a summary statement.

From Lesson 10-4

6. **Critical Thinking** If George enlarges a 3 in. × 4 in. photo so that it is 12 in. × 16 in., how will its area change?

Step 1 **Answer statement:**
The area of the new photo will be 16 times as great as that of the original photo.

Step 2 **Support:**
The dimensions of the 3 in. × 4 in. photo are multiplied by 4 to be enlarged to 12 in. × 16 in.

The area of the new photo is 16 times as great as that of the original photo.

area of original = 3 × 4 = 12 in^2

area of enlarged = 12 × 16 = 192 in^2

area of original : area of enlarged

12 : 192

1 : 16

Step 3 **Summary Statement:**
Therefore, to find the area of the enlarged photo, multiply the original area by 4^2, or 16.

Try This

Write a convincing argument to show whether or not a rectangle with whole-number dimensions can have an area of 15 m^2 and a perimeter of 15 m.

11-1 Integers and Absolute Value

Learn to identify and graph integers and find opposites.

The highest temperature recorded in the United States is 134 °F, in Death Valley, California. The lowest recorded temperature is 80° below 0 °F, in Prospect Creek, Alaska.

Vocabulary
positive number
negative number
opposites
integer
absolute value

Positive numbers are greater than 0. They may be written with a positive sign (+), but they are usually written without it. So, the highest temperature can be written as +134 °F or 134 °F.

Negative numbers are less than 0. They are always written with a negative sign (−). So, the lowest temperature is written as −80 °F.

EXAMPLE 1 Identifying Positive and Negative Numbers in the Real World

Name a positive or negative number to represent each situation.

A a gain of 20 yards in football
Positive numbers can represent *gains* or *increases*.
+20

B spending $75
Negative numbers can represent *losses* or *decreases*.
−75

C 10 feet below sea level
Negative numbers can represent values *below* or *less than* a certain value.
−10

You can graph positive and negative numbers on a number line.

Remember!
The set of whole numbers includes zero and the counting numbers. {0, 1, 2, 3, 4, ...}

On a number line, **opposites** are the same distance from 0 but on different sides of 0. Zero is its own opposite.

Integers are the set of all whole numbers and their opposites.

0 is neither negative nor positive.

594   Chapter 11 Integers

EXAMPLE 2 Graphing Integers

Graph each integer and its opposite on a number line.

A −4

+4 is the same distance from 0 as −4.

B 3

−3 is the same distance from 0 as 3.

C 0

Zero is its own opposite.

The **absolute value** of an integer is its distance from 0 on a number line. The symbol for absolute value is | |.

$|-3| = 3 \quad |3| = 3$

Reading Math

Read | 3 | as "the absolute value of 3."

Read | −3 | as "the absolute value of negative 3."

- Absolute values are never negative.
- Opposite integers have the same absolute value.
- $|0| = 0$

EXAMPLE 3 Finding Absolute Value

Use the number line to find the absolute value of each integer.

A |5|
5   5 is 5 units from 0, so |5| = 5.

B |−7|
7   −7 is 7 units from 0, so |−7| = 7.

Think and Discuss

1. **Tell** whether −3.2 is an integer. Why or why not?
2. **Give** the opposite of 14. What is the opposite of −11?
3. **Name** all the integers with an absolute value of 12.

11-1 Exercises

GUIDED PRACTICE

See Example 1 Name a positive or negative number to represent each situation.
1. an increase of 5 points
2. a loss of 15 yards

See Example 2 Graph each integer and its opposite on a number line.
3. −2
4. 1
5. −6
6. 9

See Example 3 Use the number line to find the absolute value of each integer.

−10 −9 −8 −7 −6 −5 −4 −3 −2 −1 0 +1 +2 +3 +4 +5 +6 +7 +8 +9 +10

7. |−10|
8. |6|
9. |3|
10. |−5|

INDEPENDENT PRACTICE

See Example 1 Name a positive or negative number to represent each situation.
11. earning $50
12. 20° below zero
13. 7 feet above sea level
14. a decrease of 39 points

See Example 2 Graph each integer and its opposite on a number line.
15. −5
16. 6
17. 2
18. −3
19. 9

See Example 3 Use the number line to find the absolute value of each integer.

−10 −9 −8 −7 −6 −5 −4 −3 −2 −1 0 +1 +2 +3 +4 +5 +6 +7 +8 +9 +10

20. |10|
21. |−1|
22. |−8|
23. |2|

PRACTICE AND PROBLEM SOLVING

Extra Practice See page EP23.

Write a situation that each integer could represent.
24. +49
25. −83
26. −7
27. +15
28. −2

Write the opposite of each integer.
29. −92
30. +75
31. −25
32. +1,001
33. 0

Write the absolute value of each integer.
34. |−27|
35. |105|
36. |18|
37. |−55|
38. |−1,000|

39. **Astronomy** Use the table to graph the average surface temperatures of the given planets on a number line.

Planet	Earth	Mars	Jupiter
Average Surface Temperature (°C)	15	−65	−110

40. A certain stock dropped 3 points in the stock market. Another stock gained 5 points. Write an integer to represent each stock's gain or loss.

596 Chapter 11 Integers

Earth Science

Underwater vehicles called submersibles are used to explore the deepest parts of the ocean. The Alvin, pictured above, was used to photograph and explore the Titanic in 1987.

41. **Sports** When the Mountain Lions football team returned the kickoff, they gained 45 yards. Write an integer to represent this situation.

42. **Earth Science** The Mariana Trench is the deepest part of the Pacific Ocean, reaching a depth of 10,924 meters. Write the depth in meters of the Mariana Trench as an integer.

43. **Earth Science** From June 21 to December 21, most of the United States loses 1 to 2 minutes of daylight each day. But on December 21, most of the country begins to gain 1 to 2 minutes of daylight each day. What integer could you write for a gain of 2 minutes? a loss of 2 minutes?

44. Match each temperature with the correct point on the thermometer.
    a. $-10\,°F$
    b. $5\,°F$
    c. $10\,°F$
    d. $-2\,°F$
    e. $-9\,°F$
    f. $7\,°F$

45. Which situation is least likely to be represented by -8?
    - A a temperature drop of 8 °F
    - B a depth of 8 meters
    - C a growth of 8 centimeters
    - D a time 8 years ago

46. **Write A Problem** Write a problem about the temperature rising and dropping. Start with the temperature labeled G on the thermometer. Then write an expression to represent the situation.

47. **Write About It** Is -0.5 an integer? Explain.

48. **Challenge** What are the opposites of the integers 3 units away from -8? Explain.

Test Prep and Spiral Review

49. **Multiple Choice** Which situation could the integer -50 represent?
    - A An increase of $50 in a bank account
    - B The temperature on a warm spring day
    - C The distance driven on the way to the beach
    - D A decrease of 50 employees

50. **Multiple Choice** Which integer can represent *200 years ago*?
    - F -200
    - G $200x$
    - H 200
    - J $x - 200$

Estimate by rounding to the indicated place value. (Lesson 3-2)

51. $1.892 - 0.243$; tenths
52. $13.4132 + 0.513$; tenths
53. $11.4307 - 5.2164$; thousandths

54. Hugo is filling a tub with water. The height of the water is increasing $\frac{1}{5}$ foot each minute. Use pictures to model how much the height of the water will change in 4 minutes, and then write your answer in simplest form. (Lesson 4-8)

11-2 Comparing and Ordering Integers

Learn to compare and order integers.

The table shows three golfers' scores from a golf tournament.

Player	Score
David Berganio	+6
Sergio Garcia	−16
Tiger Woods	−4

In golf, the player with the lowest score wins the game. You can compare integers to find the winner of the tournament.

Sergio Garcia

EXAMPLE 1 Comparing Integers

Use the number line to compare each pair of integers. Write < or >.

$$\leftarrow\!-5\;-4\;-3\;-2\;-1\;\;0\;\;1\;\;2\;\;3\;\;4\;\;5\!\rightarrow$$

Remember!
Numbers on a number line increase in value as you move from left to right.

A −4 ▢ 2
−4 < 2   *−4 is to the left of 2 on the number line.*

B −3 ▢ −5
−3 > −5   *−3 is to the right of −5 on the number line.*

C 0 ▢ −4
0 > −4   *0 is to the right of −4 on the number line.*

EXAMPLE 2 Ordering Integers

Order the integers in each set from least to greatest.

A 4, −2, 1

Graph the integers on the same number line.

$$\leftarrow\!-5\;-4\;-3\;-2\;-1\;\;0\;\;1\;\;2\;\;3\;\;4\;\;5\!\rightarrow$$

Then read the numbers from left to right: −2, 1, 4.

Order the integers in each set from least to greatest.

B −2, 0, 2, −5

Graph the integers on the same number line.

```
←——•——|——|——•——|——•——|——|——•——|——|——|——→
  −5 −4 −3 −2 −1  0  1  2  3  4  5
```

Then read the numbers from left to right: −5, −2, 0, 2.

EXAMPLE 3

PROBLEM SOLVING APPLICATION

At a golf tournament, David Berganio scored +6, Sergio Garcia scored −16, and Tiger Woods scored −4. One of these three players was the winner of the tournament. Who won the tournament?

1. Understand the Problem

The **answer** will be the player with the *lowest* score.
List the **important information:**

- David Berganio scored +6.
- Sergio Garcia scored −16.
- Tiger Woods scored −4.

2. Make a Plan

You can draw a diagram to order the scores from least to greatest.

3. Solve

Draw a number line and graph each player's score on it.

```
←——|——•——|——|——|——|——|——•——|——|——|——•——|——→
 −18 −16 −14 −12 −10 −8 −6 −4 −2  0  2  4  6  8
```

Sergio Garcia's score, −16, is farthest to the left, so it is the lowest score. Sergio Garcia won this tournament.

4. Look Back

Negative integers are always less than positive integers, so David Berganio cannot be the winner. Since Sergio Garcia's score of −16 is less than Tiger Woods's score of −4, Sergio Garcia won.

Sports Link

In golf, *par* is the standard number of strokes needed to hit the ball into the hole. A score of −12 means "12 strokes under par." A score of +2 means "2 strokes over par."

Think and Discuss

1. **Tell** which is greater, a negative or a positive integer. Explain.
2. **Tell** which is greater, 0 or a negative integer. Explain.
3. **Explain** how to tell which of two negative integers is greater.

11-2 Exercises

GUIDED PRACTICE

See Example 1 Use the number line to compare each pair of integers. Write < or >.

←+—+—+—+—+—+—+—+—+—+—+→
−5 −4 −3 −2 −1 0 1 2 3 4 5

1. −4 ☐ −5
2. −2 ☐ 0
3. −1 ☐ 3

See Example 2 Order the integers in each set from least to greatest.

4. 9, 0, −2
5. 7, −4, 3, −5
6. 8, −6, −1, 10

See Example 3 7. Use the table.

a. At what time was the temperature the lowest?

b. What was the highest temperature?

Time	Temperature (°F)
10:00 P.M.	1
Midnight	−4
3:30 A.M.	−6
6:00 A.M.	1

INDEPENDENT PRACTICE

See Example 1 Use the number line to compare each pair of integers. Write < or >.

←+—+—+—+—+—+—+—+—+—+—+→
−5 −4 −3 −2 −1 0 1 2 3 4 5

8. 0 ☐ 2
9. 4 ☐ −4
10. −3 ☐ −1
11. −5 ☐ 2

See Example 2 Order the integers in each set from least to greatest.

12. 11, −6, −3
13. 15, −8, 7
14. 5, −12, 0, 1
15. −9, 13, −1, −16
16. 24, −6, 7, −10, 4
17. 22, 0, −19, 8, −3

See Example 3 18. **Geography** Use the table, which shows the depths of the world's three largest oceans.

a. Which ocean is the deepest?

b. Which oceans are less than 35,000 feet deep?

Ocean	Depth (ft)
Pacific	−36,200
Atlantic	−30,246
Indian	−24,442

PRACTICE AND PROBLEM SOLVING

Extra Practice
See page EP23.

Compare. Write < or >.

19. −30 ☐ 25
20. 0 ☐ −49
21. −16 ☐ −51
22. −17 ☐ 17
23. −64 ☐ −15
24. 77 ☐ 300
25. −28 ☐ 1
26. 25 ☐ −30

Order the integers in each set from least to greatest.

27. −39, 14, 21
28. −18, −9, −31
29. 0, −26, 43, −12
30. 15, −25, −4, 31
31. −67, 82, −73, −10, 20
32. 42, −27, 69, −50, 38

33. Which set of integers is written in order from greatest to least?

   A. 0, −4, −3, −1
   B. 2, −4, 8, −16
   C. 9, −9, −10, −15
   D. −8, −7, −6, −5

34. **Earth Science** The normal high temperature in January for Barrow, Alaska, is −7 °F. The normal high temperature in January for Los Angeles is 68 °F. Compare the two temperatures using < or >.

35. **Geography** The table shows elevations for several natural features. Write the features in order from the least elevation to the greatest elevation.

Elevations of Natural Features	
Mt. Everest	29,022 ft
Mt. Rainier	14,410 ft
Kilimanjaro	19,000 ft
San Augustin Cave	−2,189 ft
Dead Sea	−1,296 ft

36. **What's the Error?** Your classmate says that 0 < −91. Explain why this is incorrect.

37. **Write About It** Explain how you would order from least to greatest three numbers that include a positive number, a negative number, and zero.

38. **Challenge** There is a missing integer from the list below. The missing integer is both the median and the mode. What is the integer? (*Hint:* There could be more than one correct answer.) 2, −10, 7, −7, 5, −5

Test Prep and Spiral Review

39. **Multiple Choice** Which set of integers is written in order from greatest to least?

   A. −3, −9, −6
   B. −3, 2, 5
   C. 2, −1, −3
   D. 4, 10, 12

40. **Short Response** The table shows the elevations relative to sea level of several cities. Order the cities from the least elevation to the greatest elevation.

City	Boston	Cincinnati	Death Valley	Salt Lake City	San Antonio
Elevation (ft)	16	483	−282	4,226	807

If the angles can form a triangle, classify it as acute, obtuse, or right. (Lesson 8-5)

41. 45°, 76°, 59°   42. 12°, 90°, 78°   43. 88°, 22°, 90°   44. 10°, 5°, 165°

Graph each integer and its opposite on a number line. (Lesson 11-1)

45. −9   46. 7   47. −2   48. 8   49. −5

11-2 Comparing and Ordering Integers

LESSON 11-2 EXTENSION
Negative Rational Numbers

Learn to compare and order negative rational numbers.

Whole numbers, decimals, fractions, percents, and integers belong to the set of *rational numbers*. A **rational number** is a number that can be written as a ratio, with any integer as the numerator, and any integer except 0 as the denominator.

rational numbers
$0.2, \frac{1}{2}, 75\%$

integers
..., –1, 0, 1, ...

whole numbers
0, 1, 2, ...

Vocabulary
rational number

EXAMPLE 1 Comparing Negative Rational Numbers

Use <, >, or = to compare each pair of numbers.

A $-\frac{2}{3}$ ■ $-\frac{1}{2}$

$-\frac{2}{3} \cdot \frac{2}{2} = -\frac{2 \cdot 2}{3 \cdot 2} = -\frac{4}{6}$

$-\frac{1}{2} \cdot \frac{3}{3} = -\frac{1 \cdot 3}{2 \cdot 3} = -\frac{3}{6}$

$-\frac{4}{6} < -\frac{3}{6}$

$-\frac{2}{3} < -\frac{1}{2}$

Write the fractions using a common denominator.

Compare.

Helpful Hint

Integers are rational numbers because they can be written using 1 as the denominator.
$-2 = \frac{-2}{1}$

B –0.2 ■ –2

–0.2

–2.0

0 is greater than –2.

–0.2 > –2

Line up the decimal points and compare from left to right.

C $-\frac{2}{5}$ ■ –0.4

$-0.4 = -\frac{4}{10} = -\frac{2}{5}$

$-\frac{2}{5} = -\frac{2}{5}$

$-\frac{2}{5} = -0.4$

Write –0.4 as a fraction in simplest form.

Compare.

602   Chapter 11 Integers

A number line can be used to place rational numbers in order.

EXAMPLE 2 **Ordering Rational Numbers**

Use a number line to write the numbers in order from least to greatest.

$-3\frac{1}{2}, 2, -1.7, -1, \frac{1}{2}$

Graph the numbers on a number line; $-3\frac{1}{2}$ is between -3 and -4, and -1.7 is between -1 and -2.

$-3\frac{1}{2}, -1.7, -1, \frac{1}{2}, 2$

EXTENSION Exercises

Use <, >, or = to compare each pair of numbers.

1. $-\frac{4}{5}$ ◼ $-\frac{5}{6}$
2. -0.8 ◼ -0.3
3. $-\frac{8}{9}$ ◼ $-\frac{5}{6}$
4. -0.85 ◼ -0.98
5. $-\frac{1}{7}$ ◼ $-\frac{1}{8}$
6. -0.99 ◼ -1
7. -1.7 ◼ $-1\frac{7}{9}$
8. $-\frac{3}{5}$ ◼ -0.6
9. -5.2 ◼ $-5\frac{1}{2}$
10. -2 ◼ -1.98
11. $-2\frac{3}{5}$ ◼ -3
12. $-\frac{1}{10}$ ◼ 0

Write the numbers in order from least to greatest.

13. $0.21, -2\frac{7}{10}, 0, -7\frac{3}{4}$
14. $2\frac{7}{20}, -5, -5\frac{3}{5}, 3.6$
15. $2.25, -4\frac{1}{10}, -3, 4\frac{3}{5}$
16. $-1\frac{12}{25}, -6.8, 3, 3.15$
17. $0.09, -2.7, -3\frac{1}{2}, \frac{4}{5}$
18. $-4.4, 0.61, -3\frac{1}{2}, -6\frac{1}{6}$
19. $2\frac{2}{5}, -8.5, -7\frac{1}{4}, 1.25$
20. $6\frac{3}{5}, -3, -3\frac{9}{10}, -3\frac{1}{3}$
21. $-2.5, -7, 4\frac{1}{5}, -8.25$
22. $-8.8, -5, -3\frac{4}{7}, -9\frac{1}{7}$

23. **What's the Error?** A student wrote on a test that $-2\frac{8}{12} > -2\frac{2}{3}$ because $8 > 2$ and $12 > 3$. What error did the student make?

24. **Challenge** Find each absolute value.

   a. $|-1.3|$
   b. $\left|-\frac{9}{10}\right|$
   c. $|-8.2|$
   d. $\left|-2\frac{6}{7}\right|$

11-3 The Coordinate Plane

Learn to locate and graph points on the coordinate plane.

Vocabulary
coordinate plane
axes
x-axis
y-axis
quadrants
origin
coordinates
x-coordinate
y-coordinate

A **coordinate plane** is formed by two number lines in a plane that intersect at right angles. The point of intersection is the zero on each number line.

- The two number lines are called the **axes**.
- The horizontal axis is called the **x-axis**.
- The vertical axis is called the **y-axis**.
- The two axes divide the coordinate plane into four **quadrants**.
- The point where the axes intersect is called the **origin**.

EXAMPLE 1 Identifying Quadrants

Name the quadrant where each point is located.

A M
Quadrant I

B J
Quadrant IV

C R
x-axis
no quadrant

Helpful Hint
Points on the axes are not in any quadrant.

An ordered pair gives the location of a point on a coordinate plane. The first number tells how far to move right (positive) or left (negative) from the origin. The second number tells how far to move up (positive) or down (negative).

The numbers in an ordered pair are called **coordinates**. The first number is called the **x-coordinate**. The second number is called the **y-coordinate**.

The ordered pair for the origin is (0, 0).

EXAMPLE 2   **Locating Points on a Coordinate Plane**

Give the coordinates of each point.

A   K

From the origin, K is 1 unit right and 4 units up.

(1, 4)

B   T

From the origin, T is 2 units left on the x-axis.

(−2, 0)

C   W

From the origin, W is 3 units left and 4 units down.

(−3, −4)

EXAMPLE 3   **Graphing Points on a Coordinate Plane**

Graph each point on a coordinate plane.

A $P(-3, -2)$

From the origin, move 3 units left and 2 units down.

B $R(0, 4)$

From the origin, move 4 units up.

C $M(3, -4)$

From the origin, move 3 units right and 4 units down.

Think and Discuss

1. **Tell** which number in an ordered pair indicates how far to move left or right from the origin and which number indicates how far to move up or down.

2. **Describe** how graphing the point (5, 4) is similar to graphing the point (5, −4). How is it different?

3. **Tell** why it is important to start at the origin when you are graphing points.

11-3 Exercises

GUIDED PRACTICE

Use the coordinate plane for Exercises 1–6.

See Example 1 Name the quadrant where each point is located.
1. T
2. U
3. B

See Example 2 Give the coordinates of each point.
4. A
5. B
6. U

See Example 3 Graph each point on a coordinate plane.
7. $E(4, 2)$
8. $F(-1, -4)$
9. $G(0, 2)$

INDEPENDENT PRACTICE

Use the coordinate plane for Exercises 10–21.

See Example 1 Name the quadrant where each point is located.
10. Q
11. X
12. H
13. Y
14. Z
15. P

See Example 2 Give the coordinates of each point.
16. P
17. R
18. Y
19. T
20. H
21. Q

See Example 3 Graph each point on a coordinate plane.
22. $L(0, 3)$
23. $M(3, -3)$
24. $S(2, 0)$
25. $V(-4, 3)$
26. $N(-2, -1)$
27. $B(4, 3)$

PRACTICE AND PROBLEM SOLVING

Extra Practice
See page EP23.

Name the quadrant where each ordered pair is located.
28. $(3, -1)$
29. $(2, 1)$
30. $(-2, 3)$
31. $(-4, -3)$
32. $\left(4\frac{1}{2}, -3\right)$
33. $\left(10, -7\frac{1}{2}\right)$
34. $\left(-6, 2\frac{1}{3}\right)$
35. $\left(-8\frac{1}{3}, -\frac{1}{2}\right)$

Graph each ordered pair.
36. $(0, -5)$
37. $(-4, -4)$
38. $(5, 0)$
39. $(3, 2)$
40. $(-2, 2)$
41. $(0, -3)$
42. $(1, -4)$
43. $(0, 0)$
44. $\left(-2\frac{1}{2}, 3\right)$
45. $\left(5, 3\frac{1}{2}\right)$
46. $\left(-4\frac{1}{3}, 0\right)$
47. $\left(0, -\frac{1}{2}\right)$

48. Graph points $A(-1, -1)$, $B(2, 1)$, $C(2, -2)$, and $D(-1, -2)$. Connect the points. What type of quadrilateral do the points form?

606 Chapter 11 Integers

Social Studies LINK

We use a coordinate system on Earth to find exact locations. The *equator* is like the *x*-axis, and the *prime meridian* is like the *y*-axis.

The lines that run east-west are *lines of latitude.* They are measured in degrees north and south of the equator.

The lines that run north-south are *lines of longitude.* They are measured in degrees east and west of the prime meridian.

49. In what country is the location 0° latitude, 10° E longitude?

50. Give the coordinates of a location in Algeria.

51. Name two countries that lie along the 30° N line of latitude.

52. Where would you be if you were located at 10° S latitude, 10° W longitude?

53. **Write About It** How is the coordinate system we use to locate places on Earth different from the coordinate plane? How is it similar?

54. **Challenge** Begin at 10° S latitude, 20° E longitude. Travel 40° north and 20° west. What country would you be in now?

Test Prep and Spiral Review

55. Multiple Choice In which quadrant is the point (−1, 2) located?

　Ⓐ Quadrant I　　Ⓑ Quadrant II　　Ⓒ Quadrant III　　Ⓓ Quadrant IV

56. Multiple Choice Which of the following coordinates is the farthest to the right of the origin on a coordinate plane?

　Ⓕ (−19, 7)　　Ⓖ (0, 12)　　Ⓗ (4, 15)　　Ⓙ (7, 0)

Write each fraction or mixed number as a decimal. (Lesson 4-4)

57. $4\frac{2}{5}$　　**58.** $\frac{9}{10}$　　**59.** $5\frac{3}{4}$　　**60.** $\frac{9}{20}$　　**61.** $\frac{1}{5}$

Compare. Write < or >. (Lesson 11-2)

62. 0 ▇ −4　　**63.** −345 ▇ 78　　**64.** −12 ▇ −6　　**65.** 14 ▇ 18

11-3 The Coordinate Plane

11-4 Transformations in the Coordinate Plane

When a marching band moves in formation, it is performing a transformation of any figure it has formed. Recall from Lesson 8-10 that there are three basic transformations. A translation moves a figure along a straight line, a reflection shows a figure's mirror image, and a rotation moves a figure around a fixed point. Remember also that in each of these basic transformations, the figure and its image are congruent.

Transformations can be shown using a coordinate plane.

EXAMPLE 1
Translating Figures in the Coordinate Plane

Translate square *ABCD* 6 units left. Give the coordinates of each vertex in the image.

Reading Math
A' is read "*A* prime." Prime notation is used to represent the point on the image that corresponds to the same point on the original figure.

Each vertex is translated 6 units left.

The vertices of the image are *A'*(−5, −1), *B'*(−5, −5), *C'*(−1, −5), and *D'*(−1, −1).

EXAMPLE 2
Reflecting Figures in the Coordinate Plane

A Reflect triangle *ABC* across the *y*-axis. Give the coordinates of each vertex in the image.

Each vertex of the image is the same distance from the *y*-axis as the corresponding vertex in the original figure.

The vertices of the image are *A'*(−2, 4), *B'*(−2, 1), and *C'*(−4, 1).

B Reflect triangle *XYZ* across the *x*-axis. Give the coordinates of each vertex in the image.

Each vertex of the image is the same distance from the x-axis as the corresponding vertex in the original figure.

Helpful Hint
A line of reflection is not limited to the *x*-axis or *y*-axis. Any line can be a line of reflection.

The vertices of the image are *X'*(–3, –2), *Y'*(3, –3), and *Z'*(4, –1).

EXAMPLE 3 Rotating Figures in the Coordinate Plane

Rotate rectangle *PQRS* 90° clockwise about the origin. Give the coordinates of each vertex in the image.

Notice that vertex Q is 4 units to the right of the origin, and vertex Q' is 4 units below the origin.

Similarly, vertex S is 3 units above the origin, and vertex S' is 3 units to the right of the origin.

The vertices of the image are *P'*(0, 0), *Q'*(0, –4), *R'*(3, –4), and *S'*(3, 0).

Think and Discuss

1. **Tell** how the *x*- and *y*-coordinates change when a figure is translated right *a* units and down *b* units.

2. **Explain** why the *x*-coordinates of the vertices of a figure do not change when the figure is reflected across the *x*-axis.

3. **Predict** the coordinates of each vertex in the image of rectangle *PQSR* from Example 3 under a 180° rotation.

11-4 Exercises

GUIDED PRACTICE

See Example 1 — Translate each figure the given number of units. Give the coordinates of each vertex in the image.

1. figure *ABCD*; 3 units up
2. figure *EFG*; 4 units left

See Example 2 — Reflect each figure across the given axis. Give the coordinates of each vertex in the image.

3. figure *ABCD*; *x*-axis
4. figure *EFG*; *y*-axis

See Example 3 — Rotate each figure the given direction and number of degrees about the origin. Give the coordinates of each vertex in the image.

5. figure *EFG*; 90° clockwise
6. figure *EFG*; 90° counterclockwise

INDEPENDENT PRACTICE

See Example 1 — Translate each figure the given number of units. Give the coordinates of each vertex in the image.

7. figure *HJKL*; 2 units left
8. figure *MNPQ*; 1 unit down

See Example 2 — Reflect each figure across the given axis. Give the coordinates of each vertex in the image.

9. figure *HJKL*; *x*-axis
10. figure *MNPQ*; *y*-axis

See Example 3 — Rotate each figure the given direction and number of degrees about the origin. Give the coordinates of each vertex in the image.

11. figure *HJKL*; 180° clockwise
12. figure *HJKL*; 90° counterclockwise

610   Chapter 11 Integers

PRACTICE AND PROBLEM SOLVING

Extra Practice
See page EP23.

Describe each transformation.

13.

14.

15.

16.

17. **Write About It** Will the image of a horizontal line be horizontal after a translation? a reflection over the x-axis? a rotation? Explain your answers.

18. **Challenge** Lara translated rhombus MNOP 2 units right and then rotated it 180° clockwise about the origin. Mike rotated rhombus MNOP 180° clockwise about the origin and then translated it 2 units right. Are the coordinates of the vertices of the two images the same? Explain.

Test Prep and Spiral Review

19. **Multiple Choice** The coordinates of the vertices of figure ABCD are A(–8, 5), B(–5, 4), C(0, 0), and D(–7, 3). The figure is reflected across the y-axis. What are the coordinates of A'?

    Ⓐ (–8, –5)   Ⓑ (8, –5)   Ⓒ (8, 5)   Ⓓ (5, 4)

20. **Short Response** Figure ABCD has vertices A(4, –1), B(0, 0), C(1, –4), and D(3, –5). Figure ABCD is rotated 180° counterclockwise about the origin. Draw figure ABCD and its image.

Solve each equation. Write the answer in simplest form. (Lesson 5-10)

21. $\frac{y}{7} = 3$ 22. $\frac{4}{5}a = \frac{1}{25}$ 23. $\frac{x}{9} = 14$ 24. $\frac{2}{5}p = 7$

CHAPTER 11 SECTION 11A

Ready To Go On?

Quiz for Lessons 11-1 Through 11-4

11-1 Integers and Absolute Value

Name a positive or negative number to represent each situation.

1. a gain of 10 yards
2. 45 feet below sea level

Write the opposite of each integer.

3. 9
4. −17
5. 1
6. −20

Write the absolute value of each integer.

7. $|7|$
8. $|-6|$
9. $|-8|$
10. $|-9|$

11-2 Comparing and Ordering Integers

Compare. Write < or >.

11. 9 ▮ −22
12. −7 ▮ 4
13. −10 ▮ −19

Order the integers in each set from least to greatest.

14. 2, −7, 14
15. 25, −9, 4, −21
16. 10, 0, −23, −17, 8

11-3 The Coordinate Plane

Use the coordinate plane for problems 17–24.

Name the quadrant where each point is located.

17. A
18. Y
19. J
20. C

Give the coordinates of each point.

21. H
22. I
23. W
24. B

Graph each point on a coordinate plane.

25. $N(-5, -2)$
26. $S(0, 4)$
27. $R(-2, 6)$
28. $M(2, 2)$

11-4 Transformations in the Coordinate Plane

Use the coordinate plane for problems 29–31.

Perform the given transformation of triangle ABC. Give the coordinates of each vertex in the image.

29. translate 6 units down
30. reflect across the y-axis
31. rotate 90° counterclockwise about point B

Focus on Problem Solving

Understand the Problem

• **Restate the question**

After reading a real-world problem (perhaps several times), look at the question in the problem. Rewrite the question as a statement in your own words. For example, if the question is "How much money did the museum earn?" you could write, "Find the amount of money the museum earned."

Now you have a simple sentence telling you what you must do. This can help you understand and remember what the problem is about. This can also help you find the necessary information in the problem.

Read the problems below. Rewrite each question as a statement in your own words.

1. Israel is one of the hottest countries in Asia. A temperature of 129 °F was once recorded there. This is the opposite of the coldest recorded temperature in Antarctica. How cold has it been in Antarctica?

2. The average recorded temperature in Fairbanks, Alaska, in January is about −10 °F. In February, the average temperature is about −4 °F. Is the average temperature lower in January or in February?

3. The south pole on Mars is made of frozen carbon dioxide, which has a temperature of −193 °F. The coldest day recorded on Earth was −129 °F, in Antarctica. Which temperature is lower?

4. The pirate Blackbeard's ship, the *Queen Anne's Revenge,* sank at Beauford Inlet, North Carolina, in 1718. In 1996, divers discovered a shipwreck believed to be the *Queen Anne's Revenge*. The ship's cannons were found 21 feet below the water's surface, and the ship's bell was found 20 feet below the surface. Were the cannons or the bell closer to the surface?

In this photo of Mars, different colors represent different temperature ranges. When the photo was taken, it was summer in the northern hemisphere and winter in the southern hemisphere.

−65 °C   −120 °C

Hands-on LAB 11-5
Model Integer Addition

Use with Lesson 11-5

Learn It Online
Lab Resources Online go.hrw.com,
keyword MR10 Lab11 Go

KEY
● = 1   ● = −1

REMEMBER
Subtracting zero from a number does not change the number's value.

Two-color counters can be used to represent integers. Yellow counters represent positive numbers and red counters represent negative numbers.

Activity

Model with two-color counters.

1 $3 + 4$ $3 + 4 = 7$

2 $-5 + (-3)$ $-5 + (-3) = -8$

One red and one yellow counter together equal zero, and are called a zero pair. Whenever you have a zero pair, you can remove it without changing the value of the model.

3 $3 + (-4)$ $3 + (-4) = -1$

Think and Discuss

1. When adding integers, would changing the order in which you add them affect the answer? Explain.

2. When can you remove counters from an addition model?

Try This

Model with two-color counters.

1. $-8 + (-4)$ 2. $-8 + 4$ 3. $8 + (-4)$ 4. $8 + 4$

614   Chapter 11 Integers

11-5 Adding Integers

Learn to add integers.

One of the world's most active volcanoes is Kilauea, in Hawaii. Kilauea's base is 9 km below sea level. The top of Kilauea is 10 km above the base of the mountain.

You can add the integers −9 and 10 to find the height of Kilauea above sea level.

Adding Integers on a Number Line
Move **right** on a number line to add a **positive** integer.
Move **left** on a number line to add a **negative** integer.

EXAMPLE 1 Writing Integer Addition

Write the addition modeled on each number line.

A

The addition modeled is $4 + 1 = 5$.

B

The addition modeled is $-2 + (-5) = -7$.

C

The addition modeled is $3 + (-8) = -5$.

Writing Math

Parentheses are used to separate addition, subtraction, multiplication, and division signs from negative integers.
$-2 + (-5) = -7$

EXAMPLE 2 Adding Integers

Find each sum.

A $6 + (-5)$

$6 + (-5) = 1$

Think:

B $-7 + 4$

$-7 + 4 = -3$

Think:

EXAMPLE 3 Evaluating Integer Expressions

Evaluate $x + 3$ for $x = -9$.

$x + 3$	*Write the expression.*
$-9 + 3$	*Substitute −9 for x.*
-6	*Add.*

Think:

EXAMPLE 4 Earth Science Application

The base of Kilauea is 9 km below sea level. The top is 10 km above the base. How high above sea level is Kilauea?

The base is **9 km below sea level** and the top is **10 km above the base**.

$-9 + 10$
1

Kilauea is 1 km above sea level.

Think and Discuss

1. **Tell** if the sum of a positive integer and −8 is greater than −8 or less than −8. Explain.

2. **Give** the sum of a number and its opposite.

11-5 Exercises

Learn It Online
Homework Help Online go.hrw.com,
keyword MR10 11-5 Go
Exercises 1–35, 41, 45, 49, 53, 55, 57

GUIDED PRACTICE

See Example 1 Write the addition modeled on the number line.

1. [number line showing 3 + 2 from 0 to 5]

See Example 2 Find each sum.

2. $-5 + 9$
3. $-3 + (-2)$
4. $8 + (-7)$
5. $10 + (-3)$
6. $-4 + (-8)$
7. $-1 + 5$

See Example 3 Evaluate $n + (-2)$ for each value of n.

8. $n = -10$
9. $n = 2$
10. $n = -2$
11. $n = -15$
12. $n = 12$
13. $n = -20$

See Example 4

14. A submarine at the water's surface dropped down 100 ft. After thirty minutes at that depth, it dove an additional 500 ft. What was its depth after the second dive?

INDEPENDENT PRACTICE

See Example 1 Write the addition modeled on each number line.

15. [number line showing 6 + (−2)]

16. [number line showing −4 + (−2)]

See Example 2 Find each sum.

17. $4 + 7$
18. $2 + (-12)$
19. $9 + (-9)$
20. $10 + (-21)$
21. $-8 + 2$
22. $-2 + 8$
23. $-1 + (-6)$
24. $-25 + (14)$

See Example 3 Evaluate $-6 + a$ for each value of a.

25. $a = -10$
26. $a = 7$
27. $a = -2$
28. $a = -6$
29. $a = 4$
30. $a = -9$
31. $a = 8$
32. $a = -20$

See Example 4

33. Jon works on a cruise ship and sleeps in a cabin that is 6 feet below sea level. The main deck is 35 feet above Jon's cabin. How far above sea level is the main deck?

34. **Recreation** Preston dives to a depth of 15 feet. He stops briefly and then dives an additional 17 feet. What is Preston's depth after his second dive?

11-5 Adding Integers 617

PRACTICE AND PROBLEM SOLVING

Extra Practice
See page EP24.

Model each addition problem on a number line.

35. $3 + (-1)$ **36.** $-2 + (-4)$ **37.** $-6 + 5$ **38.** $1 + (-2)$

39. $-1 + 6$ **40.** $5 + (-3)$ **41.** $-3 + (-1)$ **42.** $0 + (-5)$

Find each sum.

43. $-18 + 25$ **44.** $8 + (-2)$ **45.** $-5 + (-6)$ **46.** $-12 + (-7)$

47. $-6 + (-3)$ **48.** $4 + (-1)$ **49.** $20 + (-3)$ **50.** $30 + (-25)$

Evaluate each expression for the given value of the variable.

51. $x + (-3); x = 7$ **52.** $-9 + n; n = 7$ **53.** $a + 5; a = -6$

54. $m + (-2); m = -4$ **55.** $-10 + x; x = -7$ **56.** $n + 19; n = -5$

57. Earth Science The temperature at midnight was –2 °F. During the next 4 hours, a decrease of 4 °F was recorded. What was the temperature at 4 A.M.?

58. Sports In the 2001 U.S. Women's Open, Cristie Kerr had the following scores for the four rounds of golf: −1, +3, +1, and 0. What was her total score?

59. Choose a Strategy The first Roman emperor, Augustus, was born in 63 B.C.E. and died in 14 C.E. How many years did he live? (*Hint*: Years B.C.E. are like negative numbers. Years C.E. are like positive numbers. There was no year 0.)

60. Critical Thinking Will the expression $-7 + 10$ have the same sum as $10 + (-7)$? Explain your answer.

61. Write About It When adding two integers, what will the sign of the answer be when one integer is positive and the other is negative? Explain.

62. Challenge Evaluate $-3 + (-2) + (-1) + 0 + 1 + 2 + 3 + 4$. Then use this pattern to find the sum of the integers from -10 to 11 and from -100 to 101.

History Link

Augustus, originally named Octavian, ruled the Roman Empire for more than 40 years.

Test Prep and Spiral Review

63. Multiple Choice Julie earned $1,350 at her part-time job. Her paycheck showed deductions of $148.50. What was the total amount of her paycheck?

(A) $1,165.50 (B) $1,201.50 (C) $1,498.50 (D) $1,534.50

64. Multiple Choice Which sum is NOT negative?

(F) $-38 + (-24)$ (G) $-61 + 43$ (H) $-54 + 68$ (J) $-29 + 11$

65. Short Response Evaluate $b + 7$ for $b = -2, -4,$ and -8.

Find each value. (Lesson 1-2)

66. 5^3 **67.** 4^1 **68.** 9^2 **69.** 12^3 **70.** 7^4

Graph each point on a coordinate plane. (Lesson 11-3)

71. $J(5, 7)$ **72.** $M(-2, 4)$ **73.** $L(4, -3)$ **74.** $A(-1, -6)$ **75.** $W(0, 5)$

Hands-On LAB 11-6

Model Integer Subtraction

Use with Lesson 11-6

KEY
● = 1   ● = −1

REMEMBER
Adding zero to a number does not change the number's value.
● + ● = 0

Learn It Online
Lab Resources Online go.hrw.com,
keyword MR10 Lab11

Activity

Model with two-color counters.

1 3 − 2

3 − 2 = 1

2 −3 − (−2)

−3 − (−2) = −1

3 3 − (−2)

You do not have any red counters, so you cannot subtract −2. Add zero pairs until you have enough red counters to subtract.

Add 2 zero pairs.   Now you can subtract −2.

3 − (−2) = 5

Think and Discuss

1. How do you show subtraction with counters?
2. Why can you add zero pairs to a subtraction model?

Try This

Model with two-color counters.

1. 5 − 4
2. 4 − (−5)
3. −4 − 5
4. −4 − (−5)
5. 8 − 5
6. 5 − (−8)
7. −5 − 8
8. −8 − (−8)

11-6 Hands-On Lab

11-6 Subtracting Integers

Learn to subtract integers.

On a number line, integer subtraction is the opposite of integer addition. Integer subtraction "undoes" integer addition.

> **Subtracting Integers on a Number Line**
>
> Move **left** on a number line to subtract a **positive** integer.
>
> Move **right** on a number line to subtract a **negative** integer.

EXAMPLE 1 Writing Integer Subtraction

Interactivities Online

Write the subtraction modeled on each number line.

A

The subtraction modeled is $8 - 10 = -2$.

B

The subtraction modeled is $2 - (-4) = 6$.

EXAMPLE 2 Subtracting Integers

Find each difference.

A $7 - 4$

Think:

$7 - 4 = 3$

B $-8 - (-2)$

Think:

$-8 - (-2) = -6$

620 Chapter 11 Integers

EXAMPLE 3 Evaluating Integer Expressions

Evaluate $x - (-4)$ for $x = -5$.

$x - (-4)$ Write the expression.
$-5 - (-4)$ Substitute -5 for x.   Think:
-1 Subtract.

Think and Discuss

1. **Describe** the direction you would move to add a positive integer.
2. **Explain** how the answers to Example 1 help show that addition and subtraction are inverses.

11-6 Exercises

Learn It Online
Homework Help Online go.hrw.com,
keyword MR10 11-6
Exercises 1–22, 23, 25, 27, 31, 35, 37, 39

GUIDED PRACTICE

See Example 1
1. Write the subtraction modeled on the number line.

See Example 2   Find each difference.
2. $6 - 3$ 3. $3 - 6$ 4. $10 - (-4)$ 5. $-12 - (-4)$

See Example 3   Evaluate $n - (-6)$ for each value of n.
6. $n = -4$ 7. $n = 2$ 8. $n = -15$ 9. $n = 7$

INDEPENDENT PRACTICE

See Example 1
10. Write the subtraction modeled on the number line.

See Example 2   Find each difference.
11. $3 - 7$ 12. $-4 - 9$ 13. $2 - (-9)$ 14. $-22 - (-2)$

See Example 3   Evaluate $m - (-3)$ for each value of m.
15. $m = -1$ 16. $m = 7$ 17. $m = -8$ 18. $m = -5$
19. $m = 4$ 20. $m = -9$ 21. $m = -15$ 22. $m = 13$

PRACTICE AND PROBLEM SOLVING

Extra Practice
See page EP24.

Find each difference.

23. $-12 - (-6)$
24. $7 - (-3)$
25. $-4 - (-3)$
26. $8 - (-2)$
27. $19 - (-2)$
28. $-5 - 10$
29. $50 - 20$
30. $-2 - 7$

Evaluate each expression for the given value of the variable.

31. $n - (-10), n = 2$
32. $-6 - m, m = -9$
33. $x - 2, x = 6$
34. $4 - y, y = 9$
35. $j - 21, j = -17$
36. $101 - h, h = -75$

37. **Earth Science** The surface of an underground water supply was 10 m below sea level. After one year, the depth of the water supply has decreased by 9 m. How far below sea level is the water's surface now?

38. **Construction** A 200-foot column holds an oil rig platform above the ocean's surface. The column rests on the ocean floor 175 feet below sea level. How high is the platform above sea level?

39. **Earth Science** During summer 1997, NASA landed the *Pathfinder* on Mars. On July 9, *Pathfinder* reported a temperature of -1 °F on the planet's surface. On July 10, it reported a temperature of 8 °F. Find the difference between the temperature on July 10 and the temperature on July 9.

40. **What's the Error?** Ty says that $0 - (-4) = -4$. Explain why this is incorrect.

41. **Write About It** Will the difference between two negative numbers ever be positive? Use examples to support your answer.

42. **Challenge** This pyramid was built by subtracting integers. Two integers are subtracted from left to right, and their difference is centered above them. Find the missing numbers.

Test Prep and Spiral Review

43. **Multiple Choice** Evaluate $h - (-8)$ for $h = 3$.

    Ⓐ -11 Ⓑ -5 Ⓒ 5 Ⓓ 11

44. **Multiple Choice** Trina's score on a game show was -250 points. Gwen's score was -320 points. By how many points was Trina ahead of Gwen?

    Ⓕ 570 points   Ⓖ 70 points   Ⓗ -70 points   Ⓙ -570 points

Write each decimal as a percent. (Lesson 7-8)

45. 0.02
46. 0.53
47. 0.26
48. 0.44
49. 3.1

Name the quadrant where each ordered pair is located. (Lesson 11-3)

50. $(4, -6)$
51. $(-1, 5)$
52. $(2, 3)$
53. $(-2, -4)$
54. $(-10, 5)$

622 Chapter 11 Integers

11-7 Multiplying Integers

Learn to multiply integers.

You have seen that you can multiply whole numbers to count items in equally sized groups.

There are three sets of twins in the sixth grade. How many sixth graders are twins?

A set of twins is 2 people.

3 · 2 = 6   *3 sets of 2 is 6.*

So 6 students in the sixth grade are twins.

Multiplying with integers is similar.

Numbers	3 · 2	−3 · 2	3 · (−2)	−3 · (−2)
Words	3 groups of 2	the opposite of 3 groups of 2	3 groups of −2	the opposite of 3 groups of −2
Addition	2 + 2 + 2	−(2 + 2 + 2)	(−2) + (−2) + (−2)	−[(−2) + (−2) + (−2)]
Product	6	−6	−6	6

EXAMPLE 1 Multiplying Integers

Find each product.

A 4 · 3
4 · 3 = 12   *Think: 4 groups of 3*

B 2 · (−4)
2 · (−4) = −8   *Think: 2 groups of −4*

C −5 · 2
−5 · 2 = −10   *Think: the opposite of 5 groups of 2*

D −3 · (−4)
−3 · (−4) = 12   *Think: the opposite of 3 groups of −4*

Remember!
To find the opposite of a number, change the sign. The opposite of 6 is −6. The opposite of −4 is 4.

MULTIPLYING INTEGERS

If the signs are the same, the product is positive.
$$4 \cdot 3 = 12 \qquad -6 \cdot (-3) = 18$$

If the signs are different, the product is negative.
$$-2 \cdot 5 = -10 \qquad 7 \cdot (-8) = -56$$

The product of any number and 0 is 0.
$$0 \cdot 9 = 0 \qquad (-12) \cdot 0 = 0$$

EXAMPLE 2 Evaluating Integer Expressions

Evaluate $5x$ for each value of x.

A $x = -4$

$5x$ — Write the expression.
$5 \cdot (-4)$ — Substitute -4 for x.
-20 — The signs are different, so the answer is negative.

B $x = 0$

$5x$ — Write the expression.
$5 \cdot 0$ — Substitute 0 for x.
0 — Any number times 0 is 0.

Remember!
$5x$ means $5 \cdot x$.

Think and Discuss

1. Explain whether the product of two integers is greater than, less than, or between the two factors.

11-7 Exercises

GUIDED PRACTICE

See Example 1 **Find each product.**

1. $6 \cdot 4$
2. $5 \cdot (-2)$
3. $-3 \cdot 7$
4. $-2 \cdot 3$
5. $-9 \cdot (-1)$
6. $13 \cdot 0$
7. $-8 \cdot (-2)$
8. $-6 \cdot (-6)$

See Example 2 **Evaluate $3n$ for each value of n.**

9. $n = 3$
10. $n = -2$
11. $n = 11$
12. $n = -5$
13. $n = -8$
14. $n = -12$
15. $n = 6$
16. $n = 10$

INDEPENDENT PRACTICE

See Example 1 Find each product.

17. $5 \cdot 9$
18. $-7 \cdot 6$
19. $8 \cdot (-4)$
20. $-6 \cdot (-9)$
21. $-13 \cdot (-3)$
22. $4 \cdot 12$
23. $6 \cdot (-12)$
24. $-7 \cdot (-11)$

See Example 2 Evaluate $-4a$ for each value of a.

25. $a = 6$
26. $a = 12$
27. $a = 3$
28. $a = -7$
29. $a = -10$
30. $a = 7$
31. $a = -15$
32. $a = -22$

PRACTICE AND PROBLEM SOLVING

Extra Practice
See page EP24.

Evaluate each expression for the given value of the variable.

33. $n \cdot (-7);\ n = -2$
34. $-6 \cdot m;\ m = 4$
35. $9x;\ x = 6$
36. $-5m;\ m = 5$
37. $x \cdot 10;\ x = -9$
38. $-8 \cdot n;\ n = -1$

39. **Earth Science** When the moon, the sun, and Earth are in a straight line, spring tides occur on Earth. Spring tides may cause high and low tides to be two times as great as normal. If high tides at a certain location are usually 2 ft and low tides are usually -2 ft, what might the spring tides be?

40. **Critical Thinking** What number property is true for integer multiplication?

41. **What's the Error?** Ava says the value of $-6b$ when $b = -6$ is -36. What is her error? What is the correct answer?

42. **Write About It** What is the sign of the product when you multiply three negative integers? four negative integers? Use examples to explain.

43. **Challenge** Name 2 integers whose product is -36 and whose sum is 0.

Test Prep and Spiral Review

44. **Multiple Choice** During a game, Frieda scored -10 points for each question she missed. She missed 5 questions. What was the total number of points she scored on missed questions?

    (A) -50
    (B) -2
    (C) 2
    (D) 50

45. **Extended Response** What is the sign of the product when 4 negative integers are multiplied? when 5 negative integers are multiplied? Describe a rule that can be used to determine the sign of the product when the number of negative integers is even and when the number of negative integers is odd.

46. Kim cut $6\frac{1}{3}$ yards of ribbon into $\frac{1}{3}$-yard pieces. How many pieces of ribbon did Kim have? (Lesson 5-9)

Find each sum. (Lesson 11-5)

47. $3 + 6$
48. $-5 + 1$
49. $-4 + (-9)$
50. $7 + (-7)$
51. $2 + (-5)$

11-8 Dividing Integers

Learn to divide integers.

Mona is a biologist studying an endangered species of wombat. Each year she records the change in the wombat population.

Year	Change in Population
1	−2
2	−5
3	−1
4	−4

Australian wombat

One way to describe the change in the wombat population over time is to find the mean of the data in the table.

Remember!
To find the mean of a list of numbers:
1. Add all the numbers together.
2. Divide by how many numbers are in the list.
See page 288.

$$\frac{-2 + (-5) + (-1) + (-4)}{4} = \frac{-12}{4} = -12 \div 4 = \boxed{}$$

Multiplication and division are inverse operations. To solve a division problem, think of the related multiplication.

To solve $-12 \div 4$, think: What number times 4 equals -12?

$$-3 \cdot 4 = -12, \text{ so } -12 \div 4 = -3$$

The mean change in the wombat population is -3. So on average, the population **decreased by 3 wombats** per year.

EXAMPLE 1 Dividing Integers

Find each quotient.

A $12 \div (-3)$

Think: What number times -3 equals 12?
$-4 \cdot (-3) = 12$, so $12 \div (-3) = -4$.

B $-15 \div (-3)$

Think: What number times -3 equals -15?
$5 \cdot (-3) = -15$, so $-15 \div (-3) = 5$.

626 Chapter 11 Integers   Video Lesson Tutorials Online my.hrw.com

Because division is the inverse of multiplication, the rules for dividing integers are the same as the rules for multiplying integers.

DIVIDING INTEGERS

If the signs are the same, the quotient is positive.
$$24 \div 3 = 8 \qquad -6 \div (-3) = 2$$

If the signs are different, the quotient is negative.
$$-20 \div 5 = -4 \qquad 72 \div (-8) = -9$$

Zero divided by any integer equals 0.
$$\frac{0}{14} = 0 \qquad \frac{0}{-11} = 0$$

You cannot divide any integer by 0.

EXAMPLE 2 Evaluating Integer Expressions

Evaluate $\frac{x}{3}$ for each value of x.

Remember!
$\frac{x}{3}$ means $x \div 3$.

A $x = 6$

$\frac{x}{3}$ — Write the expression.

$\frac{6}{3} = 6 \div 3$ — Substitute 6 for x.

$= 2$ — The signs are the same, so the answer is positive.

B $x = -18$

$\frac{x}{3}$ — Write the expression.

$\frac{-18}{3} = -18 \div 3$ — Substitute -18 for x.

$= -6$ — The signs are different, so the answer is negative.

C $x = -12$

$\frac{x}{3}$ — Write the expression.

$\frac{-12}{3} = -12 \div 3$ — Substitute -12 for x.

$= -4$ — The signs are different, so the answer is negative.

Think and Discuss

1. **Describe** the sign of the quotient of two integers with like signs.
2. **Describe** the sign of the quotient of two integers with unlike signs.

11-8 Exercises

GUIDED PRACTICE

See Example 1 Find each quotient.

1. $64 \div 8$
2. $10 \div (-2)$
3. $-21 \div (-7)$
4. $-64 \div 2$

See Example 2 Evaluate $\frac{m}{2}$ for each value of m.

5. $m = -4$
6. $m = 20$
7. $m = -30$
8. $m = 50$

INDEPENDENT PRACTICE

See Example 1 Find each quotient.

9. $45 \div 9$
10. $-42 \div 6$
11. $32 \div (-4)$
12. $54 \div (-6)$
13. $-60 \div (-10)$
14. $-75 \div 15$
15. $22 \div 11$
16. $-48 \div (-4)$

See Example 2 Evaluate $\frac{n}{4}$ for each value of n.

17. $n = 4$
18. $n = -32$
19. $n = 12$
20. $n = -24$
21. $n = 64$
22. $n = -92$
23. $n = 56$
24. $n = -28$

PRACTICE AND PROBLEM SOLVING

Extra Practice See page EP24.

Divide.

25. $-12 \div 2$
26. $\frac{16}{-4}$
27. $-6 \div (-6)$
28. $-56 \div (-7)$
29. $\frac{-30}{-3}$
30. $-45 \div 9$
31. $\frac{-35}{5}$
32. $\frac{-63}{9}$

Evaluate each expression for the given value of the variable.

33. $n \div (-7)$; $n = -21$
34. $\frac{m}{3}$; $m = -15$
35. $\frac{x}{4}$; $x = 32$
36. $y \div (-3)$; $y = -6$
37. $\frac{a}{3}$; $a = -9$
38. $w \div (-2)$; $w = -18$
39. $-48 \div n$; $n = -8$
40. $\frac{p}{-2}$; $p = -20$
41. $j \div 9$; $j = -99$

42. The graph shows the low temperatures for 5 days in Fairbanks, Alaska.

   a. Find the mean low temperature for Monday, Tuesday, and Wednesday.
   b. Find the mean low temperature for all 5 days.
   c. **Critical Thinking** Which mean low temperature was higher? Explain.
   d. Find the range of the data.

628 Chapter 11 Integers

Life Science LINK

The Mediterranean monk seal is one of the world's rarest mammals. Monk seals have become endangered largely because divers hunt them for their skin and disturb their habitat.

Annette found this table in a science article about monk seals.

Changes in Population of Monk Seals							
Years	1971–1975	1976–1980	1981–1985	1986–1990	1991–1995	1996–2000	2001–2005
Change	550	−300	−150	−50	100	200	−100

43. a. According to the table, what was the change in the monk seal population from 1976 to 1980?
  b. What does this number mean?

44. Find the mean change per year from 1971 to 1975. (*Hint:* This is a range of 5 years, so divide by 5.) What does your answer mean?

45. Find the mean change per year from 1981 to 1990. What does your answer mean?

46. **Write About It** Why is it important to use both positive and negative numbers when tracking the changes in a population?

47. **Challenge** Suppose that there were 250 monk seals in 1971. How many were there in 2005?

Test Prep and Spiral Review

48. Multiple Choice Which quotient is greatest?

  Ⓐ $-8 \div (-2)$ Ⓑ $-10 \div 5$ Ⓒ $-10 \div (-5)$ Ⓓ $15 \div (-5)$

49. Multiple Choice The change in population for a species is recorded in the table. What is the mean of the data?

Year	1	2	3	4
Change in Population	−2	+5	−7	−4

  Ⓕ −4   Ⓗ 1
  Ⓖ −2   Ⓙ 3

Find the missing measurement for each prism. (Lesson 10-7)

50. $\ell = 9$ cm; $w = 24$ cm; $h = \underline{?}$; $V = 1{,}296$ cm³   **51.** $\ell = 8$ m; $w = \underline{?}$; $h = 13$ m; $V = 728$ cm³

Evaluate $k - (-4)$ for each value of k. (Lesson 11-6)

52. $k = -5$ **53.** $k = 7$ **54.** $k = -13$ **55.** $k = -4$ **56.** $k = 16$

Hands-on LAB 11-9

Model Integer Equations

Use with Lesson 11-9

Learn It Online
Lab Resources Online go.hrw.com,
keyword MR10 Lab11 Go

KEY
🟨 = 1
🟥 = −1
▭ = x

REMEMBER
You can add or subtract the same number on both sides of an equation.
Adding or subtracting zero does not change a number's value.

You can use algebra tiles to model equations. An equation mat represents the two sides of an equation. To find the value of the variable, get the x-tile by itself on one side of the mat. You may remove the same number of yellow tiles or the same number of red tiles from both sides.

Activity

Use algebra tiles to model and solve each equation.

1 $x + 2 = 6$

Remove 2 yellow tiles from both sides of the mat.

$x = 4$

2 $x - 3 = -5$

Use red tiles to model subtraction. Remove 3 red tiles from both sides of the mat.

$x = -2$

3 $x + 6 = 2$

Adding red tiles to both sides will allow you to remove zero pairs. If you add 6 red tiles to the left side, you must add 6 red tiles to the right side to keep the equation balanced.

Add 6 red tiles to both sides.

Now you can remove zero pairs from both sides of the mat.

$x = -4$

4 $3x = -9$

Divide each side into 3 equal groups. Remove all but one of the groups.

$x = -3$

Think and Discuss

1. In **4**, why did you divide both sides into 3 groups?

2. Why can you add zero pairs to an equation mat? Why is it not necessary to add them to both sides?

3. When you add zero to an equation, how do you know the number of red and yellow tiles to add?

4. How can you use algebra tiles to check your answers?

Try This

Use algebra tiles to model and solve each equation.

1. $x + 6 = 3$
2. $x - 1 = -8$
3. $2x = 14$
4. $4x = -8$

11-9 Hands-On Lab

11-9 Solving Integer Equations

The entrance to the Great Pyramid of Khufu is 55 ft above ground. The underground chamber is 102 ft below ground. From the entrance, what is the distance to the underground chamber?

Vocabulary
Identity Property

To solve this problem, you can use an equation containing integers.

$$55 + d = -102$$
$$\underline{-55 \qquad -55}$$
$$0 + d = -157$$
$$d = -157$$

Write the equation.
Subtract 55 from both sides to undo the addition.
Identity Property of Addition: $0 + d = d$

It is -157 ft from the entrance to the underground chamber. The sign is negative, which means you **go down 157 ft.**

The **Identity Property** for Addition allows you to simplify $d + 0$ to d in the last step of the example above.

Identity Properties			
	Words	Numbers	Algebra
	Addition: The sum of 0 and any number is the number **Multiplication:** The product of 1 and any number is the number.	$6 + 0 = 6$ $5 \cdot 1 = 5$	$d + 0 = d$ $d \cdot 1 = d$

EXAMPLE 1 Adding and Subtracting to Solve Equations

A Solve $4 + x = -2$. Check your answer.

$$4 + x = -2$$
$$\underline{-4 \qquad -4}$$
$$0 + x = -6$$
$$x = -6$$

4 is added to x.
Subtract 4 from both sides to undo the addition.
Identity Property of Addition: $0 + x = x$

Check
$$4 + x = -2$$
$$4 + (-6) \stackrel{?}{=} -2$$
$$-2 \stackrel{?}{=} -2 \checkmark$$

Write the equation.
Substitute -6 for x.
-6 is a solution.

Helpful Hint
Subtracting a number is the same as adding its opposite. To solve this equation using algebra tiles, you can add four red tiles to both sides and then remove zero pairs.

632 Chapter 11 Integers

B Solve $y - 6 = -5$. Check your answer.

$y - 6 = -5$ *6 is subtracted from y.*
$\underline{+6 \quad +6}$ *Add 6 to both sides to*
$y + 0 = 1$ *undo the subtraction.*
$y = 1$ *Identity Property of Addition: $y + 0 = y$*

Check

$y - 6 = -5$ *Write the equation.*
$1 - 6 \stackrel{?}{=} -5$ *Substitute 1 for y.*
$-5 \stackrel{?}{=} -5$ ✓   *1 is a solution.*

EXAMPLE 2 Multiplying and Dividing to Solve Equations

Solve each equation. Check your answers.

A $-3a = 15$

$\dfrac{-3a}{-3} = \dfrac{15}{-3}$ *a is multiplied by −3. Divide both sides by −3 to undo the multiplication.*

$1a = -5$
$a = -5$ *Identity Property of Multiplication: $1a = a$*

Check

$-3a = 15$ *Write the equation.*
$-3(-5) \stackrel{?}{=} 15$ *Substitute −5 for a.*
$15 \stackrel{?}{=} 15$ ✓   *−5 is a solution.*

B $\dfrac{b}{-4} = -2$

$-4 \cdot \dfrac{b}{-4} = -4 \cdot (-2)$ *b is divided by −4. Multiply both sides by −4 to undo the division.*

$1b = 8$
$b = 8$ *Identity Property of Multiplication: $1b = b$*

Check

$\dfrac{b}{-4} = -2$ *Write the equation.*
$8 \div (-4) \stackrel{?}{=} -2$ *Substitute 8 for b.*
$-2 \stackrel{?}{=} -2$ ✓   *8 is a solution.*

Think and Discuss

1. Tell what operation you would use to solve $x + 12 = -32$.

2. Tell whether the solution to $-9t = -27$ will be positive or negative without actually solving the equation.

11-9 Exercises

Learn It Online
Homework Help Online go.hrw.com,
keyword MR10 11-9
Exercises 1–32, 47, 51, 55, 57, 59, 61, 67

GUIDED PRACTICE

See Example 1 Solve each equation. Check your answers.

1. $m - 3 = 9$
2. $a - 8 = -13$
3. $z - 12 = -3$
4. $j - 2 = 7$
5. $p + 2 = -7$
6. $k - 9 = 21$
7. $g - 10 = -2$
8. $h + 15 = 25$

See Example 2

9. $-4b = 32$
10. $\frac{w}{3} = 18$
11. $5c = -35$
12. $\frac{p}{-5} = 10$
13. $6f = -36$
14. $-2c = 72$
15. $\frac{r}{10} = -90$
16. $\frac{d}{-12} = 144$

INDEPENDENT PRACTICE

See Example 1 Solve each equation. Check your answers.

17. $g - 9 = -5$
18. $v - 7 = 19$
19. $t - 13 = -27$
20. $s - 4 = -21$
21. $x + 2 = -12$
22. $y + 9 = -10$
23. $20 + w = 10$
24. $z + 15 = 50$

See Example 2

25. $6j = 48$
26. $7s = -49$
27. $\frac{a}{-2} = 26$
28. $-2r = 10$
29. $\frac{m}{-12} = 4$
30. $\frac{k}{5} = -4$
31. $u \div 6 = -10$
32. $6t = -36$

PRACTICE AND PROBLEM SOLVING

Extra Practice See page EP24.

Solve each equation. Check your answers.

33. $x - 12 = 5$
34. $w - 3 = -2$
35. $-7k = 28$
36. $g \div 7 = -2$
37. $\frac{m}{-3} = 5$
38. $a - 10 = 9$
39. $n - 19 = -22$
40. $2h = 42$
41. $13g = -39$
42. $s \div 6 = -3$
43. $24 + f = 16$
44. $q - 15 = -4$
45. $d - 26 = 7$
46. $-6c = 54$
47. $h \div (-4) = 21$
48. $7k = 70$
49. $b - 17 = 15$
50. $u - 82 = -7$
51. $-8a = -64$
52. $v + 1 = -9$
53. $\frac{t}{11} = -5$
54. $31 + j = -14$
55. $c + 23 = 10$
56. $\frac{r}{-2} = -8$
57. $15n = -60$
58. $z \div (-5) = -9$
59. $j - 20 = -23$
60. $f + 20 = -60$

61. A submarine captain sets the following diving course: dive 200 ft, stop, and then dive another 200 ft. If this pattern is continued, how many dives will be necessary to reach a location 14,000 ft below sea level?

62. **Physical Science** While exploring a cave, Lin noticed that the temperature dropped 4 °F for every 30 ft that she descended. What is Lin's depth if the temperature is 8° lower than the temperature at the surface?

63. **Sports** After two rounds in the 2001 LPGA Champions Classic, Wendy Doolan had a score of −12. Her score in the second round was −8. What was her score in the first round?

64. **Critical Thinking** If the product of a variable and a number is positive and the number is negative, what is the sign of the value of the variable?

Use the graph for Exercises 65 and 66.

65. **Life Science** Scientists have found live bacteria at elevations of 135,000 ft. This is 153,500 ft above one of the animals in the graph. Which one? (*Hint:* Solve $x + 153{,}500 = 135{,}000$.)

66. **Social Studies** The world's highest capital city is La Paz, Bolivia, with an elevation of 11,808 ft. The highest altitude that a yak has been found at is how much higher than La Paz? (*Hint:* Solve $11{,}808 + x = 20{,}000$.)

67. **Recreation** Carla is a diver. On Friday, she dove 5 times as deep as she dove on Monday. If she dove to −120 ft on Friday, how deep did she dive on Monday?

68. **Write A Problem** Write a word problem that could be solved using the equation $x - 3 = -15$.

69. **Write About It** Is the solution to $3n = -12$ positive or negative? How could you tell without solving the equation?

70. **Challenge** Find each answer.

  a. $12 \div (-3 \cdot 2) \div 2$ **b.** $12 \div (-3 \cdot 2 \div 2)$

  Why are the answers different even though the numbers are the same?

Social Studies

During the winter, yaks are able to survive in temperatures as low as −40 °F.

Test Prep and Spiral Review

71. **Multiple Choice** Kathie and her three friends each owe $24 for dinner. Solve the equation $\frac{t}{4} = 24$ to determine the total amount t of the dinner.

  Ⓐ $96   Ⓑ $28   Ⓒ $20   Ⓓ $6

72. **Short Response** David is 12 years younger than his sister Candace. David is 9 years old. Write an equation for the situation. Let c be Candace's age. Then solve the equation to find her age.

Determine if the given statements are *sometimes, always,* or *never* true. (Lesson 8-6)

73. A square is a rhombus.   74. A parallelogram is a square.

Find each product. (Lesson 11-7)

75. $5 \cdot (-7)$ 76. $-9 \cdot 9$ 77. $2 \cdot 6$ 78. $10 \cdot 0$ 79. $-8 \cdot (-4)$

11-9 Solving Integer Equations

Chapter 11 Section 11B

Ready To Go On?

Quiz for Lessons 11-5 Through 11-9

11-5 Adding Integers

Write the addition modeled on each number line.

1.
2.

Find each sum.

3. $7 + (-3)$
4. $-10 + 6$
5. $-7 + (-3)$

6. Evaluate $-5 + x$ for $x = 7$.

11-6 Subtracting Integers

Write the subtraction modeled on each number line.

7.
8.

9. Evaluate $x - (-7)$ for $x = -2$.

11-7 Multiplying Integers

Evaluate $6x$ for each value of x.

10. $x = -2$
11. $x = 1$
12. $x = -7$

Find each product.

13. $3 \cdot (-7)$
14. $-10 \cdot 8$
15. $-12 \cdot (-5)$

11-8 Dividing Integers

Evaluate $\frac{x}{4}$ for each value of x.

16. $x = -24$
17. $x = 44$
18. $x = -124$

Find each quotient.

19. $72 \div (-9)$
20. $-15 \div (-3)$
21. $-40 \div 10$

11-9 Solving Integer Equations

Solve each equation. Check your answers.

22. $5 + x = -20$
23. $3a = -27$
24. $p \div 2 = -16$
25. $c - 2 = -7$

Real-World Connections

CHAPTER 11

Shipwreck Diving The ocean floor along the New Jersey coast is dotted with shipwrecks. According to some estimates, there may be as many as 7,000 shipwrecks in the area. This makes the New Jersey coast a favorite spot among scuba divers who enjoy exploring the mysterious remains of sunken ships.

NEW JERSEY

The graph shows the depths of several shipwrecks. Use the graph for 1–3.

New Jersey Shipwrecks

Shipwreck	Depth (ft)
S. S. Mohawk	−80
Great Isaac	−90
Tolten	−95
Resor	−125
Varanger	−140

1. The wreck of the U-869 is 3 times as deep as that of the S.S. *Mohawk*. While descending to the U-869, a scuba diver stops to check her equipment every 20 feet. How many times will she check her equipment *before* reaching the U-869?

2. Carlos is diving to the *Tolten*. He dives $\frac{1}{5}$ of the distance and stops to watch a school of fish. Then he descends another 30 feet and stops to rest. How many more feet must he descend in order to reach the *Tolten*?

3. The depth of the *Eagle* is $\frac{1}{2}$ that of the *Eureka*. The *Eureka* is 15 feet closer to the surface of the water than the *Resor*. What is the depth of the *Eagle*?

Real-World Connections 637

Game Time

A Math Riddle

What coin doubles in value when half is subtracted?

To find the answer, graph each set of points. Connect each pair of points with a straight line.

1. (−8, 3) (−6, 3)
2. (−9, 1) (−7, 5)
3. (−7, 5) (−5, 1)
4. (−3, 1) (−3, 5)
5. (−1, 1) (−1, 5)
6. (−3, 3) (−1, 3)
7. (1, 1) (3, 5)
8. (3, 5) (5, 1)
9. (2, 3) (4, 3)
10. (6, 1) (6, 5)
11. (6, 1) (8, 1)
12. (9, 1) (9, 5)
13. (9, 5) (11, 5)
14. (9, 3) (11, 3)
15. (−9, −5) (−9, −1)
16. (−9, −1) (−7, −3)
17. (−7, −3) (−9, −5)
18. (−6, −1) (−6, −5)
19. (−6, −5) (−4, −5)
20. (−4, −5) (−4, −1)
21. (−4, −1) (−6, −1)
22. (−3, −1) (−3, −5)
23. (−3, −5) (−1, −5)
24. (1, −1) (1, −5)
25. (1, −5) (3, −5)
26. (4, −5) (6, −1)
27. (6, −1) (8, −5)
28. (5, −3) (7, −3)
29. (9, −5) (9, −1)
30. (9, −1) (11, −3)
31. (11, −3) (9, −3)
32. (9, −3) (11, −5)

Zero Sum

Each card contains either a positive number, a negative number, or 0. The dealer deals three cards to each player. On your turn, you may exchange one or two of your cards for new ones, or you may keep your three original cards. After everyone has had a turn, the player whose sum is closest to 0 wins the round and receives everyone's cards. The dealer deals a new round and the game continues until the dealer runs out of cards. The winner is the player with the most cards at the end of the game.

Learn It Online
Game Time Extra go.hrw.com,
keyword MR10 Games Go

A complete copy of the rules and game pieces are available online.

Materials
- business-size envelope
- ruler
- scissors
- tape
- hole punch
- chenille stem
- adding-machine tape

It's in the Bag!

PROJECT Positive-Negative Pull-Out

Pull questions and answers out of the bag to check your knowledge of integers and functions.

Directions

1. Seal the envelope. Then cut it in half.

2. Hold the envelope with the opening at the top. Lightly draw lines $\frac{3}{4}$ inch from the bottom and from each side. Fold the envelope back and forth along these lines until the envelope is flexible and easy to work with. **Figure A**

3. Put your hand into the envelope and push out the sides and bottom to form a bag. There will be two triangular points at the bottom of the bag. Tape these to the bottom so that the bag sits flat. **Figure B**

4. Make a 2-inch slit on the front of the bag about an inch from the bottom. Punch two holes at the top of each side of the bag and insert half of a chenile stem to make handles. **Figure C**

Taking Note of the Math

Starting at the end of the adding-machine tape, write a question about integers and functions, and then write the answer. After you have written several questions and answers, roll up the tape, place it in the bag, and pull the end through the slit.

It's in the Bag!

CHAPTER 11 Study Guide: Review

Vocabulary

absolute value 602	opposites 602
axes 610	origin 610
coordinate plane 610	positive number 602
coordinates 610	quadrants 610
Identity Property 632	x-axis 610
integer 602	x-coordinate 610
linear equation 646	y-axis 610
negative number 602	y-coordinate 610

Complete the sentences below with vocabulary words from the list above.

1. For the equation $y = 3x$, the __?__ is 12 when the __?__ is 4.

2. The axes separate the __?__ into four __?__.

EXAMPLES / EXERCISES

11-1 Integers and Absolute Value (pp. 594–597)

■ Name a positive or negative number to represent each situation.

15 feet below sea level −15
a bank deposit of $10 +10

■ Graph +4 on a number line.

Name a positive or negative number to represent each situation.

3. a raise of $10   4. a loss of $50

Graph each integer and its opposite on a number line.

5. −3   6. 1   7. −9   8. 0

Write the absolute value of each integer.

9. |37| 10. |−14| 11. |97| 12. |−13|

11-2 Comparing and Ordering Integers (pp. 598–601)

■ Compare −2 and 3. Write < or >.

−2 < 3   −2 is left of 3 on the number line.

Compare. Write < or >.

13. 3 ☐ 4   14. −2 ☐ 5   15. 0 ☐ 6

Order the integers in each set from least to greatest.

16. 2, −1, 4   17. −3, 0, 4   18. −6, −8, 0

640 Chapter 11 Integers

EXAMPLES

EXERCISES

11-3 The Coordinate Plane (pp. 604–607)

■ Give the coordinates of A and name the quadrant where it is located.

A is in the fourth quadrant with coordinates (2, −3).

Give the coordinates of each point.

19. A
20. C

Name the quadrant where each point is located.

21. A
22. B

11-4 Transformations in the Coordinate Plane (pp. 608–611)

■ Reflect triangle DEF across the x-axis. Give the coordinates of each vertex in the image.

The vertices of the image are D′ (−3, −1), E′ (−4, −3), and F′ (0, −2).

Perform the given transformation on each figure. Give the coordinates of each vertex in the image.

23. translate figure PRQ down 3 units
24. reflect figure WXYZ across the y-axis
25. rotate figure PQR 180° clockwise about point P.

11-5 Adding Integers (pp. 615–618)

■ Find the sum: 3 + (−2).

3 + (−2) = 1

Find each sum.

26. −4 + 2
27. 4 + (−4)
28. 3 + (−2)
29. −3 + (−2)

Evaluate $x + 3$ for each value of x.

30. $x = -20$
31. $x = 5$

32. Bactrian camels who live in the Gobi Desert must endure temperatures as low as −45 °F and as high as 100 °F in an average year. By how many degrees do the extreme temperatures in the Bactrian's habitat vary throughout the year?

EXAMPLES

EXERCISES

11-6 Subtracting Integers (pp. 620–622)

■ Evaluate $n - 4$ for $n = -1$.
$(-1) - 4 = -5$

Find each difference.

33. $-6 - 2$ 34. $5 - (-4)$
35. $-8 - (-5)$ 36. $14 - 20$

Evaluate $x - (-1)$ for each value of x.

37. $x = 12$ 38. $x = -7$

39. On December 1, the high temperature was 32 °F and the low temperature was −4 °F. What was the difference in the temperatures?

11-7 Multiplying Integers pp. (623–625)

■ Find the product: $3 \cdot (-2)$.
Think: 3 groups of −2
$3 \cdot (-2) = -6$

■ Evaluate $-2x$ for $x = -4$.
$-2(-4) = 8$

Find each product.

40. $5 \cdot (-2)$ 41. $3 \cdot 2$
42. $-3 \cdot (-2)$ 43. $-4 \cdot 2$

Evaluate $-9y$ for each value of y.

44. $y = 2$ 45. $y = -5$

46. Over the course of two golf tournaments, Alphonse averaged a score of −5 for each of the 6 rounds he played. How many strikes under par was Alphonse's combined score?

11-8 Dividing Integers (pp. 626–629)

■ $-24 \div 4$
Think: $-6 \cdot 4 = -24$
$-24 \div 4 = -6$

Find each quotient.

47. $6 \div (-2)$ 48. $9 \div 3$
49. $-14 \div (-7)$ 50. $-4 \div 2$

11-9 Solving Integer Equations (pp. 632–635)

■ Solve $x + 4 = 18$.
$x + 4 = 18$
$\underline{-4 -4}$ *Subtract 4 from both sides.*
$x = 14$

Solve each equation. Check your answers.

51. $w - 5 = -1$ 52. $\dfrac{a}{-4} = 3$
53. $2q = -14$ 54. $x + 3 = -2$

55. While touring a cavern, Marcus began in a chamber that was 35 feet above sea level. The middle of the tour was in a chamber that was 103 feet below sea level. How far did Marcus descend?

642 Chapter 11 Integers, Graphs, and Functions

Chapter Test

CHAPTER 11

Name a positive or negative number to represent each situation.

1. 30° below zero
2. a bank deposit of $75
3. a loss of 5 yards

Write the absolute value of each integer.

4. $|99|$
5. $|-115|$
6. $|-50|$
7. $|522|$

Compare. Write < or >.

8. $-4 \; \blacksquare \; 4$
9. $2 \; \blacksquare \; -9$
10. $-10 \; \blacksquare \; 8$
11. $-2 \; \blacksquare \; -12$

Order each set of integers from least to greatest.

12. $21, -19, 34$
13. $-16, -2, 13, 46$
14. $-10, 0, 25, -7, 18$

Graph each point on a coordinate plane.

15. $A(2, 3)$
16. $B(3, -2)$
17. $C(-1, 3)$
18. $D\left(-1, 2\tfrac{1}{2}\right)$
19. $E(0, 1)$

Perform the given transformation of each figure. Give the coordinates for each vertex of the image.

20. rotate figure MNOP 90° clockwise about the origin.
21. translate figure GHI 4 units up
22. reflect figure MNOP across the y-axis
23. rotate figure GHI 180° counterclockwise about point I

Add, subtract, multiply, or divide.

24. $-4 + 4$
25. $-2 - 9$
26. $-3 \cdot 8$
27. $12 \div (-3)$
28. $-48 \div (-4)$
29. $13 + (-9)$
30. $8 - (-11)$
31. $-7 \cdot (-6)$

Evaluate each expression for the given value of the variable.

32. $n + 3, n = -10$
33. $9 - x, x = -9$
34. $4m, m = -6$
35. $\dfrac{15}{a}, a = -3$
36. $(-11) + z, z = 28$
37. $w - (-8), w = 13$

Solve each equation.

38. $\dfrac{b}{7} = -3$
39. $-9 \cdot f = -81$
40. $r - 14 = -32$
41. $y + 17 = 22$

Chapter 11

Test Tackler
Standardized Test Strategies

Multiple Choice: Identifying Keywords and Context Clues

When reading a test item, pay attention to key words and context clues given in the problem statement. These clues will guide you in providing a correct response.

EXAMPLE 1

Which angle is obtuse?

A B C D

- Look for context clues. Identify what they mean.
- In this test item, **obtuse** is the context clue. It means an angle whose measure is **greater than** 90°.

Find the choice that shows an **obtuse** angle.
A: This angle's measure is 90° because it has a right angle symbol.
B: This angle's measure is greater than 90°. It is an obtuse angle.
C: This angle's measure is 180° because it is a straight angle.
D: This angle's measure is less than 90°. It is an acute angle.

The correct answer is B.

EXAMPLE 2

Kenneth makes flower deliveries along Oak Street. He starts at the flower shop on Oak Street. His first delivery is 8 blocks directly west of the shop. His second delivery takes him 4 blocks directly east of his first delivery. His third delivery takes him 5 blocks east of his second delivery. Write an expression using integers to model this situation.

F $-4 - 5 + 8$ G $8 + 4 - 5$ H $-8 - 4 - 5$ J $-8 + 4 + 5$

- Look for key words.
- In this test item, the key words are **expression** and **integers.**

Find the choice that shows the correct **integer expression** to model the situation.
F: The first delivery is 8 blocks west. This expression does not begin with -8.
G: The first delivery is 8 blocks west. This expression does not begin with -8.
H: The expression begins with -8, but 4 blocks east would be $+4$.
J: This expression's integers correctly correspond to the deliveries.

The correct answer is J.

644 Chapter 11 Integers

Hot Tip! If you do not understand what a word means, reread the sentences that surround the word and make a logical guess.

Read each test item and answer the questions that follow.

Item A
Multiple Choice Jenny is trimming the edges of a card with ribbon. The rectangular card measures 8 inches by 12 inches. How much ribbon does Jenny need to trim the card?

- Ⓐ 36 inches
- Ⓑ 40 inches
- Ⓒ 64 inches
- Ⓓ 72 inches

1. What are the dimensions of the card?
2. Which words in the problem statement are clues that you need to find the perimeter of the card?
3. When you calculate the perimeter, why are the units not given in square units?

Item B
Multiple Choice Sam has two cylinders. One cylinder has a height of 25 cm and a diameter of 8 cm. The other cylinder has a height of 15 cm and a diameter of 20 cm. What is the difference between the volumes of the two cylinders?

- Ⓕ $400\pi \, cm^3$
- Ⓖ $1,100\pi \, cm^3$
- Ⓗ $1,500\pi \, cm^3$
- Ⓙ $4,400\pi \, cm^3$

4. Make a list of the key words given in the problem statement and link each word to its mathematical meaning.
5. Which choice, if any, can be eliminated? Why?

Item C
Multiple Choice Madeline has 28 daisies and 42 violets. Find the GCF to find the greatest number of wrist corsages that can be made if each corsage has the same number of daisies and the same number of violets.

- Ⓐ 4
- Ⓑ 7
- Ⓒ 14
- Ⓓ 21

6. What is the math term that describes what is being tested?
7. Identify the keywords in this problem statement.

Item D
Multiple Choice An office supply store states that 4 out of 5 customers would recommend the store to another person. Given this information, what percent of customers would NOT recommend the office supply store to someone else?

- Ⓕ 10%
- Ⓖ 20%
- Ⓗ 40%
- Ⓙ 80%

8. What information is needed to solve this problem?
9. Which choice can be eliminated immediately? Why?
10. Write a proportion to find the percent of customers who would recommend the office store to someone else.
11. Describe two different ways to solve this problem.

Test Tackler

Cumulative Assessment, Chapters 1–11

Multiple Choice

1. Marla bought a shirt on sale for $22, which was $\frac{1}{8}$ off the original price. What decimal represents the discount received?

    A. 0.125
    B. 0.225
    C. 0.725
    D. 0.825

2. William is bringing small bottles of fruit juice for the company picnic. There are 154 people coming to the company picnic. If the drinks come in packages of 6, how many packages will William need to buy so that each guest can have 3 drinks?

    F. 20 boxes
    G. 26 boxes
    H. 75 boxes
    J. 77 boxes

3. Ashlee has 36 basketballs, 48 bean bags, and 60 flying disks. She is making playground sets for the teachers. She wants to put the same number of basketballs, bean bags, and flying disks in each set. What is the greatest number of sets she can make if she uses all of the items?

    A. 3
    B. 6
    C. 12
    D. 18

4. At 5:30 P.M., 75% of the people at company A had gone home. What fraction of people had NOT yet gone home?

    F. $\frac{3}{4}$
    G. $\frac{1}{2}$
    H. $\frac{1}{4}$
    J. $\frac{1}{25}$

5. What is the ratio of the number of students who play the drums to the number of students who play the trumpet? Give the ratio in simplest form.

School Band	
Instrument	Number of student
Drums	10
Trombone	14
Trumpet	8
Tuba	3

    A. 10 to 3
    B. 5 to 4
    C. 5 to 7
    D. 10 to 27

6. If ∠KHG and ∠JHM are congruent, what is the measure of ∠GHJ?

    F. 148°
    G. 116°
    H. 108°
    J. 96°

7. What is the reciprocal of $1\frac{3}{5}$?

    A. $-1\frac{3}{5}$
    B. $\frac{5}{8}$
    C. $\frac{8}{5}$
    D. 8

8. Find the prime factorization of 80.

    F. $2 \cdot 5^2$
    G. $2^2 \cdot 5$
    H. $2^3 \cdot 10$
    J. $2^4 \cdot 5$

9. Louie buys a baseball bat for $125, a catcher's mitt for $55, and a baseball for $3. The tax rate is 5%. If Louie gives the cashier $200, how much change will he get back?

  Ⓐ $6.15   Ⓒ $9.25
  Ⓑ $7.85   Ⓓ $10.75

10. There are 4 shows a day at the local performing arts theater. The first show starts at 10:15 A.M. Each show lasts 30 minutes, and there is a 1 hour and 30 minute break between shows. What time does the third show end?

  Ⓕ 12:15 P.M.   Ⓗ 2:45 P.M.
  Ⓖ 12:45 P.M.   Ⓙ 3:15 P.M.

HOT TIP! When adding integers, move right on a number line to add a positive number and move left on a number line to add a negative number.

Gridded Response

11. How many feet are in 8 yards?

12. Wyatt has received the following scores on his chapter spelling tests: 92, 98, 90, 97, and 92. What is the mean score of Wyatt's spelling tests?

13. Mrs. Thomas is covering the top of cardboard rectangles with foil to use in a cake display. Each rectangle is 12 in. long by 10 in. wide. How many square inches of foil will she need to cover 5 rectangles?

14. Joshua runs 35% of the way from his house to the gym. If the gym is 5 miles from Joshua's house, how many miles does Joshua run on his way to the gym?

15. What is 65 cm expressed in meters?

Short Response

S1. On Monday, the balance in Graham's checking account was $32. On Tuesday, he wrote three $18 checks. After a deposit on Wednesday, his balance was $15.

  a. Find Graham's balance on Tuesday.

  b. Write and solve an equation that can be used to find the amount of Graham's deposit. Let d = the amount of Graham's deposit. Show your work.

S2. Find the coordinates of the vertices of the square shown on the grid. Then explain how to find the new coordinates of the square after it is translated 5 units down and 3 units left.

Extended Response

E1. A store sold 44 art masks in September for $528. In October, the store sold 41 art masks for $492. In November, the store sold 38 art masks for $456. All the masks cost the same.

  a. Make a table to display the data, and then graph the data. Is the function linear? Explain your answer.

  b. Write an equation to represent the function. Tell what each variable represents.

  c. In December, the store sold 67 masks. What were the total mask sales in December?

Cumulative Assessment, Chapters 1–11

CHAPTER 12
Probability

12A Understanding Probability
12-1 Introduction to Probability
12-2 Experimental Probability
LAB Simulations
12-3 Counting Methods and Sample Spaces
12-4 Theoretical Probability

12B Using Probability
12-5 Compound Events
EXT Independent and Dependent Events
LAB Explore Permutations and Combinations
12-6 Making Predictions

Chapter Focus
- Find probability when all outcomes are equally likely.
- Use probability to make approximate predictions.

Why Learn This?

White peafowl are a color variation of the India Blue peafowl caused by a recessive gene. The chances that a peafowl will inherit the gene can be found by using probability.

Learn It Online
Chapter Project Online go.hrw.com,
keyword MR10 Ch12 Go

Are You Ready?

Vocabulary

Choose the best term from the list to complete each sentence.

1. The denominator of a fraction represents the __?__, and the numerator represents the __?__.
2. Fractions that represent the same value are __?__ fractions.
3. A __?__ is a comparison of two quantities by division.
4. Tally marks in a table show the __?__, or total, for each result.
5. A ratio of a number to 100 is called a __?__.

equivalent
frequency
part
percent
ratio
simplest form
table
whole

Complete these exercises to review skills you will need for this chapter.

Model Fractions

Write the fraction in simplest form that represents the shaded portion.

6. 7. 8.

Write Fractions as Decimals

Write each fraction as a decimal.

9. $\frac{9}{10}$ 10. $\frac{1}{2}$ 11. $\frac{12}{25}$ 12. $\frac{11}{20}$

Compare Fractions, Decimals, and Percents

Compare. Write <, >, or =.

13. 0.35 ■ 0.4   14. 0.25 ■ 25%   15. $\frac{3}{5}$ ■ 0.7   16. 0.5 ■ $\frac{23}{50}$

Write Ratios

Write each ratio.

17. blue circles to total circles
18. squares to triangles

Probability 649

CHAPTER 12

Study Guide: Preview

Where You've Been

Previously, you
- listed all possible outcomes of a probability experiment.
- used fractions to describe the results of an experiment.
- generated equivalent forms of rational numbers.

In This Chapter

You will study
- finding sample spaces using lists and tree diagrams.
- finding the probabilities of simple events and their complements.
- expressing probabilities as fractions, decimals, and percents.
- finding probabilities of compound events.

Where You're Going

You can use the skills learned in this chapter
- to find probabilities involving permutations and combinations.

Key Vocabulary/Vocabulario

complement	complemento
compound event	suceso compuesto
equally likely	igualmente probables
experiment	experimento (probabilidad)
experimental probability	probabilidad experimental
outcome	resultado (probabilidad)
prediction	predicción
probability	probabilidad
theoretical probability	probabilidad teórica

Vocabulary Connections

To become familiar with some of the vocabulary terms in the chapter, consider the following. You may refer to the chapter, the glossary, or a dictionary if you like.

1. The word *experiment* can mean "the process of testing." What do you think **experimental probability** is based on?

2. The word *compound* can mean "composed of separate elements." Do you think a **compound event** is made up of one event? Why or why not?

3. To *predict* something means to "foretell on the basis of observation, experience, or scientific reason." What do you think a **prediction** is?

4. When things are *equal*, they are of the same measure or quantity. How do you think the chances of two **equally likely** events compare?

Reading and Writing Math

CHAPTER 12

Study Strategy: Use Your Notes Effectively

Taking notes helps you understand and remember information from your textbook and lessons in class. Listed below are some steps for effectively using your notes before and after class.

Step 1: Before Class
- Review your notes from the last class.
- Then preview the next lesson and write down any questions you have.

Step 2: During Class
- Write down main ideas.
- If you miss something, leave a blank and keep taking notes. Fill in the holes later.
- Use diagrams.
- Use abbreviations, but make sure you will understand them later.

Step 3: After Class
- Fill in the holes you left during class.
- Highlight or circle the most important ideas, such as vocabulary, formulas, or procedures.
- Use your notes to quiz yourself.

Notebook contents:

Lesson 11-1: Integers and Absolute Value

How do I know if two numbers are opposites?

positive number—greater than 0; right side of number line

negative number—less than 0; left side of number line

opposites—same distance from 0 on number line

integers—whole numbers and opposites

(Number line from −5 to 5 showing negative integers on the left and positive integers on the right, with "opposites" arc between −4 and 4)

Try This

1. Look at the next lesson in your textbook. Write down some questions you have about the material in that lesson. Leave space between each question so that you can write the answers during the next class.

2. With a classmate, compare the notes you took during the last class. Are there differences in the main points that you each recorded? Brainstorm two ways you can improve your note-taking skills.

Probability

12-1 Introduction to Probability

Learn to estimate the likelihood of an event and to write and compare probabilities.

Vocabulary
probability

Interactivities Online ▶

The weather report gives a 5% chance of rain today. Will you wear your raincoat? What if the report gives a 95% chance of rain?

In this situation, you are using probability to help make a decision. **Probability** is the measure of how likely an event is to occur. In this case, both 5% and 95% are probabilities of rain.

Probabilities are written as fractions or decimals from 0 to 1 or as percents from 0% to 100%. The higher an event's probability, the more likely that event is to happen.

- Events with a probability of 0, or 0%, never happen.
- Events with a probability of 1, or 100%, always happen.
- Events with a probability of 0.5, or 50%, have the same chance of happening as of not happening.

Impossible	Unlikely	As likely as not	Likely	Certain
0		0.5		1
0%		$\frac{1}{2}$		100%
		50%		

A 95% chance of rain means rain is highly likely. A 5% chance of rain means rain is highly unlikely.

EXAMPLE 1 Estimating the Likelihood of an Event

Write *impossible, unlikely, as likely as not, likely,* or *certain* to describe each event.

Helpful Hint
A standard number cube is numbered from 1 to 6.

A The month of June has 30 days.
certain

B A coin toss comes up heads.
as likely as not

C You roll a 9 on a standard number cube.
impossible

D This spinner lands on red.
likely

652 Chapter 12 Probability

EXAMPLE 2 **Writing Probabilities**

A The weather report gives a 35% chance of rain for tomorrow. Write this probability as a decimal and as a fraction.

$35\% = 0.35$ *Write as a decimal.*

$35\% = \frac{35}{100} = \frac{7}{20}$ *Write as a fraction in simplest form.*

B The chance that Ethan is chosen to represent his class in the student council is 0.6. Write this probability as a fraction and as a percent.

$0.6 = \frac{6}{10} = \frac{3}{5}$ *Write as a fraction in simplest form.*

$0.6 = 60\%$ *Write as a percent.*

C There is a $\frac{9}{25}$ chance of getting a green gumball out of a certain machine. Write this probability as a decimal and as a percent.

$\frac{9}{25} = 9 \div 25 = 0.36$ *Write as a decimal.*

$\frac{9}{25} = \frac{9 \cdot 4}{25 \cdot 4} = \frac{36}{100} = 36\%$ *Write as a percent.*

Helpful Hint

In Example 2C, after you find the decimal form of $\frac{9}{25}$, you can use it to find the percent.

$0.36 = 36\%$

EXAMPLE 3 **Comparing Probabilities**

A On a flowering plant called the four o'clock, there is a 50% chance the flowers will be pink, a 25% chance the flowers will be white, and a 25% chance the flowers will be red. Is it more likely that the flowers will be pink or white?

Compare: 50% > 25%

The flowers are more likely to be pink than white.

B When you spin this spinner, there is a 25% chance that it will land on red, a 50% chance that it will land on yellow, and a 25% chance that it will land on blue. Is it more likely to land on red or on blue?

Compare: 25% = 25%

It is as likely to land on red as on blue.

Think and Discuss

1. **Give an example** of a situation that involves probability.

2. **Name** events that can be described by each of the following terms: *impossible, likely, as likely as not, unlikely,* and *certain.*

12-1 Exercises

GUIDED PRACTICE

See Example 1 — Write *impossible*, *unlikely*, *as likely as not*, *likely*, or *certain* to describe each event.

1. This year has 12 months.
2. You win the lottery.

See Example 2
3. Suppose that the chance of reaching into a bag of coins and selecting a quarter is 40%. Write this probability as a decimal and as a fraction.

See Example 3
4. If there are two children in a family, there is a 25% chance that both children are boys, a 25% chance that both children are girls, and a 50% chance that one child is a boy and the other is a girl. Which is more likely, that both children are boys or that one child is a boy and the other is a girl?

INDEPENDENT PRACTICE

See Example 1 — Write *impossible*, *unlikely*, *as likely as not*, *likely*, or *certain* to describe each event.

5. The spinner at right lands on green.
6. The spinner at right lands on blue.
7. You guess one winning number between 1 and 500.
8. You correctly guess one of eight winning numbers between 1 and 10.

See Example 2
9. **Sports** The chance of Jill's missing a free throw is $\frac{3}{10}$. Write this probability as a decimal and as a percent.

10. The probability of Daniel randomly selecting a long-sleeved shirt from his closet is 0.20. Write this probability as a fraction and a percent.

See Example 3
11. If you choose from a bag of mixed nuts, there is a 45% chance of choosing a peanut, a 20% chance of choosing a pecan, a 15% chance of choosing a cashew, and a 20% chance of choosing a walnut. Is it less likely that you will choose a pecan or a cashew from the bag?

PRACTICE AND PROBLEM SOLVING

Extra Practice
See page EP24.

Describe the events as *impossible*, *unlikely*, *as likely as not*, *likely*, or *certain*.

12. The probability of winning a game is $\frac{2}{3}$.
13. The probability of being chosen for a team is 0.09.
14. There is a 50% chance of snow today.
15. Your chances of being struck by lightning are $\frac{1}{2,000,000}$.
16. **Critical Thinking** Why is the event *It will be Saturday in one of the next 7 days* certain?

Life Science LINK

Each year, millions of people donate blood.

There are eight different human blood types, which are shown in the chart, along with the percent of people who have each type. It is very important that people receive the right type of blood. If they do not, their bodies will not recognize the foreign blood cells and will attack the cells.

17. How would you describe the probability of a person having AB positive blood: impossible, unlikely, as likely as not, likely, or certain? Explain.

18. If a person is randomly chosen, which blood type is he or she most likely to have?

19. If a person is randomly chosen, which blood type is he or she least likely to have?

20. Write the probability that a randomly chosen person will have A negative blood as a decimal and as a fraction in simplest form.

21. **Write About It** Blood banks especially encourage people with certain types of blood to donate. Which blood types do you think these are? Explain.

22. **Challenge** A person with AB positive blood can safely receive O, A, B, or AB blood. What is the probability that a randomly chosen person could donate blood to a person with AB positive blood?

Blood Types in the United States

- O positive, 38%
- A positive, 34%
- O negative, 7%
- B positive, 9%
- A negative, 6%
- AB positive, 3%
- B negative, 2%
- AB negative, 1%

Test Prep and Spiral Review

23. **Multiple Choice** Eddie has a $\frac{9}{20}$ chance of winning the election. What is the probability of Eddie winning the election written as a percent?

    Ⓐ 0.45   Ⓑ 0.55   Ⓒ 45%   Ⓓ 55%

24. **Gridded Response** There is a $\frac{7}{10}$ chance of rain today. What is this probability written as a decimal?

Write the prime factorization of each number. (Lesson 4-2)

25. 76   26. 12   27. 16   28. 18   29. 128

Find each missing value to the nearest hundredth. Use 3.14 for π. (Lesson 9-8)

30. $d = 2$ in.; $C = ?$ 31. $r = 5$ cm; $C = ?$ 32. $C = 28.26$ m; $d = ?$

12-2 Experimental Probability

Learn to find the experimental probability of an event.

Vocabulary
experiment
outcome
event
trial
experimental probability

An **experiment** is an activity involving chance that can have different results. Flipping a coin and spinning a spinner are examples of experiments.

The different results that can occur are called **outcomes** of the experiment. If you are flipping a coin, heads is one possible outcome.

EXAMPLE 1 Identifying Outcomes

For each experiment, identify the outcome shown.

A tossing two coins
outcome shown: heads, tails (H, T)

B rolling two number cubes
outcome shown: (3, 5)

Reading Math

Experimental probability is a way of expressing relative frequency because it compares the frequency of an event to the total number of outcomes.

An **event** is an outcome or set of outcomes. Performing an experiment is one way to estimate the probability of an event. Each repetition of the experiment is called a **trial**.

If an experiment is repeated many times, the **experimental probability** of an event is the ratio of the number of times the event occurs to the total number of trials.

Interactivities Online ▶

EXPERIMENTAL PROBABILITY

$$\text{probability} \approx \frac{\text{number of times the event occurs}}{\text{total number of trials}}$$

EXAMPLE 2 Finding Experimental Probability

For one month, Tosha recorded the time at which her school bus arrived. She organized her results in a frequency table.

Time	7:00–7:04	7:05–7:09	7:10–7:14
Frequency	8	9	3

Writing Math

The probability of an event can be written as P(event). P(blue) means "the probability that blue will be the outcome."

A Find the experimental probability that the bus will arrive between 7:00 and 7:04.

$$P(\text{between 7:00 and 7:04}) \approx \frac{\text{number of times the event occurs}}{\text{total number of trials}}$$

$$= \frac{8}{20} = \frac{2}{5}$$

B Find the experimental probability that the bus will arrive before 7:10.

$$P(\text{before 7:10}) \approx \frac{\text{number of times the event occurs}}{\text{total number of trials}}$$

$$= \frac{8+9}{20} = \frac{17}{20}$$ *Before 7:10 includes 7:00–7:04 and 7:05–7:09.*

EXAMPLE 3 Comparing Experimental Probabilities

Ian tossed a cone 30 times and recorded whether it landed on its base or on its side. Based on Ian's experiment, which way is the cone more likely to land?

Outcome	On its base	On its side
Frequency	|||| ||	|||| |||| |||| |||| |||

$P(\text{base}) \approx \frac{\text{number of times the event occurs}}{\text{total number of trials}} = \frac{7}{30}$ *Find the experimental probability of each outcome.*

$P(\text{side}) \approx \frac{\text{number of times the event occurs}}{\text{total number of trials}} = \frac{23}{30}$

$\frac{7}{30} < \frac{23}{30}$ *Compare the probabilities.*

It is more likely that the cone will land on its side.

Think and Discuss

1. **Explain** whether you and a friend will get the same experimental probability for an event if you perform the same experiment.
2. **Tell** why it is important to repeat an experiment many times.

12-2 Exercises

Learn It Online
Homework Help Online go.hrw.com,
keyword MR10 12-2
Exercises 1–8, 9, 11

GUIDED PRACTICE

See Example 1
1. Identify the outcome shown on the spinner.

Sports Josh recorded the number of hits his favorite baseball player made in each of 15 games. He organized his results in a frequency table.

Number of Hits	0	1	2	3
Frequency	4	8	2	1

See Example 2
2. Find the experimental probability that this player will get one hit in a game.

See Example 3
3. Based on Josh's results, is this player more likely to get two hits in a game or no hits in a game? How many hits will this player most likely get in a game?

INDEPENDENT PRACTICE

See Example 1
For each experiment, identify the outcome shown.

4.

5.

Jennifer has a bag of marbles. She removed one marble, recorded the color, and placed it back in the bag. She repeated this process several times and recorded her results in the table. For Exercises 6–8, use the table.

See Example 2
6. Find the experimental probability that a marble selected from the bag will be red.

7. Find the experimental probability that a marble selected from the bag will not be black.

See Example 3
8. Based on Jennifer's experiment, which color marble is she most likely to select from the bag?

Color	Frequency
White	|||||
Red	|||
Yellow	|||||
Black	||||| ||||| ||

PRACTICE AND PROBLEM SOLVING

Extra Practice
See page EP24.

Identify the outcome for each situation.

9.

10.

658 Chapter 12 Probability

11. **Weather** Janet recorded the high temperature every day in January. She recorded her results in a frequency table.

Temperature (°F)	26–35	36–45	46–55	56–65
Number of Days	10	9	11	1

    According to Janet's results, what is the probability that a day in January will be warmer than 55 °F? Describe this probability as certain, likely, as likely as not, unlikely, or impossible.

12. Mariana recorded the results of spinning a spinner with 3 sections.

Outcome	Red	Blue	Green
Spins	25	19	56

    a. Use the results in the table to find the experimental probability of the spinner landing on each color.

    b. Which section of the spinner do you think might be the greatest? Explain.

13. **Write About It** Conduct an experiment in which you toss a coin 100 times. Keep a tally of the number of times the coin shows heads. According to your results, what is the experimental probability that it will show heads? Compare your results with a classmate. Did you both get the same experimental probability? Why or why not?

14. **Challenge** Suppose you roll two number cubes and add the two numbers that come up. What do you think the most likely sum would be? (*Hint:* Perform an experiment.)

Test Prep and Spiral Review

15. **Multiple Choice** Identify the outcome shown on the spinner.

    Ⓐ blue   Ⓒ red
    Ⓑ green   Ⓓ yellow

16. **Multiple Choice** Sam plays baseball. Five of his games started at 5:00 P.M. Four started at 5:15 P.M. One started at 5:45 P.M. What is the experimental probability that his next game will start at 5:00 P.M.?

    Ⓕ $\frac{1}{10}$ Ⓖ $\frac{2}{5}$ Ⓗ $\frac{1}{2}$ Ⓙ $\frac{9}{10}$

Evaluate each expression for $x = 5$. (Lesson 2-1)

17. $x + 7$ 18. $4x$ 19. $3x + 6$ 20. $x + 5$ 21. $2x - 7$

22. Arthur has a 91% chance of making a free throw. His brother Lance has a 93% chance of making a free throw. Is it more likely that Arthur or Lance will make the free throw? (Lesson 12-1)

Hands-on Lab 12-2: Simulations

Use with Lesson 12-2

A **simulation** is a model of an experiment that would be difficult or inconvenient to actually perform. In this lab, you will conduct simulations.

Activity

A cereal company is having a contest. To win a prize, you must collect six different cards that spell *YOU WIN*. One of the six letters is put into each cereal box. The letters are divided equally among the boxes. How many boxes do you think you will have to buy to collect all six cards?

1 Since there are six different cards that are evenly distributed, you can use a number cube to simulate collecting the letters. Each of the numbers from 1 to 6 will represent a letter. A roll of the number cube will simulate buying one box of cereal, and the number rolled will represent the letter inside that box.

1	2	3	4	5	6
Y	O	U	W	I	N
/	⦀ /	////	//	//	/

2 Roll the number cube, and keep track of the numbers you roll. Continue to roll the number cube until you have rolled every number at least once.

Think and Discuss

1. Look at the results in the table above. What was the last number rolled? How do you know?
2. How many rolls did it take to get all six numbers in your simulation?
3. How many boxes of cereal do you think you would have to buy to get all six letters? If you bought this many boxes, would you be sure to win? Explain.

Try This

1. Repeat the simulation three more times. Record your results.
2. Combine your data with the data of 5 of your classmates. Find the mean number of rolls from all 6 sets of data.
3. How many boxes of cereal do you think you would have to buy to get all six letters? Is this number different from what you thought after the first simulation? Explain.

Activity 2

Amy is a basketball player who usually makes $\frac{1}{2}$ of the baskets that she attempts. Suppose she attempts 20 shots in each game. If she plays ten games, in how many games do you think she will make at least four baskets in a row?

Trial	Results
1	THTHHTTHTTHTHTTHHHTT
2	HHTTTHTHTHHHHHTTHTHT
3	HTTTHTTTHTHTTTHTTHTT
4	HTHTHTHTHTTHTHTTTTTT
5	THTTTTHHTHTHHTHTTHTT
6	HTTHTHHHHHTHHHHHHHHH
7	TTHHTTHHHTHTHHTTHTTT
8	HTTHTTHTTTHHTTHTTHTT
9	HHHTTTTTHHHHHTHHTHHT
10	HTTHHTTHHHTHHTHTHHHH

① There are two possible outcomes every time Amy shoots the ball—either she will make the basket or she will miss. Since Amy makes $\frac{1}{2}$ of her shots, you can toss a coin to simulate one shot. Let heads represent making the basket, and let tails represent missing.

② Toss the coin 20 times to simulate one game. Keep track of your results.

③ Repeat ② nine more times to simulate ten games.

Think and Discuss

1. Why does tossing a coin 20 times represent only one trial?

2. Do any of your sequences contain four or more heads in a row? How many?

3. In how many games do you think Amy will make at least four baskets in a row? Out of *every* ten games, will Amy always make at least four baskets in a row this number of times?

4. You can use your simulation to find the experimental probability that Amy will make at least four or more baskets in a row. Divide the number of trials in which the coin came up heads at least four times in a row by the total number of trials. What is the experimental probability that Amy will make at least four baskets in a row?

5. Suppose Amy made only $\frac{1}{3}$ of her shots. Would you still be able to use a coin as a simulation? Why or why not?

Try This

1. In a group of ten families that each have four children, how many families do you think will have two girls and two boys? Make a prediction, and then design and carry out a simulation to answer this question. (Assume that having a boy and having a girl are equally likely events.) Was your prediction close?

2. Use your results from the previous problem to give the experimental probability that a family with four children will have two girls and two boys.

3. Think of an experiment, and design your own simulation to model it. Present your results in a table or graph.

12-3 Counting Methods and Sample Spaces

Learn to use counting methods to find all possible outcomes.

Sample spaces are used in finding probability. The **sample space** for an experiment is all the possible outcomes. You can use { } to show sample spaces.

When you need to find many possible outcomes, you can make a tree diagram. A tree diagram is one way to organize information.

Vocabulary
sample space

EXAMPLE 1

PROBLEM SOLVING APPLICATION

In winter, Judy has a choice of two coats—a ski jacket or pea coat. She has three accessory choices—hat, scarf, or gloves. What are the different outfits Judy can wear?

1. Understand the Problem

List the **important information:**

- There are two types of coats.
- There are three accessories.

2. Make a Plan

You can draw a tree diagram to find all the possible outfits.

3. Solve

Pair the first coat with each accessory.

Pair the second coat with each accessory.

Follow each branch on the tree diagram to find all of the possible outcomes: {ski jacket and hat, ski jacket and scarf, ski jacket and gloves, pea coat and hat, pea coat and scarf, pea coat and gloves}.

4. Look Back

There are 6 branches at the end of the tree diagram. There are 6 possible outfits listed.

Another way to keep track of possible outcomes is to make an organized list.

EXAMPLE 2
Making an Organized List

Marissa is shopping for a portable MP3 player. The player comes in black, silver, and red. She can choose between models that store 120 songs or 240 songs. What are all the possible MP3 players Marissa can choose from?

black, 120 songs   *List all the players that are black.*
black, 240 songs

silver, 120 songs   *List all the players that are silver.*
silver, 240 songs

red, 120 songs   *List all the players that are red.*
red, 240 songs

The Fundamental Counting Principle is a way to find the number of outcomes in a sample space without making a list. To use the Fundamental Counting Principle, multiply the number of choices in each category.

In the example above, there are 3 colors and 2 models of MP3 players. The total number of MP3 players to choose from is $3 \cdot 2 = 6$.

EXAMPLE 3
Using the Fundamental Counting Principle

Students at Jefferson Middle School must take one fine arts class and one athletics class. The fine arts class choices are band, orchestra, choir, and art. The athletics class choices are P.E., soccer, basketball, volleyball, football, and tennis. How many possible combinations are there?

There are 4 choices for fine arts classes and 6 choices for athletics classes.

$4 \cdot 6 = 24$ *Multiply the number of choices in each category.*

There are 24 possible combinations.

Think and Discuss

1. Explain the advantages of an organized list over a random list.

2. Describe how you can check whether your list is accurate.

12-3 Exercises

Learn It Online
Homework Help Online go.hrw.com,
keyword MR10 12-3 Go
Exercises 1–6, 7, 9

GUIDED PRACTICE

See Example **1**
1. Use the ZCool Foods menu. If Carl chooses a main dish and a side dish, what are all the possible outcomes?

See Example **2**
2. **School** Patrice, Jason, and Kenya are auditioning for the school play. The director has two roles available, a doctor and a teacher. Each can be played by either a boy or a girl. What are all the possible ways the two roles can be assigned?

ZCool Foods
Main Dish: Turkey, Tacos, Pasta
Side Dishes: Fruit, Salad

See Example **3**
3. **School** Mr. Li is offering a make-up science test. He can give the test on Monday, Tuesday, or Thursday, before school, during lunch, or after school. How many different times can Mr. Li give his make-up test?

INDEPENDENT PRACTICE

See Example **1**
4. **Recreation** Use the Outdoor Club flyer. The Outdoor Club is planning its annual Spring Festival. The members must vote to choose the day of the event and the main activity. What are all the possible outcomes?

Day of Event
Saturday or Sunday
Main Activity
Foot race   Hike
Bicycle race
Swimming race
Scavenger hunt

See Example **2**
5. Greta's apartment building is protected by a security system that requires a pass code to let in residents. The code is made up of numbers from 1 to 3. The code is three digits long, and a digit cannot repeat. What are all the possible pass codes?

See Example **3**
6. **Sports** A middle school is purchasing new basketball jerseys. Each jersey will have a letter and a number on it. The possible letters are A–Z, and the possible numbers are 0–9. How many possible combinations are there?

PRACTICE AND PROBLEM SOLVING

Extra Practice
See page EP24.

7. Keisha will choose a shirt and a skirt or a pair of pants from her closet to wear to school. Find the number of different outfits she can make if she has
   a. 3 shirts, 3 pants, and 3 skirts.
   b. 7 shirts, 5 pants, and 3 skirts.

664 Chapter 12 Probability

8. Omar is redecorating his bedroom. He can choose one paint color, one border, and one type of brush.

   a. How many different combinations of paint, border, and brush are possible?

   b. If Omar found another brush that he could use, how many different combinations would be possible?

9. **Social Studies** Japanese children play a game called *Jan-Ken-Pon*. You may know it as Rock, Paper, Scissors. Two players shout at the same time, "*jan-ken-pon!*" On "*pon!*" each player shows one of three hand positions—closed fist (*gu*), open hand palm down (*pa*), or index and middle finger extended to form a V (*choki*). How many different outcomes are possible in this game?

10. **Choose a Strategy** At a meeting, each person shook hands with every other person exactly one time. There were a total of 28 handshakes. How many people were at the meeting?

11. **Write About It** Suppose you are going to choose one boy and one girl from your class for a group project. How can you find the number of possible combinations? Explain.

12. **Challenge** A sailor has five flags: blue, green, red, orange, and yellow. Suppose she wants to fly three flags, but their order is not important; red, orange, yellow is the same as yellow, orange, red. List the different combinations of flags that are possible. How many combinations are there?

Test Prep and Spiral Review

13. **Multiple Choice** A cafeteria sells 3 types of cereal and 2 types of juice for breakfast. Bo can choose 1 cereal and 1 juice. How large is the sample space?

    Ⓐ 2   Ⓑ 3   Ⓒ 6   Ⓓ 18

14. **Gridded Response** Bikes R Us sells customized bicycles. There are 5 different color frames, 2 types of tires, and 4 types of seats. How many different combinations are available for 1 frame, 1 type of tire, and 1 type of seat?

Add or subtract. Write each answer in simplest form. (Lesson 5-2)

15. $\frac{1}{3} + \frac{3}{4}$ 16. $\frac{3}{8} + \frac{2}{5}$ 17. $\frac{7}{8} - \frac{1}{4}$ 18. $\frac{5}{6} - \frac{1}{2}$

19. Use the data in the table to make a stem-and-leaf plot. (Lesson 6-9)

| Height of Sunflowers (in.) | 18 | 22 | 15 | 17 | 18 | 21 | 16 | 20 |

12-4 Theoretical Probability

Learn to find the theoretical probability and complement of an event.

Vocabulary

theoretical probability

equally likely

fair

complement

Another way to describe the probability of an event is to use **theoretical probability**. One situation in which you can use theoretical probability is when all outcomes have the same chance of occurring. In other words, the outcomes are **equally likely**.

Equally likely outcomes

There is the same chance that the spinner will land on any of these letters.

Not equally likely outcomes

There is a greater chance that the spinner will land on 1 than on any other number.

An experiment with equally likely outcomes is said to be **fair**. You can usually assume that experiments involving items such as coins and number cubes are fair.

THEORETICAL PROBABILITY

$$\text{probability} = \frac{\text{number of ways the event can occur}}{\text{total number of equally likely outcomes}}$$

EXAMPLE 1 Finding Theoretical Probability

Remember!
The sample space is heads, tails (H, T).

A What is the probability that a fair coin will land heads up?

There are two possible outcomes when flipping a coin, heads or tails. Both are equally likely because the coin is fair.

$$P(\text{heads}) = \frac{\blacksquare}{2 \text{ possible outcomes}}$$

There is only one way for the coin to land heads up.

$$P(\text{heads}) = \frac{1 \text{ way event can occur}}{2 \text{ possible outcomes}}$$

$$P(\text{heads}) = \frac{1 \text{ way event can occur}}{2 \text{ possible outcomes}} = \frac{1}{2}$$

B What is the probability of rolling a number less than 5 on a fair number cube?

There are six possible outcomes when a fair number cube is rolled: 1, 2, 3, 4, 5, or 6.

$$P(\text{less than 5}) = \frac{\square}{6 \text{ possible outcomes}}$$

There are 4 ways to roll a number less than 5: 1, 2, 3, or 4.

$$P(\text{less than 5}) = \frac{4 \text{ ways event can occur}}{6 \text{ possible outcomes}}$$

$$P(\text{less than 5}) = \frac{4 \text{ ways event can occur}}{6 \text{ possible outcomes}} = \frac{4}{6} = \frac{2}{3}$$

When you toss a coin, there are two possible outcomes: heads or tails. What is $P(\text{heads}) + P(\text{tails})$?

$$P(\text{heads}) + P(\text{tails}) = \frac{1}{2} + \frac{1}{2} = \frac{2}{2} = 1$$

The probabilities of all the outcomes in the sample space add up to 1 (or 100%, if the probabilities are given as percents).

The **complement** of an event is the set of all outcomes that are not the event.

Event	Complement of the Event
A coin landing heads up on a toss	A coin landing tails up on a toss
Rolling 5 on a number cube	Rolling 1, 2, 3, 4, or 6 on a number cube

EXAMPLE 2 Finding the Complement of an Event

Suppose there is a 10% chance of rain today. What is the probability that it will NOT rain?

In this situation, there are two possible outcomes, either it will rain or it will not rain.

$P(\text{rain}) + P(\text{not rain}) = 100\%$

$P(\text{not rain}) = 100\% - 10\%$ *Subtract.*

$P(\text{not rain}) = 90\%$

Think and Discuss

1. **Give an example** of a fair experiment. Give an example of an unfair experiment.

2. **Describe** the complement of the following situation. There is a 60% chance of snow.

12-4 Exercises

GUIDED PRACTICE

See Example 1
1. What is the probability that a fair coin will land tails up?

2. What is the probability of randomly choosing a vowel from the letters A, B, C, D, and E?

See Example 2
3. The probability that a spinner will land on blue is 26%. What is the probability that it will NOT land on blue?

4. Suppose you have an unfair number cube and the probability of rolling a 2 is 0.7. What is the probability that you will NOT roll a 2?

INDEPENDENT PRACTICE

See Example 1
5. What is the probability of rolling the number 3 on a fair number cube?

6. What is the probability of rolling a number that is a multiple of 3 on a fair number cube?

7. Find the probability that a yellow marble will be chosen from a bag that contains 3 green marbles, 2 red marbles, and 4 yellow marbles.

See Example 2
8. **Weather** Suppose there is an 81% chance of snow today. What is the probability that it will NOT snow?

9. On a game show, the chance that the spinner will land on the winning color is 0.04. Find the probability that it will NOT land on the winning color.

PRACTICE AND PROBLEM SOLVING

Extra Practice
See page EP25.

A fair number cube is rolled. Find each probability.

10. $P(4)$
11. $P(\text{not } 3)$
12. $P(1, 2, \text{or } 3)$
13. $P(\text{number greater than } 0)$
14. $P(\text{odd number})$
15. $P(\text{number divisible by } 5)$
16. $P(\text{prime number})$
17. $P(\text{negative number})$

18. **Critical Thinking** This net can be folded to make a solid figure. The solid figure can then be rolled like a number cube. Give the probability of rolling each number with the solid figure.

19. A board game has a die (singular of dice) with 12 faces. Give the probability of rolling a number that is a factor of 12.

20. **Social Studies** In a recent presidential election, the probability that an eligible person voted was about 45%. Is it more likely that an eligible person voted or did not vote?

668 Chapter 12 Probability

For Exercises 21–26, A represents an event. The probability that A will happen is given. Find the probability that A will NOT happen.

21. $P(A) = 47\%$ **22.** $P(A) = 0.9$ **23.** $P(A) = \frac{7}{12}$

24. $P(A) = \frac{5}{8}$ **25.** $P(A) = 0.23$ **26.** $P(A) = 100\%$

27. Games Mah Jong is a traditional Chinese game played with 144 decorated tiles—36 Bamboo tiles, 36 Circle tiles, 36 Character tiles, 16 Wind tiles, 12 Dragon tiles, and 8 bonus tiles. The tiles are the same shape and size, and are all blank on the back. Suppose the tiles are all placed face down and you choose one. What is the probability that you will choose a Wind tile? Write your answer as a fraction in simplest form.

Mah Jong was developed in China. Although the game's exact history is unknown, Mah Jong may be over 2,000 years old.

Nine pieces of paper with the numbers 1, 2, 2, 3, 4, 4, 5, 6, and 6 printed on them are placed in a bag. A student chooses one without looking. Compare the probabilities. Write <, >, or =.

28. $P(1)$ ▆ $P(5)$ **29.** $P(3)$ ▆ $P(2)$ **30.** $P(4)$ ▆ $P(6)$

31. $P(4)$ ▆ $P(5) + P(6)$ **32.** $P(3) + P(5)$ ▆ $P(6)$ **33.** $P(\text{less than } 3)$ ▆ $P(6)$

34. What's the Error? If you toss a cylinder, it can land on its top, on its bottom, or on its side. Your friend says that $P(\text{top}) = \frac{1}{3}$. What mistake did your friend make?

35. Write About It Toss a coin 20 times and record your results. According to your experiment, what is the probability that the coin shows tails? What is the theoretical probability that it shows tails? How do the two probabilities compare? Repeat the experiment, but this time toss the coin 50 times. Now how do the probabilities compare?

36. Challenge Suppose you perform an experiment in which you toss a fair coin and roll a fair number cube. Find the theoretical probability that heads *and* 3 will be the outcomes.

Test Prep and Spiral Review

37. Multiple Choice There is a 25% chance of snow on Friday. What is the probability that it will NOT snow on Friday?

Ⓐ 0%   Ⓑ 25%   Ⓒ 75%   Ⓓ 100%

38. Extended Response A drawer contains 6 blue socks, 4 brown socks, and 10 white socks. Arnold chooses one sock without looking. What is the probability of choosing each color sock? Compare the possibilities. Write <, >, or =.

39. Paulina will use 15 feet of ribbon to decorate baskets for her friends. If each basket requires 1.2 feet of ribbon, how many baskets can she decorate? *(Lesson 3-8)*

Find each quotient. *(Lesson 11-8)*

40. $84 \div 4$ **41.** $-25 \div 5$ **42.** $-60 \div (-20)$ **43.** $-55 \div 5$

12-4 Theoretical Probability

CHAPTER 12 SECTION 12A

Ready To Go On?

Quiz for Lessons 12-1 Through 12-4

12-1 Introduction to Probability

For Problems 1 and 2, write *impossible, unlikely, as likely as not, likely,* or *certain* to describe the event.

1. This spinner lands on blue.

2. You roll an even number on a standard number cube.

3. The chance that Mitch will win concert tickets is 0.15. Write this probability as a fraction and as a percent.

4. The chance of rain is 33% on Tuesday, 45% on Wednesday, and 35% on Thursday. On which day is it most likely to rain?

12-2 Experimental Probability

For each experiment, identify the outcome shown.

5.

6.

7. Jeremy recorded the number of times a spinner landed on each number. Based on Jeremy's experiment, on which number is the spinner most likely to land?

Outcome	1	2	3
Frequency	|||| ||	|||| |||| ||	||||	

12-3 Counting Methods and Sample Spaces

8. Mindy's Deli serves 3 kinds of pasta with 2 kinds of sauce. The different pastas are spaghetti, fettuccine, and bow tie. The different sauces are tomato and pesto. What are all the possible outcomes that include 1 pasta and 1 sauce?

9. Cynthia is choosing an outfit for the first day of class. Her choices are black or blue pants and a white, yellow, or pink shirt. How many possible combinations can she choose from?

12-4 Theoretical Probability

10. What is the probability that this spinner will land on 2?

11. What is the probability of rolling a number less than 3 on a number cube?

12. Kirk has a 33% chance of scoring in the basketball game. What is the probability that Kirk will NOT score in the game?

670 Chapter 12 Probability

Focus on Problem Solving

Look Back

• **Estimate to check that your answer is reasonable**

When you have finished solving a problem, take a minute to reread the problem. See if your answer makes sense. Make sure that your answer is reasonable given the situation in the problem.

One way to do this is to estimate the answer before you begin solving the problem. Then when you get your final answer, compare it with your original estimate. If your answer is not close to your estimate, check your work again.

Each problem below has an answer given, but it is not right. How do you know that the answer is not reasonable? Give your own estimate of the correct answer.

1 A rental car agency has 55 blue cars, 32 red cars, and 70 white cars. A customer is given a car at random. How many color outcomes are possible?

Answer: 2,100

2 A box has 120 marbles. If the probability of drawing a blue marble is $\frac{3}{8}$ and the probability of drawing a red marble is $\frac{5}{8}$, how many of each color are in the box?

Answer: 100 blue marbles and 20 red marbles

3 A store manager decides to survey one out of every ten shoppers. How many would be surveyed out of 350 shoppers?

Answer: 3 shoppers

4 Sue has just started to collect old dimes. She has six dimes from 1941, five dimes from 1932, and one dime from 1930. If she chooses one dime at random, what is the probability that it is from before 1932?

Answer: 50%

Focus on Problem Solving   **671**

12-5 Compound Events

Learn to list all the outcomes and find the theoretical probability of a compound event.

Vocabulary
compound event

If a family is going to have four children, there are 16 possibilities for the birth order of the children based on gender (boy, B, or girl, G).

BBBB, BBBG, BBGB, BBGG,
BGBB, BGBG, BGGB, BGGG,
GBBB, GBBG, GBGB, GBGG,
GGBB, GGBG, GGGB, GGGG

A **compound event** consists of two or more single events. For example, the birth of one child is a single event. The births of four children make up a compound event.

EXAMPLE 1 Finding Probabilities of Compound Events

Theresa rolls a fair number cube and then flips a fair coin.

A Find the probability that the number cube will show an odd number and that the coin will show tails.

First find all of the possible outcomes.

Number Cube

Coin		1	2	3	4	5	6
	H	1, H	2, H	3, H	4, H	5, H	6, H
	T	1, T	2, T	3, T	4, T	5, T	6, T

There are 12 possible outcomes, and all are equally likely.
Three of the outcomes have an odd number and tails:
1, T; 3, T; and 5, T.

$P(\text{odd, tails}) = \dfrac{3 \text{ ways event can occur}}{12 \text{ possible outcomes}}$

$= \dfrac{3}{12}$

$= \dfrac{1}{4}$ *Write your answer in simplest form.*

B Find the probability that the number cube will show a 2 and that the coin will show heads.

Only one outcome is 2, H.

$P(2, H) = \dfrac{1 \text{ way event can occur}}{12 \text{ possible outcomes}}$

$= \dfrac{1}{12}$

C The following experiment is going to be performed.

Step 1: Toss a fair coin. **Step 2:** Spin the spinner. **Step 3:** Choose a marble.

What is the probability that the coin will show heads, the spinner will land on orange, and a red marble will be chosen?

Coin	Spinner	Marble	Outcome
Heads	purple	red	heads, purple, red
		yellow	heads, purple, yellow
		green	heads, purple, green
	orange	red	**heads, orange, red**
		yellow	heads, orange, yellow
		green	heads, orange, green
	white	red	heads, white, red
		yellow	heads, white, yellow
		green	heads, white, green
Tails	purple	red	tails, purple, red
		yellow	tails, purple, yellow
		green	tails, purple, green
	orange	red	tails, orange, red
		yellow	tails, orange, yellow
		green	tails, orange, green
	white	red	tails, white, red
		yellow	tails, white, yellow
		green	tails, white, green

There are 18 equally likely outcomes.

$$P(\text{heads, orange, red}) = \frac{1 \text{ way event can occur}}{18 \text{ possible outcomes}}$$

$$= \frac{1}{18}$$

> **Remember!**
> You could also use the Fundamental Counting Principle to find the total possble outcomes.
> coin • spinner • marble
>   2 •   3   •   3
> = 18 total outcomes

Think and Discuss

1. Give an example of a compound event.

2. Explain any pattern you noticed while finding the number of possible outcomes in a compound event.

12-5 Compound Events **673**

12-5 Exercises

GUIDED PRACTICE

See Example 1

1. Patrick rolled a fair number cube twice. Find the probability that the number cube will show an even number both times.

2. A boy and a girl each flip a coin. What is the probability that the boy's coin will show heads and the girl's coin will show tails?

INDEPENDENT PRACTICE

See Example 1

3. If you spin the spinner twice, what is the probability that it will land on green on the first spin and on purple on the second spin?

4. What is the probability that the spinner will land on either green or purple on the first spin and yellow on the second spin?

5. What is the probability that the spinner will land on the same color twice in a row?

PRACTICE AND PROBLEM SOLVING

Extra Practice
See page EP25.

An experiment involves spinning each spinner once. Find each probability.

6. P(2 on spinner 1 and 5 on spinner 2)

7. P(not 1 on spinner 1 and not 7 on spinner 2)

8. P(even number on both spinners)

9. P(odd number on spinner 1 and even number on spinner 2)

10. P(number on spinner 2 is greater than number on spinner 1)

11. P(same number on both spinners)

12. P(a multiple of 3 on both spinners)

13. P(different number on each spinner)

14. A jar contains tiles that are numbered 1, 2, 3, 4, and 5. Danny removes a tile from the jar, replaces the tile, and draws a second tile. What is the probability that Danny will draw the same number both times?

A fair number cube is rolled, and a fair coin is tossed. Compare the probabilities. Write <, >, or =.

15. P(3 and tails) ▨ P(5 and heads)

16. P(even number and tails) ▨ P(odd number and heads)

17. P(number less than 3 and tails) ▨ P(odd number and tails)

18. P(number greater than 5 and heads) ▨ P(prime number and tails)

19. **Life Science** If a cat has 5 kittens, what is the probability that they are all female? What is the probability that they are all male? (Assume that having a male and having a female are equally likely events.)

20. **Multi-Step** The students in Jared's class have ID numbers made up of two digits from 1 through 6. The same digit can be used twice. In fact, the same digit is used twice in Jared's ID number. If Jared rolls 2 number cubes, what is the probability that he does NOT roll his ID number?

21. **What's the Error?** One of your classmates said, "If you flip a coin and roll a number cube, the probability of getting heads and a 3 is $\frac{1}{2} + \frac{1}{6} = \frac{2}{3}$." What mistake did your classmate make? Explain how to find the correct answer.

22. **Write About It** Describe a situation that involves a compound event.

23. **Challenge** You roll a number cube six times. What is the probability of rolling the numbers 1 through 6 in order?

Test Prep and Spiral Review

24. **Multiple Choice** A fair number cube is rolled twice. What is the probability that the first roll will be even and the second roll will be odd?

    Ⓐ $\frac{1}{6}$ Ⓑ $\frac{1}{4}$ Ⓒ $\frac{1}{2}$ Ⓓ $\frac{5}{6}$

25. **Multiple Choice** A fair number cube is rolled once, and a coin is flipped once. What is the probability of a 5 on the number cube and heads on the coin toss?

    Ⓕ $\frac{1}{2}$ Ⓖ $\frac{1}{4}$ Ⓗ $\frac{1}{6}$ Ⓙ $\frac{1}{12}$

Order each set of numbers from least to greatest. (Lesson 3-1)

26. 1.2, 0.445, 1.06, 0.9   27. 2.45, 2.678, 2.007, 2.02   28. 7.99, 7.999, 7.9, 7.09

29. Suppose there is a 15% chance that Cy will finish all his work before he leaves class. What is the probability that he will NOT finish? (Lesson 12-3)

LESSON 12-5 EXTENSION
Independent and Dependent Events

Learn to find the probability of independent and dependent events.

Vocabulary
independent events
dependent events

For **independent events**, the occurrence of one event has no effect on the probability that the second event will occur.

To find the probability that two independent events will occur, multiply the probabilities of the two events as follows:

Probability of Two Independent Events

$$P(A \text{ and } B) = P(A) \cdot P(B)$$

Probability of both events — Probability of first event — Probability of second event

EXAMPLE 1 Finding the Probability of Independent Events

Find the probability of rolling a 3 on a number cube and the spinner shown landing on A.

The outcome of rolling the number cube does not affect the outcome of spinning the spinner, so the events are independent.

$P(3 \text{ and } A) = P(3) \cdot P(A)$ *Use the formula.*

$= \frac{1}{6} \cdot \frac{1}{5}$ *The probability of rolling a 3 is $\frac{1}{6}$. The probability of the spinner landing on A is $\frac{1}{5}$.*

$= \frac{1}{30}$ *Multiply.*

The probability of rolling a 3 and the spinner landing on A is $\frac{1}{30}$.

Suppose you have a bag containing 3 red marbles and 2 blue marbles. You draw two marbles, one after the other. The first marble you draw affects the marbles that remain in the bag, so the two draws are *dependent events*. For **dependent events**, the occurrence of one event has an effect on the probability that the second event will occur.

To find the probability that two dependent events will occur, multiply the probabilities of the two events as follows:

Probability of Two Dependent Events

$$P(A \text{ and } B) = P(A) \cdot P(B \text{ after } A)$$

Probability of both events — Probability of first event — Probability of second event *after* the first event has occurred

EXAMPLE 2 Finding the Probability of Dependent Events

A bag contains 3 red marbles and 2 blue marbles. Find the probability of drawing a red marble and then a blue marble.

$P(\text{red and blue}) = P(\text{red}) \cdot P(\text{blue after red})$

$P(\text{red}) = \frac{3}{5}$ There are 3 red marbles out of the 5 marbles.

$P(\text{blue after red}) = \frac{2}{4} = \frac{1}{2}$ There are 4 marbles left, and 2 are blue.

$P(\text{red after blue}) = P(\text{red}) \cdot P(\text{blue after red})$

$= \frac{3}{5} \cdot \frac{1}{2} = \frac{3}{10}$ Multiply.

The probability of drawing a red marble and then a blue marble is $\frac{3}{10}$.

EXTENSION Exercises

Determine whether the events are independent or dependent.

1. Adrian chooses a baseball card from a stack. Then Jemma chooses a card from those remaining in the stack.

2. Mike draws a 7 from ten cards numbered 1 through 10. He replaces the card. Then Alison draws a 5.

Find the probability of each event for the spinners shown.

3. The spinners land on 1 and *F*.

4. The spinners land on an even number and *A*.

5. The spinners land on an odd number and *A*, *B*, *C*, or *D*.

A bag contains 4 green marbles and 6 yellow marbles. You draw a marble and put it aside. Then you draw a second marble. Find the probability of each event.

6. You draw a yellow marble and then a green marble.

7. You draw 2 green marbles.

8. **Write About It** Explain the difference between independent and dependent events.

9. **Challenge** Nicole has 10 coins in her purse: 3 pennies, 3 nickels, 2 dimes, and 2 quarters. She removes a coin from the purse and then chooses a second coin without replacing the first. What is the probability that the two coins will add up to exactly 50 cents?

Hands-on Lab 12-5: Explore Permutations and Combinations

Use with Lesson 12-5

For some compound events, the order of the outcomes matters. For three outcomes *A*, *B*, and *C*, you need to know when *A-B-C* is different from *C-B-A* and when it is considered to be the same.

Activity 1

In how many different arrangements can Ellen, Susan, and Jeffrey sit in a row?

1 In this situation, the order of the students in the different arrangements is important. "Ellen, Susan, Jeffrey" is different from "Ellen, Jeffrey, Susan." An arrangement in which order is important is called a **permutation.**

2 Write each name on 6 index cards. You will have a total of 18 cards. Show all the different ways the cards can be arranged in a row.

Arrangement	1	2	3	4	5	6
First Seat	Ellen	Ellen	Susan	Susan	Jeffrey	Jeffrey
Second Seat	Susan	Jeffrey	Jeffrey	Ellen	Susan	Ellen
Third Seat	Jeffrey	Susan	Ellen	Jeffrey	Ellen	Susan

There are 6 different ways that these three people can sit in a row.

Another way to find the number of permutations is to multiply.

First Seat   Second Seat   Third Seat

3 choices × 2 choices × 1 choice = 6 permutations

Think and Discuss

1. Think of another situation in which the order in an arrangement is important. Explain.

Try This

1. Cindy, Laurie, Marty, and Joel are running for president, vice president, secretary, and treasurer of their class. Use multiplication to find the number of different ways the election can turn out.

Activity 2

Abe, Babe, Cora, and Dora are going to work on a project in groups of 2. How many different ways can they pair off?

1 In this situation, the order in the pairs is not important. "Abe, Cora" is the same as "Cora, Abe." When order is not important, the arrangements are called **combinations.**

2 Write each name on 3 index cards. You will have a total of 12 cards. Show all pairings.

Abe	Babe		Babe	Cora		Cora	Dora
Abe	Cora		Babe	Dora			
Abe	Dora						

There are 6 different possible pairs.

Think and Discuss

Tell whether each of the following is a permutation or a combination. Explain.

1. There are 20 horses in a race. Ribbons are given for first, second, and third place. How many possible ways can the ribbons be awarded?

2. There are 20 violin players trying out for the school band and 6 players will be chosen. How many different ways could students be selected for the band?

3. Connie has 10 different barrettes. She wears 2 each day. How many ways can she choose 2 barrettes each morning?

4. Yoko belongs to a book club, and she has just received 25 new books. How many possible ways are there for them to be placed on the shelf?

Try This

1. The video club is sponsoring a double feature. How many ways can club members choose 2 movies from a list of 6 possibilities?

2. Ms. Baker must pick a team of 3 students to send to the state mathematics competition. She has decided to choose 3 students from the 5 with the highest grades in her class. Ms. Baker can either send 3 equal representatives, or she can send a captain, an assistant captain, and a secretary. Which choice results in more possible teams? Explain. Find the number of teams possible for each choice.

12-6 Making Predictions

Learn to use probability to predict events.

A **prediction** is a guess about something in the future. One way to make a prediction is to collect information by conducting a survey. The **population** is the whole group being surveyed. To save time and money, researchers often make predictions based on a **sample**, which is part of the group being surveyed. Another way to make a prediction is to use probability.

Vocabulary
prediction
population
sample

EXAMPLE 1 Using Sample Surveys to Make Predictions

Based on a sample survey, an airline claims that its flights have a 92% probability of being on time. Out of 1,000 flights, how many would you predict will be on time?

You can write a proportion. Remember that *percent* means "per hundred."

$$\frac{92}{100} = \frac{x}{1{,}000}$$ *Think: 92 out of 100 is how many out of 1,000?*

$100 \cdot x = 92 \cdot 1{,}000$ *The cross products are equal.*

$100x = 92{,}000$ *x is multiplied by 100.*

$$\frac{100x}{100} = \frac{92{,}000}{100}$$ *Divide both sides by 100 to undo the multiplication.*

$x = 920$

You can predict that about 920 of 1,000 flights will be on time.

EXAMPLE 2 Using Theoretical Probability to Make Predictions

If you roll a number cube 24 times, how many times do you expect to roll a 5?

$P(\text{rolling a 5}) = \frac{1}{6}$

$$\frac{1}{6} = \frac{x}{24}$$ *Think: 1 out of 6 is how many out of 24?*

$6 \cdot x = 1 \cdot 24$ *The cross products are equal.*

$6x = 24$ *x is multiplied by 6.*

$$\frac{6x}{6} = \frac{24}{6}$$ *Divide both sides by 6 to undo the multiplication.*

$x = 4$

You can expect to roll a 5 about 4 times.

680 Chapter 12 Probability

EXAMPLE 3

PROBLEM SOLVING APPLICATION

A stadium sells yearly parking passes. If you have a parking pass, you can park at the stadium for any event during that year.

Based on a sample group of fans, the managers of the stadium estimate that the probability that a person with a pass will attend any one event is 80%. The parking lot has 300 spaces. If the managers want the lot to be full at every event, how many passes should they sell?

1. Understand the Problem

The **answer** will be the number of parking passes they should sell. List the **important information**:
- P(person with pass attends event) = 80%
- There are 300 parking spaces.

2. Make a Plan

The managers want to fill all 300 spaces. But, on average, only 80% of parking pass holders will attend. So 80% of pass holders must equal 300. You can write an equation to find this number.

3. Solve

$$\frac{80}{100} = \frac{300}{x}$$ *Think: 80 out of 100 is 300 out of how many?*

$100 \cdot 300 = 80 \cdot x$ *The cross products are equal.*

$30{,}000 = 80x$ *x is multiplied by 80.*

$$\frac{30{,}000}{80} = \frac{80x}{80}$$ *Divide both sides by 80 to undo the multiplication.*

$375 = x$

The managers should sell 375 parking passes.

4. Look Back

If the managers sold only 300 passes, the parking lot would not usually be full because only about 80% of the people with passes will attend any one event. The managers should sell more than 300 passes, so 375 is a reasonable answer.

Think and Discuss

1. Tell whether you expect to be exactly right if you make a prediction based on a sample. Explain your answer.

12-6 Exercises

GUIDED PRACTICE

See Example 1
1. Based on a sample survey, a local newspaper states that 12% of the city's residents have volunteered at an animal shelter. Out of 5,000 residents, how many would you predict have volunteered at the animal shelter?

See Example 2
2. If you roll a fair number cube 30 times, how many times would you expect to roll a number that is a multiple of 3?

See Example 3
3. **Recreation** Airlines routinely overbook flights, which means that they sell more tickets than there are seats on the planes. Suppose an airline estimates that 93% of customers will show up for a particular flight. If the plane seats 186 people, how many tickets should the airline sell?

INDEPENDENT PRACTICE

See Example 1
4. Based on a sample survey, a local newspaper claims that 64% of the town's households receive their paper. Out of 15,000 households, how many would you predict receive the paper?

See Example 2
5. If you flip a coin 64 times, how many times do you expect the coin to show tails?

6. A bag contains 2 black chips, 5 red chips, and 4 white chips. You pick a chip from the bag, record its color, and put the chip back in the bag. If you repeat this process 99 times, how many times do you expect to remove a red chip from the bag?

See Example 3
7. **Life Science** Blood banks value type O negative blood because it can be given to people with any blood type. The director at one blood bank has a goal of 9 type O negative donors each day. If the probability that a donor has type O negative blood is 7%, how many total donations should the blood bank receive each day to reach the goal?

PRACTICE AND PROBLEM SOLVING

Extra Practice
See page EP25.

8. A sample survey of 50 people in Harrisburg indicates that 10 of them know the name of the mayor of their neighboring city.

   a. Out of 5,500 Harrisburg residents, how many would you expect to know the name of the mayor of the neighboring city?

   b. **Multi-Step** Out of 600 Harrisburg residents, how many would you predict do not know the name of the mayor of the neighboring city?

9. **Critical Thinking** A survey is being conducted as people exit a frozen yogurt store. They are being asked if they prefer frozen yogurt or ice cream. Should predictions be made about the population of the town based on the survey? Explain.

682 Chapter 12 Probability

Social Studies LINK

The Native Canadians lived in Canada before the Europeans arrived. The French were the first Europeans to settle successfully in Canada.

The graph shows the results of a survey of 400 Canadian citizens.

10. Out of 75 Canadians, how many would you predict are of French origin?

11. A random group of Canadians includes 18 Native Canadians. How many total Canadians would you predict are in the group?

12. **What's the Error?** A student said that in any group of Canadians, 20 of them will be Native Canadians. What mistake did this student make?

13. **Write About It** How could you predict the number of people of French *or* Native Canadian origin in a group of 150 Canadians?

14. **Challenge** In a group of Canadians, 15 are in the Other European origin category. Predict how many Canadians in the same group are NOT in that category.

Canadian Ethnic Groups
- Other 46
- Native Canadian 80
- British Isles origin 160
- Other European 6
- French origin 108

Test Prep and Spiral Review

15. **Multiple Choice** Jay played a game and won 24 out of 100 times. Which is the best estimate of the experimental probability of Jay winning his next game?

    (A) 5%   (B) 25%   (C) 50%   (D) 75%

16. **Multiple Choice** You roll a fair number cube 36 times. How many times do you expect to roll a 4?

    (F) 36   (G) 9   (H) 6   (J) $\frac{1}{6}$

Solve each equation. Check your answers. (Lesson 11-9)

17. $x + 10 = -2$ 18. $x - 20 = -5$ 19. $-9x = 45$ 20. $x \div (-2) = -5$

A fair number cube is rolled. Find each probability. (Lesson 12-4)

21. $P(5)$ 22. $P(\text{not } 2)$ 23. $P(3) + P(4)$ 24. $P(\text{number divisible by 3})$

Ready To Go On?

Quiz for Lessons 12-5 Through 12-6

12-5 Compound Events

Billie rolls a fair number cube and then flips a fair coin.

1. Find the probability that the number cube will show an even number and the coin will show tails.

2. Find the probability that the number cube will show a 6 and the coin will show tails.

3. Compare P(4 and heads) and P(odd number and heads). Write $<$, $>$, or $=$.

An experiment involves spinning a spinner and choosing a marble from a bag. For Problems 4–6, use the diagrams.

4. What is the probability of spinning red on the spinner and choosing a red marble from the bag?

5. What is the probability of spinning yellow and choosing a marble that is NOT yellow?

6. What is the probability of spinning a color that is NOT blue and choosing a marble that is NOT blue?

12-6 Making Predictions

7. Based on a sample survey, 26% of the local people have a pet dog. Out of 600 people, how many people do you predict will have a pet dog?

8. If you roll a number cube 54 times, how many times do you expect to roll a number less than 3?

9. Based on previous attendance, the managers for a summer concert series estimate the probability that a person will attend any one event to be 90%. The chairs set up around the stage seat 450 people. If the managers want to be at full capacity every concert, how many tickets should they sell?

10. Based on a sample survey, a newspaper states that only 45% of the local population gets the recommended amount of sleep each night. If there are 45,000 people in town, how many people are not getting enough sleep?

Real-World CONNECTIONS

CHAPTER 12

The Breaux Bridge Crawfish Festival Crawfish stew, crawfish sausage, and crawfish egg rolls are just a few of the treats offered at the Breaux Bridge Crawfish Festival. With three full days of food and music, the annual event attracts 30,000 crawfish lovers each year.

LOUISIANA

Breaux Bridge

1. One of the festival's vendors plans to give customers a chance to win a prize. Customers spin the wheel shown here and win a free sample if the wheel lands on a crawfish dish.

   a. What is the probability that a customer wins a free sample?

   b. What is the probability that a customer does not win a free sample?

2. Find the probability that two customers in a row win a free sample.

3. Find the probability that two customers in a row win a sample of crawfish stew.

4. The vendor expects to have 480 customers per day. How many customers do you predict will win a free sample each day?

5. Visitors to the festival can buy t-shirts in red, blue, green, or white. Sun visors are available in blue, green, yellow, and red. A visitor buys a t-shirt and sun visor. How many different combinations are possible?

Real-World Connections   685

Game Time

Probability Brain Teasers

Can you solve these riddles that involve probability? Watch out—some of them are tricky!

1. In Wade City, 5% of the residents have unlisted phone numbers. If you selected 100 people at random from the town's phone directory, how many of them would you predict have unlisted numbers?

2. Amanda has a drawer that contains 24 black socks and 18 white socks. If she reaches into the drawer without looking, how many socks does she have to pull out in order to be *certain* that she will have two socks of the same color?

3. Dale, Melvin, Carter, and Ken went out to eat. Each person ordered something different. When the food came, the waiter could not remember who had ordered what, so he set the plates down at random in front of the four friends. What is the probability that exactly three of the boys got what they ordered?

Round and Round and Round

This is a game for two players.

The object of this game is to determine which of the three spinners is the winning spinner (lands on the greater number most often).

Both players choose a spinner and spin at the same time. Record which spinner lands on the greater number. Repeat this 19 times, keeping track of which spinner wins each time. Repeat this process until you have played spinner A against spinner B, spinner B against spinner C, and spinner A against spinner C. Spin each pair of spinners 20 times and record the results.

Which spinner wins more often, A or B?
Which spinner wins more often, B or C?
Which spinner wins more often, A or C?
Is there anything surprising about your results?

Learn It Online
Game Time Extra go.hrw.com,
keyword MR10 Games Go

A complete copy of the rules and game pieces are available online.

Materials
- CD with case
- white paper
- scissors
- markers
- glue
- brass fastener
- large paper clip
- stapler

It's in the Bag!

PROJECT: CD Spinner

Use a CD to make a spinner. Then take notes on probability in a booklet that you store in the CD case.

Directions

1. Trace around the CD to make a circle on white paper. Divide the circle into thirds, color each third a different color, and cut out the circle. Glue the circle onto the CD. **Figure A**

2. Carefully remove the plastic CD holder from the back of the CD case. Place the CD in the holder and insert a brass fastener into the center of the CD. Bend the ends of the fastener so it stays in place, and put the holder back into the CD case. **Figure B**

3. Attach a large paper clip to the brass fastener to make a spinner. **Figure C**

4. Cut several sheets of white paper so they are $4\frac{3}{4}$ inches by $4\frac{3}{4}$ inches. Staple them together to form a booklet that fits in the cover of the CD case.

Taking Note of the Math

Use the booklet to record notes on probability. Be sure to include probabilities related to the spinner that you made.

CHAPTER 12 Study Guide: Review

Vocabulary

complement 666	population 680
compound event 672	prediction 680
equally likely 666	probability 652
event 656	sample 680
experiment 656	sample space 662
experimental probability 656	theoretical probability 666
fair 666	trial 656
outcome 656	

Complete the sentences below with vocabulary words from the list above.

1. When all outcomes have the same probability of occurring, the outcomes are ___?___.

2. A(n) ___?___ is an activity involving chance that can have different results. Each possible result is called a(n) ___?___.

3. The measure of how likely an event is to occur is the event's ___?___.

4. ___?___ is the ratio of the number of ways an event can occur to the total number of possible outcomes.

5. The set of all possible outcomes for an experiment is the ___?___.

EXAMPLES | EXERCISES

12-1 Introduction to Probability (pp. 652–655)

■ Is it *impossible, unlikely, as likely as not, likely,* or *certain* that the spinner will land on yellow?

Half of the spinner is yellow, so it is as likely to land on yellow as not.

6. Is it *impossible, unlikely, as likely as not, likely,* or *certain* that next week will have 7 days?

7. There is a 75% chance that George will win a race. Write this probability as a decimal and as a fraction.

8. Barry has a 30% chance of picking a black sock and a 50% chance of picking a white sock from his drawer. Which color sock is he more likely to pick?

688 Chapter 12 Probability

EXAMPLES

EXERCISES

12-2 Experimental Probability (pp. 656–659)

■ Margie recorded the number of times a spinner landed on each color. Based on Margie's experiment, on which color is the spinner most likely to land?

Outcomes	Red	Blue	Green
Frequency	┼┼┼┼ ┼┼┼┼ IIII	IIII	┼┼┼┼ II

$P(\text{red}) \approx \frac{14}{25}$ $P(\text{blue}) \approx \frac{4}{25}$ $P(\text{green}) \approx \frac{7}{25}$

The spinner will most likely land on red.

9. One day, the cafeteria supervisor recorded the number of students who chose each type of beverage. She organized her results in a table. Find the experimental probability that a student will choose juice.

Beverage	Juice	Milk	Water
Frequency	20	37	18

12-3 Counting Methods and Sample Spaces (pp. 662–665)

■ Liz is wrapping a gift. She can use gold or silver paper and either a red or white ribbon. From how many different combinations can Liz choose

Gold ⟨ red / white
Silver ⟨ red / white

Follow each branch to find all outcomes.
There are 4 different combinations.

10. The local restaurant has a lunch special in which you can pick an appetizer, a sandwich, and a drink. How many different lunch-special combinations are there if you have the following choices?

    appetizers: soup or salad
    sandwiches: turkey, roast beef, or ham
    drinks: juice, milk, or iced tea

12-4 Theoretical Probability (pp. 666–669)

■ What is the probability of rolling a 4 on a fair number cube?

There are six possible outcomes when a number cube is rolled: 1, 2, 3, 4, 5, or 6. All are equally likely because the number cube is fair.

$P = \frac{\text{number of ways event can occur}}{\text{total number of possible outcomes}}$

$P(4) = \frac{1 \text{ way event can occur}}{6 \text{ possible outcomes}} = \frac{1}{6}$

11. What is the probability that the spinner will land on yellow?

12. What is the probability of rolling a number greater than 3 on a fair number cube?

13. There is a 25% chance of choosing a purple marble from a bag. Find the probability of choosing a marble that is NOT purple.

Video Lesson Tutorials Online my.hrw.com

EXAMPLES

EXERCISES

12-5 Compound Events (pp. 672–675)

■ What is the probability of spinning red or blue and having the coin land heads up?

	Red	Blue	Green	White
Heads	red, H	blue, H	green, H	white, H
Tails	red, T	blue, T	green, T	white, T

There are 8 possible outcomes, and all are equally likely.

$$P(\text{red or blue, H}) = \frac{2 \text{ ways event can occur}}{8 \text{ possible outcomes}}$$

$$= \frac{2}{8} = \frac{1}{4}$$

14. Find the probability that a blue marble will be chosen, the first coin will show heads, and the second coin will show tails.

15. Jacob rolled a fair number cube, flipped a fair penny, and then flipped a fair quarter. Find the probability that the number cube will show an even number and both coins will show heads.

12-6 Making Predictions (pp. 680–683)

■ If you spin the spinner 30 times, how many times do you expect it to land on red?

$P(\text{red}) = \frac{1}{3}$

$\frac{1}{3} = \frac{x}{30}$

$3 \cdot x = 1 \cdot 30$ *The cross products are equal.*

$3x = 30$ *x is multiplied by 3.*

$\frac{3x}{3} = \frac{30}{3}$ *Divide both sides by 3 to undo the multiplication.*

$x = 10$

You can expect it to land on red about 10 times.

16. Based on a sample survey, about 2% of the items produced by a company are defective. Out of 5,000 items, how many can you predict will be defective?

17. If you roll a fair number cube 50 times, how many times can you expect to roll an even number?

18. In a sample survey, 500 teenagers indicated that 175 of them use their computers regularly. Out of 4,500 teenagers, predict how many use their computers regularly.

19. In a sample survey, 100 sixth-grade students indicated that 20 of them take music lessons. Out of 500 sixth-grade students, predict how many take music lessons.

Chapter Test

CHAPTER 12

For Items 1 and 2, write *impossible, unlikely, as likely as not, likely,* or *certain* to describe each event.

1. You roll a 3 on a standard number cube.

2. You pick a blue marble from a bag of 5 white marbles and 20 blue marbles.

3. There is a 12% chance of rain tomorrow. Write this probability as a decimal and as a fraction.

4. The probability that Mark will be selected for a scholarship is 0.8. Write this probability as a percent and as a fraction.

5. Iris asked 60 students what time they go to bed. Her results are in the table. Find the experimental probability that a student chosen at random goes to bed at 8:30 P.M.

Time (P.M.)	8:00	8:30	9:00	9:30
Frequency	12	24	18	6

6. Find the experimental probability that a student chosen at random goes to bed before 8:30 P.M.

7. Josh threw darts at a dartboard 10 times. Assume that he threw the darts randomly and did not aim. Based on his results, what is the probability that a dart will land in the center circle?

8. What is the probability of rolling an even number greater than 2 on a fair number cube?

9. The baseball game has a 64% chance of being rained out. What is the probability that it will NOT be rained out?

10. Peter has four photos to arrange in a frame. How many different ways can he arrange the photos?

11. Marsha can wear jeans or black pants with a red, blue, or white shirt. How many different outfits can she choose from?

12. If you roll a number cube 36 times, how many times do you expect to roll an even number?

13. Find the probability that you will pick a blue marble from both bags and that the spinner will land on blue.

Standardized Test Prep

Cumulative Assessment, Chapters 1–12

Multiple Choice

1. A humpback whale swimming on the water's surface dives 500 feet. It then dives another 175 feet. Which expression represents this situation?

   Ⓐ $-175 + 500$
   Ⓑ $675 - 175$
   Ⓒ $-500 - 175$
   Ⓓ $500 + 175$

2. The weather report states that there is a 60% chance of a thunderstorm. What is this probability written as a fraction in simplest form?

   Ⓕ $\frac{3}{5}$
   Ⓖ $\frac{6}{10}$
   Ⓗ $\frac{30}{60}$
   Ⓙ $\frac{60}{100}$

3. There were 18 teachers and 45 students registered to participate in a 5K walk-a-thon. Which ratio accurately compares the number of students to the number of teachers?

   Ⓐ 1:5
   Ⓑ 5:2
   Ⓒ 3:15
   Ⓓ 18:45

4. Which three-dimensional figure is a square pyramid?

   Ⓕ
   Ⓖ
   Ⓗ
   Ⓙ

5. Jason delivers newspapers. He earns $0.22 for every newspaper he delivers. He wants to buy a new printer for his computer that costs $264. If n equals the number of newspapers he delivers, which equation can be used to find the number of newspapers Jason needs to deliver in order to have enough money to buy the printer?

   Ⓐ $n - 0.22 = 264$
   Ⓑ $0.22 + n = 264$
   Ⓒ $\frac{n}{0.22} = 264$
   Ⓓ $0.22n = 264$

6. The two figures are similar. Which proportion can be used to find the missing side length?

   Ⓕ $\frac{4}{x} = \frac{18}{27}$
   Ⓖ $\frac{6}{x} = \frac{27}{4}$
   Ⓗ $\frac{6}{x} = \frac{9}{18}$
   Ⓙ $\frac{4}{x} = \frac{18}{9}$

7. Victor owns 638 model trains. He can put 24 trains in a protective case. If each case costs $5.65, how much money will Victor have to spend to put all of his model trains in cases?

   Ⓐ $135.60
   Ⓑ $146.90
   Ⓒ $152.55
   Ⓓ $158.25

8. What is 70% of 30?

   Ⓕ 0.21
   Ⓖ 2.1
   Ⓗ 21
   Ⓙ 210

9. The weights of four puppies are listed below. Which puppy is the heaviest?

Puppy	Weight (lb)
Toby	$5\frac{1}{4}$
Rusty	$5\frac{2}{5}$
Alex	$5\frac{5}{8}$
Jax	$5\frac{2}{3}$

    (A) Toby (C) Alex
    (B) Rusty (D) Jax

10. A fair number cube is rolled. What is the probability that the cube will NOT land on 4?

    (F) $\frac{1}{6}$ (H) $\frac{2}{3}$
    (G) $\frac{1}{3}$ (J) $\frac{5}{6}$

HOT TIP! A probability can be written as a decimal, fraction, or percent. Probabilities are always between 0 and 1 (or 0% and 100%). The greater the probability, the more likely the event is to occur.

Gridded Response

11. The movie *Gone with the Wind* is 3 hours and 42 minutes long. How many minutes long is the movie?

12. Nancy is stenciling 5-inch-wide stars, end-to-end, around her rectangular bedroom. Her bedroom is $12\frac{3}{4}$ feet wide and $15\frac{1}{4}$ feet long. How many whole stars will Nancy stencil?

13. The prime factorization of a number is $3^3 \times 5^2 \times 7$. What is the number?

14. Carl drives at an average rate of 60 miles per hour. How many hours will it take him to drive 240 miles?

Short Response

S1. John asked a group of teenagers how many hours of television they watch per day during the summer. He put his results in a frequency table.

Hours	2	3	4	5
Teenagers	II	UHT II	UHT I	UHT

   a. Based on this survey, what is the probability that a teenager will spend 4 hours a day watching television in the summer?

   b. John plans to ask 500 teenagers the same survey question. How many of those teenagers can he predict watch 2 hours of television per day during the summer? Explain.

S2. A restaurant offers a choice of roast beef, chicken, or fish; broccoli, carrots, or corn; and soup or salad. If you can choose one main dish, one vegetable, and one side, what are all the possible outcomes?

Extended Response

E1. There are 5 blue tiles, 7 red tiles, and 8 yellow tiles in a jar.

   a. If you pick a tile without looking, what is the probability of picking a blue tile? Express this probability as a percent, a fraction, and a decimal.

   b. If you pick a tile without looking, what is the probability of NOT picking a yellow tile? Write your answer in simplest form.

   c. You conduct an experiment in which you pick a tile out of the jar 50 different times. Each time you record the color of tile and then replace the tile before you pick another. How many times would you expect to pick a blue tile? Explain.

CHAPTER 13
Functions, Equations, and Inequalities

13A Functions
- **13-1** Tables and Functions
- **13-2** Graphing Functions
- **13-3** Slope and Rate of Change
- **LAB** Explore Linear and Nonlinear Relationships

13B Equations and Inequalities
- **13-4** Solving Two-Step Equations
- **13-5** Inequalities
- **13-6** Solving Two-Step Inequalities

Chapter Focus
- Use equations to describe relationships shown in a table.
- Solve for variables by using properties and number sense.

Why Learn This?
Functions, which show how different values are related, can be used in math to describe the real world. With fireworks, a function can show how the length of the fuse is related to the length of time before a shell explodes.

Learn It Online
Chapter Project Online go.hrw.com,
keyword MR10 Ch13 Go

Are You Ready?

Vocabulary

Choose the best term from the list to complete each sentence.

1. __?__ operations undo each other.
2. A(n) __?__ is a mathematical statement that two quantities are equivalent.
3. A(n) __?__ is a ratio that compares two quantities measured in different units.
4. A(n) __?__ of numbers is used to locate a point on a coordinate plane.

equation
ordered pair
expression
rate
inverse

Complete these exercises to review skills you will need for this chapter.

Words for Operations

Write the operation and algebraic expression for each word expression.

5. the product of 3 and t
6. 9 less than z
7. the quotient of d and 17
8. 28 more than g
9. 101 times k
10. 43 minus x

Inverse Operations

Use the inverse operation to solve each equation.

11. $x + 12 = 31$
12. $8n = 104$
13. $56 \div p = 8$
14. $t - 14 = 33$
15. $a - 82 = 7$
16. $\frac{s}{6} = 5$
17. $b + 22 = 93$
18. $15 = 3n$

Graph Ordered Pairs

Use the coordinate plane. Write the ordered pair for each point.

19. A
20. B
21. C
22. D
23. E
24. F

Functions, Equations, and Inequalities

CHAPTER 13 Study Guide: Preview

Where You've Been

Previously, you
- created and analyzed different types of graphs.
- graphed ordered pairs on the coordinate plane.
- studied ratios and rates.
- solved algebraic equations by using inverse operations.

In This Chapter

You will study
- special relationships between variables called functions.
- graphing functions on the coordinate plane.
- finding rates of change that describe functions.
- solving two-step equations.
- solving one- and two-step inequalities.

Where You're Going

You can use the skills learned in this chapter
- to find the total cost of items or services that charge by the number of units purchased.
- to analyze data and make predictions about linear functions in math and science courses.

Key Vocabulary/Vocabulario

function	función
inequality	desigualdad
input	entrada
linear equation	ecuación lineal
output	salida
rate of change	tasa de cambio
slope	pendiente

Vocabulary Connections

To become familiar with some of the vocabulary terms in the chapter, consider the following. You may refer to the chapter, the glossary, or a dictionary if you like.

1. The prefix *in-* means "not." If two numbers are part of an **inequality**, how do you think they are related to each other?

2. The words *in* and *out* are used all the time. Certain numbers in math are **inputs**, and others are **outputs**. What do you think the difference is?

3. The word *linear* is a form of the word *line*. What do you think a picture of a **linear equation** would look like if you drew it on a coordinate plane?

4. The word *slope* commonly describes something that slants upward or downward like a ski slope. In math, *slope* is used to describe a line. How might a line look different if you changed its **slope**?

Reading and Writing Math

CHAPTER 13

Study Strategy: Prepare for Your Final Exam

In your math class, you use skills that you have learned throughout the year, so most final exams cover material from the beginning of the course.

A timeline and checklist like the one shown can help you study for the final exam in an organized way.

2 weeks before the final exam I will:
- Gather my notes.
- Review lessons.
- Make a list of all formulas I will probably need to know.
- Create a practice exam using problems from the book that have answers.
- Go over any missed problems from previous tests and quizzes.
- Ask about any concepts that are difficult.

1 week before the final exam I will:
- Take the practice exam and check my answers.
- For each problem I miss, find 2 or 3 other similar problems and work them.
- Look over the *Study Guide: Review* at the end of each chapter.
- Work with a friend from class to quiz each other on formulas from my list and other major concepts.

1 day before the final exam I will:
Make sure I have:
- Sharpened pencils with erasers.
- Calculator (if allowed) with fresh batteries.
- Any other math tools I may need.
- Make sure I get a good night's sleep.

Try This

1. Create a timeline and checklist of your own to help you prepare for your final exam.

Functions, Equations, and Inequalities

13-1 Tables and Functions

Learn to use data in a table to write an equation for a function and to use the equation to find a missing value.

Vocabulary
function
input
output

A baseball pitch thrown too high, low, or wide is considered outside the strike zone. A pitcher threw a ball 4 inches too low. How far in centimeters was the ball outside the strike zone? Make a table to show how the number of centimeters increases as the number of inches increases.

Inches	Centimeters
1	2.54
2	5.08
3	7.62
4	10.16

(+1 → +2.54 between each row)

The number of centimeters is 2.54 times the number of inches. Let x represent the number of inches and y represent the number of centimeters. Then the equation $y = 2.54x$ relates centimeters to inches.

A **function** is a rule that relates two quantities so that each **input** value corresponds exactly to one **output** value.

Input 2 → Rule $y = 2.54x$ → Output 5.08

Input 4 → Rule $y = 2.54x$ → Output 10.16

When the input is 4 in., the output is 10.16 cm. So the ball was 10.16 centimeters outside the strike zone.

You can use a function table to show some of the values for a function.

EXAMPLE 1 — Writing Equations from Function Tables

Write an equation for a function that gives the values in the table. Use the equation to find the value of y for the indicated value of x.

x	3	4	5	6	7	10
y	6	8	10	12	14	▭

y is 2 times x.   *Compare x and y to find a pattern.*
$y = 2x$ *Use the pattern to write an equation.*
$y = 2(10)$ *Substitute 10 for x.*
$y = 20$ *Use your function rule to find y when x = 10.*

Helpful Hint
When all the y-values are greater than the corresponding x-values, use addition and/or multiplication in your equation.

Chapter 13 Functions, Equations, and Inequalities

You can write equations for functions that are described in words.

EXAMPLE 2

Translating Words into Math

Write an equation for the function. Tell what each variable you use represents.

The length of a rectangle is 5 times its width.
ℓ = length of rectangle   *Choose variables for the equation.*
w = width of rectangle
$\ell = 5w$ *Write an equation.*

EXAMPLE 3

PROBLEM SOLVING APPLICATION

Car washers tracked the number of cars they washed and the total amount of money they earned. They charged the same price for each car they washed. They earned $60 for 20 cars, $66 for 22 cars, and $81 for 27 cars. Write an equation for the function.

1. Understand the Problem

The **answer** will be an equation that describes the relationship between the number of cars washed and the money earned.

2. Make a Plan

You can make a table to display the data.

3. Solve

Let c be the number of cars. Let m be the amount of money earned.

c	20	22	27
m	60	66	81

m is equal to 3 times c.   *Compare c and m.*
$m = 3c$ *Write an equation.*

4. Look Back

Substitute the c and m values in the table to check that they are solutions of the equation $m = 3c$.

$m = 3c$ (20, 60) $m = 3c$ (22, 66) $m = 3c$ (27, 81)
$60 \stackrel{?}{=} 3 \cdot 20$ $66 \stackrel{?}{=} 3 \cdot 22$ $81 \stackrel{?}{=} 3 \cdot 27$
$60 \stackrel{?}{=} 60$ ✔ $66 \stackrel{?}{=} 66$ ✔ $81 \stackrel{?}{=} 81$ ✔

Think and Discuss

1. Explain how you find the y-value when the x-value is 20 for the function $y = 5x$.

13-1 Exercises

Learn It Online
Homework Help Online go.hrw.com,
keyword MR10 13-1 Go
Exercises 1–9, 11, 13, 15, 17

GUIDED PRACTICE

See Example 1 Write an equation for a function that gives the values in each table. Use the equation to find the value of y for the indicated value of x.

1.
x	1	2	3	6	9
y	7	8	9	12	■

2.
x	3	4	5	6	10
y	16	21	26	31	■

See Example 2 Write an equation for the function. Tell what each variable you use represents.

3. Jen is 6 years younger than her brother.

See Example 3
4. Brenda sells balloon bouquets. She charges the same price for each balloon in a bouquet. The cost of a bouquet with 6 balloons is $3, with 9 balloons is $4.50, and with 12 balloons is $6. Write an equation for the function.

INDEPENDENT PRACTICE

See Example 1 Write an equation for a function that gives the values in each table. Use the equation to find the value of y for the indicated value of x.

5.
x	0	1	2	5	7
y	0	4	8	20	■

6.
x	4	5	6	7	12
y	0	2	4	6	■

See Example 2 Write an equation for the function. Tell what each variable you use represents.

7. The cost of a case of bottled juices is $2 less than the cost of twelve individual bottles.

8. The population of New York is twice as large as the population of Michigan.

See Example 3
9. Oliver is playing a video game. He earns the same number of points for each prize he captures. He earned 1,050 points for 7 prizes, 1,500 points for 10 prizes, and 2,850 points for 19 prizes. Write an equation for the function.

PRACTICE AND PROBLEM SOLVING

Extra Practice
See page EP26.

Write an equation for a function that gives the values in each table, and then find the missing terms.

10.
x	−1	0	1	2	5	7
y	■	3.4	4.4	5.4	■	10.4

11.
x	2	3	5	9	11	14
y	−6	−10	−18	−34	−42	■

12.
x	20	24	28	32	36	40
y	−5	−6	−7	■	−9	−10

13.
x	−5	−3	−1	0	1	3
y	−11	−7	■	−1	1	■

14. **Multi-Step** The height of a triangle is 5 centimeters more than twice the length of its base. Write an equation relating the height of the triangle to the length of its base. Find the height when the base is 20 centimeters long.

Write an equation for each function. Define the variables that you use.

15. THE NUMERATORS — $125.00 plus $55 per hour

16. FRED'S Taxi Company — $2.50 plus $0.90 per mile

17. Multi-Step Georgia earns $6.50 per hour at a part-time job. She wants to buy a sweater that costs $58.50. Write an equation relating the number of hours she works to the amount of money she earns. Find how many hours Georgia needs to work to buy the sweater.

Use the table for Exercises 18–20.

Width (pixels)	Length (pixels)
30	95
40	125
50	155
60	185

18. Graphic Design Margo is designing a Web page displaying rectangles. Use the table to write an equation relating the width of a rectangle to the length of a rectangle. Find the length of a rectangle that has a width of 250 pixels.

19. What's the Error? Margo predicted that the length of a rectangle with a width of 100 pixels would be 310 pixels. Explain the error she made. Then find the correct length.

20. Write About It Explain how to write an equation for the data in the table.

21. Challenge Write an equation that would give the same y-values as $y = 2x + 1$ for $x = 0, 1, 2, 3$.

Test Prep and Spiral Review

22. Multiple Choice Sunny Lawn Care charges $25 per visit plus $2 per cubic foot. Which equation models this situation?

Ⓐ $y = x + 2$ Ⓑ $y = x + 25$ Ⓒ $y = 25x + 2$ Ⓓ $y = 2x + 25$

23. Multiple Choice Which is an equation for the function that gives the values in the table?

x	3	4	5	6	7
y	8	11	14	17	20

Ⓕ $y = 2x + 2$ Ⓗ $y = 2x + 6$
Ⓖ $y = 3x - 1$ Ⓙ $y = 3x + 1$

Solve each equation. Check your answers. (Lesson 3-9)

24. $4.2 + n = 6.7$ **25.** $x - 2.3 = 1.6$ **26.** $1.5w = 3.6$ **27.** $\frac{p}{4} = 1.3$

Find the volume of each cylinder using the information given. (Lesson 10-8)

28. $r = 6$ cm; $h = 6.4$ cm   **29.** $r = 5$ ft; $h = 9$ ft   **30.** $d = 7$ m; $h = 11$ m

13-2 Graphing Functions

Learn to represent linear functions using ordered pairs and graphs.

Vocabulary
linear equation

Chris is ordering art supplies online. Each canvas costs $16, and the shipping and handling charge is $6 for the whole order.

The total cost y depends on the number of canvasses x. This function is described by the equation $y = 16x + 6$.

To find solutions of an equation with two variables, first choose a replacement value for one variable and then find the value of the other variable.

EXAMPLE 1 Finding Solutions of Equations with Two Variables

Use the given x-values to write solutions of the equation $y = 16x + 6$ as ordered pairs.

Make a function table by using the given values for x to find values for y.

x	16x + 6	y
1	16(1) + 6	22
2	16(2) + 6	38
3	16(3) + 6	54
4	16(4) + 6	70

Write these solutions as ordered pairs.

(x, y)
(1, 22)
(2, 38)
(3, 54)
(4, 70)

Check if an ordered pair is a solution of an equation by putting the x and y values into the equation to see if they make it a true statement.

EXAMPLE 2 Checking Solutions of Equations with Two Variables

Determine whether the ordered pair is a solution to the given equation.

(8, 16); $y = 2x$

$y = 2x$ *Write the equation.*
$16 \stackrel{?}{=} 2(8)$ *Substitute 8 for x and 16 for y.*
$16 \stackrel{?}{=} 16$ ✔

So (8, 16) is a solution of $y = 2x$.

You can also graph the solutions of an equation on a coordinate plane. When you graph the ordered pairs of some functions, they form a straight line. The equations that express these functions are called **linear equations**.

EXAMPLE 3 Reading Solutions on Graphs

Use the graph of the linear function to find the value of *y* for the given value of *x*.

$x = 1$

Start at the origin and move 1 unit right.
Move up until you reach the graph. Move left to find the y-value on the y-axis.

When $x = 1$, $y = 3$. The ordered pair is $(1, 3)$.

EXAMPLE 4 Graphing Linear Functions

Graph the function described by the equation.

$y = 2x + 1$

Make a function table. Substitute different values for x.

Write the solutions as ordered pairs.

x	2x + 1	y
−1	2(−1) + 1	−1
0	2(0) + 1	1
1	2(1) + 1	3

(x, y)
(−1, −1)
(0, 1)
(1, 3)

Graph the ordered pairs on a coordinate plane. Draw a line through the points to represent all the values of x you could have chosen and the corresponding values of y.

Think and Discuss

1. **Explain** why the points in Example 4 are not the only points on the graph. Name two points that you did not plot.
2. **Tell** whether the equation $y = 10x - 5$ describes a linear function.

13-2 Exercises

GUIDED PRACTICE

See Example 1   Use the given x-values to write solutions of each equation as ordered pairs.

1. $y = 6x + 2$ for $x = 1, 2, 3, 4$
2. $y = -2x$ for $x = 1, 2, 3, 4$

See Example 2   Determine whether each ordered pair is a solution to the given equation.

3. $(2, 12); y = 4x$
4. $(5, 9); y = 2x - 1$

See Example 3   Use the graph of the linear function to find the value of y for each given value of x.

5. $x = 1$
6. $x = 0$
7. $x = -1$

See Example 4   Graph the function described by each equation.

8. $y = x + 3$
9. $y = 3x - 1$
10. $y = -2x + 3$

INDEPENDENT PRACTICE

See Example 1   Use the given x-values to write solutions of each equation as ordered pairs.

11. $y = -4x + 1$ for $x = 1, 2, 3, 4$
12. $y = 5x - 5$ for $x = 1, 2, 3, 4$

See Example 2   Determine whether each ordered pair is a solution to the given equation.

13. $(3, -10); y = -6x + 8$
14. $(-8, 1); y = 7x - 15$

See Example 3   Use the graph of the linear function to find the value of y for each given value of x.

15. $x = -2$
16. $x = 1$
17. $x = -3$
18. $x = 0$
19. $x = -1$
20. $x = 2$

See Example 4   Graph the function described by each equation.

21. $y = 4x + 1$
22. $y = -x - 2$
23. $y = x - 2$
24. $y = -2x - 4$
25. $y = 3x - 2$
26. $y = -x$

PRACTICE AND PROBLEM SOLVING

Extra Practice
See page EP27.

Complete each table, and then use the table to graph the function.

27. $y = x - 2$

x	-1	0	1	2
y	■	■	■	■

28. $y = 2x - 4$

x	-1	0	1	2
y	■	■	■	■

29. Which of the ordered pairs below is not a solution of $y = 4x + 9$?
    $(1, 14), (0, 9), (-1, 5), (-2, 1), (2, 17)$

704   Chapter 13 Functions, Equations, and Inequalities

Physical Science Link

Temperature can be expressed according to different scales. The Kelvin scale is divided into units called kelvins, and the Celsius scale is divided into degrees Celsius.

The table shows several temperatures recorded in degrees Celsius and their equivalent measures in kelvins.

Equivalent Temperatures

Celsius (°C)	Kelvin (K)
−100	173
−50	223
0	273
50	323
100	373

30. Write an equation for a function that gives the values in the table. Define the variables that you use.

31. Graph the function described by your equation.

32. Use your graph to find the value of y when x is 0.

33. Use your equation to find the equivalent Kelvin temperature for −54 °C.

34. Use your equation to find the equivalent Celsius temperature for 77 kelvins.

35. **What's the Question?** The answer is −273 °C. What is the question?

36. **Write About It** Explain how to use your equation to determine whether 75 °C is equivalent to 345 kelvins. Then determine whether the temperatures are equivalent.

37. **Challenge** How many ordered-pair solutions exist for the equation you wrote in Exercise 30?

A technician preserves brain cells in this tank of liquid nitrogen, which is at −196 °C, for later research.

Test Prep and Spiral Review

38. **Multiple Choice** Which of the ordered pairs is NOT a solution of $y = -5x + 10$?

    Ⓐ (−20, 6) Ⓑ (5, −15) Ⓒ (4, −10) Ⓓ (2, 0)

39. **Multiple Choice** The equation $y = 12x$ shows the number of inches y in x feet. Which ordered pair is on the graph of the equation?

    Ⓕ (−2, 24) Ⓖ (1, 13) Ⓗ (4, 48) Ⓙ (12, 1)

Find the mean of each data set. (Lesson 6-2)

40. 0, 5, 2, 3, 7, 1
41. 6, 6, 6, 6, 6, 6, 6, 6, 6
42. 2, 3, 4, 5, 6, 7, 8, 1, 9

Solve each equation. Check your answers. (Lesson 11-9)

43. $\left(\dfrac{y}{-10}\right) = 12$
44. $p + 25 = -4$
45. $j - 3 = -15$
46. $5m = -20$

13-3 Slope and Rate of Change

Learn to find rates of change and slopes.

Vocabulary
rate of change
slope

By measuring the height of a plant at the same time each day, you can determine the rate at which the plant is growing. The plant's growth is a *rate of change*.

The **rate of change** of a function is a ratio that compares the difference between two output values to the difference between the corresponding input values.

$$\text{rate of change} = \frac{\text{change in } y\text{-values}}{\text{change in } x\text{-values}}$$

In some functions the rate of change is *constant*, which means that it is the same for all x- and y-values. In other functions, the rates of change are *variable*, which means they are different for some x- and y-values.

EXAMPLE 1 — Using a Table to Identify Rates of Change

Caution!
Be careful to put the differences in y-values in the numerator and the differences in x-values in the denominator when you write a rate of change.

Tell whether the rates of change are constant or variable.

A

x	0	1	3	6	8
y	0	4	8	8	6

+1 +2 +3 +2

x	0	1	3	6	8
y	0	4	8	8	6

+4 +4 +0 −2

Find the differences between consecutive data points.

$\frac{4}{1} = 4$ $\frac{4}{2} = 2$ $\frac{0}{3} = 0$ $\frac{-2}{2} = -1$

Find each ratio of the change in y to the change in x.

The rates of change are variable.

B

x	0	1	4	6	7
y	1	2	5	7	8

+1 +3 +2 +1

x	0	1	4	6	7
y	1	2	5	7	8

+1 +3 +2 +1

Find the differences between consecutive data points.

$\frac{1}{1} = 1$ $\frac{3}{3} = 1$ $\frac{2}{2} = 1$ $\frac{1}{1} = 1$

Find each ratio of the change in y to the change in x.

The rate of change is constant.

Reading Math

Recall that a function whose graph is a straight line is a linear function.

To show rates of change on a graph, plot the data points and connect them with line segments. This graph shows the data in Example 1B.

When the rate of change is constant, the segments form a straight line. The constant rate of change of a line is its **slope**.

EXAMPLE 2 Gardening Application

Evan planted some new plants in his garden. He measured the height of the same plant each Wednesday for five weeks. The table shows the measurements Evan recorded.

Week	1	2	3	4	5
Height (cm)	3	6	9	12	15

A Determine whether the rates of change are constant or variable.

$\frac{3}{1} = 3 \quad \frac{3}{1} = 3 \quad \frac{3}{1} = 3 \quad \frac{3}{1} = 3$

The rate of change is constant.

B Graph the data and connect the points with line segments. If the rate of change is constant, find and interpret the slope.

The rate of change between any two points is 3. The slope of the line is 3.

The slope is 3. This means the plant grew 3 cm each week.

Think and Discuss

1. **Explain** how to determine the rate of change from a table of values.
2. **Tell** why rates of change in the real world usually involve two units, such as mi/h.
3. **Give an example** of a constant rate of change and a variable rate of change in the real world.

13-3 Exercises

Learn It Online
Homework Help Online go.hrw.com,
keyword MR10 13-3 Go
Exercises 1–10, 11, 15, 17

GUIDED PRACTICE

See Example 1 Tell whether the rates of change are constant or variable.

1.
x	1	3	4	7	10
y	5	15	20	35	50

2.
x	0	4	5	8	9
y	3	7	10	20	23

3.
x	1	2	4	7	12
y	6	12	18	42	54

4.
x	2	3	4	6	8
y	6	9	12	18	24

See Example 2

5. McKenzie files documents each day after school for an attorney's office. McKenzie recorded the amount of money she earned for several hours during the past week.

Number of Hours	3	7	10	12	16
Earnings	$25.50	$59.50	$85.00	$102.00	$136.00

   a. Determine whether the rates of change are constant or variable.

   b. Graph the data and connect the points with line segments. If the rate of change is constant, find and interpret the slope.

INDEPENDENT PRACTICE

See Example 1 Tell whether the rates of change are constant or variable.

6.
x	0	3	4	9	12
y	0	7.5	10	22.5	30

7.
x	0	1	2	5	7
y	0	3	6	15	21

8.
x	0	3	5	6	9
y	11	18	15	16	20

9.
x	2	3	6	7	10
y	0.2	0.3	0.6	0.7	0.1

See Example 2

10. Samantha's coach recorded the amount of time it took her to run several miles during her track workout on Thursday.

Miles	1	2	3	4	5
Minutes	6.5	13	19.5	26	32.5

   a. Determine whether the rates of change are constant or variable.

   b. Graph the data and connect the points with line segments. If the rate of change is constant, find and interpret the slope.

PRACTICE AND PROBLEM SOLVING

Extra Practice
See page EP27.

Graph each set of points and connect them with line segments. If the rate of change is constant, give the slope of the line containing the points.

11. $(-2, -5), (0, -1), (3, 5), (5, 9)$

12. $(-2, -3), (1, 1.5), (4, 6), (9, 13.5)$

13. $(-2, -8), (-1, -3), (2, 4), (6, 6)$

14. $(-1, 6), (2, 0), (3, -2), (6, -8)$

708 Chapter 13 Functions, Equations, and Inequalities

Economics

George Washington Carver discovered 300 different uses for peanuts, as well as hundreds of other uses for soybeans, pecans, and sweet potatoes.

15. Transportation The table shows the number of passengers on a bus at various times during the day. Do the data show a constant rate of change? Explain your answer.

Time	9:00 A.M.	12:00 NOON	5:00 P.M.
Passengers	50	5	49

16. Economics The graph shows the cost of peanuts.

  a. Find the rates of change between four consecutive pairs of points.

  b. If the rate of change in part **a** is constant, find and interpret the slope of the line.

17. What's the Error? A student says that the rate of change for the data in the table cannot be constant because the *y*-values do not increase by the same amount. What error did the student make?

x	0	3	4	9	12
y	0	7.5	10	22.5	30

18. Critical Thinking When are the rates of change of a function equal to the slope of the function?

19. Challenge Give a situation in which data might show both a constant and a variable rate of change.

Test Prep and Spiral Review

20. Multiple Choice What is the slope of the line?

  Ⓐ -4 Ⓑ $-\frac{1}{4}$ Ⓒ $\frac{1}{4}$ Ⓓ 4

21. Short Response Tell whether the rates of change are variable or constant. If the rate of change is constant, find the slope of the line containing the points.

x	0	2	5	7	11
y	0	2.5	6.25	8.75	13.75

Evaluate $3x^2 + 1$ for each value of *x*. *(Lesson 2-1)*

22. $x = 5$ **23.** $x = 10$ **24.** $x = 15$ **25.** $x = 20$

26. Based on a sample survey, a radio station states that 53% of the people in its broadcast area prefer country music. If 600,000 people live in the area, how many would you predict prefer country music? *(Lesson 12-6)*

13-3 Slope and Rate of Change

Hands-on Lab 13-3: Explore Linear and Nonlinear Relationships

Use with Lesson 13-3

You can learn about linear and nonlinear relationships by looking at patterns.

Activity

1 This model shows stage 1 to stage 3 of a pattern.

Stage 1   Stage 2   Stage 3

a. Use square tiles or graph paper to model stages 4, 5, and 6.

b. Record each stage and the perimeter of each figure in a table.

c. Graph the ordered pairs (x, y) from the table on a coordinate plane.

Stage (x)	Perimeter (y)
1	6
2	12
3	18
4	24
5	30
6	36

If you connected the points you graphed, you would draw a straight line. This shows that the relationship between the stage and the perimeter of the figure is linear. The equation for this line is $y = 6x$.

710   Chapter 13 Functions, Equations, and Inequalities

2 This table shows several ordered pairs in a relationship.

Stage (x)	Square Root (y)
1	1
4	2
9	3
16	4
25	5
36	6

$1 = 1 \cdot 1$ or $1 = 1^2$
$4 = 2 \cdot 2$ or $4 = 2^2$
$9 = 3 \cdot 3$ or $9 = 3^2$

The square root of 4 is 2, which is written like this: $\sqrt{4} = 2$.

a. You can model this by arranging squares in 1-by-1, 2-by-2, and 3-by-3 blocks.

b. Graph the ordered pairs (x, y) from the table on a coordinate plane.

Stage 1   Stage 4   Stage 9

If you connect the graphed points, you draw a curve. This shows that the relationship between the stage number and that number's square root is nonlinear. The equation for this curve is $y = \sqrt{x}$.

Think and Discuss

1. Explain what pattern you see in the y-values of the ordered pairs from the graph above.

Try This

Use the x-values 1, 2, 3, and 4 to find ordered pairs for each equation. Then graph the equation. Tell whether the relationship between x and y is linear or nonlinear.

1. $y = 2 + x$
2. $y = 4x$
3. $y = x^3$
4. $y = x + 4$
5. $y = x(2 + x)$
6. $y = x + x$
7. $y = 2x$
8. $y = x^2$
9. $y = 3 + 2x$

13-3 Hands-On Lab

CHAPTER 13 SECTION 13A

Ready To Go On?

Quiz for Lessons 13-1 Through 13-3

13-1 Tables and Functions

Write an equation for a function that gives the values in each table. Use the equation to find the value of y for each indicated value of x.

1.
x	2	3	4	5	8
y	7	9	11	13	▪

2.
x	1	4	5	6	8
y	▪	18	23	28	38

For Problems 3–6, write an equation for the function. Tell what each variable you use represents.

3. The number of plates is 5 less than 3 times the number of cups.

4. The time Rodney spends running is 10 minutes more than twice the time he spends stretching.

5. The height of a triangle is twice the length of its base.

6. A store manager tracked T-shirt sales. The store charges the same price for each T-shirt. On Monday, 5 shirts were sold for a total of $60. On Tuesday, 8 shirts were sold for a total of $96. On Wednesday, 11 shirts were sold for a total of $132. Write an equation for the function.

13-2 Graphing Functions

Use the given x-values to write solutions of each equation as ordered pairs.

7. $y = 4x + 6$ for $x = 1, 2, 3, 4$

8. $y = 10x - 7$ for $x = 2, 3, 4, 5$

Use the graph of the linear function at right to find the value of y for each given value of x.

9. $x = 3$
10. $x = 0$
11. $x = -1$
12. $x = -2$

Graph the function described by each equation.

13. $y = x + 5$
14. $y = 3x + 2$
15. $y = -2x$

13-3 Slope and Rate of Change

Tell whether the rates of change are constant or variable.

16.
x	0	1	2	3	4	5
y	4	5	6	7	8	9

17.
x	0	3	4	7	8	11
y	5	6	8	11	15	20

Focus on Problem Solving

Make a Plan

• **Choose a problem-solving strategy**

The following strategies can help you solve problems.

- Use a Venn Diagram
- Draw a Diagram
- Make a Model
- Guess and Test
- Work Backward
- Find a Pattern
- Make a Table
- Solve a Simpler Problem
- Use Logical Reasoning
- Make an Organized List

Tell which strategy from the list above you would use to solve each problem. Explain your choice. Then solve the problem.

1 The temperature on a winter day is −6 °F at 8:00 A.M., −4 °F at 9:00 A.M., and −2 °F at 10:00 A.M. The temperature continues to change by the same amount each hour. What is the temperature at 2:00 P.M.?

2 Caleb lives in one of the states listed in the table. His home is at an elevation of 600 feet. There is a park in his state at an elevation of 150 feet. Which state does Caleb live in?

State	Lowest Elevation (ft)	Highest Elevation (ft)
California	−282	14,494
Louisiana	−8	535
West Virginia	240	4,861

3 On a map of Nadia's town, the library is located at (2, 3), the museum is located at (1, −2), city hall is located at (−2, −3), and the aquarium is located at (−4, 2). She wants to organize a field trip to the two buildings that are closest to each other. Which two buildings should she choose?

4 In the past month, Ethan's savings account had withdrawals and deposits in the amounts of −$25, +$45, +$15, −$40, and +$60. He wants to check the receipts for one of the withdrawals and one of the deposits. How many different combinations of one withdrawal and one deposit are there?

13-4 Solving Two-Step Equations

Learn to solve two-step equations.

Derrick has saved $40 for go-cart racing. The cost of a racing license is $16, and the cost of each race is $6. To find out how many races he can afford, Derrick can solve a *two-step equation*.

Solving two-step equations is similar to solving one-step equations as done in Chapter 2. To solve two-step equations, use two inverse operations to isolate the variable.

EXAMPLE 1 Solving Two-Step Equations

Helpful Hint

Undo operations in the reverse of the Order of Operations. First undo addition or subtraction. Then undo multiplication or division.

Solve each equation.

A $5x + 8 = 43$

$5x + 8 = 43$
$\ -8 \ \ -8$ Subtract 8 from both sides to undo the addition.
$5x = 35$
$\dfrac{5x}{5} = \dfrac{35}{5}$ Divide both sides by 5 to undo the multiplication.
$x = 7$

Check $5x + 8 = 43$
$5(7) + 8 \stackrel{?}{=} 43$ Substitute 7 for x in the equation.
$35 + 8 \stackrel{?}{=} 43$
$43 \stackrel{?}{=} 43$ ✔   7 is the solution.

B $\dfrac{x}{9} - 4 = 10$

$\dfrac{x}{9} - 4 = 10$
$\phantom{\dfrac{x}{9}}\ +4 \ \ +4$ Add 4 to both sides to undo the subtraction.
$\dfrac{x}{9} = 14$
$9 \cdot \dfrac{x}{9} = 9 \cdot 14$ Multiply both sides by 9 to undo the division.
$x = 126$

Check $\dfrac{x}{9} - 4 = 10$
$\dfrac{126}{9} - 4 \stackrel{?}{=} 10$ Substitute 126 for x in the equation.
$14 - 4 \stackrel{?}{=} 10$
$10 \stackrel{?}{=} 10$ ✔   126 is the solution.

Helpful Hint

Because the fraction bar acts as a grouping symbol, the expression $\frac{x+7}{2}$ is equivalent to the expression $\frac{(x+7)}{2}$.

C
$$\frac{x+7}{2} = 30$$
$$2 \cdot \frac{x+7}{2} = 2 \cdot 30 \quad \text{Multiply both sides by 2 to undo the division.}$$
$$x + 7 = 60$$
$$\underline{-7 \quad -7} \quad \text{Subtract 7 from both sides to undo the addition.}$$
$$x = 53$$

Check
$$\frac{x+7}{2} = 30$$
$$\frac{53+7}{2} \stackrel{?}{=} 30 \quad \text{Substitute 53 for x in the equation.}$$
$$\frac{60}{2} \stackrel{?}{=} 30$$
$$30 \stackrel{?}{=} 30 \checkmark \quad \text{30 is the solution.}$$

EXAMPLE 2 Consumer Economics Application

Derrick has saved $40 for go-cart racing. The cost of a racing license is $16, and the cost of each race is $6. How many races can Derrick afford?

A Write a two-step equation to represent the situation.

Let *x* represent the number of races Derrick can afford.

cost of a race times the number of races	+	cost of license	=	total cost
6x	+	16	=	40

The equation $6x + 16 = 40$ represents the situation.

B Solve the equation.

$$6x + 16 = 40$$
$$\underline{-16 \quad -16} \quad \text{Subtract 16 from both sides.}$$
$$6x = 24 \quad \text{Simplify.}$$
$$\frac{6x}{6} = \frac{24}{6} \quad \text{Divide both sides by 6.}$$
$$x = 4$$

Derrick can afford 4 races.

Think and Discuss

1. **Give an example** of a two-step equation that could be solved by subtracting first and then multiplying.

2. **Make a conjecture** about how to solve an equation with more than two steps, such as $\frac{3x+7}{5} = 11$.

13-4 Exercises

GUIDED PRACTICE

See Example 1 Solve each equation.

1. $2x + 6 = 22$
2. $\frac{x}{7} - 4 = 2$
3. $7x - 11 = 38$
4. $\frac{x}{4} + 8 = 13$
5. $7x - 5 = 23$
6. $\frac{x}{5} - 16 = 9$
7. $\frac{x-6}{3} = 7$
8. $2x + 7 = 9$
9. $\frac{x+8}{2} = 10$
10. $\frac{x}{3} + 4 = 15$
11. $\frac{x+12}{4} = 8$
12. $3x - 15 = 3$

See Example 2

13. Zach's plant is 12 centimeters tall. If the plant continues to grow 3 centimeters each week, after how many weeks will the plant be 33 centimeters tall?

    a. Let x represent the number of weeks. Write a two-step equation to represent the situation.

    b. Solve the equation.

INDEPENDENT PRACTICE

See Example 1 Solve each equation.

14. $8x + 17 = 57$
15. $11x - 8 = 58$
16. $13 + 3x = 22$
17. $16 + \frac{x}{3} = 18$
18. $10 + \frac{x}{2} = 19$
19. $\frac{x}{7} - 4 = 6$
20. $6x - 19 = 5$
21. $2x - 17 = 7$
22. $18 + 5x = 43$
23. $\frac{x+14}{5} = 6$
24. $\frac{x}{11} - 3 = 4$
25. $\frac{x-9}{10} = 4$
26. $9x + 2 = 20$
27. $\frac{x-42}{12} = 7$
28. $4x - 20 = 4$
29. $\frac{x+1}{8} = 15$
30. $\frac{x}{4} + 5 = 9$
31. $\frac{x-13}{3} = 17$

See Example 2

32. Rachel has budgeted $180 for the debate club party. She has purchased refreshments for $84. She would also like to hire a magician. For how many hours can Rachel pay a magician?

    a. Let x represent the number of hours. Write a two-step equation to represent the situation.

    b. Solve the equation.

MAIN EVENT ENTERTAINERS
Clown $24 per hour
Juggler $21 per hour
Magician $32 per hour

PRACTICE AND PROBLEM SOLVING

Extra Practice
See page EP28.

33. Gracey purchased 6 tickets to a concert and paid a service charge of $16.50. She paid a total of $121.50. What was the cost of each ticket?

34. Forrest paid a total of $6.25 for 3 tacos and an iced tea that cost $1.45. What was the cost of each taco?

Marine Life

Elephant seals can hold their breath for more than 80 minutes and can dive to depths of almost 5,000 feet as they search for food.

Write and solve an equation for each problem.

35. Three less than four times a number is twenty-five.
36. Ten less than the quotient of a number and three is eight.
37. One more than five times a number is forty-one.
38. The product of eight and a number minus three is ninety-three.
39. Twelve more than the quotient of a number and nine is twenty.
40. **Marine Life** An elephant seal weighed 64 pounds at birth. Two weeks later the seal weighed 288 pounds. About how much weight did the seal gain each day?
    a. Let w represent the number of pounds gained each day. Write a two-step equation to represent the situation.
    b. Solve the equation.

Solve each equation.

41. $\frac{x}{2} + 0.6 = 3.4$
42. $3x - \frac{2}{5} = \frac{8}{5}$
43. $\frac{2}{3}x - 7 = 3$
44. $\frac{x}{2} + \frac{3}{7} = \frac{1}{2}$
45. $0.6x - 4.3 = 4.7$
46. $\frac{1}{4}x - \frac{1}{4} = \frac{1}{8}$

47. **Write About It** Write a two-step equation that can be solved using addition and division.

48. **What's the Error?** A student solved the equation $\frac{x}{4} + 2 = 10$ as shown at right. Explain the error the student made. What is the correct answer?

$\frac{x}{4} + 2 = 10$
$\frac{x}{4} = 8$
$x = 2$

49. **Challenge** Solve the equation $\frac{4x + 20}{8} = -1$.

Test Prep and Spiral Review

50. **Multiple Choice** Which equation does NOT have a solution of $x = 5$?
    Ⓐ $2x + 15 = 25$
    Ⓑ $3x - 12 = 3$
    Ⓒ $\frac{x}{5} + 11 = 16$
    Ⓓ $\frac{x}{5} + 11 = 12$

51. **Gridded Response** Solve the equation $7x - 19 = 44$. What is the value of x?

Order the fractions and decimals from least to greatest. (Lesson 4-4)

52. $0.3, \frac{2}{5}, \frac{1}{3}$
53. $\frac{4}{3}, 1.1, 0.95$
54. $0.99, \frac{9}{10}, \frac{10}{11}$
55. $0.5, 0.35, \frac{3}{5}$

Tell whether the rates of change are constant or variable. (Lesson 13-3)

56.
x	2	5	9	14	20
y	11	17	25	35	47

57.
x	0	2	4	6	8
y	1	4	6	4	1

13-4 Solving Two-Step Equations

13-5 Inequalities

Learn to solve one-step inequalities.

An **inequality** is a statement that two quantities are not equal. The quantities are compared by using one of the following symbols:

$$< \quad > \quad \leq \quad \geq \quad \neq$$

An inequality may contain a variable, as in $x > 3$. A **solution of an inequality** is any value of the variable that makes the statement true.

Vocabulary

inequality

solution of an inequality

x	x > 3	Solution?
0	$0 \stackrel{?}{>} 3$	No; 0 is **not** greater than 3, so 0 is not a solution.
3	$3 \stackrel{?}{>} 3$	No; 3 is **not** greater than 3, so 3 is not a solution.
4.5	$4.5 \stackrel{?}{>} 3$	Yes; 4.5 is greater than 3, so 4.5 is a solution.
12	$12 \stackrel{?}{>} 3$	Yes; 12 is greater than 3, so 12 is a solution.

The table shows that an inequality may have more than one solution. You can use a number line to show all of the solutions of an inequality.

This graph shows that any number greater than 3 is a solution of the inequality. The empty circle means that 3 is not a solution. A solid circle would indicate that 3 is a solution.

$$\longleftarrow\!\!|\!-\!\!|\!-\!\!|\!-\!\!|\!-\!\!|\!-\!\!|\!-\!\!|\!-\!\!|\!-\!\circ\!-\!\!|\!-\!\!|\!\longrightarrow$$
$$-5\; -4\; -3\; -2\; -1\;\; 0\;\; 1\;\; 2\;\; 3\;\; 4\;\; 5$$

EXAMPLE 1 Graphing Inequalities

Graph the solutions of each inequality on a number line.

A $w \leq 4$

Draw a solid circle at 4 to show that 4 is a solution. Shade to the left to show that values less than 4 are also solutions.

B $z > -2$

Draw an empty circle at -2 to show that -2 is not a solution. Shade to the right to show that values greater than -2 are solutions.

You can solve inequalities that contain addition and subtraction in the same way you solved equations.

Chapter 13 Functions, Equations, and Inequalities

EXAMPLE 2 **Solving Inequalities with Addition or Subtraction**

Solve and graph each inequality.

A $y + 7 < 9$

$$y + 7 < 9$$
$$\underline{-7 \phantom{<} -7}$$
$$y < 2$$

7 is added to y. Subtract 7 from both sides of the inequality to undo the addition.

The empty circle at 2 shows that 2 is not a solution.

B $4 \leq n - 3$

$$4 \leq n - 3$$
$$\underline{+3 +3}$$
$$7 \leq n$$

3 is subtracted from n. Add 3 to both sides of the inequality to undo the subtraction.

The solid circle at 7 shows that 7 is a solution.

Helpful Hint

In Example 2B, the inequality $7 \leq n$ can be rewritten as $n \geq 7$ to make it easier to graph the solution.

Solving inequalities that contain multiplication and division of positive numbers is similar to solving equations. However, there are special rules for negative numbers, which you will learn in future math courses.

EXAMPLE 3 **Solving Inequalities with Multiplication or Division**

Solve and graph each inequality.

A $\frac{x}{6} > 2$

$$\frac{x}{6} > 2$$
$$6 \cdot \frac{x}{6} > 6 \cdot 2$$
$$x > 12$$

x is divided by 6. Multiply both sides of the inequality by 6 to undo the division.

The empty circle at 12 shows that 12 is not a solution.

B $5p \leq 45$

$$5p \leq 45$$
$$\frac{5p}{5} \leq \frac{45}{5}$$
$$p \leq 9$$

p is multiplied by 5. Divide both sides of the inequality by 5 to undo the multiplication.

The solid circle at 9 shows that 9 is a solution.

Think and Discuss

1. **Tell** how you could check your solution to an inequality.
2. **Explain** why it is necessary to use an empty circle to graph solutions of inequalities that contain < or >.

13-5 Exercises

GUIDED PRACTICE

See Example 1 Graph the solutions of each inequality on a number line.

1. $w \leq 0$
2. $x > 5$
3. $z \geq 9$
4. $g < 4$
5. $7 < t$
6. $4 \geq q$

Solve and graph each inequality.

See Example 2
7. $y - 5 \geq 0$
8. $x + 4 < 10$
9. $s + 2 \leq 10$
10. $r + 9 \leq 23$
11. $p - 4 > 2$
12. $4 + r \leq 7$

See Example 3
13. $3t \leq 27$
14. $4x < 16$
15. $\frac{d}{6} \geq 1$
16. $\frac{x}{3} < 2$
17. $2k < 8$
18. $2p \geq 8$

INDEPENDENT PRACTICE

See Example 1 Graph the solutions of each inequality on a number line.

19. $t \geq -2$
20. $y < 10$
21. $q \leq 7$
22. $n \geq 5$
23. $-1 \leq p$
24. $f > -3$

Solve and graph each inequality.

See Example 2
25. $x + 2 > 4$
26. $y + 3 \leq 4$
27. $b + 1 > 5$
28. $g - 6 \geq 4$
29. $f - 5 \leq 2$
30. $w + 3 < 8$

See Example 3
31. $7t < 42$
32. $\frac{x}{9} < 1$
33. $\frac{y}{6} \geq 1$
34. $3a \leq 9$
35. $4h < 20$
36. $\frac{r}{2} \geq 4$

PRACTICE AND PROBLEM SOLVING

Extra Practice
See page EP28.

Write an inequality for each sentence. Then graph the solutions of your inequality on a number line.

37. c is less than or equal to two.
38. p is greater than 11.
39. 2 times r is less than 14.
40. s plus 2 is greater than or equal to 5.

41. **Geography** Rhode Island is the smallest state in the United States, with an area of 1,045 square miles. Let a represent the area of any state in the United States. Write an inequality relating a to the area of Rhode Island.

42. **Social Studies** The U.S. Constitution says that "No Person shall be a Representative who shall not have attained to the age of twenty five Years." Let a represent the age of any United States Representative. Write an inequality relating a to the minimum age of a United States Representative.

LINK

Geography

Although it is more than 6,000 ft shorter than Mt. McKinley, Pikes Peak in Colorado is the most visited mountain in North America. It attracts more than 500,000 people per year.

Solve and graph each inequality.

43. $\frac{1}{3}c < 3$
44. $b + 1.5 \geq 8.5$
45. $y + \frac{3}{4} < 1\frac{1}{2}$
46. $\frac{1}{2}x \leq 1$
47. $3.8 + k > 4.2$
48. $\frac{m}{3.2} \leq 2$

49. **Fishing** At some lakes, people who fish must throw back any trout that is less than 10 inches long. Write an inequality that represents the lengths of trout that may be kept.

50. The table shows the prices of the items that Lexi is selling as part of a fundraiser. Write two inequalities to describe the price of any item, one using the < symbol and one using the > symbol.

Fundraising Price List
$4.50, $9.75, $7.00, $5.75, $9.25, $6.50

51. **Geography** Mt. McKinley is the highest point in the United States, with an elevation of 20,320 ft. Let a represent the elevation of any other U.S. location. Write an inequality relating a to Mt. McKinley's elevation.

52. **Critical Thinking** Explain why you should graph the solutions of an inequality instead of listing them.

53. **What's the Error?** A student graphed $x > 1$ as shown. What did the student do wrong? Draw the correct graph.

54. **Write About It** Describe a situation that can be represented by an inequality. Write and graph the inequality.

55. **Challenge** A compound inequality combines two inequalities. To solve a compound inequality, write two separate inequalities and solve each inequality separately. Solve the inequality $12 < x + 2 \leq 21$.

Test Prep and Spiral Review

56. **Multiple Choice** Which value is part of the solution to the inequality $4x > 16$?

    Ⓐ $x = -4$ Ⓑ $x = 2$ Ⓒ $x = 4$ Ⓓ $x = 8$

57. **Short Response** Explain how the solution of $x + 3 = 10$ differs from the solution of $x + 3 > 10$.

Use the bar graph to answer each question. (Lesson 6-4)

58. How old are most of the students?

59. Which ages have fewer than 8 students in the class?

Convert. (Lesson 9-3)

60. 27 ft = ▧ yd
61. 15 qt = ▧ pt
62. 13 lb = ▧ oz
63. 23 c = ▧ qt

13-5 Inequalities

13-6 Solving Two-Step Inequalities

Learn to solve two-step inequalities.

Joseph wants to determine the lowest score he can earn on an exam to ensure that he gets an A in the class. He could write and solve a two-step inequality to find what score is needed.

To solve a two-step inequality, use inverse operations to "undo" the operations in the inequality one at a time.

EXAMPLE 1 Solving Two-Step Inequalities

Solve and graph each inequality.

Remember!
Undo operations in the opposite order they were applied. In Example 1A, undo addition and then undo multiplication.

A $5x + 7 \leq 62$

$$5x + 7 \leq 62$$
$$-7 -7$$
$$5x \leq 55$$

Subtract 7 from both sides of the inequality to undo the addition.

$$\frac{5x}{5} \leq \frac{55}{5}$$

Divide both sides by 5 to undo the multiplication.

$$x \leq 11$$

Place a solid circle at 11, and then shade to the left.

Check $5x + 7 \leq 62$
$$5(10) + 7 \stackrel{?}{\leq} 62$$
$$50 + 7 \stackrel{?}{\leq} 62$$
$$57 \leq 62 \checkmark$$

Substitute a value less than 11 for x.

The check supports your answer.

B $\frac{r}{2} - 6 > 10$

$$\frac{r}{2} - 6 > 10$$
$$\phantom{\frac{r}{2}} +6 +6$$
$$\frac{r}{2} > 16$$

Add 6 to both sides of the inequality to undo the subtraction.

$$2 \cdot \frac{r}{2} > 2 \cdot 16$$

Multiply both sides by 2 to undo the division.

$$r > 32$$

Place an empty circle at 32, and then shade to the right.

EXAMPLE 2

PROBLEM SOLVING APPLICATION

Joseph's scores on the first three exams in math class were 87, 96, and 98. What score can Joseph earn on the fourth exam to ensure an average of at least 90?

1. Understand the Problem

The **answer** will be the fourth exam score.

List the **important information:**

- The first three exam scores were 87, 96, and 98.
- The average needs to be at least 90.

2. Make a Plan

Write and solve an inequality. Let x equal the unknown exam score. The average of the exam scores must be greater than or equal to 90.

The sum of the scores	divided by	the number of exams	must be greater than or equal to	90
$(87 + 96 + 98 + x)$	÷	4	≥	90

3. Solve

$$\frac{87 + 96 + 98 + x}{4} \geq 90 \quad \text{Write an inequality.}$$

$$\frac{281 + x}{4} \geq 90 \quad \text{Simplify the numerator.}$$

$$4 \cdot \frac{281 + x}{4} \geq 4 \cdot 90 \quad \text{Multiply both sides of the inequality}$$
$$281 + x \geq 360 \quad \text{by 4 to undo the division.}$$

$$\underline{-281 \qquad -281} \quad \text{Subtract 281 from both sides to}$$
$$x \geq 79 \quad \text{undo the addition.}$$

Joseph must earn a 79 or greater on the fourth exam to have an average of at least 90.

4. Look Back

Make a table. Substitute values to test the inequality.

70	$\frac{87 + 96 + 98 + 70}{4} \not\geq 90$	85	$\frac{87 + 96 + 98 + 85}{4} \geq 90$
75	$\frac{87 + 96 + 98 + 75}{4} \not\geq 90$	90	$\frac{87 + 96 + 98 + 90}{4} \geq 90$

Think and Discuss

1. Describe the steps used to solve the inequality $\frac{x+3}{5} \leq 6$.

2. Make a conjecture about how you would solve the inequality $\frac{w+7}{3} \leq w - 5$.

13-6 Exercises

GUIDED PRACTICE

See Example 1 Solve and graph each inequality.

1. $2x - 9 \geq 3$
2. $5x + 16 > 41$
3. $9x + 17 \geq 44$
4. $10x - 12 < 28$
5. $\frac{x + 14}{10} \geq 2$
6. $\frac{x + 7}{3} > 4$
7. $\frac{x}{4} + 7 \leq 8$
8. $\frac{x + 2}{4} < 1$
9. $\frac{x}{5} + 12 > 15$
10. $3x - 7 > 2$
11. $\frac{x}{2} + 3 \leq 4$
12. $6x + 3 < 9$
13. $8x + 5 < 29$
14. $4x + 11 \leq 19$
15. $\frac{x}{3} - 1 < 0$
16. $\frac{x}{2} + 6 \geq 10$
17. $\frac{x}{3} + 10 < 12$
18. $\frac{x}{2} - 2 \geq 1$

See Example 2

19. A car salesman earns $700 per month plus a commission of 5% of his total sales. The salesman needs a monthly income of at least $2,800. Write and solve an inequality to find how much the salesman must sell each month.

INDEPENDENT PRACTICE

See Example 1 Solve and graph each inequality.

20. $6x + 13 > 31$
21. $9x + 5 < 59$
22. $1 + \frac{x}{8} < 2$
23. $\frac{x}{2} + 16 \geq 17$
24. $7x - 4 \leq 17$
25. $5 + 3x \leq 29$
26. $\frac{x}{5} + 1 \geq 2$
27. $12 + \frac{x}{2} > 17$
28. $24x + 16 \leq 64$
29. $11x - 12 \geq 32$
30. $5x - 14 > 21$
31. $3x + 21 \leq 27$
32. $\frac{x + 8}{6} > 2$
33. $\frac{x}{9} + 6 \leq 6$
34. $\frac{x + 7}{2} \leq 6$
35. $\frac{x}{2} + 17 > 22$
36. $7x - 15 \geq 62$
37. $\frac{x + 9}{5} < 2$

See Example 2

38. Stephanie and Melinda are driving from Cleveland to Cincinnati. So far, they have traveled 80 miles. How fast must Stephanie and Melinda drive in order to cover the remaining distance in no more than 4 hours?

PRACTICE AND PROBLEM SOLVING

Extra Practice See page EP28.

39. **Consumer Math** Peter has a budget of $120 for the Math club celebration. He wants to buy $15 worth of drinks and some pizza. Each pizza costs $12. Write and solve an inequality to determine the number of pizzas Peter can buy.

724 Chapter 13 Functions, Equations, and Inequalities

Write and solve a two-step inequality for each sentence. Then graph your solution on a number line.

40. Three times a number, decreased by five, is greater than seven.

41. A number divided by two, increased by four, is less than six.

42. Two-thirds times a number, increased by one, is less than or equal to eleven.

43. The difference of a number and two, divided by three, is greater than or equal to one.

44. **Travel** Sarah needs at least $650 for a trip to Canada. She has already saved $182 for the trip. If she earns $6.50 per hour, how many hours must she work to afford her trip?

Solve each inequality. Graph the solutions on a number line.

45. $3g - 2 \leq 4$
46. $5 + 4z > 17$
47. $\frac{x+5}{3} < 4$
48. $2 \leq 4n - 6$
49. $\frac{y-5}{10} < 3$
50. $5h - 4 \geq 6$

51. **Theater** A theater company is trying to raise at least $6,000 for new costumes and set-construction equipment. So far, they have received $4,875 in donations. If tickets to the annual Spring Revue cost $25 each, how many tickets must the company sell to reach its goal?

52. **What's the Error?** A student solved the inequality as shown. What did the student do wrong? Write the correct solution.

$$2x + 5 > 17$$
$$-5 -5$$
$$2x > 12$$
$$\frac{2x}{2} > \frac{12}{2}$$
$$x > 6$$

53. **Write About It** Compare the steps you would follow to solve an inequality to the steps you would follow to solve an equation.

54. **Challenge** What is the least whole-number solution of $2x - 3.5 > 17.7$?

Test Prep and Spiral Review

55. **Multiple Choice** Which value is NOT a solution of $3x - 10 \geq 20$?

    (A) 8   (B) 10   (C) 12   (D) 18

56. **Short Response** Explain the steps you would follow to solve and graph the inequality $5x - 12 > 13$.

Find the least common multiple (LCM). (Lesson 5-1)

57. 19 and 38
58. 12 and 34
59. 15, 20, and 48
60. 12, 18, and 20

Find the area of a rectangle with the given dimensions. (Lesson 10-1)

61. length: 5 m
    width: 1.2 m
62. length: 2 cm
    width: 17.3 cm
63. length: 15 ft
    width: 7.5 ft
64. length: 7 in.
    width: 8.25 in.

Theater

More than 45 million people in 63 cities have seen the musical theater adaptation of *The Lion King*.

Ready To Go On?

Quiz for Lessons 13-4 Through 13-6

13-4 Solving Two-Step Equations

Solve each equation.

1. $3x + 10 = 40$
2. $\frac{y + 5}{12} = 20$
3. $22z - 13 = 163$
4. $\frac{a}{5} + 3 = 7$
5. $14b + 9 = 149$
6. $\frac{c}{7} - 8 = 9$
7. $9d - 2 = 70$
8. $\frac{g - 24}{18} = 1$
9. $15h + 20 = 185$

10. Susan's parents are planning her birthday at a bowling alley. The bowling alley charges a $25 flat fee plus $3.50 for each child at the party. How many children, including Susan, can attend the party for a total cost of $60?

13-5 Inequalities

Solve and graph each inequality.

11. $s - 21 \geq 30$
12. $4 + k < 12$
13. $m + 1 < 18$
14. $\frac{n}{29} \leq 5$
15. $14p < 266$
16. $30q \leq 270$
17. $26r > 26$
18. $15j \geq 45$
19. $\frac{t}{12} \geq 7$

20. The Brazelton Middle School band is washing cars to raise money for an end-of-year trip. If the band members charge $7.50 per car, how many cars must they wash to raise at least $210?

13-6 Solving Two-Step Inequalities

Solve and graph each inequality.

21. $\frac{u}{8} + 12 < 20$
22. $16v - 13 \leq 179$
23. $8w + 10 < 18$
24. $16x - 29 \leq 243$
25. $\frac{y - 12}{14} \leq 0$
26. $\frac{x}{7} - 9 > 5$
27. $\frac{a - 5}{3} \geq 2$
28. $4b + 8 > 28$
29. $c - 6 > 18$

30. Ricardo is training to compete in a triathlon. This week, he ran 18 miles on Monday and 10 miles on Wednesday. How far must he run on Friday to average at least 15 miles for each of the three days?

726 Chapter 13 Functions, Equations, and Inequalities

Real-World Connections

CHAPTER 13

The Alaska Railroad The Alaska Railroad began in 1903 with just 51 miles of track. Today, the railroad winds through 500 miles of stunning scenery. During the summer months, the railroad is one of Alaska's top tourist attractions.

1. Kayla is taking the Denali Star train to Fairbanks. She gets on at Wasilla, which is 50 miles north of Anchorage. The table shows the time she travels and her distance from Anchorage.

    a. Describe any patterns you see in the table.

    b. Graph the function described by the table.

    c. Does the table show a linear relationship? Why or why not?

    d. Write an equation for a function that gives the values in the table.

    e. Use the equation to find the missing value of y in the table.

Time in hours (x)	0	1	2	3	4
Distance from Anchorage in miles (y)	50	80	110	140	

2. Fairbanks is 350 miles from Anchorage.

    a. Write an equation that you can solve to find out how long it takes the train to reach Fairbanks.

    b. Solve the equation.

    c. Explain how you can use your graph to find the number of hours it takes to reach Fairbanks.

Game Time

Try Angles

Solve each equation below. Then use the values of the variables to decode the answer to the question.

$47 = 2a + 33$

$\dfrac{b}{4} = 7$

$3 + 4c = 43$

$3d + 12 = 15$

$3e = 72$

$\dfrac{f + 10}{3} = 6$

$\dfrac{g}{3} + 4 = 7$

$h - 7 = 11$

$\dfrac{i + 2}{5} = 3$

$\dfrac{j + 0.5}{8} = 2$

$\dfrac{7 + k}{5} = 20$

$7l + 5 = 9$

$8m + 7 = 127$

$2n + 3 = 6$

$7o + 3 = 24$

$\dfrac{p}{9} + 5 = 11$

$\dfrac{q}{11} + 13 = 16$

$\dfrac{r}{4} - 3 = 2$

$4s - 7 = 1$

$2t + 13 = 21$

$\dfrac{u}{2} - 13 = 1$

$8v + 11 = 107$

$6w - 19 = 11$

$4x + 7 = 9$

$3y - 15 = 3$

$\dfrac{z}{10} + 1 = 11$

Why did the angle make straight A's?

$\overline{}\;\overline{}\;\overline{}\quad\overline{}\;\overline{}\;\overline{}\;\overline{}\;\overline{}\quad\overline{}\;\overline{}\;\overline{}\quad\overline{}\;\overline{}\;\overline{}\;\overline{}\;\overline{}\;\overline{}\quad\overline{}\;\overline{}\;\overline{}\;\overline{}\;\overline{}$.
4 18 24   7 1.5 9 $\frac{4}{7}$ 24   5 7 2   7 $\frac{4}{7}$ 5 7 6 2   20 13 9 18 4

24 Points

This traditional Chinese game is played using a deck of 52 cards numbered 1–13, with four of each number. The cards are shuffled, and four cards are placed face up in the center. The winner is the first player who comes up with an expression that equals 24, using each of the numbers on the four cards once.

Complete rules and a set of game cards are available online.

Materials
- magazine
- glue
- scissors
- index cards

It's in the Bag!

PROJECT **Picture Envelopes**

Make these picture-perfect envelopes in which to store your notes on the lessons of this chapter.

Directions

1. Flip through a magazine and carefully tear out six pages with full-page pictures that you like.

2. Lay one of the pages in front of you with the picture face down. Fold the page into thirds as shown, and then unfold the page. **Figure A**

3. Fold the sides in, about 1 inch, and then unfold. Cut away the four rectangles at the corners of the page. **Figure B**

4. Fold in the two middle flaps. Then fold up the bottom and glue it onto the flaps. **Figure C**

5. Cut the corners of the top section at an angle to make a flap. **Figure D**

6. Repeat the steps to make five more envelopes. Label them so that there is one for each lesson of the chapter.

Taking Note of the Math

Use index cards to take notes on the lessons of the chapter. Store the cards in the appropriate envelopes.

CHAPTER 13 Study Guide: Review

Vocabulary

function 698	output 698
inequality 718	rate of change 706
input 698	slope 707
linear equation 703	solution of an inequality 718

Complete the sentences below with vocabulary words from the list above.

1. A(n) __?__ is a statement that two values are not equal.

2. The graph of a(n) __?__ is a straight line.

3. A(n) __?__ shows relationships between quantities.

EXAMPLES

EXERCISES

13-1 Tables and Functions (pp. 698–701)

■ Write an equation for a function that gives the values in the table. Use the equation to find the value of y for the indicated value of x.

x	2	3	4	5	6	12
y	5	8	11	14	17	

y is 3 times x minus 1. *Find a pattern.*
$y = 3x - 1$ *Write an equation.*
$y = 3(12) - 1$ *Substitute 12 for x.*
$y = 36 - 1 = 35$

Write an equation for a function that gives the values in each table. Use the equation to find the value of y for each indicated value of x.

4.
x	2	3	4	5	6	8
y	6	8	10	12	14	

Write an equation to describe the function. Tell what each variable you use represents.

5. The length of a rectangle is 4 times its width.

13-2 Graphing Functions (pp. 702–705)

■ Graph the function described by the equation $y = 3x + 4$.

Make a table.   *Write as ordered pairs.*

x	3x + 4	y	(x, y)
0	3(0) + 4	4	(0, 4)
1	3(1) + 4	7	(1, 7)
2	3(2) + 4	10	(2, 10)

Graph the ordered pairs on a coordinate plane.

Use the given x-values to write solutions of each equation as ordered pairs.

6. $y = 2x + 5$ for $x = 1, 2, 3, 4$

7. $y = x + 7$ for $x = 1, 2, 3, 4$

Determine whether each ordered pair is a solution to the given equation.

8. $(3, 12)$; $y = 5x - 3$

9. $(6, 14)$; $y = x + 7$

EXAMPLES

EXERCISES

13-3 Slope and Rate of Change (pp. 706–709)

■ Tell whether the rates of change are constant or variable.

x	3	4	5	6
y	2	4	6	8

Find the differences between consecutive data points.

+1 +1 +1

x	3	4	5	6
y	2	4	6	8

+2 +2 +2

Find each ratio of the change in y to the change in x.

$\frac{2}{1} = 2$ $\frac{2}{1} = 2$ $\frac{2}{1} = 2$

The rate of change is constant.

Tell whether the rates of change are constant or variable.

10.
x	4	−5	−3	8
y	10	6	8	9

11.
x	2	10	18	26
y	3	2	1	0

12.
x	6	−7	10	0
y	10	7	4	1

13.
x	−5	1	7	13
y	−1	8	17	26

14. Marco is counting the number of cars that pass through an intersection each time the light turns green. The table shows his data. Determine whether the rates of change are constant or variable.

Time	1:00 P.M.	2:00 P.M.	3:00 P.M.	4:00 P.M.
Number of cars	5	7	4	9

13-4 Solving Two-Step Equations (pp. 714–717)

Solve each equation.

■ $3x + 5 = 23$

$3x + 5 = 23$
$-5 -5$ *Subtract 5 from both sides to undo the addition.*
$\frac{3x}{3} = \frac{18}{3}$ *Divide both sides by 3 to undo the multiplication.*
$x = 6$

■ $\frac{y}{7} - 2 = 11$

$\frac{y}{7} - 2 = 11$
$+2 +2$ *Add 2 to both sides to undo the subtraction.*
$\frac{y}{7} = 13$
$\frac{y}{7} \cdot 7 = 13 \cdot 7$ *Multiply both sides by 7 to undo the division.*
$y = 91$

Solve each equation.

15. $6z - 1 = 59$
16. $12a - 7 = 29$
17. $2b + 1 = 5$
18. $\frac{b}{5} - 11 = 4$
19. $\frac{c + 5}{11} = 55$
20. $6d - 3 = 9$
21. $2h - 9 = 7$
22. $\frac{j}{7} - 11 = 5$

23. Randall practices hitting baseballs at a batting cage in a fun park. It costs $2.00 to get into the park, plus $0.50 for each turn in the cage. If Randall has $4.50, how many turns can he take in the cage?

24. Joseph earns $40 per night delivering pizza, plus $3 for each pizza he delivers. How many pizzas must Joseph deliver in order to earn $124 in one night?

EXAMPLES

13-5 Inequalities (pp. 718–721)

Solve and graph each inequality.

■ $k - 5 > 2$

$k - 5 > 2$
$\underline{+5 \quad +5}$ Add 5 to both sides to undo the subtraction.
$k \quad\; > \quad 7$

<-1 0 1 2 3 4 5 6 7 8 9>

■ $\frac{m}{3} \geq 2$

$\frac{m}{3} \geq 2$
$3 \cdot \frac{m}{3} \geq 3 \cdot 2$ Multiply both sides by 3 to undo the division.
$m \geq 6$

<-1 0 1 2 3 4 5 6 7 8 9>

13-6 Solving Two-Step Inequalities (pp. 722–725)

Solve and graph each inequality.

■ $9y - 4 > 14$

$9y - 4 > 14$
$\underline{+4 \quad +4}$ Add 4 to both sides to undo the subtraction.
$\frac{9y}{9} > \frac{18}{9}$ Divide both sides by 9 to undo the multiplication.
$y > 2$

<-5 -4 -3 -2 -1 0 1 2 3 4 5>

■ $\frac{z}{7} + 2 \geq 3$

$\frac{z}{7} + 2 \geq 3$
$\underline{\quad -2 \quad\; -2}$ Subtract 2 from both sides to undo the addition.
$\frac{z}{7} \quad\; \geq \quad 1$
$7 \cdot \frac{z}{7} \geq 7 \cdot 1$ Multiply both sides by 7 to undo the division.
$z \geq 7$

<-1 0 1 2 3 4 5 6 7 8 9>

EXERCISES

Solve and graph each inequality.

25. $\frac{n}{6} > 5$ 26. $10p \leq 10$
27. $s + 3 \geq 8$ 28. $r - 2 > 12$
29. $\frac{q}{6} \leq 10$ 30. $u - 7 < 4$
31. $5t \leq 45$ 32. $v + 5 > 9$
33. $\frac{w}{2} > 2$ 34. $x + 6 > 9$

35. For his art class, Manny must do at least 8 projects per semester. If Manny has completed 5 projects so far this semester, how many more projects must he complete before the semester ends?

36. The debate club is selling tickets to a lecture. The auditorium can hold at most 520 people. So far, 133 tickets have been sold. How many more tickets can be sold?

Solve and graph each inequality.

37. $3a - 1 < 23$ 38. $\frac{b}{4} - 11 \leq 5$
39. $\frac{c}{11} - 1 \geq 7$ 40. $11d + 3 < 36$
41. $8g + 1 > 97$ 42. $\frac{h}{4} + 4 \geq 11$
43. $\frac{j}{11} - 3 \leq 4$ 44. $7k + 12 < 75$

45. Masey must average at least 87 on two quizzes before she can move on to the next skill level. Masey got a 90 on her first quiz. What score must she get on her second quiz in order to advance?

46. Billy wants to walk at least 28 miles this week. On Monday, he walked 8 miles. How many miles does he need to walk on each of the 4 remaining days in order to reach his goal?

Chapter 13 Functions, Equations, and Inequalities

Chapter Test

Chapter 13

Write an equation for a function that gives the values in each table. Use the equation to find the value of y for each indicated value of x.

1.
x	2	3	4	5	6	7
y		8	11	14	17	20

2.
x	1	2	3	4	5	9
y	8	10	12	14	16	

Write an equation for the function. Tell what each variable you use represents.

3. The number of buttons on the jacket is 4 more than the number of zippers.

4. The length of a parallelogram is 2 in. more than twice the height.

Use the given x-values to write solutions of each equation as ordered pairs. Then graph the function described by each equation.

5. $y = 5x - 3$ for $x = 1, 2, 3, 4$

6. $y = 2x - 3$ for $x = 0, 1, 2, 3$

Determine whether the rates of change are constant or variable.

7.
x	5	7	9	11
y	1	9	17	25

8.
x	3	8	11	14
y	−3	−1	−5	5

9. Emily is participating in a project for P.E. Every day, she walks a certain distance and keeps track of the total distance she has walked for the entire project. The table shows her data for the first five days.

Day	1	2	3	4	5
Total Distance (mi)	2	4	6	8	10

a. Determine whether the rates of change are constant or variable.

b. Graph the data and connect the points with line segments. If the rate of change is constant, find and interpret the slope.

Solve each equation.

10. $\frac{x}{12} - 15 = 39$

11. $\frac{y}{7} - 12 = 2$

12. $7z + 1 = 15$

13. A new one-year membership at Foster Golf Club costs $400. A registration fee of $100 is paid up front, and the rest is paid monthly. How much do new members pay each month?

Solve and graph each inequality.

14. $15a < 150$

15. $\frac{b}{6} \geq 4$

16. $\frac{j}{15} + 6 > 6$

17. $2k - 15 \geq 3$

18. Rudy has $6.00. Bagels cost $0.50 each, and a small container of cream cheese costs $1.50. At most, how many bagels can Rudy buy if he also buys one small container of cream cheese?

CHAPTER 13

Test Tackler
STANDARDIZED TEST STRATEGIES

Multiple Choice: Recognize Distracters

In multiple-choice items, the options that are incorrect are called *distracters*. This is an appropriate name, because these incorrect options can distract you from the correct answer.

Test writers create distracters by using common student errors. Beware! Even if the answer you get when you work the problem is one of the options, it may not be the correct answer.

EXAMPLE 1

Simplify the expression $6^2 \div 8 + 15(10 - 3)$.

- A) 26.5
- B) 106.5
- C) 109.5
- D) 151.5

Look at each option carefully.
A This is a distracter. You would get this answer if you added 15 to $(10 - 3)$, or 7. Recall that parentheses mean multiplication.
B This is a distracter. You would get this answer if you simplified 6^2 as 12.
C This is the correct answer.
D This is a distracter. You would get this answer if you multiplied 15 by 10 but not by 3.

EXAMPLE 2

What is the value of x in the equation $2x + \frac{1}{5} = \frac{3}{5}$?

- F) 1
- G) $\frac{4}{5}$
- H) $\frac{2}{5}$
- J) $\frac{1}{5}$

Look at each option carefully.
F This is a distracter. You would get this answer if you divided the right side of the equation by $\frac{2}{5}$ instead of by 2 in the final step of the solution.
G This is a distracter. You would get this answer if you multiplied the right side of the equation by 2 in the final step of the solution.
H This is a distracter. You would get this answer if you added $\frac{1}{5}$ to the right side of the equation in the first step of the solution.
J This is the correct answer.

Hot Tip! When you calculate an answer to a multiple-choice test item, try to solve the problem again with a different method to make sure your answer is correct.

Read each test problem and answer the questions that follow.

Item A
A spinner is divided into 8 equal sections numbered from 1 to 8. If the arrow is spun once, what is the probability that it will NOT land on a section numbered less than 3?

- (A) $\frac{1}{8}$
- (B) $\frac{2}{8}$
- (C) $\frac{3}{8}$
- (D) $\frac{6}{8}$

1. What common error does choice B represent?

2. Which numbers on the spinner are NOT less than 3?

3. Which is the correct answer?

Item B
Evaluate $1.5x + 2.5$ for $x = 0.5$.

- (F) 1
- (G) 3.25
- (H) 4.5
- (J) 10

4. How can you evaluate this algebraic expression?

5. What is a common error when working with decimals?

6. What common error does choice J represent?

7. Which answer is correct?

Item C
The length of a hiking trail is $6\frac{2}{3}$ miles. Along the trail there are 4 exercise stations that are evenly spaced. What is the distance between each exercise station?

- (A) $1\frac{1}{2}$ miles
- (B) $1\frac{2}{3}$ miles
- (C) $2\frac{2}{3}$ miles
- (D) $26\frac{2}{3}$ miles

8. Why can choice D be eliminated immediately? What operation was used to get this answer?

9. What error does choice C represent?

10. What operation can you use to find the correct answer?

11. Which is the correct answer?

Item D
Which is the approximate circumference of the circle below?

14 cm

- (F) 7 centimeters
- (G) 42 centimeters
- (H) 84 centimeters
- (J) 147 centimeters

12. Which answer choice can be eliminated immediately? Why?

13. What common error does choice J represent?

14. What formula can you use to find the circumference of a circle? How was this formula used incorrectly to get choice H?

Test Tackler

Cumulative Assessment, Chapter 13

Multiple Choice

1. Which number line shows the solution to $\frac{g}{2} + 6 \leq 9$?

   A, B, C, D [number lines 0–10]

2. Marcus surveyed people to find out how many siblings they had. People who responded to the survey had 0, 2, 4, 3, 1, 1, 2, 11, 3, and 3 siblings. Which number in the data set is an outlier?

   F 3
   G 6
   H 8
   J 11

3. Carla is selling some of her paintings to raise money for a new bike that costs $700. She has already raised $185. If the paintings sell for $35 each, at least how many paintings must Carla sell to have enough money to buy the bike?

   A 6 paintings
   B 9 paintings
   C 15 paintings
   D 20 paintings

4. Solve $\frac{r}{3} - 7 = 17$.

   F $r = 8$
   G $r = 27$
   H $r = 30$
   J $r = 72$

5. Which solution makes $5x - 11 = 34$ true?

   A $x = 9$
   B $x = 27$
   C $x = 45$
   D $x = 115$

6. Angle USR is congruent to angle VST. What is the measure of angle USR?

   F 19°
   G 38°
   H 71°
   J 142°

7. A landscaper is planning a circular garden. The garden will have a radius of 4 meters. What will be the circumference of the garden, to the nearest tenth? Use 3.14 for π.

   A 50.2 m
   B 25.1 m
   C 12.6 m
   D 100.4 m

8. For five days, Billy kept track of the number of customers who ate lunch at his new restaurant. If the pattern in the table continues, how many customers will eat lunch at Billy's restaurant on Friday?

Day	Number of Customers
Sunday	12
Monday	25
Tuesday	38
Wednesday	51
Thursday	64
Friday	

   F 70
   G 72
   H 75
   J 77

9. Which is not equal to 2^5?

   Ⓐ $22 + 5(5 - 2) - 5$

   Ⓑ $2(2 \times 5) + (32 - 25)$

   Ⓒ $15 + 5(5 - 2) + 2$

   Ⓓ $5 \times 2 + 22$

10. Jacques collects stamps. Currently he has 124 stamps. If Jacques collects 4 stamps a week, in how many weeks will he have 200 stamps in his collection?

    Ⓕ 19 weeks   Ⓗ 50 weeks

    Ⓖ 31 weeks   Ⓙ 81 weeks

11. Shaun wants to raise $350 for his favorite charity. For each mile he runs this month, his sponsors will donate $1. Shaun has already raised $210. If he plans to run 16 more times this month, at least how many miles should he run each time to reach his goal?

    Ⓐ 2.5 miles   Ⓒ 13.125 miles

    Ⓑ 8.75 miles Ⓓ 21.875 miles

Gridded Response

12. In the last 5 days, a bank teller helped the following numbers of customers: 81, 96, 134, 142, and 99. To the nearest whole number, what is the mean number of customers the bank teller helped?

13. How many square feet does the figure cover?

    17 ft, 11 ft, 8 ft

14. Solve $\frac{x-2}{13} = 4$.

15. While hiking in Death Valley, California, Li climbed from a depth of −70 m to the top of Dante's Peak at an elevation of 1,670 m. What was the vertical distance that Li climbed in meters?

Short Response

S1. A new ice cream shop polled several people about their favorite ice cream flavors. The graph below shows the results.

Favorite Ice Cream Flavor
- Strawberry 5%
- Mint Chocolate Chip 15%
- Vanilla 35%
- Cookies and Cream 15%
- Chocolate 30%

a. If 165 people chose mint chocolate chip as their favorite flavor, how many people chose cookies and cream?

b. What is the total number of people represented in the graph? Explain how you found your answer.

S2. A circle has a radius of 9 feet. Tom wants to draw a square with a perimeter that is larger than the circumference of the circle. At least how long should each side of the square be? Use 3.14 for π. Explain how you found your answer.

Extended Response

E1. It cost Sue and Raylene $118.50 to make 19 scarves. They want to sell the scarves for a profit of at least $100.00.

a. Write and solve an inequality to find how much they should charge for each scarf. Show your work.

b. Sue and Raylene each decide to keep one scarf. How much should they charge for each remaining scarf to earn at least $100.00 in profit?

c. How much more will each scarf cost if they each keep one, rather than selling all 19?

Student Handbook

Extra Practice **EP2**

Problem-Solving Handbook **PS1**
- Draw a Diagram PS1
- Make a Model PS2
- Guess and Test PS3
- Work Backward PS4
- Find a Pattern PS5
- Make a Table PS6
- Solve a Simpler Problem PS7
- Use Logical Reasoning PS8
- Use a Venn Diagram PS9
- Make an Organized List PS10

Skills Bank **SB1**
- Place Value—Trillions Through Thousandths SB1
- Compare and Order Whole Numbers SB1
- Round Whole Numbers and Decimals SB2
- Roman Numerals SB3
- Addition SB3
- Subtraction SB4
- Multiply Whole Numbers SB4
- Divide Whole Numbers SB5
- Divide with Zeros in the Quotient SB5
- Multiples SB6
- Inverse Properties SB6

Mental Math SB7
Fractional Part of a Region SB8
Fractional Part of a Set SB8
Like Terms SB9
Solve Equations with Variables on Both Sides SB10
The Pythagorean Theorem SB11
Sectors of Circles SB11
Exterior Angles of Polygons SB12
Relationships Between Planes SB13
Compare Units SB14
Convert Between Measurement Systems SB15
Measuring with Nonstandard Units SB16
Significant Figures SB17
Box-and-Whisker Plots SB18
Sampling and Bias SB19
Effects of Sample Size on Probability SB20

Selected Answers SA1
Glossary G2
Index I2
Formulas .... inside back cover

Extra Practice ... Chapter 1

LESSON 1-1

Estimate each sum or difference by rounding to the place value indicated.

1. 7,685 + 8,230; thousands
2. 23,218 + 37,518; ten thousands
3. 52,087 − 35,210; ten thousands
4. 292,801 − 156,127; hundred thousands
5. 14,325 + 25,629; hundreds
6. 9,210 − 396; hundreds

7. Mr. Peterson needs topsoil for his garden. His rectangular garden is 78 in. long and 48 in. wide. A bag of topsoil covers an area of 500 square inches. How many bags should Mr. Peterson buy?

8. Natalie's family is having a picnic at an amusement park. The park is 153 miles from Natalie's house. If the family drives 55 mi/h, about how long will it take them to get to the park?

LESSON 1-2

Write each expression in exponential form.

9. $5 \times 5 \times 5 \times 5 \times 5 \times 5$
10. $3 \times 3 \times 3 \times 3$
11. $10 \times 10 \times 10 \times 10 \times 10$
12. $2 \times 2 \times 2 \times 2$
13. $7 \times 7 \times 7$
14. 9×9

Find each value.

15. 5^2
16. 5^5
17. 6^3
18. 10^5
19. 9^1
20. 3^6
21. 4^3
22. 2^5

23. A certain colony of bacteria doubles in size every 5 minutes. If the colony began with 2 organisms, how many will there be after 30 minutes?

24. Patricia e-mailed a joke to 4 of her friends. Each of those friends e-mailed the joke to 4 other friends. If this pattern continues, how many people will receive the e-mail on the fifth round of e-mails?

LESSON 1-3

Simplify each expression.

25. $15 + 7 \times 3$
26. $3 \times 3^2 + 13 - 5$
27. $10 \div (3 + 2) \times 2^3 - 8$
28. $4^2 - 12 \div 3 + (7 - 5)$
29. $10 \times (25 - 11) \div 7 + 6$
30. $(3 + 6) \times 18 \div 2 + 7$

31. The sixth-grade band students sell cases of fruit for a fund-raiser. Emily sold 18 cases of oranges for $12 each, 11 cases of apples for $10 each, and 5 cases of grapefruit for $14 each. Simplify $18 \times 12 + 11 \times 10 + 5 \times 14$ to find how much money she should collect in all.

Extra Practice ... Chapter 1

LESSON 1-4

Simplify.

32. 15 + 7 + 23 + 5   **33.** 4 × 13 × 5   **34.** 34 + 16 + 22 + 18

Use the Distributive Property to find each product.

35. 5 × 54   **36.** 3 × 32   **37.** 7 × 26   **38.** 9 × 73

39. A middle school band practices for 80 minutes every day during school. How many minutes do they practice over the course of 3 weeks?

40. A store keeps track of how many people enter the store each hour. On a recent day, 13, 12, 17, and 8 people entered the store during each hour of a four-hour period. How many people entered the store during the 4 hours?

LESSON 1-5

For Exercises 46–48, choose a solution method and solve. Explain your choice.

41. The table shows the number of days it rained each month. How many days total did it rain in the year?

42. The coldest temperature in a city was 11 °F. The warmest temperature that same year was 89 °F. What is the difference between the highest and lowest temperatures?

Month	Days of Rain	Month	Days of Rain
January	6	July	15
February	5	August	9
March	7	September	17
April	14	October	14
May	12	November	8
June	10	December	5

43. Heather is a member of a dance company. She practices 14 hours a week. How many hours does she practice each year? (*Hint*: There are 52 weeks in a year.)

LESSON 1-6

Identify a pattern in each arithmetic sequence and then find the missing terms.

44. 8, 16, 24, ▨, ▨, ▨   **45.** 6, 11, 16, ▨, ▨, ▨   **46.** 100, 85, 70, ▨, ▨, ▨

47.

Position	1	2	3	4	5	6	7	8
Value of Term	1	12	23	34	45	▨	▨	▨

Identify a pattern in each sequence. Name the missing terms.

48. 496, 248, 260, ▨, 142, 71, ▨   **49.** 1, 8, 4, 32, 16, ▨, 64, 512, ▨

50. The Summer Olympic Games are held once every 4 years. The last two Summer Olympics were held in 2004 in Athens, and in 2008 in Beijing. Were Summer Olympics Games held in 1990? Explain your answer.

Extra Practice ... Chapter 2

LESSON 2-1

Evaluate each expression to find the missing values in the tables.

1.
y	23 + y
17	40
27	
37	

2.
w	w × 3 + 10
4	22
5	
6	

3.
x	x ÷ 8
40	5
48	
56	

LESSON 2-2

4. Earth has a diameter of 7,926 miles. Let d represent the diameter of the Moon, which is smaller than the diameter of Earth. Write an expression to show how much larger the diameter of Earth is than the diameter of the Moon.

Write each phrase as a numerical or algebraic expression.

5. the sum of 322 and 18
6. the product of 7 and 12
7. the quotient of n and 8
8. 14 more than x

Write two phrases for each expression.

9. (23)(6)   10. $52 - p$ 11. $y \div 4$ 12. $8 + 4$ 13. $13 \cdot m$

LESSON 2-3

Write an expression for the missing value in each table.

14.
Albert's Age	Ashley's Age
10	1
14	5
18	9
n	

15.
Hooves	Horses
16	4
12	3
8	2
n	

16. A parallelogram has a base of 4 inches. The table shows the area of the parallelogram for different heights. Write an expression that can be used to find the area of the parallelogram when its height is h inches.

Base (in.)	Height (in.)	Area (in²)
4	4	16
4	5	20
4	6	24
4	h	

Extra Practice ... Chapter 2

LESSON 2-4

Determine whether the given value of each variable is a solution.

17. $a + 15 = 34$, when $a = 17$ **18.** $t - 9 = 14$, when $t = 23$

19. Rachel says she is 5 feet tall. Her friend measured her height as 60 inches. Determine if these two measurements are equal.

LESSON 2-5

Solve each equation. Check your answers.

20. $r + 13 = 36$ **21.** $52 = 24 + n$ **22.** $6 + s = 10$

23. Towns A, B, and C are located along Main Road, as shown on the map. Town A is 34 miles from town C. Town B is 12 miles from town C. Find the distance d between town A and town B.

LESSON 2-6

Solve each equation. Check your answers.

24. $z - 9 = 5$ **25.** $v - 17 = 14$ **26.** $24 = w - 6$

27. Reggie withdrew $175 from his bank account to go shopping. After his withdrawal, there was $234 left in Reggie's account. How much money did Reggie have in his account before his withdrawal?

LESSON 2-7

Solve each equation. Check your answers.

28. $4y = 20$ **29.** $21 = 3t$ **30.** $72 = 9g$

31. The area of a rectangle is 54 in². Its width is 6 in. What is its length?

32. A squirrel can run 36 miles in 3 hours. Solve the equation $3m = 36$ to find the number of miles a squirrel can run in 1 hour.

LESSON 2-8

Solve each equation. Check your answers.

33. $\frac{n}{4} = 6$ **34.** $7 = \frac{t}{5}$ **35.** $\frac{a}{8} = 12$

36. Sydney likes to run and ride a bike for exercise. Each day, she runs for one-third the time that she rides her bike. Yesterday, Sydney ran for 15 minutes. How many minutes did she ride her bike?

Extra Practice ... Chapter 3

LESSON 3-1

Write each decimal in standard form, expanded form, and words.

1. 1.32
2. 0.6 + 0.003 + 0.0008
3. five and three thousandths

4. Joshua ran 1.45 miles, and Jasmine ran 1.5 miles. Who ran farther?

Order the decimals from least to greatest.

5. 3.89, 3.08, 3.8
6. 20.65, 20.09, 20.7
7. 0.053, 0.43, 0.340

LESSON 3-2

8. The femur is the upper leg bone, and the tibia is one of the lower leg bones. The average length of the femur is 50.5 cm, and the average length of the tibia is 43.03 cm. Estimate the total length of the leg if the bones were placed end to end.

Estimate by rounding to the indicated place value.

9. 5.856 − 1.3497; hundredths
10. 4.7609 + 7.2471; tenths

Estimate each product or quotient.

11. 20.84 ÷ 3.201
12. 31.02 × 4.91
13. 39.76 ÷ 7.94

Estimate a range for the sum.

14. 8.38 + 24.92 + 4.8
15. 38.27 + 2.99 + 15.32

LESSON 3-3

Find each sum or difference.

16. 1.65 + 4.53 + 3.2
17. 2.2 + 6.8
18. 7 − 0.6

Evaluate 6.35 − s for each value of s.

19. $s = 3.2$
20. $s = 2.108$
21. $s = 5.0421$

22. Brianna is shopping for school clothes and wants to purchase the following items: a shirt for $19.50, shoes for $35.00, a skirt for $12.39, socks for $6.99, and a pair of jeans for $19.95. Not including tax, how much money will Brianna need to purchase these items?

LESSON 3-4

Write each number in scientific notation.

23. 60,000
24. 423,800
25. 8,500,000

Write each number in standard form.

26. 5.632×10^5
27. 2.1×10^8
28. 1.425×10^4

Extra Practice ... Chapter 3

LESSON 3-5

Find each product.

29. 0.5×0.7 **30.** 0.3×0.06 **31.** 6.12×5.9

Evaluate $4x$ for each value of x.

32. $x = 2.071$ **33.** $x = 5.42$ **34.** $x = 7.85$

35. Each car tire costs $69.99. How much will 4 tires cost?

LESSON 3-6

Find each quotient.

36. $0.84 \div 6$ **37.** $11.07 \div 9$ **38.** $27.6 \div 12$

Evaluate $0.564 \div x$ for each given value of x.

39. $x = 4$ **40.** $x = 12$ **41.** $x = 2$

42. Marci pays $8.97 at the grocery store for 3 pounds of cherries. How much does each pound cost?

LESSON 3-7

Find each quotient.

43. $4.5 \div 0.9$ **44.** $59.7 \div 0.4$ **45.** $8.32 \div 8$

46. Lisa paid $13.41 for 4.5 pounds of ground chicken. How much did each pound cost?

LESSON 3-8

47. Jocelyn has 3.5 yards of ribbon. She needs 0.6 yards of ribbon to make one bow. How many bows can Jocelyn make?

48. Louie has a piece of wood that is 46.8 cm long. If he cuts the piece into 4 equal sections, how long will each section be?

LESSON 3-9

Solve each equation. Check your answer.

49. $b - 5.2 = 2.6$ **50.** $5t = 24.5$ **51.** $\frac{p}{3} = 1.8$

52. The area of a rectangle is 41 cm². Its length is 8.2 cm. What is its width?

53. The area of Henry's kitchen is 168 ft². The cost of tile is $4.62 per square foot. What is the total cost to tile the kitchen?

Extra Practice ... Chapter 4

LESSON 4-1

Tell whether each number is divisible by 2, 3, 4, 5, 6, 9, and 10.

1. 12,680
2. 174
3. 1,638
4. 735

Tell whether each number is prime or composite.

5. 97
6. 9
7. 111
8. 256

LESSON 4-2

List all of the factors of each number.

9. 28
10. 51
11. 70
12. 24

Write the prime factorization of each number.

13. 48
14. 72
15. 81
16. 150

LESSON 4-3

Find the GCF of each set of numbers.

17. 15 and 35
18. 16 and 40
19. 22 and 68
20. 6, 36, and 60
21. 27, 36, and 54
22. 14, 28, and 63

23. Alice has 42 red beads and 24 white beads. What is the greatest number of bracelets Alice can make if each bracelet has the same number of red beads and the same number of white beads and if every bead is used?

LESSON 4-4

Write each decimal as a fraction or mixed number.

24. 0.31
25. 1.9
26. 2.53
27. 0.07

Write each fraction or mixed number as a decimal.

28. $1\frac{7}{8}$
29. $\frac{5}{9}$
30. $6\frac{3}{5}$
31. $\frac{5}{6}$

Order the fractions and decimals from least to greatest.

32. $0.3, \frac{3}{5}, 0.53$
33. $0.8, 0.67, \frac{7}{8}$
34. $0.68, \frac{2}{3}, \frac{3}{4}$

LESSON 4-5

Find the missing numbers that make the fractions equivalent.

35. $\frac{4}{5} = \frac{\blacksquare}{20}$
36. $\frac{8}{12} = \frac{2}{\blacksquare}$
37. $\frac{6}{7} = \frac{\blacksquare}{28}$
38. $\frac{24}{3} = \frac{\blacksquare}{1}$

Write each fraction in simplest form.

39. $\frac{6}{10}$
40. $\frac{7}{9}$
41. $\frac{4}{16}$
42. $\frac{2}{6}$

Extra Practice ... Chapter 4

LESSON 4-6
Write each mixed number as an improper fraction.

43. $3\frac{1}{4}$
44. $6\frac{5}{7}$
45. $1\frac{2}{9}$
46. $2\frac{7}{10}$

47. Brett's favorite soup recipe calls for $\frac{14}{4}$ cups of chicken broth. Write $\frac{14}{4}$ as a mixed number.

LESSON 4-7
Compare. Write <, >, or =.

48. $\frac{2}{5}$ ■ $\frac{4}{5}$
49. $\frac{5}{6}$ ■ $\frac{7}{8}$
50. $\frac{1}{3}$ ■ $\frac{9}{27}$
51. $\frac{9}{15}$ ■ $\frac{2}{5}$

52. Natalie lives $\frac{1}{6}$ mile from school. Peter lives $\frac{3}{10}$ mile from school. Who lives closer to the school?

Order the fractions from least to greatest.

53. $\frac{3}{5}, \frac{5}{9}, \frac{4}{5}$
54. $\frac{1}{6}, \frac{3}{7}, \frac{1}{3}$
55. $\frac{1}{2}, \frac{5}{8}, \frac{7}{12}$

LESSON 4-8

56. Rose is filling a tub with water. The height of the water is increasing $\frac{1}{8}$ foot each minute. Use pictures to model how much the height of the water will change in 5 minutes, and then write your answer in simplest form.

Subtract. Write each answer in simplest form.

57. $1 - \frac{7}{9}$
58. $2\frac{5}{6} - 1\frac{1}{6}$
59. $5\frac{7}{10} - 3\frac{3}{10}$
60. $2 - \frac{3}{4}$

Evaluate each expression for $x = \frac{7}{12}$. Write each answer in simplest form.

61. $\frac{11}{12} - x$
62. $x + 1\frac{1}{12}$
63. $x - \frac{5}{12}$

LESSON 4-9
Estimate each sum or difference by rounding to 0, $\frac{1}{2}$, or 1.

64. $\frac{7}{8} + \frac{7}{15}$
65. $\frac{5}{6} + \frac{1}{11}$
66. $\frac{7}{12} - \frac{4}{9}$

Use the table for Exercises 67 and 68.

67. The table shows the number of hours each day that Michael worked. About how many hours did Michael work on Monday and Tuesday?

68. About how many more hours did he work on Thursday than on Friday?

Michael's Work Schedule	
Day	Hours Worked
Monday	$4\frac{5}{6}$
Tuesday	$5\frac{1}{4}$
Thursday	$6\frac{1}{10}$
Friday	$4\frac{5}{12}$

Extra Practice **EP9**

Extra Practice ... Chapter 5

LESSON 5-1

1. There are 18 girls on the dance team. Barrettes are sold in packs of 6. Ponytail holders are sold in packs of 2. What is the least number of packs they could buy so that each girl has a barrette and a ponytail holder and none are left over?

Find the least common multiple (LCM).

2. 9 and 15
3. 12 and 16
4. 10 and 12
5. 3, 4, and 5

LESSON 5-2

Add or subtract. Write each answer in simplest form.

6. $\frac{3}{5} + \frac{2}{3}$
7. $\frac{7}{8} - \frac{1}{6}$
8. $\frac{1}{3} + \frac{1}{2}$

9. About $\frac{1}{3}$ of the animals at the zoo are birds. The mammals make up $\frac{2}{5}$ of the zoo's population. What fraction of the zoo's animals are mammals or birds?

LESSON 5-3

Find each sum or difference. Write the answer in simplest form.

10. $18\frac{1}{3} + 16\frac{1}{6}$
11. $5\frac{3}{4} + 3\frac{5}{12}$
12. $12\frac{1}{2} - 8\frac{2}{5}$

13. Joan has a rottweiler and a Chihuahua. The rottweiler weighs $99\frac{1}{2}$ lb, and the Chihuahua weighs $3\frac{1}{4}$ lb. How much more does Joan's rottweiler weigh than her Chihuahua?

LESSON 5-4

Subtract. Write each answer in simplest form.

14. $4\frac{2}{5} - 2\frac{9}{10}$
15. $9\frac{1}{6} - 5\frac{5}{6}$
16. $6 - 1\frac{7}{12}$

17. Adam purchased a 10 lb bag of dog food. His dog ate $7\frac{1}{3}$ lb. of dog food in one week. How many pounds of dog food were left after one week?

LESSON 5-5

Solve each equation. Write the solution in simplest form.

18. $a + 5\frac{3}{10} = 9$
19. $1\frac{3}{8} = x - 2\frac{1}{4}$
20. $6\frac{5}{6} = t + 1\frac{2}{3}$

21. Taylor needs to change a lightbulb that is $12\frac{1}{3}$ feet above the floor. Without a ladder, Taylor can reach $6\frac{1}{2}$ feet. How tall must her ladder be in order for her to reach the lightbulb?

LESSON 5-6

Multiply. Write each answer in simplest form.

22. $2 \cdot \frac{1}{5}$
23. $3 \cdot \frac{1}{6}$
24. $2 \cdot \frac{2}{11}$

Extra Practice ... Chapter 5

25. There are 16 players on the baseball team. Of these players, $\frac{1}{4}$ are girls. How many girls play on the baseball team?

LESSON 5-7

Multiply. Write each answer in simplest form.

26. $\frac{1}{10} \cdot \frac{5}{6}$
27. $\frac{8}{9} \cdot \frac{3}{4}$
28. $\frac{5}{7} \cdot \frac{3}{10}$

Evaluate the expression $a \cdot \frac{1}{10}$ for each value of a. Write the answer in simplest form.

29. $a = \frac{4}{5}$
30. $a = \frac{2}{3}$
31. $a = \frac{5}{9}$

32. Camille spent $\frac{2}{5}$ of her weekly allowance on meals in restaurants. She spent $\frac{1}{2}$ of that money on pizza. What fraction of her weekly allowance did Camille spend on pizza?

LESSON 5-8

Multiply. Write each answer in simplest form.

33. $\frac{1}{4} \cdot 1\frac{2}{3}$
34. $2\frac{3}{5} \cdot \frac{1}{3}$
35. $\frac{7}{8} \cdot 1\frac{1}{3}$

Find each product. Write the answer in simplest form.

36. $1\frac{1}{3} \cdot 1\frac{3}{5}$
37. $4 \cdot 2\frac{6}{7}$
38. $\frac{2}{5}$ of $4\frac{1}{2}$

39. An art class has 18 students, and $\frac{1}{3}$ of the students are painting. How many of the students in the class are painting?

LESSON 5-9

Find the reciprocal.

40. $\frac{7}{9}$
41. $\frac{2}{13}$
42. $\frac{1}{12}$
43. $\frac{8}{5}$

Divide. Write each answer in simplest form.

44. $\frac{1}{6} \div 3$
45. $\frac{4}{7} \div 2$
46. $2\frac{1}{2} \div 1\frac{3}{4}$

47. Debbie bought $8\frac{1}{2}$ lb of ground turkey. She packed the turkey in $\frac{1}{2}$ lb containers and put them in the freezer. How many containers of ground turkey did she pack?

LESSON 5-10

Solve each equation. Write the answer in simplest form.

48. $\frac{3}{5}a = 12$
49. $6b = \frac{3}{7}$
50. $\frac{3}{8}x = 5$
51. $3s = \frac{7}{9}$
52. $\frac{5}{12}m = 3$
53. $\frac{9}{10}t = 6$

54. Joanie used $\frac{2}{3}$ of a box of invitations to invite friends to her birthday party. If she sent out 12 invitations, how many total invitations were in the box?

Extra Practice ... Chapter 6

LESSON 6-1

1. Each year a community holds a 5 km race. In 2004, 1,345 people participated in the race. In 2005, 1,415 people participated. In 2006, 1,532 people participated. In 2007, 1,607 people participated, and in 2008, 1,781 people participated. Use the data to make a table. Then use your table to describe how participation changed over time.

2. Make a table using the basketball data below. Then use your table to tell which player had the most points, rebounds, and assists.

   In 1,560 games, Kareem Abdul-Jabbar scored 38,387 points, grabbed 17,440 rebounds, and made 5,660 assists. In 897 games, Larry Bird scored 21,791 points, grabbed 8,974 rebounds, and made 5,695 assists. In 963 games, Bill Russell scored 14,522 points, grabbed 21,620 rebounds, and made 4,100 assists.

LESSON 6-2

Find the mean, median, mode, and range of each data set.

3.
Points Scored				
16	18	23	13	15

4.
Hours Worked							
37	42	43	38	39	40	45	40

LESSON 6-3

5. a. The table shows a student's test scores. Find the mean, median, and mode of the test scores.

Test Scores			
78	82	87	95

   b. On the next test the student scored a 92. Find the mean, median, and mode with the new test score.

6. The daily temperatures for the first eight days of April were 52 °F, 63 °F, 61°F, 54 °F, 52 °F, 55 °F, 68 °F, and 75°. What are the mean, median, and mode of this data set? Which one best describes the data set?

LESSON 6-4

Use the bar graph to answer each question.

7. Which type of vacation received the most votes?

8. Which types of vacations received more than 20 votes?

9. Use the data given below to make a bar graph.

Number of Days with Temperatures over 100°F			
June	3	August	14
July	5	September	7

EP12 Extra Practice

Extra Practice ... Chapter 6

LESSON 6-5

10. Use the data of students' heights to make a frequency table with intervals. Then use your frequency table to make a histogram.

Heights of Students (in.)							
63	58	48	60	60	65	56	57
56	62	61	58	59	55	64	50

11. Make a line plot of the data.

Number of Miles Biked																							
14	45	33	34	32	37	44	19	35	36	17	33	35	40	41	38	47	31	44	23	27	20	33	45	27

LESSON 6-6

Name the ordered pair for each location on the grid.

12. L 13. M 14. R

Graph and label each point on a coordinate grid.

15. $A(0, 3)$ 16. $B(5\frac{1}{2}, 3)$ 17. $C(2, 1\frac{1}{2})$

LESSON 6-7

18. Use the data in the table to make a double-line graph. Did toy sales increase or decrease for store A?

Toy Sales				
	January	March	May	July
Store A	$460	$580	$950	$1200
Store B	$520	$450	$880	$1250

LESSON 6-8

19. Explain why this bar graph is misleading.

20. What might people believe from the misleading graph?

LESSON 6-9

21. Use the data in the table to make a stem-and-leaf plot. Then use your stem-and-leaf plot to find the mean, median, and mode of the data.

Time Spent Doing Homework (min)				
15	35	60	65	15
10	35	60	20	35

LESSON 6-10

22. The table shows the shoe sizes of the female students in Mrs. Woodward's gym class. Which graph would be more appropriate to show the data—a stem-and-leaf plot or a line plot? Draw the more appropriate graph.

Shoe Sizes of Female Students															
7	8	$7\frac{1}{2}$	8	9	5	$9\frac{1}{2}$	7	$7\frac{1}{2}$	$7\frac{1}{2}$	$8\frac{1}{2}$	8	7	$6\frac{1}{2}$	7	8	10	9

Extra Practice EP13

Extra Practice ... Chapter 7

LESSON 7-1

Use the table to write each ratio.

1. cooking books to poetry books
2. biography books to total books
3. A pack of 12 pens costs $5.52. A pack of 8 pens costs $3.92. Which is the better deal?

Types of Books in Doug's Collection			
Reference	10	Comic	7
Mystery	8	Poetry	5
Biography	3	Cooking	4

LESSON 7-2

Use a table to find three equivalent ratios.

4. $\frac{2}{5}$
5. 5 to 12
6. 1:2
7. $\frac{6}{7}$

8. The table shows how many pizzas Travis Middle School orders for certain numbers of students. Predict the number of pizzas the school orders for 175 students.

Students	50	100	150	200	250
Pizzas	10	20	30	40	50

LESSON 7-3

Find the missing value in each proportion.

9. $\frac{5}{4} = \frac{n}{12}$
10. $\frac{2}{9} = \frac{4}{n}$
11. $\frac{6}{10} = \frac{n}{5}$
12. $\frac{7}{8} = \frac{21}{n}$

13. To make 2 quarts of punch, Jenny adds 16 grams of juice mix to 2 quarts of water. How much mix does Jenny need to make 3 quarts of punch?

LESSON 7-4

14. The two triangles are similar. Find the missing length y and the measure of ∠B.

LESSON 7-5

15. A telephone pole casts a shadow that is 32 yd long. At the same time, a yardstick casts a shadow that is 4 yd long. How tall is the telephone pole?

LESSON 7-6

Use the map to answer each question.

16. On the map, the distance from State College to Belmont is 2 cm. What is the actual distance between the two locations?

17. Henderson City is 83 miles from State College. How many centimeters apart should the two locations be placed on the map?

Scale: 1 cm:5 mi

Extra Practice ... Chapter 7

LESSON 7-7

Write each percent as a fraction in simplest form.

18. 50% **19.** 34% **20.** 8% **21.** 12%

22. Michael's baseball team won 85% of its games. Write 85% as a fraction in simplest form.

Write each percent as a decimal.

23. 13% **24.** 76% **25.** 5% **26.** 70%

27. At the toy store, sales increased by 26%. Write 26% as a decimal.

LESSON 7-8

Write each decimal as a percent.

28. 0.56 **29.** 0.092 **30.** 0.4 **31.** 0.735

Write each fraction as a percent.

32. $\frac{4}{5}$ **33.** $\frac{4}{25}$ **34.** $\frac{7}{16}$ **35.** $\frac{5}{8}$

36. In Mrs. Piper's class, $\frac{17}{20}$ of the students have a pet. What percent of the students in the class have pets?

LESSON 7-9

37. A theater sold a total of 570 tickets for a new movie. Of those tickets, 30% were children's tickets. How many children's tickets were sold?

38. Kathy has listened to 80% of the music on a CD. If 26 minutes have passed, how many more minutes of music are left on the CD?

39. Find 30% of 98.   **40.** Find 15% of 220.   **41.** Find 5% of 72.

LESSON 7-10

42. Ashley wants to buy a sweater regularly priced at $19.95. It is on sale for 25% off the regular price. About how much will she pay for the sweater after the discount?

43. Margo and her three friends went to dinner. The bill was $34.62. They left a tip that was 15% of the bill. About how much was the tip?

44. Patricia is buying new roller skates that cost $59.99. The sales tax rate is 7%. About how much will the total cost of the roller skates be?

Extra Practice ... Chapter 8

LESSON 8-1

Use the diagram to name each geometric figure.

1. three points
2. two lines
3. a point shared by two lines
4. a plane

Use the diagram to give a possible name to each figure.

5. three line segments
6. three ways to name the line
7. six rays
8. another name for ray XY

LESSON 8-2

Use a protractor to measure each angle. Classify each angle as acute, right, obtuse, or straight.

9.
10.
11.
12.

LESSON 8-3

Find each unknown angle measure.

13. 30°, a
14. 68°, b
15. 105°, c
16. 98°, d

LESSON 8-4

Classify each pair of lines.

17.
18.
19.
20.

EP16   *Extra Practice*

Extra Practice ... Chapter 8

LESSON 8-5

Use the diagram to find the measure of each indicated angle.

21. ∠FJH

22. ∠FJG

Classify each triangle using the given information.

23. The perimeter of the triangle is 14 in.

24. The perimeter of the triangle is 45 ft.

25. The perimeter of the triangle is 20 ft.

LESSON 8-6

Give the most descriptive name for each figure.

26. 27. 28. 29.

Complete the statement.

30. A parallelogram with four right angles can be a ___?___ or a ___?___.

31. A quadrilateral with exactly two parallel sides is a ___?___.

LESSON 8-7

Tell whether each shape is a polygon. If so, give its name and tell whether it appears to be regular or not regular.

32. 33. 34. 35.

LESSON 8-8

Identify a possible pattern. Use the pattern to draw the missing figure.

36. 37.

Extra Practice   EP17

Extra Practice ... Chapter 8

LESSON 8-9

Decide whether the figures in each pair are congruent. If not, explain.

38.

39.

LESSON 8-10

Tell whether each is a translation, rotation, or reflection.

40.

41.

42.

Draw each transformation.

43. Draw a translation 2 cm to the right.

44. Draw a 90° clockwise rotation about the point.

45. Draw a vertical reflection across the line.

LESSON 8-11

Determine whether each dashed line appears to be a line of symmetry.

46.

47.

48.

49.

Tell whether each figure has rotational symmetry.

50.

51.

52.

EP18 *Extra Practice*

Extra Practice ... Chapter 9

LESSON 9-1
What unit of measure provides the best estimate? Explain.

1. A book is about 12 ___?___ long.
2. A newborn baby weights about 8 ___?___ .
3. A small aquarium holds about 10 ___?___ of water.

LESSON 9-2
What unit of measure provides the best estimate? Explain.

4. An earthworm is about 10 ___?___ long.
5. A leaf has a mass of about 250 ___?___ .
6. The mass of a fork is about 40 ___?___ .

LESSON 9-3
Convert.

7. 156 in. = ▧ ft
8. 6 T = ▧ lb
9. 24 qt = ▧ gal
10. 13,200 ft = ▧ mi
11. 8 pt = ▧ qt
12. 33 yd = ▧ ft

13. A marathon is about 26.2 miles. How many feet long is a marathon?

LESSON 9-4

14. The height of a telephone pole is 15 meters. How many centimeters is this?

Convert.

15. A hat has a mass of about 86 g. 86 g = ▧ kg
16. A rain gauge holds about 0.5 L of water. 0.5 L = ▧ mL
17. 550 g = ▧ kg
18. 88 cm = ▧ mm
19. 1,585 m = ▧ km
20. 5,500 mg = ▧ g
21. 200 mL = ▧ L
22. 2.2 mL = ▧ L

LESSON 9-5

23. 1,095 days = ▧ yr
24. 4 min 23 s = ▧ s
25. 3 weeks = ▧ hr
26. 96 h = ▧ days
27. 78 weeks = ▧ yr
28. 1h 35 min = ▧ min

29. Rochelle's birthday party starts at 7:30 P.M. and lasts for 3 hours 45 minutes. What time does her party end?

Estimate the temperature.

30. 18° C is about ▧ ° F
31. 35° F is about ▧ ° C
32. 44° C is about ▧ ° F

Extra Practice **EP19**

Extra Practice ... Chapter 9

LESSON 9-6

Estimate the measure of ∠A in each figure. Then use a protractor to check the reasonableness of your answer.

33.

34.

35.

36. The shape of a swimming pool is shown. Find the measures of ∠A and ∠C.

LESSON 9-7

Find the perimeter of each figure.

37.

38.

Find the perimeter P of each rectangle.

39.   40.   41.

Find each unknown measure.

42. What is the value of b if the perimeter equals 82 cm?

43. What is the value of x if the perimeter equals 36?

LESSON 9-8

A carpenter is building a circular tabletop. Find the circumference by rounding π to 3.

44. What is the circumference if the diameter is 4 feet?

45. If the radius of the tabletop is 3 feet, what is its circumference?

Find each missing value to the nearest hundredth. Use 3.14 for π.

46. $C = ?$ $d = 2.8$ m

47. $r = ?$ $C = 145$ cm

EP20 Extra Practice

Extra Practice ... Chapter 10

LESSON 10-1

Find the area of each figure.

1. 7 m by 4 m rectangle
2. Parallelogram, height $1\frac{1}{4}$ cm, base $2\frac{1}{2}$ cm
3. Parallelogram, height 8.5 cm, base 13.2 cm

LESSON 10-2

Find the area of each triangle or trapezoid.

4. Triangle, height 5.5 cm, base 3 cm
5. Trapezoid, parallel sides 4 cm and 6 cm, height 2 cm
6. Triangle, legs 3 cm and 4 cm

7. A sailboat's sail is shaped like a triangle with a base of 6 feet and a height of 17 feet. What is the area of the sail?

LESSON 10-3

Find the area of each polygon.

8. Figure with dimensions 5 in., 2.5 in., 8 in., 2 in.
9. Figure with dimensions 9 ft, 15 ft, 17 ft

LESSON 10-4

10. Find how the perimeter and area of the figure change when the dimensions change.

    6 m by 9 m → 2 cm by 3 cm

LESSON 10-5

Estimate the area of each circle. Use 3 to approximate π.

11. Circle, 8 cm
12. Circle, 2.2 in.
13. Circle, 14.4 m

Find the area of each circle. Use $\frac{22}{7}$ for π.

14. Circle, 12 cm
15. Circle, 15 cm
16. Circle, 3 yd

17. A pie recipe calls for the crust to be rolled out to form a circle with a diameter of 9 in. Find the area of the dough when it is rolled out. Use 3.14 for π.

Extra Practice ... Chapter 10

LESSON 10-6

Identify the number of faces, edges, and vertices on each three-dimensional figure.

18. 19. 20.

LESSON 10-7

Find the volume of each prism.

21. 2 in., 16 in., 3 in.
22. 6.1 cm, 1.5 cm, 3.2 cm
23. 8.2 ft, 11 ft, 6 ft

LESSON 10-8

Find the volume V of each cylinder to the nearest cubic unit. Use 3.14 for π.

24. 3 cm, 8 cm
25. 10 ft, 7 ft
26. 6 in., 20 in.

27. A cylindrical rain gauge with a diameter of 2 inches is filled with rainwater to a height of 8.4 inches. Estimate the volume of the rainwater to the nearest cubic inch.

28. Find which cylinder has the greater volume. Use 3.14 for π.

   Cylinder A 8 cm, 15 cm
   Cylinder B 12 cm, 22 cm

LESSON 10-9

Find the surface area S of each three-dimensional figure. Use 3.14 for π.

29. 4 in., 5 in., 10 in.
30. 7 ft, 3 ft, 3 ft
31. 5 in., 12 in.

EP22 *Extra Practice*

Extra Practice ... Chapter 11

LESSON 11-1

Name a positive or negative number to represent each situation.

1. 120 feet below sea level
2. saving $22
3. a decrease of 5°

Graph each integer and its opposite on a number line.

4. +1
5. −5
6. −3
7. +2

Write the absolute value of each integer.

8. |−43|
9. |82|
10. |−153|
11. |39|

LESSON 11-2

Compare each pair of integers. Write < or >.

12. 15 ■ −19
13. −7 ■ −10
14. −3 ■ 7
15. −8 ■ 2

Order the integers in each set from least to greatest.

16. −6, 5, −2
17. 12, −25, 10
18. −1, −3, 4, 0

19. On Monday, the temperature was 3°C. On Tuesday, the temperature was −4°C. On Wednesday, the temperature was −1°C. On which day was the temperature the coldest?

LESSON 11-3

Name the quadrant where each point is located.

20. A
21. R
22. C
23. T

Give the coordinates of each point.

24. B
25. S
26. D
27. U

Graph each point on a coordinate plane.

28. M(2, −1)
29. W(−4, −2)
30. A(2, 3)

LESSON 11-4

Perform the given transformation of quadrilateral *ABCD*. Give the coordinates of each vertex in the image.

31. translate right 3 units
32. rotate 180° clockwise about the origin
33. reflect across the *y*-axis
34. translate down 2 units
35. rotate 270° counterclockwise about the origin
36. reflect across the *x*-axis

Extra Practice   EP23

Extra Practice ... Chapter 11

LESSON 11-5

Find each sum.

37. $14 + (-25)$ **38.** $-24 + 4$ **39.** $15 + (-14)$ **40.** $18 + (-1)$

Evaluate $y + 2$ for each value of y.

41. $y = -5$ **42.** $y = -1$ **43.** $y = 3$ **44.** $y = -8$

45. In the morning, the temperature was −3°C. By the afternoon, the temperature had risen 7°C. What was the temperature in the afternoon?

LESSON 11-6

Find each difference.

46. $-9 - 19$ **47.** $15 - (-20)$ **48.** $8 - 19$ **49.** $-20 - 20$

Evaluate $a - (-5)$ for each value of a.

50. $a = -6$ **51.** $a = 2$ **52.** $a = 1$ **53.** $a = -5$

54. Josh enters a cave at 0 feet above sea level and climbs to a height 40 feet above the entrance level. Then he descends 200 feet. At what depth is Josh now?

LESSON 11-7

Find each product.

55. $5 \cdot (-2)$ **56.** $-3 \cdot (-7)$ **57.** $-4 \cdot 4$ **58.** $8 \cdot (-9)$

Evaluate $3x$ for each value of x.

59. $x = -5$ **60.** $x = 8$ **61.** $x = -9$ **62.** $x = 0$

63. Mitchell missed 7 questions on a test. Each missed question was worth −2 points. What was the total number points he scored on missed questions?

LESSON 11-8

Find each quotient.

64. $20 \div (-4)$ **65.** $-48 \div (-6)$ **66.** $-24 \div 8$ **67.** $-18 \div (-2)$

Evaluate $\frac{n}{4}$ for each value of n.

68. $n = -36$ **69.** $n = 44$ **70.** $n = -12$ **71.** $n = -60$

72. The low temperatures for 5 consecutive days in January were −7 °F, −10 °F, 3 °F, 0 °F, and −6 °F. What was the average low temperature for these 5 days?

LESSON 11-9

Solve each equation. Check your answers.

73. $5 + y = 1$ **74.** $b - 8 = -6$ **75.** $-6 + m = -2$

76. $-6g = 30$ **77.** $-3c = -9$ **78.** $7r = -42$

79. A team of mountain climbers descended 4,000 feet to a camp that was at an altitude of 11,500 feet. At what altitude did they start?

Extra Practice ... Chapter 12

LESSON 12-1

Write *impossible*, *unlikely*, *as likely as not*, *likely*, or *certain* to describe each event.

1. picking a green marble from this bag of marbles

2. picking a red marble from this bag of marbles

3. The chance of winning a sweepstakes is 3%. Write this probability as a decimal and as a fraction.

4. A particular brand of cereal is offering a prize in each box. There is a 34% chance the toy will be a rubber ball, a 50% chance it will be a small figurine, and a 16% chance it will be a game. Is it more likely that the prize will be a rubber ball or a game?

LESSON 12-2

For each experiment, identify the outcome shown.

5.

6.

For one month, Maggie recorded the weather. She organized her results in a frequency table.

7. Find the experimental probability of cloudy weather.

8. Based on Maggie's findings, is it more likely that the weather will be cloudy or rainy?

Weather	Sunny	Cloudy	Rainy
Frequency	17	6	7

LESSON 12-3

9. Miguel is buying a new car. He has three choices for the exterior color: black, silver, or blue. He has two choices for the interior color: black or brown. What are the different color combinations Miguel can choose from?

10. For breakfast, Brianna can have oatmeal, cold cereal, or eggs and then a banana, an apple, or an orange. How many different breakfast combinations can Brianna choose from?

11. At summer camp, the campers can participate in 3 different activities each morning: hiking, swimming, and arts and crafts and 2 different activities each afternoon: tennis and biking. How many possible combinations of activities are there?

Extra Practice **EP25**

Extra Practice ... Chapter 12

LESSON 12-4

12. What is the probability of rolling an even number on a fair number cube?

13. What is the probability of randomly choosing the letter *T* from the letters *M, A, T, H, E, M, A, T, I, C, S*?

14. The weather report stated that there is a 42% chance of snow today. What is the probability that it will NOT snow?

15. During its grand opening, a store is giving away prizes. The chance of winning a prize is 0.16. Find the probability of NOT winning a prize.

LESSON 12-5

16. Find the probability of spinning red on the spinner and choosing a red marble from the bag.

17. Find the probability of spinning yellow and choosing a marble that is NOT yellow.

18. Find the probability of spinning a color that is NOT blue and choosing a marble that is NOT blue.

19. You toss two fair coins and roll a fair number cube. What is the probability that both coins will land heads up and the cube will show a number greater than 4?

LESSON 12-6

20. Based on a sample survey, a local newspaper stated that 26% of the population has a pet dog. Out of 600 people, how many people can you predict will have a pet dog?

21. If you roll a number cube 54 times, how many times do you expect to roll a number less than 3?

22. A promotion team is selling tickets for unreserved seats to a concert. The promotion team estimates that 75% of the people who purchase a ticket will attend the concert. If the stadium seats 15,000 people and the promotion team wants to have all of the seats full at the concert, how many concert tickets should they sell?

EP26 *Extra Practice*

Extra Practice ... Chapter 13

LESSON 13-1

Write an equation for a function that gives the values in each table. Use the equation to find the value of y for the indicated value of x.

1.
x	1	2	3	4	5	10
y	7	9	11	13	15	

2.
x	3	5	7	9	11	13
y	5	11	17	23	29	

Write an equation for the function. Tell what each variable you use represents.

3. The length of a rectangle is 4 cm less than 3 times its width.

4. Darren's age is 5 more than 2 times Nicole's age.

5. Madison has 13 more books than Staci.

6. The number of penguins at the zoo is 3 less than 7 times the number of giraffes.

LESSON 13-2

Use the given x-values to write solutions of each equation as ordered pairs.

7. $y = 6x + 2$ for $x = 1, 2, 3, 4$

8. $y = 5x - 9$ for $x = 2, 3, 4, 5$

Determine whether the ordered pair is a solution to the given equation.

9. $(2, 3)$; $y = x + 1$

10. $(9, 7)$; $y = 3x - 12$

11. $(0, 4)$; $y = 2x - 1$

12. $(1, 1)$; $y = x$

Graph the function described by each equation.

13. $y = 4x - 3$

14. $y = x + 1$

LESSON 13-3

Determine whether the rates of change are constant or variable.

15.
x	1	3	5	7	9
y	12	14	16	18	20

16.
x	5	8	9	13	17
y	0	3	4	8	12

17.
x	10	20	30	40	50
y	8	15	19	25	31

18.
x	28	26	18	16	8
y	35	33	25	23	15

19. Rico measured the amount of snow that fell during the day. The results are shown. Graph the points. Then find and interpret the slope.

Hour	1	2	3	4	5
Snow (in.)	1	4	7	10	13

Extra Practice ... Chapter 13

LESSON 13-4

Solve each equation.

20. $5x + 2 = 7$
21. $\frac{x+4}{3} = 7$
22. $3x - 5 = 1$
23. $\frac{x+8}{4} = 11$
24. $\frac{x-10}{2} = 13$
25. $2x - 7 = 11$
26. $\frac{x+15}{5} = 6$
27. $6x + 1 = 7$
28. $2x + 6 = 10$
29. $\frac{x+18}{9} = 2$
30. $3x + 5 = 11$
31. $\frac{x}{2} - 8 = 3$

32. Tiffany paid $45 to rent a canoe. The cost for renting the canoe was $12 per hour. Tiffany also had a coupon for $15 off the total cost. How many hours did Tiffany rent the canoe?

33. Barry measured a small tree to be 28.75 inches tall. If the tree continues to grow 2.5 inches each month, after how many months will the tree measure 84.5 centimeters tall?

LESSON 13-5

Graph the solutions to each inequality on a number line.

34. $f < 7$
35. $h \leq 2$
36. $a \leq 9$
37. $n > 4$
38. $b < 5$
39. $q \geq 6$
40. $3 < d$
41. $s > 1$

Solve each inequality. Graph the solutions on a number line.

42. $z + 3 \leq 4$
43. $3b \geq 12$
44. $x - 7 < 1$
45. $6g < 18$
46. $f + 8 > 13$
47. $\frac{v}{2} \leq 5$
48. $a - 6 \geq 0$
49. $\frac{s}{4} \geq 3$

50. Ms. Hu's science class is going on a field trip. They will be riding in vans that hold 8 people each. At least 28 students and 4 adults will be going on the trip. How many vans are needed to make the trip?

LESSON 13-6

Solve and graph each inequality.

51. $2x + 6 > 10$
52. $3x + 12 \leq 18$
53. $4x - 15 > 1$
54. $2x - 13 \leq 7$
55. $42x - 25 \geq 59$
56. $3x + 18 > 45$
57. $\frac{x+8}{5} < 6$
58. $\frac{x+35}{2} \leq 25$

Write an inequality to represent each situation. Solve the inequality.

59. Jenna makes and sells floral bouquets. She spends $25 on tools and equipment. If Jenna sells bouquets for $5 each, how many must she sell to make a profit of more than $80?

60. Brandon's three scores on a video game were 107, 210, and 176. What scores can Brandon earn on his fourth attempt to ensure an average of at least 175 points?

Draw a Diagram

When problems involve objects, distances, or places, you can **draw a diagram** to make the problem easier to understand. You will often be able to use your diagram to solve the problem.

Problem Solving Strategies

Draw a Diagram
Make a Model
Guess and Test
Work Backward
Find a Pattern
Make a Table
Solve a Simpler Problem
Use Logical Reasoning
Use a Venn Diagram
Make an Organized List

All city blocks in Sunnydale are the same size. Tina starts her paper route at the corner of two streets. She travels 8 blocks south, 13 blocks west, 8 blocks north, and 6 blocks east. How far is she from her starting point when she finishes her route?

Understand the Problem

Identify the important information.
- Each block is the same size.
- You are given Tina's route.

The answer will be the distance from her starting point.

Make a Plan

Use the information in the problem to **draw a diagram** showing Tina's route. Label her starting and ending points.

Solve

The diagram shows that at the end of Tina's route she is 13 − 6 blocks from her starting point.

13 − 6 = 7

When Tina finishes, she is 7 blocks from her starting point.

Look Back

Be sure that you have drawn your diagram correctly. Does it match the information given in the problem?

PRACTICE

1. Laurence drives a carpool to school every Monday. He starts at his house and travels 4 miles south to pick up two children. Then he drives 9 miles west to pick up two more children, and then he drives 4 miles north to pick up one more child. Finally, he drives 5 miles east to get to the school. How far does he have to travel to get back home?

2. The roots of a tree reach 12 feet into the ground. A kitten is stuck 5 feet from the top of the tree. From the treetop to the root bottom, the tree measures 32 feet. How far above the ground is the kitten?

Make a Model

If a problem involves objects, you can sometimes **make a model** using those objects or similar objects to act out the problem. This can help you understand the problem and find the solution.

Problem Solving Strategies

Draw a Diagram Make a Table
Make a Model Solve a Simpler Problem
Guess and Test Use Logical Reasoning
Work Backward Use a Venn Diagram
Find a Pattern Make an Organized List

Alice has three pieces of ribbon. Their lengths are 7 inches, 10 inches, and 12 inches. Alice does not have a ruler or scissors. How can she use these ribbons to measure a length of 15 inches?

Understand the Problem

Identify the important information.

- The ribbons are 7 inches, 10 inches, and 12 inches long.

The answer will show how to use the ribbons to measure 15 inches.

Make a Plan

Measure and cut three ribbons or strips of paper to **make a model.** One ribbon should be 7 inches long, one should be 10 inches long, and one should be 12 inches long. Try different combinations of the ribbons to form new lengths.

Solve

When you put any two ribbons together end to end, you can form lengths of 17, 19, and 22 inches. All of these are too long.

Try placing the 10-inch ribbon and the 12-inch ribbon end to end to make 22 inches. Now place the 7-inch ribbon above them. The remaining length that is **not** underneath the 7-inch ribbon will measure 15 inches.

Look Back

Use another strategy. Without using ribbon, you could have **guessed** different ways to add or subtract 7, 10, and 12. Then you could have **tested** to see if any of these gave an answer of 15:

$10 + 12 - 7 = 15$

PRACTICE

1. Find other lengths that you can measure with the three pieces of ribbon.

2. Andy stacks four cubes, one on top of the other, and paints the outside of the stack (not the bottom). How many faces of the cubes are painted?

Guess and Test

If you do not know how to solve a problem, you can always make a **guess**. Then **test** your guess using the information in the problem. Use the result to make a better guess. Repeat until you find the correct answer.

Problem Solving Strategies

Draw a Diagram
Make a Model
Guess and Test
Work Backward
Find a Pattern
Make a Table
Solve a Simpler Problem
Use Logical Reasoning
Use a Venn Diagram
Make an Organized List

There were 25 problems on a test. For each correct answer, 4 points were given. For each incorrect answer, 1 point was subtracted. Tania answered all 25 problems. Her score was 85. How many correct and incorrect answers did she have?

Understand the Problem

Identify the important information.

- There were 25 problems on the test.
- A correct answer received 4 points, and an incorrect answer lost 1 point.
- Tania answered all of the problems and her score was 85.

The answer will be the number of problems that Tania got correct and incorrect.

Make a Plan

Start with a **guess** for the number of correct answers. Then **test** to see whether the total score is 85.

Solve

Make a first guess of 20 correct answers.

Correct	Incorrect	Score	Result
20	5	$(20 \times 4) - (5 \times 1) = 80 - 5 = 75$	Too low—guess higher
23	2	$(23 \times 4) - (2 \times 1) = 92 - 2 = 90$	Too high—guess lower
22	3	$(22 \times 4) - (3 \times 1) = 88 - 3 = 85$	Correct ✓

Tania had 22 correct answers and 3 incorrect answers.

Look Back

Notice that the guesses made while solving this problem were not just "wild" guesses. Guessing and testing in an organized way will often lead you to the correct answer.

PRACTICE

1. The sum of Joe's age and his younger brother's age is 38. The difference between their ages is 8. How old are Joe and his brother?

2. Amy bought some used books for $4.95. She paid $0.50 each for some books and $0.35 each for the others. She bought fewer than 8 books at each price. How many books did Amy buy? How many cost $0.50?

Problem Solving Handbook

Work Backward

Some problems give you a sequence of information and ask you to find something that happened at the beginning. To solve a problem like this, you may want to start at the end of the problem and **work backward**.

Problem Solving Strategies

Draw a Diagram
Make a Model
Guess and Test
Work Backward
Find a Pattern
Make a Table
Solve a Simpler Problem
Use Logical Reasoning
Use a Venn Diagram
Make an Organized List

Jaclyn and her twin sister, Bailey, received money for their birthday. They used half of their money to buy a video game. Then they spent half of the money they had left on a pizza. Finally, they spent half of the remaining money to rent a movie. At the end of the day, they had $4.50. How much money did they have to start out with?

Understand the Problem

Identify the important information.

- The girls ended with $4.50.
- They spent half of their money at each of three stops.

The answer will be the amount of money they started with.

Make a Plan

Start with the amount you know the girls have left, $4.50, and **work backward** through the information given in the problem.

Solve

Jaclyn and Bailey had $4.50 at the end of the day.

They had twice that amount before renting a movie.   2 × $4.50 = $9

They had twice that amount before buying a pizza.   2 × $9 = $18

They had twice that amount before buying a video game. 2 × $18 = $36

The girls started with $36.

Look Back

Using the starting amount of $36, work from the beginning of the problem. Find the amount they spent at each location and see whether they are left with $4.50.

Start: $36
Video game: $36 ÷ 2 = $18
Pizza: $18 ÷ 2 = $9
Movie rental: $9 ÷ 2 = $4.50 ✓

PRACTICE

1. Chris is 5 years younger than Mark. Justin is half as old as Chris. Mary, who is 10, is 3 years younger than Justin. How old is Mark?

2. If you divide a mystery number by 4, add 8, and multiply by 3, you get 42. What is the mystery number?

Find a Pattern

In some problems, there is a relationship between different pieces of information. Examine this relationship and try to **find a pattern.** You can then use this pattern to find more information and the solution to the problem.

Problem Solving Strategies

Draw a Diagram Make a Table
Make a Model Solve a Simpler Problem
Guess and Test Use Logical Reasoning
Work Backward Use a Venn Diagram
Find a Pattern Make an Organized List

Students are using the pattern at right to build stairways for a model house. How many blocks are needed to build a stairway with seven steps?

Understand the Problem

The answer will be the total number of blocks in a stairway with seven steps.

Make a Plan

Try to **find a pattern** between the number of steps and the number of blocks needed.

The first step is one block. The second step is two blocks, the third step is three blocks, and the fourth step is four blocks.

Step	Number of Blocks in Step	Total Number of Blocks in Stairway
2	2	1 + 2 = 3
3	3	1 + 2 + 3 = 6
4	4	1 + 2 + 3 + 4 = 10

To find the total number of blocks, add the number of blocks in the first step, the second step, the third step, and so on.

Solve

The seventh step will be made of seven blocks. The total number of blocks will be $1 + 2 + 3 + 4 + 5 + 6 + 7 = 28$.

Look Back

Use another strategy. You can **draw a diagram** of a stairway with 7 steps. Count the number of blocks in your diagram. There are 28 blocks.

PRACTICE

1. A cereal company adds baseball cards to the 3rd box, the 6th box, the 11th box, the 18th box, and so on of each case of cereal. In a case of 40 boxes, how many boxes will have baseball cards?

2. Describe the pattern and find the missing numbers.

1; 4; 16; 64; 256; ▨; ▨; 16,384

Problem Solving Handbook   **PS5**

Make a Table

When you are given a lot of information in a problem, it may be helpful to organize that information. One way to organize information is to **make a table**.

Problem Solving Strategies

Draw a Diagram · **Make a Table**
Make a Model · Solve a Simpler Problem
Guess and Test · Use Logical Reasoning
Work Backward · Use a Venn Diagram
Find a Pattern · Make an Organized List

Mrs. Melo's students scored the following on their math test: 90, 80, 77, 78, 91, 92, 73, 62, 83, 79, 72, 85, 93, 84, 75, 68, 82, 94, 98, and 82. An A is given for 90 to 100 points, a B for 80 to 89 points, a C for 70 to 79 points, a D for 60 to 69 points, and an F for less than 60 points. Find the number of students who scored each letter grade.

Understand the Problem

Identify the important information.

- You have been given the list of scores and the letter grades that go with each score.

The answer will be the number of each letter grade.

Make a Plan

Make a table to organize the scores. Use the information in the problem to set up your table. Make one row for each letter grade.

Solve

Read through the list of scores. As you read each score, make a tally in the appropriate place in your table. There are 20 test scores, so be sure you have 20 tallies in all.

Letter Grade	Number
A (90–100)	۱۱۱۱۱ ۱
B (80–89)	۱۱۱۱۱ ۱
C (70–79)	۱۱۱۱۱ ۱
D (60–69)	۱۱
F (below 60)	

Mrs. Melo gave out six A's, six B's, six C's, two D's, and no F's.

Look Back

Use another strategy. Another way you could solve this problem is to **make an organized list.** Order the scores from least to greatest, and count how many scores are in each range.

62, 68, 72, 73, 75, 77, 78, 79, 80, 82, 82, 83, 84, 85, 90, 91, 92, 93, 94, 98
  D   C   B   A

PRACTICE

1. The debate club has 6 members. Each member will debate each of the other members exactly once. How many total debates will there be?

2. At the library, there are three story-telling sessions. Each one lasts 45 minutes, with 30 minutes between sessions. If the first session begins at 10:00 A.M., what time does the last session end?

Solve a Simpler Problem

Sometimes a problem contains large numbers or requires many steps. Try to **solve a simpler problem** that is similar. Solve the simpler problem first, and then try the same steps to solve the original problem.

Problem Solving Strategies

Draw a Diagram
Make a Model
Guess and Test
Work Backward
Find a Pattern
Make a Table
Solve a Simpler Problem
Use Logical Reasoning
Use a Venn Diagram
Make an Organized List

At the end of a soccer game, each player shakes hands with every player on the opposing team. How many handshakes are there at the end of a game between two teams that each have 20 players?

Understand the Problem

Identify the important information.

- There are 20 players on each team.
- Each player will shake hands with every player on the opposing team.

The answer will be the total number of handshakes exchanged.

Make a Plan

Solve a simpler problem. For example, suppose each team had just one player. Then there would only be one handshake between the two players. Expand the number of players to two and then three.

Solve

When there is 1 player, there is $1 \times 1 = 1$ handshake. For 2 players, there are $2 \times 2 = 4$ handshakes. And for 3 players, there are $3 \times 3 = 9$ handshakes.

Players Per Team	Diagram	Handshakes
1		1
2		4
3		9

If each team has 20 players, there will be $20 \times 20 = 400$ handshakes.

Look Back

If the pattern is correct, for 4 players there will be 16 handshakes and for 5 players there will be 25 handshakes. Complete the next two rows of the table to check these answers.

PRACTICE

1. Martha has 5 pairs of pants and 4 blouses that she can wear to school. How many different outfits can she make?

2. What is the smallest 5-digit number that can be divided by 50 with a remainder of 17?

Use Logical Reasoning

Sometimes a problem may provide clues and facts that you must use to answer a question. You can **use logical reasoning** to solve this kind of problem.

Problem Solving Strategies

Draw a Diagram
Make a Model
Guess and Test
Work Backward
Find a Pattern
Make a Table
Solve a Simpler Problem
Use Logical Reasoning
Use a Venn Diagram
Make an Organized List

Kevin, Ellie, and Jillian play three different sports. One person plays soccer, one likes to run track, and the other swims. Ellie is the sister of the swimmer. Kevin once went shopping with the swimmer and the track runner. Match each student with his or her sport.

Understand the Problem

Identify the important information.

- There are three people, and each person plays a different sport.
- Ellie is the sister of the swimmer.
- Kevin once went shopping with the swimmer and the track runner.

The answer will tell which student plays each sport.

Make a Plan

Start with clues given in the problem, and **use logical reasoning** to find the answer.

Solve

Make a table with a column for each sport and a row for each person. Work with the clues one at a time. Write "yes" in a box if the clue applies to that person. Write "no" if the clue does not apply.

	Soccer	Track	Swim
Kevin		no	no
Ellie			no
Jillian			

- Ellie is the sister of the swimmer, so she is not the swimmer.
- Kevin went shopping with the swimmer and the track runner. He is not the swimmer or the track runner.

So Kevin must be the soccer player, and Jillian must be the swimmer. This leaves Ellie as the track runner.

Look Back

Compare your answer to the clues in the problem. Make sure none of your conclusions conflict with the clues.

PRACTICE

1. Karin, Brent, and Lola each ordered a different slice of pizza: pepperoni, plain cheese, and ham-pineapple. Karin is allergic to pepperoni. Lola likes more than one topping. Which kind of pizza did each person order?

2. Leo, Jamal, and Kara are in fourth, fifth, and sixth grades. Kara is not in fourth grade. The sixth-grader is in chorus with Kara and has the same lunch time as Leo. Match the students with their grades.

Use a Venn Diagram

You can **use a Venn diagram** to display relationships among sets in a problem. Use ovals, circles, or other shapes to represent individual sets.

Problem Solving Strategies

Draw a Diagram
Make a Model
Guess and Test
Work Backward
Find a Pattern
Make a Table
Solve a Simpler Problem
Use Logical Reasoning
Use a Venn Diagram
Make an Organized List

Robert is taking a survey to see what kinds of pets students have. He found that 70 students have dogs, 45 have goldfish, and 60 have birds. Some students have two kinds of pets: 17 students have dogs and fish, 22 students have dogs and birds, and 15 students have birds and goldfish. Five students have all three kinds of pets. How many students in the survey have only birds?

Understand the Problem

List the important information.

- You know that 70 students have dogs, 45 have goldfish, and 60 have birds.

The answer will be the number of students who have only birds.

Make a Plan

Use a Venn diagram to show the sets of students who have dogs, students who have goldfish, and students who have birds.

Solve

Draw and label three overlapping circles. Work from the inside out. Write "5" in the area where all three circles overlap. This represents the number of students who have a dog, a goldfish, and a bird.

Use the information in the problem to fill in other sections of the diagram. You know that 60 students have birds, so the numbers within the bird circle will add to 60.

So 18 students have only pet birds.

Look Back

When your Venn diagram is complete, check it carefully against the information in the problem. Make sure your diagram agrees with the facts given.

PRACTICE

1. How many students have only dogs?

2. How many students have only goldfish?

Problem Solving Handbook PS9

Make an Organized List

In some problems, you will need to find how many different ways something can happen. It is often helpful to **make an organized list.** This will help you count the outcomes and be sure that you have included all of them.

Problem Solving Strategies

Draw a Diagram
Make a Model
Guess and Test
Work Backward
Find a Pattern
Make a Table
Solve a Simpler Problem
Use Logical Reasoning
Use a Venn Diagram
Make an Organized List

In a game at an amusement park, players throw 3 darts at a target to score points and win prizes. If each dart lands within the target area, how many different total scores are possible?

Understand the Problem

Identify the important information.
- A player throws three darts at the target.

The answer will be the number of different scores a player could earn.

Make a Plan

Make an organized list to determine all possible outcomes and score totals. List the value of each dart and the point total for all three darts.

Solve

You can organize your list by the number of darts that land in the center. All three darts could hit the center circle. Or, two darts could hit the center circle and the third could hit a different circle. One dart could hit the center circle, or no darts could hit the center circle.

3 Darts Hit Center	2 Darts Hit Center	1 Dart Hits Center	0 Darts Hit Center
10 + 10 + 10 = 30	10 + 10 + 5 = 25	10 + 5 + 5 = 20	5 + 5 + 5 = 15
	10 + 10 + 2 = 22	10 + 5 + 2 = 17	5 + 5 + 2 = 12
		10 + 2 + 2 = 14	5 + 2 + 2 = 9
			2 + 2 + 2 = 6

Count the different outcomes. There are 10 possible scores.

Look Back

You could have listed outcomes in random order, but because your list is organized, you can be sure that you have not missed any possibilities. Check to be sure that every score is different.

PRACTICE

1. A restaurant has three different kinds of pancakes: cinnamon, blueberry, and apple. If you order one of each kind, how many different ways can the three pancakes be stacked?

2. How many ways can you make change for a quarter using dimes, nickels, and pennies?

Skills Bank ...

Place Value—Trillions Through Thousandths

You can use a place-value chart to read and write numbers.

EXAMPLE

What is the place value of the digit 3 in 8,126,300,567.1?

The digit 3 is in the hundred-thousands place.

PRACTICE

Write the place value of the underlined digit.

1. 1<u>4</u>,536,992.1
2. 3<u>4</u>.071
3. 6,<u>1</u>90.05
4. <u>5</u>,027,549,757,202
5. 1<u>0</u>3.526
6. 3.7<u>2</u>1
7. <u>6</u>5,331,040,421
8. 75,983.00<u>9</u>

Compare and Order Whole Numbers

As you read a number line from left to right, the numbers are ordered from least to greatest.

You can use a number line and place value to compare whole numbers. Use the symbols > (is greater than) and < (is less than).

EXAMPLE

Compare. Write <, >, or =.

A 412 ▢ 418
418 is to the right of 412 on a number line.
412 < 418

B 415 ▢ 407
1 ten is greater than 0 tens.
415 > 407

PRACTICE

Compare. Write <, >, or =.

1. 419 ▢ 410
2. 9,161 ▢ 8,957
3. 5,036 ▢ 5,402
4. 617 ▢ 681
5. 700 ▢ 698
6. 1,611 ▢ 1,489

Round Whole Numbers and Decimals

You can use a number line or rounding rules to round whole numbers to the nearest 10, 100, 1,000, or 10,000.

EXAMPLE 1

Round 547 to the nearest 10.

Look at the number line.

```
      540 541 542 543 544 545 546 547 548 549 550
                                      ↑
                                     547
```

547 is closer to 550 than to 540. So 547 rounded to the nearest 10 is 550.

You can use rounding rules to round whole numbers and decimals to any place value.

ROUNDING RULES

If the digit to the right is 5 or greater, increase the digit in the rounding place by 1.

If the digit to the right is less than 5, keep the digit in the rounding place the same.

EXAMPLE 2

Round each number to the given place value.

A 12,573; thousands

12,573   *Find the digit in the thousands place.*
↑ Digit is 5 or greater. Add 1.   *Look at the digit to its right.*

12,573 rounded to the nearest 1,000 is 13,000.

B 5.16; whole number

1 < 5   So 5.16 rounds to 5.

C 13.45605; ten-thousandth

5 ≥ 5   So 13.45605 rounds to 13.4561.

PRACTICE

Round each number to the given place value.

1. 15,638; hundreds
2. 37,519; thousands
3. 9,298; tens
4. 69,504; ten thousands
5. 852; thousands
6. 33,449; hundreds
7. 3.982; tenth
8. 6.3174; hundredth
9. 1.471; whole number
10. 48.1526; hundredth
11. 5.03654; ten-thousandth
12. 0.083; tenth

Roman Numerals

Instead of using place value, as with the decimal system, combinations of letters are used to represent numbers in the Roman numeral system.

I = 1	V = 5	X = 10
L = 50	C = 100	D = 500
M = 1,000		

No letter can be written more than three times in a row. If a letter is written before a letter that represents a larger value, then subtract the first letter's value from the second letter's value.

EXAMPLE

Write each decimal number as a Roman numeral and each Roman numeral as a decimal number.

A 9
$9 = X - I = IX$

B CLV
$CLV = 100 + 50 + 5 = 155$

PRACTICE

Write each decimal number as a Roman numeral and each Roman numeral as a decimal number.

1. 12
2. 25
3. 209
4. 54
5. VIII
6. LXXII
7. XIX
8. MMIV

Addition

Addition is used to find the total of two or more quantities. The answer to an addition problem is called the *sum*.

EXAMPLE

4,617 + 5,682

Step 1: Add the ones.	**Step 2:** Add the tens.	**Step 3:** Add the hundreds. Regroup.	**Step 4:** Add the thousands.
4,617 + 5,682 9	4,617 + 5,682 99	1 4,617 + 5,682 299	1 4,617 + 5,682 10,299

The sum is 10,299.

PRACTICE

Find the sum.

1. 711 + 591
2. 2,580 + 2,345
3. 21,470 + 13,329
4. $165 + $304
5. 6,905 + 872
6. 47,231 + 3,254

Skills Bank **SB3**

Subtraction

Subtraction is used to take away one quantity from another quantity. The answer to a subtraction problem is called the *difference*.

EXAMPLE

780 − 468

Step 1: Regroup. Subtract the ones.	Step 2: Subtract the tens.	Step 3: Subtract the hundreds.
7 10 7 8̸ 0̸ − 4 6 8 ――― 2	7 10 7 8̸ 0̸ − 4 6 8 ――― 1 2	7 10 7 8̸ 0̸ − 4 6 8 ――― 3 1 2

The difference is 312.

PRACTICE

Find the difference.

1. 6,785 − 2,426
2. 3,000 − 1,930
3. 932 − 868
4. 41,003 − 22,500
5. $1,075 − $918
6. 12,035 − 640

Multiply Whole Numbers

Multiplication is used to combine groups of equal amounts. The answer to a multiplication problem is called the *product*.

EXAMPLE

105 × 214

Step 1: Think of 214 as 2 hundreds, 1 ten, and 4 ones. Multiply by 4 ones.	Step 2: Multiply by 1 ten, or 10.	Step 3: Multiply by 2 hundreds, or 200.	Step 4: Add the partial products.
2 105 × 214 ――― 420 ← 4 × 105	105 × 214 ――― 420 1050 ← 10 × 105	1 105 × 214 ――― 420 1050 21000 ← 200 × 105	105 × 214 ――― 420 1050 +21000 ――― 22,470

The product is 22,470.

PRACTICE

Find the product.

1. 350 × 112
2. 3,218 × 231
3. 187 × 136
4. 5,028 × 225
5. 642 × 428
6. 2,039 × 570

Divide Whole Numbers

Division is used to separate a quantity into equal groups. The answer to a division problem is known as the *quotient*.

EXAMPLE

$672 \div 16$

| Step 1: Write the first number inside the long division symbol and the second number to the left. Place the first digit of the quotient.

$16\overline{)672}$ 16 cannot go into 6, so try 67. | Step 2: Multiply 4 by 16, and place the product under 67.

4
$16\overline{)672}$ Subtract 64
-64 from 67.
3 | Step 3: Bring down the next digit of the dividend.

42
$16\overline{)672}$ Divide 32
$-64\downarrow$ by 16.
32
-32
0 |

The quotient is 42.

PRACTICE

Find the quotient.

1. $578 \div 34$
2. $736 \div 8$
3. $826 \div 118$
4. $945 \div 45$
5. $6,312 \div 263$
6. $5,989 \div 53$

Divide with Zeros in the Quotient

Sometimes when dividing, you need to use zeros in the quotient as placeholders.

EXAMPLE

$3,648 \div 12$

| Step 1: Divide 36 by 12 because 12 > 3.

3
$12\overline{)3,648}$ | Step 2: Place a zero in the quotient because 12 > 4.

30
$12\overline{)3,648}$
$-36\downarrow$
04 | Step 3: Bring down the 8.

304
$12\overline{)3,648}$
$-36\downarrow$
048
-48
0 |

The quotient is 304.

PRACTICE

Find the quotient.

1. $424 \div 4$
2. $5,796 \div 28$
3. $540 \div 18$
4. $7,380 \div 123$
5. $12,045 \div 3$
6. $10,626 \div 21$

Skills Bank **SB5**

Multiples

Multiples of a number can be found by multiplying the number by 1, 2, 3, and so on.

EXAMPLE

Find the first five multiples of 3.

$3 \cdot 1 = 3$	*Multiply 3 times 1.*	$3 \cdot 4 = 12$	*Multiply 3 times 4.*
$3 \cdot 2 = 6$	*Multiply 3 times 2.*	$3 \cdot 5 = 15$	*Multiply 3 times 5.*
$3 \cdot 3 = 9$	*Multiply 3 times 3.*		

The first five multiples of 3 are 3, 6, 9, 12, and 15.

PRACTICE

Find the first five multiples of each number.

1. 9   **2.** 10   **3.** 20   **4.** 15   **5.** 7   **6.** 18

Inverse Properties

Addition and multiplication follow some properties, or laws, such as the Commutative, Associative, and Distributive Properties. Knowing the inverse properties of addition and multiplication can help you evaluate expressions and solve equations.

Inverse Property of Addition	
The sum of any number and its opposite is 0.	$4 + (-4) = 0$

Inverse Property of Multiplication	
For any number except 0, the product of the number and its reciprocal is 1.	$3 \times \frac{1}{3} = 1$

EXAMPLE

Tell whether one of the inverse properties can be used to simplify the expression $3 - 4 + 4$. If so, tell which property.

$3 - 4 + 4$ *−4 and 4 are opposites.*

Yes, the Inverse Property of Addition can be used.

PRACTICE

Tell whether one of the inverse properties can be used to simplify the expression. If so, tell which property.

1. $5 \cdot 6 \cdot \frac{1}{5}$ **2.** $3(6 + (-6))$ **3.** $4 \cdot 3(-4)$

4. $2(6 - 4) + 3$ **5.** $\frac{1}{3}(2 + 1)$ **6.** $5 + 8 \cdot \frac{1}{5}$

Mental Math

You can use mental math to multiply by powers of ten.

EXAMPLE 1

4,000 × 100

> **Step 1:** Look for a basic fact using the nonzero part of the factors.
>
> $$4 \times 1 = 4$$
>
> **Step 2:** Add the number of zeros in the factors. Place that number of zeros in the product.
>
> $$4,000 \times 100 = 400,000$$

The product is 400,000.

You can use basic facts and place value to solve math problems mentally.

EXAMPLE 2

Solve mentally.

A 300 + 200

Basic fact: 3 + 2 = 5   *Think: 3 hundreds + 2 hundreds*
300 + 200 = 500

B 200 × 600

Basic fact: 2 × 6 = 12   *Think: There are four zeros in the factors,*
200 × 600 = 120,000   *so place four zeros in the product.*

PRACTICE

Multiply.

1. 600 × 100
2. 90 × 1,000
3. 2,000 × 10
4. 400 × 10
5. 10,000 × 1,000
6. 7,100 × 1,000

Solve mentally.

7. 500 + 400
8. 80 − 50
9. 700 × 30
10. 2,500 ÷ 50
11. 1,200 + 600
12. 20 × 9,000
13. 650 − 300
14. 320 ÷ 8
15. 90 × 90

Skills Bank **SB7**

Fractional Part of a Region

You can use fractions to name parts of a whole. The denominator tells how many equal parts are in the whole. The numerator tells how many of those parts are being considered.

EXAMPLE

Tell what fraction of each region is shaded.

A $\frac{1}{2}$

B $\frac{1}{3}$

C $\frac{3}{4}$

PRACTICE

Tell what fraction of each region is shaded.

1. 2. 3.

4. 5. 6.

Fractional Part of a Set

You can use fractions to name part of a set. The denominator tells how many items are in the set. The numerator tells how many of those items are being used.

EXAMPLE

Tell what fraction of each set are stars.

A 3 out of 10 shapes are stars.
$\frac{3}{10}$

B 5 out of 7 shapes are stars.
$\frac{5}{7}$

PRACTICE

Tell what fraction of each set is shaded.

1. 2. 3.

4. 5. 6.

Like Terms

Terms of an expression are the parts that are added or subtracted. A term can be a number, variable, or a product of numbers and variables. **Like terms** have the same variable raised to the same power.

Like terms often have different *coefficients*. A **coefficient** is a number multiplied by a variable. A variable written without a coefficient has a coefficient of 1. A number written with no variable is a constant. All constants are like terms.

$$x^2 - 2y + 3x + 4y + 5$$

Coefficients: $2y$, $3x$, $4y$
Constant: 5

You can combine like terms in an expression by adding their coefficients. An expression is said to be simplified if all like terms are combined.

EXAMPLES

Simplify each expression by combining like terms.

A $3x + 6x$

$(3x) + (6x)$ *Identify like terms.*
$9x$ *Add coefficients: 3 + 6 = 9.*

B $3a + 2b + a + 4b$

$(3a) + [2b] + (a) + [4b]$ *Identify like terms.*
$3a + a + 2b + 4b$ *Use the Commutative Property to group like terms.*
$4a + 6b$ *Add coefficients: 3 + 1 = 4, 2 + 4 = 6.*

C $6x + 5y + 3 - 4x + 5 - y$

$(6x) + [5y] + \triangle 3 - (4x) + \triangle 5 - [y]$ *Identify like terms.*
$6x - 4x + 5y - y + 3 + 5$ *Use the Commutative Property to group like terms.*
  Move the operation in front of each term with that term.
$2x + 4y + 8$ *Combine coefficients: 6 − 4 = 2, 5 − 1 = 4.*
  Combine constants: 3 + 5 = 8.

PRACTICE

Simplify each expression by combining like terms.

1. $5c + 2c$
2. $14d + 5 - 8d$
3. $18p + 3 - 8p - 5$
4. $5m - 15 - 20m + 5$
5. $6x - 12y + 14x + 20y$
6. $9u + 11v - 22u + 12v$
7. $5a + 11b + 5 - 2a - 5b + 6$
8. $16p + 5 + p - 3q + 6 - q$
9. $2u + v + 15u + 6v + 8 - v - 6$
10. $8x + y - 9x + 3z + 2x - 7y + z$

Solve Equations with Variables on Both Sides

You can solve equations with variables on both sides by first collecting the variables on one side of the equation and the constants on the other.

EXAMPLE

Solve each equation.

A $5x + 6 = 3x + 10$

Model the equation using algebra tiles.

You want x-tiles on only one side of the equation. Subtract three tiles from each side.

$2x + 6 = 10$

To isolate the x-tiles, subtract six 1-tiles from each side.

$2x = 4$

Divide the tiles on each side of the equation so that each x-tile is by itself.

$x = 2$

PRACTICE

Solve each equation.

1. $5x + 4 = 4x + 8$
2. $8x - 5 = 6x + 7$
3. $3x - 5 = -2x + 10$
4. $8x + 5 = 7x + 11$
5. $9x - 5 = 4x + 10$
6. $8x + 3 = 5x + 9$

The Pythagorean Theorem

The **legs** of a right triangle are the sides that form the right angle. The side opposite the right angle is the **hypotenuse**.

The Pythagorean Theorem states that the sum of the squares of the lengths of the legs is equal to the square of the length of the hypotenuse. That is, $a^2 + b^2 = c^2$.

EXAMPLE

Find the unknown length.

$$a^2 + b^2 = c^2$$
$$4^2 + b^2 = 5^2 \quad \text{Substitute 4 for a and 5 for c.}$$
$$16 + b^2 = 25 \quad \text{Simplify.}$$
$$-16 \qquad -16 \quad \text{Subtract 16 from both sides.}$$
$$b^2 = 9$$
$$\sqrt{b^2} = \sqrt{9} \quad \text{Find the positive square root of both sides.}$$
$$b = 3$$

PRACTICE

Find the unknown length.

1. (triangle with sides 13, 12, and b)
2. (triangle with sides 15, 9, and a)
3. (triangle with sides c, 12, and 16)

Sectors of Circles

A **sector** of a circle is enclosed by two radii and an arc connecting them. Given a circle of radius r and a central angle that measures $m°$, the area of the sector is $\frac{m}{360}\pi r^2$.

EXAMPLE

Find the area of the sector. Use 3.14 for π.

$$A = \frac{m}{360}\pi r^2$$
$$= \frac{90}{360} \cdot 3.14 \cdot 6^2 = 28.26 \quad \text{Substitute 90 for m and 6 for r.}$$

The area of the sector is 28.26 in^2.

PRACTICE

Find the area of each sector. Use 3.14 for π.

1. (sector: 90°, 2 cm)
2. (sector: 120°, 3 ft)
3. (sector: 60°, 12 m)

Exterior Angles of Polygons

An **interior angle** of a polygon is formed by two sides of the polygon. An **exterior angle** is formed by one side of the polygon and the extension of an adjacent side. In a triangle, each exterior angle has two *remote interior angles*. A **remote interior angle** is an interior angle that is not adjacent to the exterior angle.

The Exterior Angle Theorem states that the measure of an exterior angle of a triangle is equal to the sum of the measures of its remote interior angles.

$$m\angle 4 = m\angle 1 + m\angle 2$$

EXAMPLE 1

Find the value of *x*.

$x° + 63° = 120°$	*Use the Exterior Angle Theorem.*
$x + 63 = 120$	
$\underline{-63 \quad -63}$	*Subtract 63 from both sides.*
$x = 57$	

The Polygon Exterior Angle Sum Theorem states that the sum of the exterior angle measures, one angle at each vertex, of a convex polygon is 360°.

EXAMPLE 2

Find the value of *x*.

$x° + 30° + 75° + 80° + 55° = 360°$	*Use the Polygon Exterior Angle Sum Theorem.*
$x + 30 + 75 + 80 + 55 = 360$	
$x + 240 = 360$	*Simplify.*
$\underline{-240 \quad -240}$	*Subtract 240 from both sides.*
$x = 120$	

PRACTICE

Find the value of *x*.

1. (triangle with 65°, x°, 140°)
2. (triangle with 32°, 74°, x°)
3. (polygon with 110°, x°, 85°, 105°)
4. (polygon with x°, 70°, 78°, 72°, 66°)

Relationships Between Planes

Any two unique planes in space either intersect in a line or do not intersect at all. Two planes are parallel if they do not intersect. Two intersecting planes are perpendicular if the angle between them is a right angle.

Planes *A* and *B* are parallel.   Planes *C* and *D* are perpendicular.

EXAMPLE

In the diagram, identify all pairs of planes that appear to be parallel to each other, all pairs that appear to be perpendicular to each other, and all pairs that intersect but do not appear perpendicular to each other.

Planes *E* and *F* appear to be parallel to each other.
Planes *E* and *G* appear to be perpendicular to each other.
Planes *F* and *G* appear to be perpendicular to each other.

PRACTICE

In each diagram, identify all pairs of planes that appear to be parallel to each other, all pairs that appear to be perpendicular to each other, and all pairs that intersect but do not appear perpendicular to each other.

1.
2.
3.
4.

Skills Bank **SB13**

Compare Units

When converting area from one unit to another, you must remember that area is measured in square units.

1 ft × 1 ft square

$$1 \text{ square foot} = 1 \text{ foot} \times 1 \text{ foot}$$
$$= 12 \text{ inches} \times 12 \text{ inches}$$
$$= 144 \text{ square inches}$$

Customary Units for Area	
1 square foot (ft^2) = 144 square inches (in^2)	1 acre (a) = 4,840 square yards (yd^2)
1 square yard (yd^2) = 9 square feet (ft^2)	1 acre (a) = 43,560 square feet (ft^2)
1 square yard (yd^2) = 1,296 square inches (in^2)	1 square mile (mi^2) = 640 acres (a)

EXAMPLE 1

Which is the greater area, 3 yd^2 or 25 ft^2?

$3 \text{ yd}^2 = 3 \times 9 \text{ ft}^2 = 27 \text{ ft}^2$ *Think: 1 yd^2 = 9 ft^2*

$27 \text{ ft}^2 > 25 \text{ ft}^2$

$3 \text{ yd}^2 > 25 \text{ ft}^2$

Use the same principle to compare metric square units.

EXAMPLE 2

Which is the greater area, 5 km^2 or 5,000 m^2?

$5 \text{ km}^2 = 5 \times 1,000,000 \text{ m}^2 = 5,000,000 \text{ m}^2$ *Think: 1 km^2 = 1,000,000 m^2*

$5,000,000 \text{ m}^2 > 5,000 \text{ m}^2$

$5 \text{ km}^2 > 5,000 \text{ m}^2$

PRACTICE

Compare. Write <, >, or =.

1. 12,500 yd^2 ▓ 3 acres
2. 6 yd^2 ▓ 42 ft^2
3. 4 ft^2 ▓ 576 in^2
4. 5 yd^2 ▓ 6,500 in^2
5. 2.3 mi^2 ▓ 1,430 acres
6. 0.5 acre ▓ 21,700 ft^2
7. 30 cm^2 ▓ 3 m^2
8. 5 m^2 ▓ 75,000 cm^2
9. 6 km^2 ▓ 60 m^2
10. 100,000 cm^2 ▓ 1 km^2

Convert Between Measurement Systems

To convert between customary and metric units, you can use the following conversion factors.

Length	Mass	Capacity
1 in. = 2.54 cm	1 oz ≈ 28 g	1 fl oz ≈ 29.6 mL
1 mi. ≈ 1.6 km	1 lb ≈ 0.45 kg	1 qt ≈ 0.95 L

EXAMPLES

A How many kilometers are in 350 miles?

$350 \text{ mi} = \square \text{ km}$

$\dfrac{1 \text{ mi}}{1.6 \text{ km}} = \dfrac{350 \text{ mi}}{x \text{ km}}$ *1 mi ≈ 1.6 km. Write a proportion.*

$1 \cdot x = 1.6 \cdot 350$ *The cross products are equal.*

$x = 560$

$350 \text{ mi} \approx 560 \text{ km}$

B How many quarts does a 2-liter bottle of juice hold?

$2 \text{ L} = \square \text{ qt}$

$\dfrac{0.95 \text{ L}}{1 \text{ qt}} = \dfrac{2 \text{ L}}{x \text{ qt}}$ *1 qt ≈ 0.95 L. Write a proportion.*

$0.95 \cdot x = 1 \cdot 2$ *The cross products are equal.*

$0.95x = 2$

$\dfrac{0.95x}{0.95} = \dfrac{2}{0.95}$ *Divide both sides by 0.95 to undo the multiplication.*

$x = 2.11$

$2 \text{ L} \approx 2.11 \text{ qt}$

PRACTICE

Use the conversion factors in the table to answer each question.

1. How many grams are in 100 ounces?
2. How many kilograms are in 85 pounds?
3. How many fluid ounces are in 500 milliliters?
4. How many miles are in 30 kilometers?
5. How many centimeters are in 3 feet?
6. How many meters are in 5 miles?
7. How many quarts are in 285 liters?
8. How many kilometers are in 20 miles?

Measuring with Nonstandard Units

You can create your own units of measurement to approximate measures when you do not have standard measuring tools. You can measure distances like your stride, foot length, hand width, and finger width and use these units to estimate lengths.

Stride	Foot length	Hand width	Finger width
33 in.	10 in.	4 in.	$\frac{1}{2}$ in.

EXAMPLES

A The width of your desk is about 7 hand widths. Estimate the width of your desk in inches.

$$\frac{1 \text{ hand width}}{4 \text{ in.}} = \frac{7 \text{ hand widths}}{x \text{ in.}}$$ Set up a proportion to find the distance in inches.

$4 \times 7 = 1 \times x$ Find cross-products.

$28 = x$ Multiply.

The width of your desk is about 28 inches.

B The distance from your classroom to the library is about 24 strides. Estimate the distance from your classroom to the library in feet.

$$\frac{1 \text{ stride}}{33 \text{ in.}} = \frac{24 \text{ strides}}{x \text{ in.}}$$ Set up a proportion to find the distance in inches.

$24 \times 33 = 1 \times x$ Find cross-products.

$792 = x$ Multiply.

$792 \text{ in.} \times \frac{1 \text{ ft}}{12 \text{ in.}}$ Use a conversion factor.

66 ft

It is about 66 feet from your classroom to the library.

PRACTICE

Measure your stride, foot length, hand width, and finger width. Choose an appropriate unit for each object, and give an approximate measure for each object.

1. Width of a classroom
2. Diameter of a CD
3. Height of a classroom door
4. Height of a desk
5. Width of your textbook
6. Length of an unsharpened pencil

Significant Figures

Significant figures are the digits in a measurement that are known with certainty. When given a number, the significant figures are identified as follows:
- Nonzero digits
- Zeros at the end of a number and to the right of the decimal point
- Zeros between significant figures

Number	Significant Figures	Reasoning
230	two	The zero at the end of the number is not a significant figure because it is not to the right of the decimal point.
230.0	four	The zero at the end of the number is significant because it is to the right of the decimal point. The first zero is between significant figures.

When adding or subtracting, find the number with the least number of *digits* to the right of the decimal point. Round your answer so that it has the same number of digits to the right of the decimal.

When multiplying or dividing, find the number with the least number of *significant figures*. Round your answer so that it has that number of significant figures.

EXAMPLES

Write each answer with the appropriate number of significant figures.

A $25.3 - 7.12$

$$\begin{array}{r} 25.3 \\ -\ 7.12 \\ \hline 18.18 \end{array}$$

← 1 digit after the decimal
← 2 digits after the decimal

18.2 ← Round the difference to have one digit to the right of the decimal.

B 1.1×0.2

$$\begin{array}{r} 1.1 \\ \times\ 0.2 \\ \hline 0.22 \end{array}$$

← 2 significant figures
← 1 significant figure

0.2 ← Round the product to 1 significant figure.

PRACTICE

Determine the number of significant figures in each decimal.

1. 240
2. 0.0065
3. 210.00

Write each answer with the appropriate number of significant figures.

4. $2.3 + 2.46$
5. $12.3 - 2.54$
6. $110.5 + 10.34$
7. $22.30 - 2.04$
8. 2.5×0.4
9. $1.25 \div 0.05$
10. $4.2 \div 0.70$
11. 10×0.024
12. 4.2×0.040

Box-and-Whisker Plots

A **box-and-whisker plot** shows the distribution of data. You need five values to make a box-and-whisker plot.
- The **minimum** is the least value of the data.
- The **maximum** is the greatest value of the data.
- The **median** is the middle value of the data or the mean of the two middle values.
- The **lower quartile** is the median of the lower half of the data.
- The **upper quartile** is the median of the upper half of the data.

EXAMPLE

Use the data to make a box-and-whisker plot.

58, 60, 47, 56, 32, 78, 44, 72, 42, 35, 66

Order from least to greatest.	32, 35, 42, 44, 47, 56, 58, 60, 66, 72, 78
Find the minimum.	**32**, 35, 42, 44, 47, 56, 58, 60, 66, 72, 78
Find the maximum.	32, 35, 42, 44, 47, 56, 58, 60, 66, 72, **78**
Find the median.	32, 35, 42, 44, 47, **56**, 58, 60, 66, 72, 78
Find the lower quartile.	32, 35, **42**, 44, 47, 56, 58, 60, 66, 72, 78
Find the upper quartile.	32, 35, 42, 44, 47, 56, 58, 60, **66**, 72, 78

Step 1: Place a dot at the median, upper quartile, and lower quartile. Make a box connecting these points.

Step 2: Place a dot at the minimum and maximum.

Step 3: Connect the minimum and the maximum to the box with segments called whiskers.

PRACTICE

Use the data to make a box-and-whisker plot.

1. 8, 6, 5, 4, 12, 9, 2
2. 56, 61, 45, 55, 63, 59, 46
3. 28, 12, 35, 22, 13, 33, 33, 17, 18, 22, 25
4. 78, 85, 68, 57, 72, 63, 79, 60, 66, 52, 78

Sampling and Bias

A **population** is a group about which someone is gathering information.

A **sample** is part of a population. For example, if 6 students are chosen to represent a class of 24 students, the 6 students are a sample of the population of 24 students.

A sample is **random** if every member of the population has an equal chance of being chosen.

Bias is error that favors part of a population and/or does not accurately represent the population. Bias can occur from using a sample that is not random or from asking confusing or leading questions.

EXAMPLE

A Terence wants to know what students in his class think about the test they took. He asks all the students who sit in the back row. Explain whether the sample is random.

Since he selected only the students in the back row, other students did not have a chance to be selected. The sample is not random.

B Explain whether the following question is biased. "Do you think the corrupt mayor should be thrown out of office?"

The question is biased because it states that the mayor is corrupt, which leads people to believe that he should be thrown out of office.

C Janine wanted to know if students supported the current budget that moved funds from the athletic department to the arts department. She surveyed students on the baseball team. Explain whether the survey is biased.

The survey is biased because it samples students on the baseball team and they are not likely to want funds to be moved.

PRACTICE

Explain whether each sample is random.

1. To complete his survey, Paul placed the names of all students in his class in a hat. Then, without looking, he drew names out of the hat.
2. Dena got a list of the names and phone numbers of every senior at her school. The list was organized in alphabetical order. She surveyed the first 50 students on the list who responded to her call.

Explain whether each question is biased.

3. "Do you support the building of the new baseball stadium?"
4. "Do you support the new factory that will bring hundreds of new jobs to the community?"

5. Explain whether the survey is biased: To find out whether their customers will shop online, a store sent a survey to all shoppers on its email list.

Effects of Sample Size on Probability

Theoretical probability is a ratio of the number of ways an event can occur to the number of equally likely outcomes possible. Experimental probability is a ratio of the number of times an event does occur to the number of times an activity is performed.

As the number of trials increases, the experimental probability should get very close to the theoretical probability.

EXAMPLE

John, Sara, and Marcus flipped a coin a given number of times and recorded the results. Find the probability that the coin lands heads up in each experiment. Find the theoretical probability and compare the experimental probability to the theoretical probability.

John

Heads	14
Tails	6

Total 20

$P = \frac{14}{20} = 70\%$

Sara

Heads	22
Tails	28

Total 50

$P = \frac{22}{50} = 44\%$

Marcus

Heads	48
Tails	52

Total 100

$P = \frac{48}{100} = 48\%$

Theoretical Probability $= \frac{1}{2} = 50\%$

When more trials are performed, the experimental probability gets closer to 50%.

PRACTICE

Use the table for 1–2.

1. Color a sheet of white paper with a 10 × 10 grid as described in the table. (Each square of the grid should be large enough for a penny to fit within the square.)

2. Drop a penny onto the grid 20 times and record the color it lands on.

    a. Find the experimental probability of the penny landing on each color.
    b. Find the theoretical probability of the penny landing on each color.
    c. Compare the experimental probabilities from **a** with the theoretical probabilities from **b**.

Color	Number of Squares
Red	15
Blue	9
Green	16
Purple	5
Yellow	25

3. Combine your results with those of several classmates. Compare the experimental probabilities from the combined data to the theoretical probabilities. Explain how increasing the number of trials affected the experimental probabilities with respect to the theoretical probability.

Formulas

Volume*

Prism	$V = Bh$
Rectangular Prism	$V = Bh$ or $V = \ell wh$
Cylinder	$V = Bh$ or $V = \pi r^2 h$
Pyramid	$V = \frac{1}{3}Bh$
Cone	$V = \frac{1}{3}Bh$ or $V = \frac{1}{3}\pi r^2 h$

Surface Area*

Prism	$S = 2B + L$ or $S = 2B + Ph$
Cylinder	$S = 2B + L$ or $S = 2\pi r^2 + 2\pi rh$
Regular Pyramid	$S = B + L$ or $S = B + \frac{1}{2}P\ell$
Cone	$S = B + L$ or $S = \pi r^2 + \pi r \ell$

*B represents the area of the base of a solid figure.

Temperature

Celsius (°C)	$C = \frac{5}{9}(F - 32)$
Fahrenheit (°F)	$F = \frac{9}{5}C + 32$

Other

Diameter	$d = 2r$
Simple Interest	$I = Prt$
Pythagorean Theorem	$a^2 + b^2 = c^2$

Selected Answers

Chapter 1

1-1 Exercises

1. 7,000 3. 1,500 bottles of water
5. about 2 gallons 7. 40,000
9. 20,000 11. 40 golf balls 13. 500
15. 0 17. 11,000 19. 40,000
21. 70,000 23. 400,000 25. 10 square miles 27. 40,000 square miles 33. 400; 36 rounds to 40, and 8 rounds to 10 35. 2,615
37. 2,496 39. $1,000 + 300 + 50 + 4$
41. $400,000 + 10,000 + 6,000 + 700 + 3$

1-2 Exercises

1. 8^3 3. 6^5 5. 5^5 7. 16 9. 625
11. 343 13. 2^6 15. 8^2 17. 6^5
19. 7^7 21. 4^2 23. 243 25. 81
27. 512 29. 256 31. 144
33. $16 \times 16 \times 16$ 35. $31 \times 31 \times 31 \times 31 \times 31 \times 31$ 37. $50 \times 50 \times 50$
39. $1 \times 1 \times 1 \times 1 \times 1 \times 1 \times 1 \times 1 \times 1$ 41. $8 \times 8 \times 8 \times 8 \times 8$
43. 1,000,000 45. 6,651
47. 100,000 49. 512 51. 125
53. > 55. < 57. > 59. 1,024 cells 61. 8; 2^8, or 256 65. D
67. 8,245; 8,452; 8,732 69. 11,901; 12,681; 12,751 71. 50,000

1-3 Exercises

1. 33 3. 50 5. 4 7. $138 9. 10
11. 32 13. 14 15. 25 17. 40
19. 24 21. 1,250 pages 23. 18
25. 57 27. 1 29. 22 31. 64 33. 22
35. $(7 + 2) \times 6 - (4 - 3) = 53$
37. $5^2 - 10 + (5 + 4^2) = 36$
39. $9^2 - 2 \times (15 + 16) - 8 = 11$
41. $4^2 \times (3 - 2) \div 4 = 4$ 43. 30 m²
45. 300 m³ 49. J 51. 3,273
53. 70,007 55. 125 57. 256

1-4 Exercises

1. 40 3. 50 5. 320 7. 120 9. 156
11. 99 13. 108 15. 40 17. 50
19. 640 21. 108 23. 426 25. 138
27. 372 29. 328 31. 40 33. 60
35. 198 37. 111 39. 70 41. 70°F
43. 153 45. 198 51. 108 eggs
53. $208 59. 2,718 mi
61. 1,367,000 63. 62 65. 56

1-5 Exercises

1. paper and pencil; 364
3. calculator; 64,890 5. mental math; middle row 7. 111
9. 515,844 11. 210 13. 350
19. 936; $13 \cdot 3 = 39$; $39 \cdot 24 = 936$
21. 30 23. 12 25. Distributive Property 26. Commutative Property

1-6 Exercises

1. add 12; 60; 72; 84 3. add 11; 51; 62 5. add 7 and subtract 2; 12; 19
7. multiply by 6 and divide by 2; 9; 162 9. subtract 14; 28; 14; 0
11. add 3; 20; 23 13. add 21 and subtract 4; 41; 62; 58 15. divide by 4 and multiply by 2; 100; 25
17. 5, 14, 23, 32, 41 19a. 2018
b. 1994 c. yes; $2006 + 2(12) = 2030$ 21. subtract 4 and add 5
27. A 29. 60 31. 120

Chapter 1 Study Guide: Review

1. sequence, term 2. base, exponent 3. order of operations
4. simplify 5. 1,000 6. 6,000
7. 20,000 8. 800 9. 5^3 10. 3^5
11. 7^4 12. 8^2 13. 4^4 14. 1^3
15. 256 16. 16 17. 216 18. 27
19. 1 20. 2,401 21. 125 22. 100
23. 81 24. 59 25. 11 26. 26
27. 17 28. 5 29. 45 30. $149
31. 30 32. 520 33. 80 34. 1,080
35. 40 36. 320 37. 168 38. 135
39. 204 40. 152 41. 62°
42. Possible answer: You can use the Distributive Property to break up 14 and then use mental math; $(10 \times 5) + (4 \times 5) = 70$. 43. Possible answer: Since the numbers are so big, it is best to use a calculator; $\$8,951,056,150,180.66 \div 302,634,238 = \$29,577.14$.
44. Possible answer: Since the numbers are easy, you can use mental math; 69 °F − 41 °F = 28 °F. 45. Add 5; 24, 29.
46. Subtract 2; 13, 11. 47. Add 4 and subtract 2; 20, 22.
48. Multiply by 3; 81, 243.
49. Add 5 and subtract 2; 71, 74.

Chapter 2

2-1 Exercises

1. 56; 65 3. 24; 28; 32; 36
5. 23; 25 7a. 2 hr: 100 − 120 miles; 3 hr: 150 − 180 miles; 4 hr: 200 − 240 miles; 5 hr: 250 − 300 miles b. between 350 and 420 miles 9. 32° F; 50° F; 77° F 11. 32
13. 13 15. 8 17. 56 19. 10
21. 110 23. 24 zlotys 29. 38
31. 5^6 33. $919

2-2 Exercises

1. $4,028 − m$ 3. $15x$ 5. $\frac{p}{5}$
7. $(149)(2)$ 9. the product of 345 and 196; 345 times 196 11. the difference of d and 5; 5 less than d
13. $5x$ 15. $325 \div 25$ 17. $137 + 675$
19. $j − 14$ 21. take away 19 from 243; 243 minus 19 23. 342 multiplied by 75; the product of 342 and 75 25. the product of 45 and 23; 45 times 23 27. the difference of 228 and b; b less than 228 29. $15 \div d$ 31. $67m$
33. $678 − 319$ 37. $d \div 4$ 41. C
43. 360 45. 360 47. 8 49. 16

2-3 Exercises

1. $4n$ **3.** $5w$ **5.** $7n$ **7.** s^2 **9.** $n + 5$
11. $88n$ **13.** $n + 7$; $3n + 1$ **17.** G
19. 29 **21.** 21 **23.** 245 **25.** 126

2-4 Exercises

1. no **3.** yes **5.** yes **7.** 53 feet is equal to 636 inches. **9.** no **11.** yes
13. no **15.** yes **17.** no **19.** yes
21. 300 m is equal to 30,000 cm.
23. yes **25.** no **27.** no **29.** yes
31. no **33.** yes **35.** $17 \neq 350 \div 20$; no, they do not have the same amount of money. **37.** 6 **39.** 2
41. 3 **47.** H **49.** 9^4 **51.** 8^2

2-5 Exercises

1. $x = 36$ **3.** $n = 19$ **5.** $p = 18$
7. 6 blocks **9.** $r = 7$ **11.** $b = 25$
13. $z = 9$ **15.** $g = 16$ **17.** 6 meters
19. $n = 7$ **21.** $y = 19$ **23.** $h = 78$
25. $b = 69$ **27.** $t = 26$ **29.** $m = 22$
31. $p + 20 = 36$ **33.** 880 m **37.** B
39. 648; 798; 923 **41.** 1,036; 1,498; 2,163 **43.** 9, 7, 5

2-6 Exercises

1. $p = 17$ **3.** $a = 31$ **5.** $n = 33$
7. $y = 25$ **9.** $a = 38$ **11.** $a = 97$
13. $p = 33$ **15.** $s = 31$ **17.** $x = 36$
19. $a = 21$ **21.** $f = 14$ **23.** $r = 154$
25. $g = 143$ **27.** $m = 18$
29. 13 million **33.** D **35.** 71
37. 22 **39.** $y = 38$ **41.** $b = 56$

2-7 Exercises

1. $x = 3$ **3.** $a = 9$ **5.** $c = 11$
7. 45 feet **9.** $a = 4$ **11.** $x = 4$
13. $t = 7$ **15.** $m = 11$ **17.** 6 feet
19. $y = 9$ **21.** $y = 8$ **23.** $y = 20$
25. $z = 40$ **27.** $y = 23$ **29.** $y = 18$
31. $y = 8$ **33.** $a = 14$ **35.** $x = 3$
37. $t = 6$ **39.** 15 to 177 segments
41. 4,000 light-sensitive cells **45.** C
47. 7,000 **49.** $b = 42$ **51.** $n = 212$

2-8 Exercises

1. $y = 12$ **3.** $r = 63$ **5.** $j = 36$
7. $f = 60$ **9.** 90 min **11.** $c = 26$
13. $g = 98$ **15.** $x = 144$ **17.** $r = 81$
19. $c = 96$ **21.** $c = 165$ **23.** $c = 70$
25. $c = 60$ **27.** $\frac{w}{381} = 76$; $w = 28{,}956$ m **33.** J **35.** Add 5; 25, 30, 35 **37.** $r = 13$ **39.** $p = 9$

Chapter 2 Study Guide: Review

1. algebraic expression
2. equation **3.** variable
4. 7, 6 **5.** 6, 10 **6.** 9, 18, 27, 36
7. 30, 33, 36, 39 **8.** 75, 80, 85, 90
9. $15 + b$ **10.** 6×5 **11.** $9t$
12. $g \div 9$ **13.** the product of 4 and z; 4 times z **14.** 15 plus x; the sum of 15 and x **15.** 54 divided by 6; the quotient of 54 and 6
16. m divided by 20; the quotient of m and 20 **17.** 3 minus y; the difference of 3 and y **18.** the sum of 5,100 and 64; 64 added to 5,100
19. y minus 3; the difference of y and 3 **20.** g minus 20; the difference of g and 20 **21.** $3n + 1$
22. $n - 1$ **23.** yes **24.** no **25.** yes
26. yes **27.** $x = 6$ **28.** $n = 14$
29. $c = 29$ **30.** $y = 6$ **31.** $p = 27$
32. $w = 9$ **33.** 67 channels
34. $k = 45$ **35.** $d = 9$ **36.** $p = 63$
37. $n = 67$ **38.** $r = 14$ **39.** $w = 144$
40. 31 sports **41.** $v = 8$ **42.** $y = 9$
43. $c = 7$ **44.** $n = 2$ **45.** $s = 8$
46. $t = 10$ **47.** 50 pounds
48. $r = 42$ **49.** $t = 15$ **50.** $y = 18$
51. $n = 72$ **52.** $z = 52$
53. $b = 100$

Chapter 3

3-1 Exercises

1. $1 + 0.9 + 0.08$; one and ninety-eight hundredths
3. 0.0765; seven hundred sixty-five ten-thousandths **5.** Osmium
7. 4.09, 4.1, 4.18 **9.** $7 + 0.08 + 0.009 + 0.0003$; seven and eight hundred ninety-three ten-thousandths **11.** 7.15; $7 + 0.1 + 0.05$ **13.** the Chupaderos meteorite **15.** 1.5, 1.56, 1.62
17. nine and seven thousandths
19. ten and twenty-two thousandths **21.** one hundred forty-two and six thousand five hundred forty-one ten-thousandths **23.** ninety-two thousand, seven hundred fifty-five hundred thousandths **25.** <
27. < **29.** < **31.** three hundredths **33.** one tenth
35. 4.034, 1.43, 1.424, 1.043, 0.34
37. 652.12, 65.213, 65.135, 61.53
39. Ross 154 **41.** Alpha Centauri, Proxima Centauri **45.** C
47. 9,000 **49.** $n = 123$ **51.** $c = 52$

3-2 Exercises

1. about 12 miles **3.** 12 **5.** 5.4988
7. 120 **9.** from 44 to 46.5
11. about 450 miles **13.** 3.4
15. 5.157 **17.** 20 **19.** 6 **21.** from 14 to 17 **23.** 48 **25.** 17 **27.** $0.22, $0.10, $0.08, $0.04 **29.** $(12 \times 8) - (18 \times 4) = 24$, or about 24 cents
37. 6 inches in April, 10 inches in May, 2 inches in June **39.** $x = 69$
41. 8.009, 8.05, 8.304 **43.** 30.211, 30.709, 30.75

3-3 Exercises

1. 20.2 miles **3.** 12.65 miles
5. 5.6 **7.** 4.9 **9.** 3.55 **11.** 4.948
13. $567.38 **15.** 1.5 **17.** 18 **19.** 4.3
21. 2.3 **23.** 5.87 **25.** 9.035
27. 8.669 **29.** 0.143 **31.** 3.778
33. 3.8179 **35.** 1 **37.** 52.836
39. 29.376 **41.** 84.966 **43.** $72.42
45. 0.196 **49.** C **51.** $s = 70$
53. $t = 1{,}464$ **55.** 60

3-4 Exercises

1. 593,700 **3.** 609,120 **5.** 5.0×10^5
7. 6,793,000 **9.** 382,000
11. 278,000 **13.** 3,818,000
15. 412,900 **17.** 9.0×10^4
19. 1.607×10^6 **21.** 6.0×10^6
23. 321,100 **25.** 7,700
27. 4,030,000 **29.** 6.2×10^6

Selected Answers **SA3**

31. 123,400 **33.** 208,000 **35.** 54.3
37. 1.5×10^5 **39.** 6.52×10^2
41. 6.5342×10^4 **43.** 2.8001×10^4
45. Range: 38,000 to 120,000; possible answer: 100,000
47. $150,000 = 1.5 \times 10^5$
49. 24,600,000; 2.46×10^7 **53.** D
55. Commutative Property
57. Associative Property **59.** 1.9
61. 1.2

3-5 Exercises

1. $1.68 **3.** 0.24 **5.** 0.21 **7.** 16.52
9. 35.63 **11.** 2.59 km **13.** 0.027
15. 0.217 **17.** 0.00042 **19.** 0.012
21. 13.321 **23.** 26.04 **25.** 1.148
27. 2.5914 **29.** 0.009 **31.** 0.0612
33. 26.46 **35.** 1.6632 **37.** 0.2444
39. 4.1184 **41.** 14.06 **43.** 37.38
45. 62.1 **47.** 5.8 **49.** 4.65 pounds
51. 7.38 lb **55.** B **57.** $x = 32$
59. $t = 51$ **61.** $1 + 0.2 + 0.03$
63. $20 + 6 + 0.07$ **65.** $80 + 0.002$

3-6 Exercises

1. 0.23 **3.** 0.35 **5.** 0.078 **7.** 0.104
9. $8.82 **11.** 0.22 **13.** 0.27
15. 0.171 **17.** 0.076 **19.** 0.107
21. 1.345 **23.** 0.236 **29.** when the divisor is greater than the portion of the dividend being divided into
31. C **33.** Subtract 5; 60.
35. Alternate adding 7 and subtracting 4; 21. **37.** 20.8
39. 710,000

3-7 Exercises

1. 5 **3.** 17 **5.** 6 **7.** 54.6 mi/h **9.** 6
11. 8 **13.** 217.5 **15.** 11 **17.** 5
19. 11.6 gallons of gas **21.** 6.3
23. 191.1 **25.** 184.74 **27.** 12.2
29. 12.2 **31.** 1,270 **33.** 1,125
35. 920 **37.** 2.15×10^7 **39.** about 232 bills; about $4,640 **45.** C
47. > **49.** > **51.** 16.06 **53.** 3.12

3-8 Exercises

1. 10 belts **3.** 2.25 meters
5. 8 bunches **7.** 3 packs

13. C **15.** $y = 63$ **17.** $y = 17$
19. 9.1 **21.** 14

3-9 Exercises

1. $a = 7.1$ **3.** $c = 12.8$ **5.** $d = 3.488$
7. 60.375 m² **9.** $b = 9.3$
11. $r = 20.8$ **13.** $a = 10.7$
15. $f = 6.56$ **17.** $z = 4$
19a. 1.6 meters **b.** $14.40
21. $q = 24.7$ **23.** $b = 4.2$
25. $a = 13.9$ **27.** $z = 13$
29a. 19.5 units, 21 units
b. 50.5 units **31.** 1.9×10^6 kg
33. 9 capsules **39.** H **41.** $7z$
43. 5.1 **45.** 16.08

Chapter 3 Study Guide: Review

1. front-end estimation
2. scientific notation **3.** clustering
4. $5 + 0.6 + 0.08$; five and sixty-eight hundredths **5.** $1 + 0.007 + 0.0006$; one and seventy-six ten-thousandths **6.** $1 + 0.2 + 0.003$; one and two hundred three thousandths **7.** $20 + 3 + 0.005$; twenty-three and five thousandths
8. $70 + 1 + 0.03 + 0.008$; seventy-one and thirty-eight thousandths
9. $90 + 9 + 0.9 + 0.09 + 0.009 + 0.0009$; ninety-nine and nine thousand, nine hundred ninety-nine ten thousandths **10.** 1.12, 1.2, 1.3 **11.** 11.07, 11.17, 11.7
12. 0.033, 0.3, 0.303 **13.** 5.009, 5.5, 5.950 **14.** 101.025, 101.25, 101.52 **15.** 11.32 **16.** 2.3 **17.** 14
18. 80 **19.** 9 **20.** 2,000 **21.** 24.85
22. 5.3 **23.** 33.02 **24.** 4.9225
25. 2.58 **26.** 2.8718 **27.** 1.47
28. 6.423 **29.** $41.73 **30.** 126,000
31. 54,600 **32.** 6,700,000
33. 180,600 **34.** 5.5×10^5
35. 7.23×10^3 **36.** 1.3×10^6
37. 1.48×10^1 **38.** 30,200
39. 429,300 **40.** 1,700,000
41. 5,390 **42.** 5.04×10^7 **43.** 9.44
44. 0.865 **45.** 0.0072 **46.** 24.416
47. 0.54 **48.** 10.5148 **49.** 5,678.4 lbs **50.** 1.03 **51.** 0.72 **52.** 3.85

53. 2.59 **54.** $3.64 **55.** 8.1
56. $6.1\overline{6}$ **57.** $3.87\overline{6}$ **58.** 52.275
59. 0.75 meter **60.** 14 containers
61. 9 cars **62.** 5.5 ft **63.** $a = 13.38$
64. $y = 2.62$ **65.** $n = 2.29$
66. $p = 60.2$ **67.** $5.00

Chapter 4

4-1 Exercises

1. 2, 4 **3.** none **5.** composite
7. composite **9.** composite
11. composite **13.** 3 **15.** 3, 5, 9
17. 2, 4 **19.** 2 **21.** composite
23. prime **25.** composite
27. prime **29.** composite
31. prime **33.** no, no, no, no
35. yes, no, yes, no, no, no, no
37. True **39.** True **41.** 1, 4, or 7
43. 1, 4, or 7 **45.** 0, 3, 6, or 9
47. Prime numbers from 50 to 100 are 53, 59, 61, 67, 71, 73, 79, 83, 89, and 97. **49.** Mackinac Straits
55. D **57.** 7, 11, 15, 19, 23
59. 6, 30, 150, 750, 3,750 **61.** 30

4-2 Exercises

1. 1, 2, 3, 4, 6, 12 **3.** 1, 2, 4, 13, 26, 52 **5.** $2^4 \cdot 3$ **7.** $2 \cdot 3 \cdot 11$ **9.** 1, 2, 3, 4, 6, 8, 12, 24 **11.** 1, 2, 3, 6, 7, 14, 21, 42 **13.** 1, 67 **15.** 1, 5, 17, 85 **17.** 7^2
19. $2^2 \cdot 19$ **21.** 3^4 **23.** $2^2 \cdot 5 \cdot 7$
33a. 15 boys per team **b.** 5 teams of 9 players **35.** $3^2 \cdot 11$ **37.** $2^2 \cdot 71$
39. $2^3 \cdot 3 \cdot 5 \cdot 7$ **41.** $2^2 \cdot 5 \cdot 37$
43. $2^2 \cdot 5^2$ **45.** 7^3 **47.** Birds **53.** 60
55. 3, 5 **57.** 2, 3, 4, 5, 6, 9, 10
59. 2, 4, 5, 10 **61.** 2, 3, 4, 5, 6, 9, 10

4-3 Exercises

1. 9 **3.** 7 **5.** 6 **7.** 4 arrangements
9. 14 **11.** 2 **13.** 4 **15.** 12
17. 3 teams **19.** 12 **21.** 5 **23.** 2
25. 75 **27.** 4 **29.** 6 baskets
31. 2 **33.** 9 **35.** 6 **37.** 6 rows
39. 4 groups **43.** A **45.** $y = 27$
47. $z = 8$ **49.** $2 \times 3 \times 7$
51. 3×17 **53.** $5^2 \times 2^3$

4-3 Extension

1. intersection: empty; union: all whole numbers 3. intersection: 1, 2, 3, 4, 6, 9, 12, 18, 36; union: 1, 2, 3, 4, 6, 8, 9, 12, 18, 24, 36, 72 5. yes 7. no

4-4 Exercises

1. $\frac{3}{20}$ 3. $\frac{43}{100}$ 5. 0.4 7. 0.125 9. 0.21, $\frac{2}{3}$, 0.78 11. $\frac{1}{9}$, 0.3, 0.52 13. $5\frac{71}{100}$ 15. $3\frac{23}{100}$ 17. $2\frac{7}{10}$ 19. $6\frac{3}{10}$ 21. 1.6 23. 3.275 25. 0.375 27. 0.625 29. $\frac{1}{9}$, 0.29, $\frac{3}{8}$ 31. $\frac{1}{10}$, 0.11, 0.13 33. 0.31, $\frac{3}{7}$, 0.76 35. $90 + 2 + \frac{3}{10}$ 37. $100 + 7 + \frac{1}{10} + \frac{7}{100}$ 39. $0.1\overline{6}$; repeats 41. $0.41\overline{6}$; repeats 43. 0.8; terminates 45. $0.8\overline{3}$; repeats 47. $0.91\overline{6}$; repeats 49. > 51. < 53. < 55. < 57. $4\frac{1}{2}$, 4.48, 3.92 59. 125.25, 125.205, $125\frac{1}{5}$ 61. Jill 63. $\frac{1}{20}$ 67. D 69. 21.47 71. 23.45 73. 14 75. 16

4-5 Exercises

1. $\frac{2}{3}, \frac{8}{12}$ 3. $\frac{1}{2}, \frac{5}{10}$ 5. 25 7. 21 9. $\frac{1}{5}$ 11. $\frac{1}{4}$ 21. 15 23. 70 25. 6 27. 140 29. $\frac{1}{4}$ 31. $\frac{1}{5}$ 33. $\frac{3}{4}$ 35. $\frac{1}{2}$ 37. $\frac{3}{6} = \frac{1}{2}$ 39. $\frac{2}{3} = \frac{8}{12}$ 41. $\frac{5}{20}; \frac{1}{4}$ 43. $\frac{14}{35}, \frac{2}{5}$ 47. Baskets and wreaths are $\frac{12}{72} = \frac{1}{6}$; jewelry is $\frac{32}{72} = \frac{4}{9}$; glass and pottery are $\frac{16}{72} = \frac{2}{9}$; paintings are $\frac{12}{72} = \frac{1}{6}$. 51. B 53. $x = 45$ 55. $w = 18$ 57. $0.\overline{6}$ 59. 3.2

4-6 Exercises

1. $2\frac{2}{5}$ 3. $\frac{8}{3}$ 5. $\frac{12}{5}$ 7. $8\frac{3}{5}$ 9. $\frac{20}{9}$ 11. $\frac{13}{3}$ 13. $\frac{25}{6}$ 15. $\frac{19}{5}$ 17. 4; whole number 19. $8\frac{3}{5}$; mixed number 21. $8\frac{7}{10}$; mixed number 23. 15; whole number 25. $\frac{53}{11}$ 27. $\frac{93}{5}$ 29. 3; 5 31. 13; 9 33. 2; 10 35. $28\frac{4}{9}$ yards 37. = 39. < 41. $40\frac{1}{2}$; $50\frac{1}{2}$ 43. $\frac{9}{5}$ 49. J 51. 9,198; 10,462; 11,320

53. 37 to 39.5 55. 31 to 32.5 57. 1, 2, 3, 4, 6, 9, 12, 18, 36

4-7 Exercises

1. > 3. = 5. yes 7. $\frac{1}{4}, \frac{1}{3}, \frac{2}{5}$ 9. $\frac{1}{6}, \frac{1}{2}, \frac{2}{3}$ 11. < 13. > 15. = 17. > 19. $\frac{3}{7}, \frac{1}{2}, \frac{3}{5}$ 21. $\frac{1}{3}, \frac{3}{8}, \frac{4}{9}$ 23. $\frac{2}{3}, \frac{7}{10}, \frac{3}{4}$ 25. $\frac{1}{4}, \frac{3}{8}, \frac{2}{3}$ 27. < 29. > 31. > 33. > 35. $\frac{3}{10}, \frac{2}{5}, \frac{1}{2}$ 37. $\frac{1}{5}, \frac{7}{15}, \frac{2}{3}$ 39. $\frac{2}{5}, \frac{4}{9}, \frac{11}{15}$ 41. $\frac{5}{12}, \frac{5}{8}, \frac{3}{4}$ 43. Laura; $\frac{3}{5} > \frac{4}{7}$ 45. $1\frac{1}{8}, 1\frac{2}{5}, 3, 3\frac{2}{5}, 3\frac{4}{5}$ 47. $\frac{1}{2}, \frac{3}{4}, 3\frac{1}{15}, 3\frac{1}{10}, 3\frac{1}{5}$ 49. $3\frac{5}{7}, 4\frac{2}{3}, 4\frac{3}{4}, 5, 5\frac{1}{3}$ 59. 4.05×10^5 61. 2.3×10^7 63. $\frac{2}{21}$ 65. $\frac{2}{5}$

4-8 Exercises

1. $\frac{1}{2}$ foot 3. $7\frac{1}{7}$ 5. $5\frac{1}{6}$ 7. $\frac{2}{5}$ 9. $\frac{1}{5}$ 11. $\frac{2}{7}$ 13. $1\frac{3}{5}$ 15. $\frac{6}{5}$ or $1\frac{1}{5}$ 17. $\frac{1}{10}$ 19. $\frac{5}{8}$ 21. $\frac{14}{33}$ 23. $\frac{2}{3}$ 25. $13\frac{1}{3}$ 27. $\frac{17}{24}$ 29. $\frac{4}{9}$ 31. $\frac{5}{7}$ 33. $8\frac{2}{3}$ 35. $\frac{3}{4}$ hour 37. $1\frac{3}{5}$ hr 39. 1 foot 51. $\frac{2}{6}, \frac{3}{7}, \frac{5}{4}$ 53. $\frac{3}{10}, \frac{1}{3}, \frac{3}{8}$

4-9 Exercises

1. about 1 3. about $\frac{1}{2}$ 5. 16 miles 7. about $\frac{1}{2}$ 9. about 0 11. about $1\frac{1}{2}$ 13. about 2 15. 4 tons 17. $3\frac{1}{2}$ tons 19. > 21. < 23. > 25. about 2 27. about 3 29. about $13\frac{1}{2}$ 31. $\frac{3}{4}$ in. 33. about $9\frac{1}{2}$ in. 37. B 39. 3 41. 10 43. $n + 5$

Chapter 4 Study Guide: Review

1. improper fraction; mixed number 2. repeating decimal; terminating decimal 3. prime number; composite number 4. 2 5. 2, 3, 5, 6, 9, 10 6. 2, 3, 6, 9 7. 2, 4 8. 2, 5, 10 9. 3 10. composite 11. composite 12. prime 13. composite 14. prime 15. composite 16. composite 17. prime 18. composite 19. prime 20. 1, 2, 3, 4, 5, 6, 10, 12, 15, 20, 30, 60 21. 1, 2, 3, 4, 6, 8, 9, 12, 18, 24, 36, 72 22. 1, 29 23. 1, 2, 4, 7, 8, 14, 28, 56 24. 1, 5, 17, 85 25. 1, 71 26. $5 \cdot 13$ 27. $2 \cdot 47$ 28. $2 \cdot 5 \cdot 11$ 29. 3^4 30. $3^2 \cdot 11$ 31. $2^2 \cdot 19$ 32. $7 \cdot 11$ 33. $5 \cdot 11$ 34. $2 \cdot 23$ 35. 12 36. 25 37. 9 38. 4 39. $\frac{37}{100}$ 40. $1\frac{4}{5}$ 41. $\frac{2}{5}$ 42. 0.875 43. 0.4 44. $0.\overline{7}$ 45. Possible answer: $\frac{2}{3}, \frac{8}{12}$ 46. Possible answer: $\frac{8}{10}, \frac{16}{20}$ 47. Possible answer: $\frac{1}{4}, \frac{2}{8}$ 48. $\frac{7}{8}$ 49. $\frac{3}{10}$ 50. $\frac{7}{10}$ 51. $\frac{34}{9}$ 52. $\frac{29}{12}$ 53. $\frac{37}{7}$ 54. $3\frac{5}{6}$ 55. $3\frac{2}{5}$ 56. $5\frac{1}{8}$ 57. $3\frac{3}{4}$ 58. > 59. > 60. = 61. < 62. $\frac{3}{8}, \frac{2}{3}, \frac{7}{8}$ 63. $\frac{3}{12}, \frac{1}{3}, \frac{4}{6}$ 64. $\frac{1}{3}, \frac{3}{8}, \frac{1}{2}$ 65. $\frac{5}{8}, \frac{7}{9}, \frac{9}{10}$ 66. 1 67. $\frac{3}{4}$ 68. $\frac{3}{5}$ 69. $6\frac{5}{7}$ 70. $\frac{5}{8}$ 71. 1 72. $\frac{1}{2}$ 73. 11 74. $2\frac{1}{2}$

Chapter 5

5-1 Exercises

1. 3 packs of pencils and 4 packs of erasers 3. 36 5. 20 7. 48 9. 40 11. 63 13. 150 15. 8 17. 20 19. 18 21. 12 23. 24 25. 66 27. 60 29. 140 31. 12 33c. 12 d. Possible answer: 120, 144, 132 35. 12 and 16 37a. 120 b. 120 c. 4 41. B 43. 0.03 45. 0.24 47. > 49. > 51. $4\frac{5}{7}$

5-2 Exercises

1. $\frac{5}{12}$ ton 3. $\frac{3}{10}$ 5. $\frac{13}{14}$ 7. $\frac{1}{6}$ cup 9. $\frac{7}{12}$ 11. $\frac{9}{20}$ 13. $1\frac{2}{15}$ 15. $1\frac{1}{8}$ 17. $\frac{7}{15}$ 19. $\frac{7}{18}$ 21. $\frac{1}{3}$ 23. $\frac{28}{33}$ 25. $\frac{7}{18}$ 27. $\frac{1}{5}$ 29. $\frac{2}{2}$ or 1 31. $1\frac{1}{8}$ 33. $\frac{1}{2}$ 35. $\frac{4}{7}$ 37. $\frac{3}{4}$ 39. $\frac{7}{8}$ 41. $\frac{1}{6}$ gallon 43. $\frac{9}{40}$ lb 49. $\frac{11}{12}$ mi 51. 1.1 53. 0.125 55. > 57. >

5-3 Exercises

1. $10\frac{5}{12}$ 3. $6\frac{1}{12}$ 5. $4\frac{1}{4}$ 7. $6\frac{7}{12}$ 9. $6\frac{1}{4}$ 11. $8\frac{7}{12}$ 13. $29\frac{3}{5}$ 15. $34\frac{1}{2}$ 17. $3\frac{51}{90}$ 19. $20\frac{13}{36}$ 21. $12\frac{5}{24}$

23a. $26\frac{3}{5}$ lb **b.** $2\frac{1}{10}$ lb **c.** $11\frac{1}{10}$ lb
25. $1\frac{7}{10}$ **27.** $23\frac{3}{4}$ **29.** $13\frac{1}{4}$ **31.** $18\frac{1}{5}$
33. $\frac{1}{2}$ mi **35.** 5 **37.** $1\frac{1}{12}$ **39.** $8\frac{1}{9}$
41. 0 **43.** $9\frac{3}{8}$ km **45.** $16\frac{1}{2}$ yards
51. J **53.** $1\frac{1}{2}$ **55.** $1\frac{2}{5}$ **57.** $\frac{49}{60}$
59. $1\frac{1}{15}$

5-4 Exercises

1. $\frac{3}{4}$ **3.** $1\frac{2}{3}$ **5.** $2\frac{2}{3}$ pounds **7.** $3\frac{4}{5}$
9. $7\frac{7}{8}$ **11.** $4\frac{13}{18}$ **13.** $1\frac{4}{5}$ **15.** $6\frac{2}{3}$ pounds **17.** $1\frac{4}{9}$ **19.** $8\frac{9}{11}$ **21.** $11\frac{2}{9}$
23. $12\frac{13}{18}$ **25.** $7\frac{1}{4}$ in. **27.** $7\frac{1}{3}$
29. $3\frac{8}{11}$ **31.** $11\frac{4}{7}$ **33.** $4\frac{11}{12}$ **35.** $1\frac{5}{6}$
37. $\frac{1}{12}$ **39.** $13\frac{5}{12}$ **41.** $1\frac{1}{12}$ yards²
43. $1\frac{11}{12}$ yards² **47.** C **49.** $a = 16$
51. $z = 9$ **53.** 17 **55.** 22

5-5 Exercises

1. $4\frac{1}{2}$ **3.** $5\frac{5}{8}$ **5.** $4\frac{1}{10}$ **7.** $57\frac{3}{4}$ in.
9. $3\frac{5}{8}$ **11.** $4\frac{5}{6}$ **13.** $8\frac{7}{9}$ **15.** $6\frac{1}{4}$ feet
17. $5\frac{1}{10}$ **19.** $7\frac{9}{10}$ **21.** $\frac{1}{3}$
23. 16 ounces **25.** $\frac{3}{8}$ in. **27.** $7\frac{7}{18}$
29. $5\frac{5}{12}$ **31.** $4\frac{1}{4}$ **37.** B **39.** 12
41. 72 **43.** $\frac{7}{20}$ **45.** $7\frac{17}{30}$

5-6 Exercises

1. $\frac{8}{9}$ **3.** 3 **5.** $\frac{3}{7}$ **7.** 6 **9.** 8 **11.** 9
13. 27 boys **15.** $\frac{3}{4}$ **17.** $\frac{4}{5}$ **19.** $\frac{6}{11}$
21. 10 **23.** 6 **25.** 2 **27.** $5\frac{5}{7}$ **29.** $3\frac{5}{9}$
31. 7 **33.** 15 **35.** 5 **37.** $\frac{48}{5}$ or $9\frac{3}{5}$
39. 45 **41.** > **43.** = **45.** < **47.** >
49. $33 **51.** 165 feet tall **55.** C
57. $75 - w$ **59.** $p \div 7$ **61.** $8\frac{5}{7}$
63. $6\frac{3}{8}$

5-7 Exercises

1. $\frac{1}{6}$ **3.** $\frac{3}{7}$ **5.** $\frac{2}{15}$ **7.** $\frac{1}{20}$ **9.** $\frac{2}{21}$
11. $\frac{5}{9}$ **13.** $\frac{1}{4}$ **15.** $\frac{5}{11}$ **17.** $\frac{2}{15}$ **19.** $\frac{1}{8}$
21. $\frac{4}{27}$ **23.** $\frac{5}{48}$ **25.** $\frac{4}{15}$ **27.** $\frac{1}{14}$
29. $\frac{27}{35}$ **31.** $\frac{9}{55}$ **33.** $\frac{1}{4}$ cup **35.** <
37. > **39.** < **41a.** Multiply by $\frac{1}{4}$.
b. $\frac{1}{12}$ **43.** $\frac{3}{8}$ lb **45.** $\frac{3}{8}$ **49.** D
51. $n = 3$ **53.** $a = 13$ **55.** $\frac{4}{9}$ **57.** $\frac{4}{7}$

5-8 Exercises

1. $\frac{5}{6}$ **3.** $\frac{11}{14}$ **5.** $\frac{13}{15}$ **7.** $2\frac{1}{16}$ **9.** $21\frac{5}{7}$
11. $12\frac{7}{20}$ **13.** $\frac{15}{16}$ **15.** $\frac{7}{15}$ **17.** $1\frac{1}{18}$
19. $\frac{13}{14}$ **21.** $2\frac{2}{7}$ **23.** $15\frac{1}{2}$ **25.** $23\frac{1}{2}$
27. $3\frac{3}{5}$ **29.** $\frac{10}{27}$ **31.** $1\frac{1}{4}$ **33.** $\frac{1}{6}$
35. $13\frac{3}{4}$ **37.** $2\frac{2}{3}$ **39.** $17\frac{1}{2}$
41. $1\frac{17}{25}$ bags **45.** $1\frac{3}{7}$
47. 28 **49.** $1\frac{7}{8}$ **51.** $21\frac{3}{4}$
53. $3\frac{1}{2}$ cups of flour; 5 teaspoons of baking powder **55a.** $6\frac{1}{8}$ cups
b. $1\frac{1}{6}$ cups **c.** $1\frac{3}{4}$ teaspoons
57. 12 **59.** $1\frac{2}{3}$ **61.** 5.4×10^2
63. 5.4×10^4 **65.** $\frac{1}{2}$ **67.** 4

5-9 Exercises

1. $\frac{7}{2}$ **3.** 9 **5.** $\frac{5}{13}$ **7.** $1\frac{5}{7}$ **9.** $2\frac{1}{6}$
11. $\frac{9}{50}$ **13.** $4\frac{4}{7}$ **15.** 10 **17.** $\frac{12}{11}$
19. $\frac{11}{8}$ **21.** $\frac{7}{6}$ **23.** $\frac{4}{21}$ **25.** $1\frac{5}{14}$
27. 12 **29.** $\frac{3}{10}$ **31.** $2\frac{22}{45}$ **33.** $\frac{2}{3}$
35. $\frac{1}{40}$ **37.** $1\frac{17}{25}$ **39.** $4\frac{2}{3}$ **41.** $\frac{3}{28}$
43. 16 bags **45.** yes **47.** yes
49. $\frac{5}{2}, \frac{25}{4}$ **51.** $\frac{1}{5}, \frac{1}{5}$ **53.** The reciprocal of a fraction has the fraction's numerator as its denominator and has the fraction's denominator as its numerator. The product of a fraction and its reciprocal is 1.
55. $\frac{11}{12}$ **57.** $1\frac{1}{14}$ **59.** $41\frac{19}{75}$
61. $24\frac{2}{9}$ in. **67.** H **68.** 2; 4.32
69. 1; 9.5 **70.** 3; 16.192 **71.** 2; 0.04
73. $\frac{7}{8}$ **75.** $5\frac{13}{15}$

5-10 Exercises

1. $z = 16$ **3.** $x = 7\frac{1}{2}$ **5.** 24 **7.** $x = 9$
9. $t = \frac{1}{10}$ **11.** $y = 20$ **13.** $j = 12\frac{6}{7}$
15. $10 **17.** $y = 10$ **19.** $t = 16$
21. $b = 14$ **23.** $x = 9\frac{1}{3}$ **25.** $n = 12$
27. $y = \frac{2}{3}$ **29.** $\frac{3}{2}n = 9; n = 6$
31. 4 minutes **33.** 11 dresses
35. 20 more pages **41.** B **43.** 35
45. 2 **47.** 3 **49.** $1\frac{1}{5}$ **51.** $\frac{15}{28}$

Chapter 5 Study Guide: Review

1. reciprocals **2.** least common denominator **3.** 30 **4.** 48 **5.** 27
6. 60 **7.** 225 **8.** 660 **9.** $\frac{33}{40}$ **10.** $\frac{3}{4}$
11. $\frac{1}{15}$ **12.** $\frac{5}{24}$ **13.** $4\frac{7}{10}$ **14.** $3\frac{1}{18}$
15. $\frac{11}{30}$ **16.** $3\frac{2}{3}$ **17.** $1\frac{1}{2}$ **18.** $5\frac{2}{3}$
19. $2\frac{5}{8}$ **20.** $6\frac{13}{14}$ **21.** $1\frac{1}{8}$
22. $4\frac{3}{4}$ feet **23.** $30\frac{3}{20}$ **24.** $14\frac{11}{12}$
25. $5\frac{5}{12}$ **26.** $3\frac{4}{9}$ **27.** $5\frac{7}{15}$ **28.** $3\frac{3}{10}$
29. 7 oz **30.** $1\frac{2}{3}$ miles **31.** $5\frac{7}{7}$ **32.** $\frac{3}{4}$
33. $2\frac{4}{7}$ **34.** $2\frac{1}{2}$ **35.** 3 **36.** $1\frac{1}{5}$
37. 21 members **38.** $\frac{1}{3}$ **39.** $\frac{15}{28}$
40. $\frac{1}{10}$ **41.** $\frac{7}{25}$ **42.** $\frac{5}{81}$ **43.** $\frac{3}{14}$
44. $\frac{8}{15}$ **45.** $\frac{9}{10}$ **46.** $1\frac{1}{4}$ **47.** 2 **48.** $\frac{4}{21}$
49. $\frac{3}{20}$ **50.** $\frac{5}{9}$ **51.** 8 times
52. $a = \frac{1}{8}$ **53.** $b = 2$ **54.** $m = 17\frac{1}{2}$
55. $g = \frac{2}{15}$ **56.** $r = 10\frac{4}{5}$
57. $s = 50$ **58.** $p = \frac{1}{9}$ **59.** $j = 1\frac{53}{64}$
60. 80 inches

Chapter 6

6-1 Exercises

1.

Day	High Temperature (°F)
Mon	72
Tue	75
Wed	68
Thu	62
Fri	55

3.

Test	Grade
1st	70
2nd	75
3rd	80
4th	85
5th	90

5.

Date	Thickness (in.)
December 3	1
December 18	2
January 3	5
January 18	11
February 3	17

It became safe to ice-skate around January 10.

7. Jeffery is in sixth grade. Victoria is in seventh, and Arthur is in eighth.
11. 81 **13.** 216 **15.** 2 times 12; 2 multiplied by 12

17. m divided by 3, the quotient of m and 3

6-2 Exercises

1. mean = 22 **3.** mean = 6.5
5. mean = 57, median = 54, no mode, range = 23 **7.** range = 19, mean = 508.2, median = 508.5, mode = 500 **9.** 11 **11.** 4 **13.** 70
15. 6, 7, 12, 15, 15 **19.** C **21.** 25
23. 2 **25.** 5

6-3 Exercises

1a. mean = 4.75, median = 5, no mode **b.** mean = 10, median = 7, no mode **3.** mean = 225, median = 187.5, mode = 240; median **5.** with: mean = 738.8, median = 810, no mode without: mean = 913.25, median = 906.5, no mode **7.** mean ≈ 118.29, median = 128, no mode
13. 70 **15.** $n = \frac{9}{10}$ **17.** median: 35; no mode; range = 45

6-4 Exercises

1. green

3. Number of Students in Mr. Jones's Classes (bar graph)

5. orange

7. Days with Rainfall (bar graph)

9. 14 million mi^2
11. ≈ 8.14 million mi^2

13a. Scores of Practice Games (bar graph, Blue Squad and Green Squad)

b. Blue: mean ≈ 47.3, range = 26; Green: mean = 47.3, range = 16
c. Possible answer: The green squad; their performance is more consistent, and their scores have steadily increased over time.
17. J **19.** $\frac{1}{5}$ **21.** $2\frac{1}{3}$

6-5 Exercises

1.

Type of Instrument	
Trumpet	|||||
Drums	||
Tuba		
Trombone	|||
French horn	||||

3.

Number of Years of Each Presidential Term				
Number (Intervals)	0–3	4–7	8–11	12-15
Frequency	7	22	12	1

5.

Pets	
Dog	|||||	
Cat	|||||
Bird	||||
Fish	|||
Hamster	||

7.

Final Medal Standing at the Summer Olympic Games for the Top 25 Countries					
Number (intervals)	1–20	21–40	41–60	61–80	81–100
Frequency	14	8	3	0	2

9. histogram

11.

Populations of Australia's States and Territories	
Census	Frequency
0–999,999	3
1,000,000–1,999,999	2
2,000,000–2,999,999	0
3,000,000–3,999,999	1
4,000,000–4,999,999	1
5,000,000–5,999,999	0
6,000,000–6,999,999	1

13. no **17.** B **19.** 1 + 0.2 + 0.03; one and twenty-three hundredths
21. 20 + 6 + 0.07; twenty-six and seven-hundredths **23.** 19 **25.** 9

6-5 Extension

1. $0.00–$29.99 and $40.00–$59.99

3.

Amount ($)	Frequency	Cumulative Frequency
$0.00–$9.99	11	11
$10.00–$19.99	12	23
$20.00–$29.99	11	34
$30.00–$39.99	3	37
$40.00–$49.99	10	47
$50.00–$59.99	9	56

6-6 Exercises

1. (2, 3) **3.** (7, 6) **5.** (4, 5)
7–9. (coordinate graph showing points T and U)

11. (3, 0) **13.** (1, 4) **15.** (11, 7)
17–21. (coordinate graph showing points X, Q, P)

23. A **25.** C **27.** P **29.** (9, 8)
31. (1, 5) **33.** (9, 0) **35.** $\left(5\frac{1}{2}, 0\right)$
39. D **41.** $3^3 \times 5^2$ **43.** $2^2 \times 3^2 \times 5$
45. $\frac{3}{28}$ **47.** $\frac{3}{14}$

6-7 Exercises

1. School Enrollment (line graph, years 2005–2008)

3. 125

5. Comparison of Stock Prices (graph with Stock A and Stock B by Month)

7. 200 million

9. Soccer Team Fund-Raising Efforts (graph with Team A and Team B by Days of sales)

11. Max **15.** C **17.** $s = 18$
19. $m = 15$

6-8 Exercises

5. The vertical axis begins at 430 rather than zero. **7.** the yearly increments changed

9. Strips Significantly Better (bar graph: Strips ~1,007; Paste ~995; Paint ~997)

Paste is Most Effective (bar graph: Strips ~995; Paste ~1,010; Paint ~995)

17. Possible answer: Damon scored twice as Kyle on the test.
19. 124
21, 23. (coordinate grid with point B at (6, 2) and point D at (1, 0))

6-9 Exercises

1. Daily High Temperatures (°F)

Stems	Leaves
3	7 9
4	0 5 8
5	1 6

Key: 3|7 means 37

3. 44 **5.** 32 **7.** 34 **9.** 41 **11.** 52
13. 42 **15.** A

17. Number of Cars with One Passenger

Stems	Leaves
8	0 1 2 3 7 8 9
9	2 4 4 5 9
10	0 1 3 9
11	
12	4 5

Key: 8|0 means 80

21. 2,000 **23.** 225,971; 2,004,801; 298,500,004 **25.** $\frac{7}{4}$ **27.** 5

6-10 Exercises

1. line graph **3a.** Possible answer: Line graph; it shows change over time.
b. U.S. Population (line graph 1900–2000)

9. line plot **11.** 5 **13.** 4

Chapter 6 Study Guide: Review

1. histogram **2.** ordered pair
3. mode

4.
Snake Lengths (ft)	
Anaconda	35 ft
Diamond python	21 ft
King cobra	19 ft
Boa constrictor	16 ft

5. mean: 37; median: 38; mode: 39; range: 7 **6.** mean: 62.5; median: 50; mode: 50; range: 90 **7.** with outlier: mean ≈ 14.29; median = 11; mode = 12; without outlier: mean ≈ 10.33; median = 10.5; mode = 12
8. with outlier: mean = 31; median = 32; mode = 32; without outlier: mean = 35.75; median = 33; mode = 32 **9.** with outlier: mean ≈ 19.67; median = 14; mode = none; without outlier: mean = 13.2; median = 13; mode = none **10.** 8th grade

11. (bar graph of Grade by Subject: Math, English, History, Science)

12.
Points Scored			
Points (Intervals)	1–4	5–8	9–12
Frequency	2	3	1

13. (histogram of Frequency vs Points)

14. (4, 1) **15.** (3, 3)

16. Bookstore Sales (line graph by Month: January–April)

17. April **18.** Sales decreased from January to February and then increased from February to April. **19.** The scale starts out in increments of one mile and then it changes to 5 miles.

20. Basketball Scores

Stems	Leaves
2	0 2 6 8
3	4
4	0 4 6

Key: 2|0 means 20

21. smallest value: 20, largest value: 46, mean: 32.5, median: 31, no mode, range: 26 **22.** line graph

Chapter 7

7-1 Exercises

1. 3:10 **3.** 41:16 **5.** the 8-ounce bag **7.** 19:3 **11.** the 15 lb bag **13.** 24 to 11, 24:11 **15.** 7 to 10, 7:10 **17.** 5 to 9, 5:9 **19.** $\frac{100}{101}$, 100:101, 100 to 101 **21.** 8:5 **23.** 5:8 **25.** 8:16 **27.** Wednesday **33.** The 24-ounce box is the better deal. **35.** 3 **37.** 1 **39.** $m = \frac{11}{18}$ **41.** $h = \frac{2}{3}$

7-2 Exercises

1.
2	7
4	14
6	21
16	56

3.
96	48
48	24
24	12
12	6

5.
| 5 | 10 | 15 | 20 |
| 8 | 16 | 24 | 32 |

7.
| 24 | 12 | 6 | 3 |
| 16 | 8 | 4 | 2 |

9. 35 min

11.
8	15
16	30
24	45
32	60

13.
| 6 | 12 | 18 | 48 | 96 |
| 7 | 14 | 21 | 56 | 112 |

15.
| 11 | 22 | 33 | 44 |
| 25 | 50 | 75 | 100 |

17.
| 51 | 102 | 153 | 204 |
| 75 | 150 | 225 | 300 |

19. $\frac{8}{3}$ **21.** 24; 15 **27.** about 70,000,000 **31.** B **33.** 448.5; 447; 452; 94

7-3 Exercises

3. 7 **5.** 35 **9.** 15 **11.** 55 **13.** 2 **15.** 3 **17.** 7 **19.** 3 **21.** $\frac{21}{6}$ **23.** 72 euros, 102 Canadian dollars, 752 yuan, 408 shekels, and 1,108 Mexican pesos. **27.** C **29.** < **31.** = **33.** 4 to 9, $\frac{4}{9}$ **35.** 6:13, 6 to 13

7-4 Exercises

1. The length of the missing side is 4 cm; m∠G = 37° **3.** The length of the missing side, n, is 3 inches; m∠M = 110° **5.** sides; $\overline{AC}$ and $\overline{XY}$; $\overline{XW}$ and $\overline{AB}$; $\overline{BC}$ and $\overline{WY}$; angles: X and A; W and B; Y and C **9.** m∠H = 80°, m∠J = 80°, m∠Z = 100°; the length of $\overline{WX}$ is 5.5 yd, the length of $\overline{ZY}$ is 5.5 yd, and the length of $\overline{WZ}$ is 4 yd. **11.** No; the corresponding sides are not in proportion. **17.** G **19.** Distributive Property **21.** 5 **23.** 0.7

7-5 Exercises

1. 15 ft **3.** 18 ft **5.** 104 in. **7.** 120 m **11.** 14.2 **13.** 4.9 **15.** $8\frac{1}{4}$ **17.** $8\frac{4}{5}$

7-6 Exercises

1. 300 ft **3.** No **5.** 2.5 inches **7a.** north wall: 2 in.; west wall: 3 in.; south wall: 5 in.; east wall: 4.25 in. **9.** 336 km **17.** 64 in. **19.** 38.4 **21.** 3.87 **23.** $x = 3$ **25.** $k = 42$ **27.** $p = 1$

7-7 Exercises

1.

3.

5. $\frac{4}{5}$ **7.** $\frac{23}{25}$ **9.** 0.04 **11.** 0.64

13.

15.

17. $\frac{3}{4}$ **19.** $\frac{18}{25}$ **21.** $\frac{16}{25}$ **23.** $\frac{17}{20}$ **25.** 0.44 **27.** 0.29 **29.** 0.6 **31.** 0.07 **33.** 0.02 **35.** 0.01 **37.** 0.7 **39.** 0.37 **41.** 0.08 **43.** 0.75 **45.** 1 **47.** 0.52 **49.** $\frac{3}{20}, \frac{13}{25}, \frac{71}{100}$, 1 **51.** 11% = 0.11 **53.** No **59.** H **61.** 17 **63.** 10

7-8 Exercises

1. 39% **3.** 80% **5.** 44% **7.** 70% **9.** 60% **11.** 60% **13.** 34% **15.** 62% **17.** 30% **19.** 45% **21.** 12.5% **23.** 74% **25.** 40% **27.** 4%, $\frac{1}{25}$ **29.** 45%, $\frac{9}{20}$ **31.** 1%, $\frac{1}{100}$ **33.** 60%, $\frac{3}{5}$ **35.** 14%, $\frac{7}{50}$ **37.** 80%, 0.8 **39.** 83.33%, 0.83 **41.** 34%, 0.34 **43.** 4%, 0.04 **45.** 26.67%, 0.27 **47.** < **49.** = **51.** > **53.** < **55.** about 48%; about 52% **57.** 0.098, $\frac{7}{8}$, 90% **59.** 0.21, $\frac{7}{25}$, 38% **61.** 17%, $\frac{5}{9}$, 0.605 **67.** D **69.** $1\frac{1}{4}$ **71.** $\frac{9}{10}$ **73.** 3 ft **75.** 2.25 ft

7-9 Exercises

1. 44 T-shirts **3.** 6.72 **5.** 0.4 **7.** 37.8 **9.** 6 dolls **11.** 30 minutes **13.** 28.6 **15.** 18.2 **17.** 94.5 **19.** 2.28 **21.** 5.2 **23.** 12.32 **25.** 40.56 **27.** 31 **29.** 12 **31a.** 9 feet **b.** 108 square feet

33. 12 atoms of hydrogen, 6 atoms of carbon, and 6 atoms of oxygen **39.** $57.60 **41.** $\frac{39}{50}$ **43.** $\frac{99}{100}$ **45.** 87.5%

7-10 Exercises

1. about $7.65 **3.** about $151.20
5. about $18.75 **7.** about $11.10
9. about $55.65 **11.** Yes
13. $339.20 **19.** Music Palace CDs sell for $11.97. Awesome Sound CDs sell for $11.69. Awesome Sound has the better deal. **21.** yes
23. 3 **25.** 13 **27.** 600

7-10 Extension

1. $148.75 **3.** $32 **5.** $250 **7.** 3%
9. $367.20 **11.** $37,500

Chapter 7 Study Guide: Review

1. discount **2.** percent
3. corresponding angles
4. Possible answers: 2:4; 3:6; 6:12
5. 12 oz for $2.64
6. Possible answers:

3	6	9	12
10	20	30	40

7. Possible answers:

5	10	15	20
21	42	63	84

8. Possible answers:

15	30	45	60
7	14	21	28

9. $47.25 **10.** $n = 9$ **11.** $n = 3$
12. $n = 14$ **13.** $n = 2$ **14.** 6 cups of bananas **15.** $n =$ inches; $m\angle A = 90°$ **16.** 94 ft **17.** 43.75 miles **18.** 3 inches **19.** $\frac{3}{4}$ **20.** $\frac{3}{50}$
21. $\frac{3}{10}$ **22.** 0.08 **23.** 0.65 **24.** 0.2
25. 89.6% **26.** 70% **27.** 5.7%
28. 12% **29.** 70% **30.** 25%
31. 87.5% **32.** 80% **33.** 6.25%
34. 65% **35.** 12 **36.** 5.94
37. 117 tickets **38.** about $1.80
39. about $19.20 **40.** about $4.35
41. about $1.08

Chapter 8

8-1 Exercises

3. K **7.** $\overrightarrow{AB}$ **15.** point
19. L————M
21. Y————X→
23a. points **b.** line **c.** line segment **d.** ray **25.** $\overline{XY}, \overrightarrow{XY}, \overleftrightarrow{XY}$
29. A **31.** $k = 21$ **33.** $k = 100$
35. $3\frac{1}{4}$ **37.** $13\frac{2}{3}$ **39.** $11\frac{4}{7}$

8-2 Exercises

1. 90° **3.** 60°
5. 135°
7. 190°
9. acute **11.** $\angle G$ acute; $\angle H$ obtuse; $\angle J$ right; $\angle K$ obtuse; $\angle L$ obtuse **13.** 35°
15. 150°
17. 90°
19. 45°
21. acute **23.** $\angle A$ obtuse; $\angle B$ obtuse; $\angle C$ acute; $\angle D$ obtuse; $\angle E$ obtuse; $\angle F$ acute
25. Possible answer:
27. straight **29.** acute **35.** G
37. 40%; $\frac{2}{5}$ **39.** 90%; $\frac{9}{10}$ **41.** 3.6
43. 71.5

8-3 Exercises

1. vertical **3.** $m\angle a = 9°$
5. adjacent **7.** $m\angle c = 78°$
9. angles 1, 5, 6, 7 and 8 **11.** 108°, 108°, 72° **13.** 35° **15.** 75° **17.** 28°
19. 59° **21.** 78° **23.** 99°
25. angles C and D are congruent angles **29.** D **31.** $n = 2$
33. $p = 0.25$ **35.** straight **37.** acute

8-4 Exercises

1. intersecting **3.** perpendicular
5. skew **7.** skew **9.** parallel
13. $\overleftrightarrow{BF}, \overleftrightarrow{GH}, \overleftrightarrow{EF}, \overleftrightarrow{CG}$ **15.** $\overleftrightarrow{AB}, \overleftrightarrow{EF}, \overleftrightarrow{FG}, \overleftrightarrow{BC}$ **17.** sometimes **19.** never
25. H
27–31.
33. 33° **35.** 27°

8-5 Exercises

1. obtuse triangle **3.** 82°
5. isosceles **7.** 60° **9.** scalene
11. yes, right **13.** no **15.** yes, obtuse **19.** $1\frac{1}{6}$ ft, equilateral
29. A **31.** 0.12 **33.** 0.03 **35.** 0.76
37. M————G
39. •A

8-6 Exercises

1. rectangle **3.** square **5.** squares
7. quadrilateral **9.** parallelogram
11. trapezoid **13.** quadrilateral, parallelogram, rectangle, rhombus, (square)
15. quadrilateral, parallelogram, (rhombus) **17.** never **19.** always
21. sometimes **23.** sometimes
25. not possible **27.** not possible
35. Quadrilateral, parallelogram, rhombus; *rhombus* is the most descriptive **37.** 2, 6, 18, 54, 162
39. never

8-7 Exercises

1. polygon, hexagon, regular
3. polygon, triangle, regular
5. polygon, quadrilateral, not regular **7.** not a polygon **9.** not formed by line segments **11.** not

formed by line segments **13.** 125°
15. never **17.** sometimes **23.** c
25. c = 1.1 **27.** j = 51.54 **29.** yes; obtuse

8-8 Exercises

1.

3. Possible answer: purple, purple, red, yellow, green, yellow; red, yellow, green, yellow, purple

5.

7.

9.

The lines should be green.

13. C **15.** 81 **17.** 27 **19.** 1,024
21. $2 \cdot 5^2$ **23.** $2 \cdot 107$

8-9 Exercises

1. not congruent; different sizes
3. Figure A **5.** The figures are irregular hexagons that are not congruent.

7.

11. A **13.** y = 9 **15.** n = 8 **17.** $\frac{8}{21}$
19. $\frac{3}{8}$

8-10 Exercises

1. reflection **3.** translation
5.

7. translation
9.

13.

15. A **17.**

21. D **23.** 19 × 3 **25.** 5 + 9
27. $6\frac{71}{100}$ **29.** $2\frac{22}{25}$

8-11 Exercises

1. The line is a line of symmetry.
3. The line is a line of symmetry.
5. 3 lines of symmetry **7.** 4 lines of symmetry **9.** yes **11.** yes
13. The line is a line of symmetry.
15. 4 lines of symmetry **17.** 7 lines of symmetry **19.** no lines of symmetry **21.** yes **29.** B **31.** >
33. 24.68 **35.** 74.35

Chapter 8 Study Guide: Review

1. trapezoid **2.** polygon
3. Possible answer: $\overleftrightarrow{EC}, \overleftrightarrow{AD}$
4. Possible answer: $\overrightarrow{BC}$ **5.** acute
6. obtuse **7.** acute **8.** straight
9. b = 27° **10.** d = 98°
11. perpendicular **12.** skew
13. obtuse scalene **14.** right isosceles **15.** parallelogram
16. triangle; not regular
17. triangle; not regular
18. rectangle; not regular
19. Add 1 shaded and 1 white triangle each time. **20.** Add 1 row of circles each time.

21. not congruent; different sizes
22. congruent **23.** translation

24.

25.

26. yes; no **27.** yes; yes

Chapter 9

9-1 Exercises

1. in. **3.** gal **5.** mi **7.** qt **9.** ft
11. gal **13.** oz **17.** about 1 qt
21. $8\frac{1}{4}$ lb **27.** Possible answers: *rod*: a unit of length equal to $5\frac{1}{2}$ yards; *peck*: a dry measure of capacity equal to 8 quarts; *dram*: a very small unit of weight equal to 0.0625 ounce **29.** F **31.** 1, 3, 5, 9, 15, 45 **33.** 1, 2, 4, 5, 8, 10, 16, 20, 40, 80 **35.** acute

9-2 Exercises

1. m **3.** L **5.** about 7 cm **7.** g
9. L **11.** the width of his fist
13. km **15.** g **17.** mL **19.** Yes; possible answer: The balloon weighs 0.8 g more with the air.
23. C **25.** 8 **27.** 16 **29.** 36 **31.** 60

9-3 Exercises

1. 108 **3.** 7 **5.** 3 **7.** 8 **9.** 3 **11.** 22
13. about 24 cups **15.** 48 **17.** 2
19. 2 **21.** 6,000 **23.** 3 **25.** 20
27. < **29.** = **31.** < **33.** = **35.** >
37. about 434 yards **39a.** 9 yd
b. 324 in. **41.** 3,520; 2 **43.** 8; 16
47. 4 pints **49.** Possible answer: First, convert either the inches to feet or the feet to inches so that both lengths have the same unit. Then compare. **51.** A **53.** x = 9
55. d = 17

Selected Answers **SA11**

9-4 Exercises
1. 0.115 km 3. 0.852 5. 3,500
7. 4,400 9. 0.05 11. 0.006
13. 0.110 15. 22,500 17. 2.460
19. 9.68 21. 0.782 23. 21.6 L;
21,600 mL 25. $x = 0.23850$
27. 7,000 29. = 31. < 33. =
35. St. Louis Gateway Arch; 18 m
39. approximately 50 cups
41. 0.452 kg; 452,000 mg; 0.136 kg
43. obtuse 45. sometimes
47. never

9-5 Exercises
1. 1,200 3. $2\frac{1}{2}$ 5. 480 7. 2:15 P.M.
9. 54 11. 60 13. 4 15. 2 17. 26
19. 12:10 P.M. 21. 198
23. > 25. < 27. 480; 470
29. about 28°C 35. C 37. >
39. < 41. 5.55 43. 9.447

9-6 Exercises
1. 52°; acute 3. 90°; right 5. 45°
7. $\angle A = 150°$; $\angle B = 90°$ 9. 180°;
straight 11. 35° 13. 108° 17. 5.5°
23. 65°; acute; 65 < 90 25. 2
27. 8

9-7 Exercises
1. 2 in. 3. 40 m 5. 7 yd 7. 96 in.
9. 7 cm 11. 42 m 13. 6 in.
15. 42 in. 17. 2 km 19a. 44 ft ×
20 ft b. 128 ft 25. 24.68
27. 74.35 29. $x = 3$ 31. $k = 42$

9-8 Exercises
1. circle G, chords $\overline{EF}$ and $\overline{HI}$,
diameter $\overline{EF}$, and radii $\overline{GF}$, $\overline{GE}$,
and $\overline{GD}$ 3. 12 ft 5. 12.56 in.
7. 15 yd 9. 4.71 m 11. 0.5 in.
13. 5.75 ft, 36.11 ft 15. 5.4 in.,
2.7 in. 17. 9.42 ft 21. 48.8 cm
23. 880 revolutions 25. $\frac{10}{12}, \frac{3}{4}, \frac{1}{12}$
27. $\frac{3}{4}, \frac{5}{8}, \frac{7}{16}$ 29. 0.05 31. 1

Chapter 9 Study Guide: Review
1. perimeter; circumference
2. diameter 3. customary system

4. in.; about five widths of your
thumbs 5. mi; about 800 times 18
football fields 6. lb; about 2
loaves of bread 7. fl oz; about a
spoonful 8. $\frac{1}{8}$ in. 9. mm; about
32 times the thickness of a dime
10. mg; about 5 times the mass of
a very small insect 11. kg; about
two textbooks 12. L; about two
blender containers 13. 2 cm
14. 15,840 ft 15. 6 yd 16. 12 c
17. 3 gal 18. 8 lb 19. 4 T 20. 4 lb
21. 144 in. 22. 4 qt 23. 99 ft
24. 250 yd 25. 3,200 mL
26. 0.007 L 27. 0.342 km
28. 0.042 kg 29. 0.051 m
30. 71,000 m 31. 681,296 g
32. 1 h 33. 59,400 s
34. 105 days 35. 12:10 P.M.
36. 105° 37. Possible answer: 90°;
actual measure: 85° 38. 33.9 in.
39. 6 ft 40. 31.4 ft 41. 9 m
42. 50.24 cm 43. 11 ft

Chapter 10

10-1 Exercises
1. about 8.5 square units 3. about
6 square units 5. 100.1 in^2
7. 48 ft^2 9. 10 in^2 11. about
6 square units 13. about 4 square
units 15. 12.75 m^2 17. 260 ft^2
19. 0.75 cm^2 25. B 27. 1, 2, 4, 5,
10, 20 29. 1, 59 31. 7 ft

10-2 Exercises
1. 3 yd^2 3. 27 m^2 5. 26 ft^2
7. 88 cm^2 9. 3 ft^2 11. 72 in^2
13. 16 yd^2 15. 96 m^2
17. 5 square units 19. 15 square
units 21. 346.5 m^2 31. 175 cm^2
33. $\frac{12}{5}$ 35. $\frac{15}{2}$

10-3 Exercises
1. 2,800 m^2 3. 57 square units
5. 640 yd^2 11. 40 square units
13. $5\frac{1}{6}$ 15. $6\frac{3}{10}$ 17. 144 cm^2

10-4 Exercises
1. When the dimensions of the
square are divided by 3, the
perimeter is divided by 3, and the
area is divided by 9 or 3^2.
3. When the dimensions of the
triangle are multiplied by 4, the
perimeter is multiplied by 4, and
the area is multiplied by 16 or 4^2.
5a. 4,800 ft 5b. 280 ft, 320 ft 9. D
11. $\frac{3}{4}$ 13. $\frac{1}{2}$ 15. $\frac{13}{20}$ 17. 56 cm

10-5 Exercises
1. 48 ft^2 3. 243 in^2 5. 616 cm^2
7. 12.56 ft^2 9. 768 in^2 11. 38.5 yd^2
13. 2,464 ft^2 15. $A = 102.02$ cm^2,
$C = 35.8$ cm 17. $A = 174.28$ in^2,
$C = 46.79$ in. 19. 1.13 km^2 25. C
27. $\frac{1}{6}$ 29. $\frac{5}{18}$ 31. $\frac{3}{25}$ 33. $\frac{5}{4}$ or $1\frac{1}{4}$

10-6 Exercises
1. 5 faces, 8 edges, 5 vertices
3. 5 faces, 8 edges, 5 vertices
5. square pyramid 7. 5 faces,
9 edges, 6 vertices 9. 6 faces,
12 edges, 8 vertices 11. sphere
13. square pyramid, yes 15. cone,
no 17. B, C and D 19. B
21. true 23. true 25. 8; octagonal
pyramid 29. C 31. < 33. >
35. parallel 37. intersecting

10-7 Exercises
1. 162 cm^3 3. 10 ft^3 5. 320 ft^3
7. 1 × 1 × 10 and 2 × 5 × 1
9. 79.36 in^3 11. 54 m^3 13. 71.72 ft^3
15. 480 in^3 17. 474.375 km^3
19. 20 ft 21. 10 cm^3, 1 cm^3,
3.5 cm^3, 300 cm^3, 20 cm^3 23. pine
25. Alicia does not have gold.
29. 77.4 31. 3 33. 9

10-8 Exercises
1. 754 m^3 3. 3,140 in^3
5. Cylinder B 7. 314 ft^3 9. 31 cm^3
and 283 cm^3 11. 138 in^3 13. 4 m^3
15. 100.48 in^3 17. 1,987.03 ft^3
19. 12,560 mm^3 21. 923 ft^3
23. It cannot hold 200 cm^3 of juice

because it only has a volume of 196.25 cm³. **29.** the tomato soup can holds more soup **31.** 9, 12 **33.** 115°

10-9 Exercises

1. 94 in² **3.** 56 cm² **5.** 2,640 cm²
7. 326.56 ft² **9.** 376.8 m²
11. $16\frac{1}{2}$ m² **13.** 133 cm²
15. 11 km² **17.** 712.72 m²
21. about 96 ft² **23.** about 190 cm²
27. D **29.** $y = 11$ **31.** $y = 154$
33. $3\frac{5}{8}$ **35.** $7\frac{7}{10}$

Chapter 10 Study Guide: Review

1. polyhedron **2.** volume
3. vertex **4.** 18 ft² **5.** 7 m²
6. 12 in² **7.** 12 in² **8.** 154 in²
9. 12 cm² **10.** 30 cm² **11.** 12 ft²
12. 135 cm² **13.** 175.5 ft²
14. The perimeter is multiplied by 2, and the area is multiplied by 4 or 2^2. **15.** 78.5 ft² **16.** 200.96 cm²
17. 12.56 m² **18.** 113.04 ft²
19. 154 ft² **20.** 5 faces, 8 edges, 5 vertices; rectangular pyramid
21. 6 faces, 12 edges, 8 vertices; rectangular prism **22.** 384 cm³
23. 6,300 in³ **24.** 353 m³
25. 2,308 ft³
26. 125 m² **27.** 102 cm²

Chapter 11

11-1 Exercises

1. +5
3. [number line from −4 to 4]
5. [number line from −7 to 7]
9. 3 **11.** +50 **13.** +7 **21.** 10
23. 2 **25.** spending $83 **29.** +92
31. +25 **33.** 0 **35.** 105 **37.** 55

11-2 Exercises

1. > **3.** < **5.** −5, −4, 3, 7
7a. 3:30 A.M. **b.** 1°F **9.** > **11.** <
13. −8, 7, 15 **15.** −16, −9, −1, 13
17. −19, −3, 0, 8, 22 **19.** < **21.** >
23. < **25.** < **27.** −39, 14, 21
29. −26, −12, 0, 43
31. −73, −67, −10, 20, 82 **33.** C
35. San Augustin Cave, Dead Sea, Mr. Rainier, Kilimanjaro, Mt. Everest **39.** C **41.** acute
43. cannot form a triangle
45. [number line]
47. [number line]
49. [number line]

11-2 Extension

1. > **3.** < **5.** < **7.** > **9.** >
11. > **13.** $-7\frac{3}{4}, -2\frac{7}{10}, 0, 0.21$
15. $-4\frac{1}{10}, -3, 2.25, 4\frac{3}{5}$ **17.** $-3\frac{1}{2}$, −2.7, 0.09, $\frac{4}{5}$ **19.** −8.5, $-7\frac{1}{4}$, 1.25, $2\frac{2}{5}$
21. −8.25, −7, −2.5, $-4\frac{1}{5}$

11-3 Exercises

1. III **3.** I **5.** (1, 2)
7–9. [graph with E(4, 2), F(−1, −4)]
11. II **13.** I **15.** IV **17.** (−2, 4)
19. (4, 4) **21.** (−3, 0)
23. [graph]
25. [graph]
27. [graph]
29. I **31.** III **33.** IV **35.** III
37–47. [graph with points $(-2\frac{1}{2}, 3)$, (−2, 2), $(-4\frac{1}{3}, 0)$, (0, 0), $(0, -\frac{1}{2})$, (5, 0), $(5, 3\frac{1}{7})$, (3, 2), (−4, −4), (0, −3), (1, −4), (0, −5)]
49. Gabon **55.** B **57.** 4.4 **59.** 5.75
61. 0.2 **63.** < **65.** <

11-4 Exercises

1. $A'(1, 7)$, $B'(3, 7)$, $C'(3, 5)$, $D'(1, 5)$
3. $A'(1, -4)$, $B'(3, -4)$, $C'(3, -2)$, $D'(1, -2)$ **5.** $E'(0, 0)$, $F'(0, -3)$, $G'(-3, 0)$ **7.** $H'(-1, -2)$, $J'(2, 2)$, $K'(1, 0)$, $L'(-2, 0)$ **9.** $H'(-1, 2)$, $J'(-4, 2)$, $K'(-3, 0)$, $L'(0, 0)$
11. $H'(-1, -2)$, $J'(-4, -2)$, $K'(-3, 0)$, $L'(0, 0)$ **13.** translated up 3 units
15. reflected across the x-axis
19. C **21.** $y = 21$ **23.** $x = 126$

11-5 Exercises

1. 3 + 2 = 5 **3.** −5 **5.** 7 **7.** 4 **9.** 0
11. −17 **13.** −22 **15.** 6 + (−2) = 4
17. 11 **19.** 0 **21.** −6 **23.** −7
25. −16 **27.** −8 **29.** −2 **31.** 2
33. 29 feet
35. [number line diagram]
37. [number line diagram]

39. [number line showing +6 and −1, from −3 to 6]

41. [number line showing +(−1) and −3, from −5 to 0]

43. 7 **45.** −11 **47.** −9 **49.** 17
51. 4 **53.** −1 **55.** −17 **57.** −6°F
63. B **65.** 5, 3, −1 **67.** 4 **69.** 1,728
71–75. [coordinate plane with points J, W, L]

11-6 Exercises

1. $6 - 5 = 1$ **3.** −3 **5.** −8 **7.** 8
9. 13 **11.** −4 **13.** 11 **15.** 2
17. −5 **19.** 7 **21.** −12 **23.** −6
25. −1 **27.** 21 **29.** 30 **31.** 12
33. 4 **35.** −38 **37.** −19 m
39. 9°F **43.** D **45.** 2% **47.** 26%
49. 310% **51.** II **53.** III

11-7 Exercises

1. 24 **3.** −21 **5.** 9 **7.** 16 **9.** 9
11. 33 **13.** −24 **15.** 18 **17.** 45
19. −32 **21.** 39 **23.** −72 **25.** −24
27. −12 **29.** 40 **31.** 60 **33.** 14
35. 54 **37.** −90 **39.** 4 ft to −4 ft
45. positive; negative **47.** 9
49. −13 **51.** −3

11-8 Exercises

1. 8 **3.** 3 **5.** −2 **7.** −15 **9.** 5
11. −8 **13.** 6 **15.** 2 **17.** 1 **19.** 3
21. 16 **23.** 14 **25.** −6 **27.** 1
29. 10 **31.** −7 **33.** 3 **35.** 8
37. −3 **39.** 6 **41.** −11 **43a.** −300
b. a decrease of 300 seals from 1976 to 1980 **45.** −20 **47.** 500

48. A **49.** G **50.** 6 cm **51.** 7 m
52. −1 **53.** 11 **54.** −9 **55.** 0
56. 20

11-9 Exercises

1. $m = 12$ **3.** $z = 9$ **5.** $p = -9$
7. $g = 8$ **9.** $b = -8$ **11.** $c = -7$
13. $f = -6$ **15.** $r = -900$
17. $g = 4$ **19.** $t = -14$
21. $x = -14$ **23.** $w = -10$
25. $j = 8$ **27.** $a = -52$
29. $m = -48$ **31.** $u = -60$
33. $x = 17$ **35.** $k = -4$
37. $m = -15$ **39.** $n = -3$
41. $g = -3$ **43.** $f = -8$ **45.** $d = 33$
47. $h = -84$ **49.** $b = 32$ **51.** $a = 8$
53. $t = -55$ **55.** $c = -13$
57. $n = -4$ **59.** $j = -3$
61. 70 dives **63.** −4
65. $x = -18,500$; sponge
67. −24 ft **71.** A **73.** always
75. −35 **77.** 12 **79.** 32

Chapter 11 Study Guide: Review

1. output, input **2.** coordinate plane, quadrants **3.** +10 **4.** −50
5. [number line from −4 to 4]
6. [number line from −3 to 3]
7. [number line from −10 to 0]
8. [number line from −3 to 3]
9. 37 **10.** 14 **11.** 97 **12.** 13
13. < **14.** < **15.** <
16. −1, 2, 4 **17.** −3, 0, 4
18. −8, −6, 0 **19.** (−2, −3)
20. (1, 0) **21.** III **22.** II
23. [coordinate plane with triangle ABC]
$P'(1, -1)$, $Q'(1, 2)$, $R'(4, -1)$

24. [coordinate plane with quadrilateral WXYZ]
$W'(0, -2)$, $X'(0, -4)$, $Y'(4, -2)$, $Z'(2, -1)$

25. [coordinate plane with triangle PQR]
$P'(1, 2)$, $Q'(1, -1)$, $R'(-2, 2)$
26. −2 **27.** 0 **28.** 1 **29.** −5
30. −17 **31.** 8 **32.** 1940 **33.** −8
34. 9 **35.** −3 **36.** −6 **37.** 13
38. −6 **39.** 36 °F **40.** −10 **41.** 6
42. 6 **43.** −8 **44.** −18 **45.** 45
46. −30 **47.** −3 **48.** 3 **49.** 2
50. −2 **51.** $w = 4$ **52.** $a = -12$
53. $q = -7$ **54.** $x = -5$ **55.** 138 ft

Chapter 12

12-1 Exercises

1. certain **3.** 0.4, $\frac{2}{5}$ **5.** likely
7. unlikely **9.** 0.3, 30%
11. cashew **13.** unlikely
15. unlikely **17.** unlikely **19.** AB negative **23.** C **25.** $2^2 \cdot 19$
27. 2^4 **29.** 2^7 **31.** 31.4 cm

12-2 Exercises

1. 6 **3.** no hits; 1 hit **5.** HTH
7. $\frac{13}{25}$ **9.** yellow **11.** $\frac{1}{31}$; unlikely
15. D **17.** 12 **19.** 21 **21.** 3

12-3 Exercises

1. turkey and fruit; turkey and salad; tacos and fruit; tacos and salad; pasta and fruit; pasta and salad **3.** 9 **5.** 123, 132, 213, 231,

312, 321 **7a.** 18 **b.** 56 **9.** 9
13. C **15.** $1\frac{1}{12}$ **17.** $\frac{5}{8}$

12-4 Exercises

1. $\frac{1}{2}$ **3.** 74% **5.** $\frac{1}{6}$ **7.** $\frac{4}{9}$ **9.** 0.96
11. $\frac{5}{6}$ **13.** 1 **15.** $\frac{1}{6}$ **17.** 0 **19.** 50%
21. 53% **23.** $\frac{5}{12}$ **25.** 0.77 **27.** $\frac{1}{9}$
29. < **31.** < **33.** > **37.** C
39. 21 **41.** −5 **43.** −11

12-5 Exercises

1. $\frac{1}{4}$ **3.** $\frac{1}{9}$ **5.** $\frac{1}{3}$ **7.** $\frac{1}{2}$ **9.** $\frac{1}{3}$ **11.** 0
13. 1 **15.** = **17.** < **19.** $\frac{1}{32}$; $\frac{1}{32}$
25. J **27.** 2.007, 2.02, 2.45, 2.678
29. 85%

12-5 Extension

1. dependent **3.** $\frac{1}{24}$ **5.** $\frac{1}{3}$ **7.** $\frac{2}{15}$
9. $\frac{1}{45}$

12-6 Exercises

1. 600 **3.** 200 tickets **5.** 32 **7.** 129 donors **11.** about 90 **15.** B
17. $x = -12$ **19.** $x = -5$ **21.** $\frac{1}{6}$
23. $\frac{1}{3}$

Chapter 12 Study Guide: Review

1. equally likely **2.** experiment; outcome **3.** probability
4. theoretical probability
5. sample space **6.** certain
7. 0.75, $\frac{3}{4}$ **8.** white **9.** $\frac{20}{75} = \frac{4}{15}$
10. 18 combinations **11.** $\frac{1}{4}$ **12.** $\frac{1}{2}$
13. 75% **14.** $\frac{1}{6}$ **15.** $\frac{1}{8}$ **16.** 100 items **17.** 25 times **18.** 1,575 teenagers **19.** 100 students

Chapter 13

13-1 Exercises

1. 15 **3.** $j = b - 6$ **7.** $c = 12s - 2$
9. $p = 150m$ **11.** −54 **13.** −3; 5
15. Let c be the total cost and h be the number of hours. $c = \$125 + \$55h$ **17.** 9 hours **23.** G
25. $x = 3.9$ **27.** $p = 5.2$
29. 706.5 ft³

13-2 Exercises

1. (1, 8); (2, 14); (3, 20); (4, 26)
3. no **5.** 2 **7.** 0
9.

11. (1, −3); (2, −7); (3, −11); (4, −15) **13.** yes **15.** 1 **17.** 0
19. 2
21.

23.

25.

27. −3; −2; −1; 0 **29.** (1, 14)
31.

33. 219 kelvins **39.** H **41.** 6
43. $y = -120$ **45.** $j = -12$

13-3 Exercises

1. constant **3.** variable
7. constant **9.** variable
11.

linear; 2
13.

not linear
15. The rate of change is variable; possible answer: the rate of change from 9:00 A.M. to noon is −15 and the rate of change from noon to 5:00 P.M. is $\frac{44}{5}$. **21.** 1.25
23. 301 **25.** 1,201

13-4 Exercises

1. $x = 8$ **3.** $x = 7$ **5.** $x = 4$
7. $x = 27$ **9.** $x = 12$ **11.** $x = 20$
13a. $3x + 12 = 33$ **b.** $x = 7$; the plant will be 33 cm tall after 7 weeks **15.** $x = 6$ **17.** $x = 6$
19. $x = 70$ **21.** $x = 12$ **23.** $x = 16$
25. $x = 49$ **27.** $x = 126$
29. $x = 119$ **31.** $x = 64$
35. $4x - 3 = 25$; $x = 7$
37. $5x + 1 = 41$; $x = 8$ **41.** $x = 5.6$
43. $x = 15$ **45.** $x = 15$ **51.** 9
53. 0.95, 1.1, $\frac{4}{3}$ **55.** 0.35, 0.5, $\frac{3}{5}$
57. variable

Selected Answers **SA15**

13-5 Exercises

1. [number line: closed dot at 0, shaded left]
3. [number line: closed dot at 8, shaded left]
5. [number line: open dot at 7, shaded right]
7. $y \geq 5$; [number line]
9. $s \leq 8$; [number line]
11. $p > 6$; [number line]
13. $t \leq 9$; [number line]
15. $d \geq 6$; [number line]
17. $k < 4$; [number line]
19. $t \geq -2$; [number line]
21. $q \leq 7$; [number line]
23. $-1 \leq p$; [number line]
25. $x > 2$; [number line]
27. $b > 4$; [number line]
29. $f \leq 7$; [number line]
31. $t < 6$; [number line]
33. $y \geq 6$; [number line]
35. $h < 5$; [number line]
37. $c \leq 2$; [number line]
39. $2r < 14$; $r < 7$; [number line]
41. $a \geq 1{,}045$
43. $c < 9$; [number line]
45. $y < \frac{3}{4}$; [number line]
47. $k > -0.4$; [number line]
49. $t \geq 10$ 51. $a < 20{,}320$ 59. 16 and 20 61. 30 63. 5.75

13-6 Exercises

1. $x \geq 6$; [number line]
3. $x \geq 3$; [number line]
5. $x \geq 6$; [number line]
7. $x \leq 4$; [number line]
9. $x > 15$; [number line]
11. $x \leq 2$; [number line]
13. $x < 3$; [number line]
15. $x < 3$; [number line]
17. $x < 6$; [number line]
19a. $700 + 0.05x \geq 2{,}800$
b. $x \geq 42{,}000$; the salesman must sell \$42,000 or more.
21. $x < 6$; [number line]
23. $x \geq 2$; [number line]
25. $x \leq 8$; [number line]
27. $x > 10$; [number line]
29. $x \geq 4$; [number line]
31. $x \leq 2$; [number line]
33. $x \leq 0$; [number line]
35. $x > 10$; [number line]
37. $x < 1$; [number line]
39. $12x + 15 \leq 120$; $x \leq 8.75$; [number line]
41. $\frac{x}{2} + 4 < 6$; $x < 4$; [number line]
45. $g \leq 2$; [number line]
47. $x < 7$; [number line]
49. $y < 35$; [number line]
51. at least 45 tickets 55. A
57. 38 59. 240 61. 6 m²
63. 112.5 ft²

Chapter 13 Study Guide: Review

1. inequality 2. linear equation
3. function 4. $y = 2x + 2$; 18
5. $\ell = 4w$, ℓ = length, w = width
6. $(1, -3), (2, -1), (3, 1), (4, 3)$
7. $(1, 8), (2, 9), (3, 10), (4, 11)$
8. yes 9. no 10. variable
11. constant 12. variable
13. constant 14. variable
15. $z = 10$ 16. $a = 3$
17. $b = 2$ 18. $b = 75$
19. $c = 600$ 20. $d = 2$

21. $h = 8$ **22.** $j = 112$
23. 5 turns **24.** 28 pizzas
25. $n > 30$;
26. $p \leq 1$;
27. $s \geq 5$;
28. $r > 14$;
29. $q \leq 60$;
30. $u < 11$;
31. $t \leq 9$;
32. $v > 4$;
33. $w > 64$;
34. $x > 3$;
35. $x \geq 3$; at least 3 more projects
36. $x \leq 387$; 387 more tickets at most
37. $a < 8$;
38. $b \leq 64$;
39. $c \geq 88$;
40. $d < 3$;
41. $g > 12$;
42. $h \geq 28$;
43. $j \leq 77$;
44. $k < 9$;
45. $x \geq 84$; a score of at least 84
46. $x \geq 5$; at least 5 miles each day

Selected Answers **SA17**

Glossary/Glosario

A

ENGLISH	SPANISH	EXAMPLES
absolute value The distance of a number from zero on a number line; shown by | |. (p. 595)	**valor absoluto** Distancia a la que está un número de 0 en una recta numérica. El símbolo del valor absoluto es | |.	$\|-5\| = 5$
acute angle An angle that measures greater than 0° and less than 90°. (p. 411)	**ángulo agudo** Ángulo que mide más do 0° y menos de 90°.	
acute triangle A triangle with all angles measuring less than 90°. (p. 429)	**triángulo acutángulo** Triángulo en el que todos los ángulos miden menos de 90°.	
addend A number added to one or more other numbers to form a sum.	**sumando** Número que se suma a uno o más números para formar una suma.	In the expression $4 + 6 + 7$, the numbers 4, 6, and 7 are addends.
Addition Property of Opposites The property that states that the sum of a number and its opposite equals zero.	**Propiedad de la suma de los opuestos** Propiedad que establece que la suma de un número y su opuesto es cero.	$12 + (-12) = 0$
adjacent angles Angles in the same plane that have a common vertex and a common side. (p. 416)	**ángulos adyacentes** Ángulos en el mismo plano que comparten un vértice y un lado.	$\angle 1$ and $\angle 2$ are adjacent angles.
algebraic expression An expression that contains at least one variable. (p. 50)	**expresión algebraica** Expresión que contiene al menos una variable.	$x + 8$ $4(m - b)$
algebraic inequality An inequality that contains at least one variable.	**desigualdad algebraica** Desigualdad que contiene al menos una variable.	$x + 3 > 10$ $5a > b + 3$
alternate exterior angles For two lines intersected by a transversal, a pair of angles that lie on opposite sides of the transversal and outside the other two lines. (p. 425)	**ángulos alternos externos** Dadas dos rectas cortadas por una transversal, par de ángulos no adyacentes ubicados en los lados opuestos de la transversal y fuera de las otras dos rectas.	$\angle 4$ and $\angle 5$ are alternate exterior angles.

ENGLISH	SPANISH	EXAMPLES
alternate interior angles For two lines intersected by a transversal, a pair of nonadjacent angles that lie on opposite sides of the transversal and between the other two lines. (p. 425)	**ángulos alternos internos** Dadas dos rectas cortadas por una transversal, par de ángulos no adyacentes ubicados en los lados opuestos de la transversal y entre las otras dos rectas.	$\angle 3$ and $\angle 6$ are alternate interior angles.
angle A figure formed by two rays with a common endpoint called the vertex. (p. 410)	**ángulo** Figura formada por dos rayos con un extremo común llamado vértice.	
area The number of square units needed to cover a given surface. (p. 534)	**área** El número de unidades cuadradas que se necesitan para cubrir una superficie dada.	The area is 10 square units.
arithmetic sequence A sequence in which the terms change by the same amount each time. (p. 29)	**sucesión aritmética** Una sucesión en la que los términos cambian la misma cantidad cada vez.	The sequence 2, 5, 8, 11, 14... is an arthmetic sequence.
Associative Property of Addition The property that states that for three or more numbers, their sum is always the same, regardless of their grouping. (p. 22)	**Propiedad asociativa de la suma** Propiedad que establece que agrupar tres o más números en cualquier orden siempre da como resultado la misma suma.	$2 + 3 + 8 = (2 + 3) + 8 = 2 + (3 + 8)$
Associative Property of Multiplication The property that states that for three or more numbers, their product is always the same, regardless of their grouping. (p. 22)	**Propiedad asociativa de la multiplicación** Propiedad que establece que agrupar tres o más números en cualquier orden siempre da como resultado el mismo producto.	$2 \cdot 3 \cdot 8 = (2 \cdot 3) \cdot 8 = 2 \cdot (3 \cdot 8)$
asymmetrical Not identical on either side of a central line; not symmetrical.	**asimétrico** Que no es idéntico a ambos lados de una línea central; no simétrico.	
average The sum of the items in a set of data divided by the number of items in the set; also called *mean*.	**promedio** La suma de los elementos de un conjunto de datos dividida entre el número de elementos del conjunto. También se le llama *media*.	Data set: 4, 6, 7, 8, 10 Average: $\frac{4+6+7+8+10}{5} = \frac{35}{5} = 7$
axes The two perpendicular lines of a coordinate plane that intersect at the origin. (p. 604)	**ejes** Las dos rectas numéricas perpendiculares del plano cartesiano que se intersecan en el origen.	

Glossary/Glosario **G3**

ENGLISH	SPANISH	EXAMPLES

B

bar graph A graph that uses vertical or horizontal bars to display data. (p. 298)

gráfica de barras Gráfica en la que se usan barras verticales u horizontales para presentar datos.

base (in numeration) When a number is raised to a power, the number that is used as a factor is the base. (p. 10)

base (en numeración) Cuando un número es elevado a una potencia, el número que se usa como factor es la base.

$3^5 = 3 \cdot 3 \cdot 3 \cdot 3 \cdot 3$; 3 is the base.

base (of a polygon or three-dimensional figure) A side of a polygon; a face of a three-dimensional figure by which the figure is measured or classified. (p. 560)

base (de un polígono o figura tridimensional) Lado de un polígono; la cara de una figura tridimensional, a partir de la cual se mide o se clasifica la figura.

bisect To divide into two congruent parts.

trazar una bisectriz Dividir en dos partes congruentes.

box-and-whisker plot A graph that shows how data are distributed by using the median, quartiles, least value, and greatest value; also called a box plot. (p. SB18)

gráfica de mediana y rango Gráfica para demostrar la distribución de datos utilizando la mediana, los cuartiles y los valores menos y más grande; también llamado gráfica de caja.

break (graph) A zigzag on a horizontal or vertical scale of a graph that indicates that some of the numbers on the scale have been omitted. (p. 299)

discontinuidad (gráfica) Zig-zag en la escala horizontal o vertical de una gráfica que indica la omisión de algunos de los números de la escala.

C

capacity The amount a container can hold when filled.

capacidad Cantidad que cabe en un recipiente cuando se llena.

Celsius A metric scale for measuring temperature in which 0°C is the freezing point of water and 100°C is the boiling point of water; also called *centigrade*.

Celsius Escala métrica para medir la temperatura, en la que 0° C es el punto de congelación del agua y 100° C es el punto de ebullición. También se llama *centígrado*.

Glossary/Glosario

ENGLISH	SPANISH	EXAMPLES
center (of a circle) The point inside a circle that is the same distance from all the points on the circle. (p. 512)	**centro (de un círculo)** Punto interior de un círculo que se encuentra a la misma distancia de todos los puntos de la circunferencia.	
center (of rotation) The point about which a figure is rotated.	**centro (de una rotación)** Punto alrededor del cual se hace girar una figura.	
certain (probability) Sure to happen; having a probability of 1. (p. 652)	**seguro (probabilidad)** Que con seguridad sucederá. Representa una probabilidad de 1.	
chord A segment whose endpoints lie on a circle. (p. 512)	**cuerda** Segmento cuyos extremos se encuentran en un círculo.	
circle The set of all points in a plane that are the same distance from a given point called the center. (p. 512)	**círculo** Conjunto de todos los puntos en un plano que se encuentran a la misma distancia de un punto dado llamado centro.	
circle graph A graph that uses sections of a circle to compare parts to the whole and parts to other parts. (p. 516)	**gráfica circular** Gráfica que usa secciones de un círculo para comparar partes con el todo y con otras partes.	
circumference The distance around a circle. (p. 512)	**circunferencia** Distancia alrededor de un círculo.	
clockwise A circular movement in the direction shown.	**en el sentido de las manecillas del reloj** Movimiento circular en la dirección que se indica.	
clustering A method used to estimate a sum when all addends are close to the same value. (p. 114)	**aproximación** Método que se usa para estimar una suma cuando todos los sumandos se aproximan al mismo valor.	27, 29, 24, and 23 all cluster around 25.
combination An arrangement of items or events in which order does not matter.	**combinación** Agrupación de objetos o sucesos en la cual el orden no es importante.	For objects A, B, C, and D, there are 6 different combinations of 2 objects: AB, AC, AD, BC, BD, CD.
common denominator A denominator that is the same in two or more fractions. (p. 193)	**común denominador** Denominador que es común a dos o más fracciones.	The common denominator of $\frac{5}{8}$ and $\frac{2}{8}$ is 8.

Glossary/Glosario **G5**

ENGLISH	SPANISH	EXAMPLES
common factor A number that is a factor of two or more numbers.	**factor común** Número que es factor de dos o más números.	8 is a common factor of 16 and 40.
common multiple A number that is a multiple of each of two or more numbers.	**común múltiplo** Un número que es múltiplo de dos o más números.	15 is a common multiple of 3 and 5.
Commutative Property of Addition The property that states that two or more numbers can be added in any order without changing the sum. (p. 23)	**Propiedad conmutativa de la suma** Propiedad que establece que sumar dos o más números en cualquier orden no altera la suma.	$8 + 20 = 20 + 8$
Commutative Property of Multiplication The property that states that two or more numbers can be multiplied in any order without changing the product. (p. 23)	**Propiedad conmutativa de la multiplicación** Propiedad que establece que multiplicar dos o más números en cualquier orden no altera el producto.	$6 \cdot 12 = 12 \cdot 6$
compatible numbers Numbers that are close to the given numbers that make estimation or mental calculation easier. (p. 6)	**números compatibles** Números que están cerca de los números dados y hacen más fácil la estimación o el cálculo mental.	To estimate $7{,}957 + 5{,}009$, use the compatible numbers 8,000 and 5,000: $8{,}000 + 5{,}000 = 13{,}000$
compensation When a number in a problem is close to another number that is easier to calculate with, the easier number is used to find the answer. Then the answer is adjusted by adding to it or subtracting from it. (p. 26)	**compensación** Cuando un número de un problema está cerca de otro con el que es más fácil hacer cálculos, se usa el número más fácil para hallar la respuesta. Luego, se ajusta la respuesta sumando o restando.	
complement The set of all outcomes that are not the event. (p. 666)	**complemento** La serie de resultados que no están en el suceso.	When rolling a number cube, the complement of rolling a 3 is rolling a 1, 2, 4, 5, or 6.
complementary angles Two angles whose measures add to 90°. (p. 417)	**ángulos complementarios** Dos ángulos cuyas medidas suman 90°.	The complement of a 53° angle is a 37° angle.
composite number A number greater than 1 that has more than two whole-number factors. (p. 157)	**número compuesto** Número mayor que 1 que tiene más de dos factores que son números cabales.	4, 6, 8, and 9 are composite numbers.
compound event An event made up of two or more simple events. (p. 672)	**suceso compuesto** Suceso que consta de dos o más sucesos simples.	When tossing a coin and rolling a number cube, the event of the coin landing heads up and the number cube landing on 3 is a compound event.

ENGLISH	SPANISH	EXAMPLES
cone A three-dimensional figure with one vertex and one circular base. (p. 561)	**cono** Figura tridimensional con un vértice y una base circular.	
congruent Having the same size and shape.	**congruentes** Que tienen la misma forma y el mismo tamaño.	
congruent angles Angles that have the same measure. (p. 416)	**ángulos congruentes** Ángulos que tienen la misma medida.	m ∠ABC = m ∠DEF
congruent figures Two figures whose corresponding sides and angles are congruent. (p. 450)	**figuras congruentes** Figuras que tienen el mismo tamaño y forma.	
congruent line segments Two line segments that have the same length. (p. 430)	**segmentos congruentes** Dos segmentos que tienen la misma longitud.	
conjecture A statement that is believed to be true.	**conjetura** Enunciado que se supone verdadero.	
constant A value that does not change. (p. 50)	**constante** Valor que no cambia.	3, 0, π
coordinates The numbers of an ordered pair that locate a point on a coordinate graph. (p. 604)	**coordenadas** Los números de un par ordenado que ubican un punto en una gráfica de coordenadas.	The coordinates of B are (−2, 3).
coordinate grid A grid formed by the intersection of horizontal and vertical lines that is used to locate points. (p. 311)	**cuadrícula de coordenadas** Cuadricula formado por la intersección de líneas horizontales y líneas verticales que se usando por localizar puntos.	
coordinate plane A plane formed by the intersection of a horizontal number line called the *x*-axis and a vertical number line called the *y*-axis. (p. 604)	**plano cartesiano** Plano formado por la intersección de una recta numérica horizontal llamada eje *x* y otra vertical llamada eje *y*.	
correspondence The relationship between two or more objects that are matched.	**correspondencia** La relación entre dos o más objetos que coinciden.	

ENGLISH	SPANISH	EXAMPLES
corresponding angles (for lines) Angles in the same position formed when a third line intersects two lines. (p. 425)	**ángulos correspondientes (en líneas)** Ángulos en la misma posición formaron cuando una tercera linea interseca dos lineas.	∠1 and ∠3 are corresponding angles.
corresponding angles (in polygons) Angles in the same relative position in polygons with an equal number of sides. (p. 356)	**ángulos correspondientes (en polígonos)** Ángulos que se ubican en la misma posición relativa en polígonos que tienen el mismo número de lados.	∠A and ∠D are corresponding angles.
corresponding sides Sides in the same relative position in polygons with an equal number of sides. (p. 356)	**lados correspondientes** Lados que se ubican en la misma posición relativa en polígonos que tienen el mismo número de lados.	$\overline{AB}$ and $\overline{DE}$ are corresponding sides.
counterclockwise A circular movement in the direction shown.	**en sentido contrario a las manecillas del reloj** Movimiento circular en la dirección que se indica.	
cross product The product of numbers on the diagonal when comparing two ratios. (p. 353)	**producto cruzado** El producto de los números multiplicados en diagonal cuando se comparan dos razones.	For the proportion $\frac{2}{3} = \frac{4}{6}$, the cross products are $2 \cdot 6 = 12$ and $3 \cdot 4 = 12$.
cube (geometric figure) A rectangular prism with six congruent square faces.	**cubo (figura geométrica)** Prisma rectangular con seis caras cuadradas congruentes.	
cube (in numeration) A number raised to the third power.	**cubo (en numeración)** Número elevado a la tercera potencia.	$5^3 = 5 \cdot 5 \cdot 5 = 125$
cumulative frequency The frequency of all data values that are less than or equal to a given value. (p. 308)	**frecuencia acumulativa** Muestra el total acumulado de las frecuencias.	
customary system The measurement system often used in the United States. (p. 480)	**sistema usual de medidas** El sistema de medidas que se usa comúnmente en Estados Unidos.	inches, feet, miles, ounces, pounds, tons, cups, quarts, gallons
cylinder A three-dimensional figure with two parallel, congruent circular bases connected by a curved lateral surface. (p. 560)	**cilindro** Figura tridimensional con dos bases circulares paralelas y congruentes, unidas por una superficie lateral curva.	

ENGLISH	SPANISH	EXAMPLES

D

decagon A polygon with ten sides. | **decágono** Polígono de diez lados. | (star figure)

degree The unit of measure for angles or temperature. | **grado** Unidad de medida para ángulos y temperaturas. |

denominator The bottom number of a fraction that tells how many equal parts are in the whole. | **denominador** Número de abajo en una fracción que indica en cuántas partes iguales se divide el entero. | $\frac{3}{4}$ ← denominator

dependent events Events for which the outcome of one event affects the probability of the other. (p. 676) | **sucesos dependientes** Dos sucesos son dependientes si el resultado de uno afecta la probabilidad del otro. | A bag contains 3 red marbles and 2 blue marbles. Drawing a red marble and then drawing a blue marble without replacing the first marble is an example of dependent events.

diagonal A line segment that connects two non-adjacent vertices of a polygon. (p. 438) | **diagonal** Segmento de recta que une dos vértices no adyacentes de un polígono. |

diameter A line segment that passes through the center of a circle and has endpoints on the circle, or the length of that segment. (p. 512) | **diámetro** Segmento de recta que pasa por el centro de un círculo y tiene sus extremos en la circunferencia, o bien la longitud de ese segmento. | (circle with diameter)

difference The result when one number is subtracted from another. | **diferencia** El resultado de restar un número de otro. |

dimension The length, width, or height of a figure. | **dimensión** Longitud, ancho o altura de una figura. |

discount The amount by which the original price is reduced. (p. 384) | **descuento** Cantidad que se resta del precio original de un artículo. |

Distributive Property The property that states if you multiply a sum by a number, you will get the same result if you multiply each addend by that number and then add the products. (p. 23) | **Propiedad distributiva** Propiedad que establece que, si multiplicas una suma por un número, obtendrás el mismo resultado que si multiplicas cada sumando por ese número y luego sumas los productos. | $5(20 + 1) = 5 \cdot 20 + 5 \cdot 1$

dividend The number to be divided in a division problem. | **dividendo** Número que se divide en un problema de división. | In $8 \div 4 = 2$, 8 is the dividend.

divisible Can be divided by a number without leaving a remainder. (p. 156) | **divisible** Que se puede dividir entre un número sin dejar residuo. | 18 is divisible by 3.

Glossary/Glosario **G9**

ENGLISH	SPANISH	EXAMPLES
divisor The number you are dividing by in a division problem.	**divisor** El número entre el que se divide en un problema de división.	In $8 \div 4 = 2$, 4 is the divisor.
dodecagon A polygon with 12 sides.	**dodecágono** Polígono de 12 lados.	
double-bar graph A bar graph that compares two related sets of data. (p. 299)	**gráfica de doble barra** Gráfica de barras que compara dos conjuntos de datos relacionados.	
double-line graph A graph that shows how two related sets of data change over time. (p. 315)	**gráfica de doble línea** Gráfica lineal que muestra cómo cambian con el tiempo dos conjuntos de datos relacionados.	

E

ENGLISH	SPANISH	EXAMPLES
edge The line segment along which two faces of a polyhedron intersect. (p. 560)	**arista** Segmento de recta donde se intersecan dos caras de un poliedro.	
elements The words, numbers, or objects in a set. (p. 170)	**elementos** Palabras, números u objetos que forman un conjunto.	Elements of A: 1, 2, 3, 4
empty set A set that has no elements. (p. 170)	**conjunto vacío** Un conjunto que no tiene elementos.	
endpoint A point at the end of a line segment or ray.	**extremo** Un punto ubicado al final de un segmento de recta o rayo.	
equally likely Outcomes that have the same probability. (p. 666)	**igualmente probables** Resultados que tienen la misma probabilidad de ocurrir.	When you toss a coin, the outcomes "heads" and "tails" are equally likely.
equation A mathematical sentence that shows that two expressions are equivalent. (p. 66)	**ecuación** Enunciado matemático que indica que dos expresiones son equivalentes.	$x + 4 = 7$ $6 + 1 = 10 - 3$
equilateral triangle A triangle with three congruent sides. (p. 430)	**triángulo equilátero** Triángulo con tres lados congruentes.	
equivalent Having the same value.	**equivalentes** Que tienen el mismo valor.	

ENGLISH	SPANISH	EXAMPLES
equivalent fractions Fractions that name the same amount or part. (p. 180)	**fracciones equivalentes** Fracciones que representan la misma cantidad o parte.	$\frac{1}{2}$ and $\frac{2}{4}$ are equivalent fractions.
equivalent ratios Ratios that name the same comparison. (p. 342)	**razones equivalentes** Razones que representan la misma comparación.	1/2 and 2/4 are equivalent ratios.
estimate (n) An answer that is close to the exact answer and is found by rounding or other methods.	**estimación (s)** Una solución aproximada a la respuesta exacta que se halla mediante el redondeo u otros métodos.	
estimate (v) To find an answer close to the exact answer by rounding or other methods.	**estimar (v)** Hallar una solución aproximada a la respuesta exacta mediante el redondeo u otros métodos.	
evaluate To find the value of a numerical or algebraic expression. (p. 50)	**evaluar** Hallar el valor de una expresión numérica o algebraica.	Evaluate $2x + 7$ for $x = 3$. $2x + 7$ $2(3) + 7$ $6 + 7$ 13
even number A whole number that is divisible by two.	**número par** Un número cabal que es divisible entre dos.	
event An outcome or set of outcomes of an experiment or situation. (p. 656)	**suceso** Un resultado o una serie de resultados de un experimento o una situación.	
expanded form A number written as the sum of the values of its digits.	**forma desarrollada** Número escrito como suma de los valores de sus dígitos.	236,536 written in expanded form is 200,000 + 30,000 + 6,000 + 500 + 30 + 6.
experiment In probability, any activity based on chance. (p. 656)	**experimento** En probabilidad, cualquier actividad basada en la posibilidad.	Tossing a coin 10 times and noting the number of "heads."
experimental probability The ratio of the number of times an event occurs to the total number of trials, or times that the activity is performed. (p. 656)	**probabilidad experimental** Razón del número de veces que ocurre un suceso al número total de pruebas o al número de veces que se realiza el experimento.	Kendra attempted 27 free throws and made 16 of them. Her experimental probability of making a free throw is $\frac{\text{number made}}{\text{number attempted}} = \frac{16}{17} \approx 0.59$.
exponent The number that indicates how many times the base is used as a factor. (p. 10)	**exponente** Número que indica cuántas veces se usa la base como factor.	$2^3 = 2 \cdot 2 \cdot 2 = 8$; 3 is the exponent.
exponential form A number is in exponential form when it is written with a base and an exponent. (p. 10)	**forma exponencial** Cuando se escribe un número con una base y un exponente, está en forma exponencial.	4^2 is the exponential form for $4 \cdot 4$.
expression A mathematical phrase that contains operations, numbers, and/or variables.	**expresión** Enunciado matemático que contiene operaciones, números y/o variables.	$6x + 1$

Glossary/Glosario **G11**

ENGLISH	SPANISH	EXAMPLES
F		
face A flat surface of a polyhedron. (p. 560)	**cara** Lado plano de un poliedro.	Face (shown on a rectangular prism)
factor A number that is multiplied by another number to get a product. (p. 161)	**factor** Número que se multiplica por otro para hallar un producto.	7 is a factor of 21 since $7 \cdot 3 = 21$.
factor tree A diagram showing how a whole number breaks down into its prime factors. (p. 161)	**árbol de factores** Diagrama que muestra cómo se descompone un número cabal en sus factores primos.	12 / $3 \cdot 4$ / $2 \cdot 2$ $12 = 3 \cdot 2 \cdot 2$
Fahrenheit A temperature scale in which 32°F is the freezing point of water and 212°F is the boiling point of water.	**Fahrenheit** Escala de temperatura en la que 32° F es el punto de congelación del agua y 212° F es el punto de ebullición.	
fair When all outcomes of an experiment are equally likely, the experiment is said to be fair. (p. 666)	**justo** Se dice de un experimento donde todos los resultados posibles son igualmente probables.	When tossing a fair coin, heads and tails are equally likely. Each has a probability of $\frac{1}{2}$.
formula A rule showing relationships among quantities.	**fórmula** Regla que muestra relaciones entre cantidades.	$A = \ell w$ is the formula for the area of a rectangle.
fraction A number in the form $\frac{a}{b}$, where $b \neq 0$.	**fracción** Número escrito en la forma $\frac{a}{b}$, donde $b \neq 0$.	
frequency The number of times a data value occurs. (p. 304)	**frecuencia** Cantidad de veces que aparece el valor en un conjunto de datos.	In the data set 5, 6, 7, 8, 9, the data value 6 has a frequency of 2.
frequency table A table that lists items together according to the number of times, or frequency, that the items occur. (p. 304)	**tabla de frecuencia** Una tabla en la que se organizan los datos de acuerdo con el número de veces que aparece cada valor (o la frecuencia).	Data set: 1, 1, 2, 2, 3, 4, 5, 5, 5, 6, 6 Frequency table: <table><tr><th>Date</th><th>Frequency</th></tr><tr><td>1</td><td>2</td></tr><tr><td>2</td><td>2</td></tr><tr><td>3</td><td>1</td></tr><tr><td>4</td><td>1</td></tr><tr><td>5</td><td>3</td></tr><tr><td>6</td><td>2</td></tr></table>
front-end estimation An estimating technique in which the front digits of the addends are added. (p. 115)	**estimación por partes** Técnica en la que se suman sólo los números enteros de los sumandos. y luego se ajusta la suma para tener una estimacion mas exacta.	Estimate 25.05 + 14.671 with the sum 25 + 14 = 39. The actual value is 39 or greater.

ENGLISH	SPANISH	EXAMPLES
function An input-output relationship that has exactly one output for each input. (p. 698)	**función** Relación de entrada-salida en la que a cada valor de entrada corresponde un valor de salida.	
function table A table of ordered pairs that represent solutions of a function. (p. 698)	**tabla de función** Tabla de pares ordenados que representan soluciones de una función.	x: 3, 4, 5, 6 / y: 7, 9, 11, 13

G

ENGLISH	SPANISH	EXAMPLES
graph of an equation A graph of the set of ordered pairs that are solutions of the equation.	**gráfica de una ecuación** Gráfica del conjunto de pares ordenados que son soluciones de la ecuación.	
greatest common factor (GCF) The largest common factor of two or more given numbers. (p. 165)	**máximo común divisor (MCD)** El mayor de los factores comunes compartidos por dos o más números dados.	The GCF of 27 and 45 is 9.

H

ENGLISH	SPANISH	EXAMPLES
height In a triangle or quadrilateral, the perpendicular distance from the base to the opposite vertex or side. (p. 535) In a prism or cylinder, the perpendicular distance between the bases. (pp. 566, 577)	**altura** En un triángulo o cuadrilátero, la distancia perpendicular desde la base de la figura al vértice o lado opuesto. En un prisma o cilindro, la distancia perpendicular entre las bases.	
heptagon A seven-sided polygon.	**heptágono** Polígono de siete lados.	
hexagon A six-sided polygon.	**hexágono** Polígono de seis lados.	
histogram A bar graph that shows the frequency of data within equal intervals. (p. 305)	**histograma** Gráfica de barras que muestra la frecuencia de los datos en intervalos iguales.	Starting Salaries
hypotenuse In a right triangle, the side opposite the right angle. (p. SB11)	**hipotenusa** En un triángulo rectángulo, el lado opuesto al ángulo recto.	hypotenuse

Glossary/Glosario

ENGLISH	SPANISH	EXAMPLES
Identity Property (for Multiplication) The property that states that the product of 1 and any number is that number. (p. 632)	**Propiedad de identidad (de la multiplicación)** Propiedad que establece que el producto de 1 y cualquier número es ese número.	$5 \times 1 = 5$ $-8 \times 1 = -8$
Identity Property (for Addtion) The property that states the sum of zero and any number is that number. (p. 632)	**Propiedad de identidad (de la suma)** Propiedad que establece que la suma de cero y cualquier número es ese número.	$7 + 0 = 7$ $-9 + 0 = -9$
image A figure resulting from a transformation.	**imagen** Figura que resulta de una transformación.	
impossible (probability) Can never happen; having a probability of 0. (p. 652)	**imposible en (probabilidad)** Que no puede ocurrir. Suceso cuya probabilidad de ocurrir es 0.	
improper fraction A fraction in which the numerator is greater than or equal to the denominator. (p. 186)	**fracción impropia** Fracción cuyo numerador es mayor que o igual al denominador.	$\frac{5}{5}$ $\frac{7}{3}$
independent events Events for which the outcome of one event does not affect the probability of the other. (p. 676)	**sucesos independientes** Dos sucesos son independientes si el resultado de uno no afecta la probabilidad del otro.	A bag contains 3 red marbles and 2 blue marbles. Drawing a red marble, replacing it, and then drawing a blue marble is an example of independent events.
indirect measurement The technique of using similar figures and proportions to find a measure. (p. 360)	**medición indirecta** La técnica de usar figuras semejantes y proporciones para hallar una medida.	
inequality A mathematical sentence that shows the relationship between quantities that are not equal. (p. 718)	**desigualdad** Enunciado matemático que muestra una relación entre cantidades que no son iguales.	$5 < 8$ $5x + 2 \geq 12$
input The value substituted into an expression or function. (p. 698)	**valor de entrada** Valor que se usa para sustituir una variable en una expresión o función.	For the rule $y = 6x$, the input 4 produces an output of 24.
integer A member of the of set whole numbers and their opposites. (p. 594)	**entero** Un miembro del conjunto de los números cabales y sus opuestos.	. . . −3, −2, −1, 0, 1, 2, 3, . . .
interest The amount of money charged for borrowing or using money, or the amount of money earned by saving money. (p. 388)	**interés** Cantidad de dinero que se cobra por el préstamo o uso del dinero, o la cantidad que se gana al ahorrar dinero.	
interior angles Angles on the inner sides of two lines intersected by a third line. In the diagram, $\angle c$, $\angle d$, $\angle e$, and $\angle f$ are interior angles. (p. 425)	**ángulos internos** Ángulos en los lados internos de dos líneas intersecadas por una tercera. En el diagrama, $\angle c$, $\angle d$, $\angle e$ y $\angle f$ son ángulos internos.	

ENGLISH	SPANISH	EXAMPLES
intersecting lines Lines that cross at exactly one point. (p. 420)	**líneas secantes** Líneas que se cruzan en un solo punto.	
intersection (sets) The set of elements common to two or more sets. (p. 170)	**intersección (de conjuntos)** Conjunto de elementos comunes a dos o más conjuntos.	
interval The space between marked values on a number line or the scale of a graph.	**intervalo** El espacio entre los valores marcados en una recta numérica o en la escala de una gráfica.	
inverse operations Operations that undo each other: addition and subtraction, or multiplication and division. (p. 70)	**operaciones inversas** Operaciones que se cancelan mutuamente: suma y resta, o multiplicación y división.	
isosceles triangle A triangle with at least two congruent sides. (p. 430)	**triángulo isósceles** Triángulo que tiene al menos dos lados congruentes.	

L

ENGLISH	SPANISH	EXAMPLES
lateral surface In a cylinder, the curved surface connecting the circular bases; in a cone, the curved surface that is not a base.	**superficie lateral** En un cilindro, superficie curva que une las bases circulares; en un cono, la superficie curva que no es la base.	
least common denominator (LCD) The least common multiple of two or more denominators. (p. 224)	**mínimo común denominador (mcd)** El mínimo común múltiplo de dos o más denominadores.	The LCD of $\frac{3}{4}$ and $\frac{5}{6}$ is 12.
least common multiple (LCM) The smallest number, other than zero, that is a multiple of two or more given numbers. (p. 218)	**mínimo común múltiplo (mcm)** El menor de los múltiplos (distinto de cero) de dos o más números.	The LCM of 10 and 18 is 90.
like fractions Fractions that have the same denominator. (p. 192)	**fracciones semejantes** Fracciones que tienen el mismo denominador.	$\frac{5}{12}$ and $\frac{3}{12}$ are like fractions.
like terms Terms with the same variables raised to the same exponents. (p. SB9)	**términos semejantes** Términos con las mismas variables elevadas a los mismos exponentes.	$3a^2b^2$ and $7a^2b^2$
line A straight path that has no thickness and extends forever. (p. 406)	**línea** Trayectoria recta que no tiene ningún grueso y que se extiende por siempre.	
line graph A graph that uses line segments to show how data changes. (p. 314)	**gráfica lineal** Gráfica que muestra cómo cambian los datos mediante segmentos de recta.	Marlon's Video Game Scores

Glossary/Glosario **G15**

ENGLISH	SPANISH	EXAMPLES
line plot A number line with marks or dots that show frequency. (p. 304)	**diagrama de acumulación** Recta numérica con marcas o puntos que indican la frecuencia.	X X X X X X X X X 0 1 2 3 4 Number of pets
line of reflection A line that a figure is flipped across to create a mirror image of the original figure. (p. 453)	**línea de reflexión** Línea sobre la cual se invierte una figura para crear una imagen reflejada de la figura original.	Line of reflection
line of symmetry The imaginary "mirror" in line symmetry. (p. 457)	**eje de simetría** El <<espejo>> imaginario en la simetría axial.	
line segment A part of a line between two endpoints. (p. 407)	**segmento de recta** Parte de una línea con dos extremos.	A————B
line symmetry A figure has line symmetry if one half is a mirror-image of the other half. (p. 457)	**simetría axial** Una figura tiene simetría axial si una de sus mitades es la imagen reflejada de la otra.	
linear equation An equation whose solutions form a straight line on a coordinate plane. (p. 703)	**ecuación lineal** Ecuación en la que las soluciones forman una línea recta en un plano cartesiano.	$y = 2x + 1$

M

ENGLISH	SPANISH	EXAMPLES
mean The sum of the items in a set of data divided by the number of items in the set; also called *average*. (p. 288)	**media** La suma de todos los elementos de un conjunto de datos dividida entre el número de elementos del conjunto.	Data set: 4, 6, 7, 8, 10 Mean: $\frac{4+6+7+8+10}{5} = \frac{35}{5} = 7$
median The middle number or the mean (average) of the two middle numbers in an ordered set of data. (p. 289)	**mediana** El número intermedio o la media (el promedio) de los dos números intermedios en un conjunto ordenado de datos.	Data set: 4, 6, 7, 8, 10 Median: 7
metric system A decimal system of weights and measures that is used universally in science and commonly throughout the world. (p. 484)	**sistema métrico** Sistema decimal de pesos y medidas empleado universalmente en las ciencias y por lo general en todo el mundo.	centimeters, meters, kilometers, grams, kilograms, milliliters, liters
midpoint The point that divides a line segment into two congruent line segments.	**punto medio** El punto que divide un segmento de recta en dos segmentos de recta congruentes.	A B C B is the midpoint of $\overline{AC}$

Glossary/Glosario

ENGLISH	SPANISH	EXAMPLES
mixed number A number made up of a whole number that is not zero and a fraction. (p. 175)	**número mixto** Número compuesto por un número cabal distinto de cero y una fracción.	$5\frac{1}{8}$
mode The number or numbers that occur most frequently in a set of data; when all numbers occur with the same frequency, we say there is no mode. (p. 289)	**moda** Número o números más frecuentes en un conjunto de datos; si todos los números aparecen con la misma frecuencia, no hay moda.	Data set: 3, 5, 8, 8, 10 Mode: 8
multiple A multiple of a number is the product of the number and any nonzero whole number.	**múltiplo** El producto de un número y cualquier número cabal distinto de cero es un múltiplo de ese número.	
Multiplication Property of Zero The property that states that the product of any number and 0 is 0.	**Propiedad de multiplicación del cero** Propiedad que establece que el producto de cualquier número y 0 es 0.	$6 \times 0 = 0$ $-5 \times 0 = 0$
multiplicative inverse One of two numbers whose product is 1. (p. 260)	**inverso multiplicativo** Uno de dos números cuyo producto es igual a 1.	The multiplicative inverse of $\frac{3}{4}$ is $\frac{4}{3}$.

N

ENGLISH	SPANISH	EXAMPLES
negative number A number less than zero. (p. 594)	**número negativo** Número menor que cero.	-2 is a negative number.
net An arrangement of two-dimensional figures that can be folded to form a polyhedron. (p. 576)	**plantilla** Arreglo de figuras bidimensionales que se doblan para formar un poliedro.	
numerator The top number of a fraction that tells how many parts of a whole are being considered.	**numerador** El número de arriba de una fracción; indica cuántas partes de un entero se consideran.	$\frac{3}{4}$ ← numerator
numerical expression An expression that contains only numbers and operations. (p. 18)	**expresión numérica** Expresión que incluye sólo números y operaciones.	$(2 \cdot 3) + 1$

O

ENGLISH	SPANISH	EXAMPLES
obtuse angle An angle whose measure is greater than 90° but less than 180°. (p. 411)	**ángulo obtuso** Ángulo que mide más de 90° y menos de 180°.	
obtuse triangle A triangle containing one obtuse angle. (p. 429)	**triángulo obtusángulo** Triángulo que tiene un ángulo obtuso.	

ENGLISH	SPANISH	EXAMPLES
odd number A whole number that is not divisible by two.	**número impar** Un número cabal que no es divisible entre dos.	
opposites Two numbers that are an equal distance from zero on a number line. (p. 594)	**opuestos** Dos números que están a la misma distancia de cero en una recta numérica.	5 and −5 are opposites.
order of operations A rule for evaluating expressions: first perform the operations in parentheses, then compute powers and roots, then perform all multiplication and division from left to right, and then perform all addition and subtraction from left to right. (p. 18)	**orden de las operaciones** Regla para evaluar expresiones: primero se resuelven las operaciones entre paréntesis, luego se hallan las potencias y raíces, después todas las multiplicaciones y divisiones de izquierda a derecha y, por último, todas las sumas y restas de izquierda a derecha.	$3^2 - 12 \div 4$ $9 - 12 \div 4$ Evaluate the power. $9 - 3$ Divide. 6 Subtract.
ordered pair A pair of numbers that can be used to locate a point on a coordinate plane. (p. 311)	**par ordenado** Par de números que sirven para ubicar un punto en un plano cartesiano.	The coordinates of B are (−2, 3)
origin The point where the *x*-axis and *y*-axis intersect on the coordinate plane; (0, 0). (p. 604)	**origen** Punto de intersección entre el eje *x* y el eje *y* en un plano cartesiano: (0, 0).	
outcome A possible result of a probability experiment. (p. 656)	**resultado** Posible resultado de un experimento de probabilidad.	When rolling a number cube, the possible outcomes are 1, 2, 3, 4, 5, and 6.
outlier A value much greater or much less than the others in a data set. (p. 292)	**valor extremo** Un valor mucho mayor o menor que los demás valores de un conjunto de datos.	
output The value that results from the substitution of a given input into an expression or function. (p. 698)	**valor de salida** Valor que resulta después de sustituir un valor de entrada determinado en una expresión o función.	For the rule $y = 6x$, the input 4 produces an output of 24.
overestimate An estimate that is greater than the exact answer. (p. 6)	**estimación alta** Estimación mayor que la respuesta exacta.	100 is an overestimate for the sum $23 + 24 + 21 + 22$.

P

parallel lines Lines in a plane that do not intersect. (p. 420)	**líneas paralelas** Líneas que se encuentran en el mismo plano pero que nunca se intersecan.	

ENGLISH	SPANISH	EXAMPLES
parallelogram A quadrilateral with two pairs of parallel sides. (p. 434)	**paralelogramo** Cuadrilátero con dos pares de lados paralelos.	
pentagon A five-sided polygon.	**pentágono** Polígono de cinco lados.	
percent A ratio comparing a number to 100. (p. 371)	**porcentaje** Razón que compara un número con el número 100.	$45\% = \frac{45}{100}$
perfect square A square of a whole number.	**cuadrado perfecto** El cuadrado de un número cabal.	$5^2 = 25$, so 25 is a perfect square.
perimeter The distance around a polygon. (p. 506)	**perímetro** Distancia alrededor de un polígono.	18 ft, 6 ft, perimeter = 48 ft
permutation An arrangement of items or events in which order is important.	**permutación** Arreglo de objetos o sucesos en el que el orden es importante.	For objects A, B, and C, there are 6 different permutations: ABC, ACB, BAC, BCA, CAB, CBA.
perpendicular bisector A line that intersects a segment at its midpoint and is perpendicular to the segment.	**mediatriz** Línea que cruza un segmento en su punto medio y es perpendicular al segmento.	ℓ is the perpendicular bisector of $\overline{AB}$.
perpendicular lines Lines that intersect to form right angles. (p. 420)	**líneas perpendiculares** Líneas que al intersecarse forman ángulos rectos.	
pi (π) The ratio of the circumference of a circle to the length of its diameter; $\pi \approx 3.14$ or $\frac{22}{7}$. (p. 512)	**pi (π)** Razón de la circunferencia de un círculo a la longitud de su diámetro; $\pi \approx 3.14$ ó $\frac{22}{7}$	
plane A flat surface that has no thickness and extends forever. (p. 406)	**plano** Superficie plana que no tiene ningún grueso y que se extiende por siempre.	plane R or plane ABC
point An exact location that has no size. (p. 406)	**punto** Ubicación exacta que no tiene ningún tamaño.	point P
polygon A closed plane figure formed by three or more line segments that intersect only at their endpoints. (p. 438)	**polígono** Figura plana cerrada, formada por tres o más segmentos de recta que se intersecan sólo en sus extremos.	
polyhedron A three-dimensional figure in which all the surfaces or faces are polygons. (p. 560)	**poliedro** Figura tridimensional cuyas superficies o caras tienen forma de polígonos.	

ENGLISH	SPANISH	EXAMPLES
population The whole group being surveyed. (p. 680)	**población** El grupo completo que es objeto de estudio.	In a survey about eating habits of middle school students, the population is all middle school students.
positive number A number greater than zero. (p. 594)	**número positivo** Número mayor que cero.	2 is a positive number. $\xleftarrow{\quad}$ –4 –3 –2 –1 0 1 2 3 4 $\xrightarrow{\quad}$
power A number produced by raising a base to an exponent.	**potencia** Número que resulta al elevar una base a un exponente.	$2^3 = 8$, so 2 to the 3rd power is 8.
prediction A guess about something that will happen in the future. (p. 680)	**predicción** Pronóstico sobre algo que puede ocurrir en el futuro.	
prime factorization A number written as the product of its prime factors. (p. 161)	**factorización prima** Un número escrito como el producto de sus factores primos.	$10 = 2 \cdot 5$ $24 = 2^3 \cdot 3$
prime number A whole number greater than 1 that has exactly two factors, itself and 1. (p. 157)	**número primo** Número cabal mayor que 1 que sólo es divisible entre 1 y él mismo.	5 is prime because its only factors are 5 and 1.
principal The initial amount of money borrowed or saved. (p. 388)	**capital** Cantidad inicial de dinero depositada o recibida en préstamo.	
prism A polyhedron that has two congruent, polygon-shaped bases and other faces that are all rectangles. (p. 560)	**prisma** Poliedro con dos bases congruentes con forma de polígono y caras con forma de rectángulos.	
probability A number from 0 to 1 (or 0% to 100%) that describes how likely an event is to occur. (p. 652)	**probabilidad** Un número entre 0 y 1 (ó 0% y 100%) que describe qué tan probable es un suceso.	A bag contains 3 red marbles and 4 blue marbles. The probability of randomly choosing a red marble is $\frac{3}{7}$.
product The result when two or more numbers are multiplied.	**producto** Resultado de multiplicar dos o más números.	The product of 4 and 8 is 32.
proper fraction A fraction in which the numerator is less than the denominator. (p. 186)	**fracción propia** Fracción en la que el numerador es menor que el denominador.	$\frac{3}{4}, \frac{1}{13}, \frac{7}{8}$
proportion An equation that states that two ratios are equivalent. (p. 352)	**proporción** Ecuación que establece que dos razones son equivalentes.	$\frac{2}{3} = \frac{4}{6}$
protractor A tool for measuring angles.	**transportador** Instrumento para medir ángulos.	
pyramid A polyhedron with a polygon base and triangular sides that all meet at a common vertex. (p. 561)	**pirámide** Poliedro cuya base es un polígono; tiene caras triangulares que se juntan en un vértice común.	

ENGLISH	SPANISH	EXAMPLES

Q

quadrant The *x*- and *y*-axes divide the coordinate plane into four regions. Each region is called a quadrant. (p. 604)

cuadrante El eje *x* y el eje *y* dividen el plano cartesiano en cuatro regiones. Cada región recibe el nombre de cuadrante.

	Quadrant II	Quadrant I
	Quadrant III	Quadrant IV

quadrilateral A four-sided polygon. (p. 434)

cuadrilátero Polígono de cuatro lados.

quotient The result when one number is divided by another.

cociente Resultado de dividir un número entre otro.

In $8 \div 4 = 2$, 2 is the quotient.

R

radius A line segment with one endpoint at the center of a circle and the other endpoint on the circle, or the length of that segment. (p. 512)

radio Segmento de recta con un extremo en el centro de un círculo y el otro en la circunferencia, o bien la longitud de ese segmento.

range (in statistics) The difference between the greatest and least values in a data set. (p. 289)

rango (en estadística) Diferencia entre los valores máximo y mínimo de un conjunto de datos.

Data set: 3, 5, 7, 7, 12
Range: $12 - 3 = 9$

rate A ratio that compares two quantities measured in different units. (p. 343)

tasa Una razón que compara dos cantidades medidas en diferentes unidades.

The speed limit is 55 miles per hour or 55 mi/h.

rate of change A ratio that compares the difference between two output values to the difference between the corresponding input values. (p. 706)

tasa de cambio Razón que compara la diferencia entre dos salidas con la diferencia entre dos entrados.

The cost of mailing a letter increased from 22 cents in 1985 to 25 cents in 1988. The rate of change was
$\frac{25 - 22}{1988 - 1985} = \frac{3}{3}$
$= 1$ cent per year.

rate of interest The percent charged or earned on an amount of money; see *simple interest*. (p. 388)

tasa de interés Porcentaje que se cobra por una cantidad de dinero prestada o que se gana por una cantidad de dinero ahorrada; ver *interés simple*.

ratio A comparison of two quantities by division. (p. 342)

razón Comparación de dos cantidades mediante una división.

12 to 25, 12:25, $\frac{12}{25}$

rational number A number that can be written in the form $\frac{a}{b}$, where *a* and *b* are integers and $b \neq 0$. (p. 602)

número racional Número que se puede expresar como $\frac{a}{b}$, donde *a* y *b* son números enteros y $b \neq 0$.

3, 1.75, $0.\overline{3}$, $-\frac{2}{3}$, 0

Glossary/Glosario **G21**

ENGLISH	SPANISH	EXAMPLES
ray A part of a line that starts at one endpoint and extends forever in one direction. (p. 407)	**rayo** Parte de una línea que comienza en un extremo y se extiende siempre en una dirección.	
reciprocal One of two numbers whose product is 1. (p. 260)	**recíproco** Uno de dos números cuyo producto es igual a 1.	The reciprocal of $\frac{2}{3}$ is $\frac{3}{2}$.
rectangle A parallelogram with four right angles. (p. 434)	**rectángulo** Paralelogramo con cuatro ángulos rectos.	
rectangular prism A polyhedron whose bases are rectangles and whose other faces are rectangles.	**prisma rectangular** Poliedro cuyas bases son rectángulos y cuyas caras tienen forma de rectángulos.	
reflection A transformation of a figure that flips the figure across a line. (p. 453)	**reflexión** Transformación que ocurre cuando se invierte una figura sobre una línea.	
regular polygon A polygon with congruent sides and angles. (p. 438)	**polígono regular** Polígono con lados y ángulos congruentes.	
repeating decimal A decimal in which one or more digits repeat infinitely. (p. 176)	**decimal periódico** Decimal en el que uno o más dígitos se repiten infinitamente.	$0.75757575\ldots = 0.\overline{75}$
rhombus A parallelogram with all sides congruent. (p. 434)	**rombo** Paralelogramo en el que todos los lados son congruentes.	
right angle An angle that measures 90°. (p. 411)	**ángulo recto** Ángulo que mide exactamente 90°.	
right triangle A triangle containing a right angle. (p. 429)	**triángulo rectángulo** Triángulo que tiene un ángulo recto.	
rotation A transformation in which a figure is turned around a point. (p. 453)	**rotación** Transformación que ocurre cuando una figura gira alrededor de un punto.	
rotational symmetry A figure that can be rotated about a point by an angle less than 360° so that the image coincides with the preimage has rotational symmetry. (p. 458)	**simetría de rotación** Una figura que puede rotarse alrededor de un punto en un ángulo menor de 360° de forma tal que la imagen coincide con la imagen original que tenga simetría de rotación.	

ENGLISH	SPANISH	EXAMPLES
rounding Replacing a number with an estimate of that number to a given place value.	**redondear** Sustituir un número por una estimación de ese número hasta cierto valor posicional.	2,354 rounded to the nearest thousand is 2,000; 2,354 rounded to the nearest 100 is 2,400.

S

ENGLISH	SPANISH	EXAMPLES
sales tax A percent of the cost of an item, which is charged by governments to raise money. (p. 384)	**impuesto sobre la venta** Porcentaje del costo de un artículo que los gobiernos cobran para recaudar fondos.	
sample A part of a group being surveyed. (p. 680)	**muestra** Parte de un grupo que es objeto de estudio.	In a survey about eating habits of middle school math students, a sample is a survey of 100 randomly-chosen students.
sample space All possible outcomes of an experiment. (p. 662)	**espacio muestral** Conjunto de todos los resultados posibles de un experimento.	When rolling a number cube, the sample space is 1, 2, 3, 4, 5, 6.
scale The ratio between two sets of measurements. (p. 364)	**escala** La razón entre dos conjuntos de medidas.	1 cm: 5 mi
scale drawing A drawing that uses a scale to make an object proportionally smaller than or larger than the real object. (p. 364)	**dibujo a escala** Dibujo en el que se usa una escala para que un objeto se vea proporcionalmente mayor o menor que el objeto real al que representa.	A blueprint is an example of a scale drawing.
scale model A proportional model of a three-dimensional object.	**modelo a escala** Modelo proporcional de un objeto tridimensional.	
scalene triangle A triangle with no congruent sides. (p. 430)	**triángulo escaleno** Triángulo que no tiene lados congruentes.	
scientific notation A method of writing very large or very small numbers by using powers of 10. (p. 116)	**notación científica** Método que se usa para escribir números muy grandes o muy pequeños mediante potencias de 10.	$12{,}560{,}000{,}000{,}000 = 1.256 \times 10^{13}$
segment A part of a line made of two endpoints and all points between them. (p. 407)	**segmento** Parte de una línea que consiste en dos extremos y todos los puntos entre éstos.	
sequence An ordered list of numbers. (p. 29)	**sucesión** Lista ordenada de números.	2, 4, 6, 8, 10, . . .
set A group of items. (p. 170)	**conjunto** Un grupo de elementos.	

Glossary/Glosario

ENGLISH	SPANISH	EXAMPLES
side A line bounding a geometric figure; one of the faces forming the outside of an object.	**lado** Línea que delimita las figuras geométricas; una de las caras que forman la parte exterior de un objeto.	
significant figures The figures used to express the precision of a measurement. (p. SB17)	**dígitos significativos** Dígitos usados para expresar la precisión de una medida.	
similar Figures with the same shape but not necessarily the same size are similar. (p. 356)	**semejantes** Figuras que tienen la misma forma, pero no necesariamente el mismo tamaño.	
simple event An event consisting of only one outcome.	**suceso simple** Suceso que tiene sólo un resultado.	In the experiment of rolling a number cube, the event consisting of the outcome 3 is a simple event.
simple interest A fixed percent of the principal. It is found using the formula $I = Prt$, where P represents the principal, r the rate of interest, and t the time. (p. 388)	**interés simple** Un porcentaje fijo del capital. Se calcula con la fórmula $I = Cit$, donde C representa el capital, i, la tasa de interés y t, el tiempo.	
simplest form (of a fraction) A fraction is in simplest form when the numerator and denominator have no common factors other than 1. (p. 181)	**mínima expresión (de una fracción)** Una fracción está en su mínima expresión cuando el numerador y el denominador no tienen más factor común que 1.	Fraction: $\frac{8}{12}$ Simplest form: $\frac{2}{3}$
simplify To write a fraction or expression in simplest form. (p. 18)	**simplificar** Escribir una fracción o expresión numérica en su mínima expresión.	
simulation A model of an experiment, often one that would be too difficult or too time-consuming to actually perform. (p. 660)	**simulación** Representación de un experimento, por lo regular de uno cuya realización sería demasiado difícil o llevaría mucho tiempo.	
skew lines Lines that lie in different planes that are neither parallel nor intersecting. (p. 420)	**líneas oblicuas** Líneas que se encuentran en planos distintos, por eso no se intersecan ni son paralelas.	$\overleftrightarrow{AE}$ and $\overleftrightarrow{CD}$ are skew lines.
slope The constant rate of change of a line. (p. 707)	**pendiente** La tasa de cambio constante de una línea.	$\frac{1}{1}=1 \quad \frac{3}{3}=1 \quad \frac{2}{2}=1 \quad \frac{1}{1}=1$

ENGLISH	SPANISH	EXAMPLES
solid figure A three-dimensional figure.	**cuerpo geométrico** Figura tridimensional.	
solution of an equation A value or values that make an equation true. (p. 66)	**solución de una ecuación** Valor o valores que hacen verdadera una ecuación.	Equation: $x + 2 = 6$ Solution: $x = 4$
solution of an inequality A value or values that make an inequality true. (p. 718)	**solución de una desigualdad** Valor o valores que hacen verdadera una desigualdad.	Inequality: $x + 3 \geq 10$ Solution: $x \geq 7$
solve To find an answer or a solution.	**resolver** Hallar una respuesta o solución.	
sphere A three-dimensional figure with all points the same distance from the center. (p. 561)	**esfera** Figura tridimensional en la que todos los puntos están a la misma distancia del centro.	
square (geometry) A rectangle with four congruent sides. (p. 434)	**cuadrado (en geometría)** Rectángulo con cuatro lados congruentes.	
square (numeration) A number raised to the second power.	**cuadrado (en numeración)** Número elevado a la segunda potencia.	In 5^2, the number 5 is squared.
square number A number that is the product of a whole number and itself.	**cuadrado de un número** El producto de un número cabal multiplicado por sí mismo.	25 is a square number since $5^2 = 25$.
square root A number that is multiplied by itself to form a product is called a square root of that product. (p. 539)	**raíz cuadrada** El número que se multiplica por sí mismo para formar un producto se denomina la raíz cuadrada de ese producto.	$16 = 4 \cdot 4$ and $16 = -4 \cdot -4$, so 4 and -4 are square roots of 16.
standard form (in numeration) A number written using digits.	**forma estándar** Una forma de escribir números por medio de dígitos.	Five thousand, two hundred ten in standard form is 5,210.
stem-and-leaf plot A graph used to organize and display data so that the frequencies can be compared. (p. 322)	**diagrama de tallo y hojas** Gráfica que muestra y ordena los datos, y que sirve para comparar las frecuencias.	Stem | Leaves 3 | 2 3 4 4 7 9 4 | 0 1 5 7 7 7 8 5 | 1 2 2 3 Key: 3|2 means 3.2
straight angle An angle that measures 180°. (p. 411)	**ángulo llano** Ángulo que mide exactamente 180°.	
subset A set contained within another set. (p. 171)	**subconjunto** Conjunto que pertenece a otro conjunto.	

Glossary/Glosario **G25**

ENGLISH	SPANISH	EXAMPLES
substitute To replace a variable with a number or another expression in an algebraic expression.	**sustituir** Reemplazar una variable por un número u otra expresión en una expresión algebraica.	
sum The result when two or more numbers are added.	**suma** Resultado de sumar dos o más números.	
supplementary angles Two angles whose measures have a sum of 180°. (p. 417)	**ángulos suplementarios** Dos ángulos cuyas medidas suman 180°.	30° 150°
surface area The sum of the areas of the faces, or surfaces, of a three-dimensional figure. (p. 576)	**área total** Suma de las áreas de las caras, o superficies, de una figura tridimensional.	12 cm, 6 cm, 8 cm Surface area = $2(8)(12) + 2(8)(6) + 2(12)(6) = 432$ cm^2

T

ENGLISH	SPANISH	EXAMPLES
term (in a sequence) An element or number in a sequence. (p. 29)	**término (en una sucesión)** Elemento o número de una sucesión.	5 is the third term in the sequence 1, 3, 5, 7, 9, . . .
terminating decimal A decimal number that ends, or terminates. (p. 176)	**decimal finito** Decimal con un número determinado de posiciones decimales.	6.75
tessellation A repeating pattern of plane figures that completely cover a plane with no gaps or overlaps. (p. 462)	**teselado** Patrón repetido de figuras planas que cubren totalmente un plano sin superponerse ni dejar huecos.	
theoretical probability The ratio of the number of ways an event can occur to the total number of equally likely outcomes. (p. 666)	**probabilidad teórica** Razón del numero de las maneras que puede ocurrir un suceso al numero total de resultados igualmente probables.	When rolling a number cube, the theoretical probability of rolling a 4 is $\frac{1}{6}$.
tip The amount of money added to a bill for service; usually a percent of the bill. (p. 384)	**propina** Cantidad que se agrega al total de una factura por servicios. Por lo general, es un porcentaje del total de la factura.	
transformation A change in the size or position of a figure. (p. 453)	**transformación** Cambio en el tamaño o la posición de una figura.	

Glossary/Glosario

ENGLISH	SPANISH	EXAMPLES
translation A movement (slide) of a figure along a straight line. (p. 453)	**traslación** Desplazamiento de una figura a lo largo de una línea recta.	
trapezoid A quadrilateral with exactly one pair of parallel sides. (p. 434)	**trapecio** Cuadrilátero con un par de lados paralelos.	
tree diagram A branching diagram that shows all possible combinations or outcomes of an event. (p. 662)	**diagrama de árbol** Diagrama ramificado que muestra todas las posibles combinaciones o resultados de un suceso.	
trial Each repetition or observation of an experiment. (p. 656)	**prueba** Cada repetición u observación de un experimento.	In the experiment of rolling a number cube, each roll is one trial.
triangle A three-sided polygon.	**triángulo** Polígono de tres lados.	
Triangle Sum Theorem The theorem that states that the measures of the angles in a triangle add to 180°.	**Teorema de la suma del triángulo** Teorema que establece que las medidas de los ángulos de un triángulo suman 180°.	
triangular prism A polyhedron whose bases are triangles and whose other faces are rectangles.	**prisma triangular** Poliedro cuyas bases son triángulos y cuyas demás caras tienen forma de rectángulos.	

U

ENGLISH	SPANISH	EXAMPLES
underestimate An estimate that is less than the exact answer. (p. 6)	**estimación baja** Estimación menor que la respuesta exacta.	100 is an underestimate for the sum 26 + 29 + 31 + 27.
union The set of all elements that belong to two or more sets. (p. 170)	**unión** El conjunto de todos los elementos que pertenecen a dos o más conjuntos.	
unit conversion The process of changing one unit of measure to another.	**conversión de unidades** Proceso que consiste en cambiar una unidad de medida por otra.	
unit rate A rate in which the second quantity in the comparison is one unit. (p. 343)	**tasa unitaria** Una tasa en la que la segunda cantidad de la comparación es una unidad.	10 cm per minute
unlike fractions Fractions with different denominators. (p. 192)	**fracciones distintas** Fracciones con distinto denominador.	$\frac{3}{4}$ and $\frac{1}{2}$ are unlike fractions.

ENGLISH	SPANISH	EXAMPLES

V

variable A symbol used to represent a quantity that can change. (p. 50) | **variable** Símbolo que representa una cantidad que puede cambiar. | In the expression $2x + 3$, x is the variable.

Venn diagram A diagram that is used to show relationships between sets. (p. 170) | **diagrama de Venn** Diagrama que muestra las relaciones entre conjuntos. |

vertex On an angle or polygon, the point where two sides intersect. (p. 410) | **vértice** En un ángulo o polígono, el punto de intersección de dos lados | A is the vertex of $\angle CAB$.

vertical angles A pair of opposite congruent angles formed by intersecting lines. (p. 416) | **ángulos opuestos por el vértice** Par de ángulos opuestos congruentes formados por líneas secantes. | $\angle 1$ and $\angle 3$ are vertical angles. $\angle 2$ and $\angle 4$ are vertical angles.

volume The number of cubic units needed to fill a given space. (p. 566) | **volumen** Número de unidades cúbicas que se necesitan para llenar un espacio. | Volume $= 3 \cdot 4 \cdot 12 = 144$ ft^3

X

x-axis The horizontal axis on a coordinate plane. (p. 604) | **eje x** El eje horizontal del plano cartesiano. |

x-coordinate The first number in an ordered pair; it tells the distance to move right or left from the origin, (0, 0). (p. 604) | **coordenada x** El primer número en un par ordenado; indica la distancia que debes avanzar hacia la izquierda o hacia la derecha desde el origen, (0, 0). |

ENGLISH	SPANISH	EXAMPLES

Y

y-axis The vertical axis on a coordinate plane. (p. 604)

eje y El eje vertical del plano cartesiano.

y-coordinate The second number in an ordered pair; it tells the distance to move up or down from the origin, (0, 0). (p. 604)

coordenada y El segundo número en un par ordenado; indica la distancia que debes avanzar hacia arriba o hacia abajo desde el origen, (0, 0).

Z

zero pair A number and its opposite, which add to 0.

par nulo Un número y su opuesto, que sumados dan 0.

18 and −18

Index

A

Absolute value, 595
Acute angles, 411
Acute triangles, 429
Addition
  decimals, 110–111
    exploring, 108–109
    mental math, 111
    rounding to estimate, 104
  fractions
    estimating, 200–201
    with like denominators, 196–197
    modeling, 222–223
    with unlike denominators, 224–225
  integers, 614–616
  inverse operations, 70, 74
  mixed numbers, 196–197, 228–229
  solving equations by, 74–75, 238–239, 714–715
  solving inequalities by, 718
  whole numbers, SB3
    estimating, 6
Addition equations, 70–71
Additional data, 292–293
Adjacent angles, 416
Agriculture Link, 195
Alfred the Great, 483
Algebra
  The development of algebra skills and concepts is a central focus of this course and is found throughout this book.
  equations
    addition, solving by, 74–75
    decimal, 136–137
    division, solving by, 77–78
    fraction, 238–239, 264–265
    integer, 630–633
    linear, 703
    multiplication, solving by, 81–82
    solutions of, 66–67
    subtraction, solving by, 70–71
    two-step, 714–715
    with two variables, 702–703
  expressions
    algebraic, 50–51
    translating between tables and, 58–59
    translating between words and, 54–55
  functions, 698
    graphing, 702–703
    input and output, 698
    linear, 703, 710–711
    nonlinear, 710–711
    rate of change, 706–707
    slope, 707

  tables and, 698–699
    translating words into, 698–699
  inequalities, 718, 722–723
  properties
    Associative, 22–23
    Commutative, 22–23
    Distributive, 22–23
  proportions, 352–353
    cross products to complete, 353
    exploring, 350–351
    and indirect measurement, 360–361
    modeling, 352
    in scale drawings, 363–365
    in similar figures, 356–357
  variables, 50–51
Algebra tiles, 630–631, 632–633
Algebraic expressions
  evaluating, 50–51
  translating between tables and, 58–59
  translating between words and, 54–55
Alternate exterior angles, 425
Alternate interior angles, 425
Alvin submersible, 597
Amazon River, 54
American colonies, 314
Angle(s)
  acute, 411, 429
  adjacent, 416
  alternate exterior, 425
  alternate interior, 425
  classifying, 411
  complementary, 417
  congruent, 414–416
  corresponding, 356, 425
  drawing, 410
  exterior, SB12
  interior, SB12
  measuring, 410
  obtuse, 411, 429
  in polygons, 502–503
  right, 411, 429
  straight, 411
  supplementary, 417
  in triangles, 429, 433
  vertical, 416
Applications
  Agriculture, 195
  Archaeology, 21
  Architecture, 411, 490, 513, 541, 554, 563, 579
  Art, 117, 445, 491, 546
  Astronomy, 26–27, 102, 103, 159, 186–187, 188, 365, 596
  Biology, 348, 490
  Career, 113
  Chemistry, 383
  Construction, 622
  Consumer, 19, 218, 451
  Consumer Economics, 715
  Consumer Math, 124, 127, 128, 131, 343, 344, 380
  Cooking, 193, 257, 554
  Crafts, 240

  Earth Science, 24, 61, 83, 101, 119, 132, 295, 372, 376, 555, 597, 600, 601, 616, 618, 622, 625
  Economics, 709
  Education, 290
  Entertainment, 118, 266, 347, 378
  Games, 669
  Gardening, 707
  Geography, 76, 118, 294, 409, 490, 601, 720, 721
  Geometry, 52, 138, 163, 382
  Graphic Art, 358
  Graphic Design, 701
  Health, 104, 107, 321
  History, 73, 132, 294, 349, 483, 515, 553, 618
  Hobbies, 366, 456
  Language Arts, 377, 456
  Life Science, 13, 25, 67, 80, 119, 164, 168, 178, 189, 196, 199, 203, 217, 227, 229, 230, 231, 247, 253, 263, 265, 267, 317, 366, 372, 629, 635, 655, 675, 682
  Marine Life, 717
  Measurement, 52, 68, 133, 137, 188, 230, 235, 240, 353, 361, 452, 515, 549, 573
  Money, 53, 68, 107
  Music, 374, 461, 571
  Photography, 133
  Physical Science, 73, 82, 102, 125, 163, 421, 569, 705
  Physics, 487
  Recreation, 535, 617, 664, 682
  School, 230, 664
  Science, 57, 122, 573
  Social Studies, 9, 21, 32, 54, 56, 68, 71, 76, 134, 168, 181, 189, 224, 226, 239, 245, 292, 301, 307, 327, 355, 367, 373, 387, 432, 447, 458, 499, 537, 543, 547, 607, 635, 665, 668, 683, 720
  Sports, 27, 110, 113, 163, 178, 201, 240, 292, 294, 348, 437, 490, 492, 503, 509, 555, 597, 599, 618, 634, 654, 658
  Swimming, 113
  Technology, 381, 383
  Theater, 725
  Transportation, 709
  Weather, 284–285, 659, 668
Archaeology, 21
Architecture, 411, 490, 513, 541, 554, 563
Architecture Link, 579
Are You Ready?, 3, 47, 95, 153, 215, 281, 339, 403, 475, 531, 591, 649, 695
Area, 534
  changing dimensions, 548–549
  circles, 551–553
  comparing perimeter and, 544
  comparing units of, SB14
  composite figures, 545–546
  irregular figures, estimating, 534
  parallelograms, 534

I2 Index

rectangles, 62–63, 534–535
squares, 538–539
surface area, 576–577
trapezoids, 540
triangles, 539–540
Arithmetic sequence, 29–30
Armstrong, Lance, 492
Art, 117, 444, 445, 546
Art Link, 491
Assessment
Chapter Test, 41, 91, 147, 211, 275, 335, 397, 471, 525, 587, 643, 691, 733
Countdown to Testing, C4–C27
Cumulative Assessment, 44–45, 92–93, 150–151, 212–212, 278–279, 336–337, 400–401, 472–473, 528–529, 588–589, 646–647, 692–693, 736–737
Ready To Go On?, 14, 34, 64, 84, 114, 140, 172, 190, 204, 242, 268, 296, 328, 368, 390, 426, 448, 464, 500, 518, 556, 580, 612, 636, 670, 684, 712, 726
Real-World Connection, 35, 85, 141, 205, 269, 329, 391, 465, 519, 581, 637, 685, 727
Standardized Test Prep, 44–45, 92–93, 150–151, 212–212, 278–279, 336–337, 400–401, 472–473, 528–529, 588–589, 646–647, 692–693, 736–737
Study Guide: Preview, 4, 48, 96, 154, 216, 282, 340, 476, 532, 592, 650, 696
Study Guide: Review, 38–40, 88–90, 144–146, 208–210, 272–274, 332–334, 394–396, 468–470, 522–524, 584–586, 640–642, 688–690, 730–732
Test Tackler
Any Question Type: Use a Diagram, 526–527
Extended Response: Write Extended Responses, 398–399
Gridded Response: Write Gridded Responses, 276–277
Multiple Choice
Eliminate Answer Choices, 42–43
Identifying Keywords and Context Clues, 644–645
Recognize Distracters, 734–735
Short Response: Write Short Response, 148–149
Associative Property, 22–23
Astronomy, 26–27, 102, 159, 186–187, 188, 365, 596
Astronomy Link, 103
Atlantic Ocean, 118, 224, 600
Augustus, 618
Australia, 307, 547
Axes, 604

B

Balance scales, 66–67, 70
Bar graphs, 298-299
misleading, 318
using a spreadsheet to create, 302–303
when to use, 325
Base
of a number, 10
of a three-dimensional figure, 560
Berganio, David, 598
Bergen, Bill, 113
Bias, SB19
Biology, 348, 490
Box-and-whisker plot, SB18
Brazil, 238
Bull, Sherman, 292

C

Calculator, 142; *see also* Graphing calculator
Calories, 104
Capacity
converting units of, 488–489, 493
customary units of, 481
metric units of, 485
Cape Hatteras lighthouse, 361
Career Link, 113
Carver, George Washington, 709
Caution!, 22, 59, 77, 104, 261, 314, 323, 353, 488, 493, 502, 503, 566, 706
Celsius degrees, converting to Fahrenheit, 497
Center of a circle, 512
Centimeter, 484
Centimeter cubes, 558–559, 564–565, 566–567
Centimeter ruler, 549
Challenge
Challenge exercises are found in every lesson. Some examples: 9, 13, 21, 25, 28
Changing dimensions, 548–549
Chapter Project Online, 2, 46, 94, 152, 214, 280, 338, 402, 474, 530, 590, 648, 694
Chapter Test, 41, 91, 147, 211, 275, 335, 397, 471, 525, 587, 643, 691, 733
Chemistry, 383
Chess, 58, 456
Chicago, 364
***Children at the Ice Cream Stand* (Johnson),** 357
Choose a Strategy, 32, 69, 128, 159, 221, 241, 432, 456, 515, 573, 618, 665
Chord, 512
Circle graphs, 516–517

Circles, 512
area, 551–553
circumference, 510–511, 512–513
diameter, 512
radius, 512
sector of, SB11
Circumference, 512–513
exploring, 510–511
Classifying
angles, 411
pairs of lines, 420–421
polygons, 438–439
quadrilaterals, 434–435
three-dimensional figures, 560–561
triangles, 429–430
Coinage Act, 132
Colonies, American, 314
Colorado, 79
Combinations, 679
Common denominators, 193
Common factors, 165
Communicating Math
choose, 245
classify, 439
compare, 435, 561
describe, 7, 59, 71, 82, 123, 197, 245, 289, 299, 305, 312, 323, 326, 451, 493, 553, 567, 577, 605, 621, 627, 663, 667, 723
determine, 105, 201, 251, 421, 458
explain, 11, 19, 30, 51, 59, 75, 82, 101, 111, 117, 127, 137, 157, 162, 166, 181, 187, 193, 197, 201, 219, 225, 229, 235, 239, 245, 255, 261, 265, 285, 293, 343, 347, 357, 372, 376, 381, 385, 407, 411, 430, 445, 451, 458, 485, 489, 497, 503, 507, 513, 535, 541, 546, 549, 553, 567, 571, 599, 609, 621, 624, 657, 663, 673, 699, 703, 707, 719
give, 55, 299, 376, 417, 535, 595, 616
give an example, 27, 67, 235, 239, 319, 353, 365, 372, 381, 411, 421, 454, 481, 653, 667, 673, 707, 715
look, 176
make a conjecture, 715, 723
name, 51, 101, 251, 357, 361, 407, 439, 454, 595, 653
predict, 609
read, 11, 187
show, 111, 123
suppose, 7, 365
tell, 19, 27, 30, 55, 67, 71, 75, 78, 82, 105, 111, 117, 123, 127, 130, 134, 137, 157, 162, 166, 176, 181, 187, 193, 197, 201, 219, 225, 229, 251, 255, 265, 285, 289, 299, 312, 319, 343, 353, 372, 376, 385, 411, 430, 435, 445, 507, 513, 549, 553, 577, 595, 599, 605, 609, 616, 633, 657, 681, 703, 707, 719
use, 417
write, 372
Commutative Property, 22–23

Index **I3**

Comparing
  area and perimeter, 544
  decimals, 101
  experimental probabilities, 657
  fractions, 192–193
  integers, 598
  probabilities, 653
  rational numbers, 602–603
  units of area, SB14
  whole numbers, SB1
Compass, 511
Compatible numbers, 6
Complement, 667
Complementary angles, 417
Composite figures, 545–546
Composite numbers, 157
Compound events, 672–673
Computer
  geometry software, 433
  spreadsheet, 33, 302–303
Cone, 561
Congruent angles, 414–416
Congruent figures, 450–451
Congruent line segments, 430
Constant, 50
Constitution, U.S., 720
Construction, 622
Consumer application, 19, 218, 451
Consumer Economics, 715
Consumer Math, 124, 127, 128, 131, 343, 344, 380
Conversion factors, 488–489
Conversions
  customary units, 488–489
  metric units, 492–493
  between measurement systems, SB15
  between percents, decimals, and fractions, 379
  temperature, 497
  time, 496
Cooking, 193, 554
Cooking Link, 257
Coordinate grid, 311–312
Coordinate plane
  characteristics, 604
  graphing points on, 605
  linear functions, 703
  locating points on, 605
  quadrants, 604
  transformations on, 608–609
Coordinates, 604
Corresponding angles, 356, 425
Corresponding sides, 356
Costa Rica, 238–239
Countdown to Testing, C4–C27
Counters, 287, 288, 350–351, 614, 616, 619, 620–621
Counting methods, 662–663
Crafts, 240

Critical Thinking, 25, 56, 57, 61, 69, 128, 135, 159, 163, 167, 202, 256, 262, 267, 290, 291, 306, 307, 320, 327, 345, 358, 409, 413, 423, 432, 437, 441, 482, 491, 495, 543, 550, 555, 563, 618, 625, 628, 634, 668, 682, 709, 721
Cross products, 353
Cube, 560
Cumulative frequency, 308–309
Cup, 481, 488
Currency, 355
Customary units of measure, 480–481
  converting, 488–489
Cylinders, 560
  creating nets for, 574
  surface area, 577
  volume, 564–565, 570–571

Data
  additional, 292–293
  displays
    bar graphs, 298–299, 302–303
    box-and-whisker plots, SB18
    choosing an appropriate, 325–326
    frequency tables, 304–305
    histograms, 305
    line graphs, 314–315
    line plots, 304
    misleading, 318–319
    stem-and-leaf plots, 322–323
    tables, 284–285
  frequency distributions of, 308–309
  outliers, 292–293
  using a survey to collect, 310
Davis, Shani, 292
Davis Cup, 294
Days, 496–497
Dead Sea, 601
Death Valley, California, 594
Decagon, 438
Decimal equations, 136–137
Decimal grids, 98–99, 108–109, 120–121, 174, 175, 181
Decimals
  addition, 110–111
    exploring, 108–109
    mental math, 111
    rounding to estimate, 104
  comparing, 101
  converting between percents, fractions and, 375–376, 379
  division
    by decimals, 129–130
    exploring, 120–121
    interpreting the quotient, 133–134
    rounding to estimate, 105
    by whole numbers, 126–127
  equations, 136–137
  estimating, 104–105
  fractions and, 174–176

  modeling, 98–99
  multiplication, 122–123
    exploring, 120–121
    rounding to estimate, 105
  ordering, 101
  percents written as, 372, 375
  place value and, 100
  probability, 652–653
  reading, 100
  repeating, 176
  rounding, 104–105, SB2
  subtraction, 110–111
    exploring, 108–109
    mental math, 111
    rounding to estimate, 104
  terminating, 176
Decimeter, 484
Declaration of Independence, 294
Degrees, 410
Denominators
  common, 193
  like, adding and subtracting with, 196–197
  unlike, adding and subtracting with, 224–225
Density, 569
Dependent events, 676–677
Diagonal, 438
Diameter, 510, 512
Discounts, 384–385
Displaying data, *see* Data, displays
Distance
  converting units of, 493
  finding on maps and scale drawings, 364–365
Distributive Property, 22–23
Divisibility, 156–157
Divisible, 156
Division
  decimals
    by decimals, 129–130
    exploring, 120–121
    interpreting the quotient, 133–134
    rounding to estimate, 105
    by whole numbers, 126–127
  divisibility, 156–157
  fractions
    modeling, 258–259
    using reciprocals, 260–261
  integers, 626–627
  inverse operations, 77, 81
  mixed numbers, 260–261
  solving equations by, 77–78, 714–715
  solving inequalities by, 718
  whole numbers, SB5
    estimating, 7
  with zeros in the quotient, SB5
Division equations, 81–82
Double-bar graph, 299
Double-line graph, 315
Draw a Diagram, PS1
Drawings, scale, 363–365

I4 Index

E

Earth, 159, 365, 596
  surface covered by oceans, 224
Earth Science, 24, 61, 83, 101, 119, 132, 372, 376, 600, 601, 616, 618, 622, 625
Earth Science Link, 295, 555, 597
Economics, 709
Edge (of a three-dimensional figure), 560
Edison, Thomas, 570–571
Education, 290
Eiffel Tower, 362
El Azizia, Libya, 295
Elements of sets, 170
Elevation, 635
Empire State Building, 83
Endangered species, 164
Entertainment, 118, 266, 347
Entertainment Link, 378
Equally likely, 666
Equations
  addition, 70–71
  decimal, 136–137
  division, 81–82
  fraction, 238–239, 264–265
  integer, 630–633
  linear, 703
  multiplication, 77–78
  solutions of, 66–67
  subtraction, 74–75
  two-step, 714–715
  with two variables, 702–703
  with variables on both sides, SB10
Equator, 607
Equilateral triangles, 430
Equivalent fractions, 179–181
Equivalent ratios, 342–343
  In proportions, 350–351
  using tables to explore, 346–347
Estimation, 52, 68, 79, 119, 132, 486, 491, 499, 515, 537, 579
  decimals, 104–105
  fraction sums and differences, 200–201
  front-end, 105
  temperature, 497
  whole numbers, 6–7
Evaluate, 50
Events, 656
  complement, 667
  compound, 672–673
  dependent, 676–677
  independent, 676–677
Everest, Mount, 292
Experiment, 656
Experimental probability, 656–657
Exploring
  area and perimeter of rectangles, 62–63
  area of circles, 551
  circumference, 510–511
  decimal addition and subtraction, 108–109
  decimal multiplication and division, 120–121
  decimals and fractions, 174
  factors, 160
  fraction measurement, 184–185
  linear and nonlinear relationships, 710–711
  order of operations, 16–17
  perimeter and area, 544
  permutations and combinations, 678–679
  proportions, 350–351
  volumes of prisms and cylinders, 564–565
Exponential form, 10
Exponents, 10–11
  in order of operations, 19
Expressions
  algebraic, 50
  integer, 616, 621, 624, 627
  translating between tables and, 58–59
  translating between words and, 54–55
Extended Response, 32, 57, 132, 195, 247, 327, 387, 423, 495, 625, 669
  Write Extended Responses, 398–399
Extension
  Frequency Distribution, 308–309
  Independent and Dependent Events, 676–677
  Negative Rational Numbers, 602–603
  Sets of Numbers, 170–171
  Simple Interest, 388–389
Exterior angles, 425, SB12
Exterior Angle Theorem, SB12

F

Face (of a three-dimensional figure), 560
Factors
  common, 165
  explore, 160
  greatest common factor, 165–166
  prime factorization, 160–161
Factor tree, 161
Fahrenheit degrees, converting to Celsius, 497
Fair, 666
Fernandez, Armand, 491
Figures
  composite, area of, 545–546
  congruent, 450–451
  irregular, estimating area of, 534
  similar, 356–357, 548–549
  three-dimensional figures, see Three-dimensional figures
Find a Pattern, PS5
Flatiron Building, 540, 541
Florida, 367
Focus on Problem Solving
  Look Back, 501, 671
  Make a Plan, 297, 369, 449, 713
  Solve, 15, 115, 243, 427, 557
  Understand the Problem, 65, 173, 191, 613
Formulas, see inside back cover
Foot, 480, 488
The *Four Seasons* (Vivaldi), 241
Fraction bars, 186–187, 196–197, 222–223, 232–233, 234, 248–249, 258–259
Fraction equations
  addition and subtraction, 238–239
  multiplication and division, 264–265
Fractional part of a region, SB8
Fractional part of a set, SB8
Fractions
  addition
    estimating, 200–201
    with like denominators, 196–197
    mixed numbers, 228–229
    modeling, 222–223
    with unlike denominators, 224–225
  common denominators, 193
  comparing, 192–193
  converting between percents, decimals and, 375–376, 379
  decimals and, 174–176
  division
    mixed numbers, 260–261
    modeling, 258–259
    using reciprocals, 260–261
  equations
    addition and subtraction, 238–239
    multiplication and division, 264–265
  equivalent, 179–181
  improper, 186–187
  like fractions, 192, 196–197
  measurement and, 184–185
  multiplication, 250–251
    mixed numbers, 254–255
    modeling, 248–249
    by whole numbers, 244–245
  ordering, 193
  percents and, 371, 376
  probability, 652–653
  proper, 186
  simplest form, 181
  subtraction
    estimating, 200–201
    with like denominators, 196–197
    mixed numbers, 228–229
    modeling, 222–223
    with regrouping, 232–235
    with unlike denominators, 224–225
  unlike fractions, 192, 224–225
  using to name part of a region, SB8
  using to name part of a set, SB8
Freitag, Jacques, 488
Frequency, 304
Frequency distribution, 308–309
Frequency table
  cumulative frequency, 308–309

with intervals, 305
with tally marks, 304
Front-end estimation, 105
Functions, 698
  graphing, 702–703
  input and output, 698
  linear, 703, 710–711
  nonlinear, 710–711
  rate of change, 706–707
  slope, 707
  tables and, 698–699
Fundamental Counting Principle, 663

G

Galileo Galilei, 125
Gallon, 481, 488
Games Link, 669
Game Time
  Fraction Bingo, 270
  Fraction Riddles, 270
  The Golden Rectangle, 392
  Jumbles, 142
  Logic Puzzle, 520
  Make a Buck, 142
  Math Magic, 86
  A Math Riddle, 638
  Palindromes, 36
  Poly-Cross Puzzle, 582
  Polygon Hide-and-Seek, 582
  Probability Brain Teasers, 686
  Riddle Me This, 206
  On a Roll, 206
  Round and Round and Round, 686
  Spin-a-Million, 36
  Spinnermeania, 330
  Tangrams, 466
  A Thousand Words, 330
  Triple Play, 392
  Try Angles, 728
  24 Points, 728
  Zero Sum, 638
Game Time Extra, 36, 86, 142, 206, 270, 330, 392, 466, 520, 582, 638, 686, 728
Garcia, Sergio, 598
Gardening, 707
General Sherman, 247
Geography, 76, 118, 294, 490, 601, 720
Geography Link, 409, 721
Geometric patterns, 444–445
Geometry
  The development of geometry skills and concepts is a central focus of this course and is found throughout this book.
  angles, 410–411, 414–417, 425, 502–503
  applications, 52, 138, 163, 382
  area, 534–535, 538–541, 544–546, 548–549, 551–553
  circles, 510–513
  circumference, 510–513
  congruent figures, 450–451

cylinders, 564–565, 570–571
geometric patterns, 444–445
lines, 406, 420–421, 424–425
line segment, 406
nets, 574–577
parallelograms, 534–535
perimeter, 506–507, 544
planes, 406
points, 406
polygons, 438–439, 442–443
prisms, 564–567
pyramids, 561, 577
quadrilaterals, 434–435
rays, 407
rectangles, 62–63, 434–435, 506, 534–535, 544, 548
similar figures, 356, 360–361, 548–549
software, 433
squares, 434–435, 538–539
surface area, 574–577, 576–577
symmetry, 457–458
tessellations, 462–463
three-dimensional figures, 558–561, 574–575
transformations, 453–454, 608–609
triangles, 428–430, 433
volume, 564–567, 570–571
Geometry software, 433
George Washington Bridge, 159
Georgia Aquarium, 474
Giant squid, 85
Golden Gate Bridge, 159
Goldwater, Barry, 349
Gram, 484, 492–493
Grand Canyon, 83, 129
Graphic Art, 358
Graphic Design, 701
Graphing calculator, 16–17, 169, 379
Graphing
  functions, 702–703
  inequalities, 718
  linear functions, 703
  ordered pairs, 311–312
  points on coordinate plane, 605
  transformations, 608–609
Graphs
  bar, 298–299, 302–303
  circle, 516–517
  double-bar, 299
  double-line, 315
  histogram, 305
  line, 314–315
  misleading, 318–319
Gravitational effect, 122
Greatest common factor (GCF), 165–166
  graphing calculator to find, 169
  simplest form and, 181
Great Pyramid of Khufu, 632
Gridded Response, 21, 25, 53, 103, 119, 128, 164, 178, 237, 257, 267, 291, 295, 324, 362, 367, 409, 441, 547, 555, 569, 579, 655, 665, 709, 717
  Use a Diagram, 526–527
  Write Gridded Responses, 276–277

Grids
  coordinate, 311–312
  decimal, 98–99, 108–109, 120–121, 174, 175, 181
  ten by ten, 370, 374
Guess and Test, PS3
Gymnastics, 110

H

Hands-On Lab
  Collect Data to Explore Mean, 287
  Construct Circle Graphs, 516–517
  Construct Congruent Segments and Angles, 414–415
  Create Tessellations, 462–463
  Draw Views of Three-Dimensional Figures, 558–559
  Explore Area and Perimeter of Rectangles, 62–63
  Explore Area of Circles, 551
  Explore Circumference, 510–511
  Explore Decimal Addition and Subtraction, 108–109
  Explore Decimal Multiplication and Division, 120–121
  Explore Decimals and Fractions, 174
  Explore Factors, 160
  Explore Fraction Measurement, 184–185
  Explore Linear and Nonlinear Relationships, 710–711
  Explore Perimeter and Area, 544
  Explore Permutations and Combinations, 678–679
  Explore Proportions, 350–351
  Explore Volumes of Prisms and Cylinders, 564–565
  Intersecting Polygons, 442–443
  Model Decimals, 98–99
  Model Equivalent Fractions, 179
  Model Fraction Addition and Subtraction, 222–223
  Model Fraction Division, 258–259
  Model Fraction Multiplication, 248–249
  Model Integer Addition, 614
  Model Integer Equations, 630–631
  Model Integer Subtraction, 619
  Model Percents, 370
  Model Subtraction with Regrouping, 232–233
  Model Three-Dimensional Figures, 574–575
  Parallel Line Relationships, 424–425
  Select and Use Appropriate Measuring Tools, 478–479
  Simulations, 660–661
  Sketch Scale Drawings, 363
  Squares and Square Roots, 538–539
  Triangle Inequality, 428
  Use a Survey to Collect Data, 310
Hawaii, 56
Health, 104, 107
Health Link, 321

Helpful Hint, 29, 129, 161, 162, 166, 171, 181, 192, 197, 201, 229, 251, 292, 315, 322, 346, 364, 376, 380, 430, 492, 545, 546, 561, 577, 602, 604, 609, 632, 652, 653, 698, 714

Heptagon, 438

Hexagon, 438

Histogram, 305

History, 73, 294, 553

History Link, 132, 349, 483, 515, 618

Hobbies, 366

Hobbies Link, 456

Homework Help Online
Homework Help Online is available for every lesson. Refer to the go.hrw.com box at the beginning of every exercise set. Some examples: 8, 12, 20, 24, 27

Hot Tip!, 43, 45, 93, 149, 151, 213, 279, 337, 399, 401, 473, 527, 529, 589, 645, 647, 693, 735

Hours, 496–497

Hypotenuse, SB11

I

Iceland, 537

Improper fractions, 186

Inch, 480, 488

Independent events, 676–677

Indian Ocean, 600

Indirect measurement, 360–361

Inequalities
graphing, 718
solutions of, 718
solving by
addition and subtraction, 719
multiplication and division, 719
two-step, 722–723

Input, 698

Integer equations, 630–633

Integers, 594
absolute value, 595
addition, 615–616
modeling, 614
comparing, 598
division, 626–627
equations, 630–633
graphing, 595
multiplication, 623–624
ordering, 598–599
subtraction, 620–621
modeling, 619

Interactivities Online, 10, 29, 50, 54, 66, 71, 74, 77, 81, 100, 110, 116, 136, 156, 161, 175, 180, 186, 238, 244, 250, 254, 264, 289, 292, 311, 318, 343, 353, 356, 364, 371, 375, 380, 406, 411, 416, 420, 429, 434, 450, 453, 506, 548, 560, 566, 570, 576, 615, 620, 652, 656, 662

Interdisciplinary Link, 9, 13, 21

Interest, 388

Interest rate, 388

Interior angles, 425, SB12

International Association of Athletic Federations (IAAF), 488

International Space Station, 581

Intersecting lines, 420–421

Intersecting planes, SB13

Intersection of sets, 170–171

Inverse operations
addition and subtraction, 70, 74
multiplication and division, 77, 81

Inverse properties, SB6

Isosceles triangles, 430

It's in the Bag!
Area and Volume Suitcase, 583
CD Spinner, 687
Double-Door Fractions, Decimals, and Percents, 393
Flipping over Fractions, 271
Geometry Grab Bag, 467
Graphing According to Me, 331
Perfectly Packaged Perimeters, 521
Picture Envelopes, 729
Picture This, 37
Positive-Negative Pull-Out, 639
Projects E Z 2 C Decimals, 143
Spec-Tag-Ular Number Theory, 207
Tri-Sided Equations, 87

J

Jamaica, 499

Jan-Ken-Pon, 665

Johnson, Lyndon B., 349

Johnson, William H., 357

Jupiter, 125, 596

K

Kerr, Cristie, 618

Kilauea, 615, 616

Kilimanjaro, 601

Kilogram, 484

Kilometer, 484

L

Lab Resources Online, 16, 33, 62, 98, 108, 120, 160, 169, 174, 179, 184, 222, 232, 248, 258, 287, 310, 350, 363, 370, 379, 414, 424, 428, 433, 442, 462, 478, 510, 516, 538, 544, 551, 558, 564, 574, 614, 619, 630, 660

Labs, see Hands-On Lab; Technology Lab

Ladder diagrams
greatest common factor, 165
prime factorization, 161

Lake Superior, 490

Language Arts, 377, 456

La Paz, Bolivia, 635

Latitude, lines of, 607

Leaning Tower of Pisa, 505

Least common denominator (LCD), 226

Least common multiple (LCM), 218–219

Leg, SB11

Legend (on a map), 409

Length
converting units of, 488–489
customary units of, 480
metric units of, 484

Library of Congress, 119

Life Science, 67, 178, 196, 203, 217, 229, 230, 263, 366, 372, 635, 675, 682

Life Science Link, 13, 25, 80, 119, 164, 168, 189, 199, 227, 231, 247, 253, 265, 267, 317, 629, 655

Like denominators, 196–197

Like fractions, 192
adding and subtracting with, 196–197

Like terms, SB9

Linear equations, 703

Linear functions, 703
exploring, 710–711
graphing, 703
rate of change, 706–707
slope, 707

Line graphs, 314–315
misleading, 319
when to use, 325

Line of reflection, 453–454

Line of symmetry, 457–458

Line plot, 304

Line segments, 407
congruent, 430
constructing congruent, 414–415

Lines, 406
classifying pairs of, 420–421
intersecting, 420–421
parallel, 420–421
perpendicular, 420–421
of reflection, 453–454
skew, 420–421
of symmetry, 457–458

Link
Agriculture, 195
Architecture, 579
Art, 491
Astronomy, 103
Cooking, 257
Earth Science, 295, 555, 597
Entertainment, 378
Games, 669
Geography, 409, 721
Health, 321
History, 132, 349, 483, 515, 618
Hobbies, 456
Life Science, 13, 25, 80, 119, 164, 168, 189, 199, 227, 231, 247, 253, 265, 267, 317, 629, 655
Marine Life, 717
Money, 53
Music, 374, 461

Index **I7**

Physical Science, 73, 125, 569, 705
Science, 57
Social Studies, 9, 21, 181, 307, 355, 367, 432, 447, 499, 537, 543, 607, 635, 683
Sports, 437, 599
Technology, 383
Theater, 725
Weather, 284–285
The Lion King, 725
Liter, 485, 492–493
Little League Baseball, 163
London Eye, 139
Longitude, lines of, 607
Long-Term Parking (Fernandez), 491
Louvre Museum, 579

M

Mackinac Straits Bridge, 159
Madagascar, 267
Magellan, Ferdinand, 73
Mah Jong, 669
Make a Conjecture, 425, 442, 443, 715, 723
Make a Model, PS2
Make a Table, PS6
Make an Organized List, PS10
Manipulatives
    algebra tiles, 630–631, 632–633
    balance scales, 66–67, 70
    centimeter cubes, 558–559, 564–565, 566–567
    coins, 673
    counters, 287, 288, 350–351, 614, 616, 619, 620–621
    decimal grids, 98–99, 108–109, 120–121, 174, 175, 181
    fraction bars, 186–187, 196–197, 222–223, 224, 232–233, 234, 248–249, 258–259
    number cube, 206, 672, 676
    pattern blocks, 179
    ruler, 184–185
    spinners, 36, 330, 673, 676–677, 686, 687
    square tiles, 710–711
    ten by ten grid, 370, 374
Maps, 364–365
Maracana Municipal Stadium, 119
Mariana Trench, 597
Marine Life Link, 717
Mars, 125, 132, 596, 622
Martin, Andrew, 58
Mass
    converting units of, 493
    metric units of, 484–485
Maui, 56
Mean, 288–289
    exploring, 287

Measurement
The development of measurement skills and concepts is a central focus of this course and is found throughout this book.
    angles in polygons, 502–503
    Applications, 52, 68, 133, 137, 188, 230, 235, 240, 353, 361, 452, 515, 549
    area, 534–535, 538–541, 544–546, 548–549, 551–553
    circumference, 510–513
    converting between systems of, SB15
    converting units of, 488–489, 492–493
    customary units of, 480–481
    fractions and, 184–185
    indirect, 360–361
    metric units of, 484–485
    nonstandard units, SB16
    perimeter, 506–507
    selecting appropriate tools, 478–479
    surface area, 576–577
    temperature, 496–497
    time, 496–497
Measuring cup, 479
Median, 289
Mental math, 22–23, 111, SB7
Mercury, 61, 125, 365
Meteor Crater, 555
Meteorites, 102, 188
Meter, 484, 492–493
Metric ruler, 478, 484, 485, 510–511
Metric units of measure
    choosing appropriate units of, 484–485
    converting, 492–493
Mile, 480, 488
Milligram, 484
Milliliter, 485
Millimeter, 484
Minnehaha Waterfall, 68
Minutes, 496–497
Misleading graphs, 318–319
Mixed numbers, 175
    addition, 196–197, 228–229
    division, 260–261
    equations, 238–239, 264–265
    improper fractions and, 187
    multiplication, 254–255
    subtraction, 196–197, 228–229
    with regrouping, 232–235
Mode, 289
Modeling
    decimals, 98–99
    equivalent fractions, 179
    fraction addition and subtraction, 222–223
    fraction division, 258–259
    fraction multiplication, 248–249
    integer addition, 614
    integer equations, 630–631
    integer subtraction, 619
    percents, 370

    subtraction with regrouping, 232–233
    three-dimensional figures, 574–575
Money, 68, 107, 132
Money Link, 53
Months, 496–497
Moons of planets, 26
Moracova, Martina, 113
Mount Everest, 601
Mount McKinley, 65, 721
Mount Rainier, 76, 601
Mount Shasta, 76
Multi-Step, 13, 24, 52, 61, 69, 83, 106, 107, 113, 125, 128, 132, 135, 139, 177, 178, 195, 226, 230, 236, 253, 256, 286, 307, 313, 345, 349, 355, 378, 382, 386, 387, 419, 487, 490, 491, 494, 495, 498, 499, 555, 569, 573, 675, 682, 700, 701
Multiple Choice
Multiple Choice test items are found in every lesson. Some examples: 9, 13, 21, 25, 28
    Eliminate Answer Choices, 42–43
    Identifying Keywords and Context Clues, 644–645
    Use a Diagram, 526–527
Multiples, SB6
Multiplication
    decimals, 122–123
        exploring, 120–121
        rounding to estimate, 105
    fractions, 250–251
        modeling, 248–249
        by whole numbers, 244–245
    integers, 623–624
    inverse operations, 77, 81
    mixed numbers, 254–255
    solving equations by, 77–78, 714–715
    solving inequalities by, 718
    whole numbers, SB4
        estimating, 7
Multiplication equations, 77–78
Music, 214, 571
Music Link, 374, 461

N

NASA, 581, 622
Ndebele people, 447
Negative numbers, 594–595
Neptune, 125
Nets, 574–575, 576–577
Nevada, 543
New York City, 76
Nile River, 54
Nonagon, 438
Nonlinear functions, 710–711
Nonstandard units, SB16
Number cube, 206, 672, 676

Number line
  adding integers on, 615–616
  integers, 595, 598–599
  subtracting integers on, 620–621
Numbers
  compatible, 6
  composite, 157
  integers, *see* Integers
  mixed, *see* Mixed numbers
  negative, 594–595
  positive, 594–595
  prime, 157
  rational, 602–603
  in scientific notation, 116–117
  sets of, 170–171
  whole, *see* Whole numbers
Number theory
  divisibility, 156–157
  factors, 160–162, 165–166
  sets of numbers, 170–171
Numerical expressions, 18–19
  translating between tables and, 58–59
  translating between words and, 55

O

Oates, Kareena, 515
Obtuse angles, 411
Obtuse triangles, 429
Octagon, 438
Octavian, 618
Okeechobee, Lake, 367
Old City Market, 181
Olympic Games, 292
Online Resources, 678
  Chapter Projects Online, 2, 46, 94, 152, 214, 280, 338, 402, 474, 530, 590, 648, 694
  Game Time Extra, 36, 86, 142, 206, 270, 330, 392, 466, 520, 582, 638, 686, 728
  Homework Help Online
    Homework Help Online is available for every lesson. Refer to the go.hrw.com box at the beginning of every exercise set. Some examples: 8, 12, 20, 24, 27
  Interactivities Online, 10, 29, 50, 54, 66, 71, 74, 77, 81, 100, 110, 116, 136, 156, 161, 175, 180, 186, 238, 244, 250, 254, 264, 289, 292, 311, 318, 343, 353, 356, 364, 371, 375, 380, 406, 411, 416, 420, 429, 434, 450, 453, 506, 548, 560, 566, 570, 576, 615, 620, 652, 656, 662
  Lab Resources Online, 16, 33, 62, 98, 108, 120, 160, 169, 174, 179, 184, 222, 232, 248, 258, 287, 310, 350, 363, 370, 379, 414, 424, 428, 433, 442, 462, 478, 510, 516, 538, 544, 551, 558, 564, 574, 614, 619, 630, 660, 678

  Resources Online, 3, 14, 34, 47, 64, 84, 95, 114, 140, 153, 172, 190, 204, 215, 242, 268, 281, 296, 302, 328, 339, 368, 390, 403, 426, 448, 464, 475, 500, 518, 531, 556, 580, 591, 612, 636, 649, 670, 684, 695, 712, 726
  State Test Practice, 44, 92, 150, 212, 278, 336, 400, 472, 528, 588, 646, 692, 736
Opposites, 594
Order of operations, 16–19
Ordered pairs, 311–312
Ordering
  decimals, 101
  fractions, 193
  integers, 598–599
  rational numbers, 603
  whole numbers, SB1
Origin, 604
Ounce, 480, 481, 488
Outcomes, 656
Outlier, 292–293
Output, 698
Overestimate, 6
Overtime, 727

P

Pacific Ocean, 224, 600
Parallel lines, 420–421
  constructing, 424
Parallelograms, 434–435
  area of, 534
Pathfinder, 622
Pattern blocks, 179
Patterns, 498
  geometric, 444–445
  sequences and, 29–30, 33
Patterson, Carly, 110
Patterson, David, 73
Pei, I. M., 579
Pentagon, 438
Percent problems, 380–381
Percents, 371
  converting between decimals, fractions and, 375–376, 379
  discounts, 384–385
  modeling, 370–371
  probability, 652–653
  sales tax, 384, 385
  simple interest, 388
  tips, 384, 385
Perimeter, 506
  changing dimensions, 548–549
  comparing area and, 544
  exploring, 62–63
Permutations, 678
Perpendicular lines, 420–421
Photography, 133
Physical Science, 82, 102, 163, 421

Physical Science Link, 73, 125, 569, 705
Physics, 487
Pi, 511, 512, 552
Pike's Peak, 721
Pint, 481, 488
Place value, SB1, 100–101
Planes, 406
  coordinate, 604–605
    transformations in the, 608–609
  relationships between, SB13
Pluto, 188
Pointillism, 116
Points, 406
  graphing on coordinate plane, 605
Polygons, 438; *see also* specific polygons
  angles in, 502–503
  classifying, 438–439
  congruent, 450–451
  diagonals in, 438–439
  exterior angles of, SB12
  interior angles of, SB12
  intersecting, 442–443
  naming, 438
  perimeter of, 506–507
  quadrilaterals, 434–435
  regular, 438
  triangles, 428–430, 433
Polyhedrons, 560–561
Pony Express, 432
Population, 314, 327, 680, SB19
Population density, 294
Positive numbers, 594–595
Pound, 480, 488
Powers of ten
  converting metric units, 492–493
  scientific notation and, 116–117
Precision, 428
Predictions
  using surveys to make, 680
  using theoretical probability to make, 680
Presidents, U.S., 74
Pressure, 82
Prime factorization, 160–161
  factor tree, 161
  to find greatest common factor, 165
  to find least common multiple, 219
  ladder diagram, 161
  simplest form and, 181
Prime meridian, 607
Prime numbers, 157
Principal, 388
Prisms, 560–561
  nets, 574–575, 576–577
  surface area, 576–577
  volume, 564–567
Probability, 652–683
  combinations, 679
  comparing, 653
  complement, 667
  compound events, 672–673
  dependent events, 677

Index **19**

effects of sample size on, SB20
experimental, 656–657
independent events, 676
making predictions, 680–681
permutations, 678
sample spaces, 662–663
simulations, 660–661
theoretical, 666–667, 680

Problem solving, see Focus on Problem Solving

Problem solving is a central focus of this course and is found throughout this book.

Problem Solving Application, 11, 78, 130, 166, 265, 299, 357, 438, 489, 567, 599, 662, 681, 699, 723

Problem Solving Strategies
Draw a Diagram, PS1
Find a Pattern, PS5
Guess and Test, PS3
Make a Model, PS2
Make a Table, PS6
Make an Organized List, PS10
Solve a Simpler Problem, PS7
Use a Venn Diagram, PS9
Use Logical Reasoning, PS8
Work Backward, PS4

Proper fraction, 186

Properties
Associative, 22–23
Commutative, 22–23
Distributive, 22–23

Proportions, 352–353
converting units of measure, 489
cross products, 353
exploring, 350–351
indirect measurement, 360–361
modeling, 352
scale drawings, 363–365
similar figures, 356–357
solving, 353

Prospect Creek, Alaska, 594

Protractor, 356, 410–411, 425, 502–503, 516–517

Pyramids, 561
nets, 577
surface area, 577

Pythagorean Theorem, SB11

Q

Quadrants, 604
Quadrilaterals, 434
classifying, 434–435
Quart, 481, 488
Quartiles, SB18
Queen Anne's Revenge, 613
Quotients, interpreting, 133–134

R

Radius, 512, 551, 552

Rafting, 46
Range, 289
Rates, 343
of change, 706–707
using tables to explore, 346–347
unit, 343
Rate of change, 706–707
Ratios, 342–343
equivalent, 342–343
using tables to explore, 346–347
percents as, 371
Rational numbers, 602–603
Rays, 407
Reading and Writing Math, 5, 49, 97, 155, 217, 283, 341, 405, 477, 533, 593, 650, 697
Reading Math, 66, 67, 100, 186, 299, 304, 308, 342, 346, 352, 410, 411, 420, 439, 540, 595, 608, 656, 707
Reading Strategies, see also Reading and Writing Math
Learn Math Vocabulary, 533
Read a Lesson for Understanding, 155
Read and Interpret Graphics, 283
Read Problems for Understanding, 405
Use Your Book for Success, 5
Ready To Go On?, 14, 34, 64, 84, 114, 140, 172, 190, 204, 242, 268, 296, 328, 368, 390, 426, 448, 464, 500, 518, 556, 580, 612, 636, 670, 684, 712, 726
Reagan, Ronald, 74
Real-World Connection, 35, 85, 141, 205, 269, 329, 391, 465, 519, 581, 637, 685, 727
Reciprocals, 260–261
Recording Industry Association of America, 378
Recreation, 535, 617, 664, 682
Rectangles, 434–435
area, 62–63, 534–535
changing dimensions, 548
perimeter, 62–63, 506
Rectangular prisms, 560–561
nets, 574
drawing views of, 558
volume, 564–565, 566
Reflection, 453
on coordinate plane, 608–609
line of, 453
Regrouping, 232–235
Regular polygons, 438
Remember!, 6, 18, 105, 111, 123, 126, 127, 133, 136, 137, 156, 193, 196, 218, 219, 224, 245, 255, 264, 357, 372, 384, 444, 450, 489, 497, 594, 598, 623, 624, 626, 627, 666, 673, 722
Repeating decimals, 176
Resources Online, 3, 14, 34, 47, 64, 84, 95, 114, 140, 153, 172, 190, 204, 215, 242, 268, 296, 302, 328, 339, 368, 390, 403, 426, 448, 464, 475, 500, 518, 531, 556, 580, 591, 612, 636, 649, 670, 684, 695, 712, 726

Rhode Island, 720
Rhombuses, 434–435
Right angles, 411
Right triangles, 429
Roman Empire, 618
Roman numerals, SB3
Roosevelt, Theodore, 74
Rose, Steve, 73
Rotation, 453
on coordinate plane, 609
Rotational symmetry, 458
Rounding
decimals, 104–105, SB2
estimating by, 6–7
whole numbers, 6–7, SB2
Rulers, 179, 184–185, 478, 480–481, 484–485, 510–511, 549
Rungnado Stadium, 119

S

St. Louis Gateway Arch, 495
Sales tax, 371, 384, 385
Samples, 680
Sample size, SB20
Sample spaces, 662–663
organized lists, 663
tree diagrams, 662–663
Sampling, SB19
San Augustin Cave, 601
San Jacinto Monument, 495
Saturn, 125, 188
Scale, 364, 479
Scale drawings, 364–365
Scale factor, 363
Scale models, 338
Scalene triangles, 430
School, 230, 664
Science, 122, 573
Science Link, 57
Scientific notation, 116–117
Seconds, 496–497
Sector (of a circle), SB11
Sequences
arithmetic, 29–30
completing, 30
extending, 29–30
finding patterns in, 33
writing expression for, in a table, 59
Sequoia National Park, 247
Sets
intersection, 170–171
union, 170–171
Seurat, Georges, 116
Shakespeare, 377
Shanghai, China, 76, 338
Shea Stadium, 437
Short Response, 9, 28, 76, 107, 159, 199, 227, 257, 286, 307, 317, 321, 345, 349, 383, 437, 447, 456, 461, 487, 505, 515,

543, 573, 601, 611, 618, 635, 721, 725
Use a Diagram, 526–527
Write Short Response, 148–149
Sides, corresponding, 356
Significant figures, SB17
Similar figures, 356–357
changing dimensions, 548–549
find missing measurement in, 356
indirect measurement, 360–361
Simple interest, 388–389
Simplest form, 181
Simplify, 18–19
Simulations, 660–661
Skew lines, 420–421
Skills Bank, SB1–SB20
Slope, 707
Social Studies, 32, 54, 56, 68, 71, 76, 134, 168, 189, 224, 226, 239, 245, 292, 301, 327, 373, 387, 458, 547, 665, 668, 720
Social Studies Link, 9, 21, 181, 307, 355, 367, 432, 447, 499, 537, 543, 607, 635, 683
Solution of an equation, 66
Solution of an inequality, 718
Solve a Simpler Problem, PS7
Solving equations
by adding, 74–75
decimal, 136–137
by dividing, 77–78
fraction, 238–239, 264–265
integer, 630–633
by multiplying, 81–82
by subtracting, 70–71
two-step, 714–715
variables on both sides, SB10
South Africa, 447
South Georgia Island, 280
Speed
of light, 119
of sound, 119, 163
Spheres, 561
Spinner, 330, 673, 676–677, 686, 687
Spiral Review
Spiral Review questions are found in every lesson. Some examples: 9, 13, 21, 25, 28
Sports, 27, 110, 113, 163, 178, 201, 240, 292, 294, 348, 490, 492, 503, 509, 555, 597, 618, 634, 654, 658
Sports Link, 437, 599
Spreadsheet, 33, 302–303
Squares, 434–435
area, 538–539
Square pyramids, 561
nets, 575
Square root, 539
Square tiles, 710–711
Standardized Test Prep, 44–45, 92–93, 150–151, 212–212, 278–279, 336–337, 400–401, 472–473, 528–529, 588–589, 646–647, 692–693, 736–737

Standardized Test Strategies, see Standardized Test Prep
Star Wars, 118
State Test Practice, 44, 92, 150, 212, 278, 336, 400, 472, 528, 588, 646, 692, 736
Statue of Liberty, 360, 490
Stem-and-leaf plots, 322–323
Strahov Stadium, 119
Straight angles, 411
Student Help
Caution!, 22, 59, 77, 104, 261, 314, 323, 353, 488, 493, 502, 503, 566, 706
Helpful Hint, 29, 122, 129, 161, 162, 166, 171, 181, 192, 197, 201, 229, 251, 292, 315, 322, 346, 364, 376, 380, 430, 492, 545, 546, 561, 577, 602, 604, 609, 632, 652, 653, 698, 714
Hot Tip!, 43, 45, 93, 149, 151, 213, 279, 337, 399, 401, 473, 527, 529, 589, 645, 647, 693, 735
Reading Math, 66, 67, 100, 186, 299, 304, 308, 342, 346, 352, 410, 411, 420, 439, 540, 595, 608, 656, 707
Remember!, 6, 18, 105, 111, 123, 126, 127, 133, 136, 137, 156, 193, 196, 218, 219, 224, 245, 254, 255, 264, 357, 372, 384, 444, 450, 489, 497, 594, 598, 623, 624, 626, 627, 666, 673, 722
Writing Math, 51, 176, 615, 657
Study Guide: Preview, 4, 48, 96, 154, 216, 282, 340, 404, 476, 532, 592, 650, 696
Study Guide: Review, 38–40, 88–90, 144–146, 208–210, 272–274, 332–334, 394–396, 468–470, 522–524, 584–586, 640–642, 688–690, 730–732
Study Strategy, see also Reading and Writing Math
Make Flash Cards, 217
Prepare for Your Final Exam, 697
Use Your Notes Effectively, 651
Subtraction
decimals, 110–111
exploring, 108–109, 110–111
mental math, 111
rounding to estimate, 104
fractions
estimating, 200–201
with like denominators, 196–197
modeling, 222–223
with regrouping, 232–235
with unlike denominators, 224–225
integers, 619–621
inverse operations, 70, 74
mixed numbers, 196–197, 228–229
solving equations by, 70–71, 714–715
solving inequalities by, 718
whole numbers, SB4
estimating, 6
Subtraction equations, 74–75

A Sunday on La Grande Jatte (Seurat), 116
Supplementary angles, 417
Surface area, 576–577
Surveys, 310
making predictions using, 680
Swimming, 113
Symmetry
lines of, 457–458
rotational, 458

T

Tables
to explore equivalent ratios and rates, 346–347
frequency, 304–305
to identify rate of change, 707
making, 284–285
translating between expressions and, 58–59
functions and, 698–699
Taxes, sales, 371, 384, 385
Technology, 381
geometry software, 433
graphing calculator, 16–17, 169, 379
spreadsheet, 33, 302–303
Technology Link, 383
Technology Lab
Angles in Triangles, 433
Convert Between Percents, Decimals, and Fractions, 379
Create Bar Graphs, 302–303
Explore the Order of Operations, 16–17
Find a Pattern in Sequences, 33
Greatest Common Factor, 169
Televisions, 378
Temperature, 73, 295, 618, 628
converting, 497
estimating, 497
positive and negative numbers and, 594
Ten by ten grid, 370, 371, 374
Ten Fingers, Ten Toes, 506
Terminating decimals, 176
Tessellations, 462–463
Test Prep
Test Prep questions are found in every lesson. Some examples: 9, 13, 21, 25, 28
Test Tackler
Any Question Type: Use a Diagram, 526–527
Extended Response: Write Extended Responses, 398–399
Gridded Response: Write Gridded Responses, 276–277
Multiple Choice
Eliminate Answer Choices, 42–43
Identifying Keywords and Context Clues, 644–645

Recognize Distracters, 734–735
Short Response: Write Short Response, 148–149
Test Taking Strategy, *see* Test Tackler
Test Taking Tips, *see* Hot Tip!
Theater Link, 725
Theoretical probability, 666–667
  making predictions using, 680
Think and Discuss
  Thing and Discuss is found in every lesson. Some examples: 7, 11, 16, 17, 19
Thompson, Jennifer, 113
Three-dimensional figures, 560–561; *see also* specific three-dimensional figures
  drawing views of, 558–559
  identifying faces, edges and vertices, 560–561
  modeling, 574–577
  nets, 574–577
  surface area, 574–577
  volume, 564–567, 570–571
Tiles
  algebra tiles, 630–631, 632–633
  square tiles, 710–711
Time
  converting, 496
  elapsed, 497
  units of, 496
Tips, 384, 385
Ton, 480, 488
Too little information, 65
Too much information, 65
Tour de France, 492
Transformations, 453–454
  on coordinate plane, 608–609
Translations, 453
  on coordinate plane, 608
Transportation, 709
Trapezoids, 434–435
Tree diagram, 662–663
Trials, 656
Triangles, 429–430
  acute, 429
  angles in, 429, 433
  area, 539–540
  classifying, 429–430
  equilateral, 430
  finding measure of missing angle, 429–430
  isosceles, 430
  obtuse, 429
  right, 429
  scalene, 430
  similar, 356
    indirect measurement, 360–361

sum of angles of, 439
Triangular prisms, 566
Two-step equations, 714–715
Two-step inequalities, 722–723

U

Ulrich, Thea, 515
Underestimate, 6
Union of sets, 170–171
Unit rates, 343
U.S. Constitution, 245
U.S. Mint, 132
Unlike denominators
  adding and subtracting, 224–225, 228–229, 234–235
Unlike fractions, 192
Use a Venn Diagram, PS9
Use Logical Reasoning, PS8

V

Variables, 50
  algebraic expressions and, 50–51
Venn diagram, 170–171, PS9
Venus, 26, 125, 365
Verrazano-Narrows Bridge, 159
Vertex
  of angles, 410
  of three-dimensional figures, 560–561
Vertical angles, 416
Vivaldi, Antonio, 241
Vocabulary Connections, 4, 48, 96, 154, 216, 282, 340, 404, 476, 532, 592, 650, 696
Volume, 566
  cylinders, 564–565, 570–571
  prisms, 564–565, 566–567

W

Washington Monument, 489
Water, 352, 372, 622
  density of, 569
  Earth's surface covered by, 224
Weather, 659, 668
Weather Link, 284–285
Weeks, 496–497
Weight
  converting units of, 488–489
  customary units of, 480–481
What's the Error?, 25, 53, 76, 103, 119, 125, 132, 139, 159, 164, 168, 178, 199, 227, 237, 263, 291, 295, 307, 324, 349, 355, 358, 383, 387, 409, 413, 423, 437, 441, 487, 491, 495, 499, 505, 509, 555, 563, 601, 622, 625, 669, 675, 683, 701, 709, 717, 721, 725
What's the Question?, 9, 28, 113, 189, 231, 247, 267, 313, 321, 345, 378, 579, 705
Whole numbers
  adding, SB3
  comparing and ordering, SB1
  dividing decimals by, 126–127
  dividing whole numbers by, SB5
  estimating, 6–7
  multiplying fractions by, 244–245
  multiplying whole numbers by, SB4
  rounding, SB2
  subtracting, SB3
Wombat, 626
Woods, Tiger, 598
Words
  and math, translating between, 54–55
Work Backward, PS4
Write About It
  Write About It exercises are found in every lesson. Some examples: 9, 13, 21, 25, 28
Write a Problem, 57, 73, 83, 107, 125, 135, 195, 203, 241, 253, 327, 367, 374, 419, 483, 543, 597, 635
Writing Math, 51, 176, 615, 657
Writing Strategies. *see also* Reading and Writing Math
  Keep a Math Journal, 97
  Use Your Own Words, 49
  Write a Convincing Argument, 593
  Write a Convincing Explanation, 341

X

x-axis, 604
x-coordinate, 604

Y

Yard, 480, 488
y-axis, 604
y-coordinate, 604
Year, 496–497

Credits ...

■ Staff Credits

Bruce Albrecht, Kimberly Barr, Erik Brandon, Jennifer Cassle, Tica Chitrarachis, Lorraine Cooper, Marc Cooper, Nina Degollado, Michelle Dike, Sam Dudgeon, Kelli R. Flanagan, Stephanie Friedman, Pam Garner, Diannia Green, Jennifer Gribble, Tom Hamilton, Liz Huckestein, Sarah Hudgens, Wilonda Ieans, Jevara Jackson, Simon Key, Jane A. Kirschman, Cathy Kuhles, Jill M. Lawson, Liann Lech, Leandria Lee, Jessika Maier, Jeff Mapua, Jonathan Martindill, Virginia Messler, Erica Miller, Erin Miller, Stacey Murray, Susan Mussey, Michael Neibergall, Kim Nguyen, Sara Phelps, Chris Rankin, Theresa Reding, Manda Reid, Jane Reinig, Katie Seawell, Patricia Sinnott, Patti Smith, Victoria Smith, Melinda Steele, Jeannie Taylor, David Trevino, April Warn, Kira J. Watkins, Glenn P. Worthman, David W. Wynn

■ Photo Credits

All images HMH Photo unless otherwise noted.

Real World Connection icons: ("R"), Ingram Publishing/SuperStock; ("e"), Jupiter Images/Brand X/Alamy; ("a"), imagebroker/Alamy; ("l"), Flat Earth; ("dash"), Dex Image/Alamy; ("W"), Stockbyte/gettyimages; ("o"), Jupiter Images/Brand X/Alamy; ("r"), Iugris/Alamy; ("l"), Ian Andrews/Alamy; ("d"), VLO-IMAGES/Alamy

Table of Contents: (chapter one), age fotostock/SuperStock; (chapter two), Pat and Chuck Blackley; (chapter three), John Dunn /Icon SMI/CORBIS; (chapter four), Design Pics Inc./Alamy; (chapter five), Michelle Pedone/zefa/CORBIS, Inc.; (chapter six), Colin Monteath/Hedgehog House/Minden Pictures; (chapter seven), Ryan Pyle/None/Corbis; (chapter eight), Alan Evans/Alamy; (chapter nine), Stephen Marks/Getty Images; (chapter ten), Richard Cummins/CORBIS; (chapter eleven), China Tourism Press/The Image Bank/Getty Images; (chapter twelve), Fred Hazelhoff/FOTO NATURA/Minden Pictures; (chapter thirteen), Bruce Wheadon/Alamy

Chapter One: 2 (bkgd), age fotostock/SuperStock; 6 (tr), © Cartoon Stock; 7 (cr), Gabe Palmer/Alamy; 9 (tr), James L. Amos/CORBIS; 10 (tr), CORBIS/Bettmann; 13 (tr), CORBIS/Lester V. Bergman; 15 (br), ©Michael Dunning/Getty Images/FPG International; 19 (b), Sam Dudgeon/HRW; 21 (tr), Atlantide Phototravel/CORBIS; 21 (tc), Photos by Wendy Mimiaga, courtesy of the Crow Canyon Archaeological Center; 22 (cr), DINODIA/Art Directors & TRIP Photo Library; 22 (tc), Digital Image copyright © 2010 PhotoDisc; 25 (c), Sam Dudgeon/HRW; 25 (r), PhotoDisc - Digital Image copyright © 2004 PhotoDisc; 25 (tl), C.K. Lorenz/Photo Researchers; 26 (tr), NASA-JPL-Caltech - Voyager/digital version by Science Faction/Getty Images; 29 (tr), Victoria Smith/HRW; 35 (bl), ©Icon Sports Media, Inc./CORBIS; 35 (c), Royalty Free/CORBIS; 36 (br), Jenny Thomas/HRW; 37 (b), HRW

Chapter Two: 46 (bkgd), © Pat and Chuck Blackley; 53 (tl), Sam Dudgeon/HRW; 54 (tr), © Richard Cummins/SuperStock; 57 (all patches), NASA; 57 (all patches), NASA; 57 (tr), AP Photo/NASA; 61 (r), © Adam Woolfitt/CORBIS; 65 (b), Stock Connection Distribution/Alamy; 67 (b), Eric Nathan/Alamy; 70 (tr), Buzz Pictures/SuperStock; 73 (l), © AP IMAGES/Lisa Poole; 74 (tc), Photodisc/Getty Images; 74 (tr), Bettmann/CORBIS; 74 (cl), Wally McNamee/CORBIS; 77 (tr), Bianca Lavies/National Geographic Image Collection; 80 (tr), David Aubrey/CORBIS; 81 (tr), © Photographers Choice RF/SuperStock; 85 (c), H. Mark Weidman; 87 (b), HRW

Chapter Three: 94 (bkgd), John Dunn/Icon SMI/CORBIS; 101 (tr), Jerry Schad/Photo Researchers, Inc.; 104 (tr), David Deas /DK Stock/Getty Images; 107 (tr), Mark Tomalty/Masterfile; 110 (tr), AP Photo/John Russell; 113 (tl), Frank Siteman/Getty Images/Stone; 115 (bc), Peter Van Steen/HRW; 115 (bl), Peter Van Steen/HRW; 116 (detail), ON-PAGE CREDIT; 116 (tr), ON-PAGE CREDIT; 119 (tl), George Hall/Check Six; 122 (tr), NASA/Photo Researchers, Inc.; 125 (br), Bettmann/CORBIS; 125 (tr), CORBIS; 126 (tr), Digital Vision/Alamy; 128 (cr), Victoria Smith/HRW; 129 (tr), Mark Gibson/Gibson Stock Photography; 132 (b), Phil Schermeister/CORBIS; 133 (tr), Sam Dudgeon/HRW; 136 (t), © Greer & Associates, Inc./SuperStock; 139 (tr), SuperStock; 141 (b), Greg Probst/Corbis; 142 (cr), Jenny Thomas/HRW; 143 (b), HRW

Chapter Four: 154 (bkgd), Design Pics Inc./Alamy; 156 (tr), Barry Austin/gettyimages; 159 (l), Tetra Images/Alamy; 164 (tr), Henry Westheim Photography/Alamy; 166 (tr), Somos Images LLC/Alamy; 168 (tl), Frans Lanting/Minden Pictures; 173 (b), Digital Image copyright © 2004 PhotoDisc; 175 (tr), Doug Pensinger/Getty Images; 178 (cr), Pat Lanza/FIELD/Bruce Coleman, Inc.; 183 (cr), Wendell Metzen/Bruce Coleman, Inc.; 183 (tr), Bob Krist/CORBIS; 184 (t), Peter Van Steen/HRW; 185 (acorn), Digital Image copyright © 2004 PhotoDisc; 185 (cicada), Digital Image copyright © 2005 Artville; 185 (egg), Digital Image copyright © 2004 PhotoDisc;
185 (key), Digital Image copyright © 2005 EyeWire; 185 (penny), Digital Image copyright © 2005 EyeWire; 185 (rock), Digital Image copyright © 2004 PhotoDisc; 185 (shamrock), Digital Image copyright © 2004 PhotoDisc; 185 (shell), Digital Image copyright © 2004 PhotoDisc; 186 (tr), Frank Zullo/Photo Researchers, Inc.; 189 (tl), Science Photo Library/Photo Researchers, Inc.; 191 (b), FRANCK FIFE/AFP/Getty Images; 192 (tr), Craig Lovell/Eagle Visions Photography/Alamy; 195 (tl), Peter Van Steen/HRW; 196 (tr), Gerolf Kalt/zefa/Corbis Images; 199 (tl), Chris Sanders/Taxi/Getty Images; 200 (tr), Skip Brown/National Geographic/gettyimages; 203 (tc), Mark Moffett/Minden Pictures; 203 (tl), SuperStock; 203 (tr), Raymond A. Mendez/Animals Animals/Earth Scenes; 205 (b), James Randklev/Corbis; 206 (br), Randall Hyman/HRW; 207 (b), HRW

Chapter Five: 214 (bkgd), Michelle Pedone/zefa/CORBIS; 218 (b), Beverly Barrett/HRW; 218 (c), Beverly Barrett/HRW; 218 (tr), JUPITERIMAGES/Brand X/Alamy; 224 (t), Earth Imaging/Stone/Getty Images; 227 (br), Gerry Ellis/Minden Pictures; 227 (cl), © Eric Hosking/CORBIS; 227 (cr), Paul Chesley/National Geographic Image Collection; 227 (tr), SuperStock; 228 (tr), Frans Lanting/Minden Pictures; 229 (c), Frans Lanting/Minden Pictures; 231 (l), Kenneth Garrett/National Geographic/gettyimages; 234 (tr), JUPITERIMAGES/ Liquid Library Value/Alamy; 238 (tr), Paulo Fridman/CORBIS; 239 (cr), FABIO COLOMBINI MEDEIROS/Animals Animals/Earth Scenes; 243 (bl), Ingram Publishing/SuperStock; 247 (tr), Jeff Foott/Discovery Communications, Inc.; 253 (l), Tom McHugh/Photo Researchers, Inc.; 254 (tr), David Young-Wolff/Photographer's Choice/Getty Images; 257 (c), D. Hurst/Alamy; 260 (tr), Victoria Smith/HRW; 264 (tr), D. Hurst/Alamy; 265 (tr), Beverly Barrett/HRW; 265 (l), Juniors Bildarchiv/Alamy; 267 (tl), Frans Lanting/Minden Pictures; 269 (br), Ryan Scofield/American Royal Barbeque; 269 (bl), Steve Adams/Mira/Digital Railroad; 270 (br), Ken Karp/HRW; 271 (b), HRW

Chapter Six: 280 (bkgd), Colin Monteath/Hedgehog House/Minden Pictures; 284 (bl), Carl and Ann Purcell/Index Stock Imagery, Inc.; 284 (t), NOAA/Getty Images; 288 (t), David Young-Wolff/PhotoEdit, Inc.; 291 (r), Stockdisc Classic/Alamy; 292 (tr), Doug Pensinger/Getty Images; 295 (tr), Sergio Pitamitz/CORBIS; 295 (c), K-PHOTOS/Alamy; 297 (bc), Victoria & Albert Museum/Art Resource, NY; 297 (bl), © Index Stock/Alamy Photos; 297 (br), U.S. Department of the Interior, National Park Service, Edison National Historic Site; 297 (mp3), © PunchStock; 298 (cr), Tim Davis/Photo Researchers, Inc.; 298 (cl), Sharon Smith/Bruce Coleman, Inc.; 298 (t), SuperStock; 298 (tr), Dr. Eckart Pott/Bruce Coleman, Inc.; 304 (c), Federal Bureau of Investigation; 304 (l), Leonard Lessin/Peter Arnold; 304 (loop), © Peter Miller/Stone/Getty Images; 307 (t), Roland Seitre / Peter Arnold, Inc.; 311 (t), ON PAGE CREDIT; 314 (t), ON PAGE CREDIT; 317 (l), GK Hart/Vikki Hart/Getty Images; 318 (c), Brand X Pictures; 318 (tr), David Madison/Bruce Coleman, Inc.; 321 (c), John Bavosi/Science Photo Library/Photo Researchers, Inc.; 321 (tr), John Bavosi/Science Photo Library/Photo Researchers, Inc.; 322 (tr), GAVRYSH DIMA/GAMMA/Eyedea; 329 (b), Gene Rhoden/BRUCE COLEMAN INC.; 330 (br), Randall Hyman/HRW; 331 (b), HRW

Chapter Seven: 338 (bkgd), Ryan Pyle/None/Corbis; 342 (tr), MIKE THEILER/AFP/Getty Images; 346 (tr), AP Photo/Big Lots, Rene Macura; 349 (tl), Bettmann/CORBIS; 352 (tr), © Cartoon Stock; 355 (tc), Jeff Greenberg/PhotoEdit, Inc.; 355 (tr), Peter Adams/CORBIS; 355 (cr), Slim Plantagenate/Alamy; 355 (c), Randy Faris/CORBIS; 357 (tr), Smithsonian American Art Museum, Washington, DC / Art Resource, NY; 358 (t), Victoris Smith/HRW; 360 (t), Amanda Hall/Robert Harding World Imagery/Getty Images; 361 (tl), Thinkstock/Getty Images; 364 (tl), Richard Cummins/Lonely Planet Images; 364 (cr), Lee Snider/Photo Images/CORBIS; 366 (b), E. R. Degginger/Bruce Coleman, Inc.; 369 (br), Len Rubenstein/Index Stock Imagery, Inc.; 371 (tr), Victoria Smith/HRW; 374 (t), Erin Patrice O'Brien/Taxi/Getty Images; 378 (t), Brooks Kraft/CORBIS; 380 (tr), Sam Dudgeon/HRW; 383 (tl), Lucy Schaly/Beaver County Times/AP/Wide World Photos; 384 (tr), © Jonny Hawkins/Cartoon Stock; 387 (l), D. Hurst/Alamy; 391 (b), Walter Bibikow/Corbis; 392 (br), Ken Karp/HRW; 392 (c), © Mimmo Jodice/CORBIS; 392 (cl), © Massimo Listri/CORBIS; 392 (cr), © Gianni Dagli Orti/CORBIS; 393 (b), HRW

Chapter Eight: 402 (bkgd), Alan Evans/Alamy; 410 (tr), Courtesy of Icon Health & Fitness; 416 (c), Corbis Premium RF/Alamy; 416 (b), StockShot/Alamy; 418 (cl), Werner Forman Archive/Piers Morris Collection/Art Resource, NY; 418 (r), Peter Van Steen/HRW; 418 (tl), D. Hurst/Alamy; 418 (cr), © Barbara Cesery/SuperStock; 420 (t), © age fotostock/SuperStock; 421 (tl), Emmanuel Faure/SuperStock; 421 (tr), Peter Van Steen/HRW; 421 (cl), Victoria Smithx/HRW; 421 (cr), JUPITERIMAGES/Brand X/Alamy; 422 (t), Chloe Johnson/Alamy; 422 (c), Alex L. Fradkin/Photodisc/gettyimages; 429 (b), Iconotec/Alamy; 432 (l), on-page credit; 434 (tr), Composition 17, 1919 (oil on canvas), Doesburg, Theo van (1883-1931)/Haggs Gemeentemuseum, The Hague, Netherlands/Bridgeman Art Library; 437 (tl), David Forbert/SuperStock; 438 (bl), Digital Image copyright © 2010 PhotoDisc; 438 (cl), Digital Image copyright © 2010 PhotoDisc; 439 (t), Digital Image copyright © 2010 PhotoDisc; 440 (tc), Peter Van Steen/HRW; 440 (tl), Beverly Barrett/HRW; 440 (tr), Peter Van Steen/HRW; 440 (cl), Jeff Speed/First Light; 440 (c), Bryan Eveleigh/Alamy; 440 (cr), B E Eyley Architectural Images/Alamy; 444 (t), Robert Fried/Alamy; 445 (bl), Peter Van Steen/HRW; 445 (cr), Peter Van Steen/HRW; 446 (c), Peter Van Steen/HRW; 447 (tr), Steve Vidler/SuperStock;

449 (b), © Michael Boys/CORBIS; 450 (t), Realimage/Alamy; 452 (cl), "Sunflowers" by Mary Backer/Sam Dudgeon/HRW Photo; 452 (cr), "Sunflowers" by Mary Backer/Sam Dudgeon/HRW Photo; 452 (l), Original Artwork © "Sunflowers" by Mary Backer/Sam Dudgeon/HRW Photo; 452 (r), "Sunflowers" by Mary Backer/Sam Dudgeon/HRW Photo; 456 (l), Nik Wheeler/CORBIS; 457 (t), © Royalty Free/CORBIS; 458 (b), Dorling Kindersley/Getty Images; 459 (t), Victoria Smith/HRW; 459 (c), Victoria Smith/HRW; 461 (cr), ©corbisimages.com; 461 (t), Jon Arnold Images/Alamy; 465 (bl, cr), Patrick S. O'Donnell; 467 (b), HRW; 467 (bc), HRW

Chapter Nine: 474 (bkgd), Stephen Marks/Getty Images; 481 (b), Victoria Smith/HRW; 482 (b), HRW; 482 (t), HRW; 483 (l), Winchester Cathedral, Hampshire, UK / Bridgeman Art Library; 485 (b), Victoria Smith/HRW; 486 (b), Siede Preis/Getty Images; 486 (t), Photonica/Getty Images; 487 (r), Stephanie Friedman/HRW Photo; 488 (r), Michael Steele/Getty Images; 491 (l), © Peter Arnold, Inc.; 492 (r), AP Photo/Alessandro Trovati; 495 (tc), Taxi/Getty Images; 495 (tr), Robert Harding Picture Library Ltd / Alamy; 496 (tr), Alan Copson City Pictures / Alamy; 499 (br), Lonely Planet Images/Getty Images; 499 (cr), Alan Schein Photography/CORBIS; 499 (t), Travel-Shots/Alamy; 499 (tr), Michael S. Yamashita/CORBIS; 501 (b), Nic Hamilton/Alamy; 502 (tr), Royalty-Free/Corbis; 505 (tr), AP Photo/Fabio Muzzi; 506 (b), Victoria Smith/HRW; 506 (tr), Karl-Josef Hildenbrand/epa/CORBIS; 508 (br), Digital Image copyright © 2010 PhotoDisc; 508 (tr), © 2008 AbleStock.com/JupiterImages Corporation; 512 (c), Masterfile; 512 (tr), Masterfile; 515 (l), AP Photo/Francis Moran; 519 (cr, b), Ilene MacDonald/Alamy; 520 (br), Tim Davis/HRW Photo; 521 (b), HRW

Chapter Ten: 530 (bkgd), Richard Cummins/CORBIS; 533 (r), HRW; 534 (tr), North Wind Picture Archives; 537 (c), NASA/Science Source/Photo Researchers, Inc.; 537 (tr), Tom Till/Photographer's Choice/Getty Images; 540 (tr), Raymond Patrick/Taxi/Getty Images; 543 (tr), Shirley Richards/SuperStock; 544 (c), Victoria Smith/HRW; 548 (t), ColorBlind Images/Iconica/Getty Images; 549 (t), © 2007 Photos.com/JupiterImages Corporation; 549 (tl) © 2007 Photos.com/JupiterImages Corporation; 552 (tr), Getty Images; 555 (l), David Parker/Photo Researchers, Inc.; 555 (tr), © Tim De Waele/Photo & Co./Corbis; 557 (bl), © Omni Photo Communications Inc./Index Stock Imagery/Jupiter Images; 560 (t), Tetra Images/Alamy; 561 (b), Peter Van Steen/HRW; 561 (c), Sam Dudgeon/HRW; 561 (t), Stefano Blanchetti/CORBIS; 562 (cl), NewsCom; 562 (tc), JUPITERIMAGES/Brand X /Alamy; 562 (tr), Victoria Smith/HRW; 562 (cl), © PunchStock; 562 (bc), D. HurstAlamy; 562 (br), iStockphoto.com; 563 (cl), © CuboImages srl/Alamy; 563 (c), Alan Schein Photography/Corbis; 563 (cr), Jon Hicks/Corbis; 567 (tr), Victoria Smith/HRW; 567 (c), Victoria Smith/HRW; 567 (c), Victoria Smith/HRW; 567 (c), Victoria Smith/HRW; 567 (c), Victoria Smith/HRW; 569 (tr), Charles D. Winters/Photo Researchers, Inc.; 569 (c), Charles D. Winters/Photo Researchers, Inc.; 570 (tr), Photo by Museum of the City of New York/Byron Collection/Getty Images; 570 (tc), Underwood & Underwood/CORBIS; 576 (t), © Blend Images/Alamy; 579 (tl), Mark C. Burnett/Photo Researchers, Inc.; 581 (tc, bc), Photo by John Corbett/Courtesy of The Preservation Society of Newport County; 582 (c), Tim Davis/HRW Photo; 583 (b), HRW

Chapter Eleven: 590 (bkgd), China Tourism Press/The Image Bank/Getty Images; 594 (tl), CORBIS/Bill Ross; 594 (tr), Patrick J. Endres/AlaskaPhotographics; 597 (l), Emory Kristof/National Geographic Image Collection; 598 (t), Ian Walton/Getty Images; 599 (l), Chris Trotman/Duomo Photography; 601 (cl), © Photographers Choice RF/SuperStock ; 601 (cr), © Jon Arnold Images/SuperStock; 608 (tr), David Young-Wolff/PhotoEdit, Inc.; 613 (br), © AFP/Getty Images; 615 (tr), Pacific Stock/SuperStock; 618 (l), Robert Emmett Bright/Photo Researchers; 623 (tr), © Digital Vision/PunchStock; 626 (t), JUERGEN & CHRISTINE SOHNS/Animals Animals/Earth Scenes; 629 (cr), Francisco Marquez; 629 (tr), Jacana / Photo Researchers, Inc; 635 (l), © Macduff Everton/Getty Images; 637 (c), Herb Segars-gotosnapshot.com; 638 (br), Jenny Thomas/HRW; 639 (b), HRW

Chapter Twelve: 648 (bkgd), FRED HAZELHOFF/FOTO NATURA/Minden Pictures; 652 (tr), Victoria Smith/Harcourt; 655 (tr), Tek Image/Photo Researchers, Inc.; 656 (cl), EyeWire - Digital Image copyright © 2004 EyeWire; 656 (cr), EyeWire - Digital Image copyright © 2004 EyeWire; 658 (c), EyeWire - Digital Image copyright © 2004 EyeWire; 658 (cl), EyeWire - Digital Image copyright © 2004 EyeWire; 658 (cr), Sam Dudgeon/HRW; 658 (l), Sam Dudgeon/HRW; 667 (all), Peter Van Steen/HRW; 669 (tl), © CORBIS; 671 (b), © Jason Hawkes/Getty Images/Stone; 672 (tr), Dynamic Graphics Group/i2i/Alamy; 673 (tl), Digital Image copyright © 2004 EyeWire; 675 (r), © Pat Doyle/CORBIS; 680 (t), Peter Essick/Aurora/Getty Images; 683 (t), © Richard T. Nowitz/CORBIS; 683 (tl), Yvette Cardozo/Index Stock Imagery/Jupiter Images; 683 (tr), © Jeff Curtes/CORBIS; 683 (tr), © Reuters NewMedia Inc./CORBIS; 685 (b), John Chiasson/Liaison/Getty Images; 686 (b), Ken Karp/HRW; 687 (b), HRW; 690 (tc), Digital Image copyright © 2004 EyeWire; 690 (t), Digital Image copyright © 2004 EyeWire; 690 (tr), Digital Image copyright © 2004 EyeWire; 691 (br), ©Stockbyte - four food images; frame - Victoria Smith/HRW

Chapter Thirteen: 694 (bkgd), Bruce Wheadon/Alamy; 698 (t), Koji Aoki/Sport/Jupiterimages; 702 (t), Donald Nausbaum/Photographer's Choice RR/Getty Images; 705 (tr), Simon Fraser/MRC Unit, Newcastle General Hospital/Science Photo Library/Photo Researchers, Inc.; 706 (t), © Tom Stewart/CORBIS; 709 (tl), © Hulton Archive/Getty Images; 713 (br), Garry Black/Masterfile; 714 (t), © Nicola Gavin/Alamy; 717 (tl), Francois Gohier/Photo Researchers, Inc.; 721 (tl), © David Muench/CORBIS; 725 (tl), © Paul Miller/epa/Corbis; 727 (b), Blaine Harrington III/Alamy; 727 (cr), Greg Vaughn/Alamy; 728 (br), Jenny Thomas/HRW; 729 (b), Victoria Smith/Harcourt

Back Matter: *Student Handbook TOC:* 738 (tl) John Langford/HRW; 739 (br) Sam Dudgeon/HRW; *Problem Solving Handbook:* PS1 (c), Pictor/Alamy Photos; PS2 (bl, br), Sam Dudgeon/HRW; PS2 (tl), Victoria Smith/HRW; PS3 (tr), Charles Gupton/CORBIS; PS4 (tr), Victoria Smith/HRW; PS5 (tr), Victoria Smith/HRW; PS7 (tr), Cleo Freelance Photography/Painet Inc.; PS8 (bl, cl), Victoria Smith/HRW; PS8 (tr), Sam Dudgeon/HRW

Table of Measures

METRIC

Length
1 kilometer (km) = 1,000 meters (m)
1 meter = 100 centimeters (cm)
1 centimeter = 10 millimeters (mm)

Capacity
1 liter (L) = 1,000 milliliters (mL)

Mass
1 kilogram (kg) = 1,000 grams (g)
1 gram = 1,000 milligrams (mg)

CUSTOMARY

Length
1 mile (mi) = 5,280 feet (ft)
1 yard (yd) = 3 feet
1 foot = 12 inches (in.)

Capacity
1 gallon (gal) = 4 quarts (qt)
1 quart = 2 pints (pt)
1 pint = 2 cups (c)
1 cup = 8 fluid ounces (fl oz)

Weight
1 ton (T) = 2,000 pounds (lb)
1 pound = 16 ounces (oz)

TIME

1 year (yr) = 365 days
1 year = 12 months (mo)
1 year = 52 weeks (wk)
1 week = 7 days

1 day = 24 hours (h)
1 hour = 60 minutes (min)
1 minute = 60 seconds (s)

Formulas

Perimeter and Circumference

Square	$P = 4s$
Rectangle	$P = 2\ell + 2w$ or $P = 2(\ell + w)$
Polygon	$P =$ sum of the lengths of the sides
Circle	$C = 2\pi r$ or $C = \pi d$

Area

Square	$A = s^2$
Rectangle	$A = \ell w$ or $A = bh$
Parallelogram	$A = bh$
Triangle	$A = \frac{1}{2}bh$ or $A = \frac{bh}{2}$
Trapezoid	$A = \frac{1}{2}(b_1 + b_2)h$ or $A = \frac{(b_1 + b_2)h}{2}$
Circle	$A = \pi r^2$

Holt McDougal Online Learning

All the help you need, any time you need it.

go.hrw.com

Hundreds of videos online!

Lesson Tutorial Videos feature entertaining and enlightening videos that illustrate every example in your textbook!

Log on to www.go.hrw.com to access Holt's online resources.

Premier Online Edition
- Complete Student Edition
- **Lesson Tutorial Videos** for every example
  > Course 1: 287 videos
  > Course 2: 317 videos
  > Course 3: 341 videos
- Interactive practice with feedback

Extra Practice
- Homework Help Online
- Intervention and enrichment exercises
- State test practice

Online Tools
- Graphing calculator
- TechKeys "How-to" tutorials on graphing calculators
- Virtual Manipulatives
- Multilingual glossary

For Parents
- Parent Resources Online